D1737677

Handbook of Research on Retailer–Consumer Relationship Development

Fabio Musso
University of Urbino, Department of Economics, Society and Politics (DESP), Italy

Elena Druica
University of Bucharest, Department of Economic and Administrative Sciences, Romania

A volume in the Advances in Marketing, Customer Relationship Management, and E-Services (AMCRMES) Book Series

An Imprint of IGI Global

Managing Director:	Lindsay Johnston
Production Editor:	Jennifer Yoder
Development Editor:	Erin O'Dea
Acquisitions Editor:	Kayla Wolfe
Typesetter:	Deanna Jo Zombro
Cover Design:	Jason Mull

Published in the United States of America by
   Business Science Reference (an imprint of IGI Global)
   701 E. Chocolate Avenue
   Hershey PA 17033
   Tel: 717-533-8845
   Fax: 717-533-8661
   E-mail: cust@igi-global.com
   Web site: http://www.igi-global.com

                    Library of Congress Cataloging-in-Publication Data

Handbook of research on retailer-consumer relationship development / Fabio Musso and Elena Druica, editors.
    pages cm
  Includes bibliographical references and index.
  Summary: "This book offers a complete and updated overview of various perspectives relating to customer relationship management within the retail industry and stimulates the search for greater integration of these views in further research"-- Provided by publisher.
    ISBN 978-1-4666-6074-8 (hardcover) -- ISBN 978-1-4666-6075-5 (ebook) -- ISBN 978-1-4666-6077-9 (print & perpetual access) 1. Retail trade. 2. Customer relations. I. Musso, Fabio, 1960- II. Druica, Elena, 1971-
    HF5429.H2833 2014
    658.8'12--dc23
                        2014007824

This book is published in the IGI Global book series Advances in Marketing, Customer Relationship Management, and E-Services (AMCRMES) (ISSN: 2327-5502; eISSN: 2327-5529)

British Cataloguing in Publication Data
A Cataloguing in Publication record for this book is available from the British Library.

For electronic access to this publication, please contact: eresources@igi-global.com.

Advances in Marketing, Customer Relationship Management, and E-Services (AMCRMES) Book Series

Eldon Y. Li
National Chengchi University, Taiwan & California Polytechnic State University, USA

ISSN: 2327-5502
EISSN: 2327-5529

MISSION

Business processes, services, and communications are important factors in the management of good customer relationship, which is the foundation of any well organized business. Technology continues to play a vital role in the organization and automation of business processes for marketing, sales, and customer service. These features aid in the attraction of new clients and maintaining existing relationships.

The Advances in Marketing, Customer Relationship Management, and E-Services (AMCRMES) Book Series addresses success factors for customer relationship management, marketing, and electronic services and its performance outcomes. This collection of reference source covers aspects of consumer behavior and marketing business strategies aiming towards researchers, scholars, and practitioners in the fields of marketing management.

COVERAGE

- B2B Marketing
- CRM and Customer Trust
- CRM in Financial Services
- CRM Strategies
- Customer Relationship Management
- Data Mining and Marketing
- E-Service Innovation
- Ethical Considerations in E-Marketing
- Legal Considerations in E-Marketing
- Online Community Management and Behavior
- Relationship Marketing
- Social Networking and Marketing
- Web Mining and Marketing

IGI Global is currently accepting manuscripts for publication within this series. To submit a proposal for a volume in this series, please contact our Acquisition Editors at Acquisitions@igi-global.com or visit: http://www.igi-global.com/publish/.

Titles in this Series

For a list of additional titles in this series, please visit: www.igi-global.com

Handbook of Research on Retailer-Consumer Relationship Development
Fabio Musso (University of Urbino, Department of Economics, Society and Politics (DESP), Italy) and Elena
Druica (University of Bucharest, Department of Economic and Administrative Sciences, Romania)
Business Science Reference • copyright 2014 • 685pp • H/C (ISBN: 9781466660748) • US $380.00 (our price)

Strategies in Sports Marketing Technologies and Emerging Trends
Manuel Alonso Dos Santos (Universidad Católica de la Santísima Concepción, Chile)
Business Science Reference • copyright 2014 • 363pp • H/C (ISBN: 9781466659940) • US $235.00 (our price)

Handbook of Research on Consumerism in Business and Marketing Concepts and Practices
Hans-Ruediger Kaufmann (University of Nicosia, Cyprus & International Business School at Vilnius University,
Lithuania) and Mohammad Fateh Ali Khan Panni (City University, Bangladesh)
Business Science Reference • copyright 2014 • 668pp • H/C (ISBN: 9781466658806) • US $365.00 (our price)

Handbook of Research on Management of Cultural Products E-Relationship Marketing and Accessibility Perspectives
Lucia Aiello (Unviersitas Mercatorum, Italy)
Business Science Reference • copyright 2014 • 486pp • H/C (ISBN: 9781466650077) • US $345.00 (our price)

Marketing in the Cyber Era Strategies and Emerging Trends
Ali Ghorbani (Payame Noor University, Iran)
Business Science Reference • copyright 2014 • 357pp • H/C (ISBN: 9781466648647) • US $185.00 (our price)

Transcultural Marketing for Incremental and Radical Innovation
Bryan Christiansen (PryMarke, LLC, USA) Salih Yıldız (Gümüşhane University, Turkey) and Emel Yıldız
(Gümüşhane University, Turkey)
Business Science Reference • copyright 2014 • 588pp • H/C (ISBN: 9781466647497) • US $185.00 (our price)

Progressive Trends in Knowledge and System-Based Science for Service Innovation
Michitaka Kosaka (Japan Advanced Institute of Science and Technology, Japan) and Kunio Shirahada (Japan
Advanced Institute of Science and Technology, Japan)
Business Science Reference • copyright 2014 • 511pp • H/C (ISBN: 9781466646636) • US $185.00 (our price)

Innovations in Services Marketing and Management Strategies for Emerging Economies
Anita Goyal (Indian Institute of Management (IIM), Lucknow, India)
Business Science Reference • copyright 2014 • 331pp • H/C (ISBN: 9781466646711) • US $185.00 (our price)

DISSEMINATOR OF KNOWLEDGE

www.igi-global.com

701 E. Chocolate Ave., Hershey, PA 17033
Order online at www.igi-global.com or call 717-533-8845 x100
To place a standing order for titles released in this series, contact: cust@igi-global.com
Mon-Fri 8:00 am - 5:00 pm (est) or fax 24 hours a day 717-533-8661

List of Contributors

Table of Contents

Section 1
Consumers' Behavior, Buying Preferences, and Relationships with Retailers

Section 2
Retail Context, Store Formats, and Retail Services

Section 3
Store Atmosphere and Interaction with Consumers

Section 4
Innovation, ICT, and Social Media: The Multichannelling Challenges for Retailers

Detailed Table of Contents

Section 1
Consumers' Behavior, Buying Preferences, and Relationships with Retailers

This section offers an overview of the key issues on consumer behavior, highlighting the decision-making criteria for buying products in a context of relationships with the retailer. Together with the analysis of the main characters of consumer behavior, store loyalty, shopping experience, and the role of private label products are explored in light of consumer perceptions and changes.

Building on findings from previous research on dimensions of Consumer Perceived Values (CPVs), an Integrated Consumer Perceived Value Model comprising utilitarian, hedonic, and social values is proposed to explain observed consumer decisions (viz. purchase or do not purchase), and to provide new frontiers for consumer behaviour research. The distinguishing if not innovative features of the proposed model are: (1) it provides a framework to investigate the competing, complementary, and compensating effects of the CPV dimensions; (2) it distinguishes the CPV dimensions that affect consumer decisions specifically and those that affect consumer decisions homogeneously; and (3) while some CPVs are generated and interact serially, other CPVs could be generated and interact in parallel.

Consumer-Brand Identification (CBI) has been identified as an important antecedent of consumer-brand relationships. Consumers show positive attitudes towards brands that reflect their self-concept and are more likely to express and enhance their identity. In this sense, Consumer-Retailer Identification (CRI) represents a powerful tool for retailers to develop meaningful relationships by strengthening emotional connections with their customers. This chapter proposes a literature review of previous research on the role of consumer's self-concept in the development of retailer-customer relationships. Focusing on identity-based consumer behaviour, the chapter provides a comprehensive picture of the past research and the emerging trends on CBI and then proposes a conceptual framework of CRI.

Dong-Jin Lee, Yonsei University, South Korea
Grace B. Yu, Duksung Women's University, South Korea
M. Joseph Sirgy, Virginia Polytechnic Institute and State University, USA
Ahmet Ekici, Bilkent University, Turkey
Eda Gurel-Atay, University of Puget Sound, USA
Kenneth D. Bahn, James Madison University, USA

In this chapter, the authors make an attempt to review and integrate much of the research on shopping well-being and ill-being experiences. The integrated model identifies the antecedents of these two focal constructs in terms of situational, individual, and cultural factors. The consequences of shopping well-being and ill-being experiences on life satisfaction (or subjective well-being) are explained through a bottom-up spillover process. Managerial implications and avenues for future research are also discussed.

Amalia Duṭu, University of Pitesti, Romania

An economic crisis is an uncertainty situation with negative economic evolutions like unemployment, inflation rate increasing, freezing or decreasing of the wages, purchasing power decrease, investments value reduction, fluctuations in consumer prices, restrictions in accessing loans, and fluctuations in currency exchange rate that represent economic shocks hitting most of the consumers to some extent. During economic turbulent times, consumers are highly exposed to such risks. The present chapter is intended to explain the consumers' behaviour alteration and spending patterns in recession conditions dealing with the panic mechanism that shapes the consumers' behaviour in this particular context, analyzing it from an economic and psychological perspective. The chapter is organized in two complementary parts in an attempt to present a comprehensive picture of consumers' behaviour change in uncertainty conditions. Readers can find answers to the "HOW" question and also to the "WHY" question placed behind consumers' behaviour alterations during recession.

Arturo Z. Vásquez-Párraga, The University of Texas – Pan American, USA
Miguel Ángel Sahagún, The University of Texas – Pan American, USA
Pablo José Escobedo, The University of Texas – Pan American, USA

This chapter examines the process of how store customers become loyal to their stores. The authors pursue a theoretical and empirical research approach designed to identify and test a parsimonious model. The result is an explanation chain that incorporates relational variables, trust and commitment, satisfaction, and the moderating factors of the relational variables. The findings reveal that customer commitment is the major contributing explanation for true customer loyalty, significantly more than the contributed explanation of customer satisfaction. The cognitive moderating factors (store familiarity, store choice, customer perceived risk, and communication) and the affective moderating factors (customer opportunistic tendencies, consumer involvement, shared personal values, and shared management values) are significantly related to the core variables and thus contribute some explanation, yet their contribution is very small compared to the contribution of the core variables, thereby suggesting the significance of the core variables in the explanation of customer store loyalty.

Chapter 6

Elisa Martinelli, University of Modena and Reggio Emilia, Italy
Donata Tania Vergura, University of Parma, Italy

The chapter focuses on the role played by Private Labels (PLs) in the retailer-consumer relationship. Specifically, the results of a survey aimed at investigating the ability of a specific kind of PL, namely Premium Private Label (PPL), to improve customer loyalty to the retailer are presented. After reviewing the literature on the PLs' role in the retailer-customer relationship, a theoretical model is proposed and tested by administering a questionnaire to a sample of retail customers and then applying structural equation modeling. Four key components of PPLs' image, namely quality, assortment, access, and value, are studied as antecedents of customer satisfaction to the PPL, while customer loyalty to the PPL is considered as a mediator between customer satisfaction to the PPL and customer loyalty to the retailer. Results show that PPLs positively impact on customer loyalty to the retailer through a causal relationship driven by PPL quality and PPL value.

Section 2
Retail Context, Store Formats, and Retail Services

The second section refers to the retail context, offering an overview of the way in which formats, retail environment, and locations are changing facing new consumers' expectations and values. The shopping activity as an experience to be enriched becomes the subject of new paradigms for the retailer to offer in the combination of products, services, entertainment, and environmental values whose importance is increasing.

Chapter 7

Barbara Borusiak, Poznan University of Economics, Poland

The main aim of this chapter is to explain the mechanisms for the emergence of selected innovative formats on the basis of the existing format change theories. The chapter comprises three main parts. First, the nature of a retail format is explored and the classification of retail formats is presented. Second, four groups of theories (cyclical, conflict, environmental, and integrated theories) explaining the emergence and evolution of retail formats are analysed. Third, retail formats theories are applied in explaining the emergence of two formats: pop-up store and m-commerce. The approach involves a review of literature and the analysis of some empirical data concerning the structure of the retail trade turnover in the chosen countries.

    Jason J. Turner, Abertay University, UK
    Toni Gardner, Abertay University, UK

The aims of this exploratory research are to evaluate customer and retailer perceptions of the decline of the UK High Street and investigate the potential of the service encounter, specifically customer service, as a means to reverse this decline. The background to this research is one where the UK High Street is in decline as a result of out-of-town retailing, the growth in the use of technology and online shopping, and high business rates and rents. Using interviews in 2013 across four Scottish cities (Aberdeen, Dundee, Edinburgh, and Glasgow) with 40 retailers (national chains and independents) across the fashion, footwear, jewellery and health and beauty sectors, and 40 customers aged between 18 and 60, the chapter reveals that unlike the retailers in this study, customers are not of the opinion that an improvement in current, in some cases, "disappointing" customer service would encourage them back to the High Street. Rather customers thought solutions to the decline in the UK High Street lay in combining the appeal of online convenience and choice with the tangibility of the physical store experience.

    Kathleen L. Wolf, University of Washington, USA

Many cities and communities are working toward urban sustainability goals. Yet, retailers and merchants may not find environmental benefits to be compelling when compared to the direct costs of landscape and trees. Nonetheless, a quality outdoor environment may provide atmospherics effects that extend store appeal to the curb and heighten the positive experiences and psychological reactions of visitors while in a shopping district. A multi-study program of research shows that having a quality urban forest canopy within business districts and commercial areas can promote positive shopper perceptions and behavior. Positive responses include store image, patronage behavior, and willingness to pay more for goods and services. This chapter provides a summary of the research, connects results to psychological marketing theory, provides evidence-based design recommendations, and makes suggestions for potential future research activity.

    Patrizia de Luca, University of Trieste, Italy
    Giovanna Pegan, University of Trieste, Italy

This chapter has the aim to improve understanding of the in-store customer experience in the retail environment by analyzing the business of coffee shops in the United States market with a specific focus on American and Italian chains. After a brief overview of the managerial literature on coffee shops, the main findings of the qualitative research is presented. In particular, this chapter outlines the features of the U.S. coffee shop landscape and explores American consumers' perception of the coffee shop experience using nethnography. The results show a complex framework from the offer and the demand perspective that could also contribute to supporting coffee companies in managing customer experience strategy in the American market.

Chapter 11

Sergio Barile, Sapienza, University of Rome, Italy
Marialuisa Saviano, University of Salerno, Italy

The aim of this chapter is to highlight the necessity of a change in perspective and a new approach to Retail Service Marketing by addressing the recent challenges posed by a radical rethinking of market exchange logic using a service view. Recent Service Marketing advances are analyzed, which lead to the Service Dominant Logic proposal to take a general service view of market exchange, envisaging an emerging paradigm change. However, the key to this potential paradigm change is not yet well focused. A gap in the theoretical approach emerges that can be closed by adopting the Viable Systems Approach and the structure-system interpretation scheme. Their implications for retailing are discussed, and the key to change is emphasized. This chapter introduces a new theoretical and conceptual framework rooted in systems thinking, which recommends a Service Systems Approach to Retail Marketing.

Chapter 12

Ana Isabel Jiménez-Zarco, Open University of Catalonia, Spain
María Pilar Martínez-Ruiz, University of Castilla la Mancha, Spain
Alicia Izquierdo-Yusta, University of Burgos, Spain

This chapter examines how social and economic changes of recent years have led to a new consumer profile. Furthermore, it explores how current responsible concerns regarding consumption, as well as a greater concern for welfare sustainability and the environment, are affecting purchasing behavior. With these ideas in mind, this chapter analyses how organizations have to evolve towards a new marketing paradigm in order to link to their customers emotionally. In this regard, the evolution of the marketing concept is reviewed—departing from a Marketing 1.0 paradigm, passing through a Marketing 2.0 paradigm—in order to understand how the so-called Marketing 3.0 emerged. The chapter concludes by analyzing the different rules that guide this new approach and how companies in the distribution sector are applying them in their daily activities.

Section 3
Store Atmosphere and Interaction with Consumers

Section 3 offers an overview of store atmosphere and the interaction with consumers. In the first part (chapters 13 to 16), issues related to the store atmosphere are analyzed considering sensorial factors, the relationship with salespeople, and even taking into account security issues inside stores. The last 3 chapters of the section focus on consumers' involvement in co-creation of the retail service with reference to elements related to social responsibility and ethical/social values.

Chapter 13

Sanda Renko, University of Zagreb, Croatia

Many studies have found that within an intensely competitive market, it is difficult for retailers to gain advantages from products, prices, promotions, and location. They have to work hard to keep their stores favourable in the mind of consumers. Both practitioners and researchers recognize store atmosphere as a tool for creating value and gaining customers. This chapter provides a conceptual framework for studying the influence of store atmosphere on the store patronage. The chapter presents the main dimensions that constitute conventional retail stores' atmosphere and clarifies the manipulation of elements such as colour, lighting, signage, etc. within the store to communicate retailers' messages to customers. The topic is investigated from both retailers` and customers` perspective. The chapter concludes that both consumers and retailers prioritize functional cues in modern retailing forms.

Chapter 14

Mónica Gómez Suárez, Universidad Autónoma de Madrid, Spain
Cristina García Gumiel, Universidad Autónoma de Madrid, Spain

The main concern of this chapter is to develop a state-of-the-art of the literature referring to the use of sensorial marketing within the store. For this purpose, a deep interdisciplinary review of the theoretical and empirical works related to this discipline has been carried out. Thanks to this review, the link between some sensorial stimuli and consumer behavior has been demonstrated, but also the lack of research in some areas of study has been identified. This chapter provides a general overview of the sensorial variables used within the store by the managers, their main effects in the consumer behavior, and the most important model, the SOR model, to explain these relations. Conclusions, managerial implication, and recommendations for future research are provided.

Chapter 15

Mirian Palmeira, Federal University of Parana (UFPR), Brazil

The aim of this chapter is to identify whether frontline employees perceived themselves as having feelings of sexism, ageism, and appearance discrimination against customers in retail services. This investigation is a quantitative research, a conclusive description, and ex post facto study, which utilises a survey to collect the data and sampling by convenience. Three protocols are used (1) to format the questionnaire, (2) to produce 12 different standards combining age, gender, and appearance, and (3) to create social classification. In a previous study (Palmeira, Palmeira, & Santos, 2012), customers of different ages and genders perceived some degree of prejudice and discrimination in face-to-face retail services. Now, on the other side of the coin, frontline employees who work in Fashion and Food retailing recognise that there is prejudiced behaviour against customers, depending on their age, gender, and appearance, when providing them with face-to-face retail services. More than 95% of female and more than 64% of male attendants believe that well-dressed, young female customers are given priority when being served. Almost 80% of female and only 58% of male frontline workers believe that badly-dressed middle-aged men (not younger men) are the last to be served when there is no clear queuing process in the retail spatial area. This context strongly suggests the growing importance of an interpersonal skills training process for an organisations' staff as a way of avoiding behaviour that makes the customers think that there are prejudice and discrimination in the service process.

Chapter 16

Retailers use a number of ambient, design, and social elements with the aim of creating a unique, pleasant, and engaging Customer Shopping Experience (CSE). However, a store may be made paradoxically less attractive by the feelings of insecurity generated by the fact that the same elements can also encourage shoplifting. As a result, retailers have to balance their efforts to enhance a store's attractiveness by ensuring a high level of sales environment surveillance without interfering with the shopping experience. The aim of this chapter is to propose a conceptual framework that enriches the analysis of the development of retailer/consumer relationships by highlighting how retailers can make store surveillance simultaneously secure and appealing to shoppers. The analysis draws heavily on theoretical evidence in the marketing, environmental psychology, service, and retail management literature, and indicates that retailers' investments in store design, staff training, and technological systems can ensure adequate security levels without compromising customers' shopping experiences as long as the surveillance allows them to have direct contact with the store, its articles, and staff.

Chapter 17

This chapter focuses on strategic retailer-Non-Profit Organization (NPO) partnerships, based in North America and Europe, from a management perspective. It explores how and why these partnerships have had an impact on the retailer-consumer relationship, how they have shaped and influenced socially conscious shoppers, and how they have affected consumer trust as well as retail business practices and strategies, within the last decade. Retailer-NPO partnerships have emerged as a viable business strategy to support Corporate Social Responsibility (CSR) initiatives now commonplace among most large retail organizations. Consumers have become empowered, with the help of new social media technologies, to efficiently communicate, influence, and persuade other consumers around the globe. Therefore, consumers increasingly expect retailers to have an ethical and social responsibility to their people, products, operations, and communities. CSR practices have become integral to retailer sustainability and managing complex retailer-consumer relationships. This chapter reviews relevant theoretical frameworks, discusses the latest research findings from literature sources, and examines the industry practices (case studies) of several retailer-NPO partnerships across North America and Europe.

Chapter 18

Consumers are increasingly expressing critical stances towards corporate power and mainstream market ideology. Although the literature depicts their attitude as mainly reactive, it is emerging that there is scope, in retailing, for more proactive forms of collaboration with companies. This chapter aims to explore the outcomes in terms of new retail formulas derived from the effective interaction between retailers and engaged consumers, such as those belonging to social movements. In the analysis, the authors refer to a specific context and kind of product, namely food, which has recently been catalyzing an increasing number of concerns as expressed by consumers, eventually aggregating the interests of various social movements expressing new more ethical and sustainable market stances. In particular, the authors focus on the case of Eataly, a new venture that emerged from an ideological alliance and a mutual organizational commitment between corporate power and the Slow Food social movement. Eataly represents an interesting setting to better understand how such forms of collaboration can occur, how and to what extent the community and corporate stances mutually adjust during the process, and which types of reactions emerge from the more radical members of the social movement.

    Elena Candelo, University of Turin, Italy
    Cecilia Casalegno, University of Turin, Italy
    Chiara Civera, University of Turin, Italy

The chapter demonstrates the extent to which companies operating in the Retailing Grocery industry use Corporate Social Responsibility (CSR) as driver to enhance their brand and pursue commercial value, or to purely redefine their business priorities in accordance to evolving consumers' needs and expectations by making CSR a new concrete business model and evolving towards the concept of Corporate Shared Value (CSV). The study is addressed to analyse the matter of facts in two different European geographical areas: Italy and United Kingdom, chosen because of the peculiar approaches in companies' attitude towards CSR and CSV, ultimately. Many differences and some relevant similarities in the implementation of CSV as new strategic model between the countries have emerged, with UK showing the most formalized and standardized integration between social and economic value within its Grocer Retailer companies' business activities.

Section 4
Innovation, ICT, and Social Media: The Multichannelling Challenges for Retailers

The last section is about innovation, which for retailing is primarily in the field of Information and Communication Technologies (ICT) and the related social media development. The characteristics of ICT innovation are analyzed with reference to the effects of new social media on the interaction between retailers and consumers. Multichannelling emerges as one of the most relevant consequences of this evolution. Multichannelling and its implications for marketing, organization, and distribution strategies seems to be the next decade challenge for all the players involved in the consumer-retailer-producer interaction.

    Eleonora Pantano, University of Calabria, Italy & Eindhoven University of Technology, The
        Netherlands
    Harry Timmermans, Eindhoven University of Technology, The Netherlands

Continuous advancements in technology make available a huge number of advanced systems that enhance consumers' in-store experience and shopping activity. In fact, the introduction of in-store technologies such as self-service systems, interactive displays, digital signage, etc. has impacted the retail process in multiple ways, including client-vendor interactions. While in a traditional offline context retailers exploit the development of interpersonal relationships for increasing consumers' trust, loyalty, and satisfaction, in a technology-mediated context this process becomes more difficult. To advance our knowledge and predict the future diffusion of these technologies, it is necessary to answer the following questions: (1) to what extent do consumers trust (physical) retailers' suggestions? and (2) to what extent will consumers substitute the opinion of a physical seller with virtual recommendations? The aim of this chapter is to assess the typology of current existing relationships between vendor (retail staff) and clients, with special emphasis on consumers' trust towards their suggestions. To achieve this goal, the chapter focuses on a comparison of consumers' perception of suggestions proposed by physical friends and suggestions proposed online (e.g. through social networks). The findings provide a benchmark to evaluate current client-vendor and client-social networks relationships and enhance our understanding of the possible substitution of physical vendors by recommendations systems based on advanced technologies.

Irene Gil Saura, Universidad de Valencia, Spain
María Eugenia Ruiz Molina, Universidad de Valencia, Spain
Gloria Berenguer Contrí, Universidad de Valencia, Spain

Retailers have to operate in highly competitive environments, where innovation may become a source of sustainable competitive advantage. This chapter aims at exploring the relationship between retail innovativeness and the level of technological advancement as well as the ICT solutions implemented by store chains of four retail activities (e.g. grocery, textile, electronics, and furniture and decoration). In addition to this, the authors test the existence of significant differences in consumer perceptions and behavioral intentions between retailers perceived as high innovators and those considered low innovators. As a result, differences in consumer behaviour are found between high and low innovators that may be explained by the strong relationship between retail innovativeness and the technology implemented by the store. Notwithstanding, these findings are sensitive to the type of product sold by the store.

Sandro Castaldo, Bocconi University, Italy
Monica Grosso, EMLYON Business School, France

Internet merchants are compelled to collect personal information from customers in order to deliver goods and services effectively. However, the ease with which data can be acquired and disseminated across the Web has led to many potential customers demonstrating growing concerns about disclosing personal information. This chapter analyzes the interaction between two strategies that firms can use to alter potential customers' cost/benefit evaluation and increase information disclosure: the development of initial trust and compensation. The derived hypotheses are tested by means of two experimental studies, whose findings are compared across two different consumer target groups.

Francesca Negri, University of Parma, Italy

The Internet has revolutionized almost every facet of business and personal life. We are facing a far-reaching revolution, driven by Social Networking Sites (SNSs) where people talk about their life, purchases, and experiences. Mobile devices and tablets are replacing computers as the main access point to the Internet. Customer expectations are rising constantly with the development of new technologies. Social Media comes in many forms: blogs, media sharing sites, forums, review sites, virtual worlds, social networking sites, etc. Social Networking Sites (SNSs), the focus of this chapter, are the most disruptive social media and a key opportunity for business. Most industries recognized in that shift the potential for a more intimate and productive relationship with customers. Nowadays, retailers have no choice in whether they do social media: they only have the choice of how well they do it. Retailers need to convert browsers to buyers, and one-time customers to loyal sharing fans, so that they become advocates in the real and virtual worlds. The shift is deep: from one-way communication to conversation, and from advertising as an interruption to the interactivity in all locations. The originality of the chapter consists on its introduction of the concept of Social Networking Sites (SNSs) as an integration of the retailing marketing mix, defining its role in a marketing strategy, and providing some managerial implications for practitioners. After an introductive overview of the trend adopting a retailer point of view, four are the chapter's cornerstones: opportunities belonging from geolocation; how to plan a social media strategy; a new channel of interaction between customers and retailers: the social customer service; how to face a crisis in a Web 2.0 context. These are four brand new ways to engage consumers. This topic is relatively new and in continuous becoming, and much of interest remains to be said about it. The chapter's approach is to present what the authors believe to be the most relevant for a retailer facing a social networking challenge.

Ronan de Kervenoael, Sabanci University, Turkey & Aston University, UK
Alan Hallsworth, Portsmouth University, UK
David Tng, Singapore Institute of Management, Singapore

Geography, retailing, and power are institutionally bound up together. Within these, the authors situate their research in Clegg's work on power. Online shopping offers a growing challenge to the apparent hegemony of traditional physical retail stores' format. While novel e-formats appear regularly, blogshops in Singapore are enjoying astonishing success that has taken the large retailers by surprise. Even though there are well-developed theoretical frameworks for understanding the role of institutional entrepreneurs and other major stakeholders in bringing about change and innovation, much less attention has been paid to the role of unorganized, nonstrategic actors—such as blogshops—in catalyzing retail change. The authors explore how blogshops are perceived by consumers and how they challenge the power of other shopping formats. They use Principal Components Analysis to analyze results from a survey of 349 blogshops users. While the results show that blogshops stay true to traditional online shopping attributes, deviations occur on the concept of value. Furthermore, consumer power is counter intuitively found to be strongly present in the areas related to cultural ties, excitement, and search for individualist novelty (as opposed to mass-production), thereby encouraging researchers to think critically about emerging power behavior in media practices.

Multichannel integration in retailing is the ability of retailers to combine physical infrastructures (stores) and virtual channels (catalogues, Internet, and mobile shopping) in order to sell and distribute products and the related post-sales services. The purpose of this chapter is to investigate how shoppers perceive three different multichannel integration models in retailing: independent, database, and full-integrated models. The results of a qualitative enquiry and a quantitative survey reveal that when consumers choose among different multichannel retailers, the retailer's brand reputation, the experience with other shopping channels of the same retailer, and the Website design are the most cited factors influencing their purchasing decision. Even though findings disclose that respondents do not perceive multichannel integration as a driver of their shopping choices, the qualitative data indicates the existence of a respondents' attitude towards the multichannel integration, measured in this chapter through an exploratory and a confirmatory factor analysis in the quantitative survey.

Chapter 26

This chapter introduces the challenges that SMEs face while starting e-commerce activity in the Northern Finland context. Based on the project results, six interviews, and the preliminary outcomes of the questionnaire, this study focuses on push-pull effects to start e-commerce activities. Following this framework, the structure of this study is twofold. At first, the authors ask why a firm, which already has an existing traditional brick-and-mortar shop, would develop its business exploiting digital solutions and e-commerce. In other words, what is the attainable incremental value for this kind of firm via e-commerce? Second, what kinds of attractive possibilities will e-commerce provide for the business of the firm? Both of these perspectives are concentrated on the phase in which the firm takes in the use e-commerce activities. The authors study this phase, basing the analysis on the literature review, questionnaire, and six interviews of SME entrepreneurs. The outcomes of this chapter show the relevance of push-pull perspective in the studies about the first steps of e-commerce.

Foreword

Consumers are the most important people for any organization. They are the resources upon which the success of the businesses and other organizations depend. One of the primary goals of any retail marketing strategy should be to identify and meet the needs of the consumer. Considering consumer importance at all stages of the marketing process helps an organization to ensure greater consumer satisfaction and increase its long-term goal of repeat business.

Consumer satisfaction is at the heart of marketing. Studies over the year estimate that it costs five to ten times as much to attract new consumers as it does to keep an existing one. The relationship between the consumer and the organization is critical.

Developing good consumer relationships continues to be one of the major concerns for businesses around the world. The role and importance of providing consumer service continues to be emphasized by organizations of all sizes. Academic and practitioners alike continue to look for ways to measure and create better consumer service.

In the *Handbook of Research on Retailer-Consumer Relationship Development*, Fabio Musso and Elena Druica have edited the quintessential collection of research articles that address many of the major issues related to the study and practice of relationship between retailers and their consumers. They have brought together academics from all over the world to address the key issues for the development of successful relationships between retailers and their consumers for their different perspectives.

Section one of the book presents six chapters discussing how consumer behavior and buying preferences influence their relationships with retailers. Consumers' perceptions of value, self-congruity, well-being, and loyalty are a sample of some of the topics discussed in the initial section. The second section of the book is a series of works that examine the role of store formats and retails services on the consumer-retailer relationship. This section examines a wide variety of variables inside and outside (i.e., trees in a retail shopping area) of stores that influence the consumer experience.

The third section addresses a specific topic within a retail store that influences consumer behavior – its atmosphere. This chapter looks at attempts by retailers to enhance the consumers' experiences in the store by appealing to their senses, training employees to be unbiased when working with consumers, and showing consumers the retailers' commitment to social responsibility.

The final section of the text presents seven chapters that show how retailers can use technology to innovate in ways that improve their relationships with consumers. The integration of online sales and promotion within the traditional retail environment is the topic of five of the chapters.

Overall, this collection of writings from authors representing 15 different countries presents a diverse range of views on an important topic. It also shows the common need that exists for retailers to find ways to develop good relationships with their consumers to keep them happy and loyal.

Perry Haan
Tiffin University, USA

Perry Haan, *PhD, is Professor of Marketing and Entrepreneurship at Tiffin University in Tiffin, Ohio. Haan served as Tiffin University Dean of the School of Business from 2007-2010. Haan worked as a faculty member and administrator in higher education for the past 25 years. He has won teaching awards at three different institutions of higher learning. In 2010, he was awarded a Fellowship by the International American Association of Financial Management for his teaching and academic work in international markets. He has authored or co-authored over 60 peer-reviewed articles. He co-authored a textbook, Practical Statistics for Business. His research interests include entrepreneurship, international business, ethics, sales and sales management, education marketing, and sports marketing.*

Preface

Research on consumer behavior has traditionally focused on the analysis of decisions related to the choice of products or brand manufacturers. In more recent years, an increasing number of contributions considered this choice together with the choice of the point of sale and the retailer. Indeed, what consumers buy is a complex system of products and services, and a context in which they are delivered.

The relationship between consumers and retailers is based on economic factors, but a wide variety of non-economic elements exert an influence, both at the individual and the collective level. Interactions follow economic and social behavior norms, and social norms and codes of conduct change continuously, as a consequence of technology changes and cultural changes. Technology changes—particularly communication technologies—mainly refer to the Internet and social media development. Cultural changes refer to the convergence at the international level of income, lifestyles, and habits, on one side, and the increased mobility of people, on the other side, that favor the encounter and interaction between different cultures.

The shopping behavior is changing as well. Since shopping has become something more than a necessary activity—with leisure and entertainment components—new horizons to the development of enriched shopping experiences have been opened.

Retailers analyze and interpret such changes in a continuous effort aimed at identifying new markets and market segments. However, the responsive nature of retailers has not been emphasized. Whilst retailers operate with cultural norms and thus reflect these, they can also shape the cultural norms in many ways. Retailers' initiatives and environments are not neutral entities, and they can condition and structure consumers moods and behaviors and in some case can also influence cultural norms.

Modern techniques of retailing and new retail formats allow retailers to assume a more central role in consumers' concerns. The elements of the retail offer pay more attention to store design, ambience, and all those issues that have to do with the balance between price, service, and quality of purchased products, and also entertainment occasions for customers.

All the changes described above require an examination and updating of knowledge about the relationship between consumers and retailers. At the same time, the role of retailers must be analyzed following a multiple perspective according to issues related to consumers' behavioral dynamics, technology, communication codes and tools, social interaction, market knowledge, and social responsibility.

This book provides theoretical frameworks and the latest empirical research findings on the topics related to the changes that are occurring. Firstly, it is addressed to scholars who need an overview of the research field related to the retailer-consumer relationship in order to better contextualize their studies and receive suggestions for cross-disciplinary analyses. In addition, the book can be a tool for managers and entrepreneurs, both in the retail trade and the manufacturing sector, for upgrading their knowledge in the field and completing their perspective for a better approach to their reference markets.

Finally, the book can also be a valuable reference for local government agencies and public bodies who are in charge of the management of planning policies for the retail offer development and city center organization. This field is connected to the Town Center Management (TCM) area of interest, for which a complete knowledge of all the dynamics related to the retailer-consumer relationship is essential.

The book is divided into four sections.

The first section provides an overview of the key issues of consumers' behavior, analyzing the decision-making criteria for buying products in a context of relationships with the retailer. Together with the analysis of the main characters of consumer behavior, store loyalty, shopping experience, and the role of private label products are explored in light of consumer perceptions and changes.

The second section refers to the retail context, offering an overview of the way in which formats, retail environment, and locations are changing facing new consumers' expectations and values. The shopping activity as an experience to be enriched becomes the subject of new paradigms for the retailer to offer in the combination of products, services, entertainment, and environmental values whose importance is increasing.

In the third section, the store atmosphere and consumers' involvement in co-creation of the retail service are considered. Store atmosphere is analyzed for the way in which it exerts influence on consumers, considering sensorial factors, the relationship with salespeople, and even taking into account security issues inside stores. The consumer involvement is also analyzed regarding social responsibility and the emerging ethical issues.

The last section is about innovation, which for retailing is primarily in the field of Information and Communication Technologies (ICT) and the related social media development. The characteristics of ICT innovation are analyzed with reference to the effects of new social media on the interaction between retailers and consumers. Multichannelling emerges as one of the most relevant consequences of this evolution. Multichannelling and its implications for marketing, organization, and distribution strategies seems to be the next decade challenge for all the players involved in the consumer-retailer-producer interaction.

Chapter 1 introduces the section on consumers' behavior. The chapter titled "Customer Perceived Values and Consumer Decisions: An Explanatory Model," by Philip Y. K. Cheng, proposes an integrated value model to explain consumer decisions. The model comprises utilitarian, hedonic, and social values. It has three distinguishing features. First, the model segregates utilitarian, hedonic, and social values at the levels of products and marketing environment, respectively. Accordingly, the model can explain not only the homogeneous impact of shopping environment and marketing strategies on all the products under the same roof but also the willingness of consumers to pay higher price for the same products under a different marketing environment. Second, the model integrates all the contributing factors to the consumer decisions, which are individually identified, and their nature can be competing, complementary, or compensating. Third, the structure of the model is heteroarchical, while, since some of its dimensions are generated and interact serially, other dimensions could be generated and interact in parallel. The model provides a framework for empirical research to enhance greater understanding of the effectiveness, relative successes, and failures of various consumer marketing channels and strategies.

In Chapter 2, titled "Identity-Based Consumer Behaviour, Self-Congruity, and Retailer-Consumer Relationships: A Literature Review," Isabella Maggioni examines consumer-brand identification as an antecedent of the retailer-consumer relationship. Consumers show positive attitudes towards brands that reflect their self-concept and are more likely to express and enhance their identity. Similarly, consumer-retailer identification represents a tool for retailers to develop effective relationships by strengthening emotional connections with their customers. The chapter proposes a conceptual framework of consumer-retailer identification. The process of identification between a retailer and a customer assumes a particular connotation, and the interplay of multiple facets at different levels makes the process complex, with the store playing a key role.

The third chapter on "Shopping Well-Being and Ill-Being: Toward an Integrated Model" (by Dong-Jin Lee, Grace B. Yu, M. Joseph Sirgy, Ahmet Ekici, Eda Gurel-Atay, and Kenneth D. Bahn) makes an attempt to review and integrate the literature on shopping well-being and ill-being experiences. The study identifies the antecedents of these two constructs in terms of situational, individual, and cultural factors. The link between shopping well-being experiences and life satisfaction is explained using the bottom-up spillover theory. Satisfaction can be explained and predicted from satisfaction experienced within different life domains such as health, job, family, friends, community, material possessions, and shopping. Positive affective experiences related to shopping may be at the bottom of the satisfaction hierarchy. Shopping ill-being may adversely impact life satisfaction through the effects of compulsive shopping. Compulsive shopping causes a great deal of dissatisfaction in various life domains by usurping time, energy, and money from social life, family life, work life, spiritual life, community life. The managerial and policy implications of this integrated model are relevant. In order to increase consumer's experiences leading to shopping well-being, retailers could use the results of this analysis to develop specifically designed marketing programs. Public policy officials could also develop specific policies to encourage retailers to develop programs to increase shopping well-being and decrease shopping ill-being.

In chapter 4, Amalia Dutu analyzes consumers' behavior in a condition of economic crisis. Her chapter titled "Understanding Consumers' Behavior Change in Uncertainty Conditions: A Psychological Perspective" is intended to explain from an economic and psychological point of view the consumers' behavior alteration and spending patterns in recession conditions. Even if there are no two similar crises, and each crisis is a unique event considering generating factors, severity, evolution, outcomes, and duration, some general trends in the consumers' behavior alteration during recessions can be synthesized as follows: consumption reduction, increasing savings, migration on the demand curve, elimination/postponing of major purchases, brand loyalty shift, price priority/sensitivity, rationalization of expenses, changes in shopping places, aggressive search for options, and changing spending allocation. These alterations vary in intensity from one country to another and from one category of consumers to another in the frame of one national market.

Chapter 5 by Arturo Z. Vásquez-Parraga, Miguel Ángel Sahagún, and Pablo José Escobedo is on "Customer Store Loyalty: Process, Explanation Chain, and Moderating Factors." The chapter examines the process of how consumers become loyal to their stores. Following a theoretical and empirical research approach, findings reveal that customer commitment is the major contributor of explanation to customer loyalty, significantly more than the contributed explanation of customer satisfaction. The cognitive moderating factors (store familiarity, store choice, customer perceived risk, and communication) and the affective moderating factors (customer opportunistic tendencies, consumer involvement, shared personal values, and shared management values) are significantly related to the core variables and thus contribute some explanation. Yet, their influence is very small compared to the influence of the core variables. The key contribution of the research lies in the use of relational components (trust and commitment) in addition to transactional ones (satisfaction) and the moderating effects produced by cognitive and affective attitudes shaping or modifying the core process.

Chapter 6 by Elisa Martinelli and Donata Tania Vergura is the last chapter of the first section. The chapter, titled "Evolving the Private Label Role in the Retailer-Customer Relationship: Antecedents and Impact of Premium Private Labels on Customer Loyalty to the Retailer," focuses on the role played by private labels in the retailer-consumer relationship. The results of a survey conducted on a sample of grocery retail customers in Italy shows that premium private labels positively impact customer loyalty to the retailer through a causal relationship driven by product quality and value. Private labels emerge as a tool for strengthening the relationship with the customer, potentially acting as a vehicle for information about the value of the retailer over its competitors. This confirms the process of trading up of the private label in recent years and the role it has gained as a signal of reputation, credibility, and trust.

The second section of the book is on the retail context, store formats, and retail services. The section starts with chapter 7, authored by Barbara Borusiak and focused on "The Mechanisms for the Emergence and Evolution of Retail Formats." The chapter explains the mechanisms for rising and development of innovative formats on the basis of the existing format change theories. After exploring the nature of a retail format and presenting a classification of retail formats, the chapter analyses four groups of key theories (cyclical, conflict, environmental, and integrated) on the emergence and evolution of retail formats, focusing on two innovative formats: pop-up store and e-commerce.

Chapter 8 is titled "Critical Reflections on the Decline of the UK High Street: Exploratory Conceptual Research into the Role of the Service Encounter," by Jason J. Turner and Toni Gardner. The chapter addresses an important theme in Western countries' retailing, consolidating existing literature on the use of in-store technology to enhance the customer experience, and takes research forward in the area of the decline of the High Street and the role of customer service. The results from an exploratory research show that rather than being perceived as a threat to the High Street, the growth of online buying and customers' increased use of technology for purchasing products and services should be seen as a positive, enhancing the appeal and adding value to customers' High Street retail experience.

In chapter 9, Kathleen L. Wolf contributes knowledge about the "macro" level of consumer perception, the positive influence of the outdoor environment on buying behavior. The chapter, titled "City Trees and Consumer Response in Retail Business Districts," suggests that a quality urban forest helps to define retail place. Many marketing studies have focused on the "micro" level of product packaging and placement and indoor retail configuration. However, they failed to recognize the value of the external context in the streetscape. Yet, non-economic factors (such as atmospherics) appear to influence consumer behavior and choice on a subconscious level. Study results suggest that higher price valuations are mediated by psychological inferences of district character and product quality. Thus, creating and stewarding an urban forest canopy may enhance revenues for businesses in retail districts that offer diverse products and services. Consumer purchases can provide both compensatory returns for district-wide costs of tree planting and maintenance, as well as revenue enhancement for individual businesses. Trees and landscapes can be significant elements in place marketing.

Patrizia de Luca and Giovanna Pegan, authors of chapter 10 ("The Coffee Shop and Customer Experience: A Study of the U.S. Market"), contribute to improve understanding of the in-store customer experience in the retail environment by analyzing the business of coffee shops in the United States market with a specific focus on American and Italian chains. The chapter outlines the features of the U.S. coffee shop landscape and explores American consumers' perception of the coffee shop experience using nethnography. Results show a complex framework according both to the offer and the demand perspective that could also contribute to supporting coffee companies in managing customer experience strategies in the American market.

Chapter 11, titled "A New Systems Perspective in Retail Service Marketing," focuses on a service view to interpret the main issues related to retail marketing. Sergio Barile and Marialuisa Saviano highlight the need of a change in perspective and a new approach to retail marketing by rethinking the market exchange logic using a service view. A gap in the theoretical approach emerges that can be covered by adopting a Viable Systems Approach and a structure-system interpretation scheme.

In chapter 12, Ana Isabel Jiménez-Zarco, María Pilar Martínez-Ruiz, and Alicia Izquierdo-Yusta ("Personally Engaged with Retail Clients: Marketing 3.0 in Response to New Consumer Profiles") examine how social and economic changes of recent years have led to a new consumer profile. The chapter explores how current responsible concerns regarding consumption, as well as a greater concern for welfare sustainability and the environment, are affecting purchasing behavior. On these bases, the chapter focuses on how organizations have to evolve towards a new marketing paradigm in order to link to their customers emotionally. In this regard, the evolution of the marketing concept is reviewed in order to understand how the so-called Marketing 3.0 paradigm emerged. According to this new paradigm, companies are no longer freelance fighters but are an organization that acts as part of a loyal network of partners, where people are not just consumers. Indeed, new technologies and the development of the Internet and social networks have enabled consumers to freely express their experiences as active part of the communication system between manufacturers, retailers, and their respective markets.

Section 3 offers an overview on store atmosphere and the interaction with consumers. In the first part (chapters 13 to 16), issues related to the store atmosphere are analyzed. The last 3 chapters of the section focus on the interaction with consumers with reference to elements related to social responsibility and ethical/social values.

Chapter 13, by Sanda Renko, discusses "Atmosphere as a Store Communication Tool." The chapter provides a conceptual framework for studying the influence of store atmosphere on store patronage. The key dimensions that constitute conventional retail store atmosphere are presented, and the chapter clarifies the manipulation of elements such as color, lighting, signage, etc. within the store to communicate and exert influence on customers. The topic is investigated from both retailers` and customers` perspectives. The contribution of the study to current literature is that there is no ideal model of store atmosphere to be followed by retail managers. The possible methods that can help retailers in making store atmosphere decisions are related to prototyping, which is testing customers` acceptance of specific store environment before it is adopted throughout the whole retail chain; computer-assisted design, based on the contribution of ideas and proposals by store planners, customers, executives etc.; lab experiments, based on the subjects` response to verbal descriptions of a store in a lab setting; and videotape and slides methods to manipulate retail environments.

In the same field of store atmosphere is chapter 14 ("The Use of Sensorial Marketing in Stores: Attracting Clients through their Senses), by which Mónica Gómez Suárez and Cristina García Gumiel present a state-of-the-art of the literature referring to the use of sensorial marketing within the store. For this purpose, an interdisciplinary review of the theoretical and empirical works related to this discipline has been carried out. Results show that consumers need to feel involved and to be part of the purchasing process. When customers feel involved, they state to have an additional value. This bring one to the conclusion that the more power a company provides to its customers and the more it takes care of them, the better it is perceived.

In chapter 15, Miriam Palmeira analyses whether frontline employees in retail services perceive themselves as having feelings of sexism, ageism, and appearance discrimination against customers. In her chapter titled "Frontline Employees' Self-Perception of Ageism, Sexism, and Lookism: Comparative Analyses of Prejudice and Discrimination in Fashion and Food Retailing," the author presents a quantitative study of frontline employees working in fashion and food retailing. More than 95% of female and more than 64% of male attendants believe that well-dressed, young female customers are given priority when being served. Almost 80% of female and only 58% of male frontline workers believe that badly dressed, middle-aged men (not younger men) are the last to be served when there is no clear queuing process in the retail spatial area. This context strongly suggests the growing importance of an interpersonal skills training process for an organisations' staff as a way of avoiding behaviours that make the customers think that there is prejudice and discrimination in the service process.

Chapter 16, titled "A Dilemma for Retailers: How to Make Store Surveillance Secure and Appealing to Shoppers," by Angelo Bonfanti, proposes a conceptual framework that highlights how retailers can make store surveillance simultaneously secure and appealing to shoppers. Retailers use a number of ambient, design, and social elements with the aim of creating a unique, pleasant, and engaging customer-shopping experience. However, a store may be made less attractive in presence of feelings of insecurity or, on the opposite side, excessive control. As a result, retailers have to balance their efforts to enhance a store's attractiveness by ensuring a high level of sales environment surveillance without interfering with the shopping experience. The analysis is based on theoretical evidence in the marketing, environmental psychology, service and retail management literature, and indicates that retailers' investments in store design, staff training, and technological systems can ensure adequate security levels without compromising customers' shopping experiences.

The chapter by Janice Rudkowski (chapter 17, "Retailer-Non-Profit Organization (NPO) Partnerships: Building Trust with Socially Conscious Consumers") explores how and why strategic retailer-non-profit organization partnerships have an impact on the relationship between retailer and consumer, how they shape and influence socially conscious shoppers, and how they affect consumer trust as well as retail business practices and strategies. The chapter highlights the way in which partnerships have influenced socially conscious shoppers and the shopping environments. In some cases, they have completely transformed the retailer-led business model into a consumer-led business model. Thus, consumers' sphere of influence can involve product assortment and price, and can extend itself to sourcing, product development, and community involvement. Retailer-NPO partnerships are no longer just a strategy to generate more revenue, being part of the firm's broader Corporate Social Responsibility plan to build consumer loyalty, operate an ethical business, offer ethical and sustainable product choices, and support local and national communities.

The relationship with external ethical movements is also analyzed in chapter 18 ("Engaging Social Movements in Developing Innovative Retail Business Models") by Roberta Sebastiani and Francesca Montagnini. This chapter explores the outcomes in terms of new retail formulas derived from the interaction between retailers and engaged consumers. Results of a study based on a case study show that there is room for a coordinated effort between corporate power and collective stances, mediated by social movements. The case analyzed offers fruitful suggestions for existing retailers to rethink their business models, aligning them to the critical stances expressed by socially conscious consumers.

Chapter 19, titled "Meanings and Implications of Corporate Social Responsibility and Branding in Grocer Retailers: A Comparative Study over Italy and the UK," by Elena Candelo, Cecilia Casalegno, and Chiara Civera, considers the extent to which companies operating in the grocery retail industry use Corporate Social Responsibility as a driver to enhance their brand and redefine business priorities according to the emerging consumers' needs and expectations. The resulting business model evolves towards the concept of Corporate Shared Value (CSV).

The last section of the book is about innovation, whose characteristics are analyzed with reference to the effects of new social communication technologies on the interaction between retailers and consumers. Multichannelling emerges as one of the most relevant consequences of this evolution.

In chapter 20, Eleonora Pantano and Harry Timmermans present "An Exploratory Study of Client-Vendor Relationships for Predicting the Effects of Advanced Technology-Based Retail Scenarios." The aim of the chapter is to assess the typology of current relationships between vendor (retail staff) and clients facing the introduction of in-store technologies such as self-service systems, interactive displays, etc. Findings provide a benchmark to evaluate current client-vendor and client-social network relationships and enhance understanding of the possible substitution of physical vendors by recommendations systems based on advanced technologies.

Irene Gil Saura, María Eugenia Ruiz Molina, and Gloria Berenguer Contrí explore in chapter 21 ("Retail Innovativeness: Importance of ICT and Impact on Consumer Behaviour") the relationship between information and communication technologies innovation within retail businesses and consumer behavior. Results provide evidence about the influence of retail innovativeness on consumer behavior, enabling the identification of the most influencing technologies on customer perceptions.

Chapter 22 by Sandro Castaldo and Monica Grosso, titled "Retailer-Customers Relationships in the Online Setting: An Empirical Investigation to Overcome Privacy Concerns and Improve Information Sharing," investigates the effect of trust and compensation on information sharing, which is a prerequisite for the adoption of many new technologies. By means of two experimental studies, the authors analyze the interaction between two strategies that firms can use to alter potential customers' cost/benefit evaluation and increase information disclosure: the development of initial trust and compensation. The results show the key role of trust in increasing information sharing with e-vendors and behavioral differences between the target groups. Thanks to this study, marketers may gain a clear picture on how to manage their customer relationships in contexts where technologies actually reduce the direct contact between the firm and the client, at least in the traditional form based on interpersonal interaction.

The subject of chapter 23 is "Retail and Social Media Marketing: Innovation in the Relationship between Retailers and Consumers," by Francesca Negri. The chapter introduces the concept of Social Networking Sites as an integration of the retailing marketing mix, defining their role in a marketing strategy, and providing some managerial implications for practitioners. Mobile devices and tablets are replacing computers as the main access point to the Internet. Customer expectations are rising, supported by the development social media: blogs, media sharing sites, forums, review sites, virtual worlds, social networking sites, etc. Retailers need to convert browsers to buyers and one-time customers to loyal sharing fans so that they become advocates in the real and virtual worlds. The shift is deep: from one-way communication to conversation, and from advertising as an interruption to the interactivity in all locations.

A focus on blogshops is shown in chapter 24 by Ronan de Kervenoael, Alan Hallsworth, and David Tng. In their chapter titled "Singapore's Online Retail Deviants: Analyzing the Rise of Blogshops' Power," the authors analyze the role of unorganized, nonstrategic actors, such as blogshops, in catalyzing retail change. They explore how blogshops are perceived by consumers and how they challenge the power of other shopping formats. The results from a survey on a sample of consumers show that blogshops stay true to traditional online shopping attributes. Furthermore, consumer power is counter-intuitively found to be strongly present in the areas related to cultural ties, excitement, and search for individualist novelty (as opposed to mass-production), thereby encouraging researchers to think critically about emerging power behavior in media practices.

Chapter 25 introduces the concept of multichannelling. Daniela Andreini and Giuseppe Pedeliento in their chapter titled "Is Multichannel Integration in Retailing a Source of Competitive Advantage? A Consumer Perspective" analyze the conditions in which retailers combine physical infrastructures (stores) and virtual channels (catalogues, Internet, and mobile shopping) in order to sell and distribute products and related services. The chapter investigates how shoppers perceive 3 different multichannel integration models in retailing: independent, database, and full-integrated models. The results reveal that when consumers choose among different multichannel retailers, the retailer's brand reputation, the experience with other shopping channels of the same retailer, and the Website design are the most influential factors for purchasing decision.

On the same issue of multichannelling is chapter 26 ("About the Challenges to Start E-Commerce Activity in SMEs: Push-Pull Effects," by Rauno Rusko and Joni Pekkala). The authors analyze the challenges faced by small and medium enterprises while starting e-commerce activity, pointing out the need to combine existing traditional brick-and-mortar shops with digital solutions and e-commerce for selling products.

There are a lot of books related to relationship marketing, customer relationship management, consumer behavior, retailing, and retail management. All these fields are usually covered with reference to business-to-business relationships, to information management tools, or with perspectives limited to specific issues (e.g. consumer behavior, retailing, marketing information system, etc.). A broader view of the relationship between retailers and final consumers is missing, although it is treated as a complementary aspect. Since this book is putting together several perspectives that can be used for analyzing the retailer-consumer relationship, it covers a gap in this area, which is of interest both to retailers and manufacturers. This may stimulate the search for greater integration of these perspectives in future research, stimulating inter/multi-disciplinary approaches.

Fabio Musso
University of Urbino, Department of Economics, Society and Politics (DESP), Italy

Elena Druica
University of Bucharest, Department of Economic and Administrative Sciences, Romania

Acknowledgment

We are very grateful to many people who have been helping during the editorial work.

First, we want to thank to IGI Global for accepting this book. We don't know many of the people who evaluated our project and who made it possible for the handbook to be released. Nevertheless, we would like to mention them and express our gratitude for their support.

We would like to thank all the authors we accepted to be part of this project. They interpreted the book guidelines with great expertise and professionalism, offering analysis perspectives of great interest and full of stimuli.

A special thanks goes to the members of the Editorial Advisory Board, among whom are international experts. We are honored to have had the opportunity to collaborate with them in this project, and we are grateful to all of them for having trusted in our initiative.

We are also grateful to all the reviewers who contributed, providing to all authors useful suggestions about their manuscripts.

A special mention goes also to Erin O'Dea, Jan Travers, Kayla Wolfe, and Brett Snyder, from IGI Global for their qualified support and assistance during the whole process of publication.

We were fortunate to have Perry Haan as a collaborator. Perry provided us with an integrated vision about this book, and his involvement and support are invaluable.

Finally, we would like to thank ourselves for having worked together with the aim to give a significant contribution to knowledge in the field of retailer-consumer relationships. We are not in the position to judge whether we have achieved this goal, but we are sure that the result of our teamwork was greater than the simple sum of efforts that each of us would have been able to bear individually.

Fabio Musso
University of Urbino, Department of Economics, Society and Politics (DESP), Italy

Elena Druica
University of Bucharest, Department of Economic and Administrative Sciences, Romania

Section 1
Consumers' Behavior, Buying Preferences, and Relationships with Retailers

This section offers an overview of the key issues on consumer behavior, highlighting the decision-making criteria for buying products in a context of relationships with the retailer. Together with the analysis of the main characters of consumer behavior, store loyalty, shopping experience, and the role of private label products are explored in light of consumer perceptions and changes.

Chapter 1
Customer Perceived Values and Consumer Decisions:
An Explanatory Model

Philip Y. K. Cheng
Australian Catholic University, Australia

ABSTRACT

Building on findings from previous research on dimensions of Consumer Perceived Values (CPVs), an Integrated Consumer Perceived Value Model comprising utilitarian, hedonic, and social values is proposed to explain observed consumer decisions (viz. purchase or do not purchase), and to provide new frontiers for consumer behaviour research. The distinguishing if not innovative features of the proposed model are: (1) it provides a framework to investigate the competing, complementary, and compensating effects of the CPV dimensions; (2) it distinguishes the CPV dimensions that affect consumer decisions specifically and those that affect consumer decisions homogeneously; and (3) while some CPVs are generated and interact serially, other CPVs could be generated and interact in parallel.

INTRODUCTION

In the past decades, much of the consumer perceived value (CPV) and shopping motivation studies have investigated the CPV dimensions on consumer behaviour, viz. the CPVs have been categorised into over 20 dimensions (Rintamaki *et al.*, 2006; and Davis and Dyer, 2012 have provided surveys on these CPV dimensions). Interestingly, in spite of these developments, there is very limited literature if at all explaining consumer decisions with these CPV dimensions. Imagine this scenario. In cutting her hair, Lady A sometimes goes to a corner barber shop where the cost of a hair cut is $30. At other times, she goes to a boutique hairdresser where the cost of a hair cut is $150. How could we explain consumer decisions like this with CPV dimensions? This is the objective of the chapter, integrating utilitarian, hedonic and social CPV dimensions into a model to explain consumer decisions. These CPV dimensions have competing, complementary and compensating effects against one another; the model captures the interaction effects of these CPV dimensions, and explains consumer decisions accordingly.

DOI: 10.4018/978-1-4666-6074-8.ch001

The remainder of the chapter is organised as follows. The value concepts in consumer behaviour are first discussed, as an introduction to the utilitarian, hedonic and social values within the CPV context. Supplemented by illustrative examples, a model is then proposed to analyse consumer decisions, together with explanations of its distinguishing features and applications. Managerial implications of the model and future research directions are discussed before the conclusion.

In the context of this chapter, the term *product* encompasses both tangible products (e.g. a car, a computer, a handbag) and intangible products (viz. services such as air travel; tennis lessons; a plumber fixing a gas leak in a residential property).

BACKGROUND

Origins and Concepts of Customer Perceived Values

There could be various origins of the CPV concepts. The economic concept of experienced utility, the utility associated with pleasures of consumption or from total wealth, dated back to Daniel Bernoulli and Jeremy Bentham, could be one. Dewey's theory of valuation (1939, 1966) could be another, as Davis and Dyer (2012) explain. "Under Dewey's rubric, value flows from the fulfilment (solution) of human needs and wants. In a consumer application of this theory, the needs and wants of consumers, as they actually are and as they perceived them, motivate them to enter the marketplace for experiences and acquisitions that may result in fulfilment of those needs and wants – or what Dewey viewed as a solution seeking. When that fulfilment occurs, whether actual or perceived, the consumer then develops a value perception of the experience that is associated with the needs and wants that motivated the foray into the marketplace. That value perception feeds back into the consumer's subsequent consumption experiences" (Davis & Dyer, 2012, p. 117).

Thus, the concept of value has been playing a dominant role in explaining consumer behaviour. However, a precise definition of "value" is elusive; value conceptualizations also vary according to context. In the context of consumer behaviour, there are at least four common notions of the term "value" (Zeithaml, 1988). The simplest and common conceptualization simply equates value with price. The second and third value conceptualizations highlight the exchange process between buyers and sellers: the former represents the trade-off between costs and benefits; while the latter is more specific and sophisticated, and expresses value as a trade-off between perceived product quality and price. The fourth value conceptualization is all inclusive, equating value with an overall assessment of subjective worth of all factors that make up the complete shopping experience, not simply product acquisition. This is the value concept adopted for this chapter, and as many other researchers have done, we call this consumer perceived value (CPV).

However, this concept of CPV is too vague and general to explain consumer decisions. Therefore, as introductory and background reference, we first and briefly (i) outline the history of consumer perceived value (CPV); and (ii) explain the concepts of utilitarian, hedonic and social values, the three general but inclusive dimensions of CPV. Then, we introduce the Integrated Consumer Perceived Value Model with an embedded definition of CPV for consumer decisions.

THE CONSUMER PERCEIVED VALUE

Consumer Perceived Value Research: A Historical Perspective

Consumer behaviour studies probably start with the traditional product-acquisition explanations (e.g. Bloch & Richins, 1983). Understandably, if we still assume today that consumer decisions are based exclusively on the merits of goods and services concerned, given the sophistication of the marketing and shopping strategies that have been prevalent in the past decades, we are ignoring many other attributes and we would fail to provide realistic and adequate explanations for consumer behavior. Consequently, researchers like Babin *et al.,* (1994) segregate CPV into the concepts of utilitarian value and hedonic value, as one of the first steps to overcome the deficiencies of the simplistic product-acquisition approach. Some researchers go a bit further, and introduce the third CPV dimension of social value (e.g. Rintamaki *et al.,* 2006). Naturally, CPVs can be investigated from different perspectives, and at various depths. Rintamaki *et al.,* (2006) and Davis and Dyer (2012) have identified over 20 CPV dimensions in their surveys. For example, Sheth *et al.,* (1991) claim that consumer choice is a consequence of five independent values: functional value; social value; emotional value; epistemic value; and conditional value. Davis and Dyer (2012) propose that CPV is comprised of exchange value; personal value; and social value. Are there much differences between (i) utilitarian value on one hand, functional value, conditional value, and exchange value on the other; and (ii) hedonic value on one hand, emotional value, epistemic value, and personal value on the other? We do not think so. It seems that whatever these CPV dimensions are called, they are either the various attributes of the broad categories of *utilitarian value, hedonic value* and *social value*, respectively; or they are the same utilitarian value, hedonic value and social value identified under different terms. Therefore, for the purpose of introducing a homogeneous model to explain consumer decisions and to provide a framework for future research, we adopt a parsimonious approach – we consider the CPV dimensions that have been identified in past literature could be inclusively categorized under the general concepts of utilitarian value, hedonic value and social value, *per sec.* In another words, these three broad concepts are adequate to explain most if not all consumer behaviour that have been observed.

These three concepts – utilitarian value, hedonic value and social value – are briefly summarized and illustrated as follows. Readers are referred to the literature suggested in the Additional Reading Section for more detailed discussions and examples.

Utilitarian Value (Homo Economicus)

Under this concept, purchases and shopping experiences are the means to meet predefined ends; the motivations are primary necessity rather than recreation, as consumers seeking to satisfy their physical needs. Products like food, clothing, shelter, medical care, and electrical appliances are examples that reflect utilitarian values most. Purchase is not always necessary, as merely collecting information or surveying also generate utilitarian values.

Utilitarian values also illustrate the basic attributes of buying and selling, exchange or trading (Davis & Dyer, 2012). Price rather than quality is the primary factor in the assessment of *acquisition value.* Bargains and discounts best illustrate *transaction value.* *Efficiency value* addresses the issues of time, effort and convenience in shopping. *Choice value,* as the term implies, refers to the range of products and services available for shopping. Attempting to realize these four values, most utilitarian shoppers would strive for fastidious and consequent successful shopping. In summary, utilitarian consumer behavior can be described as deliberate, ergic, task-related, and rational, according to some scholars, Batra and Ahtola (1991), for example. One might have doubts whether a consumer is always rational and aware of what is being purchased. Still, among the utilitarian, hedonic and social CPV dimensions, consumers would be most rational in the utilitarian dimensions, relatively.

Hedonic Value (Homo Ludens)

In simplest and idealistic terms, a hedonic shopper is a person who strives for maximum net pleasure (pleasure less pain) under the given constraints. Pleasures could be for self or extended to third parties. Pleasures could also be for (i) the body and senses (e.g. chocolates; dining out; visit of brothels); (ii) the heart (e.g. buying and giving presents away as expressions of love, care, and gestures of appreciation); and (iii) the mind (e.g. going to movies and concerts; artworks; buying and wearing aesthetic jewellery to show off one's wealth and possibly social status; buying and wearing clothes outfit to show off one's attractive features of the body). If the cost of a product is considered as "pain"; then a hedonist shopper is also a utilitarian shopper from the perspective of "value for money," but with relatively more emphasis on the hedonist aspects. Understandably, if the emphasis on hedonist aspects is excessive, a hedonist shopper could over indulge in pleasures, with unfavourable consequences, physically (e.g. getting sick), financially (e.g. getting money inappropriately to sustain pleasures), and otherwise (e.g. becoming a lotus eater).

From another perspective, as illustrated by impulsive and compulsive shopping, hedonic values could be more associated with the act of shopping than the items purchased. Shopping as means of stress relief, escapism (e.g. air conditioned malls are more popular during hot days, especially in developing countries), giving oneself an instant "treat," etc, are further examples that illustrate the relative significance of the act of shopping versus the items purchased. Even without purchasing, purposeful, relaxing and pleasant shopping experiences could still provide hedonic values: one can satisfy a fantasy during window shopping by imagining what one can buy when having the money, for example. In summary, hedonic values associate with one's senses, feelings, generation of positive emotions and mitigation of negative emotions.

Social Value (Homo Faber)

We believe the following phenomenon, which is not uncommon in many developed countries, reflects the essence of (i) social value in shopping; and (ii) consumer societies. A housewife of a migrant family lives in a suburb that is highly populated by her countrymen. She could not speak the language of the country she resides in. Utilitarian shopping among the corner shops where both the sellers and customers speak her native language is the social highlight of her normal days. The items in these shops are probably more expensive than the equivalent items in the shops where only the local language is spoken, and where the clientele is more local than foreign. Yet, the housewife is willing to pay for the higher prices, as these corner shops are the centres of her outside-the-family social activities, and she feels most at home in such marketing circumstances. This corner shop environment illustrates the interactive dimension of the social values in shopping at one end of the spectrum. At the other end of the spectrum are the shopping centres with good varieties of shops, food outlets, supermarkets, cinemas, medical centres, etc, that are accessible by public transport and/ or ample parking is available. These shopping centres provide one-stop, convenient social arenas where people can meet, new friends can make, and where families can combine their shopping and leisure activities under one roof.

Apart from social interactions, social status and self esteem are the other two dimensions of social values in shopping. Some shoppers would buy only from departmental stores and not from discount stores or mass merchandisers, even though the items are exactly the same (e.g. refrigerators and washing machines of the same brands), and are cheaper with the latter. Usually or expectedly, shop assistants in departmental stores are more presentable and offer better quality customer services. The shopping ambience of departmental stores is more appealing than that of discount stores in some aspects. While these tangible differences do offer shoppers comparative appeals to buy from departmental stores, they are not all. It cannot be denied that some of the exclusive departmental shoppers are conscious of their social status and self esteem – how they like to be seen, how they like to see themselves, the identities they attempt to assign to themselves (e.g. many shoppers have the conviction that patrons of departmental stores primarily come from upper income groups, while discount stores tend to attract lower-income consumers), and the symbolic features that shopping in prestige departmental stores and boutique shops represent. In summary, the social values in shopping carry significant personal meanings and interests, on top of utilitarian and hedonic values.

The social dimensions of CPV just explained are at a micro, individualistic level; there are macro aspects as well. The example of the migrant housewife in the beginning of this section is also an example of ethnic or cultural shopping; the corner shops and their patrons are "communities" which are or can serve as agents for social integration and channels of information dissemination. These macro implications of the social dimensions of CPV would be discussed at a later section of *The Proposed CPV Model and Managerial Implications*.

An Integrated Consumer Perceived Value Model

As indicated in the Introduction, the objective of this chapter is to propose an Integrated Consumer Perceived Value (CPV) Model to explain consumer decisions, and to provide a framework to conduct CPV research in a new frontier. More specifically, the model can explain consumer phenomena like: (i) a consumer who normally shops in departmental stores buys a product from a mass merchandiser on an exceptional basis; (ii) a consumer who likes the product and has the money to buy it foregoes the purchase at the end; and (iii) a product can be sold in a brick and mortar store but not via an on-line marketing channel.

As the name implies, the Integrated Consumer Perceived Value (CPV) Model integrates utilitarian values, hedonic values, and social values into an aggregate, upon which the purchase decision is based on. The model is conceptualised in the form of a structural equation as follows:

Integrated Consumer Perceived Value of consumers towards a particular product (ICPV) = $\sum \pm$
Consumer Perceived Value associated with each of the characteristics of the product $(P_i) + \sum \pm$
Consumer Perceived Value associated with each of the characteristics of the marketing environment (M_j)

Each of the characteristics of the product and its marketing environment would have a utilitarian, a hedonic and a social CPV simultaneously, and are identified by subscripts i (for product) and j (for marketing environment). By giving each of these characteristics a separate CPV identity for its utilitarian, hedonic and social dimension, respectively, it is then feasible to consider interaction effects of the CPV dimensions and their contributions to the ultimate consumer decision. If a consumer finds a particular characteristic of the product or its marketing environment appealing in the utilitarian, hedonic or social CPV dimension, the corresponding CPV would be positive, and higher the value the more appealing the characteristic is. If a consumer finds a particular characteristic annoying or disappointing, the corresponding CPV would be negative. The CPV would be zero if the consumer finds the characteristic indifferent.

The positive and negative signs of the CPVs have two meanings. First, positive means that the characteristic increases the likelihood that the product would be purchased in the marketing environment being sold. Negative means that the characteristic decreases the likelihood that the product would be purchased. Second, the positive and negative signs reflect the competing, complementary and compensating natures of the

CPVs relative to one another. If two CPVs have the same sign (positive or negative), they are complementary with each other. If two CPVs have opposite signs, viz. one CPV has a positive sign and the other CPV has a negative sign, the CPV that has a positive sign is compensating the CPV with a negative sign. Alternatively, the CPV with a negative sign is competing with the CPV that has a positive sign. In all cases, a consumer would purchase the product only if the Integrated Consumer Perceived Value (i) is positive; and (ii) equals or is greater than the perceived value of the price. If a consumer is choosing an item from a choice set, the consumer would purchase the item with the biggest positive differential between the Integrated Consumer Perceived Value and the perceived value of its price.

Most of the CPV models have either a strictly hierarchical structure (e.g. Zeithmal, 1988; Rintamaki *et al.*, 2006) or a flat, sequential progression (e.g. Davis & Dyer, 2012). These structures imply that, categorically, one CPV dimension comes before another, or one CPV dimension is more fundamental or important (at least in terms of rankings) than the other. We are of the opinion that such interpretation of the relationships between CPV dimensions might not necessarily be true, realistic or practical, for reasons like whether we can assume all consumers are homogeneous in their decision criteria, and whether empirical validation of such interpretations are feasible. Accordingly, we propose a heteroarchical structure – we assume that each CPV dimension has the same "horizontal" position and authority, and has a theoretically equal role. The relative importance of each CPVs to the consumer decision is reflected by its contribution to the Integrated Consumer Perceived Value upon which the consumer's decision is based. The heteroarchical structure also means that while some of the CPVs could be generated and interact serially, while other CPVs could be generated and interact in parallel (viz. simultaneously).

The concept and structure of the Integrated Consumer Perceived Value Model have a number of implications. First, it explains how each of the (i) characteristics of the product; and (ii) characteristics of the marketing environment, jointly with other characteristics, has contributed to the Integrated Consumer Perceived Value and hence to the consumer decisions. Second, we are not proposing that the CPVs are represented by precise numerical values or mathematical functions. Rather, they can be fuzzy, qualitative and relative in nature. For example, Characteristic A of Product X can relate to consumers' fantasies, and therefore carries a higher hedonic CPV relative to that of Characteristic B of Product Y, which an individual can go without. Then, Product X would have a higher Integrated Consumer Perceived Value relative to that of Product Y, assuming all other things equal between the two products. Product X would then be purchased instead of Product Y. In summary, the concept of Integrated Consumer Perceived Value can add to the explanation and predictability of consumer decisions, over and beyond what individual CPVs can.

Illustrative Examples of the Integrated Consumer Perceived Value Model

In the Introduction, we ask how we could explain with CPV dimensions on consumer phenomenon like Lady A sometimes having a hair cut at the corner shop (where the cost of a hair cut is $30) and at other times with the boutique hairdresser (where the cost of a hair cut is $150). Now, we can offer an explanation to the phenomenon with the proposed model. On a particular day, Lady A just feels like having a no-frill hair cut, and considers that the CPV of a no-frill hair cut is say X. Lady A would go to the corner barber shop and not to the boutique hairdresser if X equals or is greater than $30 but less than $150. On another day, Lady A would attend a wedding reception in the evening. She would like an exquisite hair-do to be outstanding, and feels like being pampered by a hairdresser before the occasion. Lady A would go to the boutique hairdresser if she considers the CPV of having her hair-do done there is say Y, and Y equals or is greater than $150. Naturally, Y is also greater than $30, but Lady A would not go to the corner barber shop because the features associated with the CPV of Y are not available at the corner barber shop.

The following examples further illustrate how the model works with the competing, compensatory and complementary aspects.

(Positive) hedonic values associated with the product compete with the (negative) utilitarian values associated with the same product. "I like this dress, right colour and size for me. It brings out my best physical features. However, I cannot think of any occasions that I can wear the dress. Hence, it is not worth buying." In this case, the negative utilitarian values exceed the positive hedonic values. The Integrated Consumer Perceived Value is negative; hence there is no purchase.

(Positive) hedonic values associated with the product complement the (positive) social values associated with the marketing environment, and more than compensate the (negative) utilitarian values associated with the same product. "I like this dress, right colour and size for me. It brings out my best physical features. All my friends would know that this dress and the brand are only available in this shop where the rich and famous buy and then show-off their fashions. The occasions, if any, that I can wear this dress are very limited. Still, it is value for money even if I can wear this dress only once, just like the wedding dress." This illustration is an extension of the previous one. There is a purchase because both the hedonic and social values are positive, and their sum exceeds the negative utilitarian value, viz. a positive Integrated Consumer Perceived Value, which equals or is greater than the cost of the dress. The utilitarian value associated with the

dress is negative, because at the time of purchase, the buyer still does not know when she can wear the dress.

(Positive) utilitarian values associated with the product compensate the (negative) social values associated with the marketing environment. "I never buy from discount stores. I like the space, ambience and service from departmental stores. However, I will make an exception this time – the big discount this mass merchandiser offers on this new model of BBQ set is, I admit, very appealing." There is a purchase because the positive utilitarian values exceed the negative social values. The Integrated Consumer Perceived Value is positive, equals or is greater than the cost of the BBQ set.

The same model can also explain marketing phenomena like why a product can be sold in one marketing channel but not in the other, exclusively. Yet, when the product is sold in both marketing channels, the strengths of one marketing channel compensate the weakness of another marketing channel, and consequently with overall positive results. For example, many consumers would like to experience the aroma of a perfume before the first purchase. Such experience is feasible with a brick and mortar but not with an online marketing environment. Therefore, relative to the CPVs of a brick and mortar marketing environment, the CPVs of an online marketing environment are negative, so negative (suspicion on, privacy and security concerns over an online marketing channel would introduce negative CPVs) that they diminish the Integrated Consumer Perceived Value of the perfume to the extent that consumers would not purchase the perfume, if it is sold exclusively on line. In contrast, if the perfume is offered in a multi-channel shopping environment (e.g. both brick and mortar and online), the brick and mortar marketing environment offers (i) the trial of the perfume in person for the initial purchase; (ii) interactions with shop assistants and possibly with other patrons of the product; and if appropriate, (iii) fact to face and hence more speedy and effective complaints resolution. In contrast, the online marketing environment offers logistic convenience for subsequent purchases. Thus, the Integrated Consumer Perceived Value of the perfume is enhanced generally, and increases the likelihood that the perfume would be purchased in either marketing channel.

Managerial Implications

Perhaps, the most significant contribution of the proposed model is that it offers a framework for retailers, product manufacturers, and service providers to formulate their marketing strategies. With the framework, the scope of the strategies could go above and beyond the products themselves, their price and quality, and the marketing environment, on their own merits, into how one comparative weakness can be compensated by a comparative strength, and how two comparative strengths can complement each other to become a formidable strength. In another words, one does not have to compete on the same playing field as that of the competitors, but can specialise in a niche that one does best or has the most comparative advantage.

For example, consumers of the respective BIG FIVE Personalities (Neo Personality Inventory: openness to experience; conscientiousness; extroversion; agreeableness; neuroticism) would find the utilitarian, hedonic and social dimensions of the same products and marketing environments appealing in various degrees. Product manufacturers and service providers could create their brand personalities, and retailers could design their marketing environments, with particular combinations of utilitarian, hedonic and/or social CPV dimensions such that the consequent products and marketing environments appeal to targeted consumer personalities. Some of the classical examples of brand personalities matching consumer personalities are: (i) serious, intelligent, efficient; e.g. Mercedes Benz; (ii) rugged, tough, athletic; e.g. Adidas, Victoria Bitter beer; (iii) glamorous, romantic, sexy; e.g. Chanel; and (iv)

sophistication: upper class; charming; naturally high price; e.g. Louis Vuitton. As examples for marketing environments, a conservative departmental store with shop assistants wearing black and white uniforms and a trendy, no-frill retail outlet with rock and roll music reflect the same CPV dimensions at almost opposite ends of the spectrum, thus attracting different clientele. At individual levels, green conscious and price conscious consumers would assign different CPVs to the same CPV dimensions.

The contributions of the proposed model could also be demonstrated in two other perspectives.

First, comparative competition. A large discount store has cost and hence price (viz. primarily utilitarian CPV dimensions) advantages over a corner shop, because of economies of scale. However, a corner shop could exploit advantages along the social CPV dimensions with ethnic features for example. Accordingly, a corner shop could find it still viable to compete and sell the same product at a price higher that at a discount store.

Second, social contributions. Ethnic shopping contributes to communities generally in social integration and information dissemination to ethnic groups, a role traditionally undertaken by entities such as communities services providers and not-for-profit organisations. There are commercial incentives for retailers to provide ethnic shopping, as extra profits could be made from values added along the social CPV dimensions. At the same time, a government advocating multi-culturalism could provide additional incentives (e.g. subsidies or tax concessions) to promote ethnic shopping. In another words, retailers can assume a role in business and communities simultaneously.

FUTURE RESEARCH DIRECTIONS

In terms of explanatory power with respect to the apparent "irrational" consumer behaviour (e.g. impulsive and compulsive shopping) and other consumer phenomena, our proposed Integrated

Consumer Perceived Value Model is an extension of the study by Babin *et al.,* (1994), because of the incorporation of social values. In terms of refinement of utilitarian, hedonic and social values, our proposed model distinguishes these CPVs further at the levels of products and marketing environment, in comparison to the model by Rintamaki *et al.,* (2006). In contrast to Davis and Dyer's (2012) sequential CPV model and Rintamaki *et al.*'s (2006) hierarchical model, our proposed model offers a heteroarchical structure. Comparing to these three studies, our proposed model offers the concept of competing, complementary and compensating CPVs. This concept offers a more precise explanation of consumer behaviour than otherwise, viz. which of the three values – utilitarian, hedonic and social – is the determining or dominant factor in the observed consumer phenomenon, for example. Overall, the proposed model opens up new frontiers for consumer behaviour and retailer research, and humbly we offer three topics. First, investigate the competing, complementary and compensating effects of individual CPV dimensions relative to one other. For example, among supermarkets, big players have cost and hence price advantages over small players because of economies of scale and greater abundance in capital. What are the strategies along the hedonic and social CPV dimensions that the small players can adopt to fend off the predatory competition from the big players? Second, distinguish and identify how the effects of the CPV dimensions affect consumer behaviour heterogeneously (e.g. How would a green-conscious consumer and a price-conscious consumer react differently to a green version of a product that costs more relative to the original version?), and third, these CPV dimensions that affect consumer behaviour homogeneously (e.g. Music and games are homogeneous products, in the sense that both are compact discs and one compact disc is no different from another compact disc. What are the CPV dimensions that account for music and games equal successes in on-line sales?).

CONCLUSION

In this chapter, we propose an Integrated Consumer Perceived Value Model to explain consumer decisions as well as suggest new frontiers for consumer behaviour and retailer research. Although the model still employs the concepts of utilitarian, hedonic and social values as previous researchers have done, it has three distinguishing if not innovative features. First, the model segregates utilitarian, hedonic and social values at the levels of products and marketing environment, respectively. Accordingly, the model can explain not only the homogeneous impact of shopping environment and marketing strategies on all the products under the same roof, but can also explain the willingness of consumers to pay higher price for the same products under a different marketing environment, as illustrated by the examples provided earlier. Second, the concept of the proposed model acknowledges and integrates all the contributing factors to the consumer decisions, be they utilitarian, hedonic or social. These contributions are individually identified, and their nature can be competing, complementary or compensating. Consequently, the model can explain the interaction effects of the CPVs which otherwise would not be feasible. Third, the structure of the model is heteroarchical, while some of CPV dimensions are generated and interact serially, other CPV dimensions could be generated and interact in parallel. Thus, the model provides a framework for empirical research to enhance greater understanding of the effectiveness, relative successes and failures of various consumer marketing channels and strategies.

REFERENCES

Aaker, J. (1997). Dimensions of brand personality. *JMR, Journal of Marketing Research, 34*(3), 347–356. doi:10.2307/3151897

Babin, B., Darden, W., & Griffin, M. (1994). Work and/or fun: Measuring hedonic and utilitarian shopping value. *The Journal of Consumer Research, 20*(4), 644–656. doi:10.1086/209376

Batra, R., & Ahtola, O. (1991). Measuring the hedonic and utilitarian sources of consumer attitudes. *Marketing Letters, 2*, 159–170. doi:10.1007/BF00436035

Bloch, P., & Richins, L. (1983). Shopping without purchases: An investigation of consumer browsing behaviour. In R. Bagozzi, A. Tybout, & A. Arbor (Eds.), *Advances in consumer research* (pp. 389–393). Association for Consumer Research.

Costa, P. Jr, & McCrae, R. (1992). Normal personality assessment in clinical practice: The Neo Personality Inventory. *Psychological Assessment, 4*, 5–13. doi:10.1037/1040-3590.4.1.5

Davis, L., & Dyer, B. (2012). Consumers' value perceptions across retail outlets: Shopping at mass merchandisers and department stores. *International Review of Retail, Distribution and Consumer Research, 22*(2), 115–142. doi:10.1080/09593969.2011.634074

Dewey, J. (1939). Theory of valuation. In O. Neurath, R. Carnap, & C. Morris (Eds.), *International Encyclopedia of Unified Science* (pp. 1–67). Chicago, IL: The University of Chicago Press.

Dewey, J. (1966). *Theory of valuation.* Chicago, IL: The University of Chicago Press.

Rintamaki, T., Kanto, A., Kuusela, H., & Spence, M. (2006). Decomposing the value of department store shopping into utilitarian, hedonic and social dimensions: Evidence from Finland. *International Journal of Retail & Distribution Management, 34*(1), 6–24. doi:10.1108/09590550610642792

Sheth, J., Newman, B., & Gross, B. (1991). Why we buy what we buy: A theory of consumption values. *Journal of Business Research, 22*(2), 159–170. doi:10.1016/0148-2963(91)90050-8

Zeithaml, V. (1988). Consumer perceptions of price, quality, and value: A means-end model and synthesis of evidence. *Journal of Marketing, 52*(3), 2–22. doi:10.2307/1251446

ADDITIONAL READING

Arnold, M., & Reynolds, K. (2003). Hedonic shopping motivations. *Journal of Retailing, 79*(2), 77–95. doi:10.1016/S0022-4359(03)00007-1

Bloch, P., & Grady, B. (1984). Product Involvement as leisure behaviour. In T. Kinnera, & A. Arbor (Eds.), *Advances in Consumer Research* (pp. 197–202). MI: Association for Consumer Research.

Buttle, F., & Coates, M. (1984). Shopping motives. *The Service Industries Journal, 4*(1), 71–82. doi:10.1080/02642068400000007

Butz, H. Jr, & Goodstein, L. (1996). Measuring customer value: Gaining the strategic advantage. *Organizational Dynamics, 24*(3), 63–78. doi:10.1016/S0090-2616(96)90006-6

Chandon, P., Wansink, B., & Laurent, G. (2000). A benefit congruency framework of sales promotion effectiveness. *Journal of Marketing, 64*(4), 65–81. doi:10.1509/jmkg.64.4.65.18071

Cox, A., Cox, D., & Anderson, R. (2005). Reassessing the pleasures of store shopping. *Journal of Business Research, 58*(3), 250–259. doi:10.1016/S0148-2963(03)00160-7

Dodds, W., Monroe, K., & Grewal, D. (1991). Effects of price, brand, and store information on buyers' product evaluation. *JMR, Journal of Marketing Research, 28*(3), 307–320. doi:10.2307/3172866

Gale, B. (1994). *Managing customer value: Creating quality and service that customers can see.* New York, NY: The Free Press.

Hirschman, E., & Holbrook, M. (1982). Hedonic consumption: Emerging concepts, methods and propositions. *Journal of Marketing, 46*(Summer), 92–101. doi:10.2307/1251707

Holbrook, M., & Hirschman, E. (1982). The experiential aspects of consumption: Consumer fantasies, feelings, and fun. *The Journal of Consumer Research, 9*(September), 132–140. doi:10.1086/208906

Holbrook, M., & Hirschman, E. (1994). The nature of customer value: An axiology of services in the consumption experience. In R. Rust, & R. Oliver, (Ed.), Service Quality. New Directions in Theory and Practice (pp. 21-71). Sage, CA: Thousand Oaks.

Holbrook, M., & Hirschman, E. (1999). *Introduction to consumer value. Consumer Value: A Framework for Analysis and Research, Kegan Paul.* London: Routledge. doi:10.4324/9780203010679

Kantamneni, S., & Coulson, K. (1996). Measuring perceived value: Scale development and research findings from a consumer survey. *Journal of Marketing Management, 6*(2), 72–86.

Kim, S., & Chen-Yu, J. (2005). Discount store patronage: A comparison between South Korea and the United States. *Clothing & Textiles Research Journal, 23*(3), 165–179. doi:10.1177/0887302X0502300303

Mathwick, C., Malhotra, N., & Rigdon, E. (2001). Experiential value: conceptualization, measurement and application in the catalog and Internet shopping environment. *Journal of Retailing, 77*(1), 39–56. doi:10.1016/S0022-4359(00)00045-2

Mathwick, C., Malhotra, N., & Rigdon, E. (2002). The effect of dynamic retail experiences on experiential perceptions of value: An Internet and catalog comparison. *Journal of Retailing, 78*(1), 51–60. doi:10.1016/S0022-4359(01)00066-5

Monroe, K., & Chapman, J. (1987). Framing effects on buyers' subjective product evaluations. *Advances in Consumer Research. Association for Consumer Research (U. S.), 14*(1), 193–197.

Parasuraman, A., & Grewal, D. (2000). The impact of technology on the quality-value-loyalty chain: A research agenda. *Journal of the Academy of Marketing Science, 28*(1), 168–174. doi:10.1177/0092070300281015

Petrick, J. (2002). Development of a multi-dimensional scale for measuring the perceived value of a service. *Journal of Leisure Research, 34*(2), 119–134.

Pooler, J. (2003). *Why we shop: Emotional rewards and retail strategies.* Westport, CT: Praeger Publisher.

Ravald, A., & Gro¨nroos, C. (1996). The value concept and relationship marketing. *European Journal of Marketing, 30*(2), 19–30. doi:10.1108/03090569610106626

Sherry, J. Jr. (1990). Dealers and dealing in a periodic market: Informal retailing in ethnographic perspective. *Journal of Retailing, 66*(Summer), 174–200.

Sweeney, J., & Soutar, G. (2001). Consumer perceived value: the development of a multiple item scale. *Journal of Retailing, 77*(2), 203–220. doi:10.1016/S0022-4359(01)00041-0

Tauber, E. (1972). Why do people shop? *Journal of Marketing, 36*(4), 46–59. doi:10.2307/1250426

Terblance, N., & Boshoff, C. (2004). The in-store shopping experience: A comparative study of supermarket and clothing store customers. *South African Journal of Business Management, 35*(4), 1–10.

Tsai, S. (2005). Utility, cultural symbolism and emotion: A comprehensive model of brand purchase value. *International Journal of Research in Marketing*, *22*(3), 277–291. doi:10.1016/j.ijresmar.2004.11.002

Westbrook, R., & Black, W. (1985). A motivation-based shopper typology. *Journal of Retailing*, *61*(1), 78–103.

KEY TERMS AND DEFINITIONS

Consumer Decision: Decision by a consumer to purchase a product - tangible items (e.g. a fridge) or services (e.g. transportation).

Hedonic Value: A dimension of consumer perceived value associated with senses, pleasures, feelings, and emotions.

Heteroarchy: A network of elements in which each element has the same "horizontal" position and authority, and has a theoretically equal role. It is an antonym to hierarchy.

Integrated Consumer Perceived Value (ICPV): An all inclusive, abstract, aggregate value measure that a consumer perceived on a product and the marketing environment in which the product is sold. Integrated in the sense that the ICPV integrates or aggregates the utilitarian, hedonic and social values associated with the product and the marketing environment. The consumer will purchase the product if the ICPV (i) is positive; and (ii) equals or is greater than the perceived value of the price of the product.

Product: A generic term that include tangible items (e.g. a watch) and intangible services (e.g. medical care).

Social Value: A dimension of consumer perceived value associated with social interactions (particularly with those with common culture and language), social status and self esteem.

Utilitarian Value: A dimension of consumer perceived value associated with the necessities of living.

Chapter 2
Identity–Based Consumer Behaviour, Self–Congruity, and Retailer–Consumer Relationships:
A Literature Review

Isabella Maggioni
Monash University, Australia

ABSTRACT

Consumer-Brand Identification (CBI) has been identified as an important antecedent of consumer-brand relationships. Consumers show positive attitudes towards brands that reflect their self-concept and are more likely to express and enhance their identity. In this sense, Consumer-Retailer Identification (CRI) represents a powerful tool for retailers to develop meaningful relationships by strengthening emotional connections with their customers. This chapter proposes a literature review of previous research on the role of consumer's self-concept in the development of retailer-customer relationships. Focusing on identity-based consumer behaviour, the chapter provides a comprehensive picture of the past research and the emerging trends on CBI and then proposes a conceptual framework of CRI.

INTRODUCTION

Quoting Belk (1988), "we are what we have... our possessions are a major contributor to and reflection of our identities" (p. 139).

Besides providing functional benefits, brands enable experiential opportunities through their use (Holbrook, & Hirschmann, 1982; Arnould & Price, 1993). Through brands individuals can show something personal about them to others, but they can also answer to their inner desire to define themselves and to communicate who they are to the society (Shembri, Merrilees, & Kristiansen, 2010). Consumers have a natural affinity for brands that match at best their self- and social-identities and they are steadily involved in a matching process, aimed at identifying which brands are better consistent with their self-concept

DOI: 10.4018/978-1-4666-6074-8.ch002

(Sirgy et al., 1997; Sirgy et al., 2000; Reed et al., 2012; Chattaraman, Lennon, & Rudd, 2010). In particular, brands act twofold, expressing who a person is and revealing what groups a person belongs to and aligns with (Shembri, Merrilees, & Kristiansen, 2010). In this sense, brands play a key role in the communication of individuals' self-image (Belk, 1988; Arnould, & Thompson, 2005; Chattaraman, Lennon, & Rudd, 2010).

This customer-retailer identification process has been recognized to have a positive impact on both pre-purchase and post-purchase evaluations and behaviours and on the effective building and management of relationships with brands (Tuskej et al., 2013). It is argued that the identification of a customer with a retailer crucially impacts on retailer's success. Moreover, it has several managerial implications related to the promotion and to the communication of a retail brand based on the symbolic cues associated with desirable consumer identities.

Although the paramount attention given to identity-based consumption, the retail literature lacks in exploring this topic. This chapter aims at reviewing previous research on the role of consumer's self-concept in the development of brand-customer relationships, extending the consumer-brand identification theory to retail settings and proposing a theoretical framework for consumer-retailer identification. In particular, this chapter provides a comprehensive picture of the past research, as well as of the emerging trends in identity-based consumer behaviour literature. The literature review has been carried out following the recommendations of Baker (2000) and mainly considering scientific journal articles on the topics of self-concept in consumer behaviour and brand-consumer identification. This chapter also provides some insights for future research on identity-based consumer behaviour in retail settings by critically exploring the role of self-congruity and of customer-retailer identification in the development and in the management of retailer-customer relationships.

BACKGROUND

Products and brands play multiple roles in consumers' lives. According to Fournier (1991), brands and products can offer functional benefits, provide experiential opportunities through their use (Holbrook, & Hirschmann, 1982; Arnould & Price, 1993), and assist with establishing and defining consumer's identity (Levy, 1959; Belk, 1988; Solomon, 1988; Ligas, 2000; Fournier, 2009). It is argued that consumers purchase goods not just for functional reasons, but also because they represent a vehicle for self-expression, acting as an extension of one's self-concept (Levy, 1959; Belk, 1988). Starting from Levy (1959), the role of self-concept in consumer behaviour has been explored by several researchers.

Besides providing functional benefits, products enable experiential opportunities through their use and carry a variety of symbolic meanings (Keller, 1993; Levy, 1959, Helgeson & Supphellen, 2004).

In particular, brands and in general possessions can be viewed as n extension of one's self (Belk, 1988; Gardner & Levy, 1955) as symbolic meanings associated with a brand or a product help consumers in the development of a unique and visible representation of their selves (Ligas, 2000). In his study on consumers' goals and products meanings, Ligas (2000) highlights how consumers try to achieve three different levels of goals through products, namely (1) having, (2) doing, and (3) being goals.

Whereas functional product meanings correspond to consumers' having- and doing- level goals, symbolic product meanings play a key role in achieving being-level goals and doing-level goals mainly related to intangible experiences involving personal values (Ligas, 2000). Through products individuals can show something personal about them to others, but they can also answer to their inner desire to define themselves and to communicate who they are to the society (Shembri, Merrilees, & Kristiansen, 2010).

Products and brands can be considered as main contributors to the construction and to the communication to the society of one's self-concept. Considering the process of one's self-concept formation and definition, products and brands can act twofold: inward forming one's identity, and outward expressing who a person is and revealing what social groups a person aligns with (Shembri, Merrilees, & Kristiansen, 2010).

The role of self-concept in consumer behaviour has been traditionally investigated by two complementary theoretical frameworks: social identity theory (Tajfel & Turner 1986) and identity theory (Stryker 1968; Stryker&Burke, 2000).

Whereas social identity theory posits that the essence of one's self-identification relies on the membership to a social group (or groups) and also on the value and the emotional significance attached to such a membership (Tajfel & Turner, 1986), identity theory is more focused on individual behaviour and the private self, stating that identity is linked to the different social roles that a person can have in a social setting.

A subject can have multiple identities which are organized hierarchically. In this sense, customers perceive products and brands as similar or different from their selves (Kleine, Kleine, & Allen 1995) according to which kind of identity is more salient in a particular purchasing context (Arnett, German, & Hunt 2003; Bolton & Reed 2004; Oyserman 2009).

These two theories represent the theoretical foundation on which *consumer-brand identification* theory (CBI) has been conceptualized, as both explore the relationship between one's self-concept and social entities (Belk, 1988; Sirgy, 1982).

A growing body of research has focused on what is the meaning for consumers to identify with a brand and has investigated the implications of CBI for a successful brand management (Stokburger-Sauer et al., 2012; Chernev et al., 2011; Escalas & Bettman, 2003; 2009).

CBI has been linked to several other concept in consumer behaviour literature. In particular, researchers have investigated this construct in relation to brand attitude and brand attachment (Park et al., 2010), brand love (Batra, Ahuvia, & Bagozzi, 2012; Carrol & Ahuvia, 2006), and self-brand connection (Escalas & Bettman, 2003; 2009; Fournier, 2009).

According to Lam et al., (2010), CBI is defined as a psychological state in consumer's mind of perceiving, feeling and valuing the belongingness with a brand. Stokburger-Sauer et al., (2012) provide a further definition of CBI that is conceived as "a consumer's perceived state of oneness with a brand" (p. 407). Both definitions describe CBI as a "state" and set it apart from the process of comparison between one's self-concept and brand image.

However, Lam et al. (2010)'s approach, conceives CBI as a multidimensional construct, formed by three dimensions: the cognitive, the emotional and the value dimension. On the other hand, Stockburger-Sauer et al. (2012) conceptualize CBI just as a cognitive construct and distinguish it from emotional and value assessment dimensions, which can be considered as inputs or outputs of CBI.

Several researchers pointed out how consumers tend to develop positive attitudes towards brands that reflect their personality and how consumers are more willing to develop a relationship with brands that express and are also able to enhance their identity (Tuskej et al., 2013). In this sense, consumers show a natural affinity for products that match at best their self- and social- identities (Aaker, 1997; Sirgy et al., 1997; Sirgy et al., 2000; Reed et al., 2012).

Moreover, CBI has found to play a fundamental role in building and maintain consumer-brand relationships (Lam et al., 2010; Tuskej et al., 2013), showing a significant influence on buying decision making process (Ahearne et al., 2005), satisfaction (Kuenzel & Halliday, 2008), loyalty and positive word of mouth (Bhattacharya & Sen, 2003; Kim et al., 2001).

CONSUMER-BRAND IDENTIFICATION AND SELF-CONGRUITY IN RETAIL

The Drivers of Consumer-Brand Identification

Consumer-brand identification has been recognized to have positive influences on both pre-purchase and post-purchase behaviours and on the effective development and maintenance of relationships with customers (Tuskej et al., 2013). Given this crucial impact on a business success, a growing body of research has focused on the meaning of CBI and on the study of the drivers of CBI (Table 1).

Drivers of CBI have been identified as those factors that play a key role in generating and enhancing the process of identification with a particular brand. Bhattacharya and Sen (2003) relate CBI to consumer's self-concept needs and identify as primary drivers of CBI consumer's self-defining and enhancement motivations. On the other hand, Escalas and Bettman (2003; 2009) investigate CBI considering consumer's social needs, suggesting that consumers identify with brands whose identities are aligned with desirable reference groups and celebrity endorsers.

A more comprehensive perspective has been adopted by Stokburger-Sauer et al., (2012) that includes both cognitive and experiential drivers. Among the cognitive drivers of CBI, it is possible to identify three main sub-categories, which are (1) self-definition drivers, (2) self-expression

drivers, and (3) self-enhancement drivers (Bhattacharya & Sen, 2003; Stokburger-Sauer et al., 2012; Chernev et al., 2011).

Self-definition drivers reflect consumers' inner desire of define their selves and maintain a clear sense of who they are. More in detail, a wide body of research has focused on the similarity between the brand and the consumer, defining it as self-congruity, brand-self congruence, brand-self similarity (Bhattacharya & Sen, 2003; Stokburger-Sauer et al., 2012; Sirgy et al., 2000).

As consumers tend to associate human characteristics to brands (Aaker, 1997), finding themselves similar to a brand leads consumers to feel closer and to get engaged in a relationship with it.

Self-expression and self-enhancement drivers are related to consumers' "need for uniqueness" (Snyder & Fromkin, 1977; Tepper Tian et al., 2001) and help themselves to distinguish from the others and to see (or be seen) in a positive light in social settings (Bhattacharya & Sen, 2003, Belk, 1988). Individuals try to pursue social inclusion and social distinctiveness at the same time in order to affirm their identities according to the different social context in which they are in a particular moment (Thompson et al., 2006). In this sense the purchase and use of particular brands can help to socially develop, affirm and enhance consumers' identity.

Considering the experiential drivers of CBI, three additional sub-categories can be identified and include (1) affective and emotional drivers, (2) social connection and alignment drivers, and (3) experience-related drivers (Escalas & Bettman,

Table 1. Drivers of consumer – brand identification

	CONSUMER NEEDS	CBI DRIVERS	KEY REFERENCES
COGNITIVE DRIVERS	• Self-defining needs • Self-expression needs • Self-enhancement needs	• Brand-self similarity • Brand distinctiveness • Brand prestige	Bhattacharya and Sen (2003) Escalas and Bettman (2003; 2009) Stokburger-Sauer et al. (2012)
EXPERIENTIAL DRIVERS	• Affective and emotional needs • Social connection and alignment needs • Experience needs	• Brand warmth • Brand social benefits • Memorable brand experience	Escalas and Bettman (2003; 2009) Thompson et al., (2006) Stokburger-Sauer et al. (2012)

2003; 2009; Thompson et al., 2006; Stokburger-Sauer et al., 2012).

Affective and emotional drivers are related to the kind of perceptions that consumers develop by purchasing and consuming the brand. It is possible to discern between warm brands and cold brands according to the level of emotional engagement created through brand experience. Brand warmth is strictly related to product category, brand distinctiveness and brand positioning (Stokburger-Sauer et al., 2012). Warm (or emotional) brands are more likely to generate CBI than cold (or rational) brands, as they carry deeper and identity-related meanings about systems of values and beliefs that can be shared or not by consumers (Park et al., 2010, Carroll & Ahuvia, 2006).

Social connection and alignment drivers predicts CBI according to the extent to which consumers perceive interactions with a brand as a way to connect or align with reference groups in a social context. In addition to individual beliefs, brands carry social and cultural meanings (Holt, 2005; Thompson et al., 2005) and act as a device to develop social relationships with others. Literature on brand communities and consumption subcultures have shown how consumers join and coalesce into subgroups or communities in virtue of a shared brand commitment and attachment (Bagozzi et al., 2012; Thompson et al., 2006; Stokburger-Sauer, 2010). In this sense, brands that are able to provide a social benefit by increasing the social integrations of an individual, are more likely to have a stronger impact on CBI.

The last type of CBI drivers includes the experience-based ones. Regardless the frequency of use, brands can occupy a salient position in consumers' mind. Indeed, some brands are able to provide customers with extraordinary and affectively charged experiences that last in their mind for a long time. Memorable brand experiences have been recognized as an antecedent of CBI, as such brands are more likely to leave a mark in defining one's sense of self by strongly connect consumers' to a brand (Stokburger-Sauer et al., 2012).

Self-Congruity as a way to Achieve Consumer-Brand Identification

Among the drivers of CBI, brand-self similarity or self-congruity is the one that has been traditionally more investigated in consumer behaviour literature.

Literature on consumer behaviour has deeply analysed the relationship between consumers' self-concept and consumer behaviour. Starting from Levy (1959), many scholars focused their studies on the role of self-concept in consumer behaviour.

Self-concept can be defined as "the totality of the individuals' thoughts and feelings having reference to themselves as subjects as well as objects" (Malhotra, 1988). Self-concept is a multidimensional concept that comprises four dimensions, i.e. the actual self, the ideal self, the social self, and the ideal social self (Sirgy 1982; Sirgy et al., 1997).

Actual and social self-image respectively indicates "how people see themselves" and "how people think others see them" (Beerli et al, 2007; Kang et al 2012). Ideal self and ideal social self-image indicates "how people would like to see themselves" and "how people would like others to see them."

It is argue that customers choose products and brands perceptually consistent with their own self-concept (Sirgy, 1982) and while purchasing, consumers tend to evaluate a brand by matching its image with their self-concept. This is because much of the research on self-concept has tried to explain consumer behaviour in terms of congruity between a product/brand with the consumer's self-concept.

In the marketing literature, self-congruence, self-image congruence, self-congruity, brand-self similarity and image congruence are interchangeably used to refer to this construct.

Self-congruity can be defined as the degree of match/mismatch between a brand/store image and a customer's self-image (Sirgy, 1985). So, self-congruity act as a link between the self-concept and the symbolic meanings underlying products and brands (Quester, 2000) and it is strictly linked to the way in which one perceives him/her self (Parker, 2009). Self-congruity is therefore a dynamic concept that changes from situation to situation as well as a multidimensional concept.

Although its multidimensionality, very few studies attempt to investigate all the four types of self-congruity and most of them just consider actual self-congruity.

Early studies on self-congruity were undertaken in the areas of branding and mainly investigated consumers' pre-purchase evaluations such as purchase intentions (Landon, 1974), product preferences (Dolich, 1969), product choice (Malhotra, 1988) and attitudes.

Recently, self-congruity theory has been extended to model post-purchase evaluations and behaviours (Hosay & Martin, 2012), such as satisfaction, perceived quality, perceived value and loyalty (He & Mukherjee, 2007).

Although, self-congruity has been recognized as a valid and robust construct in the fields of consumer identity and symbolic consumption research (Aguirre-Rodriguez et al., 2012), several studies observe that its impact on consumer behaviour is sometimes weak and not consistent (Malhotra, 1988; Willems & Swinnen, 2011).

Indeed, consumer behaviour is a function of both symbolic and utilitarian attributes of a product/brand/store. So self-congruity framework needs to be integrated with evaluations related to functional congruity (Sirgy 1991), as scholars in many occasions simply ignored the effect of brand/product/store utilitarian attributes on consumer behaviour (Malhotra, 1988). More recent studies recommend a balanced approach considering both functional congruity and self-congruity (Willems & Swinnen, 2011).

From Consumer-Brand Identification to Consumer-Retailer Identification

Consumer-brand identification assumes particular connotations when considering retail settings. According to Aliawadi and Keller (2004) retailer brands are more multi-sensory in nature compared to products brands and can count on richer consumer experiences to develop their image and their brand equity. They can rely on a variety of tools to define their image and personality, such as servicescape variables, pricing policies, assortment mix, private labels, and location cues.

As a consequence, shoppers tend to shape stereotyped images related to retailers which act as a frame of comparison in CBI.

Moreover, shopping is a pure social activity that can impact both the individual side and the social side of one's identity. In particular, several researchers pointed out how consumers tend to develop positive attitudes towards those stores that reflect their personality (Aaker, 1997; Sirgy et al., 1997; Sirgy et al., 2000, Reed et al., 2012).

Store image is a key concept in the retailing literature that reflects shoppers' perception of a store in terms of functional and psychological attributes (Martineau, 1958). Functional attributes are concrete, tangible, and observable, whereas psychological attributes are abstract, intangible and not directly observable. Although most of the literature on store image, has primarily considered functional and utilitarian store attributes as key drivers of store loyalty, a growing body of research has increasingly shift the focus to the hedonic, symbolic and psychological cues associated with store image (Chebat et al., 2009; O'Cass & Grace, 2008; Sirgy et al., 2000; Willems & Swinnen, 2011; Yim et al., 2007).

Darden and Babin (1994) show how consumers assign affective qualities to retail stores and Helgesson and Supphellen (2004)'s study highlights that consumers can easily describe retailers and stores using human personality traits.

D'Astous and Lévesque (2003) provide a clear distinction between store image and store personality: "Whereas store image is a mental representation that encompasses all dimensions that are associated with a store, [...] store personality is restricted to those mental dimensions that correspond to human traits" (D'Astous and Lévesque, 2003, p. 456).

As for brands and products, the congruence between customer's self-concept and store image has been found to be crucial to the development of successful retailer-customer relationships (Fournier, 1998; Sirgy et al., 2000; O'Cass & Grace, 2008; Willems & Swinnen, 2011).

Research on store image and self-concept is well documented, but most of the studies focus on pre-purchase evaluations. Just a few consider post purchase behaviours and even fewer analyse the relationship between self-congruity and customer loyalty (Bellenger et al 1976, Chebat et al., 2009, He & Mukherjee, 2007, Heath & Scott, 1998, Sirgy & Samli, 1985, Willems & Swinnen 2011).

The CBI process is more complex when considering retail, as it is the result of the interplay of multiple facets related to store and retailer image. If we consider the case of retail chains and franchises, consumers evaluations can be shaped at two different levels: the particular store and the chain/the franchise/the retailer.

Consumers can be influenced in their decisions making process by both retailer corporate policies and particular store policies. For instance, a retailer whose corporate image is based on ethical and sustainable values, is expected to provide shopping experience tailored on such values, including fair trade products in the assortment and worrying about energy saving and pollution generation, as well as work environment of employees. In this sense, the interplay of retailer's policies at corporate level and at store level shape the image of a retailer. Such a multilevel perspective should be taken into account when analyzing CBI in retail settings.

Rooted in previous conceptualizations of CBI, we conceive *consumer retailer-identification* (CRI) as a psychological state in shoppers' mind, who feel a sense of belongingness with a retailer and/or with a specific store. This process can occur at store, at retailer, or at both levels, in which case may lead to a stronger effect of CRI on consumer behaviours.

Extending the CBI framework to retail contexts needs particular attention in particular considering self-congruity and retailer-self similarity.

Indeed, it is possible to identify two facets of retailer's brand image that can act as a frame of comparison with consumer's self-concept and play a key role in terms of CRI. These two facets are namely retailer (store) personality and retailer (store) user imagery.

Retailer (store) personality is one of the dimensions of brand associations in consumers' mind. Extending the concept of brand personality to retail settings, this construct can be defined as the set of human characteristics associated with a retailer (Aaker, 1997). At store level, Martineau (1958) has introduced the concept of store personality and identified some factors that contribute to its definition (layout and architecture, symbols and colours, advertising, and sales personnel). D'Astous and Levesque (2003) have then developed a scale to measure store personality, including positive and negative dimensions related to the shopping experience in a store.

The other facet that plays an important role in the assessment of congruity between a retailer and a customer is retailer (store) user imagery. As stated by Sirgy et al. (2000), "shoppers perceive stores differently in terms of the store's typical clientele or patrons" (p. 127).

The construct of user imagery refers in general to the stereotypic images of users of a product or of a store (Sirgy et al., 1997; Sirgy et al., 2000). Although the image of the typical user of a brand/store is believed to be reflective of the image of the brand/store, user-imagery and brand personality may not always be in agreement (Keller, 1998;

Phau & Lau, 2000) and there are some cases in which users' profiles is inconsistent with the personality of the brand (Aaker, 1997).

Moreover, there can be more than one type of user for the same brand (Usaki & Baloglu, 2011) and the evaluation of self-congruity can also be biased by sociological evaluations that exceed the brand domain. Helgeson and Supphellen (2004) suggest that brand personality and user imagery are two different constructs and that both have a role in the assessment of self-congruity.

Self-congruity has been recognized as a valid and robust foundation in consumer identity and symbolic consumption research (Aguierre-Rodriguez et al., 2012) and has been widely investigated in relation to pre-purchase variables, such as evaluations, preferences and intentions. Despite the richness of literature on the topic, the study of this construct related to post-purchase behaviours in retail contexts is still limited (Chebat et al., 2009; Ha & Im, 2012; O'Cass & Grace, 2008; Sirgy & Samli, 1985; Willems & Swinnen, 2011).

Towards a Theoretical Framework of Consumer – Retailer Identification

CBI has proven to be a valid tool in managing and improving the quality of consumer-brand relationships. Although the limited research on CBI in retail settings, the topic deserves more attention as it represents a powerful tool for fostering retailer-customer relationships.

Retailers should carefully consider the multiple facets implicated in the process of CRI in order to foster the positive impacts on commitment development and relationship building with their customers.

As stated before, CRI occurs with reference to two different facets of retailer image, i.e. the personality and the shopper imagery. Moreover, the identification process takes place at two different levels: the store and the retailer. Through the combination of these different facets, consumers define a stereotypic image of retailers that represents the basis for comparison in the process of CRI. Considering the positive influence of CRI on commitment, loyalty and positive word of mouth, it is also important for retailers to understand how CRI can be fostered to positively impact relational outcomes.

The role of stores deserves particular attention when focusing on CRI. The store is the most influential touch point between a retailer and its customers. In this sense it could be seen as a mighty vehicle through which convey symbolic meanings and personality traits of a retailer to consumers.

Based on previous insight we propose a framework of CRI that aims at extending CBI theory to retail setting, considering the prominent role of the store as well as the impact of retailer's corporate policies (see Figure 1).

Store cues can reinforce the establishment of CRI with favourable consequences on retailer-customer relationship quality. Among them, scholars have pointed out that particular attention should be given to atmospheric and location cues, merchandise cues, price and promotion cues (Sirgy et al., 2000) and service cues. Beside impacting on the cognitive side, by creating awareness related to a particular brand personality, stores also represent the ideal place where to promote interaction with and engagement to retail brand by working on experiential drivers of CRI.

Event marketing, product co-creation, brand communities are some of the tools that can assist retailers with delivering fascinating and vivid experiences that can turn into affectively-charged memories.

On the other hand, corporate policies can positively impact cognitive cues related to CRI by communicating key retailer values and provide specific product experiences through private labels.

Figure 1. Consumer – retailer identification: A conceptual framework

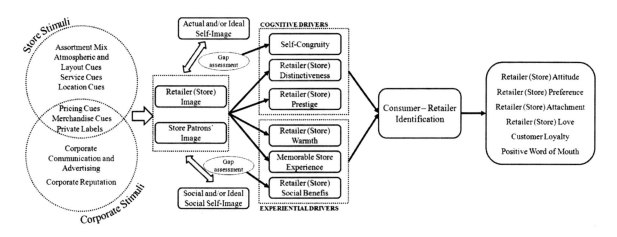

CONCLUSION AND FUTURE RESEARCH DIRECTIONS

Building sustainable retailer-consumer relationships has always been crucial for a business long-term success. Retailers are increasingly involved in the challenging establishment of meaningful relationships with their customers. In this sense, the role of retail brands should be reconsidered in the light of the growing importance of identity-based motivations in consumer behaviour. A wide body of research has identified *consumer-brand identification* theory (CBI) as a solid theoretical foundation to explore the relationship and the interactions between one's self-concept and brands. CBI has found to play a key role in developing long-term relationships with customers because of its positive impact on several attitudinal and relational constructs, such as preference, loyalty and commitment. Recently the research focus has shifted from the analysis of the outcomes of CBI to the study of its antecedent, i.e. those drivers that enhance the process of identification between a brand and a customer's self-concept. Stemming from the literature review, drivers of CBI can be classified into cognitive and experiential. Among them, self-congruity (or brand-self similarity) has been recognized as a valid and robust construct

in the fields of consumer identity and symbolic consumption research.

Despite the richness of literature on the topic, little attention has been given to the study of CBI in retail settings. We propose a theoretical framework that extends CBI to retail settings, defining it as *consumer-retailer identification*. It can be stated that the process of identification between a retailer and a customer assumes particular connotations, whose implications needs to be further investigated by researchers.

The interplay of multiple facets at different levels make CRI a more complex process in which the store has a key role to play. Stores represent the ideal places where retailers can effectively communicate their personality and engage customers through experiential drivers such as in-store events or co-creation.

In spite of the crucial role played by CBI in consumer-brand relationships, further research is needed to better understand CRI potential. Future research should focus on the role of store image and servicescape variables in impacting CBI. What is the impact of store design, music, aroma and colours on CRI? What kind of in-store events are key to improve the identification with a retailer? What is the role of merchandise mix and pricing policies in fostering CRI?

Besides focusing on the role of the store in CRI, retail brand equity and corporate branding strategy effects should deserve more attention from scholars. How corporate advertising and communication can influence CRI? What is the role of private labels?

Moreover, as shopping is a social activity, future research could also investigate CRI adopting a social-identity perspective, focusing on social benefits embedded in retail brands.

From a managerial point of view, CRI represent a powerful tool for enhancing retailer-consumer relationships. However, encouraging customers to identify with a retailer is a complex tasks that first requires a deep knowledge of who are a retailer's customers.

Monitoring customers becomes crucial and retailers should collect information not just in terms of demographics but also including personality traits, emotions, aspirations, and desires. It is important to identify which values are important to your customers and use them as a way to better define retailer positioning. The second step implies the creation of a retail brand personality based on a unique positioning align with target consumers' actual and desirable images. While defining a clear and distinctive positioning, retailers should take into account both the individual and the social side of brand personality in order to generate brand warmth, emotional engagement and to provide social benefits to their customers. Retailers should pay also particular attention to store design and layout, trying to keep it as consistent as possible and aligned with retail brand and target customers' values.

Finally, it is essential to develop an integrated and effective communication strategy, using both traditional and emerging channels, such as blogs and social networks. This kind of actions are key to facilitate the process of identification with a particular retailer, improving the degree of self-congruity with positive impacts in terms of relational outcomes.

Considering the importance of being goals and identity-based motivation in consumer behaviour, the identification with a particular retailer represents an effective driver of successful and sustainable relationships, leading consumers to develop a stronger commitment based on a solid emotional bond.

REFERENCES

Aaker, J. (1997). Dimensions of brand personality. *JMR, Journal of Marketing Research, 34,* 347–357. doi:10.2307/3151897

Aguirre-Rodriguez, A., Bosnjak, M., & Sirgy, J. M. (2012). Moderators of the self-congruity effect on consumer decision-making: a meta-analysis. *Journal of Business Research, 65,* 1179–1188. doi:10.1016/j.jbusres.2011.07.031

Ahearne, M., Bhattacharya, C. B., & Gruen, T. (2005). Antecedents and consequences of customer–company identification: expanding the role of relationship marketing. *The Journal of Applied Psychology, 90,* 574–585. doi:10.1037/0021-9010.90.3.574 PMID:15910151

Aliawadi, K. L., & Keller, K. L. (2004). Understanding retail branding: conceptual insights and research priorities. *Journal of Retailing, 80,* 331–342. doi:10.1016/j.jretai.2004.10.008

Arnett, D. B., German, S. D., & Hunt, S. D. (2003). The identity salience model of relationship marketing success: the case of nonprofit marketing. *Journal of Marketing, 67*(2), 89–105. doi:10.1509/jmkg.67.2.89.18614

Arnould, E. J., & Price, L. L. (1993). River magic: Extraordinary Experience and the extended service encounter. *The Journal of Consumer Research, 20*(1), 24–45. doi:10.1086/209331

Bagozzi, R. P., Bergami, M., Marzocchi, G., & Morandin, G. (2012). Customer–organization relationships: Development and test of a theory of extended identities. *The Journal of Applied Psychology*, *97*(1), 63–76. doi:10.1037/a0024533 PMID:21766998

Baker, M. J. (2000). Writing a literature review. *The Marketing Review*, *1*, 219–247. doi:10.1362/1469347002529189

Batra, R., Ahuvia, A., & Bagozzi, R. P. (2012). Brand Love. *Journal of Marketing*, *76*, 1–16. doi:10.1509/jm.09.0339

Beerli, A., Díaz Meneses, G., & Gil, S. M. (2007). Self-congruity and destination choice. *Annals of Tourism Research*, *34*(3), 571–587. doi:10.1016/j.annals.2007.01.005

Belk, R. W. (1988). Possessions and the extended self. *The Journal of Consumer Research*, *15*, 139–168. doi:10.1086/209154

Bhattacharya, C. B., & Sen, S. (2003). Consumer-company identification: a framework for understanding consumers' relationships with companies. *Journal of Marketing*, *67*, 76–88. doi:10.1509/jmkg.67.2.76.18609

Bolton, L. E., & Reed, A. II. (2004). Sticky priors and identification based judgments. *JMR, Journal of Marketing Research*, *41*, 397–410. doi:10.1509/jmkr.41.4.397.47019

Carroll, B. A., & Ahuvia, A. C. (2006). Some antecedents and outcomes of brand love. *Marketing Letters*, *17*(2), 79–89. doi:10.1007/s11002-006-4219-2

Chernev, A., Hamilton, R., & Gal, D. (2011). Competing for consumer identity: limits to self-expression and the perils of lifestyle branding. *Journal of Marketing*, *75*, 66–82. doi:10.1509/jmkg.75.3.66

Dolich, I. J. (1969). Congruence relationships between self images and product brands. *JMR, Journal of Marketing Research*, *6*(1), 80–84. doi:10.2307/3150001

Escalas, J. E., & Bettman, J. R. (2003). You Are What They Eat: The Influence of Reference Groups on Consumers' Connections to Brands. *Journal of Consumer Psychology*, *13*(3), 339–348. doi:10.1207/S15327663JCP1303_14

Escalas, J. E., & Bettman, J. R. (2005). Self-construal, reference groups, and brand meaning. *The Journal of Consumer Research*, *32*, 378–389. doi:10.1086/497549

Fournier, S. (1991). Meaning-based framework for the study of consumer-object relations. [Provo, UT: Association for Consumer Research.]. *Advances in Consumer Research. Association for Consumer Research (U. S.)*, *18*, 736–742.

Fournier, S. (2009). Lessons learned about consumers' relationships with brand. In *Handbook of brand relationships*. N.Y. Society for Consumer Psychology and M.E. Sharp.

Gardner, B. B., & Levy, S. J. (1955). The product and the brand. *Harvard Business Review*, *33*(2), 33–39.

He, H., & Mukherjee, A. (2007). I am, ergo I shop: does store image congruity explain shopping behaviour of Chinese consumers? *Journal of Marketing Management*, *23*(5-6), 443–460. doi:10.1362/026725707X212766

Helgeson, J. G., & Supphellen, M. (2004). A conceptual and measurement comparison of self-congruity and brand personality: The impact of socially desirable responding. *International Journal of Market Research*, *46*(2), 205–233.

Holbrook, M. B., & Hirschmann, E. C. (1982). The experiential aspects of consumption: consumer fantasies, feelings, and fun. *The Journal of Consumer Research*, *9*, 132–140. doi:10.1086/208906

Holt, D. B. (2005). How societies desire brands: Using cultural theory to explain brand symbolism. In S. Ratneshwar, & D. G. Mick (Eds.), *Inside consumption* (pp. 273–291). London: Routledge.

Hosay, S., & Martin, D. (2012). Self-image congruence in consumer behaviour. *Journal of Business Research, 65*, 685–691. doi:10.1016/j.jbusres.2011.03.015

Kang, J., Tang, L., Lee, J. Y., & Bosselman, R. H. (2012). Understanding customer behavior in name-brand Korean coffee shops: The role of self-congruity and functional congruity. *International Journal of Hospitality Management, 31*, 809–818. doi:10.1016/j.ijhm.2011.09.017

Keller, K. L. (1993). Conceptualizing, measuring, and managing customer-based brand equity. *Journal of Marketing, 57*(1), 1–22. doi:10.2307/1252054

Kim, A. C., Dongchul, H., & Aeung-Bae, P. (2001). The effect of brand personality and brand identification on brand loyalty: applying the theory of social identification. *The Japanese Psychological Research, 43*, 195–206. doi:10.1111/1468-5884.00177

Kleine, S. S., Kleine, R. E., & Allen, C. T. (1995). How is possession 'me' or 'not me'? Characterizing types and an antecedent of material possession attachment. *The Journal of Consumer Research, 22*, 327–343. doi:10.1086/209454

Kuenzel, S., & Halliday, V. S. (2008). Investigating antecedents and consequences of brand identification. *Journal of Product and Brand Management, 17*, 293–304. doi:10.1108/10610420810896059

Lam, S. K., Ahearne, M., Hu, Y., & Schillewaert, N. (2010). Resistance to brand switching when a radically new brand is introduced: a social identity theory perspective. *Journal of Marketing, 74*, 128–146. doi:10.1509/jmkg.74.6.128

Levy, S. J. (1959). Symbols for sale. *Harvard Business Review, 37*, 117–124.

Ligas, M. (2000). People, products, and pursuits: exploring the relationship between consumer goals and product meanings. *Psychology and Marketing, 17*(11), 983–1003. doi:10.1002/1520-6793(200011)17:11<983::AID-MAR4>3.0.CO;2-J

Malhotra, N. K. (1988). Self concept and product choice: an integrated perspective. *Journal of Economic Psychology, 9*, 1–28. doi:10.1016/0167-4870(88)90029-3

Oyserman, D. (2009). Identity-based motivation and consumer behaviour. *Journal of Consumer Psychology, 19*, 276–279. doi:10.1016/j.jcps.2009.06.001

Park, C. W., MacInnis, D. J., Priester, J., Eisingerich, A. B., & Iacobucci, D. (2010). Brand attachment and brand attitude strength: conceptual and empirical differentiation of two critical brand equity drivers. *Journal of Marketing, 74*, 1–17. doi:10.1509/jmkg.74.6.1

Parker, B. T. (2009). A comparison of brand personality and brand user-imagery congruence. *Journal of Consumer Marketing, 26*(3), 175–184. doi:10.1108/07363760910954118

Quester, P. G., Karunaratna, A., & Goh, L. K. (2000). Self-congruity and product evaluation: a cross-cultural study. *Journal of Consumer Marketing, 17*(6), 525–535. doi:10.1108/07363760010349939

Reed, A. II, Forehand, M. R., Puntoni, S., & Warlop, L. (2012). Identity-based consumer behaviour. *International Journal of Research in Marketing, 29*, 310–321. doi:10.1016/j.ijresmar.2012.08.002

Shembri, S., Merrilees, B., & Kristiansen, S. (2010). Brand Consumption and Narrative of the Self. *Psychology and Marketing, 27*(6), 623–638. doi:10.1002/mar.20348

Sirgy, M. J. (1982). Self-concept in consumer behavior: a critical review. *The Journal of Consumer Research, 9,* 287–300. doi:10.1086/208924

Sirgy, M. J. (1985). Using self-congruity and ideal congruity to predict purchase motivation. *Journal of Business Research, 13,* 195–206. doi:10.1016/0148-2963(85)90026-8

Sirgy, M. J., Grewal, D., & Mangleburg, T. (2000). Retail environment, self-congruity, and retail patronage: an integrative model and a research agenda. *Journal of Business Research, 49,* 127–138. doi:10.1016/S0148-2963(99)00009-0

Sirgy, M. J., Grewal, D., Mangleburg, T. F., Park, J., Chon, K., & Claiborne, C. B. etal. (1997). Assessing the predictive validity of two methods of measuring self-image congruence. *Journal of the Academy of Marketing Science, 25*(3), 229–241. doi:10.1177/0092070397253004

Sirgy, M. J., Johar, J. S., Samli, A. C., & Claiborne, C. B. (1991). Self-congruity versus functional congruity: predictors of consumer behaviour. *Journal of the Academy of Marketing Science, 19*(4), 363–375. doi:10.1007/BF02726512

Snyder, C. R., & Fromkin, H. L. (1977). Abnormality as a positive characteristic: The development and validation of a scale measuring need for uniqueness. *Journal of Abnormal Psychology, 86*(5), 518–527. doi:10.1037/0021-843X.86.5.518

Solomon, M. R. (1988). Mapping product constellations: a social categorization approach to consumption symbolism. *Psychology and Marketing, 5,* 233–258.

Stokburger-Sauer, N., Ratneshwar, S., & Sankar, S. (2012). Drivers of consumer–brand identification. *International Journal of Research in Marketing, 29,* 406–418. doi:10.1016/j.ijresmar.2012.06.001

Stryker, S. (1968). Identity Salience and Role Performance. *Journal of Marriage and the Family, 4,* 558–564. doi:10.2307/349494

Stryker, S., & Burke, P. J. (2000). The past, present, and future of an identity. *Social Psychology Quarterly, 63*(4), 284–297. doi:10.2307/2695840

Tajfel, H., & Turner, J. C. (1986). The social identity theory of inter-group behavior. In S. Worchel, & W. G. Austin (Eds.), *Psychology of intergroup relations.* Chicago, IL: Nelson-Hall.

Tepper Tian, K., Bearden, W. O., & Hunter, G. L. (2001). Consumers' need for uniqueness: scale development and validation. *The Journal of Consumer Research, 28*(1), 50–66. doi:10.1086/321947

Thompson, C. J., Rindfleisch, A., & Arsel, Z. (2006). Emotional branding and the strategic value of the Doppelgänger brand image. *Journal of Marketing, 70*(1), 50–64. doi:10.1509/jmkg.2006.70.1.50

Thomson, M., MacInnis, J. D., & Park, C. W. (2005). The ties that bind: measuring the strength of consumers' emotional attachments to brands. *Journal of Consumer Psychology, 15,* 77–91. doi:10.1207/s15327663jcp1501_10

Tuškej, U., Golob, U., & Podnar, K. (2013). The role of consumer–brand identification in building brand relationships. *Journal of Business Research, 66,* 53–59. doi:10.1016/j.jbusres.2011.07.022

Willems, K., & Swinnen, G. (2011). Am I cheap? Testing the role of store personality and self-congruity in discount retailing. *International Review of Retail, Distribution and Consumer Research, 21*(5), 513–539. doi:10.1080/09593969.2011.618888

KEY TERMS AND DEFINITIONS

Brand Distinctiveness: The ability of a brand of being recognized as unique and different from other brands, in order to address consumers' need for uniqueness at both individual and social levels.

Brand Prestige: The level of exclusivity of a brand that enables consumers to satisfy their self-enhancement needs.

Brand Social Benefits: A series of benefits provided by a brand linked to its capability to carry social and cultural meanings and to provide social interaction opportunities to consumers.

Brand Warmth: The degree to which a brand is able to arouse emotions and empathy in consumers, as being perceived as warm instead of cold.

Consumer – Brand Identification: A psychological state in consumer's mind of perceiving, feeling and valuing the belongingness with a brand.

Consumer – Retailer Identification: A psychological state in shoppers' mind, who feel a sense of belongingness with a retailer and/or with a specific store. This process may occur at store, at retailer, or at both levels, and may involve both retailer (store) personality and retailer (store) user imagery.

Memorable Brand Experience: The ability of a brand to deliver vivid and remarkable experiences originating from extraordinary consumption activities, regardless the frequency of use.

Retailer (Store) Personality: A mental representation of a retailer (store) based on human traits, such as friendly, annoying, enthusiastic, irritating, or honest.

Retailer (Store) User Imagery/Patrons' Image: The stereotypic images of users of a product or of patrons of a store. Not always the image of the typical user/patron of a brand/store is reflective of the image of the brand/store, as well as there can be more than one type of user/patron for the same brand/store.

Self – Congruity: The degree of similarity between a brand/store image and a customer's self-image.

Chapter 3
Shopping Well–Being and Ill–Being:
Toward an Integrated Model

Dong-Jin Lee
Yonsei University, South Korea

Ahmet Ekici
Bilkent University, Turkey

Grace B. Yu
Duksung Women's University, South Korea

Eda Gurel-Atay
University of Puget Sound, USA

M. Joseph Sirgy
Virginia Polytechnic Institute and State University, USA

Kenneth D. Bahn
James Madison University, USA

ABSTRACT

In this chapter, the authors make an attempt to review and integrate much of the research on shopping well-being and ill-being experiences. The integrated model identifies the antecedents of these two focal constructs in terms of situational, individual, and cultural factors. The consequences of shopping well-being and ill-being experiences on life satisfaction (or subjective well-being) are explained through a bottom-up spillover process. Managerial implications and avenues for future research are also discussed.

INTRODUCTION

Over the last several decades much research in retailing has focused on various consequences of shopping activities. One important consequence of shopping is its impact on consumer well being.

Studies found that shopping contributes to the consumer well-being providing consumers with experiences of hedonic enjoyment and satisfaction of various needs (Arnold & Reynolds, 2003, 2012; Babin, Darden, & Griffin, 1994; Timothy,

2005). Other studies found that shopping can have a negative impact on consumer well-being as in the case of compulsive buying and impulse buying (Schor, 1991; Rojek, 2006).

Despite the seemingly significant impact of shopping on consumer's lives, there is a lack of consensus on the impact of shopping on consumer well-being. There is still a need to integrate research from various disciplines to provide answers to effect of shopping on consumer well- being. The question remains. Do shopping experiences

DOI: 10.4018/978-1-4666-6074-8.ch003

have a positive or negative impact on the well-being of consumers? What are the factors affecting these negative and positive shopping experiences, which in turn influence consumer well-being? There is a great need to integrate the two diverging perspectives.

The main purpose of this chapter is, therefore, to develop a model that integrates antecedents and consequences of shopping well-being and ill-being experiences. The proposed model developed in this chapter treats shopping well-being and ill-being experiences as two distinct concepts. Shopping well-being experiences deal with the positive aspects of consumers' retail activities, whereas shopping ill-being experiences deal with the negative aspects. The integrated model identifies the antecedents of these two focal constructs in terms of situational, individual, and cultural factors. The consequences of shopping well-being and ill-being experiences on life satisfaction (or subjective well-being) are explained through a bottom-up spillover process.

Understanding those factors affecting shopping well-being experiences and shopping ill-being experiences allow policy makers and retailers develop marketing programs that can effectively enhance consumer well-being while minimizing the negative impact of programs on consumer well-being.

BACKGROUND

Positive Impact of Shopping on Consumer Well-Being

In some cases, shopping contributes to the well being of consumers by paving way to hedonic enjoyment and satisfaction of self-expressive needs. Retailing scholars have argued that shopping is associated with hedonic value (e.g, Arnold & Reynolds, 2003; 2012; Babin, Darden, & Griffin, 1994), excitement and delight (e.g., Oliver, Rust, & Varki, 1997; Wakefield & Baker, 1998),

and enjoyment (e.g., Beatty & Ferrell, 1998). Hedonic retail activities have been described as a form of "recreation" (e.g., Backstrom, 2006; Guiry, Magi, & Lutz, 2006), entertainment (e.g., Moss, 2007), or related to enthusiasm that creates emotional arousal and joy (e.g., Jin & Sternquist, 2004; Pooler, 2003).

More recently, researchers expressed interest in the idea that retail activities (i.e., shopping) help shoppers express themselves (Timothy, 2005). As such, it can be argued that shopping activities are not only hedonically enjoyable but also self-expressive in that they allow the consumer to become emotionally involved with the purchase thus serving to actualize the consumer's potential in becoming a good mother/father, wife/husband, etc. Much of this discussion is related to *shopping well-being experiences*. This construct is explicitly defined as the degree to which consumers experience hedonic enjoyment and satisfaction of self-expressive needs through their shopping activities.

Negative Impact of Shopping on Consumer Well-Being

By the same token, consumer shopping experiences have a negative impact on the overall sense of well-being of consumers. Shopping ill-being has much to do with the potential dark side of consumers' retail/shopping activities. Studies have argued that shopping may lead to compulsive buying, which creates much ill-being (Faber & O'Quinn, 1992; Hosch & Loewenstein, 1991; Kwak, Zinkman, & Crask, 2003; O'Guinn & Faber, 1989).

Compulsive shopping refers to consumers' tendency to be preoccupied with buying that is revealed through repetitive buying and a lack of impulse control over buying (Ridgeway, Kukar-Kinney, & Monroe 2008). It has been found that internet versus brick and mortar retail shopping has created a tendency toward compulsive shopping manifested in avoiding social interactions (Kukar-Kinney, Ridgway, & Monroe, 2009).

This is another example of consumers engaging in shopping behavior that reduces social interaction, which may be symptomatic of shopping ill-being. Also, the popular press opined that contemporary lifestyle encourages compulsive shopping and fosters materialism through the purposeful design and creation of desire for the acquisition of more and more material products (Benson, 2000; Faber & Christenson, 1996; Hine, 2002; Schor, 2004).

The desire to "have more" also creates a so-called "work and spend cycle" (Schor, 1991). The author argues that consumers devote more and more hours to work in order to financially and emotionally support their increased level of material acquisition. In a similar vein, Rojek (2006) argues that time spent on shopping (i.e., in the purchase of consumer goods and services) should be viewed as time taken away from more meaningful activities. In this chapter, *shopping ill-being experiences* are defined as the degree to which consumers experience impulsive buying and/or compulsive buying by overspending time, effort, and money in shopping activities.

AN INTEGRATED MODEL OF SHOPPING WELL-BEING AND ILL-BEING

The integrated model is shown in Figure 1. The model shows the two focal constructs of shopping well-being and ill-being experiences, their consequence (overall sense of well-being or life satisfaction), and their antecedents (situational, personal, and social/cultural factors).

The Impact of Shopping Well-Being and Ill-Being Experiences on Overall Life Satisfaction

With respect to *shopping well-being experiences*, there is some suggestive evidence that supports the notion that shopping activity may contribute to one's sense of well-being (Tauber, 1972).

Researchers have long recognized that the psychological life space is multi-dimensional because people segment their emotional experiences in multiple life domains such as social life, work life, family life, spiritual life, shopping life,

Figure 1. An integrated model of shopping well-being and ill-being experiences

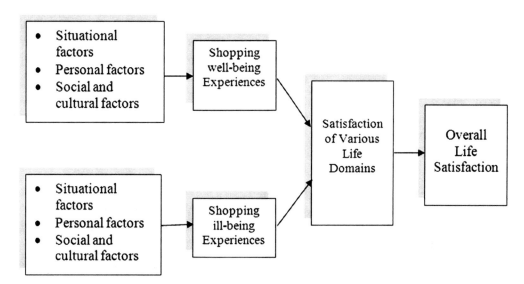

etc. (Andrews & Withey, 1976; Campbell, Converse, & Rodgers, 1976; Day, 1978; 1987; Diener, 1984). Specifically, memories related to specific kinds of experiences and feelings are stored in psychological domains that reflect primary activities. And within each life domain the person has certain value-laden beliefs (Andrews & Withey, 1976; Campbell, Converse, & Rodgers, 1976). In other words, people have multiple psychological domains housing value-laden beliefs in relation to education, family, health, job, friends, shopping, etc. Our main focus in this chapter is *positive and negatives shopping experiences affect satisfaction in the shopping life domain.*

A number of quality-of-life studies have shown that life satisfaction can be explained and predicted from satisfaction one experiences within the different life domains (Campbell, Converse, & Rodgers, 1976). For example, people may feel satisfied with life as a direct function of their satisfaction with their health, job, family, friends, community, material possessions, shopping experiences, etc.

To fully explain the relationship between the shopping well-being experiences (i.e., satisfaction with shopping life) and overall life satisfaction, we need to discuss the concepts of bottom-up spillover in the context of consumer well-being in general. *Bottom-up spillover* between consumer well-being experiences and life satisfaction is traditionally conceptualized using a satisfaction hierarchy model (Lee & Sirgy, 1995; Meadow, 1988). This model is based on research on consumer satisfaction (Aiello, Czepiel, & Rosenberg, 1977) and life satisfaction (Andrews & Withey, 1976; Campbell, Converse, & Rodgers, 1976). The basic premise is that overall life satisfaction is functionally related to satisfaction with all of life's domains and sub-domains. Most multi-attribute attitude models use bottom-up spillover logic in predicting and explaining attitude. A familiar example is brand attitude models that assume a consumer's attitude toward a product, such as a car, is a direct function of the consumer's evaluations of the various attributes of the car moderated by the belief strength associated with each attribute (Fishbein & Ajzen, 1975). Satisfaction researchers have used this same logic to conceptualize the determinants of consumer satisfaction (Aiello, Czepiel, & Rosenberg, 1977).

The essence of the bottom-up spillover model is the notion of a satisfaction hierarchy, and that positive and negative affect spill over from concrete events to life domains (e.g., shopping life, work life, leisure life, family life, social life, love life) to overall life. Thus, specific events housed in a given life domain may affect life satisfaction through a "bottom-up spillover" of affect (Diener, 1984; Sirgy, 2002; Sirgy, Kruger, Lee, & Yu, 2011). That is, satisfaction from a life domain or specific experiences within a life domain vertically spills over to more super-ordinate life domains--the affect within a life domain (or sub domain) spills over *bottom-up* to the most super-ordinate domain (life in general), influencing life satisfaction.

There are many advocates of the bottom-up approach to life satisfaction (Bharadwaj & Wilkening, 1977; Heady, Holstrom, & Wearing, 1985). Many studies have been conducted using the bottom-up approach by examining the spillover effects of satisfaction in the consumer life domain in a community context (i.e., at a macro level dealing with goods and service found in the local area, rather than dealing with a particular good or service) on life satisfaction (Sirgy et al., 2008; Lee et al., 2002). Other studies are more micro in focus. That is, studies focused on the spillover effect of satisfaction with a specific product or specific consumption experiences on life satisfaction--personal transportation (Sirgy, Lee, & Kressman, 2006), housing (e.g., Grzeskowiak, Sirgy, Lee, & Claiborne, 2006), healthcare services (e.g., Sirgy, Rahtz, & Lee, 2004; Sirgy, Hansen, & Littlefield, 1994), internet use (Sirgy, Lee, & Bae, 2006), and travel and tourism (Neal, Uysal, & Sirgy, 2004; Sirgy, Kruger, Lee, & Yu, 2011).

Based on bottom-up spillover theory, one can argue that affective experiences related to shopping (i.e., shopping well-being experiences) may be at the bottom of the satisfaction hierarchy. Satisfaction with various aspects of shopping life may influence

- Satisfaction with social life (i.e., shopping paves way to interact with friends and shopping personnel at the various stores),
- Satisfaction with family life (i.e., shopping provides goods and services to meet family consumption needs),
- Satisfaction with work life (i.e., shopping provides goods and services to help achieve work-related goals),
- Satisfaction with community life (i.e., shopping mall, shopping centers, and large stores provide a variety of venues that allows community residents to interact and feel connected), and
- Satisfaction with financial life (i.e., shopping allows consumers to shop around to find high quality brands for low prices).

The construct of *shopping ill-being experiences* has been conceptually developed (Ekici et al., 2013) but its impact on subjective well-being has not been demonstrated. One such avenue for considering shopping-ill being is that of compulsive buying as defined by Ridgway, Kukar-Kinney, and Monroe (2008). Compulsive buying may result in numerous negative consequences, such as financial problems, emotional harm (e.g., negative feelings, feeling guilty), and social and relationship problems (Faber & O'Guinn, 1992). All factors may influence shopping ill-being experiences which could lead to negative impact on consumer well-being through a bottom-up spillover effect. In other words, spending too much time shopping may detract from opportunities to engage in other activities that can enhance the sense of social well-being, family well-being, work well-being, etc. Furthermore, spending too much money on

material acquisition is likely to lead to financial debt, which may take away from spending on other goods and services essential to social well-being, family well-being, work well-being, etc.

Antecedents of Shopping Well-Being Experiences

To reiterate, *shopping well-being experiences* in this chapter is defined as the degree to which consumers experience hedonic enjoyment and satisfaction of self-expressive needs through shopping activities. Positive affect from shopping well-being experiences are likely to spillover to other life domains including social life, family life, work life, community life, and financial life. That is, shopping well-being experiences are associated with positive emotions (e.g., shopping satisfaction, shopping pleasure, shopping delight) related to shopping activities.

There are several factors that may contribute to those positive emotions, hence the sense of shopping well-being. These factors can be categorized as situational, personal, and social/cultural factors.

Situational Factors: Situational factors that positively affect shopping well-being are mostly the results of retailer-controlled activities. For instance, providing customers with in-store guidance (Gurel-Atay, Giese, & Godek, 2010), employee assistance (Puccinelli et al., 2009), or efficient store layout (Titus & Everett, 1995) may decrease the time and effort spent by customers, thus, leading to satisfying experiences in shopping life.

Indeed, it is suggested that time and effort perceptions, especially by time-strapped customers, impact how those customers assess their shopping pleasure (Baker et al., 2002). For consumers who want to browse and experience the fun side of shopping, on the other hand, retailers can create an exciting and stimulating environment. Other store atmosphere factors, such as background sound (Morin, Dube, & Chebat, 2007) or odors (Spangenberg, Crowley, & Henderson, 1996), can also be used to make the shopping experience pleasant, resulting in increased shopping well-being (Pan & Zinkhan, 2006). Retail crowding, especially spatial crowding, is another retailer-controlled factor that has an effect on shopping satisfaction, hence shopping well-being. For instance, Machleit, Eroglu, and Mantel (2000) found that when the store is crowded, the excitement of shopping and shopping satisfaction is lessened.

Stock-outs may also affect the level of shopping well-being. Fitzsimons (2000), for instance, found that consumers may enjoy shopping more when "personal commitment to the out-of-stock option is low and the stock-out leads to a decrease in the difficulty of making a product selection." In other words, when the stock-out option is not important to the consumer, and when the absence of options makes decision making easier for the consumer, consumers may experience higher levels of shopping well-being–perhaps due to the decreased amount of time and effort spent on shopping.

Personal Factors: One important personal factor that affects shopping well-being is the importance of shopping to a consumer. Consumer who perceives shopping as an important part of his/her life is more likely to feel motivated to engage in shopping activities and actually enjoy shopping (Guiry, Magi, & Lutz, 2006; Sansone & Smith, 2000). Consumers who perceive shopping as his/her part of personal identity and use shopping for self-expressiveness are likely to experience shopping well-being (Timothy, 2005).

Consumers' attitudes may also contribute to shopping well-being. For instance, people who have positive attitudes toward shopping in general, as opposed to people who dislike shopping, are more likely to have an increased level of shopping well-being experiences (Puccinelli et al., 2009). Similarly, people who have low satisfaction thresholds (Mittal & Kamakura, 2001) and a disposition toward satisfaction (Grace, 2005) are likely to have a high level of shopping well-being experiences.

Another personal factor that may affect shopping well-being is shopping efficacy, which is defined as "the degree to which one can efficiently find a particular product for which one is shopping" (Gurel-Atay, Giese, & Godek, 2008). Some people perform better at shopping; they know where to find products they are looking for and buy those items at the best prices in a reasonable amount of time. When these consumers perceive that their shopping is successful, they are likely to experience positive affect (Arnold et al., 2005). In other words, these efficient and effective consumers who feel that they do well in shopping (i.e., buy quality products at low prices) are likely to experience shopping well-being.

A related concept to shopping efficacy is the sense of time urgency (Rizkalla, 1989), or the feeling of time pressure (Gurel-Atay, Giese, & Godek, 2010). Some people are believed to be more sensitive to time and this sensitivity may affect their well-being in general and shopping well-being in particular (Rizkalla, 1989). More specifically, consumers who feel rushed are more likely to dislike shopping (Gurel-Atay, Giese, & Godek, 2010; Rizkalla, 1989), probably because rushing through the shopping process makes product choices more difficult (Dhar & Nowlis, 1999) and results in poor purchase decisions (Johnson & Payne, 1985; Park, Iyer, & Smith, 1989). Therefore, one can hypothesize that shopping efficacy may contribute to the sense of shopping well-being.

Social and Cultural Factors: Because studies on social and cultural differences in shopping well-being are at best limited, we call for future research on this topic. Previous findings in cross-cultural studies related to emotions and shopping activities can be used to generate some working hypotheses to understand how cultural factors may affect shopping well-being. For instance, because the frequency and intensity of positive emotions is stronger in Western cultures than in Asian cultures (Scollon, Diener, Oishi, & Biswas-Diener, 2004) and because Asians tend to report lower levels of well-being in general (Valenzuela, Mellers, & Strebel, 2008), it can be assumed that, compared to Non-Asians, Asians may have decreased levels of shopping well-being.

However, a contradictory finding was obtained by Morgeson et al., (2010). By using a sample of cross-industry satisfaction data from 19 nations, these authors examined the determinants of cross-national variation in customer satisfaction. The results indicated that customer satisfaction is higher for consumers in traditional societies (compared to those in secular-rational societies). In another study, Laroche et al., (2004) compared the satisfaction levels of Japan (a traditional, Asian country) consumers with US and Canada (secular-rational, Western cultures) consumers. Japanese consumers, compared to US and Canadian consumers, reported lower satisfaction ratings when performance was high and higher satisfaction ratings when performance was low. The authors believed that these results were obtained because "Japanese consumers are more conservative in their evaluations of superior service but are less critical (or more forgiving) of inferior service" (Laroche et al., 2004). These contradictory findings come from studies not directly related to shopping well-being; thus, these findings highlight the need for more cross-cultural research to understand differences in shopping well-being experiences.

Antecedents of Shopping Ill-Being Experiences

Shopping ill-being experiences is defined as the degree to which consumers experience impulsive buying and compulsive buying in shopping through overspending time, effort, and money, Here, resources (time, money, and effort) an individual invests in shopping come at the expense of time, money, and effort required in other life domains to maintain a certain level of life satisfaction. This overspending (time, money, and effort) on shopping generally result in complaints among family members, relatives/friends, and/or people at work. These complaints, in turn, contribute to a significant amount of dissatisfaction in life domains related to family life, social life, work life, and financial life.

Even though shopping well-being and shopping-ill being appears as the opposite side of the same coin, they conceptually represent different constructs. While shopping well-being essentially deals with the individual's (i.e., shopper's) positive feelings regarding shopping (that reflect the contribution of shopping to satisfaction in various life domains), shopping ill-being experiences involve the perception of the shopper to the complaints and negative feelings expressed by significant others (e.g., family members, friends and associates) about one's shopping. As noted, when an individual's shopping activities are perceived rather "compulsive" by the close friends and/or family members, these activities may adversely affect life satisfaction. This section provides an overview of the situational, personal, and socio-cultural factors that may account for shopping-ill-being.

Situational Factors: Situational factors that contribute to compulsive shopping and shopping ill-being may be classified as payment-, product-, and retailer-originated. Credit usage may be considered as payment-originated contributing to negative outcomes arising from shopping. Research suggests that the number of credit cards regularly used, as well as the amount of credit debt, are both linked to compulsive shopping (Norum, 2008; Park & Burns, 2005; Dittmar, 2005). For example, Norum's (2008) study, conducted among US college students, reports that irrational credit card use is strongly associated with compulsive buying. As the author argues, American youth have been raised in a credit card society where having money and appearing rich are very important. As a result, "the value placed on status and the acceptance of consumer debt contribute to compulsive buying" (Norum, 2008). In addition, the literature suggests that as compared to "normal" shoppers, compulsive shoppers tend to have more credit cards, less likely to use cash as a payment

33

method, and more likely to have more than one credit card to maximize their credit limit (Black, 2007; O'Guinn & Faber, 1989).

With respect to product-originated factors, research has shown that certain categories (clothing, jewelry, makeup, and collectibles with women, and electronic equipment and collectables with men) are more likely to be the target of compulsive shopping (Faber et al., 1987; Christenson et al., 1994; O'Guinn & Faber, 1989). These categories are considered as more related to self-esteem and may facilitate positive interaction with sales people, which in turn, may help increase the shopper's self-esteem but also induce the shopper to overspend (Faber et al., 1987).

In addition, design and structure of retail environment may contribute to compulsive shopping and therefore shopping-ill being experiences. Shopping environments are deliberately designed to appeal to all the senses and shoppers with higher compulsive tendencies are more likely to be affected by such design (Pooler, 2003). In fact, Mitchell et al., (2006) suggested that 89 percent of their subjects indicated that their compulsive buying episodes occur in stores. Further, Schlosser et al., (1994) reported shoppers with a compulsive tendency pay particular attention to the store "atmospherics" and be enticed by a variety of stimuli including color, sound, texture, and smell. More recent evidence suggests that today the internet provides an additional context in which compulsive shopping can be stimulated (Browne, Durrett & Wetherbe, 2004). Therefore, the design of commercial/shopping websites may encourage acquisition, compulsive behavior, and shopping ill-being.

Personal Factors: Research has indicated that people with low esteem, mood disorder, depression, compulsive hoarding, and/or impulse control disorders are more likely to demonstrate compulsive behavior (Koran, 2000; Mueller et al., 2007, O'Guinn & Faber, 1989). Although intense shopping activities may provide short-term relief from a negative emotional state (Workman &

Paper, 2010), the same activities may lead to an operant conditioned response–shopping becomes conditioned as a response to emotional distress (Falk, 1981). Other personality traits such as ability to fantasize and (low and high) arousal levels have also been linked to compulsive shopping (Black, 2007; Miller, 1980). Furthermore, research has noted that perfectionism (Nakken, 1988; Peele, 1990), impulsiveness (e.g., Christenson et al., 1994), excitement seeking (Mendelson & Mello, 1986), approval seeking (O'Guinn & Faber, 1989), and general compulsiveness (Albenese, 1988) may account for compulsive shopping.

Research has also indicated that certain demographic segments are more likely to engage in compulsive shopping which may result in shopping ill-being. Several researchers have found that women tend to score higher than men on measures of compulsive shopping (Black 1996; O'Guinn & Faber, 1989). This may occur because shopping seems to be an activity that is sex-typed (i.e., the social norm seems to be that women tend to do spend money, men tend to make money). Even though findings regarding age and income have been mixed (Christensen et al., 1994; Schlosser et al., 1994), it seems that there may be a tendency that lower socioeconomic status consumers are impacted by negative aspects of shopping to a greater extent, compared to their higher socioeconomic counterparts.

Materialism also serves as a significant predictor of compulsive shopping. The extant literature suggests that material possessions serve as surrogates for non-satisfying social relationships (Richins & Dawson, 1992). Materialistic consumers tend to place a greater importance on possessions than relationships (Belk, 1985; Dittmar, 2005), and as a result, may engage in compulsive shopping activities that may result in ill-being.

Social and Cultural Factors: Whether a person spends much time, money, and effort on shopping may be shaped by his/her social/family environment and learned consumption habits from childhood (Faber & O'Guinn, 1988; Moschis & Cox, 1998). Socio-oriented family communication patterns, as well as learned saving, spending and the use of money may affect children's attitude toward money, consumption, and shopping (Moore & Moschis, 1981). Thus, compulsive shopping habits may be learned from parents' buying habits. In addition, certain consumers may develop disruptive shopping habits in order to gain attention and obtain feelings of approval and self-esteem "during shopping and spending that they may not have received as children" (DeSarbo & Edwards, 1996, p. 240).

Other socio-cultural factors may involve the commercial environment and advertising activities, and the culture in general (Valence, d'Astous, & Fortier, 1988). Some sociologists argue that advertising is particularly responsible for the progressive transmittal of the materialistic ideal. According to McBride (1980), advertising drives individuals to irrational consumption behavior by making use of their achievement needs, by making light of people's emotions, and making use of the anxiety produced by competition (Valence et al., 1988).

Whether pathological shopping patterns (which may lead to shopping ill-being) is a "cultural" phenomena has been investigated in different cultural contexts including Germany (Scherhorn, Reisch, & Raab, 1990), Canada (d'Astous, Maltais, & Roberge, 1990), Mexico (Roberts & Sepulveda, 1999), and South Korea (Kwak, Zinkhan, & Crask, 2003). Using the *German Addictive Buying Indicator* (a measure of compulsive buying adapted from Valance et al., 1988), Scherhorn et al., (1990) reported that German consumers use the act of buying as a means of compensation for coping with stress, frustration, disappointment, distortion of autonomy, and lack of self-esteem. The "compensatory buying" (Scherhorn et al., 1990) finding is consistent with the findings of those conducted in other "western societies" such as the US and Canada (d'Astous et al., 1990).

The Mexican and the South Korean studies employed the *Diagnostic Screener for Compulsive Buying* (DSCB) developed by Faber and O'Guinn (1992). The results from these studies suggest that compulsive shopping may follow a different pattern in the US, Mexico, and South Korea. Kwak et al., (2003) explained their findings by stating that Korean consumers may decompose the concept of compulsive buying into two aspects: "financial outcomes" and "unfettered spending" (p. 167). For example, Korean consumers may "see the problems associated with physical cash flow as being separate from the impulsiveness of the behavior itself" (p. 168). American consumers do not make such this distinction. These results further suggest that even though compulsive shopping is a pervasive human phenomenon and therefore may be considered as "global" phenomenon (Kwak et al., 2003) certain cultural characteristics may shape its formation. Another multi-country study of consumers in Australia, United States, Hong Kong, Singapore, and Malaysia (Kacen & Lee, 2002) show: cultural factors such as individualism versus collectivism and independent versus interdependent self-concept may systematically influence impulsive and compulsive shopping. The study reveals, for example, that as compared to Caucasians, Asian consumers engage in less impulse purchase. "Independence" appears to play a role in certain pathological shopping behavior particularly among Caucasians--for these consumers, the more independent their self-concept, the greater the likelihood of engaging in more impulse buying.

FUTURE RESEARCH DIRECTIONS

We recommend that future research should test the links between shopping well-being and life satisfaction through the mediation effects of satisfaction in important life domains such as social life, family life, work life, community life, and financial life. The theory that could help explain this mediation effect is bottom-up spillover as discussed earlier. Similarly, guided by the same theory, future research should formally test the effect of shopping ill-being on life satisfaction as mediated by dissatisfaction in important life domains such as family life, social life, and work life.

Future research could also examine the effects of shopping efficacy, shopping involvement, and shopping convenience on shopping well-being. Similarly, future research could test the effect of environmental and situational factors affecting shopping ill-being. Additionally, future research could empirically examine the effect of materialism on shopping ill-being. In summary, future research should test the link of certain antecedents (situational, personal, and social/cultural factors), not only in relation to shopping well-being and ill-being experiences, but also in relation to domain satisfaction, and ultimately, life satisfaction. It is also important to understand which antecedent factors (situational factors, personal factors, socio-cultural-factors) have the greatest impact on shopping well-being and ill-being so that specific managerial and policy initiative can be designed to improve satisfaction with life.

CONCLUSION

We made an attempt in this chapter to review and integrate much of the research findings concerning two focal constructs: shopping well-being and ill-being. Based on the research literature, we linked the antecedents of shopping well-being and shopping ill-being through a set of situational, personal, and social/cultural factors. We also explained the link between shopping well-being/ ill-being and life satisfaction.

More specifically, we explained the link between shopping well-being experiences and life satisfaction using bottom-up spillover theory (life satisfaction can be explained and predicted from satisfaction one experiences within the different life domains such as satisfaction with health, job, family, friends, community, material possessions, and shopping). That is, positive affective experiences related to shopping (i.e., experiences related to shopping well-being) may be at the bottom of the satisfaction hierarchy. Satisfaction experiences (shopping well-being) may influence satisfaction in various life domains (social life, family life, work life, community life, and financial life) and overall life satisfaction.

Shopping ill-being may adversely impact life satisfaction through the effects of compulsive shopping. Compulsive shopping causes a great deal of dissatisfaction in various life domains by usurping time, energy, and money from social life, family life, work life, spiritual life, community life, etc. In other words, compulsive shopping serves as an opportunity cost–opportunity to enhance life satisfaction through using the time, energy, and money invested in shopping activities to other activities that can increase satisfaction in important life domains, that ultimately contribute to life satisfaction. Also, compulsive shopping may lead the shopper to debt, which in turn may prevent the shopper from acquiring needed goods and services in social life, family life, work life, etc. Material deprivation may play an important role in decreasing the sense of well-being in those life domains, which in turn may contribute significantly to life dissatisfaction.

With respect to the antecedents of shopping well-being, we identified a set of situational factors (e.g., retailer-controlled activities such as providing customers with in-store guidance, employee assistance, or efficient store layout; shopper-related activities such as store atmosphere for those who like to browse; spatial crowding; and stock-outs), personal factors (e.g., importance of shopping to a consumer, positive attitudes toward shopping in general, a disposition toward satisfaction, shopping efficacy, and sense of time urgency), social/cultural factors (e.g., Western versus Asian cultures and traditional versus secular-rational societies).

With respect to the antecedents of shopping ill-being experiences, we also identified a different set of situational, personal and social/cultural factors. Situational factors involve payment-related factors (e.g., credit use), product-related factors (e.g., clothing, jewelry, makeup, and collectibles with women, and electronic equipment and collectables with men), and retailer-related factors (shopping environment such as store design and other store atmospherics). As previously discussed in the chapter, one of the situational factors affecting shopping ill-being is the credit use. Excessive reliance on credit cards may contribute to compulsive buying and shopping ill-being. Consumers, at times, use multiple credit cards (each having credit limits well-above their income limits). Some consumers pay only the minimum due while continuing their shopping and debt accumulation. This is of course ill-advised because it is a situation that eventually wrecks havoc on their finances. To reduce the adverse consequences of credit misuse, policy makers should go beyond providing information about the optimal use of credit card. Perhaps, a public policy initiative should be undertaken to limit the total number of credit cards and/or the total amount of credits limit a consumer may have. For example, consumers' maximum credit card limit (on all cards combined) should not exceed their reported income.

Personal factors include personality traits (e.g., materialism, self-esteem, mood disorder, depression, compulsive hoarding, impulse control disorders, ability to fantasize, arousal, perfectionism, impulsiveness, excitement seeking, approval seeking, and general compulsiveness) and demographics (e.g., gender, socioeconomic status). Examples of social and cultural factors include social/family environment and learned consumption habits from childhood, socio-oriented family communication patterns, learned saving and spending, the commercial environment and advertising activities, and culture (western versus Asian).

The managerial and policy implications of this integrated model of shopping well-being and ill-being are important. In order to increase consumer's experiences leading to shopping well-being, retailers could help consumers enhance their shopping efficacy and involvement by providing additional information to make them "better" shoppers (shopping for the highest quality brand at the lowest price). Retailers could make the shopping experience more pleasant and convenient. In addition, retailers could make a concerted effort to reduce consumer experiences leading to shopping ill-being through programs that may ameliorate compulsive shopping.

In sum, retailer could use this research to develop marketing programs to increase shopping well-being and decrease shopping ill-being. Public policy officials could also develop specific policies to encourage retailers to develop programs to increase shopping well-being and decrease shopping ill-being. The research findings as summarized in this chapter should be highly instrumental in developing managerial and public policies to achieve these goals.

REFERENCES

Aiello, A. Jr, Czepiel, J. A., & Rosenberg, L. J. (1977). Scaling the heights of consumer satisfaction: an evaluation of alternative measures. In R. Day (Ed.), *Consumer satisfaction, dissatisfaction, and complaint behavior* (pp. 43–50). Bloomington, IN: Indiana University School of Business.

Albanese, P. J. (1988). The intimate relations of the consistent consumer: Psychoanalytic object relations theory applied to economics. In P. J. Albanese (Ed.), *Psychological foundations of economic behavior* (pp. 59–79). New York: Praeger.

Andrews, F. M., & Withey, S. B. (1976). *Social indicators of well-being: America's perception of life quality*. New York, NY: Plenum Press. doi:10.1007/978-1-4684-2253-5

Arnold, M. J., & Reynolds, K. E. (2003). Hedonic shopping motivations. *Journal of Retailing*, *79*(2), 77–95. doi:10.1016/S0022-4359(03)00007-1

Arnold, M. J., & Reynolds, K. E. (2012). Approach and avoidance motivation: Investigating hedonic consumption in a retail setting. *Journal of Retailing*, *88*(3), 399–411. doi:10.1016/j.jretai.2011.12.004

Arnold, M. J., Reynolds, K. E., Ponder, N., & Lueg, J. E. (2005). Customer delight in a retail context: Investigating delightful and terrible shopping experience. *Journal of Business Research*, *58*, 1132–1145. doi:10.1016/j.jbusres.2004.01.006

Babin, B. J., Darden, W. R., & Griffin, M. (1994). Work and/or fun: Measuring hedonic and utilitarian shopping value. *The Journal of Consumer Research*, *20*(4), 644–656. doi:10.1086/209376

Backstrom, K. (2006). Understanding recreational shopping: A new approach. *International Review of Retail, Distribution and Consumer Research*, *16*(2), 143–158. doi:10.1080/09593960600572167

Baker, J., Parasuraman, A., Grewal, D., & Voss, G. B. (2002). The influence of multiple store environment cues on perceived merchandise value and patronage intentions. *Journal of Marketing*, *66*(2), 120–141. doi:10.1509/jmkg.66.2.120.18470

Beatty, S. E., & Ferrell, M. E. (1998). Impulse buying: Modeling its precursors. *Journal of Retailing*, *74*(2), 169–191. doi:10.1016/S0022-4359(99)80092-X

Belk, R. W. (1985). Materialism: Trait aspects of living in the material world. *The Journal of Consumer Research*, *12*(3), 265–279. doi:10.1086/208515

Bharadwaj, L., & Wilkening, E. A. (1977). The prediction of perceived well-being. *Social Indicators Research*, *4*(1), 421–439. doi:10.1007/BF00353143

Black, D. W. (1996). Compulsive buying: A review. *The Journal of Clinical Psychiatry*, *57*, 50–55. PMID:8698681

Black, D. W. (2007). A review of compulsive buying disorder. *World Psychiatry; Official Journal of the World Psychiatric Association (WPA)*, *6*(1), 14–18. PMID:17342214

Browne, G. J., Durrett, J. R., & Wetherbe, J. C. (2004). Consumer reactions to towards clicks and bricks: Investigating buying behavior on-line and at stores. *Behaviour & Information Technology*, *23*, 237–245. doi:10.1080/0144929041000168 5411

Campbell, A., Converse, P. E., & Rodgers, W. L. (1976). *The quality of American life: perceptions, evaluations, and satisfactions*. New York, NY: Russell Sage Foundation.

Childres, T. L., Carr, C. L., Peck, J., & Carson, S. (2001). Hedonic and utilitarian motivations for online retail shopping behavior. *Journal of Retailing*, *77*, 511–535. doi:10.1016/S0022-4359(01)00056-2

Christenson, G. A., Faber, R. J., de Zwaan, M., & Raymond, N. C. (1994). Compulsive buying: Descriptive characteristics and psychiatric comorbidity. *Journal of Clinical Psychiatry*, *55*, 5-1 1.

Cross, G. (2000). *An all-consuming century: Why commercialism won in modern America*. New York: Columbia University Press.

d'Astous, A., Maltais, J., & Roberge, C. (1990). *Compulsive buying tendencies of adolescent consumers*. Paper presented at Advances in Consumer Research Conference. Provo, UT.

Day, R. L. (1978). Beyond social indicators: quality of life at the individual level. In *Marketing and the quality of life*. Chicago, IL: American Marketing Association.

Day, R. L. (1987). Relationship between life satisfaction and consumer satisfaction. In A. C. Samli (Ed.), *Marketing and quality-of-life interface* (pp. 289–311). Westport, CT: Greenwood Press.

DeSarbo, W. S., & Edwards, E. A. (1996). Typologies of compulsive buying behavior: A constrained clusterwise regression approach. *Journal of Consumer Psychology*, 5(3), 231–262. doi:10.1207/s15327663jcp0503_02

Dhar, R., & Nowlis, S. M. (1999). The effect of time pressure on consumer choice deferral. *The Journal of Consumer Research*, 25(4), 369–384. doi:10.1086/209545

Diener, E. (1984). Subjective well-being. *Psychological Bulletin*, 95, 542–575. doi:10.1037/0033-2909.95.3.542 PMID:6399758

Dittmar, H. (2005). A new look at 'compulsive buying': Self-discrepancies and materialistic values as predictors of compulsive buying tendency. *Journal of Social and Clinical Psychology*, 24(5), 832–859. doi:10.1521/jscp.2005.24.6.832

Faber, R. J., & O'Guinn, T. C. (1988). *Dysfunctional consumer socialization: A search for the roots of compulsive buying*. Paper presented at the 13th annual International Association for Research in Economic Psychology Colloquium. Leuven, Belgium.

Faber, R. J., & O'Guinn, T. C. (1992). A clinical screener for compulsive buying. *The Journal of Consumer Research*, 19, 459–469. doi:10.1086/209315

Faber, R. J., O'Guinn, T. C., & Krych, R. (1987). Compulsive consumption. In M. Wallendorf, & P. Anderson (Eds.), *Advances in consumer research* (Vol. 14, pp. 132–135). Provo, UT: Association for Consumer Research.

Falk, J. L. (1981). The environmental generation of excessive behavior. In S. J. Mule (Ed.), *Behavior in excess: An examination of volitional disorders* (pp. 313–337). New York: Free Press.

Fishbein, M., & Ajzen, I. (1975). *Belief, attitude, intention, and behavior: An introduction to theory and research*. Reading, MA: Addison-Wesley.

Fitzsimons, G. J. (2000). Consumer response to stockouts. *The Journal of Consumer Research*, 27(2), 249–266. doi:10.1086/314323

Grzeskowiak, S., Sirgy, M. J., Lee, D. J., & Claiborne, C. B. (2006). Housing well-being: Developing and validating a measure. *Social Indicators Research*, 79(3), 503–541. doi:10.1007/s11205-005-5667-4

Guiry, M., Magi, A. W., & Lutz, R. J. (2006). Defining and measuring recreational shopper identity. *Journal of the Academy of Marketing Science*, 34(1), 74–83. doi:10.1177/0092070305282042

Gurel-Atay, E., Giese, J., & Godek, J. (2008). Exploring the role of shopping efficacy on customer satisfaction and behavioral intentions. In A. Y. Lee, & D. Soman (Eds.), *NA - Advances in Consumer Research* (pp. 964–965). Duluth, MN: Association for Consumer Research.

Gurel-Atay, E., Giese, J. L., & Godek, J. (2010). Retailer evaluation: The crucial link between in-store processes and shopping outcomes. *International Review of Retail, Distribution and Consumer Research*, 20(3), 297–310. doi:10.1080/09593969.2010.491202

Headey, B., Holmstrom, E., & Wearing, A. (1985). Models of well-being and ill-being. *Social Indicators Research*, 7(3), 211–234. doi:10.1007/BF00319311

Hine, T. (2002). *I want that! How we all became shoppers*. New York: Harper Collins Press.

Hosch, S. J., & Loewenstein, G. F. (1991). Time-inconsistent preferences and consumer self-control. *The Journal of Consumer Research*, 17, 492–507. doi:10.1086/208573

Jin, B., & Sternquist, B. (2004). Shopping is truly a joy. *The Service Industries Journal*, 24(6), 1–18. doi:10.1080/0264206042000299158

Johnson, E. J., & Payne, J. W. (1985). Effort and accuracy in choice. *Management Science, 31*(4), 395–414. doi:10.1287/mnsc.31.4.395

Kacen, J. J., & Lee, J. A. (2002). The influence of culture on consumer impulsive buying behavior. *Journal of Consumer Psychology, 12*(2), 163–176. doi:10.1207/S15327663JCP1202_08

Kukar-Kinney, M., Ridgway, N. M., & Monroe, K. B. (2009). The relationship between consumers' tendencies to buy compulsively and their motivations to shop and buy on the Internet. *Journal of Retailing, 85*(3), 298–307. doi:10.1016/j.jretai.2009.05.002

Kwak, H., Zinkhan, G. M., & Crask, M. R. (2003). Diagnostic screener for compulsive buying: Applications to the USA and South Korea. *The Journal of Consumer Affairs, 37*, 161–171. doi:10.1111/j.1745-6606.2003.tb00445.x

Laroche, M., Ueltschy, L. C., Abe, S., Cleveland, M., & Yannopoulos, P. P. (2004). Service quality perceptions and customer satisfaction: Evaluating the role of culture. *Journal of International Marketing, 12*(3), 58–85. doi:10.1509/jimk.12.3.58.38100

Lee, D. J., & Sirgy, M. J. (1995). Determinants of involvement in the consumer/marketing life domain in relation to quality of life: a theoretical model and research agenda. In H. L. Meadow, M. J. Sirgy, & D. Rahtz (Eds.), *Development in quality of life studies in marketing* (pp. 13–18). Dekalb, IL: Academy of Marketing Science.

Lee, D. J., Sirgy, M. J., Larsen, V., & Wright, N. D. (2002). Developing a subjective measure of consumer well-being. *Journal of Macromarketing, 22*(2), 158–169. doi:10.1177/0276146702238219

Machleit, K. A., Eroglu, S. A., & Mantel, S. P. (2000). Perceived retail crowding and shopping satisfaction: What modifies this relationship? *Journal of Consumer Psychology, 9*(1), 29–42. doi:10.1207/s15327663jcp0901_3

McBride, S. (1980). *Many voices, one world: Communication in society, today and tomorrow.* New York: UNESCO.

McCarville, R. E., Shaw, S. M., & Ritchie, M. (2013). *Shopping as leisure: A study of avid shoppers.* World Leisure Journal.

Meadow, H. L. (1988). The satisfaction attitude hierarchy: Does marketing contribute? In S. Shapiro (Ed.), *Proceedings of the 1988 American Marketing Association Winter Educators' Conference* (pp. 482-483). Chicago, IL: American Marketing Association.

Mendelson, J., & Mello, N. (1986). *The addictive personality.* New York: Chelsea House.

Miller, D. (1998). *A theory of shopping.* New York: Cornell University Press.

Miller, P. (1980). Theoretical and practical issues in substance abuse assessment and treatment. In W. R. Miller (Ed.), *The addictive behaviors* (pp. 265–290). Oxford, UK: Paragon.

Mitchell, J. E., Burgard, M., Faber, R., Crosby, R., & De Zwaan, M. (2006). Cognitive behaviour therapy for compulsive buying disorder. *Behaviour Research and Therapy, 44*, 1859–1869. doi:10.1016/j.brat.2005.12.009 PMID:16460670

Moore, R. L., & Moschis, G. P. (1981). The role of family communication in consumer learning. *The Journal of Communication, 31*, 42–45. doi:10.1111/j.1460-2466.1981.tb00449.x

Morgeson, F. V. III, Mithas, S., Keiningham, T. L., & Aksoy, L. (2011). An investigation of the cross-national determinants of customer satisfaction. *Journal of the Academy of Marketing Science, 29*(2), 198–215. doi:10.1007/s11747-010-0232-3

Morin, S., Dube, L., & Chebat, J. C. (2007). The role of pleasant music in servicescapes: A test of the dual model of environmental perception. *Journal of Retailing, 83*(1), 115–130. doi:10.1016/j.jretai.2006.10.006

Moschis, G. P., & Cox, D. S. (1988). Deviant consumer behavior. *Advances in Consumer Research. Association for Consumer Research (U. S.)*, *16*, 732–737.

Moss, M. (2007). *Shopping as an entertainment experience*. Lanham, MD: Lexington Books.

Mueller, A., Mueller, Albert, Mertens, Silbermann, Mitchell, et al. (2007). Hoarding in a compulsive buying sample. *Behaviour Research and Therapy*, *45*(11), 2754–2763. doi:10.1016/j.brat.2007.07.012 PMID:17868641

Nakken, C. (1988). *The addictive personality: Understanding compulsion in our lives*. San Francisco: Harper & Row.

Neal, J., Sirgy, M. J., & Uysal, M. (2004). Measuring the Effect of Tourism Services on Travelers' Quality of Life: Further Validation. *Social Indicators Research*, *69*, 243–277. doi:10.1007/s11205-004-5012-3

Norum, P. (2008). The role of time preference and credit card usage in compulsive buying behavior. *International Journal of Consumer Studies*, *32*(3), 269. doi:10.1111/j.1470-6431.2008.00678.x

O'Guinn, T. C., & Faber, R. J. (1989). Compulsive buying: A phenomenological exploration. *The Journal of Consumer Research*, *16*, 147–157. doi:10.1086/209204

Oliver, R. L., Rust, R. T., & Varki, S. (1997). Customer delight: Foundations, findings, and managerial insight. *Journal of Retailing*, *73*(3), 311–336. doi:10.1016/S0022-4359(97)90021-X

Pan, Y., & Zinkhan, G. M. (2006). Determinants of retail patronage: A meta-analytical perspective. *Journal of Retailing*, *82*(3), 229–243. doi:10.1016/j.jretai.2005.11.008

Park, C. W., Iyer, E. S., & Smith, D. C. (1989). The effects of situational factors on in-store grocery shopping behavior: The role of store environment and time available for shopping. *The Journal of Consumer Research*, *15*(4), 422–433. doi:10.1086/209182

Park, H.-J., & Burns, L. D. (2005). Fashion orientation, credit card use, and compulsive buying. *Journal of Consumer Marketing*, *22*(2/3), 135–141. doi:10.1108/07363760510595959

Peele, S. (1990). The meaning of addiction: Compulsive experience and its interpretation. Lexington, MA: Lexington.

Pooler, J. (2003). *Why we shop: Emotional rewards and retail strategies*. London: Praeger Publishers.

Prus, R., & Dawson, L. (1991). Shop 'til you drop: Shopping as recreational and laborious activity. *Canadian Journal of Sociology*, *16*(2), 145–164. doi:10.2307/3341271

Puccinelli, N. M., Goodstein, R. C., Grewal, D., Price, R., Raghubir, P., & Stewart, D. (2009). Customer experience management in retailing: Understanding the buying process. *Journal of Retailing*, *85*(1), 15–30. doi:10.1016/j.jretai.2008.11.003

Richins, M. L., & Dawson, S. (1992). A consumer values orientation for materialism and its measurement: Scale development and validation. *The Journal of Consumer Research*, *19*, 303–316. doi:10.1086/209304

Ridgeway, N. M., Kukar-Kinney, M., & Monroe, K. B. (2008). An expanded conceptualization and a new measure of compulsive buying. *The Journal of Consumer Research*, *35*(4), 622–639. doi:10.1086/591108

Rizkalla, A. N. (1989). Sense of time urgency and consumer well-being: Testing alternative causal models. In T. K. Srull (Ed.), *NA - Advances in Consumer Research* (pp. 180–188). Provo, UT: Association for Consumer Research.

Roberts, J. A., & Sepulveda, C. J. M. (1999). Money attitudes and compulsive buying: An exploratory investigation of the emerging consumer culture in Mexico. *Journal of International Consumer Marketing, 11*(4), 53–74. doi:10.1300/J046v11n04_04

Rojek, C. (2006). Representation. In C. Rojek, S. M. Shaw, & A. J. Veal (Eds.), *A handbook of leisure studies* (pp. 459–474). London, UK: Palgrave-Macmillan. doi:10.1057/9780230625181

Sansone, C., & Smith, J. L. (2000). Interest and self-regulation: The relation between having to and wanting to. In C. Sansone, & J. M. Harackiewicz (Eds.), *Intrinsic and extrinsic motivation: The search for optimal motivation and performance* (pp. 343–374). San Diego, CA: American Press. doi:10.1016/B978-012619070-0/50034-9

Scherhorn, G., Reisch, L. A., & Raab, G. (1990). Addictive buying in West Germany: An empirical study. *Journal of Consumer Policy, 13*, 355–387. doi:10.1007/BF00412336

Schlosser, S., Black, D. W., Repertinger, S., & Freet, D. (1994). Compulsive buying: Demography, phenomenology, and comorbidity in 46 subjects. *General Hospital Psychiatry, 16*, 205–212. doi:10.1016/0163-8343(94)90103-1 PMID:8063088

Schor, J. B. (1991). *The overworked American: The unexpected decline of leisure*. New York: Basic Books.

Schor, J. B. (2004). *Born to buy*. New York: Scribner.

Scollon, C. N., Diener, E., Oishi, S., & Biswas-Diener, R. (2004). Emotions across cultures and methods. *Journal of Cross-Cultural Psychology, 35*(3), 304–326. doi:10.1177/0022022104264124

Sirgy, M. J. (2002). *The psychology of quality of life*. Dordrecht, The Netherlands: Kluwer Academic Publishers. doi:10.1007/978-94-015-9904-7

Sirgy, M. J., Hansen, D. E., & Littlefield, J. E. (1994). Does hospital satisfaction affect life satisfaction? *Journal of Macromarketing, 14*, 36–46. doi:10.1177/027614679401400204

Sirgy, M. J., Kruger, S. P., Lee, D. J., & Yu, G. B. (2011). How does a travel trip affect tourists' life satisfaction? *Journal of Travel Research, 50*(3), 261–275. doi:10.1177/0047287510362784

Sirgy, M. J., Lee, D. J., & Bae, J. (2006). Developing a subjective measure of internet well-being: Nomological validation. *Social Indicators Research, 78*(2), 205–249. doi:10.1007/s11205-005-8209-1

Sirgy, M. J., Lee, D. J., Grzeskowiak, G., Chebat, J.-C., Johar, J. S., Herman, A., & Montana, J. (2008). An extension and further Validation of a community-based consumer well-being measure. *Journal of Macromarketing, 28*(3), 243–257. doi:10.1177/0276146708320447

Sirgy, M. J., Lee, D. J., & Kressmann, F. (2006). A need-based measure of consumer well-being (CWB) in relation to personal transportation: Nomological validation. *Social Indicators Research, 79*(2), 337–367. doi:10.1007/s11205-005-4920-1

Sirgy, M. J., Rahtz, D., & Lee, D. J. (2004). Further validation and extension of the quality of life community healthcare model and measures. *Social Indicators Research, 69*(2), 167–198. doi:10.1023/B:SOCI.0000033592.58120.9b

Spangenberg, E. R., Crowley, A. E., & Henderson, P. (1996). Improving the store environment: Do olfactory cues affect evaluations and behaviors? *Journal of Marketing*, *60*(2), 67–80. doi:10.2307/1251931

Stebbins, R. A. (2006). Shopping as leisure, obligation, and community. *Leisure*, *30*(2), 467–474. doi:10.1080/14927713.2006.9651367

Tauber, E. M. (1972). Why do people shop? *Journal of Marketing*, *36*(4), 46–49. doi:10.2307/1250426

Timothy, D. (2005). *Shopping, tourism, retailing, and leisure*. Toronto, Canada: Channel View Publications.

Titus, P., & Everett, P. B. (1995). The consumer retail search process: A conceptual model and research agenda. *Journal of the Academy of Marketing Science*, *23*(2), 106–119. doi:10.1177/0092070395232003

Valence, G., d'Astous, A., & Fortier, L. (1988). Compulsive buying: Concept and measurement. *Journal of Consumer Policy*, *11*, 419–433. doi:10.1007/BF00411854

Valenzuela, A., Mellers, B., & Strebel, J. (2008). Cross cultural differences in delight. In A. Y. Lee, & D. Soman (Eds.), *NA - Advances in Consumer Research* (pp. 678–679). Duluth, MN: Association for Consumer Research.

Wakefield, K. L., & Baker, J. (1998). Excitement at the mall: Determinants and effects on shopping response. *Journal of Retailing*, *74*(4), 515–539. doi:10.1016/S0022-4359(99)80106-7

Wanger, T. (2007). Shopping motivation revised: A means-end chain analytical perspective. *International Journal of Retail & Distribution Management*, *35*(7), 569–582. doi:10.1108/09590550710755949

Workman, L., & Paper, D. (2010). Compulsive buying: A theoretical framework. *The Journal of Business Inquiry*, *9*(1), 89–126.

ADDITIONAL READING

Chebat, J.-C., El-Hedhli, K., & Sirgy, M. J. (2009). How does shopper-based mall equity generate mall loyalty? A conceptual model and empirical evidence. *Journal of Retailing and Consumer Services*, *16*(1), 50–60. doi:10.1016/j.jretconser.2008.08.003

Chebat, J.-C., Sirgy, M. J., & Grzeskowiak, S. (2010). How can shopping mall management best capture mall image? *Journal of Business Research*, *63*(7), 735–740. doi:10.1016/j.jbusres.2009.05.009

El-Hedhli, K., Chebat, J-C. (in press). Shopping well-being: Construct, antecedents, and consequences. *Journal of Business Research* (published online July 29, 2011).

Lee, D.-J., & Sirgy, M. J. (2012). Consumer well-being (CWB), Various conceptualizations and measures. In K. C. Land, A. C. Michalos, & M. J. Sirgy (Eds.), *Handbook of Social Indicators and Quality of Life* (pp. 331–354). Dordrecht: Springer Publishers. doi:10.1007/978-94-007-2421-1_15

Lee, D.-J., Sirgy, M. J., Wright, N. D., & Larsen, V. (2002). Developing a subjective measure of consumer well-being. *Journal of Macromarketing*, *22*(2), 158–169. doi:10.1177/0276146702238219

Sirgy, M. J. (2012). *The psychology of quality of life: Hedonic well-being, life satisfaction, and eudaimonia* (2nd ed.). Dordrecht, Netherlands: Springer Publishers. doi:10.1007/978-94-007-4405-9

Sirgy, M. J., Lee, D.-J., & Rahtz, D. (2007). Research in consumer well-being (CWB), An overview of the field and introduction to the special issue. *Journal of Macromarketing*, *27*(4), 341–349. doi:10.1177/0276146707307212

KEY TERMS AND DEFINITIONS

Bottom-Up Spillover: The notion of a satisfaction hierarchy, and that positive and negative affect spill over from concrete events to life domains (e.g., shopping life, work life, leisure life, family life, social life, love life) to overall life.

Compulsive Buying: The consumers' tendency to be preoccupied with buying manifested through repetitive buying and lack of impulse control in shopping.

Hedonic Enjoyment in Shopping: The degree to which shopping experiences are associated with increased positive emotions and decreased negative emotions.

Life Satisfaction: A global assessment of a person's quality of life.

Materialism: People who are materialistic lace much value of the material life compared to other life domains such as family life, work life, community life, and spiritual life.

Self-Expressiveness in Shopping: The extent to which shopping activities help the shopper express his or her own social identity.

Shopping Ill-Being: The degree to which consumers experience overspending of time, energy, and money in their shopping.

Shopping Well-Being: The degree to which consumers experience hedonic enjoyment and satisfaction of self-expressive needs through shopping activities.

Chapter 4
Understanding Consumers' Behaviour Change in Uncertainty Conditions:
A Psychological Perspective

Amalia Duţu
University of Pitesti, Romania

ABSTRACT

An economic crisis is an uncertainty situation with negative economic evolutions like unemployment, inflation rate increasing, freezing or decreasing of the wages, purchasing power decrease, investments value reduction, fluctuations in consumer prices, restrictions in accessing loans, and fluctuations in currency exchange rate that represent economic shocks hitting most of the consumers to some extent. During economic turbulent times, consumers are highly exposed to such risks. The present chapter is intended to explain the consumers' behaviour alteration and spending patterns in recession conditions dealing with the panic mechanism that shapes the consumers' behaviour in this particular context, analyzing it from an economic and psychological perspective. The chapter is organized in two complementary parts in an attempt to present a comprehensive picture of consumers' behaviour change in uncertainty conditions. Readers can find answers to the "HOW" question and also to the "WHY" question placed behind consumers' behaviour alterations during recession.

INTRODUCTION

Since 2007, the global economy has entered a period of profound restructuring, the world facing one of the worst economic crisis in its history. It is amazing how fast the financial crisis that started in the U.S. turned into an economic global crisis. The rapid expansion of the economic crisis worldwide, confirms the acceleration of the globalization process and the interdependencies existing between national economies at present. The current economic crisis is considered an unprecedented event for the world, its unique character being supported by several aspects, including its severity and global nature. If the confidence crisis that followed the financial crisis played an

DOI: 10.4018/978-1-4666-6074-8.ch004

important role in turning the financial crisis into an economic one, the acceleration of economic globalization and increasing interdependence in economy have contributed significantly to the expansion of global economic crisis by domino and contagion effects.

Throughout the time, analysts and researches indentified different causes for each important economic crisis episode, a common point being the emotion. At the conference "Crisis of Confidence. The Recession and the Economy of Fear" held in 2009, sponsored by the University of Pennsylvania's Department of Psychiatry and the Psychoanalytic Center, there was emphasized the following aspect: "The emotion not only led America into the present economic crisis but it could also keep it there." David M. Sachs, training and supervising analyst at Psychoanalytic Center of Philadelphia stated that "the economic crisis is not one of concern but one of confidence." In this respect, Nobel economist Stiglitz (2008) claimed that the financial crisis emerged from a catastrophic collapse of confidence. At the same time, Ron Anderson (2009) asked some questions in an article posted on his blog: "Have you noticed that in general, people provide only economic explanations to the present crisis? Have you noticed the majority arguments are built on economic and political elements and only on a small scale on psychological ones?." Generally, recessions lead to unemployment problems, therefore, incomes fall, consumer confidence decreases, and all these lead to a raise in uncertainty about the future (Kay, 2010).

Looking at the present global economic turmoil, the transformation mechanism of the financial crisis in an economic one spread worldwide is based on the fact that a certain type of crisis generated the emergence of another type of crisis, the key driver to this emergence being the emotion. The core mechanism of this phenomenon is considered the "economy of fear." Due to the exposure to the uncertainty and economic shocks the emotional response of consumers to the effects of the financial crisis determined the decrease of their confidence in brands, companies, sectors of activity, and in the anti-crisis measures taken by governments. In other words, the negative emotional response determined the appearance of confidence crisis which is associated with the alteration of consumption and spending allocation, people considering savings as a proper reaction to the uncertainty of their existence. Fear of the future, unfavorable changes in price elasticity, hard value and cost benefits gain in importance, compressed time preference, financing becomes more important and safety becomes a higher priority. Consumers choose saving their money instead of spending it (Simon, 2009). The fall in consumer spending leads to a decrease in aggregate demand and therefore lower economic growth. The fall in consumer spending leads to a decrease in aggregate demand and therefore, lowers economic growth. This had as a consequence market contractions and their structure alterations, generating the classical overproduction crisis, but also the prologue of the economic crisis. Thus, the new market situation is characterized as the "age of thrift" which has radically changed customer purchase behaviour providing an environment dominated by public skepticism and lack of trust in business and in marketing offers (Piercy et al., 2010). This is supported by the evolution of Consumer Confidence Index (CCI) which, according to Nielsen Global Confidence Index Report 2008 has experienced significant decreases in all national markets in which it was measured, in some national markets taping an absolute record of decrease. In the first half of 2009, CCI continued to decline in 48 of the 50 monitored countries (see Box 1).

In this context, important drivers of the individuals' behaviour changes are emotions and psychological factors. Confronted with economic shocks, consumers adapt themselves to the situation through adjustment of purchase behaviour and spending allocation. Actually, during the last few years consumers "learnt" how to live from "adjustment to adjustment" on all national mar-

Box 1. Market mood: The "voice" of consumers

> "There will be no spending for a long time; we have cut up all our credit cards."
>
> "The economic crisis has made me curtail my spending habits. In the future, I will continue to hold off on my spending until the economy gets better."
>
> "The economy is scary."
>
> "If people stay calm and not give into their fear, we will be okay"

Source: The Nielsen Company – Consumer Reaction to the Banking Crisis, Comments about Economy, October, 30, 2008, http://www.claritas.com/eDownloads/webinar/Nielsen-Claritas-Webinar-Consumer-Reaction-Banking-Crisis-103008.pdf

kets. Therefore, in recession context companies have to operate on volatile markets, characterized by contractions and important changes in their structures this phenomena being correlated with consumer behaviour alterations. That is why understanding the psychology of the crisis and the panic mechanism behind it is very useful in elaborating the recovery strategies and in determining people's post-crisis behaviour. The present chapter is intended to explain the consumer behaviour alteration and spending patterns in uncertainty conditions (economic crisis) dealing with the panic mechanism that shapes the consumer's behaviour in this particular context, analyzing it from an economic and psychological perspective. Thus, the main objectives of the chapters are:

- To present the results to an extensive literature review regarding consumers behaviour change in the context of different crisis episodes in order to identify some patterns of purchase alteration and shopping behaviour,
- To explain the panic mechanism behind the economic behaviour alteration through the model of consumer behaviour change in uncertainty conditions,
- To present a model of psychological market segmentation and a consumers typology regarding behaviour alteration, a sociological and psychological profile.

In order to fulfill the objectives of the chapter, an extensive literature review in both the field of economic crisis and consumer's behaviour in uncertainty situations, and in risk theory and consumers psychology was conducted.

The chapter is organized into two complementary parts in the attempt to present a comprehensive picture of consumer's behaviour change in uncertainty conditions. Readers can find answers to the "HOW" question but also to "WHY" question behind consumers behaviour alterations during recession. The present chapter will display the patterns of consumer's behaviour change based on previous experiences but also based on present meltdown. On the other hand, this chapter is grounded on the results of research conducted during 2009-2012, in the field of consumer behaviour and consumer psychology. Thus, the chapter presents how the panic mechanism works and how the psychological factors are linked with behaviour alteration and the spending allocation.

THE *HOW* QUESTIONS: HOW DOES CONSUMERS BEHAVIOUR CHANGE IN CRISIS CONDITIONS? WHAT DO EMPIRICAL FINDINGS SHOW?

In one study Dutt and Padmanabhan's (2009) identified 435 currency crises episodes across 195 countries over the period 1960 to 2006. Thereby, at international level, there are different studies achieved in the context of various economic crisis periods, some of them having as a purpose, the identification of core changes occurred in consumers' behaviour and in spending allocation as a result of the exposure to economic shocks generated by the recession. Anyway, should be noted that until present crisis episode only a few researcher were focusing on the topic adopting various manners of approaching.

The first relevant study belongs to Kelly and Schewe (1974), who analyzed the reaction of American consumers to the stagflation during 1973 to 1974 in the context of 1973 oil crisis. The main directions that they followed in the analysis were: consumption vs. savings, postponing important purchases, extensive credit usage, and change of lifestyle. Also, Shama (1980) analyzed this change in case of New York consumers and found that the recession conducted to changes in consumers' motivations, values, attitudes and expectations. Thus, the core changes identified by these researchers were: the desire to buy less (the decrease of consumption desire), the postponing of long-lasting product purchase, the focus on comparing the products and an extension of purchase duration, the change of purchase habits and the elimination of waste and the usage of promotion coupons. For durable goods, consumers were focusing on product utility and price. Also, they started to use cheaper products such as private labels, saved less and used more loans.

Many researchers examined the consumers' reaction to economic impacts generated by the Latin American crises. Latin America's crises hit households hard. For instance, in the 1980s, real wages in Argentina and Mexico fell by nearly 40 percent, while poverty increased by more than 30 percent. In Chile, real wages shrank by about 15 percent and unemployment rose by 9 percentage points within a year. In the 1995–1996 crisis, real wages in Mexico fell by more than 30 percent. In Argentina, unemployment rose by 6 percentage points and remained at around 18 percent of the

work force for more than two years (The world Bank, 1998). In an interesting approach Friszbain et al., (2003) identified more types of strategies adopted by households in Argentina during 2001 to 2002, the most difficult period in the history of this country. The strategies identified by them were separated in groups according to the type of household response to the economic crisis. The first group of strategies called adaptive strategies covers in fact, a reactive response of the household with a view to quantitative and qualitative consumption. The second group of strategies called active strategies, engender a proactive response of the household, focusing on home goods production for selling, entrance on the labor market of a new member of the household, at least one member of the family begins to work longer hours, at least one member of the family emigrated or relocated permanently in another city, another province, etc. The third group of strategies called social network, consists essentially in searching for living support provided by people outside the household. The above mentioned authors explored the relation between the strategies identified and the type of economic shock experienced by the household, and found that there was a direct connection in between and the change of household behaviour is correlated with the wealth and number of members of the respective household. Robles et al., (2002) identified, in the context of the same crisis episode, the following changes in Argentinean consumers' behaviour: the avoidance of long term financial commitments by leaving out major purchases: cars, houses, holidays, etc., the re-evaluation of consumption mix by increasing expenses for basic products, the change of purchase habits by guiding the consumers toward self-service, discount outlets and hypermarkets, the search for a favorable quality-price balance. McKenzie (2004) found in an interesting study that although consumers bought less after the devaluation, they shopped more days. This increase in shopping frequency occurred over a wider variety of channels, and was almost entirely through increased shopping for priced products. The share of expenditure allocated to premium brand products fell for all parts of the expenditure distribution, suggesting that consumers were also reducing the quality of their goods purchased during the crisis. In broad lines, the same main directions in consumers' behaviour change were identified by Zurawicki and Braidon (2005) in a research made with the purpose to identify middle-class Argentinean consumers' reaction between 2001 and 2002.

The Asian crisis that affected the entire region that followed after a very long boom period, taking by surprise all consumers, represented main topic for many empirical studies. In a paper that provided the background for discussions during the Asia Development Forum held in March 1998 in Manila, adopting a social perspective Tamar Manuelyan Atinc and Michael Walton (1998), described different strategies adopted by people in order to survive and underline the cutting down on household expenditure using some impressive examples as in slum areas, people reported cutting down from three meals per day to two, or even one. In Indonesia and the Philippines (Mindanao), teachers reported that children were eating less before coming to school in the mornings and buying less from vendors and that this was affecting students' ability to concentrate. Ang et al., (2000) identified the following behavioural changes within the Asian crisis: a lower consumption for all product categories and waste riddance, the search for extra information, the substitution of products, the buying of home products rather than foreign products, the choice of discount and neighborhood shops. Also, Kang and Sawada (2008) analyzed how the credit crunch in Korea in the late 1990s affected household behaviour and welfare. They found that, Korean households reduced consumption of luxury items while maintaining food, education and health related expenditures in order to deal with the negative shocks of the 1997 credit crunch. Also, there are empirical evidences that households have cut back spending on "deferrable" items (such as clothing, household furniture and

similar semidurables) while maintaining real expenditures on foods in Indonesia during 1997-1998 (Frankenberg et. al., 2002).

The nowadays recession without precedent in the entire world, called consumers attention upon revising their behaviour and budget allocation. A great number of empirical studies were conducted from different perspective in many countries beginning with 2008, in order to identify the national patterns of consumers behaviour change.

Quelch and Jocz (2009), presented in one of the first studies during the present crisis episode, the shifts in consumers psychology and habits adopting psychological market segmentation approach. They described three different consumers groups presenting different patterns alterations: The slam-on-the-brakes segment, which feels the hardest hit, reduces all types of spending, Pained-but-patient consumers, who constitute the largest segment, also economize in each area, though less aggressively, Comfortably well-off individuals consume at near-prerecession levels but become a little more selective (and less conspicuous) about their purchases, Live-for-today consumers pretty much carry on as usual, responding to the recession mainly by extending their timetables for making major purchases. Also, these authors, argued that all consumers, no matter the segment prioritize consumption by sorting products and services into some certain categories: essentials (central to survival or well-being), treats (justifiable), postponables (can be put off), and expendables (unnecessary or unjustifiable). A close approach was used by Urbonavicius and Pikturnien (2009) in Lithuanian context, who identified six types of consumers' response associated to behaviour change:

1. To continue with the same behaviour without any change – this type of behaviour does not imply changes at the level of high income consumers who do not undergo but very scarcely the effects of the crisis;

2.   To reduce spending in order to survive – this type of response implies significant alterations of consumers' behaviour by a blunt reduction of the quantity and quality of the products;

3.   To reduce spending in order to make some savings – is a feature of the consumers whose budgets were not significantly affected but choose to become cautious for purchases that are not essentially necessary and they prefer to save money;

4.   To concentrate on short-term increase of life quality, as long as it can be afforded – this type of response characterizes the category of young people free of financial and social obligations;

5.   To improve life quality by consuming more products and services – this response implies the increase of consumption of certain categories of products and services, increase stimulated by the decrease of prices for different products; and

6.   Improve life quality by consuming better quality products and services – this response means that consumers are driven towards better quality products

In different studies conducted in European countries there was reported some similar shifts in consumers' behaviour. Thus, in Slovakian context, Chebeň and Hudáčková (2010), identified six main features that describe changes in consumer behaviour during economic crisis: reduction of spending on less necessary goods, price became the main factor in decision-making, increased use of discounts and price reductions, delaying larger purchases ad infinitum, reducing consumers' loyalty to brands, more rational decisions. The change of consumer behaviour pattern was not very different in Romanian consumers' case compared with others European consumers (Pandelica & Pandelica, 2011). The most important change was the elimination or postponing of the major purchases. Concurrently, Romanian' consumers focused on spending optimization, first of all, because they engaged in an extra information searching process and on the other hand, because they focused on the best quality-price ratio. Even if the price seemed to be more important in the process of choosing the products, the quality of products remained an important issue. The core tendency regarding spending allocation was the rationalization of expenses, by keeping the expenses at almost the same level for strictly necessary products (basic food products) and decreasing the expenses for almost all the other categories of products and services. Thus, the Romanian' consumers, spent almost the same amounts on basic food products, water, gas, electricity, pharmaceutical and medical care products. They spent significantly less on journeys, holidays, leisure, appliances and tools (household appliances, electronics, furniture, etc.), alcoholic drinks and tobacco, magazines, newspapers, books. Polish consumers (Jasiulewicz, 2011) were forced to use their savings, drastically reduce their expenditures, ask relatives for help or take extra work. At the same time, a significant reallocation of consumption expenditures was visible. Poles spent more especially on foodstuffs and smaller consumption of some goods (alcoholic beverages, cigarettes, books, recreation, services, clothes and shoes) was connected with the attempt of expenditures limitation. Expenditures limitation in households caused by economic crisis determinate a change in Polish consumers' lifestyle. They spend less on their pleasures such as holiday trips, entertainment, meals outside home, services associated with caring for body and beauty. Every fifth respondent chooses public transport instead of car reduces consumption of electricity, gas and water and limits paid services associated with the house and its surroundings in order to save some money. The crises negatively affects the Polish consumers mood and their perception on future taking into account that high concern dominated and pessimistic attitudes like panic and depression were identified among respondents.

Flatters and Willmott (2009) in an article published in Harvard Business Review presented different patterns of behavoiur change of American consumers:

1. A demand for simplicity meaning that during recession consumers are used to limited offers and they tend to simplify their demand,
2. Discretionary thrift taking into account that even the rich people are economizing, although they don't have to. They revealed their dissatisfaction with excess consumption. They started to recycle, buy used goods and teach their children simple and traditional values,
3. Mercurial consumption dealing with the fact that consumers are "agile" and they act fast in response to price change having the ability to switch brands looking for the least price sacrificing the quality and loyalty.

Nie et. al. (2010) identified, in their turn, the impact of the financial crisis on consumer behaviour in China context, as follows:

1. Consumer confidence declined, spending budget significantly reduced, as the uncertainty of economic development and job security increase, consumer confidence index in China fall 94.5 in march 2008 to 86 in march 2009, which was the lowest point in last few years. Chinese consumers spent less in the household products, personal care products, food and drink. Meanwhile they buy less in the area of leisure and entertainment, and postpone buy large goods;
2. Chinese consumers became more rational and sensitive to price, they chose domestic brands instead foreign brands and put emphasis on product efficacy, durability. Consumers pay more attention on price and quality than on style, brand and service. In addition, more consumers are beginning

to get access to shops and make Internet research when they are shopping;
3. The change of consumers' shopping places dealing with the fact that online shopping is more and more attractive to consumers.

In India Kondawar and Jadhav (2012) underlined the fact that the consumers psychology and behaviour has changed greatly in the financial crisis, the main shifts reported were:

1. Decline in consumers' expectations regarding income, resulting in lack of consuming confidence,
2. Rational consumer behaviour replaced the impulse buying behaviour as Indians consumers become more and more rational, and purchasing decisions are prudent every time,
3. The price sensitivity of consumers increased, as India's consumers in the process of decision-making are engaging in addition search of information and make an additional effort in price decision-making. Also Mansoor and Jalal (2011) found in case of Bahraini consumers a shift from expensive to inexpensive substitute, a shift from luxury to essential, a shift from huge quantities to small quantities and a shift from consumption to saving.

As one can notice, at international level, there are many studies that provide empirical insights regarding behaviour alteration in various recessions. In every recession marketers find themselves in poorly charted waters because no two downturns are exactly alike (Quelech & Jocz, 2009). In spite of the differences that are obvious, based on the results of different international studies conducted in several contexts (crisis episodes, countries, regions), a synthesis can be traced according to the Box 2.

Box 2. The consumers' behaviour alteration during the recession period

---

The consumption reduction - a less wastefully consumer

In the context of recession there is a significant decrease of consumption desire. Because of the economic shocks exposure generated by the economic turmoil and because of the uncertainty associated with these, consumers tend to consume less. Consumption reduction is associated to savings increase or to survival. Consumers revealed their dissatisfaction with excess consumption and tend to turn to the simplicity in their consumption. Also, they reevaluate what actually is necessary and essential, even if the essential meaning vary from one country to another and is modeled by economic, cultural and social factors. During recession consumers rediscovered their capacity to control and reduce the consumption dealing with the shift from huge quantities to small quantities and the appearance of WHY behind the buying (It is really necessary?). Consumers are turning to the economic good sense and "wisdom." This alteration was reported in all country case studies. Nonetheless, the consumption decrease varies as intensity across countries but also across different groups of consumers in the frame of one national market. Concurrently, the consumption reduction varies across different categories of products and services.

Increasing savings – a more prudent consumer

In recession, people tend to consider savings as a proper reaction to the uncertainty of their existence. Thus, this tendency is correlated with uncertainty and economic shocks exposure (unemployment, decreasing of income, loosing job stability etc.). Still, the empirical findings are mixed in this sense. As a result, in some countries even if some categories of consumers spent less they didn't increase savings during recession because of the higher inflation and prices during the period as well as because of freezing or decrease of incomes, being forced to use their savings in order to survive. On the other hand, in some countries even rich people saved up, although they didn't have to. This tendency was reported by some country case studies.

Migration on the demand curve – the reduction of quality

In the recession period consumers tend to migrate on the demand curve switching brands: from premium or middle products to cheaper products. They buy generic brand products and replace expensive goods by substitutes or cheaper ones. This alteration in consumers' behaviour was reported in all national markets but the migration rate varies from one country to another, on one hand, and from a category of consumer to another, on the other hand.

Elimination/postponing of major purchases - a caution consumer

In economic stressful times consumers have eliminated or postponed the major purchases (durable goods). Even if the level of income permit such purchases, consumers stay cautious and eliminate what is not strictly necessary, because of the uncertainty of economic evolutions that generates financial and job insecurity. This shift in consumers' behaviour was presented in many country case studies even if this trend varies among national markets and across different groups of consumers within one national market.

Brand loyalty shift – a less loyal consumer

The consumers become more agile and they are less loyal because of financial pressure but also because of changes in values, attitudes and things that matters. Taking into account that in economic downturn the consumers are less confident in brands they easily change their favorite brand and location for shopping focusing on price, price reductions, price-quality ratio. This shift in consumers' behaviour has been found in many countries, especially during present crisis episode.

Price comes first/Price sensitivity – more sensitive

Price became the main factor in decision-making. Thus, consumers become price sensitive and act fast in response to price change which is correlated with the shift from expensive to inexpensive substitute, and shift from luxury to essential. This alteration in consumers' behaviour was reported in all national market.

The rationalization of the consumption and expenses – a more pragmatic consumer

On the one hand the rationalization refers to keeping the expenses at almost the same level for strictly necessary products (essentials) and decreasing the expenses for almost all the other categories of products and services. On the other hand this tendency refers to best value for money. Even if in the context of the economic turmoil price seems to be more important in the process of choosing the products, the quality of products remained an important issue. Thus, the consumer wants to pay less but he/she also wants the maximum of the quality for the price. The rationalization process is correlated with the extra search for information in the buying process (a better informed consumer). Thus, crisis has brought a more rational and selective shopping behaviours on all national markets.

Aggressive search for options – a better informed consumer

In recession periods consumers engaged in an extra information searching process, allocate more time in finding information and options because they are focusing on the best quality-price ratio. Thus, they attach great importance to the collection of information on buying and value product performance information, Consumers are wiser and better informed and they have "discovered" a lot of options and the power to use it.

Shifts in emphasize on different attributes – the change in the "Why" behind the buying

As consumers become more rational they put a greater emphasize on other product attributes. It is about the shift from image, style, brand and "nice to have" to the best value for money and a more focus on efficiency, durability, necessity etc.

---

continued on following page

Box 2. Continued

Changes in shopping place

During recessions consumers increased use of discounts and price reductions and they turn towards discount and neighborhood shops. At the same time, online shopping became more attractive to consumers. Many country case studies reported similar shifts.

Changing in spending allocation – quantities reduction

In economic hard times consumers reevaluate their purchasing basket and reallocate the consumption expenditures among products and service categories. The general tendency is keeping the expenses at almost the same level comparing with pre-crisis period for strictly necessary products but also other products and services considered essentials and decreasing the expenses for almost all the other categories of products and services, considered non-essentials. Of course, the essential meaning varies to a certain extent from one country to another and it was basically reevaluated. Regarding the spending allocation for basic food products, the results of countries' case studies are mixed. On one hand, there are countries where these expresses remained almost on the same level or increased. On the other hand, in some countries were reported the decrease of the expenses for such products. Still, in many case studies conducted in United States, Europe and Asia, there was a common point, respectively an important decrease of the expenditures for some certain categories such as: journeys, holidays, leisure, house maintenance and improvement, household appliances, electronics, furniture, etc.

Source: Author's synthesis based on different country case studies

HOW Should Retailers Respond in the Context of Consumer' Behaviour Shifts?

The change of consumers' behaviour during recession is directly reflected in the "wallet share," the "shopping basket" and on the shelves of the retailers. As a result, retailers need to revise their strategies to meet the new type of customer and his particular behaviour shift. It can be presume that the most important for any retailer or consumer driven business in such turbulent times is to think and act for their customers. Customer values and behaviour changed dramatically during the downturn as the synthesis shows (Box 2). It is therefore possible that retailers' products and service offerings may become unaligned with demand. What strategies and tactics can help retailers to survive, and even thrive, during an economic storm? A synthesis of the most important shifts regarding strategies and operations adopted by retailers in order to handle the difficult economic period can be traced (see Box 3).

Regarding consumers' response in recession, Goldmen (2003) referred to the effects of the destructive emotions, Quelech and Jocz (2009) considered the response of the consumers in present economic context was an emotional one and Perriman et. all. (2010) noted aspects such as perceived risk, fear about buying, or hard tan-

gible advantages become more important, while image and "nice to have" attributes moved into the background. In uncertainty times the customers' fear for the future deeply impacts on their behaviour thus, the customers that companies thought they had in the pre-recession times, can be almost unrecognizable during downturn. Even if at the international level we can find answers for the question: "HOW does consumers' behaviour change in crisis conditions?" and even if many researchers have pointed out that consumers response in such a context was rather emotional, at the international level we can find only some fragmented answers to the "WHY" behind the consumers' behaviour change. In uncertainty times it is very important that companies, including retailers, to understand how their clients react and why people behave like that. Such an understanding should represent the starting point in planning the response of the organization. Thus, the companies have to penetrate into their clients' minds and the reshaping process of strategies and tactics during recession should start with a deep understanding of the internal processes that conducted to individual behaviour shifts. During my studies I have found that in some international studies conducted in economic turmoil periods, researchers explored the link between economical status of the individual or of the household

Box 3. The retailers' response regarding consumer behaviour alteration

---

1. New retail formats in response to consumers' movement towards discount and neighborhood formats.

As I noted in the first part of the chapter, the consumer behaviour shift during the last few years call the retailers to the reevaluation of the retail format (new developments and design). Taking into account the changes regarding shopping place (formats) and the price sensitivity, retailers should focus on smaller discount formats and on the online formats that are two important trends that flourished during the recession.

- *Shop formats need to be thoroughly reviewed* considering that consumers tend to migrate towards smaller formats, neighborhood formats and discount formats.
- *Innovative retail formats should be developed - online and virtual retail formats*

In the context of the economic crisis, proximity development is a certain trend driven by consumers' behaviour shifts. The proximity becomes an important factor for intermediary buying (refill). This trend emerged from the new reality of the last few years: smaller basket per visit and increased shopping frequency. Also, the smaller proximity formats offer some certain advantages: time economization (shopping after work hours), simplicity and a diversified range of products, shopping in smaller formats provide a better control over shopping budgets compared with shopping in hypermarket format. Thus the frequency of the "refill" purchases has increased. As a response to these shifts in the consumers behaviour the big retailers reacted in Romania, by developing smaller formats and proximity formats: PROFI – 160 smaller formats, MEGA IMAGE – 150 smaller formats, BILLA – 73 smaller formats, CAREFFOUR MARKETS – 69 smaller formats/CAREFFOUR EXPERESS – 33 shops, PROFI CITY – 8 shops, PROFI LOCO – the new concept implemented in rural area (according to Alina Bondoc, Romania CBD Team Leader, P&G)

On the other hand, there are many reasons why, especially in crisis context consumers are shopping online. This is not a new trend but was intensified by the economic crisis. Shopping online can offer consumers greater product choice opportunity, more price transparency and a better basis of comparison in searching options. The first retailer from FMCG industry that introduced the online format was the British company Tesco PLC in 1997. So, this format is not new and its development is not a crisis response. But, in the last few years it is obvious that this trend has accelerated and many retailers adopted and developed such formats. Let's have a look around online retail formats developed in the last few years: In 2011 Tesco developed the first concept of the virtual shop that was not located in the commercial surface. Thus, in many stations of the South Chorea subway, Tesco put digital billboards which display shelves with different products that exist in the offer of Home Plus. Each product has a QR code which is scanned with mobile phone, and the product goes into the shopping basket. In 2012, the concept was extended on the British market. Also, in 2012 Tesco launched online formats in Czech Republic followed shortly by Slovakia and Poland. In the online shop consumers can find an offer containing up to 20.000 products covering many food and non-food categories. In 2010 Auchan Group developed a business division for e-commerce. In 2012, The Belgian Group Delhaize re-lunched its online platform DelhaizeDirect.be, and open Delhaize Direct-Cube a virtual shop in the central Railway Station from Bruxelles, containing up to 300 articles. The German Group REWE entered in 2011 in online commerce and lunched REWE on-line.

Obviously during the crisis retailers have focused in their business strategies on the development of the innovative retail formats in order to be closer by the consumers. A new wave in this strategy has been adopted and this trend will continue in the future, but we can conclude that this wave was intensified in the last few years. On the other hand the modernization of the traditional formats and the development of the smaller proximity formats were accelerated in the last few years.

2. The assortments review in response to the shifts in the consumers' purchasing habits and changes in spending allocation.

Looking at the behaviour change at the clusters level presented in Box 2 and 4, the identified pattern is common but the intensity of behaviour shift vary on a certain extent from one cluster to another, country by country. Also, regarding spending allocation patterns, it is obviously that some products categories are more affected then others in the "wallet share" and in the "shopping basket." In this context, those retailers with a high share of non-food products were more affected. The assortments reduction in order to cope with these shifts was one of the strategic directions adopted by retailers. Also, the range optimization is a strategic direction adopted in order to cope with consumers' behaviour change.

3. Value for money - Own brand strategy and different tactics

According to David Bradbury, Assistant Treasure, Minister Assistant for Financial Services and Superannuation and Minister for Competition Policy and Consumer Affairs, Australian Government (2013) in the global crisis we have seen the rise of so called "cautious consumers." Consumers are increasingly aware of global economic difficulties and concerned about global economic uncertainty. These cautious consumers have been saving more and spending less than they may have before the global crisis. And when making their spending decisions, these cautious consumers are also more aggressively seeking out value for money. If you combine this lower propensity to spend with the fact that consumers now expect more for their money, this represent a challenge for the retail sector. As it was pointed out in this chapter (Box 2) during recession consumers tend to migrate on the demand curve looking for affordable products and good deals putting a great emphasis on value for money. These tendencies towards "professionalization of shopping" call the retailers to adjust their offerings and to develop the private label ranges. This strategy of growth and diversification, especially in economic difficult times, was adopted by many retailers taking into account that these brands are no longer perceived as "low-cost option." If in Vest Europe the increase of market share for private labels is off, the levels varying country by country, in Eastern Europe the share of private labels continue to grow. The success of this growth strategy during the crisis was supported by the development of multiple retail formats, making these labels affordable and easy to find. On the other hand, different tactics were adopted in order to manage the "value for money" search by consumers. The packaging was one of these. For instance, in the last few years consumers could find products in bigger packages with lower price per unit or smaller packages with better prices or even a small reduction in quantity of the package for the same price. The usage of the promotional package containing complementary products with a lower price per unit represented a used tactic in this sense. It is important to note that, even if price becomes the first criterion for consumers' choice, according to the results of my research presented in the Box 3, but also in other international studies, consumers are looking for the best value that can obtain for the paid price. Thereby a decrease in quality in order to maintain price is not a very good option.

---

continued on following page

Box 3. Continued

---

4. Focusing on rebuilding of the loyalty

In economic turmoil period consumers are less loyal they change the favorite brand and shopping location focusing on price, price reductions, and price-quality ratio optimization. Thus, the best price becomes the main factor influencing the choice of brands and shopping place. Anyway, should be note that according to Global Survey of Loyalty Sentiment, Nielsen, at the global level, there is a higher degree of loyalty for the retailer (74%) compared to brand loyalty which recorded a mean around 61%. We can conclude that the tendency to switch the brands is higher than the tendency to switch the shopping place.

In this context the adaptation of fidelity programs and schemes are very important. Anyway the simple schemes are suitable in the context of economic turbulence when the trust degree is on the lowest level. If a fidelity program is not free on costs and simple to be accessed, the consumers will not follow the scheme. On the other hand, the retailers should communicate all the benefits of the participation in the program. The usage of the on-line communication to presents the benefits of such programs may be very efficient in such turbulent period.

5. Being empathic with the customers

Being hit by the consequences of the economic crisis, consumer confidence in brands was affected. In difficult economic times is very important to be emphatic with the customers' economic situation. Different tactics were adopted in this sense. For instance the development of offerings and solutions around the idea of economizing and the communication of this idea is a way to tell customer that you are thinking about his/her problems and you find solutions for this. All the solutions adopted in this line should be communicated as "we are thinking solutions for your problems." On the other hand, the messages should be focused on real benefits and attributes of the products. Also using cross-promotional on the shelves for the products that are no longer on the purchasing list during recession and the additional signalization of the products within the shop may be a good tactic to help consumers to find solutions.

Source: Author's synthesis based on in-depth-interviews and different reviewed studies

and behavioural shifts, underling the existence of significant relationships in between.

Taking into account the fact that in many international studies it was pointed out that emotions and panic feeling were "catalysts" of the behaviour alteration; in 2009 I started a research project with the purpose to explore this link. Thus, the study was an exploratory one, based on the premise that psychological factors play an important role in the consumers' behaviour change in nowadays economic crisis (uncertain conditions). Therefore, its purpose was to examine the causal relationship that develops between psychological factors considered within the developed conceptual model and the consumers' behaviour alterations. The final purpose of the study was to offer an additional insight regarding consumers' behaviour change in uncertainty context, a complementary approach to those based on economical factors.

THE *WHY* QUESTION: THE PANIC MECHANISM: WHY DID CONSUMERS BEHAVE LIKE THAT?

In order to frame the panic mechanism behind the change of consumers' behaviour, and to identify how panic feeling works, I was started from a broader context with the purpose to determine the core factors that generate the change of consumers' behaviour in uncertainty context as recession. There was analyzed several studies that was done in the context of various types of crises: recession, food security crisis - contamination with salmonella, avian flu, terrorism crisis (USA, 2001), public health security crisis - AH1N1/swine flu, 2009. Thus, there was considered different types of uncertainties that generate risks and stress exposure. Also, most of these uncertainties were unique events, so there was no past previous context to allow people to place such events.

The purpose of this analysis was to identify to what extent these situations with negative impact on people (risk and stress generating situations) display some common aspects. The results of the analysis pointed out that obviously each crisis is unique event and no crisis is similar to another as no two similar crisis are alike considering generating factors, severity, evolution, outcomes etc. But, it was established the fact that in all these uncertainty situations with risk and stress exposure the psychological factors play an important role in determining the change of human behaviour with consequences over economic and financial behaviour, health status and social capital. Thus, in order to frame the conceptual model regarding the change of consumers' behaviour in risk-generating situations (uncertainty) it was started from the premise that risk perception and risk aversion are important internal drivers of behaviour change in economic turbulent times.

Risk concept is a commune denomination, very often used nowadays in various circumstances: finance, insurance, economic behaviour, strategy, investments, economic trends, public health, terrorism, food security and so on. As Hillson and Webster (2004) point out, there is a great range of definitions for risk-concept in the academic literature. Even among risk practitioners in the various professional bodies there is an ongoing debate about the subject matter at the heart of their discipline. Also there is a huge variation in the general literature, reflecting the lack of official agreement on the basic definition of risk (Hillson & Webster, 2006).

According to Slovic at. al. (2004) there are three fundamentals ways of seeing risk: risk as feeling that capture the instinctive and intuitive reaction to danger, risk as analysis that brings logic, reason and scientific deliberation to bear on hazard management and risk as politics. In psychology, risk is defined as a subjective construct influenced by how the event is interpreted (Weber, 2004). Risks lead many people to think only about threats, that is, those uncertainties that if they occur would result in an undesirable outcome. In this line each risk can be seen as uncertainty, which can be expressed as 'probability' or 'likelihood'; and how much it matters, expressed as 'impact' or 'consequence'. Holton (2004) argues that there are two ingredients that are needed for risk to exist. The first is uncertainty about the potential outcomes from an experiment and the other is that the outcomes have to matter in terms of providing utility. Thus, risk can be seen as the product of the probability of an event occurring, that is viewed as undesirable, and an assessment of the expected harm from the event occurring

Nevertheless, there is consensus within various approaches as to the fact that risks is associated with uncertainty and generates consequences. A recession, in general is considered as uncertainty and a risk generating situation with significant effects on individuals, labeled as economic shocks, representing the external factors of the behaviour change or stimuli. Zurawicki and Braidot (2004) defined the economic crisis from consumers' perspective as the most traumatizing event that affects family's life and brings a sudden and substantial deterioration of economic situation. Akerlof and Shiller (2009) emphasized that a growing number of economists recognized that a psychological perspective is necessary in economic analysis in recession. Thus, in the recession context environmental factors like unemployment, inflation raise, the freezing or decrease of income, the decrease of purchasing power, the decrease of deposits, the loss of job stability represent economic shocks that individuals have to cope, risks respectively, as long as such evolutions represent "uncertainties that matter" (Hillson & Murray-Webter, 2006) having important effects on individuals' lives. These economic shocks labeled as risks in the panic framework were considered external stimuli that generate the individual behaviour change (catalysts of change). For instance, some consumers postponed the major purchases during the last few years even if the level of income provided the solvability for such purchases, but the fear of unknown made them cautious. In the framing process there was a great emphasis on exploring and understanding the mental structures and processes which mediate between these stimuli and individual response (as economic behaviour). Also these risks become the main stressors that are correlated with the directions of behaviour alterations, but also with health status and social relationships (Pandelică & Pandelică, 2011; 2012). For instance, in the study that I conducted in 2010 in Romania, I have found that the most important stressors during analyzed period were essentially of economic nature. The hierarchy regarding the stressors was:

1. The evolution of national economy,
2. The financial status,
3. The decreasing of the purchasing power,
4. The fear of the unemployment,
5. The capacity to ensure a decent living for the family.

An interesting aspect was the fact that media and the way in which it was reflected the evolution of economic crisis was pointed out as an important stressor by Romanians. This interesting aspect sustains what it is already known that in some situations, media has the tendency to exaggerate when they present the effects of the economic crisis, delivering scenarios that make people agitated. Between all these stressors and measured directions of behaviour change were identified direct relations of causality (Pandelică & Pandelică, 2011; 2012).

According to specialized literature different things matter to different people to a different extent in different circumstances. So, risk perception and risk aversion vary on a spectrum. Thus, each risk is perceived and interpreted (represented) differently by each and every individual, which is the assessment of the situational context, controllability of estimated effects, and confidence in these estimations (Sitkin & Weingart, 1995). According to Slovic et. al. (2004) people support their judgments not only on what they are thinking but also on how they feel about it. If their feeling are favorable they tend to estimate risk as low, if their feelings towards it are unfavorable, then they tend to estimate the opposite – high risk. Thus, risk perception is the interpretation that an individual makes with a view to the chances to be exposed to risk content (Pennnings et. al., 2002), the assessment of risk content and the capacity to control the exposure. For instance, perception over unemployment is an interpretation of the extent to which the individual considers himself liable to unemployment, the estimated outcomes of this situation and the control degree of this situation. This interpretation is generating fear of

unemployment and the emotion of job stability loss. The highest values of this perception the highest behaviour alterations. Thus, this personal interpretation generates emotions such as anxiety, depression, stress, fury, fear etc. In a summary of potential emotions in relation to perception of risk and risk attitude Hillson (2008) reviewed such affective factors like: *Fear* (dread, worry, concern…) of the consequences of something happening, *Hate* (dislike, disgust…) - I don't want it/want less of it, *Sadness* (depressed, morbid…) - life is bad, more bad things are probable.

Consequently, each individual likes/dislikes, tolerate/do not tolerate in a certain measure the risk-generating situation, reflecting each person's risk-attitude and that leads to certain feelings such as panic, confidence/lack of confidence in brands, companies, government, media, future. Risk attitude is a chosen response to uncertainty that matters, influenced by perception (Hillson & Webter, 2006). Perception drives risk attitude, which in turn affects the quality of decisions made under conditions of uncertainty. For instance, being risk adverse means uncomfortable with uncertainty, the desire to avoid or reduce threats and to exploit opportunities to remove or to limit the uncertainty. We can think of a person with a high perception of unemployment (low job stability) and a low toleration regarding this situation which decides to consume less and to save more based on the assumption to manage the possible unemployment period. Indeed, in my study I have found that there is a significant relationship between the two psychological factors considered in my model – risk perception and risk aversion, but also, between these factors and all measured directions of consumers' behaviour change (the migration on the demand curve, the postponing/elimination of the major purchases, the aggressive search of options in choosing products, in the process of product choice the price comes first, in the process of product choice the quality comes first, the trial of new innovative products) taking into account that I have found a direct relation of causality in between (Pandelică & Pandelică, 2011; 2012). Thus, risk aversion is a hypothetical construction reflecting whether the individual likes or dislikes, tolerate or not tolerate risk-generating situation. So, risk aversion is a mental projection of a certain situation (Hillson & Webter, 2006).

Thereby, in recession context the change of individual' behaviour is determined by risk perception regarding the risk exposure (the effects of economic crisis) and risk aversion regarding the evolution of national economic situation (risk generating situation). Also, in the uncertainty context the extent to which an individual considers that he/she will manage the risk exposure play an important role in alternating the behaviour (Figure1).

Certainly not all individuals are alike, they do not react identically in a risk-generating situation,

Figure 1. Conceptual model regarding the change of consumers' behaviour in risk-generating situations (uncertainty)
Source: Author's work (further development of the "Conceptual model regarding the change of consumer's behavior in risk-generating situations," Pandelica and Pandelica, 2011).

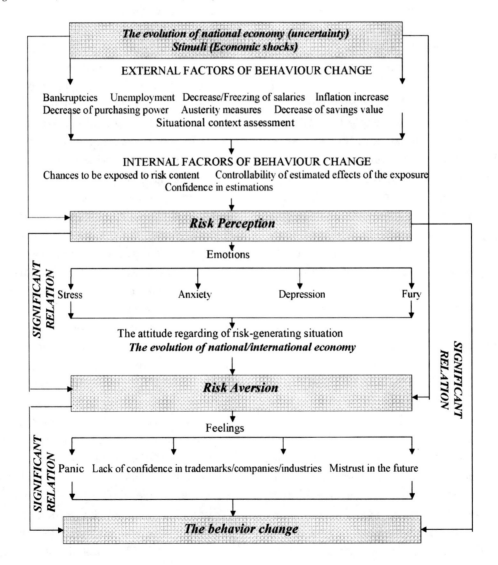

such as recession because their perceptions over risk generating situations are varying on a great extent function of: the estimation of the chances to be exposed to risk content, the assessment of risk content (effects) and the capacity to control the exposure but also by the presence or lack of previous experience in a similar situation. Attitude towards risk is correlated with the risk perception and the two internal psychological factors of the consumer behaviour change vary on a certain scale. Thus, the change of consumers' behaviour is not expected to have the same intensity and follow the same patterns, and the consequences of risk exposure to have the same intensity in all cases. Starting from the models presented by Pennings et al., (2002) and Lusk and Coble (2005) regarding consumers' reaction in risk conditions, in my approach the consumers behaviour was decomposed in two psychological dimensions (internal factors - risk perception and risk aversion) considering the manner in which they interact in order to obtain a clearer image of the behaviour change in recession. According to Quelch (2009) the segmentation scheme that companies have been using prior to the recession is obsolete, and that most companies need to go out and re-talk to their customers and re-frame their segmentation approach. The traditional ways

Figure 2. Conceptual model regarding the psychological segmentation of the market based on internal factors of behaviour – risk perception and risk aversion (MS = market segment; CCI = Consumer Confidence Index)
Source: Author's personal work (further development of the "Conceptual model regarding the psychological segmentation of the market" developed by Pandelica and Pandelica (2011) using Pennings et. al (2002), Lusk and Coble (2005) models).

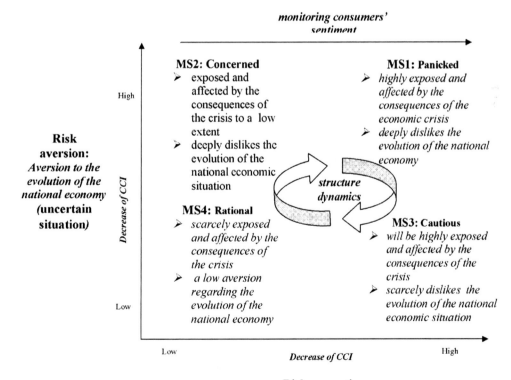

that companies segment their customers – maybe by lifestyle, demographics– aren't necessarily as relevant as segmenting them according to their emotional reaction to the downturn.

The Structure Dynamics

During recession the structure of the market has a certain dynamic and the dimension of the four segments is varying from one national market to another, according to:

1. The severity of the economic crisis effects (S),
2. Experience/lack of experience of some previous economic turbulent times in the relatively recent history of the national economy (E),
3. The moment on the crisis curve (phase) (T) the moment when the government adopted the austerity measures and the severity of these measures (MA),
4. Cultural factors (CF).

For instance, when people interpret the content of a risk in order to evaluate how bad the situational context is, they use their previous experiences gained during turbulent economic periods. When such a previous period was experienced in the recent history of a national economy, the consumers' response to the uncertainty will be based on a learning lesson; thereby they tend to assess the gravity of the situation more "correctly." When there isn't such a background experience, the consumers will have the tendency "to project the worst of their fears" (Ron Anderson, 2009) in order to make this evaluation. Thus, their response to crisis will be an emotional one taking into account that there is no past background to allow them to place such events. This was emphasized by Zurawicki and Braidon (2004) in their research paper that analyzed the middle-class consumers' reaction in the context of the Crisis in Argentina (2001-2002). They underlined that in the case of Asian Crisis (1997-1998) the consumer was taken

by surprise considering that nobody anticipated the crisis that followed after a long period of economic development; thus, the consumers had no previous context to rely on. On the other hand, Argentinean consumers accumulated experience regarding the "correct" reaction in recession conditions taking into account the economic reforms of the 1990s envisaging the liberalization of the markets that led to a decrease of life standard and change of consumers' behaviour. Therefore, they were in a much better position for a "correct evaluation" of the gravity of the situation in the context of 2001-2002 crisis. In nowadays crisis episode, as it already was mentioned, in many countries consumers faced with unprecedented situation and their reaction is based on emotions.

Also, the dimension of the four segments is altering according to the evolution of the economic crisis (phases) – entering into recession, the bad situation of the national economy, the climax of the recession, the signs of recovery and full overcoming of the crisis (classical curve). During these phases, risk perception and risk-generating situation aversion alter in time according to this evolution. Bombol M. (2011) has made attempts to systematize the consumers behaviours in the various stages of crisis: The first stage (2008) was characterized by limitation of unnecessary pleasure goods purchasing, emotional purchases controlling, denying the necessity of conscious reduction in consumption; The second stage (2009) brought another shifts in consumers behaviour like: substitution of more expensive products with cheaper, postponing expensive purchases for later, reducing the unnecessary expenses; and The third stage (2010) characterized by getting used to the crisis, ostentatious savings and bigger consumer awareness. The stages correspond to different shifts in behaviour alteration and to different phases on the crisis curve. Also, should be noted that in the recession period there is a process of learning. Thus, consumers learnt to one phase to another how to manage the situation and how to live from "adjustment to adjustment."

Likewise, the dimensions of the segments vary from one national market to another according to the severity of the effects of the economic crisis (how badly the national economy was affected). Not least, considering that in economic crisis periods, the pessimism grows in accordance with the reaction of the government through anti-crisis measures, the dimensions of the four segments vary according to the moment when the austerity measures were adopted and to the severity of these measures. For instance, in Greece case, the austerity measures conducted to general strikes and violent riots. At the same time, Romanian government adopted the most severe austerity measures in the European Union by the end of May, 2010 which contributed to the lowest consumer confidence index values in July 2010 that represented the highest diminishing during the last ten years according to a study made by GfK (2010). In spite of the fact that the austerity measures were more sever in the Romania case compared with Greece, the people reaction was moderated. This can be explained by the uncertainty avoidance index that characterizes the two cultures. Thus, according to the Hofstede (2004) study, Greece is the most risk avoidance culture recording a UAI (Uncertainty Avoidance Index) of 112, while Romania recorded a UAI of 90. As Gärling et. al. (2009) emphasized, the way people behave, their attitudes and values, and the way they perceive themselves, are functions of cultural, historical, and political influence. Considering the austerity measures as external stimuli which generate people reaction, their response will be determinate by the individual capacity to cope with unpredictability, and as Hofstede (2004) demonstrated this capacity varies to one culture to another.

FUTURE RESEARCH DIRECTIONS

During recessions important research questions were concerned academic scholars but also marketing managers and practitioners, such as: How deep are the shifts in consumers' behaviour during recessions? What are the patterns of behaviour alteration and spending allocation during reces-

Table 1. The centroids of the final clusters generated by SPSS

Psychological factors	Clusters			
	Cluster 1	Cluster 2	Cluster 3	Cluster 4
Perception regarding the exposure to the outcomes of the crisis generated by the evolution of the national economy	4.38	2.42	3.70	1.67
Aversion to the evolution of the national economy	4.70	4.64	2.43	2.33

Source: Author's work - data analysis with SPSS

Table 2. Clusters membership and dimension (Romanian market, 2010)

Clusters	Number of Cases	Percent	Profile
Cluster 1	282	53.51%	The Panicked
Cluster 2	145	27.51%	The Concerned
Cluster 3	67	12.72%	The Cautious
Cluster 4	33	6.26%	The Rational
Total	**527**	**100%**	**100%**

Source: Author's work - data analysis with SPSS

Box 4. Psychological market segmentation: Romanian Case*

Even if optimistic forecasts were delivered by different analysts regarding Romania's economic evolution in 2010 as well as Romania's government optimism, Romanians were more pessimistic regarding this issue at the beginning of 2010. This was sustained by the fact that a great majority (89.4%) of respondents acknowledge that Romania will not overcome the recession in 2010 and 90.3% thought that there will be no improvement of the national economic situation in the next six months.

In order to identify psychological market segmentation in Romanian case, K-means cluster analysis was used, the number of initial clusters (established according to the conceptual model of psychological segmentation presented in Figure 2) was 4.

CLUSTERS PROFILING

The Panicked

Profile: *The Panicked are those consumers considering that within the next six months they will be highly affected by the consequences of the economic crisis and they dislike the evolution of the national economy on a great extent. This cluster is made up of employees with a low and medium income (53,5%); retired persons and unemployed persons considering that out of 67 of the respondents 49 are Panicked who acknowledged that they were affected by unemployment in the last six months. An interesting aspect is that 20.3% from the respondents professing that they were not affected by the effects of the recession are 'panicked'. Thus, in this cluster are concentrated those who were already exposed to the risk content but also those who have a high perception about the exposure of risks in the next period. Most of the Panicked are individuals with a low level of income and education and they come from rural area considering that 67.0% of the respondents coming from rural area on the entire sample are concentrated on this cluster.*

Behaviour Shifts: main tendency within this cluster was a significant reduction in consumption. This was done in order to survive (69.86%). The majority of *Panicked* consumers changed the favorite products/brands with some cheaper ones (67.02%) and eliminated/postponed most of their important purchases (90.78%). Time allotted for information gathering and aggressive searching for comparative options and thus, for the best choice increased during purchasing (80.50%). In the decision making process most of them took into account the best/affordable of all prices (87.23%) but also, the quality (54.96%). It is obvious that within this segment, there is a decrease of consumption from both a quantity and quality point of view. At the same time, an important part of the *Panicked* consumers approached a more rational behaviour not only by eliminating the products that are not strictly necessary but considering a deeper analysis of the quality-price balance. The migration on the demand curve can be associated with the relatively low degree of confidence in brands at the level of this cluster.

The Concerned

Profile: *The Concerned are those consumers thinking that in the next six months they will be scarcely affected by the consequences of the recession and the evolution of the national economic situation is deeply dissatisfactory. The membership to this cluster is diverse: employees with medium income (66,2%), students (17,9%), entrepreneurs/freelancers (10,3%), retired persons (11%). Still the commune features are present, taking into account that the majority of the concerned have high education and graduated high-school (41,4%), a higher education institution (41,4%) or postgraduation courses (6.2%), and most of them are coming from the urban area.*

Behaviour Shifts: within this cluster there were identified two distinct tendencies regarding consumption vs. savings. On the one hand 50.34% of its members acknowledged that, in the last six months compared to the previous period, they had a lower consumption for most of them with the purpose of saving money, on the other hand, 44.66% of the concerned consumers preserved the level of consumption by decreasing their savings. Anyway the central tendency was towards saving. Only a minority (11.03%) of the members of this cluster migrated to the lower level of the demand curve; a great number of them kept on buying their preferred products/trademarks or they changed them only in some circumstances (categories of products). Only 43.45% of the *Concerned* consumers eliminated/postponed the purchase of important items. Unlike the 'panicked', only 48.9% of the Concerned allotted more time for information and comparison of offers in the decision-making process. Within this process, quality comes first (79.31%) and then comes the price (40.69%). One can notice that the decrease of consumption was made through means of eliminating the unnecessary products, preserving though the quality of the products and services consumed. Thus, in this cluster the main tendency was the reduction of quantity but not necessary the reduction of the quality. Should be noted that at the level of this cluster the degree of confidence in brands is relative high and this can be associated with a low migration on the demand curve and a relative high brand loyalty.

The Cautious

Profile: *The Cautious are those consumers thinking that within the next six months they will be highly exposed to the consequences of the recession and the evolution of the national economic situation scarcely displeases them (low risk aversion). This cluster encompasses employees (67,3%) with a medium and high monthly income as well as entrepreneurs considering that 18,4% from the total number of entrepreneurs of the sample belong to this cluster. The presence of entrepreneurs shows the impact of the recession on business environment and the difficult problems they have to cope with for surviving in the context of economic turbulence. Also some common features can be traced on the level of this cluster taking into account that most of cautions graduated high-school (55.2%), and higher education institutions (28,4%) and come from urban area.*

Behaviour Shifts: this cluster also displayed two major tendencies relatively balanced regarding consumption vs. savings. On the one hand, 47.70% of the *Cautious* acknowledged that they reduced consumption for the purpose of saving, while 52.30% preserved their consumption through decreasing their savings in order to achieve that. Anyway the central tendency was the reduction of saving for consumption purpose. Only a minority of the members of this cluster migrated to the lower curve of demand (32.4%), the majority part kept on purchasing the favorite products and brands. The majority of the *Cautious* eliminated/postponed major purchases (50.75%) and engaged in an extra search of information for purchasing process (55.22%) searching for the best choice options. For the *Cautious*, the quality comes first (71.64%) and then the price (59.70%) in the decision-making process for products. An interesting result is the slightly intense alteration in case of this cluster compared with the previous cluster. This intense alteration is not a necessary linked with the level of income but with risk perception which is higher comparing with previous group. If we compare the *Cautious* with the *Concerned*, a more rational behaviour is visible. The *Cautious* eliminated the unnecessary purchases on a greater extent and were focusing on a higher extent on the quality-price ratio optimization. The empirical measurement of the degree of confidence in brands presented a slightly lower mean value in case of *Cautious* compared to concerned and this can explain the higher shift regarding the migration on the demand curve and the slightly lower brand loyalty in case of this cluster.

continued on following page

Box 4. Continued

The Rational

Profile: *The Rational are those consumers thinking that within the next six months they will be scarcely affected by the consequences of the recession and have a low aversion regarding the evolution of the national economy. The respondents belonging to this cluster are employees with a high monthly income as well as those who professed that they were not affected by the consequences of the recession. Most of the Rational come from urban areas (95,6%) and graduated high school (40,0%) and a higher education institution (48,9%).*

Behaviour Shifts: the main tendency at the level of this cluster is preserving the consumption, considering that 63.70% of them preserved their level of consumption in the last six months compared to the previous period; 27.3% of them decreasing their savings in order to sustain the consumption. An important majority of the *Rational* kept on purchasing favorite products and brands migrating to the lower curve of demand only in some situations. At the same time, the majority of the members of this cluster made big purchases during the analyzed period (69.70%). Generally, the *Rational* did no allocated more time for information when making choices as they relied more on quality (84.85%) than on price (39.39%). One can notice that within this segment, there are no important changes in consumers' behaviour. There is, still, a slight difference or rationalization through a decrease of unnecessary purchases. At the level of this cluster it was registered the highest level of trust in brands, generally rational being loyal consumers.

*The purpose of the study was to analyze the causal relationship between the psychological factors considered as independent variables and some dependent variables: consumers' behaviour, health status, stress generating factors, social and family relationships (social capital), degree confidence in the context of nowadays economic crisis. In order to achieve the purpose of this study, a consumer survey was conducted during April, 2010 at the level of a 527 Romanian consumers' sample.

Source: Synthesis of author's research findings, Pandelică and Pandelică (2011).

sion? There will be permanent shifts after the recession will be overcome?

The present chapter focused on finding steady empirical answers to the following research question: "HOW does consumers' behaviour change in crisis conditions?" and "WHY did consumers behave like that?," adopting a psychological perspective. In the future the main research question that I intend to focus is: WHAT is the pattern of reversing consumer behaviour in the post-crisis period?

CONCLUSION

An economic crisis is an uncertainty situation with negative economic evolutions like unemployment, inflation rate increasing, freezing or decreasing of the wages, purchasing power decrease, investments value reduction, fluctuations in consumer prices, restrictions in loan accessing, fluctuations in currency exchange rate that represent economic shocks hitting consumers. During economic turbulent times consumers are highly expose to the content of these risks and thus an economic crisis is considered one of the most traumatizing events that affects family's life and brings a sudden and

substantial deterioration of economic situation of the household. Nevertheless, such economic evolutions represent "uncertainties that matter" that are correlated with consumers' behaviour change. Behaviour alteration during recession follows different patterns depending on external factor (exposure to the economic shocks) and internal factors (psychological ones – risk perception and risk attitude regarding the uncertainty situation).

The empirical studies conducted in different contexts (recession episodes, countries, regions) provided empirical insights regarding behaviour alteration in various recessions. Even if during this chapter it was clearly mentioned that there are no two similar crisis, taking into account that each crisis is a unique event considering generating factors, severity, evolution, outcomes, duration and so forth, the extensive literature review conducted in the background permitted to synthesize some general trends in the consumers behaviour alteration during recession, as follows: the consumption reduction, increasing savings, migration on the demand curve, elimination/postponing of major purchases, brand loyalty shift, price comes first/price sensitivity, rationalization of the consumption and expenses, changes in shopping place, aggressive search for options, shifts in emphasize on different attributes, changing in spending allocation. Anyway, these alterations vary as intensity from one country to another, but also from one category of consumers to another in the frame of one national market. During the recession consumers "learn" how to live from "adjustment to adjustment," the lesson of survival and to find their own way in the turmoil. On this path consumers become smarter, agile, more caution, less wastefully, less loyal, turn to simplicity, more pragmatic, more rational and less emotional to the advertising content, better informed

If we admit that psychology of the crisis is an important component of a recession and that psychological factors play an important part in the alteration of consumer's behaviour, then it becomes an essential condition for companies to know and understand these aspects in order to handle the crisis successfully. In uncertain conditions, like economic crisis, there is a direct causality relationship between risk perception, risk aversion and all the dimensions of consumers' behaviour change Therefore, it is important for marketing managers to have a closer look upon the WAY behind people's behaviour in such conditions. Further on, in recessions by decomposing consumers' behaviour in the two psychological components using a psychological model of market segmentation, the companies can get a more comprehensive image of the way their clients react in crisis conditions than if they used demographic or psychographic criteria such as: income, sex, lifestyle and so on.

In this chapter it is provided a new perspective for approaching consumers' behaviour in recession conditions based on empirical support, opening new directions for research. On the other hand marketing practitioners can find a comprehensive image about the manner in which consumers react and behave in uncertainty contexts like recessions.

REFERENCES

Akerlof, G., & Shiller, R. (2009). *Animal Spirit: How Human Psychology Drives the Economy, and Why It Matters for Global Capitalism*. Princeton University Press.

Ang, S. H. (2001). Personality Influences on Consumption: Insight from the Asian Economic Crisis. *Journal of International Consumer Marketing*, *13*(1), 5–21. doi:10.1300/J046v13n01_02

Ang, S. H., Leong, S. M., & Kotler, P. (2000). The Asian apocalypse: crisis marketing. *Long Range Planning*, *33*(1), 97–119. doi:10.1016/S0024-6301(99)00100-4

Atinc, M., & Walton, M. (1998). *Social Consequences of the East Asian Financial Crisis*. Retrieved Jun 16, 2013, from http://citeseerx.ist.psu.edu/viewdoc/download?doi=10.1.1.198.2871&rep=rep1&type=pdf

Chebeň, J., & Hudáčková, L. C. (2010). *Influence of the Global Economic Crisis on Consumer Behaviour in Slovakia*. Retrieved Jun 16, 2013, from http://vz.fmv.vse.cz/wp-content/uploads/9_2010.pdf

Dutt, P., & Padmanabhan, V. (2009). *When to Hit the Panic Button? Impact of Currency Crisis on Consumer Behaviours*. Retrieved May 7, 2011, from http://faculty.edu/dutt/Research/Paddy_Pushan.pdf

Duygan, B. (2005). *Aggregate Shocks, Idiosyncratic Risk, and Durable Goods Purchases: Evidence from Turkey's 1994 Financial Crisis*. European University Institute Finance and Consumption Program. Retrieved Jun 16, 2013, from http://www.econbiz.de/en/search/detailed-view/doc/all/aggregate-shocks-idiosyncratic-risk-and-durable-goods-purchases-evidence-from-turkeys-1994-financial-crisis-duygan-burcu/10005069449/?no_cache=1

Fiszbein, A., Giovagnoli, P. I., & Adúriz, I. (2003). The Argentinean crisis and its impact on household welfare. *CEPAL Review*, *79*, 143–158.

Flatters, P., & Willmott, M. (2009). Understanding the post-recession consumers. *Harvard Business Review*, *7*(8), 106–112.

Frankenberg, E., James, P., & Duncan, T. (2003). Economic Shocks, Wealth, and Welfare. *The Journal of Human Resources*, *38*(2), 280–321. doi:10.2307/1558746

Garling, T., Kirchler, E., Lewis, A., & van Raaij, F. (2009). Psychology, Financial Decision Making, and Financial Crisis. *Psychological Science in the Public Interest*, *10*, 1–47. doi:10.1177/1529100610378437

Global Consumer Confidence, Concerns and Spending. (2009). *A global Nielsen consumer report.* Retrieved from http://pt.nielsen.com/documents/tr_0905NelsenGlobalConsumerCon fidenceReport1stHalf09.pdf

Global Consumer Confidence, Concerns and Spending. (2010). *A global Nielsen consumer report.* Retrieved from http://lk.nielsen.com/site/documents/CCI1stQuater10.pdf

Goleman, D. (2003). *Destructive Emotions.* London: Bloomsbury Publishing PLC.

Hillson, D., & Webster, R. (2004). Understanding and managing risk attitude. In *Proceedings of 7th Annual Risk Conference.* Retrieved April 22, 2010, from http://www.kent.ac.uk/scarr/events/finalpapers/Hillson%20%2B%20Murray-Webster.pdf

Hillson, D., & Webster, R. (2006). *Managing Risk Attitude using Emotional Literacy.* Retrieved April 22, 2013, from http://www.ashgate.com/pdf/white_papers/Gower_White_Paper_Managing_Risk_Attitude_Emotional_Literacy.pdf

Hofstede, G. (2004). *Hofstede Dimension Data Matrix.* Retrieved August 22, 2010, from http://www.geerthofstede.nl

Hofstede, G., & McCrae, R. (2004). Personality and culture revisited: linking traits and dimensions of culture. *Cross-Cultural Research*, *38*(1), 52–88. doi:10.1177/1069397103259443

Holton, G. (2004). Defining Risk. *Financial Analysts Journal*, *60*(6), 19–25. doi:10.2469/faj.v60.n6.2669

Jasiulewicz, A. (2011). Economic Crisis Influence on the Polish Consumer Behaviour. In *Overcoming the Crisis: Economic and Financial Developments in Asia and Europe*, (pp. 77-88). Retrieved June, 24, from http://www.hippocampus.si/ISBN/978-961-6832-32-8/papers/jasiulewicz.pdf

Kang, S. J., & Sawada, Y. (2008). Credit crunch and household welfare, the case of the Korean financial crisis. *The Japanese Economic Review*, *59*, 438–458. doi:10.1111/j.1468-5876.2008.00429.x

Kay, M. (2010). Marketing During a Recession: Social Effects and Marketing Opportunities. In *Proceedings of the Northeast Business & Economics Association*, (pp. 587-589). Academic Press.

Kelley, E., & Schewe, L. (1975). Buyer behaviour in a stagflation-shortages economy. *Journal of Marketing*, *39*, 44–60. doi:10.2307/1250114

Kondawar, D., & Jadhav, P. (2012). Global economic crisis & consumer behavior. *ABHINAV*, *1*(12), 82–87.

Lusk, J. L., & Coble, K. H. (2005). Risk Perceptions, Risk Preference and Acceptance of Risky Food. *American Journal of Agricultural Economics*, *87*(2), 393–421. doi:10.1111/j.1467-8276.2005.00730.x

Mansoor, D., & Jalal, A. (2011). The Global Business Crisis and Consumer Behaviour: Kingdom of Bahrain as a Case Study. *International Journal of Business and Management*, *6*(1), 104–115.

Miller, D., & Reilly, J. (1994). *Food scares in the media.* Glasgow University Media Group. Retrieved April 04, 2010, from http://www.dmiller.info/food-scares-in-the-media

Nie, B., Zhao, F., & Yu, J. (2010). *The Impact of the Financial Crisis on Consumer Behaviour and the Implications of Retail Revolution*. Retrieved July, 08, 2013, from http://www.seiofbluemountain.com/upload/product/201008/2010shcyx06a12.pdf

Nielsen Company. (2008, October 30). *Consumer Reaction to the Banking Crisis, Comments about Economy*. Retrieved from http://www.claritas.com/eDownloads/webinar/Nielsen-Claritas-Webinar-Consumer-Reaction-Banking-Crisis-103008.pdf

Pandelica, A., & Pandelica, I. (2011). The change of consumers' behaviour in crisis conditions: A psychological approach to the empirical evidence from Romania. *African Journal of Business Management, 5*(28), 11399–11412.

Pennings, J., Wansink, B., & Meulenberg, M. (2002). A Note on Modeling Consumer Reaction to a Crisis: The Case of the Mad Cow Disease. *International Journal of Research in Marketing, 19*, 91–100. doi:10.1016/S0167-8116(02)00050-2

Perner, L. (2008). *Consumer behaviour: the psychology of marketing*. Univ. of Southern California. Retrieved Jun 6, 2013, from http://www.consumerpsychologist

Perriman, H., Ramsaran-Fowdar, R., & Baguant, P. (2010). The impact of the global financial crisis on consumer behavior. In Z. Haqq (Ed.), *Proceedings of Annual London Business Research Conference*. Retrieved July, 18, 2013, from http://www.wbiconpro.com/06-Priya.pdf

Piercy, N. F., Cravens, D. W., & Lane, N. (2010). Marketing Out Of The Recession: Recovery Is Coming, But Things Will Never Be The Same Again. *Marketing Review, 10*(1), 3–23. doi:10.1362/146934710X488915

Quelch, J., & Jocz, K. (2009). How to market in a Downturn. *Harvard Business Review*. Retrieved February 8, 2010, from http://hbr.harvardbusiness.org/2009/04/how-tomarket-in-a-downturn/ar/1

Robles, F., Simon, F., & Haar, J. (2002). *Winning strategies for the new Latin markets*. Financial Times/Prentice Hall.

Shama, A. (1978). Management and Consumers in Era of Stagflation. *Journal of Marketing, 42*(3), 43–52. doi:10.2307/1250533

Shama, A. (1980). *Marketing in a slow growth economy: the impact of stagflation on consumer psychology*. New York: Praeger Publishers.

Simon, H. (2009). The crisis and customer behaviour: eight quick solutions. *Journal of Customer Behaviour, 8*(2), 177–186. doi:10.1362/147539209X459796

Sitkin, S., & Weingart, L. (1995). Determinants of risky decision making behaviour: A test of mediating role of risk perception and propensity. *Academy of Management Journal, 38*, 1573–1592. doi:10.2307/256844

Slovic, P., Finucane, M., Peters, E., & MacGregor, D. (2004). Risk as Analysis and Risk as Feeling: Some Thoughts about Affect, Reason, Risk and Rationality. *Risk Analysis, 24*(2), 311–322. doi:10.1111/j.0272-4332.2004.00433.x PMID:15078302

Stiglitz, J. (2008, September 16). The fruit of hypocrisy. *The Guardian*. Retrieved February 10, 2010, from http://www.guardian.co.uk/commentisfree/2008/sep/16/economics.wallstreet

Urbonavicius, S., & Pikturnien, I. (2010). Consumer in the face of economic crisis: Evidence from two generations in Lithuania. *Economics and Management, 15*, 827–834.

Weber, E., & Milliman, R. (1997). Perceived risk attitudes: Relating risk perception to risky choice. *Management Science, 43*, 123–144. doi:10.1287/mnsc.43.2.123

World Health Organization. (2011). *Impact of economic crises on mental health*. Retrieved from http://www.euro.who.int/data/assets/pdf_file/0008/134999/e94837.pdf

Zurawicki, L., & Braidot, N. (2005). Consumer during the crisis: responses from the middle class in Argentina. *Journal of Business Research, 58*(8), 1100–1109. doi:10.1016/j.jbusres.2004.03.005

ADDITIONAL READING

American Generations: Who They Are and How They Live, 7th Ed., New Strategist Publications, Inc., June 2010.

Asia, E. The road to recovery. *The International Bank for Reconstruction and Development/The world Bank, 1998, Washington, D.C.* Available at http://irving.vassar.edu/faculty/dk/Roadto%20 Recovery.pdf

Bohlen, C., & Mihas, N. (2010). How the recession has changed US consumer behaviour. *The McKinsey Quarterly, 1,* 17–20.

Brand, J. E., Becca, L., & William, T. G. (2008). Effects of Layoffs and Plant Closings on Depression among Older Workers. *Research on Aging, 30*(6), 701–721. doi:10.1177/0164027508322574 PMID:20011238

Brand, J. E., & Burgard, S. A. (2008). Job Displacement and Social Participation over the Life Course: Findings for a Cohort of Joiners. *Social Forces, 87*(1), 211–242. doi:10.1353/sof.0.0083

Brenner, M. H., & Mooney, A. (1983). Unemployment and health in the context of economic change. *Social Science & Medicine, 17*(16), 1125–1138. doi:10.1016/0277-9536(83)90005-9 PMID:6623119

Hands, W. (2010). Economics, psychology and the history of consumer choice theory. *Cambridge Journal of Economics, 34*(4), 633–648. doi:10.1093/cje/bep045

Hillson, D.A. (2002). What is risk? Towards a common definition. *Journal of the UK Institute of Risk*, April 2002, 11-12.

Jin, H. J., & Koo, W. W. (2003). The effects of the BSE Outbreak in Japan on Consumer Preferences. *European Review of Agriculture Economics, 30*(2), 173–192. doi:10.1093/erae/30.2.173

Kalogeras, N., Pennings, J., & Koert, V. (2008). Consumer Food Safety Risk Attitudes and Perceptions over time: The Case of BSE Crisis. *12th Congress of the European Association of Agricultural Economists.*

Kittiprapas, S. (2002). Social Impacts of Financial and Economic Crisis in Thailand, *EADN Regional Project on the Social Impact of the Asian Financial Crisis.* Available at http://www.eadn.org/So-cial%20Impacts%20of%20Financial%20and%20 Economic%20Crisis%20in%20Thailand.pdf.

Kwak, I., Song, Y., & Kim, K. (1999). The financial crisis effects on the family life: A comparison between before and after IME. *Journal of Korean Home Economics Association*, (17), 121-137.

McKenzie, D. J. (2006). The Consumer Response to the Mexican Peso Crisis. *Economic Development and Cultural Change, 55*(1), 139–172. doi:10.1086/505721

Mining the U.S. Generation Gaps. *The Nielsen Company*, March 2010. Available at: http://blog.nielsen.com/nielsenwire/consumer/mining-the-u-s-generation-gaps/.

Pandelică, A., Diaconu, M., & Pandelică, I. (2012). Individual Behaviour Change Through Economic Shocks Exposure. Empirical Evidence from Romania. *The Journal of American Academy of Business, Cambridge, 18*(1).

Pandelică, A., & Pandelică, I. (2011). The effects of the economic crisis over consumers' behaviour. Empirical evidences from Romanian. *Marketing From Information to Decision, 4,* 347–356.

Pandelică, I., Pandelică, A., & Dabu, B. (2010). The Response of Organizations in Crisis Conditions. *Journal of American Academy of Business, Cambridge, 1*(2).

Percy, C. (2009). Forces of change: shopper behaviour. Re-shaping the future of grocery. *Retail Digest, Fall 2009*, 48-57.

Pernia, E. M., & Knowles, J. C. (1998). Assessing the social impact of the financial crisis in Asia, Asian Development Bank, *Economics and Development Resource Center, EDRC Briefing Notes*, Number 6. Available at http://aric.adb.org/pdf/edrcbn/edrcbn06.pdf

Saad, L. (2009). U.S. Flue Fear Abates, Precautionary Steps Still Sparse. Available at: http://www.gallup.com/poll/118156/Swine-Flu-Fear-Abates-Precautionary-Seps-Still-Sparse.html.

Shao, C. (2009). The Impact of Financial Crisis on Consumer Buying Behaviour. *Marketing Management Garden*, 6, 114–352.

Stegaroiu, C., & Stegaroiu, V. (2010). The algorithm for the development of global financial crisis. *African Journal of Business Management*, *4*(19), 4183–4190.

Sutherland, A. (1997). Fiscal crises and aggregate demand: can high public debt reverse the effects of fiscal policy? *Journal of Public Economics*, *65*(2), 147–162. doi:10.1016/S0047-2727(97)00027-3

Wansink, B. (2004). Consumer Reaction to Food Safety Crisis. *Advances in Food and Nutrition Research*, *48*, 103–150. doi:10.1016/S1043-4526(04)48002-4 PMID:15498694

KEY TERMS AND DEFINITIONS

Behaviour Alteration: Reflected by the shifts in consumers behaviour during economic turbulent times being associated to some certain directions: consumption decrease, spending decrease and changes in spending allocation, the migration on the demand curve, switching brands, elimination/postponing of major purchases, brand loyalty decrease, shifts in decision-making process, a higher emphasis on information process, price sensitivity, rationalization of the consumption and expenses, changes in shopping place, shifts in emphasize on different attributes, changing in spending allocation etc.

Economic Shock Exposure: The effective confrontation with the effects of risks generated by the evolution of national economy during recession (unemployment, inflation rate increasing, freezing or decreasing of the wages, purchasing power decrease, investments value reduction etc.) but also the fear regarding the probability of being exposed. For instance, the loss of job security is not so visible like unemployment experience, but is a very stressful experience, sometimes more stressful than the unemployment itself. The individual preoccupied by job stability is exposed to a higher stress because of the anticipation of the outcomes generated by the possible unemployment and thus by the ambiguity of the future. The effects of this exposure are visible on a short term at the emotional level (anxiety, depression, exhaustion, lack of concentration).

Economic Turbulent Times: Economic downturn periods characterized by volatility, uncertainty and change, structural brakes and shift phases. Changes are fast and directions of economic change are not very clear.

Panic Mechanism: The frame reflecting the external behavioural factors representing stimuli (risk content exposure), the internal behaviour factors reflected by risk perception and risk aversion, the relations established between these factors and how these factors have modeled individual behaviour in uncertainty contexts. In this mechanism emotions and feelings play an important role in the relations established between factors.

Risk Aversion in Recession Context (Uncertainty): An individual reflection of the way of thinking and feeling regarding the evolution of national economy during downturn, being a chosen response towards uncertainty shaped by emotions: stress, anger, fury, depression etc. Thus, risk aversion varies on a certain scale between two bipolar attributes: liked on a great extent - disliked on a great extent.

Risk Perception in Recession Context (Uncertainty): Represents the personal interpretation that individuals make regarding the exposure of the risks generated by the evolution of national economy. This is a personal assessment of the chances to be exposed to certain risk, the assessment of risk content (effects), the capacity to control the exposure and confidence in these estimations. Thus risk perception varies on a certain scale.

Uncertainty Associated to Recession: Reflected by the unpredictability of economic evolutions at micro and macro level, lack of visibility regarding this evolutions, and the risks generated by these evolutions with both social and economic consequences on people, affecting the quality of life, the health status of the population and the family financial situation, but also the social relationships and "capital loss."

Chapter 5
Customer Store Loyalty:
Process, Explanation Chain, and Moderating Factors

Arturo Z. Vásquez-Párraga
The University of Texas – Pan American, USA

Miguel Ángel Sahagún
The University of Texas – Pan American, USA

Pablo José Escobedo
The University of Texas – Pan American, USA

ABSTRACT

This chapter examines the process of how store customers become loyal to their stores. The authors pursue a theoretical and empirical research approach designed to identify and test a parsimonious model. The result is an explanation chain that incorporates relational variables, trust and commitment, satisfaction, and the moderating factors of the relational variables. The findings reveal that customer commitment is the major contributing explanation for true customer loyalty, significantly more than the contributed explanation of customer satisfaction. The cognitive moderating factors (store familiarity, store choice, customer perceived risk, and communication) and the affective moderating factors (customer opportunistic tendencies, consumer involvement, shared personal values, and shared management values) are significantly related to the core variables and thus contribute some explanation, yet their contribution is very small compared to the contribution of the core variables, thereby suggesting the significance of the core variables in the explanation of customer store loyalty.

INTRODUCTION

Customers can more easily identify themselves with brands on the basis of successful positioning and effective fitting of product values to consumer needs. Notwithstanding, customers may not follow the same process when becoming loyal to stores where many brands, some of them competing with each other, may complicate the B to C relationships and, thus, the way store customers become loyal.

This study aims at examining anew the entire process of how store customers become loyal to

DOI: 10.4018/978-1-4666-6074-8.ch005

their stores. We not only describe the process but also attempt to explain it on the basis of empirical research. Our study of customer store loyalty focuses on the explanation of true loyalty, the understanding of a core process generating customer loyalty on the basis of relational components in addition to transactional ones, and the moderating effects produced by cognitive and affective attitudes shaping or modifying the core process. Our research uses a sample of multicultural store customers experiencing a variety of stores. The presence of large stores, like supermarkets, versus small and more customized stores, like specialized stores, allows for a variety of situations facilitating a more realistic study context.

We first introduce and discuss the conceptual framework that provides the basis to propose a conceptual model. We then present the research method and the results obtained, discuss the findings, and derive some research and managerial implications. We finally offer suggestions for future research, managerial implications, and the study conclusions.

CONCEPTUAL FRAMEWORK

The conceptual framework of this study focuses on true loyalty, the core process store customers use to achieve it, and the moderating forces and attitudes intervening in the process either as shapers of a common path in customer loyalty formation or modifiers of specific paths in customer loyalty implementation.

Customer Store Loyalty

Store customers develop loyalty in various representations. Some of these refer to behavior, such as going to the same store every week because the store is close to the consumer's home, and others reflect attitudes such as cognitive and affective attitudes. Past studies have focused on behavioral loyalty and helped build customer loy-

alty programs that encourage customers to repeat purchase in the same stores. Loyalty programs do not attempt to proactively influence customer attitudes. Customer loyalty involves human behavior and attitudes, "a favorable correspondence between relative attitude and repeat patronage" (Dick & Basu, 1994).

Thus, following Dick and Basu (1994) and Oliver (2010), this study examines customer loyalty in its three phases, cognitive, affective, and behavioral. Behavior and attitudes operate in unison to generate customer store loyalty, true loyalty. True loyalty requires a meaningful presence of both positive attitudes and behavioral experience in consumers. The absence of attitudes limits the human experience to "spurious" loyalty and the absence of behavioral experience limits the attitudes to "latent" loyalty (Dick & Basu, 1994). "Spurious" loyalty is often represented or exemplified by repeat purchase and customer retention–themes that have been the focal point of abundant research.

Customer Satisfaction

Satisfaction is an evaluative, affective, or emotional response that evolves with the experience a consumer has with a good or service over a period of time (Oliver & Swan, 1989). Store customers experience satisfaction in more than one way (Oliver, 2010). They can be satisfied with the products they buy but fundamentally they may be satisfied with the transaction they are involved in when acquiring the product. Satisfaction is a cumulative construct that includes not only satisfaction with specific products and services but also with the various aspects of the transaction and the organization such as the interaction with employees and the physical facilities. Yet, transaction satisfaction is different from consumption satisfaction (Oliver, 2010) and both are different from competing satisfaction (Vásquez-Párraga & Alonso, 2000). Transaction satisfaction occurs during the interaction between the customer and the store personnel. Consumption satisfaction relates to satisfaction with the product and may occur after the purchase is completed. Finally, competing satisfaction is generated by other stores to which customers can switch. In order to comprehensibly study customer satisfaction with stores we must include transaction and competing customer satisfactions.

In addition, the literature mentions brand satisfaction or satisfaction with the brand (Oliver, 2010). Granted, brand satisfaction may also deal with all three types of satisfaction but depends much more on consumption satisfaction than on transaction and competing satisfaction. Furthermore, stores may carry private brands which can be compared to national brands also available at the store. However, this comparison alone is another subject.

Customer Satisfaction: Loyalty Relationship

According to Oliver (1993), "a satisfactory purchase experience would appear to be one requirement for the type of continued interest in a product that may lead to repeat purchasing." Moreover, "customer loyalty is a deeply held commitment to rebuy or repatronize a preferred product or service consistently in the future, thereby causing repetitive same-brand or same brand-set purchasing, despite situational influences and marketing efforts that have the potential to cause switching behavior" (Oliver, 2010). Accordingly, previous research has emphasized the role of customer satisfaction in the formation and evolution of customer loyalty and considered the satisfaction-loyalty linkage a solid explanation (Hallowell, 1996; Heskett, Jones, Loveman, Sasser & Schlesinger, 1994; Reicheheld, 1996).

Customer satisfaction alone can be the result of a good transaction. Repeated purchases increase the number of transactions and therefore generate loyalty (Bolton, Lemon & Verhoef, 2004; Chiou & Droge, 2006). The customer loyalty these authors

investigate is spurious loyalty, a concept related to repeated purchase. Spurious loyalty is fundamentally behavioral and relies on transactions, such as those promoted by existing loyalty programs.

From Transactional to Relational Exchanges

Actual experiences of store customers, however, do not validate a simple customer satisfaction-loyalty path in the formation of loyalty. Instead, store customers seem to follow a more complex path, one in which relational components are present and often dominate the transactional ones in the experienced core process. Satisfaction with the transaction requires relational interactions; true loyalty is both behavioral and attitudinal; more importantly, attitudinal loyalty requires generating relational approaches. All these requirements force the researcher to look elsewhere for a meaningful explanation of how customer loyalty is generated and sustained.

Moreover, recent research has found that customer satisfaction and loyalty are only indirectly related (Miranda, Konya & Havrila, 2005; Sivadas & Baker-Prewitt, 2000), that store loyalty cannot be generated by satisfaction alone as other predictors are better and stronger than satisfaction (Kumar, Pozza & Ganesh, 2013), and that, therefore, there is a more complex process involved in the generation of customer loyalty (Vásquez-Párraga & Alonso, 2000).

Role of Trust and Commitment

The explanation of customer store loyalty requires an integrated explanation of the core process and the identification of moderating factors intervening in either the formation of the process or the sustenance of the process, or both. Empirical research shows that customers rely on both relations and transactions on their way to becoming loyal (Oliver, 2010). Key transactions include the purchase process and the resulting customer satisfaction. Key relational processes include trust and commitment exchanges. Both transactions and relational processes are revealed in the loyalty path used by store customers (Carpenter, 2007; De Wulf, Odekerken-Schroder, & Iacobucci, 2001; Rafiq, Fulford & Lu, 2013), hotel guests (Zamora, Vásquez-Párraga, Morales & Cisternas, 2004), airline travelers (Bravo, Vásquez-Párraga & Zamora, 2005), and land-transportation travelers (Zamora, Vásquez-Párraga, Rodriguez & Gonzalez, 2011). Additional relational variables are examined in other studies such as word-of-mouth communication (Sivadas & Baker-Prewitt, 2000).

CONCEPTUAL MODEL

Four cornerstone concepts are adopted in our conceptual model representing the core process of customer store formation, that is, how store customers become loyal to their stores. These concepts are customer satisfaction, trust, commitment, and loyalty, all four sequentially linked to constitute an explanation chain. An explanation chain includes key variables used to offer a parsimonious explanation of a sought outcome or phenomenon

(Hunt, 2010). The proposed explanation for store loyalty starts with customer satisfaction, which in turn generates customer trust that is followed by customer commitment to a relationship, which in turn results in customer loyalty. Thus, customer store loyalty can be defined as the end result of customers and providers achieving successful relationships of trust and commitment after an initial satisfactory encounter (Vásquez-Párraga & Alonso, 2000).

In addition, this conceptual model (Vásquez-Alonso (V-A) approach) examines the moderating effects of relevant cognitive and affective attitudes impacting on the relational variables, trust and commitment (Vásquez-Párraga & Alonso, 2000). The cognitive factors include store familiarity, store choice, customer perceived risk, and communication. The affective factors include customer opportunistic tendencies, consumer involvement, shared personal values, and shared management values. A complete map of how the core variables are linked in an explanation chain and how the cognitive and affective factors moderate the role of trust or commitment in the explanation chain is shown in Figure 1.

Figure 1. Antecedents of customer loyalty: Model
Source: Adapted from Vásquez-Párraga and Alonso, 2000.

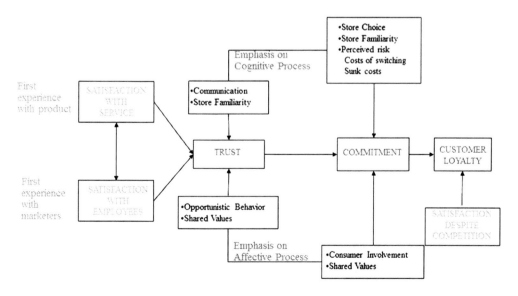

METHODOLOGY

Research Design

Our research methodology is designed to test a core process and its moderating factors in the formation of customer store loyalty. The core process is relational and includes an explanation chain as follows, and the moderating factors reflect the cognitive and affective influences therein. For the core process, the mediation of two key relational variables, trust and commitment, is incorporated in the customary satisfaction-loyalty linkage. Thus, the core process consists of an explanation chain that starts with satisfaction, which influences trust. Trust is essentially linked to commitment as per previous literature, and commitment is the immediate antecedent of loyalty: Satisfaction → trust → commitment → customer loyalty.

The moderating factors reflect the cognitive and affective attitudes impacting the way the key relational variables, trust and commitment, work. Adopting the V-A approach, the following cognitive factors are included: store choice, store familiarity, perceived risk, and communication between the customer and the company. Similarly, we include the following affective factors: company opportunism, consumer involvement with the service, shared personal values, and shared management values.

Measurement

Table 1 presents the core constructs and their dimensions, if any, with corresponding items, reliability coefficients and average variance explained. The four core constructs are measured as follows. Satisfaction is a second-order factor resulting from three separate constructs: consumption satisfaction, transaction satisfaction and competitive satisfaction, each one consisting of four items. Trust is measured using six items previously tested in similar research. Commitment is also measured using five items previously tested.

Customer loyalty is a second-order factor resulting from three separate constructs: cognitive loyalty, affective loyalty, and behavioral loyalty, each one consisting of five items. Items and their loading into the expected constructs are shown in Table 1.

Table 2 presents the cognitive and affective moderators of trust and commitment, each one with corresponding items, reliability coefficients and average variance explained. The four cognitive moderators include customer perceived risk, store familiarity, store choice, and communication, and all are measured using five items per construct. The three affective moderators include customer opportunistic propensity, consumer involvement, and shared values with the retailer, and all are measured using five items per construct as shown in Table 2.

Both the cognitive and affective attitudes moderate the effect of either trust on commitment or commitment on loyalty, as shown in Figure 1.

Sample

In order to implement the survey, adult consumers were approached in a geographical area where 1) consumers experience grocery stores carrying either national or local or both types of brands and 2) different requirements to achieve customer satisfaction in the short-term and gain customer loyalty, trust, and commitment in the long-term can be scrutinized. Only adults who reported having shopping experience were interviewed. The approached overall sample included 467 store customers: about 60% were women, 44% were married, and 44% were older than 30 years.

RESULTS AND DISCUSSION

Core Constructs

The results were examined in various steps. First, exploratory factor analyses were performed to find the aimed constructs. Then, using maxi-

Table 1. Core constructs: Confirmatory factor analysis

Constructs and Items	Factor Loadings
Cognitive Loyalty (α =.799, AVE = 55.878%)	
(Lo_C1) Once I get to know a grocery store, I tend to use that store more often	.696
(Lo_C2) For the time being, I am not looking for an alternative store	.681
(Lo_C3) When I decide to stay with a store, I make sure that the store is adequate to my needs	.820
(Lo_C4) I am loyal to my grocery store because personnel at this store is very knowledgeable	.767
(Lo_C5) Client loyalty in grocery stores is based on good personal reasons and experiences	.766
Affective Loyalty (α =.874, AVE = 66.898%)	
(Lo_A1) Once I get used to a store, I hate to switch	.768
(Lo_A2) I feel a strong loyalty to my favorite store	.865
(Lo_A3) I have developed some sort of emotional connection with my favorite store	.807
(Lo_A4) Continued service from my favorite store gives me peace of mind	.812
(Lo_A5) I'd like to have my current favorite store as my permanent store	.835
Inner Behavioral Loyalty (α =.851, AVE = 69.809%)	
(Lo_BI1) Even though grocery stores are available in many brands, I always use the same one	.819
(Lo_BI2) If I like a grocery store, I rarely switch from it just to try something different	.749
(Lo_BI3) I have been with my favorite store for a long time	.890
(Lo_BI4) I plan to continue relying on my favorite store for a long time	.876
Outer Behavioral Loyalty (α =.842, AVE = 86.354%)	
(Lo_BO1) I say positive things about my favorite store to others	.929
(Lo_BO2) I encourage friends and relatives to use my favorite store	.929
Commitment (α =.910, AVE = 73.824%)	
(Comt1) I am proud to be a client of my favorite grocery store	.899
(Comt2) I feel a sense of belonging to my store	.908
(Comt3) As far I am concerned no one could choose a better grocery store	.864
(Comt4) I am very confident about the success of my store	.821
(Comt5) I feel that I have a personal relationship with my grocery store	.811
Trust (α =.900, AVE = 66.027%)	
(Trust1) I have complete faith in the integrity of the personnel at my store	.825
(Trust2) I feel quite confident that my store will always try to treat me fairly	.871
(Trust3) My grocery store has been frank in dealing with me	.810
(Trust4) My store would never try to gain an advantage by deceiving its clients	.834
(Trust5) My grocery store is trustworthy	.845
(Trust6) I am sure that the offerings at my favorite grocery store are valuable ones	.719
Satisfaction with Service (α =.909, AVE = 79.039%)	
(Sat_S1) This is one of the best experiences with a grocery store I have ever had	.833
(Sat_S2) This grocery store is exactly what I need	.911
(Sat_S3) This grocery store has worked out as well as I thought it would	.912
(Sat_S4) This grocery store has adequately fulfilled my expectations	.898
Satisfaction with Employees (α =.872, AVE = 72.405%)	
(Sat_E1) Employees at my current grocery store give me personal attention	.853
(Sat_E2) Employees at my current grocery store know what they are doing	.859
(Sat_E3) Employees at my grocery store are never too busy to respond to client requests promptly	.869
(Sat_E4) Employees from my favorite grocery store are polite	.822
Satisfaction Despite Competition (α =.900, AVE = 76.957%)	
(Sat_C1) Compared to the other stores, my grocery store offers the best products	.877
(Sat_C2) Compared to the other stores, my grocery store has the best reputation	.882
(Sat_C3) Compared to the other stores, my stores give customers the best satisfaction overall	.896
(Sat_C4) I am satisfied with my decision to choose this store over all the other stores	.854

α = Cronbach coefficient alpha.

AVE = average variance extracted

Table 2. Moderating factors: Confirmatory factor analysis

Constructs and Items	Factor Loadings
Product Choice (α =.695, AVE = 45.296%)	
I know that there are several possible alternatives to my favorite grocery store	.646
Before I selected my grocery store, I knew about several alternatives	.756
I often check about new possible alternatives to my current grocery store	.657
The prices at my favorite store are competitive	.655
More and more people and companies are starting business in retailing	.644
Product Familiarity (α =.867, AVE = 65.749%)	
Compared to other people, I know a lot about grocery stores	.837
Compared to most of my friends, I know a lot about grocery stores	.839
I am familiar with many products offered by my favorite store	.822
I know a lot about selecting products and services made available by grocery stores	.843
I have a clear idea about what grocery stores should offer in order for me to get maximum satisfaction	.705
Opportunism (α =.861, AVE = 64.609%)	
To accomplish its own objectives, my store might not provide me with the best benefits available	.750
To accomplish its own objectives, my store sometimes promises to do things without actually delivering them	.804
My grocery store sometimes pretends that a service is of value to me, when in fact the store is looking out for itself	.871
I think that my store does not care about me	.831
My grocery store only cares about the money I pay	.757
Perceived Risk (α =.855, AVE = 63.628%)	
I am concerned about making a mistake in choosing a grocery store	.769
The decision to choose a grocery store involves high risk	.854
If I have to switch my current store, I might lose some benefits I have already earned	.838
I think that there is a hidden cost if I switch my current store	.834
Switching among stores involves a cost in terms of time and effort	.681
Communication (α =.853, AVE = 63.537%)	
My store keeps me informed of new products	.697
My store clearly explains the product features when I ask	.822
When I make suggestions, the personnel working at my store always listens to my suggestions	.827
If I want to, I can have detailed conversations regarding products and prices with personnel from my store	.856
As far as I know, my store cares about receiving feedback from its customers	.774
Consumer Involvement (α =.894, AVE = 70.447%)	
I have great interest in grocery stores	.856
Grocery stores are fascinating	.882
I have a compulsive need to know more about grocery stores	.848
I like to make comparisons between grocery stores	.757
I like to talk to my friends about grocery stores	.848
Shared Personal Values (α =.761, AVE = 32.437%)	
In this business, unethical behaviors shouldn't be tolerated	.884
In this business, using unethical advertising cannot be justified	.876
Shared Management Values (α =.723, AVE = 48.260%)	
In order to succeed in this business, it is not necessary to compromise one's ethics	.554
In this business, unethical behaviors shouldn't be tolerated	.753
In this business, using unethical advertising cannot be justified	.779
The way opportunistic stores try to get new customers is unethical	.679
It is unethical to call a competitor's customers and try to convince them to switch stores	.686

α = Cronbach coefficient alpha.

AVE = average variance extracted

mum likelihood factor analysis, it was found that all items loaded in the targeted constructs. Table 1 shows the core constructs including the items measured, their factor loadings, their reli-ability coefficients (α), and the average variance explained (AVE). The items representing cognitive, affective and behavioral loyalty loaded as expected in corresponding constructs, with the exception of behavioral loyalty which split in two components, an inner and an outer tendency of behavioral loyalty as best described by the items themselves (see Table 1). The split of behavioral loyalty into inner and outer constructs is factual and is not reported in the literature. The four constructs reflecting customer loyalty (cognitive, affective, inner behavioral, and outer behavioral) show high reliability coefficients (above .80) and acceptable average variances explained (Hair, Black, Babin & Anderson, 2010).

The relational core constructs, trust and commitment, showed to be unidimensional and have all measured items loaded into the corresponding constructs with reliability coefficients above .90 and average variance explained above 67 percent. The last construct, customer satisfaction, is a second-order factor resulting from the three types of satisfaction (with the service, with employees, and despite competition). All items measuring satisfaction loaded as expected with reliability coefficients above .87 and average variance explained above 72 percent.

Moderating Factors

Table 2 shows the confirmatory factor analysis performed for the moderating factors. All items loaded acceptably into the expected construct and all constructs have high reliability coefficients (above .70) and acceptable average variances explained.

Correlations

Table 3 exhibits a correlation matrix among all constructs to examine the extent to which the construct are related. All correlations are positive and significant among the core constructs (coefficients vary from .597 to .746). All cognitive factors are positively and significantly related to each other and to the other variables with very few exceptions. Store choice is positively and significantly related to all variables. Store familiarity, perceived risk, and communication are also positively and significantly related to all variables except opportunism (with store familiarity) and shared personal

Table 3. Correlation matrix

Variable	1	2	3	4	5	6	7	8	9	10	11	12
1. Loyalty	1.00											
2. Commitment	.715**	1.00										
3. Trust	.636**	.746**	1.00									
4. Satisfaction	.597**	.625**	.670**	1.00								
5. Opportunism	-.179**	-.121**	-.257**	-.261**	1.00							
6. Shared P. Values	.158**	.077	.196**	.221**	-.097*	1.00						
7. Shared M. Values	.134**	.200**	.202**	.281**	-.018	.340**	1.00					
8. Communication	.460**	.525**	.565**	.629**	-.219**	.080	.286**	1.00				
9. Store Familiarity	.501**	.509**	.458**	.524**	-.022	.154**	.203**	.489**	1.00			
10. Store Choice	.223**	.333**	.321**	.228**	.282**	.159**	.196**	.248**	.333**	1.00		
11. Perceived Risk	.196**	.350**	.186**	.239**	.282**	-.028	.188**	.335**	.327**	.223**	1.00	
12. C. Involvement	.263**	.421**	.276**	.294**	.117*	-.025	.222**	.517**	.499**	.267**	.570**	1.00

**Correlation is significant at the 0.01 level (2-tailed).

* Correlation is significant at the 0.05 level (2-tailed).

values (with perceived risk and communication). Similarly, all affective factors are significantly related to all variables, with three variables showing a positive relation and one (opportunism) a negative relation. Correlations are negative between opportunism and the core variables, as expected, and also negative with the moderating variables except store choice and perceived risk. Consumer involvement, shared personal values, and shared management values are positively and significantly related to all variables except shared personal values (involvement), commitment (shared personal values), and opportunism (shared management values).

Regression

Table 4 summarizes the results of a multi-regression analysis showing the effects of the core variables on customer loyalty and the effects of the moderating variables interacting with the relational variables, trust and commitment.

Model 1 accounts for the basic explanation chain (presented in research design) in which only core variables participate. The resulting R^2 is .555 to which commitment is the major contributor, followed by satisfaction and trust. Model 2 incorporates the moderating factors in the regression with a .027 increase in the explanation and only four

Table 4. Regression results: Explanation chain and moderating factors

Dependent Variable:	MODEL 1[a]		MODEL 2[b]		MODEL 3[c]	
Customer Loyalty	b	t-value	b	t-value	b	t-value
Constant	21.391***	7.446	22.307***	5.461	-8.393	-.460
Commitment	1.321***	10.098	1.390***	10.010	1.397***	2.345
Trust	.360***	2.737	.268**	1.959	1.281*	1.780
Satisfaction	.278***	4.647	.194***	2.886	.201***	2.973
Opportunism			-.016	-.168	-.041	-.088
Shared Personal Values			.352*	1.842	2.433***	3.085
Shared Management Values			-.168*	-1.804	-.249	-.560
Communication			.103	.775	.415	.846
Store Familiarity			.513***	4.193	-.086	-.159
Store Choice			-.159	-1.265	.015	.038
Perceived Risk			-.082	-.849	.042	.096
Consumer Involvement			-.172*	-1.783	.469	1.238
Trust x Opportunism					.000	.006
Trust x Shared Personal Values					-.072***	-2.841
Trust x Shared Management Values					.014	.651
Trust x Communication					-.011	-.706
Trust x Store Familiarity					-.013	-.570
Commitment x Consumer Involvement					-.027*	-1.774
Commitment x Shared Mgt. Values					-.013	-.570
Commitment x Store Familiarity					.041*	1.831
Commitment x Store Choice					-.006	-.374
Commitment x Perceived Risk					-.003	-.213

continued on following page

Table 4. Continued

Dependent Variable:	MODEL 1[a]		MODEL 2[b]		MODEL 3[c]	
Customer Loyalty	b	t-value	b	t-value	b	t-value
R^2	.555		.582		.597	
F	192.513		57.496		31.399	
ΔR^2			.027		.015	

[a]Core variable effects
[b]Moderating variable effects
[c]Two-way interaction effects
*p<.10, **p<.05, ***p<.01 (one-tailed test for hypothesized relationships).

variables contributing significantly: store familiarity and, to a lesser extent, consumer involvement and shared personal and management values. Finally, Model 3 includes two-way interaction terms between core variables and moderating variables. The result is a net increase of .015 in the R^2 with only one significant though negative interaction

between opportunism and trust. Models 2 and 3 contribute a total $\Delta R^2 = .042$.

The overall regression results reveal that the large effects of satisfaction, trust, and commitment, formed in an explanation chain, on customer loyalty, the dependent variable, clearly overwhelm the small effects of the moderating variables. These results do not deny the importance of other

Figure 2. Customer store loyalty: SEM results

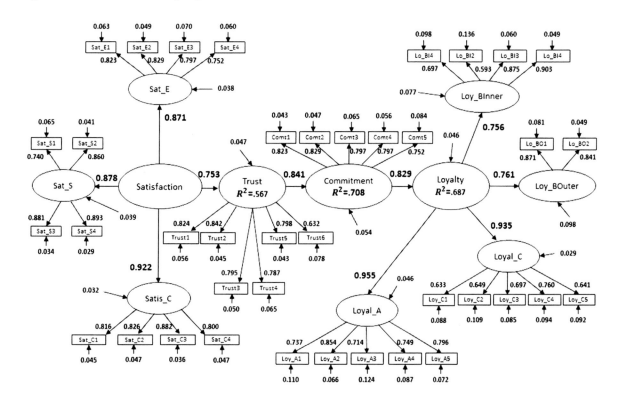

variables in the process of generating customer store loyalty; on the contrary, they highlight the importance of the core variables in the explanation chain as the central forces shaping the formation and sustenance process of customer store loyalty.

SEM Results

A structural equation model is presented to estimate the simultaneous relationships and the measurement errors occurring in the explanation chain. Figure 2 shows the well-fitted second-order constructs of loyalty and satisfaction and the result-

ing overall fit of the model representing the explanation chain. Customer loyalty is a second-order factor derived from four dimensions: cognitive loyalty, affective loyalty, inner behavioral loyalty, and outer behavioral loyalty. Customer satisfaction is also a second-order factor derived from three types of satisfaction: service satisfaction, transaction satisfaction, and competing satisfaction. The R^2 obtained for customer loyalty using SEM is higher ($R^2 = .687$) than the coefficient estimated using SPSS ($R^2 = .555$) mainly because of the simultaneous effects.

Table 5. SEM results

Measurement Parameter Estimates (Standardized)							
Factor Loadings				**Error Variances**			
λSat_E1	.823***	λLo_BI1	.697***	εSat_E1	.063***	εLo_BI1	.098***
λSat_E2	.829***	λLo_BI2	.593***	εSat_E2	.049***	εLo_BI2	.136***
λSat_E3	.797***	λLo_BI3	.875***	εSat_E3	.070***	εLo_BI3	.060***
λSat_E4	.752***	λLo_BI4	.903***	εSat_E4	.060***	εLo_BI4	.049***
λSat_S1	.740***	λLo_BO1	.871***	εSat_S1	.065***	εLo_BO1	.081***
λSat_S2	.860***	λLo_BO2	.841***	εSat_S2	.041***	εLo_BO2	.049***
λSat_S3	.881***	λLo_A1	.737***	εSat_S3	.034***	εLo_A1	.110***
λSat_S4	.893***	λLo_A2	.854***	εSat_S4	.029***	εLo_A2	.066***
λSat_C1	.816***	λLo_A3	.714***	εSat_C1	.045***	εLo_A3	.124***
λSat_C2	.826***	λLo_A4	.749***	εSat_C2	.047***	εLo_A4	.087***
λSat_C3	.882***	λLo_A5	.796***	εSat_C3	.036***	εLo_A5	.072***
λSat_C4	.800***	λLo_C1	.633***	εSat_C4	.047***	εLo_C1	.088***
λTrust1	.824***	λLo_C2	.649***	εTrust1	.056***	εLo_C2	.109***
λTrust2	.842***	λLo_C3	.697***	εTrust2	.045***	εLo_C3	.085***
λTrust3	.795***	λLo_C4	.760***	εTrust3	.050***	εLo_C4	.094***
λTrust4	.787***	λLo_C5	.641***	εTrust4	.065***	εLo_C5	.094***
λTrust5	.798***			εTrust5	.043***		
λTrust6	.632***			εTrust6	.078***		
λComt1	.823***			εComt1	.043***		
λComt2	.829***			εComt2	.047***		
λComt3	.797***			εComt3	.065***		
λComt4	.797***			εComt4	.056***		
λComt5	.752***			εComt5	.084***		

continued on following page

Table 5. Continued

Measurement Parameter Estimates (Standardized)				
Structural Parameter Estimates	**Gamma (γ 's)**			
γSatisfaction-Trust	.753			
γTrust-Commitment	.841			
γCommitment-Loyalty	.829			
Second Order Factors	**Gamma (γ 's)**		**Second Order Factors**	**Gamma (γ 's)**
γLoyalty-Loy_BInner	.756		γSatisfaction-Sat_E	.871
γLoyalty-Loy_BOuter	.761		γSatisfaction-Sat_S	.878
γLoyalty-Loyal_A	.955		γSatisfaction-Sat_C	.922
γLoyalty-Loyal_C	.935			
Explained Variances:	R^2Trust =.567	R^2Commitment =.708		R^2Loyalty =.687
Goodness of Fit:				
X^2(692) = 1791.282, p =.000				
RMSEA =.063				
NNFI =.899				
CFI =.905				
SRMR =.069				

***p<.001 (two-tailed)

Table 5 summarizes the results obtained using SEM. All factor loadings are above .40 as required for item retention and all structural parameter estimates are higher than .70 (Hair et al., 2010). The model fit measures are within the thresholds required (higher than .9 for fit indices; lower than .08 for residuals - Hair et al., 2010): CFI=.905, NNFI=.899, Chi Squared (692) = 1,791.281 at p =.000, RMSEA=.063, and SRMR=.069. Both, Figure 2 and Table 5 also show the explained variances of trust (R^2 =.567), commitment (R^2 =.708) and loyalty (R^2 =.687), denoting high levels of explanation that derive from these variables alone. Table 4 explores additional variables (moderating variables) and the interaction effects between the core variables and the moderating variables and shows that these additional variables and interactions do not add sizable explanation to the model (ΔR^2 =.042).

FUTURE RESEARCH DIRECTIONS

In spite of the well-supported findings in this research, additional research is needed on consumers in different contexts and with other characteristics, other moderating factors or the same factors under different conditions. Because our explanation chain can be rivaled by other explanations, other frameworks and other explanation proposals can be generated and tested for validity, reliability and parsimony.

MANAGERIAL IMPLICATIONS

There are managerial implications of this research on the understanding and practice of loyalty development among store customers. Store managers will benefit from knowing that customer satisfaction alone will not generate customer loyalty in the long-term primarily because transactions alone (repeated purchase, spurious loyalty) do not guarantee stable consumer attitudes in the presence of competition. In today's complex environment of increasing competition and innovation among stores, managers will learn to achieve "true" customer loyalty by pursuing the relational path of trust and commitment immediately after attaining customer store satisfaction. Managers will also learn to use knowledge about the role of some moderating factors, such as store familiarity, consumer involvement, or shared personal values, on trust and commitment.

CONCLUSION

This study aimed at examining anew the entire process of how store customers become loyal to their stores. In order to accomplish this objective, we pursued theoretical and empirical research aimed at identifying and testing a parsimonious model. A core process of customer loyalty formation was defined and modeled as an explanation chain that incorporates key variables used to offer a parsimonious explanation of customer true loyalty as follows: store loyalty starts with customer satisfaction, which in turn generates customer trust that is followed by customer commitment to a relationship, which in turn results in customer loyalty. Phrased succinctly, customer store loyalty is the end result of customers and providers achieving successful relationships of trust and commitment after an initial satisfactory encounter.

The key contribution of our research lies in the use of relational components (trust and commitment) in addition to transactional ones (satisfaction) and the moderating effects produced by cognitive and affective attitudes shaping or modifying the core process. The findings demonstrate that customer commitment is the major contributor of explanation to customer loyalty, significantly more than the contributed explanation of customer satisfaction.

The cognitive moderating factors (store familiarity, store choice, customer perceived risk, and communication) and the affective moderating factors (customer opportunistic tendencies, consumer involvement, and shared personal values and shared management values) are significantly related to the core variables and thus contribute an explanation; yet their contribution is very small ($\Delta R^2 = .042$) in comparison to the contribution of the core variables ($R^2 = .687$).

REFERENCES

Bolton, R. N., Lemon, K. N., & Verhoef, P. C. (2004). The theoretical underpinnings of customer asset management: A framework and propositions for future research. *Journal of the Academy of Marketing Science, 32*(3), 271–292. doi:10.1177/0092070304263341

Bravo, M., Vásquez-Párraga, A. Z., & Zamora, J. (2005). Loyalty in the air: Real and fictitious factors in the formation of loyalty of airline passengers. *Studies and Perspectives in Tourism, 14*(2), 101–126.

Carpenter, J. M. (2008). Consumer shopping value, satisfaction and loyalty in discount retailing. *Journal of Retailing and Consumer Services, 15*, 358–363. doi:10.1016/j.jretconser.2007.08.003

Chiou, J. S., & Droge, C. (2006). Service quality, trust, specific asset investment, and expertise: Direct and indirect effects in a satisfaction-loyalty framework. *Journal of the Academy of Marketing Science, 34*(4), 613–627. doi:10.1177/0092070306286934

De Wulf, K., Odekerken-Schroder, G., & Iacobucci, D. (2001). Investments in consumer relationships: A cross-country and cross-industry exploration. *Journal of Marketing, 65*, 33–50. doi:10.1509/jmkg.65.4.33.18386

Dick, A. S., & Basu, K. (1994). Customer loyalty: Toward an integrated conceptual framework. *Journal of the Academy of Marketing Science, 22*, 99–113. doi:10.1177/0092070394222001

Hair, J., Black, W., Babin, B., & Anderson, R. (2010). *Multivariate data analysis* (7th ed.). Upper Saddle River, NJ: Pearson Prentice Hall.

Hallowell, R. (1996). The relationships of customer satisfaction, customer loyalty, and profitability: An empirical study. *International Journal of Service Industry Management, 7*(4), 27–42. doi:10.1108/09564239610129931

Heskett, J. L., Jones, T. O., Loveman, G. W., Sasser, W. E. Jr, & Schlesinger, L. A. (1994, March-April). Putting the service profit chain to work. *Harvard Business Review*.

Hunt, S. D. (2010). *Marketing Theory: Foundations, Controversy, Strategy, Resource-Advantage Theory*. Armonk, NY: M.E. Sharpe.

Kumar, V., Pozza, I. D., & Ganesh, J. (2013). Revisiting the satisfaction-loyalty relationship: Empirical generalizations and directions for future research. *Journal of Retailing, 89*(3), 246–262. doi:10.1016/j.jretai.2013.02.001

Miranda, M. J., Konya, L., & Havrila, I. (2005). Shoppers' satisfaction levels are not the only key to store loyalty. *Marketing Intelligence & Planning, 23*(2), 220–232. doi:10.1108/02634500510589958

Oliver, R. L. (1993). Cognitive, affective, and attribute bases of the satisfaction response. *The Journal of Consumer Research, 20*, 418–430. doi:10.1086/209358

Oliver, R. L. (1999). Whence consumer loyalty? *Journal of Marketing, 63*, 33–44. doi:10.2307/1252099

Oliver, R. L. (2010). *Satisfaction: A Behavioral Perspective on the Consumer* (2nd ed.). Armond, NY: M.E. Sharpe.

Oliver, R. L., & Swan, J. E. (1989). Equity and disconfirmation perceptions as influences on merchant and product satisfaction. *The Journal of Consumer Research, 16*, 372–383. doi:10.1086/209223

Rafiq, M., Fulford, H., & Lu, X. (2013). Building customer loyalty in online retailing: The role of relationship quality. *Journal of Marketing Management, 29*(3-4), 494–517. doi:10.1080/0267257X.2012.737356

Reichheld, F. F. (1996). *The Loyalty Effect*. Boston: Harvard Business School Press.

Sivadas, E., & Baker-Prewitt, J. L. (2000). An examination of the relationship between service quality, customer satisfaction, and store loyalty. *International Journal of Retail and Distribution Management, 28*(2), 73–82. doi:10.1108/09590550010315223

Vásquez-Párraga, A. Z., & Alonso, S. (2000). Antecedents of customer loyalty for strategic intent. In J. P. Workman Jr, & W. D. Perreault (Eds.), *Marketing Theory and Applications*. Chicago: American Marketing Association.

Zamora, J., Vásquez-Párraga, A. Z., Morales, F., & Cisternas, C. (2004). Formation process of guest loyalty: Theory and an empirical test. *Studies and Perspectives in Tourism, 13*(3-4), 197–221.

Zamora, J., Vásquez-Párraga, A. Z., Rodriguez, A., & Gonzalez, A. (2011). Road travelers' motivations and loyalty: Train versus bus services. *Journal of Travel & Tourism Marketing, 28*, 541–555. doi:10.1080/10548408.2011.588119

ADDITIONAL READING

Ailawadi, K. L., Pauwels, K., & Steenkamp, J.-B. E. M. (2008). Private-label use and store loyalty. *Journal of Marketing, 72*, 19–30. doi:10.1509/jmkg.72.6.19

Bustos-Reyes, C. A., & Gonzalez-Benito, O. (2008). Store and store format loyalty measures based on budget allocation. *Journal of Business Research*, *61*, 1015–1025. doi:10.1016/j.jbusres.2007.03.008

Chen, Y.-H., Wang, X., Wang, Y.-Y., & Tsai, S.-C. (2010). The moderating effect of retailer image on customers' satisfaction-loyalty link. Paper presented at the 2010 7th. International Conference on Service Systems and Service Management (ICSSSM), Taichung, Taiwan: Asia University.

Davies, G. (1992). The two ways in which retailers can be brands. *International Journal of Retail and Distribution Management*, *20*(2), 70–76. doi:10.1108/09590559210009312

Evanschitzky, H., & Wunderlich, M. (2006). An examination of moderator effects in the four-stage loyalty model. *Journal of Service Research*, *8*(4), 330–345. doi:10.1177/1094670506286325

Fullerton, G. (2005). The service quality-loyalty relationship in retail services: Does commitment matter? *Journal of Retailing and Consumer Services*, *12*(2), 99–111. doi:10.1016/j.jretconser.2004.04.001

Juhl, H. J., Kristensen, K., & Ostergaard, P. (2002). Customer satisfaction in European food retailing. *Journal of Retailing and Consumer Services*, *9*(6), 327–334. doi:10.1016/S0969-6989(02)00014-0

Kim, H., & Niehm, L. S. (2009). The impact of Website quality on information quality, value, and loyalty intentions in apparel retailing. *Journal of Interactive Marketing*, *23*, 221–233. doi:10.1016/j.intmar.2009.04.009

Knox, S. D., & Denison, T. J. (2000). Store loyalty: Its impact on retail revenue. An empirical study of purchasing behavior in the U.K. *Journal of Retailing and Consumer Services*, *7*(1), 33–45. doi:10.1016/S0969-6989(98)00033-2

Kristensen, K., Juhl, H. J., & Ostergaard, P. (2001). Customer satisfaction: Some results for European retailing. *Total Quality Management*, *12*(7&8), 890–897. doi:10.1080/09544120100000012

Lee, W.-I., Chang, C.-Y., & Liu, Y.-L. (2010). Exploring customers' store loyalty using the means-end chain approach. *Journal of Retailing and Consumer Services*, *17*, 395–405. doi:10.1016/j.jretconser.2010.04.001

Mitchell, V.-W., & Kiral, R. H. (1998). Primary and secondary store loyal customer perceptions of grocery retailers. *British Food Journal*, *100*(7), 312–319. doi:10.1108/00070709810242109

Murgulets, L., Eklof, J., Dukeov, I., & Selivanova, I. (2002). Customer satisfaction and retention in transition economies. *Total Quality Management*, *12*(7&8), 1037–1046.

Piron, F. (2001). Effects of service and communication initiatives on retail grocery consumers' loyalty. *Singapore Management Review*, 45-60.

Sawmong, S., & Ogenyy, O. (2004). The store loyalty of the U.K.'s retail consumers. *The Journal of American Academy of Business, Cambridge*, September, 503-509.

Spiggle, S., & Sewall, M. A. (1987). A choice sets model of retail selection. *Journal of Marketing*, *51*(April), 97–111. doi:10.2307/1251132

Stark, M., & Ebenkamp, B. (1999)... *Brandweek*, *40*(28), 16–17.

Straughan, R. D., & Albers-Miller, N. D. (2001). An International Investigation of Cultural and Demographic Effects on Domestic Retail Loyalty. *International Marketing Review*, *18*(5), 521–541. doi:10.1108/EUM0000000006044

Torres, E., Vásquez-Párraga, A. Z., & Barra, C. (2009). The path of patient loyalty and the role of doctor reputation. *Health Marketing Quarterly*, *26*(3), 183–197. doi:10.1080/07359680903263565 PMID:19813122

Wong, A. (2004). The role of emotional satisfaction in service encounters. *Managing Service Quality*, *14*(5), 365–376. doi:10.1108/09604520410557976

Wong, A., & Sohal, A. (2003a). Service quality and customer loyalty perspectives on two levels of retail relationships. *Journal of Services Marketing*, *17*(5), 495–513. doi:10.1108/08876040310486285

Wong, A., & Sohal, A. (2003b). A critical incident approach to the examination of customer relationship management in a retail chain: An exploratory study. *Qualitative Marketing Research: An International Journal*, *6*(4), 248–262. doi:10.1108/13522750310495337

KEY TERMS AND DEFINITIONS

Customer Commitment: Customer's engagement or continuing obligation to buy or use the same product or company.

Customer Satisfaction: Customer's fulfillment or gratification for buying or using a product or company.

Customer Store Loyalty Explanation Chain: The process of customer loyalty is explained using three antecedents in a sequential order as follows: it starts with customer satisfaction, which influences trust. Trust is essentially linked to commitment as per previous literature, and commitment is the immediate antecedent of customer loyalty: Satisfaction → trust → commitment → customer loyalty.

Customer Store Loyalty: Long-term loyalty relationship of customers to their stores.

Customer Trust: Customer's confidence in a product or person or company.

Store Customer: Buyers and users of store products.

Vásquez-Alonso (A-V) Approach: Refers to the conceptual model designed to explain customer store loyalty using four core variables (customer satisfaction, trust, commitment, and loyalty) to account for the main effects, four cognitive variables (store familiarity, store choice, customer perceived risk, and communication) to moderate the effects of trust and commitment, and four affective variables (customer opportunism, consumer involvement, customer shared personal values, and customer shared management values) to moderate the effects of trust and commitment.

Chapter 6

Evolving the Private Label Role in the Retailer– Customer Relationship:
Antecedents and Impact of Premium Private Labels on Customer Loyalty to the Retailer

Elisa Martinelli
University of Modena and Reggio Emilia, Italy

Donata Tania Vergura
University of Parma, Italy

ABSTRACT

The chapter focuses on the role played by Private Labels (PLs) in the retailer-consumer relationship. Specifically, the results of a survey aimed at investigating the ability of a specific kind of PL, namely Premium Private Label (PPL), to improve customer loyalty to the retailer are presented. After reviewing the literature on the PLs' role in the retailer-customer relationship, a theoretical model is proposed and tested by administering a questionnaire to a sample of retail customers and then applying structural equation modeling. Four key components of PPLs' image, namely quality, assortment, access, and value, are studied as antecedents of customer satisfaction to the PPL, while customer loyalty to the PPL is considered as a mediator between customer satisfaction to the PPL and customer loyalty to the retailer. Results show that PPLs positively impact on customer loyalty to the retailer through a causal relationship driven by PPL quality and PPL value.

INTRODUCTION

Private labels (PLs), also named as store brands or retail brands, are generally brands owned, controlled, and sold exclusively by one retailer under its own brand name (Sethuraman & Cole, 1999). The PL importance in the grocery sector has enormously increased over the past two decades, especially within Europe's shoppers. The Private Label Manufacturers Association (PLMA, 2012)

DOI: 10.4018/978-1-4666-6074-8.ch006

states that PLs now account for 40% or more of the products sold in six countries: Switzerland (53%), Spain (49%), United Kingdom (47%), Portugal (43%), Germany (41%) and Belgium (40%). In Italy, where the study reported in this chapter was conducted, PLs possess a lower market share, equals to 20%, but show increasingly higher rates of growth (SymphonyIRI Group, 2012).

PLs have grown in availability and market share, thanks to the following driving factors: firstly, the increasing level of concentration in retailing, which enables grocery chains to offer own brands, as this policy requires economies of scale to be purposed; secondly, a much more positive consumer's attitude towards PLs in general, thanks to an increase in their quality perceptions (Steenkamp, Van Heerde, & Geyskens, 2010); thirdly, their price convenience in comparison with national brands (NB), factor particularly critical during the current economic crisis that has contributed to consolidate the PL as a purchasing reference (Nielsen, 2011) and to increase its value. In 2011, the European PL food market reached €436 billion (PlanetRetail, 2011).

Traditionally, these products have been generally positioned as low price/good value for money offerings as for the perceived quality differential with NBs. But the PL role has greatly evolved over time: the width of PL offerings has enlarged and these products are now present not only in almost any Fast Moving Consumer Goods (FMCG) category, but also in the non-food ones (e.g. clothes, appliances, etc.) and in services (travel booking, broadband communications, etc.). At the same time, the depth of PLs offerings has increased and different lines of store brands have been introduced by retailers in order to satisfy consumers' demands in different market segments (Sayman & Raju, 2004). New types of PLs are now present on the shelves and some of them are explicitly directed at significantly improving perceived quality as they tend to use the same creation codes as NBs (Burt, 2000). On the basis of positioning differ-

entiation, store brands can now be divided into 2-tier (Yang & Wang, 2010) or 3-tier (Lamey, Deleersnyder, Dekimpe, & Steenkamp, 2007) PLs. Under this strategy, Premium Private Labels (PPL) are gaining an increasing interest. In Italy their market share accounts for 5.1% of PLs and they show a strong market potential. PPLs are defined as "consumer products, produced by or on behalf of retailers with high quality and priced close to national brands, that contribute to differentiating the retailer from its competitors" (Huang & Huddleston, 2009, p. 978). Examples are Tesco's "Finest" in UK, Loblaw's "President's Choice" in Canada, Esselunga's "Top" in Italy. In order to achieve a "premium" positioning for their products, retailers are investing in appealing packaging and in advertisement on the media, as well as in store brand retail outlets (Lincoln & Thomassen, 2008).

Within this context, the present chapter focuses on the role played by PLs in the retailer-consumer relationship and presents the results of a survey aimed at investigating the ability of PPLs to improve retailer brand loyalty. As a matter of fact, PPLs are an important tool that grocery retailers are recently using to upgrade the chain's image and strengthen customer loyalty to the retailer as a brand. Consequently, it would be useful to give support to this strategy verifying the role of PPLs in the formation of customer loyalty to the retailer as extant literature does not provide sufficient empirical proof of this relationship. Moreover, the present literature lack in verifying the determinants of customer satisfaction with PPLs. Hence, our research questions are as follows: does customer loyalty to the PPL transform into customer loyalty to the retailer? Which are the PPL characteristics that impact on customer satisfaction with PPLs? Does customer satisfaction with PPL translate in customer loyalty to the PPL? And ultimately: does this loyalty to the PPL transfer to customer loyalty to the retailer? To address these issues, this paper proposes a theoretical model, testing it on the data collected administering a questionnaire to a sample of 299 Italian retail customers, interviewed through an in-store survey.

This chapter would make the following contributions to the extant literature. First of all, it systematically outlines the evolution of the literature on the role of PLs in the retailer-consumer relationship, aiming at becoming a reference for tracing the achievements of the extant literature on the topic. Secondly, it specifically examines and investigates the role of PPLs in the process of developing customer loyalty to the retailer, filling in the gap of knowledge of the extant literature on this topic. From this point of view, it would give scientific support of the importance of PPLs in building customer satisfaction and loyalty for these kind of products, and in so doing gaining customer loyalty to the retail chain. This chapter would also contribute to extend the knowledge of retail managers and consultants on PLs and customer loyalty in retail contexts. Moreover, the reading of this chapter would provide retail managers and consultants with the knowledge of PPLs cues in which to invest in order to satisfy customers and gain their preferences.

From a structural point of view the chapter is organised as follows. After reviewing the literature on the role played by PLs in the retailer-consumer relationship, the chapter would explain the conceptual framework and the hypotheses underpinning the study. Then, the methodology is presented, describing the sample and the data collection procedure adopted, together with the measurements employed. Subsequently, results are depicted and discussed, followed by some reflections on possible further research directions. Final conclusions and remarks end the work.

BACKGROUND

Previous research on PLs is broad in scope and established around several different issues. Three are the main areas of study: the contribution of PLs

to retailer sales and profitability; the impact of PLs in the supplier-retailer relationship; the role played by PLs in the retailer-consumer relationship. This paragraph would concentrate on the latter study area, as raising matter of research interest, reviewing the extant literature on this topic.

Early studies on PLs dated back to mid-1960s, when PLs appeared on the market as "generic" products, and were mainly descriptive. The initial focus was on understanding buyers' profile in terms of demographic and psychographic characteristics (e.g. Burger & Scott, 1972; Coe, 1971; Dick, Jain & Richardson, 1995; 1996; Frank & Boyd, 1965; Murphy, 1978; Myers, 1967). Burger and Scott (1972) highlighted that PLs buyers encompass all socio-economic groups, and Frank and Boyd (1965) evidenced that people prone to buy PLs do not differ in their socio-economic and consumption characteristics from people who buy NBs. Myers (1967) and Szymanski and Busch (1987) suggested that individual characteristics are not indicative of PLs preferences. In sum, these studies generally failed to determine consistent consumer profiles, leading a number of scholars to address an ongoing interest to this theme. Thus, several authors focused on the relationship between PL proneness and purchase and socio-demographic characteristics, namely age (Putsis & Cotterill, 1999; Sethuraman & Cole, 1999), gender (Sethuraman & Cole, 1999), income level (Baltas & Argouslidis, 2007; Dhar & Hoch, 1997; Richardson, Jain, & Dick, 1996), size of the household (Richardson et al., 1996), level of education (Binkley, Eales, Jekanowski, & Dooley, 2001), and ethnicity (Putsis & Cotterill, 1999). However, the results obtained are mixed and do not enable to derive common beliefs on the characteristics of PLs buyers.

Since the mid-eighties, with the advent of scanner data and the increasing application of analytical models in marketing, there has been an upsurge in the number of studies dealing with PLs and the research interest raised also on other streams relative to consumer perceptions of PLs and behavioral patterns. Specifically, PLs became the research object and sought to understand what are consumer preferences towards PLs versus NBs (Quelch & Harding 1996; Raju, Sethuraman, & Dhar, 1995; Sethruraman & Cole, 1999), which are the product attributes of greatest interest to consumers (Baltas, 1997; Baltas, Doyle, & Dyson, 1997; Glynn & Chen, 2009; McNeill & Wyeth, 2011; Mieres, Martin & Gutierrez, 2006) and which other factors impact on PLs proneness. Dekimpe, Steenkamp, Mellens, and Vanden Abeele (1997) showed that PLs cause a decline in consumers NB loyalty. Traditionally, the consumer's preference for a NB over a PL often relates to the higher perceived purchasing risk carried by the latter (Batra & Sinha, 2000; Liljander, Polsa, & van Riel, 2009). This is an influencing factor emerged also in previous studies. For example, Bettman (1974) found variables reflecting lower perceived risk and greater information to be associated with PL proneness, as well as Livesey and Lennon (1978) highlighted the importance of consumer experience with PLs and perceived risk. The focus was particularly placed on PLs quality differential. But while during '80ies studies evidenced that consumers perceived these products as being of relatively poor quality and consequently they tend to be unwilling to purchase them (Bellizzi, Krueckeberg, Hamilton, & Martin, 1981; Cunningham, Hardy, & Imperia, 1982; Richardson, Dick, & Jain, 1994), in the following decade consumers' perceptions of PLs started to improve. As the PL has evolved over time, the actual and perceived product quality gap with NB is decreasing (Hoch & Banerji, 1993; Quelch & Harding, 1996; Batra & Sinha, 2000). The following other influencing factors were researched. Bellizzi et al., (1981) found that store-brand prone consumers are less sensitive to brands and advertising. Accordingly, Baltas (1997) profiled PL purchasers as price cautious, shopping frequent and familiar with PLs, but not promotion sensitive consumers. Richardson et al., (1996)

identified familiarity with store brands, extrinsic cues usage in product evaluation, perceived quality variation, perceived risk and perceived value for money as factors influencing PL proneness. Miquel, Caplliure and Aldas-Manzano (2002) demonstrated that greater involvement leads to better knowledge, which in turn increases store brand proneness. This resulted to be more category specific than consumer specific (Sethuraman & Cole, 1999) as PLs tend to gain higher share in less-promoted categories with a small number of brands, and when the price differential with national brands is large (Dhar & Hoch, 1998; Hoch & Banerji, 1993). Consumers' evaluations of PLs depend not only on product attributes, but also on store image (Semeijn, van Riel, & Ambrosini, 2004; Vahie & Paswan, 2006).

In the new millennium, the interest for the role of intrinsic and extrinsic PL cues as determinants or moderators of shopping habits continued, but the extant literature gave also increasing attention to consumers' attitude towards PL products (e.g. De Wulf, Odekerken-Schroëder, Goedertier, & Van Ossel, 2005; Liu & Wang, 2008; Garretson, Fisher, & Burton, 2002; Collins-Dodd & Lindley, 2003), and to the relationship between PLs and store loyalty (Ailawadi, Pauwels, & Steenkamp, 2008; Binninger, 2008; Corstjens & Lal, 2000; Dhar, Hoch, & Kumar, 2001; González-Benito & Martos-Partal, 2012; Martenson, 2007; Richardson et al., 1996; Steenkamp & Dekimpe, 1997). But results are mixed: the relationship may be nonlinear, possibly even nonmonotonic. Ailawadi and Harlam (2004) found that medium PL users contribute more than light users or non-users of PLs to retailer sales and profits, but heavy PL users contribute less than medium users. In any case, a few authors have dealt directly with PLs by addressing consumer loyalty. This is why this chapter would focus on this topic. The following paragraph describes the conceptual framework used in the study and its hypotheses.

CONCEPTUAL FRAMEWORK AND HYPOTHESES

Retailers offer PLs for three main reasons: firstly, they can boost their margins and sales (Hoch & Banerji, 1993); secondly, they can increase their contractual power with NB manufacturers (Narasimhan & Wilcox, 1998); thirdly, they can obtain customer loyalty (Steenkamp & Dekimpe, 1997).

From the early 1990s on, customer loyalty has become a key concept in marketing studies. The benefits that companies can get from customer loyalty are well documented in the literature. Loyal customers are less sensitive to price (Krishnamurthi & Raj, 1991) and to the promotional policies and offerings of competitors (Jensen & Hansen, 2006). Moreover, they act as information channel for the brand, leading to a beneficial word-of-mouth (Shoemaker & Lewis, 1999). Maintain loyal customers is less costly than acquiring new ones (Reichheld, 1993), especially in mature and competitive markets (Ehrenberg & Goodhardt, 2000), as grocery retailing is nowadays. In this sector, pursuing customer loyalty has become an objective of strategic importance (Flavián, Martínez, & Polo, 2001; Jensen, 2011). In the last decade, retailers experienced multi-loyalty and variety-seeking behaviors by consumers, making assortments and products key factors in building customer loyalty (East, Harris, Wittson, & Lomax, 1995; Odekerken-Schroëder, de Wulf, Kasper, Kleijnen, Hoekstra, & Commandeur, 2001).

The prevailing literature on customer loyalty in retail settings investigated the relationship at a store level (Bloemer & De Ruyter, 1998; Sirohi, McLaughlin, & Wittink, 1998; Sivadas & Baker-Prewitt, 2000), while attempts to examine this relationship at the retailer level are more contemporary and reply to the call for more research on issues related to the retail brand equity perspective made recently by relevant scholars (Ailawadi & Keller, 2004; Burt, 2000; Burt & Davies, 2010). Consequently, this study would consider a conceptualisation of customer loyalty in relation to the retailer as a brand. In particular, it will focus on the behavioural dimension of customer loyalty as intended in a conative sense.

Traditionally, a PL has been considered as a brand extension of a retailer as the parent brand (e.g. Aaker & Keller, 1990; Völckner & Sattler, 2006). In this perspective, the success of a PL depends on the transfer of store equity to the PL. But also the inverse could be true as PLs are perceived today as brands per se.

Empirical evidence on the relationship between PL purchase and store loyalty has been explored, corroborating a positive correlation between PL use and store loyalty (Ailawadi, Neslin & Gedenk, 2001; Corstjens & Lal, 2000; Kumar & Steenkamp, 2007). And as Corstjens and Lal (2000) analytically demonstrated that store brands can generate retail differentiation, store loyalty and store profitability only if the quality of the store brand is sufficiently high, this paper would focus on the highest tier of PLs, that is: PPLs. Kumar and Steenkamp (2007, p. 41) emphasized that, "the emergence of the 'premium' [PL] is one of the hottest trends in retailing." Because of their higher positioning and role, PPLs should be particularly prone to develop customer loyalty not only to the store, but also to the retailer, at the chain level. But this is an issue that the extant literature did not empirically address in depth so far. Binninger (2008) showed that PL satisfaction and loyalty influence store loyalty but the author did not distinguish between PL-tiers and focused on customer loyalty to the store, not to the retailer. Kremer and Viot (2012) evidenced that store brands contribute to the retailer image, but they excluded to verify this impact at the PPL level. Huang and Huddleston (2009) addressed theoretically the impact of PPL on customer loyalty, but did not confirm it empirically.

An attitudinal loyalty perspective is employed in this study. As the extant literature evidenced that customer satisfaction is one of the main determinants of customer loyalty to products or stores (Oliver, 1999; Garbarino & Johnson,

1999; Jones & Suh, 2000), a model in which customer loyalty is measured through intentions to repurchase the PPL and to repurchase from the retailer is proposed (Macintosh & Lockshin, 1997; Delgado-Ballester, Munuera-Alemàn, & Yagüe-Guillén, 2003). This link has also been verified in distribution contexts, namely in the grocery one (Bloemer & De Ruyter, 1998; Noordhoff, Pauwels & Odekerken-Schröder, 2004). Likewise, while numerous authors are questioning the intricate and deterministic link between satisfaction and loyalty (Kamakura, Mittal, de Rose, & Mazzon, 2002; Kumar, dalla Pozza & Ganesh, 2013), those two measures still remains massively important at the corporate level.

Our model is also addressed at measuring the impact of some main components of PPL image on the sequence analyzed. Four variables are observed, namely: perceived quality, assortment, access and value.

The quality of a product plays a crucial role in consumers' preferences, their satisfaction level and purchase decisions (Raju, Srinivasan, & Lal, 1990; Parasuraman, Zeithaml & Berry, 1996). It affects also a brand's performance (Aaker, 2004) and the decision to select the store in which to purchase (Pan & Zinkhan, 2006). PLs perceived quality is here defined in terms of product performance and the consistency of performance over time with respect to intrinsic attributes (Richardson et al., 1996). Researchers have suggested that the principal reason for the growth of PLs has been their improved quality (Hoch & Banerji, 1993). Perceived merchandise quality was found to positively influence customer satisfaction (Bagozzi, 1992; Babakus, Bienstock, & Van Scotter, 2004). Therefore, the same relationship can be postulated when the product under observation is the PPL.

HP1: PPL quality is an antecedent of customer satisfaction with the PPL.

PLs have been recognized for their capacity to increase perceived assortment variety (Nies &

Natter, 2012). This is particularly true for high-quality and specialty PLs lines since these are more unique than value PLs. PPLs are extending to an increasing number of product categories; consequently the PPL assortment, intended as the retailer's offer of a broad and complete range of products under the PL brand name, can influence the level of customer satisfaction. Sayman & Raju (2004) suggested that store brands have been introduced by retailers in order to satisfy consumers' demand in different market segments; consequently, we can postulate that PPL assortment can positively affect the level of satisfaction that a consumer can get from PPLs.

HP2: PPL assortment is an antecedent of customer satisfaction with the PPL.

In addition, since not only improvements in quality but also in packaging/features (Choi & Coughlan, 2002) and in the way retailers are evidencing PLs in-store are increasingly characterizing the growth of these store brands, PPL access, defined here as the easiness to locate these products into the store and on the shelves, would be considered as the third antecedent of customer satisfaction with the PPL.

HP3: PPL access is an antecedent of customer satisfaction with the PPL.

As stated in the previous paragraph, issues of quality and pricing of PLs relative to NBs have been a dominant focus of research in this literature. From this point of view, PPLs are high quality products and their price tend to communicate this value. In this work, PPL value is intended as the perceived quality of a product in relation to the price paid for that product (Zeithaml, 1988). As it has been suggested that where consumers balance price and quality there is a more favorable attitude and perception toward PLs, it is possible to postulate a positive and direct effect of PPL value on customer satisfaction with the PPL.

HP4: PPL value is an antecedent of customer satisfaction with the PPL.

Customers who are satisfied with a brand are likely to buy it again in order to simplify their brand choice decisions and diminish uncertainty (Bloemer & Kasper, 1995). However, "researchers have commonly neglected the possibility that consumers have strong preferences for or even feel loyal toward a particular PL [...] Empirical evidence, on the contrary, increasingly suggests that at least some PLs command loyal customer bases" (Nies & Natter, 2012, p. 280). Veloutsou, Gioulistanis & Moutinho (2004) found that customer loyalty occurs when consumers are satisfied with the PL. Consequently, the following hypothesis could be postulated:

HP5: Customer satisfaction with the PPL positively impacts on customer loyalty to the PPL.

A consumer who is loyal to a PL will have a more favorable perception of the overall retailer brand (De Wulf et al., 2005). Consumers who profess to be loyal to a specific PL are likely to be more loyal to the retailer from whom they bought the PL (Binninger, 2008; Steenkamp & Dekimpe, 1997; Uncles & Ellis, 1989). It could thus posit that PPL loyalty has a positive impact on customer loyalty to the retailer as a brand:

HP6: Customer loyalty to the PPL is an antecedent of customer loyalty to the retailer.

METHODOLOGY

Sample and Data Collection

The survey was conducted in a grocery retailing context. Data were collected administering a structured questionnaire to a convenience sample of 299 retail customers approached while exiting two stores located in different Italian towns and regions (Parma in Emilia Romagna and Florence in Tuscany) and belonging to two of the main grocery retailers operating in the country. Both retailers have a 3-tier PL policy. The decision to administer the questionnaire in different stores/retailers responds to the opportunity to avoid possible distortions due to the specific positioning of a certain retailer/store.

Data were gathered within a period of two weeks on different days and at different times in order to collect the greatest likely variety of buying models.

The sample is mainly composed of women (70%). Overall, 36% of respondents are aged between 36 and 50, while 35% are aged over 50. The level of education is quite high: half of the sample (50%) completed the high-school; 35% are graduated or post-graduated; 2% left school after the primary level and a further 12% after the secondary level. The prevalent employment condition is full-time worker (57%), while 25% of the respondents are part-time workers or retired (15%). Family composition is diversified: 22% are single, 6% live in a family of 5 or more members and the remaining live in families from 2 to 4 components. The annual net income does not exceed 36,000 euros for the 48% of the sample, while the income of 41% ranged from 36,000 to 70,000 euros. Only 10% earned more than 70,000 euros a year.

Measurements

The measurements used were identified on the basis of a literature review (Table 1).

Customer satisfaction has been measured in a "backward looking" perspective (Vesel & Zabkar, 2010). This is based on the belief that customers become loyal when they develop a cumulative satisfaction through a series of positive service encounters with the retail brand (Garbarino & Johnson, 1999; Oliver, 1999). In this sense, satisfaction results from the retailer's performance that a customer has so far experienced (Gustafsson,

Table 1. Constructs and items used in the questionnaire

Constructs	Items	References
PPL quality	The PPL "X" offers high quality products	Adapted from Kremer & Viot (2012)
	I like the PPL "X" products	
	I can be certain of the quality of PPL "X" products	
PPL assortment	The PPL "X" offers the products I search for	
	The PPL "X" offers a broad range of products	
	Within the PPL "X" I always find what I need	
PPL access	PPL "X" products are well positioned on the shelves	
	PPL "X" products are easy to find into the store	
PPL value	PPL "X" products offer good value for money	
	PPL "X" products prices are fair	
Customer satisfaction with the PPL (CS PPL)	I am satisfied with the PPL "X" products.	Garbarino & Johnson (1999)
	Overall, the PPL "X" satisfies my needs	
Customer loyalty to the PPL (CL PPL)	I will continue to buy the PPL "X" products.	Chaudhuri & Holbrook (2001); Sirohi et al., (1998)
	I will buy again the PPL "X" next time I go shopping	
	I am willing to buy again the PPL "X" products.	
Customer loyalty to the retailer (CL R)	I will shop again at this retailer.	Sivadas & Baker-Prewitt (2000)
	I intend to continue shopping at this retailer.	
	Should I need to do shopping again, I will return at this retailer.	

Johnson & Ross, 2005), rather than an assessment of the last transaction-specific experience of satisfaction or dissatisfaction. As a matter of fact, marketing literature evidenced the better predictability of the former perspective rather than the latter (Jones & Suh, 2000).

Customer loyalty to the PPL and to the retailer is intended in a conative way, such as "a brand-specific commitment to repurchase" (Oliver, 1999, p. 35). In retailing context, this construct can be measured through behavioural intentions indicators such as intention to repurchase in a store (Macintosh & Lockshin, 1997; Sivadas & Baker-Prewitt, 2000).

Structural Equation Modeling (SEM) was used to synthesize the latent variables hypothesized, to identify the path of relationships between them, and to estimate the parameters of structural models (Bollen, 1989; Hair, Black, Babin, Anderson, & Tatham, 2005).

RESULTS

Descriptive Statistics

Results (Table 2) show that consumer perception of the components of PPL image is very good (1–7 Likert scale). All four components (quality, assortment, access and value) achieve high scores, with the access items rated as best. Also customer satisfaction toward the PPL is high, as well as stated intentions to rebuy PPL products and to repurchase from the retailer. Correlation analyses revealed that the observed variables are positively related to each another (see also Table 4 in the Appendix).

Analysis of the Proposed Model

Reliability was assessed as internal consistency using Cronbach's alpha coefficient and item-total

Table 2. Descriptive statistics for the observed variables

Constructs	Variables	Mean	Std. Dev.
PPL quality	MQ1	5.62	1.731
	MQ2	5.98	1.565
	MQ3	5.80	1.585
PPL assortment	MA1	4.65	2.084
	MA2	5.26	1.792
	MA3	4.65	2.058
PPL access	ML1	6.19	1.482
	ML2	6.23	1.471
PPL value	MPr1	5.34	1.796
	MPr2	5.22	1.853
CS PPL	CS1	5.64	1.885
	CS2	5.63	1.881
CL PPL	I1	5.75	1.841
	I2	4.80	2.218
	I3	5.73	1.851
CL R	INT1	6.46	1.361
	INT2	6.41	1.454
	INT3	6.40	1.447

correlation. The alpha index is much greater than the threshold value of 0.70 (Nunnally & Bernstein, 1994) for each scale (α PPL quality = 0.88; α PPL assortment = 0.91; α PPL access = 0.97; α PPL value = 0.95; α CS PLL = 0.97; α CL PPL = 0.88; α CL R = 0.97) and all items had a high item-total correlation, indicating their capability to measure the construct.

Structural equation modeling with maximum likelihood method was employed to estimate the parameters for testing the proposed model. The data were analyzed in Lisrel 8.80. To scale the latent variables, the first factor loading for each of them was set to 1.

The findings show that the model in Figure.1 fits the data acceptably well (χ^2 = 402.154; df = 123; CFI = 0.976; NNFI = 0.970; RMSEA = 0.085, p = 0.000; SRMR = 0.063), according to Hu and Bentler (1995) and Browne and Cudeck

(1993). All factor loadings for the observed variables are significant (Table 3).

Since the Cronbach's alpha to assess the internal consistency of measures suffers from some weaknesses (Miller, 1995; Raykov, 1998; Schmitt, 1996), two additional construct reliability indices were calculated, namely Composite Reliability (CR) and the Average Variance Extracted (AVE) (Hair et al., 2005). The recommended cut-off points for the adequacy of the two indices are 0.70 for CR (Steenkamp & van Trijp, 1991) and 0.50 for AVE (Fornell & Larcker, 1981). As shown in Table 3 they are well above the threshold values.

Results show that PPLs positively contribute to customer loyalty toward the retailer. The four components of PPL image in total explained 63% of the variance in customer satisfaction toward PPL, but only quality (β =.673, p <.01) and value (β =.133, p <.05) have a statistically significant regression coefficient. Thus, H1 and H4 are supported. The effects of PPL assortment and access, instead, are not significant, leading us to reject H2 and H3.

At the same time, the results of structural equation modeling indicate that CS PPL increases customer loyalty to PPL products (β =.966, p <.01; R^2 = 0.93). Also the prediction path from CL PPL to CL R was statistically significant (β =.443, p <.01; R^2 = 0.20), confirming that the first construct mediates the effect of customer satisfaction on retailer repurchase intentions. Thus, H5 and H6 are supported. Figure 1 shows the tested structural model with standardized coefficients.

DISCUSSION

PLs play an important role in retail strategy and understanding PL purchase behavior is a critical issue for both scholars and marketers. The review of the literature on the role of PLs in the retailer customer-relationship evidenced that there is an increasing and recent interest in understanding the way in which customer loyalty can be affected

Table 3. Factor loadings

	PPL Quality	PPL Assortment	PPL Access	PPL Value	CS PPL	CL PPL	CL R
MQ1	0.721						
MQ2	0.918						
MQ3	0.892						
MA1		0.951					
MA2		0.741					
MA3		0.943					
ML1			0.965				
ML2			0.980				
PR1				0.954			
PR2				0.940			
CS1					0.982		
CS2					0.957		
I1						0.986	
I2						0.634	
I3						0.975	
INT1							0.951
INT2							0.995
INT3							0.996
Construct reliability	0.88	0.91	0.97	0.95	0.97	0.91	0.99
AVE	0.72	0.78	0.95	0.90	0.94	0.77	0.96

$p < .01$

Figure 1. Structural model with standardized coefficients

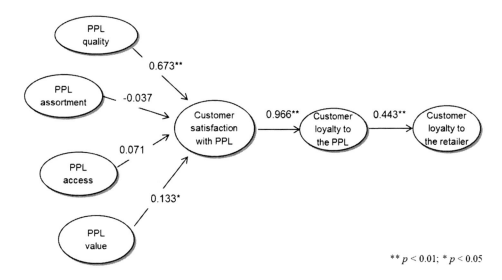

** $p < 0.01$; * $p < 0.05$

by PLs. In fact, in the first part of the chapter it has been pointed out that many authors call for supplementary research on this theme.

This work contributes to the body of knowledge in this area by focusing on a specific PL tier, namely PPLs, and empirically examining their role as activator of customer loyalty. The results offer a new contribution to the interpretation of the marketing role of PLs. Descriptive findings evidenced that the image possessed by PPLs and perceived by customers in terms of quality, assortment, access and value obtained high scores from the retail customers interviewed, confirming the good evaluation and image developed by these products. But the following structural model tested showed that only quality and value resulted in impacting customer satisfaction and by this way customer loyalty to the PPL and then from to the retailer. So, PPLs can strengthen the relationship that a consumer has with a retailer but only after that customer loyalty to the PPL brand has emerged.

These findings may help retailers in their decisions regarding PPL correct market positioning. The importance given to the PPL quality demonstrates that the retailer brand is evaluated not only for its value for money, but also on the basis of its intrinsic characteristic. As a consequence, retailers should emphasize the efforts placed on quality control process to maintain more consistent levels of quality as well as on improving them. Objective tests revealed that there is often little, if any, quality difference between PLs and NBs (Apelbaum, Gerstner, & Naik, 2003), and Steenkamp et al., (2010) found that, on average, the perceived quality gap is small too. Thus, retailers should make an effort to stress the quality perception and rightly communicate it in their store chain. Investment in high quality, in fact, means investment in image (Burt, 2000). At the same time, it is worth rending evident the positive price image (fair and good value for money) of these products in comparison with NBs. In this regard, the price gap between

the two brand types represents a strategic choice that goes beyond category boundaries since the PL price contributes to create the price image of the retailer and leads the consumer to choose it. On the contrary, retailers do not need to be particularly preoccupied of extending the PPL to every category and accurate in assigning good shelves space to PPL products. These factors do not increase customer satisfaction and lack in developing customer loyalty.

In conclusion, PPLs emerge as a tool that could contribute to strengthening the relationship with the retailer, potentially acting as a vehicle for information about the value of the retailer over its competitors. This confirms the process of trading up of the PL in recent years and the role it has gained as a signal of reputation, credibility and trust. Therefore, PLs and, in particular, PPLs can represent a mean to establish lasting relationships with customers.

FUTURE RESEARCH DIRECTIONS

PLs are experiencing a terrific growth of popularity between consumers. The current economic crisis push this tendency. Not only their market share behaves countercyclically, but it has been recently evidenced that part of the boost in PL share during contractions is permanent (Lamey, Deleersnyder, Steenkamp, & Dekimpe, 2012). As a consequence, this area of study would continue to raise its importance in the future, maintaining high the interest on the enduring battle with NBs and on consumer factors affecting PLs success. But also other topics are raising. Hyman, Kopf, & Lee, (2010) evidenced three possible areas of further research: 1) inter-country differences in PLs usage in order to investigate, for example, the effect of national culture on PL purchase; 2) the social benefits and social costs of PLs; 3) the factors that contribute to PLs retailers' comparative advantage with niche consumer groups.

CONCLUSION

The chapter has highlighted the growing role played today by PLs in the retailer-consumer relationship and reviewed the main literature on this theme, stating an increasing and recent interest of PL studies for the link with customer loyalty. In this perspective, the chapter has also reported the results of a study aimed at specifically focus on PPLs as literature lacks in empirically demonstrating their contribution to customer loyalty. Findings reached this goal: PPLs can positively impact on customer loyalty to the retailer, measured through intentions to repurchase the PPL, through a causal relationship driven by PPL quality and PPL value and mediated by satisfaction and loyalty to the PPL.

However, despite the contribution made by the study conducted, some limitations affect its relevance. Firstly, the survey relates to a generic concept of PPL, although previous literature found differences in the impact of PLs depending of the product category. Secondly, the loyalty construct investigated is measured as attitudinal while also behavioural loyalty should be included to measure true loyalty (Dick & Basu, 1994). Moreover, there are other important constructs forming part of the satisfaction-loyalty framework which were not included in this study, such as trust and commitment (Morgan & Hunt, 1994). Other variables can then impact or moderate the effect of PPL on customer loyalty, such as PL attitude, level of familiarity, customer involvement. For instance, the relationship between customer satisfaction and repurchase behavior has been found to be contingent on the mediating effects of convenience, competitive intensity, customer involvement, and household income (Seiders, Voss, Grewal, & Godfrey, 2005). Finally, it has been taken for granted the interviewees' ability to distinguish between different PL tiers.

REFERENCES

Aaker, D. A. (2004). *Brand Portfolio Strategy: Creating Relevance, Differentiation, Energy, Leverage and Clarity*. Free Press.

Aaker, D. A., & Keller, K. L. (1990). Consumer evaluation of brand extensions. *Journal of Marketing*, *54*(1), 27–41. doi:10.2307/1252171

Ailawadi, K., & Keller, K. L. (2004). Understanding retail branding: conceptual insights and research priorities. *Journal of Retailing*, *80*(4), 331–342. doi:10.1016/j.jretai.2004.10.008

Ailawadi, K., Pauwels, K., & Steenkamp, J.-B. (2008). Private-label use and store loyalty. *Journal of Marketing*, *72*(6), 19–30. doi:10.1509/jmkg.72.6.19

Ailawadi, K. L., & Harlam, B. (2004). An empirical analysis of the determinants of retail margins: the role of store brand share. *Journal of Marketing*, *68*(1), 147–166. doi:10.1509/jmkg.68.1.147.24027

Ailawadi, K. L., Neslin, S. A., & Gedenk, K. (2001). Pursuing the value-conscious consumer: store brands versus national brand promotions. *Journal of Marketing*, *65*(1), 71–89. doi:10.1509/jmkg.65.1.71.18132

Apelbaum, E., Gerstner, E., & Naik, P. A. (2003). The Effects of Expert Quality Evaluations Versus Brand Name on Price Premiums. *Journal of Product and Brand Management*, *12*(2–3), 154–165. doi:10.1108/10610420310476915

Babakus, E., Bienstock, C. C., & Van Scotter, J. R. (2004). Linking Perceived Quality and Customer Satisfaction to Store Traffic and Revenue Growth. *Decision Sciences*, *35*(4), 713–737. doi:10.1111/j.1540-5915.2004.02671.x

Bagozzi, R. P. (1992). The self-regulation of attitudes, intentions, and behavior. *Social Psychology Quarterly*, *55*(2), 178–204. doi:10.2307/2786945

Baltas, G. (1997). Determinants of store brand choice: a behavioral analysis. *Journal of Product and Brand Management, 6*(5), 315–324. doi:10.1108/10610429710179480

Baltas, G., & Argouslidis, P. C. (2007). Consumer characteristics and demand for store brands. *International Journal of Retail & Distribution Management, 35*(5), 328–341. doi:10.1108/09590550710743708

Baltas, G., Doyle, P., & Dyson, P. (1997). A model of consumer choice for national vs store brands. *The Journal of the Operational Research Society, 48*(10), 988–995. doi:10.1057/palgrave.jors.2600454

Batra, R., & Sinha, I. (2000). Consumer-level factors moderating the success of private label brands. *Journal of Retailing, 76*(2), 175–191. doi:10.1016/S0022-4359(00)00027-0

Bellizzi, J. A., Krueckeberg, H. F., Hamilton, J. R., & Martin, W. A. (1981). Consumer Perceptions of National, Private, and Generic Brands. *Journal of Retailing, 57*(4), 56–70.

Bettman, J. R. (1974). Relationship of information-processing attitude structures to private brand purchasing behavior. *The Journal of Applied Psychology, 59*(1), 79–83. doi:10.1037/h0035817

Binkley, J., Eales, M., Jekanowski, M., & Dooley, R. (2001). Competitive behavior of national brands: the case of orange juice. *Agribusiness, 17*, 139–160. doi:10.1002/1520-6297(200124)17:1<139::AID-AGR1007>3.0.CO;2-4

Binninger, A. S. (2008). Exploring the relationships between retail brands and consumer store loyalty. *International Journal of Retail & Distribution Management, 36*(2), 94–110. doi:10.1108/09590550810853057

Bloemer, J., & De Ruyter, K. (1998). On the relationship between store image, store satisfaction and store loyalty. *European Journal of Marketing, 32*(5/6), 499–513. doi:10.1108/03090569810216118

Bloemer, J. M., & Kasper, H. D. (1995). The complex relationship between consumer satisfaction and brand loyalty. *Journal of Economic Psychology, 16*, 311–329. doi:10.1016/0167-4870(95)00007-B

Bollen, K. A. (1989). *Structural Equations with Latent Variables*. New York, NY: Wiley Interscience.

Browne, M. W., & Cudeck, R. (1993). Alternative ways of assessing model fit. In K. A. Bollen, & J. S. Long (Eds.), *Testing structural equation models*. Newbury Park, CA: Sage Publications.

Burger, P. C., & Schott, B. (1972). Can private brand buyers be identified? *JMR, Journal of Marketing Research, 9*, 219–222. doi:10.2307/3149961

Burt, S. (2000). The strategic role of retail brands in British grocery retailing. *European Journal of Marketing, 34*(8), 875–890. doi:10.1108/03090560010331351

Burt, S. L., & Davies, K. (2010). From the retail brand to the retail-er as a brand: themes and issues in retail branding research. *International Journal of Retail & Distribution Management, 38*(11/12), 865–878. doi:10.1108/09590551011085957

Chaudhuri, A., & Holbrook, M. B. (2001). The chain of effects from brand trust and brand affect to brand performance: the role of brand loyalty. *Journal of Marketing, 65*(2), 81–93. doi:10.1509/jmkg.65.2.81.18255

Choi, S. T., & Coughlan, A. T. (2006). Private label positioning: quality versus feature differentiation from the national brand. *Journal of Retailing, 82*(2), 79–93. doi:10.1016/j.jretai.2006.02.005

Coe, B. D. (1971). Private versus national preference among lower and middle-income consumers. *Journal of Retailing, 4,* 61–72.

Collins-Dodd, C., & Lindley, T. (2003). Store brands and retail differentiation: the influence of store image and store brand attitude on store brand own perceptions. *Journal of Retailing and Consumer Services, 10*(4), 345–352. doi:10.1016/S0969-6989(02)00054-1

Corstjens, M., & Lal, R. (2000). Building store loyalty through store brands. *JMR, Journal of Marketing Research, 37*(3), 281–291. doi:10.1509/jmkr.37.3.281.18781

Cunningham, I., Hardy, A. P., & Imperia, G. (1982). Generic Brands Versus National Brands and Store Brands. *Journal of Advertising Research, 22,* 25–32.

De Wulf, K., Odekerken-Schroëder, G., Goedertier, F., & Van Ossel, G. (2005). Consumer perceptions of store brands versus national brands. *Journal of Consumer Marketing, 22*(4), 223–232. doi:10.1108/07363760510605335

Dekimpe, M. G., Steenkamp, J. B. E. M., Mellens, M., & Vanden Abeele, P. (1997). Decline and variability in brand loyalty. *International Journal of Research in Marketing, 14*(5), 405–420. doi:10.1016/S0167-8116(97)00020-7

Delgado-Ballester, E., Munuera-Alemàn, J. L., & Yagüe-Guillén, M. J. (2003). Development and validation of a brand trust scale. *International Journal of Market Research, 45*(1), 35–53.

Dhar, S. K., & Hoch, S. J. (1997). Why store brand penetration varies by retailer. *Marketing Science, 16,* 208–227. doi:10.1287/mksc.16.3.208

Dhar, S. K., Hoch, S. J., & Kumar, N. (2001). Effective category management depends on the role of the category. *Journal of Retailing, 77*(2), 165–184. doi:10.1016/S0022-4359(01)00045-8

Dick, A. S., & Basu, K. (1994). Customer loyalty: toward an integrated conceptual framework. *Journal of the Academy of Marketing Science, 22*(2), 99–113. doi:10.1177/0092070394222001

Dick, A. S., Jain, A. K., & Richardson, P. (1995). Correlates of store brand proneness: some empirical observations. *Journal of Product and Brand Management, 4*(4), 15–22. doi:10.1108/10610429510097663

Dick, A. S., Jain, A. K., & Richardson, P. (1996). How consumers evaluate store brands. *Journal of Product and Brand Management, 5*(2), 19–28. doi:10.1108/10610429610119405

East, R., Harris, P., Wittson, G., & Lomax, W. (1995). Loyalty to supermarkets. *International Review of Retail, Distribution and Consumer Research, 5,* 99–109. doi:10.1080/09593969500000006

Ehrenberg, A. S. C., & Goodhardt, G. J. (2000). New brands: near instant loyalty. *Journal of Marketing Management, 16,* 607–617. doi:10.1362/026725700785045912

Flavián, C., Martínez, E., & Polo, Y. (2001). Loyalty to grocery stores in the Spanish market of the 1990s. *Journal of Retailing and Consumer Services, 8*(2), 85–93. doi:10.1016/S0969-6989(99)00028-4

Fornell, C., & Larcker, D. F. (1981). Evaluating structural equation models with unobservable variables and measurement error. *JMR, Journal of Marketing Research, 18*(1), 39–50. doi:10.2307/3151312

Frank, R. E., & Boyd, H. W. (1965). Are private-brand prone grocery customers really different? *JMR, Journal of Marketing Research, 4,* 27–35.

Garbarino, E., & Johnson, M. S. (1999). The different roles of satisfaction, trust and commitment in customer relationships. *Journal of Marketing, 63*(2), 70–87. doi:10.2307/1251946

Garretson, J., Fisher, D., & Burton, S. (2002). Antecedents of private label attitude and brand promotion attitude: similarities and differences. *Journal of Retailing, 78*(2), 91–99. doi:10.1016/S0022-4359(02)00071-4

Glynn, M. S., & Chen, S. (2009). Consumer-factors moderating private label brand success: further empirical results. *International Journal of Retail & Distribution Management, 37*(11), 896–914. doi:10.1108/09590550910999343

González-Benito, O., & Martos-Partal, M. (2012). Role of retailer positioning and product category on the relationship between store brand consumption and store loyalty. *Journal of Retailing, 88*(2), 236–249. doi:10.1016/j.jretai.2011.05.003

Gustafsson, A., Johnson, D. M., & Ross, I. (2005). The effects of customer satisfaction, relationship commitment, dimensions, and triggers on customer retention. *Journal of Marketing, 69*(4), 210–218. doi:10.1509/jmkg.2005.69.4.210

Hair, J. F., Black, W. C., Babin, B., Anderson, R. E., & Tatham, R. L. (2005). *Multivariate Data Analysis* (6th ed.). Englewood Cliffs, NJ: Prentice Hall.

Hoch, S. J., & Banerji, S. (1993). When Do Private Labels Succeed? *Sloan Management Review, 34,* 57–67.

Hu, L. T., & Bentler, P. M. (1995). Evaluating model fit. In R. H. Hoyle (Ed.), *Structural equation modeling: concepts, issues, and applications.* Thousand Oaks, CA: Sage Publications.

Huang, Y., & Huddleston, P. (2009). Retailer premium own-brands: creating customer loyalty through own-brand products advantage. *International Journal of Retail & Distribution Management, 37*(11), 975–992. doi:10.1108/09590550910999389

Hyman, M. R., Kopf, D. A., & Lee, D. (2010). Review of literature – future research suggestions: private label brands: benefits, success factors and future research. *Journal of Brand Management, 17*(5), 368–389. doi:10.1057/bm.2009.33

Jensen, J. M. (2011). Consumer loyalty on the grocery product market: an empirical application of Dick and Basu's framework. *Journal of Consumer Marketing, 28*(5), 333–343. doi:10.1108/07363761111149983

Jensen, J. M., & Hansen, T. (2006). An empirical examination of brand loyalty. *Journal of Product and Brand Management, 15*(7), 442–449. doi:10.1108/10610420610712829

Jones, M. A., & Suh, J. (2000). Transaction-specific satisfaction and overall satisfaction: an empirical analysis. *Journal of Services Marketing, 14*(2), 147–159. doi:10.1108/08876040010371555

Kamakura, W. A., Mittal, V., de Rose, F., & Mazzon, J. A. (2002). Assessing the Service-Profit Chain. *Marketing Science, 21*(3), 294–317. doi:10.1287/mksc.21.3.294.140

Kremer, F., & Viot, C. (2012). How store brands build retailer brand image. *International Journal of Retail & Distribution Management, 40*(7), 528–543. doi:10.1108/09590551211239846

Krishnamurthi, L., & Raj, S. P. (1991). An empirical analysis of the relationship between brand loyalty and consumer price elasticity. *Marketing Science, 10,* 172–183. doi:10.1287/mksc.10.2.172

Kumar, N., & Steenkamp, J.-B. E. M. (2007). *Private Label Strategy.* Cambridge, MA: Harvard Business School Press.

Kumar, V., Dalla Pozza, I., & Ganesh, J. (2013). Revisiting the satisfaction–loyalty relationship: Empirical generalizations and directions for future research. *Journal of Retailing, 89*(3), 246–262. doi:10.1016/j.jretai.2013.02.001

Lamey, L., Deleersnyder, B., Dekimpe, M. J., & Steenkamp, J.-B. E. M. (2007). How Business Cycles Contribute to Private-Label Success: Evidence from the United States and Europe. *Journal of Marketing, 71*(1), 1–15. doi:10.1509/jmkg.71.1.1

Lamey, L., Deleersnyder, B., Steenkamp, J.-B. E. M., & Dekimpe, M. J. (2012). The Effect of Business-Cycle Fluctuations on Private-Label Share: What Has Marketing Conduct Got to Do with It? *Journal of Marketing, 76*, 1–19. doi:10.1509/jm.09.0320

Liljander, V., Polsa, P., & van Riel, A. (2009). Modelling consumer responses to an apparel store brand: store image as a risk reducer. *Journal of Retailing and Consumer Services, 16*(4), 281–290. doi:10.1016/j.jretconser.2009.02.005

Lincoln, K., & Thomassen, L. (2008). *Private label: Turning the retail threat into your biggest opportunity.* London: Kogan Page.

Liu, T. C., & Wang, C. Y. (2008). Factors affecting attitudes toward private labels and promoted brands. *Journal of Marketing Management, 24*(3-4), 283–298. doi:10.1362/026725708X306103

Livesey, F., & Lennon, P. (1978). Factors affecting consumers' choice between manufacturer brands and retailer own labels. *European Journal of Marketing, 12*(2), 158–170. doi:10.1108/EUM0000000004965

Macintosh, G., & Lockshin, L. S. (1997). Retail relationships and store loyalty: a multi-level perspective. *International Journal of Research in Marketing, 14*, 487–497. doi:10.1016/S0167-8116(97)00030-X

Martenson, R. (2007). Corporate brand image, satisfaction and store loyalty: a study of the store as a brand, store brands and manufacturer brands. *International Journal of Retail & Distribution Management, 35*(7), 544–555. doi:10.1108/09590550710755921

McNeill, L., & Wyeth, E. (2011). The private label grocery choice: consumer drivers to purchase. *International Review of Retail, Distribution and Consumer Research, 21*(1), 95–109. doi:10.1080/09593969.2011.537822

Mieres, C. G., Martin, A. M., & Gutierrez, J. A. T. (2006). Influence of perceived risk on store brand proneness. *International Journal of Retail & Distribution Management, 34*(10), 761–772. doi:10.1108/09590550610691347

Miller, M. B. (1995). Coefficient alpha: introduction from the perspectives of classical test theory and structural equation modeling. *Structural Equation Modeling, 2*(3), 255–273. doi:10.1080/10705519509540013

Miquel, S., Caplliure, E. M., & Aldas-Manzano, J. (2002). The effect of personal involvement on the decision to buy store brands. *Journal of Product and Brand Management, 11*(1), 6–18. doi:10.1108/10610420210419513

Morgan, R. M., & Hunt, S. D. (1994). The commitment-trust theory of relationship marketing. *Journal of Marketing, 58*, 20–38. doi:10.2307/1252308

Murphy, P. E. (1978). The effect of social class on brand and price consciousness for supermarket products. *Journal of Retailing, 54*, 33–42, 89.

Myers, J. G. (1967). Determinants of private brand attitude. *JMR, Journal of Marketing Research, 4*(1), 73–81. doi:10.2307/3150168

Narasimhan, C., & Wilcox, R. (1998). Private labels and the channel relationship: A cross-category analysis. *The Journal of Business, 71*(4), 573–600. doi:10.1086/209757

Nielsen. (2011). *Global Private Label Report: The Rise of the Value-Conscious Shopper.* Retrieved from http://www.nielsen.com/us/en/newswire/2011/global-private-label-report-the-rise-of-the-value-conscious-shopper.html

Nies, S., & Natter, M. (2012). Does Private Label Quality Influence Consumers' Decision on Where to Shop? *Psychology and Marketing, 29*(4), 279–292. doi:10.1002/mar.20521

Noordhoff, C., Pauwels, P., & Odekerken-Schröder, G. (2004). The effect of customer card programs: A comparative study in Singapore and The Netherlands. *International Journal of Service Industry Management, 15*(4), 351–364. doi:10.1108/09564230410552040

Nunnally, J. C., & Bernstein, I. H. (1994). *Psychometric theory* (3rd ed.). New York: McGraw-Hill.

Odekerken-Schroëder, G., de Wulf, K., Kasper, H., Kleijnen, M., Hoekstra, J., & Commandeur, H. (2001). The impact of quality on store loyalty: a contingency approach. *Total Quality Management, 12*(3), 307–322. doi:10.1080/09544120120034474

Oliver, R. L. (1999). Whence customer loyalty? *Journal of Marketing, 63,* 33–44. doi:10.2307/1252099

Pan, Y., & Zinkhan, G. M. (2006). Determinants of Retailing Patronage: A Meta-analytical Perspective. *Journal of Retailing, 82*(3), 229–243. doi:10.1016/j.jretai.2005.11.008

Parasuraman, A., Zeithaml, V. A., & Berry, L. L. (1996). The behavorial consequences of service quality. *Journal of Marketing, 60,* 31–46. doi:10.2307/1251929

PlanetRetail. (2011). *Country report Western Europe.* London: Author.

PLMA (Private Label Manufacturer's Association). (2012). *Private Label Today.* Retrieved May 15, 2013, from http://plmainternational.com/en/private_label12_en.htm

Putsis, W. P. Jr, & Cotterill, R. W. (1999). Share, price and category expenditure – geographic market effects and private labels. *Managerial and Decision Economics, 20*(4), 175–187. doi:10.1002/(SICI)1099-1468(199906)20:4<175::AID-MDE928>3.0.CO;2-I

Quelch, J., & Harding, D. (1996). Brands versus private labels: fighting to win. *Harvard Business Review, 74*(1), 99–109.

Raju, J., Sethuraman, R., & Dhar, S. (1995). National Brand: Store Brand Price Differential and Store Brand Market Share. *Pricing Strategy and Practice, 3*(2), 17–24.

Raju, J. S., Srinivasan, V., & Lal, R. (1990). The effects of brand loyalty on competitive price promotional strategies. *Management Science, 36*(3), 276–304. doi:10.1287/mnsc.36.3.276

Raykov, T. (1998). Coefficient alpha and composite reliability with interrelated nonhomogeneous items. *Applied Psychological Measurement, 22*(4), 375–385. doi:10.1177/014662169802200407

Reichheld, F. (1993). Loyalty-based management. *Harvard Business Review, 71*(2), 64–73. PMID:10124634

Richardson, P. S., Dick, A. S., & Jain, A. K. (1994). Extrinsic and intrinsic cue effects on perceptions of store brand quality. *Journal of Marketing, 58*(4), 28–36. doi:10.2307/1251914

Richardson, P. S., Jain, A. K., & Dick, A. (1996). Household Store Brand Proneness: A Framework. *Journal of Retailing, 72*(2), 159–185. doi:10.1016/S0022-4359(96)90012-3

Sayman, S., & Raju, J. S. (2004). Investigating the cross-category effects of store brands. *Review of Industrial Organization, 24*(2), 129–141. doi:10.1023/B:REIO.0000033349.67467.b7

Schmitt, N. (1996). Uses and abuses of coefficient alpha. *Psychological Assessment, 8*(4), 250–353. doi:10.1037/1040-3590.8.4.350

Seiders, K., Voss, G. B., Grewal, D., & Godfrey, A. L. (2005). Do satisfied customers buy more? Examining moderating influences in a retailing context. *Journal of Marketing, 69*(4), 26–43. doi:10.1509/jmkg.2005.69.4.26

Semeijn, J., van Riel, A. C. R., & Ambrosini, A. B. (2004). Consumer evaluations of store brands: effects of store image and product attributes. *Journal of Retailing and Consumer Services*, *11*(4), 247–258. doi:10.1016/S0969-6989(03)00051-1

Sethuraman, R., & Cole, C. (1999). Factors influencing the price premiums that consumers pay for national brands over store brands. *Journal of Product and Brand Management*, *8*(4), 340–351. doi:10.1108/10610429910284319

Shoemaker, S., & Lewis, R. C. (1999). Customer loyalty: the future of hospitality marketing. *International Journal of Hospitality Management*, *18*, 345–370. doi:10.1016/S0278-4319(99)00042-0

Sirohi, N. E., McLaughlin, W., & Wittink, D. R. (1998). A model of consumer perceptions and store loyalty intentions for a supermarket retailer. *Journal of Retailing*, *74*(2), 223–245. doi:10.1016/S0022-4359(99)80094-3

Sivadas, E., & Baker-Prewitt, J. L. (2000). An examination of the relationship between service quality, customer satisfaction, and store loyalty. *International Journal of Retail & Distribution Management*, *28*(2), 73–82. doi:10.1108/09590550010315223

Steenkamp, J. B., & van Trijp, H. (1991). The use of LISREL in validating marketing constructs. *International Journal of Research in Marketing*, *8*(4), 283–299. doi:10.1016/0167-8116(91)90027-5

Steenkamp, J.-B. E. M., & Dekimpe, M. G. (1997). The increasing power of store brands: building loyalty and market share. *Long Range Planning*, *30*(6), 917–930. doi:10.1016/S0024-6301(97)00077-0

Steenkamp, J. B. E. M., Van Heerde, H., & Geyskens, I. (2010). What makes consumers willing to pay a price premium for national brands over private labels? *JMR, Journal of Marketing Research*, *47*(6), 1011–1024. doi:10.1509/jmkr.47.6.1011

SymphonyIRIgroup. (2012). *Le Private Label in Europa- 2012*. Esiste un limite alla crescita, Ottobre.

Szymanski, D. M., & Busch, P. S. (1987). Identifying the generics-prone consumer: a meta-analysis. *JMR, Journal of Marketing Research*, *24*, 425–431. doi:10.2307/3151391

Uncles, M. D., & Ellis, K. (1989). The buying of own labels. *European Journal of Marketing*, *23*(3), 57–70. doi:10.1108/EUM0000000000561

Vahie, A., & Paswan, A. (2006). Private label brand image: its relationship with store image and national brand. *International Journal of Retail and Distribution Management*, *34*(1), 67–84. doi:10.1108/09590550610642828

Veloutsou, C., Gioulistanis, E., & Moutinho, L. (2004). Own labels choice criteria and perceived characteristics in Greece and Scotland: factors influencing the willingness to buy. *Journal of Product and Brand Management*, *13*(4/5), 228–241. doi:10.1108/10610420410546943

Vesel, P., & Zabkar, V. (2010). Comprehension of relationship quality in the retail environment. *Managing Service Quality*, *20*(3), 213–235. doi:10.1108/09604521011041952

Völckner, F., & Sattler, H. (2006). Drivers of Brand Extension Success. *Journal of Marketing*, *70*(2), 18–34. doi:10.1509/jmkg.70.2.18

Yang, D., & Wang, X. (2010). The effects of 2-tier store brands' perceived quality, perceived value, brand knowledge, and attitude on store loyalty. *Frontiers of Business Research in China*, *4*(1), 1–28. doi:10.1007/s11782-010-0001-7

Zeithaml, V. A. (1988). Consumer perceptions of price, quality, and value: a means-end model and synthesis of evidence. *Journal of Marketing*, *52*, 2–22. doi:10.2307/1251446

ADDITIONAL READING

Anselmsson, J., & Johansson, U. (2007). Corporate social responsibility and the positioning of grocery brands. *International Journal of Retail & Distribution Management.*, *35*(10), 835–856. doi:10.1108/09590550710820702

Anselmsson, J., Johansson, U., Maranon, A., & Persson, N. (2008). The penetration of retailer brands and the impact on consumer prices – a study based on household expenditures for 35 grocery categories. *Journal of Retailing and Consumer Services*, *15*(1), 42–51. doi:10.1016/j.jretconser.2007.03.001

Arce-Urrida, M., & Cebollada, J. (2012). Private labels and national brands across online and offline channels. *Management Decision*, *50*(10), 1772–1789. doi:10.1108/00251741211279594

Bao, Y., Bao, Y., & Sheng, S. (2011). Motivating purchase of private brands: Effects of store image, product signatureness, and quality variation. *Journal of Business Research*, *64*, 220–226. doi:10.1016/j.jbusres.2010.02.007

Bergès-Sennou, F., Bontems, P., & Réquillart, V. (2004). Economics of private labels: a survey of literature. *Journal of Agricultural & Food Industrial Organization*, *2*(1), 1–25. doi:10.2202/1542-0485.1037

Bonfrer, A., & Chintagunta, P. K. (2004). Store brands: who buys them and what happens to retail prices when they are introduced? *Review of Industrial Organization*, *24*(2), 195–218. doi:10.1023/B:REIO.0000033352.19694.4a

Burton, S., Lichtenstein, D. R., Netemeyer, R. G., & Garretson, J. A. (1998). A scale for measuring attitude toward private label products and an examination of its psychological and behavioral correlates. *Journal of the Academy of Marketing Science*, *26*(4), 293–306. doi:10.1177/0092070398264003

Cataluña, F., Garcia, A., & Phau, I. (2006). 'The influence of price and brand loyalty on store brands versus national brands'. *International Review of Retail, Distribution and Consumer Research*, *16*, 433–452. doi:10.1080/09593960600844236

Dunne, D., & Narasimhan, C. (1999). The new appeal of store brands. *Harvard Business Review*, *77*(3), 41–48. PMID:10387771

El-Amir, A., & Burt, S. (2010). Towards modelling the retailer brand from a sociological perspective: a social construction of the grocery store from a customer standpoint. *Journal of Brand Management*, *17*(6), 429–445. doi:10.1057/bm.2009.36

Erdem, T., Zhao, Y., & Valenzuela, A. (2004). Performance of store brands: a cross-country analysis of consumer store-brand preferences, perceptions, and risk. *JMR, Journal of Marketing Research*, *41*(1), 86–100. doi:10.1509/jmkr.41.1.86.25087

Fitzell, P. (2003), Private label marketing in 21st century: store brands/exclusive brands on the cutting edge, Global Books, New York, NY.

Kara, A., Rojas-Méndez, J. I., Kucukemiroglu, O., & Harcar, T. (2009). Consumer preferences of store brands: role of prior experiences and value consciousness. *Journal of Targeting. Measurement and Analysis for Marketing*, *17*(2), 127–137. doi:10.1057/jt.2009.6

Keith, L., & Thomassen, L. (2008). *Private label: Turning the retail brand threat into your biggest opportunity.* Kogan Page.

Kumar, N., & Steenkamp, J.-B. (2007). *Private label strategy: How to meet the store brand challenge.* Boston, MA: Harvard Business Press.

Luijten, T., & Reijnders, W. (2009). The development of store brands and the store as a brand in supermarkets in The Netherlands. *International Review of Retail, Distribution and Consumer Research*, *19*(1), 45–58. doi:10.1080/09593960902781268

Manzur, E., Olavarrieta, S., Hidalgo, P., Farías, P., & Uribe, R. (2011). Store brand and national brand promotion attitudes antecedents. *Journal of Business Research, 64,* 286–291. doi:10.1016/j.jbusres.2009.11.014

Narasimhan, C., & Wilcox, R. T. (1998). Private labels and the channel relationship: a cross-category analysis. *The Journal of Business, 71*(4), 573–600. doi:10.1086/209757

Neidell, L. A., Boone, L. E., & Cagley, J. W. (1984). Consumer responses to generic products. *Journal of the Academy of Marketing Science, 12,* 161–176. doi:10.1007/BF02721806

Nenycz-Thiel, M., & Romaniuk, J. (2009). Perceptual categorization of private labels and national brands. *Journal of Product and Brand Management, 18*(4), 251–261. doi:10.1108/10610420910972774

Omar, E. (1996). Grocery purchase behaviour for national and own-label brands. *The Service Industries Journal, 16*(1), 58–66. doi:10.1080/02642069600000006

Palmeira, M.M., & Thomas, D. (2011). Two-tier store brands: The benefic impact of a value brand on perceptions of a premium brand, *87*(4), 540-548.

Richardson, P. S. (1997). Are store brands perceived to be just another brand? *Journal of Product and Brand Management, 6*(6), 388–404. doi:10.1108/10610429710190432

Soberman, D. A., & Parker, P. M. (2006). The economics of quality-equivalent store brands. *International Journal of Research in Marketing, 23,* 125–139. doi:10.1016/j.ijresmar.2005.09.008

Uusitalo, U. (2001). Consumer perceptions of grocery retail formats and brands. *International Journal of Retail & Distribution Management, 29*(5), 214–225. doi:10.1108/09590550110390995

Whelan, S., & Davies, G. (2006). Profiling consumers of own brands and national brands using human personality. *Journal of Retailing and Consumer Services, 13*(5), 393–402. doi:10.1016/j.jretconser.2006.02.004

Zielke, S., & Dobbelstein, T. (2007). Customer's willingness to purchase new store brands. *Journal of Product and Brand Management, 16*(2), 112–121. doi:10.1108/10610420710739982

KEY TERMS AND DEFINITIONS

Customer Loyalty: Likelihood of a customer to continue to purchase in the retailer's chain stores.

Customer Satisfaction: Ability of a product/service to meet/exceed consumer expectations.

Groceries: Food and non-food products widely distributed and relatively inexpensive, purchased frequently and with minimum of effort.

Grocery Retailer: Retailer who possesses a number of stores (store chain).

Premium Private Label: PL with high quality and priced close to national brands.

Private Label: Brand owned, controlled and sold exclusively by one retailer under its brand name.

Structural Equation Modeling (SEM): A statistical technique for testing and estimating causal relations.

APPENDIX

Table 4. Correlation matrix between observed variables

	MQ1	MQ2	MQ3	MA1	MA2	MA3	ML1	ML2	MPr1	MPr2	I1	I2	I3	CS3	CS4	INT1	INT2
MQ2	.620																
MQ3	.697	.820															
MA1	.479	.409	.472														
MA2	.563	.567	.612	.692													
MA3	.422	.375	.423	.901	.691												
ML1	.564	.651	.605	.326	.424	.298											
ML2	.556	.664	.590	.324	.409	.312	.946										
MPr1	.406	.509	.473	.458	.490	.476	.410	.462									
MPr2	.455	.505	.466	.466	.501	.467	.374	.400	.897								
I1	.453	.735	.630	.329	.426	.290	.583	.615	.466	.460							
I2	.293	.438	.411	.316	.331	.280	.328	.359	.389	.378	.621						
I3	.429	.714	.614	.336	.429	.309	.552	.580	.498	.483	.962	.621					
CS3	.510	.727	.652	.416	.530	.385	.544	.566	.498	.521	.912	.610	.892				
CS4	.471	.764	.684	.385	.487	.354	.583	.606	.519	.501	.923	.594	.907	.926			
INT1	.186	.275	.265	.193	.270	.163	.261	.309	.211	.152	.451	.314	.440	.426	.445		
INT2	.160	.270	.256	.182	.300	.188	.224	.270	.244	.189	.437	.290	.429	.414	.429	.946	
INT3	.158	.266	.253	.192	.301	.197	.227	.274	.260	.202	.431	.279	.423	.407	.424	.947	.990

$p < .01$

Section 2
Retail Context, Store Formats, and Retail Services

The second section refers to the retail context, offering an overview of the way in which formats, retail environment, and locations are changing facing new consumers' expectations and values. The shopping activity as an experience to be enriched becomes the subject of new paradigms for the retailer to offer in the combination of products, services, entertainment, and environmental values whose importance is increasing.

Chapter 7
The Mechanisms for the Emergence and Evolution of Retail Formats

Barbara Borusiak
Poznan University of Economics, Poland

ABSTRACT

The main aim of this chapter is to explain the mechanisms for the emergence of selected innovative formats on the basis of the existing format change theories. The chapter comprises three main parts. First, the nature of a retail format is explored and the classification of retail formats is presented. Second, four groups of theories (cyclical, conflict, environmental, and integrated theories) explaining the emergence and evolution of retail formats are analysed. Third, retail formats theories are applied in explaining the emergence of two formats: pop-up store and m-commerce. The approach involves a review of literature and the analysis of some empirical data concerning the structure of the retail trade turnover in the chosen countries.

INTRODUCTION

A retail format is one of the fundamental concepts in the retail sector, being a synthesis of the marketing strategy of a commercial company. The choice of retail format determines the choice of enterprise resources which are necessary to perform the sales function. Thus the decision regarding the choice of format by means of which a company operates on the market is one of the fundamental decisions that a retailer has to make, and it has far-reaching consequences (Yu & Ramanathan, 2008). This applies particularly to store-based retailing.

The resources necessary to run them are capital-intensive (Dragun, 2004) and significantly specific in the context of the types of asset specificity distinguished by Williamson (1991). This means that the growing dynamics of market phenomena and the evolution of economic structures increases the level of risk for retailers connected with their choice of retail format. The retail formats which exist today are characterised by unprecedented variability: new formats are appearing, existing formats are evolving, and their life-cycles are becoming significantly shorter (Davidson et al., 1976; McGoldrick & Davies, 1995).

DOI: 10.4018/978-1-4666-6074-8.ch007

The aim of this chapter is to explain the mechanisms for the emergence of innovative formats on the basis of existing theories of format change. Therefore, the chapter presents the conceptualisation of a retail format, a critical analysis of the four groups of theories relating to format change (cyclical, conflict, environmental and integrated theories), as well as the mechanisms for the emergence of new formats based on the examples of pop-up stores and m-commerce. In order to explain these phenomena an integrated theoretical approach has been adopted. The chapter also indicates some probable new fields of research and new formats which are likely to appear in the retail trade.

CONCEPTUALISATION OF A RETAIL FORMAT

The Nature of a Retail Format

The need for clarifying the nature of a retail format stems from the fact that there is some ambiguity regarding the interpretation of this notion in the scientific literature (Reynolds et al., 2007). As a starting point for the conceptualisation of a retail format the essence of the product of a retail company must be explained. This product is a service, and the basis for the service is a set of goods, which is the range of products on offer. This means that a retailer's product is a service which is based on a set of products originating outside the retail sector. Essentially, it is the service element that provides the added value generated by a retail company (Dawson, 2000). This product is intended for two groups of recipients: the basic, traditional group of buyers being consumers; and the second group of recipients being producers. To individual customers a retailer offers access to goods manufactured in a variety of sectors, i.e. it offers in one place a bundle of relationships between the retailer and manufacturers (usually numerous, though this is not a necessary condition). To producers a retailer

offers access to individual consumers in the form of a bundle of relationships with individual buyers (Walter et al., 2001). In other words, the essence of a retailer's product is offering usability in the form of access to manufacturers (and in the case of producers – access to consumers) whose products are offered to the consumer in a convenient form in terms of configuration, location, time and volume, with favourable terms of service and payment (in the latter case convenience ought to treated as the result of the competitive situation in a given sector, which depends on the number of participants and the intensity of competition).

A retailer's product, when considered structurally, has a very complex nature: it is defined by a number of components such as the form of the product assortment (in terms of dimensions such as depth, width and the criteria for its creation); and the conditions in which it is offered (location, time, presentation, range of services, price level, forms of payment, how customers receive goods). This product meets two types of buyers' needs. The first type are needs which to be satisfied require a product from the product range of a shop. The other type of needs are to a large extent independent from the product assortment of a shop. These are social needs (related to contact with people, developing interpersonal relations, a sense of belonging to a group, and building one's position in it); aesthetic needs (being in a place with a visually attractive interior); educational needs (learning new patterns of consumption, discovering innovative products and their applications); and needs connected with spending leisure time, either by doing shopping itself or by taking advantage of an 'entertainment package' offered especially by shopping centres, which includes exhibitions, shows, competitions etc. (Fiore & Kim, 2007).

The considerable complexity of a retailer's product means that, taking into account the actual transactions between a retailer and a customer, the product is highly individualised, which is typical of service products. On the other hand, it is essential to ensure mass (and also economical) access to goods, which prompts retailers to standardise products. An aggregated and standardised designation for the product/service of a commercial enterprise is the retail format, which is a specific manner for conducting sales, both store-based and non-store. Different retail formats are characterised by a specific configuration of such marketing strategy instruments as product and service assortment, pricing policy, the location and manner of offering products, as well as the type and configuration of the resources used (Reynolds et al., 2007; Zentes et. al., 2007; Tiwari, 2009).

Classification of Retail Formats

In order to better understand the nature of retail formats a classification of formats will be presented, as some formats are well-established whereas others are innovative formats, sometimes poorly structured. Several systems of retail format classification have been developed by governmental institutions. Some of these include the American Standard Industrial Classification (SIC) code, the International Standard Industrial Classification of all Economic Activities (ISIC) of the United Nations or the NACE (Nomenclature statistique des Activites economiques dans la Communaute Europeenne) of the European Union (Zentes et al., 2007). These classifications, however, focus mainly on the type of goods sold and have little relevance for researchers and practitioners in the retail sector. The classification of retail whereas in practice formats proposed here (Table 1) takes into account a multitude of criteria and is based on a set of marketing strategy instruments; the most important of which are product assortment for store-based formats (Guy, 1998), and the method of communicating with customers for non-store formats. The presented formats are of great importance in economic practice, although they do not exhaust the set of existing formats. In particular this applies to the 'specialists' category of non-grocery store-based retail formats, where only a few examples are listed, there is a large variety of them. This is because more and more new product selection criteria are used; namely, the criteria of raw materials and technological relatedness of products are replaced by market criteria such as the target group or a specific type of need. The classification also does not mention store-based retail formats which cannot be clearly defined as grocery or non-grocery, which results from the fact that the formula of the format is highly flexible in terms of the products on offer. These include, for example, concept stores and pop-up stores.

Table 1. Classification of retail formats

Store-Based Retail Formats	Non-Store Retail Formats
Grocery: • convenience stores • discount stores • forecourt stores • hypermarkets/superstores • supermarkets • small grocers • food/drink specialists	**Internet Retailing:** • e-stores/e-commerce • m-stores/m-commerce • online auctions • group buying • social commerce

Non-Grocery:
• speciality stores (for example: apparel specialists, electronics and appliance specialists, health and beauty specialists)
  • mixed retailers
    o department stores
    o variety store
    o mass merchandisers
    o warehouse clubs
	Other Non-Store Retailing:
	• direct selling
	• television home shopping channels
	• mail orders catalogues
	• vending
	• market stands

THE THEORIES OF THE EMERGENCE AND EVOLUTION OF FORMATS

Classification of Theories

The retail format is a dynamic conceptual category; new formats appear, existing ones evolve, and some cease to exist (McNair, 1958; Hollander, 1966; Dreesman, 1968; Swan, 1974; Davidson et al., 1976; Kaufman, 1985; Brown, 1987; 1990; 1991; Rousey & Morganosky, 1996; Takei et al., 2006). The changeability of store formats as a manifestation of certain concepts of market operations has repeatedly been the subject of research and a number of theories have been developed to account for it. Their classification is presented in Table 2.

A multiplicity of theories for explaining certain phenomenon is not unusual in management sciences. It applies even to very basic concepts such as an enterprise. The existence of multiple theories relating to a certain area is usually connected with a large diversity of studied objects as well as the complexity and significance of an issue, which justifies the numerous attempts at explaining it. In the case under discussion such attempts are understandable: investors want to know which retail formats provide the best chance for success and how to design portfolios of formats. Therefore, what questions should the theory of formats answer? The most fundamental one has already been formulated, but it can be broken down into several specific questions:

1. Why and in what form do new formats emerge?
2. In what direction and at what speed do existing formats evolve? What does this depend on, that is;
3. What is the impact of the environment (macro- and micro-environment) on existing and potential formats? Does this impact have the nature of feedback? How do the resources of a company influence this process?

Table 2. Theories explaining the changes in retail formats

Groups of Theories	Theory	Representative Authors
Cyclical Theories	The wheel of retailing theory	McNair (1958)
	The retail accordion theory	Hollander (1966)
	The three wheels of retailing theory	Izraeli (1973)
	The format life cycle theory	Davidson, Bates, Bass (1976)
	The concept of the "big middle"	Levy, Grewal, Peterson, Connolly (2005)
Conflict Theories	The dialectical theory	Swan (1974) Maronick, Walker (1974) Stern, El-Ansary (1977) Kaufman (1985)
Environmental Theories	The theory of natural selection/evolution	Dreesman (1968) Markin, Duncan (1981)
	The adaptation theory	Michael, Kim (2005) Takei, Kudo, Miyata, Ito (2006)
	The survival of the fattest theory	Hanappi (2004)
Integrated Theories	Environmental-cyclical	Kaynak (1979)
	Cycle-conflict	Gist (1968)
	Environment-cycle-conflict	Beem, Oxenfeldt (1966)

Source: Adapted from Brown, 1991, Anitsal and Anitsal 2011.

The following section of the chapter will present an analysis of the format theories developed to-date in order to assess their explanatory value.

Cyclical Theories

Chronologically, the first concept which attempted to explain the mechanisms for the emergence and changes to formats was the Wheel of Retailing theory (McNair, 1958). According to this theory, innovative formats are characterised by low cost, which justifies low profit margins and consequently low prices. Over time, however, the standard of the services offered by such enterprises increases as retailers wish to expand their business and attract more customers. This leads to an increase in operating costs and prices and thus offers opportunities for new competitors to enter the market with low-cost and low-price strategy. The format in a mature stage becomes low effective and vulnerable to new competitors which enter the market with low prices and at low costs.

The Wheel of Retailing theory is based on four basic premises:

- There are many price-sensitive buyers who are willing to forego a higher standard of service, a wider product range and a convenient location if in return they get lower prices. However, there are also buyers who are sensitive to prestige and the standard of service;
- Price-sensitive individual consumers are not very loyal, which means that they are prepared to change shops if they find a retailer who offers lower prices;
- New entrants in the retail sector are able to operate with lower operating costs than existing companies;
- Changes in the concept of a store's operations through improving standards (a shift in the wheel of retailing) aim to enhance the shop's image, expand the target group and consequently increase turnover.

McNair proposed the Wheel of Retailing theory to explain the changeability of the format of department stores in the United States. Later this model was positively verified based on the examples of other formats: supermarkets (Bucklin, 1972), off-price retailers (Kaikati, 1985), and discount stores (Perrigot et al., 2007); the phenomenon of improving standards in respect of products and services is noticeable in their evolution. However, one can find examples in the history of the development of commercial enterprises where a new enterprise offered high standards and this is why it gained approval from buyers. The Wheel of Retailing theory does not explain this phenomenon. Thus it is not universal and this is one of its shortcomings which has prompted criticism of this theory (Hollander, 1960; Goldman, 1975; Kaynak, 1979; Brown, 1990; Davies, 1999). In addition, it does not offer a detailed explanation as regards the causes for the emergence of new formats or the mechanisms of format evolution. Its greatest merit is an attempt to address the issue of the form of a new format; however, the answer is limited to indicating only one possible scenario which involves implementing a low-cost strategy and targeting price-sensitive buyers. These shortcomings prompted researchers to persevere in their efforts.

Nearly ten years later another attempt was undertaken by Hollander (1966), who proposed a different concept for explaining format changes based on the idea of cyclical fluctuations. According to the so-called Retail Accordion theory, in the subsequent stages of the development of this sector the formats which emerge and gain an advantage are those which alternate between specialisation and universalisation of their product and service structure. In this case the extent of explaining the complexity of the issues related to the emergence and evolution of formats is therefore limited as it identifies the sources of innovation and the direction of format evolution in respect of only one feature describing a format: the width of product assortment. Additionally, studies conducted in British, German, French and Italian markets (Hart, 1999; Cardinali 2009) show the two tendencies mentioned above occur simultaneously only in relation to different formats. On the one hand, the range of products offered by, for example, discount stores expands; on the other hand, super- and hypermarkets tend to limit their product range. This means that this theory also has a limited explanatory value. Comparing it to the previous one, one can say that it attempts to answer the same questions, and although the answer is not a fully satisfactory one, it is worth noting that this theory identifies two different sources of innovation and the potential directions of format evolution.

The evolution of ideas and accumulation of knowledge are manifested in another proposal – Israeli's Three Wheels of Retailing theory (1973). The author incorporated elements of previous theories and created a concept according to which there exist two alternative sources of innovation as regards new formats: low costs linked with low standards, and very high standards which require high costs. Their further evolution proceeds along familiar lines: the low-cost format strives to raise its standards of service, which leads to an increase in costs and prices; the opposite happens in the case of a format where the initial standards are high. An important advantage of the Three Wheels of Retailing concept is that it indicates a variety of inter-format interactions, or inter-format competition, which leads on the one hand to the convergence of existing formats, and on the other hand to the emergence of new formats in an attempt to be different from existing ones. Therefore, it can be concluded that this concept has many points in common with the attempts at explaining the issue of format change on the basis of conflict theories, which will be discussed in the subsequent section of this chapter.

The idea of cyclical fluctuations is also the basis for the Retail Format Life Cycle theory (Davidson et al., 1976). It was developed as a response to the criticisms relating to the Wheel of Retailing concept, in particular with regard to its two limitations:

- The Wheel of Retailing theory focuses on costs and the related margin level; as a result it cannot be applied to account for new formats which are not price-oriented (e.g. convenience store),
- The Wheel of Retailing concept does not examine the regularities in terms of the pace of change; it only indicates the direction of change (namely in a one-dimensional way).

The Life Cycle concept, however, is not in opposition to the Wheel of Retailing theory; rather, it is its extension which tries to explain the complex nature of format innovation and to determine the pace of the change. The fundamental thesis of the Life Cycle theory is that a format has a life cycle similar to that of a material product. This life cycle consists of four basic stages:

- **Innovation:** The stage when a new format appears which has some unique characteristics that distinguish it from the formats already in the market and that help it gain a considerable advantage. The advantage is a result of a number of factors: a better cost position, which leads to a better price offer; a specific product assortment configuration; and a range of commercial services provided (location, service methods, forms of payment, opening hours, additional services). The innovative features are a result of spotting gaps in the market which the existing formats have not been able to fill. At this stage, if a format successfully fills a gap in the market a substantial increase in sales revenues follows (which proves that the novelty has been accepted by customers); profitability, however, is relatively low because this is a learning stage on the one hand, and a stage for creating the scale of operations on the other;

- **Growth:** During the second stage of the life cycle there is a significant increase in revenues as well as profitability. As approval for the new format grows (the share of the market increases), traditional formats begin to lose ground in the market, which prompts them to try and modify their own formats. Usually, however, the modification is only partial and concerns only one parameter of the format, e.g. the price level. This means that the modification is either insufficient (the essence of innovation of new formats lies in the composition of constituent features) or impossible to maintain in the long term (lowering the prices without lowering costs is possible only over a relatively short period of time);

- **Maturity:** This is the third stage in the life cycle of a format during which the growth rate decreases and the sales revenues stabilise as a result of growing problems related to managing an expanded and complex organisation and an excessively developed sales network in a given market (disproportionate to its size). This causes the phenomenon of cannibalisation; competition with new formats is increasing. The result is a decline in the profitability of an enterprise;

- **Decline:** The last stage in the life cycle, which can be delayed through some modifications and improvements. However, this does not mean that it is always possible to prevent the stage of decline, which is characterised by a drop in market share, a decrease in profitability (to even below zero) and generally being unable to effectively compete with other players.

An analysis of empirical data which describe the history of format development (presented in Table 3) makes it possible to formulate a conclusion that the life cycle of formats is becoming shorter, and this seems to be one of the particular, sector-specific symptoms of the growing dynamics of change in the economy as a whole.

The theory of the Life Cycle of Formats contains much more universal ideas relating to the features of innovative formats compared to previous theories, in which innovation was based on the dichotomy low standard – low cost, high standard – high cost. The authors also indicated the source of innovation, which are the observations of buyers leading to spotting gaps in the market. An unquestionable advantage of the Life Cycle concept is the empirically confirmed increase in the rate of change of formats. Nevertheless, questions arise about the determinants of the duration of a format's life cycle. This is connected, among others, with the observation which indicates a

Table 3. Life cycle duration of selected formats

Store Format	Approximate Date of Origin	Approximate Date of Achieving Maximum Market Share	Approximate Cycle Duration Until Maturity
Department Store	1860	1940	80
Variety Store	1924	1968	44
Supermarket	1930	1965	35
Hypermarket	1965	1995	30
Discount Store	1970	2000	30

Source: Davidson et. al., 1976, McGoldrick and Davies, 1995.

renaissance of discount stores in the wake of the world economic crisis which started in 2008.

In relation to the Format Life Cycle Theory, a new concept was proposed fairly recently - the concept of the "big middle" (Levy et al., 2005). According to this theory new formats emerge as 'low-price' or 'innovative', and there are two other groups of formats. The "big middle" comprises a group of retailers whose formats have the best price-to-quality ratio. This gives them a good market position and allows them to implement economies of scale. The fourth group are formats which are threatened with demise because of an unsatisfactory ratio between the prices and value proposition. This concept originated in the United States and was verified there. Undoubtedly, there is also a need to do so in relation to other markets.

Conflict Theories

A different approach to explaining the issue of format change was used in the Conflict theories. According to these theories, conflict between existing and new formats is the driving force behind changes in the retail sector. The source of this conflict is competition between old and new, innovation, which is considered (Schumpeter 1950) to be the most inherent feature of a capitalist economy and its principal driving force. The emergence of innovative formats forces the existing formats to respond. The response to innovation is a process whose nature has been repeatedly studied, also in relation to the retail sector. One of the first researchers who explored this issue was Gist (1968), according to whom conflicts between retail companies is a driving force behind the changes which occur in the reality of the commercial world. The conflict occurs as a result of introducing innovation in the operations of different players, either those who already are on the market or new market entrants. Swan (1974) proposed an adaptation of Parsons and Smelser's model of social change, in which he identified seven stages of the process of

change. Another model is the concept created by Fink, Baek and Taddeo, adapted for the purposes of distribution channels by Stern and El-Ansary (1977), which indicates four stages in the action-reaction sequence: shock, retreat (defensive action), acceptance and adaptation. A more profound analysis of the process of creating innovation and the responses to it is based on Hegelian dialectic (Maronick & Walker, 1974; Kaufman, 1985). This explains development as a natural consequence of the appearance of an original idea (thesis), its negation (antithesis) and a result in the form of a synthesis. A newly-created format in a conceptual sense is an antithesis of an existing format (thesis). The imitation effect (mutual adaptation) which occurs between the two leads to the emergence of another format (synthesis), which later becomes the thesis. In this way it is possible to explain the emergence of a number of formats such as department stores, discount stores, discount department stores, hypermarkets, discount hypermarkets and other so-called hybrid formats (Cardinali, 2009). It ought to be stressed that in comparison to the Wheel of Retailing theory or the Format Life Cycle theory, the Conflict theory has contributed a lot more to the understanding of how new formats emerge by identifying two basic mechanisms: a conceptualisation of a format through negating or reversing the characteristics of existing formats, and new formats becoming similar to existing ones. Thus, the Conflict theory has given rise to the development of a multi-element Environmental theory of new format emergence.

Environmental Theories

Environmental theories are a group of theories which focus on the impact of exterior factors and phenomena on a format and on the format's adaptive changes (Anitsal & Anitsal, 2011). They include such theories as the Adaptation theory, the Natural Selection theory and the Survival of the Fattest theory.

The Adaptation theory assumes that changes in the business environment are reflected in internal changes. In a sense this is a continuation of the dialectic approach as adaptation is a common feature of both those theories, though in the Environmental theory adaptation means adapting to a nominally greater number of factors which influence the operations of a company (format holder). The main assertion of this theory states that all the changes which occur in the market environment (macro- and micro-) of a company are reflected in the existing structure of the retail trade (Brown, 1987, Michael & Kim, 2005). Innovative formats will emerge (or rather, will be effective) if the operating conditions are favourable and/or if they have the ability to adapt; however, the most significant are social changes (the number, size, geographical distribution and income of households; the level of education and urbanisation), technological changes, legal changes, as well as the intensity of competition (Takei et al., 2006). For example, department stores would not have appeared in mid-19th century if it had not been for the development of the middle class, the development of public transport systems, the invention of lifts, as well as the customers' readiness to accept the fixed price policy. The supermarket, on the other hand, is a consequence of the Great Depression, the introduction of refrigerators onto the market, the popularisation of cars, the emergence of new packaging technologies (developed for the army during World War 1) and an increase in literacy (Bates, 1989). The origins of the discount store date back to the late 1940s, the time of the postwar reconstruction of Europe (Perrigot et al., 2007). The 1970s, the time of the great energy crisis, mark the beginning of the great expansion of discount stores.

By analogy to Darwinian evolutionism based on the principle of natural selection it can be said that the formats which are best adapted to changes in the operating conditions achieve greater efficiency in market services, have a better market position and contribute to the growth of commercial enterprises. In contrast, formats which are not modified according to changes in the environment are replaced by others, which are better suited to the current conditions. This mechanism very well explains the multiplicity and diversity of retail formats (Markin & Duncan, 1981).

Another environmental theory is the Survival of the Fattest theory (Hanappi, 2004). According to this theory, larger and stronger organisms have a greater chance of surviving in the business environment than smaller ones. In the case of the retail sector, however, there is insufficient evidence to support such a view. This applies to both retail formats and individual trading companies. It is possible to indicate many large, significant formats which are currently in decline (e.g. department stores) or in crisis (e.g. hypermarkets). The same applies to commercial enterprises, as evidenced by the failure of Walmart in Germany or the bankruptcy of Praktiker AG (declared on 11th July 2013).

Integrative Theories

The theories presented above are not mutually exclusive. They describe the process of format evolution from different perspectives and often have limited explanatory properties: they are suitable for describing the changes of selected formats, on selected markets and at specific stages of development. Cyclical theories point to the sources of innovation and the internal evolution of formats; conflict theories indicate inter-format interactions; environmental theories attach particular importance to external conditions and the ability of formats to adapt to them under pain of death (as in the case of department stores). Thus, none of them provides a comprehensive explanation of institutional changes in the retail sector. This is why adopting an integrated approach may be the solution and combined theories have been proposed. Three such proposals ought to be mentioned:

- Environmental-cyclical theories, whose authors point out that cyclical changes occur consequent on the occurrence of favourable environmental conditions (Kaynak, 1979), which seems obvious (particularly as one of the elements of this theory is identifying the causes of increases in the level of commercial services, costs, profit margins and prices). The Wheel of Retailing theory cannot be considered in isolation, separated from actual operating conditions, because it is a generalisation of a historical analysis.
- Cycle-conflict – an attempt at integrating the cyclical approach and the conflict approach which was undertaken by Gist (1968), the author of the dialectical theory of retail, who indicated that mature formats are the thesis, innovative formats are the antithesis, and the synthesis is a result of their mutual adjustment.
- Environment-cycle-conflict.

An integrated approach to the phenomenon of retail format evolution has been proposed by Agergaard, Olsen and Allpass (1970). According to this concept, the pattern of development resembles a spiral rather than a cycle. The theory assumes that the modification of a format (particularly in the direction of higher standards) automatically creates a vacuum in which new formats can appear. But because in the meantime the operating conditions have changed, innovative formats introduced at different times vary from one another. According to this theory, the convenience store is a more sophisticated version of the earlier corner shop. Also, discount stores are cheaper forms of supermarkets, and off-price stores are a modification of discount stores. The principal reason for these changes is economic growth, whose rate determines the pace of format change. This theory does not take into account other factors (e.g. technological or legal) which may promote or restrict the development of some formats.

A slightly different approach to format change is presented by Beem and Oxenfeld (1966). In their view, these changes (in a historical perspective) can be explained by distinguishing two types of cycles: long and short. Long cycles begin when new innovative formats emerge and span their entire life cycle. From the beginning of their existence new formats are observed by other market participants and it is not long before the imitation effect occurs: imitators appear that want to use the same solutions for achieving a competitive advantage. The decreasing distance forces the innovator, but also the imitator, to look for distinguishing features for their operations. Short cycles pertain to just such intra-format changes.

EXAMPLES OF INNOVATIVE RETAIL FORMATS AND AN ATTEMPT AT EXPLAINING THEIR ORIGINS

In the current structure of the retail sector store-based retail formats play a dominant role in terms of generating turnover. According to Euromonitor International data for 2012, for example, in the United States 88.97% of the turnover in retail trade was generated by such formats, in Great Britain – 88.43%, in Japan – 89.23% and in South Korea – 80.41%. It must be noted, however, that in the years 2007-2012 the most dynamic section of retail sales was online trading (for example, in the United States total retail sales increased by 5.6% and retail sales on the Internet increased by 73.2%; the respective figures for Great Britain are 11.5% and 113.7%, and for South Korea 32.8% and 93.2%). The process of new format emergence applies to both store-based and non-store based retailing. Let us look at the mechanism for the emergence of two innovative formats in the light of the previously presented theories relating to format emergence and change: the pop-up store and m-commerce.

The most important feature of the pop-up store is the temporariness of its existence. This statement lends support to cyclical theories as well as reflecting dialectical processes in change. The contemporary pop-up store is essentially a version of itinerant trade which existed at the dawn of commerce. It originated as a result of a division of labour in society and the emergence of agents who professionally engaged in sales activities. After centuries of development in the retail sector, which throughout this time sought to produce stationary points of sale, here again has emerged a format which by definition is temporary. In a way, this is a negation of the current standard which favours running a business for a long time. Such solutions, up to now considered the most desirable, were justified on the one hand by the relatively costly and time-consuming process of accumulating resources and the need for obtaining the benefits of those efforts. On the other hand, the longer the duration of the operations, the greater the chance of creating brand value and providing the customers with the comfort of repeat visits. However, in the post-modern era nothing remains the same; the modern reality is fluid and based on perpetual change (Bauman, 2007). Stability is not necessarily a virtue; novelty gains in value. A pop-up store does not last long – from several days to several months, usually around a month (Surchi, 2011). The first such shops appeared in Great Britain in 2003, then also in the US, Italy and France. In their most innovative form they operate as ordinary shops, but they can also operate as stands in shopping centres, itinerant sales points (e.g. on buses), or online shops (Surchi, 2011).

Describing the mechanism for the emergence of pop-up stores requires taking into account environmental factors. The most significant one is the evolution in customer behaviour. There are more and more customers who expect more from retailing than a good quality to price ratio for a product (Florida, 2002). Consumers increasingly desire products that express their unique, personal identity (Kim et al., 2010). They expect innovation, surprises, new products (Barnes & Lea-Greenwood, 2006). This is particularly noticeable

in the fashion industry. At the same time, more and products are subject to fashion, not only clothes and accessories but also home and garden furnishings, toys, sporting goods, cars, houses, and even pets. Fast fashion, a phenomenon which originated in the apparel industry, perfectly fits this trend. The precursors of applying this concept in business are considered to be Inditex and H&M. The essence of this concept is a radical reduction in the time of preparing a collection and shortening the entire life cycle. In pre-fast fashion days, the period between designing and manufacturing clothing was approximately six months; in the fast fashion era this cycle lasts four weeks or less (Mihm, 2010). Products are marketed at high frequency, and the batches are relatively small. This is intended to generate the effect of uniqueness, which in many cases encourages a customer to make an instant purchase rather that postpone it till later. Products are designed for a relatively short period of use. The fact that they are fashionable means that they are 'stigmatised' as belonging to a particular season by their colour, fabric and style. As a result, there is a high level of recurring demand among new-fashion buyers, which leads to a growth in revenues and an increase in the market power of the companies which apply this concept. It ought to be added that for manufacturers the pop-up store is not only a format for selling goods, i.e. an element in the distribution channel, but also a method of testing new products and an ambient marketing instrument.

An important factor is also the development of companies which offer the resources necessary to set up a shop. Creating a pop-up store is like creating a virtual organisation; it requires a venue (often in a location with the highest flow of buyers), furnishings and employees for a short-term project. A particular role in this process is played by Internet portals which function as intermediaries (e.g. commercial space exchanges)

A possible reason for the success of pop-up stores can be (according to the Theory of Natural Selection) the fact that they are better adapted to the environment than other formats. In this case it can be concluded that the pop-up store is a synthesis of 'push' actions from producers seeking more effective ways of distribution and market communication, and 'pull' actions relating to customer expectations. A catalyst for this reaction are the markets for resources which are necessary for a retail company to open a shop. Such a configuration of factors bodes well for the future of the pop-up store.

It is worth noting that in comparison to earlier formats, the approach to determining the sources for the innovativeness of pop-up stores is non-standard (which to a large extent corresponds to the findings of the Format Life Cycle theory). So far, they have been traced to such features of shops as product assortment, sales area, price level and range of services. New shops have opened which offered lower prices in contrast to higher ones; were bigger in contrast to smaller ones; or were more general in contrast to more specialised ones. The pop-up store, in essence, is different from the vast majority of existing retail formats. It is like a comet or an ephemeron whose transience attracts the attention of surprise-hungry consumers. The example of the pop-up store shows that consumers do not always expect shops to offer lower prices, greater convenience or a higher standard of service. The range of their expectations is much wider, although they themselves might not be aware of some of them. This issue is a potentially attractive area of research.

The second format which has been selected for this analysis is mobile commerce (m-commerce). It is difficult to pinpoint the date of origin of this format. The most important determinant of its development was smartphones launch. In 2007 Apple launched the first model of iPhone, followed by similar devices marketed by Nokia, Samsung, HTC and Motorola. In 2008 the first Android-powered phones appeared. This marked the beginning of an exponential increase in the number of applications which served various purposes: providing entertainment, comparing prices, searching for

products or places (e.g. shops or cash machines), preparing shopping lists, conducting transactions, making payments, as well as many others.

M-commerce is quite broadly defined as all activities related to a (potential) commercial transaction conducted through computer-mediated networks with the help of mobile devices – mainly mobile phones and personal data assistants (PDAs) (Tarasewich, 2002; Tiwari et al., 2006). These activities include:

- Providing information to a consumer and acquiring information by a consumer;
- Creating a real-time interaction between a retailer and a consumer, used by any type of retailer, including bricks-and-mortar (Yang, 2010),
- Purchasing goods and services via a mobile phone or another mobile device (Clarke, 2001).

A separate retail format exists when transactions are made with the help of a mobile device. In many ways m-commerce is largely similar to standard online commerce, it is a modification of it (from the perspective of both the customer and the seller). Its main feature is that it offers the convenience of remote access to a range of products. However, the features of m-commerce are more advanced in comparison to those of online shops which can be accessed from a desktop PC; these are (Liao et al., 1999; Shin & Shim, 2002; Gilbert & Han, 2005; Yang, 2010):

- Personalised products which take into account not only customer profiles and the time context but also the spatial context of interaction;
- Access to products anytime and anywhere. Purchases can be made both in shops which offer goods on a Website and from those which offer their products in the public space (as in the case of Tesco in South Korea). This option means that a customer

can make a purchase not only when they feel like doing so, but also when they are away from their PC and are subject to forced inactivity, for example waiting for a tram or sitting in a dentist's waiting room.

The source of innovation for m-commerce is providing customers with constant (continuous and ubiquitous) contact with retailers – total contact. Potentially, it is also a highly expansive format. In the current practice of format operations it was usually the consumer who initiated contact by going to a shop or an online shop's Website. M-commerce allows a retailer to be more active and take the initiative as regards offering products. At the same time, this feature has caused some legal controversy (particularly relating to ensuring customer privacy). M-commerce is a format the development of which is a consequence of the 'push' impact on the part of smartphone and smartphone application suppliers as well as retailers and banks. This format is characterised by a high degree of technological advancement and the process of its adaptation is dependent on the adaptation of technology. This is influenced on the one hand by the perceived usefulness of the technology, and on the other by its perceived ease of use (Venkatesh & Davis, 1996). Thus the question remains to what extent consumers are and will be inclined to use m-commerce. Many studies have been conducted worldwide to determine the attitudes of consumers towards mobile marketing (Broeckelman, 2010; Yang, 2010; Persaud & Azhar, 2012; Wells et al., 2012). Their findings indicate significant cultural differences in this respect. The issue of acceptance for the new format has not been studied very thoroughly yet, but here cultural differences also seem to be quite noticeable (Su & Adams, 2010). The factors relating to the acceptance of the m-commerce format by consumers from different countries will certainly be the subject of ample research in the future.

CONCLUSION AND EMERGING ISSUES

An effective explanation for the emergence of new formats requires an integrated theoretical approach. Undoubtedly, just like in the case of all social phenomena, nothing happens without a reason, which means that it is necessary to determine the strength and direction of the influencing factors. These factors are diverse because they are related to different kinds of processes (social, technological, economic, sector-specific) and have different types of impact (push and pull). The effectiveness of new format emergence depends on the degree of adaptation to these conditions; the better the adaptation, the greater the chances of development. The sources of innovation are also significant as innovation is the sine qua non for the emergence of a new format: there must me something that distinguishes the new from the old. A potential list of such sources does not exist, and in the search for new ones a non-linear approach is becoming evident, which probably means that not all new formats need be based on existing ones, being their modification or opposite.

A common element of the two innovative formats presented, the pop-up store and m-commerce, is time as a criterion behind their emergence. Time, which is a strictly non-renewable resource, is the source of innovation for both pop-up stores and m-commerce, though in different ways. M-commerce is an answer to the pragmatism of customers, who want to save time. The pop-up store is a format which accelerates the pace of change, thus dynamising the passage of time.

In the near future more new formats are certain to appear. These will most probably include further modifications of online stores, for example a format which will make it possible to do automated shopping, without customer participation. In this format orders will be generated by an intelligent refrigerator or other household appliance.

A solution which may revolutionise online commerce may be a shop which instead of selling real products will offer products in a digital form. This will require the popularisation of 3D printers. Such devices already make it possible to print a variety of goods, ranging from simple plastic items (e.g. building blocks for children) to very complex structures (such as human body parts for transplantation). A significant drop in the price of this type of printer may lead to their widespread use by consumers, who instead of purchasing products in a physical form will buy templates for the printers. In this way consumers will be able to customise the goods they buy and acquire them almost immediately after becoming aware of their needs.

However, it is almost certain that new store-based retail formats will also emerge. In many developed countries the formats belonging to this category have dominated the retail trade and there are no indications that they may cease to exist in the foreseeable future. The phenomenon which promotes the emergence of new store-based formats is the internationalisation of commercial enterprises. Also, new formats are bound to emerge which will be a synthesis of stationary and online retailing, using augmented reality technology. Thankfully, there are no limits to the ingenuity of entrepreneurs.

REFERENCES

Agergaard, E., Olsen, P. A., & Allpass, J. (1970). The interaction between retailing and the urban center structure: A theory of spiral movement. *Environment and Planning, 2*, 55–71. doi:10.1068/a020055

Anitsal, I., & Anitsal, M. M. (2011). Emergence of Entrepreneurial Retail Forms. *Academy of Entrepreneurship Journal, 17*(2), 1–17.

Barnes, L., & Lea-Greenwood, G. (2006). Fast fashioning the supply chain: shaping the research agenda. *Journal of Fashion Marketing and Management, 10*(3), 259–271. doi:10.1108/13612020610679259

Bates, A. D. (1989). The Extended Specialty Store: A Strategic Opportunity for the 1990s. *Journal of Retailing, 65*(3), 379–389.

Bauman, Z. (2007). *Liquid Times: Living in an Age of Uncertainty.* Cambridge, MA: Polity Press.

Beem, E. R., & Oxenfeldt, A. R. (1966). A Diversity Theory for Market Processes in Food Retailing. *Journal of Farm Economics, 48*, 69–95. doi:10.2307/1236319

Broeckelmann, P. (2010). Exploring consumers' reactions towards innovative mobile services. *Qualitative Market Research: An International Journal, 13*(4), 414–429. doi:10.1108/13522751011078827

Brown, S. (1987). Institutional Change in Retailing: A Review and Synthesis. *European Journal of Marketing, 21*(6), 5–36. doi:10.1108/EUM0000000004701

Brown, S. (1990). The Wheel of Retailing: Past and Future. *Journal of Retailing, 66*(2), 143–149.

Brown, S. (1991). Variations on a Marketing Enigma: The Wheel of Retailing Theory. *Journal of Marketing Management, 7*(2), 131–155. doi:10.1080/0267257X.1991.9964146

Bucklin, L. P. (1972). *Competition and Evolution in the Distributive Trades.* Englewood Cliffs, NJ: Prentice Hall.

Cardinali, M. G. (2009). The strategic options of modern retailers in the development of new formats. In *Proceedings of XV European Association of Education and Research in Commercial Distribution Conference* (pp. 1-28), Guildford, UK: Surrey University.

Clarke, I. I. (2001). Emerging value propositions for m-commerce. *The Journal of Business Strategy, 18*(2), 133–149.

Davidson, W. R., Bates, A. D., & Bass, S. J. (1976, November-December). The Retail Life Cycle. *Harvard Business Review*, 89–96.

Davies, G. (1999). The Evolution of Marks and Spencer. *The Service Industries Journal, 19*(3), 60–73. doi:10.1080/02642069900000030

Dawson, J. (2000). Viewpoint: Retailer Power, Manufacturer Power, Competition and Some Questions of Economic Analysis. *International Journal of Retail & Distribution Management, 28*(1), 5–8. doi:10.1108/09590550010306700

Dragun, D. (2004). The financial implications of retail strategy. In J. Reynolds, & C. Cuthbertson (Eds.), *Retail strategy: The view from the bridge.* Oxford, UK: Elsevier Butterworth-Heinemann. doi:10.1016/B978-0-7506-5696-2.50009-X

Dreesman, A. C. R. (1968). Patterns of Evolution in Retailing. *Journal of Retailing, 44*, 64–81.

Fiore, A. M., & Kim, J. (2007). An integrative framework capturing experiential and utilitarian shopping experience. *International Journal of Retail & Distribution Management, 35*(6-7), 421–442. doi:10.1108/09590550710750313

Florida, R. (2002). *The Rise of the Creative Class.* New York: Basic Books.

Gilbert, L. A., & Han, H. (2005). Understanding mobile data services adoption: demography, attitudes or needs? *Technological Forecasting and Social Change, 72*, 327–337. doi:10.1016/j.techfore.2004.08.007

Gist, R. R. (1968). *Retailing: Concepts and decisions.* New York: Wiley.

Goldman, A. (1975). The role of trading up in the development of the retailing system. *Journal of Marketing, 39*(1), 54–62. doi:10.2307/1250803

Guy, C. M. (1998). Classifications of retail stores and shopping centres: some methodological issues. *GeoJournal, 45*, 255–264. doi:10.1023/A:1006960414161

Hanappi, H. (2004). *The Survival of the Fattest: Evolution of needs, lust and social value in a long-run perspective.* Paper presented at the European Association for Evolutionary Political Economy Conference. Crete.

Hart, C. (1999). The Retail Accordion and Assortment Strategies: an Explanatory Study. *International Review of Retail, Distribution and Consumer Research, 9*(2), 111–126. doi:10.1080/095939699342598

Hollander, S. C. (1960). The Wheel of Retailing. *Journal of Marketing, 25*(1), 37–42. doi:10.2307/1249121

Hollander, S. C. (1966). Notes on the Retail Accordion. *Journal of Retailing, 43*, 24–40.

Izraeli, D. (1973). The Three Wheels of Retailing: A Theoretical Note. *European Journal of Marketing, 7*(1), 70–74. doi:10.1108/EUM0000000005101

Kaikati, J. D. (1985). Don't discount off-price retailers. *Harvard Business Review, 63*(3), 85–92.

Kaufman, S. (1985). Coping with Rapid Retail Evolution. *Journal of Consumer Marketing, 2*(1), 17–27. doi:10.1108/eb038817

Kaynak, E. (1979). A refined approach to the wheel of retailing. *European Journal of Marketing, 13*(7), 237–245. doi:10.1108/EUM0000000004957

Kim, H., Fiore, A. M., Niehm, L. S., & Jeong, M. (2010). Psychographic characteristics affecting behavioral intentions towards pop-up retail. *International Journal of Retail & Distribution Management, 38*(2), 133–154. doi:10.1108/09590551011020138

Levy, M., Grewal, D., Peterson, R. A., & Connolly, B. (2005). The concept of the big middle. *Journal of Retailing, 81*(2), 83–88. doi:10.1016/j.jretai.2005.04.001

Liao, S., Shao, I. P., Wang, H., & Chen, A. (1999). The adoption of virtual banking: an empirical study. *International Journal of Information Management, 19*(1), 63–74. doi:10.1016/S0268-4012(98)00047-4

Markin, R. J., & Duncan, C. P. (1981). The Transformation of Retailing Institutions: Beyond the Wheel of Retailing and Life Cycle Theories. *Journal of Macromarketing, 1*(1), 58–66. doi:10.1177/027614678100100110

Maronick, T. J., & Walker, B. J. (1974). The dialectic evolution of retailing. In B. Greenberg (Ed.), *Proceedings of the Southern Marketing Association.* Atlanta, GA: Georgia State University.

McGoldrick, P. J., & Davies, G. (Eds.). (1995). *International Retailing: Trends and Strategies.* Glasgow, UK: Pitman Publishing.

McNair, M. P. (1958). Significant Trends and Development in the Postwar Period. In A. B. Smith (Ed.), *Competitive Distribution in a Free, High-level Economy and its Implications for the University.* Pittsburgh, PA: University of Pittsburgh Press.

Michael, S. C., & Kim, S. M. (2005). The organizational ecology of retailing: A historical perspective. *Journal of Retailing, 81*(2), 113–123. doi:10.1016/j.jretai.2005.03.005

Mihm, B. (2010). Fast Fasion In A Flat World: Global Sourcing Strategies. *International Business & Economics Research Journal, 9*(6), 55–63.

Perrigot, R., Basset, G., & Cliquet, G. (2007). Does the retailing wheel still work? The case of the hard discount stores in France. In J. Zentes, D. Morschett, & H. Schramm-Klein (Eds.), *XIV European Association of Education and Research in Commercial Distribution Conference Proceedings* (pp. 1328-1353). Saarbruecken, Germany: Saarland University.

Persaud, A., & Azhar, I. (2012). Innovative Mobile Marketing via Smartphones: Are Consumers Ready? *Marketing Intelligence & Planning, 30*(4), 418–443. doi:10.1108/02634501211231883

Reynolds, J., Howard, E., Cuthbertson, C., & Hristov, L. (2007). Perspectives on retail format innovation: relating theory and practice. *International Journal of Retail & Distribution Management, 35*(8), 647–660. doi:10.1108/09590550710758630

Rousey, S. P., & Morganosky, M. A. (1996). Retail format change in US markets. *International Journal of Retail & Distribution Management, 24*(3), 8–16. doi:10.1108/09590559610147883

Schumpeter, J. A. (1950). *Capitalism, Socialism and Democracy.* New York: Harper & Brothers Publishers.

Shin, G., & Shim, S. S. Y. (2002). A service management framework for m-commerce applications. *Mobile Networks and Applications, 7*(3), 199–212. doi:10.1023/A:1014574628967

Stern, L. W., & El-Ansary, A. I. (1977). *Marketing Channels.* Englewood Cliffs, NJ: Prentice Hall.

Su, Q., & Adams, C. (2010). *Consumers' Attitude Toward Mobile Commerce: A Model to Capture the Cultural and Environment Influences.* Hershey, PA: IGI Global.

Surchi, M. (2011). The temporary store: a new marketing tool for fashion brands. *Journal of Fashion Marketing and Management, 15*(2), 257–270. doi:10.1108/13612021111132672

Swan, J. E. (1974). A Functional Analysis of Innovation in Distribution Channels. *Journal of Retailing, 50*(1), 9–23.

Takei, H., Kudo, K., Miyata, T., & Ito, Y. (2006). Adaptive Strategies for Japan's Retail Industry Facing a Turning Point. *Nomura Research Institute Papers, 110*, 1–13.

Tarasewich, P. (2002). Issues in mobile e-commerce. *Communications of the Association for Information Systems, 8*, 41–64.

Tiwari, R., Buse, S., & Herstatt, C. (2006, September-October). From electronic to mobile commerce: Opportunities through technology convergence for business services. *Tech Monitor*, 38-45.

Tiwari, R. S. (2009). *Retail Management, Retail Concepts and Practices*. Mumbai: Global Media.

Venkatesh, V., & Davis, F. D. (1996). A model of the antecedents of perceived ease of use: development and test. *Decision Sciences, 27*(3), 451–481. doi:10.1111/j.1540-5915.1996.tb01822.x

Walter, A., Ritter, T., & Gemunden, H. G. (2001). Value Creation in Buyer-Seller Relationships: Theoretical Considerations and Empirical Results from a Supplier's Perspective. *Industrial Marketing Management, 30*, 365–377. doi:10.1016/S0019-8501(01)00156-0

Wells, R., Kleshinski, C. E., & Lau, T. (2012). Attitudes Toward and Behavioral Intensions to Adopt Mobile Marketing, Comparisons of Gen Y in the United States, France and China. *International Journal of Mobile Marketing, 7*(2), 5–24.

Williamson, S. C. (1991). Comparative Economic Organization: The Analysis of Discrete Structural Alternatives. *Administrative Science Quarterly, 36*(2), 269–296. doi:10.2307/2393356

Yang, K. (2010). Determinants of US consumer mobile shopping services adoption, implications for designing mobile shopping services. *Journal of Consumer Marketing, 27*(3), 262–270. doi:10.1108/07363761011038338

Yu, W., & Ramanathan, R. (2008). An assessment of operational efficiencies in the UK retail sector. *International Journal of Retail & Distribution Management, 36*(11), 861–882. doi:10.1108/09590550810911656

Zentes, J., Morschett, D., & Schramm-Klein, H. (2007). *Strategic Retail Management: Text and International Cases*. Wiesbaden, Germany: Gabler.

ADDITIONAL READING

Baek, J. (2005). How Does the Global Retailer Localize Its Format? *Journal of Global Marketing, 18*(1-2), 151–166. doi:10.1300/J042v18n01_09

Bhardwaj, V., & Fairhurst, A. (2010). Fast fashion: response to changes in the fashion industry. *International Review of Retail, Distribution and Consumer Research, 20*(1), 165–173. doi:10.1080/09593960903498300

Chan, F. T. S., & Chong, A. Y.-L. (2013). Analysis of the determinants of consumers' m-commerce usage activities. *Online Information Review, 37*(3), 443–461. doi:10.1108/OIR-01-2012-0012

Colla, E. (2004). The Outlook for European Grocery Retailing: Competition and Format Development. *International Review of Retail, Distribution and Consumer Research, 14*(1), 47–69. doi:10.1080/0959396032000154293

Colla, E., & Lapoule, P. (2012). E-commerce: exploring the critical success factors. *International Journal of Retail & Distribution Management, 40*(11), 842–864. doi:10.1108/09590551211267601

Dawson, J. (2005). New cultures, new strategies, new formats and new relationships in European retailing: some implications for Asia. *Journal of Global Marketing, 18*(1-2), 73–97. doi:10.1300/J042v18n01_05

Doherty, N. F., & Ellis-Chadwick, F. (2010). Internet retailing: the past, the present and the future. *International Journal of Retail & Distribution Management, 38*(11/12), 943–965. doi:10.1108/09590551011086000

Hajli, M. (2012). A research framework for social commerce adoption. *Information Management & Computer Security, 21*(3), 144–154. doi:10.1108/IMCS-04-2012-0024

Hino, H. (2010). Antecedents of supermarket formats' adoption and usage: A study in the context of non-western customers. *Journal of Retailing and Customer Services, 17*(1), 61–72. doi:10.1016/j.jretconser.2009.09.005

Jhamb, D., & Kiran, R. (2012). Emerging Retail Formats and It's Attributes: An Insight to Convenient Shopping. *Global Journal of Management and Business Research, 12*(2), 63–71.

Kandampully, J. (Ed.). (2012). *Service Management. The New Paradigm in Retailing*. New York: Springer.

Kim, S.-H., & Kincade, D. H. (2006). The Model for the Evolution of Retail Institution Types. *Journal of the Korean Society of Clothing and Textiles, 30*(12), 1661–1671.

Kumar, S., Eidem, J., & Perdomo, D. N. (2012). Clash of the e-commerce titans. A new paradigm for consumer purchase process improvement. *International Journal of Productivity and Performance Management, 61*(7), 805–830. doi:10.1108/17410401211263872

Lowe, M., & Wrigley, N. (2009). Innovation in retail internationalization: Tesco in the USA. *International Review of Retail, Distribution and Consumer Research, 19*(4), 331–347. doi:10.1080/09593960903331337

Musso, F. (2010). Innovation in Marketing Channels. *Symphonya. Emerging Issues in Management, 1*, 25–44.

Payton, P. (2007). New Formats from New Retailers: Breakthrough Concepts from the US. *European Retail Digest, 55*, 17–25.

Pearson, D., Henryks, J., Trott, A., Jones, P., Parker, G., Dumaresq, D., & Dyball, R. (2011). Local food: understanding consumer motivations in innovative retail formats. *British Food Journal, 113*(7), 886–899. doi:10.1108/00070701111148414

Picot-Coupey, K. (2012). Pop-up stores as a foreign operation mode for retailers. *University of Rennes1 & University of Caen Working Paper, 41*, 1-30. From http://crem.univ-rennes1.fr/wp/2012/201241.pdf

Pomodoro, S. (2013). Temporary retail in fashion system: an explorative study. *Journal of Fashion Marketing and Management, 17*(3), 341–352. doi:10.1108/JFMM-07-2012-0033

Reutterer, T., & Teller, C. (2009). Store format choice and shopping trip types. *International Journal of Retail & Distribution Management, 37*(8), 695–710. doi:10.1108/09590550910966196

Runfola, A., & Guercini, S. (2013). Fast fashion companies coping with internationalization: driving the change or changing the model? *Journal of Fashion Marketing and Management, 17*(2), 190–205. doi:10.1108/JFMM-10-2011-0075

Stephen, A. T., & Toubia, O. (2010). Deriving Value from Social Commerce Networks. *JMR, Journal of Marketing Research, 47*, 215–228. doi:10.1509/jmkr.47.2.215

Tordjman, A. (1994). European Retailing. Convergences, Differences and Perspectives. *International Journal of Retail & Distribution Management*, *22*(5), 3–19. doi:10.1108/09590559410067299

Wood, S., Lowe, M., & Wrigley, N. (2010). Conceptualising innovative customer-facing responses to planning regulation: The UK food retailers. *The Service Industries Journal*, *30*(12), 1967–1990. doi:10.1080/02642060903191124

Young, K., & Kim, H.-Y. (2012). Mobile shopping motivation: an application of multiple discriminant analysis. *International Journal of Retail & Distribution Management*, *40*(10), 778–789. doi:10.1108/09590551211263182

KEY TERMS AND DEFINITIONS

Adaptation Theory: Assumes that changes in the business environment are reflected in internal changes. The main assertion of this theory states that all the changes which occur in the market environment (macro- and micro-) of a company are reflected in the existing structure of the retail trade.

Conflict Theories: According to them, conflict between existing and new formats is the driving force behind changes in the retail sector.

M-Commerce: An Internet retailing format based on the possibility of making transactions via mobile devices such as smartphones and personal data assistants.

Pop-Up Store: A temporary retail outlet which sells short lines of goods and/or unique products.

Retail Accordion Theory: In the subsequent stages of the development of retail sector the formats which emerge and gain an advantage are those which alternate between specialisation and universalisation of their product and service structure.

Retail Format Life Cycle Theory: Refers to the succession of identifiable stages a retail format goes through over time: innovation, growth, maturity and decline.

Retail Format: An aggregated and standardised designation of a retailer's product which denotes a certain way of conducting sales, both in the store-based and non-store form. Retail formats are described in terms of marketing strategy instruments such as product and service assortment, pricing policy, the location and manner of offering products, as well as the type and configuration of the resources used.

Retailer's Product: A service which to consumers offers access to products which originate outside the trade sector, and to suppliers – access to the consumer market. A retailer's product, when considered structurally, has a very complex nature: it is defined by a number of components such as the form of the product assortment (in terms of dimensions such as depth, width and the criteria for its creation); and the conditions in which it is offered (location, time, presentation, range of services, price level, forms of payment, how customers receive goods).

Wheel of Retailing Theory: Concept explaining the mechanisms for the emergence and changes to retail formats. It suggests that new retail formats often start as discount store and then improve their service to get better position on the market.

Chapter 8
Critical Reflections on the Decline of the UK High Street:
Exploratory Conceptual Research into the Role of the Service Encounter

Jason J. Turner
Abertay University, UK

Toni Gardner
Abertay University, UK

ABSTRACT

The aims of this exploratory research are to evaluate customer and retailer perceptions of the decline of the UK High Street[1] and investigate the potential of the service encounter, specifically customer service, as a means to reverse this decline. The background to this research is one where the UK High Street is in decline as a result of out-of-town retailing, the growth in the use of technology and online shopping, and high business rates and rents (Bignell & Lefty, 2013; Bamfield, 2013; Milliken, 2012; Poulter, 2012; Hall, 2011; Portas, 2011). Using interviews in 2013 across four Scottish cities (Aberdeen, Dundee, Edinburgh, and Glasgow) with 40 retailers (national chains and independents) across the fashion, footwear, jewellery and health and beauty sectors, and 40 customers aged between 18 and 60, the chapter reveals that unlike the retailers in this study, customers are not of the opinion that an improvement in current, in some cases, "disappointing" customer service would encourage them back to the High Street. Rather customers thought solutions to the decline in the UK High Street lay in combining the appeal of online convenience and choice with the tangibility of the physical store experience.

INTRODUCTION

The decline of the UK High Street (a typical High Street is illustrated in Figures 1 and 2) has been a much discussed topic in the UK media and academic community not only because of its importance to UK retailing and the changing nature of the UK consumer but also because of its negative impact on community cohesion (Cooper, cited in Hill, 2013). The reasons for and the consequences of the decline in the UK High Street have been well documented with a number of key

DOI: 10.4018/978-1-4666-6074-8.ch008

themes emerging from the literature, specifically: that the number of empty shops on the High Street has continued to increase year on year to reach around 46,000 in 2013 (Turner-Mitchell, 2012) which has either contributed to or is as a result of customers increased use of the Internet and more recently mobile devices (Milliken, 2012; O'Reilly, 2012) to purchase products and services; that customers seek convenience, choice and as a result of the current recession, value for money, which is arguably better facilitated by online and out-of-town retailing (Bignell & Lefty, 2013; Bamfield, 2013; Milliken, 2012; Poulter, 2012; Portas, 2011; Hall, 2011). A number of solutions have been suggested, with Portas (2011) in her 'Review into the future of our High Streets' making 28 recommendations which focused on non-digital solutions, specifically High Street management, the need to change existing legislation to address barriers to retailers ability to change the use of existing retail spaces and reduce current business rates which are considered high by many retailers. Leroux & Ralph (2013) proposed the need for High Street retailers to embrace the click-and-collect concept and Findlay (2013) proposed the need for High Street retailers to better connect, particularly emotionally, with customers. Using qualitative research through interviews in Scotland's four major cities (Aberdeen, Dundee, Edinburgh and Glasgow) with 40 retailers (20 national chains and 20 independents) representing the fashion, footwear, jewellery and health and beauty sectors and 40 customers (20 aged 18-30 and 20 aged 31 and over), this exploratory research will evaluate customer and retailer perceptions of the decline of the UK High Street and investigate, amongst other measures, the potential of the service encounter, specifically customer service as a means to reverse this decline. Clearly enhancing the service encounter is not the only solution to reverse the UK High Street decline, however making the in-store experience more appealing to customers presents retailers with an opportunity to exploit something which is not readily available online

and may encourage customers to shop in the High Street as well as online rather than increasingly just shopping online.

BACKGROUND

'The UK High Street is in crisis' is a common media headline in recent years and reflects a key theme in UK retailing, namely the decline of the High Street, the reasons for this decline and suggestions on how to arrest this decline. Although there are other themes facing today's UK retailer such as internationalisation and understanding new markets to facilitate expansion (Smith, 2013); control over stock and optimal planning to meet the demands of an increasingly more informed customer (Smith, 2013), many of the key themes in retail are related to the decline of the High Street. The high rents and associated costs to the

Figure 1. Glasgow High Street (© 2014, Toni Gardner; used with permission)

Figure 2. Dundee High Street (© 2013a, James Kelly; used with permission)

physical store (Department for Communities & Local Government, 2013; Smith, 2013; Portas, 2011) have made it increasingly difficult to stay competitive offline and has therefore presented retailers with dilemmas, do they continue to increase their online presence and if so will this come at the expense of the customer experience offline? Can the in-store experience be combined with online convenience? Due to the increase in online shopping (Bamfield, 2013; Westbrook, 2013) the need to understand the customer and how they shop both online and in-store has become increasingly important, a theme reflected in the need to have the correct product assortment which appeals to online and in-store customers and reinforced by the fact that customers are now more price aware due to comparative Websites and promotions being more transparent and traceable (Smith, 2013).

The decline of the UK High Street is in contrast to the majority of European countries where customers "still prefer to visit their local shops and town centres rather than buy products online or shop at out-of-town retail venues" (Briggs, 2013,

para.1). According to EMEA (2013) although online shopping is becoming increasingly popular amongst European customers "when it comes to buying clothing or grocery most European consumers still prefer the convenience of local shops and town centres" (p.4). Such research indicates that the decline of the High Street is perhaps particular to the UK but that does not mean that other nations will not be affected by this retail theme in the future. When the research reviews the literature we can observe that customers across Europe seek convenience and are increasingly using the Internet to make their retail purchases (Anon, 2013a; Cotterill, 2013; EMEA, 2013; Roland Berger, 2013; Sikora, 2013) which are similar to trends in the UK and therefore it is not too much of a stretch to hypothesize that the European town centre could follow a similar decline, being used predominantly for showrooming (Butler, 2013; Roland Berger, 2013) as customers with higher expectations seek more retail choice and added value (Anon, 2013a) from their shopping experience. Such a trend would arguably be to the detriment of the respective communities, creating a negative impact both psychologically and socially on the community feel in their towns and cities (Hill, 2013).

According to Hall (2011) "Britain's shops and High Streets are in crisis due to the economic downturn and the continued growth in the number of out-of-town shopping centres, supermarkets and retail parks, which are attracting custom away from town centres" (para.8). Such a perspective has merit; low wage rises and inflation have arguably led to a lack of consumer spending and low growth (Moulds, 2013; Cooper, 2012) which has in turn, had a negative effect on High Street footfall, duration of visit and spend. High business rates and rents for retailers amounting to more than £7bn a year (Ruddick, 2013) has led Portas (2011) to argue that in order to drive consumers to the High Street there needs to be a degree of free parking provision and reduced business rates (Anon, 2013b; Portas, 2011). Currently legislation does not make it easy to change the use from empty properties to housing, crèches or gyms (Minton, et al., 2013) which in turn contributes to a difficult trading environment for retailers on the High Street which has seen the number of 'voids' or store vacancies increase from 5.4% in 2008 to 14.1% in March 2013 (Bamfield, 2013) and the number of store closures reach 3,936 in 2012 (Neate & Moulds, 2012) with a further one in five stores anticipated to close by 2018 (Glenday, 2013).

Although Hall (2011) has identified key economic issues contributing to the High Street decline, research should also take into account the growth in technology which has built on the influence of out-of-town retailing in changing the shopping behaviour of the UK consumer. Retailers such as HMV, Blockbuster, Republic and Jessops arguably failed to adapt to changes in consumer behaviour and the importance of the online component in the retail offer (Bignell & Lefty, 2013) and have since gone into administration (it should be noted however, that HMV have since emerged from administration). When the

research refers to online, it does not simply mean online competition, with online retail argued to amount to 21.5% of retail sales by 2018 (Bamfield, 2013), the research is also referring to the retailers use of their own Website "to drive footfall, as 96 per cent of shoppers use the Internet for research before buying products offline" (O'Reilly, 2012, para.3). More recently, this trend in not just confined to Websites, "almost a third (32 per cent) of shoppers in the UK have used their mobile to locate a retailers nearest store" (O'Reilly, 2012, para.3). The increased use of technology can and has influenced consumer buying behaviour in how we shop, where we shop and when we shop (Poulter, 2012) with convenience the key value proposition (Miller, 2013; Newman, 2012).

Customers are increasingly shopping online and via mobile devices with online retail spend currently accounting for 12.7% of total retail spending and anticipated to increase to 21.5% by 2018 (Bamfield, 2013; Westbrook, 2013). In other words, the way individuals shop is beginning to change, 'showrooming' is a phrase associated to a growing number of UK consumers who research their purchase online, compare the prices of the competition, search for other information, then use the store to experience or trial the product before making their final purchase which could be online or offline (Butler, 2013; Roland Berger, 2013; Warman, 2013; Wearn, 2013; Oates, 2011). Today's customers are now more informed than ever before, have their needs anticipated, are able to shop how they want and when they want, have access to customer reviews and recommendations, and online interactive tools like augmented reality (Ramaswamy, 2013; Poulter, 2012) and desire convenience (Miller, 2013; Newman, 2012). According to Portas (2011) "an increasing number of shops are falling by the wayside as they fail to meet the expectations of today's increasingly sophisticated, time-poor yet experience-rich, consumer" (p.9). However that is not to say that other motivations to shopping no longer apply. As argued by the Chief Executive of Kurt Geiger, (cited in

Turner-Mitchell, 2012) "people will always want to go to the high street because they want to discover things and they want to be with people in a bustling environment" (para.15). In other words, for some, shopping is both a recreational experience and a means for social interaction (Rohm & Swaminathan, 2004; Brown, Pope & Voges, 2003; Sit, Merrilees & Birch, 2003).

ISSUES, CONTROVERSIES, PROBLEMS

Today's typical UK High Street is said to have lost its identity, characterised by charity, payday and betting shops (Dominiczak, 2013), (illustrated in Figure 3), although it should be noted that there are variations in the degree of problems facing the High Street depending on which part of the country is being examined (Bennison, Warnaby & Pal, 2010). Retailers who operate on the High Street, but also have an online presence, have observed online sales out performing that of their bricks-and-mortar stores (Geddes, 2011), a trend which will continue unless the High Street adapt to changes in consumers motivations to and expectations for shopping (Findlay, 2013).

Figure 3. High Street decline (© 2013b, James Kelly; used with permission)

An individual can have a number of motivations for shopping, they could be motivated by convenience; the need for immediate possession; to seek variety; for information; as a recreational experience or for social interaction (Rohm & Swaminathan, 2004; Sit, Merrilees & Birch, 2003). Today's customer is considered time poor, desires choice, is price sensitive and wants to shop when it is convenient for them (Sampson, 2013), a trend accelerated by smart phones and mobile devices (Milliken, 2012).

When we examine these motivations in the context of the UK High Street the current problems and possible solutions become clearer. The High Street could potentially exploit those shopping motivations, creating a more inviting and customer focused environment, as "you can't try on a dress over the Internet" (Turner-Mitchell, 2012, para.15). Equally the High Street could embed technological advancements into their offer to increase their appeal to those shoppers motivated by convenience and immediate possession (Rohm & Swaminathan, 2004), using mediums such as multi and omni-channel retailing, smart devices and click-and-collect services (Chahal, 2013; Wallop, 2013; Whiteaker, 2012; Dennis, Harris & Sandhu, 2002) to enhance the customer encounter and service experience.

What the High Street needs to be is "lively, dynamic, exciting social places that gives a sense of belonging and trust to a community" (Portas, 2011, p.3). If customers are shopping online because of convenience, choice and price then High Street retailers need to provide an experience which is either not available online, specifically a comfortable, stimulating and hassle free shopping experience (Etsell & Hinton, 2013; Findlay, 2013; Potter, 2013) or compliments the online experience (Reimers & Clulow, 2009) to offer a more diverse and convenient way to service customers (Steiner, 2013) and encourage them back to the High Street and potentially allow for increased dwell time and spend.

The Portas (2011) review highlights the increasingly competitive environment facing the High Street and has given rise to the aims of this study, to evaluate customer and retailer perceptions of the decline of the UK High Street and to examine the role of the service encounter as a possible solution to the decline of the High Street in the UK. By service encounter the research does not simply mean the provision of excellent customer service, it means the creation of a unique in-store experience which customers cannot experience online with the retailer-customer interface at its centre. This research is advocating that the High Street incorporates new technology and approaches such as click-and-collect (Minton, et al., 2013; O'Brien, 2013; Quinn, 2013; Wallop, 2013; Langston, 2012; Whiteaker, 2012) to both operate in parallel and compete with online and out-of-town competition and provide customers with a reason to return to the High Street based on convenience, choice and a value added customer service encounter.

Harnessing Technology

Incorporating technology is one possible solution to the decline of the High Street with several technologies capable of enhancing the customer experience and engaging consumers to want to return to offline shopping. As boundaries between online and offline shopping continue to be blurred, mediums such as augmented reality, location based technology and magic mirrors will further "support the convergence of [the] online and physical" (Withers & De Judicibus, 2013, para.5) retail environment. Retailer and fashion brand Burberry has already designed its flagship London store "into a bricks-and-mortar version of a Website...a clear statement to the world that, for Burberry, digital now comes first" (Cartner-Morley, 2012, para.5) and Oasis is equipping staff with iPads to save customers queuing at the tills (Fisher, 2012). Saving customers time and fitting in with the 'convenience' mentality is

increasingly being used in the High Street with electronic and machine assisted services providing customers with a feeling of autonomy and control, convenience (Lee, et al., 2010; Dabholkar, Bobbitt & Lee, 2003; Fitzsimmons, 2003; Meuter, et al., 2000) and less time spent queuing which is directly related to customer satisfaction with the retailer (Muller, 2008). By combining "the best of both online and offline retail" (Chahal, 2013, para.19) customer needs may be satisfied more effectively, however retailers should be aware that customers' expectations may also rise as a result.

The Service Encounter

The application of technology to the retail environment has the potential to enhance the customer experience, allowing staff more time to focus on the customer (Shields, 2013). However just using technology to replicate the online experience may not necessarily enhance the customer experience, rather technology must compliment the strengths of the offline experience, in particular the service encounter.

Customers patronise retailers for a number of reasons, it could be because of employees (Smith, et al., 2004; Wong, 2004; Swan, et al., 1999; Saunders, et al., 1992), customer service (Butcher, et al., 2001; Heskett, et al., 1997; Javalgi & Moberg, 1997), brands (De Wulf, et al., 2005; Barnes, 2003; Rundle-Thiele & MacKay, 2001; Ewing, 2000; Baldinger & Ruben, 1996; Day, 1969; Cunningham, 1956) and/or environmental factors such as the store, its atmospherics and its location (Miranda, et al., 2005; Sit, Merrilees & Birch, 2003). These studies underline the importance of the customer experience and the need for retailers to deliver a quality and relationship enhancing service (Wong & Sohal, 2006; Wong & Sohal, 2003). However given the decline in customer footfall on the High Street and the requirement to reduce costs to compete with online shopping, High Street retailers face a predicament and the "need to strike a balance between reducing costs and improving the customer experience" (Bishop, 2013, para. 15). Currently the offline experience is not as convenient as it is online so in order for retailers to encourage customers to the High Street retailers should perhaps emphasise the experience and enhance the personal approach (Butler, 2013). In the past customers were only able to receive a more personalised experience offline, now-a-days, through technology and the ability of online retailers and/or retailers with an online presence to capture customer data for profiling purposes, online retailers are also able to offer personalisation. Therefore High Street retailers have to provide customers with "value, service, entertainment and experience, [however] the average High Street has in many cases simply failed to deliver" (Portas, 2011, p. 2).

SOLUTIONS AND RECOMMENDATIONS

The research used qualitative interviews and quota sampling with 40 retailers (20 independents and 20 national chains) representing the fashion, footwear, jewellery and health and beauty sectors and 40 customers (20 males and females aged 18-30 and 20 males and females aged 31 and over) across the 4 Scottish cities (Aberdeen, Dundee, Edinburgh and Glasgow). Both retailers and customers were approached to participate in person, with the researcher explaining the research and ethical considerations directly to the respective store manager and then seeking permission to discuss the research with customers. There was a relatively high refusal rate, with 1 in 4 retailers and 1 in 5 customers unable to make the time commitment to be interviewed, those who agreed to participate provided their contact details and were contacted via telephone to arrange a convenient time and location for the interviews to take place.

In order to address the aims of this research, the analysis and discussion of the qualitative data is divided into three main sections based on the themes to emerge from the interviews with retailers and customers. The first section investigates retailers and customers perceptions of the High Street and their opinions on why the High Street has declined. The second section examines perceptions of the role technology can play in encouraging customers back to the High Street. The third section evaluates perceptions on whether the service encounter can play a role in encouraging customers to return to the High Street and reverse the current decline. Throughout this chapter representative quotes from retailers and customers and illustrative analysis will be used to evaluate the themes to emerge from the research.

Shopping Behaviour on the High Street

Customer Perspectives

All customers were asked in the first instance to provide their opinions on the typical 'High Street' and in the second instance on the 'High Street' to which they were most familiar, in order to identify whether opinions were specific to a particular city High Street or generalisable across Scotland. It should be noted that in terms of customer perspectives there were no variations between responses based on age, gender or city. There was however variations in responses among retailers in terms of the city and whether they were a national chain or independent, these variations are commented on throughout the qualitative analysis.

Prior to examining responses to questions relating to the specific themes of this research, customers were asked three classification questions relating to their shopping behaviour on the High Street. Firstly, customers were asked how often they shopped on the High Street; responses varied, ranging from every day to five times a year. There was no clear pattern, with customers all having individual High Street shopping frequencies, although the majority of customers shopped every two weeks to once per month. Secondly, customers were asked at what times of day they shopped on the High Street, similarly to the earlier question, there was no clear pattern of responses, although the majority shopped between 12 and 3 during the weekday. What these responses inform the research is that the frequency of visit to the High Street was not particularly high, with those visits predominantly by city centre workers shopping during their lunch-break. Thirdly, customers were asked what products/services they shopped for on the High Street, similarly to previous responses, there was no clear pattern of responses. Reasons for High Street patronage included shopping for clothing, toiletries, prescriptions, food and cards, with the majority frequenting the High Street for toiletries (including perfume and cosmetics) and clothing, specifically the trying on of clothes, but not necessarily purchasing them. Rather, these customers would appear to use the physical store for showrooming (Butler, 2013; Roland Berger, 2013; Warman, 2013; Wearn, 2013; Oates, 2011).

Retailer Perspectives

When retailers were asked at what times customers usually patronised their store, similarly to the responses from customers, they varied with no clear pattern. Retailers stated that shopping depended on the time of year and the type of retailer they were but when asked to give a specific time the majority of retailers stated between 12 and 3 and 4 and 6, with the national chains selecting both time slots and the independent retailers selecting the time slot between 12 and 3 as the time when customers usually patronise their store. The fact that the majority of retailers provided a similar response to the majority of customers indicated a degree of synergy between the retailer and the customer and interestingly all retailers thought their opening hours were appropriate to their customers needs based on footfall and the opening hours of their competitors. However this raises an interesting point around retailers' response

to customer demand and whether they dictate demand through their opening hours with customers shopping, predominantly during their lunch; when the retailers are open rather than when they would prefer to shop.

This issue of the retailer meeting the needs of the customer was further examined when the research asked retailers whether they carried out market research to better understand their customers. The national chains agreed that they carried out market research through a variety of different mediums, including online and in-store surveys, focus and listening groups and competitions. The majority of independent retailers did not carry out market research not because they did not see the benefits but because of the time associated with carrying out such research. The extent to which the lack of market research impacts on an independent retailers understanding and meeting the demands of customers will be investigated throughout the chapter beginning with customer and retailer perceptions of the High Street decline.

The High Street Decline

A summary of the themes to emerge from interviews with customers and retailers regarding the decline of the High Street are illustrated in Table 1.

Customer Perspectives

The majority of customers agreed that the High Street has declined, with a representative quote being:

Yes, the number of empty shops has increased and there are more and more pound shops[2] alongside similar type fashion stores.

A number of customers made the distinction that this decline was particularly acute in the High Street of smaller towns and cities. Only one customer disagreed with the statement, indicating:

Table 1. Summary of themes to emerge from the findings: The decline of the High Street

Theme	Customers	National Chains	Independents
The High Street decline – has the High Street declined?	The majority of customers agreed that the High Street was in decline.	All national chains agreed that the High Street was in decline.	All independent retailers agreed that the High Street was in decline.
The High Street decline – why has the High Street declined?	The majority of customers thought the High Street has declined because of the Internet, offering choice and convenience to customers.	There was no clear pattern of responses with retailers citing the Internet, limited parking, the economy, the weather, business rates, the media and limited facilities as reasons for the High Street decline.	There was no clear pattern of responses with retailers citing the Internet, limited parking, the economy, the weather, business rates, the media and limited facilities as reasons for the High Street decline.

No [pause] for me it hasn't especially declined it's just online shopping that is more and more important but without it necessarily making [the] High Street decline.

From these customer perspectives one could argue that the High Street has lost its appeal and identity, characterised by charity stores, pound shops and betting shops (Dominiczak, 2013) with many similar fashion stores, arguably motivating customers to patronise online retailers for convenience and variety (Rohm & Swaminathan, 2004). Interestingly, customers could be partly to blame for this lack of an engaging environment because of their choosing online retailers over the High Street, i.e. if customers do not patronise the High Street businesses close which presents as ever declining customer offer, further exacerbating the cycle of decline.

Retailer Perspectives

All retailers, not just the majority, like the majority of customers, who were interviewed agreed that the High Street has declined, with a typical response being:

Yes, the number of empty shops has increased [pause] footfall has decreased, the High Street has changed a fair bit over the past 10 years.

It should also be noted that a number of retailers indicated that although they thought the majority of High Streets were in decline they did not think all offline retailers were in decline, indicating that those retailers who provided customers with a positive customer encounter and experience, giving them what they wanted when they wanted it both online and in-store, have proved successful. In other words by combining "the best of both online and offline retail" (Chahal, 2013, para. 19) some retailers have managed to prosper which perhaps provides some insight into a solution to the decline of the High Street which will be investigated later in the chapter.

Why the High Street has Declined

Customer Perspectives

When asked 'Why do you feel the High Street has declined?' the majority of customers felt the Internet was principally to blame, a medium better placed to meet customers demand for convenience and choice. A typical response was:

I think it declined because of the Internet [pause] I think the Internet gives a lot of choice [and] I also think the opening hours on the High Street aren't suitable to modern day life.

A minority of customers were of the opinion that out-of-town retailing has influenced the decline of the High Street also citing the variables convenience and choice as reasons why customers patronise out-of-town retailers in favour of the High Street. A typical response was:

Retail parks have certainly influenced the decline [pause] they have longer opening hours, good parking and more choice.

Customer responses reflect the literature with Bignell & Lefty (2013); Bamfield (2013); Milliken (2012); Poulter (2012); Hall (2011); and Portas (2011) citing the reasons for the decline of the High Street being the increased use of the Internet, mobile devices and out-of-town retailing, with customers motivated by convenience, choice and value for money. To verify this observation, customers were asked for their reasons for shopping online and although no clear pattern emerged, the majority of respondents stated choice and convenience, with a typical response being:

Two major reasons really, choice and convenience. I like to sit and browse for clothes and dictate when it's going to be sent to me.

A number of customers cited price as well as the ability to compare prices as their reasons for shopping online with a minority of customers simply stating the ability to compare prices or habit as their reasons for shopping online. Typical responses were:

It's cheaper to buy online, you don't have to pay to park the car and you can compare prices, [pause] you feel you are getting a good deal buying online 'cos they don't have the overheads.

I can compare prices just by going store to store or using comparison Websites, this way I know I'm getting the best deal.

It was an interesting finding that some customers thought products were cheaper online because they believed that High Street retailers had higher overheads (specifically rent and rates) and may be perceived as even less competitive when the associated travel costs are added on (although it should be noted that such costs are usually negated when one factors in delivery charges from online retailers). A further interesting finding is that some customers were motivated to purchase online because of the ability to compare prices, providing them with relevant information (Rohm & Swaminathan, 2004) and in part reassuring them that they are making the correct buying decision. Those reasons, along with the variables choice and/or convenience, appear to indicate that alternatives to the High Street, namely the Internet and out-of-town retailing were in a better position to provide customers with what they wanted, when they wanted it (O'Reilly, 2012; Portas, 2011; Hall, 2011). A point illustrated by a customer's quote "most High Street shops are closed when I finish work."

Retailer Perspectives

When the research asked retailers why the High Street has declined, similarly to the majority of customers, some retailers cited the increased popularity of online shopping and the development of out-of-town retailing as the reasons for the decline, with typical responses being:

Customers believe they get a better deal online, I guess they feel it's more convenient and they get time to shop around.

Parking is a big issue on the High Street, its expensive and a bit limited so given the choice I think people go out-of-town or stay at home [pause] its convenience I guess.

However there was no clear pattern of responses with a number of retailers giving a number of secondary reasons for the decline of the High Street, some of which were supported by the literature and included the economy (Hall, 2011), the weather, parking (Anon, 2013b; Portas, 2011), business rates (Hill, 2013; Ruddick, 2013; Portas, 2011), the media and a lack of town centre activities. In contrast to customers, retailers saw the decline of the High Street as a more complex issue with a number of interrelated variables. The majority of national chains stated that the reasons for the decline were related to the High Street itself, its definition and which city the High Street was in, with Glasgow argued to be in a better position than Aberdeen, Dundee or Edinburgh, if the High Street was referring to Buchanan Street (considered by national chains and independents in Glasgow as the High Street in Glasgow). The majority of retailers (both independents and national chains) cited more than one reason in their response to why the High Street has declined, summarised by the quote:

The recession has had an effect, [pause] which is made worse by the media and weather. If customers buy online its convenient, delivered to their door without having to worry about parking.

These responses from retailers and customers provide some insight into the first part of the research equation, namely why the High Street has declined, revealing the main themes of the appeal of online retailing, providing convenience and choice and the repelling aspects of the High Street, lacking variety of retailers, appeal, identity (Dominiczak, 2013), convenient opening hours and parking (Anon, 2013b; Portas, 2011). In order to address the second part of the research equation, the factors which would encourage customers back to the High Street, customers and retailers were asked a series of questions relating to proposed solutions, specifically around the service encounter and the improved use of in-store technology.

Encouraging Customers Back to the High Street

Retailer Perspectives

Retailers were asked which retail measures could be incorporated to make customers patronise the High Street more frequently. When the research analysed the responses there was no clear pattern with the majority of retailers citing more than one measure specifically free parking particularly during the evenings, more variety of retailers, i.e. retailers to compliment the concentration of clothing stores and from the retailers in Dundee who argued better quality retailers, i.e. more branded retailers which are available in other cities. A typical response was:

I would say free parking and more choice as that is something that the online environment offers [pause] we as retailers on the High Street are struggling to offer the same choice at the same price as online as with them you don't have to pay parking as well.

A number of independents provided the unhelpful response, "offering something which isn't available online," when prompted to specify which features, they responded that they did not know.

To ascertain what retailers thought they as a store on the High Street could do to make the High Street more appealing and encourage increased customer footfall, the majority stated an improved, more welcoming and transparent customer service with a representative quote being:

Continue to listen to the customer and deliver high standards of customer service.

Only one retailer provided a different response and emphasised their brand pull and the need to be supported by High Street management. This retailer said:

We would say our brand would pull custom to the High Street [we] just need more help from the centre or high street management.

These findings indicate that retailers do not see one specific measure as a means to encourage customers back to the High Street although the majority see free parking (Anon, 2013b; Portas, 2011), retail variety and improved customer service (Butcher, et al., 2001; Heskett, et al., 1997; Javalgi & Moberg, 1997) as measures to make the High Street more appealing. The extent to which retailers and customers agree that these measures will reverse the decline of the High Street will be investigated later in the chapter.

The Role of Technology

A summary of the themes to emerge from interviews with customers and retailers regarding the role of technology in reversing the decline of the High Street are illustrated in Table 2.

Customer Perspectives

The majority of customers shopped online, predominantly using a laptop or PC; however a large proportion used mobile technology (tablet and/or mobile phones) in conjunction with a laptop or PC to shop. The main reasons for using mobile technology for shopping was convenience, being able to shop on their terms and not those imposed by the opening hours of High Street retailers, a point which was eluded to earlier in the context of shopping behaviour. When asked if customers would be 'more likely to use a retailer which had both an online and offline presence than a retailer which only had an offline presence' the majority indicated they would, principally for the reasons of convenience, having the ability to return products purchased online, choice, and to shop according to their needs and shopping context. A typical response was:

It would be a good mix of the online and offline benefits. Most people shop offline to try on products, if you included the convenience of online shopping then more people would shop in the High Street.

The majority of customers agreed that they would use click-and-collect and that if more High Street retailers incorporated such a facility into their offer they would be more likely to frequent

Table 2. Summary of themes to emerge from the findings: Encouraging customers back to the High Street using technology

Theme	Customers	National Chains	Independents
Encouraging customers back to the High Street – the role of technology and the impact of the Internet.	The majority of customers shopped online because of convenience.	All national chains agreed that the Internet and subsequently online buying had a significant impact on the decline of the High Street.	All independents agreed that the Internet and subsequently online buying had a significant impact on the decline of the High Street.
Encouraging customers back to the High Street – the role of technology in-store.	The majority of customers were more likely to use a retailer which had both an online and offline presence because of convenience. The majority of customers agreed they would frequent the High Street more often if retailers incorporated facilities such as click-and-collect.	All national chains agreed that the use of technology in-store could reverse the decline of the High Street with the caveat that the technology would have to add value to the customer experience.	The majority of independent retailers thought the use of technology in-store could reverse the decline of the High Street with the caveat that the technology would have to add value to the customer experience.

the High Street. The majority of respondents would also frequent the High Street more often if technology in general was included into the offline experience, specific technology which would make High Street shopping more convenient with quicker access to information. A typical response was:

If shops in the High Street had click-and-collect or have other facilities which made shopping easier I would shop there more often [pause] you know have touch screen technology and things.

Given a customer's motivation for convenience (Miller, 2013; Sampson, 2013; Newman, 2012; Rohm & Swaminathan, 2004) and their increased use of technology (Bamfield, 2013; Minton, et al., 2013; O'Brien, 2013; Quinn, 2013; Wallop, 2013; Westbrook, 2013; Langston, 2012; Whiteaker, 2012) it would appear that if High Street retailers were to include more technology features in-store, specifically click-and-collect (Minton, et al., 2013; O'Brien, 2013; Quinn, 2013; Langston, 2012; Whiteaker, 2012) and have an online presence (Bamfield, 2013; O'Reilly, 2012) customers would return to the High Street due to them having a choice and their shopping experience being made more convenient (Turner-Mitchell, 2012; Reimers & Clulow, 2009).

Retailer Perspectives

When retailers were asked about the role of technology on the decline of the High Street all retailers agreed that the Internet and subsequently online buying had a significant impact. A typical response was:

It's becoming increasingly difficult to compete with online retailers as a [High Street] retailer.

However when retailers were asked whether offline retailers use of technology could reverse this decline and increase customer visits to the High Street, opinion was divided. The majority of retailers indicated that it would depend on the type of technology with the integration of technology purely for the sake of it viewed as not necessarily adding value to the customer experience; those retailers who agreed with the statement indicated that it could support the current offer, with a representative quote being:

It would help customers compare prices or specific products [pause] it would benefit them to have that information available offline and may mean that they visit the High Street more frequently as they know that they're always getting the best offer and price.

A minority of retailers (all were independents) indicated that the embedding of technology into offline retail would make no difference to the frequency of customer visits to the High Street with a typical response being:

No, I don't think it would make a difference, it's not something that affects the customer experience currently.

Such a response from the minority of independent retailers would appear to run contrary to customer opinion and the perspectives of the majority of retailers in this research and also the literature which is of the opinion that customers do use technology and if given the opportunity to use it offline would do so (Minton, et al., 2013; O'Brien, 2013; Quinn, 2013; Wallop, 2013; Warman, 2013; Wearn, 2013; Langston, 2012; Whiteaker, 2012). The national chains had already integrated technology into their offer with all retailers having a Website which allowed customers to purchase online and some also offered home delivery, iPads and/or a click-and-collect service. All the national chains acknowledged their use of technology as "helpful" to both enhancing the customer experience and their profitability.

These responses from retailers and customers provide some insight into the second part of the research equation, how to encourage customers back to the High Street. The main themes to emerge were that customers would patronise the High Street more often if technological measures were incorporated which made shopping more convenient and accessible. The majority of retailers agreed that the use of technology offline could reverse the decline of the High Street but with the reservation that retailers have to be selective in the technology they use. Interestingly this was the first time national chains and independents differed significantly in their responses, with a minority of retailers, (all independents), stating that the embedding of technology into offline retail would make no difference to the frequency of customer's visits to the High Street. The extent to which opinion differed between customers and retailers with regards to the service encounter and whether an improved customer service could reverse the decline of the High Street will be investigated in the next section.

The Role of Customer Service

A summary of the themes to emerge from interviews with customers and retailers regarding the role of customer service in reversing the decline of the High Street are illustrated in Table 3.

Customer Perspectives

Having established that the role of technology was important to customers online and potentially offline behaviour, customers were then asked how important customer service was to their shopping experience. All customers agreed that customer service was important to them, with responses ranging from very important to pretty important. A typical response was:

It's important because I like to know that if I go into a shop I will get help and assistance.

Interestingly a number of customers indicated that they were not always satisfied with the levels of customer service in the High Street, using phrases

Table 3. Summary of themes to emerge from the findings: Encouraging customers back to the High Street using customer service

Theme	Customers	National Chains	Independents
Encouraging customers back to the High Street – the role of customer service.	All customers agreed that customer service was important to their shopping experience. The majority of customers did not agree that customer service was the main reason for their frequenting the High Street.	The majority of national chains agreed that customer service was the main reason for customers frequenting the High Street.	The majority of independents agreed that customer service was the main reason for customers frequenting the High Street.
Encouraging customers back to the High Street – the role of customer service, improved or even excellent customer service.	An equal proportion of customers agreed and disagreed that improved or even excellent customer service would encourage them to frequent the High Street more often.	The majority of national chains agreed that improved or even excellent customer service would increase customers frequenting the High Street.	The majority of independents agreed that improved or even excellent customer service would increase customers frequenting the High Street.
Encouraging customers back to the High Street – the role of customer service, comparing online and in-store customer service.	The majority of customers did not think the High Street offered better customer service in contrast to online customer service but that the High Street did make products tangible in contrast to online retailing.		

such as "unhelpful," "rude," "obviously having a bad day" to describe their experience of customer service and the staff in High Street retailers. This theme of being disgruntled with customer service in the High Street is supported when we assess responses to the question 'Is customer service the main reason for you patronising the High Street?' with the majority of customers stating no, it was not the main reason, a typical response was:

It's not the main reason [pause] trying on products and just the experience of shopping are more important reasons.

It would appear that although customer service is viewed as important to customers, it was not the main reason for their patronising the High Street, in fact when asked whether improved or even excellent customer service would increase the frequency of their visits, opinion was divided evenly, however it should be noted that many of those who agreed with the statement ('Would improved or even excellent customer service make you frequent the High Street more often?') included a caveat, stating that it would only make a difference if it were in conjunction with improvements in convenience, choice, price and rewards for repeat custom. For those customers who disagreed with the statement, arguing that price, choice and convenience were more important, a representative quote was:

I don't think so, to me convenience is more important and if the High Street just improve customer service buying online still is cheaper, has more choice and is more convenient.

For those customers who thought improved or even excellent customer service would increase their visits a representative quote was:

Yeah, it would make me go back [pause] customer service is important and excellent customer service is more important than anything, [pause] well as important as choice and price.

Customers intimated that customer service was important, capable of providing them with assistance and support (Butcher, et al., 2001; Heskett, et al., 1997; Javalgi & Moberg, 1997). However customers felt that customer service on the High Street was currently lacking these elements, instead being characterised by "rude" and "unhelpful staff," an issue compounded by a High Street already lacking atmosphere and emotional connection (Findlay, 2013). Customer service was not considered the main reason for their patronising of the High Street and even if the current levels were improved to 'excellent' it would not influence the majority of customers to return to the High Street either in favour of or in parallel with online shopping given the appeal of convenience and choice available online.

Retailer Perspectives

When retailers were asked whether customer service was the main reason for customers shopping in the High Street, the majority agreed indicating that staff interaction and interacting with the products add to the customer experience, with a typical response being:

It's often interactions with staff that help make that [the shopping] experience enjoyable.

A minority of retailers (including both national chains and independents) stated that customer service was but one factor, with other issues such as product range, store layout and location and environmental factors inhibiting a customer's patronage of the High Street, with a typical response being:

There are too many factors that stop customers from shopping on the High Street [pause] I'm not even sure customers think of customer service when they shop on the High Street.

To continue this theme of customer service and in contrast to the perspectives of customers, the majority of retailers stated that the delivery of improved or even excellent customer service would increase the frequency of customers patronising the High Street, with a typical response being:

Better and consistent customers service would get customers back to the High Street as its giving customers something they don't get online.

An interesting finding was revealed when the research compares the perspectives of retailers and customers. The majority of retailers (both national chains and independents) were of the opinion that customer service was the main reason why customers patronised the High Street whereas the majority of customers disagreed citing factors such as trying products on and the shopping experience as more important. It would appear that even though customers valued customer service, some felt that the customer service provided by offline retailers could be improved and was neither the main reason for their patronising the High Street nor would it encourage them to visit the High Street more often even if customer service was improved or even excellent. This mismatch of opinion goes some way to addressing the issue of the decline of the High Street and is a common theme to emerge from this research, that the needs of customers are not being met, with some retailers, specifically independents, appearing not to address the factors which drive and could potentially increase customer footfall to the High Street. This issue facing these independents is compounded by the fact raised earlier in the chapter that the majority of these retailers do not conduct market research and are perhaps at a disadvantage when it comes to having a holistic understanding of the customer.

High Street and Online Customer Service Compared: Customer Perspectives

To ascertain perceptions of online customer service in contrast to the customer service on the High Street customers were asked the question 'Does online shopping offer the same level of customer service as the High Street?' The majority of customers thought the High Street did not necessarily provide better customer service but being face-to-face was more suitable for dealing with customer complaints and aftercare, with a typical response being:

I don't think you can really compare [pause] customer service online is good [pause] and the in-store customer service is generally OK. I guess the main difference is the fact that in-store the service is face-to-face.

However it should be noted that a number of customers stated that customers shop online for convenience, choice and price comparisons as well as price competitiveness and that customer service was not a major reason for their shopping online, with a representative quote being:

You don't shop online for the service, you shop for convenience, price and choice [pause] you don't really think about getting poor customer service online [pause] I guess the only way you could get bad customer service is if the wrong product arrived or it was damaged.

It would appear that the majority of customers thought the High Street did not necessarily provide better customer service when compared to online retailers, with many customers adding the caveat that when shopping online customer service was not the main or even secondary reason why they preferred to shop online (Miller, 2013; Newman, 2012; Rohm & Swaminathan, 2004). Customers argued that improved customer service would not encourage customers back to the High Street nor was it the main reason for their patronage of the High Street. To this end customers were asked what the High Street could offer customers that online retailers could not as a way of encouraging customers back to the High Street. The majority of customers discussed the tangible factors, and similarly to issues discussed earlier in the chapter, the ability to touch, see and try on the products, with a typical response being:

You get to see what the product looks like in store rather than seeing a picture of it online [pause] you get to try it on or try it out.

It is worth noting that a minority of customers stated that the High Street were better placed to encourage impulse buying, although they acknowledged that online retailers could also encourage customers to buy on impulse. A representative quote was:

When you browse the store on the High Street the layout sometimes throws up things which you might not have seen online unless you searched for it.

Customers were of the opinion that improved customer service would not encourage them back to the High Street, nor were they of the opinion that the High Street provided a better customer service when compared to online retailers, with the added reservation that it was convenience and not customer service which motivated them to shop online (Bamfield, 2013; Bignell & Lefty, 2013; Miller, 2013; Milliken, 2012; Newman, 2012; Poulter, 2012; Portas, 2011; Hall, 2011). This finding underlines the point made earlier that offline retailers have to make the in-store shopping experience more convenient, accessible and engaging for customers in order to increase customer footfall to the High Street, providing unique selling points and differentiating itself from online shopping.

SUMMARY DISCUSSION

The results from the interviews with customers and retailers (national chains and independents) assist in explaining the decline of the High Street and address the potential of the service encounter, specifically customer service as a means to reverse the decline. Key issues have been identified which either inhibit customers shopping on the High Street and/or encourage them to shop online, which include the offline opening hours, which customers felt could be more flexible and reflective of changing consumption patterns rather than have customers shop when retailers want them to shop, parking (Anon, 2013b; Portas, 2011) and business rates (Hill, 2013; Portas, 2011). Convenience either individually or in conjunction with choice and price were identified as key motivators in customers shopping behaviour (Bamfield, 2013; Bignell & Lefty, 2013; Miller, 2013; Sampson, 2013; Milliken, 2012; Newman, 2012; Poulter, 2012; Hall, 2011; Reimers & Clulow, 2009). It would appear that customers have become used to the benefits of online shopping (Minton, et al., 2013; O'Brien, 2013; Quinn, 2013; Wallop, 2013; Warman, 2013; Wearn, 2013; Langston, 2012; O'Reilly, 2012; Whiteaker, 2012), which may have raised their expectations with regards to High Street retailers, expectations which are not being addressed as well as they are online or at least not well enough to make them stop shopping online and return to the High Street. However this does not mean that the High Street no longer has a place in UK retailing. Customers intimated that they preferred retailers who had an online and offline presence as it accommodated their motivation for convenience and to receive support in terms of trying products on (Butler, 2013; Roland Berger, 2013; Warman, 2013; Wearn, 2013; Turner-Mitchell, 2012; Oates, 2011) return products, pick up products through click-and-collect and receive face-to-face sales support. The role of customer service in encouraging customers back to the High Street was seen as less influential, although many retailers thought it was the main reason and a possible solution to reversing the decline of the High Street. According to a number of customers, the current service encounter and customer service is characterised by "rude" and "unhelpful staff" which does little to enhance a High Street which already lacks identity (Dominiczak, 2013) atmosphere and emotional connection (Findlay, 2013).

FUTURE RESEARCH DIRECTIONS

As a result of this exploratory study, there are future areas for research both conceptually and theoretically. The first area for future research is with regard to conducting a comparative study with cities in England in an attempt to understand if the findings from this research in Scotland are generalisable. This research would reveal common themes in customer and retailer perspectives and enable the construction of a framework around which we can better understand and evaluate viable solutions to the decline of the UK High Street.

A second area for future research is to investigate the possible lessons UK offline retailers could learn from their European counterparts. As European customers tend to patronise town centres and local shops (Briggs, 2013; EMEA, 2013) despite increased shopping online, further research would be useful to investigate whether there is a formulae or particular measures which UK retailers could implement in order to reverse the decline of the High Street.

A third area for future research is to investigate the particular role of technology in reviving the UK High Street. Based on the findings from this research, customers did appreciate the High Street as a means of realising the tangible dimensions of the shopping experience, being able to try on products, particularly clothing following and/ or preceding an online search, a practice called showrooming (Butler, 2013; Roland Berger, 2013;

Warman, 2013; Wearn, 2013; Oates, 2011). However these customers did not necessarily purchase those products offline following the showrooming practice. Future research could evaluate how retailers could 'fuse together' technology and the store environment to encourage customers to patronise the High Street more frequently and more importantly to buy in-store instead of online.

CONCLUSION

This research addresses an important theme in UK retailing, consolidating existing literature on the use of in-store technology to enhance the customer experience, and takes research forward in the area of the decline of the High Street and the role of customer service. The qualitative research found that the majority of customers frequented the High Street every two weeks to once per month which was not particularly high and that those visits were predominantly by city centre workers shopping during their lunch-breaks, mainly for toiletries and clothing. The reasons for their lack of shopping on the High Streets of Aberdeen, Dundee, Edinburgh and Glasgow were summed up in their reasons for the decline of the High Street and the factors which would encourage them to return, that online retailers provide better choice, convenience and the ability to compare prices which are usually more competitive than those on the High Street. Unlike the retailers in this study, customers were not of the opinion that an improvement in current, in some cases, 'disappointing' customer service would encourage them back to the High Street. Rather customers thought solutions to the decline of the UK High Street lay in combining the convenience and choice of online retail with the tangibility of the offline retailer experience. The research contends that the increased integration of technology into High Street stores should be seen as a means to enable more focus on providing an enhanced customer experience (Chahal, 2013; Shields, 2013). The results from the exploratory research show that rather than being perceived as a threat to the High Street, the growth of online buying and customers increased use of technology for purchasing products and services should be seen as a positive, enhancing the appeal and adding value to customers High Street retail experience.

REFERENCES

Anon. (2013a). European Consumers Want Choices and Convenience When Shopping Online. *ComScore*. Retrieved October 27, 2013, from http://pressroom.ups.com/Press+Releases/Current+Press+Releases/ci.European+Consumers+Want+Choices+And+Convenience+When+Shopping+Online.print

Anon. (2013b). Majority care about high street decline, but parking prevents use. *AMT*. Retrieved October 27, 2013, from http://towns.org.uk/2013/06/10/majority-care-about-high-street-decline-but-parking-prevents-use/

Baldinger, A. L., & Ruben, J. (1996). Brand loyalty: The link between attitude and behaviour. *Journal of Advertising Research*, *36*(2), 22–34.

Bamfield, J. A. N. (2013). *Retail futures 2018: Shop numbers, online and the High Street, A guide to retailing in 2018*. Nottingham, UK: Centre for Retail Research.

Barnes, J. G. (2003). Establishing meaningful customer relationships: why some companies and brands mean more to their customers. *Managing Service Quality*, *13*(3), 178–186. doi:10.1108/09604520310476445

Bennison, D., Warnaby, G., & Pal, J. (2010). Local shopping in the UK: Towards a synthesis of business and place. *International Journal of Retail & Distribution Management*, *38*(11/12), 846–864. doi:10.1108/09590551011085948

Bignell, P., & Lefty, M. (2013). High Street blues: the slow death of retail Britain. *The Independent*. Retrieved March 27, 2013, from http://www.independent.co.uk/news/business/analysis-and-features/high-street-blues-the-slow-death-of-retail-britain-8458766.html

Bishop, D. (2013). Customer service lessons from the High Street. *The Marketing Donut*. Retrieved August 6, 2013, from http://www.marketingdonut.co.uk/marketing/customer-care/understanding-your-customers/customer-service-lessons-from-the-high-street

Briggs, F. (2013). Local shops and town centres are top choice for European shoppers, CBRE finds. *Retailtimes*. Retrieved October 27, 2013, from http://retailtimes.co.uk/local-shops-and-town-centres-are-top-choice-for-european-shoppers-cbre-finds/#

Brown, M., Pope, N., & Voges, K. (2003). Buying or Browsing? An exploration of shopping orientations and online purchase intention. *European Journal of Marketing*, *37*(11/12), 1666–1684. doi:10.1108/03090560310495401

Butcher, K. et al. (2001). Evaluative and relational influences on service loyalty. *International Journal of Service Industry Management*, *12*(4), 310–327. doi:10.1108/09564230110405253

Butler, M. (2013). Showrooming: are retailers ready to embrace it? *The Guardian*. Retrieved June 8, 2013, from http://www.guardian.co.uk/media-network/media-network-blog/2013/may/09/showrooming-retail-solution-e-commerce

Cartner-Morley, J. (2012). Burberry designs flagship London shop to resemble its Website. *The Guardian*. Retrieved June 8, 2013, from http://www.theguardian.com/fashion/2012/sep/12/burberry-london-shop-Website

Chahal, M. (2013). Open all hours: the future of the High Street. *Marketing Week*. Retrieved March 27, 2013, from http://www.marketingweek.co.uk/trends/open-all-hours-the-future-of-the-high-street/4005606.article

Cooper, K. (2012). High Street plunges into triples dip. *The Sunday Times*. Retrieved March 27, 2013, from http://www.thesundaytimes.co.uk/sto/business/Retail_and_leisure/article1184780.ee

Cotterill, S. (2013). 43% of Europeans shop online. *InternetRetailer*. Retrieved October 27, 2013, from http://www.Internetretailer.com/2012/06/07/43-europeans-shop-online

Cunningham, R. M. (1956). Brand loyalty- What, where, how much. *Harvard Business Review*, *34*, 116–128.

Dabholkar, P. A., Bobbitt, L. M., & Lee, E.-J. (2003). Understanding consumer motivation and behaviour related to self-scanning in retailing. *International Journal of Service Industry Management*, *14*(1), 59–95. doi:10.1108/09564230310465994

Day, G. S. (1969). A two-dimensional concept of brand loyalty. *Journal of Advertising Research*, *9*, 29–35.

De Wulf, K. et al. (2005). Consumer perceptions of store brands versus national brands. *Journal of Consumer Marketing*, *22*(4), 223–232. doi:10.1108/07363760510605335

Dennis, C., Harris, L., & Sandhu, B. (2002). From bricks to clicks: Understanding the e-consumer. *Qualitative Market Research: An International Journal*, *5*(4), 281–290. doi:10.1108/13522750210443236

Department for Communities and Local Government. (2013). *The Future of High Streets: Progress since the Portas Review*. London: Crown.

Dominiczak, P. (2013). Pay day lenders 'could replace independent shops' in High Street reforms. *The Telegraph*. Retrieved August 6, 2013, from http://www.telegraph.co.uk/lifestyle/reinvent-the-high-street/10088028/Pay-day-lenders-could-replace-independent-shops-in-high-street-reforms.html

EMEA. (2013). *How we shop: Inside the minds of Europe's consumers. EMEA*. London: CBRE Ltd.

Etsell, C., & Hinton, M. (2013). How the UK will shop: 2013. *Verdict in Association with SAS*. Retrieved August 6, 2013, from http://www.siicex.gob.pe/siicex/documentosportal/alertas/documento/doc/773247859rad0250B.pdf

Ewing, M. T. (2000). Brand and retailer loyalty: Past behaviour and future intentions. *Journal of Product and Brand Management*, *9*(2), 120–127. doi:10.1108/10610420010322161

Findlay, D. (2013). High Street retailers must rediscover that emotional connection with customers. *Marketing Magazine*. Retrieved August 6, 2013, from http://www.marketingmagazine.co.uk/article/1186124/high-street-retailers-rediscover-

Fisher, L. (2012). Top retailers at channel crossroads. *Marketing Magazine*. Retrieved March 27, 2013, from http://www.marketingweek.co.uk/trends/top-retailers-at-channel-crossroads/4003348.article

Fitzsimmons, J. A. (2003). Is self-service the future of services? *Managing Service Quality*, *13*(6), 443–444. doi:10.1108/09604520310506496

Gardner, T. (2014). *Glasgow High Street* [Image]. Retrieved from Toni Gardner.

Geddes, I. (2011). The store of the future: The new role of the store in a multichannel environment. *Deloitte*. Retrieved August 6, 2013, from http://www.deloitte.com/assets/Dcom-UnitedKingdom/Local%20Assets/Documents/Industries/Consumer%20Business/uk-cb-store-of-the-future-report.pdf

Glenday, J. (2013). Study warns one in five High Street shops could be shuttered by 2018. *The Drum.* Retrieved March 27, 2013, from http://www. thedrum.com/news/2013/05/28/study-warns-one-five-high-street-shops-could-be-shuttered-2018

Hall, J. (2011). Mary Portas: High Streets destined to 'disappear forever'. *The Telegraph.* Retrieved March 20, 2013, from http://www.telegraph. co.uk/finance/newsbysector/retailandconsumer/8951411/Mary-Portas-high-streets-destined-to-disappear-forever.html

Heskett, J. L. et al. (1997). *The service profit chain: How leading companies link profit and growth to loyalty, satisfaction and value.* New York: The Free Press.

Hill, J. (2013). High Street chain store closures soar, says research. *BBC News Business.* Retrieved November 15, 2013, from http://www.bbc.co.uk/news/business-21611772

Javalgi, R., & Moberg, C. (1997). Service loyalty: Implications for service providers. *Journal of Services Marketing, 11*(3), 165–179. doi:10.1108/08876049710168663

Kelly, J. (2013a). *Dundee High Street* [Image]. Retrieved from James Kelly.

Kelly, J. (2013b). *High Street decline* [Image]. Retrieved from James Kelly.

Langston, P. (2012). Will click and collect save the High Street? *Retail Week.* Retrieved June 9, 2013, from http://www.retail-week.com/multichannel/comment-will-click-and-collect-save-the-high-street/5039566.article

Lee, H. J. et al. (2010). The influence of consumer traits and demographics on intention to use retail self-service checkouts. *Marketing Intelligence & Planning, 28*(1), 46–58. doi:10.1108/02634501011014606

Leroux, M., & Ralph, A. (2013). Retailers will shine if customers can click and collect. *The Times.* Retrieved March 14, 2013, from http://www. thetimes.co.uk/tto/business/industries/retailing/article3660985.ece

Meuter, M. L. et al. (2000). Self-service technologies: understanding customer satisfaction with technology-based service encounters. *Journal of Marketing, 64*, 50–64. doi:10.1509/jmkg.64.3.50.18024

Miller, G. (2013). Is the prime reason customers shop online price or convenience? Which one? Are you sure? *The Retail Intelligence Company.* Retrieved August 12, 2013, from http://upstreamcommerce.com/blog/2013/08/07/ptime-reason-customers-shop-online-

Milliken, J. (2012). Mobile phones are changing the world of retail – at a remarkable rate. *The Guardian.* Retrieved March 20, 2013, from http://www.guardian.co.uk/media-network/media-network-blog/2012/jun/26/mobile-retail-technology-consumer

Minton, A., et al. (2013). How can we save the High Street? *The Guardian.* Retrieved June 9, 2013, from http://www.guardian.co.uk/commentisfree/2013/jan/15/how-can-we-save-high-street

Miranda, M. J. et al. (2005). Shoppers' satisfaction levels are not the only key to store loyalty. *Marketing Intelligence & Planning, 23*(2), 220–232. doi:10.1108/02634500510589958

Moulds, J. (2013). UK GDP shrank by 0.3% in fourth quarter. *The Guardian.* Retrieved March 27, 2013, from http://www.guardian.co.uk/business/2013/jan/25/uk-gdp-crunch-time-osborne

Muller, A. (2008, December) Self-service shopping: Advantages for both retailers and customers. *The Retail Digest*, 50-53.

Neate, R., & Moulds, J. (2012). More High Street name will collapse in New Year, warns retail body. *The Guardian*. Retrieved March 27, 2013, from http://www.guardian.co.uk/business/2012/dec/31/high-street-names-collapse-new-year

Newman, M. (2012). Customers want convenience. *RetailWeek*. Retrieved August 12, 2013, from http://www.retail-week.com/comment/customers-want-convenience/5033060.article

O'Brien, P. (2013). Click and collect cannot save the High Street analyst. *InternetRetailing*. Retrieved June 9, 2013, from http://Internetretailing.net/2013/04/click-and-collect-cannot-save-the-high-street-analyst/

O'Reilly, L. (2012). Digital will save the High Street. *Marketing Week*. Retrieved March 27, 2013, from http://www.marketingweek.co.uk/news/digital-will-save-the-high-street/4004029.article

Oates, D. (2011). The changing face of UK retail in today's multi-channel world. *An Experian white paper*. Retrieved March 27, 2013, from http://www.experian.co.uk/assets/business-strategies/white-papers/RWC-whitepaper2.pdf

Portas, M. (2011). The Portas Review: An independent review into the future of our High Streets. *BIS*. Retrieved March 27, 2013, from http://www.bis.gov.uk/assets/BISCore/business-sectors/docs/p/11-1434-portas-review-future-of-high-streets.pdf

Potter, B. (2013). The future High Streets forum launches: Why no mention of digital? *Econsultancy*. Retrieved August 6, 2013, from http://econsultancy.com/uk/blog/62483-the-future-high-streets-forum-launches-why-no-mention-of-digital

Poulter, S. (2012). Dying High Street shops where up to a third is empty. *The Daily Mail*. Retrieved March 27, 2013, from http://www.dailymail.co.uk/news/article-2097383/Dying-high-streets-shops-empty.html

Quinn, I. (2013). Independent stores 'should team up on click & collect offers'. *The Grocer*. Retrieved June 9, 2013, from http://www.thegrocer.co.uk/companies/independent-stores-should-team-up-on-click-and-collect-offers/343174.article

Ramaswamy, S. (2013). Shopping then and now: Five ways retail has changed and how businesses can adapt. *Google Think Insights*. Retrieved August 6, 2013, from http://www.google.com/think/articles/five-ways-retail-has-changed-and-how-business

Reimers, V., & Clulow, V. (2009). Retail centres: It's time to make them convenient. *International Journal of Retail & Distribution Management, 37*(7), 541–562. doi:10.1108/09590550910964594

Rohm, A. J., & Swaminathan, V. (2004). A typology of online shoppers based on shopping motivations. *Journal of Business Research, 57*, 748–757. doi:10.1016/S0148-2963(02)00351-X

Roland Berger. (2013). What the customer really wants. *Roland Berger*. Retrieved October 27, 2013, from http://www.rolandberger.com/press_releases/513-press_archive2013_sc_content/What_the_customer_really_wants.html

Ruddick, G. (2013). Government should freeze business rates for two years to help the High Street. *The Telegraph*. Retrieved March 27, 2013, from http://www.telegraph.co.uk/finance/newsbysector/retailandconsumer/10069475/Government-should-freeze-business-rates-for-two-years-to-help-high-street.html

Rundle-Thiele, S., & MacKay, M. M. (2001). Assessing the performance of brand loyalty measures. *Journal of Services Marketing, 15*(7), 529–546. doi:10.1108/EUM0000000006210

Sampson, J. (2013). Why the High Street isn't dying. *Huffington Post*. Retrieved March 27, 2013, from http://www.huffingtonpost.co.uk/josie-sampson/why-the-high-street-isnt-dying_b_2811337.html?icid=hp_search_art

Saunders, D. et al. (1992). Employee voice to supervisors. *Employee Responsibilities and Rights Journal, 5*, 241–259. doi:10.1007/BF01385051

Shields, R. (2013). Google touts retail solutions. *Marketing Week.* Retrieved March 27, 2013, from http://www.marketingweek.co.uk/news/google-touts-retail-solutions/4005513.article

Sikora, D. (2013). Online or Offline Shopping? Its Not Either or Neither–It's Both. *Insights.* Retrieved October 27, 2013, from http://insights.wired.com/profiles/blogs/online-or-offline-shopping-it-s-not-either-or-neither-it-s-both#axzz2ixud0ZSn

Sit, J., Merrilees, B., & Birch, D. (2003). Entertainment-seeking shopping centre patrons: The missing segments. *International Journal of Retail & Distribution Management, 31*(2), 80–94. doi:10.1108/09590550310461985

Smith, A. et al. (2004). Delivering customer loyalty schemes in retailing: Exploring the employee dimension. *International Journal of Retail & Distribution Management, 32*(4), 190–204. doi:10.1108/09590550410528962

Smith, K. (2013). 6 challenges retailers face. *EDIDT.* Retrieved November 11, 2013, from http://editd.com/blog/2013/04/6-challenges-retailers-face/

Steiner, R. (2013). No stopping the online shopping revolution as 'omni-channel' retailers offer more options than ever before. *Thisismoney.* Retrieved June 6, 2013, from http://www.thisismoney.co.uk/money/markets/article-2317260/The-omni-channel-online-shopping-revolution.html

Swan, J. E. et al. (1999). Customer trust in a salesperson: An integrative review and meta-analysis of the empirical literature. *Journal of Business Research, 44*(2), 93–107. doi:10.1016/S0148-2963(97)00244-0

Turner-Mitchell, P. (2012). Don't abandon retail: People will always want the High Street. *The Guardian.* Retrieved August 6, 2013, from http://www.theguardian.com/uk/the-northerner/2012/sep/21/manchester-salford-high-street-retail-mary-portas-shops

Wallop, H. (2013). Click and collect- the new way to go shopping. *The Telegraph.* Retrieved March 27, 2013, from http://www.telegraph.co.uk/finance/newsbysector/retailandconsumer/9785532/Click-and-collect-the-new-way-to-go-shopping.html

Warman, M. (2013). The future of shopping: From high street to iStreet. *The Telegraph.* Retrieved August 6, 2013, from http://www.telegraph.co.uk/technology/news/9821702/The-future-of-shopping-from-h...

Wearn, R. (2013). Online shops take stock and move into the High Street. *BBC News.* Retrieved August 8, 2013, from http://www.bbc.co.uk/news/business-22404652?print=true

Westbrook, T. (2013). High Street needs e-tail therapy: Lack of vision as much to blame for retailers' failures as the rise of e-commerce. *Insight.* Retrieved August 6, 2013, from http://www.cio.co.uk/insight/strategy/high-street-needs-e-tail-therapy/

Whiteaker, J. (2012). Feature: Is the UK a click & collect nation? *Retailgazette.* Retrieved August 6, 2013, from http://www.retailgazette.co.uk/articles/23311-feature-is-the-uk-a-click-collect-nation

Withers, C., & De Judicibus, D. (2013). Augmented Aisles: the online invasion. *The Guardian.* Retrieved June 6, 2013, from http://www.guardian.co.uk/media-network/media-network-blog/2013/mar/14/online-technology-high-street-innovation

Wong, A. (2004). The role of emotional satisfaction in service encounters. *Managing Service Quality*, *14*(5), 365–376. doi:10.1108/09604520410557976

Wong, A., & Sohal, A. S. (2003). Service quality and customer loyalty perspectives on two levels of retail relationships. *Journal of Services Marketing*, *17*(5), 495–513. doi:10.1108/08876040310486285

Wong, A., & Sohal, A. S. (2006). Understanding the quality of relationships in consumer services. *International Journal of Quality & Reliability Management*, *23*(3), 244–264. doi:10.1108/02656710610648215

ADDITIONAL READING

Allies & Morrison Urban Practitioners. (2013). The Changing Face of the High Street: Decline and Revival. *English Heritage*, 1-68. Retrieved October 27, 2013, from http://www.english-heritage.org.uk/publications/changing-face-high-street-decline-revival/773_130604_final_retail_and_town_centre.pdf

Anon. (2012). Making it click: Retailers are striving to combine the advantages of physical shops with the benefits of online selling. *Economist*. Retrieved October 27, 2013, from http://www.economist.com/node/21548236

Anon. (2013). The UK High Street: The decline of a British institution. *The Grocer*. Retrieved October 27, 2013, from http://www.thegrocer.co.uk/reports-and-advice/third-party-reports/the-uk-high-street-the-decline-of-a-british-institution/348613.article

Anon. (2013). Shopper Discounts and Rewards | how the British high street could be saved. *Shopperdiscountsrewards*. Retrieved October 27, 2013, from: http://shopperdiscountsrewards.org/2013/09/05/queen-of-shops-mary-portas-discusses-uk-high-street-report/

Anon. (2013). The future of high streets. *LSE*. Retrieved October 27, 2013, from: http://www.lse.ac.uk/researchAndExpertise/researchHighlights/Economy/HighStreets.aspx

Anon. (2013). There's no place like the mall: US shoppers unplug. *Nielsen*. Retrieved October 27, 2013, from http://www.nielsen.com/us/en/newswire/2013/there_s-no-place-like-the-mall--u-s--shoppers-unplug.html

Anon. (2013). Online, Offline, or Both? How German brick-and-mortar retailers tackle the online challenge. *Roland Berger*. Retrieved October 27, 2013, from http://www.rolandberger.com/media/news/2013-03-01-rbsc-news-Online_or_offline_or_both.html

Bacon, J. (2013). Rebooting Britain's high streets. *MarketingWeek*. Retrieved October 27, 2013, from http://www.marketingweek.co.uk/trends/rebooting-britains-high-streets/4006739.article

Ellis, R. (2011). High Street Retail Units. *CBRE*, 1-7. Retrieved October 27, 2013, from http://www.cbre.eu/portal/pls/portal/res_rep.show_report?report_id=1776

Greenfield, R. (2013). The only Place People Shop Online Is Amazon. *TheWire*. Retrieved October 27, 2013, from http://www.theatlanticwire.com/business/2013/08/only-place-people-shop-online-amazon/68823/

Grimsey, B., et al. (2013). The Grimsey Review: An Alternative Future for the High Street. *Grimsey Review*, 1-59. Retrieved October 27, 2013, from http://www.vanishinghighstreet.com/wp-content/uploads/2013/09/GrimseyReview04.092.pdf

Hall, J., & Ruddick, G. (2013). Half of high street retailers in danger of closing down. *The Telegraph*. Retrieved October 27, 2013, from http://www.telegraph.co.uk/finance/newsbysector/retailandconsumer/10278443/Half-of-high-street-retailers-in-danger-of-closing-down.html

Jordan, J. (2012). The death of the American Shopping mall. *The Atlantic Cities Place Matters*. Retrieved October 27, 2013, from http://www.theatlanticcities.com/jobs-and-economy/2012/12/death-american-shopping-mall/4252/

Kennedy, S. (2013). Can the British high street reinvent itself? *Channel4*. Retrieved October 27, 2013, from http://blogs.channel4.com/siobhan-kennedy/british-high-street-reinvent/342

Rhodes, C. (2013). The Retail Industry. *House of Commons Library*, 1-12. Retrieved October 27, 2013, from http://www.parliament.uk/briefing-papers/SN06186.pdf

Roberts, N. (2013). Clicks versus Bricks: The Battle for the High Street. *Insead*. Retrieved October 27, 2013, from http://knowledge.insead.edu/business-finance/marketing/clicks-versus-bricks-the-battle-for-the-high-street-2442

Schutte, S. (2013). Innovation can reverse the decline of the high street. *Realbusiness*. Retrieved October 27, 2013, from http://realbusiness.co.uk/article/24474-innovation-can-reverse-the-decline-of-the-high-street

Swinney, P., & Sivaev, D. (2013). Beyond the High Street: Why our city centres really matter. *Centreforcities*, 1-47. Retrieved October 27, 2013, from http://www.centreforcities.org/assets/files/2013/13-09-09-Beyond-the-High-Streets.pdf

Titley, C., et al. (2012). Future of the High Street. *Institute of Engineering & Technology*, 7(5), Retrieved October 27, 2013, from http://eandt.theiet.org/magazine/2012/05/future-high-street.cfm

Turrow, J., Feldman, L., & Meltzer, K. (2005). Open to Exploitation: America's Shoppers Online and Offline. *University of Pennsylvania*, 1-39. Retrieved October 27, 2013, from http://repository.upenn.edu/cgi/viewcontent.cgi?article=1035&context=asc_papers

KEY TERMS AND DEFINITIONS

Click-and-Collect: A process which allows customers to order (and pay for) a product online and collect in-store or (in some cases) from a selection of designated locations at a time convenient to them.

Customer Service: The support and/or advice provided by a company and its personnel to customers purchasing or using its products or services.

Decline of the UK High Street: The situation which has seen an increase in vacant premises on UK High Streets and customers increasingly favouring shopping online and out-of-town for their goods and services.

In-Store Technology: The use and application of technology such as touchscreen kiosks, screens and interactive mirrors, QR codes, ipads, video screens and click-and-collect facilities in-store.

Online Shopping: The process where customers can purchase or browse goods and services from a seller via the internet.

Service Encounter: A customers interaction with a service provider.

ENDNOTES

[1] The main street of a UK town or city which has a variety of retailers usually including banks and eateries.

[2] A retailer which sells a variety of low cost household goods.

Chapter 9
City Trees and Consumer Response in Retail Business Districts

Kathleen L. Wolf
University of Washington, USA

ABSTRACT

Many cities and communities are working toward urban sustainability goals. Yet, retailers and merchants may not find environmental benefits to be compelling when compared to the direct costs of landscape and trees. Nonetheless, a quality outdoor environment may provide atmospherics effects that extend store appeal to the curb and heighten the positive experiences and psychological reactions of visitors while in a shopping district. A multi-study program of research shows that having a quality urban forest canopy within business districts and commercial areas can promote positive shopper perceptions and behavior. Positive responses include store image, patronage behavior, and willingness to pay more for goods and services. This chapter provides a summary of the research, connects results to psychological marketing theory, provides evidence-based design recommendations, and makes suggestions for potential future research activity.

INTRODUCTION

In recent decades researchers have explored the connections between store environments and shopper activity. Many retailers and merchants use evidence-based strategies to enhance shoppers' experiences. Interior design, product integration and placement, the appearance and behavior of sales associates, and even the choice of background music are implemented and tweaked to influence consumer behavior. Retail establishments from small independent shops to chain department stores work to make the shopping environment alluring, comfortable, and profitable.

Meanwhile, gardeners and philosophers have celebrated the pleasures of trees and nature for centuries, noting the role of plants in aesthetics, cultural symbolism, and therapy. Recent research confirms the benefits that people gain from nature experiences. However, the two research pursuits – investigations of human experiences of retail place and studies of nature settings – have rarely intersected.

DOI: 10.4018/978-1-4666-6074-8.ch009

City trees provide many environmental benefits such as clean air and water, reduced heat island effects, and reduced energy usage. Yet merchants often do not find such benefits compelling. To address the more direct interests of retailers a series of studies has explored both business peoples' attitudes about trees and shopper response to urban forest canopy. The research results make the case for the importance of business investment in a tree program, in order to address urban sustainability, but more importantly, to enhance the appeal and success of business centers in cities and towns.

This chapter builds the case for the importance of having trees and quality landscapes in retail settings. The first sections address the broader issues of urban sustainability, retail settings, and recent research about urban forest benefits. A background section then presents the psychological theory about people's response to place, retail settings, and nature. A program of research studies has explored how business district visitors respond to city trees; key findings are summarized. A research discussion section is followed by guidelines for urban forest planning in contemporary shopping environments. This presentation of theory and research presents several research opportunities, the focus of the last section in the chapter.

ISSUE: RETAIL ENVIRONMENTS AND SUSTAINABILITY

Local governments are increasingly interested in pursuing urban sustainability goals. Science, technology, and professional best practices have evolved to integrate natural systems and elements into the basic functions of cities and towns. Yet not all property owners are necessarily committed to ecology and landscape development for the sake of sustainability. For instance shop owners within the retail and commercial districts of cities often lament the dis-services of street trees and vegetation, calling out the costs and annoyances of blocked signs, debris, and sidewalk damage. These practical concerns often lead to plans and practices that preclude plantings, in the belief that open, clear streets provide optimal shopping environments.

The basis of consumer behavior has changed in recent decades. While the retailer-consumer relationship still involves rational economic transactions, it also includes a variety of non-economic factors. Shopping has become much more than an activity of necessity, and now has leisure and entertainment components. The aspects of the retail environment that attract customers and encourage them to purchase are not fully understood. Behavioral economics and neuromarketing are emerging fields of study that pursue better understanding of economic and retail behavior.

Facing competition from online and big box competitors, many merchants in local and neighborhood shopping districts give greater attention to the quality of experience in their shop and customer service. Curiously, in many instances the attention to retail experience and place does not extend beyond the front door. On approach a customer encounters blank walls, barren sidewalks, and large paved areas devoted to parking. The appealing retail experience that is carefully cultivated within the store is often absent at the curb and other outdoor areas of the business district or site.

Central business districts are the retail and civic centers of many urban neighborhoods and smaller cities. As business associations implement district improvements and strategies to attract and retain shoppers, some retailers may overlook the importance of a quality streetscape on visitors' encounters with a business district. The direct costs of an urban forest improvement program can be readily tallied; assessing the consumer response benefits is more difficult. Yet, trees and landscape are playing an ever more important role in urban quality of life.

BACKGROUND: BENEFITS AND FUNCTIONS OF URBAN FORESTRY

Aesthetics and beauty are probably the most commonly described benefits of city trees, parks, and gardens. Tree plantings have historically been an important element of beautification programs in cities throughout the world. Yet recent science indicates that decisions to plant and manage trees should not be based only on aesthetics, as urban forestry and greening provide many citywide benefits. Here are key findings from recent research.

Ecosystem Services

The term *ecosystem services* (ES) has evolved to describe the full scope of nature's contributions to human health and welfare. ES are defined as those conditions and processes by which natural ecosystems sustain and fulfill human life. Economists have used the concept of ecosystem services for decades, but it really gained momentum in the 1990s after a key paper was published in the journal *Nature* (Costanza et al., 1997). The article defined ES and tackled the ambitious goal of providing an economic estimate, suggesting that all services across the planet tallied up to an average annual value of USD $33 trillion.

Natural assets, such as forests, agricultural lands, shorelines, and seas, have been the sources of essential and economically valuable goods and services throughout human history. Products such as timber, grains, and fish are readily bought and sold in markets. ES also includes natural systems benefits that have economic consequences, but setting their values is more difficult. Examples include flood protection, pollinator activity, natural filtering of potable water, and climate stability. Generally, ecosystem services arise from broad systems of ecological components, processes, and functions, but the term specifically signifies aspects of ecosystems that are valued by people. Recent research in urban forestry and urban ecology has yielded important insights about the functions of natural systems within cities.

Environmental Benefits

Trees are major contributors of environmental services (Chen & Jim, 2008; Wolf, 2013). Trees modify local microclimate to improve living conditions, including changes in solar radiation, wind speed, air temperature, relative humidity, and re-radiation from paved areas. Urban greening also improves air quality, as plant foliage enables beneficial gaseous exchange and intercepts polluting particles. Urban vegetation positively affects water quantity and quality, as the pervious soils of planted areas allow infiltration of precipitation, reducing runoff and increasing groundwater recharge. Soils and vegetation can also retain water pollutants, thus improving water quality by mitigating nonpoint source pollution. Climate and energy effects are additional benefits. Strategically placed trees within residential areas can reduce heat gain, thus reducing household energy consumption. Scaling up, areas of substantial tree canopy across a city can produce an oasis effect in hot climates, contributing to mitigation of the urban heat island effect, perhaps a more immediate threat in some cities than climate change.

Health and Well-Being Benefits

Many environmental services have health consequences, such as provision of clean air and water. In addition, nearly 40 years of research across multiple social science disciplines points to important psychosocial benefits (Wolf, 2008a; Wolf, 2012). Having trees and nature in cities satisfies basic human needs, improves livability, and enhances quality of life. Nature provides beauty and aesthetics in built environments, but is also profoundly important to human health and well-being. The evidence spans social scales from individual response to person-to-person interactions, to neighborhoods, to organizations, and to various types of communities. The studies document how nature contributes to human performance and functioning in everyday life, and address some of the most urgent issues of contemporary society, such as education performance, public health costs, therapy for emotional and physical disabilities (such as those experienced by veterans returning from deployment), and mental functioning of the growing elderly population.

While the experience of nature is not a panacea for the ills of society, extensive psychosocial research suggests that natural settings enable a positive response, better functioning, and healing. The Green Cities: Good Health Website (www. green health.washington.edu) is a catalog of research about these social, economic, and cultural benefits, also termed ecosystem services (2013a). More than 2,800 peer-reviewed publications have been collected and sorted into topical themes. This knowledge shows why planning and management of urban forests, and urban greening more generally, are important to improve social capital and provide better human habitat.

BACKGROUND: PSYCHOLOGY OF ECONOMICS, RETAIL, AND NATURE

Shopping behavior is based on complex psychological interactions, and the physical environment can influence consumer motivations. Here are some of the psychological dynamics of consumer purchasing, including the role of physical environments. While city trees and landscapes provide wide-reaching benefits, the following concepts suggest how the experience of nature might contribute to consumer behavior in retail settings.

Psychology of Economics

Exciting new research and theory development has shifted how economists, financial planners,

and retailers think about a person's financial and purchasing actions. New perspectives about people and finances address actual (rather than assumed) behaviors and their psychological basis.

Behavioral Economics

The standard (neoclassical) economic analysis assumes that each person behaves in ways that maximize his or her individual self-interest, and does so by carrying out a fully rational analysis of all available options. This 'rational man' assumption has emphasized efficiencies in economic choices, yet recent research suggests that the premise has many shortfalls that can lead to unrealistic economic analysis and policy-making (Kahneman, 2003). Behavioral economics is a rapidly growing sub-discipline that seeks to increase the explanatory and predictive power of economic theory by providing it with more psychologically plausible foundations (Lambert, 2006). Early behavioral economists tended to emphasize the role of cognitive types of errors (such as framing effects and time discounting) in suboptimal decision-making. Recent research, however, points to the important role of affect in judgment and choice. Beliefs, emotions, and heuristics are at least partly responsible for expressions of human behavior. In addition, humans show enormous sensitivity to social influence, including attention to personal identity, social proof, and social learning. Within the last two decades assumptions about the sources of economic choice have diversified, and theorists are considering a broader potential range of influences on economic behavior.

Neuromarketing

Neuromarketing is the application of neuroscience and brain scanning in the context of economic behavior (Lewis & Bridger, 2005). This new applied field attempts to better understand how economic behavior is expressed within the complex interacting neural systems of the human brain. Brain imaging has been used to evaluate response to video clips and TV advertisements, study decision-making among shoppers, and test the likely impacts of political advertising during elections. Though a relatively new science, neuromarketing research confirms the experimental observations of behavioral economics, showing that decision making can be understood as a process of resolution of different interacting, and often competing, specialized neural systems.

The brain has two key subsystems. The combined limbic and paralimbic system rules the intuitive and affective parts of our psyches and functions unconsciously. The analytic system of the frontal and parietal cortexes controls conscious thinking, such as information processing and future-oriented reasoning. Interaction of the limbic and analytic systems governs human decision-making. People appreciate their cognitive abilities, but the brain has been dependent on instinctual responses for millions of years, thus the most ancient part of our brain known as the R-complex or the reptilian brain, influences much of our behavior. This all suggests that emotions play a significant role in consumer choice mechanisms and at times there may even be disconnect between conscious reasoning and preference expressions (Morin, 2011).

Place and Environmental Psychology

Behavioral economics and neuromarketing acknowledge that economic behavior is supported by a variety of unexpected processes, in addition to rational choice analysis. Humans are remarkably efficient information processors, constantly seeking to make sense of the physical cues around them. Some of the earliest studies in environmental psychology explored how people comprehend place and built settings.

Person/Environment Interactions

Social scientists distinguish the physical-tangible aspects of an environment from interpersonal and sociocultural connections. For instance, some person/environment research is premised on stimulus-response assumptions, that is, immediate reaction to prompts in our surroundings. On the other hand, an interactional perspective (Stokols, 1978) suggests that response to environments arises from a person's myriad assessments of a physical setting. Observers interpret rather literal characteristics of a place to make judgments of function (e.g. school vs. hospital) or wayfinding (i.e. how to efficiently navigate a space). Observers also make connotative or inferential judgments about the quality or character of a place and the people who inhabit it (Nasar, 1998). People cognitively overlay physical form with meanings or representations, integrating mediating information gained from observers' prior experiences, social learning, and attitudes.

Social Psychology

The discipline of social psychology also offers insights for understanding the cognitive processes of place-based consumer response. Social psychology is defined by Brehm et al., (1999) as "the scientific study of how individuals think, feel, and behave in regard to other people and how individuals' thoughts, feelings, and behaviors are affected by other people." Social perceivers assemble various bits of information, and mediated by perceiver dispositions, form impressions of others. Leyens and Fiske, (1994) note that, "people continuously build impression theories and use them in their commerce with other people." Observed traits are the indirect cues used to interpret feelings, personality, character and likely behaviors. Diverse information about a person is integrated to form a coherent impression and guide decisions about how to interact with a person. Rapid cognitive assessment is the basis for inference and evaluation of new acquaintances. Built settings may evoke similar evaluative responses, as suggested by the research presented later in this chapter.

Retail Psychology

Shopping and purchasing involve complex cognitive processes, some of which the consumer is aware of while others are nonconscious (Veryzer, 1999). Brick-and-mortar retailers rely on the tangible, physical setting of their business to attract consumers to their products and services. Stimulus response marketing and retail science studies have mostly focused on store interiors. Might the streetscape and a lush tree canopy generate similar responses?

Atmospherics

Marketing researchers have explored the 'atmospherics' attributes of products and stores and have evaluated their role in consumer behavior. For instance, effects of store elements of music, lighting, color, scent, layout, signage and service staff are complex (Lam, 2001). Store environments can affect shoppers' behaviors through responses of emotion, cognition, and physiological state. Pleasant store settings are significant predictors of willingness to spend time in a store and of intentions to spend more money than originally planned (Donovan et al., 1994). Interior elements contribute to store image; for instance classical music and soft lighting are associated with a high quality image. Evaluations are also influenced by elements that are perceived as cues of level of service, merchandise quality, and general characterization of store types. Actual environmental conditions, such as temperature and noise levels, affect one's sense of comfort and can influence the amount of time spent in a particular environment.

Store Image

Retail cognitions include inferences and impressions of product or store quality that shoppers make upon experiencing store-based cues. A related cognitive dimension is store image, that is, the way in which a store is defined in the shopper's mind, including not only a store's functional qualities but also its aura or psychological attributes. An array of attributes that contribute to store image was identified by Lindquist (1975) and included physical facilities. Store image can influence a buyer's mood, and thus enhance affiliative behaviors within the store; e.g., spending more time and money than planned, and intention to revisit (Smith & Sherman, 1993). Whereas intentional cognitive factors may largely account for store selection and for planned purchases within the store, emotional reaction to the store's environment may influence unplanned purchasing, extra spending, and time spent inside the store.

Nature Psychology

Behavioral economics, supported by neuroscience studies, acknowledges the broader set of potential influences on everyday consumer behavior. Place and retail psychology studies confirm that perceptions about a shopping place (and associated behavior) are informed by physical features and place ambience, such as light, sound, and color. The role of nature in the perceptual mix has rarely been addressed in marketing research, yet studies in environmental psychology and allied disciplines show consistent positive human response to nature, trees, and landscapes.

Landscape Preference

Psychological assessments of urban landscapes indicate that aesthetic response is more than a mere reaction to what is beautiful or pleasant, but is one expression of a complex array of perceptual and cognitive processes (Kaplan & Kaplan, 1989).

Imbedded within visual preferences are reactions to cues that help one to make sense of an environment. Response to visual attributes is rarely neutral; there are often associated judgments and behaviors. Urban scenes containing trees (particularly large ones) are consistently highly preferred (Dilley & Wolf, 2013). Some investigations have assessed response of people to particular trees in close proximity. Others have evaluated the general meaning and values that trees represent for people in urban environments. Generally positive responses to the urban forest are associated with higher property values in those communities with large trees. Also, natural amenities positively influence the publics' perceptions of urban place and function. The general public rates the benefits of urban trees highly (Lohr et al., 2004).

Biophilia

Another recent and emergent theory about human behavior is *biophilia* (Kellert & Wilson, 1993). The term refers to the innate emotional affiliation with natural processes and elements (such as trees and gardens) expressed by the human species. Biophilia is claimed to be the result of human evolution in natural environments, and our dependence on natural systems for food, water, shelter, and other basic needs. Although it is still uncertain as to what extent biophilia is hard-wired, numerous studies across a variety of disciplines (e.g. psychology, sociology, geography, anthropology, public health, epidemiology, and others) point to nature's beneficial effects. Humans respond positively to natural elements within cities in terms of affect, cognition, and physiology (Wolf, 2008a).

RESEARCH: TREES AND RETAIL BEHAVIOR

Urban forest managers and advocates can now reference an abundance of studies that document the environmental services that urban forests provide. Yet business people often don't consider such evidence to be relevant to the bottom line. What can justify investment in tree planting and management in the retail streetscape? Merchants are interested in the potential return from green investment.

The theory and concepts presented in the background section converge on the realization that consumer behavior is an expression of complex psychological interactions – not simply rational analysis – and that outdoor place and nature are probable influences. Premised on these ideas a series of studies explored the psychosocial response of shoppers to outdoor consumer environments (Wolf, 2004a; Wolf, 2005a). Surveys were used to evaluate how business district visitors respond to the presence of quality urban forest canopy.

A set of research questions guided each of the studies. We asked what might be the relationship between urban forest canopy, and:

- Visual quality, or the degree to which people judge a setting as pleasing and desirable;
- Place perceptions, meaning the mental representations or assumptions that one infers from an outdoor setting;
- Patronage behavior, including the stated frequency and duration of shopping actions, such as length of a visit, and;
- Price perceptions, represented by consumers' willingness-to-pay for products and services.

Additional questions explored attitudes about benefits and annoyances that consumers may associate with trees, and how business people may differ from consumers in their preferences and attitudes toward trees. An overview of the results follows, with emphasis on the four core questions.

Methods

Each study involved two sampling approaches. Sampling of retail environments included the "main street" business districts of large (Wolf, 2003a), mid-size (Wolf, 2004b) and small cities (Wolf, 2005b). Districts were selected based on architectural characteristics, status of revitalization programs, and socio-economic status of neighboring residential areas. Respondent sampling across the studies typically included randomly selected nearby visitors from within a buffer distance of the targeted business districts, and included people from multiple U.S. cities. Replicate studies also evaluated commercial areas adjacent to freeway roadsides (Wolf, 2003b; Wolf, 2006) and small malls (Wolf, 2008b; Wolf, 2009a). Local collaborators made it possible for our research teams to sample business districts and associated users throughout the United States; their efforts were greatly appreciated.

Cited articles report the peer-reviewed, primary research and can be accessed for more detailed descriptions of methods. Generally, all surveys started with a preference rating exercise, presenting a set of images that depicted streetscapes with varying forest character, while minimizing the variation of other visual content. Each survey also contained streetscape scenarios "with trees" or "without trees," and questions about a respondent's projected shopping behavior while viewing one of the settings. Measures included rating scales as well as categorical responses. Surveys were randomly distributed among respondents by mail or during sidewalk intercepts. Analysis methods were also similar across each of the surveys. Preference means were calculated for each of the images (up to 35 visual stimuli per study), then image categories were prepared using factor analysis. For each of the scenarios, responses variables sets were first tallied, then combined using data reduction methods such as factor analysis to understand underlying categories. Finally, responses were compared for differences between commercial streetscape settings "with" or "without" trees. When appropriate, comparisons were also made between respondent subgroups, generally based on demographics.

Results and Findings

The results of the research program can help local resource managers and merchants to better understand, and reconcile, the tensions that are often associated with trees in consumer environments. This results summary reports trends and consistencies across the multi-study research program; again, details of findings pertaining to the respective urban retail settings can be found in the prior citations. Figures and tables present examples of findings within single studies, as well as across the different settings. Data analysis generally revealed consistently positive associations between streetscapes having trees, and consumer preferences, perceptions, and behavior.

Visual Quality

Image preference ratings sorted into three to five visual categories per study (each containing at least two images), with mean ratings ranging from 1.65 to 4.00 on rating scales from 1 to 5. Figures 1 and 2 show sample category images and mean preference responses across the studies. Within each study, consumer ratings increased steadily with the presence of trees. Images depicting business district settings having tidy sidewalks and quality buildings, but no trees, were at the low end of the scores. Images having well-tended, large trees received the highest landscape preference ratings, even though plants obscured other visual elements (such as historic buildings and signs).

Place Perceptions

While viewing one retail scenario (randomly presented), each respondent was asked to rate his or her level of agreement with statements about

Figure 1. Image preference categories and mean ratings across multiple studies
Means (standard deviations) for categories from small +, midsize ++, and large cities +++.
Means for a total of 13 categories ranged from 1.65 to 4.00 on a rating scale of 1 to 5 (more information available in Wolf, 2005a).

High	**Medium**	**Low**
Green Streets ++ mean 4.00 (0.60)	Enclosed Sidewalk + mean 3.32 (0.83)	Dominant Buildings ++ mean 1.98 (0.71)
Pocket Parks + mean 3.72 (0.77)	Naturalistic +++ mean 3.17 (1.04)	Sparse Vegetation +++ mean 1.95 (0.61)
Formal Foliage +++ mean 3.70 (0.70)	Buffered Building ++ mean 3.13 (1.00)	No Trees + mean 1.65 (0.72)

the place using Likert scaled variables. Means for categories of items were compared between the forested and 'no tree' conditions (Table 1). Again, trees were associated with higher ratings of 'amenity' and 'visual quality' across the studies. Moving beyond the obvious visual content, the respondents made inferences about the settings. For instance, positive scores for maintenance were given to districts with trees, despite efforts to present the same level of building care and street tidiness in the study images. Respondents also attributed social traits and characteristics to in-store experiences. Judgments of products and merchants were more positive in forested places. This was also the case for inferences about product value,

product quality, and merchant responsiveness. It seems that favorable expectations of shopping experiences are initiated long before a consumer enters the door of a shop.

Patronage Behavior

Study participants stated their patronage behavior with respect to travel to the business district, visitation patterns, and willingness-to-pay for parking while considering the streetscape scenarios. Responses were analyzed to evaluate the relationship between reported intentions and streetscape character. Responses on most patronage variables, across each main street study were found to be

Figure 2. Summary of image preference categories and mean ratings across multiple studies
Source study for category: + small city, ++ midsize city, +++ large city (more information available in Wolf, 2005a).

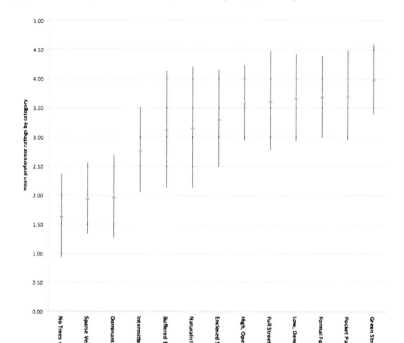

Table 1. Mean ratings for place perceptions categories across multiple study settings

Settings Perception Category	Large Cities*		Small Cities**	
	No Trees	**With Trees**	**No Trees**	**With Trees**
Amenity and Comfort	3.00 (1.28)	5.69 (1.05)	3.8 (1.62)	5.8 (0.91)
Maintenance and Upkeep	4.27 (1.39)	5.94 (0.87)		
Merchant Interaction	4.24 (0.98)	4.90 (0.94)	4.4 (1.14)	4.9 (0.97)
Quality of Products	3.59 (1.07)	5.00 (1.14)		

Likert rating scale: 1=strongly disagree, 4=neutral, and 7=strongly agree. Reported values are mean (standard deviation).
Means were compared on perception categories by urban forest condition within different sized cities.
Statistical significance: *one-way analysis of variance, p<0.000; ** independent samples t-test, p <0.000

significantly higher for "with trees" as compared to "without trees" conditions (Table 2). A distinct pattern of response was evident. Responses for settings "without trees" appeared concentrated at the lower end of each of the patronage variable's values, while streetscapes "with trees" seemed to generate higher value responses. For example, respondents claimed they would travel farther to visit a business district having trees in both large and small cities. This could translate to an expanded trade area radius that adds thousands of people within urban population centers. Once there, survey respondents claimed they would stay longer, which may lead to greater sales revenues (Underhill, 1999).

Table 2. Summary of patronage behavior responses across multiple study settings

Reatail Setting Patronage	Large Cities with Trees	Mid-Sized City with Trees	Small Cities with Trees
Travel Time	*more time		
Travel Distance	*greater distance		*greater distance
Duration of Visit	*more time	^more time	*more time
Frequency of Visits	*more frequent	^more frequent	*more frequent
Parking Fee WTP	*higher fee		*higher fee

Interval or categorical data were collected for each patronage variable.

WTP = willingness to pay, or respondent stated price.

Comparisons are between 'with tree' and 'no tree' district conditions across different city sizes using Pearson's X^2 and Cramer's V tests, statistical significance: $*p<0.000$, $^p<0.001$.

For details see: large cities – Wolf, 2003a; mid-sized city – Wolf, 2004b; small cities – Wolf, 2005b.

Product Pricing

A pricing assessment was done using contingent valuation to understand the impact of streetscape trees on price perceptions. Respondents were presented with a list of goods and services and were asked to state prices for each. The list contained products within different product classes that were supposedly offered for sale in the setting. Table 3 lists respondents' valuations, and demonstrates the positive price effect associated with the presence of trees. There was some variability of price response between different sized cities, yet trees appeared to be consistently associated with higher price points. When standardized across all product categories and scenarios, the amenity margin for the presence of trees was 12% for large cities and 9% for small cities. The variation by city size may have been due to greater public appreciation for trees in big cities, may reflect differences in local economies of big versus small cities, or may be due to the economic downturn in the US that occurred in the period between the two studies.

Demographics Comparisons

Surveys included demographics questions. Survey participants in the large and small city studies were generally slightly older, somewhat more affluent, and less culturally diverse than the general U.S.

Table 3. Summary of patronage behavior responses across multiple study settings

Setting Product Class	Large Cities *		Small Cities **	
	No Trees	With Trees	No Trees	With Trees
Convenience	8.98 (2.74)	13.78 (5.00)	5.93 (3.09)	7.48 (4.54)
Shopping	33.52 (11.49)	47.36 (18.54)	69.42 (42.41)	92.22 (59.76)
Specialty	51.88 (18.30)	73.24 (30.79)	63.96 (26.78)	74.32 (30.70)

Mean (standard deviation) indicate comparisons on product classes by urban forest conditions for large cities (Wolf, 2003a) and small (Wolf, 2005b).

Values are $U.S., and indicate willingness to pay using respondent determined and open-ended pricing scales. Statistical significance: *one-way ANOVA, $p<0.000$; **independent samples t-tests, $p<0.005$.

Product classes (Kinnear et al., 1995):

1. Convenience goods are widely available and purchased with little deliberation,
2. Shopping goods are purchased after planning and comparison and are selectively distributed, and
3. Specialty goods have high brand recognition and consumer loyalty thus little comparison shopping is done before purchase.

populace. Respondents in Athens, the mid-size city, were younger and had reduced household incomes, which is not surprising for a college town. Despite demographic differences among participants, the consistency of responses across all studies was remarkable; green shopping districts were consistently preferred (Wolf, 2007).

DISCUSSION: NATURE, SHOPPING ENVIRONMENTS, AND CONSUMER RESPONSE

A four concept framework guided the trees and retail research program - visual quality, place perceptions, patronage behavior, and price perceptions. The results demonstrate the potential value gained from a green consumer environment. The product pricing responses have been of greatest interest to merchant audiences, but other measures yield insights as to why shoppers may be willing to pay more for products in central business districts that have a quality urban forest. It is important to note that each of the studies asked participants to indicate their responses to entire districts, each having a unified character throughout, and not to individual merchants or shops that may or may not have fronting trees. Investing in district wide urban forestry improvements provide the perceptual richness and sense of place that trees can generate.

Looking across the research results we can infer why the research studies indicated consistent retail behavior responses in business districts across a continent and located in cities of different sizes. First, there is nearly forty years of evidence about the positive responses of people to experiences of nearby nature, that is, the everyday trees, gardens, and green spaces within cities, and one expression of the evidence is a biophilia hypothesis. The emergence of behavioral economics, supported by the objective observational brain imaging of neuromarketing, indicates that individuals' decisions about purchases, personal finance, and investment

are influenced by a broader spectrum of factors than has been acknowledged by the 'rational man' model, with emotion playing a key role.

The premises of person/environment interactions interject the possibility that physical form and the built environment can inform not only cognition, but may also evoke emotion through the symbols or representations of place, or the relative ease or frustration with which a person negotiates a space. Social psychological concepts of "social attribution" and "impression formation" readily translate to consumer/environment interactions. The positive responses to urban forest canopy in business districts is likely due to both the literal presence of trees as nature elements, and the emotional or cognitive sensations associated with movement through a pleasant consumer environment.

While behavioral economics attempts to articulate the underlying dynamics of macroeconomics, it does so by way of the cumulative effects of millions of individuals' decisions. Most of the studies and emerging principles of behavioral economics consider psychological functions of the individual, or social response where one interacts with individuals or small groups. Economic theory has rarely explored the role of one's physical environment in financial decision-making and behavior. Few studies have analyzed the relationships between the attributes of one's surroundings and how one considers, then acts on decision inputs, and how that changes across settings. For instance, might local climate or the conditions of one's neighborhood be associated with financial behavior patterns?

Even fewer studies have explored the interaction of biophilia and commerce (Joye et al., 2010). It appears that trees are a significant atmospheric element of the business street, and are one of the first attributes of a business district that a visitor encounters. External conditions deserve greater attention, as store and shopping center exteriors present initial perceptual cues to consumers. Features such as storefronts, entrances, display windows, building architecture, and parking lot character can create favorable or negative impressions that affect the frequency of return, amount spent during a visit, types of products purchased, and time spent at the shopping venue. These place elements must appeal to the shopper to induce approach behaviors for a retail store or service to be successful (Wolf, 2013b). In turn perceived service quality, emotional satisfaction, and positive image are key drivers of customer loyalty and recommendation (Ladhari, 2011).

RECOMMENDATIONS: TREES AND PLACE DESIGN

Trees and business research included interviews with independent merchants and managers of chain stores. The potential environmental benefits of having trees near their storefronts were of minimal interest to most. Rather, many called out the direct costs of tree planting and management, such as irrigation and pruning, leaf and debris removal, and infrastructure damage such as roots causing cracked sidewalks.

There are best practices and management strategies that alleviate such annoyances, optimize the benefits of city trees, and promote urban forest health. A comprehensive plan provides long-term guidance and continuity of care for trees that can live for decades. Good planning is more likely to support landscaping that can create positive shopper experiences, as a plan helps garner support from community members, boosts fundraising opportunities, and ensures that details are thought through. Following planning and planting, ongoing maintenance will ensure maximum benefit and cost control.

Trees are living resources that change in character and form over many years. This dynamic, living design element offers opportunities, but also can create tensions in the built environment. Here are guidelines for integrating trees into the retail streetscape (Wolf, 2009b).

Creating Place

Each tree species or cultivar has a distinct mature form, size, and other attributes. Plant selections can "brand" a place through subtle, yet observable, distinctions of texture, seasonal color, and plant massing (Figure 3). Within a shopping district diverse tree groupings and arrangement help a person distinguish sub-zones, thereby providing cues for orientation and wayfinding. Working within a selected plant palette, a landscape designer can promote variety within unity, creating a place perceived to be coherent overall and having distinctive features. Conventional planting patterns are one tree per every 30 linear feet (or more) of sidewalk. Variations on this basic pattern make a shopping district more interesting and unique. For instance, double rows of trees can be planted if sidewalks are wide enough. Mixed species provide interesting visual patterns. Understory plantings of flowers and shrubs add color and focal points.

Order and Tidiness

Survey respondents preferred scenes where vegetation is presented in patterns, and where there is order within the street scene. Careful and routine maintenance is also important as tidiness improves preference ratings across all landscapes. Again, there is more to this than meets the eye; during interviews shoppers claimed that the level of care for plants in the sidewalk zone provided cues about the level of care and customer service they might expect from nearby merchants.

Store Visibility and Trees

Merchants often express concerns about trees and visibility of their signs, awnings, and storefronts. Extra attention to design is needed to prevent such conflicts. Certain design principles can alleviate visibility issues. First, tree species choice is important. Trees with a more open and airy canopy, rather than a thick, dense canopy will permit bet-

Figure 3. Retail place-making using trees and accessory vegetation: Chicago, IL; Seattle, WA; Austin, TX (photo credits: Kathleen Wolf)

ter views. Tree species with a mature height that is ultimately higher than sign heights are good choices. There are additional precautions as a tree grows. Ongoing maintenance should include pruning to guide the shape of the tree's canopy and remove any limbs that might be hazards. As the tree grows, the canopy can be "limbed up" to raise branches and foliage above signs and storefronts. The canopy can also be opened up with selective pruning to allow sunlight to filter down to the sidewalk, making the street more pleasant for pedestrians. Tree topping is not the answer as it causes a flush of new branch and leaf growth that becomes a more dense visual obstruction. Repeated shearing of treetops causes poor tree health in the long run.

Signage and storefront design may also reduce visual conflicts. Color and materials choices for signs should contrast with foliage, drawing the eye to visual accents. Monument signage can be used to consolidate multiple scattered signs into a single streetside structure that is readily seen and understood. Perhaps "iconic" signage, using quickly interpreted symbols for goods and services, could be placed, reducing the need for multiple, large, highly individualized signs that take more time for passing motorists to comprehend. Indeed, traffic-calming approaches may

be another solution, as drivers moving through a business district at high speeds may not notice signs no matter how visible.

Create Social Spaces

Shopping is often a social and recreational experience, shared with family or friends. Outdoor seating areas should be given careful thought. Randomly placed benches on the sidewalk may not be comfortable or visually appealing. Benches and custom seating can wrap around a tree pit or planter to give customers a sense of shelter while watching activity on the street. Trees and planters can also be used to perceptually break up a large paved area into a series of "rooms," making the space feel more human in scale and welcoming (Figure 4). Such small spaces offer places of respite for extended district stays, or can be used for outdoor dining.

FUTURE RESEARCH DIRECTIONS

As cities pursue more sustainable practices, there is greater attention to urban forestry, park systems for health, green infrastructure, and other nature-based policies or programs. This book focuses on

Figure 4. Trees and accessory vegetation serve to separate and define subspaces within retail environments: Charlotte, NC; Seattle, WA; Arlington, VA (photo credits: Kathleen Wolf)

one land use and activity within the broader context of cities – retail environments. While taking up far less land than other land uses in the typical city (such as residential or even transportation) the quality and character of a community's retail centers reflect the identity of a place. There are two general domains of research opportunities that have direct consequences for retail settings and urban sustainability.

Trees, Vegetation and Retail Behavior

The results concerning retail perceptions, patronage, and willingness-to-pay are all based on self-report data. These outcomes could be validated in several ways. First, the studies relied on stated pricing and behavior; revealed willingness-to-pay studies rely on the actual price paid for market goods that have a specified level of an environmental attribute. A consumer price index approach that compares prices of a "basket of goods and services" across multiple places having or not having trees would be a more objective assessment of any amenity margin in retail pricing. Also, hedonic pricing could be used to capture value increments by comparing cohorts of districts that are similar, but differ on the character and quality of urban forest conditions. A natural experiment could be conducted in a single business district having trees if they are removed within a short time frame (e.g. following an ice storm or due to insect damage). Another important validation would be

to compare actual on-site visual preference ratings with those expressed for photographic images. The self-report studies were conducted in urban neighborhood and 'main street' business districts; validation of the measures could be extended to other settings, such as malls of various sizes and indoor settings.

From a marketing perspective shoppers are diverse in goal orientation, socio-economic status, and retail product interests. Three general shopping motivations have been differentiated: functional, experiential, and social (Geuens et al., 2001). Individuals may have a prevailing motivational type, yet various shopping trips may be situational and connect to different motivations. An interesting marketing perspective is to empirically test how any specific shopping motivation or type of shopping is supported by streetscape characteristics, particularly tree canopy. Also, are there specific landscape attributes that both support the shopper's intentions, and increase satisfaction with the product or service after the return home?

Urban Forest Health and Sustainability

The studies found that large trees were associated with the highest business district approval ratings, yet the built conditions of retail settings often present challenges that restrict tree growth. Paved areas have elevated ambient temperatures that can stress trees (and humans). Other challenges include limited root and canopy volumes, compacted and low nutrient soils, water stress, and interactions with utilities. Pedestrians and passing vehicles pose daily risks in terms of tree damage and health. Additional research and technology development is needed to generate better knowledge about how to integrate trees into commercial settings, as well as all urban land use zones. While the general concepts of traditional forest management apply to city trees, the needs of particular urban circumstances (such as central business districts) merit dedicated science and best management practices.

Successful urban forest management entails direct costs while benefits are less readily measured, thus a process for benefit/cost analysis is another research opportunity. Forest planting, pruning, and care costs can be easily estimated. Results of the studies presented here could be used to calculate tentative fiscal benefits, and then used to estimate net value of trees in business districts, thereby determining a reasonable investment plan to support trees whose level of benefit increases over decades.

The presence of trees within retail environments suggests several research questions about sustainability, with consequences that extend beyond the immediate district. Merchant or business associations are instrumental in creating high quality green shopping areas, as improvements must be implemented across an entire district or mall. Once active in landscape improvements (and observing likely positive return on investment) might merchant associations be more inclined to commit to other district-wide (or city level) sustainability practices? Also, building owners are increasingly seeking sustainability certifications (such as LEED or SITES). Might forest management be included in their public messaging about green business practices, thus appealing to shoppers of certain demographics? Finally, might high quality, flourishing trees in retail centers provide models of best species choice and best practices that shoppers can transfer to their homes, and perhaps contribute to citywide tree canopy goals with

new plantings? The potential behavior transfer of satisfying retail experiences to more generalized behaviors that contribute to urban sustainability sets up several intriguing research questions.

CONCLUSION

Consumer purchasing represents about two-thirds of the economic activity of the United States, and is a substantial economic influence in most nations. Merchants in urban business districts now face competitive pressure from regional malls, big box retailers and e-tailers. Marketing and consumer outreach serve multiple purposes, first attracting the attention and visitation of shoppers and, once people have arrived, helping to shape the character and quality of the shopping experience. While many conditions contribute to consumer perceptions of attractive, desirable shopping settings, the results of our research program suggests that a quality urban forest helps to define retail place. Many marketing studies have focused on the "micro" level of product packaging and placement, or indoor retail configuration. This study contributes information about the "macro" level of consumer perception, that is the positive influences of the outdoor environment on consumer choice and behavior.

Business people may fail to recognize the value of trees in the streetscape, or may judge costs (e.g., reduced patronage due to sign blockage, sidewalk debris) to be greater than potential economic gains. Yet non-economic factors (such as atmospherics) appear to influence consumer behavior and choice on a subconscious level. Business people, focusing on direct costs, can overlook potential place-marketing benefits of urban nature. Study results suggest that higher price valuations are mediated by psychological inferences of district character and product quality. Thus, creating and stewarding an urban forest canopy may enhance revenues for businesses in retail districts that offer diverse products and services. Consumer purchases provide both compensatory returns for district-wide costs of tree planting and maintenance, as well as revenue enhancement for individual businesses.

A comprehensive measurement approach was used in studies of retail business districts located in diverse city settings to better understand consumer perceptions and behavior in the presence of trees. Statistically significant differences were found on four groups of measures – visual quality, place perceptions, shopper patronage and product pricing – with forested districts having higher ratings and values. It is important to note that the highest ratings were granted to places having full, mature tree canopy, indicating careful maintenance across decades. City trees provide environmental benefits, the usual justification for urban forestry investment, and are an important concern as the public gains greater interest in urban sustainability. These studies demonstrate that trees serve other functions, particularly for retail and commercial interests. Trees and landscapes can be significant elements in place marketing. Economists have noted that shopping was once a utilitarian activity to fulfill needs and wants, but today's shoppers are pursuing places that offer social, memorable experiences. Trees help create place and connect to deeply felt preferences and appreciations that people have for nature. The urban forest can be an important part of the vibrant, satisfying places that shoppers enjoy.

ACKNOWLEDGMENT

Partial support for the research about consumer response to business districts was provided by the USDA Forest Service, Urban and Community Forestry Program, on recommendation of the (U.S.) National Urban and Community Forestry Advisory Council. Additional writing support was provided by the USDA Forest Service, Pacific Northwest Research Station.

REFERENCES

Brehm, S. S., Kassin, S. M., & Fein, S. (1999). *Social psychology*. New York, NY: Houghton Mifflin.

Chen, W. Y., & Jim, C. Y. (2008). Assessment and valuation of the ecosystem services provided by urban forests. In M. M. Carreiro, Y. C. Song, & J. Wu (Eds.), *Ecology, planning, and management of urban forests* (pp. 53–83). New York, NY: Springer. doi:10.1007/978-0-387-71425-7_5

Costanza, R., d'Arge, R., De Groot, R., Farber, S., Grasso, M., & Hannon, B. etal. (1997). The value of the world's ecosystem services and natural capital. *Nature*, *387*(6630), 253–260. doi:10.1038/387253a0

Dilley, J., & Wolf, K. L. (2013). Homeowner interactions with residential trees in urban areas. *Arboriculture and Urban Forestry*, *39*(6), 267–277.

Donovan, R. J., Rossiter, J. R., Marcoolyn, G., & Nesdale, A. (1994). Store atmosphere and purchasing behavior. *Journal of Retailing*, *70*(3), 283–294. doi:10.1016/0022-4359(94)90037-X

Geuens, M., Brengman, M., & S'Jegers, R. (2001). An exploratory study of grocery shopping motivations. In A. Groeppel-Klien, & F.-R. Esch (Eds.), *European advances in consumer research* (vol. 5, pp. 135-140). Provo, UT: Association for Consumer Research.

Joye, Y., Willems, Brengman, & Wolf, K. (2010). The effects of urban retail greenery on consumer experience: Reviewing the evidence from a restorative perspective. *Urban Forestry & Urban Greening*, *9*, 57–64. doi:10.1016/j.ufug.2009.10.001

Kahneman, D. (2003). Maps of bounded rationality: Psychology for behavioral economics. *The American Economic Review*, *93*(5), 1449–1475. doi:10.1257/000282803322655392

Kaplan, R., & Kaplan, S. (1989). *The experience of nature: A psychological perspective.* New York, NY: Cambridge University Press.

Kellert, S. R., & Wilson, E. O. (Eds.). (1993). *The biophilia hypothesis.* Washington, DC: Island Press.

Kinnear, T. C., Bernhardt, K. L., & Krentler, K. A. (1995). *Principles of marketing.* New York, NY: Harper Collins.

Ladhari, R., Souiden, N., & Ladhari, I. (2011). Determinants of loyalty and recommendation: the role of perceived service quality, emotional satisfaction and image. *Journal of Financial Services Marketing, 16*(2), 111–124. doi:10.1057/fsm.2011.10

Lam, S. Y. (2001). The effects of store environment on shopping behaviors: a critical review. *Advances in Consumer Research. Association for Consumer Research (U. S.), 28*, 190–197.

Lambert, C. (2006). The marketplace of perceptions. *Harvard Magazine, 108*(4), 50–60.

Lewis, D., & Bridger, D. (2005). Market researchers make increasing use of brain imaging. *Advances in Clinical Neuroscience & Rehabilitation, 5*(3), 36–37.

Leyens, J. P., & Fiske, S. T. (1994). Impression formation: From recitals to symphonie fantastique. In P. G. Devine, D. L. Hamilton, & T. M. Ostrom (Eds.), *Social cognition: Impact on social psychology.* San Diego, CA: Academic Press.

Lindquist, J. D. (1975). Meaning of image: A survey of empirical and hypothetical evidence. *Journal of Retailing, 50*(4), 29–38.

Lohr, V. I., Pearson-Mims, C. H., Tarnai, J., & Dillman, D. (2004). How urban residents rate and rank the benefits and problems associated with trees in cities. *Journal of Arboriculture, 30*(1), 28–35.

Morin, C. (2011). Neuromarketing: The new science of consumer behavior. *Society, 48*(2), 131–135. doi:10.1007/s12115-010-9408-1

Nasar, J. L. (1998). *The evaluative image of the city.* Thousand Oaks, CA: Sage Publications.

Smith, R. B., & Sherman, E. (1993). Effects of store image and mood on consumer behavior: a theoretical and empirical analysis. In L. McAlister, & M. L. Rothschild (Eds.), *Advances in Consumer Research* (Vol. 20). Provo, UT: Association for Consumer Research.

Stokols, D. (1978). Environmental psychology. *Annual Review of Psychology, 29*, 253–259. doi:10.1146/annurev.ps.29.020178.001345 PMID:341781

Underhill, P. (1999). *Why we buy: the science of shopping.* New York: Simon and Schuster.

Veryzer, R. W. (1999). A nonconscious processing explanation of consumer response to product design. *Psychology and Marketing, 16*(6), 497–522. doi:10.1002/(SICI)1520-6793(199909)16:6<497::AID-MAR4>3.0.CO;2-Z

Wolf, K. (2003a). Public response to the urban forest in inner-city business districts. *Journal of Arboriculture, 29*(3), 117–126.

Wolf, K. L. (2003b). Freeway roadside management: The urban forest beyond the white line. *Journal of Arboriculture, 29*(3), 127–136.

Wolf, K. L. (2004a). Nature in the retail environment: Comparing consumer and business response to urban forest conditions. *Landscape Journal, 23*(1), 40–51. doi:10.3368/lj.23.1.40

Wolf, K. L. (2004b). Trees and business district preferences: A case study of Athens, Georgia, US. *Journal of Arboriculture, 30*(6), 336–346.

Wolf, K. L. (2005a). Business district streetscapes, trees, and consumer response. *Journal of Forestry*, *103*(8), 396–400.

Wolf, K. L. (2005b). Trees in the small city retail business district: Comparing resident and visitor perceptions. *Journal of Forestry*, *103*(8), 390–395.

Wolf, K. L. (2006). Assessing public response to the freeway roadside: Urban forestry and context sensitive solutions. *Transportation Research Record*, *1984*, 102–111. doi:10.3141/1984-12

Wolf, K. L. (2007). The environmental psychology of trees. *International Council of Shopping Centers Research Review*, *14*(3), 39–43.

Wolf, K. L. (2008a). Metro nature: its functions, benefits and values. In E. L. Birch, & S. M. Wachter (Eds.), *Growing greener cities: Urban sustainability in the twenty-first century* (pp. 294–315). Philadelphia, PA: University of Pennsylvania Press.

Wolf, K. L. (2008b). Community context and strip mall retail: Public response to the roadside landscape. *Transportation Research Record*, *2060*, 95–103. doi:10.3141/2060-11

Wolf, K. L. (2009a). Strip malls, city trees, and community values. *Arboriculture & Urban Forestry*, *35*(1), 33–40.

Wolf, K. L. (2009b). Trees mean business: city trees and the retail streetscape. *Main Street News*, *263*, 1–9.

Wolf, K. L. (2012). The changing importance of ecosystem services across the landscape gradient. In D. N. Laband, B. G. Lockaby, & W. C. Zipperer (Eds.), *Urban-rural interfaces: Linking people and nature* (pp. 127–146). Madison, WI: Soil Science Society of America.

Wolf, K. L. (2013a). Why do we need trees? Let's talk about ecosystem services. *Arborist News*, *22*(4), 32–35.

Wolf, K. L. (2013b). The urban forest. *Communities & Banking*, *24*(2), 25–27.

ADDITIONAL READING

Beatley, T. (2010). *Biophilic cities: Integrating nature into urban design and planning*. Washington, D.C.: Island Press.

Bratman, G. N., Hamilton, J. P., & Daily, G. C. (2012). The impacts of nature experience on human cognitive function and mental health. *Annals of the New York Academy of Sciences*, *1249*, 118–136. doi:10.1111/j.1749-6632.2011.06400.x PMID:22320203

Campbell, L., & Wiesen, A. (2009). *Restorative commons: Creating health and well-being through urban landscapes*. Gen. Tech. Rep. NRS-P-39. Newtown Square, PA: USDA Forest Service, Northern Research Station.

Donovan, G. H., & Butry, D. T. (2010). Trees in the city: valuing street trees in Portland, Oregon. *Landscape and Urban Planning*, *94*(2), 77–83. doi:10.1016/j.landurbplan.2009.07.019

Donovan, G. H., & Butry, D. T. (2011). The effect of urban trees on the rental price of single-family homes in Portland, Oregon. *Urban Forestry & Urban Greening*, *10*, 163–168. doi:10.1016/j.ufug.2011.05.007

Donovan, G. H., & Prestemon, J. P. (2012). The effect of trees on crime in Portland, Oregon. *Environment and Behavior*, *44*(1), 3–30. doi:10.1177/0013916510383238

Johnston, M., & Percival, G. (Eds.). (2012). *Trees, people and the built environment: Proceedings of the urban trees research conference 13-14 April 2011*. Edinburgh, Scotland: Forestry Commission.

Kaplan, R., & Kaplan, S. (1989). *The experience of nature: A psychological perspective*. New York, NY: Cambridge University Press.

Kaplan, R., Kaplan, S., & Ryan, R. L. (1998). *With people in mind: Design and management of everyday nature.* Washington, D.C.: Island Press.

Kaplan, S. (1995). The urban forest as a source of psychological well-being. In G. A. Bradley (Ed.), *Urban forest landscapes: Integrating multidisciplinary perspectives* (pp. 17–40). Seattle, WA: University of Washington Press.

Kuo, F. E. (2003). The role of arboriculture in a healthy social ecology. *Journal of Arboriculture, 29*(3), 148–155.

Kuo, F. E., Bacaicoa, M., & Sullivan, W. C. (1998). Transforming inner-city landscapes: Trees, sense of safety, and preference. *Environment and Behavior, 30*(1), 28–59. doi:10.1177/0013916598301002

Kuo, F. E. M. (2010). *Parks and other green environments: Essential components of a healthy human habitat.* Ashburn, VA: National Recreation and Park Association.

Lottrup, L. (2012). *Workplace greenery: Use, preferences, and health benefits of green outdoor environments at workplaces.* Frederiksberg, Denmark: Copenhagen University.

Matsuoka, R. H., & Kaplan, R. (2008). People needs in the urban landscape: Analysis of landscape and urban planning contributions. *Landscape and Urban Planning, 84*(1), 7–19. doi:10.1016/j.landurbplan.2007.09.009

Nilsson, K., Sangster, M., Gallis, C., Hartig, T., de Vries, S., & Seeland, K. (Eds.). (2011). *Forests, trees and human health.* Springer Verlag. doi:10.1007/978-90-481-9806-1

Payton, S., Lindsey, G., Wilson, J., Ottensmann, J. R., & Man, J. (2008). Valuing the benefits of the urban forest: A spatial hedonic approach. *Journal of Environmental Planning and Management, 51*(6), 717–736. doi:10.1080/09640560802423509

Platt, R. H. (2004). Toward ecological cities: Adapting to the 21st century metropolis. *Environment, 46*(5), 10–27. doi:10.1080/00139150409604388

Sander, H., Polasky, S., & Haight, R. G. (2010). The value of urban tree cover: a hedonic property price model in Ramsey and Dakota Counties, Minnesota, USA. *Ecological Economics, 69*(8), 1646–1656. doi:10.1016/j.ecolecon.2010.03.011

Thomas, K., & Geller, L. (Eds.). (2013). *Urban forestry: Toward an ecosystem services research agenda.* Washington, D.C.: The National Academies Press.

Thompson, C., & Aspinall, P. A. (2011). Natural environments and their impact on activity, health, and quality of life. *Applied Psychology: Health and Well-Being, 3*(3), 230–260.

Tsunetsugu, Y., Park, B. J., & Miyazaki, Y. (2010). Trends in research related to shinrin-yoku (taking in the forest atmosphere or forest bathing) in Japan. *Environmental Health and Preventive Medicine, 15*(1), 27–37. doi:10.1007/s12199-009-0091-z PMID:19585091

Tyrväinen, L. (1997). The amenity value of the urban forest: An application of the hedonic pricing method. *Landscape and Urban Planning, 37*(3-4), 211–222. doi:10.1016/S0169-2046(97)80005-9

Tyrväinen, L., & Pauleit, S. etal. (2005). Benefits and uses of urban forests and trees. In C. C. Konijnendijk, K. Nilsson, T. B. Randrup, & J. Schipperijn (Eds.), *Urban forests and trees* (pp. 81–114). Berlin: Springer-Verlag. doi:10.1007/3-540-27684-X_5

Ulrich, R. S. (1986). Human responses to vegetation and landscapes. *Landscape and Urban Planning, 13*, 29–44. doi:10.1016/0169-2046(86)90005-8

Van den Berg, A. E., Hartig, T., & Staats, H. (2007). Preference for nature in urbanized societies: Stress, restoration, and the pursuit of sustainability. *The Journal of Social Issues, 63*(1), 79–96. doi:10.1111/j.1540-4560.2007.00497.x

Wachter, S. M., & Wong, G. (2008). What is a tree worth? Green-city strategies, signaling and housing prices. *Real Estate Economics, 36*(2), 213–239. doi:10.1111/j.1540-6229.2008.00212.x

Wilson, E. O. (1984). *Biophilia: The human bond with other species.* Cambridge, MA: Harvard University Press.

KEY TERMS AND DEFINITIONS

Biophilia: A hypothesis about the innate and durable human attraction to nature due to an evolutionary history of reliance on landscape for basic needs, now expressed as fascination and aesthetic enjoyment when experiencing nature.

Environmental Psychology: A field of research and practical applications, based on contributions of multiple disciplines, concerning the interplay of humans and physical settings, and the mutual benefits that can result. Settings can include natural environments, built places, and any particular places (such as offices or hospitals) where human function is dependent on physical factors.

Green Infrastructure: Using natural systems and their ecological functions to replace, augment, or supplement more traditional gray infrastructure in urban settings, in order to achieve more cost-effective and sustainable management of air and water quality.

Landscape Preference: A field of study spanning nearly 40 years that demonstrates the general and consistent positive response of humans to certain landscape elements and their arrangements, with large trees and park-like settings being particularly favored.

Metro Nature Services: The array of human benefits provided by the experience of nearby nature in cities – including positive cognitive, emotional, and physiological outcomes – demonstrated by nearly 40 years of research and indicating that trees, parks, and gardens in cities serve broader purposes than aesthetics and beautification.

Nature Atmospherics: An understanding of how trees, gardens, and landscapes, as an ambient feature in retail settings, play a role in shopping environment appeal and consumer behavior.

Urban Forestry: The care and management of trees in urbanized environments (including streets, parks, open spaces, and within all public and private land uses) for aesthetic, environmental, economic, and public health functions and benefits.

Chapter 10
The Coffee Shop and Customer Experience:
A Study of the U.S. Market

Patrizia de Luca
University of Trieste, Italy

Giovanna Pegan
University of Trieste, Italy

ABSTRACT

This chapter has the aim to improve understanding of the in-store customer experience in the retail environment by analyzing the business of coffee shops in the United States market with a specific focus on American and Italian chains. After a brief overview of the managerial literature on coffee shops, the main findings of the qualitative research is presented. In particular, this chapter outlines the features of the U.S. coffee shop landscape and explores American consumers' perception of the coffee shop experience using nethnography. The results show a complex framework from the offer and the demand perspective that could also contribute to supporting coffee companies in managing customer experience strategy in the American market.

INTRODUCTION

Coffee companies face a continuously evolving perspective on consumption in which new lifestyle trends create different competitive fields and new key factors. One of the most relevant trends is the growing development of out-of-home consumption; new coffee consumption occasions have emerged outside the home in several developed markets and in emerging markets (Gilmore, 2004; IBISWorld, 2013; OIFB-Osservatorio Internazio-

nale Food Beverage, 2013; Wong, 2010). Further, the cultural hybridization created by opening new market perspectives has helped modify the architecture of the spaces dedicated to clients who are more refined and therefore ask for higher quality. As places, ways, and moments of consumption evolve, bars and similar places become aggregation sites. This suggests new ways of considering outdoor consumption. Today, pleasure and leisure play an important role in consumer culture (Belk, Guliz & Soren, 2003; Hirschman & Holbrook,

DOI: 10.4018/978-1-4666-6074-8.ch010

1982), and often "consumers enjoy leisure away from home and work in 'third places' such as cafés" (Karababa & Ger, 2010, p. 737). In other words, coffee shops have assumed a particular role in affecting sociocultural behavior and the consumption landscape in international markets (Agrawal, 2009; Thompson & Arsel, 2004).

Recently, the managerial literature on coffee and coffee shops has emphasized the importance of deepening the coffee shop experience in different contexts to understand its main drivers in creating a delightful coffee experience (Sathish & Venkatesakumar, 2011; Yu & Fang, 2009). As Pine and Gilmore (1998) emphasized, "consumers unquestionably desire experiences, and more and more businesses are responding by explicitly designing and promoting them" (p. 97). The literature recognizes the key role that a customer experience plays in determining the competitive success of a company in all industries (Carù & Cova, 2003; Hirschman & Holbrook, 1982; Pine & Gilmore, 1999; Resciniti, 2004; Schmitt, 1999; Verhoef et al., 2009). In particular, creating a memorable customer experience is a strategic objective in the retailing business. As several authors have pointed out, to manage the customers' experience, retailers should understand what the experience actually means to them and which marketing tools could be relevant to influence this experience (Grewal, Baker, Levy & Voss, 2003; Naylor, Kleiser, Baker & Yorkston, 2008). According to a recent study:

The customer experience construct is holistic in nature and involves the customer's cognitive, affective, emotional, social and physical responses to the retailer. This experience is created not only by those elements which the retailer can control (e.g., service interface, retail atmosphere, assortment, price), but also by elements that are out of the retailer's control (e.g., influence of others, purpose of shopping) (Verhoef et al., 2009, p. 32).

In this perspective, creating the customer experience could depend on different elements, such as the social environment (i.e., reference group, tribes, service personnel), service interface (i.e., service persons, technology supports), retail atmosphere (i.e., design, scents, temperature, music), assortment (i.e., quality, uniqueness, variety), price (i.e., level, promotions), retail brand, and previous customer experiences in the same or alternative channels. Situation moderators (type of store, location, season, competition) and consumer moderators (task orientation, goals, socio-demographic aspects, attitudes, and so on) could also affect customer experience (Verhoef et al., 2009). Despite acknowledging the customer experience in retail businesses, some studies have highlighted the risk that management techniques may incur when standardized and unnatural products are offered. This could contrast with the original idea that sees, in the "personal" dimension, the customer as an active co-creator of the same experience (Gentile, Spiller & Noci, 2007). In addition, in the managerial coffee shop literature scholars have emphasized the problem of competing brands offering an increasingly similar café experience and the threat of a "me too" perception (Agrawal, 2009). In summary, several authors pointed out the scarcity of research on the customer experience and agreed on the need for more studies on this topic (Gentile et al., 2007; Verhoef et al., 2009).

In this framework, the goal of this chapter is to improve understanding of the in-store customer experience by analyzing the specific retail context of U.S. coffee shops. In the chapter, after a brief overview of the existing managerial literature on coffee shops, the findings of a qualitative study, focused on American and Italian coffee chains, are presented. In particular, this chapter outlines the features of the U.S. coffee shop landscape and American consumers' perception of the coffee shop experience by using nethnography. This study also contributes to supporting coffee companies in managing their customer experience strategy in the American market.

This research focused on such a specific product/market for several reasons. Coffee is one of the most consumed beverages worldwide (Ponte, 2002). Over the past few years, coffee chains have become increasingly popular among customers who enjoy having their coffee away from home. Coffee shops play a relevant role in portraying the new social and cultural geography of coffee in different countries (Brando, 2013; Thompson & Arsel, 2004). Coffee shop chains and independent coffee and snack shops compete with other segments of the hospitality industry such as limited-service restaurants for customers' "eating out budget" (Statista, 2013). The American market represents one of the most important markets for coffee consumption in terms of out-of home consumption: *Specialist coffee shops* chains recorded 5% growth in 2011, the highest segment of cafés/bars (Euromonitor International, 2012). Today, this segment has 42% of the total coffee and snack shops market with US$29 billion in revenue (IBISWorld, 2013; Statista, 2013; Statistic Brain, 2013). In the American market, coffee consumption styles are corrupted by different cultural influences, such as European coffee culture, in particular Italian espresso culture. As several researchers have pointed out, Italian coffee culture in the international consumptionscape is acknowledged all over the world (Bertoldi, Giachino & Marenco, 2012; de Luca & Pegan, 2012; De Toni & Tracogna, 2005), and Italy is considered the *archetype of a coffee consuming nation* (Kjeldegard & Ostberg, 2007, p. 181). Further, "the consumption of Italian-style espresso-based beverages outside the home is widespread, and many of these beverages are drunk in branded coffee shop outlets, based on a format popularized in the United States" (Morris, 2013).

BACKGROUND

Origins and Development of the Coffee Shops

Coffee shops, or coffee houses, are establishments where coffee is the main beverage offered although food and other beverages are also available, especially nonalcoholic beverages, as well as specialty snacks. The products are usually consumed on-site, but they can be purchased to go. Their development potential comes mainly from their ability to assume different meanings according to the different needs of different customers. The coffee shop is first a point of purchase and consumption, but can also be a place to meet friends, read, surf the Net, take a break, and so on (de Luca & Pegan, 2013; Kjeldgaard & Ostberg, 2007). As a public space across various disciplines, the coffee shop has generated much attention in the literature as scholars have reflected on the recent and relevant success of international coffee chains. Thus, the literature on coffee shops across the centuries and their various international contexts is growing. However, not enough studies have examined the different forms in different contexts (for example, the English coffee house, the French café, the Italian coffee bar) and the reason why these forms have succeeded or failed in different eras (Morris, 2012).

Coffee shops were established first in Istanbul in the 16th century and then in Europe, starting in large cities such as London, Vienna, and Paris. In Italy, the espresso bar became the dominant model. Espresso coffee has become synonymous with Italy, as for other beverages that use it as a base, for example, cappuccino and caffè latte (Morris, 2012). For centuries, coffee shops have occupied the center of urban life, fostering a distinctive social as well as consumption culture that has played an important role in the political, financial, scientific, and literary fields, particularly during the 18th century (Calhoun, 2008; Markman, 2006).

The phenomenon of coffee shops spread to northern Europe where Scandinavia has the highest per-capita coffee consumption (Kjeldgaard & Ostberg, 2007). In the United States, coffee shops were established by the initiative of Italian American immigrant communities in major cities such as New York, Boston, and San Francisco, where the shops rapidly spread, particularly on the West Coast by non-Italian entrepreneurs. In 1971, Starbucks was established in Seattle. Starbucks standardized and diffused coffee culture worldwide, especially espresso culture. However, the company's development has slowed in the last few years because of a new counterculture of consumption dominated by an anti-Starbucks discourse (Clark, 2009; Thompson & Arsel, 2004).

Coffee culture has spread to Asia, especially China and India, as part of new lifestyles and shopping trends mostly because of the globalization of large, fast-growing Western chains, such as Café Coffee Day, the leading café chain in India (Agrawal, 2009; Brando, 2013).

Today, there are two main business models for coffee shops. Large standardized chains are widespread on national or global levels with centralized choices at the corporate level and develop through direct investment in proprietary stores and/or through franchising. Independent, locally owned coffee shops often specialize in specific types of coffee (green, fair trade, and *gourmet*) and services. Thanks to differentiation, local coffee shops are able to compete with the largest chains (WiseGeek, 2013).

Different types of coffee shops coexist in markets. They are not easy to distinguish one from the other, because of the natural and mutual influence of different cultural models. For example, in an analysis of the Scandinavian area, Kjeldgaard and Ostberg (2007) highlighted three coffee culture styles in the local market: "Americana," "Culinaria," and "Viennese." "Americana" is strongly influenced by Starbucks' strategic choices. "Culinaria" refers to different kinds of authenticity of the place of origin where the style of Italian bars

and French *brasseries* is predominant. "Viennese" is linked to the style of historic cafés in central Europe that originated in Vienna in the 19th century. Apart from these main models, which over time have been differently characterized in some areas and countries, other coffee shops were created for specific targets and then spread to a wider public. "Internet cafés" and "maid cafés" are examples of this trend. Internet cafés were established to offer Internet and Wi-Fi services to their customers (The Economist, 2003), whereas the maid café is a themed bar established at the beginning of the 21st century in Japan for customers keen on comic strips and animation. Maid cafés then spread to other targets and outside national borders. Other popular café formats are common in different international markets such as the mix offered by Café Coffee Day in India (Agrawal, 2009). "Lounge cafés" combine the style and luxury of a lounge with the lively environment and comfort of a café, "Garden cafés" offer customers the joy of being served pots of coffee in a green landscape. "Music cafés" give customers the choice of playing their favorite songs packs on digital audio jukeboxes or watching their favorite music videos on video jukeboxes. "Book cafés" cater to lovers of reading who have the opportunity to live a complete coffee experience. "Highway cafés" provide travelers a cool and comfortable place to sit and relax with coffee and snacks before hitting the road again.

The Theoretical Framework

New lifestyle and consumption trends can shape different competitive fields and create new key factors in different industries. One of the most relevant trends is the development of out-of-home consumption. In this context, new coffee consumption occasions have emerged outside the home in several developed and emerging markets (Gilmore, 2004; IBISWorld, 2013; OIFB, 2013; Wong, 2010), and the coffee shop has assumed a specific role in affecting the sociocultural and consumption landscape of international markets

(Brando, 2013; Thompson & Arsel, 2004; Wong, 2010).

In recent years, some literature contributions analyzed coffee shops from different managerial points of view (Table 1). Their focus has been analyzing case studies and field research in different countries. The case studies considered leading companies, such as the American Starbucks and the Indian Café Coffee Day, and have usually analyzed them from a managerial perspective. Qualitative and/or quantitative research has been conducted in a small number of countries, such as the United States, Scandinavian countries, India, and Taiwan. In particular, emerging markets have become interesting contexts for research considering their rapid socioeconomic transformations and new trends in consumption culture.

The main managerial studies on coffee shops analyzed consumption culture, globalization vs. glocalization, authenticity, and customer experience. Regarding the first aspect, studies on coffee have dealt with contemporary consumer cultures across the world. The academic discussion in the literature of globalization and "glocalization" has aimed at studying whether consumer cultures are becoming homogenized or whether they are still

Table 1. Recent studies of coffee shops

Authors	Key words	Research Objectives/Main Findings	Research Area/Method	Suggestions for Future Research
Thompson & Arsel (2004)	Hegemonic brandscape, Glocalization, Starbucks, Anti-corporate experiences	They investigate the ways in which global brands structure these expressions of cultural heterogeneity and consumers' corresponding experiences of glocalization. They develop the construct of the hegemonic brandscape, supporting two distinctive forms of local coffee shop experience through which consumers forge aestheticized (café flaneurs) and politicized (oppositional localists) anti-corporate identifications.	United States Qualitative research Interviews coffee shops Hermeneutical approach	Not made explicit
Kjeldgaard & Ostberg (2007)	Scandinavian market, Coffee culture styles, Globalization, Glocalization. Authenticity	Mapping the cultural terrain that structures the possible meanings and practices of coffee cultural consumption: 1. Explore how the hegemonic brandscape may operate in a cultural context outside North America by exploring coffee cultural discourses in the Scandinavian context. 2. Namely, to explore whether there is such a thing as a specific Scandinavian consumer culture that interacts with global structures in the process of glocalization.	Scandinavia (Sweden and Denmark) Qualitative research Primary and secondary data Ethnography Interviews Qualitative data analysis	To explore how the hegemonic brandscape may operate in a cultural context outside North America, in different countries.
Agrawal (2009)	Café chain, Café market in India, Café Coffee Day, Brand positioning, Building distinct brand identity, Specialist coffee chain	The case describes the journey of Café Coffee Day and the beginning of café culture in India. The problem of competing brands offering an increasingly similar café experience and the threat of a "me too" perception are highlighted.	India Case study Qualitative analysis	The problem of competing brands offering an increasingly similar café experience and the threat of a "me too" perception are highlighted.

continued on following page

Table 1. Continued

Authors	Key words	Research Objectives/Main Findings	Research Area/Method	Suggestions for Future Research
Yu & Fang (2009)	Quality, Experience economy, Maslow's theory, One-to-one marketing	Relative impacts of product quality, service quality, and experience quality on customer perceived value and intention to shop in the future, for a coffee shop market. Pine and Gilmore's framework of an experience economy is not always true. The relative importance of product, service, and experience changes over the income levels and the frequency of consumption.	Taiwan Quantitative and qualitative data. Questionnaire 147 Starbucks coffee customers	The qualitative data suggest the analysis of more potential factors determining perceived value, such as price, location, and branding; a closer examination of positive and negative contextual experiences since they are stated by customers as the top liked and disliked items.
Karababa & Ger (2010)	Coffee house, Ottoman society, consumption culture, leisure consumption	This study supports and extends two broader theoretical claims: 1) Consumption resolves the tension between the individual's pursuit of pleasure and morality. 2) Market cultures are co-created through discursive negotiations and practices.	Ottoman coffeehouses. Anthropological-historical approach. Leisure consumption among male consumers	Not made explicit
Sathish & Venkatesakumar (2011)	Customer experience, Satisfaction, Loyalty, Café Coffee Day, India	The study attempts to find the effects of various dimensions influencing the Customer Experience, thus creating a coffee experience and a sense of satisfaction in visiting a Café Coffee Day store. It develops a conceptual framework for managing the customer experience and an instrument for measuring the experience.	India Quantitative research 200 well-structured questionnaires	Further research is needed to explore and deepen the understanding of the nature of drivers and their interdependency, their significance in creating delightful customer experiences of this nature.
Bertoldi, Giachino, & Marenco (2012)	Brand, Coffee market, Cross-cultural studies, Food and drink products, India	The aim is to investigate brand strategies implemented by food and beverage firms going international and to determine how to build the brand strategy for entering emerging markets through acquisitions.	India Case study Lavazza company Qualitative approach	Improvements can be made to the framework by using other case studies.
Seaford, Culp, & Brooks (2012)	Marketing and branding, Brand equity, Brand positioning, Starbucks	The case of Starbucks is designed for students.	United States Case study	Not made explicit

characterized by a high degree of heterogeneity (Kjeldgaard & Ostberg, 2007; Thompson & Arsel, 2004). In the view of the supporters of the homogenization perspective, transnational corporations colonize local cultures through global brands (Falk, 1999; Ritzer, 1998). Contrary to this homogenization thesis are anthropological studies that affirmed consumers often adapt the meanings of global brands to their own purposes and fit the global brands into local cultural and social lifestyle models. According to this approach, the relation between global brands and local cultures produces heterogeneity as global brands take on various localized meanings (Ger & Belk, 1996; Hannerz, 1996).

Generally, these theorists have suggested that local cultures and the forces of globalization are completely interpenetrated. Therefore, the effects of globalization on everyday cultural life are more accurately described as a process of "glocalization" (Robertson, 1995; Wilk, 1995). To theorize these aspects of "glocalization," Thompson and Arsel (2004) developed the concept of the hegemonic brandscape. This is a "cultural system of servicescapes that are linked together and structured by a discursive, symbolic and competitive relationships to a dominant (market-driving) experiential brand" (Thompson & Arsel, 2004, p. 632). In this way, the hegemonic brandscape drives an experience economy market and, by functioning as a cultural model that consumers act, think, and feel through, also shapes consumer lifestyles and identities.

As emphasized in the literature on coffee shops, authenticity is another crucial aspect (Gilmore & Pine, 2007). Grayson and Martinec (2004) and Peirce (1998) distinguished between "indexical and iconic authenticity." The term "authentic" is sometimes used to describe something that is thought not to be a copy or an imitation. An object is deemed authentic when it is believed to be "the original" or "the real thing": In this case, authors use the term "indexical authenticity." Alternatively, in the case of "iconic authenticity," the term "authentic" is sometimes used to refer to something whose physical manifestation is "indexically authentic."[1] Kjeldgaard and Ostberg's (2007) contribution to the coffee shop field is quite interesting. Using this perspective, they analyzed coffee shops in the Scandinavian market. In the case of coffee shops, the term indexical authenticity implies that the retail outlet has a factual and spatiotemporal link with something else. Indexicality thus distinguishes "the real thing" from its copies. The authors suggested, for example, that an Italian-style café can achieve indexical authenticity if the coffee is served by immigrants from Italy or if the coffee beans are an Italian brand. Iconic authenticity, however, refers

to situations in which the physical manifestation resembles something indexically authentic. In their opinion, a Starbuckified coffee shop is perceived as iconically authentic if in the consumer's experience the coffee shop is similar to coffee shops found overseas (Kjeldgaard & Ostberg, 2007, pp. 180–181). In any case, iconic and indexical authenticities are not mutually exclusive, and authenticity is not inherent in an object. Authenticity is better understood as an assessment made by a particular evaluator in a particular context (Grayson & Martinec, 2004). For example, many coffee shops in Stockholm have names such as Sosta, Tintarella di Luna, and Molto. They feature baristas from Italy or at least baristas who are fluent in Italian to reinforce their Italianness. In this way, they emphasized that they "just are" as opposed to other places that are "trying to be." "Hence they are mustering a legitimacy rooted in indexical authenticity. Whether they are successful in this endeavor is an entirely different story" (Kjeldgaard & Ostberg, 2007, p. 182).

Finally, as highlighted by various authors, the role of the customer experience appears particularly relevant for the coffee shop business (Michelli, 2007; Ponte, 2002; Sathish & Venkatesakumar, 2011; Yu & Fang, 2009). During the last few decades, the customer experience has been the focus of many studies in marketing and management (Carù & Cova, 2003; Holbrook & Hirschman, 1982; Pine & Gilmore, 1999; Resciniti, 2004; Schmitt, 1999), and is recognized as a key factor in creating customer value and a fundamental element in the competitive confrontation of any company (Smith & Wheeler, 2002). Different definitions of customer experience have been proposed. Customer experience is the result of a collection of emotions, feelings, and behaviors that arise during the entire decision-making and consumption process through a series of integrated relationships among people, objects, processes, and atmosphere (Pine & Gilmore, 1999). The customer experience is particularly important in the retailing business where the store atmosphere represents a basic multi-sensorial communication vehicle (Andersson & Mossberg, 2004; de Luca, 2000, 2009; de Luca & Vianelli, 2004; Donovan & Rossiter, 1982; Grewal, Baker, Levy & Voss, 2003; Kotler, 1973; Machleit & Eroglu, 2000; Zarantonello, 2009). However, this experience is created not only by the elements the retailer can control, such as the store atmosphere, assortment, price, and service interface, but also by elements that are outside the retailer's control (Verhoef et al., 2009, p. 32). Additional elements, most of all situation moderators (type of store, location, consumption culture, competition, economic climate) and consumer moderators (task orientation, goals, sociodemographic aspects, attitudes), should be considered in the process of creating the customer experience (Verhoef et al., 2009). Studies have also highlighted the risk that management techniques may incur when standardized and unnatural products are offered, which contrasts the original conception that sees the customer as an active co-creator of the same experience (Gentile et al., 2007). To preserve the authentic character of products and services, the offer should be anchored in space and time by linking it with the social or individual values of the historical tradition of a certain territorial panorama. In this regard, some authors have discussed the "Mediterranean" approach (often opposed to the "American" one), which is based on several aspects, such as the strong connection with the history and the traditions of the territory, the association with communities or tribes of consumption where feelings and passions are shared, the celebration of rites regarding the products, the attention to symbolic details, and the need for authenticity (Carù & Cova, 2003; Corciolani, 2010).

From these insights, managerial literature contributions on coffee shops pointed out important critical factors when the coffee shop experience is designed: the problem of competing brands offering an increasingly similar café experience and the threat of a "me too" perception (Agrawal, 2009); the relative importance of products, service, and contextual experience depending on different aspects, such as income levels and the frequency of consumption (Yu & Fang, 2009); the need for a closer examination of positive and negative contextual experiences since they are stated by customers as the top liked and disliked items (Yu & Fang, 2009); and a deeper understanding of the nature of drivers and their interdependency, their significance in creating delightful customer experiences (Sathish & Venkatesakumar, 2011).

RESEARCH ON AMERICAN AND ITALIAN COFFEE SHOPS IN THE U.S. MARKET

Research Objective and Method

The purpose of this research is to improve understanding of the in-store customer experience in the retail environment, by analyzing the business of coffee shops in the U.S. market, with a specific focus on American and Italian chains. In particular, this chapter aims to outline the features of the coffee-shop landscape in the United States and to analyze consumers' perception of the coffee shop experience within relevant online communities of American coffee consumers using netnography. This specific research method was used considering that "as value shifts to experiences, the market is becoming a forum for conversation and interactions between consumers, consumers' communities and firms" (Prahalad & Ramaswamy, 2004). These interactions between customer and firm represent the place of value creation. Informed, active, and networked consumers increasingly co-create this value with companies. This knowledge is relevant to support coffee companies in managing their customer experience strategy in the American market.

This research focused on a specific product/ market for several reasons:

- The recent development of out-of-home consumption and the role played by coffee shops in portraying the new social and cultural geography of coffee in various international markets (Brando, 2013; Statista, 2013; Thompson & Arsel, 2004);
- The role that the American market plays in coffee consumption (Euromonitor International, 2012; Statistic Brain, 2013);
- The particular relevance of Italian coffee culture in the international consumption-scape (Bertoldi et al., 2012; de Luca & Pegan, 2012; De Toni & Tracogna, 2005; Kjeldegard & Ostberg, 2007; Morris, 2012).

Regarding the methodology, a qualitative research was conducted to combine different data sources and analytical methods (Denzin & Lincoln, 1998) to study the coffee shop phenomenon in more depth. The collection and analytical processes integrated secondary and primary data gathered from specialized publications company and branch Web sites, and online communities of American consumers. The research was developed in several phases:

1. Identification and selection of coffee shops in the American market;
2. Identification of Italian coffee shop chains already present in the American market;
3. Arrangement of synthetic sheets with ex ante coding based on the literature of competitive analysis and customer experience;
4. Ex post coding after new relevant information came to light during the qualitative analysis of the data; and
5. Integration of secondary data with a nethnographic[2] research on online communities of American coffee consumers.

Findings and Discussion

The Coffee Shop Landscape in the United States

In recent years, the phenomenon of coffee shops in the United States has gained relevance particularly in metropolitan areas, such as Seattle, New York, San Francisco (Altmann, 2007; E-Imports, 2012; NYCEDC-New York City Economic Development Corporation, 2013). The general field of coffee and snack shops[3] (US$29 billion in the first half of 2013) is divided into different segments of which coffee shops are the most relevant with 42% of the total market. Chains dominate: In more than 21,000 *specialist coffee shops,* 13,000 are *specialist coffee shop chains,* and the remainder (more than 8,000) are *independent specialist coffee shops* (Euromonitor International, 2012; IBISWorld, 2013; SBDC- Small Business Development Center, 2012).

Regarding market concentration, the two leading companies, Starbucks Corporation and Dunkin' Brands Inc., cover more than 60% of the outdoor consumption market with 36.7% and 24.6% of the market, respectively (IBISWorld, 2013). The first four companies reached 64.8%, and there is a considerable gap between the two leaders and the others. Recently, however, specialized chains have gone through a critical period with the shutdown of coffee shops caused by the diffused decrease in earnings and therefore of outdoor consumption. For example, since the beginning of the financial crisis, Starbucks has shut down approximately 1,000 stores in the United States alone. However, this trend has been partially counterbalanced by new openings in emerging markets (Euromonitor International, 2012). The presence of local, smaller, independent coffee shops is growing in importance. The "mom-and-pop coffee shops," "gourmet coffee," and the initiatives linked to the particular phenomenon of "third wave coffee"[4] are usually oriented toward niche products (de Luca

& Pegan, 2012; Gold, 2008). The consumer, who is becoming more sophisticated and careful about personal health and higher quality, is increasingly interested in select and niche offers (*premium coffee, fair trade,* and *organic coffee*) within the entire consumption experience (products, services, and shop environment). This tendency has also been registered by large standardized companies, such as Starbucks and Caribou Coffee. In addition to having expanded their selections, these companies have undertaken initiatives oriented toward projecting coffee shops that, unlike in the traditional systems of product offering, reflect a personalized atmosphere. In these coffee shops, consumers have an experience that is similar to those typically offered by local, independent coffee shops.

In 2012, the volume of coffee sales in the on-trade market demonstrated a development rate of 2% (Euromonitor International, 2013), which was slower than before. On the one hand, in the past, new challenging lifestyles boosted outdoor consumption and thus the development of coffee shops and other channels of trade. On the other hand, the recent economic crisis affected domestic consumption precipitating a move toward savings and an increased concern about the *value for money* in general (IBISWorld, 2013).

The competitive framework was developed through identifying and selecting coffee shops in the United States, considering the relevant chains in the market.[5] The collected data were classified in summary sheets with an ex ante coding process based on the literature in terms of competitive analysis and customer experience. Ex post coding was performed after new relevant information emerged from the qualitative analysis of the data. Some determinant characteristics were considered: country and year of origin, type of growth, number of sale points, presence in foreign markets, assortment, service, atmosphere, local community support, mission, and other distinctive features.

For what concerns the American market of coffee shops, by examining only American chains with more than five sale points (24 chains) and all the Italian chains in the United States (seven chains), 31 coffee shop brands were analyzed (Table 2). The companies began to enter the U.S. market in the 1960s. The growth strategies are based on direct investment and franchising systems; in several cases, the strategies were combined. The two leader companies have more than 10,000 coffee shops (Starbucks and Dunkin' Donuts) and the other four more than 500 (McCafé, The Coffee Bean & Tea Leaf, Caribou Coffee, and Seattle's Best Coffee). These main companies have also an international presence.

The seven Italian companies (Table 2), initially established as coffee roasters, gradually integrated with the development of coffee shop chains. The companies' cities of origins are all located in the central-northern part of Italy. In all the cited cases, the growth strategy is based on franchising. The number of Italian coffee shops in the U.S. market is very small, fewer than 10 in all cases.

Table 2. Main coffee shop chains in the U.S. market (2013)

Country of Origin	Coffee Shop Chains in the United States
United States	Starbucks Corporation, Dunkin' Donuts, Au Bon Pain, Biggby Coffee, Blue Bottle Coffee, Blue State Coffee, Caribou Coffee, The Coffee Bean & Tea Leaf, Coffee Beanery, Crazy Mocha Coffee Company, Dunn Bros Coffee, Gimme! Coffee, Intelligentsia Coffee & Tea, It's A Grind Coffee House, Jittery Joe's, McCafé, Peet's Coffee & Tea, PJ's Coffee of New Orleans, Port City Java, Seattle's Best Coffee, SPoT Coffee, Stumptown Coffee Roasters, Tully's Coffee, Chock Full o'Nuts
Italy	Caffè Vergnano, Espressamente Illy, Espression Lavazza, Lino's Coffee, Mokarabia Coffee Bar, Saquella Espresso Club, Segafredo Zanetti Espresso.

Source: adapted from de Luca and Pegan (2013).

In addition to mapping, analysis of the secondary data, which were collected from different sources (company Web sites, specialized Web sites, and specific publications), yielded key points of the programmed positioning of the players in the United States. The three main models of coffee shops were identified: the "American global model," the "American independent model," and the "Italian model."

The "American global model" consists of big groups with large and widespread market distribution, such as Starbucks and Dunkin' Donuts, or chains inspired by these companies. They are characterized by increased standardization of the demand and an atmosphere with a great assortment of products of quality standards that are often certified. Other service features include high logistics (e.g., open 24 hours) and technology (e.g., payment by mobile phone), a strong bond with the local community (initiatives to support specific projects), and participation in philanthropic initiatives that have social or environmental goals.

The "American independent model" is an expression of the commercial initiatives directed to a niche market that is expanding and usually sustains an anti-corporate counter-consumerism culture (Thompson & Arsel, 2004). This model is characterized by small, independent companies and small chains that cater to specific local consumption cultures. These include "third wave coffee" members such as Intelligentsia, Blue Bottle Coffee, and Stumptown Coffee Roasters.

The "Italian model" is represented by companies that entered the U.S. market with the aim of diffusing an authentic espresso culture by proposing a multi-sensorial experience in terms of product, service, and atmosphere. Their communication is mainly focused on the authenticity of the made-in-Italy brand with the aim of offering coffee customers an experience of the "Italian lifestyle." Italian coffee shop chains want to deliver the uniqueness and exclusivity of Italian style, in terms of not only the high quality of the product but also the in-store environment. Ambient conditions, interior design, and physical and social factors (i.e., friendliness of the baristas) are marketing tools used to create a delightful coffee shop experience for customers. Today, the seven Italian chains present in the U.S. market are characterized by limited distribution coverage.

American Consumers' Perception of the Coffee Shop Experience

To understand the consumer perceptions of the coffee shop experience in the United States, a nethnographic research was conducted (Kozinets, 2002, 2010) in relevant online communities of American coffee consumers. To guarantee the plurality of the opinions expressed, only online communities *created by consumers* with more than 5,000 users were considered (Kozinets, 2002), not those *created for consumers* by the same companies such as Facebook pages or other social networks[6] (Bartoccini & Di Fraia, 2004). The focus was on discussions that have emerged since 2010. Three forums[7] were selected. Discussion posts from 2010 until the beginning of August 2013 were examined. After the first phase of study and comprehension of the language of the different forums, the data collected (fragments of posts or posts in their original language[8]) within the object of the research were organized for data publication and to be a source. The collected data were then analyzed to determine findings that were relevant to the market study. With the analysis of short spontaneous stories in the posts, there has been a will to capture several consumption experiences that people had in coffee shops. The data are not generalized because they are based on the opinions of subjects in a restricted and specific category of American consumers, such as coffee lovers, in some cases *baristas,* who love talking about the beverage and about coffee shops in online communities. The collected data expressed a significant variety of "voices" that are important for better understanding this particular consumption experience and the U.S. coffee shop landscape from a consumer perspective.

In Table 3, a brief overview of the main findings of this nethnographic research is presented. The main concepts that came to light from this qualitative study of the posts and the principal theoretical categories to which the main features of the analyzed concepts can be related are emphasized. The qualitative analysis of the posts showed several determinants of the holistic customer experience (Verhoef et al., 2009). In particular, the coffee shop atmosphere (design, furniture, music), assortment (quality of coffee, variety, uniqueness), service interface (customization), social environment (baristas), coffee culture, and coffee shop models and chains seem to be relevant drivers of the coffee shop experience. Further, posts pointed out the importance of the store environment in influencing the coffee shop customer experience (Donovan & Rossiter, 1982; Naylor et al., 2008).

The online discussions emphasized that the coffee shop is perceived as a leisure place where people can relax and spend time alone or in good company. In other words, the analysis revealed a predisposition for small places that have a high-quality product and service and are relaxing (*my favorite coffee shop is a small, family owned shop where they pay attention to providing good [fresh] coffee and excellent customer service, relaxing atmosphere*). According to these posts, this perception appears very common in the market (*If there were two shops with equally good coffee, and one was owned by a giant corporation...If you don't trust your palate, and you don't really know which is better, I would imagine most people would feel better supporting the smaller shop*).

This conception of the coffee shop experience affects customer expectations of the in-store physical setting. Simple lines, warm colors, and comfortable chairs or couches are preferred to modern and innovative design pieces.

A significant component of the atmosphere is the background music (Millman, 1982) because it affects the mood: Music should be adapted to the daytime (*there are times in the morning that would benefit from a more silent atmosphere … at night you can get a great vibe going playing the right stuff at a good level*). Consumers also indicated that music should not disturb customers (*I don't like a lot of distracting noise, and I'm sure many of the customers feel the same..... Little crowd noise should be low volume music*). Even if the different elements of the store atmosphere (Kotler, 1973) seem to represent a relevant influencer of customer experience for other consumers, the quality of this experience is most of all determined by the product: *The coffee should be what people remember*. The coffee shop customer experience should be designed by focusing on the product, because a coffee shop should always convey a passion for coffee. In this perspective, the quality of the coffee is a determinant to deliver a satisfying experience and is the key to success (*Always remember focus on the coffee and work on improving it every day*).

Further, according to the acknowledgement of the role of the assortment as a determinant of the customer experience (Baker et al., 2002; Huffman & Kahn, 1998; Janakiraman, Meyer & Morales, 2006), several combinations of food and espresso seem to be appreciated (*Biscotti seems to be a favorite and some find a grilled nutella sandwich... Homemade biscuits, muffins*). Someone talks about the importance of adapting to local customer needs as a way of promoting differentiation (*what you offer should be based on local cultural needs...look around at other neighboring shops and try for something different and unique*).

Several consumers emphasized the importance of details in the service, for example, offering coffee in ceramic cups to *bring out the truest flavor of the coffee*. To solve the problem of take-out coffee, which dominates buying practices in the United States and imposes paper cups, new initiatives are emerging (*the trend now is a rebate or incentive for customers when they brought*

Table 3. Main topics from nethnographic analysis

Examples of Meaningful Posts	Main Topics	Category of Topics
"My favorite coffee shop is a small, family owned shop where they pay attention to providing good (fresh) coffee and excellent customer service, relaxing atmosphere" "If there were two shops with equally good coffee, and one was owned by a giant corporation... If you don't trust your palate, and you don't really know which is better, I would imagine most people would feel better supporting the smaller shop" "There are times in the morning that would benefit from a more silent atmosphere ... at night you can get a great vibe going playing the right stuff at a good level"	Relaxing place / Familiar place / Comfortable chairs and couches / Background music / Warm colors	Coffee shop atmosphere
"The coffee should be what people remember" "Always remember focus on the coffee and work on improving it every day" "I've seen some interesting combinations of food and espresso.. Biscotti seems to be a favorite and some find a grilled nutella sandwich right for the occasion" "What you offer should be based on local cultural needs...look around at other neighboring shops and try for something different and unique"	High quality coffee / Freshness and Goodness / Assortment / Adaptation to local needs	Product and assortment
"Making drinks is easy, making every customers feel welcome and appreciated is the real challenge in a café" "It's watching for the customer's mood... Remembering or making the effort to discover their tastes and preferences" "Every customer should be acknowledged when they walk in and made to feel like they are VIP guests"	Customization / Competence / Welcome / Kindness / Cups / Differentiation	Service interface and Social environment
"Third wave roaster cafe: high-end coffees, compete in barista competition, give coffee classes...a deeper way to approach coffee than before"	Third wave coffee	Coffee consumption culture
"I like the Italian style of stand-up bars for a quick espresso" "...I would guess that France, Italy and Spain would be great places to research some ideas..European countries are well known for their exquisite cuisine, fine wines and of course, the best espresso(in the world perhaps?) Not to put us down, but to say that we could certainly take a lesson from places where coffee & cafes are an important part of their culture" "I think what works in the European Cafe will not always work here in America and the reverse probably holds true.".Coffee culture has developed on very different lines in America from Italy"	European/Italian coffee culture / European/Italian versus American coffee style/ culture	
"Sturbucks is one of the biggest paradoxes in coffee.. the problem is the standardization... Sturbucks wants their coffee to taste the same everywhere" "I think Sturbucks has done a great job of getting North Americans to realize there is more to coffee than Dunkin' Donuts, etc. As a result, I think they've been instrumental in creating a market for this third wave of high-quality espresso we're experiencing here now" "Intelligentsia is the really good artisanal third wave espresso...I like Blue Bottle because they are always very engaged with you"	Multinational chains Starbucks model / Small chains / Artisanal coffee / Third wave coffee/ espresso	Coffee shop models and chains
"I've tried Illy USA out a couple of times, you may want to look at them and their customer service is superb! Hope this helps!...There's an Illy in the Hard Rock, and a Lavazza somewhere else on the strip...If there's no third wave places, these may be your best bet"	Italian chains	
"Espressamente Illy at The Palazzo is.....really bad... Lino's is from Italy and is a multinational coffee café, much like an embryonic Starbucks" "I tried Espressamente Illy in the Palazzo. It was ok, but the layout of their store is incredibly annoying..."		

in their own mugs or cups). In any case, as suggested in the literature, the social component and the service interface (Baker et al., 2002; Verhoef et al., 2009) are relevant in affecting purchasing behavior and customer experience. Reception, kindness, and the competence of servers, who are coffee professionals, were expressed as crucial elements of the quality of the delivered service (*every customer should be acknowledged when they walk in and made to feel like they are VIP guests*). A good coffee should always come with good service (*I'd think that the places here that don't do both will eventually fail when people realize they don't need to put up with poor service to get good quality coffee*). One post emphasized that the real competitive challenge is to create a unique service (*Making drinks is easy, making every customers feel welcome and appreciated is the real challenge in a café*). This concept was also confirmed by consumers/professionals who stated that attention to an individual customer is the key factor for successful coffee shops (*It's watching for the customer's mood... Remembering or making the effort to discover their tastes and preferences*).

The new coffee shop trends in the United States are largely inspired by specific coffee consumption cultures and coffee shop models. According to Kjeldgaard and Ostberg (2007), in this study the analysis of the posts pointed out three coffee shop models that affect the customer experience: the American global model of the "Starbuckified" chains, the American independent model of the "third wave coffee," and the Italian model. The phenomenon of "third wave coffee," for example, has modified the perception of coffee from a commodity to an experience (Pine & Gilmore, 1999) just like wine, music, and art. Nevertheless, there is no single definition of the term (*third wave roaster cafe: high-end coffees, compete in barista competition, give coffee classes...a deeper way to approach coffee than before*). However, according to several users, the phenomenon is now diffused (*it is used to distinguish canned*

mass-market coffee from large chain coffee shops and, in turn, the large chain coffee shops from the independent and micro-chain roasters and retailers ... love it or hate it, it's beyond absurdity to think this term invented by elite coffee bars and is used only by a tiny clique). Recognition of the superiority of European and Italian coffee cultures emerged clearly from the posts (*I enjoy the cafes of Italy- the types of pastries and food they offer as well as the quality of the coffee and service. ...I like the Italian style of stand-up bars for a quick espresso....European countries are well known for their exquisite cuisine, fine wines and of course, the best espressos*). The appreciation for Europe's ancient, embedded tradition of espresso coffee should be considered to improve the coffee shop experience in the United States (*we could certainly take lesson from places where coffee & cafes are an important part of their culture. ... I actually love a lot of the design ideas that I see on my trips there*). This leading role is remarkable (*a primary difference between espresso in Italy and espresso in the US is that in Italy you have to work hard to find a bad espresso while in the US you have to work hard to find good espresso*). Some posts expressed the wish that there could be a diffusion of the Italian coffee shop style in the United States for economic purposes as well (*I like the Italian style of stand-up bars for a quick espresso. 90 cents Euro for a shot. Wish more places in the USA were like that*). In some cases, the same consumers are conscious that a consumption culture linked to the country of origin is not always transferable in another market (*I think what works in the European Cafe will not always work here in America and the reverse probably holds true*). This post noted that the *coffee culture has developed on very different lines in America from Italy*. Furthermore, American consumption culture is tied to continuous changes in the market. Regarding the American chains from the discussions in the online communities, a coffee shop landscape emerged that is characterized by the polarization of judgments, more positive toward small chains–particularly "third wave coffee" such as Stumptown Coffee Roasters, Blue Bottle Coffee, and Gimme–more negative about multinational chains such as Starbucks. There is a general appreciation for the first coffee shops that offered their customers an all-around quality coffee experience (*Intelligentsia is the really good artisanal third wave espresso…I like Blue Bottle because they are always very engaged with you*). In opposition, many posts expressed negative opinions about the experience had in big chains such as Starbucks (*everything in wrong…the espresso is awful…the super autos make a flat tasting drink…..Starbucks is to coffee what McDonalds is to casual dining acceptable and readily available but the baseline for quality…I can't even tolerate the smell…all baristas are incompetent…S. is one of the biggest paradoxes in coffee.. the problem is the standardization…S. wants their coffee to taste the same everywhere*). Regarding the Italian coffee brands in the U.S. market,[9] the analysis found a polarization of positive comments and behaviors (*I've tried Illy USA out a couple of times, you may want to look at them and their customer service is superb! Hope this helps!... There's an Illy in the Hard Rock, and a Lavazza somewhere else on the strip…If there's no third wave places, these may be your best bet*). In other cases, the judgment was not favorable, indicating the risk that dissatisfaction can create a chain of negative comments, especially if the source is a specialist consumer as well as an opinion leader (*Espressamente Illy at The Palazzo is…..really bad… Lino's is from Italy and is a multinational coffee café, much like an embryonic Starbucks (in more ways than one). […] The cup had no nose and thin cream. The taste was nutty, then bitter, then chocolate. The strength of the flavors was thin, suggesting stale*). Even if the quality of the made-in-Italy product is recognized, other elements such as the atmosphere of the specific Italian coffee shop or the service, cannot always meet the target (*I tried Espressamente Illy in the Palazzo. It was ok, but the layout of their store*

is incredibly annoying…The barista attempted a latte art pour but it didn't work out. Couldn't do it under the pressure).

From the brief discussion by consumers, a problem emerges, especially for Italian chains, in the relation between projected and perceived experience (as are sum of the experiential dimensions of the product, service, and atmosphere) that can lead to an unclear competitive positioning (Kotler, 1973; Grewal et al., 2003). In particular, if from the offer side–as previously highlighted–the communication focusing on emphasizing the value of an authentic espresso culture by proposing a multi-sensorial experience, from the consumer perspective the perceived experience sometimes can be badly influenced by managing choices that are incoherent with the programmed positioning.

CONCLUSION

The findings of our qualitative research on American and Italian chains in the United States have highlighted a complex framework from an offer and demand point of view. Thus, we point out observations from a theoretical and managerial perspective.

From a theoretical point of view, the collected data expressed a significant variety of "voices" that led to better understanding of the main drivers of the customer experience in a particular retail environment, such as coffee shops, underlying its holistic nature. In particular, our first findings support the importance of focusing not only on the factors that retailers can control but also on moderators' factors that are out of their control. Regarding the first type of factors (which can be controlled by the retailers), our results emphasized the role of the product, the service, and the store environment in influencing the coffee shopper experience. Further, several moderators factors were revealed, for example, the type of store, the coffee culture consumption, the competitive scenario. First, the quality of the product, especially its goodness and freshness, represents a fundamental driver of a memorable coffee shop experience for the customer. However, different store dimensions, such as ambience, design, and social environment (Baker, 1987; Bitner, 1992) are perceived to be relevant by the U.S. online consumer communities in affecting their experience. In particular, consumers emphasized furniture, interior design, and music as background characteristics influencing their mood and the experience they had in a specific coffee shop. According to Baker (1987), in the posts analyzed, consumers emphasized the relevance of the social component of the store environment, interpreted most of all as the competence and kindness of baristas. A customized service is considered a key factor when delivering a rewarding experience to customers. Further, according to Kotler (1973), the in-store atmosphere becomes a more relevant marketing tool as the number of competitive outlets increase (as in the U.S. coffee shops markets), when the difference of the product and its price is low, when the products are intended for specific lifestyle groups, such as highly involved coffee lovers in online communities.

From a managerial perspective, coffee manufacturers and coffee retailers should have to deeply understand what their customers need and desire in order to design an effective in-store atmosphere and customer experience (Gentile et al., 2007; Kotler, 1973; Yu & Fang, 2009). Further, they should consider that this experience is variable because it can be affected by the frequency of consumption of the product, the context, and the target. This knowledge of the market could be an essential tool for improving the positioning of coffee brands in the U.S. market. Referring to the specific case of Italian coffee shop chains, the U.S. market could present some threats. First, the economic crisis has reduced purchasing power and increased concern about value for money, which is affecting the out-of-home consumption. Further, other threats emerge from the "American global

model," that dominates the market and influences consumption culture. However, opportunities for Italian companies could come from the new trends of the "third wave coffee" and the "American independent model." Indeed the growing customer interest in high-quality coffee, craftsmanship, and desire for authenticity of the coffee shop could increase the value of the made-in-Italy brand and of the Italian lifestyle experience. These findings improve the knowledge of the way in which Italian coffee companies (often divided between the standardized offer and the promise of authenticity) could successfully face competition in foreign markets. According to the authenticity approach in the marketing and management literature (Beverland, 2006; Carù & Cova, 2003; Gilmore & Pine, 2007), Italian companies should reinforce their strengths focusing on well-established traditions in coffee products and atmosphere. Indeed, the creation of a successful consumption experience needs to ground a specific offer in space and time, reflecting an authentic atmosphere through active co-creation with the customer. However, a problem could arise because of competing brands offering an increasingly similar café experience and the threat of a "me too" perception (Agrawal, 2009). In these consumption experiences, companies should also pay attention to the social dimension of the atmosphere (relationships among customers and among customers and salespersons) in coffee shops. Italian coffee companies should also overcome weaknesses by keeping their promise of authenticity (i.e., authentic Italian espresso) and coherence in all the different sides of their offer. In this way, the gap between the quality of the product and the quality of service sometimes perceived by American consumers should be reduced. Even in the U.S. market, which Italian companies entered several years ago, the positive Italian espresso image cannot be taken for granted. The made-in-Italy brand requires constant and accurate monitoring of the market (Bertoli & Resciniti, 2012; de Luca, Vianelli, & Marzano, 2013; Vianelli, de Luca, &

Pegan, 2012). Focusing on the product alone is not sufficient. Competitive success could come, above all, from knowledge of the market and from the ability to build a long-term relationship with customers in international markets.

FUTURE RESEARCH DIRECTIONS

This study highlights several aspects that should be addressed in future research. First, the perception of American consumers could be investigated in depth through different qualitative research methods, not only through online consumer communities. For example, focus groups or in-depth face-to-face interviews could produce deeper understanding of the coffee shop customer experience, its drivers, and their interdependency. With the aim of improving the analysis of the customer perception, quantitative research could also be developed in the U.S. market. In order to enhance the analysis of the coffee shop industry in the offer perspective, in-depth interviews with coffee companies and case studies could be conducted. In particular, focusing on Italian coffee brands, there is a need for a closer examination of the marketing tools the brands used to keep their promise of authenticity (i.e., authentic Italian espresso) and coherence in all aspects of their offer strategy (i.e., store atmosphere) in the U.S. market. Further, it would be useful to extend the research to other relevant markets for made-in-Italy brands, such as emerging ones.

ACKNOWLEDGMENT

This research project has been supported by the University of Trieste (Italy) under the PRIN (Progetti di Ricerca di Interesse Nazionale) Programme 2009 sponsored by Ministry of Education, Universities and Research (Italy).

REFERENCES

Agrawal, R. (2009). Threat of a me too perception: a case of Café Coffee Day. *The Marketing Review*, *9*(3), 251–271. doi:10.1362/146934709X467811

Altmann, M. (2007). *Coffee Shop Industry – A Strategic Analysis. Scholarly Research Paper Katz-Graduate School of Business Pittsburgh/ USA Doc. N. V111348*. Retrieved August 19, 2013, from http://www.grin.com

Andersson, T. D., & Mossberg, L. (2004). The dining experience: do restaurants satisfy customer needs? *Food Service Technology*, *4*(4), 171–177. doi:10.1111/j.1471-5740.2004.00105.x

Baker, J. (1987). The Role of the Environment in the Marketing Service: The Consumer Perspective. In J. A. Czepiel, C. A. Congram, & J. Shanahan (Eds.), *The Services Challenge: Integrating for Competitive Advantage* (pp. 79–84). Chicago: American Marketing Association.

Baker, J., Parasuraman, A., Grewal, D., & Voss, G. (2002). The influence of multiple store environment cues on perceived merchandise value and patronage intentions. *Journal of Marketing*, *66*, 120–141. doi:10.1509/jmkg.66.2.120.18470

Bartoccini, E., & Di Fraia, G. (2004). Le comunità virtuali come ambienti. In e-Research: Internet per la ricerca sociale e di mercato. Roma: Laterza.

Beckmann, S. C., & Roy Langer, C. (2005). *Netnography: Rich insights from online research*. Retrieved August 20, 2013, from http://frontpage.cbs.dk/insights/pdf/670005_beckmann_langer_full_version.pdf

Belk, R. W., Guliz, G., & Soren, A. (2003). The Fire of Desire: A Multisited Inquiry into Consumer Passion. *The Journal of Consumer Research*, *30*, 326–352. doi:10.1086/378613

Bertoldi, G., Giachino, C., & Marenco, S. (2012). Bringing gourmet coffee to India: lessons of an Italian firm in an emerging market. *Business Strategy Review*, *33*, 32–43. doi:10.1108/02756661211282777

Bertoli, G., & Resciniti, R. (Eds.). (2012). *International Marketing and the Country of Origin Effect*. Cheltenham, UK: Edward Elgar.

Beverland, M. B. (2006). The real thing: branding authenticity in the luxury wine trade. *Journal of Business Research*, *59*(2), 251–258. doi:10.1016/j.jbusres.2005.04.007

Bitner, M. J. (1992). Servicescapes: The Impact of Physical Surroundings on Customers and Employees. *Journal of Marketing*, *56*(2), 57–71. doi:10.2307/1252042

Brando, C. H. J. (2013). Trends in new coffee consuming markets – Out of Home consumption. *P&A International Marketing*. Retrieved April 20, 2013, from http://www.ico.org/event_pdfs/seminar-consumption/peamarketing-e.pdf

Business Monitor International (BMI). (2013). *United States Food & Drink Report 2013*. BMI.

Calhoun, B. (2008). Shaping the Public Sphere: English Coffeehouses and French Salons and the Age of the Enlightenment. *Colgate Academic Review*, *3*, 74–99.

Carù, A., & Cova, B. (2003). Revisiting Consumption Experience: A More Humble but Complete View of the Concept. *Marketing Theory*, *3*(2). doi:10.1177/14705931030032004

Clark, T. (2009). *Starbucks: Il buono e il cattivo del caffè*. Milano: Egea.

Corciolani, M. (2010). *La ricerca di autenticità nei processi di consumo*. Pisa: Edizioni PLUS.

de Luca, P. (2000). Gli effetti dell'atmosfera del punto vendita sul comportamento d'acquisto del consumatore: verifica empirica di un modello di psicologia ambientale. *Industria & Distribuzione*, *2*, 11–22.

de Luca, P. (2009). Atmosfera del punto vendita ed esperienza di shopping nel commercio al dettaglio. In S. Sciarelli & R. Vona (Eds.), Management della distribuzione commerciale: Elementi di economia e gestione delle imprese commerciali. Milano: McGraw-Hill.

de Luca, P., & Pegan, G. (2012). *La percezione del Made in Italy sui mercati internazionali: primi risultati di una ricerca netnografica sulle comunità online di consumatori di caffè*. Paper presented at IX Convegno Annuale della SIM - Società Italiana di Marketing. Benevento, Italy.

de Luca, P., & Pegan, G. (2013). *I coffee shop italiani nel quadro competitivo internazionale: una ricerca qualitativa sul mercato USA*. Paper presented at X° Convegno Annuale della SIM - Società Italiana di Marketing. Milano, Italy.

de Luca, P., & Vianelli, D. (2004). Coinvolgimento del consumatore e valutazione dell'atmosfera del punto vendita. *Micro&Macro Marketing*, *3*, 581–594.

de Luca, P., Vianelli, D., & Marzano, F. C. (2013). Entry Strategies and Distribution Channels of Italian SMEs in the Chinese Market. In B. Christiansen., E. Turkina & N.Williams N. (Eds.), Cultural and Technological Influences on Global Business. Hershey, PA: IGI Global.

De Toni, A. F., & Tracogna, A. (2005). *L'industria del caffè: Analisi di settore, casi di eccellenza e sistemi territoriali: Il caso Trieste*. Milano: Il Sole 24 Ore.

Denzin, N. K., & Lincoln, Y. S. (1998). *Collecting and interpreting qualitative materials*. Thousand Oaks, CA: Sage Publications.

Donovan, R. J., & Rossiter, J. R. (1982). Store Atmosphere: An Environmental Psychology Approach. *Journal of Retailing*, *58*, 34–57.

Douglas, M., & Isherwood, B. (1984). *Il mondo delle cose. Oggetti, valori, consumo*. Bologna: Il Mulino.

E-Imports. (2012). *Coffee Statistics*. Retrieved May 5, 2013, from http://www.e-importz.com/Support/specialty_coffee.htm

Economist. (2003). *Coffee Houses: The Internet in a cup*. Retrieved August 19, 2013, from http://www.economist.com/node/2281736/print

Euromonitor International. (2012). *Cafés/Bars in the US*. Author.

Euromonitor International. (2013). *Coffee in the US*. Retrieved August 8, 2013, from http://www.euromonitor.com/coffee-in-the-us/report

Falk, R. (1999). *Predatory Globalization: Critique*. Cambridge, MA: Polity Press.

Gentile, C., Spiller, N., & Noci, G. (2007). How to Sustain the Customer Experience: An Overview of Experience Components that Co-create Value With the Customer. *European Management Journal*, *25*(5), 395–410. doi:10.1016/j.emj.2007.08.005

Ger, G., & Belk, R. W. (1996). Cross-cultural Differences in Materialism. *Journal of Economic Psychology*, *17*(1), 55–77. doi:10.1016/0167-4870(95)00035-6

Gilmore, J. (2004). *Quantitative Trends in the North American Coffee Market 2004, Datamonitor Inc*. Paper presented at the 93rd National Coffee Association Conference. Dana Point, CA.

Gilmore, J. H., & Pine, B. J. II. (2007). *Authenticity: What consumers really want*. Boston: Harvard Business School Press.

Gold, J. (2008, March 12). La Mill: The Latest Buzz. *LA Weekly*.

Grayson, K., & Martinec, R. (2004). Consumer Perceptions of Iconicity and Indexicality and Their Influence on Assessments of Authentic Market Offerings. *The Journal of Consumer Research*, *31*(2), 296–312. doi:10.1086/422109

Grewal, D., Baker, J., Levy, M., & Voss, G. B. (2003). The effects of wait expectations and store atmosphere evaluations on patronage intentions in service-intensive retail stores. *Journal of Retailing*, *79*, 259–268. doi:10.1016/j.jretai.2003.09.006

Hannerz, U. (1996). *Transnational Connections*. New York: Routledge.

Hirschman, E. C., & Holbrook, M. B. (1982). Hedonic Consumption: Emerging Concepts, Methods and Propositions. *Journal of Marketing*, *46*, 92–101. doi:10.2307/1251707

Huffman, C., & Kahn, B. E. (1998). Variety for Sale: Mass Customization of Mass Confusion. *Journal of Retailing*, *74*(4), 491–513. doi:10.1016/S0022-4359(99)80105-5

IBISWorld. (2013). Coffee & Snack Shops in the US. *IBISWorld Industry Report 72221b*. Retrieved August 20, 2013, from www.ibisworld.com

Janakiraman, N., Meyer, R. J., & Morales, A. C. (2006). Spillover Effects: How Consumers Respond to Unaspected Changes in Price and Quality. *The Journal of Consumer Research*, *33*, 361–369. doi:10.1086/508440

Karababa, E., & Ger, G. (2010). Early Modern Ottoman Coffeehouse Culture and the Formation of the Consumer Subject. *The Journal of Consumer Research*, *37*, 737–760. doi:10.1086/656422

Kjeldegard, D., & Ostberg, J. (2007). Coffee Grounds and the Global Cup: Glocal Consumer Culture in Scandinavia. *Consumption. Markets and Culture*, *10*(2), 175–187. doi:10.1080/10253860701256281

Kotler, P. (1973). Atmospherics as a marketing tool. *Journal of Retailing*, *49*, 48–64.

Kozinets, R. (2002, February). The field behind the screen: Using netnography for marketing research in online communities. *JMR, Journal of Marketing Research*, 61–72. doi:10.1509/jmkr.39.1.61.18935

Kozinets, R. (2010). *Netnography: Doing ethnographic research online.* Thousand Oaks, CA: Sage Publications.

Lévi-Strauss, C. (1992). *Antropologia strutturale.* Milano: Mondadori.

Machleit, K. A., Eroglu, S., & Powell Mantel, S. (2000). Perceived Retail Crowding and Shopping Satisfaction: What Modifies This Relationship? *Journal of Consumer Psychology, 9,* 29–42. doi:10.1207/s15327663jcp0901_3

Markman, E. (2006). *The Coffee House: A Cultural History.* London: Weidenfeld and Nicolson.

Michelli, J. (2007). *The Starbucks Experience: 5 Principles for Turning Ordinary Into Extraordinary.* New York: McGraw Hill.

Millman, R. E. (1982). Using background music to affect the behavior of supermarkets shoppers. *Journal of Marketing, 46,* 86–91. doi:10.2307/1251706

Morris, J. (2012). *Coffee House Formats Compared.* Paper presented at the CHORD Conference Retailing and Distribution History. Wolverhampton, UK.

Morris, J. (2013). Why Espresso? Explaining changes in European coffee preferences from a production of culture perspective. *European Review of History: Revue europeenne d'histoire, 20*(5), 881-901.

Naylor, G., Kleiser, S. B., Baker, J., & Yorkston, E. (2008). Using Transformational Appeals to Enhance the Retail Experience. *Journal of Retailing, 84*(1), 49–57. doi:10.1016/j.jretai.2008.01.001

NYCEDC-New York City Economic Department Corporation. (2013). *Coffee and tea in New York City.* Retrieved May 30, 2013, from http://www.nycedc.com/blog-entry/coffee-and-tea-new-york-city

OIFB-Osservatorio Internazionale Food Beverage. (2013). *Globalizzazione dei consumi.* Retrieved May 10, 2013, from http://www.oifb.com/index.php?option=com_content&view=article&id=109

Pegan, G., & Vianelli, D. (2013). *Il ruolo degli importatori nella valorizzazione del country of origin: un'indagine qualitativa sul vino italiano nel mercato statunitense.* Paper presented at X° Convegno Annuale della Società Italiana di Marketing Smart-Life: Dall'innovazione tecnologica al mercato. Milan, Italy.

Peirce, C. S. (1998). *Collected Papers of Charles Sanders Peirce.* Bristol, UK: Thoemmes.

Pine, J. B. II, & Gilmore, J. H. (1998, July-August). Welcome to the Experience Economy. *Harvard Business Review,* 97–105. PMID:10181589

Pine, J. B. II, & Gilmore, J. H. (1999). *The Experience Economy.* Boston: Harvard Business School Press.

Ponte, S. (2002). The 'Latte Revolution'? Regulation, Markets and Consumption in the Global Coffee Chain. *World Development, 30*(7), 1099–1122. doi:10.1016/S0305-750X(02)00032-3

Prahalad, C. K., & Ramaswamy, V. (2004). Co-creation experiences: The next practice in value creation. *Journal of Interactive Marketing, 18*(3), 5–14. doi:10.1002/dir.20015

Resciniti, R. (2004). *Il marketing orientato all'esperienza: L'intrattenimento nella relazione con il consumatore.* Napoli: Edizioni Scientifiche Italiane.

Ritzer, G. (1998). *The McDonaldization Thesis.* London: Sage.

Robertson, R. (1995). Glocalization: Time-Space and Homogeneity-Heterogeneity. In M. Featherstone, S. Lash, & R. Robertson (Eds.), *Global Modernities* (pp. 25–44). London: Sage. doi:10.4135/9781446250563.n2

Sathish, A. S., & Venkatesakumar, R. (2011). Coffee Experience and Drivers of Satisfaction, Loyalty in a Coffee outlet – With specially reference to Café Coffee Day. *Journal of Contemporary Management Research, 5*(2), 1–13.

SBDCN-Small Business Development Center Network. (2012). *Coffee Shop Business Overview & Trends 2012.* Retrieved May 10, 2013, from http://www.sbdcnet.org/small-business-research-reports/coffee-shop-2012

Schmitt, B. H. (1999). *Experiential Marketing.* New York: The Free Press.

Seaford, B. C., Culp, R. C., & Brooks, B. W. (2012). Starbucks: Maintaining A Clear Position. *Journal of the International Academy for Case Studies, 18*(3), 39–57.

Smith, S., & Wheeler, J. (2002). *Managing the Customer Experience: Turning Customers into Advocates.* Harlow, UK: Prentice Hall.

Statista. (2013). *Market share of the leading coffee chains in the United States in 2011.* Retrieved May 9, 2013, from http://www.statista.com/statistics/250166/market-share-of-major-us-coffee-shops

Statistic Brain. (2013). *Coffee Drinking Statistics.* Retrieved May 11, 2013, from http://www.statisticbrain.com/coffee-drinking-statistics

Thompson, C. J., & Arsel, Z. (2004). The Starbucks Brandscape and Consumers' (Anti-Corporate) Experiences of Glocalization. *The Journal of Consumer Research, 31,* 631–643. doi:10.1086/425098

Verhoef, P. C., Lemon, K. N., Parasuraman, A., Roggeveen, A., Tsiros, M., & Schlesinger, L. A. (2009). Customer Experience Creation: Determinants, Dynamics and Management. *Journal of Retailing, 85*(1), 31–41. doi:10.1016/j.jretai.2008.11.001

Vianelli, D., de Luca, P., & Pegan, G. (2012). *Modalità d'entrata e scelte distributive del made in Italy in Cina.* Milano: Franco Angeli.

Wilk, R. (1995). Learning to Be Local in Belize: Global Systems of Common Difference. In D. Miller (Ed.), *Worlds Apart: Modernity Through the Prism of the Local* (pp. 110–131). London: Routledge.

WiseGeek. (2013). *What is a coffee shop.* Retrieved August 19, 2013, from http://www.wisegeek.org/what-is-a-coffee-shop.htm

Wong, J. (2010). *Aussie café culture accounts for 'biggest growth in coffee AFN March 4.* Retrieved August 25, 2013, from http://www.ausfoodnews.com.au/2010/03/04/aussie-cafe-culture-accounts-for-biggest-growth-in-coffee.html

Yu, H., & Fang, W. (2009). Relative impact from products quality, service quality, and experience quality on customer perceived value and intention to shop for the coffee shop market. *Total Quality Management, 20*(11), 1273–1285. doi:10.1080/14783360802351587

Zarantonello, L. (2009). Gli spazi di consumo temporanei: un'analisi esplorativa attraverso cinque casi di studio. *Micro & Macro Marketing, 18*(1), 19–40.

ADDITIONAL READING

Alon, I., Jaffe, E., & Vianelli, D. (2013). *Global Marketing: Contemporay Theory, Practice, and Cases.* New York: McGraw-Hill Higher Education.

Arnould, E. J., & Thompson, C. J. (2005). Consumer culture theory (CCT), Twenty years of research. *The Journal of Consumer Research, 31*(4), 868–883. doi:10.1086/426626

Bador, O., Bucci, A., & Cova, B. (1993). Societing: Managerial response to European aestheticization. *European Management Journal*, Special Issue EAP 20th Anniversary, 48-55.

Badot, O., & Cova, B. (2008). The Myopia of New Marketing Panaceas: The case for Rebuilding our Discipline. *Journal of Marketing Management*, 24(1/2), 205–219. doi:10.1362/026725708X274000

Bauman, Z. (1998). *Globalization: The human consequences*. New York: Columbia University Press.

Beverland, M. B. (2009). *Building brand authenticity: 7 habits of iconic brands*. Basingstoke: Palgrave MacMIllan.

Carù, A., & Cova, B. (2007). *Consuming experience*. Oxon: Routledge.

Christiansen, B., Turkina, E., & Williams, N. (Ed.) (2013). Cultural and Technological Influences on Global Business. Hershey, US: Business Science Reference (IGI Global).

Dalli, D., Romani, S., & Gistri, G. (2006). Brand Dislike: Representing the Negative Side of Consumer Preferences. *Advances in Consumer Research. Association for Consumer Research (U. S.)*, 33, 87–95.

de Mooij, M. (2011). *Consumer Behavior and Culture: Consequences for Global Marketing and Advertising*. Thousand Oaks, US: Sage.

Di Fraia, G. (2004). e-Research. Internet per la ricerca sociale e di mercato. Roma: Laterza.

Goulding, C. (2005). Grounded theory, ethnography and phenomenology. A comparative analysis of three qualitative strategies for marketing research. *European Journal of Marketing*, 39(3/4), 294–308. doi:10.1108/03090560510581782

Healy, M., Beverland, M., Oppewal, H., & Sands, S. (2007). Understanding Retail Experiences - The case for Ethnography. *International Journal of Market Research*, 49(6), 751–779.

Huffman, C., Ratneshwar, S., & Mick, D. G. (2000). *The why of consumption: Contemporary perspective on consumer motives*. New York: Routledge.

Kozinets, R. V. (2002). Can Consumers Escape the Market? Emancipatory Illuminations from Burning Man. *The Journal of Consumer Research*, 29.

Levy, M., & Weitz, B. A. (2006). *Retail Management*. New York: McGraw-Hill College.

Lonsway, B. (2009). *Making Leisure Work: Architecture and the Experience Economy*. Oxford: Routledge Press.

Muradian, R., & Pelupessy, W. (2005). Governing the coffee chain: The role of voluntary regulatory Systems. *World Development*, 33(12), 2029–2044. doi:10.1016/j.worlddev.2005.06.007

Pendergrast, M. (2010). *Uncommon Grounds: The History of Coffee and How It Transformed Our World*. New York: Basic Books.

Petermans, A., & Van Cleempoel, K. (2010). Designing a retail store environment for the mature market: a European perspective. *Journal of Interior Design*, 35(2), 21–36. doi:10.1111/j.1939-1668.2009.01036.x

Satin, M. (2010). *Coffee Talk: The Stimulating Story of the World's Most Popular Brew*. New York: Prometheus Books.

Sherry, J. F. (1998). *Servicescapes: The concept of place in contemporary markets*. Chicago: NTC Business.

Thurston, R. W., Morris, J., & Steiman, S. (2013). *Coffee. A Comprehensive Guide to the Bean, the Beverage, and the Industry*. Rowman & Littlefield Publishers.

Yin, R. K. (2009). Case study research: Design and methods (4thed.). Thousand Oaks, CA: Sage.

Yin, R. K. (2011). *Qualitative Research from start to finish.* New York: The Guilford Press.

KEY TERMS AND DEFINITIONS

Coffee Shop: Establishments where coffee is the main beverage offered although food and other beverages are also available, especially nonalcoholic beverages and specialty snacks.

Customer Experience: A holistic concept that expresses the result of a collection of emotions, feelings, and behaviors that arise during the entire decision-making and consumption process through a series of integrated relationships among people, objects, processes, and atmosphere.

Nethnography: Ethnography applied to the Web. This recognized method is frequently applied in the latest social and marketing research, usually to observe the complex underlying symbolic world of buying behavior and to explain consumers' action-structured paths.

Online Community: A social network of individuals interacting through social media, with the aim of pursuing mutual interests or goals. It potentially crosses geographic and political boundaries.

Qualitative Research: The aim to gather an in-depth understanding of human behavior and the reasons at the basis of such behavior. It investigates above all the why and how of decision making and expresses all the different facets of the considered phenomenon. Thus, smaller focused samples are used instead of large samples. Consequently, qualitative research produces information for specific cases and is not generalizable.

Store Atmosphere: The system of physical and social dimensions of a retail store affecting consumer perception and behavior.

Third Wave Coffee: Part of the specialty coffee movement. It refers to a current movement to produce high-quality coffee, and consider coffee as an artisanal foodstuff rather than a commodity. The term refers chiefly to the American phenomenon since the 1990s and continuing today. Similar movements exist in other countries, such as Australia, New Zealand, and Scandinavia.

ENDNOTES

[1] Authors have sometimes distinguished this sense of authenticity from indexical "authenticity" by using phrases such as "authentic reproduction" or "authentic recreation" (Grayson & Martinec, 2004).

[2] Nethnography, which is ethnography applied to the Web, is a recognized method frequently applied in the latest social and marketing research (Kozinets, 2010). This method is used to observe the complex underlying symbolic world of buying behavior and to explain consumers' action-structured paths. The application of nethnography to marketing research derives from the recognition that goods have a meaning that goes beyond their immediate function and are used in the production processes of sense, involving communication from single users and from social groups (Douglas & Isherwood, 1984; Lévi-Strauss, 1992).

[3] The coffee and snack shops industry is composed of establishments that prepare or serve coffee and other nonalcoholic beverages and specialty snacks including ice cream, frozen yogurt, cookies, donuts, bagels, juices, smoothies, and sodas. Products may be consumed on-site or to go. This industry contains the following segments: coffee shops, donut shops, ice cream shops, bagel shops, cookie shops, frozen yogurt shops, and other snack shops (IBISWorld, 2013).

[4] Gold (2008) said, "We are now in the third wave of coffee connoisseurship, where beans are sourced from farms instead of countries,

roasting is about bringing out rather than incinerating the unique characteristics of each bean, and the flavor is clean and hard and pure."

5   Many sources were used to identify and select the coffee shops: www.thedailymeal. com, www.usatoday.com, www.bloomberg. com, www.franchisehelp.com, http://eater. com

6   The choice of eliminating some types of communities was determined by the decision not to choose *a priori* consumers who would demonstrate positive behavior toward specific coffee shop chains or coffee brands, such as on Facebook fan pages.

7   The aim was to gather the opinions of forum users that were as spontaneous as possible.

We decided not to use a participant nethnographic method, where the researcher figures in the community (Beckmann, 2005). However, to conduct ethical nethnography, preserving the anonymity of the users, we decided to eliminate the names of the forums.

8   To conduct ethical nethnography in this research, we decided not to report nicknames and complete original posts, only determinant fragments in the analysis (Kozinets, 2010).

9   Regarding Italian coffee shop chains, analysis of the forums considered only a limited number of explicit quotations that referred to the Illy, Lavazza, and Lino's Coffee chains.

Chapter 11
A New Systems Perspective in Retail Service Marketing

Sergio Barile
Sapienza, University of Rome, Italy

Marialuisa Saviano
University of Salerno, Italy

ABSTRACT

The aim of this chapter is to highlight the necessity of a change in perspective and a new approach to Retail Service Marketing by addressing the recent challenges posed by a radical rethinking of market exchange logic using a service view. Recent Service Marketing advances are analyzed, which lead to the Service Dominant Logic proposal to take a general service view of market exchange, envisaging an emerging paradigm change. However, the key to this potential paradigm change is not yet well focused. A gap in the theoretical approach emerges that can be closed by adopting the Viable Systems Approach and the structure-system interpretation scheme. Their implications for retailing are discussed, and the key to change is emphasized. This chapter introduces a new theoretical and conceptual framework rooted in systems thinking, which recommends a Service Systems Approach to Retail Marketing.

INTRODUCTION

Service marketing on the one hand, and retail marketing on the other, have fueled a growing interest by scholars and practitioners in recent decades and given rise to relevant, worldwide research streams. Despite apparent theoretical and practical connections between the two areas of interest, little attention has been devoted to combining their respective theoretical advances. Conversely, with appropriate integration, as suggested by Bateson since 1985 and more recently,

although implicitly, by Lusch, Vargo and O' Brien (2007), the two fields can gain significant benefits from one another.

Accordingly, we focus on the inner "service" nature of retailing and argue that a relevant contribution can emerge by integrating recent advances into the theoretical context of Service Marketing, with particular reference to the Service-Dominant Logic (SDL) proposal (Lusch & Vargo, 2006; Vargo & Lusch, 2006; 2008) and the wider view of Service Science (SS) (Maglio & Spohrer, 2008; Spohrer, Maglio, Bailey & Gruhl, 2007). With this

DOI: 10.4018/978-1-4666-6074-8.ch011

aim, we discuss this possible theoretical integration by adopting the general perspective of the Viable Systems Approach (*vSA*) (Barile, 2000; 2008; 2009; Golinelli, 2000, 2010; Various Authors, 2011) as a methodological reference useful to highlight convergences and potential advances.

The evolutionary pathway traced by marketing theory in recent decades shows a series of changes in perspective that have led to a shift in focus from selling goods to establishing solid relationships with customers and, more recently, to developing a general service logic in the market exchange. This evolution has been theorized as leading from a Goods-Dominant Logic (GDL) to a Service-Dominant Logic (SDL) of market exchange (Lusch & Vargo, 2006). The key step in this evolution was first identified by the Relationship Marketing research stream (Gummesson, 2002), which understands the need to develop and maintain good relationships with customers both to build a solid basis for market exchange and to overcome transactional logic.

Interpreted through the lens of the *vSA*, this evolution clearly reflects the need to overcome the traditional reductionist view of marketing, creating the basis for a new general theory of exchange. When focus is on goods, on products to manufacture, sell, distribute, deliver to customers, attention generally falls on their features (especially the physical ones) and is diverted away from the reason for which they are manufactured, sold, distributed, delivered, etc.: *to serve* the needs of people or organizations, solving their problems. Perspective needs to be changed by recovering the original "service" purpose.

In this context, the need for a systems view capable of strengthening the understanding of emerging requirements of the current market scenario clearly reveals a research gap that must be closed (Barile, Pels, Polese & Saviano, 2012). By adopting the perspective of systems thinking, the traditional reductionist view still appears to dominate over the interpretative approach both in business research and in management. This is particularly true in the case of retailing, in which, despite relevant recent theoretical and practical advances, the traditional view, excessively focused on "goods to sell" instead of "service to propose," still dominates in most cases. Although technically paid for offering a service, in actual fact, many retailers reveal to still play a mere operative role in making a manufacturers' products assortment accessible to consumers. This can be true even when many additional services are offered with the aim of enhancing the value delivered by retailers to customers.

Through the integration of the SDL and SS theoretical proposals, the general framework of the *vSA* can offer interpretation schemes useful to read the evolution of the retail marketing approach, identifying key elements of analysis that show what we call the "paradox" of GDL in retail marketing as a specific expression of what we consider the more general "structural" management approach that has dominated in the industrial era. Mainly concerned about the design and engineering of the system's *structure*, the industrial era paradigm does not adequately focus on the dynamic and interactional nature of the *system* functioning. Focus on structure is sufficient to implement effective systems until the environment remains stable. With the increase of complexity it is necessary to govern the system's dynamics in order to ensure the achievement of planned goals.

The adoption of the *vSA* structure-system dual perspective (Barile & Saviano, 2011) as a lens to investigate retail management can reveal a persistent dominance of a view excessively focused on physical, functional and objective aspects of the entire retail offering system. This dominance appears when the service process dynamics, especially the ones of cognitive nature, are disregarded and attention is only on the design of the structure. In such limited view, a transactional logic, in which focus is on the object of the market exchange rather than on the process, generally appears to characterize the retailer-consumer relationship.

By integrating the SDL and SS scientific proposals within the *vSA* general framework, a wider relational context appears in which all interacting actors, whether sellers or clients, are viewed as resource integrators connected within a value cocreation relationship network on the basis of a mutual agreement to reciprocate value propositions (Golinelli, Barile, Saviano & Polese, 2012).

So as not to be confused with traditional "service*s*" marketing as an approach to market services rather than products, the new "service" logic has the merit of understanding the need both to rethink the approach to marketing and to definitively overcome the limits of traditional transactional logic. In this respect, we argue that although the relationship marketing approach has taken a decisive step away from the traditional goods-focused view, a further step needs to be taken to recognize that the shift from relationship to interaction requires a different (systems and dynamic) perspective and a consistent management approach.

The new service logic, based on the value cocreation view (Vargo, Maglio & Akaka, 2008), appears to go beyond the well-known experiential approach (Schmitt, 1999) and, in the *vSA* perspective, as we will argue hereafter, is revealed to have an inner systemic nature. Retailing can be a privileged context of analysis of the new service approach (Martinelli, 2009), revealing that a gap still emerges, theoretically and practically, when considering the implications of this systemic nature. Both from a theoretical and a practical perspective, in fact, when in the definition and design of the retailer offering system, the focus remains on the structural and physical aspects of space management and merchandising, what can happen when customers begin to interact with the offering system is often neglected. In a competitive environment of growing complexity, to be aware of the dynamics of emergence of the system from the structure and of its potential outcomes is fundamental.

The *vSA* methodology can help navigate and accomplish the evolutionary pathway of retail marketing by building on the theoretical assumptions of systems thinking and by working on a systems and service view that focuses on its interactional, contextual and cocreational nature. The discussion of this proposal is the aim of this chapter. Some empirical evidence about the marketing approach evolution and the shift from a transactional to a service-dominant logic which confirm a growing emphasis on relationships and networks with customers and other stakeholders are discussed by Brodie (2009).

In such a context, the adoption of a systems approach in retailing can methodologically contribute to more effectively address challenges and requirements of the current fast changing scenario, where decision makers experience conditions of growing complexity. Further empirical research is however required to give evidence of this potential contribution and to develop specific models and lines of action.

The chapter starts by introducing recent research advances in the service and marketing literature that we believe to be relevant to rethinking the retail marketing approach. These proposals are reinterpreted by adopting the *vSA* lens to emphasize key trends in retail marketing. The chapter proceeds by describing the most important stages of marketing's evolution in recent decades, analyzing their implications for retailing. Finally, it outlines the key elements of a systems approach to Retail Service Marketing and future research trends.

THEORETICAL BACKGROUND: TOWARD AN INTEGRATED SERVICE SYSTEMS MARKETING PERSPECTIVE

In recent decades, by building upon the reciprocal recognition of a strong convergence in their respective theoretical assumptions and conceptual premises, SDL and SS have fostered fruitful research collaborations among various scientific communities. Advancing this collaboration and recognizing the collaborating communities' common roots in systems thinking, an integrated line of thought has been developed within the *vSA* research domain that can significantly contribute to the advancement of Service Marketing and offer new insights for rethinking the retail marketing approach.

Since the study of marketing began, marketing scholars have performed several research stages that have progressively broadened the scope of the field, often leading scholars and practitioners to anticipate theoretical advances relevant to a wider management domain.

The Relationship Marketing View

We must recall the contributions of European scholars to business-to-business (B2B) research and the network perspective (Håkansson & Snehota, 1995), along with the key steps of relationships and service identified by the Nordic School (Grönroos, 1994), which significantly contributed to the advancement of the discipline and caused a change in perspective by focusing on relations, first from a one-to-one and then from a many-to-many perspective (Gummesson, 2004). Many-to-many marketing can be intended to develop from Relationship Marketing (RM) (Gummesson, 2002) and Customer Relationship Management (CRM) (Barry & Linoff, 1999; Payne & Frow, 2005) to utilize the network properties of marketing, widening the view from the dyadic level of supplier-customer relationship to a whole relational-network view.

The relational view of marketing in the context of retailing has fostered a change in the store management approach highlighting relevant opportunities for customer retention not only by introducing fidelity cards but also by creating attractive environments through effective store design, servicescape and space management choices (Bitner, 1992; Castaldo & Mauri, 2008).

The Service-Dominant Logic and Service Science View

Following these main trends, proponents of SDL and SS have opened their views to a worldwide discussion (Gummesson, Mele & Polese, 2009) and have become the "pillars" of the "Naples Forum on Service" (see www.naplesforumonservice.it), which has the aim of integrating resource knowledge of service by drawing on a potential scientific collaboration based on the mutual coherence of their respective scientific propositions (Barile, Montella & Saviano, 2012; Barile & Polese, 2010; Gummesson, Mele & Polese, 2011; Spohrer, Golinelli, Piciocchi & Bassano, 2010).

SDL is defined as a mindset that has a unified understanding of market exchange. "The foundational proposition of S-D logic is that organizations, markets, and society are fundamentally concerned with exchange of service–the applications of competences (knowledge and skills) for the benefit of a party. That is, *service is exchanged for service*; all firms are service firms; all markets are centered on the exchange of service, and all economies and societies are service based. Consequently, marketing thought and practice should be grounded in service logic, principles and theories" (Retrieved July 20, 2013, from http://sdlogic.net/).

The wider perspective of SS (a short version of Service Science, Management and Engineering and Design, SSMED) has contributed by abstracting a science from the study of service systems. The aim is to valorize multidisciplinary approaches to service and integrate them into a transdisciplinary body of knowledge, including Information Technology (IT), Operational Management (OM), Marketing (MKT), Human Resource (HR), and Engineering (ENG), by calling for collaboration by a broad range of academic institutions and practitioners, giving rise to a potentially wider convergence of thought (IfM & IBM, 2008).

The Research Gap

Since retail was first developed as a discipline, there has been a recognized need for a marketing approach aimed at understanding what consumers really want and expect from the stores in which they shop (Fram, 1965; Greenley & Shipley, 1988; Walker, 1975). By closing the gap between manufacturers and consumers, retailing has always shown that it has a highly innovative capability of instigating a commercial revolution and inverting the dynamic of power in the distributor-manufacturer relationship (Varaldo & Dalli, 1989). This relational view has characterized the theoretical perspective of a significant Italian research stream aimed at understanding the main trends and innovation pathways of the evolution of marketing channels (Barile, 1996; Barile & Pastore, 2002; Castaldo, 2001; Fornari, 2012; Lugli, 1976; Musso, 2010; Pastore, 1996; Pellegrini, 2008; Saviano, 2003; Vaccà, 1963; Varaldo, 1971; Varaldo & Fornari, 1998).

Today, many scholars and researchers are convinced that it is time for a new paradigm in retailing. In a research review paper published in Journal of Retailing, Grewal and Levy evidenced that the "service success strategies" was chosen as one of the four categories of retailing topics that can have the potential for the greatest contribution in retailing research (Grewal, 2009, p. 522). A concrete proposal derives from the adoption of the service marketing and management perspectives in the context of retailing (Kandampully, 2012a; Lusch, Vargo & O'Brien, 2007). This proposal focuses on: the customer's retail service experience, the use of information technology in supply chain management, store management and market intelligence (Kandampully, 2012b; Kim & Kandampully, 2012).

A significant step has been taken in recognizing the relevance of customer *context* to defining the correct offering strategy (Barnes & Wright, 2012) and to implementing the *cocreational* view by considering both the strong interconnections of the employees and customers' perspectives on achieving loyalty (Keiningham, Aksoy & Williams, 2012). From our perspective, however, the paradigmatic change these scholars and researchers aim to accomplish is in place but is still not well focused. In fact, although customer experience and Information and Communication Technology (ICT) are relevant elements of the required change, and a more holistic view has been adopted, together with relevant aspects that the research should deepen (Verhoef et al., 2009), we think that the proper focus is the manner in which the customer's role in the process is changing and/or should change (Sorescu et al., 2011). In other words, focus should shift on the dynamics of the process of interaction with the retail offering system.

The Interpretative Contribution of the Viable Systems Approach

Through the lens of the *vSA*, we can identify key aspects for a deeper rethinking of the retail marketing approach. In recent decades, building on traditional Italian studies that originally suggested a systems approach to business governance (Saraceno, 1970), the Italian research community has contributed the *vSA* (Barile, 2000; 2009; Barile, Pels, Polese & Saviano, 2012; Golinelli, 2000; 2010; http://en.wikipedia.org/wiki/Viable_systems_approach), which is essentially a methodology for the governance and study of social and business phenomena rooted in systems thinking and built upon an updated version of the Viable System Model by Stafford Beer (1972). In a nutshell, according to *vSA*, a viable system is an open system capable of surviving in its context by dynamically establishing harmonic (consonant) relationship with other viable entities with which it needs to interact in order to gain access to resources relevant for its functioning and survival. When consonant relationships are established, a resonant outcome (value) can be achieved during interaction (Barile & Saviano, 2011).

One of the main contributions of the *vSA* lies in overcoming the limits of the traditional analytical approach, taking into account business's true systemic nature and functioning, along with social phenomena. This advance has been formalized in the "structure-system" general interpretation scheme (Barile & Saviano, 2010; 2011). According to this dual perspective, observers and decision makers should distinguish between a *Structure-Based View* (StBV)–a static observation perspective that focuses on parts, functions and relations and is useful for objectively describing a phenomenon–and a *Systems-Based View* (SyBV)–a dynamic perspective that focuses on finalities, roles and interaction and is necessary to interpret the functioning of a system (Golinelli, Barile, Saviano & Polese, 2012). Thus, a view focused on parts is inadequate to understand the whole, because relevant systemic properties emerge from interaction.

In the context of marketing, the shift from parts to relations has been accomplished by Relationship Marketing, which has established the potential paradigm change and put the focus on relationships. However, a further step needs to be accomplished by shifting the focus to interaction. This is what SDL has done with its theoretical proposal of a new "service-logic."

From a *vSA* view, GDL takes a more general structure-based approach, and the shift towards SDL could mean a shift toward a more general systems-based logic (Barile & Saviano 2010; Golinelli, Barile, Saviano & Polese, 2012). A service structure represents that which appears from the static observation of a service system. To envision the service system that emerges from a structure, we should focus on interaction processes

The new service logic addresses the traditional problem of the product-service distinction, overcoming the limits of a "negative" description of services as non-material, non-tangible, non-storable, non-separable and non-standardizable product. In the context of retailing, this view has been characterized by the application of the prod-

uct marketing mix (4Ps) framework (McCarthy, 1964) to retailing (Chai, 2009). A significant effort has been necessary to clarify the differences, first, between product and service marketing, and second, between service and retail marketing. Of course, it is useful to analyze key elements of the retailing mix by referencing the 4Ps to recognize the relevant peculiarities of retail as a service and to apply marketing at an operative level. However, more strategic reasoning is needed to overcome the limits of such an approach and definitively address the issue of the "negative" definition of service. The solution of adding Ps to the 4 in existence (Lovelock & Wirtz, 2004), while capturing aspects that characterize service, remains anchored to the need to refer to *product* marketing to qualify *service* marketing. Conversely, SDL introduces a new concept of service that is no longer the "non-material" version of the product but instead is a concept with positive characteristics that expresses a more radical change in the cultural approach to market exchange.

Therefore, the shifts in perspective accomplished first by relationship marketing and later by SDL may direct marketing science toward a general *theory of interaction* based on the adoption of a systems approach (Golinelli, Barile, Spohrer & Bassano, 2010; Golinelli, Barile, Saviano & Polese, 2012).

On the basis of this theoretical introduction, we develop a scheme of synthesis in which the main steps of the marketing evolutionary pathway, as well as key aspects of each of the theoretical proposals, which we consider relevant as references for rethinking how to approach retailing, are synthesized in the light of the *vSA*, as illustrated in Table 1.

As we will clarify in the next section, with the interpretative support of the *vSA*, we essentially propose to accomplish a theoretical advance by using the systems view to identify the culmination of the described evolutionary pathway of marketing.

Table 1. Service- and systems-based scientific paradigms of marketing

Scientific Communities		Paradigms	Focus
Structure-Based View (StBV)	RM	Relationship	Relations
	MtoM	Network Relationship	Relations
VSA		Structure-Systems & Viable Systems	Relations/Interaction
Systems-Based View (SyBV)	S-DL	Service-Logic of Marketing & Value Co-Creation	Interaction
	SS	Service Systems Management Engineering and Design	Interaction

Source: Adapted from Golinelli, Barile, Saviano & Polese, 2010, p. 130).

Recognizing the need for a systems approach of management, it has been very correctly argued that "most enterprises, including retail organizations, are organized to manage compartmentalized tasks and activities and, thus, when a problem occurs the focus is on the local concern and not on fixing the systemic problem" (Lusch, Vargo & O' Brien, 2007, p. 10).

A Retail Marketing Rethinking from a Service Systems View

In this section, we will analyze the evolution of the marketing approach in the context of retailing, discussing the potential contribution of service marketing interpreted from a *vSA* perspective.

Three main evolutionary stages of the marketing approach can be summarized by considering the key aspects under focus as follows:

1. A first stage, in which the focus shifts initially from production to products and then to markets and clients (the advent of marketing).
2. A second stage, in which the focus shifts to relations (the era of relationship marketing).
3. A third stage, in which the focus shifts to interaction (the emerging marketing paradigm change).

The first phase of marketing evolution occurs after a long period of paying attention to the production process. The focus is on "objects" to sell and deliver to customers, who are essentially consumers of goods and products. Value is incorporated into the goods through the production process and is "destroyed" by customers through the consumption process. This is the time of one-sided focus on the manufacturing sector, in which distribution is only the "fourth" of the famous Marketing "Ps," a manufacturer's operative decision to choose the most efficient solution to deliver products to customers. The retail service essentially consists in giving consumers physical access to a variety of products. The retailers' role is still viewed from the perspective of the manufacturer. The prevalent nature of this commercial service is logistic and the distinction between goods and services is net. Services are viewed as accessories to a product offering.

When competition begins to grow, companies are forced to accomplish their first relevant shift in focus from the industrial organization of production to the investigation of markets in search of the best competitive conditions. The focus progressively shifts first to the market and later to the client, who becomes the gravitational center of interest and whose satisfaction is of primary concern. The role of service becomes more relevant and helps to differentiate offerings; scholars begin to re-evaluate the traditional distinction between goods and services and to define a new general approach to marketing.

From a *vSA* perspective, the limits of the traditional reductionist view become apparent, but focus simply shifts from one part of the market relationship to the other, and a transactional logic still dominates (Barile & Saviano, 2012). This is evident in the context of retailing, although the service provider and client are physically connected. What appears clear is that the physical connection between the two is not sufficient to generate an effective interaction.

The second stage of marketing evolution can be identified as the introduction of relationship marketing that has also opened the view to the relevant contribution of network theory (Costabile, 2001; Grandinetti, 2008; Grönroos, 1994; Gummesson & Polese, 2009; Storbacka & Nenonen, 2009). The shift of focus to relationships is the expression of a paradigmatic marketing change in which companies understand that what is relevant is not simply to sell goods to consumers but also, and primarily, to develop and maintain good relationships with them (Andreassen & Olsen, 2012).

In practice, the marketing approach has evolved from one-party centricity (supplier or customer) to two-party centricity (customer-supplier) and to early versions of multiparty centricity (network) (Golinelli, Barile, Saviano & Polese, 2012; Gummesson, Mele & Polese, 2011). In fact, as soon as the relational view disclosed the new approach, it became possible to understand that the relational context that has developed can (and should) be observed at a wider network level.

This need to widen the view appears clear from a *vSA*: the openness in the systemic functioning of social organizations implies a view extended to the whole operative context of the system, considering multiple sets of influences of the various entities (suprasystems) with which the organizations establish relations. In this respect, Gummesson's many-to-many marketing theoretical proposal represents a relevant advance (Gummesson, 2002; 2004).

In this new scenario, which seems to mark a key step in the evolution of marketing, the *vSA* perspective highlights an important point: although it may appear that companies begin to definitively understand that goods and products are just means to satisfy needs, often the focus remains on them as objects and the potential benefits of the relationship marketing approach are not well exploited. In such cases, the traditional transactional scheme still dominates, reducing the impact of change. This shift in relations indeed represents a revolutionary change, not simply a way to make business more profitable. It implies a change in a company's value systems and general schemes. In a few words, the relational view should better help to definitively overcome transactional logic. It would be a great contradiction to adopt the relational approach to speculative aims. Only short-term results would be achieved, threatening the long-term survival of the firm.

Unfortunately, the context of retailing is full of evidence of such contradictory (although not always intentional) behavior (see Box 1).

Moreover, retailers in general, influenced by the physical view of the retail system's structure (assortment, equipment, space, etc.) too often still think in terms of selling *goods* in a manner that is far from a true service logic. This is what we mean when we talk about *the paradox of a GDL*

Box 1. The example of fidelity cards

Let us consider the case of fidelity cards (Castaldo & Cillo, 2001; Ziliani, 2010). They represent a good example of how superficial the adoption of a relational approach may be. Fidelity cards were designed with the goal of making loyal customers. We know that the first step for obtaining loyalty is customer satisfaction, but we also know that the behavioral dimension (repurchase) is a necessary but not sufficient condition to make loyal customers: it is the cognitive dimension of trust that qualifies full loyalty (Barnes and Wright, 2012; Castaldo, 2001; Chattaraman, 2012; Costabile, 2001). When retailers use fidelity cards as a means to merely keep a customer linked to the company by leveraging on the logic of "advantage," they reveal to be still anchored to a transactional logic. They simply try to speculate on the relationship with customers. This behavior can provide only a short-term advantage and the business model appears not to vary.

in retailing. Of course, we specifically refer to less-innovative retail companies. There are many examples of retailers that take a very advanced approach to marketing. Nevertheless, the mere adoption of innovative solutions does not imply overcome a goods-dominant logic, and the focus may be still be excessively placed on goods.

From a *vSA* view, these considerations lead to the thought that although the evolutionary stage represents a turning point in the evolution of marketing, because it is a passage essential to stimulate the emergence of the exchange paradigm, it is common to observe permanent dominant schemes.

In fact, we currently observe a scenario in which tradition and innovation coexist not so much because they complete an offering system useful for satisfying different market expectations but primarily because traditional, dominant approaches are difficult to eradicate.

With respect to the next step of marketing evolution, authors have focused on different aspects that qualify the emerging paradigm change (Castaldo, 2001; Costabile, 2001; Grönroos, 1994; 2011). Many authors put emphasis on the technological aspect as that which is the most revolutionary. Indeed, ICT is relevant to retailing and has radically changed the business models of the so-called new economy. It cannot be denied that ICT has also made possible a dramatic rethinking of the marketing and communications approaches helping to structurally design service systems.

The third evolutionary phase is, in fact, also identified as a phase of the so-called marketing 2.0 or 3.0 (Kotler, Kartajaya & Setiawan, 2010), recognizing relevant trends, and making possible a more dynamic and interactive use of technology. However, we would direct attention not only on the *technological* change that characterizes this stage but mainly on the *methodological* change, in actual fact promoted by SDL, which, integrated with the wider perspective of a science of service systems (Service Science), can truly build the foundation for a *paradigm* change in marketing as well as in management. In this sense, what we

identify as characterizing this third stage is a new focus on *interaction*.

Although not explicitly central, interaction is a key point in the SDL theoretical proposal, which embraces a general view of service in which the various actors, as resource integrators, interact on the basis of mutual agreement on reciprocal value propositions and generate value in a contextual and dynamic manner (Grönroos, 2011; Kim & Kandampully, 2012; Lusch & Vargo, 2006; Valdani, 2009; Vargo & Lusch, 2006). Value is no longer incorporated into the product or service but instead *emerges* during the interaction process (Golinelli, Barile, Saviano & Polese, 2012).

Interaction is the key element of a service logic consistent with the systemic functioning of business and social phenomena; it captures the inner rule of market exchange by focusing on its true dynamic nature. From our perspective, the change is from a static, structural view to a dynamic, systems view of market exchange.

In the context of retailing, what we can observe on the basis of our framework is particularly interesting. In the traditional view, the retail exchange phase represents the "last mile" of a long chain effort aimed at creating value to be recognized by the market. A linear sequential logic characterizes a flow of subsequent market exchanges from manufacturing to distribution to consumption. The focus is clearly on:

- A physical flow of goods and products;
- A sequential and linear view of this flow;
- An accessory role of services as value added to goods along the flow;
- A space and time separation of the various phases;
- A struggle to align progressive outcomes with the expectations of the various actors involved in the process;
- A key, but final stage of retailing as the place where demand and supply meet.

There have been several theoretical advances that lead to the reconsideration of this conventional channel view of market exchanges.

Retail Service Systems' designers should be aware that the design of the retail system's structure is only a necessary condition to obtain a retail system. A retail store is designed as a structure, but functions as an open system. This openness implies that unexpected interactions may arise and the implemented system may significantly diverge from the designed one. Scholars wonder why assortment planning is so difficult for retailers (Mantrala et al., 2009). As Mantrala et al., explain, when retailers conduct product assortment planning (PAP), they determine the variety of merchandise, the depth of merchandise, and the Service level or the amount of inventory to allocate to each stock-keeping unit. They argued then that "despite longstanding recognition of its importance, no dominant PAP solution exists, and theoretical and decision support models address only some of the factors that complicate assortment planning" (Mantrala et al., 2009, p. 71). To us, the point is that this *complication* is not much a matter of variety management, but of variability governance. What makes the assortment composition successful is the alignment with customers' needs and expectations. These latter, however, continuously change, and consequently retailing performance is affected by the huge variability of markets. So, the main challenge for retailers is the emerging uncertainty which is due to increasing complexity and makes their offering structure continuously inadequate. This challenge suggests retailers to better focus on what dynamically happens when customers visit their stores. The key to change of the current evolutionary phase of marketing may be in the systems approach.

In this scenario, retailing, as both a specific area of marketing (particularly relevant with respect to the discussed aspects) and as a relevant sector of the economy, represents one of the most interesting research subjects to which the new service logic, under the wider view of systems thinking, can be applied. We believe that significant advances can be drawn from the adoption of a systems approach to retailing. To this end, the theoretical contribution of SDL and SS is significant and allows progress to accelerate. Indeed, many signals can be observed in the more recent literature on retailing, which suggests better exploration and exploitation of the contribution of systems thinking.

These are the aims of the *vSA*. The adoption of the *vSA* by retailing, through the introduced theoretical proposals, can offer insights useful to both researchers and practitioners.

Accordingly, in next section, we focus on the main issues that we believe are relevant to allow a theoretical and practical benefit from the adoption of a systems approach in retail marketing.

A Retail Service Systems Marketing Approach

Following the evolutionary trend that began with RM and continued with SDL, through the adoption of the *vSA*, it is possible to focus on the key elements of the systems perspective on retail service marketing.

First, it is useful to clarify what we mean by "retail service marketing." We mean the application of the new "service logic" to retail marketing. We consider retail as a service not in the traditional sense of the word, that is, as opposed to "product," but instead in the sense of the new service logic as applied to the specific context of the retailer-consumer relationship that we reinterpret through the lens of *vSA*.

The conceptual elements upon which we focus attention essentially derive from our shift of focus from the structural to the systemic aspects of the retail offering process. As underlined, although in general, the focus is on the tangible and physical elements of the service process, and intangibility is viewed as a problem to overcome by making the service process more "visible" and "tangible," we change the perspective and see the intangibility of service as an opportunity.

In the new era of dematerialization, decision makers and practitioners should become more familiar with the view of intangibility as an invisible but relevant dimension of any type of service process even when the object of exchange is a product. In fact, from our perspective, a product is "a standardized service process 'collapsed' into a physical object's structure, which needs to be made 'alive' through a service system to express its potential value" (Saviano, 2013).

Starting from this definition, we view retail as a service system whose main function is to create the conditions for value to emerge from a market exchange context both on the side of the manufacturer-retailer relationship and on the side of the retailer-consumer relationship. The physical elements of the service system only represent the visible part of the process. The outcome only partially depends upon these elements. There are invisible elements, such information and, in general, all of the cognitive and emotional human processes, which have a relevant impact on determining the system's outcome and can be disregarded in a structure-dominant view.

Therefore, focus shifts from the traditional components of a store's assortment, equipment, space, communication tools, etc., that configure the retail system's structure, to the retail system's service process. As clarified, this shift does not absolutely intend to neglect the structural aspects that represent the necessary conditions for a service system to emerge. We only warn they are not also sufficient conditions! We essentially suggest integrating into the retail view the systemic aspects of service, whose observation implies a change in perspective from a static (structural) to a dynamic (systems) view.

In the past decade, several steps have been taken towards a change in perspective in the approach to retail marketing which more resolutely takes the point of view of customers (see Box 2).

From a *vSA* view, this change means to more decisively act upon the cognitive aspects of interaction. In this respect, as we will see hereafter, the SDL notions of operant and operand resources become relevant and direct to a knowledge-based view of the retailer-consumer interaction, interpreted as a cognitive rather than a behavioral process.

Therefore, by adopting the *vSA* integrated with SDL and SS basic principles, retailing, like any other type of service process, can be reinterpreted as a "service system" in which people, resources and information are organized to participate in a process through which each involved actor achieve his/her own goals. The system, indeed, is viewed by each actor from his/her own perspective. Therefore, the manufacturer will see the system as a means for making profits through selling products; the retailer will see it as a means for making profits through selling a service; and the consumer will see it as a means to satisfy his/her own needs. All of the actors participate in a common process whose outcome should satisfy all expectations to make the whole system successfully survive.

The retailer-consumer relationship view significantly varies because they are concretely seen as *partners* in a common process. This is the key point of *co*creation (Rodie & Kleine, 2000; Wieland, Polese, Vargo & Lusch, 2012). Value is no longer incorporated into products and goods and transferred through them. It dynamically emerges from interaction among involved resources and is

Box 2. Examples of change in perspective

As an example of a customer-centered perspective, let us consider the re-combining of assortment variety by exploiting purchasing and consumption processes' complementarities, which has represented a very important step in rethinking the retail marketing offering approach (Castaldo, 2001). Consider, again, the distinction between the notions of space and place that have captured the relevance of making a physical "space" a meaningful "place," by shifting from the objective and physical features of a space to the subjective and cognitive dimensions of a place.

subjectively evaluated by each interacting actor. In this sense, it is *interactional, subjective, emergent* and *contextual*.

Cocreation may imply but does not coincide with coproduction. They differ as to the type and degree of participation of the customer in the process. According to Lusch, Vargo and O' Brien (2007), co-production is not new to retailing and the retailer has considerable control and influence over customer experiences. Thus the retailer should be a vital participant in the co-creation and co-production of customer experiences (see Box 3).

In a research paper aimed at empirically investigating how interaction and coproduction (in online environment) affect customer co-creation and engagement perception, Blasco, Hernandez and Jimenez (2011) stated the critical role of co-production and interactions in shaping consumer behavior. They demonstrated that coproduction plays a leading role in co-creation of value processes, as it is the main influence on perceived value co-creation, while interaction is the main driver of engagement perception. They conclude that in the context of the online purchase scenario, coproduction has a leading role in the co-creation

of value perception and is a key variable to enhance customer experience.

The interactional, subjective, emergent and contextual nature of value, requires attention to be placed not only on the design of the system's structure but also, and mainly, on the governance of emerging interaction. It is fundamental to be aware of the fact that according to the retailer's perspective, it is the structure of the system that is designed, not precisely the system/s that will emerge. Once designed, the retail system structure should be managed and the system dynamics governed in order to achieve the planned goals.

As in the general view of *vSA*, the management of the retail structure is relevant to efficiency targets, whereas the governance of the system is mainly relevant to effectiveness targets (Barile, Saviano, Polese & Di Nauta, 2013). Given that, as mentioned, many systems can emerge from the same structure, governance action is necessary to ensure that the desired system will emerge from the designed structure.

As a practical implication, our interpretative framework essentially suggests to distinguish between the structure and the systems perspective when managing retailing as well as any other kind of organization (see Box 4).

Box 3. The example of IKEA

The case of IKEA furniture represents one of the most effective examples of coproduction. Customers participate in the service production by taking on the final stage of the assembly process of products' components. It is not also an example of cocreation because the final stage of the process implies only an executive participation, which, although requiring the use of certain skills of the customer, does not go beyond a pre-designed and standardized process.

Box 4. The retail assortment as a systemic context

As an example, let's compare what happens to the same product unit when it is sold directly by manufacturer to market or distributed through a retail channel. In the first case, it more probably arrives to the consumer with its original marketing positioning. In the second case, it is inevitably subject to the retailer's merchandising strategies (layout and display) and becomes a component of a whole assortment structure, so resulting in comparative relationship with a defined set of different product units. This systemic context through which the single product unit will be seen and evaluated by customers will probably change its original marketing positioning to acquire the one that emerges from the customer perspective when he/she interacts with the whole assortment and offering system. This subjective perception is also influenced by interaction with other components of the offering system, such as the sales personnel, the other customers visiting the store during the same time, and even the customer's past experiences. The outcome of these multiple interactions is inevitably emergent and often unexpected.

The process of emergence of the system from the structure may give rise to unexpected outcomes (Barile, Saviano, Polese & Di Nauta, 2012). This is particularly true in the context of retailing, where it is common to observe an iterative approach in which a retail system's structure is progressively adapted to the market's changing needs and expectations. A store's identity is progressively defined by the market. Only very innovative retailers are capable of imposing their identity, creating market trends and driving change. Instead, many stores struggle to remain viable by dynamically becoming what consumers really need. The *vSa* notion of *viability* recalls here the three systemic conditions that characterize a viable system–openness, contextualization and dynamism–capable of surviving in a certain environment.

All of these aspects suggest constant monitoring of the dynamic process of the retailer-consumer relational experience, i.e., their interactions. In this respect, the concept of experience should be seen as the way in which customers participate in the process and contribute to co-creating its outcome. Although experiential marketing has emphasized the relevance of these aspects, we argue, as repeatedly stated, that a further step is necessary. The experiential marketing approach, particularly in the context of retailing and from a merchandising perspective, has focused attention on environmental elements of the retail context by suggesting designing stores that enhance the customer experience (Chattaraman, 2012). However, in many cases, even in the case escaping experiences (Pine & Gilmore, 1999), customers can remain passive in the process and instead of being valorized as actors in the process, are often absorbed into the system, sometimes even losing their behavioral awareness.

Conversely, from our service systems perspective, customers, as central actors in the retail process, should not simply be involved in a predefined scenario following scripts as though they were on a stage, as suggested by the experiential paradigm (Pine & Gilmore, 1999). They should

concretely cocreate the scenario by actively participating in the process, both behaviorally and, in particular, cognitively. The way in which they should participate in the system is a core aspect of the integrated *vSa*-SDL view. Accordingly, the focus is on:

- Actors as operant (systemic) resources;
- Goods, equipments, spaces, etc. as operand resources;
- Service as the application of a system's knowledge to the benefit of others;
- Interaction as a knowledge-based process;
- Value as an outcome emerging from a co-creation process.

As suggested by SDL, with reference to any type of service system, we can say that retailers and consumers are both key actors in the retail service system and act as "operant" resources. An operant resource is a resource employed to act on other operand or operant resources. Operand resources are resources upon which an operation or act is performed to produce an effect. (Constantin & Lusch, 1994, p. 144). Considering that service is intended as the application of an operant resource's knowledge to the benefit of others, it appears clear that the value which will emerge from interaction between retailers' offering and consumers will significantly depend on the contribution of the customers' knowledge and competences. In this sense, retailers and consumers can cocreate the value (see Box 5).

Generalizing the view of retailers and consumers as operant resources, the traditional functional view of the retailer, on one hand, and the consumer, on the other hand, appears less relevant compared to the "roles" they effectively play in the process as "resource integrators" which contribute to value creation. This is the essence of the shift from a structure to a systems view: although having specific functions in the market relationships (one is a retailer, the other one is a consumer), they can

Box 5. The example of Eataly

The case of Eataly is a good example of retailer-consumer cocreation. Eataly is an innovative retail formula that entered the Italian food market in 2007, creatively combining "retailtment" and "edutainment" concepts both implying a central role of customers' participation and experience. The key to success of this formula lays in a harmonic fusion of traditions, culture and values in a place where customers can not only buy and eat high quality food, but also learn about them. Eataly combines the quality excellence and the atmosphere of small traditional shops and the logics of modern retail (shops size, managerial strategy, supply chain and category management, and self service inside the shop). Different processes enrich the customer experience defined as "eatertainment" (Montagnini & Sebastiani, 2009, p. 7). The learning process, integrated with the retail sale and restaurant services, implies participation and engagement of customers in interaction whose outcome significantly depends on their knowledge contribution.

play different roles according to the kind and degree of participation in the process.

The systemic implications of participation are often disregarded in actual fact: the outcome of the retail service system process is not the service or the experience or the store itself, as variously stated in the traditional view. The system's outcome is what each interacting actor subjectively derives from the participation in the process. The system in action is not only that of the retailer that delivers the service. It is the system that emerges from the retailer-consumer relationship when they interact. The outcome of such a system cannot be totally prepacked or predefined. Only value propositions can be predefined. This aspect commonly appears as a limit, especially for large corporations whose main concern is achieving efficiency through standardization. Here lies the primary challenge of the emerging retail paradigm: to combine the efficiency of standardization with the effectiveness of differentiation. Given that, according to *vSA*, different systems can emerge from the same structure, the structure-system interpretation scheme would suggest that it is possible to standardize the basic elements and processes of an operative structure and differentiate the emerging systems. Next, SDL would add that the best way to effectively differentiate the emerging systems is to allow customers to cocreate the process according to their needs: the emerging system will leverage on the customers' knowledge resources to make the system not only different but concretely customized. In this sense, as finally suggested by the SS literature, a retailer's offering can be viewed as a "platform" for service, i.e., a structure from which the service system will emerge thanks to interaction with all of the involved actors. Thus, the store should become a service platform designed to facilitate the retailer-consumer interaction (as well as interaction with other involved actors), and to allow value to be cocreated by them (see Box 6).

Therefore, to understand what makes a retail service system's outcome effective, implies a knowledge of what makes *interaction* effective as a value cocreation process. By building on the definition of service "as the application of specialized competences (operant resources–knowledge and skills), through deeds, processes, and performances for the benefit of another entity or the entity itself" (Vargo & Lusch, 2008), we focus

Box 6. The example of Apple

The Apple's consumer and retail marketing approach represents the best example of an SDL-based systems approach to retail marketing. What exactly is the key to success of Apple? When we think of Apple, it is actually difficult to distinguish traditional manufacturer-retailer-consumer functions from the various and often overlapping roles that are dynamically played by each actor involved in the whole market process. Who has the key role? The manufacturers, the developers, the retailers or even the users, especially when they contribute to the development of new apps? Still, when Apple's engineers develop a new product they make them for themselves, that is they think as if they were users. Actually they are users. We can affirm that Apple is a creator of very innovative technology-based service platforms for communication whose contents are dynamically cocreated by the various actors involved in the network and that the store is central to the whole system. This appears to us to be the key to success of Apple.

on the non physical and less-visible processes of retail service systems, which are essentially of a cognitive nature. Thus, a model is required for the analysis of retail interaction processes that gives evidence of the cognitive aspects that lie behind behaviors, i.e., of the way that knowledge characterizes this process. In fact, the retail relationship starts only when the customer is both cognitively and behaviorally exposed to the store offering system. This interaction should be viewed as a cognitive process.

vSA proposes a model that generalizes the representation of any viable system as an *information variety* qualifying its knowledge identity as multidimensionally defined not only by information units but also by interpretation schemes and, most importantly, by the categorical values that progressively sediment during the system's life. By adopting this model, the process can be read in terms of interaction among information varieties: it initially implies a sensorial perception through which only selected "items" are captured by the interacting actors; these selected items then pass to a subsequent phase in which they are filtered by the interpretation schemes and absorbed by the system so making its initial variety to vary producing responsive behaviors. The categorical values play a decisive role in this process by allowing or preventing interaction and by determining its final outcome. The *vSA* methodological framework offers further elements and concepts to deepen these aspects and to develop consistent models of action, providing a support to the retail marketing decision-making process. To deepen these aspects, the reader should refer to the main *vSA* literature (www.asvsa.org).

FUTURE RESEARCH DIRECTIONS

Numerous implications can derive from the proposed view of Retail Service Marketing, whose insights can be shared among practitioners and should be empirically investigated to develop adequate models, techniques and tools of action or to appropriately adapt the existing ones. New innovation pathways are to be developed consistently with emerging market requirements (Musso, 2010; van Riel, 2012).

By building upon the above-mentioned research contributions in the theoretical context of service marketing and SS, from the general perspective of the *vSA*, this chapter opens a research line aimed at valorizing the potential contribution of an integrated service and systems view to retail marketing advances.

Although several research efforts in the last decade have made significant advances, we argue that a gap still exists, which may be closed developing the interpretative approach of a systems thinking view of the new service logic. By adopting the *vSA* structure-system perspective in particular, the paradigm of the retailer-consumer relationship can be reinterpreted, distinguishing between structural problems, which involve problem solving related to components, functions and relations, and systems issues, which involve decision making related to actors, roles and interaction, offering insights useful to effectively address the challenges of the evolving scenario.

CONCLUDING REMARKS

The purpose of this chapter is to propose a new service systems view, highlighting its potential interpretative contribution to the advancement of both theoretical and practical approaches to retail marketing. We limit our discussion to the introduction of the integrated *vSA*-SDL framework for stimulating a rethinking of an approach to retail marketing that appears to us still to suffer from a view excessively focused on the objective, structural and physical aspects of retailing.

The key points of our view are summarized as follows:

- Those items that are traditionally included in store design and retail service offerings are considered as a set of *operand resources* that configure the *structure* of the service system organized by the retailer;
- Retail service systems are managed by and through active *operant resources*;
- The retail service system's *structure* includes customers and other actors as external (operant) resources integrators;
- The retail service system is activated through *interaction*;
- The retail service system's outcome emerges from a *cocreation* process.

These points suggest the deepening of several aspects of what we have called a *Retail Service System* by benefitting from the contribution of several research perspectives that have more or less explicitly common roots in systems thinking. Therefore, we believe that scholars and practitioners should better explore and exploit these common roots that are often only superficially considered, without deepening their main implications.

REFERENCES

Andreassen, T. W., & Olsen, L. L. (2012). Customer Service: Does It Matter? In J. Kandampully (Ed.), *Service Management: The New Paradigm in Retailing*. New York: Springer. doi:10.1007/978-1-4614-1554-1_3

Barile, S. (1996). *Le formule di distribuzione al dettaglio*. Padova, Italy: Cedam.

Barile, S. (2000). *Contributi sul pensiero sistemico in Economia d'Impresa*. Salerno, Italy: Arnia.

Barile, S. (2008). *L'impresa come sistema: Contributi sull'Approccio Sistemico Vitale (ASv)* (2nd ed.). Torino, Italy: Giappichelli.

Barile, S. (2009). *Management sistemico vitale*. Torino, Italy: Giappichelli.

Barile, S., Montella, M., & Saviano, M. (2012). A Service-Based Systems View of Cultural Heritage. *Journal of Business Market Management*, 5(2), 106–136.

Barile, S., & Pastore, A. (2002). Forme, caratteri e divenire sistemico dei rapporti con la distribuzione ed il consumo. In G. M. Golinelli (Ed.), *L'approccio sistemico al governo dell'impresa*, (vol. 3, pp. 187-225). Padova, Italy: Cedam.

Barile, S., Pels, J., Polese, F., & Saviano, M. (2012). An Introduction to the Viable Systems Approach and its Contribution to Marketing. *Journal of Business Market Management*, 5(2), 54–78.

Barile, S., & Polese, F. (2010). Linking the viable system and many-to-many network approaches to service-dominant logic and service science. *International Journal of Quality and Service Science*, 2(1), 23–42. doi:10.1108/17566691011026586

Barile, S., & Saviano, M. (2010). *S-DL, VSA and SS – Highlighting Convergences*. Paper presented at the International CooperLink Workshop the emerging Perspective of Service Science for Management and Marketing Studies. Naples, Italy.

Barile, S., & Saviano, M. (2011). Foundations of systems thinking: the structure-system paradigm. In *Contributions to theoretical and practical advances in management: A Viable Systems Approach (vSA)* (pp. 1–26). Avellino, Italy: International Printing.

Barile, S., & Saviano, M. (2012). Oltre la partnership: un cambiamento di prospettiva. In S. Esposito De Falco, & C. Gatti (Eds.), *La consonanza nel governo dell'impresa: Profili teorici e applicazioni*. Milano, Italy: Franco Angeli.

Barile, S., Saviano, M., Polese, F., & Di Nauta, P. (2012). Reflections on Service Systems Boundaries: A Viable Systems Perspective: The case of the London Borough of Sutton. *European Journal of Management*, 30, 451–465. doi:10.1016/j.emj.2012.05.004

Barile, S., Saviano, M., Polese, F., & Di Nauta, P. (2013). Il rapporto impresa-territorio tra efficienza locale, Efficacia di contesto e sostenibilità ambientale. *Sinergie, 90,* 25–49.

Barnes, J. G., & Wright, J. W. (2012). A Framework for Applying Customer Insight and Context to the Development of a Shopping Experience Strategy. In J. Kandampully (Ed.), *Service Management: The New Paradigm in Retailing* (pp. 43–65). New York: Springer. doi:10.1007/978-1-4614-1554-1_4

Bateson, J. E. G. (1985). Retailing and Services Marketing: Friends or Foes? *Journal of Retailing, 61*(4), 11–13.

Beer, S. (1972). *Brain of the firm: a development in management cybernetics.* Herder and Herder.

Berry, M., & Linoff, G. (1999). *Mastering Data Mining: The Art and Science of Customer Relationship Management.* New York: John Wiley & Sons, Inc.

Bitner, M. J. (1992). Servicescapes: The Impact of Physical Surroundings on Customers and Employees. *Journal of Marketing, 5*(6), 57–71. doi:10.2307/1252042

Blasco, L., Hernandez, B., & Jimenez, J. (2011). Co-creation processes and engagement: an empirical approach. In E. Gummesson, C. Mele, & F. Polese (Eds.), *Service Dominant logic, Network & Systems Theory and Service Science.* Napoli, Italy: Giannini.

Brodie, R. (2009). Empirical Evidence about the Service Dominant Logic. In E. Gummesson, C. Mele, & F. Polese (Eds.), *Service science, S-D logic and network theory.* Napoli, Italy: Giannini.

Castaldo, S. (Ed.). (2001). *Retailing & innovazione.* Milano, Italy: Egea.

Castaldo, S., & Cillo, P. (2001). Le strategie di accrescimento delle risorse fiduciarie nel retailing: il ruolo delle carte fedeltà. *Industria & Distribuzione, 1,* 33–45.

Castaldo, S., & Mauri, C. (Eds.). (2008). *Store Management.* Milano, Italy: Franco Angeli.

Chai, L. G. (2009). A Review of Marketing Mix: 4Ps or More? *International Journal of Marketing Studies, 1*(1), 1–14.

Chattaraman, V. (2012). Multicultural Consumers and the Retail Service Experience. In J. Kandampully (Ed.), *Service Management: The New Paradigm in Retailing.* New York: Springer. doi:10.1007/978-1-4614-1554-1_10

Constantin, J. A., & Lusch, R. F. (1994). *Understanding resource management: How to deploy your people, products, and processes for maximum productivity.* Paper presented at The Planning Forum. Oxford, OH.

Costabile, M. (2001). *Il capitale relazionale.* Milano, Italy: McGraw-Hill.

Fornari, D. (2012). *New factors in channel relationships.* Milano, Italy: Egea.

Fram, E. H. (1965). Application of the Marketing Concept to Retailing. *Journal of Retailing, 41*(2), 19–26.

Golinelli, G. M. (2000). *L'approccio sistemico al governo dell'impresa: La dinamica evolutiva del sistema impresa tra economia e finanza* (Vol. 2). Padova, Italy: Cedam.

Golinelli, G. M. (2010). *Viable Systems Approach (*VSA*): Governing Business Dynamics.* Padova, Italy: CEDAM Kluwer.

Golinelli, G. M., Barile, S., Saviano, M., & Polese, F. (2012). Perspective Shifts in Marketing: Toward a Paradigm Change? *Service Science, 4*(2), 121–134. doi:10.1287/serv.1120.0015

Golinelli, G. M., Barile, S., Spohrer, J., & Bassano, C. (2010). *The Evolving Dynamics of Service Co-creation in a Viable Systems Perspective.* Paper presented at the 13th Toulon-Verona Conference. Coimbra, Portugal.

Grandinetti, R. (Ed.). (2008). *Marketing: Mercati, prodotti e relazioni*. Roma, Italy: Carocci.

Greenley, G. E., & Shipley, D. D. (1988). An Empirical Overview of Marketing by Retailing Organisations. *Service Industries Journal, 8*(1), 49–66. doi:10.1080/02642068800000005

Grewal, D., & Levy, M. (2009). Emerging Issues in Retailing Research. *Journal of Retailing, 85*(4), 522–526. doi:10.1016/j.jretai.2009.09.007

Grönroos, C. (1994). Quo vadis, marketing? Towards a relationship marketing paradigm. *Journal of Marketing Management, 10*(4), 347–360. doi:10.1080/0267257X.1994.9964283

Grönroos, C. (2011). A service perspective in business relationships: The value creation and marketing interface. *Industrial Marketing Management, 40*(1), 240–247. doi:10.1016/j.indmarman.2010.06.036

Gummesson, E. (2002). *Total Relationship Marketing*. Oxford, UK: Butterworth-Heinemann.

Gummesson, E. (2004). *Many-to-Many Marketing*. Malmö, Sweden: Liber.

Gummesson, E., Mele, C., & Polese, F. (2009). Service science, S-D logic and network theory: Integrating the perspectives for a new research agenda. In E. Gummesson, C. Mele, & F. Polese (Eds.), *Service science, S-D logic and network theory*. Napoli, Italy: Giannini.

Gummesson, E., Mele, C., & Polese, F. (2011). Integrating the 3 Pillars of the 2011 Naples Forum on Service: S-D logic, Network & Systems Theory and Service Science. In E. Gummesson, C. Mele, & F. Polese (Eds.), *Service-Dominant Logic, Network & Systems Theory and Service Science*. Napoli, Italy: Giannini.

Gummesson, E., & Polese, F. (2009). B2B Is Not an Island. *Journal of Business and Industrial Marketing, 24*(5/6), 337–350. doi:10.1108/08858620910966228

Håkansson, H., & Snehota, I. (1995). *Developing Relationships in Business Marketing*. London, UK: Routledge.

IfM & IBM. (2008). *Succeeding through Service Innovation: A Service Perspective for Education, Research, Business and Government*. Cambridge, UK: University of Cambridge Institute for Manufacturing.

Kandampully, J. (Ed.). (2012a). *Service Management: The New Paradigm in Retailing*. New York: Springer. doi:10.1007/978-1-4614-1554-1

Kandampully, J. (2012b). Service as the New Paradigm in Retailing. In J. Kandampully (Ed.), *Service Management: The New Paradigm in Retailing* (pp. 1–6). New York: Springer. doi:10.1007/978-1-4614-1554-1_1

Keiningham, T. L., Aksoy, L., & Williams, L. (2012). Why Loyalty Matters in Retailing. In J. Kandampully (Ed.), *Service Management: The New Paradigm in Retailing* (pp. 67–82). New York: Springer. doi:10.1007/978-1-4614-1554-1_5

Kim, M., & Kandampully, J. (2012). The Service Imperative in the Retailing Industry. In J. Kandampully (Ed.), *Service Management: The New Paradigm in Retailing* (pp. 7–24). New York: Springer. doi:10.1007/978-1-4614-1554-1_2

Kotler, P., Kartajaya, H., & Setiawan, I. (2010). *Marketing 3.0: From Products to Customers to the Human Spirit*. John Wiley & Sons Inc. doi:10.1002/9781118257883

Lovelock, C., & Wirtz, J. (2004). *Services Marketing: People, Technology, Strategy*. Prentice Hall, Pearson.

Lugli, G. (1976). *Economia della distribuzione commerciale*. Milano, Italy: Giuffrè.

Lusch, R. F., Vargo, L. S., & O'Brien, M. (2007). Competing through service: Insights from service-dominant logic. *Journal of Retailing, 83*(1), 5–18. doi:10.1016/j.jretai.2006.10.002

Lusch, R. F., & Vargo, S. L. (Eds.). (2006). *The Service-Dominant Logic of Marketing - Dialog, Debate, and Directions*. Armonk: ME Sharpe.

Maglio, P. P., & Spohrer, J. (2008). Fundamentals of service science. *Journal of the Academy of Marketing Science, 36*(1), 18–20. doi:10.1007/s11747-007-0058-9

Mantrala, M. K., Levy, M., Kahn, B. E., Fox, E. J., Gaidarev, P., Dankworth, B., & Shah, D. (2009). Why is Assortment Planning so Difficult for Retailers? A Framework and Research Agenda. *Journal of Retailing, 85*(1), 71–83. doi:10.1016/j.jretai.2008.11.006

Martinelli, E. (2009). Service-dominant logic and retail convergence. In E. Gummesson, C. Mele, & F. Polese (Eds.), *Service science, S-D logic and network theory*. Napoli, Italy: Giannini.

McCarthy, E. J. (1964). *Basic Marketing: A Managerial Approach*. Richard D. Irwin.

Musso, F. (2010). Innovation in Marketing Channels: Relationships, Technology, Channel Structure. *Symphonya: Emerging Issues in Management, 1*, 1–19.

Pastore, A. (1996). *I nuovi rapporti tra industria e distribuzione*. Padova, Italy: Cedam.

Payne, A., & Frow, P. (2005). A Strategic Framework for Customer Relationship Management. *Journal of Marketing, 69*, 167–176. doi:10.1509/jmkg.2005.69.4.167

Pellegrini, L. (2008). I rapporti industria-distribuzione: modelli integrati e ricerca di cooperazione. *Economia e Politica Industriale, 3*, 12–31.

Pine, J., & Gilmore, J. (1999). *The Experience Economy*. Boston: Harvard Business School Press.

Rodie, A. R., & Kleine, S. S. (2000). Customer Participation in Services Production and Delivery. In T. A. Swartz, & D. Iacobucci (Eds.), *Handbook of Services Marketing and Management*. Thousand Oaks, CA: Sage Publications. doi:10.4135/9781452231327.n10

Saraceno, P. (1970). La gestione dell'impresa alla luce dell'analisi dei sistemi. *Ricerche economiche, 3/4*, 256-273.

Saviano, M. (2001). Il fenomeno della globalizzazione verso un'interpretazione in chiave sistemica vitale. *Esperienze d'Impresa, 1*, 41–68.

Saviano, M. (2003). *Analisi sistemico vitale della distribuzione commerciale*. Torino, Italy: Giappichelli.

Saviano, M. (2013). *The Viable Systems Approach (vSA), what it is, what it is not*. Paper presented at the 2013 Naples Forum on Service-Service Dominant logic, Network & Systems Theory and Service Science: integrating three perspectives for a new service agenda. Ischia, Italy.

Schmitt, B. (1999). Experiential Marketing. *Journal of Marketing Management, 15*(1-3), 53–67. doi:10.1362/026725799784870496

Sorescu, A., Frambach, R. T., Singh, J., Rangaswamy, A., & Bridges, C. (2011). Innovations in Retail Business Models. *Journal of Retailing, 87S*(1), S3–S16. doi:10.1016/j.jretai.2011.04.005

Spohrer, J., Golinelli, G. M., Piciocchi, P., & Bassano, C. (2010). An Integrated SS-VSA Analysis of Changing Job Roles. *Service Science, 2*(1), 1–20. doi:10.1287/serv.2.1_2.1

Spohrer, J., Maglio, P. P., Bailey, J., & Gruhl, D. (2007). Steps Toward a Science of Service Systems. *Computer, 40*, 71–77. doi:10.1109/MC.2007.33

Storbacka, K., & Nenonen, S. (2009). Customer relationships and the heterogeneity of firm performance. *Journal of Business and Industrial Marketing, 24*(5/6), 360–372. doi:10.1108/08858620910966246

Vaccà, S. (1963). *I rapporti industria-distribuzione nei mercati dei beni di consumo.* Milano, Italy: Giuffrè.

Valdani, E. (2009). *Cliente & Service Management.* Milano, Italy: Egea.

van Riel, A. C. R. (2012). Strategic Service Innovation Management in Retailing. In J. Kandampully (Ed.), *Service Management: The New Paradigm in Retailing* (pp. 83–95). New York: Springer. doi:10.1007/978-1-4614-1554-1_6

Varaldo, R. (1971). *Potere e conflitti nei canali di distribuzione.* Pisa, Italy: Editrice tecnico scientifica.

Varaldo, R., & Dalli, D. (1989). Le relazioni strategiche tra Industria e Distribuzione. *Sinergie, 19,* 13–48.

Varaldo, R., & Fornari, D. (1998). La evoluzione dei rapporti industria-distribuzione. Dalla cooperazione al conflitto. *Sinergie, 46,* 21–49.

Vargo, S. L., & Lusch, R. F. (2006). Service-Dominant Logic: What it is, What it is not, What it might be. In R. F. Lusch, & S. L. Vargo (Eds.), *The Service-Dominant Logic of Marketing: Dialog, Debate, and Directions.* Armonk: M.E. Sharpe.

Vargo, S. L., & Lusch, R. F. (2008). Why service? *Journal of the Academy of Marketing Science, 36,* 25–38. doi:10.1007/s11747-007-0068-7

Vargo, S. L., Maglio, P. P., & Akaka, M. A. (2008). On value and value co-creation: A service systems and service logic perspective. *European Management Journal, 26*(3), 145–152. doi:10.1016/j.emj.2008.04.003

Various Authors. (2011). *Contributions to theoretical and practical advances in management: A Viable Systems Approach (vSA).* Avellino, Italy: International Printing.

Verhoef, P. C., Lemon, K. M., Parasuraman, A., Roggeveen, A., Tsiros, M., & Schlesinger, L. A. (2009). Customer Experience Creation: Determinants, Dynamics and Management Strategies. *Journal of Retailing, 85*(1), 31–41. doi:10.1016/j.jretai.2008.11.001

von Bertalanffy, L. (1968). *General System Theory: Foundations, Development, Applications.* New York: George Braziller.

Walker, W. G. (1975). Marketing research is important in retailing, now, more than ever. *Marketing News, 8*(17), 9.

Wieland, H., Polese, F., Vargo, S. L., & Lusch, R. F. (2012). Toward a Service (Eco)Systems Perspective on Value Creation. *International Journal of Service Science, Management, Engineering, and Technology, 3*(3), 12–25. doi:10.4018/jssmet.2012070102

Ziliani, C. (2010, Spring). Loyalty marketing in Italy: a decade of customer cards and clubs in food retailing. *Retail Digest,* 54-57.

ADDITIONAL READING

Barile, S. (2009, July). *The dynamic of information varieties in the processes of decision Making.* Paper presented at Proceedings of the 13th World Multi-Conference on Systemics, Cybernetics and Informatics: WMSCI, Florida.

Barile, S., & Polese, F. (2010). Linking Viable Systems Approach and Many-to-Many Network Approach to Service-Dominant Logic and Service Science. *International Journal of Quality and Service Sciences, 2*(1), 23–42. doi:10.1108/17566691011026586

Barile, S., & Polese, F. (2011). The Viable Systems Approach and its potential contribution to marketing theory. In *Various Authors, Contributions to theoretical and practical evidences in management. A Viable Systems Approach (vSA)* (pp. 139–173). Avellino, Italy: International Printing. doi:10.2139/ssrn.1919686

Barile, S., & Saviano, M. (2010). A New Perspective of Systems Complexity in Service Science. *Impresa, Ambiente. Management, 4*(3), 375–414.

Bessom, R. M., Jackson, Jr., & Donald, W. (1975). Service Retailing: A Strategic Marketing Approach. *Journal of Retailing, 51*(2), 75–84.

Bogdanov, A. (1980). *Essays in Tektology: The General Science of Organization. Seaside.* Intersystems Publications.

Brown, S. (1991). Variations on a Marketing Enigma: The Wheel of Retailing Theory. *Journal of Marketing Management, 7*(2), 131–155. doi:10.1080/0267257X.1991.9964146

Capra, F. (1997). *The web of life.* New York: Doubleday-Anchor Book.

Capra, F. (2002). *The Hidden Connections.* London: HarperCollins.

Christopher, W. F. (2007). *Holistic Management - Managing What Matters for Company Success.* Hoboken: Wiley-Interscience.

Edvardsson, B., Tronvoll, B., & Gruber, T. (2011). Expanding understanding of service exchange and value co-creation: A social construction approach. *Journal of the Academy of Marketing Science, 39*(2), 327–339. doi:10.1007/s11747-010-0200-y

Emery, F. E., & Trist, E. L. (1960). Socio-technical Systems. In W. C. Churchman, & M. Verhulst (Eds.), *Management Science, Models and Techniques.* New York: Pergamon.

Grönroos, C. (2006). What can a service logic offer to marketing theory? In R. F. Lusch, & S. L. Vargo (Eds.), *The Service-Dominant Logic of Marketing: Dialog, Debate, and Directions* (pp. 320–333). Armonk, NY: M.E. Sharpe.

Grönroos, C. (2009). *Towards Service Logic: The Unique Contribution of Value Co-Creation.* Helsinki: Hanken School of Economics.

Gummesson, E. (2006). Many-to-Many Marketing as Grand Theory: a Nordic school Contribution. In R. F. Lusch, & S. L. Vargo (Eds.), *Toward a Service-Dominant Logic of Marketing-Dialog, Debate, and Directions.* Armonk: ME Sharpe.

Gummesson, E., Lusch, R. F., & Vargo, S. L. (2010). Transitioning from Service Management to Service-Dominant Logic: Observations and Recommendations. *Special Issue of the International Journal of Quality and Service Sciences, 2*(1), 8–22. doi:10.1108/17566691011026577

Kotler, P., & Levy, S. J. (1969). Broadening the Concept of Marketing. *Journal of Marketing, 33*(1), 10–15. doi:10.2307/1248740 PMID:12309673

Lusch, R. F. (2007). Marketing's Evolving Identity: Defining Our Future. *Journal of Public Policy & Marketing, 26*(2), 261–268. doi:10.1509/jppm.26.2.261

Lusch, R. F., Vargo, S. L., & Tanniru, M. (2010). Service, value networks and learning. *Journal of the Academy of Marketing Science, 38*, 19–31. doi:10.1007/s11747-008-0131-z

Mele, C., Pels, J., & Polese, F. (2010). A Brief Review of Systems Theories and Their Managerial Applications. *Service Science, 2*(1/2), 126–135. doi:10.1287/serv.2.1_2.126

Pels, J., & Brodie, R. (2012). Value Co-creation: Using a Viable Systems Approach to Draw Implications from Organizational Theories. *Mercati & Competitività, 2*, 19–38.

Spohrer, J., Anderson, L., Pass, N., & Ager, T. (2009). Service Science and S-D Logic. In E. Gummesson, C. Mele, & F. Polese (Eds.), *Service science, S-D logic and network theory*. Napoli, Italy: Giannini.

Spohrer, J., & Maglio, P. P. (2009). Service Science: Toward a Smarter Planet. In G. Salvendy, & W. Karwowski (Eds.), *Introduction to service engineering*. Hoboken, NY: Wiley. doi:10.1002/9780470569627.ch1

Vargo, S. L. (2008). Customer Integration and Value Creation: Paradigmatic Traps and Perspectives. *Journal of Service Research, 11*(2), 211–221. doi:10.1177/1094670508324260

Vargo, S. L., & Lusch, R. F. (2004). Evolving to a new dominant logic for marketing. *Journal of Marketing, 68*(1), 1–17. doi:10.1509/jmkg.68.1.1.24036

Walker, W. G. (1975). Marketing research is important in retailing, now, more than ever. *Marketing News, 8*(17), 9.

Zeithaml, V. A., Parasuraman, A., & Berry, L. L. (1985). Problems and Strategies in Service Marketing. *Journal of Marketing, 49*, 33–46. doi:10.2307/1251563

KEY TERMS AND DEFINITIONS

Retail Service Marketing: A theoretical and practical area of marketing that integrates a general service logic in the retail marketing approach.

Service-Dominant Logic: A mindset for a unified understanding of the market exchange and the nature of organizations, markets and society. Its foundational proposition is that organizations, markets, and society are fundamentally concerned with exchange of service intended as the applications of competences (knowledge and skills) for the benefit of a party (http://sdlogic.net/).

Service Science Management Engineering and Design (also Service Science): An interdisciplinary approach to the study, design, and implementation of services systems intended as complex organization of people, technologies and shared information.

Service Structure: An organized set of people, technologies, other organizations and shared information designed to perform specific service functions.

Service System: A service structure in action finalized to the achievement of a goal (delivering value to other interested entities through service).

Value Co Creation: A view of value as an outcome emerging from an interaction process among several actors in which each of them participates as a resource integrator.

Viable Systems Approach (vSA)**:** A business governance and research methodology rooted in systems thinking and developed on the basis of an updated version of the Stafford Beer's Viable System Model (http://en.wikipedia.org/wiki/Viable_systems_approach). It is adopted and further developed by the ASvSA (Associazione per la ricerca sui Sistemi Vitali) research community (http://www.asvsa.org/index.php/en/).

Chapter 12
Personally Engaged with Retail Clients:
Marketing 3.0 in Response to New Consumer Profiles

Ana Isabel Jiménez-Zarco
Open University of Catalonia, Spain

María Pilar Martínez-Ruiz
University of Castilla la Mancha, Spain

Alicia Izquierdo-Yusta
University of Burgos, Spain

ABSTRACT

This chapter examines how social and economic changes of recent years have led to a new consumer profile. Furthermore, it explores how current responsible concerns regarding consumption, as well as a greater concern for welfare sustainability and the environment, are affecting purchasing behavior. With these ideas in mind, this chapter analyses how organizations have to evolve towards a new marketing paradigm in order to link to their customers emotionally. In this regard, the evolution of the marketing concept is reviewed–departing from a Marketing 1.0 paradigm, passing through a Marketing 2.0 paradigm–in order to understand how the so-called Marketing 3.0 emerged. The chapter concludes by analyzing the different rules that guide this new approach and how companies in the distribution sector are applying them in their daily activities.

INTRODUCTION

Companies in both the public and private sector continue to explore not only new ways to influence the decisions of individual consumers but also to look to gain the heart and minds of the consumers. That has become a challenge in a new context where the increasingly visible emerging social and economic trends also point the way to alternative, more sustainable forms of living, creating and consuming.

DOI: 10.4018/978-1-4666-6074-8.ch012

The new consumer exhibits a socially responsible buying and consumption behavior. As this is a demanding and informed consumer, he/she has more power with respect the company, being able to participate actively in the development of certain business processes. In this context, companies must reconsider how they appeal to their clients. Developing new formulae to achieve their active participation, as well as their emotional engagement, is essential for a companies' survival and the key might be Marketing 3.0. This shift is especially crucial for retail companies which have recently suffered growing competition, due largely to the global and technological environment where they now operate (e.g., Kacker, 1986; Ghemawat, 2007; Coe & Wrigley, 2009; Corstjens & Lal, 2012).

In line with these notions, this chapter seeks to offer evidence regarding the ways that companies use to enhance their relationship with consumers, considering the new consumer profile. With these ideas in mind, we revise the philosophy and strategic changes exhibited by retail companies to better serve their consumers. We also present a discussion of Marketing 3.0 - one of the primary changes companies are undertaking to serve their customers.

This chapter concludes with some key conclusions and managerial recommendations for retail companies. For example, companies must know the main factors, which contribute to the success of modern retail businesses. Likewise, we indicate how the combination of these types of factors together with the decrease in average household income, the greater penetration of mobile Internet applications and social media, give rise to a demand for products adapted to more sustainable, responsible lifestyles and the appropriate use of resources. Thus, active consumer participation can enable the development of processes and business that are both economical and more socially sustainable, as well as more efficient and more appropriate in terms of best fitting consumers' needs.

THE NEW ECONOMIC AND SOCIAL CONTEXT: DEFINING THE NEW CONSUMER PROFILE

We are experiencing a time of significant changes. The world is going through a period of rapid and unexpected turbulence. The recent financial meltdown has increased the level of poverty and unemployment, thus reducing the rate of growth of developed countries. Meanwhile, economic power has been shifting to countries in the East, which are experiencing higher rates of growth. Moreover, climate change and rising pollution are forcing countries to limit the emission of carbon dioxide into the atmosphere, which is also imposing a higher burden on business.

These changes have a profound impact on the economic and social context. But it is true that their effect have been enhanced by two other factors such as: new technological development and the globalization process.

Technological advances have brought about huge changes in consumers, markets and society in general. Thus, since the end of the last century, information technology has been introduced into the market and further developed into what it is considered as a new-wave technology.

Technology

As technology evolves, consumers and especially businesses and other organizations adopt it in order to develop their activities. The application goes beyond the development of commercial activities in the network which, known as electronic-marketing or e-marketing, is based on the use of ICT in the field of marketing. Companies implant complex technological applications, which collect, analyze, store and distribute information, which is used in decision-making processes: systems, which ultimately constitute the heart of the intelligence system of the organization.

To a large extent these changes are caused by connectivity, interactivity and information processing capacity, thus enabling the use of technology. The first two characteristics are more typical of Information Technology and communication, and particularly the Internet, and the third is more suitable for certain types of software designed for collection, processing and analysis.

In this sense, it is seen that, on the one hand, people and organizations are more than ever inter-connected. This allows them to share a virtual space with global reach in order to obtain information, to communicate, interact and exchange information, knowledge or any other product, thus overcoming the time and space barriers. On the other hand, the high degree of interactivity which is possible by means of the communications with these technologies allows the different actors involved in the value creation process - in particular the consumers – to develop a more active role in their relationship with the company (McAfee, 2009). In this line, Copeland & Malik (2005) show that new technology enables connectivity and interactivity of individuals and groups, as well as facilitating the spread of word-of-mouth information sharing. As a consequence, technology becomes a tool that allows individuals to express themselves and collaborate with others. In this situation, people can create new ideas, entertain themselves and consume them. New wave technology enables people to change from being consumers to prosumers.

Finally, technology allows organizations to access and treat quickly a large amount of information that is key to their decision-making processes (McAfee, 2006). In this regard, there are many companies, which have installed information systems to capture orders, processes and communicate information effectively and efficiently. Some systems, such as CRM, allow the company to monitor and measure contact with their customers. It stores customers´ data and therewith automates connection, according to the information it holds. This value is added to the offer made by the company, to differentiate the brand from its competitors and improve the quality of care dispensed to the

customer. However, others systems such as ERP (Enterprise Resource Planning) provide integral information, facilitating the flow of information between departments or activities of the company.

Technology makes it possible to deal directly with clients, as well as meeting and talking to them. Companies can even use technology to establish direct and collaborative client relationships. But, as we shall see, technology also implies the loss of power of the company with respect to consumers. Thus, the consumers´ role is changing due to the intensive use of new technologies. Consumers are no longer isolated individuals: rather, they are connected with one another. In making decisions, they are no longer unaware but informed. They are no longer passive but active in giving useful feedback to companies (Prahalad & Ramaswamy, 2004)

The Globalization Process

Globalization is the second element that drives the new social and economic age. It is totally influenced by technology, due the fact that information technology enables the exchange of information between nations, corporations and individuals throughout the world.

Like technology, globalization reaches everyone around the world and creates an interlinked economy. But unlike technology, globalization is a force that stimulates imbalance and creates paradoxes that have a direct impact on firms´ and individuals' behavioural change.

Basically, the principal effect of globalization is the change in the way of thinking that people and companies have. Thus, people search for a sense of continuity in their lives, instead of being anxious and bearing conflicting, intertwined values in their minds. People search for connection with others and begin to blend into their local community and society. Yet a sense of direction is also essential in times of paradox as people start to unite in support of social causes or begin to have a greater awareness and concern about poverty, injustice, environmental sustainability, community responsibility and social purpose.

Another globalization effect is that companies are now competing to be seen as providing continuity, connection and direction. According to Holt (2004), companies, and especially their brands, seek to address social, economic and environmental issues in as a way of engaging with society.

The New Consumer Profile: Do Companies Need a New Marketing Concept?

The aforementioned changes, particularly evident in Western societies, are favoring a change in individuals´ purchasing and consumption trends.

In countries like China, India and Brazil, high GDP growth rates have allowed the development of a strong middle class, characterized by a markedly consumer behavior while in Europe and the U.S. this consumption model is being strongly questioned (Majfud, 2009). Consumerism involves accumulation, purchase or consumption of goods and services considered nonessential. The same is considered a direct consequence of a social and economic model that promotes the acquisition of wealth as a sign of social status and prestige. In recent years, consumerism has been seen as one of the causes of the economic, social and environmental crisis that we are experiencing. This indicates that the mass consumption that has characterized firms since the 1950s has severely compromised the natural resources and ecological balance, while favoring social and economic imbalance between the north and south.

In response, there are new social and cultural trends emerging that advocate sustainable development, as well as environmental and responsible consumption. In the markets, their impact is evidenced by: (a) the development of new business models in companies; (b) a strong concern for society regarding the responsibility of organizations as social agents, and (c) the emergence of a new consumer model.

The new consumer is characterized by being responsible: that is to say, they are concerned about consuming what they need in a sustainable, responsible manner. For such a consumer, buying also involves a range of economic, social and environmental processes. This is a type of individual who, at the time of purchasing, questions what is expendable and what is not whilst judging their own financial ability to purchase. Moreover, in relation to the product or service, these consumers not only take the decision to buy based on price or quality (Bostman, 2010), they also respect the environment and care about the fact that manufacturing companies or service providers respect human rights and principles of social justice.

Access to technology has led to the emergence of such consumers. ICT, especially the Internet, allow them to provide a means for information, but also to communicate and disseminate their opinions and experiences. This demanding and informed consumer is not only limited to searching for information online about products and the companies that sell them. They also have enough capacity and power to be heard and to demand certain kind of behavior from firms (Mourali &Yang, 2013).

As the report prepared by Insider in 2012 notes, the consumer has more power than ever and is extremely important for businesses.

We live in a world where everything is just a click away. The Internet has conditioned us to expect information and services on demand at anytime, anywhere – and often free. It has also given us the power to share our experiences immediately, at the touch of a button. The consumer, rather than the brand, controls the interaction. As consumers, we do not need advertisers to speak directly to us anymore; through social media and our mobiles, we can instantly share recommendations and content with our friends. We can also turn to the opinions of strangers via the ratings and reviews of social commerce to help us determine which products and services we buy. Brands need to work harder to make themselves heard.

As well as reframing the individual's identity (e.g., by interacting with others, role-playing, learning and testing of one's social skills), technology can enhance empowerment of the individual through increasing self-efficiency and skills (Amichai-Hamburger et al., 2008). This latter form of empowering is especially relevant for the new consumers, because it offers a new ability to play a more important role in the process of companies' value creation.

This behavior is determined by the desire which the individual demonstrates to know whether the products are produced efficiently, or if the company is sustainable in terms of economic, social and environmental terms. This process is referred to as co-creation and can occur in a variety of contexts (Bolton & Saxena-Iyer, 2009).

The collaboration of the consumer in the development of certain processes is especially interesting for certain companies. One context in particular where consumer co-creation is increasingly vital is the area of new product development (NPD). In this regard, it is important to take into account the fact that, independently of the loss of control over certain activities which it can represent, the company finds important benefits in the development of co-creation processes. Cost-efficient and interaction opportunities offered have made co-creation a suitable means of creating value and improving the overall success of new products. In that case, consumers are able and willing to provide ideas for new goods or services that may fulfill needs that have not yet been met by the market or might improve on existing offerings (Ernst et al., 2010). Hauser et al. (2006) show that successful NPD depends on in-depth understanding of consumer needs and product development efforts that meet those needs (Hauser et al., 2006) and, in particular, ideas generated through co-creation that will more closely mirror consumer needs.

Many businesses positively regard this kind of behavior by the consumer. Some companies even consider that the participation of the customer should take place in all phases of product innovation (Ernst et al.,2010). However, as pointed out by Etgar (2008), consumers often vary greatly in their interest and ability to participate usefully in co-creation tasks. Thus, there are only some segments of consumers who might be especially willing and able to participate in co-creation activities. These include innovators (the lead users) emergent consumers and market mavens.

At a strategic level, companies establish two types of objectives:

1. That the number of consumers with which they have a close relationship is high.
2. That the relation established, aside from having a behavioral dimension (a collaborative behavior) also has an affective dimension.

Currently, reaching the hearts and minds of a large number of consumers is critical for businesses and especially in the field of marketing, it is a key factor. However, the values and motivations that characterize the new consumer are different from a decade ago: this raises the need for a new marketing concept best suited to the reality of the current situation.

MARKETING EVOLUTION: FROM MARKETING 1.0 TO MARKETING 3.0

During the last four decades, marketing has evolved through three stages that we call Marketing 1.0, 2.0, and 3.0. Nowadays, only a few companies are moving into Marketing 3.0, even though it involves a great opportunity to adapt the company to the new social and economic environment.

As we can see in the next section, the evolution of marketing is based around three major disciplines: product management, customer management and brand management. This continuous change responds to the marketing discipline's need to adaptation to different eras of human lives. Thus, in the 1950s and 1960s it was focused on product management and in the 1970s and the 1980s it evolved towards consumer management. The discipline of brand management was added at the end of the 1990s, and at the beginning of the 2000s.

The First Marketing Steps of Marketing: Marketing 1.0 and Marketing 2.0

In the early 1950s, the manufacturing sector was the centre of the developed economies. In such an environment, marketing was viewed as just one of several important functions supporting production, along with finance and human resources.

The marketing function is the sole responsibility of specialists who comprise the marketing department. They are responsible for guiding the company towards customer satisfaction. The treatment given to clients is carried out by means of the actions contained in the marketing mix program. The basic objective is that customers choose the products of the company (Sánchez et al., 2000). Ultimately, this approach focuses on the product itself and is aimed at winning new customers, while not worrying too much about their further treatment. The marketing mix is the cornerstone on which the transactional marketing approach is based. Thus, the idea is that the marketer uses 4 basic tools in order to act on its mass market (Grönroos, 1994)

The 1970s and 1980s were a turbulent time. Western economies were in crisis. For companies generating demand was harder, and required more than four Ps. The increased offer, the maturity and fragmentation of the markets, the intensification and globalization of competition and the rapid pace of technological development substantially altered the competitive landscape of enterprises.

The new reality forced a change in companies´ strategy and their conception of the environment,

so a new marketing approach to understanding and providing solutions to the challenges faced (Grönroos, 2000).

Marketing professionals were forced to think harder and create better marketing concepts in order to give a response to new consumer profiles. Also, during this time, consumers became smarter buyers. In consumers' minds, many products had a distinct positioning due to the fact that they were viewed as different and superior from the rest of the products in the market. Other variables, such as people, processes, physical evidence, public opinion or political power had to be considered in marketing strategy (Boom & Bitner, 1981).

To stimulate product demand, marketing needs to evolve from purely tactical – marketing 1.0 - to a more strategic level. Now Marketing 2.0, also known as relational marketing, will be discussed. Relationship marketing not only promotes a new way of understanding the markets, it also provides a new way to deal with and act with regard to the agents that form them. In its new understanding of reality:

1. The market passes from being analyzed from the traditional and simple dyadic perspective between two parties or agents, to a different one in which every relationship is considered a network.

2. The consumer is seen as an increasingly sophisticated agent who refuses to be anonymous and requires a personalized treatment.

3. The relationship-marketing technology is considered to go beyond the stage of automation for cost savings, so that now it begins to reinforce each other and:

4. Customer loyalty has become a priority for present-day companies.

The concept of value is of great importance as the center of the design of the corporate competitive strategy. Offering customers more value than the competition becomes the only way to attract and keep their loyalty. In this sense, the existence of an in-depth knowledge and personal attention to customers becomes a priority. This is only possible if the organization as a whole and all its resources are managed towards the market and to customer satisfaction. Competitive strategies based on the use of company resources outperforming competitors in service levels, prices, adaptation, and/or creating and delivering other benefits of a psychological and social nature (security, confidence, etc...) are sought (Grönroos, 1994). The way to do that is by creating a superior value for the customer and to keep it linked to the organization.

The actions most commonly developed for these purposes are: on the one hand, permanently enriching the content of the commercial offer through the joint delivery of products and customer services (Grönroos, 2000); on the other hand, to jointly develop a long-term behavior that is conducive to maintaining a relationship with the customer, where in addition to the above, benefits of a psychological and social nature are delivered, at the same time reducing sacrifices associated with the process of exchange and relationship for the consumer.

For the company, these actions have serious implications that go beyond the development of a new product concept, or a change in the way of understanding the act of consumption developed by the subject. The concept of marketing is altered by modifying their processes and management.

To adopt a relationship-oriented marketing implies a profound process of change for the company which goes beyond the goal of setting objectives focused on client development or the development of marketing practices which seek their loyalty. The focus on relationships is a new way of thinking about marketing activity, as well as to understanding the market and the activities which the agents who comprise it develop. The main implications of adopting such an orientation lead to relations for the organization, including those listed and discussed:

1. The active participation of consumers in the business;
2. The importance of the concept of value, which is at the center of business strategy;
3. The change in the concept of supply and the act of consumption;
4. Consideration of long-term relationships as a means to creating and conveying value, and
5. The concept of marketing as a process that affects and involves the whole enterprise.

Table 1 shows the main differences between 1.0 and 2.0 marketing approaches.

Marketing 2.0 initiates the consumer oriented era. That approach implicitly assumes the view that consumers are passive targets of marketing campaigns. Unfortunately, nowadays people are not passive and wish to be treated as simple con-

Table 1. Main differences between transactional marketing and relational marketing principals

Transactional Marketing	Relational Marketing
Focused on individual sales.	Focused on retaining customers.
Oriented to product characteristics.	Oriented to product benefits.
Providing a short-term view.	Providing a long-term vision.
Little emphasis on customer service.	Great emphasis on customer service.
Low commitment to customers.	High level of commitment to the customer.
Moderate level of customer contact.	
Quality focused essentially on the product	Quality is a common shared concern

Source: Sánchez et al. (2000).

sumers. They are playing an active role in their social and economic context, and their concerns regarding human problems leads them to look for solutions to their worries with respect to how to make the globalized world a better place. Therefore, they seek products which offer not only a social and emotional service but also a benefit for humanity in general.

Marketers must change their approach and focus on the values that the product, brands or companies can offer consumers in particular, and the world, in general. We are witnessing the rise of Marketing 3.0 or the values-driven era, where people are not treated simply as consumers, and marketers approach them as whole human beings with minds, hearts and spirits. Meanwhile companies have to address their deepest needs for social, economic and environmental justice in their mission, vision and values. Their aim is to provide solutions in order to address problems in society.

The Axes of Marketing 3.0

Marketing 3.0 places the concept of marketing in the area of human aspirations, values and spirit. It believes that consumers are complete human beings whose other needs and hopes should never be neglected. This new marketing view complements emotional marketing with human spirit marketing. Thus, marketing practices are very much influenced by changes in consumer behaviour and attitude. It is a more sophisticated form of the consumer-centric orientation where the consumer demands more collaborative, cultural and spiritual marketing approaches.

The axes of marketing 3.0 are thus defined by the three principal changes which – as we previously saw – characterize the new social and economic context: new technology development, globalization and new consumer profile. It is a marketing where companies: (a) understand community issues that relate to their business; (b) have defined perfectly what they are, why they are in

business and what they want to become: in other words, what is the corporate mission, objectives and vision; and have to invite consumers to participate in the development of the product and communication of the company.

As Figure 1 shows, marketing 3.0 is a collaborative, cultural and spiritual marketing.

Collaborative marketing is the first building block of Marketing 3.0. Companies practicing Marketing 3.0 aim to change the world. They cannot do it alone. In the interlinked economy, they must collaborate with one another, with their shareholders, with their channel partners, with their employees and with their consumers. Marketing 3.0 is a collaboration of business entities with similar sets of values and desires. On the other hand, cultural marketing is the second building block of Marketing 3.0. It is an approach that addresses the concerns and desires of global citizens. Companies practicing Marketing 3.0 should understand community issues that relates to their business and puts them at the heart of company's business model. Marketing 3.0 demonstrates its concern for the communities around it: communities of consumers, employees, channel partners and shareholders.

Finally, the spiritual or human spirit marketing, from the company's point of view, is the third building block of marketing. Thus, like creative people, companies should think about their self-actualization beyond their material objectives. They should know what they want to become and give expression to their corporate mission, vision and values. Only in this way will the business performance be the result of the consumer's appreciation of these companies' contributions to human well-being.

Marketing 3.0 in the Supply Sector

Marketing 3.0 has reached the retail sector. In fact, we are at the dawn of the next profound power shift in the retail supply chain and unlike past generations of retailers, this time it is shifting to

Figure 1. Three changes that lead to Marketing 3.0
Source: Kotler et al. (2010)

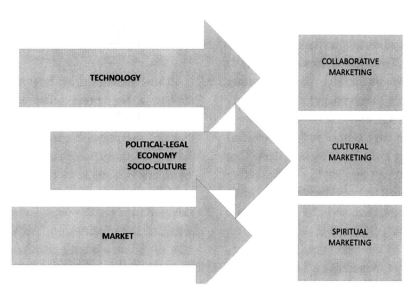

the individual shopper. This shift portends massive transformation in how the industry produces and distributes products, goes to market and measures success.

The first signs of change can be observed in the mid-1990s, when two significant trends reached a tipping point and began to converge. The first tendency was a rapid consolidation in the fast-moving consumer goods retail channel. The net result was fewer, bigger retailers, which controlled a high marker share.

These larger retail firms leveraged their size and buying power into a more forceful position when dealing with the consumer goods manufacturers. In addition, these retailers used their newfound size to adopt some of the same sophisticated marketing skills formerly the province of the national brands while also funding development of strategic private label programs. Such events began the shift of power in the supply chain to the retailers and away from the manufacturers.

The second trend is the development and rapid growth of loyalty programs within many retail channels. Together with the creation of customer loyalty, these programs seek to obtain information regarding the end customer. It can be highlighted that an important part of the loyalty programs launched by the retailers have failed with respect to cultivating the loyalty of the customer, although it has enabled them to obtain a great deal of information about the customer. This fact, together with the maturity and consolidation of the distribution sector per se, effectively led to the power change within the distribution chain, thus falling into the hands of the retailers.

Kotler et al (2010) show that suppliers play an essential role in the consolidation of Marketing 3.0. But, as these authors highlight, suppliers play a dual role in this process, given that they are hybrids of companies, consumers and employees. First, they are channel partners of the producer companies: in fact, they are the consumers with needs and wants to be served. Thus, they become collaborators, cultural change agents and creative partners for companies at the same time. But, also, suppliers are companies with their own mission, vision, value and business models. Thus, they sell to end-users and form the consumer interface.

Supplier as Companies' Collaborator

In marketing 3.0 the power belongs to consumers. Unfortunately, not all companies have direct access to the consumers. Growth requires a company to have channel partners manage their consumer interface. Therefore, the company becomes highly dependent on the distributors to market its values, especially when a large part of product or brand marketing strategy is designed by suppliers. That is why, for the correct application of marketing 3.0, companies need to consider: (a) the correct selection of the partner, and (b) the strategic management of the relationship.

With respect to the first step, Kotler et al., (2010) propose that in marketing 3.0 the channel partner selection requires a complex process of *mirroring the purpose-identity-values*. That supposes that companies should consider and select potential partners which have identical objectives-identity and values. Thus, companies need to know what is the overall objective of a potential partner (as a purpose); identify its character (identity), and be involved and share the same beliefs that the channel partner (values).

Experience such as those of Zara or Mango show us how one way to obtain the "symbiosis" between the companies and the suppliers is through a "franchise" distribution model. In that way, the company owner can look for people who have the same interests, values and objects that he/she has. Another possibility is creating direct touch point with the consumer. In this case, although this model is fully dependent on the partners who make up the distribution channel, at least companies can create and maintain a direct contact with consumers in order to market their values and interests.

Sharing values is a key element in the success of the company-supplier relationship. Thus, Rackham et al. (1996) recommend that before starting the partnership, both partners assess whether both of them:

1. Desire a win-to-win strategy;
2. Uphold a high quality standard.
3. Have unique values that are compatible with the other ones.

These authors show how a good partnership creates a horizontal relationship, where each partner should derive an equitable benefit from the collaboration. Further, when both entities have the same approach to quality, the creation of alliances is made more possible.

The second step for company marketing is to develop the correct process of strategic management of the relationship. We should remember that suppliers not only distribute the products to the market, but also provide a consumer touch point, and market the company or brand values.

In some sectors, such as the IT industry, the distributor is more important than the manufacture. That is why the concept of company-supplier integration is particularly important for obtaining consumer loyalty. Company-supplier integration usually starts from basic cooperation between them, especially in retail promotion. As the relationship strengthens, they start to integrate with other members. This process involves regular information sharing and joint strategic planning but also confidence, commitment and cooperation between both entities.

Marketing 3.0 in the Retail Sector: Applying Kotler's Ten Golden Rules

Suppliers are companies with their own mission, vision, value and business models. Thus, in order to adapt to the new economic and social context, they should focus on marketing 3.0.

Previously, we have seen that marketing 3.0 implies that company values are totally integrated in marketing. The company wants puts into practice a series of values and they give the company its personality and purpose. And at this level, any separation between marketing and values is not acceptable.

In order to guarantee the maximal level of integration between them, Kotler et al., (2010) propose ten golden rules that companies have to apply in the development of marketing strategies (see Table 2).

In this section, we not only present these rule but also offer some examples of companies which have applied them.

Rule 1: Treat your customer with love and your competitors with respect

Today's marketing seeks to develop sustainable competitive advantages based on consumers. One way to create them is "loving customers." In business, love the customers means winning their satisfaction and loyalty through giving them great value and touching their emotions and spirit.

For instance, Hollister Co is a Californian lifestyle brand created by Abercrombie & Fitch Co. The concept was originally designed to attract consumers aged 14–18, who like beach and surf culture. This brand has a lower price point than the parent brand, given that it is inspired of image of casual clothes.

Hollister California pursues the technique of "walking self-marketing," where in wearing an item of clothing with the brand's name initials, results in direct advertising. The Hollister labelled shopping bag carried out of the store produces a similar effect. As a result, the company has not relied on media marketing to communicate its desired look and appeal. The brand's marketing images and the sepia toned images provide Hollister's campaigns with a vintage feel that is adequate to their fictional date of establishment and the lifestyle promoted by the brand. Moreover, Hollister stores are designed to simulate the appearance of vintage beach shacks. Hollister Co. stores have their own monthly playlist, which is packed with surfer inspired tunes to set the whole beach shack mood and played at a fairly high vol-

Table 2. Marketing 3.0 golden rules

1. Love your consumers and respect your competitors
2. Be sensitive to change, be ready to transform
3. Guard your name, be clear about who you are
4. Customers are diverse, go first to those who can benefit most from you
5. Always offer a good package at a fair price
6. Always make yourself available, spread the good news
7. Get your customers, keep and grow them
8. Whatever your business it is service business
9. Always refine your business process in terms of quality, cost and delivery
10. Gather relevant information, but use wisdom in making your final decision

Source. Kotler et al. (2010)

ume through many strategically placed speakers throughout the store.

To respect competitors is essential in this new environment. They enlarge the whole market and guarantee the "perfect" balance between offer and demand. Without any kind of competitors, industry will grow slowly and imbalanced.

In certain situations, such as internationalisation, or developing new products or processes, competitors can become good partners. This business strategy, called coopetition, is based on a combination of cooperation and competition, derived from an understanding that business competitors can benefit when they work together. Thus, companies interact with a partial congruence of interests. They cooperate with each other to create greater value than would be obtained compared to the value created without interaction, and struggle to achieve competitive advantage. Often coopetition takes place when companies that are in the same market work together in the exploration of knowledge and research of new products, at the same time that they compete for market-share of their products and in the exploitation of the knowledge created. In this case, the interactions occur simultaneously and on different levels in the value chain.

For instance, this is the case of the arrangement between PSA Peugeot, Citroën and Toyota to share components for a new city car - simultaneously sold as the Peugeot 107, the Toyota Aygo, and the Citroën C1, where companies save money on shared costs while remaining fiercely competitive in other areas. Several advantages can be foreseen, such as cost reductions, resource complementarity and knowledge and technological transfer.

Rule 2: When times change, change with them

The business landscape keeps changing. In this context consumers are more demanding and better informed. At the same time, competitors increase in number and get smarter. They are more proactive and develop more sophisticated and valued product in order to satisfy consumers' needs and desires.

If a company is not sensitive to this context, and cannot anticipate these changes, it will become obsolete and eventually die. A company needs to pay attention to changes which it notices in its business and markets. It must try to spot trends it can turn into new sales opportunities, before its competitors. The first company who is able to identify an emerging trend and take action often becomes the market leader in their sector.

For example, many small businesses, such as Paz Elorza (http://www.pazelorza.com/) have taken advantage of the Internet since its beginning. They used it to attract new customers they weren't reaching off-line and to capture customers from competitors who didn't yet recognize the business potential of a Web site.

In that case, this company have not made sudden major changes in their business to exploit a new emerging trend. Instead, they have added something new to their business, like online shopping, a blog or presence in some social network like instegram, Facebook and twitter where they can be in direct contact with their most "technological" clients. Their marketing strategy seeks to reach new consumers' profiles. But also, they don't want to alienate the other traditional customers who aren't ready to adapt to the new online trend.

Rule 3: Make your values clear, enhance your brand reputation

In marketing, brand reputation is everything. In fact, it is the basis of a company's sustainability and credibility. As Aaker (1996) shows, if two products are similar in terms of physical appearance, quality or components, people will tend to purchase other indicators, such as brand. Thus, it is probable that people buy the one that has the stronger brand reputation. A company must make its brand positioning and differentiation clear to its target market.

Sometimes, the way to differentiate the brand is not attaching it to a product or service features, but rather, linking the brand to certain emotional or personal benefits which the client can receive through its consumption.

For example, some companies link their brand with environmental protection, ethical behaviour, or the defence of certain vulnerable groups. That is the case of Carrefour which, in 1997, decided to work in partnership with the IFHR (International Federation for Human Rights) to implement a wide-ranging programme aimed at ensuring that their suppliers used neither child nor forced labour and that they adhered to appropriate standards of employee welfare. Furthermore, owing to the current political climate in that country, they have also stopped buying goods produced in Myanmar (Burma).

Rule 4: Focus on those whom you can bring the most benefit

Segmentation is one of the most important strategies in marketing 3.0. Companies do not need to address the whole market. For them it is better to concentrate on those segments that are more stable, attractive and interesting for: where people are ready to buy and benefit from the purchase and relationship.

For instance, DIR (http://www.dir.cat) is a pioneer in promoting sports and a healthy lifestyle, offering the latest innovations in fitness, wellness and health. With over 30 years of experience, currently DIR has 17 fitness clubs in Barcelona and Sant Cugat del Vallès and 80,000 members who will have at their disposal pools, golf, boxing, yoga, paddle tennis, Pilates, wellness, nutrition and beauty services among many other facilities. They will also find many sports and social activities for singles and athletes.

DIR's mission is to improve the citizens´ quality of life, offering the benefits of a healthy lifestyle. DiR's goal is to continue to lead the industry of fitness and health in Barcelona, providing quality and innovative services which will benefit the well-being of people.

Over the last two years, DIR has developed a joint promotion with some gourmet restaurants within its geographical area. All the businesses have in common that they cater to young professionals and business executives in the same town. Thus, the restaurants' menu includes several special dishes recommended by the health club's nutritionist. They also distributed discount membership coupons for the club. Their advertising also mentioned the affiliation in order to attract health conscious customers who often avoid food prepared in gourmet restaurants. Meanwhile, DIR's monthly newsletters included a reprint of the restaurant's healthy new menu items recommended by the clubs' nutritionist. They also distributed the restaurant's discount coupons to their members.

Rule 5: Set fair prices to reflect your quality

True marketing 3.0 is a fair marketing, where price and product must match, when a good price-quality relationship exists.

SETEM Madrid, created in 1991, organizes Solidarity Camps in different countries, as well as carrying out Education for development workshops. Since 1995, the organization has undergone a major growth thanks to information campaigns such as the *Clean Clothes Campaign*, based on *education for development* activities and introducing Fair Trade to Spanish society. Nowadays, SETEM also focuses on *ethical finances for development*. In 1996, SETEM Madrid opened one of the largest fair trade shops in Spain promoting the development of farmers and craftsmen from Southern Countries by selling a wide range of products and encouraging sensible consumption.

Rule 6: Help your customers to find you

In today's global knowledge economy, people can have complete access to information through the Internet. However, there are socio-cultural differences between people, which means that they have different levels of access to technology. Companies that can straddle the divide will grow their consumer base.

For instance, Paz Elorza makes use of some social networks like Instagram, Facebook and twitter where they can be in direct contact with their most "technological" clients. Heineken Professional is a good example of how ICT enables brand not to have to use intermediaries professionally in the distribution channel, the creation of content and services in the hospitality industry and catering.

Rule 7: Obtain customers and keep them for life

A company has consumers with which it needs to maintain a good relationship. To do that, a company has to know its consumers´ personality, and what their needs, preferences and behaviour are. Then their business will grow. This is one of the principles of consumer relationship management. Thus, offering rational and emotional satisfaction is the best way to attract and maintain the correct consumers.

The sharing economy has gained a lot of momentum recently: it has moved from being a niche to a global reality and an economic phenomenon. Some companies have been created as a result of the sharing economy movement: BlaBlaCar is one of them. BlaBlaCar is a true community market based on trust which connects drivers who have empty seats in their cars to passengers looking for a ride.

BlaBlaCar transports over 550,000 passengers every month creating an entirely new, people-powered, transport network, with a dedicated customer service, a state of the art Web and mobile platform and a fast-growing community of users highly implicated with the company. BlaBlaCar is making travel social, money-saving and more efficient for millions of members across Europe.

Trust, safety and insurance are the three important ways in which BlaBlaCar creates the environment for a secure car sharing community. First, member identities are authenticated. Second, the community is self-regulating, using profiles and ratings to evaluate members and vet those that do not respect the BlaBlaCar spirit of positive community collaboration. Third, BlaBlaCar has a dedicated Member Relations team, available every day to support users.

Rule 8: Every business is a service business, because every product delivers a service

Nowadays, offer is more than a product, it is a complete set of products and services that companies give to their consumers. Thus, whatever the company business, a company has to serve its clients. Service must become a service provider's calling, and never be considered a duty. If a company serves its consumers sincerely and with complete empathy, they take away a positive memory from this experience.

Tesco PLC (LSE: TSCO) is a British multinational grocery and general merchandise retailer headquartered in Cheshunt, Hertfordshire, England, United Kingdom. It is the second-largest retailer in the world measured by profits (after Wal-Mart) and the third-largest retailer in the world measured by revenue (after Walmart and Carrefour). It has stores in 14 countries throughout

Asia, Europe and North America and is the grocery market leader in the UK (where it has a market share of around 30%), Malaysia, the Republic of Ireland and Thailand.

Tesco is characterized by offering an excellent sales service to its customers. In 1996 Tesco created Tesco Customer Service Centres, as a place that serves up excellent customer service. Nowadays, Tesco has two Customer Service Centres based in Dundee and Cardiff and over 1,800 staff who reply on average to 1.5 million contacts from customers across the UK. Tesco teams respond to both customers and stores queries, which could be about anything from its products or its consumer service in its stores – and they do so by telephone, letter and email.

Tesco also has resident technical experts at the Tesco Technical Support team, who are there to offer help and advice on any technical issues customers may have with their electrical items – whether they have been bought online or in store.

Rule 9: Every day improve your business process in every way

Honesty is one of the most valued qualities in business. And for that reason, companies must always fulfill their promises to customers and suppliers, as well as never engaging in deceit with regard to quality, delivery time or price.

National Public Radio (NPR) is a privately and publicly funded non-profit membership media organization that serves as a national syndicator to a network of 900 public radio stations in the United States. According to Forbes (2011), NPR is a great example of a company that is honest with its customers. The station takes time at the end of most programs to share listener feedback on past shows. They share the glowing reviews, of course, but they also share customer outrage, disbelief and disappointment. What's more, when NPR has made headlines for less than desirable reasons, the organization has reported its own bad news as if it were any other media outlet, rather than shifting the focus. These actions - which many companies might be afraid to take - only serve to underscore the affinity that subscribers and listeners have for the station.

Rule 10: In the decision making process consider all the information, but also use wisdom

Gather relevant information about the environment, help companies to satisfy the market where they compete, as well as the different agents with which they interact. But accumulated knowledge is not enough to make decisions. In this process, it is necessary that they also consider the experience accumulated over the years. As Kotler et al (2010) show, marketers will be able to swiftly make correct decisions, supported by their maturity of spirit and clarity of heart, in other words, by the wisdom that they inherently have.

Certain past experiences form the basis for decision making. For example, in the late 1980s the Caixa began to fund projects to eliminate poverty. Currently, Caixa" Foundation therefore promotes diverse initiatives in different areas to foster the social inclusion of the most disadvantaged sectors so that the people in them may enjoy a better life. In particular, through CaixaProinfancia they help improve the social and economic situation of families with 0 to 16 year-old children in order to prevent the perpetuation of poverty from one generation to the next.

This program is promoted and coordinated through over 350 social institutions which work in a network and see to implementing it in different Spanish cities. CaixaProinfancia helps children's social and educational development with measures intended both to give psychological and educational support and to consolidate activities in open centres, children's camps and summer schools. It also provides economic resources to cover basic needs in childhood (food, hygiene and school equipment). Since the start of the programme, they have helped over 200.000 children throughout Spain.

CONCLUSION

Marketing 3.0 has come about as a response to several factors: new technological developments, problems caused by globalization and the interest of people to express their creativity, values and spirituality. In this context, companies, as active agents in the environment, must demonstrate social responsibility through the development of actions in favour of the community, all with the aim of positioning itself as companies whose brands have respect and admiration.

Marketing 3.0 is focused on the person, not as a contradiction of the previous marketing vision, but as a refinement of it. It is the evolution from Marketing 1.0, based on the product and which appeals to the "reason" of the customer via rational arguments and passes to Marketing 2.0 which focused on customers and aimed to get to the heart of the customers (marketing oriented relations) and the Marketing 3.0 is know their customers, to be concerned about them (their emotions, their feelings, their concerns) and co-create products with them.

Companies which currently correctly apply marketing 3.0 are those which have been good at marketing 1.0 and 2.0. The marketing of the future means that companies no longer are freelance fighters, but an organization that acts as part of a loyal network of partners, where people are not just consumers, but "whole persons" with "human spirit" who want to make the world a better place.

New technologies and the development of the Internet and social networks have enabled customers to express freely their business and consumer experiences. This is not the most creative advertising, if the values of the company are not credible and not part of their DNA. Marketing 3.0 aims to create new ways of reaching customers who respect the values and which respect the employees, partners, distributors and suppliers so that they feel that they are truly part of the public services.

Suppliers play an essential role in the consolidation of Marketing 3.0. As Kotler et al (2010) show, they are hybrids of companies, consumers and employees. First of all, they are channel partners of the producer companies: in fact, they are the consumers with needs and wants to be served. And for that reason, they become collaborators, cultural change agents and creative partners for companies at the same time, but also the suppliers are companies with their own mission, vision, values and business models. In fact, they sell to end-users and form the consumer interface.

Given the complex nature of the distributors, we can see currently how the application of marketing 3.0 in the field of distribution is manifested in events such as: a retailer that leverages Web-based technologies to efficiently and effectively provide personalized ad flyers to each of its shoppers, communicated across multiple digital channels and delivered automatically into the transaction at checkout – realizing increased sales, shopping visits and customer retention through the power of brand image. Or a collaborative marketing portal enabling supply chain partners to create content and promotions, enabling actionable collaboration at a shopper level, with different shopper segments receiving different marketing initiatives across different channels, and closing the loop by providing effectiveness measures for each, from ad flyer to e-mail to kiosk interaction.

As a conclusion, we should note that suppliers' values and behaviours are changing. To provide the maximum level of value to their customers in particular, and society, in general, has become a priority. But the new consumer generation is much more attuned to social issues and concerns. Therefore, they seek to provide not only functional benefits, but also social ones. The change from marketing 1.0 to marketing 3.0 can help them to become open companies, and improve their relations with the rest of social agents. Marketing 3.0 is the first step to being human and social-centred and still be profitable at the same time.

REFERENCES

Aaker, D. A. (1996). *Building Strong Brands*. Free Press.

Bolton, R. N., & Saxena-Iyer, S. (2009). Interactive Services: A Framework, Synthesis and Research Directions. *Journal of Interactive Marketing*, *23*(1), 91–104. doi:10.1016/j.intmar.2008.11.002

Botsman, R., & Rogers, R. (2010). *What's mine is yours: How collaborative consumption is changing the way we live*. Harper Collins Publisher.

Coe, N. M., & Wrigley, N. (2009). *The Globalization of Retailing* (Vol. 1-2). Cheltenham, MA: Edward Elgar Publishing Ltd.

Copeland, M. V., & Malik, O. (2005, July). How to Ride the Fifth Wave. *Business 2.0*.

Corstjens, M., & Lal, R. (2012). Retail Doesn't Cross Borders: Here's Why and What to Do About It. *Harvard Business Review*, *90*(4), 104–111. PMID:22299510

Ernst, H., Hoyer, Krafft, & Soll. (2010). *Consumer Idea Generation*. Vallendar.

Etgar, M. (2008). A Descriptive Model of the Consumer Co-Production Process. *Journal of the Academy of Marketing Science*, *36*, 97–108. doi:10.1007/s11747-007-0061-1

Feick, L., & Price. (1987). The Market Maven: A Diffuser of Marketplace Information. *Journal of Marketing*, *51*(1), 83–97. doi:10.2307/1251146

Forbes. (2011). *Steps to More Honest Business*. Retrieved from http://www.forbes.com/sites/thebigenoughcompany/2011/09/21/3-steps-to-a-more-honest-business/

Ghemawat, P. (2007). Managing Differences: The Central Challenge of Global Strategy. *Harvard Business Review*, *85*(3), 58–68. PMID:17348170

Hauser, J., Tellis, G. J., & Griffin, A. (2006). Research on Innovation: A Review and Agenda for Marketing Science. *Marketing Science, 25,* 686–717. doi:10.1287/mksc.1050.0144

Hoffman, D. L., Kopalle, & Novak. (2010). The ''Right'' Consumers for Better Concepts: Identifying and Using Consumers High in Emergent Nature to Further Develop New Product Concepts. *JMR, Journal of Marketing Research.* doi:10.1509/jmkr.47.5.854

Holt, D. B. (2004). *How Brands Become Icons: The Principles of Cultural Branding.* Boston: Harvard Business School Press.

Hoyer, W. D., Chandy, R., Dorotic, M., Kraff, M., & Singh, S. S. (2010). Consumer Cocreation in New Product Development. *Journal of Service Research, 13*(3), 283–296. doi:10.1177/1094670510375604

Insider. (2012). *White paper.* Retrieved from http://www.mediacom.com/media/2088012/mediacom%20the%20insider_the%20empowered%20consumer_whitepaper.pdf

Kacker, M. (1986). Coming to Terms with Global Retailing. *International Marketing Review, 3*(1), 7. doi:10.1108/eb008295

Kotler, P., Kartajaya, H., & Setiawan, I. (2010). *Marketing 3.0: From Products To Customers To The Human Spirit.* New York: John Wiley & Sons Inc. doi:10.1002/9781118257883

Magnusson, P. R., Matthing, & Kristensson. (2003). Managing User Involvement in Service Innovation: Experiments With Innovating End Users. *Journal of Service Research, 6*(2), 111–124. doi:10.1177/1094670503257028

Majfud, J. (2009). The pandemic of consumerism. *UN chronicle.* Retrieved from http://institucional.us.es/araucaria/otras_res/2009_11/resegna_1109_6.htm#_ftn1

McAfee, A. (2006). Enterprise 2.0: The Dawn of Emergence Collaboration. *MIT Sloan Management Review, 47*(3), 21–28.

McAfee, A. (2009). *Enterprise 2.0: New Collaborative Tools for Your Organization's Toughest Challenges.* Boston: Harvard Business Press.

Moore, G. (1991). *Crossing the Chasm: Marketing and Selling High-Tech Products to Mainstream Customers.* New York, NY: Harper Business Essentials.

Mourali, M., & Yang, Z. (2013). The Dual Role Of Power In Resisting Social Influence. *The Journal of Consumer Research, 40*(3), 539–554. doi:10.1086/671139

Nambisan, S., & Baron. (2009). Virtual Customer Environments: Testing a Model of Voluntary Participation in Value Co-creation Activities. *Journal of Product Innovation Management, 26*(4), 388–406. doi:10.1111/j.1540-5885.2009.00667.x

O'Hern, M. S., & Rindfleisch. (2009). Customer Co-Creation: A Typology and Research Agenda. *Review of Marketing Research, 6,* 84–106.

Ogawa, S., & Piller. (2006). Reducing the Risks of New Product Development. *Sloan Management Review, 47,* 65–72.

Prahalad, C. K., & Ramaswamy, V. (2004). *The Future of Competition: Co-creating Unique Value with Consumers.* Boston: Harvard Business School Press.

von Hippel, E. (1986). Lead Users: A Source of Novel Product Concepts. *Management Science, 32,* 791–805. doi:10.1287/mnsc.32.7.791

Zohar, D. (1990). *The Quantum Self: Human Nature and Consciousness Defined by the New Physics.* New York: Quill.

ADDITIONAL READING

Bagozzi, R. P. (1995). Reflections on Relationship Marketing in Consumer Markets. *Journal of the Academy of Marketing Science*, 23(4), 272–277. doi:10.1177/009207039502300406

Baran, R., Zerres, C., & Zerres, M. (2008). Customer Relationship Management (CRM). Disponible en Web: http://bookboon.com/es/customer-relationship-management-ebook

Cook, N. (2008). *Enterprise 2.0: How Social Software Will Change the Future of Work*. Hampshire, England: Gower Publishing.

Dyche, J., & Levy, A. (2006). *Customer Data Integration: Reaching a Single Version of the Truth (SAS Institute Inc.)*. Hoboken, New Jersey: John Wiley & Sons, Inc.

Gartner Research Inc. (2003). *Building Business Benefits From CMR. Executive Report*. Stamford, CT: Gartner, Inc.

Grönroos, C. (1989). Defining Marketing: a Market-oriented Approach. *European Journal of Marketing*, 23(1), 54–58.

Grönroos, C. (1994a). Quo Vadis, Marketing? Toward a Relationship Marketing Paradigm. *Journal of Marketing Management*, 10, 347–360. doi:10.1080/0267257X.1994.9964283

Grönroos, C. (1994b). Form Marketing Mix to the Relationship Marketing Toward a Paradigm Shift in Marketing. *Asia-Australian Marketing Journal*, 2(1), 1.

Gummesson, E. (1987). Marketing- A long term interactive relationship. *Long Range Planning*, 20(4), 10–20. doi:10.1016/0024-6301(87)90151-8

Huang, Z., & Benyoucef, M. (2012). From e-commerce to social commerce: A close look at design features. *Electronic Commerce Research and Applications*, 12(4), 246–259. doi:10.1016/j.elerap.2012.12.003

Ravald, A., Grönross, C. (1996), The Value Concept and Relationship Marketing, European Journal of Marketing, 30(1)1: 19-30.

Spekman, R. E. (1988). Strategic Supplier Selection: Understanding Long-Tern Buyer Relationships. *Business Horizons*, (July/August): 75–81. doi:10.1016/0007-6813(88)90072-9

Zhou, L., Zhang, P., & Zimmermann, H.-S. (2013). Social Commerce Research: An integrated view. Electronic Cmmerce Research and Application. Online available on http://melody.syr.edu/pzhang/publications/ECRA_13_Zhou_etal_Social_Commerce.pdf

KEY TERMS AND DEFINITIONS

Co-Creation: A business strategy focus on consumer experience and interactive relationships. Co-creation allows and encourages a more active involvement from the consumer to create a value-rich experience.

Collaborative Consumption: A global concept that involves sharing, bartering, lending, trading, renting, gifting, and swapping goods instead of buying them. This concept has been in communities for thousands of years, but has recently gained popularity in the United States and Europe.

Collaborative Social Media: Term used to refer to digital media that enables broad-range participation where the distinctions between production, consumption and design are dissolved.

Consumer Empowerment: A mental state usually accompanied by a physical act which enables a consumer or a group of consumers to put into effect their own choices through demonstrating their needs, wants and demands in their decision-making with other individuals or organisational bodies in the marketplace.

Expressive Social Media: Term used to refer to digital media that allows people to freely express their ideas, tastes, preferences, opinions, etc.

Globalization: The worldwide movement toward economic, financial, trade and communication integration. Globalization implies the opening of local and nationalistic perspectives to a broader outlook of an interconnected and interdependent world with free transfer of capital, goods, and services across national frontiers.

Perceived Value: An assessment of the worth of a good or service. The product value assessed by a business when setting a price for a particular product can depend on its production costs, its overall market value and the value of the product as perceived by a targeted group of consumer.

Section 3
Store Atmosphere and Interaction with Consumers

Section 3 offers an overview of store atmosphere and the interaction with consumers. In the first part (chapters 13 to 16), issues related to the store atmosphere are analyzed considering sensorial factors, the relationship with salespeople, and even taking into account security issues inside stores. The last 3 chapters of the section focus on consumers' involvement in co-creation of the retail service with reference to elements related to social responsibility and ethical/social values.

Chapter 13
Atmosphere as a Store Communication Tool

Sanda Renko
University of Zagreb, Croatia

ABSTRACT

Many studies have found that within an intensely competitive market, it is difficult for retailers to gain advantages from products, prices, promotions, and location. They have to work hard to keep their stores favourable in the mind of consumers. Both practitioners and researchers recognize store atmosphere as a tool for creating value and gaining customers. This chapter provides a conceptual framework for studying the influence of store atmosphere on the store patronage. The chapter presents the main dimensions that constitute conventional retail stores' atmosphere and clarifies the manipulation of elements such as colour, lighting, signage, etc. within the store to communicate retailers' messages to customers. The topic is investigated from both retailers` and customers` perspective. The chapter concludes that both consumers and retailers prioritize functional cues in modern retailing forms.

INTRODUCTION

As customers become more sophisticated and better informed (McDonald et al., 2000), retailing is much less about the sale of products and services, and much more about the communication with customers and creation of relationships with them. Many customers even form impression of a retailer even before entering its stores or just after entering, but prior examining its merchandise and prices (Berman & Evans, 2010). Retailers are finding increasingly difficult to create a differential advantage on the basis of products, price, promotion and location (Baker et al., 1992; Gou-Fong Liaw, 2007). There is a growing movement

against the same of corporate, globalized retail design and the urge to create an individualized shopping experience is a major trend around the world (Dowdy, 2008,). Retailers are trying to define the manner in which they could differentiate themselves on the market and attract customers better than their competitors.

Many studies (e.g. Donovan & Rositer, 1982; Foxall, 1997; Levy & Weitz, 2012) found that the store environment significantly influenced consumer's in-store behaviour in ways they might not be aware. Tai and Fung (1997) revealed that atmospheric cues had a variety of physical and physiological effects on people with causal effects on their buying behaviour.

DOI: 10.4018/978-1-4666-6074-8.ch013

A store`s environment is comprised of a vast array of separate elements (such as colour, music, lighting, scent, etc.) which are highly interrelated and work together synergistically to affect consumers (Olahut et al., 2012, p. 319). It is a multidimensional concept comprising the store's physical characteristics, such as architecture, layout, signs and displays, colours, lighting, temperature, sounds and smells (Levy & Weitz, 2012).

Retailers may use them to provide consumers a positive shopping experience, to keep their stores favourable in the mind of consumers and to control them as well. Those elements form the part of the store atmosphere (Newman & Cullen, 2002) and enhance the customers` perception of the store. The communication process between store and its customers begins with its exterior and it continues within a store relying on colour, music, texture, aroma, lighting, etc. Moreover, they are also elements of a retailer`s communication mix and play an important role in creating and reinforcing a retailer`s brand image (Levy & Weitz, 2012). The retailer aims its communication through atmosphere to improve customers' perceptions of the store in order to increase store loyalty; to improve customers attitudes to the store in order to increase store visits, etc. Olahut et al., (2012) observed that store atmosphere „influences all aspects of the retailing business, including aspects such as the customer`s decisions on where to go for shopping, consumer`s perceptions of store image, quality of merchandise and service, buyers behaviours of the amount of time and money spent at the store, in fact the consumer`s overall satisfaction with the retail store"(p. 318).

Kotler and Keller (2006) argue that every store must embody a planned atmosphere that suits the target market and draws consumers toward purchase. Consumers purchase a total product, consisting of not simply the physical item but also the packaging, after-sales services, advertising, image and the atmosphere of the store (Kotler & Keller, 2006). Kotler (1973) points out that "in

some cases, atmosphere is the primary product" (p. 48). Creating an atmosphere in a store focusing on one element is difficult, because it involves a combination of music, colours, crowding and other stimuli (Buckley, 1987). Accordingly, this chapter will clarify the manipulation of elements such as colour, lighting, signage, etc. within the store to communicate retailer`s messages to customers. The main objective of this chapter is to present main dimensions which constitute conventional retail stores atmosphere. Additionally, the objective of the chapter is to provide a conceptual framework for studying the effects of store atmosphere in attracting customers to purchase in a particular store, because „the degree to which a retailer is able to get into the head of their customer will determine how successful these sort of strategy (i.e. store atmosphere) are" (Newman & Cullen, 2002, p. 266).

In an attempt to explain the holistic and multidimensional character of the atmosphere, the review of the elements of store atmosphere was conducted, too. For the purpose of getting better insight into the importance of atmosphere as the silent sales person (Reddy & Reddy, 2012), it has been explored in the selected retail context of the Republic of Croatia. Croatia is the Southeast European country with modern retailing forms (supermarkets, hypermarkets and discounters) which accounted for 76 per cent of grocery sales in 2011 (Nielsen Q1 Reports, 2012). Top 10 retailers hold almost 80 per cent of the Croatian market, similar to situations on the markets of the developed Central and East European countries. A research study included both retailers` and customers` perspective. Following the structure of the chapter, the discussion of the results, conclusion and future research possibilities are given. Emphasis is placed on the managerial implications, as retailers must be certain that their stores are up-to-date and portray an image that is appealing to their target markets (Baker et al., 1992, p. 446).

THEORETICAL BACKGROUND

In this section, the historical development of the concept of atmosphere and variations in the meaning of the concept in general are given. Moreover, key dimensions of the store atmosphere with their specific cues are explained. In such a way, a comprehensive framework necessary for understanding the concept of store atmosphere is provided.

Development of the Concept

Although Kotler (1973-1974) is often mentioned as the first who use and define the term, Olahut et al., (2012) note that a novelist Emil Zola was the first author who had described the relevance of atmosphere inside a department store (p. 318).

According to Kotler (1973-1974), historical perspective of the concept of atmosphere can be traced back to ancient Greece when magnificent temples were created in honour of their gods.

Medieval cathedrals and renaissance palaces were designed to produce specific feelings and reactions among people. Trade included barter transactions and selling at open markets. The development of first stores (in the second half of the 18th and at beginning of the 19th century) has started to draw retailers` attention to the space where the products are bought and/or consumed. However, at the beginning, retailers focused to make functional service spaces.

The first shopkeepers tried to lure consumers into their stores either by ostentatiously exhibiting their names or by displaying products in their windows or on tables in the street, providing that they were open for business and proud of their produce (Morgan, 2008, p. 11).

Along with the rapid development of new store formats, there has been growing recognition that product, services and salesmen are not enough to increase sales, extend consumer's time spend in the store, etc. They realized that "consumers respond to more than just the core product or service being offered when making purchase decisions" (Billings, 1990, p. 1) and that "the decision to enter a particular store, how much time to spend inside, and to buy or not to buy is heavily influenced by the shopping environment and its effect on customers` emotions" (Bohl, 2012, p. 1). De Farias (2010) suggests that until the 80's, buyers were thought to be exclusively rational beings, whose purchasing choices were made after a logical processing of available information into a stream that came from the detection of a problem to their satisfaction with the purchase (Solomon, 2008). McGoldrick (2002) adds that "in the 1980s and 1990s, there was much emphasis upon store design, used as a powerful weapon in the quest to achieve image differentiation. In the 2000s, store environments are now also a key element in the competition between physical and electronic shopping alternatives" (p. 453).

Different Aspects of the Concept

It should be noted that the shopping environment has been widely discussed in the scientific literature, not only under the term atmosphere, but also as an important part of the overall merchandising strategy (Kotler, 1973-1974; Markin et al., 1976), as one component of store image (Cox & Brittain, 2004; Dunne et al., 2002), as servicescapes (Arnould et al., 1998; Bitner, 1992), and as store ambience (Dakoumi Hamrouni & Touzi, 2011).

Eroglu et al., (2001) have been at the forefront in introducing the concept of Web or e-atmospherics, which has been motivated an emerging body of research (Burke, 2002; Dailey, 2004; de Kervenoael et al., 2008; Manganari et al., 2009). Although considerable variations exist among researchers concerning the term of store atmosphere, actual definitions are similar in a way that they highlight the combination of retail environmental cues.

Kotler (1973-1974) defined the term atmospherics as "the conscious designing of space to create certain effects in buyers. More specifically, atmospherics is the effort to design buying environments to produce specific emotional effects in the buyer that enhance his purchase probability." (p. 50). Banat and Wanderbori (2012) and Baker et al., (2003) consider store atmosphere as the design of an environment by stimulation of the five senses. According to Berman and Evans (2010) atmosphere refers to "the store`s physical characteristics that project an image to customers" (p. 508). The same authors used an excellent term to express the meaning of the atmosphere in general, as follows: "it is personality of a store…" (p. 508).

Markin et al., (1976, p. 43) concluded that store environment „is never neutral. The retail store is a bundle of cues, messages and suggestions which communicate to shoppers." Baker et al., (1992) found out that ambience cues and social cues interact with each other to influence customers` pleasure and arousal in the store environment. Additionally, arousal and pleasure may mediate the effects of store environment on customers` willingness to buy. Pleasure is associated with the amount of money spent and affinity for the store, whereas arousal is associated with money spent in the store, and the number of items purchased in the store (Sherman et al., 1997). According to Foxall (1997), "atmospherics are facets of environmental design which influence consumer behaviour by creating attention, by communicating a store image and level of service to potential buyers, and by stimulating affective responses" (p. 506). Espinoza et al., (2004) tested comprehensive causal model of the influence of atmosphere cues on consumers` perceptions of a store and their willingness to buy in a particular store. Grewal et al., (2003) investigated the relative importance of wait expectations and store atmosphere evaluations on patronage intentions. They argue that "in the eyes of customers, there is nothing positive about having to wait" (p. 265). Accordingly, perceptions of customer density and expectations of the wait had a negative effect on store atmosphere.

As psychologists have studied environment-behaviour relationships, a research stream known as "environmental psychology" was developed. Mehrabian and Russel (1974) explained that this psychological discipline was concerned with "(1) the direct impact of physical stimuli on human emotions and (2) the effect of the physical stimuli on a variety of behaviours, such as work performance or social interaction" (p. 4). Turley and Milliman (2000) start their comprehensive review of atmospheric effects on shopping behaviour with the description of the Mehrabian-Russel model. The model relies on a Stimulus-Organism-Response (S-O-R) paradigm, which assumes that the atmosphere is the stimulus (S) that causes a consumer`s evaluation (O) and causes some behavioural responses (R) (Turley & Milliman, 2000). Donovan and Rossiter (1982) and Baker et al., (1992) were the first to employ the S-O-R model to study the impact of store atmosphere on customers` perception and patronage decision (Chen & Hsieh, 2011, p. 10055). They found that pleasure resulting from exposure to store atmosphere influenced such in-store behaviours as spending levels, amount of time spent in the store, and willingness to visit the store again.

Key Dimensions of the Concept

The concept of atmosphere is, by definition, holistic (Massara, 2003, p. 47). It's the overall experience that matters more than any single aspect of the environment. Therefore, in explaining the effects of the store atmosphere on shoppers, Massara (2003) addresses to the system theory which suggests that the whole is rarely equal to the sum of the single constituent parts.

Kotler`s conclusion (1973-1974) that atmosphere is apprehended through four senses – sight, smell, sound and touch – has led to quite a few discussions about the number of key dimensions, variables, cues, or elements of an atmosphere, respectively. Kotler (1973-1974) specified four dimensions of an atmosphere as follows (p. 51):

- The main visual dimensions: colour, brightness, size, and shapes;
- The main aural dimensions: volume, and pitch;
- The main olfactory dimensions: scent, and freshness;
- The main tactile dimensions: softness, smoothness, and temperature.

Bitner (1992) considered that store environment consists of three dimensions:

- Ambient conditions: background music, noise, temperature, lighting and odour, etc.;
- Spatial layout and functionality: the layout of equipment, facilities, furniture, etc.;
- Signs, symbols and artefacts: signboards, decorations.

Berman and Evans (2010) divided atmospheric elements or stimuli into four categories:

- The exterior of the store: marquee, entrances, windows, lighting, and construction materials;
- General interior: flooring, bright, colour, scents, sounds, store fixtures, wall textures, and dressing facilities;
- The layout and design variables: allocation of floor space, classification of store offerings, determination of a traffic-flow pattern, determination of space needs, mapping out in-store locations, and arrangement of individual products;
- The point-of-purchase and decoration variables: various types of the point-of-purchase displays.

As a framework for examining the key atmospheric elements explored by various authors, we use the modified version of Massara (2003) approach and divide atmospheric into three categories: variables of the external environment, variables of the interior of the store, and human variables.

The External Variables

This category includes the storefront, entrances, display windows, building architecture, the surrounding area, and parking (Newman & Cullen, 2002, p. 246; Turley & Milliman, 2000, p. 195). Dunne et al., (2002) add signage which is critical to attracting passing shoppers, providing them with information, and enticing them to enter the store.

The review of literature shows a lack of studies analysing effects of external variables on shopping behaviour. The best impression was given by Olahut et al., (2012) who said that "even though the external variables are the first set of cues in consumers` view, studies on the exterior of the store are the worst represented atmospheric elements in marketing literature" (p. 325). Sen et al., (2002) examined the effects of window displays on decision to visit a store, while Cornelius et al., (2010), Oh and Petrie (2012) paid more attention to storefront displays and innovative displays. In their study about the influence of selected physical components of the urban environment on consumers` behavioural intentions, De Nisco and Warnaby (2013) considered parking facilities as a variable related to urban space layout and functionality. It must be noted that Turley and Milliman (2000) point out that in the situation of poorly managed external stimuli „generally speaking the rest of the atmosphere may not matter" (p.195).

The Interior Variables

This category includes lighting and colour, scents and sounds, temperature, cleanliness, displays, signs, layout, music, etc. A wide range of literature on effects of interior atmospheric cues on customer behaviour exists. Mostly, studies explored the effects of specific atmospheric cues separately.

In such a way, literature review suggests that *music* can lead to more positive evaluation of the store environment (Baker et al., 1992; Bailey & Areni, 2006; Dube & Morin, 2001; Hui et al., 1997; Grewal et al., 2003; Yalch & Spangenberg, 2000). Music can influence both conscious and unconscious customer action (Oakes, 2003). The type and the tempo of music could create an atmosphere and manipulate shopping behaviour. Soothing, peaceful classical music, with the constant tempo was found to create positive moods and pleasurable atmosphere (Baker et al., 1992; Milliman, 1986). Moreover, classical background music usually communicates a sophisticated, upper class atmosphere Areni & Kim, 1993), and any retailer wishing to convey a high prestige and high price image, should consider classical background music (Yalch & Spangenberg, 1990). "If consumers are seeking sophistication, then in-store cues must suggest, and even facilitate that experience" (Areni & Kim, 1993, p. 338). North et al., (1999) found the relationship between music and customers` product selection.

Studies of the effects of *scent and odour* have concentrated on three aspects (Olahut et al., 2012, p. 329):

1. The scent`s congruency with the product sold in the store (Mattila & Wirtz, 2001);
2. The presence of a scent (Morrin & Ratneshwar, 2000); and
3. The pleasantness of a scent (Morrin & Ratneshwar, 2000).

When scent is not congruent with the targeted product, customers have been shown to spend less time processing information about products (Peck & Childers, 2008). Banat and Wandebori (2012) point out that scent has a large impact on customer`s mood and emotions, positive impact on customer`s level of excitement and satisfaction with the shopping experience (p. 85), while having an unpleasant scent may result in negative affective or behaviour responses (Morrin & Ratneshwar,

2000). Spangenberg et al., (1996) point out that consumers` exposure to pleasant scents affects their overall time and expenditures spent in the store, and products purchased, as well.

Other atmospheric cues which have attracted research interest are *lighting and colours*. Their primary functions are to highlight merchandise and to enable effective business operations within the store, as well as to promote products. Many studies have shown the effect of colour on shopping behaviour (e.g. Ellis & Ficek, 2001; Babin et al., 2003, Chebat & Morrin, 2007). However, Varley (2001) points out that „although some retailers have embraced a colour into their corporate design and carried this through into the store design successfully, many retailers restrict the use of colour in the store to trim and signage, using neutral colours and materials for much of the store interior" (p. 158). Babin et al., (2003) suggested that lighting and colour combinations affect consumers` cognitive representation and affective reaction. Lighting could positively influence customer-shopping behaviour (Hulten et al., 2008) and the number of items examined and handled (Olahut et al., 2012). Customers` preferences for lighting levels differ in various situations. Softer lighting tends to create a more relaxing, pleasant mood than does brighter lights. Summers and Hebert (2001) investigated the amount of time at display, the number of items touched, and purchased in two lighting conditions: ambient lighting only and ambient lighting plus supplemental display lighting.

According to Olahut et al., (2012), studies how variables such as *traffic flow, layout*, location of departments, and allocation of merchandise within departments impact the emotional states of customers and their behaviour are missing. Newman et al., (2003) are among the rare ones who investigated the importance of customers` reactions to the layout of merchandise in the store. Bohl (2012) concluded that „most research in this area has dealt with the subject of store layout as a means to provide customer space to shop easily or to control traffic flow on the floor" (p. 10). Countryman and Jang (2006) considered furnishings as an important part of the physical environment, which has received very little attention in the literature on atmospheric.

While measuring the effect of store design and store atmosphere towards customer sales per visit of the concept store in Indonesia Banat and Wandebori (2012) found out that fixture and *display* product arrangement had the most effect on increasing sales per visit.

The Human Variables

This category considers the human interaction with employees or other customers. There is the literature stream that attempts to further the theoretical and empirical understanding of human variables in the creation of an atmosphere (e.g. Baker et al., 1992; Heide & Grønhaug, 2006; Massara, 2003; Turley & Milliman, 2000). According to Baker et al., (1992), social factors represent the "people" component of the environment, including both store employees and customers. Turley and Milliman (2000) included human variables comprising customer crowding and density, privacy, customer characteristics, personnel/employee characteristics, and employee uniforms (p. 197). In general, two major groups of researches on the human variables can be identified. The first group is related to store employees, their number, appearance, and behaviour which could affect a customers` perception of the service level within a retail store (Baker et al., 1992; Bitner, 1992; Turley & Milliman, 2000; etc.). Hu and Jasper (2006) found out that consumers had a more favourable attitude toward merchandise and service quality and felt more aroused or pleased with a store where more social cues were present.

The number of employees should be in accordance with the setting requirements, because more employees in a store could ensure a store functioning properly. When the number of employees in a store is less than the setting requires, it is likely to

assume that customers should wait and could be provided with the lower service level. The other group of studies on human variables examined other customers in the store are perceived in the context of crowding and density. According to Stokos (1972), physical density is associated with the number of people per unit area, while crowding refers to the negative psychological reactions to density (Grewal et al., 2003, p. 261). On the other hand, Machleit et al., (1994) are making difference between human and spatial crowding. Literature review (Machleit et al., 1994; Grewal et al., 2003) suggests that a high level of customer density may result in more negative store atmosphere evaluation. Grewal et al., (2003) point out that "atmospherics can make customers less aware of their wait because they are either distracted and/ or entertained" (p. 265).

It should be pointed out that there are a small number of studies which have proven holistic character of the concept of store atmosphere and have examined the interaction between atmospheric variables. There are the worth mentioning works of the Baker et al. (1992; 1994; 2002), Eroglu et al., (2005), Mower et al. (2012), and Teller and Dennis (2012) who realized that "it is important for the atmospheric elements to work together" (Levy & Weitz, 2012, p. 490) in order to have a positive impact on buying behaviour and customer satisfaction.

Baker et al., (1992) examined the effects of two retail atmospheric factors: ambience cues (lighting and music), and social cues (number/ friendliness of employees) on customers` pleasure, arousal, and willingness to buy. In their later work, Baker et al., (2002) focused on the interaction between store design, employees and music on the retail store perception. Teller and Dennis (2012) showed that interaction between music and aroma affected the pleasure and time spent in the store. Eroglu et al., (2005) investigated the effects of retail density and music tempo, and their impact on shopper responses. In order to fill a gap in external atmospheric literature, Mower et al., (2012) investigated the influence of window displays and landscaping on customers' responses towards an apparel boutique.

Yoo et al., (1998) examine how various characteristics of retail environments influence consumers' emotional responses in the shopping environment, and how these emotions, in turn, influence consumers' store attitudes. In their construct, store atmosphere included design, lighting, air quality in the store, inside decoration and music. However, the results of their study show that store atmosphere had no pronounced effect on either positive or negative shoppers' emotions while shopping in department stores.

METHODOLOGY

For the purpose of this chapter, a research study examining the impact of store atmosphere on customers' intentions to purchase in a particular type of grocery stores was given from both retailers' and customers' perspective. Moreover, the study considered the rating of store atmosphere among other salient store attributes, such as price, product range and quality, services, etc.

The decision to conduct study in various store types was mostly induced by the fact that different store formats want to play different roles, because they specialize in some form of values. For example, discount stores or supermarkets prioritize functional cues and to provide mainly utilitarian value. In specialty stores customers expect both utilitarian and hedonic values. Retailers could choose various combinations of these factors according to their needs. Many researchers investigated the importance of store atmosphere in the context of specific store types (e.g. Grewal et al., (2003) tested their conceptual model in a jewellery store; Baker et al., (1992) conducted an experiment in a lab setting which presented videotape version of a retail card and gift stores; Grayson and McNeill (2009) assessed the use and importance of atmospheric elements in the bar

environment). In general, researchers conclude that stores could be designed to create experience their customers prefer.

As mentioned before, the two-phase study included a qualitative and a quantitative approach: 1) the quantitative study on the sample of Croatian consumers in order to understand the rating of the atmosphere among other salient store attributes and what atmospheric cues consumers consider important for purchasing fast moving consumer goods; 2) the qualitative study among senior managers of retail companies operating on the Croatian market in order to find out whether retailers are aware of the relationships between the environment and customer purchasing behaviour.

Sampling Procedure

The first phase consists of a survey method used for collecting data from the sample of consumers when shopping for small quantities of fast moving consumer goods (i.e. everyday shopping) in various types of grocery stores in the city of Zagreb (time period November 2012 – March 2013). As non-approval to conduct the research within the store was given by retailers, 250 respondents were approached while they were leaving the store and were asked to answer the questions in the questionnaire. In order to reduce the non-response rate to a minimum, the educational purpose of the research was explained. Also, anonymity and confidentiality of the responses in the introduction of the questionnaire were stressed. The investigation was conducted by 10 undergraduate students of the Faculty of Economics and Business in Zagreb.

Table 1 summarizes the profile of the 250 interviewees, who participated in the research. As can be seen from Table 1, all the "basic" dimensions that portray the respondents' profile, namely gender, age, education, and employment status have percentages that indicate a satisfactory level of representativeness.

The second phase of the study consisted of in-depth interviews with six senior managers in

Table 1. Respondents' profile

	Percentage
Gender	
Female	58.2
Male	41.8
Age (Years)	
18-24	18.8
25-34	35.6
35-44	21.2
45-54	18.0
55-64	6.4
65+	0
Education	
Unfinished Elementary	0
Elementary	11.2
3 years-High school	39.6
Secondary/High	37.6
College/University	11.6
Occupation/Employment status	
Not employed	12.4
Pensioners	2.6
Housewives	9.8
Students	9.8
Managers	7.4
Clerk	9.2
Industrial workers	23.2
Farmers	2.4
Businessmen	20.4
Others	2.8

retail companies operating on the Croatian market. The interviews were conducted by phone in June 2013. They lasted on average about 15-20 minutes and were transcribed. Similar to Coltman (2007), pre-survey telephone calls were made at each company to identify whether they would be prepared to participate in the survey. In order to avoid unnecessary vast of time, the research instrument was sent to each company few days before interviewing.

Research Instruments' Design

In the first phase, the research was based on the face-to-face interviewing with a highly structured questionnaire which consisted of three parts. Part I required respondents to indicate the importance of store attributes when shopping for small quantities of fast moving consumer goods (i.e. „everyday shopping"). Store attributes were selected on the basis of the relevant literature analysis (McGoldrick, 2002). Respondents were asked to rank those store attributes from 1 to 6 (1 = the most important store attribute, to 6 = the least important store attribute). Moreover, as literature suggests (Massara, 2003) that customers have processed store atmosphere more specifically depending on their past and present experience, at the beginning of the questionnaire respondents were asked about their previous knowledge about the store, and the frequency of shopping in particular store.

Part II of the research instrument consisted of 20 statements related to customer evaluation of store atmospheric cues and their respond to particular atmospheric cues in a store (measured by the relationship between store atmospheric cues and customer`s purchasing decisions). The statements are based on a review of the pertinent literature on store atmospherics (e.g. Baker et al., 2002; Berman & Evans, 2010; Chen & Hsieh, 2011; Summers & Hebert, 2001; Turley & Milliman, 2000). A five-point Likert-type scale (from 5=strongly agree to 1=strongly disagree) was used to investigate attitudes of respondents related to each statement. Part III of the questionnaire consisted of characteristics of the sample (Table 1): gender, age, education, and employment status.

The collected data were analyzed using SPSS. Except from descriptive statistics calculations, significance of the findings was explored using Pearson correlation coefficient and chi-square tests, depending on the various types of combination of variables that occurred. Before using items for further analysis, testing the reliability with Cronbach's Alpha coefficient was conducted. The value of 0.78 and 0.72 respectively, suggested very good internal consistency reliability for scales used in this research (the recommended standard of 0.7 has been suggested by Nunnally (1978)). The p values were calculated to examine the level of statistical relationship between pairs of variables. The objectives were obtained using the conventional significance level of 0.05.

In the second phase, the research consisted of in-depth interviews with retail managers. The research instrument comprised questions about retailers' understanding of the effects and benefits of developing store atmosphere, whether retail companies operating on the Croatian market developed some environmental programming, or whether interior designers, architects, or landscapers were involved in creating the atmosphere of their stores, etc.

RESULTS

In accordance with the research methods, the analyses, as well as the results, first refer to the study on the sample of customers, then to the study among retail companies. What follows is a short discussion of investigated themes and some interpretations.

The Importance of Store Atmosphere from Customers' Point of View

The largest percentage of the sample consists of respondents who were shopping in supermarkets (51 per cent of respondents) and small convenience stores (45 per cent of respondents). Small number of respondents was being approached while shopping in hypermarkets and discount stores (4 per cent of respondents) because those store types usually are not located near the residence of

customers allowing them to make everyday shopping. Due to the fact that research was conducted in Zagreb, which is the capital of Croatia, those results were as expected. Namely, as the capital of the country, Zagreb is experiencing the highest retailing concentration and largest number of retail stores as well.

The analysis of the frequency of shopping in a particular store suggests that 71 per cent of respondents are making purchase of fast moving consumer goods on a daily basis. 9 per cent of respondents answered that they are doing it 4-5 times a week, while 13 per cent of respondents are shopping for small quantities of fast moving consumer goods 2-3 times a week. Those results imply that respondents have previous knowledge about the store and those results should be taken into consideration while discussing the results in Table 2.

The direct evaluation of store attributes (six store attributes were isolated and respondents were asked to evaluate them) suggests that price has the highest average score (mean=2.03). The atmosphere of a store is at the bottom of the Table 2 for all types of grocery stores. In such a way, we agreed with Dunne et al., (2002) who said that one of the cues a customers used in determining a retailer's image was retailer's prices (p. 371). In other words, prices aid and influence Croatian consumers (either consciously or unconsciously) in creating an image of the store. The possible explanation lies in the effects of global crisis

Table 2. The rating of store attributes for small shopping (1=the most important attribute; 6=the less important attribute)

Rank	Attribute	Mean (All Store Types)	Small Convenience Stores	Super-Markets	Hyper-Markets	Discount Stores
1	Price	2.03	2.12	1.96	1.62	1.50
2	Product range and quality	3.23	3.32	3.15	3.39	3.39
3	Services	3.48	3.36	3.81	3.85	3.56
4	Location	3.50	3.46	3.44	3.85	3.78
5	Personnel	4.45	4.31	4.64	4.77	5.06
6	Atmosphere	5.54	5.53	5.61	5.69	5.33

which began in 2008 and still has been evident in Croatia. Moreover, there is lower standard of living in Croatia which implies the price superiority.

However, such a forced-choice measure when respondents are forced to rank something they have not necessarily thought of, cannot deny the importance of store atmosphere. Three things should be considered:

1. Respondents are familiar with the specific store;
2. The research was conducted on the sample of respondents who usually shop in supermarkets;
3. "Grocery sector (supermarkets, discount outlets, and so on) could be expected to provide mainly utilitarian value, prioritizing functional cues and managing aesthetic-ambience cues" (Massara, 2003, p. 52).

The analysis of the statements related to the store atmospheric (Table 3) shows that general interior variables, such as cleanliness of the store, layout and display are very important for Croatian consumers. However, there are no high scores for colour, music, lighting, etc. The reason for such results lies in the previously explanation that grocery stores prioritize functionality. At the same time, they raise a question of retailers` interest in creating and maintaining unique in-store "experience" as a key differentiator. According to Table 3, surrounding area and available parking are

external variables that have impact on customers` decision to purchase in a particular store. In other words, Croatian consumers prefer variables related to convenience and ease access to the store. It is in accordance with the findings of De Nisco and Warnaby (2013) who found the link between store exterior and repatronage intentions.

To determine the direction and the strength of the relationship between atmospheric cues and the consumers' store patronage, correlation analysis was conducted. However, only moderate to weak positive associations (Table 4) were found (with the correlation significant at the 0.05 level) (in identifying the strength of the relationship Dancey and Reidy (2002) were followed). Namely, retailers who take care about product displays and the cleanliness of their stores are successful in attracting customers to make purchase in their stores. Also, the more retailers exposure their customers to pleasant scents, the more positive customers` satisfaction with the shopping experience will be. Additionally, overall in-store atmosphere of particular stores has positive correlation with customer store choice decision, and better in-store atmosphere leads to positive customer shopping behaviour. As we can see, the highest correlation coefficient with consumer satisfaction is shown by merchandise carried in the store, as well as store atmosphere which caused customers to feel pleasantly in the store. Accordingly, we conclude that mentioned attributes has the greatest influence on consumer satisfaction.

Table 3. Top atmospheric cues

Item	Mean	St. Deviation
Cleanliness of the store space	4.40	0.775
Displaying the merchandise in the store	4.33	0.882
Cleanliness and engagement of the store personnel	4.30	0.868
Product displays on the shelves	4.28	0.922
Price displays	4.03	1.030
Layout and circulation through the store	3.85	1.144
Parking availability	3.78	1.497
Pleasant scents	3.74	1.083
Surrounding area	3.12	1.259
Lighting and colours combination	2.73	1.597
Background music	2.06	1.341

Table 4. Correlation coefficient (the strongest relationships)

Services	Pearson Correlation Coefficients
Product display	0.350**
Cleanliness	0.332**
Scents	0.313**
Overall in-store atmosphere	0.310**

** Correlation is significant at the 0.05 level (2-tailed)

The Importance of Store Atmosphere from Retailers' Point of View

The findings of the interview among retail managers reveal that they are trying to ensure visibility and accessibility of the products and suitability of merchandise, price and value as well. It could be concluded that majority of investigated retail companies still underestimate the potential of using atmosphere as a marketing tool. They do not use services of interior designers, architects, or landscapers to create their in-store environment. Rather, retailer`s marketing department or visual merchandisers are responsible for creating and managing in-store environment. Retailers that operate on the Croatian market are still much concerned with the tangible products, focusing their interest on practical and functional dimensions, while neglecting the aesthetic factor in purchase behaviour.

They point out that the presentation of the merchandise is the critical factor planning the store environment. The merchandise presentation must hold customers` attention, be easy to browse and buy. Some retail chains consisting of supermarkets and hypermarkets have their space management programmes or virtual store software that provides retailers with the layout and the design of their stores.

LIMITATIONS AND FUTURE RESEARCH DIRECTION

Similar to any research, this study provides some useful findings but it has some limitations which have to be taken into account through future researches. First, this study used actual consumers in actual marketplaces as subjects, with the purpose of studying the influence and stimulation that multiple environmental cues have on consumers. However, the research was conducted outside of the store environment, after the actual shopping experience, and it was difficult to recall customers` emotional responses to a particular atmosphere. In order to improve findings of the research, an experiment (which could take a place in the lab or in "simulated store") could be included. In such experiments respondents could be exposed to different levels of environmental cues in order to analyse their impact on consumers and their decision to shop in particular stores. Gilboa and Rafaeli (2003) point out that laboratory methods are preferred to enable control over multiple intervening variables such as noise, odour, interactions with employees or other consumers, etc.

Next limitation of this study is related to the fact that respondents have previous knowledge about the store. Namely, Sherman et al., (1997) indicate that consumers deliberately choose to shop in stores that induce positive moods, so the relative effects of the store`s atmosphere may be difficult to determine without a pre-testing.

Additionally, there are various atmospheric cues included in the questionnaire design, but the examination of their interaction is missing. Because the research was conducted at the point of purchase, there is no way to assess the effects of some other variables. Therefore, we propose to further investigate the role of past and present experience that customers had with the store, because it could affect their perception of the in-store environmental cues and their approach behaviour.

Moreover, the study included retail managers trying to integrate both consumers` and retailers` point of view. As both samples were small, capturing only respondents in the capital of the country, generalizations from this study is limited. Future research should include more representative sample.

CONCLUSION

This chapter extends existing literature on retail store atmospherics by integrating both consumers` and retailers` point of view. In making their purchase decision, consumers respond to more than simply the tangible product or service being offered (Kotler, 1073-1974) and store environmental factors can influence their subjective feelings experienced in the store and influence the shopping intention, consumption amount, perceived quality, satisfaction and shopping value (Babin & Attaway, 2000). On the other side, retailers need a framework which provides them with insights on how to improve customers` perceptions of the store in order to increase store loyalty; to improve customer`s attitudes to the store in order to increase store visits, etc.

The study provides an exploratory examination of the impact of store atmosphere on customers` intentions to purchase in a particular type of grocery stores from both perspectives of retailers that operate on the Croatian market and Croatian customers` perspective. The study among retailers reveals that retail managers still do not understand the contribution of atmosphere on consumer responses. They are implementing activities in the store environment mostly based on their past experience, not on some research data. Although literature confirmed (Massara, 2003) that goods, price and services are losing their potential for differentiation, investigated retailers pointed

out price as the most important store attribute. However, though study among retailers points out their interest on practical and functional dimensions of the store environment, the findings of the study among Croatian customers propose some suggestions that retailers can take as references while creating their strategies. Firstly, the study shows that in grocery types of stores, which provide mainly utilitarian value, the overall in-store atmosphere is significantly correlated with store patronage, too. According to such conclusion that atmosphere in general positively affects customer approaching behaviour, grocery retailers should keep in mind that the retail experience must deliver value if it is to turn a one-time visitor into a repeat customer (De Farias, 2010). Secondly, the findings of the research among customers underline that Croatian customers highly evaluate general interior variables, such as cleanliness of the store, which do not require large retailer`s investments. In such a way, those findings are contradictory to retailers` debate about whether it is reasonable to invest in atmospheric cues. However, retailers should carefully determine the appropriate mix of environmental factors that may influence customers` patronage decision. Additionally, the results showed that external variables, such as surrounding area, and parking contribute to the overall customer experience. Once again, findings are related to convenience and ease access to the store. As such, they suggest retailers of what specific elements of external environment are most significant to enhance the store patronage.

This study contributes to current literature proving that there is no ideal model of store atmosphere to be followed or copied by managers of a retail or service environment. There a number of possible methods (Baker et al., 1992, p. 447) that can help retailers in making store atmosphere decisions:

1. **The Prototype:** Which is testing customers` acceptance of specific store environment before it is adopted throughout the whole

retail chain (the most expensive and time consuming method);

2. **Computer Assisted Design (CAD) Method:** Which is based on the drawing on computers with input of store planners, customers, executives etc.;

3. **A lab Experiment:** Which is based on the subjects` respond to verbal descriptions of a store in a lab setting;

4. A videotape method and using slides to manipulate retail environments.

REFERENCES

Areni, C. S., & Kim, D. (1993). The Influence of Background Music on Shopping Behavior: Classical Versus Top-Forty Music in a Wine Store. *Advances in Consumer Research. Association for Consumer Research (U. S.), 20,* 336–340.

Arnould, E. J., Price, L. L., & Tierney, P. (1998). Communicative staging of the Wilderness serviceescape. *The Service Industries Journal, 18*(3), 90–115. doi:10.1080/02642069800000034

Babin, B. J., & Attaway, J. S. (2000). Atmospheric affect as a tool for creating value and gaining share of customer. *Journal of Business Research, 49,* 91–99. doi:10.1016/S0148-2963(99)00011-9

Babin, B. J., Hardesty, D. M., & Suter, T. A. (2003). Colour and shopping intentions: The intervening effect of price pairness and perceived affect. *Journal of Business Research, 56,* 541–551. doi:10.1016/S0148-2963(01)00246-6

Bailey, N., & Areni, C. S. (2006). When a few minutes sound like a lifetime: Does atmospheric music expand or contract perceived time? *Journal of Retailing, 82*(3), 189–202. doi:10.1016/j.jretai.2006.05.003

Baker, J., Grewal, D., Levy, M., & Voss, G. (2003). Wait Expectations, Store Atmosphere and Store Patronage Intentions. *Journal of Retailing, 79*(4), 259–268. doi:10.1016/j.jretai.2003.09.006

Baker, J., Grewal, D., & Parasuraman, A. (1994). The Influence of Store Environment on Quality Inferences and Store Image. *Journal of the Academy of Marketing Science, 22*(4), 328–339. doi:10.1177/0092070394224002

Baker, J., Levy, M., & Grewal, D. (1992). An Experimental Approach to Making Retail Store Environmental Decisions. *Journal of Retailing, 68*(4), 445–460.

Baker, J., Parasuraman, A., Grewal, D., & Voss, G. B. (2002). The Influence of Multiple Store Environment Cues on Perceived Merchandise Value and Patronage Intentions. *Journal of Marketing, 66,* 120–141. doi:10.1509/jmkg.66.2.120.18470

Banat, A., & Wandebori, H. (2012). Store Design and Store Atmosphere Effect on Customer Sales per Visit. In *Proceedings of Planetary Scientific Research Center Proceeding of the 2nd International Conference on Business, Economics, Management and Behavioural Sciences.* Retrieved June 30, 2013, from http://psrcentre.org/images/extraimages/1012545.pdf

Berman, B., & Evans, J. R. (2010). *Retail Management: A Strategic Approach* (11th ed.). Pearson Education, Inc.

Billings, W. L. (1990). Effects of Store Atmosphere on Shopping Behaviour. *Honors Projects.* Retrieved June 30, 2013, from http://digitalcommons.iwu.edu/busadmin_honproj/16

Bitner, M. J. (1992). Servicescapes: the impact of physical surroundings on customers and employees. *Journal of Marketing, 56*(2), 57–71. doi:10.2307/1252042

Bohl, P. (2012). The effects of store atmosphere on shopping behaviour – A literature review. *Corvinus Marketing Studies, 1.*

Buckley, P. G. (1987). The Internal Atmosphere of a Retail Store. *Advances in Consumer Research. Association for Consumer Research (U. S.), 14*(1), 568.

Burke, R. R. (2002). Technology and customer interface: What consumers want in the physical and virtual store. *Journal of the Academy of Marketing Science, 30*(4), 411–432. doi:10.1177/009207002236914

Chebat, J.-C., & Morrin, M. (2007). Colors and cultures: exploring the effects of mall decor on consumer perceptions. *Journal of Business Research, 60*(3), 189–196. doi:10.1016/j.jbusres.2006.11.003

Chen, H.-S., & Hsieh, T. (2011). The effect of atmosphere on customer perceptions and customer behaviour responses in chain store supermarkets. *African Journal of Business Management, 5*(24), 10054–10066.

Coltman, T. (2007). Why build a customer relationship management capability? *The Journal of Strategic Information Systems, 16*, 301–320. doi:10.1016/j.jsis.2007.05.001

Cornelius, B., Natter, M., & Faure, C. (2010). How store front displays influence retail store image. *Journal of Retailing and Consumer Services, 17*, 143–151. doi:10.1016/j.jretconser.2009.11.004

Countryman, C. C., & Jang, S. (2006). The effects of atmospheric elements on customer impression: the case of hotel lobbies. *International Journal of Contemporary Hospitality Management, 18*(7), 534–545. doi:10.1108/09596110610702968

Cox, R., & Brittain, P. (2004). *Retailing: An introduction*. Financial Times, Prentice Hall.

Dailey, L. (2004). Navigational web atmospherics: Explaining the influence of restrictive navigation cues. *Journal of Business Research, 57*(7), 795–803. doi:10.1016/S0148-2963(02)00364-8

Dakoumi Hamrouni, A., & Touzi, M. (2011). Technique of collage for store design atmospherics. *Qualitative Market Research: An International Journal, 14*(3), 304–323. doi:10.1108/13522751111137523

Dancey, C. P., & Reidy, J. (2002). *Statistics Without Maths for Psychology* (2nd ed.). Pearson Education Ltd.

De Farias, S. A. (2010). *Store Atmospherics and Experiential Marketing: a conceptual framework and research propositions for an extraordinary customer experience*. Retrieved October 30, 2013, from http://www.anpad.org.br/diversos/trabalhos/EMA/ema_2010/2010_EMA27.pdf

De Kervenoael, R., Aykac, D. S. O., & Bisson, C. (2008). The influence of social E-Atmospherics in practice: A website content analysis perspective. In *Proceedings of the 7th International Congress, Marketing Trend*. Retrieved June 30, 2013, from http://research.sabanciuniv.edu/7430/

De Nisco, A., & Warnaby, G. (2013). Shopping in downtown. The effect of urban environment on service quality perception and behavioural intentions. *International Journal of Retail & Distribution Management, 41*(9), 654–670. doi:10.1108/IJRDM-05-2013-0106

Donovan, R. J., & Rossiter, J. R. (1982). Store Atmosphere: An Environmental Psychology Approach. *Journal of Retailing, 58*, 34–57.

Dowdy, C. (2008). *One-off: Independent Retail Design*. Laurence King Publishing Ltd.

Dube, L., & Morin, S. (2001). Background music pleasure and store evaluation Intensity effects and psychological mechanism. *Journal of Business Research, 54*, 107–113. doi:10.1016/S0148-2963(99)00092-2

Dunne, P. M., Lusch, R. F., & Griffith, D. A. (2002). Retailing (4th ed.). South-Western, Thomson Learning.

Ellis, L., & Ficek, C. (2001). Colour preferences according to gender and sexual orientation. *Personality and Individual Differences, 31*, 1375–1379. doi:10.1016/S0191-8869(00)00231-2

Eroglu, S. A., Machleit, K. A., & Chebat, J. C. (2005). The Interaction of Retail Density and Music Tempo: Effects on Shopper Responses. *Psychology and Marketing, 22*(7), 577–589. doi:10.1002/mar.20074

Eroglu, S. A., Machleit, K. A., & Davis, L. M. (2001). Atmospheric qualities of online retailing: a conceptual model and implications. *Journal of Business Research, 54*(2), 177–184. doi:10.1016/S0148-2963(99)00087-9

Espinoza, F., Liberali, G., & D'Angelo, A. C. (2004). Testing the influence of retail atmosphere on store choice criteria, perceived values, and patronage intentions. *American Marketing Association (AMA) Winter Educators` Conference Proceedings, 15*, 120-125.

Foxall, G. R. (1997). The Emotional Texture of Consumer Environments: A Systematic Approach to Atmospherics. *Journal of Economic Psychology, 18*(4), 505–523. doi:10.1016/S0167-4870(97)00021-4

Gilboa, S., & Rafaeli, A. (2003). Store Environment, Emotions and Approach Behavior: Applying Environmental Aesthetics to Retailing. *International Review of Retail, Distribution and Consumer Research, 13*(2), 195–211. doi:10.1080/0959396032000069568

Grayson, R. A. S., & McNeill, L. S. (2009). Using atmospheric elements in service retailing: understanding the bar environment. *Journal of Services Marketing, 23*(7), 517–527. doi:10.1108/08876040910995301

Grewal, D., Baker, J., Levy, M., & Voss, G. B. (2003). The effects of wait expectations and store atmosphere evaluations on patronage intentions in service-intensive retail stores. *Journal of Retailing, 79*, 259–268. doi:10.1016/j.jretai.2003.09.006

Heide, M., & GrØnhaug, K. (2006). Atmosphere: Conceptual Issues and Implications for hospitality management. *Scandinavian Journal of Hospitality and Tourism, 6*(4), 271–286. doi:10.1080/15022250600979515

Hu, H., & Jasper, C. R. (2006). Social cues in the store environment and their impact on store image. *International Journal of Retail and Distribution Management, 34*(1), 25–48. doi:10.1108/09590550610642800

Hui, M. K., Laurette, D., & Chebat, J.-C. (1997). The impact of music on consumers` reactions to waiting for services. *Journal of Retailing, 73*(1), 87–104. doi:10.1016/S0022-4359(97)90016-6

Hulten, B., Broweus, N., & van Dijk, M. (2008). *Sensory Marketing*. Palgrave Macmillan.

Kotler, P. (1973-1974). Atmospherics as a Marketing Tool. *Journal of Retailing, 49*(4), 48–64.

Kotler, P., & Keller, K. L. (2006). *Marketing Management* (12th ed.). Pearson Education, Inc.

Levy, M., & Weitz, B. A. (2012). *Retailing Management* (8th ed.). McGraw-Hill/Irwin.

Liaw. (2007). *The Influence of Multiple Store Environment Cues on Shopping Mood and Patronage Satisfaction*. Paper presented at the 7th Global Conference on Business & Economics. Rome, Italy.

Machleit, K. A., Kellaris, J. J., & Eroglu, S. A. (1994). Human versus spatial dimensions of crowding perceptions in retail environments: A note on their measurement and effect on shopper satisfaction. *Marketing Letters, 5*(2), 183–194. doi:10.1007/BF00994108

Manganari, E. E., Siomkos, G. J., & Vrechopoulos, A. P. (2009). Store atmosphere in web retailing. *European Journal of Marketing, 43*(9/10), 1140–1153. doi:10.1108/03090560910976401

Markin, R. J., Lillis, C. M., & Narayana, C. L. (1976). Social-psychological significance of store space. *Journal of Retailing, 52*(1), 43–54.

Massara, F. (2003). Store atmosphere: still a fledgling art. *ECR Journal, 3*(2), 47–52.

Mattila, A. S., & Wirtz, J. (2001). Congruency of scent and music as a driver of in-store evaluations and behaviour. *Journal of Retailing, 77*(2), 273–289. doi:10.1016/S0022-4359(01)00042-2

McDonald, M., Rogers, B., & Woodburn, D. (2000). *Key Customers: How to Manage them Profitably.* Butterworth-Heinemann.

McGoldrick, P. (2002). *Retail Marketing.* McGraw-Hill Education.

Mehrabian, A., & Russel, J. A. (1974). *An approach to environmental psychology.* Cambridge, MA: MIT Press.

Milliman, R. (1986). The influence of background music on the behaviour of restaurant patrons. *The Journal of Consumer Research, 13,* 286–289. doi:10.1086/209068

Morgan, T. (2008). *Visual Merchandising: Window and in-store displays for retail.* Laurence King Publishing.

Morrin, M., & Ratneshwar, S. (2000). The effects of retail store environment on retailer performance. *Journal of Business Research, 49,* 167–181. doi:10.1016/S0148-2963(99)00005-3

Mower, J. F., Kim, M., & Childs, M. L. (2012). Exterior atmospherics and consumer behaviour: Influence of landscaping and window display. *Journal of Fashion Marketing and Management, 16*(4), 442–453. doi:10.1108/13612021211265836

Newman, A., Foxall, J., & Gordon, R. (2003). In-store customer behaviour in the fashion sector: some emerging methodological and theoretical directions. *International Journal of Retail & Distribution Management, 31*(11), 591–600. doi:10.1108/09590550310503311

Newman, A. J., & Cullen, P. (2002). *Retailing: environment & operations.* Thomson Learning.

North, A. C., Hargreaves, D. J., & McKendrick, J. (1999). The Influence of In-Store Music on Wine Selections. American Psychological Association, 217-275.

Nunnally, J. C. (1978). *Psychometric theory.* McGraw-Hill.

Oakes, S. (2003). *Psychology and Marketing.* McGraw-Hill.

Oh, H., & Petrie, J. (2012). How do storefront window displays influence entering decisions of clothing stores? *Journal of Retailing and Consumer Services, 19,* 27–35. doi:10.1016/j.jretconser.2011.08.003

Olahut, M. R., El-Murad, J., & Plaias, I. (2012). Store atmosphere: Conceptual Issues and It`s Impact on Shopping Behaviour. In *Proceedings of International Conference Marketing – from information to decision,* (pp. 317-343). Academic Press.

Peck, J., & Childers, T. (2008). If it Tastes, Smells, Sounds, and Feels Like a Duck, then it must be a …: Effects of sensory factors on consumer behaviours. In *Handbook of Consumer Psychology.* Psychology Press.

Reddy, B. K., & Reddy, J. S. (2012). Atmospherics: a silent sales person in organized retailing. *International Journal of Sales. Retailing and Marketing, 1*(1), 23–29.

Sen, S., Block, L. G., & Chandran, S. (2002). Window displays and consumer shopping decisions. *Journal of Retailing and Consumer Services, 9,* 277–290. doi:10.1016/S0969-6989(01)00037-6

Sherman, E., Mathur, A., & Belk Smith, R. (1997). Store Environment and Consumer Purchase Behaviour: Mediating Role of Consumer Emotions. *Psychology and Marketing*, *14*(4), 361–378. doi:10.1002/(SICI)1520-6793(199707)14:4<361::AID-MAR4>3.0.CO;2-7

Solomon, M. R. (2008). *Consumer Behavior: buying, having and being* (8th ed.). Prentice Hall.

Spangenberg, E. R., Crowley, A. E., & Henderson, P. W. (1996). Improving the Store Environment: Do Olfactory Cues Affect Evaluations and Behaviours? *Journal of Marketing*, *60*, 67–80. doi:10.2307/1251931

Stokos, D. (1972). On the distinction between density and crowding: some implications for future research. *Psychological Review*, *79*(3), 275–277. doi:10.1037/h0032706 PMID:5056743

Summers, T., & Hebert, P. (2001). Shedding Some Light on Store Atmospherics: Influence of Illumination on Consumer Behaviour. *Journal of Business Research*, *54*, 145–150. doi:10.1016/S0148-2963(99)00082-X

Tai, H. C., & Fung, A. M. C. (1997). Application of an environmental psychology model to in-store buying behavior. *International Review of Retail, Distribution and Consumer Research*, *7*(4), 311–337. doi:10.1080/095939697342914

Teller, C., & Dennis, C. (2012). The Effect of Ambient Scent on Consumers' Perception, Emotions and Behaviour – a Critical Review. *Journal of Marketing Management*, *28*(1/2), 14–36. doi:10.1080/0267257X.2011.560719

Turley, L. W., & Milliman, R. E. (2000). Atmospheric effects on shopping behaviour: A review of the experimental evidence. *Journal of Business Research*, *49*, 193–211. doi:10.1016/S0148-2963(99)00010-7

Varley, R. (2001). *Retail Product Management: Buying and Merchandising*. Routledge. doi:10.4324/9780203358603

Yalch, R., & Spangenberg, E. (1990). Effects of Store Music on Shopping Behaviour. *Journal of Services Marketing*, *4*, 31–39. doi:10.1108/EUM0000000002502

Yalch, R., & Spangenberg, E. (2000). The Effects of Music in a Retail Setting on Real and Perceived Shopping Times. *Journal of Business Research*, *49*, 139–147. doi:10.1016/S0148-2963(99)00003-X

Yoo, C., Park, J., & MacInnis, D. J. (1998). Effects of Store Characteristics and In-Store Emotional Experiences on Store Attitude. *Journal of Business Research*, *42*, 253–263. doi:10.1016/S0148-2963(97)00122-7

ADDITIONAL READING

Backstrom, K., & Johansson, U. (2006). Creating and consuming experiences in retail store environments: Comparing retailer and consumer perspectives. *Journal of Retailing and Consumer Services*, *13*(6), 417–430. doi:10.1016/j.jretconser.2006.02.005

Berry, L. L., Carbone, L. P., & Haeckel, S. H. (2002) Managing the total customer experience, *Sloan Management Review*, Spring.

Bost, E. (1987). *Ladenatmosphare und Konsumentenverhalten (Retail atmospherics and consumer behaviour)*. Heidelberg: Physica-Verlag. doi:10.1007/978-3-642-51471-5

Chebat, J.-C., & Dube, L. (2000). Evolution and challenges facing retail atmospherics: the apprentice sorcerer is dying. *Journal of Business Research*, *49*, 89–90. doi:10.1016/S0148-2963(99)00012-0 d' Astous, A. (2000). Irritating aspects of the shopping environment. *Journal of Business Research, 49*(2), 149–156. doi:10.1016/S0148-2963(99)00002-8

Lewis, M., & Haviland, J. M. (1993). *Handbook of emotions*. New York: McGraw Hill.

Puccinelli, N. M., Goodstein, R. C., Grewal, D., Price, R., Raghubir, P., & Stewart, D. (2009). Customer experience management in retailing: understanding the buying process. *Journal of Retailing, 85*(1), 15–30. doi:10.1016/j.jretai.2008.11.003

Shiv, B., & Fedorikhin, A. (1999). Heart and mind in conflict, the interplay of affect and cognition in consumer decision making. *The Journal of Consumer Research, 26*, 278–292. doi:10.1086/209563

Turley, L. W., & Chebat, J.-C. (2002). Liking retail strategy, atmospheric design and shopping behavior. *Journal of Marketing Management, 18*, 125–144. doi:10.1362/0267257022775891

Walsh, W. B., Craik, K. H., & Price, R. H. (2000). *Person-Environment Psychology: New Directions and Perspectives*. Mahwah, New Jersey: Lawrence Erlbaum Associates.

Wilson, M. (2005). Atmosphere key to well-being. *Chain Store Age, 81*(10), 94.

Wirtz, J., Mattila, A. S., & Tan, R. L. P. (2000). The Moderating Role of Target-Arousal on the Impact of Affect on Satisfaction – an Examination in the Context of Service Experiences. *Journal of Retailing, 76*(3), 347–365. doi:10.1016/S0022-4359(00)00031-2

KEY TERMS AND DEFINITIONS

Atmospherics: The conscious designing of space to create certain effects in buyers; the effort to design buying environments to produce specific emotional effects in the buyer that enhance his purchase probability.

Atmospheric Cues: Key dimensions (variables or elements) of an atmosphere such as colour, scent, layout, music, lighting, etc.

Emotion: The oral expression of feelings and personal, subjective psychological state. When people experience external stimuli and produce a feeling reaction, an emotional reaction is produced.

Holistic Approach: Approach that addresses to the system theory which suggests that the whole is rarely equal to the sum of the single contituent parts.

Mood: Emotional response produced by external stimulation, which in turn induces psychological change and response.

Store Atmosphere: The design of in-store environment by stimulation of the five senses; the store's physical characteristics that project an image to customers.

Chapter 14
The Use of Sensorial Marketing in Stores:
Attracting Clients through their Senses

Mónica Gómez Suárez
Universidad Autónoma de Madrid, Spain

Cristina García Gumiel
Universidad Autónoma de Madrid, Spain

ABSTRACT

The main concern of this chapter is to develop a state-of-the-art of the literature referring to the use of sensorial marketing within the store. For this purpose, a deep interdisciplinary review of the theoretical and empirical works related to this discipline has been carried out. Thanks to this review, the link between some sensorial stimuli and consumer behavior has been demonstrated, but also the lack of research in some areas of study has been identified. This chapter provides a general overview of the sensorial variables used within the store by the managers, their main effects in the consumer behavior, and the most important model, the SOR model, to explain these relations. Conclusions, managerial implication, and recommendations for future research are provided.

INTRODUCTION

In the last decades, the classic tools used by managers to encourage sales and change customers' attitudes or behaviors within the store were the so-called 4p's: product, price, promotion and placement. Managers are much more concerned now about other type of variables related to the retail environment and atmosphere.

As early as the beginning of the last century, when big schemes based on self-service system such as supermarkets and hypermarkets appeared on the scene, store managers became aware of the importance of variables such as the image. They start to feel the need of having a perfect arrangement of the products in the point-of-sale, giving rise to a new concept in marketing: merchandising. Merchandising is understood as a group of

DOI: 10.4018/978-1-4666-6074-8.ch014

techniques that promote the sales of goods in retail, helping customers in their purchasing process thanks to a good presentation of their products, its environment and the use of the space in a profitable way (Zorrilla, 2000).

However, taking into consideration the high level of competition in the retail market due to the arrival of new shops, the *online shopping* and also the evolution of the consumer behaviors, managers had to find new formulas apart from the merchandising techniques to differentiate themselves. These new formulas refer to the creation of different ambiences and experiences for the customers within the store.

As Wright, Newman, and Dennis (2006) said, "for decades, marketers and researchers have been aware that shopping is not just a matter of obtaining tangible products, but also about experience and enjoyment." The result of this was the birth of a new discipline in marketing: sensorial marketing. The sensorial marketing is defined as the utilization of stimuli and elements which customers perceive by means of the senses, this is, sight, hearing, touch, smell and taste, to create specific ambiences (Gómez & García, 2010).

What seems clear right now is that customers feel the need of making the most of their time. They prefer to spend their free-time with leisure activities in which the hedonic component is high, what perfectly fits with the creation of experiences and atmospheres within the store using the sensorial marketing.

In this chapter, a review of the main literature related to sensorial marketing will be provided. For that purpose, an interdisciplinary approach by means of the analysis of empirical/experimental papers from different disciplines such as marketing, psychology and other behavioral sciences, has been carried out.

As a result, the main sensorial variables and the effect of its manipulation in consumer behaviors will be explained. Gaps in the literature and future areas of research will be also identified.

BACKGROUND

Sensorial marketing, as explained above, refers to the manipulation of some elements by retailers which are related to human senses, in order to create specific atmospheres. This promotes the development of key performance indicators, such as the duration of visit or the money spent in the store.

Although the use of the physical setting to create atmospheric impact as a form of marketing communications can be traced as far back as 1908 when the American Telegraph and Telephone (AT&T) Company used the visual impact of its organization's building' (Wright, Newman, & Dennis, 2006) as a tool. So it was in the beginning of the nineties when the potential of the atmospheric effects in retail become evident.

In relation with the origin of the atmosphere concept, it goes back to the creation of the environmental psychology. According with the psychology science, "psychologists have determined that the physical environment has an effect on human behavior and this branch of psychology has become known as environmental psychology" (Countryman & Jang, 2006). Also Mehrabian and Russell (1974) described it as "the direct impact of physical stimuli on human emotions and the effect on physical stimuli on a variety of behaviors, such as work performance or social interaction."

Taking into consideration this premise, Kotler (1973) stated that if the physical environment had an effect on human behavior, it would also influence the behavior or individuals in consumer settings such as retail stores (Countryman & Jang, 2006), giving rise to the atmosphere's concept. He defined it as "the intentional control of ambient variables with the purpose of getting a concrete customer's response" (Turley & Milliman, 2000).

Since then, various academic works have been published relating to this area. From the theoretical point of view, there are several typologies of ambient variables. In our opinion, Baker (1986), Bitner (1992) and Turley and Milliman (2000) have developed the most explanatory models. Table 1 shows a resume of the most outstanding sensorial variables.

SENSORIAL VARIABLES AND THEORETICAL MODEL

Sensorial Variables

The most important variables described above have been classified into three groups to facilitate its explanation. These three groups are: visual, auditory and kinetic variables (Gómez & García, 2012).

This section will be dedicated to the explanation of the variables included into these three groups and the effect they may have in the consumer behavior, stressing color, music and scent for being the most quoted in recent studies.

Also the main theoretical model to explain the link between the stimuli and the consumer reactions will be provided.

Visual Variables

The most important *visual variables* are the interior/exterior design, colors and lighting (Gómez & García, 2012).

Table 1. Synthesis of the most important atmosphere variables

Author	Dimension	Elements
Kotler (1973)	Visual	Color, brightness, size, shapes
	Aural	Volume, pitch
	Olfactory	Scent, freshness
	Tactile	Softness, smoothness, temperature
Belk (1975)	Physical Surroundings	Location, decor, sounds, aromas, lighting, weather and visible configurations of merchandise
	Social Surroundings	Other persons present, their characteristics, their apparent roles and interpersonal interactions
	Temporal perspective	Time
	Task Definition	Intent or requirement to select, shop for, or obtain info about a general or specific purchase
	Antecedent States	Momentary moods (i.e. anxiety, hostility, excitation) or momentary conditions (i.e. fatigue, illness)
Baker (1986)	Ambient	Air quality, temperature, humidity, loudspeakers, arousal, cleanliness, lighting
	Design	Esthetic: architectural, design, materials, colors, accessories. Functional: floor design, space, informative elements
	Social	Number and variety of consumers, workers' behavior
Bitner (1992)	Ambient Condition	Lighting, temperature, noise, arousal, music
	Space and Function	Exhibition, shape, size, spatial relation between machinery, equipment and furniture. Function makes reference to the ability of facilitate the objectives' development and achievement
Turley & Milliman (2000)	Exterior Design	Signs, shop fronts, entrances, facades, exterior design
	Ambient Conditions	Music, arousal, lighting, temperature, cleanliness
	Functional Interior Design	Interior route, furniture and equipment, accessibility
	Esthetic Interior Design	Architecture, design, style, materials, colors, information elements
	Social Dimension	Customers and employees

Source: Gómez and García (2012)

The *exterior design* has into account the architectural aspects, facades, doors, sizes, forms, shop fronts and any other element from the exterior that attract people to the interior of the shop. Once the customer is inside, decoration, merchandising and organization become relevant, this is, the interior design.

Related to *interior design*, there are two different aspects: practical and esthetic. The first one refers to the aspect focused on improving the purchasing process, such as the layout of the store or the way the products are displayed and the second one refers to the style and ornaments (Zorrilla, 2002).

Gilboa and Rafaeli (2003) mention also two important aspects related to the design: the order and the ambient complexity. Order refers to the congruency, clarity, legibility and coherence. The ambient complexity is related to the diversity, variety, ornaments and amount of information shown. These variables are important because the complexity generates visual wealth while order organizes diversity reducing uncertain scenarios and increasing the consumer's interest towards the store. This creates a feeling of approach and a bigger probability of buying (Gómez & García, 2010).

A poor interior design generates negative responses in consumers, such as discomfort and irritation, increasing the probability of not visit the store any more. However, having into account that interior design affects the affective and cognitive status, a positive design can be a differentiated element from competitors (Castro & Navarro, 2003).

Color is capable to create physiological reactions in consumers, both physical (observed by means of the blood pressure, sweating, heart and breathing rates and blinking) and emotional. This tool is one of the preferred within the professional environment because of its easy implementation and small cost (Sierra et al., 2000).

Color can be used by managers to increases or decrease the hunger, to change the emotional state, to calm down customers or to reduce the sensation of wait time. In fact, sixty-two to ninety percentage of the time spent by a person choosing a product is because of its color (Singh, 2006).

Depending of cultural behaviors and individual characteristics, people may show different reactions to same colors, but in general, warm colors -red, orange, yellow- are associated to lively moods, vitality, joy and adventure, while cold colors -blue, green- are associated with peace, calm, relax, happiness and love (see Table 2) (Gómez & García, 2010).

In the last decades, different authors have studied the influence of specific colors. Table 3 shows a resume of the main characteristics of primary colors.

Lighting is important not only in the way the product is perceived but also to attract customers to the store. For that reason, lights' orientation must be focus towards the interior and not to the exterior, to avoid blinding people where they are walking in front of the shop. In powerful lighting condition, clients tend to analyze a bigger number of products than they do with soft illumination (Areni & Kim, 1994).

Table 2. Influence of color within the store environment

Behavior	Warm Colors	Cold Colors
Attraction to the store	More attraction to the exterior	More attraction to the interior
Product perception	Original, new, avant-garde	Classic
Time spent or buying speed	Low: causing pressure, discomfort and negative attitude in customers	High: causing a pleasant atmosphere and comfort to customers
Purchasing levels	Low due to the small time spent within the store	High due to the big time spent within the store

Source: Gómez and García (2010)

Table 3. Primary color's main characteristics

Color	Characteristics	Author/s
Red	Biggerpsycho-physiologicalactivation	Wilson, 1966
	Bigger brain's function affection	Clynes and Kohn, 1968
	Associated with adjectives such as active, rebel, assertive	Aaronson, 1970
Yellow	Associated with good mood, joy, rejoicing	Sharpe, 1974
	More persistent moods	Schaie and Heiss, 1964
	Known as the brain's color	Sierra et al., 2000
Blue	Considered like the coldest color	Sierra et al., 2000
	Associated with calm, tranquility, lack of feelings	Schaie, and Heiss, 1964
	Transmits controls about emotions and behaviors	Sierra et al., 2000
Green	Associated with security, calm, freshness, youth	Sierra et al., 2000

Source: Gómez and García (2012)

Auditory Variables

In terms of auditory variables, *music* has been one of the elements more analyzed. The scientific research about music started in Germany, in the second half of the XIX century, being at the beginning of XX century when American physiologists became interested. First studies were based on the differences of incorporating music in a commercial advertisement or not. Some years later, the use of music within the store started to be analyzed by marketers (Kellaris & Rice, 1993), thanks to the technology progress and the capacity to analyze some musical elements beyond the mere presence or absence of music.

Even thought, most research about this variable has been made in the advertisement area. Yalch and Spangenberg (1993) state that music is an environmental variable particularly attractive since its manipulation is not expensive and can be easily changed in relation to the targets addressed. Giving the importance of this factor, a magazine called "Marketing Through Music" has been created and devoted to analyzing its different uses.

Music influences the consumer's emotional responses. It generates pleasure, interest and improvements in the customer's mood. As a result, this positive mood creates also positives behaviors towards the ambient. Depending on the specific mood created, the time spent in the store can be higher or lower and also the perception of it. This perception can accelerate or decelerate the time and the money spent (Gómez & García, 2010).

However, there are still some auditory elements whose effects have not been studied enough. For example, characteristics such as rhythm, voice's pitch or tempo have an important lack of research. According to Bruner (1990), there is not a definitive taxonomy of musical elements. The definition of each element varies depending on the author and also the importance assigned to each element. Same element can be considered as principal in a taxonomy and secondary in other. This author proposes a musical element's taxonomy and the emotional expressions associated to each element, being tempo, tone and texture the most important elements. Table 4 shows a definition of each element for a better understanding.

A deep revision of the literature about this area shows that the studies with empirical contrast undertaken for analyzing the effects of these factors are mainly based on time and texture, specifically in tempo, rhythm and intensity.

Tempo has been studied extensively. In a field study, Milliman (1986) concludes that when tempo is slow, traffic within the store is also low and

Table 4. Musical elements' definitions

Time	Rhythm	Pattern or placement of sounds in time and beats in music.
	Tempo	Speed or rate at which a rhythm progresses
	Phrasing	Length of time a note sounds in comparison with the rhythmic period it occupies
Pitch	Melody	Sequence of notes that forms a musical phrase, like a sentence. The horizontal progression of music
	Mode	Series of notes, arranged in a scale of ascending pitch, which provides the tonal substance of a song
	Harmony	Vertical progression of music. Notes played together to form chords and other sonorities. Provides support to the melody and directs the listener towards important structural points.
Texture	Timbre	Quality of sound that distinguishes one voice or instrument from another.
	Volume	Intensity. It contributes to the texture of music
	Instrumentation	Art of weaving together the unique sonic properties of multiple instrument to produce the complex textural fabric of a musical work

Source: Own elaboration based on Bruner (1990)

consequently, the money spent is bigger. Chebat et al. (2001), show that when tempo is high, the cognitive activity turns more difficult, increasing the excitation levels, so the information is processed worse and a decrease in the memory levels is generated.

Regarding rhythm, the lower it is, the higher number of people buying (Milliman, 1986). Staccato music causes energetic sensations, while legato music is perceived as more relaxing and calmer (Bruner, 1990).

Intensity also creates differences in the customers' responses. The general conclusion is that when the volume is high, people spend less time in the store. However there is not any significant effect related to the level of sales (Sierra et al., 2000).

Apart from the three elements above, tempo, rhythm and intensity, there is another set of factors not referred to its own characteristics but to the relationship with the consumer's response. In particular, familiarity with the music, the involvement and the consistency of the message may have an effect on this response.

When music is familiar, consumers perceive they have spent more time in the store; however they spend more time when music is unfamiliar (Yalch & Spangenberg, 2000). In the context of the involvement, when it is low, music increases the receptivity to the brand; however it distracts those whose involvement is cognitive (Park & Young, 1986). Regarding congruency, according Kellaris et al.,(1993), when music is consistent, it increases attention and brand recall. When music draws attention but is inconsistent, people pay less attention to the message and a negative influence on the memory is created.

On the other hand, we must take into account the possible effect of the musical elements in the emotional states, because people assign emotional meanings to music, experimenting affective reactions (Bruner, 1990). An example of this is that fast music is considered as happier than slow music. Kellaris and Kent (1992) identified same basic properties that Bruner did and three possible responses: pleasure, arousal and surprise.

Regarding the influence of the music in the emotional states, Dubé and Morin (2001) demonstrate empirically that there is no relationship between the specific mood generated by music and the influence on perceptions and evaluations of the store, or purchase intention (Alpert et al., 2005). However, when music is used to evoke congruent emotions with the type of purchase (lively/sad) and with the symbolic meaning of the product, the probability of purchasing increased. Lively music generates happier moods. However, sad music increases the purchasing intention (Bruner, 1990).

Broekemier et al. (2008) show a direct effect on the purchasing intention depending on the type of music, happy or sad, and if it likes to the customers. The purchasing intention is higher when people are exposed to music they know and also they like.

Other important aspect when analyzing the effects of music is the characteristics of people, as there are empirical studies which show that depending on the characteristics of the listener, the responses generated to the same stimulus may be different (Kellaris & Rice, 1993). Men and women have different hearing sensitivity, and this difference is one of the reasons why women respond worse to a loud or intense music than men (Kellaris & Rice, 1993). Other reason to explain why women respond worse to loud music, is because people respond more positively to objects that are consistent with the concept they have of themselves, so it is possible that the loud music is not well received by women as it can be perceived as less consistent with femininity (Kellaris & Rice, 1993).

Age is another factor which moderates environmental stimuli, having the possibility of influences people's evaluations and their behavior. Yalch and Spangenberg (1990) demonstrate the effects of age on the perception of time within the store, so young people perceive that they spend more time when background music, as happened with adults to foreground music.

The responses to certain stimuli also vary depending on the culture. There is a strong relationship between musical tastes and cultural background and/or ethnicity (Morier, 2005).

To close this section referred to music, the Table 5 shows a description of emotions produced by different musical elements.

Kinetic Variables

Kinetic variables refer to scent, taste, touch and density (Gómez & García, 2010). Among them, the *scent* is the only variable able to bring memories to customers, thanks to its link with the limbic system, responsible for the emotions

Table 5. Musical characteristics for producing various emotional expressions

Musical Element	Emotional Expression				
	Serious	**Sad**	**Sentimental**	**Serene**	**Humorous**
Mode	Major	Minor	Minor	Major	Major
Tempo	Slow	Slow	Slow	Slow	Fast
Pitch	Low	Low	Medium	Medium	High
Rhythm	Firm	Firm	Flowing	Flowing	Flowing
Harmony	Consonant	Dissonant	Consonant	Consonant	Consonant
Volume	Medium	Soft	Soft	Soft	Medium
	Happy	**Exciting**	**Majestic**	**Frightening**	
Mode	Major	Major	Major	Minor	
Tempo	Fast	Fast	Medium	Slow	
Pitch	High	Medium	Medium	Low	
Rhythm	Flowing	Uneven	Firm	Uneven	
Harmony	Consonant	Dissonant	Dissonant	Dissonant	
Volume	Medium	Loud	Loud	Varied	

Source: Bruner (1990)

and memories (Ward et al., 2003) and also to its direct connection with the tonsil (responsible of emotions) and the sea-horse (responsible of the memory). For this reason, olfactory memory allows people to remember not only moments but emotions (Annett, 1996).

One example of the importance given to this sense is the creation of a non-lucrative organization, The Olfactory Research Fund. Its objective is to support research projects directed to analyze the impact of scents in the perceptions (Chebat & Michon, 2003)

The most interesting scent is the one which comes from the store as a whole and not from a particular product, because the environmental scent is able to cause general reactions about all products in the consumers, including those which do not have any particular smell (Gulas & Bloch, 1995). In recent years, studies have focused on environmental odors, and not the ones coming from a particular object. However, previous studies were based on the scents of particular products (Peck & Childers, 2007).

In spite of its importance, scent has been less studied (Sierra et al., 2000) than other variables because of its complexity, different structure and organization (Gómez & Rozano, 2008). Most of the works about scent are related to these three dimensions: scent affective qualities -pleasant versus unpleasant-, scent activation qualities -physiological effects- and scent intensity -strong versus soft-, being the first one the most studied. In general, the measurement of the affective qualities has been done by means of an approach-avoidance's behavior, while physiological effects generated by means of the activation qualities, have been measured by electroencephalograms and breathing's analysis.

According to Gulas and Bloch (1995), there are some scent' characteristics that make it perceived as pleasant or not. Physiological aspects are essential in generating consumer responses and so are the memories or past experiences associated to the specific scent.

When the aroma is pleasant, an approximation behavior is generated, whereas when it is not, it produces avoidance feelings (Bone & Elle, 1999). A pleasant aroma can affect our perceptions about products and even about people. So, aromas of lavender, basil, cinnamon and citrus create calm and relaxation, while the mint, thyme and rosemary generate energy. Ginger, cardamom, licorice and chocolate, raise romanticism, while roses fight depression states (Hunter, 1995; Amodio, 1998).

Spangenberg et al., (2013) have shown in a recent research that "a simple (i.e., more easily processed) scent led to increased ease of cognitive processing and increased actual spending, whereas a more complex scent had no such effect." In the field study, when people were exposed to a thoroughgoing basil and green tea aroma, their spending basket dropped, but it was not the case when the scent was a single orange aroma.

Aroma can affect the spending time perceived in the store, the evaluation of it and its products (generating behaviors of approach or avoidance) and the money spent. However, there are several studies that show the inconsistency of the relationship between aroma and spending basket (Sierra et al., 2000), since sometimes this relationship is positive and sometimes it does not exist (Spangenberg et al., 1996).

As far as *taste* is concerned, this variable has been studied not only for launching of new products, brands, or packaging, but also to analyze product experiences (Peck & Childers, 2007).

One of the most common methods to evaluate flavors is called triangle test. Consumers are asked to identify three flavors, two of which are identical and the third different. The question in this approach is whether consumers really discriminate tastes, or they are just guessing. Another discrimination test is the one in which consumers make several paired comparisons, choose their favorite couples. After that, the consistency of these choices is analyzed to determine their discrimination capacity. A third method is the preference rank procedure in which customers have to rank samples of three flavors, one different from the other two, from highest to lowest preference. If the subject placed the flavor that is different as the best or the worst, has made a correct choice regardless of the preference (Peck & Childers, 2007).

Another kinetic variable is *touch*, the less studied variable in the marketing field (Peck & Childers, 2007). The information obtained through this sense is important for the evaluation of products, because depending on the information about the material properties of the object such as texture, softness, temperature and weight, the perception will be (Klatzky & Lederman, 1992).

The consumer's responses may differ depending on the material property evaluated. For instance, the sensations generated when consumers assess the smoothness of a product are not the same than when its weight is evaluated. When one or more of these properties vary, consumers feel more motivated to touch the product before buying, because contact with the products cause consumer confidence and a better evaluation (Peck & Childers, 2003).

The last kinetic variable, *density*, is related with more than one human sense because it is influenced by noise, temperature an even by store colors. It refers to the number of people located in a concrete space, being an objective or a perceptional measurement. It is important to differentiate density and agglomeration. Density refers to a physical relation which indicates the distribution of people in a specific space, while agglomeration is produced when people perceive their movement constrained because of the lack of space (Sierra et al., 2000).

When density turns to agglomeration, customers may feel stressed or confused, activating these responses: to pay less attention to stimulus, to decrease the decision's time, to look for less products, to evaluate only known products, to reduce the visit time and to avoid interacting with other people, both customers and employees.

Theoretical Model

Regarding theoretical models, most of them attempt to explain the influence of the factors previously seen in the consumer behavior. They are usually based on the model of Mehrabian and Russell (1974) extracted from the environmental psychology: the *SOR paradigm* (Stimulus-Organism-Response). Some relevant studies such as the ones done by Donovan and Rossiter (1982), Sherman and Smith (1986) and Anderson (1986), follow this model.

The S–O–R framework (see Figure 1) assumes that the environment contains some stimuli (S) which cause changes to people's interior or organism states (O), which generate approach or avoidance responses (R) (Vieira, 2013).

Sherman and Belk (1997) explain that "this framework consists of antecedents (the attributes of the environment), the intervening emotional state, and a taxonomy of outcomes based on the approach-avoidance concept suggested by Wundt (1905)."

The *stimulus* is defined in the model as that which affects the internal mood of the person, being described in the consumer behavior's field as those external factors associated with a pending decision. According to Sherman and Belk (1997), the conceptualization of the stimulus as something which evokes the action even intensifying it, has been accepted and incorporated to the literature.

The *organism* is defined as those internal processes and structures that intervene between the external stimulus to people and their actions, reactions or responses, being these internal processes the result of perceptions, psychological factors, feelings and thoughts (Bagozzi, 1986). Following this definition, emotional state can be conceptualized as the organism variable. According to Mehrabian and Russell (1974) it can be measured by these three factors/categories: pleasure-displeasure, arousal-non arousal, and dominance-submissiveness this latter dimension is

Figure 1. S-O-R framework

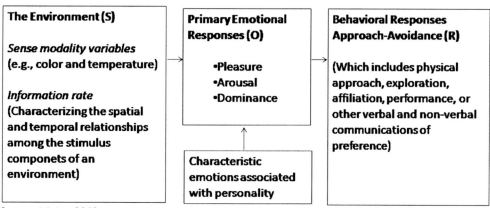

Source: Vieira. 2013

not always included in the empirical models since it is not totally predictive (Sherman & Belk, 1997).

The *response* is defined by Bagozzi (1986) as the outcome or final action: the reaction of consumers, including psychological reactions such as attitudes and/or behavioral reactions.

As it has been described, emotions are an important part of the SOR model. The theoretical contributions in the last two decades have taken emotions into consideration within the marketing field, since it has been demonstrated that they can influence consumer behavior (Matos & San Martin, 2007). Although there is not a general definition of this variable (Matos & San Martin, 2007), they can be defined as a complex set of interactions among subjective and objective factors, influenced by neural and hormonal systems, which can generate:

- Affective experiences such as feelings of activation, pleasure or displeasure,
- Cognitive processes such as perception and evaluations,
- Physiological adjustments' activation or
- A behavior that usually, but not always, is expressive, directed to a goal and adaptive (Bigné & Andreu, 2004).

Despite of the intensive efforts of many authors, until few years ago there was not any acceptable classification of the affective system, necessary to define a particular science (Diaz & Flores, 2001). According to these authors, the problem is the lack of awareness about what and how many the emotions are, and also the lack of an empirical base to develop a classification.

For many authors, the reason for this problem is conceptual and semantic. A concept is associated with the features of an object, and this association generates the meaning of the word. This seems clear to the terms which describe physical external events to the person, but it is not clear to describe mental processes such as emotions. Other authors however, show their disagreement with this argument, because the words for emotions are not referred to inaccessible spectrum, but to a sequence of events that prepare the organism to respond to a series of stimuli (Diaz & Flores, 2001).

Although some classification have been found in the literature review, such as the DES scale proposed by Izard (1977), the Plutchik scale (1980) and the PAD scale developed by Mehrabian and Russell (1974). The scale we explain in this paper will be the PAD scale by Mehrabian and Russell since it is the most quoted and used by researchers.

The acronym PAD comes through these three dimensions: pleasure-displeasure, arousal-nonarousal and dominance-submissiveness (Mehrabian & Russell, 1974).

Its key propositions are derived as follows. First, the PAD dimensions characterize all emotional states. Second, emotional states include moods, feelings, and any other feeling-related concepts. Third, the PAD dimensions are bipolar, indicating that the presence of pleasure excludes the possibility of displeasure (Huang, 2001).

The dimension of pleasure can be measured using a semantic differential scale (descriptive scale of bipolar adjectives) or observing behaviors such as smile, any kind of facial expression, gesture, positive sentence or even the tone of voice, so that we can measure the degree of happiness and joy the person has (Vaccaro, 2001). Arousal, defined as "an affective property (dimension) ranging from sleep to frantic excitement" (Mehrabian & Russell (1974), varies along a single dimension from a calm state to a frenetic one (Bigné & Andreu, 2004) being able to be measured by blood pressure, eye dilation, skin temperature, breathing, heart rate, etc. (Vaccaro, 2001). Dominance, considered as the weakest part of the model in the empirical research (Vieira, 2013), refers to the degree in which a person feels unrestricted or free to act (Bigné & Andreu, 2004). This scale consists of eighteen semantic differential items, six of them to measure the pleasure, six for the arousal and six for the dominance.

FUTURE RESEARCH DIRECTIONS

The variables coming from sensorial marketing are commonly used by retailers as a managerial solution to create good atmospheres for their consumers; although its effectiveness is hardly ever measured. Academic research has analyzed the results of its implementation but usually by

means of laboratory experiments, not in a real environment. Despite of the suitability of this method to examine the phenomena under study isolating relevant variables, this type of analysis leaves out important elements that may affect the buying process, such as customer interaction with employees or other customers. For this reason, further research analysis this phenomena within real environment is recommended.

Regarding the theoretical models found in the literature review, the most quoted is the SOR paradigm. Even though it has been challenged by several authors, who state that stimuli like smell do not follow the stages proposed by this model, because the aroma is able to generate direct consumer responses without interfering with emotions. According to Lazarus (1991) there are some works based in this emotional-cognitive model done by Spangenbert et al.,(1996), Morrin and Ratneshwar (2000) and Chebat and Michon (2003), which demonstrate how the scent does not affect the emotional state. Also Bone and Scholder (1998) conclude that the aroma may produce certain effects without causing changes in the emotional state or mood; simply the pleasant/unpleasant characteristics of the aroma are transferred to the object (Chebat & Michon, 2003). Bone and Ellen (1999) conduct also a review of the literature concluding that only sixteen percentage of the published papers show an influence on emotional states after the exposition to stimulus such as the aroma.

Further research should be done to analyze scent separately from the model and to incorporate variables that we consider essential to analyze consumer behavior which are not included in the initial model such as: antecedent's states, people characteristics (gender, age, culture, social class, etc.), previous experiences and unexpected events

As a final remark, future empirical research is recommended to cover the gaps we have highlighted in this chapter, not only in real environments but also regarding the measure of the effects that the interaction of some of these elements have in the consumers' behavior, since there are few studies which measure their impact when they act together within the retail environment.

CONCLUSION

In the last years the phenomenon of the sensorial marketing has pervaded in the organizations. Even being a discipline studied from almost one century, is now when companies make reference to new terms such as experience, atmosphere or environment, not used before. Colors, music, aromas enter the scene to generate differentiation and involvement, with the objective of creating good mood in customers, improving the performance of the store.

Consumers need to feel involved with the brand and to be part of the purchasing process. Studies have shown that when customers feel involved, they state to have an additional value. The consumer empowerment have come researchers to the conclusion that the more power a company provides to its customers and the more they take care of them, the better is perceived. Customers prefer companies which improve their purchasing process and their stay (Wright et al., 2006).

In this chapter, considered as a first step for future research, we have reviewed the use of different environmental variables to improve the stay of customers in the store. In relation with the consumer behavior caused by the use of these specific variables related to the senses, we have seen that there are variables or stimulus that have been less studied than others, such as smell or touch. Even in the case of a variable deeply studied, like music, the research shows gaps under exploring.

We have also analyzed the most quoted theoretical model, SOR, which explains the relation among stimulus, the emotional states and the consumer responses. Despite of the limitations of this model, its use has been accepted in the marketing field and consumer behavior.

After this review, a theoretical and empirical model that covers the existing gaps identified in the literature due to the lack of study in some sensorial variables and in the field of emotions should be formulated in a further paper.

REFERENCES

Alpert, J. I., Alpert, M. I., & Maltz, E. N. (2005). Purchase occasion influence on the role of music in advertising. *Journal of Business Research*, *58*(3), 369–376. doi:10.1016/S0148-2963(03)00101-2

Amodio, L. V. (1998). Mood makers: an in-depth look at how scents claim to boost your spirit and de-stress your nerves. *Good Housekeeping (New York, N.Y.)*, *227*(5), 53–55.

Anderson, P. (1986). Personality, perceptions and emotion-state factors in approach-avoidance behaviours in the store environment. In *Proceedings of AMA*, (pp. 35-39). Chicago: American Marketing Association.

Annett, J. (1996). Olfactory memory: A case study in cognitive psychology. *The Journal of Psychology*, *130*(3), 309–319. doi:10.1080/00223980.1996.9915012 PMID:8667286

Areni, C. S., & Kim, D. (1994). The influence of in-store lighting on consumers' examination of merchandise in a wine store. *International Journal of Research in Marketing*, *11*(2), 117–125. doi:10.1016/0167-8116(94)90023-X

Baker, J. (1986). *The Role of Environment in Marketing Services: The Consumer Perspective in The Services Challenge: Integrating for Competitive Advantage*. Chicago, IL: American Marketing Association.

Bigné, J. E., & Andreu, L. (2004). Modelo cognitivo-afectivo de la satisfacción en servicios de ocio y turismo. *Cuadernos de Economía y Dirección de la Empresa*, *21*, 89–120.

Bitner, M. J. (1992). Servicescapes: the impact of Physical Surroundings on Customers and Employees. *Journal of Marketing, 56*(2), 57–71. doi:10.2307/1252042

Bone, P. F., & Ellen, P. S. (1999). Scents in the marketplace: explaining a fraction of olfaction. *Journal of Retailing, 75*(2), 243–262. doi:10.1016/S0022-4359(99)00007-X

Bone, P. F., & Scholder, E. P. (1998). Does it matter if it smells? Olfactory stimuli as advertising executional cues. *Journal of Advertising, 27*(4), 29–40. doi:10.1080/00913367.1998.10673567

Broekemier, G., Marquardt, R., & Gentry, J. W. (2008). An exploration of happy/sad and like/disliked music effects on shopping intentions in a women's clothing store service setting. *Journal of Services Marketing, 22*(1), 59–67. doi:10.1108/08876040810851969

Bruner, G. C. II. (1990). Music, mood and marketing. *Journal of Marketing, 54*(4), 94–104. doi:10.2307/1251762

Castro, E., & Navarro, A. (2003, March-April). Disposición del punto de venta. *Distribución y Consumo*, 5-22.

Chebat, J. C., Chebat, B. G., & Vaillant, D. (2001). Environmental background music and in-store selling. *Journal of Business Research, 54*, 115–123. doi:10.1016/S0148-2963(99)00089-2

Chebat, J. C., & Michon, R. (2003). Impact of ambient odors on mall shoppers' emotions, cognition, and spending, a test of competitive causal theories. *Journal of Business Research, 56*, 529–539. doi:10.1016/S0148-2963(01)00247-8

Countryman, C. C., & Jang, S. (2006). The effects of atmospheric elements on customer impression: the case of hotel lobbies. *International Journal of Contemporary Hospitality Management, 18*(7), 534–545. doi:10.1108/09596110610702968

Díaz, L., & Flores, E. (2001). La estructura de la emoción humana: un modelo cromático del sistema afectivo. *Salud Mental, 24*(4), 20–35.

Donovan, R., & Rossiter, J. (1982). Store atmosphere: an environmental psychology approach. *Journal of Retailing, 58*, 34–57.

Dubé, L., & Morin, S. (2001). Background music pleasure and store evaluation: intensity effects and psychological mechanisms. *Journal of Business Research, 54*(2), 107–113. doi:10.1016/S0148-2963(99)00092-2

Gilboa, S., & Rafaeli, A. (2003). Store environment, emotions and approach behaviour: applying environmental aesthetics to retailing. *International Review of Retail, Distribution and Consumer Research, 13*(2), 195–211. doi:10.1080/0959396032000069568

Gómez, M., & García, C. (2010). *Nuevas tendencias en el punto de venta: el marketing sensorial. Distribución comercial y comportamiento del consumidor, Ramón Areces Foundation.* University of Oviedo.

Gómez, M., & García, C. (2012, March-April). Marketing sensorial: cómo desarrollar la atmósfera del establecimiento comercial. *Distribución y Consumo*, 30-39.

Gómez, M., & Rozano, M. (2008). La influencia del aroma en la percepción del establecimiento comercial. *Revista Portuguesa de Marketing, 23*(2), 59–68.

Gulas, C. S., & Bloch, P. H. (1995). Right under our noses: ambient scent and consumer responses. *Journal of Business and Psychology, 10*(1), 87–98. doi:10.1007/BF02249272

Huang, M. (2001). The theory of emotions in marketing. *Journal of Business and Psychology, 16*(2), 239–247. doi:10.1023/A:1011109200392

Hunter, B. T. (1995). The sales appeal of scents (using synthetic food scents to increase sales). *Consumer Research Magazine, 78*(10), 8–10.

Izard, C. E. (1977). *Human emotions.* New York: Plenum Press. doi:10.1007/978-1-4899-2209-0

Kellaris, J. J., & Kent, R. J. (1992). The influence of music on consumer's temporal perceptions: does time fly when you're having fun? *Journal of Consumer Psychology, 1*(4), 365–379. doi:10.1016/S1057-7408(08)80060-5

Kellaris, J. J., & Rice, R. C. (1993). The influence on tempo, loudness, and gender of listener on responses to music. *Psychology and Marketing, 10*(1), 15–28. doi:10.1002/mar.4220100103

Klatzky, R. L., & Lederman, S. J. (1992). Stages of manual exploration in haptic object identification. *Perception & Psychophysics, 52*(6), 661–670. doi:10.3758/BF03211702 PMID:1287570

Matos, F., & San Martin, S. (2007). La confianza, la intención de compra, la reputación y las emociones en la relación del consumidor con la marca: aplicación al caso de la marca Mundo Maya-México. In *Nuevas tendencias en dirección de empresas.* Departamento de Economía y Administración de Empresas, Universidad de Burgos.

Mehrabian, A., & Russell, J. A. (1974). *An approach to environmental psychology.* Cambridge, MA: MIT Press.

Milliman, R. E. (1986). The influence of background music on the behaviour of restaurant patrons. *The Journal of Consumer Research, 13*(2), 286–289. doi:10.1086/209068

Morier, M. (2005). *The sweet sound and smell of success: consumer perceptions as mediators of the interactive effects of music and scent on purchasing behaviour in a shopping mall.* (Thesis). Universidad de Concordia, Montreal, Canada.

Morrin, M., & Ratneshwar, S. (2000). The impact of ambient scent on evaluation, attention and memory for familiar and unfamiliar brands. *Journal of Business Research, 49,* 157–165. doi:10.1016/S0148-2963(99)00006-5

Park, C. W., & Young, S. M. (1986). Consumer response to television commercials: the impact of involvement and background music on bran attitude formation. *JMR, Journal of Marketing Research, 23*(1), 11–24. doi:10.2307/3151772

Peck, J., & Childers, T. L. (2003). Individual differences in haptic information processing: the need for touch scale. *The Journal of Consumer Research, 30*(3), 430–442. doi:10.1086/378619

Peck, J., & Childers, T. L. (2007). If it tastes, smells, sounds, and feels like a duck, then it must be a…: effects of sensory factors on consumer behaviours. In F. Kardes, C. Haugtvedt, & P. Herr (Eds.), *Handbook of Consumer Psychology.* Mahwah, NJ: Erlbaum.

Plutchik, R. (1980). *Emotion: a psycho evolutionary synthesis.* New York: Harper & Row.

Sherman, E., & Belk, S. R. (1997). Store environment and consumer purchase behavior: mediating role of consumer emotions. *Psychology and Marketing, 14*(4), 361–378. doi:10.1002/(SICI)1520-6793(199707)14:4<361::AID-MAR4>3.0.CO;2-7

Sherman, E., & Smith, R. B. (1986). Mood states of shoppers and store image: promising interactions and possible behavioural effects. In P. Anderson (Ed.), *Advances on consumer research.* Provo, UT: Association for Consumer Research.

Sierra, D. B., Alier, E., & Falces, C. (2000). Los efectos de las variables ambientales sobre la conducta del consumidor. *Distribución y Consumo, 54,* 5–23.

Singh, S. (2006). Impact of color on marketing. *Management Decision*, *44*(6), 783–789. doi:10.1108/00251740610673332

Spangenberg, E., Herramann, A., Zidansek, M., & Sprott, D. (2013). The Power of Simplicity: Processing Fluency and the Effects of Olfactory Cues on Retail Sales. *Journal of Retailing*, *89*(1), 30–43. doi:10.1016/j.jretai.2012.08.002

Spangenberg, E. R., Crowley, A. E., & Henderson, P. W. (1996). Improving the store environment: do olfactory cues affect evaluations and behaviors. *Journal of Marketing*, *60*, 67–80. doi:10.2307/1251931

Turley, L. W., & Milliman, R. E. (2000). Atmospheric Effects on Shopping Behaviour: A Review of the Experimental Evidence. *Journal of Business Research*, *49*(2), 193–211. doi:10.1016/S0148-2963(99)00010-7

Vaccaro, V. (2001). *In-store music's influence on consumers responses: the development and test of a music-retail environment model.* (Thesis). City University, New York.

Vieira, V. A. (2013). Stimuli-Organism-Response Framework: a meta-analytic review in the store environment. *Journal of Business Research*, *66*(9), 1420–1426. doi:10.1016/j.jbusres.2012.05.009

Ward, P., Davies, B., & Kooijman, D. (2003). Ambient smell and the retail environment: relating olfaction research to consumer behavior. *Journal of Business and Management*, *9*(3), 289–302.

Wright, L. T., Newman, A., & Dennis, C. (2006). Enhancing consumer empowerment. *European Journal of Marketing*, *40*(9/10), 925–935. doi:10.1108/03090560610680934

Yalch, R., & Spangenberg, E. (1990). Effects of store music on shopping behaviour. *Journal of Services Marketing*, *4*, 31–39. doi:10.1108/EUM0000000002502

Yalch, R., & Spangenberg, E. (1993). Using store music for retail zoning: a field experiment. *Advances in Consumer Research. Association for Consumer Research (U. S.)*, *20*, 632–636.

Yalch, R., & Spangenberg, E. (2000). The effects of music in a retail setting on real and perceived shopping times. *Journal of Business Research*, *49*, 139–147. doi:10.1016/S0148-2963(99)00003-X

Zorrilla, P. (2000). Política de merchandising en la empresa de distribución detallista. In Marketing En Sectores Específicos. editorial Pirámide.

ADDITIONAL READING

Alpert, J. I., & Alpert, M. I. (1988). Background music as an influence in consumer mood and advertising responses. *Advances in Consumer Research. Association for Consumer Research (U. S.)*, 16.

Alpert, J. I., & Alpert, M. I. (1990). Music influences on mood and purchase intentions. *Psychology and Marketing*, *7*(2), 109–133. doi:10.1002/mar.4220070204

Andreu, L., Bigné, J. E., Chumpitaz, R., Mttila, S. A., & Swaen, V. (2005), 'Effects of perceived retail environment on consumption emotions, satisfaction and behavioural intentions: a comparison between shopping centres and traditional retailing', World Marketing Conference, Muenster, Germany.

Antonides, G., Verhoef, P. C., & Van Aalst, M. (2002). Consumer perception and evaluation of waiting time: a field experiment. *Journal of Consumer Psychology*, *12*(3), 193–202. doi:10.1207/S15327663JCP1203_02

Areni, C. S., & Kim, D. (1994). 'The influence of in-store lighting on consumers' examination of merchandise in a wine store'. *International Journal of Research in Marketing*, *11*(2), 117–125. doi:10.1016/0167-8116(94)90023-X

Baker, J., Parasuraman, A., Grewal, D., & Voss, G. B. (2002). The influence of multiple store environment cues on perceived merchandise value and patronage intentions. *Journal of Marketing, 66*(abril), 120–141. doi:10.1509/jmkg.66.2.120.18470

Chattopadhyay, A., Dahl, D. W., Ritchie, R. J. B., & Shahin, K. N. (2003). Hearing voices: the impact of announcer speech characteristics on consumer response to broadcast advertising. *Journal of Consumer Psychology, 12*(3), 198–204. doi:10.1207/S15327663JCP1303_02

Diez de Castro, E., & Navarro, A. (2003). Disposición del punto de venta. *Distribución y Consumo, 13*(68), 5–22.

Grohol, J. (2005), 'Percepcion', http://psychcentral.com/psypsych/Perception.

Jain, R., & Bagdare, S. (2011). 'Music and consumption experience: a review'. *International Journal of Retail & Distribution Management, 39*(4), 289–302. doi:10.1108/09590551111117554

Kirby, A. E., & Kent, A. M. (2000). Architecture as brand: store design and brand identity. *Journal of Product & Grand Management, 19*(6), 432–439. doi:10.1108/10610421011085749

Knasko, S., Gilbert, A. N., & Sabini, J. (1990). 'Emotional state, physical well-being and performance in the presence of feigned ambient odor'. *The Journal of Applied Psychology, 20*(16), 1345–1357.

Krishna, A. (2012). An integrative review of sensory marketing: engaging the senses to affect perception, judgment and behaviour. *Journal of Consumer Psychology, 22*(3), 332–351. doi:10.1016/j.jcps.2011.08.003

Law, D., Wong, C., & Yip, J. (2012). 'How does visual merchandising affect consumer affective response? An intimate apparel experience'. *European Journal of Marketing, 46*, 112–113. doi:10.1108/03090561211189266

LeHew, M. L. A., Burgess, B., & Wesley, S. (2002). Expanding the loyalty concept to include preference for a shopping mall. *International Review of Retail, Distribution and Consumer Research, 12*(3), 225–236. doi:10.1080/09593960210139643

Lorig, T. S. (2001), 'Compendium of olfactory research, Explorations in Aroma-Chology: Investigation the sense of smell and human response to odors' (1995-2000), Dubuque, IW: Kendall-Hunt Publishing Company

Mattila, A. S., & Wirtz, J. (2001). Conguency of scent and music as a driver of in-store evaluations and behaviour. *Journal of Retailing, 77*, 273–289. doi:10.1016/S0022-4359(01)00042-2

McCabe, D. B., & Nowlis, S. M. (2003). The effect of examining actual products or product descriptions on consumer preference. *Journal of Consumer Psychology, 13*(4), 431–439. doi:10.1207/S15327663JCP1304_10

Michon, R. (2004), 'Creating business enterprise value with mall atmospherics: impact of ambient odors on mall shopers' emotions, cognition and spending', thesis, Commercial Studies School, Montreal University.

Summers, T., & Hebert, P. (2001). Shedding some light in store atmosphere, influence of illumination on consumer behaviour. *Journal of Business Research, 54*, 145–150. doi:10.1016/S0148-2963(99)00082-X

KEY TERMS AND DEFINITIONS

Atmosphere: Specific ambient created in a store by means of the utilization of sensorial elements such as colors, light or music.

Merchandising: Groups of techniques used in a store with the purpose of improving the image of the products sold.

Organism: Component of the SOR model which analyses the emotional states of customer when they are impacted by sensorial elements or stimulus.

PAD: Taxonomy to measure emotions composed by three dimensions: pleasure-displeasure, arousal-nonarousal and dominance-submissiveness.

Response: Component of the SOR model which measures the reaction a consumer has after being impacted by stimulus.

Sensorial Marketing: Marketing discipline which studies the responses of customers when they are impacted by the manipulation of variables that can be perceived by the five human senses.

Sensorial Variables: Elements or factors perceived through the five human senses which are manipulated to cause a reaction in the consumer.

SOR Model: Theoretical model which explains the relation among the stimulus (S) the customer receive, what emotions they feel in their organism (O), and their responses or attitudes (R).

Stimuli: Component of the SOR model which explores the external elements manipulated by managers to generate a response in the consumer. These external elements are perceived through the human senses.

Chapter 15

Frontline Employees' Self-Perception of Ageism, Sexism, and Lookism:
Comparative Analyses of Prejudice and Discrimination in Fashion and Food Retailing

Mirian Palmeira
Federal University of Parana (UFPR), Brazil

ABSTRACT

The aim of this chapter is to identify whether frontline employees perceived themselves as having feelings of sexism, ageism, and appearance discrimination against customers in retail services. This investigation is a quantitative research, a conclusive description (Gil, 2002), and ex post facto study, which utilises a survey to collect the data and sampling by convenience. Three protocols are used (1) to format the questionnaire, (2) to produce 12 different standards combining age, gender, and appearance, and (3) to create social classification (Rattam, 1998). In a previous study (Palmeira, Palmeira, & Santos, 2012), customers of different ages and genders perceived some degree of prejudice and discrimination in face-to-face retail services. Now, on the other side of the coin, frontline employees who work in Fashion and Food retailing recognise that there is prejudiced behaviour against customers, depending on their age, gender, and appearance, when providing them with face-to-face retail services. More than 95% of female and more than 64% of male attendants believe that well-dressed, young female customers are given priority when being served. Almost 80% of female and only 58% of male frontline workers believe that badly-dressed middle-aged men (not younger men) are the last to be served when there is no clear queuing process in the retail spatial area. This context strongly suggests the growing importance of an interpersonal skills training process for an organisations' staff as a way of avoiding behaviour that makes the customers think that there are prejudice and discrimination in the service process, as well as ASL development (T&D against Ageism, Sexism, and Lookism) being part of the strategic statements.

DOI: 10.4018/978-1-4666-6074-8.ch015

INTRODUCTION

In a previous work (Palmeira, Palmeira & Santos, 2012), there is an analysis of how customers perceived prejudice and discrimination from frontline employees during the face-to-face retail service process. They believe that somebody else receives the staff's attention before them even if they were the first to arrive in the retail spatial environment. They have a perception of some degree of prejudice and discrimination because there is always somebody else to be served before them. There are some different responses depending on age and gender. The respondents indicated a list of retail businesses they usually frequent, such as fashion shops, shoe shops, restaurants, fast food restaurants, IT stores, and so on. To produce this research, the frontline employees of the types of retail companies with the highest scores are interviewed about their self-perception of ageism, sexism and lookism against customers, and they admit that this type of bias does indeed exist in both the Fashion and Food retail sectors. Considering this context, the research problem and the objectives are set.

Research Problem

Do frontline employees perceive themselves as having feelings of sexism, ageism and lookism against customers in Fashion and Food Retailing?

Objectives

Central Objective: To identify whether frontline employees perceived themselves as having feelings of sexism, ageism and lookism against customers in Fashion and Food Retailing.

Operational Objectives:
- To describe the characteristics of the frontline employees that provide face-to-face retail services (age, gender, social class and job rank) in Fashion and Food Retailing;
- To evaluate the impact of the sector on the frontline employees' self-perception of ageism, sexism, and lookism;
- To evaluate whether frontline employees perceive the use of an inner self-discretionary system to provide service to different kind of customers, considering age, gender and appearance (first customer *versus* last customer to receive attention).
- To evaluate the self-perception of prejudice related to age, gender and appearance against customers (ASL Syndrome – Palmeira, Palmeira, & Santos, 2012).

BACKGROUND

The subjects of this research are presented in four groups of concepts and theories: frontline employees; prejudice and discrimination; ageism, sexism and lookism; and retailing. They are of great importance when it comes to helping retail companies to realise that their frontline employees can show some kind of behaviour that produces a prejudiced approach toward customers, at least in the eyes of the customers themselves. Moreover, perception is sometimes more important than reality, especially in retail services.

Frontline Employees

Frontline employees are any kind of people that interact directly with customers. Some authors consider the groups that make contact by telephone and/or by Internet as frontline employees, working, for example, in call centres, clothing retail, financial organisations and supermarkets (LaRosa & Campbell, 2010; Kerfoot & Korczynski, 2005; Robertson, 2003). Nevertheless, face-to-face contact in the same spatial environment is unique. Any other forms of contact (by phone, e-mail or through companies' Web site) do not provide a possibility of seeing the customer's phenotype and his/her physical characteristics in full. For this study, frontline employees are the staff that provide face-to-face retail services to customers in the spatial environment area.

Frontline employees are one of the key factors to customer satisfaction and they classify customers (Bettencourt & Gwinner, 1996). Staff are trained to improve different kind of skills related to the business and how to provide services. Commonly, technical capacities (information of how things work, hierarchy, etc.) are developed. Nevertheless, the "soft" competences (interpersonal skills, customers' rapport, open mind for the different, kindness, politeness, people's person skills, etc.) are taken for granted. Commitment is also frequently forgotten in T&D (Elmadağ, Ellinger & Franke, 2008). It is more unpredictable the companies focus the T&D (Training and Development) programmes for frontline employees on competences to avoid prejudiced attitudes and behaviours, such as ageism, sexism and lookism against different people, especially customers. The front staff in retail companies are seen as the Brand (LaRosa & Campbell, 2010) in face-to-face encounters. In the author's point-of-view, if a business fails to prepare its employees to provide the best service without prejudice and discrimination, the brand is tarnished in the eyes of customers.

Psychology and sociology are fields that can contribute to understanding the interaction between frontline employees and their customers. Sometimes this interaction does not produce the best results for anyone (neither satisfaction for customers nor survival and profits for companies) because there is some bias of prejudice (or frontline staff behave under some bias of prejudice) related to customers' age, gender and appearance. It may be that ageism, sexism and/or negative approach against customer's appearance are part of the face-to-face retail environment.

Prejudice and Discrimination

"The sociological concepts and theories can contribute to the Marketing and Retail fields especially to help to improve the interaction between customers and frontline employees. It is a huge problem for retail companies when there is a combination of different elements of prejudice and discrimination on the part of the staff against the customers because of their age, gender, and/or appearance" (Palmeira, Palmeira & Santos, 2012).

Prejudice can be defined as "learned beliefs and values that lead an individual or group of individuals to be biased for or against members of a particular group. Prejudice is therefore about what people think and is not necessarily translated into actions" (Haralambos & Holborn, 2008, pp. 168). On the other hand, discrimination is a clear unfavourable action towards a person considering one's age (Ageism), gender (Sexism), and appearance (Lookism) (Palmeira, Santos & Palmeira, 2012). Race and religion are linked with these themes because phenotype and faith's elements are visible and can produce different reactions of prejudice and discrimination.

Ageism, Sexism, and Lookism

There are some important definitions that can help to understand how interactions in retail lead to failure for all parties. The idea is to attempt to avoid these problems if the management understands how the dynamics between staff and customers works. Ageism, Sexism and Lookism (appearance bias) are strongly linked concepts because they can produce different kinds of personal damage due to various levels of prejudice and discrimination against individuals and their groups.

The first definition that is crucial to the subject is the concept of *ageism*, which is related to "discrimination, or the holding of irrational or prejudicial views about individuals or groups, based on their age. It involves stereotypical assumptions about a person or group's physical or mental capacities and is often associated with derogatory language. Most commonly these are applied to the elderly" (Scott & Marshall, 2009:11).

There are concerns related to ageism in the workplace (Hsiang-Fei & Sheng-Hshiung, 2011; Brennan et all, 2007). The public sector attempts to produce laws against age discrimination (Adams, 2004:219). *Nevertheless, it seems that retail companies do not believe that the frontline employees have an age bias against prospects and customers* (Kwong-Leung, 2000).

Since World War II, businesses have been formatted mainly to suit the young segments. The staff are prepared to provide service to youths (Thompson & Thompson, 2007). The population is growing older in the first quarter of the 21st century. Companies, especially those in retail, should be adapting their structure and the minds of their staff to serve older customers. A huge challenge is to avoid many biases when frontline employees face customers of a different phenotype and age of their own, without any prejudice or age discrimination.

It is important to study these subjects, because the mankind is getting older (Schirrmacher, 2004) and the retail structure is still formatted to provide service for the younger people (Thompson & Thompson, 2007). The retailers should prepare their professionals to face these phenomena that already started in the beginning of the XXI century second decade. The social psychology field is very concerned how the institutions are not prepared to serve a growing number of aging people (Abrams, 2005; Abrams et. al., 2011).

The second important definition for this study is *sexism*, which is linked to the concept of sex discrimination. Sexism is "unfair discrimination on the basis of sex. [...] Sexism occurs at different levels, from the individual to the institutionalised, but all forms combine to preserve inequality. Normally sex discrimination operates against women and in favour of men" (Scott & Marshall, 2009:686). Sexism reproduces "social inequalities based on race, gender and class" (Williams, 2006).

Sexism has been described as the practice of domination of women. It is a practice that is supported in many different ways that are critical to our socialization into our sex roles, and therefore makes this domination acceptable in society – through language, visual association, media representation, and stereotyping, especially on the basis of the mothering/caring role of women. Sexism is important also because all women experience it in different ways, depending upon their social and economic situation – within the family and in jobs – and it limits the ways in which women seek to actualize their potential (Rai, 2010).

There are many studies on sexism, but the main focus is on the workplace (Dirks, 2004; Prasad, Prasad & Mir, 2011).

The third group of concepts is related to *lookism*, which is one of the elements that can produce some kind of prejudice and discrimination based on the person's appearance, and it brings much concern to the companies that decide to format orientations to the staff when they provide services to different customers, making employees recognise diversity (Oxford Brookes University, 2007). The other more common approach is related to the staff's attire or standards and appearance policy (City of Riverside, California, 2006). "There is growing evidence of corporate demand for employees who have aesthetic qualities that can be deployed in marketing and branding strategies" (Waring, 2011), giving preference to those who "look good" or present the "right look." These strategies are "exclusory and may cause harm in the same way as other discriminatory practices" (Waring, 2011). *This concern is related to the workplace and the issue impacts behaviour among peers.* The field of psychology has studied appearance and the distress experienced by a proportion of the general population (Rumsey & Harcourt, 2005). People realise that they are evaluated by their appearance in different situations of life and most of the time the results of this 'evaluation' are against them. Kligman and Graham (1986) present some questionable statements related to appearance in the elderly, such as "elderly persons who preserve a youthful appearance (look young for their age) are likely to be more optimistic, more outgoing and more social. [...] Cosmetics can help the elderly attain some of the benefits enjoyed by the physically attractive." This may be seen as approach of the Eighties, when the concerns of prejudice linked to appearance were not as important as they are today.

Women are more concerned with physical appearance and have lower appearance self-esteem than men (Pliner, Chaiken & Flett, 1990). On the other hand, Frith and Gleeson (2004) believe that men are "increasingly dissatisfied with their appearance." Jasper and Klassen (1990) conducted a study on "stereotypical beliefs about obese men and women" and how the perception of bodily appearance can have many impacts for retailing and consumer issues. Pentecost and Andrews (2010) studied "the influence of demographic (e.g. gender and generational cohort) and psychographic (e.g. fashion fanship, attitudes and impulse buying) drivers on frequency and levels of expenditure on fashion purchases" and concluded that "females purchase more often and were significantly different from males in yearly expenditure." These are some situations that show how lookism push people to concern about appearance and how they try to have the "right" look, but none of the research had studied prejudice and discrimination in customers and frontline employees' interactions.

To understand how ageism, sexism and lookism can be damaging to face-to-face retail services, it is useful to know about Fashion and Food retailing.

Retailing

"Retailing is predominantly a domestic market activity. The total business of the vast majority of retailers is done within one particular country and in many cases, within one specific region or district" (Bruce, Moore & Birtwistle, 2004,). Retailing can be defined as a group of activities that involves "the process of selling products and services directly to the customer as a way of fulfilling one's personal needs" (Parente, 2000, p.22). Retailing is not only the purchase of goods, but is also related to the services process to the customer. Some examples are medical clinics, fitness centres, restaurants and libraries (Lovelock & Wright, 2007). These are also retailing activities. Some are done by phone, mail, on the Internet and door-to-door.

A retailer is the business unit that purchases goods from manufacturers, wholesalers and any other dealers and sells them directly to the customer (Andrade, Palmeira & Kato, 2010). The basic characteristic of retail companies is the sale of goods and services to customers irrespective of the kind of business or the place where their actions take place. Retailers try to sell their "flags," or brands, or concepts, which are responsible for the companies' image and their positioning among their stakeholders.

There are different types of retailers: the more traditional ones, such as the grocery retailers, specialty shops, department stores, supermarkets, convenience stores, discount stores and shopping malls, among other types (Reynolds & Cuthbertson, 2004; Kotler & Keller, 2006), as well as medical clinics, fitness centres, restaurants, libraries, leisure retailing and many other new formats (Lovelock & Wright, 2007), especially those related to e-commerce and online retailing. There is a group of retailer types that focuses on different ways to achieve customer loyalty (Reynolds & Cuthbertson, 2004), related to access, price, brand and assortment. If the issue is price, the retail organisation is named a Budget retailer. The Value retailer attempts to offer "everything to everybody's strategy" which is very risky but also involves the largest potential markets. The Quality retailer offers accessibility and its retail brand. And, finally, there is the Luxury retailer that focuses on its retail brand and category assortment (Reynolds & Cuthbertson, 2004).

Fashion Retailing is a very important part of the fashion supply chain that goes from the manufacturers to the consumer. It is the group of companies that "sell the merchandise to the ultimate consumer" (Solomon & Rabolt, 2009\). According to Solomon and Rabolt (2009), there are different price lines in the sector that classify businesses depending on the quality level and price of their goods. The first group is the Haute Couture or *High Fashion* that is defined as 'fine sewing', very high-quality and custom-made. The second group is called *Prêt-à-porter* that includes expensive lines, but is much affordable and casual in style. The third group is the *Designer* one where the professionals develop secondary lines called bridge lines, made of lesser-quality fabric or licensed to another manufacturer. The fourth group includes *better goods* with lower prices, good quality of a lesser-known brand or name. The fifth group comprises *moderate goods* with lower prices and quality than better products and sold in department stores and specialty shops. And finally, last but not least, the sixth group, made up of *budget goods* with the lowest price-quality approach, usually offered at discount stores or by mass merchandisers.

When it comes to timing as the focus of the analyses, there are two groups of fashion retailers, the traditional ones that have a seasonal time span of 3 to 6 months, such as the fall/winter or spring/summer season. The other group is made up of fast fashion retailers. "Fast fashion is the term that is used to represent the various strategies that fashion companies use in order to respond commercially to the latest fashion trends." [...] The younger fashion market shrinks the design to retail cycle to as little as 4 weeks making the top fashion designers available to the mass market in the same season" (Bruce, Moore, & Birtwistle, 2004).

Different types of businesses are part of *Food Retailing*. Parente (2000) classifies the activities of retailing in three distinct groups: food retailing, non-food, and services. The first includes pubs, groceries, bakeries, express stores, convenience shops, markets, traditional supermarkets, hypermarkets and shopping clubs. In the second group, there are the specialty shops, the department stores, the design products shops, the discount stores, and the outlets. And in the third group, services are included, such as clinics, beauty parlours, laundry services, shoe repair, movies, hotels, dinners and restaurants, to name only a few. The reason to highlight the Parente's classification in this section is because it focuses on the importance of Food retailing, comparing the other two groups. The second set represents the more traditional types of retailers and the third one embodies retail services.

The main focus of this chapter is the fashion and food retailing businesses that have spatial/physical retail environment and offer face-to-face customer experiences. They can also have all new information technologies, but they should include a physical space where customers come and get in touch with the frontline employees. *Self-service retail business is not part of the research, because the frontline employees' role is very limited.* In this study, Fashion retailing includes traditional clothing store formats as well as fast fashion shops, ranging from budget to designer prices lines. It does not include Couture and Haute Couture (Solomon & Rabolt, 2009). And Food retailing includes restaurants, fast food outlets and pubs, offering processed and prepared food and a variety of soft drinks and beverages directly to the customers. This classification maintains the same categories of a previous study (Palmeira, Palmeira & Santos, 2012) and it helps to reduce the complexity of the current survey.

In the next section, the methodology is presented.

RESEARCH METHODOLOGY

Methodology is produced to research prejudice and discrimination phenomena in fashion and food retailing. The approach includes a number of aspects (Gil, 2002; Malhotra, 2001; Siegel & Castellan, 2006, Mattar, 2007): the nature of the research, the population and sampling and the limitations of the study.

The Nature of the Research

This investigation is a quantitative study, a conclusive description (Gil, 2002) and *ex post facto* study, which utilises a survey to collect the data. Three protocols are used:

1. To format the questionnaire;
2. To produce 12 different standards combining age, gender and appearance; and
3. To create social classification (Rattam, 1998) based on the level of formal education, income, spatial residential area, size of residence and occupation.

The Rattam social classification Model (Rattam, 1998) is based on the idea that formal education level, size of residence, and occupation are more important than income in order to format consumer behaviour and to classify the segments as A, B, C, D and E. The protocol is used to identify in which segment the respondents are classified. Communication with the respondents is face-to-face. The researcher supplies the questionnaires, the respondents answer the questions and they return the document to the researcher as soon as they have filled in the forms.

Simple statistical analyses are used to describe the frontline employees' profile and some cross tabs analyses to produce their responses. The results of self-perception of ageism, sexism and appearance discrimination in face-to-face retail services from the frontline employees' point-of-view (Table 7) are measured on 5-point Likert-type scales (+2 = strongly agree, for positive statements, and -2 = strongly disagree, for negative statements) (Mattar, 2007; Ferguson, 1941). The format of the scales is adapted from the Fishbein Multiattribute Model scales (Engel, Blackwell & Miniard, 1990). The acquired data are organised into tables and simple statistical analysis made it possible to describe the characteristics of the frontline employees and some of their responses. Neither the SPSS nor the Mann-Whitney tests are used to organise the data, but they could be applied when working with larger samples (Wonnacott & Wonnacott, 1981). The data collected are organised to meet the operational objectives of this chapter. This criterion formats the presentation of the results.

Population and Sampling

The population of the research is made up of all Brazilian frontline employees that work in Fashion (clothes, shoes and accessories) and Food Retailing (Restaurants, Fast food luncheon and pubs). The *sample is selected by convenience* in the Curitiba metropolitan area, Parana State, Brazil. The respondents are frontline employees (sales people, attendants, waiters and bartenders). Table 1 shows some of the respondents' characteristics. The survey is conducted from October 2011 to January 2012.

Although a random sample is technically more superior to produce precise results that explain the population, there are reasons to select the sample by convenience (Mattar, 2007):

Table 1. Sampling characteristics

Gender	Fashion	Food	Total	%
Male	11	06	17	42
Female	17	06	23	58
Total	28	12	40	100

Source: survey, 2012.

1. There is not available database to list the population's members and to produce a random sample;
2. The subjects of ageism, sexism and lookism are taboos, and many potential respondents avoid answering the key-questions of the questionnaire, making all the process very time-consuming to fill in the 40 forms, because it is necessary to search for another respondents; and
3. The financial and human resources are limited to use a random sampling process.

Research Limitations

This type of study explains the results only for the sample units. The real sample is smaller than the forecasted one (40 instead of 100 units). One of the reasons for this is that the subjects "prejudice and discrimination" are taboo. The respondents are reluctant to express their opinion concerning this subject. This results in a smaller quantity of sample units. The kind of sampling that is used limits the conclusions. The results only apply to the respondents. The low number of respondents restricts the possibilities for statistical analysis. The surveys are conducted in the Southern Hemisphere, where the consuming profile is different from the type of purchasing in the Northern Hemisphere (BAM, 2012). The presentation of the results is restricted due to the format of this chapter.

RESULTS

The information related to the frontline employees' self-perception of ageism, sexism and lookism in face-to-face retail services is presented in three sections:

1. The profile of the respondents that provide face-to-face retail services;
2. The perception of the use of an inner self-discretionary system to provide service to different kind of customers, considering age, gender and appearance (first customer *versus* last customer to receive attention); and
3. The evaluation of the self-perception of prejudice and discrimination related to age, gender and appearance against customers (ASL Syndrome – Palmeira, Palmeira & Santos 2012).

The impact of the sector on the frontline employees' self-perception of ageism, sexism and lookism is seen in all sections.

The Profile of the Frontline Employees that Provide Face-to-Face Retail Services

The majority of the respondents are young: 64.71% of females and 81.82% of males from Fashion retailing; and 83.33% for both female and male from Food retailing. Based on Rattam (1998), considering level of formal education, income, neighbourhood, size of residence and occupation, the Fashion staff are from social group B (64.71% of females and 63.64% of males) and the Food employees are from class C (100% of females and males). The main job rank is the position of salesperson (94.12% of the females and 90.91% of the males in Fashion retailing) and the rank of attendant (100% of females) and waiters (66.67% of males) is from the Food sector (Table 2).

The results that show the impact of the sector on the frontline employees' self-perception of ageism, sexism, and lookism are presented in the following tables. Self-perception of prejudice and discrimination is everywhere, at different levels.

Table 2. The frontline employees' profile

Frontline Employees' Characteristics	FASHION				FOOD				FASHION and FOOD			
Age	Female	Male	% F	% M	Female	Male	% F	% M	Female	% F	Male	% M
up to 20	0	0	0.00	0.00	1	0	16.67	0.00	1	4.5	0	0.00
21-25	11	9	64.71	81.82	5	5	83.33	83.33	16	69.57	14	82.35
26-30	4	1	23.53	9.09	0	1	0.00	16.67	4	17.39	2	11.76
31-35	1	1	5.88	9.09	0	0	0.00	0.00	1	4.35	1	5.88
36-40	1	0	5.88	0.00	0	0	0.00	0.00	1	4.35	0	0.00
Total	17	11	100.00	100.00	6	6	100.00	100.00	23	100.00	17	100.00
Social Classification	Female	Male	% F	% M	Female	Male	% F	% M	Female	% F	Male	% M
B	11	7	64.71	63.64	0	0	0.00	0.00	11	47.83	7	41.18
C	6	4	35.29	36.36	6	6	100.00	100.00	12	52.17	10	58.82
Total	17	11	100.00	100.00	6	6	100.00	100.00	23	100.00	17	100.00
Job Rank	Female	Male	% F	% M	Female	Male	% F	% M	Female	% F	Male	% M
Salesperson	16	10	94.12	90.91	0	0	0.00	0.00	16	69.57	10	58.82
Attendant	1	1	5.88	9.09	6	1	100.00	16.67	7	30.43	2	11.76
Waiter	0	0	0.00	0.00	0	4	0.00	66.67	0	0.00	4	23.53
Bartender	0	0	0.00	0.00	0	1	0.00	16.67	0	0.00	1	5.88
Total	17	11	100.00	100.00	6	6	100.00	100.00	23	100.00	17	100.00

Source: survey, 2012.

The Perception of the use of an Inner Self-Discretionary System to Provide Service to Different Kind of Customers, Considering Age, Gender, and Appearance (First Customer *vs*. Last Customer to Receive Attention)

The results can be analysed in three different groups of information. The first presents how the frontline employees make rankings showing who is going to be the first person to receive the attention of frontline male employees in the retail spatial environment. The second group presents who is going to be the last customer to be served by the staff, and the third group shows whether the order of preference (or prejudice) changes if the staff are female.

Ranking of the First Customer to Receive Frontline Employees' Attention

The female attendants of both types of retailing, Fashion and Food, perceive that well-dressed young female customers receive face-to-face retail services prior everybody else if the server is male. The masculine gender has a different opinion, especially those in Food retailing. They believe that young well-dressed males attract the frontline employees' attention beforehand (Table 3).

Ranking of the Last Customer to Receive Frontline Male Attendants' Attention

To the female frontline employees, the last customer to receive the service is a badly-dressed

Table 3. The first person to receive the attention of the frontline male employees in face-to-face retail services as perceived by the frontline staff

Elements			FASHION					FOOD					FASHION and FOOD			
Gender	Age	Appear	Female	Male	% F	% M	Female	Male	% F	% M	Female	Male	% F	% M
Fem	Young	Well-dressed	16	9	94.12	81.82	6	2	100.00	33.33	22	11	95.65	64.71
Fem	Young	Badly-dressed	0	0	0.00	0.00	0	0	0.00	0.00	0	0	0.00	0.00
Fem	Mature	Well-dressed	0	1	0.00	9.09	0	0	0.00	0.00	0	1	0.00	5.88
Fem	Mature	Badly-dressed	1	0	5.88	0.00	0	0	0.00	0.00	1	0	4.35	0.00
Fem	Middle Age	Well-dressed	0	0	0.00	0.00	0	0	0.00	0.00	0	0	0.00	0.00
Fem	Middle Age	Badly-dressed	0	0	0.00	0.00	0	0	0.00	0.00	0	0	0.00	0.00
Masc	Young	Well-dressed	0	1	0.00	9.09	0	4	0.00	66.67	0	5	0.00	29.41
Masc	Young	Badly-dressed	0	0	0.00	0.00	0	0	0.00	0.00	0	0	0.00	0.00
Masc	Mature	Well-dressed	0	0	0.00	0.00	0	0	0.00	0.00	0	0	0.00	0.00
Masc	Mature	Badly-dressed	0	0	0.00	0.00	0	0	0.00	0.00	0	0	0.00	0.00
Masc	Middle Age	Well-dressed	0	0	0.00	0.00	0	0	0.00	0.00	0	0	0.00	0.00
Masc	Middle Age	Badly-dressed	0	0	0.00	0.00	0	0	0.00	0.00	0	0	0.00	0.00
		Total	17	11	100.00	100.00	6	6	100.00	100.00	23	17	100.00	100.00

Source: survey, 2012.

middle-age man. Therefore, gender produces a higher response than the type of retailing. To male frontline employees in Fashion, responses are similar to the female reactions. On the other hand, in Food retailing, the male staff believe that badly-dressed middle-age women are the last to be served (50% of the responses) (Table 4).

The Order of Preference (or Discrimination) Remains the Same in the Case of Female Staff

Both male and female frontline employees believe that the order of preference remains the same if the staff that provide the service are male or female. Actually, this is more a case of prejudice than preference, as the situation does not equalise service to customers due to their age, gender or appearance. It seems that the type of retailing does not produce different trends to these responses (Table 5).

The Evaluation of the Self-Perception of Ageism, Sexism, and Appearance Discrimination against Customers from the Frontline Employees' Point-of-View on Likert Scales

As shown in Table 6, there are 14 different statements to identify the self-perception of prejudice and discrimination in face-to-face retail services on the part of frontline staff. These phrases are used in the questionnaires to double-check whether this perception does indeed exist.

After gathering all the information from the respondents, it is necessary to calculate the scores for each of the 14 statements, to create the Likert scales' graphic elements, producing an index based on each item score, which help to visualise the extension of prejudice and discrimination related to ageism, sexism and lookism. For example:

Score of the 14th statement = [(freq1x+2) + (freq2x+1) + (freq3x-1) + (freq4x-2)]/total freq

Considering:
For positive statements

Freq1: multiply the score of position 1 by the weight +2 for "strongly agree" opinion;
Freq2: multiply the score of position 2 by the weight +1 for "agree opinion";

For negative statements

Freq3: multiply the score of position 3 by the weight -1 for "disagree opinion";
Freq4: multiply the score of position 4 by the weight -2 for "strongly disagree" opinion;
Total Freq: the statement's total frequency

Table 7 shows the table that includes the answers of the six groups of age and gender and the information to produce the Likert Scale, related to the 14 statements.

The results show that the type of retailing (Fashion or Food), rather than only gender, has an impact on the frontline employees' self-perception of ageism, sexism and lookism. According to Table 7, there are different numbers for every statement, within each type of retailing and in the gender response. In some cells, the results are neutral (0.000). This means that the values of agreement of a particular statement (2, 3, and 11) are neutralised by the values of disagreement. It does not mean that there is no ageism, sexism or lookism. It can mean that there is no self-perception of them. If there is no impact of the type of retailing on the frontline employees' self-perception of prejudice and discrimination at all, the results should produce the same value in all cells, which is not the case.

Some analyses can be made:

1. There are different self-perceptions of prejudice and discrimination among females

Table 4. The last person to receive the attention of the frontline male employees in the face-to-face retail services as perceived by the customers

Gender	Age	Appear	FASHION				FOOD				FASHION and FOOD			
			Female	% F	Male	% M	Female	% F	Male	% M	Female	% F	Male	% M
Fem	Young	Well-dressed	0	0.00	0	0.00	0	0.00	0	0.00	0	0.00	0	0.00
Fem	Young	Badly-dressed	0	0.00	0	0.00	0	0.00	0	0.00	0	0.00	0	0.00
Fem	Mature	Well-dressed	0	0.00	0	0.00	0	0.00	0	0.00	0	0.00	0	0.00
Fem	Mature	Badly-dressed	0	0.00	0	0.00	0	0.00	1	16.67	0	0.00	1	5.88
Fem	Middle Age	Well-dressed	0	0.00	0	0.00	0	0.00	1	16.67	0	0.00	1	5.88
Fem	Middle Age	Badly-dressed	0	0.00	0	0.00	0	0.00	3	50.00	0	0.00	3	17.65
Masc	Young	Well-dressed	0	0.00	0	0.00	0	0.00	0	0.00	0	0.00	0	0.00
Masc	Young	Badly-dressed	2	11.76	1	9.09	0	0.00	0	0.00	2	8.70	1	5.88
Masc	Mature	Well-dressed	0	0.00	0	0.00	0	0.00	0	0.00	0	0.00	0	0.00
Masc	Mature	Badly-dressed	0	0.00	1	9.09	0	0.00	0	0.00	0	0.00	1	5.88
Masc	Middle Age	Well-dressed	2	11.76	0	0.00	1	16.67	0	0.00	3	13.04	0	0.00
Masc	Middle Age	Badly-dressed	13	76.47	9	81.82	5	83.33	1	16.67	18	78.26	10	58.82
		Total	17	100.00	11	100.00	6	100.00	6	100.00	23	100.00	17	100.00

Source: survey, 2012.

Table 5. Order of preference if the staff are female

The order of preference remains the same if the staff are female		FASHION				FOOD				FASHION and FOOD			
		Female	Male	% F	% M	Female	Male	% F	% M	Female	% F	Male	% M
YES		13	10	76.47	90.91	6	6	100.00	100.00	19	82.61	16	94.12
NO		4	1	23.53	9.09	0	0	0.00	0.00	4	17.39	1	5.88
	Total	17	11	100.00	100.00	6	6	100.00	100.00	23	100.00	17	100.00

Source: survey, 2012.

Table 6. Statements of the Likert scale

N.	Statements
1	Well-dressed younger women receive the face-to-face retail services prior to everybody else if there is not a clear queuing process in the retail spatial environment area.
2	The frontline male employees are nicer to younger female customers.
3	The frontline female workers are nicer to younger male customers.
4	The frontline female workers are nicer to younger female customers.
5	The frontline female workers are nicer to mature female customers.
6	The frontline female workers are nicer to middle-aged female customers.
7	The frontline female workers are nicer to mature male customers.
8	The frontline female workers are nicer to middle-aged male customers.
9	The frontline male employees treat the mature female customers better than the others.
10	The frontline male employees treat the middle-aged female customers better than the others.
11	The frontline male employees treat the mature male customers better than the others.
12	Middle-aged female customers are going to be the last to receive face-to-face retail services if there is not a clear queuing system
13	The male staff provide better treatment to young male customers.
14	The male staff provide better treatment to middle-aged male customers.

of Fashion and Food retailing (1.4706 and -0.1667) in statement 1 ("well-dressed younger women receive the face-to-face retail services prior to everybody else if there is not a clear queuing process in the retail spatial environment area"), as well as in statement 2 (1.4118 to Fashion and 0.000 to Food) which mentions that "the frontline male employees are nicer to younger female customers."

2. The female and male genders of Fashion retailing have almost an opposite perception

of the female and male gender in the Food sector related to statement 5 ("the frontline female workers are nicer to mature female customers"). Fashion female frontline employees have a score of 0.8235 and Food female staff -0.8333. The Fashion male employees have a result of 0.7273 and those in the Food sector have -1.5000.

3. Concerning statements 7 ("the frontline female workers are nicer to mature male customers") and 8 (the frontline female workers are nicer to middle-aged male customers")

Table 7. Self-perception of ageism, sexism and lookism (ASL Syndrome) against customers in the face-to-face retail services from the frontline employees' point-of-view on a Likert scale

Elements			FASHION		FOOD		FASHION and FOOD	
Statements	Attendant	Customers	F	M	F	M	F	M
1	No indication of gender	Fem/Young Well-dressed	1.4706	1.2727	-0.1667	**0.0000**	1.0435	0.8235
2	Male	Fem/Young	1.4118	1.2727	**0.0000**	0.8333	1.0435	1.1176
3	Female	Male/Young	0.8235	1.3636	**0.0000**	-1.0000	0.6087	0.5294
4	Female	Female/Young	1.2353	1.4545	-0.1667	-1.3333	0.8696	0.4706
5	Female	Female/Mature	0.8235	0.7273	-0.8333	-1.5000	0.3913	-0.0588
6	Female	Female/Old	0.8824	1.0909	-0.5000	-1.5000	0.5217	0.1765
7	Female	Male/Mature	-0.1176	-0.4545	-1.0000	-0.8333	-0.3478	-0.5882
8	Female	Male/Old	-0.4118	-0.8182	-1.1667	-0.8333	-0.6087	-0.8235
9	Male	Female/Mature	0.7647	1.1818	-0.6667	-0.1667	0.3913	0.7059
10	Male	Female/Old	0.5882	0.6364	-0.3333	-0.3333	0.3478	0.4118
11	Male	Male/Mature	-0.2941	0.3636	-0.1667	-0.5000	-0.2609	**0.0000**
12	No indication of gender	Female/Old attended at the last	-0.7059	-1.0000	-0.5000	0.3333	-0.6522	-0.5294
13	Male	Male/Young	-1.1765	-0.5455	-0.5000	0.5000	-1.0000	-0.1765
14	Male	Male/Old	-0.9412	-0.3636	-0.8333	1.0000	-0.9130	0.1176

Source: survey, 2012.

the staff have the same trend of disagreement for all recipients.

4. Regarding statement 13 ("the male staff provide a better treatment to young male customers"), the employees in Food retailing have opposite perceptions (-0.5000 for females and 0.5000 for males).

In short, the higher levels (higher than 1.000) of self-perception of ageism, sexism and lookism are found in statements 1, 2 and 4 in the Fashion female group, and in statements 1, 2, 3, 4, 5 and 9 in the Fashion male group. On the other hand, the lowest level of self-perception of ASL bias (lower than -1.000) is in the Food retailing: females on statements 7 and 8, and males on 3, 4, 5, and 6. An isolated situation is statement 14 according to male staff, who show a self-perception

of prejudice and discrimination with a level of 1.000, probably meaning that the Food retailing male group believes that "the male staff provide better treatment to middle-aged male customers."

The data in Table 7 show the Likert Scales that can be visualised in Figure 1, on the following page. The Likert Scales show the profile of the frontline employees' self-perception of sexism, ageism and appearance bias in the different groups within the types of retailing and between genders. The higher the scores (1.000 and up to 2.000), the higher the perception of prejudice and discrimination; the lower the scores (-1.000 to -2.000), the lower the perception.

In the next section, conclusions recommendations and contributions, managerial implications and final issues are presented.

Figure 1. Likert scales

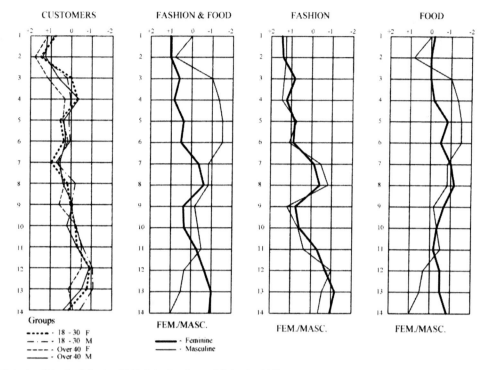

CUSTOMERS   FASHION & FOOD   FASHION   FOOD

Groups
- - - - - - 18 - 30 F
— · — · - 18 - 30 M
- - - - - - Over 40 F
————— - Over 40 M

FEM./MASC.
———— - Feminine
———— - Masculine

FEM./MASC.   FEM./MASC.

Palmeira, Palmeira & Santos, 2012; Palmeira, Santos & Palmeira, 2012.

CONCLUSION, RECOMMENDATIONS AND CONTRIBUTIONS, MANAGERIAL IMPLICATIONS, AND FINAL ISSUES

Conclusion

The results of this study contain information concerning frontline employees' self-perception of ASL bias, which may be summarised as follows: the majority of the respondents are young: 64.71% of females and 81.82% of males from Fashion retailing; and 83.33% for both female and male from Food retailing. The Fashion front staff are from social group B (64.71% of females and 63.64% of males) and the Food employees are from class C (100% of females and males). The main job rank is that of salesperson (94.12% of the females and 90.91% of the males from Fashion retailing) and in the Food sector they are attendants

(100% of females) and waiters (66.67% of males). The female frontline workers from Fashion and Food retailing perceive that well-dressed young women receive face-to-face retail services prior to everybody else if the server is male (94.12% in Fashion and 100% in the Food sector), although the masculine gender has a different opinion, especially in Food retailing; they believe that young well-dressed males receive the frontline employees' attention beforehand. To the female frontline employees, the last customer to receive the service is a badly-dressed middle-age man (76.47%). Therefore, gender produces a higher response than the type of retailing. To male frontline employees in Fashion, the responses are in line with the female reactions, in 81.82% of the responses. On the other hand, in Food retailing, the male staff believe that badly-dressed middle-age women are the last to be served (50% of the responses). Both male and female frontline employees believe that the order of preference remains the same if the staff that provide the service are male or female (76.47% of females and 90.91% of males from the Fashion sector, and 100% for both females and males in Food retailing).

The results from the Likert Scales show that there is an impact of the sector on the frontline employees' self-perception of ageism, sexism and lookism. Self-perception of prejudice and discrimination is everywhere, at different levels. An overall conclusion is that the frontline employees admit that there is ASL bias in both types of retailing, Fashion and Food, but they do not consider themselves guilty of ageism, sexism and lookism against customers. Through this study, there is no way to confirm what they believe about themselves, but the method makes it possible to show that people usually judge the context, in the case, the workplace, through the vision of their own point-of-view and experiences. Thus, if someone interprets something or somebody else in a certain light, it may mean that the respondent would behave the way he or she had judged somebody else.

Recommendations and Contributions

The recommendations for the retail companies are to create conditions for ASL self-consciousness by the frontline staff to avoid prejudiced behaviour against customers and to develop some ASL T&D (training and development) to, at least, reduce ageism, sexism and lookism in the workplace, especially in the retail spatial environment. These contents should be part of the organisation's strategic statements.

The main contribution of this study is the generation of a methodology, using Likert's scales, that sheds some light on subjects such as ageism, sexism and lookism in a spatial environment, during the frontline employees and the customers' interactions. The Likert's scales have been very useful in the study of social phenomena, since

1932 (Ferguson, 1941). It is simple to format and to use. What is new in the present situation, it is used to help to understand "taboo" subjects in Retailing, such as prejudice, discrimination, ageism, sexism and lookism. People refuse they exist and do not want to talk about them.

Managerial Implications

Prejudice and discrimination and ASL Syndrome should be of concern of every kind of retailing. If the frontline employees have prejudice behaviour against customers, the latter would not feel comfortable to shop in the retailers premises. The consequences are very clear: no purchase, no gain. So, the companies should be willing to prepare their frontline staff to welcome the customers in the service spaces.

Final Issues

Considering the results, some final issues come to mind. They should be answered in the near future to help format the retail companies' strategies, the way they are going to train and develop their frontline employees and how they provide services to their customers:

1. Customers and frontline employees are mainly from different social classifications. Does the difference affect theirs mutual perception in such a way as to produce prejudice and discrimination? Customers are from social class B and frontline employees are mainly C, considering the level of formal education, income, spatial residential area, size of residence and occupation, as it is explained in the Methodology of this chapter (Rattam, 1998). In emergent countries, there is a huge gap between social classes, not only because of differences in income and purchase power, but mainly because of educational levels and the chances of social mobility. The upper classes put their

children in private schools so they can apply for public universities. The working class children study in public schools, but cannot apply for the federal universities because of the massive competition and if they can go into higher education, they go to private colleges paying monthly fees. The "B" class people compromise their income because they can afford to pay a mortgage with high interest rates. For the "C" class segment, it is very hard to buy their own house, even with the existence of social government housing programmes, such as "your home, your life" in Brazil and council houses. The "C" class wishes to graduate to the "B" class and the "B" class is afraid of being forced down to the "C" class. These statements are very useful to summarise and visualise the differences of behaviour between the two groups and the latent resentment that can produce prejudice and discrimination.

2. Do well-trained staff behave properly with the customers and avoid ASL bias? Is T&D efficient enough to avoid ASL bias? The retail companies provide T&D to new employees in terms of technical skills, but they very seldom offer training to improve behavioural competences, especially those that help to avoid ASL Syndrome. Therefore, although T&D against ASL bias is necessary and should be part of an organisation's strategic statements, it is still difficult to predict its effectiveness because real cases are very difficult to find and analyse.

3. In the Northern Hemisphere, the retail spatial environment area is losing importance to the business compared with the growing sales levels of online shopping directly from companies' Websites. Firms are closing down their branches on the High Street (BAM, 2012). Will this also be the case in the Southern Hemisphere, where going shopping is still a form of leisure and where many customers do not trust online shopping? Now

and in the years to come, it is better to adapt a business to the profile of local customers. It is more difficult and expensive to push a retail model to emergent countries. Many shopping malls have being built in recent years (Chase, 2012), even after the 2008 credit crunch, to provide leisure activities as options for customers in their spare time in the Southern Hemisphere, including services such as cinemas, food squares, children's playgrounds, carwashes, spas, and, of course, different kinds of stores, especially fashion shops. This context shows the importance of the frontline employees' role, because the face-to-face interactions are still there. So, well-trained and committed staff can provide the service with lower chance of prejudiced behaviour against customers of different age, gender and appearance.

4. Prejudice and discrimination are "taboo" subjects. How should the respondents be dealt with in order to avoid "insincere" responses to the survey? Projective techniques (Creswell, 1998) and neural tests (Plassman et al., 2007) can be useful to obtain more "genuine" answers, although the latter are more complex and expensive to apply.

FUTURE RESEARCH DIRECTIONS

This study can be useful for improving the knowledge of the self-perception of ageism, sexism and lookism in face-to-face retail services. Its format and its methodology can be used to research different kinds of organisations, especially in the retail and service industries. Future studies can analyse other groups of employees from different professional and social status in order to improve the comparative analyses and their results. It is also possible to include cross-cultural-anthropological-marketing analyses of the ASL phenomenon. And the use of the Mann-Whitney test, larger samples and random sampling can improve the quality of the results. It seems that there are many possibilities for developing knowledge concerning prejudice and discrimination in face-to-face retail services.

REFERENCES

Abrams, D. (2005, September 6). You're considered old when you reach 49. *Evening Standard*.

Abrams, D., Russell, P. S., Vouclair, C.-M., & Swift, H. (2011). Ageism in Europe – Findings from the European Social Survey. *European Research Group on Attitudes to Age Report*. Retrieved November 30th, 2013, from http://www.ageuk. org.uk/Documents/EN-GB/For-professionals/ ageism_across_europe_report_interactive. pdf?dtrk=true

Adams, S. J. (2004). Age discrimination legislation and the employment of older workers. *Labour Economics, 11*, 219–241. doi:10.1016/j. labeco.2003.06.001

Andrade, C. F., Palmeira, M., & Kato, H. T. (2010). Private Brands and Brazilian Supermarkets. In *Proceedings of British Academy of Management Conference*. Sheffield, UK: BAM.

Bettencourt, L., & Gwinner, K. (1996). Customization of the service experience: the role of the frontline employee. *International Journal of Service Industry Management, 7*(2), 3–20. doi:10.1108/09564239610113442

Brennan, C., Carmichael, F., & Ingham, B. (2007). Ageism and Employment: A Survey of the Literature in the Context of Current Research Agendas. *University of Salford, European Social Fund project on Ageism and Employment*. Retrieved February 12th, 2012, from http://www.mams.salford.ac.uk/PWO/Projects?Ageism-Employment

British Academy of Management (BAM). (2012). The Future of the Retail Fashion Store: Setting a New Research Agenda. *Retail Fashion Seminar*. British Academy of Management.

Bruce, Moore, & Birtwistle. (2004). *International Retail Marketing – a case study approach*. Oxford, UK: Elsevier.

Chase, S. (2012). The rise of the Mall in Brazil. *The Globe and Mail*. Retrieved August, 25, 2013, from http://www.theglobeandmail.com/ report-on-business/international-business/latin-american-business/the-rise-of-the-mall-in-brazil/ article593004/

Dirks, D. (2004). *It comes with the territory: Women Restaurant Workers' Experiences of Sexual Harassment and Sexual Objectification*. (Unpublished doctoral dissertation). Graduate School of the University of Florida.

Elmadağ, A. B., Ellinger, A. E., & Franke, G. R. (2008). Antecedents and Consequences of Frontline Service Employee Commitment to Service Quality. *The Journal of Marketing Theory and Practice, 16*(2), 95–110. doi:10.2753/MTP1069-6679160201

Engel, J., Blackwell, R., & Miniard, P. (1990). *Consumer Behavior*. Orlando, FL: The Dryden Press.

Ferguson, L. W. (1941). A Study of the Likert Technique of Attitude Scale Construction. *Mead Project*. Department of Psycology, University of Connecticut. Retrieved November 24th, 2013, from http://www.brocku.ca/MeadProject/sup/ Ferguson_1941.html

Frith, H., & Gleeson, G. (2004). Clothing and Embodiment: Men Managing Body Image and Appearance. *Psychology of Men & Masculinity, 5*(1), 40–48. doi:10.1037/1524-9220.5.1.40

Gil, A. C. (2002). *Como elaborar projetos de pesquisa* [How to do research projects]. Sao Paulo: Atlas. (in Portuguese)

Haralambos, M., & Holborn, M. (2008). *Sociology – Themes and perspectives*. London, UK: Collins.

Hsiang-Fei, L., & Sheng-Hshiung, T. (2011). Customers' perceptions of service quality: do servers' age stereotypes matter? *International Journal of Hospitality Management, 30*, 283–289. doi:10.1016/j.ijhm.2010.09.002

Jasper, C., & Klassen, M. (1990). Stereotypical Beliefs about Appearance: implications for retailing and consumer issues. *Perceptual and Motor Skills, 71*, 519–528. doi:10.2466/pms.1990.71.2.519 PMID:2251085

Kerfoot, D., & Korczynski, M. (2005). Gender and Service: New Directions for the Study of 'Front-line' Service Work. *Gender, Work and Organization, 12*(5), 387–399. doi:10.1111/j.1468-0432.2005.00280.x

Kligman, A. M., & Graham, J. A. (1986). *The Psychology of Appearance in the Elderly*. Retrieved February 12th, 2012, from http://www.ncbi.nlm.nih.gov/pubmed/3521995

Kotler, P., & Keller, K. L. (2006). *Administracao de Marketing* [Marketing Management]. Sao Paulo: Pearson Prentice Hall. (in Portuguese)

Kwong-Leung, T. (2000). Ageism and Sexism at Work: The Middle-Aged Women of Hong Kong. *Gender, Technology and Development, 4*(2), 225–253. doi:10.1177/097185240000400203 PMID:12179949

LaRosa, C., & Campbell, J. (2010). *Your Frontline Employees Are Your Brand: How Do You Hire The Right Ones?* Retrieved February 12th, 2012, from http://www.fastcodesign.com/1665464/your-frontline-employees-are-your-brand-how-do-you-hire-the-right-ones

Lovelock, C., & Wright, L. (2007). *Servicos: marketing e gestao* [Services: marketing and management]. Sao Paulo: Saraiva. (in Portuguese)

Malhotra, N. K. (2001). *Pesquisa de marketing: uma orientacao aplicada* [Marketing Research: an applied approach]. Porto Alegre: Bookman. (in Portuguese)

Mattar, F. N. (2007). *Pesquisa de Marketing* [Marketing Research]. Sao Paulo: Atlas. (in Portuguese)

Oxford Brookes University. (2007). *Unit 23 Recognise diversity when delivering customer service*. Retrieved February 12th, 2012, from http://www.brookes.ac.uk/services/ocsld/staffcourses/nvq/standards/customer_service/level2/unit23.html

Palmeira, M., Palmeira, D., & Santos, C. (2012). A Perception of Prejudice in the Face-to-face Retail Services: comparative analyses of age and gender. *International Journal of Applied Behavioral Economics, 1*(4), 22–40. doi:10.4018/ijabe.2012100103

Palmeira, M., Santos, C., & Palmeira, D. (2012). Frontline Employees' Self-perception of Ageism, Sexism, and Appearance Discrimination – comparative analysis in Fashion and Food Retailing. In *Proceedings of British Academy of Management Conference*. Cardiff, UK: BAM.

Parente, J. (2000). *Varejo no Brasil – Gestao e Estrategia* [Retailing in Brazil – Management and Strategy]. Atlas. (in Portuguese)

Pentecost, R., & Andrews, L. (2010). Fashion retailing and the bottom line: The effects of generational cohorts, gender, fashion fanship, attitudes and impulse buying on fashion expenditure. *Journal of Retailing and Consumer Services, 17*(1), 43–52. doi:10.1016/j.jretconser.2009.09.003

Plassman, H. ODoherty, J., Shiv, B, & Rangel, A. (2007). Marketing actions can modulate neural representations of experienced pleasantness. *Proceedings of the National Academy of Sciences of the United States of America, 105*(3), 1050-1054.

Pliner, P., Chaiken, S., & Flett, G. (1990). *Gender Differences in Concern with Body Weight and Physical Appearance Over the Life Span*. Retrieved February 12th, 2012, from http://psp.sagepub.com/content/16/2/263.short

Prasad, A., Prasad, P., & Mir, R. (2011). One mirror in another: Managing diversity and the discourse of fashion. *Human Relations*, *64*(5), 703–724. doi:10.1177/0018726710386511

Rai, S. (2010). *Oxford dictionary or Politics*. Retrieved February 12th, 2012 from http://www.answers.com/topic/sexism

Rattam, E. (1998). *Novo modelo de estratifica-cao socioeconomica para marketing e pesquisas de marketing*. [New Social Classification Approach for Marketing and Marketing Research] (In Portuguese). Retrieved July 1st, 2008, from http://www.anpad.org.br/enanpad/1998/dwn/enanpad1998-mkt-27.pdf

Reynolds, J., & Cuthbertson, C. (2004). *Retail Strategy – the view from the bridge*. Oxford, UK: Elsevier Butterwork-Heinemann.

Riverside, City of. (2006). *City Report*. California - USA.

Robertson, J. (2003). *Knowledge management for front-line staff*. Retrieved February 12th, 2012, from http://www.steptwo.com.au/papers/kmc_frontline/index.html

Rumsey, N., & Harcourt, D. (2005). *The Psychology of Appearance*. Retrieved February 12th, 2012, from http://www.lavoisier.fr/livre/notice.asp?id=O22WA3AR3LLOWE

Schirrmacher, F. (2004). *A Revolucao dos Idosos* [The Methuselah Complot]. Rio de Janeiro, Brazil: Campus/Elsevier. (in Portuguese)

Scott, J., & Marshall, G. (2009). *Oxford dictionary of sociology* (3rd ed.). Oxford, UK: Oxford University Press. doi:10.1093/acref/9780199553008.001.0001

Siegel, S., & Castellan, J. Jr. (2006). *Estatistica Nao-parametricapara ciencias do comportamento* [Nonparametric Statistics for the Behavioral Sciences]. Porto Alegre: Bookman. (in Portuguese)

Solomon, M. R., & Rabolt, N. J. (2009). *Consumer Behavior in Fashion*. Pearson Education.

Thompson, N. J., & Thompson, K. E. (2007). Marketing and the Ageing Consumer Population: the Future is Not as Clear as the Past. In *Proceedings of British Academy of Management Conference*. Warwick, UK: BAM.

Waring, P. (2011). Keeping up appearances: Aesthetic Labour and Discrimination Law. *The Journal of Industrial Relations*, *53*(2), 193–207. doi:10.1177/0022185610397141

Williams, C. (2006). Shopping as Symbolic Interaction: race, class, and gender in the Toy Store. *Symbolic Interaction*, *28*(4), 459–472. doi:10.1525/si.2005.28.4.459

Wonnacott, T. H., & Wonnacott, R. J. (1981). *Estatistica Aplicada A Economia e a Administracao* [Applied Statistics for Economy and Business]. Rio de Janeiro, Brazil: LTC Publishers. (in Portuguese)

ADDITIONAL READING

Baral, R., & Bhargava, S. (2011). Examining the Moderating Influence of Gender on the relationships between Work-Family Antecedents and Work-Family Enrichment. Gender in Management: An International Journal, vol 26 issue 2.

Brakus, J. J., Schmitt, B. H., & Zarantonello, L. (2009). Brand Experience: what is it? How is it measured? Does it affect loyalty? *Journal of Marketing*, *73*(May), 52–68. doi:10.1509/jmkg.73.3.52

Bytheway, B. (2007). Age Prejudice and Discrimination. *Encyclopaedia of Sociology* [Online]. Retrieved Feb 1st from www.sociologyencyclopedia.com.

Del Rio, M. L., Garcia, T., Varela, C., & Benito, L. (2010). Service orientation and Quality. *European Marketing Academy Conference – EMAC 2010*, Copenhagen, Denmark.

Delcourt, C., Van Riel, A., & Van Birgelen, M. (2010). Linking Frontline Employees' Emotional Intelligence to Customer Perceptions in a Service Delivery Context. European Institute of Retailing and Services Sciences Conference – EIRASS 2009, Toronto, Canada.

Eisend, M. (2010). Investigating the Relationship between Gender Stereotyping in Advertising and Gender-related Values in Society. *European Marketing Academy Conference – EMAC 2010*, Copenhagen, Denmark.

Garcia, T., & Grande, I. (2009). Factors Affecting Buying Behaviour and Food Expenses in the Spanish Aging People. European Institute of Retailing and Services Sciences Conference – EIRASS 2009, Toronto, Canada.

Johnson, L. (2008). Re-placing gender? Reflections on 15 years of Gender, Place and Culture. *Gender, Place and Culture, 15*(6), 561–574. doi:10.1080/09663690802518412

Ogbonna, E., & Harris, L. C. (2009). Motives for Service Sabotage: An Empirical Study of Front-Line Worker Behaviors. European Institute of Retailing and Services Sciences Conference – EIRASS 2009, Toronto, Canada.

Palmeira, M., Semprebom, E., Ferrari, J., Formaggi, L., Kruger, E., Lima, L., & Barreto, S. (2009). Experiential Marketing in Bookstores. British Academy of Management Conference – BAM 2009. Brighton, UK.

Schmitt, B. H. (2003). *Customer Experience Management: A revolutionary approach to connecting with your customer*. New Jersey: John Wiley & Sons Inc.

Shaw, C. (2007). *The DNA of Customer Experience how emotions drive value*. New York: Palgrave MacMillan. doi:10.1057/9780230210813

Teller, C. (2009). Examining the Moderating Impact of Gender on Consumers' Retail Agglomeration Patronage Behavior. European Institute of Retailing and Services Sciences Conference – EIRASS 2009, Toronto, Canada.

Yeganeh, H., & May, D. (2011). Cultural Values and Gender Gap: A Cross National Analysis. Gender in Management: An International Journal, vol. 26 issue 2.

KEY TERMS AND DEFINITIONS

Ageism: Prejudice or discrimination against individuals or groups, based on their age.

Discrimination: A clear unfavourable action towards a person or groups considering one's age (Ageism), and/or gender (Sexism), and/or appearance (Lookism).

Fashion Retailing: Group of companies, part of the fashion supply chain that goes from the manufacturers to the consumer, offering fashion goods and services, through traditional seasonal spans and/or fast fashion timing, ranging from budget to designer price lines.

Food Retailing: Group of companies which includes restaurants, fast food outlets and pubs, offering processed and prepared food and a variety of soft drinks and beverages directly to the customers.

Frontline Employees: Any kind of people that interact directly with customers.

Lookism: Prejudice or discrimination against individuals or groups, based on their appearance.

Prejudice: Learned beliefs and values that lead an individual or group of individuals to be biased for or against members of particular group.

Retailing: Group of activities that involves the process of selling products and services directly to the customer as a way of fulfilling one's personal needs.

Sexism: Prejudice or discrimination against individuals or groups, based on their gender.

Spatial Retail Environment: Retailer area that includes a physical space where customers come into contact with frontline employees.

Chapter 16
A Dilemma for Retailers:
How to Make Store Surveillance Secure and Appealing to Shoppers

Angelo Bonfanti
University of Verona, Italy

ABSTRACT

Retailers use a number of ambient, design, and social elements with the aim of creating a unique, pleasant, and engaging Customer Shopping Experience (CSE). However, a store may be made paradoxically less attractive by the feelings of insecurity generated by the fact that the same elements can also encourage shoplifting. As a result, retailers have to balance their efforts to enhance a store's attractiveness by ensuring a high level of sales environment surveillance without interfering with the shopping experience. The aim of this chapter is to propose a conceptual framework that enriches the analysis of the development of retailer/consumer relationships by highlighting how retailers can make store surveillance simultaneously secure and appealing to shoppers. The analysis draws heavily on theoretical evidence in the marketing, environmental psychology, service, and retail management literature, and indicates that retailers' investments in store design, staff training, and technological systems can ensure adequate security levels without compromising customers' shopping experiences as long as the surveillance allows them to have direct contact with the store, its articles, and staff.

INTRODUCTION

Retailers acknowledge the importance of using a store's environment to create a unique customer experience (e.g. Turley & Milliman, 2000) that will make a shopping expedition pleasant and engaging, positively influence customer shopping behaviour, and increase sales. By incorporating atmospheric elements in the retail environment (Kotler, 1973; Hamrouni & Touzi, 2011), stores induce specific emotional effects that enhance the likelihood of customer purchases and the possibility of creating long-lasting consumer relationships (Babin & Attaway, 2000). Stores have become emotional places (e.g. Arnold & Reynolds, 2003; Borghini et al., 2009): stock assortments, visual merchandising, category management and all of the structural, sensorial and social characteristics of store design help to create a specific atmosphere and stimulate involvement (see Mehrabian &

DOI: 10.4018/978-1-4666-6074-8.ch016

Russell, 1974; Donovan & Rossiter, 1982; Baker, 1986; Berman & Evans, 1995; Turley & Milliman, 2000; Turley & Chebat, 2002). Enhancing the customer shopping experience (CSE) by means of exciting trade types and activities can have a significant magnetic attraction for shoppers (Ooi & Sim, 2007).

However, such strategic choices can have opposite effects on customer behaviour: a pleasant and comfortable store environment is greatly appreciated but, although open merchandising improves the shopping experience and increases sales, it can also encourage shoplifting (Phillips et al., 2005) and generally lead to increased retail shrinkage. "Shrinkage" or "shrink" is "stock loss from crime or waste expressed as a percentage of retail sales" as defined by the Global Retail Theft Barometer (GRTB, 2007), an annual study of the cost of merchandise theft and availability for the global retail industry. The 2012-2013 edition was funded by Checkpoint Systems (global leader in merchandise availability solutions for the retail industry, including loss prevention and merchandise visibility) and was undertaken in 2013 by Euromonitor International (world leader in strategy research for consumer markets). The data of this survey of 160,000 stores in 16 countries show that shrinkage amounted to more than $112 billion in 2012 (about 1.4% of global retail sales) and, with the global economic crisis still under way in 2013, remains a pressing problem that transversally involves all continents and markets. The lowest shrink rates were recorded in Japan (1% of retail sales), followed by Hong Kong, Australia and Germany (1.1%). The US and China came in at 1.5% of retail sales. The highest rates were recorded in Brazil and Mexico (1.6%). Shrinkage has four main causes (Bamfield, 2012): a) shoplifting by customers, including organised crime (41% in 2012); b) theft by dishonest employees (30%); c) in-house and administrative errors, including price, process or accounting errors (21%); and d) fraud by suppliers/manufacturers

(9%). Shrinkage affects shoppers in a number of ways, including reduced on-shelf availability, reduced assortments, defensive merchandising, and economic losses: every year, retail thefts cost each Italian family €144.00, each European family €145.00, and each global family €101.00. This cost is an "invisible tax" paid by consumers (Thornton, 1992), although it is not necessarily applied by all retailers because it depends on the business policies of the individual chain, and the criteria and margins on which they base their product sale prices. However, if it is applied, it is a substantial burden on families especially at times of financial constraints.

As shoplifting is the main cause of shrinkage, it is clearly important for retailers to keep ahead of dishonest customers and monitor shoplifters' intentions in order to obtain the most from their security investments. However, this raises the important question as to whether store surveillance is compatible with customer satisfaction, which means that retailers must seek an appropriate compromise between the need to protect their stores against shoplifting and the need to minimise the impact of this protection on their customers' shopping experience. In other words, they have to try to enhance the store's attractiveness by ensuring a high level of sales environment surveillance.

The aim of this chapter is to propose a conceptual framework that highlights what retailers can do to maintain a high level of sales environment security and merchandise protection measures, and still satisfy their customers' experiential expectations. It contributes to enriching the analysis of the development of retailer/consumer relationships by highlighting the importance for retailers of creating a system of store surveillance that is secure against shoplifting and appealing for shoppers in three ways: it reviews the main publications that provide useful information concerning a store's attractiveness and surveillance; it proposes a conceptual framework for considering how retailers can enhance their CSE and ensure store security by considering shoppers' perceptions of in-store surveillance solutions; finally, it suggests some guidance for retail managers and indicates directions for future research.

The analysis draws heavily on theoretical evidence, although identifying the papers that provide significant insights into store surveillance from a CSE perspective proved to be a laborious task because store surveillance and CSE issues are usually analysed separately. The review was therefore extended to include many contributions in the marketing, environmental psychology, retailing and service management literature. However, although some aspects relating to security solutions were found, they were often occasional and intermittent. The study especially considers the retailers' point of view, but information concerning shoppers' perceptions of store surveillance was taken not only from the literature, but also from a Nielsen research institute study carried out in 2010 and entitled "Perception of the protection and security elements of products," which was commissioned by Checkpoint Systems in order to discover the opinions of Portuguese consumers aged between 25 and 55 years.

BACKGROUND: STORE ATTRACTIVENESS AND SURVEILLANCE

Over the last thirty years or so, the development of various marketing approaches has marked the evolution of the relationship between business and the marketplace by concentrating on customer experiences (Holbrook & Hirschmann, 1982) and store management in a CSE perspective (Grewal et al., 2009). The theories of experiential marketing (O'Sullivan & Spangler, 1998; Schmitt, 1999a; b; 2003) and experience economy (Pine & Gilmore, 1999; 2002) developed from the end of the 1990s are particularly important, and explore the concept of customer experiences from various points of view (e.g. Brunetti, 2004):

1. Product-experience, when a product is enriched in such a manner that it becomes an experience (Schmitt, 1999a);
2. Experience-product, when the experience becomes a product; and
3. Experiential shopping, when a business sets up its point of sale in order to attract visitors by means of aesthetic, sensory and emotional stimuli (Pine & Gilmore, 2002).

These approaches lead retailers to compete by means of experiential and spectacular elements (Hollenbeck et al., 2008). In addition, business recognition of the importance of the affective component (Donovan & Rossiter, 1982) induces consumer to shop for hedonistic as well as utilitarian purposes (Hirschmann & Holbrook, 1982; Batra & Athola, 1990; Mano & Oliver, 1993; Boedeker, 1995; Tauber, 1995; Jones, 1999; Bäckström & Johansson, 2006). The hedonistic activity is related to the pleasure and engagement of visiting a store and shopping for products that offer sensory gratification (Babin et al., 1994; Arnold & Reynolds, 2003), and pleasurable in-store experiences are characterised by intrinsic satisfaction, perceived freedom, entertainment and escapism (Babin et al., 1994; Jones, 1999; Sit et al., 2003).

By offering functional and hedonistic added value to CSE, retailers can make it more memorable and attractive. Historically, the marketing, service and retailing management literature has considered customer experience a holistic construct that involves customers' cognitive, affective, emotional, sensorial, social and physical responses. According to Schmitt (1999a,b), "the experiential modules to be managed in Experiential Marketing include sensory experiences (sense), affective experiences (feel), creative cognitive experiences (think), physical experiences, behaviours and lifestyles (act), and social-identity experiences that result from relating to a reference group or culture (relate)." Retailers can stimulate one or more modules by means of experience providers (ExPro) (Schmitt, 1999b) such as communications, visual identity, product presentation (e.g. product design, packaging, display and brand character), co-branding (e.g. event marketing and sponsorships, product placement), the store itself, a Web'site and the new media, and their sales staff.

Protection and safety are important utilitarian benefits (Fiore & Kim, 2007): customers are more likely to shop in stores that provide a safe and secure environment (Cowper, 1992; Coleman, 2006), and are not associated with concerns about safety (Overstreet & Clodfelter, 1995). Some studies have also pointed out that, if customers do not feel safe and comfortable when shopping, they are unlikely to spend their time or their money on it (Kajalo & Lindblom, 2010b), sales are depressed and profits lost (Chapman & Templar, 2006). It can be assumed that a store will not be attractive for shoppers if they perceive insecurity and fear-arousing stimuli. Retailers therefore also have to ensure that their store environment security solutions and product protection measures guarantee a high level of surveillance in order to make their stores appealing to shoppers.

HOW TO MAKE STORE SURVEILLANCE SECURE AND APPEALING TO SHOPPERS

Store management requires retailers to satisfy a two-fold need: they need to create an attractive shopping experience that is capable of meeting their customers' latent sensorial, emotional and psychological expectations without encouraging shoplifting, and they need to ensure a level of surveillance that simultaneously protects the store against thieves for shoppers. Effective sales environment surveillance therefore has to be seen as a means of enhancing a store's attractiveness and, to do this, they need to consider shoppers' perceptions of in-store surveillance solutions in terms of CSE and security in order to understand

their positive and negative effects on the development of retailer/consumer relationships.

The conceptual framework shown in Figure 1 integrates these needs by suggesting surveillance solutions that are secure and appealing to shoppers, such as store design, staff training and technological systems, as discussed below.

How Retailers Can Enhance CSE

Retailers can enhance CSE by improving its more controllable elements, such as store atmosphere, service interfaces, assortments and prices (Verhoef et al., 2009). As consumers' in-store experiences are created as a result of interactions with all of the elements of a store (Bäckström & Johansson, 2006), retailers can leverage on the store environment (or "servicescape," Bitner, 1992) by manipulating these in three dimensions (Baker, 1986):

1. Ambient factors based on the senses of individual consumers (sight, sound, smell and touch);
2. Design elements, including functional and aesthetic aspects such as the layout, design and décor of the store (Baker et al., 2002); and
3. Social characteristics, or the people component of the space in which interpersonal interactions (Moye & Kincade, 2002) take place in the form of customer-to-customer and customer-to-staff interactions.

One of the areas that has received most attention in the service marketing literature (particularly in retail settings) concerns atmospheric variables (Hamrouni & Touzi, 2011) such as music, scent, temperature, lighting, noise and the quality of the air (for an overview, see Naylor et al., 2008). Kotler (1973) defined what he called "atmospherics" as "the effort to design buying environments to produce specific emotional effects in the buyer that enhance his purchase probability." It specifically includes all of the controllable ele-

Figure 1. Making store surveillance secure and appealing to shoppers

RETAILERS

ENHANCING THE CUSTOMER SHOPPING EXPERIENCE
to enhance store attractiveness by means of:
- ambient factors (especially the senses of individual consumers)
- store design factors such as layout, display and visual merchandising (e.g. multimedia merchandising technology)
- social factors such as relationships with personnel staff

ENSURING THE STORE SECURITY
to ensure a high level of sales environment and merchandise security by means of various forms of store surveillance that involve:
- store design elements (ensuring suitable interior lighting with no dark zones, reducing crowding, generating larger interior spaces, creating greater visibility by adjusting equipment layouts, adopting effective product displays)
- locking and security systems (displaying products in closed cabinets, showcases or counters; using empty packages containing a note to be exchanged for the product itself; attaching chains to products)
- personnel training
- technological developments (EAS and RFID systems; source tagging)

SHOPPERS' PERCEPTIONS OF STORE SURVEILLANCE SOLUTIONS
- a sales environment which offers a sense of security, transparency and trust when they shopping is positively perceived
- a store which produces a sense of distrust and intimidation, discomfort and embarrassment, frustration and sense of prohibition is adversely perceived

MAKING STORE SURVEILLANCE SECURE AND APPEALING TO SHOPPERS
Retailers have to use store design elements, personnel training and technological development systems wisely and discreetly as possible because they:
- provide safe and reliable high-level protection of store and its articles
- increase customers' sense of security
- limit shoplifting and external aggression
- stimulate trust and a desire to shop in honest shoppers
- positively influence store attractiveness, customers' behavior and shopping expeditions
- stimulate direct contact with store and its articles
- allow customers to stay freely and peacefully in the store for as long as possible

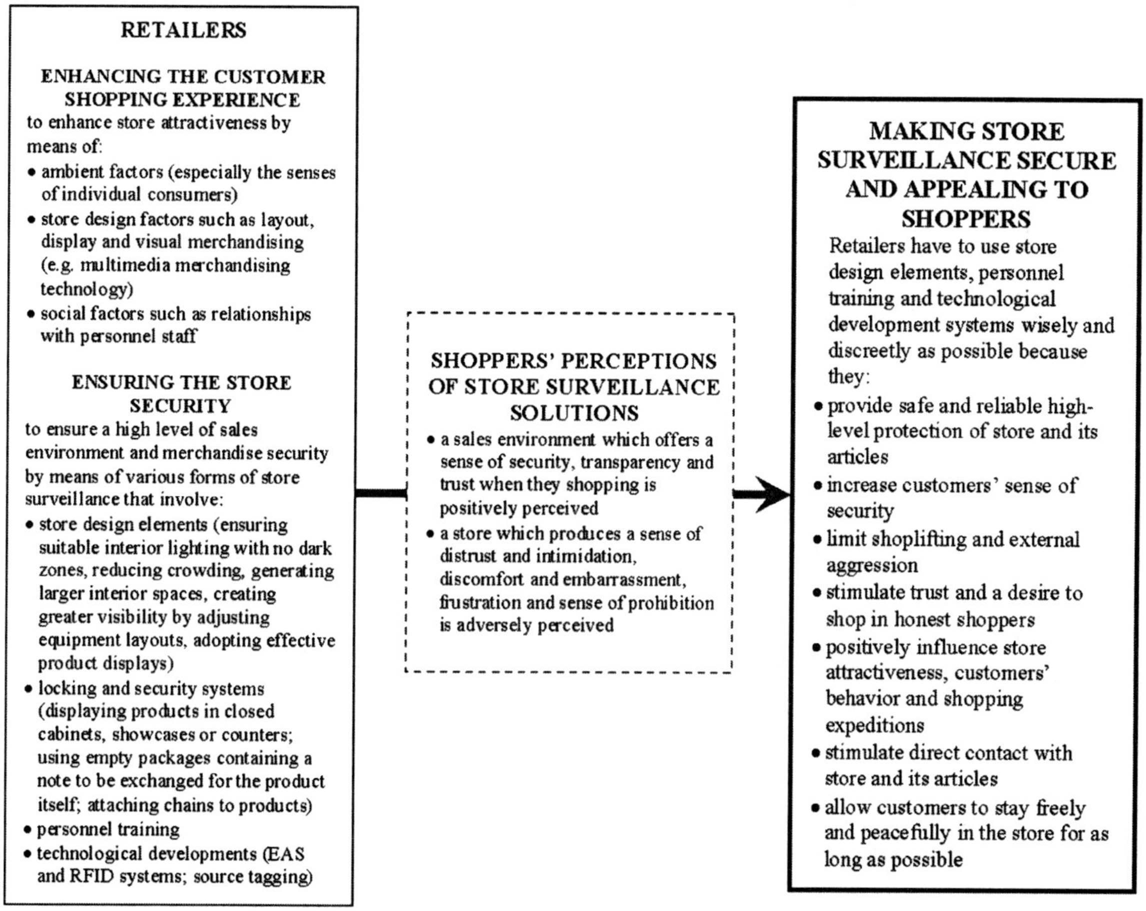

ments or stimuli within the service environment that influence emotional reactions, and therefore have an impact on behaviour (Milliman & Fugate, 1993; Spangenberg et al., 1996; Foxall, 1997; Turley & Chebat, 2002; Vieira, 2013). To use the stimulus-organism-response paradigm and pleasure-arousal-dominance model of environmental psychology (Mehrabian & Russell, 1974; Donovan & Rossiter, 1982; Bellizzi & Hite, 1992; Babin & Darden, 1995; Fiore & Kim, 2007), the environment includes the stimuli that invoke in an individual (organism) a desire to approach/avoid it (response). Essentially, a positive atmosphere can lead to approach behaviours that imply a longer stay in the store accompanied by greater expenditure or an increased propensity for impulse

buying (Donovan & Rossiter, 1982; Sherman et al., 1997; Spies et al., 1997; Foxall & Greenley, 1999; 2000), whereas a negative atmosphere may lead to avoidance behaviours such as a wish to leave the store or a sense of dissatisfaction (Donovan & Rossiter, 1982; Turley & Milliman, 2000). Environmental stimuli also have an impact on the mood of consumers (Spies et al., 1997), who are sensitive to even very small changes in the retail atmosphere (Turley & Milliman, 2000; Turley & Chebat, 2002).

Retailers can also leverage on store design, which includes all of the factors that can affect customers' perceptions of a retail environment (Bitner, 1992; Turley & Milliman 2000), from the tangible elements within it, such as equipment, furnishings, interior decoration, signage (e.g. Bonfanti, 2013), visual merchandising (e.g. Law et al., 2012), décor, store layout and display, to its external architecture and window displays. Every element of store design affects shoppers' behaviour by influencing their emotional, cognitive and physiological state, and can therefore induce customers to enter a store or not, affect the likelihood of their approaching or avoiding a product, and stimulate or limit their propensity to buy (e.g. Buttle, 1984; Lam, 2001).

In terms of the social dimension, customers' shopping experiences can be physically, emotionally and cognitively influenced by their interactions with the people in the store (personnel and other customers). Service marketing and management studies have highlighted the fact that, during service encounters, customer/staff interactions are crucial in creating customer satisfaction and service quality (e.g. Grönroos, 2000; Gummesson, 2002). Store staff play a crucial role in anticipating customer expectations, creating customer-oriented value, and building emotional bonds for lifetime relationships (Bitner, 1992). Staff attributes may signal service quality (Baker et al., 2002): for example, knowledgeable staff capable of solving problems and handling claims play a critical role in delivering a higher quality experience to retail customers (Bagdare, 2012). An ability to listen is also important in order to be able to empathise with customers (Stock & Hoyer, 2005): retail personnel can actively develop trust by perceiving, interpreting and responding to their needs. The social dimension has also been investigated in terms of crowding (e.g. Machleit et al., 1994), which shoppers generally perceive as an unpleasant experience (Hui & Bateson, 1991). Too few or too many staff can negatively affect customer experiences (Baker, 1965), and reduce shopper satisfaction (Machleit et al., 2000). Furthermore, in addition to creating psychological stress and limiting freedom (Brehm, 1966), a crowded store can encourage dishonest customers to steal (Fullerton & Punj, 1993).

How Retailers Can Ensure Store Security

Dishonest customers are led to steal if they believe it is easy to do and that they are not likely to be discovered (Tonglet, 2002; Kulas et al., 2007). It is possible that more people decide to attempt shoplifting during a recession, but the triggering factor is always based on the individual's calculation of the risk-reward ratio. Shoplifters who have been successful once are more likely to feel safer and be inclined to try again. The risk-reward ratio is also much higher in countries whose legal systems are weak in punishing retail thefts.

In order to protect their stores from such customers, retailers can invest in various methods of surveillance and shoplifting prevention (Dawson, 1993; Overstreet & Clodfelter, 1995; Tonglet & Bamfield, 1997; Gill et al., 1999; Fullerton & Punj, 2004; Hayes and Blackwood, 2006; Kajalo & Lindblom, 2010a; Hayes & Downs, 2011; Hayes et al., 2011; Kajalo & Lindblom, 2011a; Lindblom & Kajalo 2011). The solutions that have been most frequently described in the literature are sophisticated closed-circuit television (CCTV) surveillance systems, motion detectors, high-tech scanners, electronic article surveillance (EAS) devices and radio-frequency identification (RFId) tags, floor security personnel and shop detectives. Lindblom and Kajalo (2011) distinguish formal surveillance (guard patrols, CCTV, motion detector devices, and other surveillance systems) and informal surveillance (physical features, activities and people).

In brief, the main forms of store surveillance are store design elements, locking and security systems, security personnel, and technological systems.

As store design plays a very direct role in affecting customers' in-store behaviour (McGoldrick, 1990), retailers can eliminate the opportunity of stealing by making some changes to the store atmosphere, layout and display. They can organise their stores in such a way as to create suitable interior lighting (Burns et al., 2010), eliminate dark zones, reduce crowding (especially at checkout counters) (Fullerton & Punj, 1993), and generate larger interior spaces. Some give the store greater visibility by adjusting equipment layouts (Wellhoff & Masson, 2005): for example, it is good practice to eliminate areas in which shoplifters can hide while they are stealing, and use gondolas that are not too tall and preferably transparent. It is also important to make effective use of product displays by putting the products that are most subject to theft at display levels that are the least comfortable for shoplifters (although retailers must also make sure that the products do not simultaneously become less accessible to honest customers). It is appropriate to avoid displaying expensive and vulnerable products near store exits or in blind spots that are not overseen by security officers, salespeople or electronic surveillance (Gill, 2007; Lindblom & Kajalo, 2011). In this way, retailers can prevent shoplifting by creating a store design that stimulates non-fraudulent customer behaviour without limiting themselves to installing security cameras.

Many stores also make widespread use of locking and security systems, including displaying articles in closed cabinets, showcases or counters; using empty packages that only contain a voucher to be exchanged for the actual article; or attaching chains to particularly costly and/or branded articles such as consumer electronics (e.g. mp3 players, and the latest-generation mobile phones and tablets), cosmetics, perfumes, jewellery, photography items, or quality alcoholic beverages such as champagne.

The use of security personnel to protect property (sworn guards, rangers or other uniformed staff) is a useful means of reducing shoplifting and crime (Cozens et al., 2005), especially in large retail businesses and during particular times of the year such as Christmas, when the number of thefts increases sharply (GRTB, 2011). Security personnel primarily act as human deterrents, satisfy customers by creating a sensation of safety in the store, and represent a physical reference point for customers in the case of unpleasant incidents (Pretious et al., 1995). Security staff monitor what takes place in the store, and report all relevant events to sales managers. In addition, sales assistants must obviously be appropriately trained in how to remove an anti-shoplifting tag without damaging the article.

The main technological systems are: a) EAS and RFId tags, including rigid and cardboard labels that can be applied in the store or during the production/distribution process (source tagging); and b) anti-shoplifting EAS and RFId antennas, software and accessories. RFId tags in particular satisfy many of the retailers' expectations (e.g. Jones et al., 2004; Lai et al., 2005; Hingley et al., 2007; Sellitto et al., 2007; Rekik et al., 2009; Azevedo & Carvalho, 2012) because:

1. They are easy to use (they can be applied to various types of articles and are easily deactivated);
2. They are reliable (they do not usually generate false alarms);
3. They detect a large proportion of articles subject to shoplifting (although very small, the labels can be remotely detected even in the case of a large entry/exit passageway);
4. They are high quality (they respond effectively and efficiently during the detection phases regardless of the position of the antenna); and
5. The better product display they allow increases the possibility of sales.

All of these solutions are capable of storing data in special electronic devices and answering remote queries from fixed or portable "radio-frequency readers," which communicate information including warning notices of shoplifting by malicious customers (Jones et al., 2004). Source tagging, which involves applying anti-shoplifting EAS tags during the production or packaging phases, is gaining widespread acceptance because it strengthens retailer/supplier partnerships (Varaldo & Dalli, 2003). It has many advantages for retailers (Bonfanti et al., 2013) because it:

1. Optimises costs by eliminating store tagging procedures;
2. Allows the self-service display of an increasing number of items;
3. Avoids the non-homogeneous application of tags or the need to use large tags because of the difficulty of tagging in the store;
4. Reduces the problem of tampering by customers at the store;
5. Avoids damaging the image of the product, and the better packaging increases quality;
6. Improves article display because the security element becomes an integral part of the product itself; and
7. Allows sales personnel to dedicate more time to customer assistance and offering customers better service because they are not engaged in labelling/tagging or monitoring criminal activities.

Shoppers' Perceptions and Effects on the Retailer-Consumer Relationship

The in-store security system chosen by retailers can be positively or adversely perceived by consumers depending on how it emotionally affects their shopping experience. Consequently, retailers should invest in solutions that induce positive emotions in their customers. Table 1 shows shoppers' perceptions of the principal in-store surveillance systems.

Table 1. Shoppers' perceptions of store surveillance solutions

Emotions Perceived by Shoppers		In-Store Elements Perceived by Shoppers	Store Surveillance Solutions
POSITIVE	Sense of Security	• Shopping in a vagrant- and aggression-free environment • Shopping in a clean and sufficiently lit sales environment • Store not associated with concerns about safety • Entering a welcoming and reassuringly open sales environment • Not having limitations on in-store freedom • Being able to take articles directly from accessible displays • Seeing in-store security personnel as important physical and relational reference points for preventing the actions of thieves and delinquents • Not feeling constantly watched	Security Tags Antennas Security Personnel
	Transparency	• Being able to examine and test articles freely • Being able to carry articles to the checkout counter • Buying articles with visible security elements (possibly recorded on the packaging) • Buying articles with the clear identification of functions of security solutions	Security Tags
	Trust	• Being able to hold and inspect products physically • Being able to pick up, touch, interact with, and choose displayed articles • Being able to evaluate articles and learn about their characteristics • Shopping in a conversational environment	Security Tags Security Personnel
NEGATIVE	Distrust and Intimidation	• Feeling of being in an uncomfortable store • Feeling of being under constant surveillance	Security Cameras Security Personnel Warning Signs
	Discomfort and Embarrassment	Being stopped because alarm system triggered by non-deactivated security tags (unprofessional staff or technical failures)	Security Tags Security Personnel
	Frustration and Sense of Prohibition	Not being able to touch articles	Locking and Security Systems

Consumers positively perceive a sales environment that offers a sense of security (Cowper, 1992) because they like to feel safe when shopping (Coleman, 2006), and do not want concerns about safety keeping them away from a store (Overstreet & Clodfelter, 1995). They therefore understand and agree with the use of security devices in shops. They also perceive the greater vulnerability of retailers in times of economic crisis and expect that some shops with a high level of theft may try to seek a form of compensation by practising higher prices (Nielsen, 2010).

Store surveillance solutions that allow consumers to shop in a clean, vagrant- and aggression-free environment with sufficient lighting (Burns et al., 2010), and do not limit their in-store freedom (Brehm, 1966) create a positive feeling of greater security and protection, and increase transparency and trust. In other words, consumers have a positive perception of the in-store use of EAS and RFId tags, antennas, and security personnel.

The use of EAS and RFId tags and antennas, the protection methods most widely accepted by consumers (Nielsen, 2010), allows customers to enter a welcoming and reassuring open sales environment in which the articles on sale are freely available in accessible displays. Consumers can take the articles directly from the display, examine them, test them (wear them, feel them), and then carry them to the checkout counter. In addition, they prefer the choice of some stores to install the antennas in checkout areas in such a way that they merge with the sales environment. Antennas are frequently integrated in advertising panels in such a way that they avoid intimidating customers while simultaneously informing them about products, promotions and other marketing initiatives as soon as they enter a store. The presence of in-store of security personnel provides an important physical and relational reference point for preventing the action of thieves and delinquents in shops, and guarantees that the situation is being monitored (Pretious et al., 1995).

Security tags give consumers a sense of transparency (Nielsen, 2010). They tend to appreciate visible security elements that clearly identify their function, and want to know whether an article contains a security tag or not. If the tag is not visible, its existence should be indicated by means of a symbol or message on the packaging. However, some visible labels may cover relevant information, and it is important that they do not interfere with a consumer's decision-making process. A number of consumers essentially argue that the purpose of any security system should be to dissuade people from stealing rather than to catch and punish them (Nielsen, 2010): it is therefore important that it is preventive, dissuasive, and educational rather than punitive in nature.

This also reinforces their level of trust, which can be increased by means of the principle "free to touch, free to take": in order to create a superior shopping experience, consumers want to touch and interact with retail articles (Grohmann et al., 2007; Hultén, 2012); hold and inspect products physically (Krishna & Morrin, 2008); pick up, touch and choose from displayed products (McCabe & Nowlis, 2003); and be able to learn about and evaluate a product's characteristics (McCabe & Nowlis, 2003; Peck & Childers, 2003). Conversational environments also reinforce the building of trust (Bunker & Ball, 2006) and control shrinkage (DiLonardo, 2004): face-to-face communications between staff and customers increases cooperation and trust (Naquin & Paulson, 2003; Ferrin et al., 2007, 2008), and staff assistance (and/or staff security) can monitor that nobody is stealing (Phillips et al., 2005).

A number of security systems have negative effects on CSE because of the adverse emotions they arouse in honest customers, such as distrust (Friend et al., 2010), intimidation (Tonglet, 2000; Kajalo & Lindblom, 2010b), discomfort, embarrassment, frustration and a sense of prohibition (Citrin et al., 2003; Peck & Childers, 2003). Numerous security cameras, uniformed guards patrolling a store, and warning signs can create distrust and intimidation because customers feel they are constantly being watched (Jones, 1999). Security tags that are not deactivated at a checkout counter (because of unprofessional staff or technical problems) activate the alarm system when even an innocent customer passes by, and can give rise to feelings of discomfort and embarrassment: when an alarm sounds, customers are required to show their purchases to security personnel, answer probing questions and, above all, are likely to be viewed as thieves by other shoppers. Frustration and a sense of prohibition are generated by locking and security systems that prevent customers from touching articles.

IMPLICATIONS FOR STORE MANAGERS

The results of this study have a number of practical implications for managers who want to reinforce retailer/consumer relationships by means of an adequate level of security without interfering with CSE.

First of all, retailers should use store design elements, security personnel and technological systems (e.g. EAS and RFId tags) wisely and as discreetly as possible (Coleman, 2006; Kajalo & Lindblom, 2011a) because they:

- Provide safe and reliable high-level protection of the store and its merchandise;
- Increase customers' sense of security;
- Limit shoplifting and external aggression;
- Stimulate the trust and desire to shop of honest customers;
- Positively influence a store's attractiveness, customers' behaviour and shopping expeditions;
- Stimulate direct contact with articles; and
- Allow customers to stay freely and peacefully in the store for as long as possible.

Retail managers should create a store that is not perceived by customers as "armoured" because this does not encourage them to shop peacefully and freely. Customers need to be allowed have direct contact with the sales environment, its products and store personnel, which means retailers need to invest in store design, technological solutions and staff training.

Even moderate changes in store design can restrict shoplifting (O'Shea & Awwad-Rafferty, 2009). Taking a cue from frequent visits to other grocery and non-grocery stores as customers, retail managers can create a greater sense of freedom by eliminating metal detector barriers from store entryways/exits and connecting special anti-shoplifting tags to detectors hung from the ceiling or totally concealed. Alternatively, they can create observation booths overlooking sales areas: rooms occupied by one or more employees that are often positioned behind mirrors and that give a good overall view of the entire store. Such booths are also often equipped with CCTV screens.

Another means of making customers feel at ease inside a store is to use technological solutions that allow them to interact with the merchandise. Any servicescape element between customers and products puts a brake on the purchasing process (Bitner, 1992) because customers are forced to turn to sales staff in order to look at the products closely, and are often also required to do so in their presence. Keeping an article in a protective showcase or keeper, or bound with chains, limits its attractiveness and the degree of emotional involvement experienced by customers during a purchase. Customers perceive the physical environment through their senses (Soars, 2009), and so it is crucial to give them an opportunity to make direct contact with freely displayed articles: seeing, touching, feeling and perceiving an article are necessary conditions underlying a sale. The role of a product is to stimulate shoppers' emotions and, when they cannot touch it, they become frustrated. The opportunity to touch a product influences customers emotionally and creates a more personal purchase. It is crucial for store managers to generate active interactions between customers and products as this encourages both intentional and unplanned purchases (Citrin et al., 2003; Peck & Wiggins, 2006), and is a means of leveraging sales. Taking a cue from personal experience, some stores provide multimedia merchandising technology on their shelves: customers who lift products protected by a free-to-touch system activate a product-specific video containing operating/functional information, and do not have to waste time searching for sales personnel.

The success of the store design and technological solutions not only depends on their quality and effectiveness, but also on how they are managed. Store staff can play an important role by relationally interacting with in-store customers. As (potential) thieves try to avoid observation and do not like stores with interacting personnel, the relational skill of sales staff is fundamental. Possible practical solutions include asking customers whether they would like the article in their size or an alternative product, and controlling the number of articles taken into and out of fitting rooms by assisting customers in trying them on. Furthermore, asking a customer in a fitting room whether the size or colour of an article is right may interrupt attempted shoplifting or increase sales. All store employees should be motivated to pay attention to customers who may be thieves. Lindblom and Kajalo (2011) noted that informal surveillance (mainly alert employees) is more effective than formal surveillance (e.g. technological measures, guard patrols, rangers and other uniformed staff).

Investing in staff training is important for two main reasons:

- Trained and motivated staff play an important role in reducing all kinds of unwanted behaviour (Kajalo & Lindblom, 2010a); and

- The behaviour of staff is difficult to imitate because of the relational element involved in their role which, unlike the impersonal aspects of a service, is very personal in nature (Grönroos, 2000; Baccarani et al., 2010).

Stores that only invest in innovative technological solutions cannot guarantee in-store security and an effective CSE. Some retailers have doubts about the effectiveness of RFId tags because they are easily obscured by the human body and may therefore fail to trigger shoplifting detection barriers. Furthermore, patented and standardised technological solutions are also easily accessible to shoplifters, who can thus discover ways of circumventing them. It is therefore essential to combine anti-shoplifting systems with trained and motivated staff.

In order to increase employees' motivation, managers can implement incentive programmes for personnel who discover thefts committed by shoplifters or their colleagues. However, the amount of the reward must be carefully determined because, if it is too small, the programme will not work and, if it is too large, the programme may become too expensive. Theft prevention activities by employees should also be supported by training courses, workshops, films, literature, and lessons about the many and constantly changing methods of shoplifting, and the laws governing their detection and prevention. A cashier who suspects that a paying customer has something hidden may ask whether he has anything else to declare when paying: it is surprising how often shoplifters interpret this simple question as an announcement of discovery. An employee can achieve the same effect by asking a customer who has just furtively put an object into his pocket whether he can be of help in looking for the product.

FUTURE RESEARCH DIRECTIONS

The conceptual framework proposed in this study suggests a number of future research directions concerning grocery and non-grocery shopping.

There is still a lack of empirical research into how to make store surveillance secure and appealing to customers, and the present study can be considered a first step towards bridging this gap.

This study only considers the retailers' perspective and does not make a direct analysis of customers/shoppers, but it would be useful to determine the customers' point of view for purposes of comparison. It would also be interesting to analyse the needs of customers, for example by using the model of Kano (1984) to distinguish implicit (or indifferent), expected (or must-be) and latent (or attractive) needs that are respectively considered by customers as obvious, expected and unexpected. After all, customers' expectations (and particularly exceeding them) are key determinants of their consumption experience in terms of satisfaction, delight and loyalty (e.g. Kotler, 2000; Ofir & Simonson, 2007).

Another promising area for further research is to test shoppers' perceptions of the store surveillance systems proposed in the conceptual framework of this study by using the in-store elements described in Table 1 as research items.

In addition, it is possible compare perceptions with expectations using the confirmation/disconfirmation paradigm (Oliver, 1980; Churchill & Surprenant, 1982). Significant findings may also come from comparing the differences between younger and elderly customers.

It would also be interesting to study the role played by in-store communications in creating a store surveillance system that is appealing for shoppers. In-store communications cannot be limited to providing commercial information (essentially about merchandise and services), but should also be aimed at meeting those intangible expectations that have an impact on experiential shopping in order to increase customer interaction and engagement.

Finally, considering both in-store communication and ethical aspects, it would be useful to examine how managers can try to prevent shoplifting by appealing to the civil consciousness of customers in- and out-of-store communications aimed at encouraging them to report any theft they see and making them more aware that shoplifters harm not only the retailer, but also other customers and the entire community. In this sense surveillance solutions should not simply be strategically placed traps designed to capture shoplifters, but measures aimed at discouraging dishonesty.

CONCLUSION

It is not enough for retailers to rely on simple and functional store surveillance systems that are only designed to ensure a high level of security, they must also satisfy their customers in terms of their shopping experience. Stores are no longer points of purchase and sales, but have been transformed into relational places in which customers live a multi-sensory experience, and experience an emotional engagement.

The aim of this study was to explore the contribution that appealing store surveillance systems can make to developing retailer/customer relationships. Its initial analysis of the marketing, service and retailing literature concerning customer shopping experiences, store surveillance, and gaps in store attractiveness made it possible to consider surveillance solutions from the perspective of CSE. It then analysed how retailers can make store surveillance appealing by investing in store design elements, security personnel and technological systems. The experience economy and experiential marketing studies have shown that it is fundamental that shoppers be given an opportunity to move freely and peacefully in the sales environment, and actively interact with the store and its products: seeing, touching, feeling and perceiving articles are necessary conditions underlying any sale. Shopping is not simply an act of consumption but also includes interactions with product assortments, ambient elements, and the social dimension.

As a result, the study highlights the fact that retailers' investments in store design, staff training and technological systems can give stores adequate security levels without compromising their customers' shopping experience provided that the store surveillance system allows customers to have direct contacts with the store, its articles and staff. A truly successful shop should be customer-centred in all aspects of its management, and offer an enhanced, memorable, engaging and distinctive shopping experience. In-store surveillance also influences CSE because it emotionally touches customers.

REFERENCES

Arnold, M., & Reynolds, K. E. (2003). Hedonic Shopping Motivations. *Journal of Retailing*, *79*(2), 77–95. doi:10.1016/S0022-4359(03)00007-1

Azevedo, S. G., & Carvalho, H. (2012). Contribution of RFId Technology to Better Management of Fashion Supply Chains. *International Journal of Retail & Distribution Management*, *40*(2), 128–156. doi:10.1108/09590551211201874

Babin, B. J., & Attaway, J. S. (2000). Atmospheric as tool for creating value and gaining share of customer. *Journal of Business Research*, *49*(2), 91–99. doi:10.1016/S0148-2963(99)00011-9

Babin, B. J., & Darden, R. D. (1995). Consumer Self-Regulation in a Retail Environment. *Journal of Retailing*, *71*(1), 47–70. doi:10.1016/0022-4359(95)90012-8

Babin, B. J., Darden, W. R., & Griffin, M. (1994). Work and/or Fun: Measuring Hedonic and Utilitarian Shopping Value. *The Journal of Consumer Research*, *20*(4), 644–656. doi:10.1086/209376

Baccarani, C., Ugolini, M., & Bonfanti, A. (2010). *A Conceptual Service Quality Map: The Value of a Wide Opened Perspective*. Paper presented at the Organizational Excellence in Service, 13th Toulon-Verona Conference. Coimbra, Portugal.

Bäckström, K., & Johansson, U. (2006). Creating and Consuming Experiences in Retail Store Environments: Comparing Retailer and Consumer Perspectives. *Journal of Retailing and Consumer Services*, *13*(6), 417–430. doi:10.1016/j.jretconser.2006.02.005

Bagdare, S. (2012). Managing Employee Effectiveness for Retail Customer Experience. *Asia Pacific Marketing Review*, *1*(1), 98–106.

Baker, J. (1986). The Role of the Environment in Marketing Services: The Consumer Perspective. In J. A. Czepiel, C. A. Congram, & J. Shanahan (Eds.), *The Services Challenge: Integrating for Competitive Advantage* (pp. 79–84). Chicago: American Marketing Association.

Baker, J. A., Parasuraman, A., Grewal, D., & Voss, G. B. (2002). The Influence of Multiple Store Environment Cues on Perceived Merchandise Value and Patronage Intentions. *Journal of Marketing*, *66*(2), 120–141. doi:10.1509/jmkg.66.2.120.18470

Baker, R. G. (1965). Explorations in Ecological Psychology. *The American Psychologist*, *20*(1), 1–14. doi:10.1037/h0021697 PMID:14251988

Bamfield, J. A. N. (2012). *Shopping and crime*. New York: Palgrave Macmillan. doi:10.1057/9780230393554

Batra, R., & Ahtola, O. T. (1990). Measuring the Hedonic and Utilitarian Sources of Consumer Attitudes. *Marketing Letters*, *2*, 159–170. doi:10.1007/BF00436035

Bellizzi, J. A., & Hite, R. E. (1992). Environment Color, Consumer Feelings, and Purchase Likelihood. *Psychology and Marketing*, *9*, 347–363. doi:10.1002/mar.4220090502

Berman, B., & Evans, J. R. (1995). *Retail Management*. Englewood Cliffs, NJ: Prentice-Hall, Inc.

Bitner, M. J. (1992). Servicescapes: The Impact of Physical Surroundings on Customers and Employees. *Journal of Marketing*, *56*, 57–71. doi:10.2307/1252042

Boedeker, M. (1995). New-Type and Traditional Shoppers: A Comparison of two Major Consumer Groups. *International Journal of Retail & Distribution Management*, *23*(3), 17–26. doi:10.1108/09590559510083966

Bonfanti, A. (2013). Towards an Approach to Signage Management Quality (SMQ). *Journal of Services Marketing*, *27*(4), 312–321. doi:10.1108/08876041311330780

Bonfanti, A., Centomo, N., & De Stefani, E. (2013). Checkpoint Systems: prevenire i furti nei punti vendita. *Micro & Macro Marketing*, *3*, 549–574.

Borghini, S., Diamond, N., Kozinets, R. K., McGrath, M. A., Muñiz, A. M. Jr, & Sherry, J. F. Jr. (2009). Why are Themed Brand Stores so Powerful? Retail Brand Ideology at American Girl Place. *Journal of Retailing*, *85*(3), 363–375. doi:10.1016/j.jretai.2009.05.003

Brehm, J. A. (1966). *Theory of Psychological Reactance*. New York: Academic Press.

Brunetti, F. (2004). *Pervasività d'Impresa e Relazioni di Mercato: Quale Futuro?* Torino: Giappichelli.

Bunker, M. P., & Ball, D. (2006). Causes and Consequences of Grudge-Holding in Service Relationships. *Journal of Services Marketing*, *22*(1), 37–47. doi:10.1108/08876040810851941

Burns, D. J., Manolis, C., & Keep, W. W. (2010). Fear of Crime on Shopping Intentions: An Examination. *International Journal of Retail & Distribution Management*, *38*(1), 45–56. doi:10.1108/09590551011016322

Buttle, F. (1984). Merchandising. *European Journal of Marketing*, *18*(6-7), 104–124. doi:10.1108/EUM0000000004795

Chapman, P., & Templar, S. (2006). Scoping the Contextual Issues that Influence Shrinkage Measurement. *International Journal of Retail & Distribution Management*, *34*(11), 860–872. doi:10.1108/09590550610710255

Churchill, G. A., & Surprenant, C. (1982). An Investigation into Determinants of Customer Satisfaction. *JMR, Journal of Marketing Research*, *19*, 491–504. doi:10.2307/3151722

Citrin, A. V., Stern, D. E., Spangenberg, E. R., & Clark, M. J. (2003). Consumer Need for Tactile Input: An Internet Retailing Challenge. *Journal of Business Research*, *56*(11), 915–922. doi:10.1016/S0148-2963(01)00278-8

Coleman, P. (2006). *Shopping Environments: Evolution, Planning and Design*. Architectural Press.

Cowper, R. J. (1992). Shopping Centre Management for the 'Nineties'. *Property Management*, *10*(4), 329–337. doi:10.1108/02637479210030466

Cozens, P., Saville, G., & Hillier, D. (2005). Crime Prevention through Environmental Design (CPTED), Are View and Modern Bibliography. *Journal of Property Management*, *23*(5), 328–356. doi:10.1108/02637470510631483

Dawson, S. (1993). Consumer Responses to Electronic Article Surveillance Alarms. *Journal of Retailing*, *69*(3), 353–362. doi:10.1016/0022-4359(93)90011-7

DiLonardo, R. L. (2004). Got an Eye on Your Inventory? *Aftermarket Business*, *114*(12), 34–38.

Donovan, R. J., & Rossiter, J. R. (1982). Store Atmosphere: An Environmental Psychology Approach. *Journal of Retailing*, *58*(1), 34–57.

Ferrin, D. L., Bligh, M. C., & Kohles, J. C. (2007). Can I Trust You to Trust Me? A Theory of Trust, Monitoring, and Cooperation in Interpersonal and Intergroup Relationships. *Group & Organization Management, 32*(4), 465–499. doi:10.1177/1059601106293960

Ferrin, D. L., Bligh, M. C., & Kohles, J. C. (2008). It Takes Two to Tango: An Interdependence Analysis of the Spiraling of Perceived Trustworthiness and Cooperation in Interpersonal and Intergroup Relationships. *Organizational Behavior and Human Decision Processes, 107*(2), 161–178. doi:10.1016/j.obhdp.2008.02.012

Fiore, A. M., & Kim, J. (2007). An Integrative Framework Capturing Experiential and Utilitarian Shopping Experience. *International Journal of Retail & Distribution Management, 35*(6), 421–442. doi:10.1108/09590550710750313

Foxall, G. (1997). Affective Responses to Consumer Situations. *International Review of Retail, Distribution and Consumer Research, 7*(3), 191–225. doi:10.1080/095939697342996

Foxall, G. R., & Greenley, G. E. (1999). Consumers' Emotional Responses to Service Environments. *Journal of Business Research, 46*(2), 149–158. doi:10.1016/S0148-2963(98)00018-6

Foxall, G. R., & Greenley, G. E. (2000). Predicting and Explaining Responses to Consumer Environments: An Empirical Test and Theoretical Extension of the Behavioural Perspective Model. *The Service Industries Journal, 20*(2), 39–63. doi:10.1080/02642060000000019

Friend, L. A., Costley, C. L., & Brown, C. (2010). Spirals of Distrust vs Spirals of Trust in Retail Customer Service: Consumers as Victims or Allies. *Journal of Services Marketing, 24*(6), 458–467. doi:10.1108/08876041011072573

Fullerton, R., & Punj, G. (1993). Choosing to Misbehave: A Structural Model of Aberrant Consumer Behavior. *Advances in Consumer Research. Association for Consumer Research (U. S.), 20*, 570–574.

Fullerton, R. A., & Punj, G. N. (2004). Repercussions of Promoting an Ideology of Consumption: Consumer Misbehavior. *Journal of Business Research, 57*(11), 1239–1249. doi:10.1016/S0148-2963(02)00455-1

Gill, M. (2007). *Shoplifters on Shop Theft: Implications for Retailers*. Leicester, UK: Perpetuity Research & Consultancy International.

Gill, M., Bilby, C., & Turbin, V. (1999). Retail Security: Understanding what Deters Shop Thieves. *Journal of Security Administration, 22*(1), 29–39.

Grewal, D., Levy, M., & Kumar, V. (2009). Customer Experience Management in Retailing: An Organizing Framework. *Journal of Retailing, 85*(1), 1–14. doi:10.1016/j.jretai.2009.01.001

Grohmann, B., Spangenberg, E., & Sprott, D. (2007). The Influence of Tactile Input on the Evaluation of Retail Product Offerings. *Journal of Retailing, 83*(2), 237–245. doi:10.1016/j.jretai.2006.09.001

Grönroos, C. (2000). *Service Management and Marketing: A Consumer Relationship Management Approach*. Chichester, UK: John Wiley & Sons.

GRTB. (2007). *The Global Retail Theft Barometer*. Nottingham, UK: Centre for Retail Research.

GRTB. (2011). *The Global Retail Theft Barometer*. Nottingham, UK: Centre for Retail Research.

Gummesson, E. (2002). *Total Relationship Marketing*. Oxford, UK: Butterworth-Heinemann.

Hamrouni, A. D., & Touzi, M. (2011). Technique of Collage for Store Design Atmospherics. *Qualitative Market Research: An International Journal, 14*(3), 304–323. doi:10.1108/13522751111137523

Hayes, R., & Blackwood, R. (2006). Evaluating the Effects of EAS on Product Sales and Loss: Results of a Large-Scale Field Experiment. *Security Journal, 19*(4), 262–276. doi:10.1057/palgrave.sj.8350025

Hayes, R., & Downs, D. M. (2011). Controlling Retail Theft with CCTV Domes, CCTV Public View Monitors, and Protective Containers: A Randomized Controlled Trial. *Security Journal, 24*(3), 237–250. doi:10.1057/sj.2011.12

Hayes, R., Johns, T., Scicchitano, M., Downs, D., & Pietrawska, B. (2011). Evaluating the Effects of Protective Keeper Boxes on 'Hot Product' Loss and Sales: A Randomized Controlled Trial. *Security Journal, 24*(3), 357–369. doi:10.1057/sj.2011.2

Hingley, M., Taylor, S., & Ellis, C. (2007). Radio Frequency Identification Tagging. Supplier Attitudes to Implementation in the Grocery Retail Sector. *International Journal of Retail & Distribution Management, 35*(10), 803–820. doi:10.1108/09590550710820685

Hirschman, E. C., & Holbrook, M. B. (1982). Hedonic Consumption: Emerging Concepts, Methods and Propositions. *Journal of Marketing, 46*(3), 92–101. doi:10.2307/1251707

Holbrook, M. B., & Hirschman, E. C. (1982). The Experiential Aspects of Consumption: Consumer Fantasies, Feelings, and Fun. *The Journal of Consumer Research, 9*(2), 132–140. doi:10.1086/208906

Hollenbeck, C. R., Peters, C., & Zinkhan, G. M. (2008). Retail Spectacles and Brand Meaning: Insights from a Brand Museum Case Study. *Journal of Retailing, 84*(3), 334–353. doi:10.1016/j.jretai.2008.05.003

Hui, M. K., & Bateson, J. E. G. (1991). Perceived Control and the Effects of Crowding and Consumer Choice on the Service Experience. *The Journal of Consumer Research, 18*(2), 174–184. doi:10.1086/209250

Hultén, B. (2012). Sensory Cues and Shoppers' Touching Behaviour: The Case of IKEA. *International Journal of Retail & Distribution Management, 40*(4), 273–289. doi:10.1108/09590551211211774

Jones, M. A. (1999). Entertaining Shopping Experiences: An Exploratory Investigation. *Journal of Retailing and Consumer Services, 6*(3), 129–139. doi:10.1016/S0969-6989(98)00028-9

Jones, P., Clarke-Hill, C., Shears, P., Comfort, D., & Hillier, D. (2004). Radio Frequency Identification in the UK: Opportunities and Challenges. *International Journal of Retail & Distribution Management, 32*(3), 164–171. doi:10.1108/09590550410524957

Kajalo, S., & Lindblom, A. (2010a). The Perceived Effectiveness of Surveillance in Reducing Crime at Shopping Centers in Finland. *Property Management, 28*(1), 47–59. doi:10.1108/02637471011017172

Kajalo, S., & Lindblom, A. (2010b). Surveillance Investments in Store Environment and Sense of Security. *Facilities, 28*(9/10), 465–474. doi:10.1108/02632771011057198

Kajalo, S., & Lindblom, A. (2011a). Effectiveness of Formal and Informal Surveillance in Reducing Crime at Grocery Stores. *Journal of Small Business and Enterprise Development, 18*(1), 157–169. doi:10.1108/14626001111106488

Kano, N., Seraku, N., Takahashi, F., & Tsuji, S. (1984). Attractive Quality and Must-Be Quality. *Journal of Japanese Society for Quality Control, 14*(2), 39–48.

Kotler, P. (1973). Atmospherics as a Marketing Tool. *Journal of Retailing, 49*(4), 48–64.

Kotler, P. (2000). *Marketing Management: Analysis, Planning, Implementation, and Control* (10th ed.). Upper Saddle River, NJ: Prentice Hall.

Krishna, A., & Morrin, M. (2008). Does Touch Affect Taste? The Perceptual Transfer of Product Container Haptic Cues. *The Journal of Consumer Research, 34*(6), 807–818. doi:10.1086/523286

Kulas, J. T., Mcinnerney, J. E., Demuth, R. F., & Jadwinski, V. (2007). Employee Satisfaction and Theft: Testing Climate Perceptions as a Mediator. *The Journal of Psychology, 141*(4), 389–402. doi:10.3200/JRLP.141.4.389-402 PMID:17725072

Lai, F., Hutchinson, J., & Zhang, G. (2005). Radio Frequency Identification (RFID) in China: Opportunities and Challenges. *International Journal of Retail & Distribution Management, 33*(12), 905–916. doi:10.1108/09590550510634639

Lam, S. Y. (2001). The Effects of Store Environment on Shopping Behaviors: A Critical Review. *Advances in Consumer Research. Association for Consumer Research (U. S.), 28*(1), 190–197.

Law, D., Wong, C., & Yip, J. (2012). How does Visual Merchandising Affect Consumer Affective Response? An Intimate Apparel Experience. *European Journal of Marketing, 46*(1/2), 112–133. doi:10.1108/03090561211189266

Lindblom, A., & Kajalo, S. (2011). The Use and Effectiveness of Formal and Informal Surveillance in Reducing Shoplifting: A Survey in Sweden, Norway, and Finland. *International Review of Retail, Distribution and Consumer Research, 21*(2), 111–128. doi:10.1080/09593969.2011.562677

Machleit, K. A., Eroglu, S. A., & Powell Mantel, S. (2000). Perceived Retail Crowding and Shopping Satisfaction: What Modifies this Relationship? *Journal of Consumer Psychology, 9*(1), 29–42. doi:10.1207/s15327663jcp0901_3

Machleit, K. A., Kellaris, J. J., & Eroglu, S. A. (1994). Human versus Spatial Dimensions of Crowding Perceptions in Retail Environments: A Note on the Measurement and Effect on Shopper Satisfaction. *Marketing Letters, 5*(2), 183–194. doi:10.1007/BF00994108

Mano, H., & Oliver, R. L. (1993). Assessing the Dimensionality and Structure of the Consumption Experience: Evaluation, Feeling, and Satisfaction. *The Journal of Consumer Research, 20*(3), 451–466. doi:10.1086/209361

McCabe, D. B., & Nowlis, S. (2003). The Effect of Examining Actual Products or Product Descriptions on Consumer Preference. *Journal of Consumer Psychology, 13*(4), 431–439. doi:10.1207/S15327663JCP1304_10

McGoldrick, P. J. (1990). *Retail Marketing*. London: McGraw-Hill.

Mehrabian, A., & Russell, J. A. (1974). *An Approach to Environmental Psychology*. Cambridge, MA: MIT Press.

Milliman, R., & Fugate, D. (1993). Atmospherics as an Emerging Influence in the Design of Exchange Environments. *Journal of Marketing Management, 3*(1), 66–75.

Moye, L., & Kincade, D. H. (2002). Influence of Usage Situations and Consumer Shopping Orientations on the Importance of the Retail Store Environment. *International Review of Retail, Distribution and Consumer Research, 12*(1), 59–79. doi:10.1080/09593960110103823

Naquin, C. E., & Paulson, G. D. (2003). Online Bargaining and Interpersonal Trust. *The Journal of Applied Psychology, 88*(1), 113–120. doi:10.1037/0021-9010.88.1.113 PMID:12675399

Naylor, G., Kleiser, S. B., Baker, J., & Yorkston, E. (2008). Using Transformational Appeals to Enhance the Retail Experience. *Journal of Retailing, 84*(1), 49–57. doi:10.1016/j.jretai.2008.01.001

Nielsen. (2010). *Perception of the Protection & Security Elements of Products*. Neilsen.

O'Shea, L. S., & Awwad-Rafferty, R. (2009). *Design and Security in the Built Environment*. New York: Fairchild Books.

O'Sullivan, E., & Spanger, K. J. (1998). *Experience Marketing. Strategies for the New Millennium. State College*. PA: Venturing Publishing.

Ofir, C., & Simonson, I. (2007). The Effect of Stating Expectations on Customer Satisfaction and Shopping Experience. *JMR, Journal of Marketing Research*, *44*, 164–174. doi:10.1509/jmkr.44.1.164

Oliver, R. L. (1980). A Cognitive Model of the Antecedents and Consequences of Satisfaction Decisions. *JMR, Journal of Marketing Research*, *17*, 460–469. doi:10.2307/3150499

Ooi, J., & Sim, L.-L. (2007). The Magnetism of Suburban Shopping Centers: Do Size and Cineplex Matter? *Journal of Property Investment & Finance*, *25*(2), 111–135. doi:10.1108/14635780710733816

Overstreet, J., & Clodfelter, R. (1995). Safety and Security Concerns of Shopping Center Consumers and the Effect of these Concerns on Shopping Behavior. *Journal of Shopping Center Research*, *2*(1), 91–109.

Peck, J., & Childers, T. L. (2003). To Have and to Hold: The Influence of Haptic Information on Product Judgements. *Journal of Marketing*, *67*, 35–48. doi:10.1509/jmkg.67.2.35.18612

Peck, J., & Wiggins, J. (2006). It just Feels Good: Customers' Affective Response to Touch and its Influence on Persuasion. *Journal of Marketing*, *70*, 56–69. doi:10.1509/jmkg.70.4.56

Phillips, S., Alexander, A., & Shaw, G. (2005). Consumer Misbehavior: The Rise of Self-Service Grocery Retailing and Shoplifting in the United Kingdom c. 1950-1970. *Journal of Macromarketing*, *25*(1), 66–75. doi:10.1177/0276146705275715

Pine, B. J. II, & Gilmore, J. H. (1999). *The Experience Economy: Work is Theatre & Every Business a Stage*. Boston: Harvard Business School Press.

Pine, B. J. II, & Gilmore, J. H. (2002). Customer Experience Places: The New Offering Frontier. *Strategy and Leadership*, *30*(4), 4–11. doi:10.1108/10878570210435306

Pretious, M., Stewart, R., & Logan, D. (1995). Retail Security: A Survey of Methods and Management in Dundee. *International Journal of Retail & Distribution Management*, *23*(9), 28–35. doi:10.1108/09590559510098681

Rekik, Y., Sahin, E., & Dallery, Y. (2009). Inventory Inaccuracy in Retail Stores due to Theft: An Analysis of the Benefits of RFID. *International Journal of Production Economics*, *118*(1), 189–198. doi:10.1016/j.ijpe.2008.08.048

Schmitt, B. H. (1999a). Experiential Marketing. *Journal of Marketing Management*, *15*(1-3), 53–67. doi:10.1362/026725799784870496

Schmitt, B. H. (1999b). *Experiential Marketing: How to Get Customers to SENSE, FEEL, THINK, ACT and RELATE to Your Company and Brands*. New York: The Free Press.

Schmitt, B. H. (2003). *Customer Experience Management*. Wiley & Sons.

Sellitto, C., Burgess, S., & Hawking, P. (2007). Information Quality Attributes Associated with RFID-Derived Benefits in the Retail Supply Chain. *International Journal of Retail & Distribution Management*, *35*(1), 69–87. doi:10.1108/09590550710722350

Sherman, E., Mathur, A., & Smith, R. B. (1997). Store Environment and Consumer Purchase Behavior: Mediating Role of Consumer Emotions. *Psychology and Marketing*, *14*(4), 361–379. doi:10.1002/(SICI)1520-6793(199707)14:4<361::AID-MAR4>3.0.CO;2-7

Sit, J., Merrilees, B., & Birch, D. (2003). Entertainment-Seeking Shopping Centre Patrons: The Missing Segments. *International Journal of Retail & Distribution Management, 31*(2), 80–94. doi:10.1108/09590550310461985

Soars, B. (2009). Driving Sales through Shoppers' Sense of Sound, Sight, Smell and Touch. *International Journal of Retail & Distribution Management, 37*(3), 286–298. doi:10.1108/09590550910941535

Spangenberg, E., Crowley, A., & Henderson, P. (1996). Improving the Store Environment: Do Olfactory Cues Affect Evaluations and Behaviors? *Journal of Marketing, 60*(2), 67–80. doi:10.2307/1251931

Spies, K., Hesse, F., & Loesch, K. (1997). Store Atmosphere, Mood and Purchasing Behavior. *International Journal of Research in Marketing, 14*(1), 1–17. doi:10.1016/S0167-8116(96)00015-8

Stock, R. M., & Hoyer, W. D. (2005). An Attitude-Behavior Model of Salespeople's Customer Orientation. *Journal of the Academy of Marketing Science, 33*(4), 536–552. doi:10.1177/0092070305276368

Tauber, E. M. (1995). Why do People Shop? *Marketing Management, 4*(2), 58–60.

Thornton, J. (1992, February). Shoplifting - girls who steal. *Seventeen*, 86-87.

Tonglet, M. (2000). Consumer Misbehaviour: Consumers' Perceptions of Shoplifting and Retail Security. *Security Journal, 13*(4), 107–122. doi:10.1057/palgrave.sj.8340063

Tonglet, M. (2002). Consumer Misbehaviour: An Exploratory Study of Shoplifting. *Journal of Consumer Behaviour, 1*(4), 336–354. doi:10.1002/cb.79

Tonglet, M., & Bamfield, J. (1997). Controlling Shop Crime in Britain: Costs and Trends. *International Journal of Retail & Distribution Management, 25*(9), 293–300. doi:10.1108/09590559710185772

Turley, L. W., & Chebat, J. C. (2002). Linking Retail Strategy, Atmospheric Design and Shopping Behaviour. *Journal of Marketing Management, 18*(1/2), 125–144. doi:10.1362/0267257022775891

Turley, L. W., & Milliman, R. E. (2000). Atmospheric Effects on Shopping Behavior: A Review of the Experimental Evidence. *Journal of Business Research, 49*(2), 193–211. doi:10.1016/S0148-2963(99)00010-7

Varaldo, R., & Dalli, D. (2003). Le relazioni strategiche tra industria e distribuzione. *Sinergie, 61-62*, 255–297.

Verhoef, P. C., Lemonb, K. N., Parasuraman, A., Roggeveen, A., Tsiros, M., & Schlesinger, L. A. (2009). Customer Experience Creation: Determinants, Dynamics and Management Strategies. *Journal of Retailing, 85*(1), 31–41. doi:10.1016/j.jretai.2008.11.001

Vieira, V. A. (2013). Stimuli-Organism-Response Framework: A Meta-Analytic Review in the Store Environment. *Journal of Business Research, 66*(9), 1420–1426. doi:10.1016/j.jbusres.2012.05.009

Wellhoff, A., & Masson, J. E. (2005). *Le Merchandising: Bases, Techniques, Nouvelles Tendances*. Paris: Dunod.

ADDITIONAL READING

Baccarani, C., & Golinelli, G. M. (2009). *Leadership for Excellence in Services. Sinergie, 78*(Gennaio-Aprile). VII-XVI.

Bagdare, S. (2013). Antecedents of Retail Customer Experience. *Journal of Marketing Communications*, 8(3), 45–51.

Bamfield, J. (2004). Shrinkage, Shoplifting and the Cost of Retail Crime in Europe: A Cross-Sectional Analysis of Major Retailers in 16 European Countries. *International Journal of Retail & Distribution Management*, 32(5), 235–241. doi:10.1108/09590550410699233

Codeluppi, V. (2000). *Lo Spettacolo della Merce. I Luoghi del Consumo dai Passages a Disney World*. Milano: Bompiani.

Danziger, P. N. (2006). *Shopping. Why we Love it and how Retailers Can Create the Ultimate Customer Shopping Experience*. Chicago: Kaplan Publishing.

Deepak, J. (2011). Shop Lifting - An Exploratory Study of Jammu City. *Advances in Management*, 4(8), 57–65.

Fabris, G. (2003). *Il Nuovo Consumatore: Verso il Postmoderno*. Milano: FrancoAngeli.

Hirschman, E. C., & Stern, B. B. (1999). The Roles of Emotion in Consumer Research. *Advances in Consumer Research. Association for Consumer Research (U. S.)*, 26(1), 4–11.

Kajalo, S., & Lindblom, A. (2010c). How Retail Entrepreneurs Perceive the Link Between Surveillance, Feeling of Security, and Competitiveness of the Retail Store? A Structural Model Approach. *Journal of Retailing and Consumer Services*, 17(4), 300–305. doi:10.1016/j.jretconser.2010.03.001

Kajalo, S., & Lindblom, A. (2011b). An Empirical Analysis of Retail Entrepreneurs' Approaches to Prevent Shoplifting. *Security Journal*, 24(4), 269–282. doi:10.1057/sj.2010.3

Kajalo, S., & Lindblom, A. (2012). Evaluating the Effects of Formal and Informal Surveillance: A Retailer's View. In Proceedings of ASBBS Annual Conference (pp. 461-471), 19(1), Las Vegas.

Martínez, L. (2004). *The Retail Manager's Guide to Crime & Loss Prevention: Protecting your Business from Theft, Fraud and Violence*. Flushing, NY: Looseleaf Law Publications, Inc.

Mitchell, V.-W., & Chan, J. K. L. (2002). Investigating UK Consumers' Unethical Attitudes and Behaviours. *Journal of Marketing Management*, 18(1/2), 5–26. doi:10.1362/0267257022775873

Soscia, I. (2009). *Emozioni & Consumo*. Milano: Egea.

Ugolini, M., & Vigolo, V. (2009). Managing Relationships with Potential Employees: An Empirical Approach to Employer Brand. *Sinergie, Quaderni*, 16(Dicembre), 87-108.

Underhill, P. (1999). *Why we Buy. The Science of Shopping*. New York: Simon & Schuster.

KEY TERMS AND DEFINITIONS

Electronic Tags: Technological surveillance solutions applied to products by store personnel or suppliers (source tagging).

Experiential Shopping: The retailers' offer of an attractive shopping experience that is capable of meeting in-store customers' latent sensorial, emotional and psychological expectations.

In-Store Active Interaction: Opportunity for customers to touch, examine, and test merchandise freely, thus increasing their interest in a product and creating a personal purchase, as well as to receive high levels of relational service quality by store personnel.

Relational Service Quality: Store employees show courtesy, uncommon attention and passion in the way they serve and care for their customers.

Retail Store Design: The set of elements planned by retailers in order to attract in-store customers: these may be functional (layout, comfort and privacy) or aesthetic (architecture, sales equipment, colours, product displays).

Secure and Appealing Store Surveillance: Sales environment solutions and merchandise protection measures adopted by retailers in order to ensure a high level of store security while satisfying shoppers' needs and expectations.

Shoplifting Prevention: Retailers' strategy for discouraging thieves and anticipating possible thefts in the sales environment.

Store Security Personnel: Sworn guards, rangers or other uniformed staff trained to monitor the sales environment and make it safe, as well as to deter casual thieves.

Store Security Solutions: Store and merchandises protection measures and techniques adopted by retailers in order to create a secure and safe sales environment and protect against theft, shoplifting, vandalism, and organised crime.

Chapter 17
Retailer–Non–Profit Organization (NPO) Partnerships:
Building Trust with Socially Conscious Consumers

Janice Rudkowski
Helianthus Consulting, Canada & Ryerson University, Canada

ABSTRACT

This chapter focuses on strategic retailer-Non-Profit Organization (NPO) partnerships, based in North America and Europe, from a management perspective. It explores how and why these partnerships have had an impact on the retailer-consumer relationship, how they have shaped and influenced socially conscious shoppers, and how they have affected consumer trust as well as retail business practices and strategies, within the last decade. Retailer-NPO partnerships have emerged as a viable business strategy to support Corporate Social Responsibility (CSR) initiatives now commonplace among most large retail organizations. Consumers have become empowered, with the help of new social media technologies, to efficiently communicate, influence, and persuade other consumers around the globe. Therefore, consumers increasingly expect retailers to have an ethical and social responsibility to their people, products, operations, and communities. CSR practices have become integral to retailer sustainability and managing complex retailer-consumer relationships. This chapter reviews relevant theoretical frameworks, discusses the latest research findings from literature sources, and examines the industry practices (case studies) of several retailer-NPO partnerships across North America and Europe.

INTRODUCTION

The role of retail organizations and how they are perceived by society has changed and evolved over time. It is important to understand where and why these key shifts occurred throughout recent history, to provide context and understanding to the strategy behind retailer-NPO partnerships. By examining some of the shifting consumer behaviours that stemmed from economic, social, environmental

DOI: 10.4018/978-1-4666-6074-8.ch017

and/or global issues during the last 40 years, we can better understand how the retailer-consumer relationship has changed and why retailer-NPO partnerships have emerged as a viable business strategy to support CSR initiatives among large retailers throughout North America and Europe. Highlights from a thorough and relevant literature review that focused on key retail industry influences and impacts throughout the past four decades is examined throughout this chapter introduction.

Historically, the role of a retail business has been fairly simple: sell goods and/or services to the consumer at a profit thereby positively contributing to the economy. Basically, the retailer's role was that of an economic contributor. Fast-forward to present day and retailers have a much more complex and varied role, not only in terms of how they *contribute* to the economy, but more importantly, how they (and their coveted brands) are *perceived* by the communities in which they operate. This dramatic shift - from the retailer as *economic contributor* to the retailer as *social arbiter* - did not occur overnight. There have been incremental shifts in consumer behaviours over the last 40 years that have forever transformed the role of retail organizations within the economy and how they are perceived within society.

Retail in the 1970s

An example of a significant economic change was the inflation that followed the energy crisis of 1974 which introduced new retail sectors (ie. home improvement and DIY), more competitive prices, and greater product selection (Walters, 1981). The 1970s represented an explosion of growth for retailers like Walmart, for example, who for the first time had national presence with 51 stores across the United States and began trading on the New York Stock Exchange (Walmart, 2013). These economic and social changes, therefore contributed to shifting consumer behaviours including having access to more categories and products as well as cheaper prices.

Retail in the 1980s

The 1980s were defined by excessive wealth (ie. higher levels of disposable income) so retail business practices were motivated more by profit during this time period rather than consumer demand for retailer contribution to altruistic environmental or social causes. If retailers were participating in environmental or social activities, they tended to advertise them through traditional media or by publishing stakeholder reports, but these reported activities were not linked to corporate performance and lacked a set of acceptable standards against which performance could be measured (Min-young, Fairhurst & Wesley, 2009). In an effort to increase sales, satisfy shareholders and conquer new markets, a small group of large retailers from North America and Europe embraced retail internationalization strategies, and paved the way for other retailers to follow suit a decade later (Alexandru & Cristian, 2008). This decade of excess signified a shift in power within the retailer-consumer relationship; for the first time consumers held the balance of power, demanding more for less in an internationally competitive environment.

Retail in the 1990s

The 1990s saw yet another major shift with further retail internationalization (RI) as well as market consolidation. Metro Group AG, for example, a leading European food retailer, was formed in 1996 as the result of a merger between three leading German companies and continued to expand its international presence with stores in Romania and China during this decade (Metro Group AG, 2013). US-based Walmart also continued along the retail internationalization path in the 1990s and opened its first stores in Canada, China and the UK (Walmart, 2013).

It was not just increased selection, competitive prices and globalization that influenced the retailer-consumer relationship. The retailer-consumer relationship also changed as consumer awareness of prominent social issues and causes, like AIDS/HIV, piqued. The increased internationalization of the retail industry encouraged retailers to invest heavily in marketing and advertising to build their brands on a global scale. As a result, globally recognized retailer brands from the United States and Europe like Walmart, Target, Tesco and Carrefour emerged in the 1990s. Retailers tried to regain their dominance in their saturated home markets, but consumer purchasing power and global influence ruled the day (Alexandru & Cristian, 2008).

Retailers' mounting competitive and social pressures brought on by retail internationalization and increasing consumer demands led to the creation of corporate community relations (CCR) functions in the mid-1990s (Altman, 1998). CCR would influence and expand the definition of corporate citizenship, paving the way for the cause marketing mavericks of the 1980s such as McDonald's Ronald McDonald House and Lenscrafters' Gift of Sight Program to become mainstream business practices by the end of the 1990s (Ferguson & Goldman, 2010). Consumers' wants and needs were not only driving demand during this time, they were directly influencing retailers' local, global, economic *and* social business strategies.

Retail in the 2000s

As Dawar and Stornelli (2013) stated, "Perhaps the largest change in the grocery retail industry during the past 30 years has been the explosion of consumer data." (p. 85). Retailers continued to innovate and refine their strategies according to the traditional marketing mix dimensions of price, place, promotion, and product, but because of the trends in big data they also sought new growth opportunities by mining, analyzing and leveraging consumer data, information and insights. Retailers such as Tesco and Kroger have leveraged consumer data by connecting information about transactions with information about individual consumers, "… thereby enabling them to know who buys what, when and what price," (Dawar & Stornelli, 2013).

From the arrival of the Internet in the mid-1990s to its exponential growth in household penetration rates from the early 2000s through to present day, never before have consumers had such rapid and easy access to information, news and events. As a result, consumers demand more transparent retailer business practices, more value for their money, and an even better shopping experience. Consumers also scrutinize retailers' business practices with respect to their environmental practices, social activism and involvement in their communities. "What began as a simple way to build brand affinity has become a consumer expectation in an era in which sustainable and ethical consumer choices are more important than ever before" (Ferguson & Goldman, 2010).

Retailers, out of necessity, recognized that if they were not being socially or environmentally responsible, they were at risk of losing or alienating their consumers. Retailers wanting to "do good," sought partnerships with non-profit organizations (NPO) to improve the viability and visibility of this aspect of their business. The retailer-NPO partnership therefore emerged as an innovative business strategy to achieve growth objectives and differentiate a brand from its competition. Ferguson and Goldman (2010) stated, "What started as a pioneering effort by forward-thinking companies in the 1980s has gone mainstream (today), as millions of consumers now choose brand relationships based on alignment with specific causes" (p. 284).

Chapter Objectives

This chapter explores the implications and challenges of, and opportunities for, retailer-NPO partnerships, particularly as they affect the retailer-consumer relationship. A thorough literature review and industry examples from across Europe and North America support this exploration.

The specific objectives of this chapter are to:

1. Explain the changing role of retail business in society and how it has evolved within the past 40 years;
2. Define corporate social responsibility (CSR) and cause related marketing (CRM);
3. Describe the impact of the Internet and social media communications on the retailer-consumer relationship;
4. Define the retailer-NPO partnership;
5. Explain the concept of retailer-NPO partnership reciprocity;
6. Recommend four steps for the retailer-NPO partnership selection process and describe its significance;
7. Give best practice examples of European and North American retailer-NPO partnerships;
8. Summarize the conflicts and challenges within the retailer-NPO partnership; and
9. Discuss future research directions and trends in retailer-NPO partnerships.

BACKGROUND

In today's highly competitive and complex retail environment, it is no longer simply just about getting the right product to the right consumer at the right time, place, and price. Retailers, in their quest for growth and sustainability, have had to innovate, re-invent and adopt new business models and practices to win consumers' trust and be successful in the modern age of retailing.

To understand how retailers have evolved over time, it is important to examine the frameworks that have been used to help them develop their business and marketing strategies, from traditional to more modern approaches.

The traditional "4 P's" approach to the marketing mix (McCarthy, 1960): Product, Price, Place (or Distribution) and Promotion, has been in practice since the 1960's and has evolved due to increased competition, choice, and consumer demand and expectation. The 4 P's themselves replaced the 4 C's of Customer Value, Cost, Communication, and Convenience in the mid-2000s (Kotler, 2005) and the 4 A's of Awareness, Affordability, Acceptability, and Accessibility (Sheth, 2012) emerged in 2012. Most recently, the SAVE framework of Solution, Access, Value, and Education (Ettenson, Conrado & Knowles, 2013) has enjoyed popularity. These marketing frameworks help retailers effectively position their organizations for growth and thus they must continue to change and evolve.

Retail businesses, like marketing frameworks, have had to evolve and adapt to survive. Selecting the right product used to be as simple as considering factors such as: quality, quantity and assortment. Today, selecting the right product involves an extremely complex assessment of consumer needs and behaviours. Corporate social responsibility (CSR) strategies have given rise to newer strategies retailers have employed to differentiate themselves beyond product, price, place (ie. new channels) and promotion.

As retailers adapt to the global marketplace, multi-channel competition, and increased consumer expectations, every aspect of the retail business needs to be scrutinized and assessed, from product selection, pricing, promotions, store environment and shopping experience to distribution channels, supply chains, operations, recruitment, financial management and governance. Operating a successful retail business now involves, for example, an assessment of various suppliers and their sourcing and manufacturing processes, as well as checking certifications (ie. organic, gluten free, 100% cotton, Made in USA etc).

RETAILER-NPO PARTNERSHIPS

The Changing Role of Retail Business in Society

Retail businesses are increasingly under the microscope, now more than ever. Increased access to information and new and emerging technologies has produced consumers who are well-informed and who leverage their knowledge to make purchasing decisions they feel reflect their values. This has put increased pressure on retailers to make deliberate, socially-conscious business decisions. This may mean sourcing produce from local farmers, ensuring safe working environments in third-party production facilities, building energy-efficient spaces, or partnering with organizations representing social causes important to consumers. These decisions profit society, but they also come at a cost.

Ferguson and Goldman (2010) stated that, "cause sponsorship spending will rise to $1.57 billion in 2009, up from $988 million just five years ago and only $120 million back in 1990" (p. 284). This is a significant finding because it demonstrates not only the mass-scale of retailer-NPO partnerships, but also the increased investments that retailers have continued to make into CSR strategies. When analyzing results of an investment or campaign, retailers should consider return on investment (ROI) and overall impact. A 2008 Aberdeen Group benchmarking study, for example, (that tied green initiatives in retail to bottom-line improvement) revealed that green best-in-class retailers realized a 20 percent decrease in energy costs and a 5 percent decrease in merchandise costs (Ferguson & Goldman, 2010).

As Amato and Amato (2012) noted, "The past 20 years witnessed the emergence of philanthropy as an important component of retail strategy with recent contribution rates outpacing those of non-retailers" (p. 435). Retailers' interests in giving back may come as a result of their business model; one that requires constant and direct interaction with its consumers. Yet, their desire to give not only benefits the causes they support, but it can also spur sales revenue from cause-related merchandise and enhance the retailer's brand and reputation (Amato & Amato, 2012). So, in supporting a charitable cause, how can a retailer yield the appropriate profits to offset the required outputs (such as monetary donations, donations in kind or employee time)? The is a complex question that warrants further discussion and exploration into the topics of corporate social responsibility and cause-related marketing to better grasp its explanation, as examined in the next section.

Corporate Social Responsibility and Cause-Related Marketing

CSR and CRM were once little-known terms, but are now commonplace among large retail organizations across North America and Europe. These two concepts are also now thought of as integral to managing any successful retail business.

- **Corporate Social Responsibility (CSR):** Refers to all of the activities and initiatives a business undertakes to operate in a socially, economically, ethically, and environmentally sustainable manner.
- **Cause-Related Marketing (CRM):** Refers to the marketing-specific activities and initiatives that occur based on the cooperative efforts between businesses and non-profit organizations and is seen as a way for the profit-based businesses to establish long-term differentiation from competitors and to add value to their brands (Lafferty, Goldsmith, & Hult, 2004).

How does a retail organization build a CSR strategy? As an initial step in defining its corporate citizenship commitments, the retailer must first establish a broad CSR strategy that incorporates 4 key factors: people (suppliers, customers, employees); product (quality, content and origin);

environment (responsible manufacturing and operations facilities and practices); and community (local and regional involvement). Then specific CRM activities or initiatives are selected to support the CSR strategies. Retailers that have incorporated CSR and/or CRM into their practices demonstrate they value people and communities, not just the bottom line.

Why would a retailer want to adopt CSR into their business practices? When a CSR program or CRM campaign is executed well, retailers reap many rewards. Their organization becomes an "employer of choice," thereby improving recruitment and retention rates. For example, Hess et al., (2002) found that allowing employees to volunteer produced a greater reputational value than monetary gifts (Amato & Amato 2012). According to the 2008 Edelman Goodpurpose study, 63 percent of consumers think companies spend too much on marketing and advertising and should invest more for a "good cause" (Edelman, 2008). CSR and CRM efforts provide retailers with the opportunity to build more meaningful relationships and expand their customer base, which in turn can generate more sales and revenue. Retailers who partner with NPOs build strong, sustainable brands and bolster their company's reputation in the long term. Amato & Amato (2012) concluded that, "… philanthropy enhances corporate image or reputation" (p.446). Thus, these research findings allow for the conclusion that retail organizations adopt CSR and CRM into their business practices as a strategic and deliberate brand building strategy.

Impact of Customer-Retailer Communications on Retailer-Consumer Relationships

Communications between retailers and consumers have changed dramatically over the last decade, and this is important because it has forever impacted the retailer-consumer relationship. The Internet has allowed consumers to interact with each other, and with retailers, both immediately and publicly. Before the Internet, lodging a complaint, for example, via a retailer's customer service department involved talking directly to a store manager, writing a letter and mailing it, or discussing the matter over the phone with a customer service representative. Today, customer service departments have developed multiple channels for consumers who wish to get in touch with retailers. Consumers can contact retailers in person or by letter, telephone, email, Twitter, Facebook, LinkedIn, online chat, (and other various social media networks and platforms) or by publicizing their grievances through their own social media networks and contacts.

Anyone can now launch an online petition through Websites designed for this purpose. In 2007, 26-year-old Ben Rattray launched www. change.org and in the interim six years it has helped 40 million consumers launch upwards of 1000 petitions a day. Many petitions on this site have convinced retailers to change their business practices and strategies. But it's not just adult consumers who are putting the pressure on retailers to be more socially conscious. Children and young adults are also vocal advocates for positive social change. One particularly powerful petition was launched by a 10-year old named Mia Hansen who persuaded Jamba Juice to stop using Styrofoam cups and replace them with a more environmentally-friendly option. Benjamin O'Keefe, 18, gained 75,000 signatures to convince teen retailer Abercrombie & Fitch to offer larger size clothing. In May of 2013, his persuasive petition landed him an in-person meeting with the company CEO to discuss ways to make the brand more inclusive (Bluestein, 2013).

Before social media and online petitions existed, consumers had to go to considerable effort to launch a complaint. Retailers could decide *when* they would respond to the complaint and *how* they would address it. The discussion could remain somewhat confidential as word-of-mouth was slower to reach the media, let alone a global audience. Today, lodging a complaint about a retailer can be as simple as composing a 140-character Tweet that is instantly distributed to millions of current or potential customers. As a result, most retailers now have a significant online presence, not only through their corporate Website, but also through various social media channels. These allow retailers to monitor and track consumer perceptions and discussions, and to proactively address issues that could be gaining momentum amid the online chatter.

Retailer-NPO Partnerships

CSR is not just about sourcing environmentally-friendly products or manufacturing in safe and ethical facilities, it is also about supporting a community, local or global. This could mean that a retailer would give back to the community in which it operates by partnering with a local charity or NPO that is meaningful to its consumers.

- **Retailer-NPO Partnerships:** refer to a unique, mutually advantageous, and often exclusive relationship that is established to achieve specific objectives and is driven by a set of common goals.

Why would a retailer want to partner with an NPO? A retailer partners with an NPO to acquire new customers, increase customer loyalty, enhance the customers' shopping experience, and build a socially-conscious brand. The NPO partners with a retailer to build greater awareness of its cause, earn donations, broaden its donor base, and recruit volunteers. While these goals may appear to have little in common, they are in fact complementary and, in some cases, interdependent. Because a retailer's customer base is likely different than an NPO's donor base, a successfully leveraged partnership can grow the number of customers *and* donors and develop into a mutually beneficial partnership.

Retailer-NPO Partnerships: A Reciprocal Relationship

In theory, the retailer-NPO partnership should be mutually beneficial or reciprocal. In reality, this is rarely the case. This is largely due to the fact that there are many more NPOs in the marketplace (supply) than there are retail organizations that are able to donate resources, money, or employee time (demand), therefore the supply-demand ratio is more in favour of the retailer. Large retailers are also very busy organizations under significant amounts of pressure from shareholders and stakeholders to deliver short-term sales and meet revenue goals.

Given this hypothesis that a retailer-NPO partnership should be reciprocal, and given the fact that retailer-NPO partnerships provide potential benefits to each party, a comparison and contrast of retailer and NPO goals and contributions is illustrated in Table 1.

Retailer-NPO Partnership: Roles and Responsibilities

Generally in the retailer-NPO relationship, the balance of power resides with the retailer, so the notion of a reciprocal relationship is more theory than reality. In fact, as one study found, "…social campaigns are tailored around the needs of the corporation, and NPOs are essentially on trial until they can convince their corporate partners about the value of the relationship" (Liston-Heyes, 2010, p. 91). This study implies a severe imbalance in power between the retailer and NPO. Most retailer-NPO partnerships today are initiated by the retailer to meet its CSR goals, as this research supports.

Large-scale retailers now have CSR plans that are developed by CSR departments with dedicated staff, but are driven and endorsed by the organization's leadership team, and embedded within its business model (including supply chain systems and operations). CSR departments often have formal reporting structures to ensure there is a

Table 1. A comparison and contrast of retailer and NPO goals and contributions

Retailer Goals	NPO Contributions
Acquire new customers.	Donors and supporters.
Enhance reputation.	Meaningful and worthy cause.
Enhance shopping experience.	In-store promotional materials.
Build socially-conscious brand.	Association with a reputable, meaningful and worthy organization.
NPO Goals	**Retailer Contributions**
Build awareness of cause.	Customers, store locations and promotional/advertising opportunities.
Build donor base.	Current customer base.
Build volunteer base.	Customer or employee time.
Increase donations.	In-kind product donations (surplus production or facilities) and on-site customer donations.

Source: Janice Rudkowski, Helianthus Consulting 2013

dedicated and qualified team of people who have the right skills and experience to manage the plan.

Retailer-NPO partnerships tend to start as short-term projects and only grow into long-term relationships if and when they are proven successful. It takes time to build trust in a volatile retail marketplace and to prove to the retailer that its demands can be met. As retailer-NPO partnerships become more common, they may be viewed with scepticism by customers who suspect the retailer is motivated more by profit motives (Barone, Norman & Miyazaki, 2007).

It is critical retailers take great care when considering this branding strategy and when selecting a suitable NPO partner. Given that there are many different kinds and sizes of NPOs and charities in the marketplace, a retailer must choose a partner that matches its goals and mission. A poor match could have detrimental effects on the retailer's, and the NPO's, short and long-term brand reputation. The retailer's messaging should also be sincere and their connection to the local community evident before a campaign is undertaken.

Retailer-NPO Partnerships: The Selection Process

There are several steps that retailers may take to find, assess, and select the right NPO partner depending on their goals and objectives as well as stakeholder and shareholder expectations. As Barone, Norton and Miyazaki (2007) stated, "...as cause-related marketing becomes more common, retailers must be strategic in deciding when and how to implement this strategy if it is to provide a basis for meaningful differentiation" (p. 437). Partnering with an NPO requires an investment of time and resources, therefore it is critical that the partnership be mutually beneficial, promote synergies, and accomplish shared objectives.

There are numerous approaches that a retailer could take to select the right NPO partner. The following 4-step approach is proposed by the author after a thorough literature review examining multiple retailer practices with the following hypothesis: a simple, straight forward and practical approach would likely be easiest to implement. The four step process below demonstrates the author's recommended approach for retailers when selecting an NPO partner:

1. Establish Clear Goals and Align with Company Mission

It is essential that a retailer have clearly articulated goals and a mission for its business. There should also be clear goals established for its staff and community. Once these goals are in place, partnering with an NPO can be assessed as one strategy among many that might meet these goals. A recent report published by the Centre for Corporate Citizenship (Carroll School of Management within Boston College) concluded that, "…companies that align corporate citizenship strategies with overall corporate strategy are more likely to achieve important business objectives" (p. 1). The same study concluded that companies that made short-term investments were unlikely to realize the same gains as those that had made longer-term investments in CSR strategies.

The retailer's customers should be able to see a clear and credible connection between it and its cause and the cause must be relevant to them, otherwise the efforts and investment will not provide the expected returns. Therefore, the retailer-NPO partnership must make sense to all parties involved: the retailer (including leadership and the team), the NPO, and the retailer's customers (Hoeffler & Keller, 2002). For example, it may make sense for a food retailer to align with organizations that address childhood obesity or that provides food to the less fortunate. A clothing retailer may focus on organizations that lobby for sustainable cotton farming practices or fair labour laws.

NPOs support a variety of causes including the arts, culture, sports, recreation, education, health, animal welfare, disaster relief, social services and the environment to name just a few. There are also several different types of NPOs (charities, foundations etc.), each with its own unique business model, fundraising ability, capacity and mission. NPOs can also be global, national, or local in scope. Therefore, it is also important that a retailer consider an NPO's other associations to ensure there are no conflicts of interest or potential areas of controversy when considering an NPO and its partnership potential.

2. Establish Leadership Backing and Team Buy-In

When considering an NPO, the cause that the NPO stands for must resonate with, and be embraced by, both the retailer's leadership team and its employees. Sainsbury's, a UK food retailer, for example, demonstrated its commitment to CSR in 1989 when it created recyclable carrier bags, a program it initiated long before other retailers did or consumers thought to demand it. To create team buy-in, Sainsbury's established a program called "Tell Justin" in which personnel wrote directly to CEO Justin King with their CSR ideas. Initiatives such as Active Kids and Million Meal Appeal came out of this innovative internal communications program (Smith, 2013).

Ideally, the retailers' leadership team and staff should discuss, explore, evaluate, and select the NPO so that buy-in and support for the campaign's activities is more likely to be secured. Team buy-in also establishes camaraderie and community within the organization, which can enhance internal recruitment and retention rates and ensure the partnership has longevity, thus setting the partnership up for additional value creation.

3. Research, Evaluate, and Compare Options

Retailers must research, evaluate and compare options. As mentioned earlier, there are many different types of NPO's so it is important to narrow down the selection and evaluate the strengths, weaknesses, opportunities and threats of each one. Because the majority of NPOs are fundraising organizations, they are subject to scrutiny by donors and potential partners, therefore, they have to make their business operations and information transparent and accessible. As a result, there are an abundance of online tools available to help facilitate the retailer's research and evaluation process. Charity Navigator (www.charitynavigator.org) and GuideStar (www.guidestar.org), for example, are two US-based evaluator tools that allow access to financial reports as well as star ratings (Hall, 2013). Organizations such as GiveWell (www.givewell.com) and Imagine Canada (www.imaginecanada.com), which publishes *Sector Monitor Reports*, provide in-depth research on charities and industry best practices. Retailers should leverage these research tools to select an NPO that not only aligns with their goals, but also demonstrates prudent financial management, a credible reputation and strong governance track record.

4. Assess Fit and Synergies

After the goals and mission have been clearly articulated; the options have been well researched, evaluated and compared; leadership has been aligned; and team buy-in has been achieved; synergies between the two players can be further identified. It is less common for retailers to partner with newly-established, controversial causes or projects, as there will likely be too little evidence to safely make the case (Liston-Heyes, 2010). Most retailers look for well-established organizations with causes that garner broad and positive appeal, to maximize and leverage the value from the partnership.

Finding the right fit is critical because both parties need to contribute resources for the partnership to succeed. One study found that when a customer has a positive attitude toward the cause, the fit between the retailer and the cause becomes less of a strategic issue (Barone, Norman, & Miyazaki, 2007). While the assessment should confirm the reputable operation of the NPO, and its fit with the retailer's mission, the synergies will only arise once the teams have met each other and established an initial rapport.

Retailer-NPO Partnerships: Industry Best Practices across North America and Europe

To truly understand the complexity, nuances and best practices of retailer-NPO partnerships retail industry case studies from across North America and Europe have been explored in this section.

For a large retailer such as Walmart, for example, selecting a charitable partner begins with a clearly defined CSR strategy. Walmart's CSR strategy, for example, revolves around four key pillars: Environment, People, Ethical Sourcing, and Community. It partners at both the local and national levels, supporting grassroots community events as well as national fundraising and awareness campaigns. In Canada, Walmart has strategically selected four key NPO partners – Children's Miracle Network, Breakfast Clubs of Canada, Evergreen, and the Canadian Red Cross. The missions of these four NPOs strategically align with Walmart's broader organizational goals and mission (Walmart, 2013).

The Chronicle of Philanthropy conducts an annual survey in which they ask 300 of the top revenue-producing American companies, according to the Fortune 500 rankings, about their charitable contributions. They received data from 106 of them in 2012, as companies are not required by law to disclose this type of information. *The Chronicle* also asked survey respondents about their giving plans for 2013. More than three-quarters of corporate leaders said they expect their giving budgets to be about the same this year; 16% said they will give more; and 6% plan to donate less (Smith, 2013).

Two retailers ranked among America's top 10 most generous companies with Walmart at second place and Target at ninth. Walmart, which has held the top spot for 7 consecutive times, gave over $311 million in cash and $755 million in products to over 50,000 charities worldwide. Their 2012 charitable giving amounts to 4.5% of their 2011 pre-tax profits. They are forecasted to give more in 2013. Target donated $147 million in cash and $76 million in products, amounting to 5.0% of their 2011 pre-tax profits. They declined to provide a forecast for 2013. (Smith, 2013).

In another industry best practice example the Delhaize Group, a Belgian company that operates food supermarkets in 8 countries across 3 continents, was recently recognized for its partnership with the World Wildlife Federation (WWF), promising to source only fish that were 100% sustainable (European Corporate Social Responsibility Award Scheme, 2013). Increasing media focus on the issues related to overfishing offered Dalhaize an opportunity to step forward and support the WWF and adapt its supply chain operations accordingly.

Retailers large and small across the world connect with their communities by partnering with NPOs and supporting various environmental and social causes. Understanding their charitable giving practices helps to provide further understanding and context around the retailer-NPO partnership relationship. Table 2 lists the top 5 largest retailers in the world, their country of origin, their sector, charitable focus and how much they donated to charitable organizations in 2012.

Retailer-NPO Partnerships: Conflict and Challenges

There are many challenges and conflicts in managing retailer-NPO partnerships. One of the biggest challenges retailers face in managing NPO relationships is the pressure from stakeholders, shareholders, and/or upper management, to deliver short-term results (Dowden, 2013). Yet a retailer-NPO partnership, according to one study, must focus on long-term versus short-term goals in order for the "...cause relating marketing benefits to materialize into financial gains" (Liston-Heyes, 2010, p. 90). The same study also states that NPOs, "...appear to resent corporate partners

Table 2. Charitable giving among the top 5 largest retailers in the world

Retailer	Country of Origin	Sector	Charitable/Social Focus	Giving $ (2012)
Walmart	USA	Hypermarket/Supercenter/Superstore	Walmart Foundation (core areas of focus: Hunger Relief and Healthy Eating, Sustainability, Women's Economic Empowerment and Career Opportunity)	$311 Million (USD) in cash; $755 Million USD in product donations (Walmart, 2013).
Carrefour S.A.	France	Hypermarket/Supercenter/Superstore	Fondation d'Enterprise Carrefour (36 projects focused on Emergency Aid and Food Programs)	$4.5 Million Euros (Carrefour SA, 2013).
Tesco PLC	UK	Hypermarket/Supercenter/Superstore	Tesco Charity Trust (local, national and international level)	$2 Million UK Pounds (year ending February, 2012) (Tesco PLC, 2013).
Metro AG	Germany	Cash and Carry/Wholesale Club	Various	N/A (Metro AG, 2013).
The Kroger Co.	USA	Supermarket	Alliance with Feeding America	$700 Million USD funding; $7 Million in donated food (since 2006). Donated the equivalent of 200 million meals in 2012 (The Kroger Co., 2013).

Source: Deloitte and Stores Media, 2013

who are easily swayed by shifts in the short-term popularity of their causes, although they admit that some firms (retail ones in particular) actively prefer short-term campaigns and a rapid turnover of endorsements," (Liston-Heyes, 2010, p. 90). The retail sector has often been volatile, subject to shifting trends and rapidly changing consumer preferences, but despite this, it must not succumb to short-term thinking with respect to its CSR strategies.

Retailers have always understood the benefit of adjusting their product assortment to suit local tastes, so partnering with regional or local NPOs to support their communities is a logical extension of this practice. The best example of this is a neighbourhood hardware store sponsoring a local sports team. Large retailers, however, must address *both* long-term national planning concerns and the fact that their stores operate in local communities. As a result, they support both national charities and local ones. National NPOs are strategically aligned with the retailer's goals and mission, while the local NPOs support grassroots efforts.

Liston-Heyes (2010) found that, "...the diversity of social causes that a firm supports is related to its product range. Firms with a narrow product range will generally endorse fewer causes than those with a more diversified or seasonal product range" (p. 88). Retailers who compete in many different product categories will need a broader range of causes to match these.

Delivering a CSR strategy requires financial investment, resources, and/or employee time, all of which will affect the retailer's bottom line. Establishing and maintaining strategic retailer-NPO partnerships requires management's commitment because significant human, capital, and financial resources will be required to achieve its desired goals. The retailer must find ways to offset these costs by successfully operating the partnership.

This investment can present challenges if the retailer already operates with low profit margins. Increasing retail prices to offset the cost of the partnership is not a good solution since it can also result in reduced sales volumes. Higher retail prices can also result in consumers switching to competitors, thus risking consumer loyalty and trust. Boston College's Carroll School of Management and Centre for Corporate Citizenship's *The State of Corporate Citizenship 2012* report found that executives from solely business-to-consumer companies (as in the retail sector) expressed the least confidence in the likelihood of CSR campaigns to generate shareholder returns, anticipating consumers' reluctance to pay more for socially or environmentally conscious products (Centre for Corporate Citizenship, 2012). This comment supports the need for retailers to do their due diligence if and when they decide to partner with an NPO.

While some consumers are very supportive of retailer-NPO partnerships, others are quick to criticize the efforts. The issue of cannibalization of the cause itself, for example, can exist and its critics argue that, "...selling products – whether red (to support HIV/AIDS), pink (to support Breast Cancer) or green (to support environmental justice) – can shift consumer behaviour away from giving directly to the cause" (Ferguson & Goldman, 2012). Because of the trend of correlating causes with colours, the shopping environment and its cause-related merchandise can also transform the consumer perception of a specific cause from credible to commercial. Consumers can get very fatigued by too many or conflicting messages within the retail shopping environment, resulting in the creation of backlash Websites such as "Sick of Pink" (www.sickofpink.com) as well as negative word of mouth. Poor execution of retailer/NPO partnerships activities within the shopping environment can therefore have negative long term effects on both the retailer's and NPO's brand reputation.

FUTURE RESEARCH DIRECTIONS AND TRENDS

Just as the 4 P's, 4 C's and 4 A's have evolved, so too will retailer-NPO partnerships and CSR strategies. Retailers will continue to expand their CSR efforts with even more focus on issues that are important to their consumers, stakeholders, and shareholders. Consumer expectations demand retailers to revisit their CSR strategies to ensure they align with the social values of the communities in which their stores operate. If executed properly, CSR is less an utopian ideal than a pragmatic and sustainable business strategy.

Retailer-NPO partnerships will likely evolve from predominantly short-term relationships into longer-term relationships, since these provide greater opportunity to benefit from the investment. They will likely also involve even tighter links to the retailer's, and its staff's, goals while ensuring that, "…top management embodies and lives the values and beliefs inherent in corporate citizenship" (Dowden, 2013).

NPOs will adopt savvier marketing practices, business frameworks, strategies, and best practices to become more sophisticated, selective, and sought after so that they can attain a greater balance of power within the retailer-NPO partnership. Instead of retailers approaching and selecting prospective NPO partners, the NPOs may soon have significant brand power themselves and invite retailers to submit proposals to partner with them.

Retailers will need to be especially attuned to issues that arise online, and address them proactively, rather than waiting for the consumer to reach out to them. Retailers will also want to explore other ways to leverage NPO relationships and better integrate them into their organizations. Consumers may also be more directly involved in the assessment and selection of prospective NPOs down the road, allowing retailers to select partners who resonate with their stakeholders and who provide added value and positive contribution to their communities. In 2009, Target employed a consumer involvement strategy when they launched their "…Bullseye Gives program, a two-week long May campaign on their Facebook page that encouraged consumers to help decide how ten different charities should receive $3million in donations," (Ferguson & Goldman, 2012).

"Companies are becoming much more strategic in their philanthropy," states Peter Panepento, *The Chronicle of Philanthropy*'s assistant managing editor. "Instead of simply giving out grants and cutting checks, many big companies are instead looking to support philanthropic programs that closely align with their corporate goals and are looking for nonprofit partners that are able to show results. This poses challenges for some nonprofits, but it offers some great advantages to groups that are able to demonstrate that they will be good stewards of corporate investments in their work" (Smith, 2013).

The concept of charity retailing will also continue to trend as evidenced by the UK-based Charity Retail Association that boasts over 370 members and between them over 7500 stores (Charity Retail Association, 2013). A charity retailer, which is quite a modern concept, is an organization that only sells merchandise that directly benefits or supports a specific cause or several causes. Bernand and Marie-France Cohen of Paris, France opened up their charity retail store Merci (meaning thank you in French), in 2009 as a way to "pay it forward." The store, which combines home, beauty, fashion, and garden categories in addition to a café/restaurant established an endowment fund "…to finance acts of human development, particularly in the education area" (Merci, 2013). Merci works with well-known fashion designers such as Chloe and Stella McCartney as well as less-known designers to act as an incubator to produce fresh and innovative ideas and designs. (Peterson, 2012). The increasing popularity of charity retailing will likely mean more intense competition for non-charity retailers, as they each vie for consumers' loyalty, dollars and social interests.

Retailers' communication and reporting of socially responsible activity is a significant opportunity. A study by Min-young, Fairhurst & Wesley (2009), which analyzed the top 100 US retailers' CSR practices, discovered that just over one-half of the Top 100 retailers mentioned CSR on their Websites (p. 146). Consumers actively search for information on corporate social values (Anselmsson & Johansson, 2007), therefore retailers should examine additional ways to better leverage their Websites to communicate and "… disseminate their social responsibility information and facilitate more interactivity with their customers, employees and other stakeholders" (Min-young, Fairhurst & Wesley, 2009).

Finally, retailers' standards for measurement and reporting of socially responsible activities will need to improve. Min-young, Fairhurst & Wesley (2009) found that "currently, some US retailers have adopted socially responsible practices into their companies, but only a handful of examples are common public knowledge" (p. 142.). Many large organizations currently utilize their annual reports and Websites to communicate their accomplishments, from financial, environmental and societal vantage points. With increasing consumer demands and knowledge, their reporting will need to become more sophisticated and include, "third-party certification reports by bodies accredited to certify against social or environmental standards" (Min-young, Fairhurst & Wesley, 2009). Retailers' stakeholders and shareholders will also likely increase their pressures for results. These compounding demands will drive retailers to develop and adopt better and more transparent methods to monitor and measure the impact of their environmental and social activities, and better link them to corporate performance.

CONCLUSION

Retailer-NPO partnerships have profoundly influenced socially-conscious shoppers and the shopping environments in which they make purchases. Since consumers are increasingly well-informed and empowered, this new reality that has completely transformed the *retailer-led* business model into a *consumer-led* business model. The consumers' sphere of influence, therefore, not only determines product assortment and price, it extends to sourcing, product development and community involvement.

Retailer-NPO partnerships are no longer just a strategy to generate more revenue, they are part of the firm's broader CSR plan to build consumer loyalty, operate an ethical business, offer ethical and sustainable product choices and support local and national communities. Socially, environmentally and ethically sound business practices are therefore not just a trend; they are a business imperative (Ferguson & Goldman, 2012).

As retailers continue to integrate CSR and CRM best practices into their business models and operations, they will need to be more strategic about their charitable giving and partnership selections to ensure the partners they select provide value. Consumers view socially-responsible and transparent business practices as the new expected standard of operating a retail business today.

REFERENCES

Alexandru, P. N., & Cristian, D. D. (2008). Tendencies of internationalization in retailing. *The Journal of the Faculty of Economics*, *4*(1), 1099–1105.

Altman, B. W. (1998). Corporate Community Relations in the 1990s: A Study of Transformation. *Business & Society*, *37*(2), 221–227. doi:10.1177/000765039803700205

Amato, L. H., & Amato, C. H. (2012). Retail Philanthropy: Firm Size, Industry, and Business Cycle. *Journal of Business Ethics*, *1*(7), 435–448. doi:10.1007/s10551-011-1048-x

Anselmsson, J., & Johansson, U. (2007). Corporate social responsibility and the positioning of grocery brands. *International Journal of Retail and Distribution Management, 35*(10), 835–856. doi:10.1108/09590550710820702

Barone, M. J., Norman, A. T., & Miyazaki, A. D. (2007). Consumer response to retailer use of cause-related marketing: Is more fit better? *Journal of Retailing, 83,* 437–445. doi:10.1016/j.jretai.2007.03.006

Bluestein, A. (2013, September). You sign, companies listen. *Fast Company,* 34-36.

Brown, S., & Burt, S. (1992). Retail Internationalization: Past Imperfect, Future Imperative. *European Journal of Marketing, 26*(8-9), 80.

Carrefour, S. A. (2013). *Corporate Website.* Retrieved on August 15, 2013 from http://www.fondation-carrefour.org

Centre for Corporate Citizenship. (2012). Commitment to value: The state of corporate citizenship 2012 highlights. *Boston College Carroll School of Management.* Retrieved on July 31, 2013 from www.bccorporatecitizenship.org

Charity Retail Association. (2013). *Corporate Website.* Retrieved on August 29, 2103 from http://www.charityretail.org.uk

Dawar, N., & Stornelli, J. (2013). Rebuilding the relationship between manufacturers and retailers. *MIT Sloan Management Review, 54*(2), 83–90.

Deloitte & Stores Media. (2013). 2012 Top 250 Global Retailers. *16ᵗʰ Annual Global Powers of Retailing Report.* Retrieved on August 25, 2013 from http://www.stores.org/2012/Top-250-List

Dowden, C. (2013, August 8). Is it better for business to actually do good or to just look like it's doing good? *Financial Post.* Retrieved August 10, 2013 from http://business.financialpost.com/2013/08/09/is-it-better-for-business-to-actually-do-good-or-to-just-look-like-its-doing-good/

Ettenson, R., Conrado, E., & Knowles, J. (2013). Rethinking the 4 Ps. *Harvard Business Review, 91*(1), 26.

European Corporate Social Responsibility Award Scheme. (2013). *Corporate website.* Retrieved on August 30, 2013 from www.europeancsrawards.eu

Ferguson, R., & Goldman, S. M. (2010). The Cause Manifesto. *Journal of Consumer Marketing, 27*(3), 283–287. doi:10.1108/07363761011038356

Hall, J. (2013, June 12). Four tips for giving to the right nonprofit. *Forbes.* Retrieved on August 7, 2013 from http://www.forbes.com/sites/johnhall/2013/06/12/4-tips-for-choosing-a-philanthropic-partner/

Hoeffler, S., & Keller, K. L. (2002). Building brand equity through corporate societal marketing. *Journal of Public Policy & Marketing, 21,* 78–89. doi:10.1509/jppm.21.1.78.17600

Kotler, P. (2005). *According to Kotler: the world's foremost authority on marketing answers your questions.* New York, NY: Amacon.

Lafferty, B. A., Goldsmith, R. E., & Hult, G. I. (2004). The impact of the alliance on the partners: A look at cause-brand alliances. *Psychology and Marketing, 21,* 509–531. doi:10.1002/mar.20017

Liston-Heyes, C., & Liu, G. (2010). Cause-related marketing in the retail and finance sectors. *Nonprofit and Voluntary Sector Quarterly, 39*(1), 77–96. doi:10.1177/0899764008326680

McCarthy, E. J. (1960). *Basic marketing: A managerial approach.* Chicago, IL: Richard D. Irwin.

Merci. (2013). *Corporate Website.* Retrieved on August 29, 2013 from http://www.merci-merci.com

Metro Group AG. (2013). *Corporate Website.* Retrieved on August 25, 2013 from http://www.metrogroup.de

Min-Young, L., Fairhurst, A., & Wesley, S. (2009). Corporate Social Responsibility: A Review of the Top 100 US Retailers. *Corporate Reputation Review, 12*(2), 140–158. doi:10.1057/crr.2009.10

Peterson, P. (2012). Merci: a Parisian store to be thankful for. *Huffington Post*. Retrieved on August 28, 2013 from http://www.huffingtonpost.com/pam-peterson/merci-paris-store_b_2276982.html

Sheth, J., & Sisodia, R. (2012). *The 4 As of marketing: Creating value for customer, company and society*. New York, NY: Routledge.

Smith, J. (2013, July 16). America's most generous companies. *Forbes*. Retrieved on August 29, 2013 from http://www.forbes.com/sites/jacquelynsmith/2013/07/16/americas-most-generous-companies/

Smith, N. (2013, June 5). Corporate social responsibility: Power to the people. *Marketing Week*. Retrieved on August 23, 2013 from http://www.marketingweek.co.uk/trends/corporate-social-responsibility-power-to-the-people/4006810.article

Tesco, P. L. C. (2013). *Corporate Website*. Retrieved on August 22, 2013 from http://www.tescoplc.com

The Kroger Co. (2013). *Corporate Website*. Retrieved on August 16, 2013 from http://www.kroger.com

Walmart. (2013). *Corporate Website*. Retrieved on August 2, 2013 from http://corporate.walmart.com

Walters, D. (1981). The 1970s in retailing: a retrospective view. *International Journal of Retail & Distribution Management, 9*(2), 8–15. doi:10.1108/eb018090

ADDITIONAL READING

Anonymous. (2008). Do supermarkets need CSR policies more than other retailers? *Marketing*, May 21, 24.

Anonymous. (2010). Safeway Inc. announces FishWise partnership. *Business Wire*, January 26.

Anonymous. (2012). Total wine & more and the century council create unique partnership with Tampa Bay-area officials to promote responsible holiday celebrations. *PR Newswire*, November 27.

Bondy, K. (2008). The paradox of power in CSR: A case study on implementation. *Journal of Business Ethics, 82*(2), 307–323. doi:10.1007/s10551-008-9889-7

Daw, J. S., Cone, C., Darigan Merenda, K., & Erhard, A. (2011). *Breakthrough non-profit branding: Seven principles to power extraordinary results*. Hoboken, NJ: John Wiley & Sons Inc.

De Wulf, K., Gaby, G., Goedertier, F., & Gino, V. O. (2005). Consumer perceptions of store brands versus national brands. *Journal of Consumer Marketing, 22*(4), 223–232. doi:10.1108/07363760510605335

Doherty, B. (2011). Resource advantage theory and fair trade social enterprises. *Journal of Strategic Marketing, 19*(4), 357–380. doi:10.1080/0965254X.2011.581379

Dutta, K., & Singh, S. (2013). Customer perception of CSR and its impact on retailer evaluation and purchase intention in India. *Journal of Service Research, 13*(1), 111.

Edelman. (2012). *Edelman Goodpurpose 2012 global consumer survey*. Presentation. Retrieved on June 1, 2013, from http://www.slideshare.net/EdelmanInsights/global-deck-2012-edelman-goodpurpose-study

Forseter, M. (1995). From the four P's to the multiple C's. *Chain Store Age Executive with Shopping Center Age, 71*(5), 12.

Goi, C. L. (2009). A review of Marketing Mix: 4Ps or More? *International Journal of Marketing Studies, 1*(1), 2–15. doi:10.5539/ijms.v1n1p2

Hernandez, T., & Simmons, J. (2006). Evolving retail landscapes: power retail in Canada. *The Canadian Geographer*, *50*(4), 465–486. doi:10.1111/j.1541-0064.2006.00158.x

Lee, Y. I., & Trim, P. R. J. (2006). Retail marketing strategy: the role of marketing intelligence, relationship marketing and trust. *Marketing Intelligence & Planning*, *24*(7), 730–745. doi:10.1108/02634500610711888

Mattos, M. (2011). Bringing CSR into focus. *Strategy,* May, 20.

Mejri, C. A., Bhatli, D., & Benhallam, M. (2012). Why art thou resisting? Consumer resistance to the 'citizen argument' of retailers. *International Journal of Market Research*, *54*(5), 707. doi:10.2501/IJMR-54-5-707-721

Minakakis, G. (2012). Retailers need corporate social responsibility strategy. *The Vancouver Sun*, May 25, 2012. Retrieved on August 7, 2013 from http://www.georgeminakakis.com/wp-content/uploads/2012/11/VancouverSun_article.pdf

Mohin, T. (2012). The top 10 trends in CSR for 2012. *Forbes,* January 18, 2012. Retrieved on August 12, 2013 from http://www.forbes.com/sites/forbesleadershipforum/2012/01/18/the-top-10-trends-in-csr-for-2012/

Perry, P. (2012). Exploring the influence of national cultural context on CSR implementation. *Journal of Fashion Marketing and Management*, *16*(2), 141–160. doi:10.1108/13612021211222806

Porter, M.E., & Kramer, M.R. (2011). Creating Shared Value. *Harvard Business Review*, January-February, HBR Reprint R1101C, 1-17.

Rampl, L. V., Eberhardt, T., Schütte, R., & Kenning, P. (2012). Consumer trust in food retailers: conceptual framework and empirical evidence. *International Journal of Retail & Distribution Management*, *40*(4), 254–272. doi:10.1108/09590551211211765

Roberts, K. (2013). *The changing role of business and society.* Blog Post, n.d. Retrieved on June 2, 2012 from http://jsdaw.com/blog/.

Shaw, H. (2006). CSR in the community: Redefining the social role of the supermarket giants. *Social Responsibility Journal*, *2*(2), 216–222. doi:10.1108/eb059277

Skarmeas, D., & Leonidou, C. N. (2013). When consumers doubt, watch out! The role of CSR skepticism. *Journal of Business Research*, *66*(10), 1831. doi:10.1016/j.jbusres.2013.02.004

Vlachos, P. A. (2012). Corporate social performance and consumer-retailer emotional attachment. *European Journal of Marketing*, *46*(11/12), 1559–1580. doi:10.1108/03090561211259989

Zboja, J. J., & Voorhees, C. M. (2006). The impact of brand trust and satisfaction on retailer repurchase intentions. *Journal of Services Marketing*, *20*(6), 381–390. doi:10.1108/08876040610691275

KEY TERMS AND DEFINITIONS

Cause-Related Marketing (CRM): Refers to the marketing-specific activities and initiatives that occur based on the cooperative efforts of business and non-profit organizations and is seen as a way for the retailer to establish long-term differentiation from competitors and to add value to their brand (Lafferty, Goldsmith, & Hult, 2004).

Charity Retailer: A charity retailer is an organization that only sells merchandise that directly benefits or supports a specific cause or several causes.

Corporate Community Relations (CCR): Refers to the specialized function within a retail operation dedicated to building relations with the businesses, people and charitable organizations within the community where a retailer operates.

Corporate Social Responsibility (CSR): Refers to all of the activities and initiatives a retailer undertakes to operate in a socially, economically, ethically, and environmentally sustainable manner.

Customer: An individual or group of individuals that is part of a target market, and purchases a firm's products or services.

NPO: An acronym that stands for Non-Profit Organization.

Retail Internationalization (RI): Refers to the expansion of a retailer's stores or outlets into other countries or territories outside of their country of origin.

Retailer-NPO Partnerships: Refer to a unique, mutually advantageous, and often ex-clusive relationship that is established to achieve specific objectives and is driven by a set of common goals.

Shareholders: Refers to individuals or groups of individuals who hold shares (ie. partial ownership) of a publicly traded company.

Stakeholders: Refers to individuals or groups of individuals who have some type of interest or concern in a public, private or non-profit company or business. Examples of stakeholders are: customers, suppliers, partners, service providers, industry thought leaders or funders.

Chapter 18
Engaging Social Movements in Developing Innovative Retail Business Models

Roberta Sebastiani
Università Cattolica del Sacro Cuore, Italy

Francesca Montagnini
University of Milan-Bicocca, Italy

ABSTRACT

Consumers are increasingly expressing critical stances towards corporate power and mainstream market ideology. Although the literature depicts their attitude as mainly reactive, it is emerging that there is scope, in retailing, for more proactive forms of collaboration with companies. This chapter aims to explore the outcomes in terms of new retail formulas derived from the effective interaction between retailers and engaged consumers, such as those belonging to social movements. In the analysis, the authors refer to a specific context and kind of product, namely food, which has recently been catalyzing an increasing number of concerns as expressed by consumers, eventually aggregating the interests of various social movements expressing new more ethical and sustainable market stances. In particular, the authors focus on the case of Eataly, a new venture that emerged from an ideological alliance and a mutual organizational commitment between corporate power and the Slow Food social movement. Eataly represents an interesting setting to better understand how such forms of collaboration can occur, how and to what extent the community and corporate stances mutually adjust during the process, and which types of reactions emerge from the more radical members of the social movement.

INTRODUCTION

Recent research into food production, distribution, and consumption suggests that ideology and counter-culture are important factors affecting consumers' choices in terms of where food is bought as well as the kind of food chosen (Thompson & Coskuner-Balli, 2007). Food consumption is also increasingly driven by explicit and implicit symbolic arguments. Symbols seem to be attached to particular foods, their manufacturing and preparation methods, and eating patterns

DOI: 10.4018/978-1-4666-6074-8.ch018

(Kniazeva & Venkatesh, 2007). Among these symbolic arguments, fairness and authenticity of the relationship between demand and supply are growing in importance (Arnould & Price, 2000; Holt, 2002).

Meanwhile, corporate initiatives are often challenged by emerging counter-cultural movements that have adopted critical stances toward corporate power and market ideology. The counter-culture concept refers to a coherent system of norms and values that not only differ from those of the dominant system, but also comprise at least one norm or value that calls for commitment to cultural change–that is, a transformation of the dominant system of norms and values (Desmond et al., 2000). A counter-cultural movement typically involves criticism or rejection of currently powerful institutions, with accompanying hope for a better life or a new society. As new consumption ideologies emerge, extant business initiatives are criticized (Hollenbeck & Zinkhan, 2010); consequently, they are sometimes "transformed" (Kozinets & Handelman, 2004), and new market opportunities are created (Carducci, 2006; Heath & Potter, 2005).

Consumers, who often emerge as small and marginal movements (but are well rooted in the history of consumption communities), tend to demand special attention for their ideological values and expectations. The more consumers detach from the traditional market offerings–particularly in terms of food production and distribution–the more room that is left for new and more sustainable business models (Schaefer & Crane, 2005), some of which depend on actual consumers' engagement (Moraes et al., 2010). Ultimately, consumers resist extant supply modes and their ideological discourses to achieve a more genuine consumption style (product attributes, value chain properties, store environment, etc.). As corporate strategies become more responsive to these individual consumer and aggregate attitudes, retailers are among the first forced to change due to their direct interactions with final consumers as they act at the end of the supply chain.

An interesting example of this evolution is represented by Eataly, an innovative chain of food distribution co-projected and co-designed by the Slow Food consumer movement. As highlighted in its manifesto, "Eataly is an alliance of small-scale producers, who have been making the finest foods and beverages in limited quantities for generations. They have joined together to offer quality products at sustainable prices. Direct from the producer to the consumer with no middlemen: Eataly offers quality food, selected in collaboration with Slow Food" (www.eataly.it). Meanwhile, the global Slow Food movement, involving millions of people in more than 160 countries, is devoted to protecting and supporting authentic food culture by adopting a commitment to community and the environment. This movement was founded in Italy in 1989 to counteract fast food and a fast life, as well as the disappearance of local food traditions, by promoting "good, clean, and fair" food. These adjectives represent the pillars of the Slow Food philosophy. "Good" refers to the idea that a fresh and flavorsome seasonal diet satisfies the senses and is part of the local culture. "Clean" is related to food production and consumption that does not harm the environment, animal welfare, or human health. "Fair" refers to accessible prices for consumers and fair conditions and pay for producers. The Slow Food movement's main objectives are to spread taste education, connect producers and consumers of excellent foods through events and initiatives, and build new communities of quality food supporters that can, through their food choices, collectively influence how food is cultivated, produced, and distributed.

This chapter focuses on Eataly, which emerged from an ideological alliance and mutual organizational commitment between corporate power and a social movement. The discussion includes how this venture came about and the extent of consumer involvement in its development, which are particularly interesting. The case study's original and innovative dimension is twofold. First, the dialectic relationship between the company and the consumers, aggregated in the social movement, began before the launch of the new business. Second, Eataly and the Slow Food movement were mutually and significantly involved at the organizational and managerial levels to ensure that the business and ideological expectations were satisfactorily integrated. From the beginning–even before the opening of Eataly–the company sought to introduce the Slow Food counter-culture's core values and issues into the new venture's design and implementation process.

The Eataly case can be approached as a form of "active" resistance in which, through the Slow Food movement's participation in the new venture, consumers not only criticize, resist, and/or detach or react to the market, but are also directly involved in its transformation as collective agents. In this sense, new social movements can be considered not only as "identity oriented"–that is, emerging as a means for social and cultural identification (Hollenbeck & Zinkhan, 2010)–but also as agents of change of a proactive nature. Thus, what emerges is a new form of prosumerism (Kotler, 1986) that goes beyond the individual level to encompass the collective level.

The aim of this chapter is to investigate the way in which the market transformation occurred and the new venture in retailing was developed. In particular, the objective of this research is to understand how and to what extent the community and corporate stances have been mutually adjusted. Finally, we will consider whether the community (and its more radical members) has accepted this form of compromise with the market ideology.

THEORETICAL BACKGROUND

Consumers' criticism of and resistance to the extant culture and dominant ideology in food production, distribution, and consumption are becoming increasingly important considerations. Counter-cultural and social movements' actions interpret this consumer quest for authenticity

and sustainability. In the literature, their roles are depicted as mainly reactive, but there is room for a more proactive market stance. In particular, anti-consumption is considered to be one of the most common forms of detachment that alienates consumers from markets. As Lee et al., (2009, p. 145) noted, "anti-consumption research focuses on reasons against consumption [...] reasons for avoiding a product or brand." For example, voluntary simplicity implies that, as responsible consumers, we should consume less in order to reduce the waste of resources as well as foster more sustainable development (Ballantine & Creery, 2010; Cherrier, 2007; 2009b).

Nevertheless, as far as food consumption is concerned, consumers must eat; if they do not buy a specific item, they will buy something else. Anti-consumption studies, along with consumer resistance theories (Cherrier, 2009b), help us understand that any single act of avoidance as well as a more complex avoidance strategy implies some form of identity construction activity based on both negative and positive consumption practices (Cherrier, 2007). In other words, when consumers choose not to consume a good or a brand, they will choose to consume something else, and both of these activities are integrated into a process of identity construction (Newholm & Shaw 2007). According to Micheletti (2003) when these decisions are inspired by ethical concerns, we can speak of political consumerism–a perspective recently applied to the study of boycott (critical, negative) and buycott (constructive, positive) behaviors (Neilson, 2010).

Individual acts of anti-consumption and/or resistance can be perceived as forms of identity construction activities as well as forms of collective action when they converge toward counter-cultures (Desmond et al., 2000; Thompson & Coskuner-Balli, 2007) or new social movements (Buechler, 2010). In both cases, collective action aims to criticize extant culture and dominant ideology, giving members a sense of new and resistant collective identity. According to Hollenbeck and Zinkhan (2010, p. 328), new social movements' goals can be classified into four main areas: fighting for an identity, gaining autonomy, radicalizing modern values, and transforming the individual person. These objectives are (a) mainly of a critical nature (they strive to highlight what goes wrong in society) and (b) directed toward the emancipation of their members (basically by providing self-improvement strategies and tools). Social movements can also possess transformative properties whenever they react to corporate market strategies, forcing companies to change their conduct. In general, they can be seen as a critical stance arising from the society, influencing the market process in a reactive fashion.

As individuals and as members of a social movement, consumers engage in the market process (Peñaloza & Venkatesh, 2006; Sebastiani et al., 2013) by supporting the segments, channels, and companies that seem or prove compatible with their ideological strategy (Newholm & Shaw, 2007; Holt, 2002). This process resembles the reproduction-resistance dialectic described in Arnould and Thompson's (2005) review. Consumers contribute to the development of new initiatives as customers, withholding their money from outlets that they do not like and spending it at companies offering progressive business models. In addition to the money, they play an active role in creating the value of the goods and brands in which they are interested (Firat & Venkatesh, 1995). This process of value construction mediated by meanings and symbols has been observed in its positive, constructive dimension, but it can also be viewed from a critical, deconstructive point of view (Cova & Dalli, 2009). Consumer resistance is a form of co-creation when it moves resources away from a specific market/segment and takes them elsewhere, which usually happens at the consumption community level (Cova et al., 2007); as individual consumers cannot influence corporate power, communities do.

In some cases, communities have taken resources from the market and developed peer-to-peer or social production modes (Dalli & Corciolani, 2008; Kozinets, 2007) as well as they have taken old and/or rejected products back to the market (Leigh et al., 2006). In other cases, communities have criticized corporate activities, forcing them to change (Hollenbeck & Zinkhan, 2010; Kozinets & Handelman, 2004). The case presented in this chapter is slightly different from extant theories of both counter-cultures and social movements because Slow Food has played a constructive, constitutive, committed role in the development of new business. In this sense, this chapter provides a new perspective from which to analyze the relationship between corporate power and critical consumers and movements. The market's transformation does not necessarily rely upon the traditional market-mediated action and reaction between companies and consumers, although the possibility exists to negotiate and co-design new and more sustainable forms of production, distribution, and consumption.

In Figure 1(A), we compare the traditional and simplest condition in which companies' strategies point to consumers who react positively or negatively. Based on these reactions, companies adapt their strategies.

In Figure 1(B), movements develop aggregating individual consumer initiatives; they can be supportive or critical, and they can have an effect on companies' strategies. Even in this case, the process is reactive in nature. Figure 1(C) represents the Eataly and Slow Food case, highlighting how the company and the movement interact to develop a more appropriate combination of goods, services, and ideological stances to be delivered to consumers who, in turn, react accordingly (Sebastiani et al., 2013).

In the following paragraphs we conduct an in-depth investigation of how the venture has been developed and how the community and corporate stances have been adjusted. We also check whether and how the community (and its more radical members) has accepted this form of compromise between the market and society.

Figure 1. New relationships among companies, consumers and movements

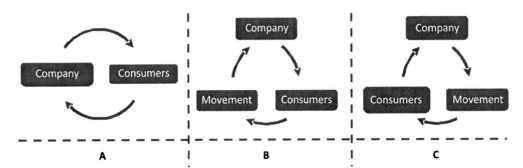

METHODOLOGY AND EMPIRICAL SETTING

Methods

Given our research aims, we opted to use a mixed methods design (Creswell, 2003; Creswell & Plano Clark, 2007) that combined both quantitative and qualitative methods. Among the four purposes for multiple methods designs (development, initiation, complementarity, interpretation) (Tashakkori & Teddlie, 1998), we adopted the initiation design, which–according to Davis et al., (2010)–draws on the outcomes of a preliminary study to inform a second study conducted using a different method. The weights of the methods adopted are unequal. The less weighted method is instrumental to the research inception whereas the second method assumes a primary role in the development of the main study.

In the first stage of our research, we seek to develop a general overview of customers' attitudes and perceptions of the new venture as well as its fit with the widespread counter-cultural movement, Slow Food, and its values. We developed a survey based on a random sampling of Eataly customers. Data were collected at Eataly's Turin branch over a three-day period during the week immediately before the Christmas holidays. The time and place for data gathering were selected due to the need to ensure a good flow of heterogeneous customers (at that time, only the Turin

store had been opened for several months). The structured interviews were articulated using open-ended questions organized in four main sections: personal data; aim and time spent for the visit, evaluation of the shop environment, and products and services; personal opinions about the coherence between Eataly's declared mission and values; and the actual offering setting). Three hundred customers were interviewed at the Turin branch's point of sale: 53% were male, distributed across ages, classes, education backgrounds, and employment, with a slight bias toward educated profiles and professional jobs (compared to the national population). Of the 300 customers, 40 (13%) were members of the Slow Food movement. Approximately 100 people were shopping at Eataly for the first time, while another 100 shop once a month or more in the store.

In the second research stage, we delved deeper into the relationship among Eataly, its customers, and the Slow Food movement. We investigated the alignment among the values underlying the movement, Eataly's business idea and its actual perception by the customers (whether they belonged to the Slow Food movement or not), and how the movement and the corporate power have been mutually adjusted when developing the new venture. In this stage, data were collected from six sources. First, in-store observations were conducted at the Turin and Milan shops, performed independently by the three researchers from the last months of 2008 until the end of 2012. These observations were individually recorded through notes and photographs, thereby allowing for the identification of the stores' features in terms of layout, atmosphere, and internal communication. Second, 50 semi-structured interviews were conducted with both regular and occasional customers in the two shops. Third, 10 in-depth interviews were conducted with customers, both Slow Food members and non-members; they were interviewed in the stores and at their homes. Fourth, 5 in-depth interviews with Slow Food managers and Eataly managers and employees were conducted as we were not only interested in considering the customer's perspective, but also wanted to compare it with the company's and the Slow Food movement's voices. Fifth, forums, blogs, and Facebook pages were used to obtain data on customers' attitudes toward Eataly. More than 350 discussions as well as comments on public blogs or forums were analyzed. Each discussion was considered independently and analyzed in its entirety. Approximately 60 were deemed to be relevant to our investigation (e.g., authenticity, sustainability, and countercultural movement) and analyzed further. Finally, secondary data on both Slow Food and Eataly (books, Websites, internal data) were collected for analysis.

Each interview, blog, or forum post was transcribed (resulting in 143 pages) and analyzed separately by each of the three researchers. The data were further coded and analyzed in tabular displays, using the main constructs from the literature (Spiggle, 1994). The adoption of a multiple method approach, the use of multiple data sources, and the triangulation among the three researchers strengthen the validity of the research findings.

The Eataly Formula

Eataly was founded by Oscar Farinetti in 2007 when he decided to transfer his experience in consumer electronics into a new retail concept, inspired by the changes affecting the sensitivity of conscious customers, as reflected by the

Slow Food movement and its principles. Eataly promotes products that are good and tasty, clean (because the company respects raw materials and guarantees transparent and traditional production processes), and fair (to ensure adequate margins for producers and affordable prices for customers). At Eataly, consumers can find an innovative combination of food shopping, restaurants, and training areas. Eataly defines itself as "the world's biggest food and wine market, where [people can] buy, taste, and learn about high-quality foods" (www.eataly.it). According to the founder, Eataly is a place where one can eat, buy, and learn at the same time. In contrast with other business models, Eataly neither enlarges the retailer core business with new services (as retailers have been doing over the past few years), nor aspires to enter the restaurant and fast food service business.

The success of the adopted business model is evident by the constant opening of new shops in both Italy and abroad (Milan, Rome, Bologna, Bari, and Genoa as well as Tokyo and New York), and Eataly is expected to have 25 branches by 2015.

MAIN FINDINGS

In this section, we present some of the main findings emerging from our two-stage research. In particular, we focus on the way in which the company and the movement collaborated and mutually adjusted to pursue a new venture. Moreover, we pinpoint how and to what extent the transformation was perceived by consumers and whether the community (and its more radical members) has accepted this form of compromise between the market and society.

The Movement's Constructive Role in Defining the Retail Formula and the Shopping Experience

The Slow Food movement has played a relevant role in establishing the Eataly business formula's main features. Eataly managers and Slow Food delegates spent more than two years working together to establish the main values and characteristics of the business models. Members of the social movement and Eataly shared the opportunity to create a new retailing formula able to enter the market, mediating between the mass market retail practices and the market niche of traditional snobbish boutiques of quality food. According to the narratives collected through the interviews with both Eataly and Slow Food managers, since the beginning, the interactions between Eataly and Slow Food have been an essential feature of the business formula.

By expressing its social role as a cultural movement, Slow Food members actively participated in the definition of the Eataly business idea and its operative interpretation. In this sense, the team promoted an assortment that was the result of their collection of suggestions from numerous Slow Food members from various local branches all over the world, called "Condotta." Moreover, the codes of conduct to select the main Eataly suppliers were co-developed.

The collaboration continued over time in order to associate other small producers of great food and wine who share the same concept of high quality at the core of the project. In keeping with the sustainability criterion of reducing transportation costs (kilometer zero), fresh produce is sourced from the surrounding areas. Where possible, the same logic applies to different categories as well as to the Japan and New York branches. In a sense, the made-in-Italy character and its apparent appeal to foreign markets are replaced by a different discourse that relates to fair and sustainable food production and distribution. Nowadays, a Slow Food representative still works at the Eataly headquarters to supervise new supplier selection during the company's territorial expansion in order to ensure continuity between Slow Food values and Eataly's assortments. As the heart of this collaboration, there is a strong sharing of intents between the movement and Eataly. The

opportunity to participate in generating a retailing solution that could fit modern distribution logics as well as the high quality of small boutiques help the Slow Food movement extend its principles to a larger mainstream market.

The stores' layouts and atmosphere were projected to support the common values belonging to Eataly and the Slow Food movement, drawing inspiration from the Tokyo fish market, the Berlin KaDeWe, Disneyland Paris, and the Paris Grand Épicerie as well as small biological markets. Many areas were built to re-create the atmospheres of traditional markets, with many stalls in which customers can touch, smell, and choose food. Educational areas and restaurants emphasize the communal nature of the consumption experience (Beverland & Farrelly, 2010) and foster wholesome food values. The shop is located in an old factory that previously produced Carpano, a traditional brand of spirits, thereby providing a good example of industrial restructuring. In the building, 11,000 square meters are dedicated to 11 small thematic restaurants (focused on cheese, pasta, ice-cream, etc.), 2500 square meters to sales (food, books, cooking tools, etc.), and 3200 square meters to educational areas, the Carpano Museum, and the conference room.

The in-store observations and interviews indicated how Eataly seeks to provide a fusion of traditions, cultures, and values embedded in a respectful relationship with food. Internal communication, which has a didactic bent, seeks to develop a sustainable, fair, and reliable relationship with the customer (McCraken, 1986; Mick & Buhl, 1992; Ballantyne, 2004). Shopping bags are made of fabric and are designed for re-use. There are no coupons or fidelity cards. There are no numbered tickets to facilitate queuing at the service counters. All of these characteristics are the result of the close interaction with the Slow Food movement and its philosophy. The partnership was not limited to the selection of products, but it expanded to include the choices in terms of communication in the market. The Slow Food team directly participated in the debate that generated the contents of the in-store communication (focused mainly on informing and educating the customers), thereby affecting the values transmitted through it, which are coherent with the Slow Food principles.

Aligning Consumers' Stances and Market Offering System

According to results of the survey, the respondents valued Eataly's range of products most, followed by the innovativeness of the initiative, the atmosphere, and the staff. Respondents' reasons for shopping at Eataly are ranked as follows:

1. Sustainability,
2. Slow Food certification,
3. Presentation and supplementary product information,
4. Staff support,
5. Product trials, and
6. Price.

From this perspective, Eataly is an attractive opportunity for consumers interested in the intrinsic qualities of food, its sustainability, and the support of critical consumption movements (e.g., Slow Food), adding further value to this offering through certification, even if they are not movement members.

Moreover, during the second stage of the research (in particular, interviews with consumers), it emerged that Eataly customers are well aware of the trade-off between resistance and mainstream marketing. Many consumers consider Eataly to be a compromise between radical forms of political consumption and innovative versions of a traditional supermarket. Some judge it positively whereas others do not. Generally speaking, Eataly's customers do not trust the commonly accepted mass market food distribution. They want authentic, local, sustainable, and ideologically acceptable produce, and they rely upon various

institutions when making purchases, including trade shows, purchase groups, and movements (e.g., Slow Food).

It is evident that consumers seek both the intrinsic properties of goods (Grayson & Martinec, 2004) and the more general properties of the production and consumption process (Beverland & Farrelly, 2010). Therefore, not only the products attract customers to Eataly, but also their involvement in the process that makes them feel as if the business differs from ordinary supermarkets. In this sense, there is a co-creative dimension in this process that appears coherent with the project developed by Eataly and the social movement. In order to appreciate the authenticity of what they buy, consumers need to be involved in a process in which they play an active role, feeling as if they are purchasing directly from the original producer (Arnould & Price, 2000; Grönroos, 2008).

Ultimately, the active involvement of a social movement, such as Slow Food, has enabled individuals and the movement itself to exert a significant influence on the adaptation of a mainstream formula to ethical stances.

Community, Movement Values, and Critical Consumers

During the exploratory stage, it was found that Eataly's loyal customers strongly identify with one another but they disidentify with traditional supermarket customers. Such associative/dissociative thoughts help define loyal Eataly customers' attitudes as well as those of customers who are more critical (Arnould & Price, 2000; McDonald et al., 2006; Rumbo, 2002). The important point here is that these perceptions and expectations are combined with the interaction between customers and the movement on one hand and the company on the other to generate a collaboration among Eataly, the Slow Food movement, and individual consumers – albeit at different levels and stages in the process – that created a new market form strongly rooted in ideology (Newholm & Shaw,

2007; Moraes et al., 2010). The research highlights that consumers' participation in and adhesion to the new venture are an individual matter empowered by this collective dimension.

However, the survey conducted in the first stage of our study identified discrepancies between Eataly's offerings and Slow Food members' broad perspective. Although no significant differences exist in the evaluation of the offerings' specific aspects (e.g., the sustainability of products) between Slow Food members and non-members, the former critically analyze the overall Eataly format. Only 30% of them believe that the Eataly formula is truly representative of the Slow Food philosophy, while approximately 90% of non-members think that the philosophy and the offering are compatible.

Examining the reasons for these results in greater depth, the second stage of our research pointed out that many critical customers visiting Eataly perceived ineffectiveness compared to other institutions, scarcity of sustainability, and excessive business exploitation in the Eataly formula. This appears coherent with findings from previous studies (Bekin et al., 2005; Dalli & Corciolani, 2008; Thompson & Sinha, 2008), which indicated that radical community members do not accept the purist form of commercialization, even if it can generate more attention for critical consumption among mainstream consumers (Kozinets & Handelman, 2004).

The literature holds that, under similar conditions (Thompson & Coskuner-Balli, 2007), community members have the power to counteract corporate co-options by moving their consumption practices away from the market. With respect to Eataly, the situation is slightly different as the community is intimately connected to the company and detachment from it does not seem possible or likely. However, some rigorous Slow Food members do visit Eataly, even if only occasionally, and seem to be pleased by the positive outcomes of this venture in the mainstream market in terms of a new sensitivity to food culture and value expressed by traditional consumers. In a sense, it

seems that transformation occurs in both corporate activities and counter-cultural movements (Dalli & Corciolani, 2008), in which a process of the moderation of radical thinking arises given the positive trade-off between the loss of some of the original rigor while gaining a more emancipated, genuine, and sustainable consumption mode by mainstream consumers as well as a more authentic food production mode. Nevertheless, some of these "radical" consumers maintain their beliefs and rely on purchasing groups and individual practices to pursue authenticity and sustainability in its purest form.

CONCLUSION AND FURTHER RESEARCH

Eataly represents the result of an innovative partnership between corporate power and a consumer movement that directly supports and validates the company's market offerings. Figure 2 summarizes Eataly's early history, highlighting the evolution of the relationship with individual consumers, the *social movement*, and its more radical members.

As highlighted in our research, the originality of Eataly's offering system is grounded in various elements–namely, product properties, strong relationships with small local manufacturers, reliance on traditional production and consumption practices, and ideological determinants. Consumers' stances find a response in two of Eataly's main dimensions: the intrinsic properties of goods and the process of consumer involvement in the process of "creating" authentic consumption and shopping experiences (Arnould & Price, 2000; Beverland & Farrelly, 2010; Grayson & Martinec, 2004). Our data indicated that both of these dimensions are important and dependent on one another.

Eataly is a unique case of an innovative business model induced by anti-consumption. In this case, detachment from mainstream marketing and distribution has turned into a new venture supported and validated by consumers both directly

Figure 2. The evolution of Eataly

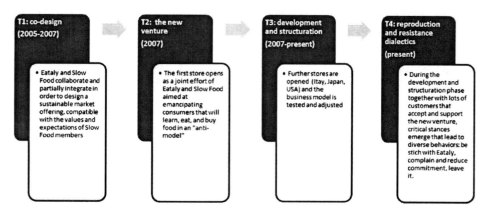

(as customers) and indirectly (as members of the Slow Food movement). Data show how important this involvement is for consumers' identity projects as they feel committed and identify with Eataly as both a form of resistance toward mainstream marketing and distribution as well as a form of constructive involvement in the new venture (Ballantine & Creery, 2010; Cherrier, 2007, 2009a).

In this sense, Eataly appears to be an original and promising form of corporate-movement interaction when compared to those addressed in the literature (Thompson & Coskuner-Balli, 2007). In fact, the co-evolution of Eataly and the Slow Food movement in this initiative has involved the company's adaptation to Slow Food members' expectations as well to Slow Food executives' explicit requirements. As a result, Eataly can attract a mixed group of customers by educating ordinary consumers and Slow Food members. Yet some of the more radical Slow Food members and highly critical consumers take issue with Eataly's commercial nature and distance themselves from it, even if they occasionally acknowledge its positive effects in terms of mainstream consumers' education toward a more authentic and sustainable model of consumption. Contrary to other cases considered in the literature (Thompson & Coskuner-Balli, 2007), only individual detachment occurs, whereas the movement (Slow Food) as a whole is still well integrated into the Eataly initiative.

The original point of the Eataly case is that this divergence does not emerge as a juxtapositioning of the community and corporate power, as was the case in previous studies, but as one group in the community on one side while the rest of the community together with the company is on the other side. This result is preliminary, and we have improved our research design to better understand the power discourse developing under the surface of an original and successful alliance between a critical movement and a company.

As highlighted in the previous sections, the Eataly experience shows that there is room for a coordinated effort between corporate power and collective stances, mediated by social movements, with regard to critical consumption. It is possible to mediate between a profit-and-loss logic and a socio-cultural demand for authentic and sustainable food (Sebastiani et al., 2013). At Eataly, this occurs at the expense of some rigor within the organization of the shop, and radical Slow Food members see problems in the mainstreaming process and in this formula's elitist image. However, ethical consumers have the opportunity (and the convenience) to find the right products in the same context without cruising the countryside in a search for authentic food. Indeed, a growing number of mainstream consumers have the opportunity to obtain sustainable products and appreciate the benefits of more ethically minded consumption. The case analyzed offers fruitful suggestions for existing retailers as well, as they can look at Eataly's experience to rethink their business models, aligning them more with critical stances expressed by social movements.

Ultimately, Eataly's study thus far suggests that there are opportunities for movements and companies to collaborate not only on the development of new business ventures with more critical concerns, but also on the business model transformation of existing retailers, which could lead to consumers' expectations being met at various levels, such as the intrinsic properties of goods and services, consumer involvement in the co-production of the shopping experience, and community certification and support. However, this experience shows that–even in these conditions–some consumers have expressed criticism and detachment. The questions that still need to be answered are related to the medium and long-term effects of such criticism within the community: Will dissatisfied members of the social movement question their participation in and support of it? Will they quit? Will they reduce their involvement and turn their attention toward other forms of collective action? More time and further research efforts are necessary to answer these questions.

REFERENCES

Arnould, E. J., & Price, L. L. (2000). Authenticating Acts and Authoritative Performances: Questing for Self and Community. In D. G. Mick, S. Ratneshwar, & C. Huffman (Eds.), *The Why of Consumption: Contemporary Perspectives on Consumer Motives, Goals and Desires* (pp. 140–163). London: Routledge.

Arnould, E. J., & Thompson, C. J. (2005). Consumer Culture Theory (Cct), Twenty Years of Research. *The Journal of Consumer Research, 31*(4), 868–882. doi:10.1086/426626

Ballantine, P. W., & Creery, S. (2010). The Consumption and Disposition Behaviour of Voluntary Simplifiers. *Journal of Consumer Behaviour, 9*(1), 45–56. doi:10.1002/cb.302

Ballantyne, D. (2004). Dialogue and its role in the development of relationship specific knowledge. *Journal of Business and Industrial Marketing, 19*(2), 114–123. doi:10.1108/08858620410523990

Bekin, C., Carrigan, M., & Szmigin, I. (2005). Defying Marketing Sovereignty: Voluntary Simplicity at New Consumption Communities. *Qualitative Market Research: An International Journal, 8*(4), 413–429. doi:10.1108/13522750510619779

Beverland, M. B., & Farrelly, F. J. (2010). The Quest for Authenticity in Consumption: Consumers' Purposive Choice of Authentic Cues to Shape Experienced Outcomes. *The Journal of Consumer Research, 36*(5), 838–856. doi:10.1086/615047

Buechler, S. M. (2010). *Understanding Social Movements: Theories from the Classical Era to the Present*. Boulder, CO: Paradigm Publishers.

Carducci, V. (2006). Culture Jamming: A Sociological Perspective. *Journal of Consumer Culture, 6*(1), 116–139. doi:10.1177/1469540506062722

Cherrier, H. (2007). Ethical Consumption Practices: Co-Production of Self-Expression and Social Recognition. *Journal of Consumer Behaviour, 6*(5), 321–335. doi:10.1002/cb.224

Cherrier, H. (2009a). Anti-Consumption Discourses and Consumer-Resistant Identities. *Journal of Business Research, 62*(2), 181–190. doi:10.1016/j.jbusres.2008.01.025

Cherrier, H. (2009b). Disposal and Simple Living: Exploring the Circulation of Goods and the Development of Sacred Consumption. *Journal of Consumer Behaviour, 8*(6), 327–339. doi:10.1002/cb.297

Cova, B., & Dalli, D. (2009). Working Consumers: The Next Step in Marketing Theory? *Marketing Theory*, *9*(3), 315–339. doi:10.1177/1470593109338144

Cova, B., Kozinets, R. V., & Shankar, A. (Eds.). (2007). *Consumer Tribes*. Burlington, MA: Butterworth-Heinemann.

Creswell, J. W. (2003). *Research Design: Qualitative, Quantitative, and Mixed Method Approaches*. Thousand Oaks, CA: Sage Publications.

Creswell, J. W., & Plano Clark, V. L. (2007). *Designing and Conducting Mixed Methods Research*. Thousand Oaks, CA: Sage Publications.

Dalli, D., & Corciolani, M. (2008). Collective Forms of Resistance: The Transformative Power of Moderate Communities: Evidence from the Bookcrossing Case. *International Journal of Market Research*, *50*(6), 757–775. doi:10.2501/S1470785308200195

Davis, D. F., Golicic, S. L., & Boerstler, C. N. (2010). Benefits and Challenges of Conducting Multiple Methods Research in Marketing. *Journal of the Academy of Marketing Science*, *39*(3), 467–479. doi:10.1007/s11747-010-0204-7

Desmond, J., McDonagh, P., & O'Donohoe, S. (2000). Counter-Culture and Consumer Society. *Consumption. Markets & Culture*, *4*(4), 241–279. doi:10.1080/10253866.2000.9670358

Firat, A. F., & Venkatesh, A. (1995). Liberatory Postmodernism and the Reenchantment of Consumption. *The Journal of Consumer Research*, *22*(3), 239–267. doi:10.1086/209448

Grayson, K., & Martinec, R. (2004). Consumer Perceptions of Iconicity and Indexicality and Their Influence on Assessments of Authentic Market Offerings. *The Journal of Consumer Research*, *31*(2), 296–312. doi:10.1086/422109

Grönroos, C. (2008). Service Logic Revisited: Who Creates Value? And Who Co-Creates? *European Business Review*, *20*(4), 298–314. doi:10.1108/09555340810886585

Heath, J., & Potter, A. (2005). *Nations of Rebels: How the Counter Culture Became Consumer Culture*. New York: Harper Business.

Hollenbeck, C. R., & Zinkhan, G. M. (2010). Anti-Brand Communities, Negotiation of Brand Meaning, and the Learning Process: The Case of Wal-Mart. *Consumption. Markets & Culture*, *13*(3), 325–345. doi:10.1080/10253861003787056

Holt, D. B. (2002). Why Do Brands Cause Trouble? A Dialectical Theory of Consumer Culture and Branding. *The Journal of Consumer Research*, *29*(1), 70–90. doi:10.1086/339922

Kniazeva, M., & Venkatesh, A. (2007). Food for Thought: A Study of Food Consumption in Postmodern Us Culture. *Journal of Consumer Behaviour*, *6*(6), 419–435. doi:10.1002/cb.232

Kotler, P. (1986). The prosumer movement: A new challenge for marketers. *Advances in Consumer Research. Association for Consumer Research (U. S.)*, *13*(1), 510–513.

Kozinets, R. V. (2007). Inno-Tribes: Star Trek as Wikimedia. In B. Cova, R. V. Kozinets, & A. Shankar (Eds.), *Consumer Tribes*. Burlington, MA: Butterwoth -Heinemann.

Kozinets, R. V., & Handelman, J. M. (2004). Adversaries of Consumption: Consumer Movements, Activism, and Ideology. *The Journal of Consumer Research*, *31*(3), 691–704. doi:10.1086/425104

Lee, M. S. W., Fernandez, K. V., & Hyman, M. R. (2009). Anti-Consumption: An Overview and Research Agenda. *Journal of Business Research*, *62*(2), 145–147. doi:10.1016/j.jbusres.2008.01.021

Leigh, T. W., Peters, C., & Shelton, J. (2006). The Consumer Quest for Authenticity: The Multiplicity of Meanings within the Mg Subculture of Consumption. *Journal of the Academy of Marketing Science, 34*(4), 481–493. doi:10.1177/0092070306288403

McCracken, G. (1986). Culture and Consumption: A Theoretical Account of the Structure and Movement of the Cultural Meaning of Consumer Goods. *The Journal of Consumer Research, 13*(1), 71–84. doi:10.1086/209048

McDonald, S., Oates, C. J., Young, C. W., & Hwang, K. (2006). Toward Sustainable Consumption: Researching Voluntary Simplifiers. *Psychology and Marketing, 23*(6), 515–534. doi:10.1002/mar.20132

Micheletti, M. (2003). *Political Virtue and Shopping: Individuals, Consumerism, and Collective Action.* New York: Palgrave Macmillan. doi:10.1057/9781403973764

Mick, D. G., & Buhl, C. (1992). A Meaning-Based Model of Advertising Experiences. *The Journal of Consumer Research, 19*(3), 317–338. doi:10.1086/209305

Moraes, C., Szmigin, I., & Carrigan, M. (2010). Living Production-Engaged Alternatives: An Examination of New Consumption Communities. *Consumption Markets & Culture, 13*(3), 273–298. doi:10.1080/10253861003787015

Neilson, L. A. (2010). Boycott or Buycott? Understanding Political Consumerism. *Journal of Consumer Behaviour, 9*(3), 214–227. doi:10.1002/cb.313

Newholm, T., & Shaw, D. (2007). Studying the Ethical Consumer: A Review of Research. *Journal of Consumer Behaviour, 6*(5), 253–270. doi:10.1002/cb.225

Peñaloza, L., & Venkatesh, A. (2006). Further Evolving the New Dominant Logic of Marketing: From Services to the Social Construction of Markets. *Marketing Theory, 6*(3), 299–316. doi:10.1177/1470593106066789

Rumbo, J. D. (2002). Consumer Resistance in a World of Advertising Clutter: The Case of Adbusters. *Psychology and Marketing, 19*(2), 127–148. doi:10.1002/mar.10006

Schaefer, A., & Crane, A. (2005). Addressing Sustainability and Consumption. *Journal of Macromarketing, 25*(1), 76–92. doi:10.1177/0276146705274987

Sebastiani, R., Montagnini, F., & Dalli, D. (2013). Ethical Consumption and New Business Models in the Food Industry: Evidence from the Eataly Case. *Journal of Business Ethics, 114*(3), 473–488. doi:10.1007/s10551-012-1343-1

Spiggle, S. (1994). Analysis and Interpretation of Qualitative Data in Consumer Research. *The Journal of Consumer Research, 21*(3), 491. doi:10.1086/209413

Tashakkori, A., & Teddlie, C. (1998). *Mixed Methodology: Combining Qualitative and Quantitative Approaches.* Thousand Oaks, CA: Sage Publication.

Thompson, C. J., & Coskuner-Balli, G. (2007). Countervailing Market Responses to Corporate Co-Optation and the Ideological Recruitment of Consumption Communities. *The Journal of Consumer Research, 34*(2), 135–152. doi:10.1086/519143

Thompson, S. A., & Sinha, R. K. (2008). Brand Communities and New Product Adoption: The Influence and Limits of Oppositional Loyalty. *Journal of Marketing, 72*(6), 65–80. doi:10.1509/jmkg.72.6.65

ADDITIONAL READING

Askegaard, S., & Kjeldgaard, D. (2007). Here, There, and Everywhere: Place Branding and Gastronomical Globalization in a Macromarketing Perspective. *Journal of Macromarketing, 27*(2), 138–147. doi:10.1177/0276146707300068

Bardhi, F., Ostberg, J., & Bengtsson, A. (2010). Negotiating Cultural Boundaries: Food, Travel and Consumer Identities. *Consumption. Markets & Culture, 13*(2), 133–157. doi:10.1080/10253860903562148

den Hond, F., & de Bakker, F. G. A. (2007). Ideologically motivated activism: How activist groups influence corporate social change activities. *Academy of Management Review, 32*(3), 901–924. doi:10.5465/AMR.2007.25275682

Denegri-Knott, J., Zwick, D., & Schroeder, J. E. (2006). Mapping consumer power: An integrative framework for marketing and consumer research. *European Journal of Marketing, 40*(9–10), 950–971. doi:10.1108/03090560610680952

Farinetti, O. (2009). *Coccode*. Milano: Giunti.

Ger, G. (1999). Localizing in the Global Village: Local Firms Competing in Global Markets. *California Management Review, 41*(4), 64–83. doi:10.2307/41166010

Hollenbeck, C. R., & Zinkhan, G. M. (2006). Consumer Activism on the Internet: The Role of Anti-Brand Communities. *Advances in Consumer Research. Association for Consumer Research (U. S.), 33*(1), 479–485.

Holzer, B. (2006). Political consumerism between individual choice and collective action: Social movements, role mobilization and signalling. *International Journal of Consumer Studies, 30*(5), 405–415. doi:10.1111/j.1470-6431.2006.00538.x

Kozinets, R. V., Handelman, J. M., & Lee, M. S. W. (2010). Don't Read This, or, Who Cares What the Hell Anti-Consumption Is, Anyways? *Consumption Markets & Culture, 13*(3), 225–233. doi:10.1080/10253861003786918

Micheletti, M., Føllesdal, A., & Stolle, D. (2004). *Politics, Products, and Markets: Exploring Political Consumerism Past and Present*. New Brunswick, N.J.: Transaction Publishers.

Muñiz, A. M., & Schau, H. J. (2005). Religiosity in the Abandoned Apple Newton Brand Community. *The Journal of Consumer Research, 31*(4), 737–747. doi:10.1086/426607

Peterson, R. A. (2005). In Search of Authenticity. *Journal of Management Studies, 42*(5), 1083–1098. doi:10.1111/j.1467-6486.2005.00533.x

Petrini, C. (2005). *Buono, pulito e giusto: Principi di nuova gastronomia*. Torino: Einaudi.

Petrini, C., & Padovani, G. (2006). *Slow Food Revolution: A New Culture for Eating and Living*. New York: Rizzoli.

Pietrykowski, B. (2009). *The Political Economy of Consumer Behaviour: Contesting Consumption*. New York: Routledge.

Shankar, A., Cherrier, H., & Canniford, R. (2006). Consumer Empowerment: A Foucauldian Interpretation. *European Journal of Marketing, 40*(9/10), 1013–1030. doi:10.1108/03090560610680989

Sims, R. (2009). Food, Place and Authenticity: Local Food and the Sustainable Tourism Experience. *Journal of Sustainable Tourism, 17*, 321–336. doi:10.1080/09669580802359293

Tencati, A., & Zslonai, L. (2012). Collaborative enterprise and sustainability: The case of slow food. *Journal of Business Ethics, 110*(3), 345–354. doi:10.1007/s10551-011-1178-1

Thompson, C. J. (2004). Marketplace Mythology and Discourses of Power. *The Journal of Consumer Research, 31*(1), 162–180. doi:10.1086/383432

Wilk, R. R. (2006). *Fast Food/Slow Food: The Cultural Economy of the Global Food System.* Lanham, MD: Altamira Press.

KEY TERMS AND DEFINITIONS

Business Model Innovation: Innovation regarding one or more interlocked constituent parts of a business model–customer value proposition, profit model, key processes and/or key resources.

Collective Identity: Individual's cognitive, moral and emotional connection with a broader community that may form part of a personal identity.

Counter-Culture: Coherent system of norms and values that not only differ from those of the dominant system, but also comprise at least one norm or value that calls for commitment to cultural change – that is, a transformation of the dominant system of norms and values.

Customer Experience: The internal and subjective response customers have to any direct or indirect contact with a company. It is holistic in nature and involves the customer's cognitive, affective, emotional, social and physical responses to multiple stimuli that are only partially under the company's control.

Eataly: New retail concept founded by Oscar Farinetti in 2007 in collaboration with Slow Food. Its original formula allows consumers to be active participants in an innovative food and beverage experience where they shop, taste and learn about high quality traditional Italian food products and beverages along with local produce and artisanal products.

Slow Food: Social movement founded in Italy in 1989 to counteract fast food and a fast life, as well as the disappearance of local food traditions, by promoting "good, clean, and fair" food.

Social Movement: Collectivity acting with some continuity to promote or resist a change in the society or organization of which it is a part.

Chapter 19
Meanings and Implications of Corporate Social Responsibility and Branding in Grocer Retailers:
A Comparative Study over Italy and the UK

Elena Candelo
University of Turin, Italy

Cecilia Casalegno
University of Turin, Italy

Chiara Civera
University of Turin, Italy

ABSTRACT

The chapter demonstrates the extent to which companies operating in the Retailing Grocery industry use Corporate Social Responsibility (CSR) as driver to enhance their brand and pursue commercial value, or to purely redefine their business priorities in accordance to evolving consumers' needs and expectations by making CSR a new concrete business model and evolving towards the concept of Corporate Shared Value (CSV). The study is addressed to analyse the matter of facts in two different European geographical areas: Italy and United Kingdom, chosen because of the peculiar approaches in companies' attitude towards CSR and CSV, ultimately. Many differences and some relevant similarities in the implementation of CSV as new strategic model between the countries have emerged, with UK showing the most formalized and standardized integration between social and economic value within its Grocer Retailer companies' business activities.

DOI: 10.4018/978-1-4666-6074-8.ch019

BACKGROUND

Many authors consider responsible, ethical, philanthropic and sustainable behaviours to be effective routes companies can take to reach their markets and meet their consumers' needs successfully (Torres *et al.,* 2012; De Pedro & Gilabert, 2012; Vallaster *et al.,* 2012; Kuepfer & Papula, 2010; Macleod, 2001; Mohr *et al.,* 2001). All the actions conducted within the above mentioned fields are commonly defined with the name of Corporate Social Responsibility (defined within the chapter to as CSR) and have started being actively implemented by companies for the last three decades. As the for-profit world has started realizing the importance of playing a role as good citizen in the society (Carrol, 1991; Ahmed & Machold, 2004) and adjusting their whole organizational culture (Schein, 2010; Pringle *et al.,* 1988) according to a responsible way of doing business that creates value also for the society, the concept of Corporate Social Responsibility has evolved towards the creation of Corporate Shared Value (defined within the chapter to as CSV) (Porter & Kramer, 2011).

Implementing a model based on Corporate Shared Value means for companies undertaking a set of profitable activities that move beyond the trade-off between business and social concerns, to buster companies' competitiveness while improving at the same time economic value and the conditions of the society their activities directly or indirectly impact on (Porter & Kramer, 2011). In order to share the value they create, companies need to communicate their responsible, ethical, philanthropic and sustainable actions in a coherent way and integrate CSV with the other marketing activities that include branding, and so set up an *Integrated marketing communication* strategy (Schultz *et al.,* 1993; Krugman *et al.,* 1994; Duncan & Mulhern, 2004; Belch, Belch, 2009).

The necessity of integrating communication levers is perceived by companies as the most effective and strategic way to recognize their business a

reason to exist, and this is undisputed especially in crisis periods (Casalegno *et al.,* 2012), when new concerns drive consumers towards more responsible and coherent choices, as far as both economic and intrinsic value of products and companies are concerned. In the specific case of Grocer Retailers, for instance, consumers are nowadays looking for tangible benefits belonging to the implementation of Corporate Shared Value: when CSV domain directly affects their actual experience with the company or company's private labels they tend to modify their shopping behaviour (trendwatching. com) and may be willing to pay higher prices if the purchase is justified by a good cause (Cause Related Marketing) (Demetriou, Papasolomou, & Vrontis, 2009) or the product simply acts in the best interest of society.

It is here that the relation between branding and Corporate Social Responsibility becomes crucial to understand the way in which companies are actually implementing the model of Corporate Shared Value. IN particular, whether CSR activities actually and purely aim at improving both society wellbeing and economic conditions or they are just addressed to help differentiating strategically companies' image related to their business operations (La Cour & Kromann, 2011) and obtain the competitive advantages (Porter & Kramer, 2002) for maximizing their profits (Friedman, 1970). In particular, which activities carried out within CSR really belong to the pure altruism of individuals running the company (Maple, 2008) and which ones just represent "an intellectual sloppy and trendy diversion from rigorous economic and institutional analysis" (Robins, 2005)?

INTRODUCTION

The general aim of the chapter is to analyse the meanings and innovative implications of Corporate Social Responsibility (CSR) strategies and policies adopted by grocer Retailers operating in two different European countries: Italy and United

Kingdom. In particular, the study seeks to serve three main purposes:

- To analyze the relation between Corporate Social Responsibility and Branding within companies' *Integrated marketing communication* strategy and therefore, to explore the real nature and implications of CSR strategies, which can be connected to the brand equity enhancement, to a pure altruistic and social vision or just to a mix of the two as practical redefinition of business priorities defined to as Corporate Shared Value;
- To highlight how CSR has evolved towards the concept of Corporate Shared Value and, according to an extensive review of the literature, build a framework on CSV which groups together and describes the set of mixed activities undertaken by companies with the aim of combining and improving both social and economic value at the same time;
- To investigate the extent to which Grocer Retailers are evolving towards the implementation of Corporate Shared Value by considering also its level of integration within companies' brand and business strategies and compare the matter of facts between Italy and the United Kingdom.

The chapter follows the deductive approach of research, whose logic is to start with theoretical assumptions that are going to be accepted or rejected by the empirical evidence (Bryaman, 2004). Accordingly, the study is structured and divided in three main parts with the purpose of accomplish the objectives of the research.

The first part titled "CSR and communication" includes an extensive review of the literature that describes the relation between Corporate Social Responsibility and branding and points out their interaction within the Integrated marketing communication strategy that leads to the evolutionary

model of Corporate Shared Value. The aim of this section is to underline the impact of CSR as communication strategy that permeates multiple and mixed communication channels, including the physical one (the point of sale), with different meanings, purposes and implications, for the business itself and the reference audience or stakeholders.

The second part "The evolution of Corporate Social Responsibility: Corporate Shared Value as new strategic model" is designed and addressed to analyse the evolution Corporate Social Responsibility theory towards the model of Corporate Shared Value. Moreover, to draw a standardized and common framework of Corporate Shared Value based on several academic and business sources and researches; it will include all the activities companies carry out within social and economic purposes in order to figure out which ones of them are more to enhance the brand image and which others are, in fact, built to serve social purpose while reaching *shared value*. The framework seeks to be comprehensive of all the activities conducted with both social and economic intents and therefore includes all the original and traditional activities always identified with the name of Corporate Social Responsibility, it reclassifies them in different dimensions and adds also products, services and processes development as actions leading to the shared value creation.

In particular, the scheme of Corporate Shared Value - identified within the chapter with the name of *"CSV dimensions and activities"* - takes into account three main dimensions:

- **Accountability:** Referred to how companies communicate and give evidence of their behaviour towards Corporate Social Responsibility;
- **Corporate Philanthropy:** It includes all the activities carried out in order to respond to the community needs by supporting third sector projects of social interest;

- **Ethics and Sustainability:** It is the dimension strictly related to the combination of environmental, societal and ethical concerns in processes, goods/products and services development.

The Corporate Shared Value framework has been built with the double intent of:

- OFFERING a better understanding over the real meanings of each activity, which is generally and simply defined under the name of CSR, but is, in fact, part of a more complex strategy with multiple objectives, some of which are clearly connected to a commercial and economic return;
- WORKING as standardized scheme to be applied to each of the Grocer Retailers operating in the countries at issue and part of the investigated sample in order to analyse their attitude and reasons driving towards the implementation of a Corporate Shared Value model.

As output of the literature review, the scheme on "CSV dimensions and activities" will function as tool to build the case studies for the practical observations.

Eventually, the third and last part titled "A compared analysis between United Kingdom and Italy" is addressed to the empirical analysis on a sample of six (6) Grocer Retailer companies, three (3) operating in Italy and three (3) from UK chosen among the biggest within the countries and the most involved (top spenders) in Corporate Philanthropy and investigated through the *case study* method of research (Yin, 2003). The aim is to investigate their behaviours and attitudes towards Corporate Shared Value and test whether the assumptions emerged from the literature review

are valid or not, depending on the specificities of the companies at issue and varying from country to country. The comparative analysis between the two countries strives to underline how socio-economic situation, institutional and historical settings, culture, religion, beliefs, preferences, and availability of information affect Grocer Retailers' approach towards Corporate Social Responsibility, Philanthropy and Corporate Shared Value ultimately, regarding chosen activities, the communication of them and the real purposes behind them. Italy and United Kingdom are peculiar so, because despite the general settings of the two present quite similar features in terms, for instance, of population and gross domestic product, the cultural environment in which CSR and philanthropy have been developed looks quite different and interesting.

The theoretical framework on *CSV dimensions and activities* will be applied to each of the investigated Grocer Retailer, in order to give an overview of the implemented activities and the reasons that drive their choices. The case study for each company will be designed and developed by gathering qualitative information to investigate, such as: the characterizations of CSR policy including its level of formalization, the governance and structure of CSR within the company, the CSV adopted activities and objectives, the meaning and purposes of their strategy for Philanthropy including tools implemented to pursue it.

The chapter is designed to function both as theoretical framework for describing the innovative approach of Corporate Shared Value and understanding the implications coming from the inclusion of such model within the business strategy, and as empirical analysis, with the intent of using the developed theory to investigate Grocer Retailers' CSV approach by comparing the matter of facts between Italy and the UK.

CSR AND COMMUNICATION

Communicating through Corporate Social Responsibility

As primary goal of any business, consumers influence and, are affected by, companies' values, beliefs, behaviours and their communication ultimately. Many factors (such as globalization, fast development of information and communication technologies, economic and financial crisis) have contributed, on one hand, to increase consumers' awareness and expectations towards products and services they buy and, on the other hand, have pushed companies to re-think about their offer, their social and environmental impacts and to build a new system of values which responds to the reference community and the society at large.

According to the 2013 Consumer Trend Report (2), nowadays products are asked to give back a specific set of expected and shared values. They need to be more than transparent to their audience, to become "naked" in communicating concrete and tangible benefits that go beyond the merely purpose a product is supposed to serve. "Brands' wishes will be consumers' command" (Consumer Trend Report, 2013) and, in this sense, consumers keep driving companies' choices in the establishment of a new vision, new business models, products and services and coherent ways of advertising and creating marketing campaigns. The necessity of building up a coherent and integrated communication strategy is a feeling shared among all the stakeholders as extended audience of any corporation (Kliatchko, 2008). Consequently, companies need to leverage on constant factors and communicate simultaneously to different targets with different schemes; in other words, to create a synergy among communication channels (Belch & Belch, 2009), because the effect resulting from their integration is more powerful than any single undertaken communication action.

As a result, coherence represents the driver of communication and helps creating the expected reputation for companies; according to this perspective, over the last three decades Corporate Social Responsibility (CSR) has started playing also this role, to become one of the most effective internal and external way of communicating homogenization and alignment between activities and values within any company's business strategy.

As the Figure 1 shows, CSR (here defined as "ethics") is used to share principles and beliefs outside and inside the company; it is addressed to an ideal level involving the entire group of stakeholders, to the interpersonal one strictly

Figure 1. Ethics in companies' communication
Source: adapted from Casalegno, 2012

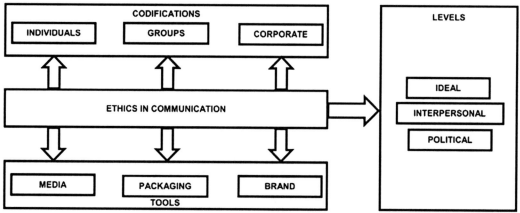

connected to the sharing of company's values and, eventually, to the political sphere in which CSR actually becomes a driver for companies' strategic and practical decisions.

As far as CSR communication tools and means are concerned, the brand, the packaging and the media constitutes the major vehicles to run a coherent communication campaign in which principles and shared values can represent effective levers for competitive advantage and can likewise talk to an audience that is not simply persuaded by paid communication activities - such as the advertising, for instance - but more and more by the ethical characterizations and social concerns contained in products and expressed by companies. Accordingly, consumers are positively affected by companies that are able to transform their communication strategy into an integrated model addressed both to commercial purposes and social improvements (Kliatchko, 2008).

Therefore, since the brand is certainly one of the main levers companies own to communicate their shared values to the reference society and stakeholders, the next paragraph is addressed to theoretically demonstrate the configuration of a brand strategy when it is intended to establish a valuable relation with Corporate Social Responsibility.

Successful Brand Strategies Incorporate Corporate Social Responsibility

The growing need of companies to differentiate themselves from competitors and build their own reputation by improving customer loyalty, combined with changes in the technological and social environment imposes profound changes in brand strategies. These changes determine the need to rethink strategies, actions and tools to manage the brand image and make it successful.

The growth in the number of branded products and the consequent growth of the intensity of communication activities increase the difficulty of differentiating products by leveraging on tangible items. Companies hold consumers through a brand image, due to the extreme difficulty in winning them over through completely new products (Aaker, 1996). In some cases the difference between the various offers of the same product (of various companies) is minimal and brand becomes the only factor of differentiation. It is therefore necessary to understand the reasons why consumers give their preference to a brand among the many offers available. First of all, a brand that offers values and communicates principles behind companies' activities in addition to the merely intrinsic tangible characteristics of the product, is able to create more loyalty among customers than the simple product does (Aaker, 2004b).

Therefore, it seems evident that consumers obtain a number of intangible benefits (such as identification, gratification and, social acceptance) from the brand, whose importance is often superior to the purpose of the product itself. Brand becomes a vehicle to influence the perception of quality and to add value to the product.

The success of a company's brand (Blombäck et al., 2012) is determined by a set of requirements (Aaker, 2004a; 2009; Balmer, 2008), which include Corporate Social Responsibility in accordance to a changing world perspective. Basically, companies connect the brand with the new trends arising among the society in general: environmental, social and economic sustainability are part of them. It is then extremely necessary to have consistency between the values associated with the brand and those transmitted by the behaviour of the company as a whole; any dystonia between companies' behaviour and brand identity is at risk of being immediately put in evidence and used against the company itself, with negative repercussions both on the brand image and on the customers' loyalty to the brand.

Evidence shows that a large proportion of consumers in Western markets (Allen & Root, 2004) bases their opinion on the brand considering also company's ethics, environmental impacts and Corporate Social Responsibility, confirming that brand reputation is as important as brand awareness to create a coherent identity (Aaker, 1996; 2009; Wheeler, 2009; Christodoulides *et al.*, 2011). Accordingly, as a system connected and tied to its environment, the company needs to create a relationship between corporate brand and the community the target belongs to. Brand is required to receive a kind of social legitimacy (Werther & Chandler, 2005) and this happens when the company is aligned to the behaviour rules built over time by the society and commonly accepted. It is here that Corporate Social Responsibility and brand appear to be closely interconnected.

CSR affects both the social legitimacy and the stakeholders perceptions thus impacts on the financial results of the company (Werther & Chandler, 2005). In this sense, profit maximization and CSR seem to become increasingly interconnected as well: social concerns incorporated into the brand strategies of the company allow the company itself to sustain its competitive advantages on a long term.

From the brand strategy point of view, the activities carried out within CSR should somehow be made visible inside and outside the company to create brand associations. The ways are numerous. Not necessarily the choice is communicating through the media, but in many the generation of a positive word-of-mouth represent a free and effective solution. This is the case of strategic philanthropy (Porter & Kramer, 2002) that companies implement to get visibility and benefit in a win-win situation (for the companies and for the social cause they are supporting).

Building a relationship between brand and CSR is important to strengthen customers' loyalty but, considering CSR popularity and complexity, isn't it time for it to become more than just a set of values to be communicated through the brand and become, instead, translated in a new strategic model as natural outcome of companies' social concerns and consumers' expectations?

THE EVOLUTION OF CORPORATE SOCIAL RESPONSIBILITY: CORPORATE SHARED VALUE AS NEW STRATEGIC MODEL

As a set of non-business oriented actions addressed to temporarily improve companies' behaviour and give them a voice within the social debate, Corporate Social Responsibility is not a new concept for them. Nowadays CSR is largely being strengthened to include a concrete set of tools and planned activities addressed to solve social and environmental issues with positive repercussions on the reference community and ultimately on the existent and potential consumers, focusing also on the financial sustainability every company strives for. It is, in other words, a new way of positioning business and relations with community by using ethical drivers (Macleod, 2001; Mohr *et al.*, 2001; Kuepfer & Papula, 2010).

Corporate Social Responsibility is becoming part of companies' main mission and therefore the strategy seems to embrace more complicated levers and activities that deal at the same time with social, economic and commercial purposes. The issue is whether this ethical and social actions combined with the business strategy can actually be considered a new business model for companies or just an effective lever of marketing and communication (La Kour & Kromann, 2011; Maple, 2008; Porter & Kramer, 2002; Robins, 2005).

Reasons driving Corporate Social Responsibility to a new business model development raise issues of different kind and the dilemma is not of an easy solution: what appears clear is that CSR needs to impose itself as a new *corporate mindset* with its own strategic implications (Kim *et al.*, 2011); in other words, it needs to evolve towards a Corporate Shared Value (CSV) model implementation (Porter & Kramer, 2011).

Despite the multiple conceptualizations of CSR and the fact that a single definition has yet to be accepted (Vallaster *et al.*, 2012), it is possible to refer to one that describes the authors' perception toward CSR as a "a cross-functioning management tool which aims at achieving long term goals by fostering voluntary companies' multi-stakeholders relationships" (Freeman & Phillips, 2002; Civera & Musso, 2012).

Starting from the above definition, the authors have tried to enrich the meaning of CSR towards CSV by grouping together all the traditional activities carried out within the name of CSR (Civera & Musso, 2012) and add those more connected to the company's business activities, which have a clear social purpose as well (such the ethical products development).

As the Table 1 shows, the three main dimensions of Corporate Shared Value include the activities generally implemented by companies when developing social and ethical strategies that also have profitable goals:

- **Accountability:** It refers to how companies communicate and give evidence of their behaviour concerning different subjects such as quality, environment, occupational safety and health, human rights and social responsibility through the voluntary adoption of International Standards and Norms or the Adherence to National or International Standards.

- **Corporate Philanthropy:** It includes all the activities carried out in order to respond to the community needs by supporting third sector's projects of social interest, from simply cash donation, employees' volunteering, Cause Related Marketing and so on. It is the dimension that, more than the others, can actually bring social and economic goals into alignment and improve companies' long-term business prospects depending on the type of tools chosen to support good causes; this is why the empirical analysis will focus mainly on Corporate Philanthropy in order to respond to the research question.

- **Ethics and Sustainability:** It is strictly related to the combination of environmental, societal and ethical concerns in processes, goods/products and services development by making the best use of Research and Development and Innovation as tools to make the difference among the competitive arena.

Among the spectrum of the above CSV initiatives, Philanthropy is considered a growing activity (Liu & Ko, 2011) and accordingly, one of the major dimensions (Kim *et al.*, 2011) to explain

Table 1. CSV dimensions and activities

Dimensions	Accountability	Philanthropy	Ethics and Sustainability
Activities	• Sustainability and Social Reports • Code of Ethics • Adherence to National and International Standards • Norms and Standards implementation: • UNI EN ISO 9001:2008 on Quality Management System Requirements • UNI EN ISO 14001 on Environmental Management Standard • OHSAS 18001 on Occupational Health and Safety Assessment Series • SA8000: Social Accountability and Human Rights • ISO 26000:2010 on Sustainable Development and Social Responsibility	• Cash and in kind supports • Sponsorships • Cause Related Marketing • Staff Involvement: payroll giving and volunteering • Corporate Foundations creation • Investments in specific projects in response to specific needs	• Development and implementation of ethical products and services • Fair trade products • Ethical funds or investments • Micro finance • Eco and Environmental-friendly products • Sustainable processes: energy saving, recycling, searching for alternative energy sources and resources • Policies and Rules issued for certain types of stakeholders • Supply chain and employees involvement in CSR tools adoption

Source: Adapted from Civera & Musso, 2012

CSV. Focusing on it gives a better understanding of whether the company benefits from commercial advantages deriving by CSR and branding interconnection or its aim is to purely foster community well-being by adopting a new strategic model of CSV. Corporate philanthropy consists of several activities aiming at building relationships with Third Sector Organizations: from the simply cash donations and investments in specific projects of social interest to the sponsorships and partnerships (Baur & Schmitz, 2012; Liu & Ko, 2011) and Cause Related Marketing. In the context of philanthropy, it clearly appears that, the more the philanthropic activities are connected to the image and the brand of the company, the more the company can mutually benefit from them and apparent philanthropy can be perceived as a form of public relations or advertising and promotion (Porter & Kramer, 2002). Cause Related Marketing (CRM) represents the clearest example of this: consumers' behaviour are expected to increase in loyalty (Sen & Bhattacharya, 2001) and the image of the company will benefit of better reputation among stakeholders (Brammer & Pavelin, 2006), while making CSR a new business model and creating, accordingly, a Shared Value.

In this sense, saying that investments in CSV under the form of philanthropic investments – and in particular in activities which can make the company increase its visibility on the market – have positive impact on the long-term competitive advantage of differentiating products and services (Porter, 1980; Demetriou *et al.,* 2009) is an understatement.

Given the theoretical framework, the aim of the chapter is to investigate if and how the big move towards Corporate Shared Value implementation - as innovative and more formalized way of thinking CSR - is being undertaken by companies, in the context of Italy and United Kingdom.

A COMPARATIVE ANALYSIS BETWEEN UNITED KINGDOM AND ITALY

UK and Italy: Peculiarities in their Attitude towards CSR and Philanthropy

Reasons, use and implications of CSR hugely vary from country to country and across sectors (Brammer & Pavelin, 2006). Many factors, such as socio-economic situation, institutional and historical settings (CGAP, 2011) culture, religion, beliefs, preferences, and availability of information really affect both the individual and the corporate behaviour towards ethics and philanthropy, regarding CSV chosen activities, the communication of them, the frequency and amount of donations to charities and the typology of relationships with them.

As far as the general setting of the two countries at issue is concerned, Italy and United Kingdom present quite similar features: first of all the population, which is estimated to be 60.1 million in Italy and 61.9 million in UK (United Nation, 2010) and secondly the gross domestic product of the two countries is quite comparable. The International Monetary Fund estimates UK GPD for the year 2010 to be equal to billion €1.700 and Italy GDP for 2010 at billion €1.707.

What looks quite different is the cultural environment in which attitudes towards CSR in general and philanthropy in particular have been developed.

The case of United Kingdom, for instance, is very representative of a country that has a strong tradition of charitable behaviour mainly due to third sector more formal development. The reasons can be found in historical evidence, which reveals how important the role of business philanthropy has been during the years in building and maintaining the social and economic wealth of UK society (CGAP, 2011). Within the growth and the weight of third sector in UK as part of "social welfare provision in response to social, economic and political needs" (CGAP, 2011) profit oriented companies have taken a part in this development by seeking to achieve both their primary goal and the ones of the societal benefit through their charitable support.

In Italy, on the other hand, culturally the growth and the weight of philanthropy has always been more connected to the pressure and the influence of religion, which has played a significant role even in the political debate and process towards the creation of a welfare-state. Philanthropic activities have been characterized by far less visibility when compared to UK and US activities during the last decades (Assifero, 2010). Today within the growth of Corporate Social Responsibility and increasing concerns about whether or not businesses can be conducive to society well being, Porter's *strategic donation and philanthropy* is gaining in importance both from the quantitative and the qualitative side. This may be the reason why Italian companies are seeking now, to introduce these practices as more formalized part of their core business activities.

Investments in CSR are generally positive and increasing in both of the countries. Reasons of investing still differ. The first "Report on Social Responsibility and Competitiveness" shows that in Italy the concepts of CSR and corporate philanthropy are still seen as related to the idea of improving brand image (RGA, 2009) rather than achieving social purposes through the implementation of a new strategic vision. The percentage of CSR communication has increased in both of the countries since 2008 and is surely representative of an ongoing and increasing attitude towards CSR communication. Furthermore, Italy suffers of a lack of CSR managers: 58,9% of the Italian companies does not have a formal CSR manager

in their organizational chart and the management is often addressed to people in charge of other functions (such as human resources, marketing and communication) (Altis, ISVI, 2006).

Companies make an extensive use of all the philanthropic tools with differences underlying and anticipating at a first glance what the findings emerged from our empirical analysis will reveal. Cash donations and employees involvement in philanthropic activities is far more popular in the UK, when, oppositely, Italian companies make large use of Cause Related Marketing and sponsorships (Osservatorio Socialis, 2010; Lillya, 2011).

By analysing the attitude toward CRS and Philanthropy in the context of Italy and the UK emerged that one of the most involved sector in these kinds of investments and concerns over the community is the Retail Grocery one.

Research Method and Considered Sample

The research has been developed by following the deductive approach of study that represents the commonest view of the nature of the relationship between theory and empirical research (Bryman, 2004). All theories, hypothesis and assumptions emerged from the literature review on Corporate Social Responsibility, Brand Communication and Corporate Shared Value have been confirmed or partly rejected through the empirical analyses conducted on a sample of six (6) companies among Retail Grocery sectors, three (3) operating in Italy and three (3) in the UK.

The sample of companies has been investigated over the extent to which their Corporate Social Responsibility programmes (with a great focus on Philanthropy) are becoming new business strategies connected to the Corporate Shared Value implementation, independent on the marketing and communication activities. The *comparative case studies* method of research has been used because of three different reasons.

First of all, the use of a *comparative study* has been necessary and required in order to be able to compare two different situations, which are in this case, referred to two different geographical contexts: Italy and United Kingdom.

Secondly, the *case study* methodology involves an extensive examination of the setting (it could be a community, an organization, a company, a single peculiar event) when a holistic and in-depth investigation is needed.

Eventually, in the case at issue, the existence of three out of three conditions that justify the *case study* implementation (Yin, 2003) has driven the choice:

1. When the focus of the study is to answer "how" and "why" questions: one of the purpose of the research is to respond to "how" companies implement CSV reasons why of doing so;
2. When the researcher cannot manipulate any behaviour among the people involved in the study: the present study does not involved people; companies have been – in fact – investigated through the analysis of their strategies and communication available on the Websites and published reports;
3. When contextual conditions are believed to be relevant to the phenomenon under study: in this case the different geographical countries to which they belong are relevant to the study; they affect companies' behaviours and how they set up actions within Corporate Shared Value.

The information from the Websites and the published reports of each company has been collected at a single point in time (T1). The collection of information has aimed at detecting certain criteria addressed to produce a standardized framework to consistently respond to the research question.

In particular, information on each company have been gathered around:

- Company general information and financials;
- Characterizations of the CSR policy including its level of formalization
- Governance and structure of CSR within the company;
- Description of CSR adopted activities;
- Focus on the strategy for Philanthropy including tools implemented to pursue it.

The information has been gathered through a careful analysis of the companies' Websites, in particular of the sections dedicated to Social Responsibility, Sustainability and Ethics (present in all the companies' Websites at issue), and through a precise reading and studying of the Reports published in the field of CSR and Philanthropy (such as Social Report, Code of Ethics, Code of Conduct, and so on) available on the Website as well.

Companies operating in the Retail Grocery sector, both in Italy and the UK, are the most involved in Corporate Philanthropy; accordingly, the gathered data are effectively compared.

A total of six (6) companies have been empirically analysed. Table 2 summarizes the sample.

Some precise criteria have been used to choose the sample and have varied depending on the geographical context the company belongs to.

As far as the UK Retailers are concerned, two criteria have been applied: the identification of the largest Grocery Retailers in the UK (among the categories Hypermarket and Supermarket) and – among the largest – the choice of the most

Table2. Summary of the UK and Italian companies' sample

Italian Retail Grocery Sector	UK Retail Grocery Sector
Coop Italia	Tesco PLC
Conad Consorzio Nazionale Dettaglianti	J Sainsbury PLC
Esselunga SpA	Co-operative Food Ltd

involved in Corporate Philanthropy. As a result, according to the ranking reported on the Website retailindustry.com, the "Guide to UK Company Giving" (Lillya, 2011) and the book "Top 3000 Charities 2012/2013" (Caritas Data, 2012) (3), which ranks the top 200 donors per community investments, the sample is here composed by: Tesco PLC Sainsbury's, and Co-operative Group (Food division).

For the Italian companies, because of the lack of data over the top corporate spenders in Corporate Philanthropy, the three largest Italian Grocery Retailers (in the category Hypermarket and Supermarket) according to the ranking reported by retailindustry.com have been picked up: Coop Italia (ranked at the 47th position), Conad Consorzio Nazionale Dettaglianti Soc. Coop. s.r.l. (67th position), and Esselunga SpA (115th position out of 250 Retailers).

KEY FINDINGS AND CONCLUSION

Given the premises that the UK and the Italian contexts can be considered quite similar and comparable when it comes to the economic, demographic and geographic factors, the empirical analysis of the peculiarities of each company at issue has led to formulate a various scenario, where many differences and some relevant similarities in CSV implementation as innovative strategy between the two countries and between the sectors emerged.

The conclusion will be drawn on the basis of the criteria used for the design of the case studies: characterizations of the Corporate Social Responsibility programmes, features of CSR Governance, typology of CSR tools used, description of the strategy for Philanthropy.

In both of the Italian and the UK contexts CSV implementation seems to represent the most effective response to the on-going challenges and changes companies and societies are facing all over the world. By having a look at the general

core and business strategy as far as Retail Grocery sector is concerned, it immediately and clearly emerges that all of them include ethics, sustainable and responsible aims or strategic objectives in the mission, values or Strategic Plan they set up for pursuing their main and core business purpose. This tendency underlines a very relevant shift of topics and issues in companies' concerns. Especially in sectors like Retail Grocery they have started perceiving the responsibility of their activities and the impact they can have on consumers' perceptions and choices.

Accordingly, CSV comes out naturally from the general business strategy, as at the heart of companies' decisions and as core values driving all the activities each company aims to implement.

As far as the Governance of CSR is concerned, a big difference between the UK and the Italian contexts emerges. The 3 analysed players in the UK (Tesco, Sainsbury's and Co-operative Food) appear to be much more formalized in the setting up of an ad-hoc Unit or Committee for CSR, belonging to the Group's Board and Chairman, with the task of giving a formal approval to the most relevant actions and statements published in the field of CSR. All the companies provide a dedicated Unit or Committee or Group involved in implementing CSR both strategically and at an operational level by pursuing concrete activities.

The spread of CSV activities is high in all the analysed companies, no matter the country. Each player counts on different adopted tools to pursue its CSV strategy and activities in the accountability and ethics and sustainability dimensions.

At the opposite, the similarities emerging in CSV activities implementation as far as accountability and ethics and sustainability are concerned, are not – in fact – reflected in the strategy for Philanthropy. The extent to which Philanthropy is considered a proper strategic move is different between the countries. The general tendency suggests that Philanthropy is becoming (or there is an explicit declaration of doing it) a real and concrete innovative strategy within the whole business strategy, as to show that concerns about communities and societies' well being need to be strategically implemented in corporates decisions. Despite this tendency, huge differences in the strategic way of pursuing philanthropic activities emerge between Italy and the UK. In general, Philanthropy appears to be more formally implemented and standardized programme are more likely to be set up in the UK context, with projects having a longer gestation and life cycle and creating more loyal relationships. Clear plans describing the economic and financial efforts in the community investments and the results achievement for projects carried out over the past years are more common among UK players. Philanthropy, similarly to CSR, represents – for them – a concrete strategy, which needs to be embedded by the whole company. This statement might justify why the technique of involving employees to volunteer and/or to fundraise for charities partnering with the company is greatly used in the UK context more than in Italy.

On one hand, the policy standardization is higher in the UK. On the other hand, a common tendency of making a use of Philanthropy as a commercial tool to obtain economic advantages and positive return on image and brand equity seems to belong to all the players; the use of Cause Related Marketing is common to all the analysed Grocer Retailers. This means that, no matter the country, pursuing a commercial return on philanthropic investments is a fact even for those Italian companies that do not implement any formal and standardized policy or strategy for Philanthropy. The only small difference in this common tendency is that, in some cases, companies based in the UK clearly admit and communicate to their stakeholders which activities are carried out for a commercial purpose.

Table 3 summarizes the results described above, identifying each considered player with the acronym Gr (standing for Grocery).

Evidence shows that CSV can really be considered a driver of both marketing communication in order to increase brand equity and awareness and of social concerns implementation to make the whole company's communication homogeneous and coherent with the values and beliefs characterizing its culture.

The intangible asset represented by the reputation a company creates is the basis for improving brand strategy. The use of this asset in branding - if managed and shared - creates a virtuous cycle building trust and increasing the equity of the brand. Accordingly, CSV incorporates brand and Corporate Social Responsibility strategies to improve the social impact, the market perception and the commercial performance of a company and its products by combining in those tangible and intangible attributes, values, symbols and social issues.

What emerges as common to all the companies part of the sample is the fact that they all go beyond to the simple CSR like a random combination of communication and non-business oriented actions

Table 3. Findings summary

Investigated Areas	Italy			United Kingdom		
Spread of CSR in accordance with the current issues	Gr1	Gr2	Gr3	Gr4	Gr5	Gr6
CSR Governance – Formalization				Gr4	Gr5	Gr6
CSR Accountability		Gr2	Gr3	Gr4	Gr5	Gr6
Philanthropy – Formal implementation				Gr4	Gr5	Gr6
Philanthropy – Employees volunteering	Gr1			Gr4	Gr5	Gr6
Philanthropy – Cause Related Marketing	Gr1	Gr2	Gr3	Gr4	Gr5	Gr6
Philanthropy – Commercial purposes				Gr4		

addressed to the community; they are actually starting implementing the innovative model of CSV which combines brand and social concerns in a formalized and strategic way in order to have positive impact both on financials and the community itself.

This kind of mixed social activities and marketing communication are driven by and are addressed to the internal and external customers, which have the power to strengthen the process and make CSR and brand merge into the innovative model of Corporate Shared Value (CSV), as the highest level of strategy formalization for companies.

Like a virtuous circle (Figure 2), the implementation of such innovative model as strategic lever can bring companies to the achievement of benefits impacting both externally and internally, aligning brand and social concerns in order to make the company a *value to share*.

FURTHER RESEARCH DIRECTIONS

Since the present research is focused on two Countries and one specific industrial sector within the category of retailing, next steps might consider a wider geographical area and the analysis of various sectors. The geographic areas of immediate concern in relation to these emerging trends are the Mediterranean countries and the Anglo-Saxon ones, considering cultural and sociological analogies, peculiarities and differences explained before in the chapter regarding consumers' behaviours in Italy and UK respectively.

As far as additional analysis of different sectors is concerned, an interesting contrast to the retail grocery can be represented by the distribution strategies of luxury goods. Given that individuals polarize their preferences in both consumer goods and luxury goods markets because of interconnected different reasons, further researches might be focused on figuring out the meanings and implications of Corporate Shared Value innovative strategies among retailing sectors differing hugely between each other: consumer and luxury goods, to see whether the strategies for CSR and branding differ.

Eventually, it would be useful to investigate the same issues, taking into account the perception and the points of view of consumers through an in-depth empirical analysis.

Figure 2. Innovative strategy virtuous circle

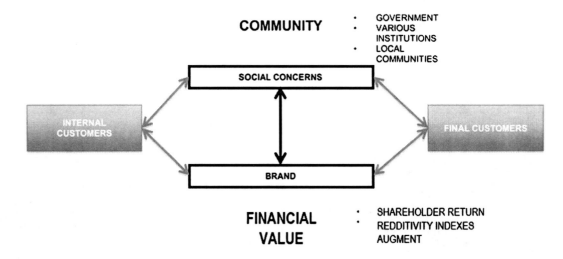

REFERENCES

Aaker, D. A. (1996). *Building Strong Brands*. New York: The Free Press.

Aaker, D. A. (2004a). Leveraging the Corporate Brand. *California Management Review, 46*(3), 6–18. doi:10.2307/41166218

Aaker, D. A. (2004b). *Brand Portfolio Strategy*. New York: The Free Press.

Aaker, D. A. (2009). *Strategic Market Management*. New York: Wiley.

Ahmed, P. K., & Machold, S. (2004). The quality and ethics connection: toward virtuous organizations. *Total Quality Management & Business Excellence, 15*(4), 527–545. doi:10.1080/1478336042000183604

Allen, J., & Root, J. (2004, September 7). The new brand tax. *Wall Street Journal*.

Altis, I. (2006). *CSR Manager within Italian companies*. Third Report on Corporate Social Responsibility in Italy.

ASSIFERO. (2010). *La filantropia istituzionale in Italia*. Le fondazioni private di erogazione: Crescita e Ruolo [Institutional Philanthropy in Italy. Private Foundations: Development and Role] Report.

Balmer, J. M. T. (2008). Identity based views of the corporation: Insights from corporate identity, organisational identity, social identity, visual identity, corporate brand identity and corporate image. *European Journal of Marketing, 42*(9/10), 879–906. doi:10.1108/03090560810891055

Baur, D., & Schmitz, P. H. (2012). Corporations and NGOs: When Accountability Leads to Co-optation. *Journal of Business Ethics, 106*, 9–21. doi:10.1007/s10551-011-1057-9

Belch, G. E., & Belch, M. A. (2009). *Advertising and Promotion: An Integrated marketing communication Perspective*. New York: McGraw-Hill.

Blombäck, A., & Ramírez-Pasillas, M. (2012). Exploring the logics of corporate brand identity formation. *Corporate Communications: An International Journal, 17*(1), 7–28. doi:10.1108/13563281211196335

Brammer, S. J., & Pavelin, S. (2006). Corporate Reputation and Social Performance: The Importance of Fit. *Journal of Management Studies, 43*(3), 435–455. doi:10.1111/j.1467-6486.2006.00597.x

Bryaman, A. (2004). *Social Research Methods*. Oxford University Press.

Caritas Data. (2012). *Top 3000 Charities 2012*. London: Sarasin & Partners.

Carrol, A. B. (1991). The pyramid of corporate social responsibility: toward the moral management of organizational stakeholders. *Business Horizons, 34*, 39–48. doi:10.1016/0007-6813(91)90005-G

Casalegno, C., Pellicelli, M., & Civera, C. (2012). Social Values and Ethics for Communicating the Corporate Identity. *The China Business Review, 11*(7), 656–671.

CGAP (Center for Charitable Giving and Philanthropy). (2011). How generous is the UK? Charitable giving in the context of household spending. *Tom McKenzie and Katie Pharoah, CGAP Briefing Note 7*.

Christodoulides, G., Jevons, C., & Blackshaw, P. (2011). The voice of the consumer speaks forcefully in brand identity: user-generated content forces smart marketers to listen. *Journal of Advertising Research, 51*(1), 101–111. doi:10.2501/JAR-51-1-101-111

Civera, C., & Musso, G. (2012). Corporate Social Responsibility and Social Economy: A closer look on financial tools into the Italian Context. In Instrumentos Solidarios en tiempo de crisis. Bosch Editor and Santander Universidades.

Demetriou, M., Papasolomou, I., & Vrontis, D. (2009). Cause-related Marketing: Building the corporate image while supporting worthwhile causes. *Journal of Brand Management, 17*, 266–278. doi:10.1057/bm.2009.9

Duncan, T., & Mulhern, F. (2004). *A White Paper on the Status, Scope and Future of IMC*. New York: McGraw-Hill.

Freeman, R. E., & Phillips, R. A. (2002). Stakeholder theory: a libertarian defence. *Business Ethics Quarterly, 12*(3), 331–333. doi:10.2307/3858020

Friedman, M. (1970). The social responsibility of firms is to increase its profits. *New York Times Magazine*.

Guilt Free Consumption. (2013). Retrieved from http://www.trendwatching.com

Kim, N., Cho, E., Kim, Y., & Lee, M. (2011). Developing an effective strategic mix of corporate philanthropy. *The Service Industries Journal, 31*(7), 1049–1062. doi:10.1080/02642060903079428

Kliatchko, J. (2008). Revisiting the IMC construct: a revised definition and four pillars. *International Journal of Advertising, 27*(1), 133–160.

Krugman, D. M., Reid, L. N., Dunn, S. W., & Barban, A. M. (1994). *Advertising: Its Role in Modern Marketing*. Fort Worth, TX: Dryden Press.

Kuepfer, J., & Papula, J. (2010). Corporate social responsibility–the dilemmas behind the popular concept and how to best address them! *International Journal of Sustainable Society, 2*(3), 291–305. doi:10.1504/IJSSOC.2010.034765

La Cour, A., & Kromann, J. (2011). Euphemisms and hypocrisy in corporate philanthropy. *Business Ethics (Oxford, England), 20*(3), 267–279. doi:10.1111/j.1467-8608.2011.01627.x

Lillya, D. (2011). *The guide to UK Corporate Giving* (8th ed.). DSC.

Liu, G., & Ko, W. W. (2011). An analysis of cause-related marketing implementation strategies through social alliance: Partnership conditions and strategic objectives. *Journal of Business Ethics, 100*(2), 253–281. doi:10.1007/s10551-010-0679-7

Macleod, S. (2001). Why worry about CSR. *Strategic Communication Management, 5*(5), 8–9.

Maple, P. (2008). The Spectrum of Philanthropy. *Caritas London, 5*, 34–36.

Mohr, B. A., Webb, D. J., & Harris, K. E. (2001). Do consumers expect companies to be socially responsible? The impact of corporate social responsibility on buying behavior. *The Journal of Consumer Affairs, 35*(1), 45–72. doi:10.1111/j.1745-6606.2001.tb00102.x

Osservatorio Socialis. (2010). *L'impegno sociale delle aziende in Italia*. [The social effort in Italian Companies]. Report.

Porter, M. (1980). *Competitive Strategy*. New York: Free Press.

Porter, M., & Kramer, M. (2011). Creating Shared Value: How to reinvent capitalism and unleash a wave of innovation and growth. *Harvard Business Review, 89*(1/2), 62–77.

Porter, M., & Kramer, R. M. (2002). The Competitive Advantage of Corporate Philanthropy. *Harvard Business Review, 80*(12), 57–68. PMID:12510538

Pringle, C. D., Jannings, D. F., & Longeneckr, J. G. (1988). *Managing Organizations: Functions and Behaviors*. Columbus, OH: Merrill.

RGA. (2009). *Etica o etichetta? Primo report su responsabilità sociale e competitività*. [Ethics or brand? Firts report on social responsibility and competitiveness]. Report.

Robins, F. (2005). The Future of Corporate Social Responsibility. *Asian Business & Management*, *4*, 95–115. doi:10.1057/palgrave.abm.9200125

Schein, E. (2010). *Organizational culture and leadership*. Wiley and Sons.

Schultz, D. E., Tannenbaum, S. I., & Lauterborn, R. F. (1993). *Integrated marketing communications*. Chicago: NTC Business.

Sen, S., & Bhattacharya, C. B. (2001). Does doing good always lead to doing better? Consumer reactions to corporate social responsibility. *JMR, Journal of Marketing Research*, *38*(2), 225–243. doi:10.1509/jmkr.38.2.225.18838

Torres, A., Bijmolt, T., Tribo', J., & Verhoef, P. (2012). Generating global brand equity through corporate social responsibility to key stakeholders. *International Journal of Research in Marketing*, *29*(1), 13–24. doi:10.1016/j.ijresmar.2011.10.002

Vallaster, C., Lindgreen, A., & Maon, F. (2012). Strategically Leveraging Corporate Social Responsibility: A Corporate Brand Perspective. *California Management Review*, *54*(3), 34–60. doi:10.1525/cmr.2012.54.3.34

Werther, W. B., & Chandler, B. (2005). Strategic corporate social responsibility as global brand insurance. *Business Horizons*, *48*, 317–324. doi:10.1016/j.bushor.2004.11.009

Werther, W. B., & Chandler, B. (2005). Strategic corporate social responsibility as global brand insurance. *Business Horizons*, *48*, 317–324. doi:10.1016/j.bushor.2004.11.009

Wheeler, A. (2009). *Designing Brand Identity: An Essential Guide for the Whole Branding Team*. Wiley.

Yin, R. K. (2003). *Case study research: Design and methods* (3rd ed.). Thousand Oaks, CA: Sage.

ADDITIONAL READING

Beckett, R. (2004). Communication Ethics: Principle and Practice. *Journal of Communication Management*, *8*(1), 41–52. doi:10.1108/13632540410807538

Belch, G. E., & Belch, M. A. (2003). *Advertising and Promotion. An Integrated marketing communication Perspective*. New York: McGraw-Hill.

Bernstein, S. R. (1951). Good Taste in Advertising. *Harvard Business Review*, *29*(3), 42–50.

Berry, L. L. (1981). The Employee as a Customer. *Journal of Retail Banking*, *31*(1), 33–44.

Brown, T., & Wyatt, J. (2010). Design thinking for social innovation. *Stanford Social Innovation Review*, *8*(1), 30–35.

Cachon, G. P., & Fisher, M. (2000). Supply chain inventory management and the value of shared information. *Management Science*, *46*(8), 1032–1048. doi:10.1287/mnsc.46.8.1032.12029

Grönroos, C. (2001). Service management and marketing (Vol. 2). New York^ eNY NY: Wiley.

Groom, S. A., & Frei, F. (2008). Integrated marketing communication. *Communication research trends*, *27*(4), 3-19.

Kenneway, M. (2006). Branding for libraries: communicating your value to increase reader awareness and usage of the library service. *Serials: The Journal for the Serials Community*, *19*(2), 120–126. doi:10.1629/19120

Kitchen, P. J., & Burgmann, I. (2004). *Integrated marketing communication*. John Wiley & Sons, Ltd.

Kok, M. (Ed.). (2002). *Global warming and social innovation: the challenge of a climate neutral society*. Earthscan.

Lane Keller, K. (2001). Mastering the marketing communications mix: Micro and macro perspectives on Integrated marketing communication programs.

Lopez-De-Pedro, J. M., & Rimbau-Gilabert, E. (2012). Stakeholder Approach: What Effects Should We Take into Account in Contemporary Societies? *Journal of Business Ethics, 107*(2), 147–158. doi:10.1007/s10551-011-1029-0

Luo, X., & Bhattacharya, C. B. (2006). Corporate social responsibility, customer satisfaction, and market value. *Journal of Marketing*, 1–18. doi:10.1509/jmkg.70.4.1

MacCallum, D. (Ed.). (2009). *Social innovation and territorial development*. Ashgate Publishing.

McWilliams, A., & Siegel, D. (2001). Corporate social responsibility: A theory of the firm perspective. *Academy of Management Review, 26*(1), 117–127.

Nelson, P. (1974). Advertising as information. *The Journal of Political Economy, 82*(4), 729–754. doi:10.1086/260231

Norris, D. G. (1992). Ingredient branding: a strategy option with multiple beneficiaries. *Journal of Consumer Marketing, 9*(3), 19–31. doi:10.1108/07363769210035206

Pickton, D., & Broderick, A. (2005). Integrated marketing communications.

Pruzan, P., & Thyssen, O. (1990). Conflict and consensus: Ethics as a shared value horizon for strategic planning. *Human Systems Management, 9*(3), 135–151.

Rossiter, J. R., & Percy, L. (1987). *Advertising and promotion management*. McGraw-Hill Book Company.

Sabel, C. F. (1996). Ireland: local partnerships and social innovation. Organisation for Economic Co-operation and Development.

Schultz, D. E. (1992). Integrated marketing communications. *Journal of Promotion Management, 1*(1), 99–104. doi:10.1300/J057v01n01_07

Sen, S., Bhattacharya, C. B., & Korschun, D. (2006). The role of corporate social responsibility in strengthening multiple stakeholder relationships: a field experiment. *Journal of the Academy of Marketing Science, 34*(2), 158–166. doi:10.1177/0092070305284978

Smith, N. C. (2003). Corporate social responsibility: Not whether, but how. *Center for Marketing Working Paper*, (03-701).

Walker, C., Pharoah, C., Marmolejo, M., & Lillya, D. (2012). *UK corporate citizenship in the 21st century*.

Walton, T. (2005). Identifying the Creative Frontiers in Consumer Products and Branding. *Design Management Review, 16*(2), 6–9. doi:10.1111/j.1948-7169.2005.tb00186.x

Weitzer, D., & Darroch, J. (2009). Why Moral Failures Precede Financial Crises. *Critical Perspectives on International Business, 5*(1/2), 6–13. doi:10.1108/17422040910938640

KEY TERMS AND DEFINITIONS

Branding: The strategy used to create a unique name and image for a product in consumers' mind.

Cause Related Marketing: A commercial activity in which businesses and charities form a partnership with each other to market an image, service or product for mutual benefit.

Corporate Shared Value: A set of profitable activities that aim at improving at the same time both the economic value and the conditions of the society companies' activities directly or indirectly affect.

Corporate Social Responsibility: The sum of policies concerning a corporate self-regulation integrated in its business model.

Ethics and Sustainability: The combination of environmental, societal and ethical concerns in processes, goods/products and services development.

Integrated Marketing Communication: The strategy of communicating simultaneously to different targets with different schemes in order to create a synergy among communication channels so that the effect resulting from their integration will be more powerful than any single undertaken communication action.

Philanthropy: Consists of several activities aiming at building relationships with third sector organizations. From the simply cash donations and investments in specific projects of social interest to the sponsorship of development and some cause related marketing activities.

ENDNOTES

1. The Authors own full responsibility of the contents of the paper. Anyway paragraphs named 'Background', 'Introduction' and 'Key findings and conclusion' have been attributed to Professor Candelo, Dr. Casalegno and Dr. Civera; while paragraphs named 'Successful brand strategies incorporate Corporate Social Responsibility' and 'Further research direction' must be attributed to Professor Elena Candelo. Paragraphs named 'Communicating through Corporate Social Responsibility' and 'UK and Italy: peculiarities in their attitude towards CSR and Philanthropy' are attributed to Dr. Cecilia Casalegno. Eventually, paragraphs named 'The evolution of Corporate Social Responsibility: Corporate Shared Value as new strategic model' and 'Research method and considered sample' must be attributed to Dr. Chiara Civera.

2. For the full report see trendwatching.com, last access 28th of August 2013.

3. 2011 Worldwide community investments: Tesco PLC (£ 64.3 million), Sainsbury's (£ 25 million), and Co-operative Group (£ 7 million cash donations).

Section 4
Innovation, ICT, and Social Media:
The Multichannelling Challenges for Retailers

The last section is about innovation, which for retailing is primarily in the field of Information and Communication Technologies (ICT) and the related social media development. The characteristics of ICT innovation are analyzed with reference to the effects of new social media on the interaction between retailers and consumers. Multichannelling emerges as one of the most relevant consequences of this evolution. Multichannelling and its implications for marketing, organization, and distribution strategies seems to be the next decade challenge for all the players involved in the consumer-retailer-producer interaction.

Chapter 20
An Exploratory Study of Client-Vendor Relationships for Predicting the Effects of Advanced Technology-Based Retail Scenarios

Eleonora Pantano
University of Calabria, Italy & Eindhoven University of Technology, The Netherlands

Harry Timmermans
Eindhoven University of Technology, The Netherlands

ABSTRACT

Continuous advancements in technology make available a huge number of advanced systems that enhance consumers' in-store experience and shopping activity. In fact, the introduction of in-store technologies such as self-service systems, interactive displays, digital signage, etc. has impacted the retail process in multiple ways, including client-vendor interactions. While in a traditional offline context retailers exploit the development of interpersonal relationships for increasing consumers' trust, loyalty, and satisfaction, in a technology-mediated context this process becomes more difficult. To advance our knowledge and predict the future diffusion of these technologies, it is necessary to answer the following questions: (1) to what extent do consumers trust (physical) retailers' suggestions? and (2) to what extent will consumers substitute the opinion of a physical seller with virtual recommendations? The aim of this chapter is to assess the typology of current existing relationships between vendor (retail staff) and clients, with special emphasis on consumers' trust towards their suggestions. To achieve this goal, the chapter focuses on a comparison of consumers' perception of suggestions proposed by physical friends and suggestions proposed online (e.g. through social networks). The findings provide a benchmark to evaluate current client-vendor and client-social networks relationships and enhance our understanding of the possible substitution of physical vendors by recommendations systems based on advanced technologies.

DOI: 10.4018/978-1-4666-6074-8.ch020

INTRODUCTION

Advances in technology constantly affect modern retailing. The development and implementation of a large number of tools influence consumers' shopping experiences and activity (Lee & Qualls, 2010; Pantano & Timmermans, 2011). Most technologies (i.e. high customized automatic services such as recommenders systems, interactive virtual sellers, etc.) may be integrated with real (physical) stores to provide new efficient in-store services (i.e. smart trolley that integrate context-aware systems for achieving consumer's position and suggesting routes for reaching some products) (Reitberger et al., 2007; Black et al., 2009). Currently, the development of new tools tends to concentrate on integrating consumer experience across channels. Thus, a likely next step will be the integration of social networks into physical stores.

Several studies examined antecedents of consumer adoption of these new technologies (Davis, 1989; Venkatesh et al., 2003; O'Brien, 2010; Bock et al.; 2012; Venkatesh et al., 2012; Toufaily et al., in press.), mainly by identifying utilitarian factors (e.g., usefulness of the technology), social aspects (e.g., social pressure of reference group), hedonic needs and personal traits (e.g., personal innovativeness), for predicting diffusion and consumers' effective usage. In contrast, research on employees' acceptance is still scarce (Lee & Qualls, 2010).

Despite the fact in-store technologies did not significantly change the traditional five steps of the decision-making process (need recognition, search for information, pre-purchase evaluation, purchase/consumption, post consumption evaluation) nor store format (Desinger et al., 2010; Pantano & Naccarato, 2010), they did change stores in terms of layout, atmosphere, product display, in-store experience (in terms of quality and quantity of delivered services), access to products and information, and client-vendor relationships (Vasquez Casielles et al., 2005; Boeck & Wamba,

2008; Black et al., 2009; Pantano, 2013). While in a traditional offline context, retailers stimulate development of interpersonal relationships to increase consumer loyalty and satisfaction and to influence consumer decision-making process (e.g., Wagner et al., 2003; Sun et al., 2009; Gaur et al., 2012; Yang, 2013; Drollinger & Comer, 2013), especially in the case of novice consumers (Wagner et al., 2003), in advanced systems-based retail environments, this process becomes more difficult as self-service technologies may substitute the physical seller. In fact, the new technologies change client-vendor relationships by providing new ways for providing suggestions and recommendations about possible purchases, comparisons of products, payment, etc. without the seller's direct assistance. Examples are automatic self-check-in desks in the airports and automatic cash desks in supermarkets (Vasquez Casielles et al., 2005; Boeck & Wamba, 2008; Zhu et al., 2013). As a consequence, interpersonal interactions become less frequent. In the online context, this problem is partially solved by providing social presence cues (i.e. avatars replacing sellers, employees, staff) and increasing the realism of the interactivity of the interface (Roy et al., 2001; Hassanein & Head, 2007). Thus, new technologies raise new questions about the relationship between the consumer and the seller (Keeling et al., 2013):

1. To what extent do consumers trust retailers' recommendations?
2. To what extent will consumers substitute recommendations of physical sellers with virtual recommendations?

The aim of this study is to assess the relationship between vendor (retail staff) and clients, with emphasis on consumers' trust towards retailers' suggestions. Moreover, consumer perceptions of suggestions and other recommendations will be compared against those of social networks users. The findings will provide data for benchmarking the evaluation of current client-vendor relationships and client-social networks users in the context of recommendations. In particular, these results will help investigating the possible (total) substitution of physical vendors for advanced systems.

BACKGROUND

A substantial amount of prior research has identified the most important seller's skills for sales success: listening skills, ability to adapt sales style to different situations and clients, and verbal communication skills (Marshall et al., 2003; Drollinger & Comer, 2013). There is also empirical evidence that listening skill of salespersons are positively related to consumer trust towards the salesperson. The ability to truly understand buyers' needs creates trust (Cicala et al., 2012; Drollinger & Comer, 2013). These skills are instrumental in building strong relationships with consumers. The importance of strong relationships in strong sales performance has been demonstrated in multiple research projects (e.g., Palmatier et al., 2006; Poon et al., 2012). For these reasons, the goal of a professional, high-performance seller is not only to achieve good sales performance, but also to build and maintain strong relationships with customers (e.g., Plouffe et al., 2010; Gaur et al., 2012), based on effective communication, information sharing, trust, consumer satisfaction, and cost reduction (Yang, 2013). In this context, Boeck and Wamba (2008) argued that the key dimensions of client-vendor relationships are

1. Communication and information sharing between the parties,
2. Cooperation on the final service, and
3. Trust between the parties.

Concerning (1) communication and information sharing between parties, client-vendor interactions involve information transfer

- From vendor to client, through communication of information related to products, promotions, and suggestions and recommendations of products; and
- From client to vendor by requesting some products and indicating preferences (Teo, 2012).

Knowledge (familiarity) of both product and vendor enables reducing social uncertainty while increasing the understanding of the situation (Sharma, 2001; Jiang et al., 2008). Vendor's knowledge transfer to a client enhances a deeper understanding of product characteristics, which is critical in making a better choice, while vendors can exploit the information obtained from clients to develop a greater understanding of market trends and improve its marketing strategies. Moreover, information sharing is based on willingness to share knowledge and on client's trust in vendors' knowledge (Teo, 2012).

The cooperation between the parties captures the actions needed to achieve a common goal (Palmatier et al., 2006; Boeck & Wamba, 2008). In the client-vendor relationship context, the common goal is the purchase. To achieve this goal the seller supports and provides information to allow the consumer to make a choice that retailers the consumer's needs. From this interaction, the vendor is also able to measure consumer satisfaction, perspective, needs and experience (Andreu et al., 2010). As a consequence, during the interaction, the vendor is able to adapt his selling tactics to better meet the consumers' needs. Hence, there is a sort of cooperation between consumer and vendor to co-create added value to the final service (Palmatier et al., 2006). The new technologies provide innovative tools for supporting cooperation between retailers and consumers, by increasing the value of the experience and the quality and quantity of knowledge shared (Boeck & Wamba, 2008).

As for trust between client and vendor, one party should have confidence in the reliability and integrity in the other party involved in the exchange (Morgan & Hunt, 1994; Twing-Knowng et al., 2013). The concept of trust has been examined from different perspectives. Previous studies seem to have focused on three main categories of trust: trust as expectancy, trust as a risk reducing mechanism, and trust as commitment (Kennedy et al., 2001). Moreover, trust has been studied from a cognitive or an affective perspective (Johnson & Grayson, 2005). Trust can be considered as the "confidence in an exchange partner's reliability and integrity" (Morgan & Hunt, 1994). The salesperson expertise and competences influence consumers' trust in vendor, store, brand and/or firm (Sun & Lin, 2010) by taking into account that high pressure selling tactics might limit trust development (Du & Fan, 2006). Trust is necessary especially in conditions under uncertainty such as during the shopping activity, when the trust in salesperson acts as a mechanism for reducing emerging risk (Ruimei et al., 2012; Teo, 2012; Twing-Knowng et al., 2013). Moreover, the level of perceived trust further measures the intensity of relationship marketing (commitment) between the partners involved in the exchange (Sun & Ling, 2010; Lee & Trim, 2006). From the cognitive perspective, trust emerges from the knowledge that allows consumers to make estimations concerning the way the salesperson will fulfil his/her duties; whereas from the affective point of view, trust involves the feeling of security and strengths of the relationship between client and vendor.

The increasing attention paid to trust in the online channel has motivated researchers to differentiate between the mechanisms involved in the online and offline context. Trust in the offline context (physical stores) is different from the online context (e-commerce, Web stores, etc.) for several reasons: the physical distance between vendor and client, presence of simultaneous time and space, presence of human attributes, feedback and learning capabilities (Mukherjee &

Nath, 2007). In fact, the online context involves increased perceived risk triggered by the absence of physical contact with the vendor (Ruimei et al., 2012; Rafiq et al., 2013). The online channel, with emphasis on social networks, offers an easy accessible and free (virtual) space where users can meet other users and share their knowledge. This space is a valuable source of information for consumers and firms alike. It allows investigating the interactions among users as part of electronic word-of-mouth communication (Utz et al., 2012; Cheung & Thadani, 2012). Several studies have highlighted consumers' attitudes towards the use of social networks for collecting information to enhance purchasing decisions by trusting online users' comments more than information posted by representatives of the firm (Dou et al., 2012).

A new physical store enriched with advanced technologies differs from both traditional and online points of sale. Consequently, reflecting on client's trust in the vendor in this retail setting represents a new challenge in developing retail strategies. Another important issue that arises is to analyse client behavior in this new retail environment. The present chapter aims at filling this gap in the literature by analysing client-vendors relationships and their consequences in this emerging *hybrid* environment.

RESEARCH METHODOLOGY

The present study is part of a larger project on developing a new technology that can be integrated in stores enabling the combination of the advantages of these innovative systems for retailing and the benefits of social networks. The main purpose of this larger project is to better understand consumers' trust in both technology and vendor during the purchasing decision in order to predict the adoption of this future technology. Consistent with this aim, the paper focuses on the following key research questions:

RQ1: To what extent do consumers trust (physical) vendors' suggestions?

RQ2: To what extent are consumers willing to substitute the opinion of a physical seller with (virtual) friends' recommendations?

To achieve our goal, we conducted a quantitative analysis based on survey data. In particular, the measurement of trust involves 8 items based on a five-point Likert scale, ranging from 1 (totally disagree) to 5 (totally agree). Five of these items concern the relationship with vendors, while 3 relate to trust in social networks. In addition, a question is asked about gender, and another question is about the connection to Internet and social networks. The sample consists of 319 respondents between 20 and 30 years old, randomly recruited from the University of Calabria between March and April 2013.

Main Findings

Females represent the majority of the sample (77%). Noteworthy data is related to respondents' ownership of a smartphone: 62% of the sample has a smartphone (including iPhone and iPad), whereas 38% has only a traditional mobile phone (without Internet connection). For each variable (trust in vendor's suggestions and trust in eWOM through social network), Cronbach's alpha was calculated. Results shown in Table indicated that

calculated values exceed the recommended minimum acceptable value of .7. Furthermore, we calculated the mean scores and standard deviation of the items measuring the various aspects of trust in vendor suggestions and friends' recommendations online (electronic word-of-mouth communication or eWOM) through social networks (Table 1).

Vendors typically have experience and deep knowledge about available products, which they might share with clients. Furthermore, they are able to suggest and influence consumers' purchasing decisions. Consequently, consumers are able to access this knowledge by asking suggestions and opinions. Our findings show to what extent consumers say they take into account vendor suggestions (mean= 2.83), ask for their suggestions (mean = 2.97), appreciate these suggestions (mean = 2.85), (ask their help while choosing (mean= 2.50), and trust their opinions (mean = 2.57). These results suggest that consumers are only moderately interacting with (physical) vendors, and consider vendor's suggestions. One reason may be consumers' limited trust in their suggestions.

The second aspect under investigation refers to consumers' trust in the opinions shared through social networks, such as Facebook. Despite the large availability of information on products, services and brands in the social networks and consumers' usage of this information (mean= 3.37), they usually do not believe in the opinions shared through this channel (mean= 2.53). Like-

Table 1. Consumers' trust in vendor and friends suggestions through social networks

	Cronbach's alpha		Mean	S.D.
Trust in vendor's suggestions	.820	Taking into account vendor suggestions	2.83	0.91
		Asking for vendor suggestions	2.97	1.09
		Appreciating vendors suggestions	2.85	1.02
		Asking vendor help before choosing	2.50	1.02
		Trusting in vendor opinion while purchasing	2.57	0.92
Trust in eWOM through social networks	.801	Believing in others' opinion shared through social networks	2.53	0.98
		Trusting in information retrieved through social networks	2.22	0.91
		Using social networks for retrieving information before purchasing	3.37	1.10

wise, they do not trust the information retrieved through social networks (mean= 2.22). Perhaps, clients do not attribute a high importance to this information because they do not need it, or because they consider the possibility to manipulate these online judgments by third parts (such as firms' representatives). Hence, these results show consumers' limited willingness to trust other's suggestions, both offline (vendors) and online (recommendations shared through internet).

Solutions and Recommendations

Client-seller successful relationships are mainly based on consumers' trust towards the vendor (Lee & Trim, 2006; Sun & Ling, 2010; Ruimei et al., 2012; Teo, 2012; Twing-Knowng et al., 2013), as well as consumers' need of employee's support for the purchase decision (Rafiq et al., 2013; Ruimei et al., 2012). Our findings show consumers need limited input by vendors, due to client's

1. Limited trust in their suggestions and opinion,
2. Low appreciation of vendors' support, and
3. Scarce need of support while shopping.

A justification may be the characteristics of our sample. Our respondents are youth (20-30 years old), who may be considered experienced buyers due to the large use and interest in new technologies as an informative source (Wagner et al.; 2003; Jiang et al., 2008). Past studies have highlighted the large use of Internet for collecting information on products and comparing goods and services, as well as for consulting reviews by young adults. Hence, consumers' past knowledge of products and brands excludes (or strongly limits) the need of interaction with a physical seller.

Although new technologies allow transferring knowledge from vendors to consumers in an easy and fast way (Teo, 2012), results in table 2 indicate that consumers may occasionally ask opinions for their purchasing, especially when new or unknown products are involved. Our results further show that the trust between client and vendor is generally low (mean < 3.0), providing empirical evidence that current (young) clients-vendors relationships are weak. Therefore, interactions with vendors may be very few and not significant. However, vendors should encourage clients to interact with them and use their knowledge about available products and services, and benefit from their recommendations. In this way, vendors can participate to the clients' purchasing decision, influence it, understand consumers' decision-making process and increase their knowledge about their behaviour. To achieve this goal, vendors need to improve their selling skills and obtain consumers' interest and trust.

The second aspect emerging from our analysis concerns clients' trust in others' opinions accessed through social networks. Although past studies have highlighted the importance of trust in technology for predicting its future adoption (Du & Fan, 2006; Jiang et al., 2008) and consumers' trust in eWOM through social networks (Utz et al., 2012; Cheung & Thadani, 2012), our results show limited trust in eWOM. In fact, users may often access to this medium for retrieving information on products and brands/firms (since the mean is slightly above 3), but they do not completely trust this kind of information. A reason may be increasing consumers' consciousness of firms' possibility to manipulate online reviews. Consumers may occasionally reach friends through social network tools when they need their suggestions when they are not physically present at the point of sale. In fact, connecting through Facebook for accessing others' opinion involves a wide range of different opinions, which can be expressed by a wide range of users (e.g. colleagues, friends, familiars, etc.). Similarly, some privacy concerns may be involved in the online sharing process, making available to a huge audience, personal behaviour.

FUTURE RESEARCH DIRECTIONS

The research shows to what extent advanced technologies may replace traditional client-vendor relationships for the youth (20-30 years old) in case of a new system that is based on the integration of social networks at the points of sale. Since young consumers are usually not interested in vendors' opinions, nor in opinions shared online through social networks, the impact of this specific technology seems limited. Hence, research on the development of the best technology-based innovation for enhancing traditional point of sale is still in progress. Future research might focus on the definition of these requirements by better understanding consumers' tacit and explicit knowledge and their effective usage of the advanced technologies currently available in the stores.

Similarly, a new technology able to support consumers' decision processes at the point of sale might substitute traditional vendors, by better meeting consumers' requests. In fact, retailers should enhance their absorptive capacity concerning consumers' interests and preferences, as well as their capabilities to better reply to consumers' demand. In this way, retailers will be able to preserve and maintain the collaboration with clients.

Moreover, a new question emerges concerning retailers' need of innovating: to what extent should retailers be *adopters* or *pioneers* for achieving competitive advantages in the new innovative scenario? Future studies should focus on investigating the best conditions for adopting and the best ones for developing new technologies to be introduced at the points of sale by analyzing the costs and risks involved in the innovation process. Hence, more tools and methods for supporting retailers in this direction are still needed.

Although past studies have highlighted the importance of others' opinion while shopping, our results showed consumers' limited interest in asking suggestions through social networks at the point of sale. One reason may be the still limited

consumer interest in accessing social networks for achieving information from the stores. In fact, they largely use phone calls or the emerging *whatsapp* chat[1] for achieving friends' opinions while shopping in the store instead of consulting social networks. For this reason, a new technology based on the integration of social networks and new technologies for the physical points of sale may fail in meeting consumers' preferences, whereas another technology more oriented to suggesting the most popular brands and products (according to personal profiles) might better fit market expectations. For instance, the new technology could exploit the social network for proposing a sort of popularity index instead of a tool for asking strangers' suggestions. Preliminary prototypes of this technology have been already introduced in South America through particular crutches with a count of the number of people who touched that item, but these are still mostly unknown in Europe. Hence, further improvements in technology could focus on the best strategy for integrating systems for evaluating the popularity of a certain product in real-time in order to make potential customers aware of the social acceptance of the future purchase and to support their decision making process.

CONCLUSION

Although the introduction of advanced technologies at the points of sale is reducing the number of interactions between clients and vendors (Vasquez Casielles et al., 2005; Boeck & Wamba, 2008; Teo, 2012; Zhu et al., 2013), their relationships still provide benefits for both actors (Reitberger et al., 2007; Black et al., 2009; Lee & Qualls, 2010; Pantano & Timmermans, 2011). Our research investigates the possible integration of social networks at traditional points of sale for developing a new technology able to support consumer decision-making process. Results shows that consumers have limited trust in vendor's suggestions and social networks. The use of advanced technologies based on the integration of social networks at the point of sale provides new services for consumers, but reduces or eliminates the cooperation between vendor and client with negative consequences for the cooperation for the final service.

Findings suggest limited trust in suggestions of vendors, who are (partially) involved in the decision process only for new/unknown products. For this reason, we may expect that a new technology (a new recommender system) might substitute physical vendors' suggestions by providing detailed and useful information for these kinds of products. Furthermore, these technologies exclude vendors' influence in the consumer decision-making process, which usually takes place in a traditional retail environment (Sharma, 2001; Sun et al., 2009). As a consequence, the vendor's capability to acquire knowledge from consumers is replaced by a system able to collect and manage emerging data. Moreover, consumers' consciousness of vendors' influence on their purchase decision might increase the sense of corporate control and guidance, by reducing their attitude towards shopping at a certain point of sale. To avoid this critical issue, vendors should enhance their ability and skills for catching consumers' interests and interact with them, for instance by using advanced technology as supporting tool (not as a substitute). Hence, a new technology should take into account both the consumers' and vendors' point of view, in order to be an integrative tool for both actors.

In conclusion, integrating a new technology based on the use of social networks at the point of sale would make the (physical) shopping experience *more social* by creating social interactions with consumers not physically present in the store. Although consumers need friends' opinions before purchasing, they may substitute the real presence with a *virtual* one, which could be involved through several new technologies (not limited to the integration with social networks). In fact, sociality is still an important aspect of shopping activity, which could be reinforced through several advanced systems for attracting consumers to the physical point of sale.

REFERENCES

Andreu, L., Sanchez, I., & Mele, C. (2010). Value co-creation among retailers and consumers: new insights into the furniture market. *Journal of Retailing and Consumer Services*, *17*(4), 241–250. doi:10.1016/j.jretconser.2010.02.001

Black, D., Clemmensen, N. J., & Skov, M. B. (2009). Supporting the supermarket shopping experience through a context-aware shopping trolley. In *Proceedings of the 21th Annual Conference on the Australian Computer-Human Interaction* (pp. 33-40). ACM Press.

Bock, G.-W., Lee, J., Kuan, H.-H., & Kim, J.-H. (2012). The progression of online trust in the multi-channel retailer context and the role of product uncertainty. *Decision Support Systems*, *53*(1), 97–107. doi:10.1016/j.dss.2011.12.007

Boeck, H., & Wamba, S. F. (2008). RFID and buyer-seller relationships in the retail supply chain. *International Journal of Retail & Distribution Management*, *36*(6), 433–460. doi:10.1108/09590550810873929

Cheung, C. M. K., & Thadani, D. R. (2012). The impact of electronic word-of-mouth communication: a literature analysis and integrative model. *Decision Support Systems*, *54*(1), 461–470. doi:10.1016/j.dss.2012.06.008

Cicala, J. E., Smith, R. K., & Bush, A. J. (2012). What makes sales presentations effective- a buyer-seller perspective. *Journal of Business and Industrial Marketing*, *27*(2), 78–88. doi:10.1108/08858621211196958

Davis, F. D. (1989). Perceived usefulness, perceived ease of use, and user acceptance of information technology. *Management Information Systems Quarterly, 13*, 319–340. doi:10.2307/249008

Desinger, C., Dekhil, M., Ghosh, R., Jain, J., & Hsu, M. (2010). Transforming retail customer shopping experiences using mobile devices, open architectures, and operational business intelligence. HP Laboratories, 36.

Dou, X., Walden, J. A., Lee, S., & Lee, J. Y. (2012). Does source matter? Examining source effects in online product reviews. *Computers in Human Behavior, 28*(5), 1555–1563. doi:10.1016/j.chb.2012.03.015

Drollinger, T., & Comer, L. B. (2013). Salesperson's listening ability as an antecedent to relationship selling. *Journal of Business and Industrial Marketing, 28*(1), 50–59. doi:10.1108/08858621311285714

Du, J.-G., & Fan, X.-C. (2006). A model of salesperson's trust and satisfaction based on the high-priced products selling in retailing. In *Proceedings of the international conference on management science and engineering* (1055-1060). Academic Press.

Gaur, S. S., Herjanto, H., & Bathula, H. (2012). Does buyer–seller similarity affect buyer satisfaction with the seller firm? *International Review of Retail, Distribution and Consumer Research, 22*(3), 315–335. doi:10.1080/09593969.2012.682597

Hassanein, K., & Head, M. (2007). Manipulating perceived social presence through the web interface and its impact on attitude towards online shopping. *International Journal of Human-Computer Studies, 65*(8), 689–708. doi:10.1016/j.ijhcs.2006.11.018

Jiang, J.-C., Chen, C.-A., & Wang, C.-C. (2008). Knowledge and trust in e-consumers' online shopping behavior. In *Proceedings of the International Symposium on Electronic Commerce and Security* (pp. 652-656). IEEE.

Johnson, D., & Grayson, K. (2005). Cognitive and affective trust in service relationships. *Journal of Business Research, 58*(4), 500–507. doi:10.1016/S0148-2963(03)00140-1

Kennedy, M.S., & Ferrell, L.K., Thorne, & LeClair, D. (2001). Consumers' trust of salesperson and manufacturer: an empirical study. *Journal of Business Research, 51*, 73–86. doi:10.1016/S0148-2963(99)00039-9

Lee, J., & Qualls, W. J. (2010). A dynamic process of buyer-seller technology adoption. *Journal of Business and Industrial Marketing, 25*(3), 220–228. doi:10.1108/08858621011027812

Lee, Y.-I., & Trim, P. R. J. (2006). Retail marketing strategy: the role of marketing intelligence, relationship marketing and trust. *Marketing Intelligence & Planning, 24*(7), 730–745. doi:10.1108/02634500610711888

Marshall, G. W., Goebel, D. J., & Moncrief, W. C. (2003). Hiring for success at the buyer-seller interface. *Journal of Business Research, 56*, 247–255. doi:10.1016/S0148-2963(02)00435-6

Morgan, R. M., & Hunt, S. D. (1994). The Commitment–Trust Theory of Relationship Marketing. *Journal of Marketing, 58*, 20–38. doi:10.2307/1252308

Mukherjee, A., & Nath, P. (2007). Role of electronic trust in online retailing: A re-examination of the commitment-trust theory. *European Journal of Marketing, 41*(9/10), 1173–1202. doi:10.1108/03090560710773390

O' Brien, H. L. (2010). The influence of hedonic and utilitarian motivations on user engagement: the case of online shopping experiences. *Interacting with Computers, 22*, 344–352. doi:10.1016/j.intcom.2010.04.001

Palmatier, R. W., Dant, R. P., Grewal, D., & Evans, K. R. (2006). Factors influencing the effectiveness of relationship marketing: a meta-analysis. *Journal of Marketing, 70*, 136–153. doi:10.1509/jmkg.70.4.136

Pantano, E. (2013). Ubiquitous retailing innovative scenario: from the fixed point of sale to the flexible ubiquitous store. *Journal of Technology Management and Innovation, 8*(2), 84–92. doi:10.4067/S0718-27242013000200007

Pantano, E., & Naccarato, G. (2010). Entertainment in Retailing: the influences of advanced technologies. *Journal of Retailing and Consumer Services, 17*(3), 200–204. doi:10.1016/j.jretconser.2010.03.010

Pantano, E., & Timmermans, H. J. P. (2011). *Advanced Technologies Management for Retailing: Frameworks and Cases.* IGI Global. doi:10.4018/978-1-60960-738-8

Plouffe, C. R., Sridharan, S., & Barclay, D. W. (2010). Exploratory navigation and salesperson performance: investigating selected antecedents and boundary conditions in high-technology and financial services contexts. *Industrial Marketing Management, 39*(4), 538–550. doi:10.1016/j.indmarman.2009.02.003

Poon, P., Albaum, G., & Chan, P. S.-F. (2012). Managing trust in direct selling relationships. *Marketing Intelligence & Planning, 30*(5), 588–603. doi:10.1108/02634501211251070

Rafiq, M., Fulford, H., & Lu, X. (2013). Building customer loyalty in online retailing: The role of relationship quality. *Journal of Marketing Management, 29*(3-4), 494–517. doi:10.1080/0267257X.2012.737356

Reitberger, W., Obermair, C., Ploderer, B., Meschtscherjakov, A., & Tscheligi, A. (2007). Enhancing the shopping experience with ambient displays: a field study in a retail store. *Lecture Notes in Computer Science, 4794*, 314–331. doi:10.1007/978-3-540-76652-0_19

Roy, M., Dewit, O., & Aubert, B. A. (2001). The impact of interface usability on trust in web retailers. *Internet Research: Electronic Networking Applications and Policy, 11*(5), 388–398. doi:10.1108/10662240110410165

Ruimei, W., Shengxiong, W., Tianzhen, W., & Xiling, Z. (2012). Customers e-trust for online retailers: a case in China. In *Proceedings of the 8th International Conference on Computational Intelligence and Security* (pp. 573-577). IEEE Computer Society Press.

Sharma, A. (2001). Consumer decision-making, salespeople's adaptive selling and retail performance. *Journal of Business Research, 54*, 125–129. doi:10.1016/S0148-2963(99)00090-9

Sun, P.-C., & Lin, C.-M. (2010). Building customer trust and loyalty: an empirical study in a retailing context. *The Service Industries Journal, 30*(9), 1439–1455. doi:10.1080/02642060802621478

Sun, T., Tai, Z., & Tsai, K.-C. (2009). The role of interdependent self-construal in consumers' susceptibility to retail salespersons' influence: a hierarchical approach. *Journal of Retailing and Consumer Services, 16*(5), 360–366. doi:10.1016/j.jretconser.2009.04.002

Toufaily, E., Souiden, N., & Ladhari, R. (in press). Consumer trust toward retail websites: comparison between pure click and click-and-brick retailers. *Journal of Retailing and Consumer Services.*

Twing-Kwong, S., Albaum, L. G., & Fullgrabe, L. (2013). Trust in customer-salesperson relationship in China's retail sector. *International Journal of Retail & Distribution Management, 41*(3), 226–248. doi:10.1108/09590551311306264

Utz, S., Kerkhof, P., & van den Bos, J. (2012). Consumer rule: how consumer reviews influence perceived trustworthiness of online stores. *Electronic Commerce Research and Applications, 11*(1), 49–58. doi:10.1016/j.elerap.2011.07.010

Vásquez Casielles, R., Suárez Álvarez, L., & Díaz Martín, A. M. (2005). Trust as a key factor in successful relationships between consumers and retail service providers. *The Service Industries Journal, 25*(1), 83–101. doi:10.1080/0264206042000302423

Venkatesh, V., Morris, M. G., Davis, G. B., & Davis, F. D. (2003). User Acceptance of Information Technology: Toward a Unified View. *Management Information Systems Quarterly, 27*(3), 425–478.

Venkatesh, V., Thong, J. Y. L., & Xu, X. (2012). Consumer acceptance and use of information technology: extending the unified theory of acceptance and use of technology. *Management Information Systems Quarterly, 36*(1), 157–178.

Wagner, J. A., Klein, N. M., & Keith, J. E. (2003). Buyer-seller relationships and selling effectiveness: the moderating influence of buyer expertise and product competitive position. *Journal of Business Research, 56*, 295–302. doi:10.1016/S0148-2963(02)00441-1

Yang, J. (2013). Harnessing value in knowledge management for performance in buyer–supplier collaboration. *International Journal of Production Research, 51*(7), 1984–1991. doi:10.1080/00207543.2012.701774

Zhu, Z., Nakata, C., Sivakumar, K., & Grewal, D. (2013). Fix it or leave it? Customer recovery from self-service technology failure. *Journal of Retailing, 89*(1), 15–29. doi:10.1016/j.jretai.2012.10.004

ADDITIONAL READING

Bennet, R., & Savani, S. (2011). Retailers' preparedness for the introduction of third wave (ubiquitous) computing applications: A survey of UK companies. *International Journal of Retail and Distribution Management, 39*(5), 306–325. doi:10.1108/09590551111130748

Bonner, J. M. (2010). Customer interactivity and new product performance: Moderating effects of product newness and product embeddedness. *Industrial Marketing Management, 39*, 485–492. doi:10.1016/j.indmarman.2008.11.006

Borgers, A., Brouwer, M., Kunen, T., Jessurun, J. J., & Janssen, I. I. (2010). A virtual reality tool to measure shoppers' tenant mix preferences. *Computers, Environment and Urban Systems, 34*(5), 377–388. doi:10.1016/j.compenvurbsys.2010.04.002

Borgers, A., & Vosters, C. (2011). Assessing preferences for mega shopping centres: a conjoint measurement approach. *Journal of Retailing and Consumer Services, 18*(4), 322–332. doi:10.1016/j.jretconser.2011.02.006

Di Stefano, G., Bambardella, A., & Verona, G. (2012). Technology push and demand pull perspectives in innovation studies: current findings and future research directions. *Research Policy, 41*, 1283–1295. doi:10.1016/j.respol.2012.03.021

Hsiao, C.-C., Yen, H. J. R., & Li, E. Y. (2012). Exploring consumer value of multichannel shopping: a perspective of means-end theory. *Internet Research, 22*(3), 318–339. doi:10.1108/10662241211235671

Hsu, M.-H., Ju, T. L., Yen, C.-H., & Chang, C.-M. (2007). Knowledge sharing behavior in virtual communities: the relationship between trust, self-efficacy, and outcome expectations. *International Journal of Human-Computer Studies*, *65*, 153–169. doi:10.1016/j.ijhcs.2006.09.003

Kasiri, N., Sharda, R., & Hardrave, B. (2012). A balanced scorecard for item-level RFID in the retail sector: a Delphi study. *European Journal of Information Systems*, *21*(3), 255–267. doi:10.1057/ejis.2011.33

Kourouthanassis, P. E., Giaglis, G. M., & Vrechopoulos, A. P. (2007). Enhancing user experience through pervasive information systems: the case of pervasive retailing. *International Journal of Information Management*, *27*, 319–335. doi:10.1016/j.ijinfomgt.2007.04.005

Lin, Y., Jessrun, J., De Vries, B., & Timmermans, H. (2011). Motivate: context aware mobile application for activity recommendation. *Lecture Notes in Computer Science*, *7040*, 210–214. doi:10.1007/978-3-642-25167-2_27

Moiseeva, A., & Timmermans, H. (2010). Imputing relevant information from multi-day GPS tracers for retail planning and management using data fusion and context-sensitive learning. *Journal of Retailing and Consumer Services*, *17*(3), 189–199. doi:10.1016/j.jretconser.2010.03.011

O'Cass, A., & Carlson, J. (2012). An e-retailing assessment of perceived website-service innovativeness: implications for website quality evaluations, trust, loyalty and word of mouth. *Australasian Marketing Journal*, *20*, 28–36. doi:10.1016/j.ausmj.2011.10.012

Oh, L.-B., Teo, H.-H., & Sambamurthy, V. (2012). The effects of retail channel integration through the use of information technologies on firm performance. *Journal of Operations Management*, *30*(5), 368–381. doi:10.1016/j.jom.2012.03.001

Pantano, E., & Di Pietro, L. (2012). Understanding consumer's acceptance of technology-based innovations in retailing. *Journal of Technology Management & Innovation*, *7*(4), 1–19. doi:10.4067/S0718-27242012000400001

Pantano, E., Iazzolino, G., & Migliano, G. (2013). Obsolescence risk in advanced technologies for retailing: a management perspective. *Journal of Retailing and Consumer Services*, *20*(1), 225–233. doi:10.1016/j.jretconser.2013.01.002

Pantano, E., & Servidio, R. (2012). Modeling innovative points of sales through virtual and immersive technologies. *Journal of Retailing and Consumer Services*, *19*(3), 279–286. doi:10.1016/j.jretconser.2012.02.002

Pantano, E., & Viassone, M. (in press). Demand pull and technology push perspective in technology-based innovations for the points of sale: the retailers evaluation. *Journal of Retailing and Consumer Services*.

Papagiannidis, S., Pantano, E., See-to, E., & Bourlakis, M. (in press). Modelling the determinants of a simulated experience in a virtual retail store and users' product purchasing intentions. *Journal of Marketing Management*.

Park, J., Gunn, F., & Han, S.-L. (2012). Multidimensional trust building in e-retailing: Cross-cultural differences in trust formation and implications for perceived risk. *Journal of Retailing and Consumer Services*, *19*, 304–312. doi:10.1016/j.jretconser.2012.03.003

Rasouli, S., & Timmermans, H. (2013). Assessment of model uncertainty in destinations and travel forecasts of models of complex spatial shopping behavior. *Journal of Retailing and Consumer Services*, *20*(2), 139–146. doi:10.1016/j.jretconser.2012.05.001

KEY TERMS AND DEFINITIONS

Client-Vendor Relationships: The interactions between buyer and seller. The strong client-vendor relationships have positive effects on the subsequent seller performance, in terms of sales growth, profits, share of market and share of voice, etc.. The key dimensions of client-vendor relationships are (i) the communication and information sharing between the parties, (ii) the cooperation on the final service, and (iii) the trust between the parties.

Electronic Word-of-Mouth Communication (eWOM): Part of word-of-mouth (informal communication among individuals) held online. Several studies identified the important of eWOM in consumers' purchasing decisions, as well as in firms' marketing strategies development by providing frequently updated information on market trends.

Innovation Management: The management of a possible innovation, which can be a product of an organizational innovation. It can be measured in terms of innovation diffusion, main characteristics, impact for the society and Management Innovation index.

Knowledge Transfer (from Vendor to Client and vice versa): From a consumers' point of view, the knowledge (familiarity) of both product and vendor is able to reduce the social uncertainty while increasing the understanding of the situation (Jiang et al., 2008). After vendor's knowledge transfer to client, the client is able to develop a deeper understanding of the products characteristics useful for making a better choice. While vendor can exploit the information achieved from clients to develop a greater understanding of market trends and improve the marketing strategies. In particular, the information sharing is based willingness to share knowledge of both consumers and vendors, as well as on client's trust in vendors' knowledge (Teo, 2012).

Seller Skills: The most important seller's skills for sales success mainly consist of listening skills, ability to adapt sales style according to the different situations/clients, and communication skills (in terms of verb communication skills). In particular, the listening skill of salesperson is positively related to consumers' trust towards the salesperson, due to the emerging ability in deeply understanding the buyer's needs and his/her point of view.

Technology Management: The management of the use of technology for human's benefits, in terms of planning, design, optimization, control of a technological product, process or service, as well as the evaluation and prediction of users' acceptance and adoption.

Trust: It exists when one party has confidence in the reliability and integrity in the other party involved in the exchange. Generally, trust can be considered as the "confidence in an exchange partner's reliability and integrity" (Morgan & Hunt, 1994). Trust further measures the intensity of relationship marketing (commitment) between the partners involved in a certain exchange.

ENDNOTES

[1]   *Whatsapp* is an emerging cross-platform mobile messaging app for mobile phones (e.g. iPhone, Android, etc.), for freely sending texts, videos and audio to memorized contacts.

Chapter 21

Retail Innovativeness:
Importance of ICT and Impact on Consumer Behaviour

Irene Gil Saura
Universidad de Valencia, Spain

María Eugenia Ruiz Molina
Universidad de Valencia, Spain

Gloria Berenguer Contrí
Universidad de Valencia, Spain

ABSTRACT

Retailers have to operate in highly competitive environments, where innovation may become a source of sustainable competitive advantage. This chapter aims at exploring the relationship between retail innovativeness and the level of technological advancement as well as the ICT solutions implemented by store chains of four retail activities (e.g. grocery, textile, electronics, and furniture and decoration). In addition to this, the authors test the existence of significant differences in consumer perceptions and behavioral intentions between retailers perceived as high innovators and those considered low innovators. As a result, differences in consumer behaviour are found between high and low innovators that may be explained by the strong relationship between retail innovativeness and the technology implemented by the store. Notwithstanding, these findings are sensitive to the type of product sold by the store.

INTRODUCTION

Retail innovativeness, defined as the extent to which retailers in the local market adopt new merchandising or service ideas (Homburg et al., 2002), is a topic that has received scarce attention in the marketing literature up to date. In particular, innovation in marketing channels has been discussed in reference to specific areas of innovation or to single categories of subjects within channels (Musso, 2010). Most of contributions have focused on innovation in retailing as 'product innovation' for distribution companies (Dawson, 2001; Dupuis, 2000; Castaldo, 2001), or as innovation in the supply chain (Musso, 2010). In this sense, the interest of researchers has focused

DOI: 10.4018/978-1-4666-6074-8.ch021

on technological issues, particularly those relating to information and communication technologies (ICT). However, to the best of our knowledge, little attention has been paid to the relationship between retail innovativeness and several ICT implemented by retailers or to the implications of retail innovativeness on consumer behavior.

In highly competitive environments, there may be great pressure for individual retailers to be innovative. Empirical strategy research based on contingency theory has suggested that the level of dynamism in the environment created through innovativeness is a key driver of a company's strategic decisions (Miller 1988; Miller & Dröge 1986). Given the classical merchandising orientation of many retailers (Mulhern, 1997; Homburg et al., 2002), one promising way for a firm to innovate is by implementing ICT to enhance their service-oriented business strategy. Notwithstanding, there may be differences in the importance of ICT for retail innovativeness across retailers depending on the store assortment. In this sense, following Berry and Barnes' (1987) typology, there is a distinction between high-touch retailers, i.e. characterized by a high level of personal contact with customers through personal selling and advice and customized services, and low-touch retailers which emphasize the use of self-service technologies. Since self-service is the sales system in most of the grocery, clothing and footwear retailers, we expect some ICT solutions, e.g. self-service technologies, to be used to a greater extent. On the other hand, for durable goods retailers, i.e. electronics/electrical appliances and furniture/decoration, higher customer involvement is expected in the purchase process and sales systems based on customization and personal selling. Thus, we understand that according to the type of product distributed by the retailer, there is a different degree of contact between customers and vendors and, thus, there may well be differences in the level of use of retailer technology depending on the type of retail activity.

Therefore, the aims of this paper are, first, to explore the relationship between retail innovativeness and the retailer's level of technological advancement and, second, to test the existence of significant differences in consumer perceptions and behavioral intentions between retailers perceived as high innovators and those considered as low innovators. In order to take into consideration the existence of potential differences due to the retailer's assortment, four types of store chains are analyzed: grocery, textile, electronics and furniture and decoration.

BACKGROUND

In recent decades, the innovation processes in marketing channels have occurred with high intensity and speed, particularly explained by advances in technology that allowed the adoption of more efficient organizational solutions (Musso, 2010). Referring to marketing channels, the concept of innovation must be seen as a strategic activity for both industrial and distribution firms to acquire a competitive advantage along the distribution channel, and as a changing process of the economic function of the distribution systems. As a result of these processes, an increased competitiveness for all firms in the channel has emerged. Technology – in particular, ICT -, social changes and new behavioral patterns of the final demand, have stimulated innovations in retailing.

Following Ryssel et al. (2004: 198), information and communication technology (ICT) is "a term that encompasses all forms of technology utilized to create, capture, manipulate, communicate, exchange, present, and use information in its various forms (business data, voice conversations, still images, motion pictures, multimedia presentations," etc.). In the relationships with the final consumer, there is a wide catalogue of technological innovations – e.g. checkout technologies, electronic and mobile payment systems, distance selling, self-service technologies, etc. – that have not been uniformly implemented by retailers.

In the field of retailing, in addition to retail innovativeness, branding has been pointed out as an important source of differentiation (Jinfeng & Zhilong, 2009). In particular, it begins to be highlighted the importance of building brand equity linked to the store, thus emerging in the literature the concept of retailer equity (Pappu & Quester, 2006b) or store equity (Hartman & Spiro, 2005). In spite of the wide research on product brand equity, the literature shows a very recent interest for the analysis of the brand equity concept in the field of retailing, being a limited number of contributions aimed at defining the content of this construct (Hartman & Spiro, 2005; Pappu & Quester, 2006a, Jinfeng & Zhilong, 2009, Swoboda et al., 2009). These studies are not conclusive about the nature of store brand equity, nor on the variables that contribute to its formation (Jinfeng & Zhilong, 2009). According to an extensive literature review conducted, we examine the influence of retail innovativeness on the store equity dimensions most frequently pointed out by research in this field, i.e. loyalty towards the establishment, awareness, service quality, product quality and perceived value. In particular, we propose to examine the existence of differences between high and low innovative retailers regarding customer perceptions on store brand equity, loyalty towards the establishment, awareness, service quality, product quality, and perceived value.

Last, regarding the consequents of store equity, behavioral intentions are examined. According to the theory of planned behavior proposed by Ajzen and Fishbein (1980), there is a relationship between beliefs, attitudes and behavioral intentions with respect to an object, so that attitude formation is based on beliefs about an object and that behavioral intentions are derived from attitudes. In the context of retailing, it has been pointed out that behavioral intentions are shaped by store-related information (Grewal et al., 1998). In particular, consumers'

beliefs about the physical attractiveness of a store has a high correlation with patronage intentions (Darden et al., 1983; Baker et al., 2002; Mohan et al., 2012). In turn, empirical evidence have been found supporting the importance of behavioral intentions as predictors of behavioral outcomes (Shamma & Hassan, 2009). There are some studies that operationalise behavioral intentions as a one dimensional construct (Cronin & Taylor, 1992), while others identify several dimensions such as repeat purchase intention and word of mouth (Zeithaml et al., 1996).

THEORETICAL FRAMEWORK AND HYPOTHESES

In order to achieve the proposed objectives, we assume as a point of departure the conceptualization of store equity or retailer equity by Arnett et al.,(2003), since it seems to gather the most relevant contributions about the dimensions of store equity. According to these authors, the dimensions of store brand equity or retailer equity are loyalty towards the establishment, awareness, service quality, product quality and perceived value. In addition to this, Arnett et al., (2003) indicate the existence of a significant positive influence of store equity on consumer behavioral intentions towards the store, the latter being understood as the intention to repeat purchase and positive word-of-mouth communications (Oliver, 1993). Other studies have found support for the positive influence of store equity on the intention to recommend the store (Swoboda et al., 2009) and to pay a premium price for the retailer's products (Netemeyer et al., 2004). It is in this theoretical framework (Figure 1) that we aim at exploring the influence of ICT on the customer perception of retail innovativeness and testing the existence of significant differences in customer perceptions of store equity and their behavioral intentions towards the store depending on the level of the retailer innovativeness.

Figure 1. Theoretical framework
Source: Authors' proposal

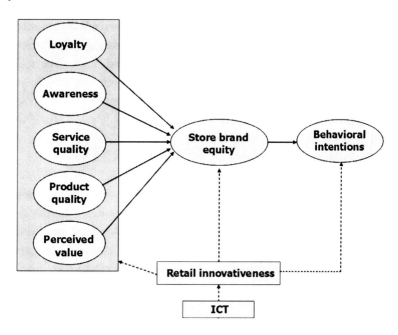

First, according to Musso (2010), innovation in marketing channels may be analyzed following three different approaches: technological perspective, relational perspective and structural perspective. In the technological perspective, Musso (2010) identifies a series of technology solutions as the most important fronts of technological innovation in the *relationships with the final consumer, i.e.* checkout technologies, dynamic pricing, electronic and mobile payment systems, distance selling, and Self-Service Technologies.

In this sense, we expect that consumer perception of retail innovativeness will depend on the technology solutions implemented by the store and, thus, we posit:

H1: Perceived advancement and customer satisfaction with retailer's ICT are antecedents of the customer's perception about the retailer innovativeness.

H2: Retailer innovativeness is positively related to the use of the most recent ICT solutions by the retailer.

Innovation involves two main words: trendy and popular (Wang et al., 2008) that are able to create and enhance value for the customers (Aaker, 2007). In this sense, we expect that the most innovative retailers enjoy superior store brand awareness.

In addition to this, according to the relational perspective of innovation in marketing channels pointed out by Musso (2010), innovation can occur in relationships with end-customers through *customer care initiatives*, i.e., all activities aimed at strengthening the relationship with the end user, such as the use of loyalty cards. In this sense, retail innovativeness is expected to influence consumer perceptions on retailer equity and behavioral intentions.

Following Grewal et al., (2010), retailers try to innovate in order to increase the value of the consumer shopping experience. This can be instrumented through enhancing service quality, since augmenting products with services has been considered as a major way retailers have of gaining differentiation in competitive markets (Homburg et al., 2002).

Regarding product quality, Fuller (2004) classifies product releases, ranking each class according to its degree of innovation, i.e. line extensions, repositioning, new form or new size, new formula for an existing product, new packaging, innovative products and creative products. Retailer's innovativeness has been associated to its capacity to release new products and, in this line, Anselmsson and Johansson (2009) provides evidence about a significant positive relationship between growth in the retailer market share in a category and level of innovativeness in the category. The authors conclude that companies could allocate resources for more creative products although it might mean fewer new product releases.

All above mentioned allow us to enunciate the following hypotheses:

H3: Retailer brand equity (global assessment as well as its dimensions – loyalty, awareness, service quality, product quality and perceived value-) is better for the most innovative retailers in comparison to the least innovative retailers.

H4: Behavioral intentions are more positive towards the store for the most innovative retailers in comparison to the least innovative retailers.

Last, since self-service is the sales system in most of the grocery, clothing and footwear retailers, we expect that innovative retailers according to the technological will be more appreciated by the consumers of these industries. On the other hand, for durable goods retailers, i.e. electronics/electrical appliances and furniture/decoration, higher customer involvement is expected in the purchase process and sales systems based on customization and personal selling. Thus, we understand that according to the type of product distributed by the retailer, there is a different degree of contact between customers and vendors and, thus, there may well be differences in the impact of retail innovativeness depending on the type of retail activity.

H5: The differences in the evaluation of retailer brand equity, behavioral intentions and perceived advancement of the retailer's ICT between the most innovative retailers and the least innovative retailers is higher for low touch retailers in comparison to high touch retailers.

METHODOLOGY

In order to obtain the information needed to achieve the above mentioned aims, a personal survey is performed. A questionnaire is developed to gather information on consumer perceptions about the variables selected, i.e. retailer's relationship innovativeness, store brand equity, loyalty towards the establishment, awareness, service quality, product quality, perceived value, behavioral intentions, retailer's technology advancement, intensity of use of ICT and customer satisfaction with retailer's technology.

In particular, the items to measure retail innovativeness are adapted from Homburg et al., (2002). Thus, we understand retail innovativeness as the extent to which the retailer's proneness to adopt new merchandising or service ideas, conceptualized as a multi-item construct that refers to the number of innovations adopted, the time of adoption, and the consistency of adoption over time.

The retailer brand equity scale is adapted from Shen (2010), while items for measuring loyalty, awareness and service quality are adapted from Arnett et al., (2003). Product quality and perceived value are measured through the items adapted from Sweeney and Soutar (2001), whereas the items for measuring behavioral intentions are adapted from Shen (2010) and Gelbrich (2011). Last, the level of perceived advancement of the retailer's ICT is measured through the items adapted from Wu et al., (2006), while the catalogue of information and communication technologies is elaborated from Musso (2010) and proposed by the authors. Finally, satisfaction with the retailer's technology has been measured as an overall assessment based on total consumer experience through a single item that, in absence of an ad-hoc scale in the literature, it has been proposed by the authors. All items are measured in a 7-point Likert scale, ranking from 1 (strongly disagree) to 7 (strongly agree).

The analyses are performed for four retail activities. In particular, we study two retail sectors of personal consumer goods (grocery and clothing/footwear) and two types of retailers of home durable goods (electronics and electrical appliances, and furniture and decoration). The choice of these four sectors is effected in order to distinguish the potential differences due to retail innovativeness across high-touch and low-touch retailers, according to the Berry and Barnes' (1987) typology. Respondents are asked to assess the items referring to retail chains they have just visited. A total of 13 store brands have been selected because of their product assortment and their position among most prominent retail brands in Europe (Interbrand, 2011) and in the Spanish market (BICE, 2011). Retailing industry in the European Union, and in particular, in Spain, is currently experienced deeply changes due to economic crisis, increasing competition and changing patterns of consumer behavior, partly due to technology evolution (Sánchez Pérez et al., 2011). In the case of the Spanish retailing industry, 2008 was already a period of recession, although retail trade still represented 15.43% of the services industry and its contribution to the Gross Added Value was 10.39%, that has experienced a continuous fall since the year 2000 (Velarde Fuentes, 2011). This downwards trend together with the increasing competition justifies the interest of analysing the role of retail innovativeness on customer perceptions and behavioral intentions in the Spanish retailing setting.

Regarding the sampling procedure, in order to obtain a representative sample, a simple random sampling procedure is followed. A total of 820 valid questionnaires were collected at the exit of several stores in a region in Spain in the period January-February 2013. Table 1 shows the main characteristics of the consumer sample.

From the data collected, first, linear regressions are estimated to assess the existence of causal relationships (Bagozzi, 1980; Creswell, 2009), being the dependent variable retail innovativeness and the independent variables the retailer's level of technological advancement and the customer satisfaction with the retailer's technology, respectively. In addition to this, correlations between retail innovativeness and several information and communications technologies are calculated.

Last, differences between the most and the least innovating retailers are tested through ANOVA analysis. The most innovative retailers are those showing mean scores for the retail innovativeness scale higher than the median value (i.e. 4), while low innovators are those scoring less than 4. Retailers showing an average retail innovativeness score of exactly 4 are eliminated in order to avoid

Table 1. Sample description

Consumer Characteristics	Frequency	%
Gender		
Male	293	35.7
Female	527	64.3
Age		
18-25 years old	151	18.4
26-35 years old	163	19.9
36-45 years old	184	22.4
46-55 years old	164	20.0
56-65 years old	114	13.9
More than 65 years old	44	5.4
Educational Level		
No studies	14	1.7
Primary studies	125	15.2
Secondary studies	286	34.9
University studies	386	47.1
No answer	9	1.1
Labour Status		
Student	123	15.0
Housewife	67	8.2
Unemployed	102	12.4
Pensioner	76	9.3
Employer	72	8.8
Employee	380	46.3

potential biases. All analyses are performed for the total sample as well as for each of the four retail activities under consideration – i.e. grocery, textile, electronics and decoration.

RESULTS

As a previous step to testing our hypotheses, a confirmatory factor analysis was performed that provided acceptable values for the reliability of the scales, measured through the composite reliability and the Cronbach's coefficient alpha for all the constructs) as well as for the extracted variances, being all the standardised factor loadings statistically significant for all the items. All this allows us to confirm the convergent validity of the model (Table 2).

Additionally, we have estimated the correlations between constructs and the confidence intervals as described by Anderson and Gerbing, 1988). The results of this analysis allow us to confirm the discriminant validity, Table 3).

Table 2. Confirmatory factor analysis results

Construct	Item	Standardized Factor Loading (st. error)	t	Cronbach's α	Composite Reliability	Average Variance Extracted
Loyalty	**L1:** I consider myself to be loyal to this store.	0.760	-	0.921	0.923	0.750
	L2: When buying this type of product, this store is my first choice.	0.898 (0.041)	28.681*			
	L3: I will not buy from other retailer if I can buy the same item at this store.	0.892 (0.041)	25.094*			
	L4: Even when items are available from other retailers, I tend to buy from this store.	0.906 (0.041)	26.486*			
Awareness	**A1:** I am aware of [store name] stores.	0.666	-	0.892	0.894	0.681
	A2: I can recognize [store name] stores among other competing stores.	0.847 (0.060)	16.010*			
	A3: Some characteristics of [store name] stores come to mind quickly.	0.915 (0.057)	19.719*			
	A4: I have difficulty in imagining [store name] stores in my mind.	0.853 (0.055)	18.255*			
Service Quality	**SQ1:** This store provides excellent service to its customers.	0.881	-	0.865	0.865	0.762
	SQ2: This store performs service right the first time.	0.865 (0.036)	28.306*			
Product Quality	**PQ1:** The items in this store have consistent quality.	0.866	-	0.917	0.921	0.797
	PQ2: The items in this store have an acceptable standard of quality.	0.956 (0.029)	37.660*			
	PQ3: The items in this store would perform consistently.	0.852 (0.033)	26.123*			

continued on following page

Table 2. Continued

Construct	Item	Standardized Factor Loading (st. error)	t	Cronbach's α	Composite Reliability	Average Variance Extracted
Perceived Value	**PV1:** The items in this store are reasonably priced.	0.841	-	0.889	0.893	0.678
	PV2: The items in this store offer value for money.	0.845 (0.039)	25.026*			
	PV3: The items in this store are good product s for the price.	0.905 (0.042)	26.238*			
	VP4: The items in this store would be economical.	0.687 (0.042)	22.644*			
Retailer Brand Equity	**RE1:** I choose this store instead of any other store, even if they are the same	0.905	-	0.968	0.968	0.883
	RE2: Even if another store has the same features as this store, I would prefer to this store.	0.960 (0.024)	45.236*			
	RE3: If there is another store as good as this store, I prefer to this store.	0.957 (0.025)	41.745*			
	RE4: It seems smarter to choose this store.	0.935 (0.027)	40.216*			
Behavioral Intentions	**BI1:** I would like to come to this store again.	0.698	-	0.868	0.878	0.605
	BI2: I would like to buy this store, even if the price in this store increases.	0.417 (0.072)	11.161*			
	BI3: I would like to recommend this store to a friend/relative.	0.881 (0.084)	17.598*			
	BI4: If my friends ask me for advice, I would recommend this retail outlet.	0.936 (0.086)	18.021*			
	BI5: I would advice others to buy this type of product from this retail outlet.	0.844 (0.087)	17.486*			
Perceived Advancement of Retailer's ICT	**T1:** This STORE invests in technology.	0.839	-	0.833	0.861	0.632
	T2: This STORE has the most advanced technology.	0.947 (0.034)	34.038*			
	T3: In comparison to its competitors, this STORE'S technology is more advanced.	0.908 (0.038)	29.473*			
	T4: This STORE considers my opinion as a customer on decisions involving IT coordination and development in order to improve services and to better satisfy my needs as a client.	0.320 (0.046)	8.795*			

Chi-square Satorra-Bentler: 1071.82; degrees of freedom: 377; CFI: 0.945; IFI: 0.945; Bentler-Bonett NNFI: 0.937; RMSEA: 0.053.

Once checked the reliability and validity of the scales used in this research, in order to achieve the first aim of this paper, we explore the relationship between retailer's innovativeness and retailer's level of technological advancement as well as customer satisfaction with the retailer's technology. Since the correlation between customer perceptions about retailer's level of technological advancement and satisfaction with the retailer's technology is very strong (i.e. 0.627), two regres-

Table 3. Means, standard deviations and correlations between constructs

Construct	Mean	St. dev.	Correlations							
			F1	F2	F3	F4	F5	F6	F7	F8
F1: Loyalty	3.998	1.666		0.500 (0.32, 0.68)	0.563 (0.39, -0.73)	0.444 (0.29, 0.60)	0.434 (0.28, 0.59)	0.736 (0.53, 0.94)	0.643 (0.48, 0.80)	0.191 (0.03, 0.36)
F2: Awareness	5.709	1.370			0.475 (0.32, 0.63)	0.409 (0.26, 0.56)	0.317 (0.19, 0.45)	0.408 (0.25, 0.57)	0.424 (0.30, 0.55)	0.192 (0.07, 0.32)
F3: Service Quality	5.458	1.335				0.623 (0.46, 0.79)	0.517 (0.36, -0.68)	0.548 (0.38, 0.72)	0.630 (0.48, -0.78)	0.376 (0.22, -0.53)
F4: Product Quality	5.560	1.245					0.454 (0.31, 0.60)	0.434 (0.28, 0.58)	0.547 (0.41, 0.68)	0.409 (0.26, 0.56)
F5: Perceived Value	4.999	1.385						0.408 (0.26, 0.56)	0.513 (0.39, 0.64)	0.140 (0.00, 0.28)
F6: Retailer Brand Equity	4.187	1.644							0.644 (0.49, 0.80)	0.255 (0.09, 0.42)
F7: Behavioral Intentions	4.556	1.629								0.344 (0.22, 0.47)
F8: Perceived Advancement of Retailer's ICT	3.886	1.675								

sions are calculated separately to avoid multicollinearity. Estimations are calculated for the total sample and for each retail activity (Table 4).

In general, there are significant positive correlations between retail innovativeness and customer perceptions about the level of advancement of the retailer's ICT solutions ($p < 0.05$). Additionally, there is a direct significant relationship between customer satisfaction with the retailer's technology and retail innovativeness. Therefore, store innovativeness and technology implemented seems to be closely related.

Notwithstanding, there is no significant relationship found consumer satisfaction with the retailer's technology and retail innovativeness for clothing and footwear retailers. From these results we infer that retail patrons of these stores do not consider retail innovativeness as so closely related with technology. Maybe in this industry retail innovativeness is linked to staff practices or policies not requiring the use of technology. Thus, we find support for Hypotheses 1 and 2 excepting for apparel retailers.

In order to identify the store technologies most related with the consumer's perception of the retailer's innovativeness (defined as the retailer's proneness to adopt new merchandising or service ideas -number of innovations adopted, time of adoption, and consistency of adoption over time), correlations are calculated between retail innovativeness scores and the store intensity of use of several ICT solutions (Table 5).

For the total sample, the highest correlations with retail innovativeness are observed for the retailer's Website, followed by screens for projecting images, multimedia kiosks, activity in social media and mobile apps, being all of them positive and significant at $p < 0.01$. In contrast, self-service technologies do not hold any significant linear relationship with retail innovativeness.

Having a look at correlations for each retail industry and technology, credit/debit card payment, the retailer's Website and mobile apps hold significant positive relationships with retail innovativeness for all groups regardless product assortment ($p < 0.01$).

However, the relationship between retailer's technology and innovativeness seems to be strongly influenced by product assortment. In particular, self-service technologies are positively and significantly related with retail innovativeness for grocery stores ($p < 0.05$), whereas no linear relationship is found for the rest of activity sectors.

In addition to this, while all ICT solutions are positively and significantly correlated to retail innovativeness for grocery retailers, only some of them seem to be relevant for the rest of store chains. Furthermore, the relative importance of each technology differs across retail activities. In the case of grocery store chains, video surveillance is the ICT most related to retail innovativeness, followed by store brand Website and activity in social media ($p < 0.01$).

Table 4. Linear regression estimations of retail innovativeness on perceived advancement and customer satisfaction with retailer's ICT

Variables	Total N=820	Grocery N=300	Clothing/Footw. N=180	Electronics N=180	Furnit./Deco. N=160
Constant	2.29[a]	2.01[a]	3.21[a]	2.51[a]	4.10[a]
Perceived advancement of retailer's ICT	0.50[a]	0.44[a]	0.26[b]	0.45[a]	0.27[a]
R^2	0.159[a]	0.130[a]	0.036[b]	0.083[a]	0.067[a]
Constant	2.44[a]	2.19[a]	3.45[a]	2.55[a]	4.12[a]
Satisfaction with the retailer's ICT	0.36[a]	0.28[a]	0.14	0.37[a]	0.23[a]
R^2	0.083[a]	0.060[a]	0.014	0.053[a]	0.058[a]

[a, b, c]Statistically significant at 1%, 5% and 10%, respectively.

Table 5. Correlations between retail innovativeness and retailer's use of ICT solutions

Items	Total N=820	Grocery N=300	Clothing/Footw. N=180	Electronics N=180	Furnit./Deco. N=160
1. Credit/debit card payment	0.24[a]	0.24[a]	0.20[a]	0.20[a]	0.32[a]
2. Retailer card payment	0.12[a]	0.11[b]	0.15[c]	-0.01	0.13[c]
3. Mobile payment	0.18[a]	0.15[b]	0.11	0.25[a]	0.13[c]
4. Web site	0.32[a]	0.26[a]	0.22[a]	0.30[a]	0.27[a]
5. E-mail	0.24[a]	0.16[a]	0.22[a]	0.14[c]	0.11
6. Phone	0.24[a]	0.25[a]	0.16[b]	0.15[b]	0.23[a]
7. Self-service technologies	0.05	0.13[b]	-0.05	0.07	0.13
8. Photoelectric cells	0.15[a]	0.22[a]	0.09	0.14[c]	0.40[a]
9. Piped music	0.24[a]	0.18[a]	0.25[a]	0.11	0.28[a]
10. Screens for projecting images	0.30[a]	0.24[a]	0.05	0.22[a]	0.23[a]
11. Multimedia kiosks	0.30[a]	0.20[a]	0.17[b]	0.19[b]	0.27[a]
12. Video surveillance	0.26[a]	0.29[a]	0.20[a]	0.10	0.26[a]
13. In-store wi-fi	0.26[a]	0.22[a]	0.18[b]	0.17[b]	0.09
14. Mobile apps	0.27[a]	0.25[a]	0.20[a]	0.19[a]	0.22[a]
15. Loyalty program	0.18[a]	0.20[a]	0.30[a]	0.06[a]	0.15[c]
16. Activity in social media (Facebook, Twitter, blogs)	0.28[a]	0.26[a]	0.26[a]	0.19[b]	0.22[a]

[a, b, c] Statistically significant at 1%, 5% and 10%, respectively.

For apparel retailers, retailer's loyalty program, activity in social media and piped music are the ICT solutions that contribute to retail innovativeness perception at a greater extent. In contrast, the use of mobile payment, self-service technologies, photoelectric cells, and screens for projecting images, is not significantly associated with the perceived retail innovativeness for this group of stores.

Regarding stores selling electronics, on one side, technologies strongly linked to retail innovativeness are retailer's Website, mobile payment and screens for projecting images. On the other side, retailer card payment, self-service technologies, piped music and video surveillance do not hold any significant relationship with retail innovativeness.

Last, for furniture and decoration retailers, retail innovativeness is mainly related to some solutions such as photoelectric cells, credit card payment, piped music, the retailer's Website and multimedia kiosks. However, other ICT applications such as e-mail for contacting with the retailer, self-service technologies and in-store wi-fi are not significantly related to retail innovativeness in this industry.

Second, in order to test the existence of differences in consumer behavior between low innovators and high innovators, retailers are divided in two groups according to the consumer perception of the retailer's innovativeness. The median value of retailer's innovativeness is 4, and those retailers scoring less than 4 have been classified as "low innovators" while retailers scoring more than 4 are considered as "high innovators" (retailers scoring exactly the median value are excluded from the study in order to avoid potential biases). Mean values are calculated for both groups regarding consumer attitudes and behavioral intentions. Differences between low and high innovators are tested through an ANOVA analysis. Results are shown in Table 6.

High innovators show higher scores than low innovators in all variables. These differences are significant for all variables excepting perceived value. Thus, retailers perceived as high innovators are also considered as more technologically advanced than low innovators. In addition to this, high innovators enjoy higher levels of customer loyalty and awareness. Their service and product are considered of superior quality in comparison to low innovators. All in all, retailer brand equity shows significantly higher scores for the most in-novative retailers, and consumer behavioral intentions are more favourable towards these retailers in comparison to low innovators.

In order to take into consideration the existence of different patterns due to the retailer's assort-ment, four types of store chains are analyzed: grocery, textile, electronics and furniture and decoration. Table 7 shows mean values and the results of the ANOVA analysis for grocery and clothing/footwear retailers.

For both grocery and apparel retailers, high innovators show higher scores than low inno-vators. Notwithstanding, different patterns are

Table 6. Mean values and ANOVA test for low and high innovators: Total sample

Construct	Low Innovators N=285 (42.2%)	High Innovators N=391 (57.8%)	F	p-value
Perceived advancement of retailer's ICT	3.32	4.35	105.6	0.000
Loyalty	3.83	4.23	9.8	0.002
Awareness	5.53	5.90	17.2	0.000
Service quality	5.21	5.67	21.8	0.000
Product quality	5.24	5.82	42.4	0.000
Perceived value	4.84	5.07	5.97	0.015
Retailer brand equity	3.90	4.46	21.4	0.000
Behavioral intentions	4.28	4.82	29.2	0.000

Table 7. Mean values and ANOVA test for low and high innovators: Grocery and clothing/footwear

Construct	Grocery				Clothing/Footwear			
	Low Innovators N=150 (61.5%)	High Innovators N=94 (38.5%)	F	p-value	Low Innovators N=64 (46.4%)	High Innovators N=74 (53.6%)	F	p-value
Perceived advancement of retailer's ICT	2.94	3.90	32.0	0.000	3.23	3.54	2.5	0.116
Loyalty	3.85	4.13	1.5	0.216	3.57	3.77	0.6	0.458
Awareness	5.51	5.98	9.2	0.003	5.44	5.89	5.2	0.024
Service quality	5.08	5.77	14.6	0.000	5.03	5.45	4.0	0.048
Product quality	5.13	6.00	30.0	0.000	5.05	5.11	0.1	0.778
Perceived value	4.99	5.61	17.4	0.000	4.76	5.07	2.5	0.114
Retailer brand equity	3.72	4.28	6.5	0.011	3.90	4.09	0.6	0.454
Behavioral intentions	4.14	4.87	17.1	0.000	4.33	4.49	0.5	0.492

observed in these types of retail chains regarding the significance of differences between high and low innovators. Regarding grocery retailers, high innovators show significantly higher assessments for all constructs excepting loyalty. Thus, ICT of highly innovative retailers are perceived as more advanced than those of low innovators, and consumer awareness and perceptions about retailer's service quality, product quality, value, retailer brand equity and behavioral intentions are significantly better for high innovators in comparison to low innovators.

On the other side, for apparel stores, differences between low and high innovators are only significant at $p<0.05$ for consumer awareness and service quality. Therefore, retail innovativeness for fashion store chains seems to be related only to retailer brand notoriety.

Similarly, mean values and ANOVA tests are calculated for electronics and furniture/decoration retailers (Table 8).

Again, high innovators show significantly higher scores than low innovators for all constructs. Notwithstanding, differences are only significant for some constructs, not being exactly the same for electronics and furniture/decoration retailers. In

particular, for electronics store chains, significant differences are observed between low and high innovators regarding the consumer's perception of advancement of the retailer's ICT solutions ($p < 0.01$). In this sense, ICT implemented by highly innovative retailers are perceived as more advanced than those used by low innovators. In addition to this, product quality of high innovators is significantly higher in comparison to low innovators ($p < 0.05$). Differences between the two groups of electronics retailers are only significant at $p < 0.10$ for retailer brand equity.

Last, for stores selling furniture and decoration items, ICT implemented by highly innovative retailers are perceived as significantly more advanced than those of low innovators ($p < 0.01$). Differences between highly and poorly innovative home furnishing retailers are also significant for behavioral intentions ($p < 0.10$), but not for the rest of constructs. Therefore, we only find partial support to Hypotheses 3 and 4, since the existence of differences between high and low innovators in consumer attitudes and behavioral intentions seems to be strongly related to the product assortment commercialized by the store.

Table 8. Mean values and ANOVA test for low and high innovators: Electronics and furniture/decoration

Construct	Electronics				Furniture/Decoration			
	Low Innovators N=55 (36.2%)	High Innovators N=97 (63.8%)	*F*	p-value	Low Innovators N=16 (11.3%)	High Innovators N=126 (88.7%)	*F*	p-value
Perceived advancement of retailer's ICT	4.38	5.01	12.7	0.001	3.67	4.63	10.7	0.001
Loyalty	3.97	4.35	1.9	0.164	4.25	4.49	0.4	0.553
Awareness	5.62	5.74	0.4	0.514	5.72	5.96	0.7	0.422
Service quality	5.58	5.65	0.2	0.694	5.81	5.71	0.1	0.747
Product quality	5.62	6.00	6.3	0.013	5.82	5.96	0.4	0.549
Perceived value	4.51	4.47	0.04	0.845	4.89	5.13	0.5	0.476
Retailer brand equity	4.21	4.66	2.9	0.088	4.45	4.67	0.3	0.589
Behavioral intentions	4.57	4.68	0.3	0.562	4.50	5.10	3.4	0.066

SOLUTIONS AND RECOMMENDATIONS

The retailers' efforts to invest in technology seem to be strongly related to retail innovativeness. In general, retail innovativeness strongly depends on the customer perception of the retailer's level of technological advancement as well as the customer satisfaction with the retailer's technology. Notwithstanding, regarding the latter, apparel retailers do not show a significant relationship between customer satisfaction with the store technology and customer perception of retail innovativeness. This finding could be explained in the sense that apparel innovative retailers are not appreciated because of their investment in technology but due to their fresh and creative practices, or their original design.

Furthermore, for some retail activities such as apparel and electronics, there are no significant differences in consumer behavioral intentions towards the retailer between highly innovative retailers and low innovators. Variety seeking or deal proneness could explain this differentiated behaviour in comparison to other retail industries. A question that may arise here is whether investing in ICT and projecting an image of innovative retailers might be worth the effort for these store chains.

In spite of these issues, we consider that, given the intense competition in the retail industry as well as the entry of new incumbents due to the trend of retail internationalization, retail innovativeness is an important issue and ICT may constitute a useful tool to build an image of innovative store.

FUTURE RESEARCH DIRECTIONS

The findings of this study are expected to pave the way for future investigations that can be conducted to capture the extent and effects of the changes that occur, as a result of innovation. In this sense, the present paper has tested the existence of significant differences in consumer behaviour between low and high innovators, as well as linear relationships between retail innovativeness and consumer perceptions of retailer's ICT. Further research should explore the sense of these relationships and check the causality of retail innovativeness on several constructs related to customer attitudes and behavioral intentions, as well as customer perceptions of the retailer's ICT investments.

Notwithstanding, future studies should overcome some of the methodological limitations of the present research. In this sense, even if using a single item for measuring customer satisfaction is not uncommon in services marketing literature (e.g. Mittal & Gera, 2013), further research should develop a multi-item scale for measuring satisfaction with the retailer's technology.

Furthermore, due to the increasing popularity of some ICT solutions in retailing and, in particular, mobile apps such as QR codes (Okazaki et al., 2013), further refinement is required in the catalogue of technology solutions in future studies.

In addition to this, since there is a great concern in the literature discussing the Technology Acceptance Model about the existence of cultural differences in technology usage and its potential impact on purchase intentions (Pookulangara & Koesler, 2011), we consider that the results obtained could be partly country-specific and, therefore, this study should be replicated in other geographical settings.

Last, technology leapfrogging in many developing countries is expected to ameliorate the digital divide with the most developed countries. This study could be also replicated for these emerging economies, thus providing relevant managerial implications for international retailers. Notwithstanding, in marketing channels of these countries where the informal economy still represents an important weight in the retailing industry, legal, privacy and ethical issues may arise and should be taken into consideration.

CONCLUSION

The analyses performed aim to provide evidence about the influence of retail innovativeness on consumer behaviour as well as to enable us to identify the information and communication technologies most influencing customer perceptions about retailer's innovativeness in each retail activity – i.e. grocery, textile, electronics and decoration.

Regarding the relationship between retail innovativeness and consumer behavior, store brand equity and its dimensions (i.e. loyalty, awareness, service quality, product quality and perceived value) are significantly higher for highly innovative retailers in comparison to low innovators only for grocery stores. Behavioral intentions towards the retailer are more positive for highly innovative retailers only for grocery and home furnishing retailers, while no significant differences are found between high and low innovators for apparel and electronics retailers. Thus, grocery and home furnishing retailers should make an effort to convey an image of innovative retailer to create brand equity and improve the consumer behavioral intentions towards the retailer.

In order to build an image of highly innovative retailer, while some ICT solutions –e.g. credit/debit card payment, the retailer's Website and mobile apps- seem to be commonly related to store innovativeness, other technologies are quite product-specific. In this sense, each retailer should define its priorities depending on its product assortment. In particular, for grocery retailers, video surveillance is the ICT most related to retail innovativeness, while for apparel store chains, retailer's loyalty program, activity in social media and piped music to create a store atmosphere are those solutions showing the highest correlations with retail innovativeness. Technologies related to the Internet and mobile communications, such as retailer's Website and m-payment are those that show the strongest correlations with retail innovativeness for electronics store chains, whereas

for furniture and decoration retailers, those ICT solutions that help to create an innovative image of the store are those that contribute to enhance the hedonic experience of the customer in the store, such as photoelectric cells, piped music and multimedia kiosks.

Therefore, customer purchase motivations and needs play an important influence in the relative relevance of each ICT solution depending on the type of retail activity. Thus, the concept of "retail innovativeness" may be understood in a different way by consumers in different types of stores, and retailers should be aware of these differences in order to create an image that reinforces their retailer store equity.

MANAGERIAL IMPLICATIONS

As above mentioned, we consider that in the current hypercompetitive environment, retail innovativeness may be a key factor in the retail store differentiation strategy and technology may help retail managers to build an image of innovative store. In this sense, Zalando and Apple have been cited as examples of retailers that have been able to innovate, inspiring the market with new ideas and new touch points, taking advantage of technology to make life easier for their consumers (Manasseh et al., 2012). Similarly, it has been pointed out that customers often appreciate not only the functional benefits of a physical store but also the overall experience it offers, distinguishing those retailers with unusual and exciting store atmospherics that add value to their shopping experience (Grewal et al., 2010).

Some examples of these retailers identified as innovators are Starbucks, or hypermarket chains such as Carrefour or Metro, that have implemented self-scanning devices and check-out systems enabling the consumer to pay without a cashier and thus saving time in their routinary purchases (Kraft & Mantrala, 2010).

The main problem with being known as an innovative retailer is that it forces the store managers to continuously implement new fresh and exciting ideas, since otherwise consumers may start to view the retailer as old-fashioned.

ACKNOWLEDGMENT

This research has been financed by the Spanish Ministry of Education and Science (Project ref.: ECO2010-17475).

REFERENCES

Aaker, D. A. (2007). Innovation: Brand it or lose it. *California Management Review, 50*(1), 8–24. doi:10.2307/41166414

Anderson, J. C., & Gerbing, D. W. (1988). Structural equation modelling in practice: a review and recommended two-step approach. *Psychological Bulletin, 103*, 411–423. doi:10.1037/0033-2909.103.3.411

Anselmsson, J., & Johansson, U. (2009). Retailer brands and the impact on innovativeness in the grocery market. *Journal of Marketing Management, 25*(1-2), 75–95. doi:10.1362/026725709X410043

Arnett, D. B., Laverie, D. A., & Meiers, A. (2003). Developing parsimonious retailer equity indexes using partial least squares analysis: a method and applications. *Journal of Retailing, 79*, 161–170. doi:10.1016/S0022-4359(03)00036-8

Bagozzi, R. P. (1980). *Causal Models in Marketing*. New York: Wiley.

Baker, J., Parasuraman, A., Grewal, D., & Voss, G. B. (2002). The influence of multiple store environment cues on perceived merchandise value and patronage intentions. *Journal of Marketing, 66*(2), 120–141. doi:10.1509/jmkg.66.2.120.18470

Berry, L. L., & Barnes, J. A. (1987). Retail Positioning Strategies in the USA. In G. Johnson (Ed.), *Business Strategy and Retailing* (pp. 107–115). Chichester, UK: John Wiley and Son Ltd.

Boletín Información Comercial Española (BICE). (2011). La distribución comercial en España en 2010. *Boletín Económico de ICE, 3015.* Retrieved August 3, 2013, from http://www.revistasice.com/es-ES/BICE/Paginas/ultimo-boletin.aspx?numero=3015

Castaldo, S. (Ed.). (2001). *Retailing & innovazione*. Milano: Egea.

Creswell, J. W. (2009). Research design: Qualitative, quantitative, and mixed methods approaches. *Sage (Atlanta, Ga.).*

Cronin, J. J., & Taylor, S. A. (1992). Measuring service quality: A reexamination and extension. *Journal of Marketing, 56*(3), 55–68. doi:10.2307/1252296

Darden, W. R., Erdem, O., & Darden, D. K. (1983). A Comparison and Test of Three Causal Models of Patronage Intentions. In W. R. Darden, & R. F. Lusch (Eds.), *Patronage Behavior and Retail Management*. New York: North-Holland.

Dawson, J. A. (2001). Is there a New Commerce in Europe? *International Review of Retail, Distribution and Consumer Research, 11*(3), 287–299. doi:10.1080/713770598

Dupuis, M. (2000). *Retail Innovation: Towards a Framework of Analysis*. Paper presented at the EAERCD Conference on Retail Innovation. Barcelona.

Gelbrich, K. (2011). I Have Paid Less Than You! The Emotional and Behavioral Consequences of Advantaged Price Inequality. *Journal of Retailing, 87*(2), 207–224. doi:10.1016/j.jretai.2011.03.003

Grewal, D., Krishnan, R., Baker, J., & Borin, N. (1998). The effect of store name, brand name and price discounts on consumers' evaluations and purchase intentions. *Journal of Retailing, 74*(3), 331–352. doi:10.1016/S0022-4359(99)80099-2

Grewal, D., Krishnan, R., Levy, M., & Munger, J. (2010). Retail success and key drivers. In *Retailing in the 21st Century* (pp. 15–30). Springer. doi:10.1007/978-3-540-72003-4_2

Hartman, K. B., & Spiro, R. L. (2005). Recapturing store image in customer-based store equity: a construct conceptualization. *Journal of Business Research, 58*, 1112–1120. doi:10.1016/j.jbusres.2004.01.008

Homburg, C., Hoyer, W. D., & Fassnacht, M. (2002). Service Orientation of a Retailer's Business Strategy: Dimensions, Antecedents, and Performance Outcomes. *Journal of Marketing, 66*(4), 86–101. doi:10.1509/jmkg.66.4.86.18511

Interbrand. (2011). *Best global brands.* Retrieved August 3, 2013, from http://www.interbrand.com/es/best-global-brands/Best-Global-Brands-2011.aspx

Jinfeng, W., & Zhilong, T. (2009). The impact of selected store image dimensions on retailer equity: Evidence from 10 Chinese hypermarkets. *Journal of Retailing and Consumer Services, 16*, 486–494. doi:10.1016/j.jretconser.2009.08.002

Krafft, M., & Mantrala, M. K. (Eds.). (2010). *Retailing in the 21st century: current and future trends.* Springer. doi:10.1007/978-3-540-72003-4

Manasseh, T., Müller-Sarmiento, P., Reuter, H., von Faber-Castell, C., & Pallua, C. (2012). Customer Inspiration–A Key Lever for Growth in European Retail. *Marketing Review St. Gallen, 29*(5), 16–21. doi:10.1365/s11621-012-0159-9

Miller, D. (1988). Relating Porter's Business Strategies to Environment and Structure: Analysis and Performance Implications. *Academy of Management Journal, 31*(2), 280–308. doi:10.2307/256549

Miller, D., & Dröge, C. (1986). Psychological and Traditional Determinants of Structure. *Administrative Science Quarterly, 31*(4), 539–560. doi:10.2307/2392963

Mittal, S., & Gera, R. (2013). Relationship between service quality dimensions and behavioural intentions: An SEM study of public sector retail banking customers in India. *Journal of Service Research, 12*(2), 147–171.

Mohan, G., Sivakumaran, B., & Sharma, P. (2012). Store environment's impact on variety seeking behavior. *Journal of Retailing and Consumer Services, 19*(4), 419–428. doi:10.1016/j.jretconser.2012.04.003

Mulhern, F. J. (1997). Retail Marketing: From Distribution to Integration. *International Journal of Research in Marketing, 14*(2), 103–124. doi:10.1016/S0167-8116(96)00031-6

Musso, F. (2010). Innovation in Marketing Channels. *Emerging Issues in Management, 1.*

Netemeyer, R. G., Krishnan, B., Pullig, C., Wang, G., Yagci, M., & Dean, D. et al. (2004). Developing and validating measures of facets of customer-based brand equity. *Journal of Business Research, 57*, 209–224. doi:10.1016/S0148-2963(01)00303-4

Okazaki, S., Navarro, A., & Campo, S. (2013). Media integration of QR code: a preliminary exploration. *Journal of Electronic Commerce Research, 14*(2), 137–148.

Oliver, R. L. (1993). Cognitive, affective, attribute bases of the satisfaction response. *The Journal of Consumer Research, 20*(3), 418–430. doi:10.1086/209358

Oliver, R. L. (1997). *Satisfaction: A behavioral perspective on the consumer.* New York, NY: McGraw-Hill.

Pappu, R., & Quester, P. (2006). A consumer-based method for retailer equity measurement: Results of an empirical study. *Journal of Retailing and Consumer Services, 13,* 317–329. doi:10.1016/j.jretconser.2005.10.002

Pappu, R., & Quester, P. (2006). Does customer satisfaction lead to improved brand equity? An empirical examination of two categories of retail brands. *Journal of Product and Brand Management, 15*(1), 4–14. doi:10.1108/10610420610650837

Ryssel, R., Ritter, T., & Gemunden, H. G. (2004). The impact of information technology deployment on trust, commitment and value creation in business relationships. *Journal of Business and Industrial Marketing, 19*(3), 197–207. doi:10.1108/08858620410531333

Sánchez Pérez, M., Estrella Ramón, A. M., Ruiz Real, J. L., & García Ramírez, A. (2011). Retailing in Europe: Situation and trends. *Revista de Estudios Empresariales, 2,* 67–95.

Shen, P. (2010). A Study on the Multi-Dimensional Relationship Between Consumer Shopping Value and Retailer Brand Equity. In *Proceedings of Marketing Science Innovations and Economic Development - Proceedings of 2010 Summit International Marketing Science and Management Technology Conference* (pp. 128-132). Retrieved August 3, 2013, from http://www.seiofbluemountain.com/upload/product/201008/2010shcyx02a9.pdf

Sweeney, J. C., & Soutar, G. N. (2001). Consumer perceived value: The development of a multiple item scale. *Journal of Retailing, 77*(2), 203–220. doi:10.1016/S0022-4359(01)00041-0

Swoboda, B., Haelsig, F., Schramm-Klein, H., & Morschett, D. (2009). Moderating role of involvement in building a retail brand. *International Journal of Retail & Distribution Management, 37*(11), 952–974. doi:10.1108/09590550910999370

Velarde Fuertes, J. (2011). Problemática actual de la distribución comercial española (un estado de la cuestión). *ICADE. Revista cuatrimestral de las Facultades de Derecho y Ciencias Económicas y Empresariales, 83-84,* 393-411.

Wang, H., Wei, Y., & Yu, C. (2008). Global brand equity model: combining customer-based with product-market outcome approaches. *Journal of Product and Brand Management, 17*(5), 305–316. doi:10.1108/10610420810896068

Wu, F., Yeniyurt, S., Kim, D., & Cavusgil, S. T. (2006). The impact of information technology on supply chain capabilities and firm performance: A resource-based view. *Industrial Marketing Management, 35*(4), 493–504. doi:10.1016/j.indmarman.2005.05.003

ADDITIONAL READING

Ailawadi, K. L., & Keller, K. L. (2004). Understanding retail branding: conceptual insights and research priorities. *Journal of Retailing, 80*(4), 331–342. doi:10.1016/j.jretai.2004.10.008

Beristain, J. J., & Zorrilla, P. (2011). The relationship between store image and store brand equity: A conceptual framework and evidence from hypermarkets. *Journal of Retailing and Consumer Services, 18,* 562–574. doi:10.1016/j.jretconser.2011.08.005

Chebat, J., El Hedhli, K., & Sirgy, M. J. (2009). How does shopper-based mall equity generate mall loyalty? A conceptual model and empirical evidence. *Journal of Retailing and Consumer Services, 16,* 50–60. doi:10.1016/j.jretconser.2008.08.003

El Hedhli, K., & Chebat, J. (2009). Developing and validating a psychometric shopper-based mall equity measure. *Journal of Business Research, 62*, 581–587. doi:10.1016/j.jbusres.2008.05.016

Fleck, N., & Nabec, L. (2010). L'enseigne: un capital pour le distributeur. *Management & Avenir, 38*(8), 14–32. doi:10.3917/mav.038.0014

Fuller, G. W. (2004). *New Food Product Development – From Concept to Marketplace* (2nd ed.). Florida: CRC Press B. C.

Ganesan, S., George, M., Jap, S., Palmatier, R. W., & Weitz, B. (2009). Supply Chain Management and Retailer Performance: Emerging Trends, Issues, and Implications for Research and Practice. *Journal of Retailing, 85*(1), 84–94. doi:10.1016/j.jretai.2008.12.001

Grewal, D., Levy, M., & Kumar, V. (2009). Customer Experience Management in Retailing: An Organizing Framework. *Journal of Retailing, 85*(1), 1–14. doi:10.1016/j.jretai.2009.01.001

Hsiao, J.-M. M. (2010). Building Competitive Advantage Through Innovative Reverse Logistics Capabilities. *Operations and Supply Chain Management, 3*(2), 70–82.

Hu, Y., & Zhao, S. (2010). A Case Study of Online Retail Innovation System On Alibaba Taobao. In IEEE Computer Society, *2010 International Conference on E-Business and E-Government* (224-227). Washington, DC: IEEE Computer Society.

Jara, M. (2009). Le capital-marque des marques de distributeurs: Une approche conceptuelle differenciée. *Revue Française du Marketing, 221*(1/5), 47-61.

Jara, M., & Cliquet, G. (2012). Retail brand equity: Conceptualization and measurement. *Journal of Retailing and Consumer Services, 19*, 140–149. doi:10.1016/j.jretconser.2011.11.003

Keller, K. L. (1993). Conceptualizing, measuring, and managing customer-based brand equity. *Journal of Marketing, 57*(January), 1–22. doi:10.2307/1252054

Kruger, H., & Fourie, L. C. H. (2003). An investigation into the uniformity and non-uniformity of online/offline retail brand building in South Africa. *South African Journal of Business Management, 34*(4), 27–34.

Laczniak, R. N., DeCarlo, T. E., & Motley, C. M. (1996). Retail equity perceptions and consumers' processing of negative word-of-mouth communication. *Journal of Marketing Theory and Practice, 4*(4), 37–48.

Martenson, R. (2007). Corporate brand image, satisfaction and store loyalty. A study of the store as a brand, store brands and manufacturer brands. *International Journal of Retail & Distribution Management, 35*(7), 544–555. doi:10.1108/09590550710755921

Musso, F. (2012). Technology in Marketing Channels: Present and Future Drivers of Innovation. [IJABE]. *International Journal of Applied Behavioral Economics, 1*(2), 41–51. doi:10.4018/ijabe.2012040104

Netemeyer, R. G., Krishnan, B., Pullig, C., Wang, G., Yagci, M., & Dean, D. et al. (2004). Developing and validating measures of facets of customer-based brand equity. *Journal of Business Research, 57*, 209–224. doi:10.1016/S0148-2963(01)00303-4

Pappu, R., & Quester, P. G. (2008). Does brand equity vary between department stores and clothing stores? Results of an empirical investigation. *Journal of Product and Brand Management, 17*(7), 425–435. doi:10.1108/10610420810916335

Pappu, R., Quester, P. G., & Cooksey, R. W. (2005). Consumer-based brand equity: improving the measurement – empirical evidence. *Journal of Product and Brand Management, 14*(3), 143–154. doi:10.1108/10610420510601012

Shamma, H. M., & Hassan, S. S. (2009). Customer and non-customer perspectives for examining corporate reputation. *Journal of Product and Brand Management, 18*(5), 326–337. doi:10.1108/10610420910981800

UNIDO. (2002). Innovation and learning in global value chains. In *Industrial Development Reports 2002/2003* (105-115). Retrieved August 3, 2013, from http://www.unido.org/fileadmin/user_media/Publications/Research_and_statistics/Branch_publications/Research_and_Policy/Files/Reports/Flagship_Reports/IDR/Industrial%20Development%20Report%202002-2003.pdf

Willems, K., & Swinnen, G. (2008). From successful differentiation in retailing to store equity. In Kooij, Dorien (Ed.) *Proceedings of the PhD Research in Business Economics and Management Conference 2008*. The Netherlands Organization for Researchers in Business Economics and Management (NOBEM). Retrieved August 3, 2013, from http://doclib.uhasselt.be/dspace/bitstream/1942/9447/1/PREBEM%20abstract%20.pdf.

Zeithaml, V., Berry, L. L., & Parasuraman, A. (1996). The Behavioral Consequences of Service Quality. *Journal of Marketing, 60*(April), 31–46. doi:10.2307/1251929

Zhang, X. M., Shen, N. L., & Mao, X. P. (2011). Model of Collaborative Knowledge Innovation with Distributor Participation in Supply Chain. *Advanced Materials Research, 201-203*, 773–778. doi:10.4028/www.scientific.net/AMR.201-203.773

KEY TERMS AND DEFINITIONS

Awareness: In the context of retailing, retailer brand awareness is the extent to which a retailer's name is familiar to consumers.

Behavioral Intentions: In the context of retailing, this concept can be defined as the consumer willingness to develop some categories of behaviors such as referrals, price sensitivity, repurchase, complaining behavior, loyalty and word of mouth (Zeithaml et al., 1996).

Information and Communication Technologies: Solutions used to create, record, manipulate, communicate, exchange, present, and use information – e.g. data, conversations, images, videos, etc.

Loyalty: Following Oliver, 1997; p. 392), retailer loyalty consists on "a deeply held commitment to rebuy or repatronize a preferred product or service consistently in the future, despite situational influences and marketing efforts having the potential to cause switching behavior."

Perceived Value: "Consumers' overall assessment of the utility of a product based on perceptions of what is received and what is given" (Zeithaml, 1988, p. 14).

Retail Innovativeness: According to the definition of Homburg et al., (2002), it is the degree to which retailers in the local market adopt new merchandising or service ideas.

Retailer Brand Equity: Hartman and Spiro (2005, p. 1114) define store equity as "the differential effect of store knowledge on customer response to the marketing of the store." Furthermore, Jinfeng and Zhilong (2009, p. 487) refer to retailer equity as "the incremental utility or value added to a retailer by its brand name," stressing an essential task of establishing the brand being identified and generating a differential response.

Retailer Product and Service Quality: Retailer perceived quality is defined as consumer's judgment about a retailer's overall excellence or superiority on the perception of goods and services (Pappu & Quester, 2006a; b).

Chapter 22

Retailer–Customers Relationships in the Online Setting:
An Empirical Investigation to Overcome Privacy Concerns and Improve Information Sharing

Sandro Castaldo
Bocconi University, Italy

Monica Grosso
EMLYON Business School, France

ABSTRACT

Internet merchants are compelled to collect personal information from customers in order to deliver goods and services effectively. However, the ease with which data can be acquired and disseminated across the Web has led to many potential customers demonstrating growing concerns about disclosing personal information. This chapter analyzes the interaction between two strategies that firms can use to alter potential customers' cost/benefit evaluation and increase information disclosure: the development of initial trust and compensation. The derived hypotheses are tested by means of two experimental studies, whose findings are compared across two different consumer target groups.

INTRODUCTION

Over the last years, a number of significant technological developments in multimedia - computing power, digital television, the internet/intranet, IP-based services, and terrestrial and satellite mobile communications - have had a profound impact on society. This ICT evolution has provided customers with tools to search for information, with innovative ways to shop and consume, as well as to interact with family and friends, firms, and institutions.

Firms have been afforded new sales and customer relationship development opportunities,

DOI: 10.4018/978-1-4666-6074-8.ch022

as they can acquire a vast quantity and variety of customer data (Cespedes & Smith, 1993; DeCew, 1997). However, realizing all these opportunities requires overcoming the main barrier to new technology adoption: the perceived risk of sharing personal information due to the lack of controls to safeguard it. The increasing interaction opportunities and low cost data exchanges – enriching the content of such interactions – that new technologies allow, also reduce control over the use of exchanged data: anonymous and unknown parties may use this data. Consequently, the ease with which data can be acquired and disseminated and the peculiarities of high-tech settings have led to growing concerns regarding whether and how consumers can safeguard their privacy (e.g., Culnan, 1993; Milne & Gordon, 1993; Milne, 2000; Phelps, Novak, & Ferrell, 1999). It is therefore not surprising that policy makers, customers, and firms – those developing new technologies and those adopting them – are paying increasing attention to privacy issues.

In this chapter, we focus on the online setting, which requires a strong flow of information to operate effectively. Online retailing cannot function at all unless firms receive extremely sensitive customer information: names, street addresses, and credit card numbers among others. Furthermore, online transactions often do not involve goods and money being exchanged simultaneously. The spatial and temporal separation between customers and e-vendors, as well as the information asymmetry between the parties (Hee-Woomg, Xu, & Koh, 2004) means that customers do not truly know what an online firm will do with their personal information. As a consequence, a key question that concerns industry, academics, and policy makers alike is: How do online consumers respond to constant requests for information? A growing debate has emerged on how consumers protect themselves against privacy invasion threats and how they have consequently modified their online behavior. Customers' "protecting behaviors" (e.g., Milne & Boza, 1999; Sheehan

& Hoy, 2000; Raman & Pashupati, 2005) seem to be aimed at reducing the information they share with online firms.

Customers are reluctant to share their data, but firms prefer customers to use self-service technologies, such as the Web, as they lead to cost savings. E-commerce has enabled retailers to enter a foreign market at lower costs than required to open physical stores. Nevertheless, cost savings and international expansion are not the only reasons for retail companies to encourage the use of alternative electronic channels: they are also extremely flexible, allowing firms to optimize their marketing information mix to automatically suggest complementary products and to implement relationship-friendly tools, such as product comparison guides (Viswanathan, 2005). Furthermore, companies can use online channels to complete and complement their local brick-and-mortar business (Steinfield, 2004). Therefore, a growing number of traditional retailers currently pursue multichannel strategies (Müller-Lankenau, Wehmeyer, & Klein, 2005), as multi-channel shoppers have a higher purchase volume and are more profitable (Venkatesan, Kumar, & Ravishankar, 2007).

E-tailers will miss all the above-mentioned opportunities unless they find a way to increase customers' information sharing. This chapter's objective is to help companies achieve this by providing recommendations derived from the results of previous studies based on self-disclosure theories (Premazzi, et al., 2010a; Premazzi, Castaldo, Hofacker, & Grosso, 2010b). We specifically examine the effects that initial trust and compensation – two relevant antecedents of sharing information with (unknown) e-vendors – have on two different customer segments as revealed in an experimental research project. This research contributes to the literature development in several ways. First, this study not only investigates the main effects of the two key antecedents of information sharing, but also their interaction. This is relevant because, although trust and compensation have been identified within self-disclosure theories, previous studies have mainly investigated these two antecedents separately. However, e-tailers could simultaneously leverage both within their relationship management strategy. Second, we analyze these two variables' roles not only regarding customers' willingness to divulge information, which was the dependent variable in most prior research, but also with regard to measuring their actual information sharing behavior toward e-marketers. This is relevant as previous research (Premazzi et al., 20120a; 2010b) has proven that the dependent variable measurement used (declared willingness or real behavior) influences the results, which can differ. Third, we investigate the role of different types of compensation and their interaction with trust. The literature on the topic has identified several types of incentives (monetary/non-monetary; certain/lottery, etc.). This study's results could thus vary according to the type of compensation offered, which will increase the managerial implications emerging from them. Finally, unlike the majority of experimental studies, the study sample is not solely composed of students, but also includes a sample of older, actively working people. Although students are an e-population target, companies wanting to target their offers at a more mature market (less interested in saving money) need to understand how this segment reacts to their trust and compensation strategies.

BACKGROUND

Information privacy can be defined as the "individual's ability to control when, how, and to what extent his or her personal information is communicated to others" (Son & Kim, 2008, p. 504). Information privacy concerns refer "to the individual's subjective views of fairness within the context of information privacy" (Malhotra, Kim, & Agarwal, 2004, p. 337). Information privacy concerns stem from the fear of losing control over one's personal data, which refers to the possible intentional or unintentional mismanagement of personal data submitted online. There is a wide range of possible privacy infringements: the company collecting data might use it for purposes that the customer did not explicitly authorize, for instance, by selling this information to third parties unknown to the customer; hackers can steal or tamper with personal data; and databases might contain errors that can affect the user negatively.

The literature has identified two key dimensions of privacy concerns: the collection and use (Castañeda & Montoro, 2007; Malhotra, et al., 2004; Rifon, LaRose, & Choi, 2005). Collection concerns refer to apprehension concerning the way in which data is collected. The diffusion of mechanisms that collect online data automatically, such as software cookies that Websites provide, gives new relevance to this dimension. Use concerns refer to apprehensiveness regarding how online entities use the data they collect. The extant literature demonstrates that privacy concerns affect a variety of behaviors, including the provision of personal information. Son and Kim (2008) investigate the effects of privacy concerns on information protection behavior, such as refusal to provide data and misrepresentation. Malhotra et al., (2004) consider privacy concerns an antecedent of the behavioral intention to provide personal information online.

How can online companies overcome privacy concerns and increase customers' information sharing? Self-disclosure theories can help answer this question. These theories suggest that consumers' willingness to disclose personal information is based on their assessments of the costs/risks and benefits (Andrade, Kaltcheva, & Weitz, 2002). While collecting personal information from customers is essential for electronic commerce viability, it has both risk and benefit implications for individuals (Hui, Teo, & Lee, 2007). E-companies could therefore use a number of approaches to alter this cost-benefit trade-off and, consequently, encourage consumers to participate in self-disclosure (Andrade et al., 2002).

Building consumers' trust and offering compensation for disclosing information are among the most cited approaches to overcoming this hurdle. Trust reduces potential consumers' perceived risk and, therefore, the cost of information sharing (Jarvenpaa & Tractinsky, 1999), while incentives increase the benefit, as they represent a reward in exchange for personal information (Andrade et al., 2002; Hui et al., 2007). The main gap in this literature stream is that previous studies have mainly dealt with intention (Castañeda & Montoro, 2007; Malhotra et al., 2004; Rifon et al., 2005; Son & Kim, 2008) rather than actual behavior with regard to personal information sharing. Consumers' intended actions differ from what they actually do, also with respect to privacy-related issues (e.g., Norberg, Horne, & Horne, 2007). Hence, attitudinal studies may not reflect the whole story. Response styles and social desirability are among many well-known problems with attitudinal surveys (Aaker, Kumar, & Day, 2001). In particular, social desirability implies that subjects tend to produce responses that put them in the most desirable light possible; in this case, by perhaps not admitting that their privacy and trust can somehow be "bought" by means of incentives.

Premazzi et al., (2010a; 2010b) has shown that the intention to provide personal data and actual behavior are not necessarily consistent. More research is thus needed on the actual behavior of online customers in a realistic setting. In order to contribute to filling this gap, we measure people's actual behavior with regard to providing personal data and compare our findings with their intention to provide this. This is only possible in a controlled experimental research like the one proposed in this chapter. The use of surveys has actually been a common element in many studies on responses to privacy invasion. The problem of a research design using surveys is threefold. First, surveys just measure past or intentional behavior, not actual and present behavior. Second, this methodology tends to heighten privacy concerns,

because respondents are sensitized to the topic since they are forced to focus on it. Finally, some research suggests that many consumers ignore the implications of privacy invasion either due to denial (Raman & Pashupati, 2005), or due to the way in which choices are presented (Johnson, Bellman, & Lohse, 2002). According to this view, consumers may not be aware of the implications of sharing their information with an online Web site, nor might they be able to predict their behavior in a survey context.

A controlled experimental research requires a homogeneous sample to avoid different characteristics of the sample biasing the study results. In experimental studies, students are usually the natural sample, as researchers find them more convenient to use. Even if students – given their high usage of virtual technologies – may be the target of many e-commerce Websites, we believe that focusing only on their behavior is reductive. We therefore suggest covering the main gap in experimental research (sampling) by comparing our results, derived from a different sample, with the traditional sample composed of students. Our sample comprises also more mature people with an own income, who are expected to behave differently (namely being more concerned with privacy-related issues) than students.

In the next sections, we therefore frame our hypothesis on both potential customers' willingness to share their information and on their actual information sharing.

Privacy Concerns, Trust, and Information Sharing

Privacy concerns are an attitude that the customer holds, but they only partially explain the customer's final behavior, since contextual factors are also at stake. Some authors have even suggested that privacy concerns themselves are contextual by nature (Sheehan & Hoy, 2000), further anchoring the user's behavior to the situation he or she experiences online. Contingent factors, which are based on a Website's specific features, can be used to actualize or neutralize privacy concerns. For instance, if users with privacy concerns – for example, they have a negative attitude toward the data collection methods and treatment on the internet – come across an e-commerce vendor that lacks the basic marks of trust – such as seals, certifications, and/or an overall appearance that guarantee the vendor's reliability –, they are unlikely to provide data and conclude a transaction. However, should such users come across a Website that they believe to be trustworthy, their concerns may be pacified and they may make a purchase. Before making a transaction, users therefore make an overall evaluation of the Website and the company behind it. All of the Website's and vendor's features influence prospective clients' trust in the specific Website.

Trust is the most relevant specific attitude that users can have towards a Website. The extant literature has employed trust, in its various conceptualizations, as a key variable to explain users' behavior (Castañeda & Montoro, 2007; Malhotra et al., 2004; Premazzi et al., 2010a; 2010b; Rifon et al., 2005; Schlosser, Barnett White, & Lloyd, 2006). Customers cannot fully forecast or control companies' behavior. Once a company has been given data, the customer cannot control what it will do with it. In some cases, the customers may not even know that a breach of privacy has occurred. This risky circumstance is typical of a relationship that should be based on trust (Castaldo, 2007; Moorman, Zaltman, & Deshpandé, 1992); that is, a situation in which a subject has to rely on another subject whose behavior he or she cannot fully control or affect, which may be harmful to him or her. Although separate concepts, trust and privacy concerns are conceptually tied to one another as both refer to an external party's potentially damaging behavior. Privacy concerns refer to the online environment in general, while trust is specific to a given Website or e-vendor. Malhotra et al., (2004) show that privacy concerns affect behavioral intention

directly and indirectly through trusting beliefs. However, their study does not refer to a specific Website, but to general trusting beliefs in online companies. Castañeda and Montoro (2007) use a Webpage for their study, but they measure trust in Websites in general. This type of study can create overlaps between privacy concerns and trust, which are distinct concepts. Therefore, they state that "further research should examine not only privacy concerns at a general level but also perceived problems within a particular context" (Malhotra et al., 2004, p. 351). Our research tries to fill this gap by measuring trust in a specific company rather than trust in general and by using privacy concerns as a control variable, given its strong link with the key variables investigated in the study.

Research has indicated that individuals' familiarity with the entity (such as a Website) collecting information will influence their willingness to share information (Sheehan, 2005). Individuals interacting with Websites with which they are familiar tend to be more willing to share private information. Their familiarity also gives them a chance to see how their information is being used or misused. There is strong consensus that trust is critical in exchanges involving interdependence, uncertainty, and risk (Milne & Boza, 1999), which is often the case in online relationships and information exchanges.

A lack of trust has been identified as one of the greatest barriers to internet transactions (e.g., Hoffman, Novak, & Peralta, 1999). If information is shared, the marketer has access to consumers' personal information, which harbors an inherent risk that the information may be misused or shared inappropriately. However, if consumers trusts the entity collecting information, their privacy concerns are likely to be pacified (Milne & Boza, 1999) and their information disclosure will be maximized (Grabner-Krauter, 2002).

With respect to database marketing, Milne and Boza (1999) examined consumers' sense of privacy and found that, under certain circumstances, building trust is more effective than efforts to reduce concerns. In this context, people's willingness to disclose information has been found to be dependent on how much they trust the requesting organization (Schoenbachler & Gordon, 2002). Gefen, Karahanna, and Straub (2003), and Hoffman (1999) arrive at a similar result with respect to online settings.

The conceptualization of online trust refers to previous research mainly conducted in the off-line environment, but adapting this to a virtual setting. Specifically, McKnight et al., (2002) identified four aspects that anchor the concept of trust: a disposition to trust (a general willingness to trust others), institution-based trust (perceptions of the internet environment), trusting beliefs (perceptions of the Web vendor) and trusting intention (an intention to engage in trust-based relationships with a Web vendor).

A peculiarity of trust in the online sector that emerges from the literature is its multi-dimensionality. Previous studies have showed that online shoppers simultaneously trust or distrust (Harris & Goode, 2004): e-vendors (e.g., Fukuyama, 1995; Urban et al., 2000); payment systems (e.g., Hoffman et al., 1999), and the very nature of the internet as well as online shopping per se (e.g., Hoffman, 1999; Schoder &Yin, 2000). In this study, we refer to trust as the trusting belief and trusting intention that a shopper develops towards a specific e-vendor.

Many studies on online trust have focused on trust building in the relationship's initial period, thus referring to a sort of initial trust. In the e-commerce context, most online retailers face the challenge of initiating consumer trust prior to online transactions, because online shoppers perceive these as more risky than traditional channels of distribution (Van den Poel & Leunis, 1999) and are therefore less likely to make such transactions. The initial period is indeed critical because consumers decide very quickly whether or not to make an online transaction; if online

retailers fail to convince customers to overcome the initial trust barrier, all their subsequent efforts will be in vain (McNight et al., 2004). Overcoming the initial trust barriers is even more difficult for small online retailers, due to their general lack of a national reputation and impressive size, the two most frequently suggested antecedents of consumer trust (Doney & Cannon, 1997; Jarvenpaa & Tractinsky, 1999). Consequently, we focus on initial trust in this study.

McNight et al., (2004) investigated the elements allowing online retailers to create initial trust by distinguishing two stages of the initial relationship: the introductory stage and the exploratory stage. During the introductory stage, users have not yet experienced a specific Website and are still trying to assess it and the Web business on the basis of second-hand information on what it offers. Users who decide to use the site enter the exploratory stage. In the exploratory stage, consumers have obtained some (though limited) first-hand, credible information, creating a stage characterized by limited familiarity. The authors' study showed that both dispositional trust and institution-based trust are important factors that initially relate to trust in an e-business. Furthermore, a disposition to trust, structural assurance, and reputation advertising affected each type of trust during both stages. Assurance icons, which are signaling devices, had little effect on the level of consumer trust in the Web vendor. The reputation advertising treatment worked well, even though it was only given in the introductory stage and not repeated in the exploratory stage, as the icons were. The significant results of reputation advertising agree with past research, which has shown that perceived reputation is a powerful predictor of trust (e.g., Jarvenpaa et al., 2000). Second-hand reputation advertising appears to provide the site with a credibility that is difficult to achieve with third party endorsements.

Based on this literature review on trust and information disclosure, our first hypothesis posits:

H₁: The higher consumers' initial trust, the higher (a) their willingness to provide information and (b) their behavioral information sharing.

Incentive and Information Sharing

Companies might use compensations (or incentives) to induce consumers to disclose information. Incentives may include various forms of compensation or rewards. Research has found that using incentives as a means to announce that personal data is being collected (Sheehan & Hoy, 2000) eliminates some consumer privacy concerns up front, particularly in situations such as market research (Milne & Gordon, 1993). The use of an incentive indicates a mutually beneficial exchange (Sheehan & Hoy, 2000). People often consider the nature of the benefit being offered in exchange for information when deciding whether an activity violates their personal privacy. Previous studies have pointed out that consumers are aware that not all relationships are mutually beneficial and, consequently, that they do not want to enter into long-term relationships with certain organizations (Szmigin & Bourne, 1998; Phelps et al., 2000). Receiving various forms of incentives also supports Milne and Gordon's (1993) supposition that some people are willing to give up a degree of privacy to obtain the products and services they want. As Sheehan and Hoy (2000) point out, consumers may not mind receiving unsolicited marketing communications about products and services in which they are interested, even if some of their personal information is used to identify them as prospective clients.

There is empirical evidence that consumers receiving tangible benefits, such as discounts, access to Websites, future savings, and rewards, may be less concerned with privacy because they feel an equal exchange has been established (Goodwin, 1991). Compensations can, however, also be either certain (e.g., a discount or a gift) or uncertain (e.g., a lottery ticket). Previous research has found that certain compensation for information disclosure is more effective than uncertain compensation (Premazzi et al., 2010b). We therefore focus on certain compensation of which there are two types: monetary compensation in the form of coupons for online purchases (Deutschen, De Ruyter, Wetzels, & Ooterveld, 2004) and non-monetary compensation in the form of gifts. As consumers can use monetary incentives flexibly, they are considered more enticing than gifts of the same value (Deutskens et al., 2004), which leads to the contention that monetary compensation is the most effective incentive. Hence, we posit the following hypothesis:

H₂ₐ, H₂ᵦ: Willingness to provide information (H₂ₐ) and actual sharing behavior (H₂ᵦ) will be higher if monetary compensation is offered, followed by a gift as compensation, and will be less if no compensation is offered.

In an exploratory experimental study, Andrade et al., (2002) examined the effects of developing a reputation for trustworthiness by providing a comprehensive privacy policy, and overcoming consumer concerns by offering rewards for disclosing personal information. They found that the comprehensiveness of the privacy policy and the company's reputation reduce the level of concern, while offering a reward increases it. They argue that "the subjective assessment of the concern over disclosure in the place of a behavioral measure of actual disclosure presents a weakness" (p. 352). En, Hock-Hai, and Wen (2006) found a highly positive relationship between a company's reputation and online consumers' willingness to accurately reveal their personal information. They also found that reputation has a moderating influence on the effects that rewards and privacy guarantees have on people's willingness to share their information.

Building on these previous findings, Premazzi et al., (2010a; 2010b) suggest that trust could be a moderating variable affecting the relationship between compensation and information disclosure. In particular, they propose that, by offering them compensation when the level of trust is already high, individuals will be more inclined to provide information online. Initial trust is therefore the key element when starting an online transaction; we therefore assume that the benefits of initial trust – in terms of a reduced perceived risk – will provide the necessary condition for increasing people's willingness to disclose information. Conversely, in a situation in which there is a lack of trust, we expect incentives to have a smaller effect on information disclosure.

We thus suggest that trusting individuals will be more inclined to provide information online if they are offered compensation or incentives. Specifically we posit:

H_{3a}, H_{3b}: In a high trust condition, subjects will be more willing to provide information (H_{3a}) if offered compensation than if not offered compensation. Conversely, the impact of compensation will be lower in a low trust condition. The same will hold true with respect to actual behavior (H_{3b}).

The hypothesized relationships were empirically investigated in two separate laboratory experiments that differed regarding the type of sample used in order to reflect the different customer segments that online retail companies may target. As previously mentioned, we used students, as well as employed people between the ages of 35 and 64, as target groups. The assumption behind the choice of two target groups is twofold: first, since students are more familiar with and skilled in respect of IT than older people, they may show

differences in their online behavior; second, since students often do not have an income, this could influence the effect of the incentives for information sharing.

EXPERIMENTAL STUDIES

Study 1: Design and Procedure

The study has a 2 (initial trust: high vs. low) x 3 (incentive: no incentive, monetary and non-monetary compensation) between-subject design. As mentioned, the sample for this study was composed of students, who are generally responsible for a key segment of online purchases. Data was collected from 163 undergraduate and graduate of an Italian management school. Table 1 shows the details of the sample division between the six experimental cells.

Subjects were recruited under the pretext of participating in consumer opinion market research for a (fictitious) UK mobile phone service provider that was said to be considering entering new competitive markets, including the Italian one. By definition, the initial trust manipulation required the participants not to be familiar with the firm used in the study. After asking the participants whether they had knowledge of the fictitious company, two (not included in the sample description of Table 1) were excluded from the sample because they claimed to know the company.

During the experiment, the participants were first given a short pamphlet describing the company profile. At this stage, their trust was

Table 1. Study 1: The number of participants in each experimental cell

		Incentive Condition			Total
		No Incentive	**Monetary Incentive**	**Non-Monetary Incentive**	
Initial Trust Condition	Low Trust	29	28	25	**82**
	High Trust	27	29	25	**81**
	Total	**56**	**57**	**50**	**163**

manipulated. We prepared two different versions of the pamphlet with different descriptions of the fictitious company. The description consisted of excerpts of articles on this company from the online version of The Wall Street Journal, which is considered a well-known and credible source. A company rating was also included. The same format and type of content were used in the two versions; the main difference was between the companies' profiles. In the high trust condition, the company was said to have the best network performance, the highest J.D. Power customer-satisfaction rating, the highest mobile connection success rate, and to have been upgraded by S&P, implying that it had a stable outlook. In contrast, in the low trust condition, the company was described as delivering inadequate customer service, had the lowest J.D. Power customer-satisfaction rating, and its sales growth was stagnant. In addition, the company was described as having been downgraded by S&P. The subjects' trust was therefore manipulated by leveraging the firm's reputation, which is considered the main antecedent of initial trust in the literature (Jarvenpaa, Tractinsky, & Vitale, 2000; Koufaris & Hampton-Sosa, 2004; McKnight et al., 2004). The pamphlet was written in English and all the participants were screened for English proficiency.

The subjects were randomly assigned to one of three of the (fictional) company's beta Websites, each reflecting one of the incentive conditions. They were instructed to examine the site closely. All three sites contained online features that one might expect from a mobile phone services company (i.e. pages devoted to plans, services, models, accessories, etc.).

After the subjects had seen their assigned Website, they were instructed to proceed to the registration page and provide information that the company might need if it wanted to contact them. This registration page asked them to provide personal information and financial data: their name, address, city, state, zip code, e-mail, phone number,

Italian social security number, credit card type, number, and its expiry date.

At this stage, the compensation manipulation occurred. In the "no incentive" condition, the subjects were simply required to provide the data indicated above. In the "monetary incentive" condition, they were informed that, after registration, they would receive a coupon worth €20 for one of the main retail chains selling electronic products in Italy. In the "non-monetary incentive" condition, the participants were informed that they would receive wireless headphones worth €20 as a gift. Once the task had been completed, the participants were asked to fill out a questionnaire containing questions measuring the dependent variable, willingness to provide information online, as well as the trust manipulation check and three control variables (covariates) – privacy concern, attitude toward online shopping, and attitude toward the product category (mobile phones).

Study 1: Variables Measures

Dependent Variables: As mentioned, we measured two dependent variables: willingness to provide information and behavioral information sharing. The willingness to provide information was measured as the average score for a multi-item question. The participants rated their willingness to provide six different types of personal data, using a seven-point scale (1 = no willingness, 7 = high willingness).

"Behavioral information sharing" was measured as follows: first, we computed how much information the subjects had provided the experimental Website as the sum of the number of identifying information items (name, address, zip code, citizenship, phone number, e-mail address, SSN and credit card expiry date, type, and number). Hence, we calculated a variable "N_provided." As the provision of false or incomplete information is a relevant issue in online information sharing (Sheehan & Hoy, 1999; Premazzi et al., 2010a;

2010b), we matched all the data provided with the questionnaire data, creating a dummy variable with a value of 1 for each data item if the provided information was true, and zero if it was false. We subsequently computed the sum of the true data items, and obtained the variable "N_matches." Finally, our dependent variable, behavioral information sharing, was computed as the mean between the two mentioned variables (Premazzi et al., 2010a; 2010b). The higher the mean, the more information the participant shared.

Covariates: These variables were measured using an 11-item index with each item comprising a seven-point (1 = strongly disagree, 7 = strongly agree) scale. The items were factorized to create a single measure for each variable (Table 2).

Trust: During the manipulation check, trust was measured using a seven-point (1 = strongly disagree, 7 = strongly agree) multi-item scale (Premazzi et al., 2010a; 2010b). The items were factor analyzed to create a single measure of trust (Cronbach's alpha = 0.949).

Study 1: Results

Tests were conducted to ensure that statistical assumptions associated with the analysis of variance (ANOVA) and the analysis of covariance (ANCOVA) had been met. Levene's test of equality of error variance was not rejected. In addition, tests were conducted to ensure there was no interaction effect between the covariate and any of the three other factors, which indicated that the assumption of the covariance regression coefficients' homogeneity had not been violated.

Table 2. Study 1: Cronbach's alpha for the co-variates' scales

Variable	Alpha
Privacy Concern	0.868
Attitude Toward Online Shopping	0.749
Commitment to Mobile Phone Services	0.839

A one-way ANOVA was used to check the trust manipulation. Participants in the high trust condition group reported a significantly higher level of trust than those in the low trust condition (M_{HIGH} = 4.697, M_{LOW} = 3.55; $F(1, 161)$= 85.152, p=0.000).

To test H_{1a}, H_{2a}, and H_{3a}, we conducted a factorial analysis of covariance (ANCOVA), using trust and incentive as independent variables, and willingness to disclose information as the dependent variable. Attitude toward online shopping, commitment to mobile phone services, and privacy concern were used as covariates. The only significant covariate that emerged was attitude toward online shopping; consequently, we re-ran the analysis with just that covariate. The beta parameter was 0.312, implying a positive relationship between the attitude toward online shopping and willingness to provide information (Table 3). These results show (Figure 1) that only the main effect of compensation is significant at 10% ($M_{NO INC.}$ = 3.375, $M_{NON MONETARY INC.}$ = 3.75, $M_{MONETARY INC.}$ = 3.84), thus confirming H_{2a}. The main effect of trust and the interaction effect between trust and compensation are not significant, meaning that both H_{1a} and H_{3a} are rejected.

The same procedure was followed, using behavioral information sharing as the dependent variable, to test our H_{1b}, H_{2b}, and H_{3b}. In this case too, the only significant covariate was attitude toward online shopping. The beta parameter was 0.423, implying a positive relationship – stronger than in the previous case – between attitude toward online shopping and behavioral information sharing (Table 4).

The main effects of trust (M_{HIGH} = 3.73, M_{LOW} = 2.85) and incentive ($M_{NO INC.}$ = 2.51, $M_{NON MONETARY INC.}$ = 3.2, $M_{MONETARY INC.}$ = 4.13) are all significant at 5%, thus confirming H_{1b} and H_{2b}. The interaction effect between trust and compensation is significant at 10%, as illustrated in Figure 2. However, H_{3b} is not supported as – contrary to the prediction – the incentive has a higher effect in the low trust condition than in the high trust condition.

Table 3. Study 1: GLM results of willingness to provide information

Source	df	Mean Square	F-Value	P-Value
Trust (T)	1	0.131	0.095	0.758
Incentive (I)	2	3.428	2.487	0.086
Attitude Toward Online Shopping	1	9.548	6.928	0.009
T*I	2	0.060	0.044	0.957
Error	154	1.378		

Figure 1. Study 1: Results of willingness to provide information

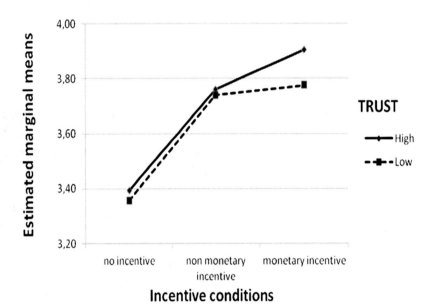

Table 4. Study 1: GLM results of information sharing

Source	df	Mean Square	F-Value	P-Value
Trust (T)	1	18.318	8.706	0.004
Incentive (I)	2	36.451	17.324	0.000
Attitude Toward Online Shopping *	1	18.276	8.686	0.004
T*I	2	5.185	2.464	0.088
Error	156	2.104		

* Attitude toward online shopping was used as a covariate.

Figure 2. Study 1: Results of behavioral information sharing

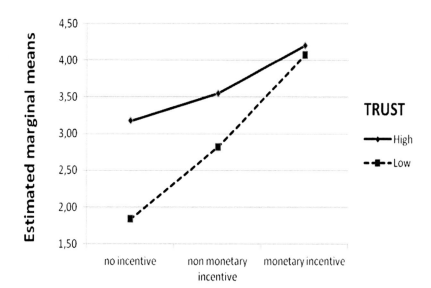

Study 2: Design and Procedure

Study 2 used the same procedure as Study 1. The only difference is that its 178 participants were not students, but working people – hence, earning an income – aged between 35 and 64 years; 47.6% of these participants were female, while 52.4% were male (Table 5).

The measures were the same as in Study 1; the scales' reliabilities are shown in Table 6.

Study 2: Results

Again Levene's test of error variance equality was not rejected and the assumption of the covariance regression coefficients' homogeneity had not been violated. A one-way ANOVA was used to check the trust manipulation. Participants in the high trust condition group reported a higher level of trust than those in the low trust condition (M_{HIGH} = 4.6046, M_{LOW} = 4.2237; F(1, 185)= 8.217, p=0.005).

As in Study 1, we conducted a factorial analysis of covariance (ANCOVA), using willingness to provide information as the dependent variable. All the covariates now emerged as significant. The beta parameter for privacy concerns was -0.245, while commitment to mobile phones was -0.284 and attitude toward online shopping was 0.371. This implies that privacy concerns and commitment to mobile phone services had a negative effect, while attitude toward online shopping had a stronger,

Table 5. Study 2: The number of participants in each experimental cell

		Incentive Condition			Total
		No Incentive	Monetary Incentive	Non-Monetary Incentive	
Trust Condition	Low Trust	30	32	33	95
	High Trust	28	31	33	92
	Total	58	63	66	187

Table 6. Study 2: Cronbach's alpha of the scales

Variable	Alpha
Privacy concern	0.903
Attitude Toward Online Shopping	0.879
Commitment to Mobile Phone Services	0.847
Trust	0.873

positive effect on the willingness to provide information. Table 6 shows the results of the analysis. The main effects of trust and compensation were not significant, meaning that both H_{1a} and H_{2a} are rejected (Table 7). Only the interaction effect of compensation and trust (Figure 3) is significant at 5%, but does not follow the predicted pattern; therefore, H_{3a} is not supported.

Table 7. Study 2: GLM results of willingness to provide information

Source	df	Mean Square	F-Value	P-Value
Trust (T)	1	.370	.236	0.627
Incentive (I)	2	1.127	.719	0.489
Attitude Toward Online Shopping *	1	25.257	16.6117	0.000
Commitment to Mobile Phones*	1	15.288	9.756	0.002
Privacy Concern*	1	10.023	6.396	0.12
T*I	2	8.283	5.285	0.006
Error	178	1.567		

* Attitude toward online shopping, commitment to mobile phones, and privacy concern were used as covariates.

Figure 3. Study 2: Results of willingness to provide information

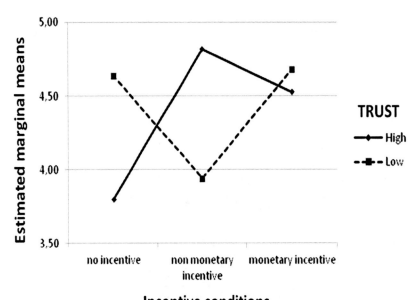

We used the same procedure to measure be-havioral information sharing (Table 8). None of the covariates were significant this time.

When behavioral information sharing is taken into consideration, the main effect of trust (M_{HIGH} = 7.56, M_{LOW} = 8.027) is significant at 10%, but in the opposite direction than H_{1b} predicted, while the main effect of compensation ($M_{NO\,INC.}$ = 7.376, $M_{NON\,MONETARY\,INC.}$ = 8.140, $M_{MONETARY\,COMP.}$ = 7.873) and the interaction effect are both sig-nificant at 5%. These results confirm H_{2b} and H_{3b}, and disconfirm H_{1b}. The interaction effect between trust and incentive is illustrated in Figure 4. Even though the interaction effect is significant at 5%, this once again does not confirm the hypothesized relationship.

DISCUSSION

The aim of our study was to empirically investigate the effect of trust and incentives on information sharing with e-tailers to help the latter exploit the opportunities made possible by the online set-ting. To overcome previous studies' limitations, we measured behavioral information sharing in addition to attitudinal information sharing. Our study showed that the results of the willingness to provide information (attitudinal measure) diverge from those based on the actual disclosure behavior (behavioral measure). Consumers' asserted actions may differ from what they actually do when facing a particular situation that entails some risk. The difference between the results of the attitudinal

Table 8. Study 2: GLM results of behavioral information disclosure

Source	df	Mean Square	F-Value	P-Value
Trust (T)	1	11.319	3.794	0.053
Incentive (I)	2	9.129	3.128	0.046
T*I	2	20.039	6.718	0.002
Error	181	2.983		

Figure 4. Study 2: Results of behavioral information sharing

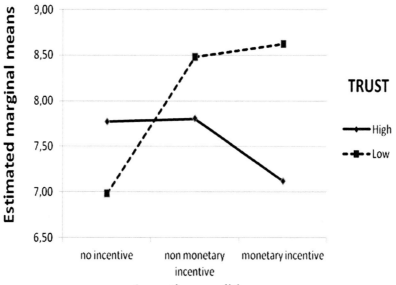

and behavioral data, which we obtained when we tested H$_1$, H$_2$, and H$_3$, confirms the relevance of not only relying on willingness measures as many studies do.

We thus concentrate on the actual information disclosure to discuss the study's theoretical contribution. Contrary to our expectations, compensation appears to be more useful for improving information disclosure in the low trust condition than in the high trust condition (see Figures 2 and 4). This is consistent with Hui et al.,'s (2007) results, according to which compensation can offset the lack of privacy assurance, implying a sort of "tradability" of privacy. Here, compensation seems to offset the lack of initial trust in information disclosure.

However, these results do not mean that initial trust plays no role. If no compensation is offered, trust always allows higher disclosure of information. This implies that creating trust by using immaterial resources could be a valuable approach with which firms can increase consumers' disclosure. While many online operators invest their resources in creating increasingly innovative compensation systems in order to increase their relationship with Website visitors, this strategy – besides being costly – could also be ineffective if customers' trust is already high.

Finally, the difference between the results obtained from the two samples implies that consumers' characteristics could be a promising variable that affects various strategies' effectiveness regarding information disclosure and which should be considered in future theoretical developments.

FUTURE RESEARCH DIRECTIONS

There are many future research directions on the topic of privacy issues with regard to new technology adoption in retailing. The starting point for future research would be to design further studies meant to overcome the limitation of the described studies. Therefore, future studies should be more

cautious when trying to generalize their results and more investigations are needed to enlarge their scope.

Our studies focused on only one e-tailing format and a specific retail setting (mobile phones and services). Different results may be obtained with other e-tailing contexts, involving different types of goods and services. We also focused on the early stage of the firm-customer relationship, considering a virtual company establishing a presence (the Website) in a foreign country. It could be interesting to investigate the relationship between the same constructs in the context of multi-channel firms, including both physical and other direct channels. Moreover, our study was carried out in only one country, Italy. Replication in other countries might be interesting. As En et al., (2006) noted, privacy concerns and attitudes toward providing information online may vary with the political, economic, legal, and cultural contexts. For a retailer exploiting online settings, the physical distance becomes less relevant (owing to technology), but the cultural distance might turn out to be of paramount importance.

Furthermore, although we attempted to make it representative of a real site, we used a fictitious Website. Although we chose to present a site offering products and services that would at least be of moderate interest to most people (selling mobile phones and related services), it is possible that the site was not of interest to all the participants. We assumed that the participants would have at least a little interest in such products and services, especially in Italy, where the market is relatively saturated and expenditure on mobile services is very high.

In respect of trust, we only used firm reputation to manipulate trust, but there are many other factors that might contribute to establishing trust in a retailer. These may include the experience with the retailer, or the perception of opportunistic behaviors. Real companies could also be considered in order to investigate the effects of brand equity on the dynamic of trust. Collaborating with a real retailer may contribute to closing the potential gap between academic research and managerial practice.

Moreover, the study focused on individual trust in online firms. However, e-trust is a multi-level construct. A peculiarity of the online setting is that it does not simply involve trust between the customer and the vendor (investigated here), but also between the buyer and the transaction medium – the technology – and the internet environment (e.g., Harris & Goode, 2004; Lee & Turban, 2002; McKnight, Choudhury, & Kacmar, 2002; Shankar, Urban, & Sultan, 2002). It would thus be interesting to consider other levels of trust (e.g., technology trust and institutional trust) in addition to considering different antecedents of trust in a vendor.

Finally, other technology-based retail settings, besides the online setting, are still vastly unexplored areas for research on privacy concerns. A starting point could be investigating new retail media increasing their market shares due to their synergies with PC-based online settings, such as the mobile setting. Mobile devices are becoming increasingly relevant marketing and retailing tools, as they not only allow the customer to be contacted at any time, but also allow ever greater customization than the "traditional" online context (on the PC). However, this characteristic, which is the main opportunity for marketers using this medium, is also the main obstacle to its diffusion to consumers. Contacting customers on their mobile device could be considered a greater privacy invasion. Moreover, sharing personal data over a mobile phone could raise a greater privacy concern than when the same actions occur on a PC.

We cannot infer that the results that hold for e-commerce also hold for m-commerce. We therefore suggest that future research should investigate the differences between customers' behavior toward these two media forms. A starting point would be to conduct a study similar to the one described in this chapter, but one that includes the media through which the customer and firm interact as another independent variable.

CONCLUSION

The aim of our study was to empirically investigate the effect of trust and compensation on information sharing, which is a prerequisite for many new technologies' adoption. The studies described here focused on the online setting, and are meant to be starting point for future research in other technology-based retail settings. In particular, we used a fictional retailer in the mobile phone business selling products and services to end customers. Building on previous studies, and to overcome a common limitation, we measured behavioral information sharing, not just attitudinal information sharing.

The results of our two experimental studies show the key role of trust in increasing information sharing with e-vendors and behavioral differences between the target groups. If future studies support our findings, marketers may gain a clear picture of how to manage their customer relationships in contexts where technologies actually reduce the direct contact between the firm and the client, at least in the traditional form based on interpersonal interaction. This paradox is a key challenge for retailers who decide to invest in new technologies.

Managerial Implications

The aim of this study was to leverage some theoretical gaps to point out managerial implications for companies interested in increasing their sales online. In this study, we consider overcoming privacy concern as the main way companies can reach this objective. The literature suggests two strategies that practitioners can utilize: leveraging trust, or providing customers with compensation for increasing their information disclosure, a necessary condition to sell online. In this study we tested both to analyze their interaction and to provide insights for practitioners.

The first interesting results from a managerial point of view is that if no compensation is offered, trust always allows higher disclosure of information.

This implies that creating trust by using immaterial resources could be a valuable approach with which firms can increase consumers' disclosure. While many online operators invest their resources in creating increasingly innovative compensation systems in order to increase their relationship with Website visitors, this strategy – besides being costly – could also be ineffective if customers' trust is already high. Compensation is not, after all, effective in increasing information disclosure when trust is already high and therefore serves no purpose after a successful trust creating strategy.

The key question is therefore: how can managers increase their potential customers' trust? Since we focus on the trust in an online vendor in this research, we suggest that firms' efforts should be directed toward leveraging e-trust antecedents in the company and its Website. The most important antecedents identified in the literature are: perceived reputation (Jarvenpaa et al., 2000; Yoon, 2002; Pavlou, 2003; Hee-Woong et al., 2004; Koufaris & Hampton-Sosa, 2004), navigation and user-friendliness (Koufaris & Hampton-Sosa, 2004; Newholm, McGoldrick, Keeling, Macaulay, & Doherty, 2004; Bart, Shankar, Sultan, & Urban, 2005), error-freeness (Newholm et al., 2004; Bart et al., 2005), site design (Shneiderman, 2000), the presence of a virtual advisor (Urban, Sultan, & Qualls, 2000; Hee-Woong et al., 2004; Bart et al., 2005), and of a community (Luo, 2002; Newholm et al., 2004).

Another interesting element in terms of managerial implications is the differences in the results between the two studies, which are based on different targets groups. This suggests that firms should define their strategies according to the main target group that they address. If the target group comprises working people with an income, monetary incentives could impact firms perceived as trustworthy negatively at first, as this may undermine potential customers' initial trust and lessen their willingness to disclose information. Conversely, monetary incentive is the most effective strategy if the main target group is

younger and composed of students. This results is based on the basics of marketing segmentation and targeting, which also proves to be relevant in the online sector.

REFERENCES

Aaker, D. A., Kumar, V., & Day, G. S. (2001). *Marketing Research* (7th ed.). New York: John Wiley and Sons.

Andrade, E. B., Kaltcheva, V., & Weitz, B. (2002). Self-Disclosure on the Web: The Impact of Privacy Policy, Reward and Company Reputation. *Advances in Consumer Research. Association for Consumer Research (U. S.)*, 29(1), 350–353.

Bart, Y., Shankar, V., Sultan, F., & Urban, G. L. (2005). Are The Drivers And Role Of Online Trust The Same For All Web Sites And Consumers? A Large-Scale Exploratory Empirical Study. *Journal of Marketing*, 69(4), 133–152. doi:10.1509/jmkg.2005.69.4.133

Castaldo, S. (2007). *Trust in Marketing Relationships*. Cheltenham, UK: Edward Elgar. doi:10.4337/9781847208576

Castañeda, A. J., & Montoro, F. J. (2007). The effect of Internet General Privacy Concern on Customer Behavior. *Electronic Commerce Research*, 7(2), 117–141. doi:10.1007/s10660-007-9000-y

Cespedes, F. V., & Smith, H. J. (1993). Database Marketing: New Rules for Policy and Practice. *Sloan Management Review*, 34(4), 8–12.

Culnan, M. J. (1993). How Did They Get My Name? An Exploratory Investigation Of Consumer Attitudes Toward Secondary Information Use. *Management Information Systems Quarterly*, 17(3), 341–363. doi:10.2307/249775

DeCew, J. (1997). *In Pursuit of Privacy: Law, Ethics, and the Rise of Technology*. Ithaca, NY: Cornell University Press.

Deutschen, E., De Ruyter, K., Wetzels, M., & Ooterveld, P. (2004). Response Rate and Response Quality of Internet-Based Surveys: An Experimental Study. *Marketing Letters*, *15*(1), 21–36. doi:10.1023/B:MARK.0000021968.86465.00

Doney, P. M., & Cannon, J. P. (1997). An examination of the nature of trust in buyer-seller relationships. *Journal of Marketing*, *61*(2), 35–51. doi:10.2307/1251829

En, X., Hock-Hai, T., & Wen, W. (2006). Volunteering Personal Information On The Internet: Effects Of Reputation, Privacy Notices, And Rewards On Online Consumer Behavior. *Marketing Letters*, *17*(1), 61–74. doi:10.1007/s11002-006-4147-1

Fukuyama, F. (1995). *Trust: The Social Virtues and the Creation of Prosperity*. New York: Free Press.

Gefen, D., Karahanna, E., & Straub, D. W. (2003). Trust and TAM in online shopping: An integrated model. *Management Information Systems Quarterly*, *27*(1), 51–90.

Goodwin, C. (1991). Privacy: Recognition of a Consumer Right. *Journal of Public Policy & Marketing*, *10*(1), 149–166.

Grabner-Kraeuter, S. (2002). The Role of Consumers' Trust in Online-Shopping. *Journal of Business Ethics*, *39*(1-2), 43–50. doi:10.1023/A:1016323815802

Harris, L. C., & Goode, M. M. H. (2004). The Four Levels Of Loyalty And The Pivotal Role Of Trust: A Study Of Online Service Dynamics. *Journal of Retailing*, *80*(2), 139–158. doi:10.1016/j.jretai.2004.04.002

Hee-Woomg, K., Xu, Y., & Koh, J. (2004). A Comparison of Online Trust Building Factors Between Potential Customers and Repeat Customers. *Journal of the Association for Information Systems*, *5*(10), 392–420.

Hoffman, D. (1999). Information privacy in the marketspace: implications for the commercial uses of anonymity on the web. *The Information Society*, *15*(2), 129–140. doi:10.1080/019722499128583

Hoffman, D., Novak, T. P., & Peralta, M. A. (1999). Building Consumer Trust Online Environment: The Case For Information Privacy. *Communications of the ACM*, *42*(4), 80–85. doi:10.1145/299157.299175

Hui, K. L., Teo, H. H., & Lee, S. Y. T. (2007). The value of privacy assurance: an exploratory field experiment. *Management Information Systems Quarterly*, *31*(1), 19–33.

Jarvenpaa, S. L., Tractinsky, J., & Vitale, M. (2000). Consumer Trust In An Internet Store. *Information Technology Management*, *1*(1/2), 45–71. doi:10.1023/A:1019104520776

Jarvenpaa, S. L., & Tractinsky, N. (1999). Consumer trust in an internet store: a cross-cultural validation. *Journal of Computer-Mediated Communication*, *5*(2), 1–35.

Johnson, E. J., Bellman, S., & Lohse, G. L. (2002). Defaults, framing, and privacy: Why opting in opting out. *Marketing Letters*, *13*(1), 5–15. doi:10.1023/A:1015044207315

Koufaris, M., & Hampton-Sosa, W. (2004). The Development Of Initial Trust In An Online Company By New Customers. *Information & Management*, *41*(3), 377–397. doi:10.1016/j.im.2003.08.004

Lee, M. K. O., & Turban, E. (2002). A Trust Model for Consumer Internet Shopping. *International Journal of Electronic Commerce*, *6*(1), 75–91. doi:10.1023/A:1013340118965

Luo, X. (2002). Trust Production And Privacy Concerns On The Internet: A Framework Based On Relationship Marketing And Social Exchange Theory. *Industrial Marketing Management*, *31*(2), 111–118. doi:10.1016/S0019-8501(01)00182-1

Malhotra, N. K., Kim, S. S., & Agarwal, J. (2004). Internet Users' Information Privacy Concerns (IUIPC), the Construct, the Scale, and a Causal Model. *Information Systems Research*, *15*(4), 336–355. doi:10.1287/isre.1040.0032

McKnight, D. H., Choudhury, V., & Kacmar, C. (2002). The Impact of Initial Consumer Trust on Intention to Transact with a WebSite: A Trust Building Model. *The Journal of Strategic Information Systems*, *13*(4), 297–323. doi:10.1016/S0963-8687(02)00020-3

McKnight, D. H., Kacmar, C., & Choudhury, V. (2004). Shifting Factors and the Ineffectiveness of Third Party Assurance Seals: A Two-Stage Model of Initial Trust in a Web Business. *Electronic Markets*, *14*(3), 252–266. doi:10.1080/1019678042000245263

Milne, G. R. (2000). Privacy And Ethical Issues In Database/Interactive Marketing And Public Policy: A Research Framework And Overview Of The Special Issue. *Journal of Public Policy & Marketing*, *19*(1), 1–6. doi:10.1509/jppm.19.1.1.16934

Milne, G. R., & Boza, M. E. (1999). Trust and Concern in Consumers' Perceptions of Marketing Information Management Practices. *Journal of Interactive Marketing*, *13*(1), 5–24. doi:10.1002/(SICI)1520-6653(199924)13:1<5::AID-DIR2>3.0.CO;2-9

Milne, G. R., & Gordon, M. E. (1993). Direct Mail Privacy-Efficiency Trade-offs Within an Implied Social Contract Framework. *Journal of Public Policy & Marketing*, *12*(2), 206–215.

Moorman, C., Zaltman, G., & Deshpandé, R. (1992). Relationships Between Providers and Users of Market Research: The Dynamisc of Trust Within and Between Organizations. *JMR, Journal of Marketing Research*, *29*(3), 314–328. doi:10.2307/3172742

Müller-Lankenau, C., Wehmeyer, K., & Klein, S. (2005). Multi-Channel Strategies: Capturing and Exploring Diversity in the European Retail Grocery Industry. *International Journal of Electronic Commerce*, *10*(2), 85–122. doi:10.2753/JEC1086-4415100204

Newholm, T., McGoldrick, P., Keeling, K., Macaulay, L., & Doherty, J. (2004). Multi-story trust and online retailer strategies. *International Review of Retail, Distribution and Consumer Research*, *14*(4), 437–456. doi:10.1080/0959396042000260889

Norberg, P. A., Horne, D. R., & Horne, D. A. (2007). The Privacy Paradox: Personal Information Disclosure Intentions versus Behaviors. *The Journal of Consumer Affairs*, *41*(1), 100–126. doi:10.1111/j.1745-6606.2006.00070.x

Pavlou, P. A. (2003). Consumer Acceptance Of Electronic Commerce - Integrating Trust And Risk With The Technology Acceptance Model. *International Journal of Electronic Commerce*, *7*(3), 69–103.

Phelps, J., Nowak, G. J., & Ferrell, E. (2000). Privacy Concerns and Consumer Willingness to Provide Personal Information. *Journal of Public Policy & Marketing*, *19*(1), 27–4. doi:10.1509/jppm.19.1.27.16941

Premazzi, K., Castaldo, S., Grosso, M., Raman, P., Brudvig, S., & Hofacker, C. (2010a). Customer information sharing with e-vendors: The role of initial trust and incentives. *International Journal of Electronic Commerce*, *14*(3), 63–91. doi:10.2753/JEC1086-4415140304

Premazzi, K., Castaldo, S., Hofacker, C., & Grosso, M. (2010b). Supporting retailers to exploit online settings for internationalization: the different role of trust and compensation. *Journal of Retailing and Consumer Services*, *17*(3), 229–240. doi:10.1016/j.jretconser.2010.03.006

Raman, P., & Pashupati, K. (2005). Online Privacy: Consumer Concerns and Technological Competence. In S. Krishnamurthy (Ed.), *Contemporary Research in E-Marketing* (pp. 200–225). Hershey, PA: Idea Group Publishing.

Rifon, N. J., LaRose, R., & Choi, S. M. (2005). Your Privacy Is Sealed: Effects of Web Privacy Seals on Trust and Personal Disclosures. *The Journal of Consumer Affairs, 39*(2), 339–362. doi:10.1111/j.1745-6606.2005.00018.x

Schlosser, A. E., White, T. B., & Lloyd, S. M. (2006). Converting Web Site Visitors into Buyers: how Web Site Investment Increases Consumer Trusting Beliefs and Online Purchase Intentions. *Journal of Marketing, 70*(2), 133–148. doi:10.1509/jmkg.70.2.133

Schoder, D., & Yin, P. L. (2000). Building firm trust online. *Communications of the ACM, 43*(12), 73–79. doi:10.1145/355112.355127

Schoenbachler, D. D., & Gordon, G. L. (2002). Trust and Customer Willingness to Provide Information in Database-Driven Relationship Marketing. *Journal of Interactive Marketing, 16*(3), 2–16. doi:10.1002/dir.10033

Shankar, V., Urban, G. L., & Sultan, F. (2002). Online Trust: A Stakeholder Perspective, Concepts, Implications and Future Directions. *The Journal of Strategic Information Systems, 11*(4), 325–344. doi:10.1016/S0963-8687(02)00022-7

Sheehan, K. B. (2005). Public Opinions of Online Privacy: Definitions, Assessment and Implications for Industry and Public Policy. In S. Krishnamurthy (Ed.), *Contemporary Research in E-Marketing* (pp. 186–199). Idea Group Publishing.

Sheehan, K. B., & Hoy, M. G. (1999). Flaming, Complaining, Abstaining: How Online Users Respond to Privacy Concerns. *Journal of Advertising, 28*(3), 37–51. doi:10.1080/00913367.1999.10673588

Sheehan, K. B., & Hoy, M. G. (2000). Dimensions of Privacy Concern among Online Consumers. *Journal of Public Policy & Marketing, 19*(1), 62–73. doi:10.1509/jppm.19.1.62.16949

Shneiderman, B. (2000). Designing Trust Into Online Experiences. *Communications of the ACM, 43*(12), 57–59. doi:10.1145/355112.355124

Son, J.-Y., & Kim, S. S. (2008). Internet Users' Information Privacy-Protective Responses: A Taxonomy and A Nomological Model. *Management Information Systems Quarterly, 32*(3), 503–529.

Steinfield, C. (2004). The Missing Link: Connecting Physical And Virtual Channels Through Click & Mortar Electronic Commerce. In K. Stanoevska-Slabeva (Ed.), *Digital Economy* (pp. 141–157). Anspruch und Wirklichkeit. doi:10.1007/978-3-642-17032-4_10

Szmigin, I., & Bourne, H. (1998). Consumer Equity in Relationship Marketing. *Journal of Consumer Marketing, 15*(6), 544–557. doi:10.1108/07363769810240545

Urban, G. L., Sultan, F., & Qualls, W. J. (2000). Placing trust at the center of your internet strategy. *Sloan Management Review, 42*(1), 39–48.

Van den Poel, D., & Leunis, J. (1999). Consumer acceptance of the internet as a channel of distribution. *Journal of Business Research, 45*(3), 249–256. doi:10.1016/S0148-2963(97)00236-1

Venkatesan, R., Kumar, V., & Ravishankar, N. (2007). Multichannel Shopping: Causes and Consequences. *Journal of Marketing, 71*(2), 114–132. doi:10.1509/jmkg.71.2.114

Viswanathan, S. (2005). Competing across Technology-Differentiated Channels: The Impact of Network Externalities and Switching Costs. *Management Science, 51*(3), 483–496. doi:10.1287/mnsc.1040.0338

Yoon, S. J. (2002). The Antecedents And Consequences Of Trust In Online Purchase Decisions. *Journal of Interactive Marketing, 16*(2), 47–63. doi:10.1002/dir.10008

ADDITIONAL READING

Everard, A., & Galletta, D. F. (2005). How Presentation Flaws Affect Perceived Site Quality, Trust, and Intention to Purchase from an Online Store. *Journal of Management Information Systems, 22*(3), 55–95.

Hong, W., & Thong, J. Y. L. (2013). Internet Privacy Concerns: An Integrated Conceptualization And Four Empirical Studies. *Management Information Systems Quarterly, 37*(1), 275–298.

Im, S., Lee, D. H., Taylor, C. R., & D'Orazio, C. (2008). The influence of consumer self-disclosure on web sites on advertising response. *Journal of Interactive Advertising, 9*(1), 87–106. doi:10.1080/15252019.2008.10722146

Long, G., Hogg, M. K., Hartley, M., & Angold, S. J. (1999). Relationship Marketing And Privacy: Exploring The Thresholds. *Journal of Marketing Practice: Applied Marketing Science, 5*(1), 4–20. doi:10.1108/EUM0000000004548

Milne, G. R., & Culnan, M. J. (2004). Strategies for Reducing Online Privacy Risks: why Consumers Read (or Don't Read) Online Privacy Notices. *Journal of Interactive Marketing, 18*(3), 15–29. doi:10.1002/dir.20009

Miyazaki, A. D., & Krishnamurthy, S. (2002). Internet Seals of Approval: Effects on Online Privacy Policies and Consumer Perceptions. *The Journal of Consumer Affairs, 36*(1), 28–49. doi:10.1111/j.1745-6606.2002.tb00419.x

Nowak, G. J., & Phelps, J. (1997). Direct Marketing And The Use Of Individual-Level Consumer Information: Determining How And When Privacy Matters. *Journal of Direct Marketing, 11*(4), 94–108. doi:10.1002/(SICI)1522-7138(199723)11:4<94::AID-DIR11>3.0.CO;2-F

Otto, J. R., & Chung, Q. B. (2000). A Framework For Cyber-Enhanced Retailing: Integrating E-Commerce Retailing With Brick-And-Mortar Retailing. *Electronic Markets, 10*(3), 185–191. doi:10.1080/10196780050177099

Pagani, M. (2007). A vicarious innovativeness scale in the domain of 3G mobile services: integrating the Domain Specific Innovativeness Scale with psychological and rational indicators. *Technology Analysis and Strategic Management, 19*(6), 709–728. doi:10.1080/09537320701711207

Pagani, M. (2008). A Value-Choice model to forecast market consequences of 3G mobile service design decisions. *International Journal of Mobile Marketing, 3*(1), 23–31.

Phelps, J. E., D'Souza, G., & Nowak, G. J. (2001). Antecedents And Consequences Of Consumer Privacy Concerns: An Empirical Investigation. *Journal of Interactive Marketing, 15*(4), 2–17. doi:10.1002/dir.1019

Premazzi, K. Castaldo, S., Hofacker, C., & Grosso, M. (2010). Trust in on line customer-firm interaction: a literature review and directions for research. In D. Latusek Dominika & A. Gerbasi Alexandra (Eds.) Trust and Technology in a Ubiquitous Modern Environment (pp. 287-303), IGI Global.

Reibstein, D. J. (2002). What Attracts Customers to Online Stores, and What Keeps Them Coming Back? *Journal of the Academy of Marketing Science, 30*(4), 465–47. doi:10.1177/009207002236918

Rust, R. T., & Kannan, P. K. (2003). e-Service: A New Paradigm for Business in the Electronic Environment. *Communications of the ACM, 46*(6), 37–44. doi:10.1145/777313.777336

Sawhney, M., & Zabin, J. (2002). Managing and Measuring Relationship Equity in the Network Economy. *Journal of the Academy of Marketing Science, 30*(4), 313–333. doi:10.1177/009207002236908

Sayre, S., & Horne, D. A. (2000). Trading Secrets for Savings: How Concerned Are Consumers about a Privacy Threat from Club Cards? *Advances in Consumer Research. Association for Consumer Research (U. S.), 27*(1), 151–155.

Smith, H. J., Milberg, S. J., & Burke, S. J. (1996). Information Privacy: Measuring Individuals' Concerns About Organizational Practices. *Management Information Systems Quarterly, 20*(2), 167–196. doi:10.2307/249477

Steinfield, C., Bouwman, H., & Adelaar, T. (2002). The Dynamics of Click-and-Mortar ElectronicCommerce: Opportunities and Management Strategies. *International Journal of Electronic Commerce, 7*(1), 93–119.

Wang, S., Beatty, S. E., & Foxx, W. (2004). Signalling the trustworthiness of small online retailers. *Journal of Interactive Marketing, 18*(1), 53–69. doi:10.1002/dir.10071

Ying-Chao, L., J., Chend, L.S.L., Huanga, W. H., Ming-Sung Chenga, J., & Shih-Tse Wangb, E. (2008). Do extrinsic cues affect purchase risk at international e-tailers: The mediating effect of perceived e-tailer service quality. *Journal of Retailing and Consumer Services, 15*(5), 420–428. doi:10.1016/j.jretconser.2007.11.001

KEY TERMS AND DEFINITIONS

ANCOVA: Multivariate data analysis technique used in experimental research that allows researcher to test for the significant difference between the means of the dependent variable in the different experimental groups when controlling for the results of the covariate variables.

ANOVA: Multivariate data analysis technique used in experimental research that allows researcher to test for the significant difference between the means of the dependent variable in the different experimental groups.

Covariate Variable: A variable that could influence the effect of the independent variable on the dependent variable in experimental research; it is therefore measured and its results are controlled for to determine the "pure" causal effect.

Incentive or Compensation: Something firms give to customers in exchange for providing their personal data; it may take several forms (money, gift, etc.).

Information and Communication Technologies (ICT): ICTs are meant to increase information exchange and communication between geographically separated parties, but they also increase many users' privacy concerns.

Privacy Concern: Concern about the safeguarding and usage of personal data provided to an entity (such as a firm).

Trust: A subject's (the trustor) belief that another subject (the trustee) will act according to his or her expectations during a risky situation over which he or she has no control.

Chapter 23
Retail and Social Media Marketing:
Innovation in the Relationship between Retailers and Consumers

Francesca Negri
University of Parma, Italy

ABSTRACT

The Internet has revolutionized almost every facet of business and personal life. We are facing a far-reaching revolution, driven by Social Networking Sites (SNSs) where people talk about their life, purchases, and experiences. Mobile devices and tablets are replacing computers as the main access point to the Internet. Customer expectations are rising constantly with the development of new technologies. Social Media comes in many forms: blogs, media sharing sites, forums, review sites, virtual worlds, social networking sites, etc. Social Networking Sites (SNSs), the focus of this chapter, are the most disruptive social media and a key opportunity for business. Most industries recognized in that shift the potential for a more intimate and productive relationship with customers. Nowadays, retailers have no choice in whether they do social media: they only have the choice of how well they do it. Retailers need to convert browsers to buyers, and one-time customers to loyal sharing fans, so that they become advocates in the real and virtual worlds. The shift is deep: from one-way communication to conversation, and from advertising as an interruption to the interactivity in all locations. The originality of the chapter consists on its introduction of the concept of Social Networking Sites (SNSs) as an integration of the retailing marketing mix, defining its role in a marketing strategy, and providing some managerial implications for practitioners. After an introductive overview of the trend adopting a retailer point of view, four are the chapter's cornerstones: opportunities belonging from geolocation; how to plan a social media strategy; a new channel of interaction between customers and retailers: the social customer service; how to face a crisis in a Web 2.0 context. These are four brand new ways to engage consumers. This topic is relatively new and in continuous becoming, and much of interest remains to be said about it. The chapter's approach is to present what the authors believe to be the most relevant for a retailer facing a social networking challenge.

DOI: 10.4018/978-1-4666-6074-8.ch023

INTRODUCTION

The purpose of the Chapter is to highlight the innovation in the relationship between shoppers and retailers: Web 2.0 permits the retailers to engage customers on Social Networking Sites (SNSs). The new contest determines new rules, opportunities and threats in engaging customers.

Something has changed. Web 2.0 is a set of economic, social, and technology trends that collectively form the basis for the next generation of the Internet, a more mature, distinctive medium characterized by user participation, openness, and network effects. Qualman (2013) defines Socialnomics as "the value created and shared via Social Media and its efficient influence on outcomes economic, political, relational, etc.). Or, more simply put, it's word of mouth on digital steroids."

There is need to investigate the managerial and organizational implications of engaging with consumers in various ways through SNSs. This Chapter therefore makes an exploratory investigation into the new interactions between retailers, shoppers, and consumers.

The interactive capabilities of SNSs can be used to engage the shopper as customer in many ways, and it is imperative for retailers and academics to learn about the role of Social Media in this new context.

Providing detailed description and a general overview of the trend, the chapter identifies the role of social networks in retailer marketing strategy through a review of existing literature, recent data provided by eminent Research Institutes (MGI, Nielsen, eMarketer, et al.) and empirical research findings from the Author's research process.

BACKGROUND

The trend toward networked applications is accelerating, and Social Media Marketing is at the moment an important topic of conversation amongst academics and researchers.

Kozinets (2010) states that our social worlds are going digital. Everyday 2.23 billion people around the world go online (cmo.com), and many express their feelings and experiences about products and services through Social Media. Internet users spend 23% time online social networking. Many contributions (McKinsey Global Institute, 2012; Nielsen, 2012; Hinchcliffe & Kim, 2012) underline the far-reaching opportunities belonging from social challenge. So businesses and social researchers are finding that to understand society they must follow people's social activities and encounters on the Internet and Social Networking Sites. Andzulis, Panagopoulos and Rapp (2012) state that "companies today are wrestling with how to adopt Social Media into their business models and strategy" (p. 306).

But in spite of the expansion of Social Media, there is a paucity of research and academic literature on the role Social Media play in the retailing mix. From a business perspective, the lack of a strategic approach represents a significant barrier to effective engagement with Social Media.

"Web 2.0," the Web constructed by users themselves through blogs, communities and file sharing was first referred to in 2004 by Tim O'Reilly (Doherty et al., 2010). It is a context based on sharing platforms (blogs, YouTube, Flickr,...) and platforms hosting Social Networking Sites (Facebook, Myspace, Ning,...). In the words of Tim O'Reilly (2006 "Web 2.0 is much more than just pasting a new user interface onto an old application. It's a way of thinking, a new perspective on the entire business of software - from concept through delivery, from marketing through support. Web 2.0 thrives on network effects: databases that get richer the more people interact with them, applications that are smarter the more people use them, marketing that is driven by user stories and experiences, and applications that interact with each other to form a broader computing platform." Blogs, social networks like Facebook, and microblogging platforms like Twitter are simply technologies that foster communication, sharing, and collaboration (Barefoot et al. 2010). Or more precisely, Facebook, Linkedin, Twitter, Myspace and so on are not Social Networks themselves, but the tools and the platforms that allow people to manage and to expand their Social Network online. "With millions of people around the world, from an ever widening age profile, spending ever more time communicating with their "friends" via sites, such as Facebook, it is very likely that the power of social networking will continue to expand, and have a far greater affect on the modern consumers' online shopping behaviour" (Doherty et al., 2010).

In order to describe the context of the new relationship between businesses and customers, it is useful to refer to the POEM Model proposed by Forrester Research (Corcoran, 2009). POEM stands for Paid, Owned and Earned Media and shows the different ways a brand can reach its audience. Shown below, the POEM Model adapted to retailing companies.

Paid media: All advertising bought by retailers on digital or traditional media, e.g. TV and radio campaigns, display ads and paid search, or the house organ and flyers diffusion. Content is entirely controlled by the retailer and communication flows only in one direction, from retailer to audience, with no opportunity for interaction. This type of advertising is very expensive, and is showing a progressive loss of effectiveness. Paid media is a channel that can be controlled, but response rates and credibility are declining very fast. On the other hand, no other type of media can guarantee the same immediacy and scale.

Owned media: All points of contacts and exposures owned and controlled by the retailer. In a digital context, the most important owned medium is often the Website. In a Social Media panorama, owned media can be official Facebook and Twitter accounts and brand blogs. Retailers' mobile APPs and games are owned media too. Owned media create brand portability: retailers can extend brand presence beyond their own Website online through Social Media sites and communities. These new contexts are built for longer-term relationships with customers, in a bid for two-way conversation. The retailer writes a post on the Facebook page, and the fans can reply, share and comment, positively or negatively. Many customers enjoy engaging with their brand through long-term relationships through Social Media sites (Harris & Dennis, 2011; Gummerus et al., 2012). Owned media consists essentially of social content strategy.

Earned media: Gives visibility through people and customer comments, shares and recommendations. In this case, the customers become the channel. Earned media consist essentially of consumer comments and reviews, viral video views, etc. A retailer's tweet is owned media, but if the tweet is retweeted by a loyal customer it becomes earned media. This is the most credible form of media, but from the retailer point of view it also represents the biggest opportunity and threat. Social Media has also created a new currency, "social currency," referring to the concept of influence. This is the era of "value to many," where the customers is the real king. "Social Media is the mechanism that allows users to avoid information indigestion" (Qualman, 2013): people want to know what peers think about products and services, and it doesn't matter if they are friends or unknown people "met" on Social Networking Sites. The "Like" button allows users to share things/brands/places they like, and seek approval from others within their network (Walker Naylor et al., 2012). Influencing the buyer in no longer sufficient: retailers need to influence the potential buyer's network, through this kind of advocate customer. Zarrella found (2010) that many rating and review sites initially allowed users to post anonymously. But over time, many, such as TripAdvisor and Amazon, have incorporated a reputation system where users or their individual reviews can be rated on a scale of usefulness or accuracy. Recently, a new kind of review site has emerged that combines local ratings with social networking features, like the popular site Yelp.com.

Exists also the possibility to pay or sell with a tweet (paywithatweet.com): people sell and buy products through the value of their social networks. Every time people pay with a tweet, their social friends see information about the product. And the product soon becomes known.

Earned media are free for retailers. Customer word of mouth (WOM) is spontaneous and voluntary, as well as being the most reliable (Harvey et al, 2011). Earned media are a gift.

On the other hand, WOM can sometimes be negative, and difficult or impossible to control. Retailers need to learn to respond, and consider carefully when it is appropriate or useful to stimulate earned media through WOM marketing. Measuring the ROI of earned media is difficult and requires continuous monitoring.

Paid, Owned and Earned media work best when used together, but retailers need to make the hard choice of what to include and what not to include, especially when budgets are tight. They are in any case a supplement to more traditional trade and in store marketing, and not a substitute.

Table 1 shows how retailers are committed in Social Networking Sites: between the top ten companies most talked about on Facebook, as

Table 1. Top ten companies most talked about on Facebook

Brand	People Talking about them on Facebook
Coca-Cola	1.04 m
Avon	929k
Walmart	757k
Disney	737k
Samsung Mobile	634k
Intel	588k
Bud Light	504k
Guarana Antarctica	494k
NBA	477k
Visa	470k

Source, Richter (2013)

of August 19, 2013 (Richter, 2013), Walmart is the third.

The table shows clearly that people are talking about Walmart, a FMCG retailer. And although Walmart is the biggest retailer in the world, it would be hard to define it as a "lovebrand." So Social Networking Sites now represent a big opportunity, as well as a threat, for other retailers and chains, because customers are yet talking about them online, and an increasing numbers of customers are accessing retail information on-the-go, using mobile phones, and looking for a more personal and relevant experience.

ENGAGING CUSTOMERS ON SOCIAL NETWORKING SITES: CHALLENGES FOR RETAILERS

How Social Networking Sites are contributing to innovate in retailing? The answer is shown in the Table 2 that highlights the disruptive elements as well as the opportunities and threats.

The most important components and elements of the table will be analyzed in depth in the further pages.

Social Networking Sites (SNSs)

Boyd and Ellison (2007) define "social network sites as Web-based services that allow individuals to (1) construct a public or semi-public profile within a bounded system, (2) articulate a list of other users with whom they share a connection, and (3) view and traverse their list of connections and those made by others within the system."

Social networking is one element of the "Web 2.0" environment, and adapting it to retail, retailers will face increasingly intense pressure from consumers to deliver a more authentic dialogue and provide opportunities to both customize the interface and allow consumers to generate their own content (Wirtz et al., 2010). In an increasingly competitive retail environment, successful

Table 2. Challenges and innovation in retailing

Traditional Relationship	Challenges for Retailers	Innovation in Retailing
Touch point: store, Website.	Touch point: store, Website and **Social Media**.	New opportunities of engagement trough integration online/ in store marketing (geolocation). Retailers need to be where customers are, setting a Social Networking plan. Threat: a low-cost but high-energy strategy.
From Communication *Top down* (one to many)	**To** Conversation *Top down* (one to many) *Peer to peer* (many to many) *Bottom up* (many to one)	The conversation is personal, bidirectional, very fast. User Generated Contents become Social Currency. Retailers need to plan a Social Customer Care (social caring) to match the interactive and real time conversations.
Focused on Company.	Focused on **People**.	Retailers must listen and monitor conversations. Contents must be engaging, not spamming.
Retailers owned media and contents.	Retailers **share** contents. Contents are **created** by customers. Customers are media.	Threat: loss of control. Retailers need a Crisis Management planning.
Relationship not mediated by technology.	**Portable devices** are very important in the customer shopping experience.	Retailers need to consider mobile and tablet as part oh their retailing mix: the new relationship is mediated by mobile devices.

retailers are finding new ways to connect with their customers in order to drive sales, loyalty and customer awareness (Negri, 2011).

The dozens of practitioner articles on SNSs agree on several points (Andzulis et al., 2012): first, they are important. Second, "the balance of power has moved, inexorably, and forever, from the company to the customer" (Baer, 2010). And last, but not least, they require resources in terms of money and people, integration and deep commitment. Practitioner articles do not point out that a Social Media strategy is not a medley of disjointed tactics and promotional operations.

Many retailers, such as Walmart, Inditex Zara, Amazon, Best Buy, and Abercrombie & Fitch are now managing Social Media Marketing through Facebook or Twitter. This section describes some of the most important Social Networking Sites, and discusses how to create a Social Media Marketing Plan, with the use of key performance indicators.

The social network Website *Facebook* was launched in 2004 at Harvard University by Mark Elliot Zuckerberg and now has more than 1 billion members worldwide. Facebook's mission is "to give people the power to share and make the world more open and connected." Millions of people around the world use Facebook everyday to keep up with friends, upload photos, share links and videos, and learn more about the people they meet and the products/services they buy. Facebook Inc. began selling stock to the public and trading on the NASDAQ on May 18, 2012. Most of Facebook's revenue comes from advertising.

Twitter is a Website owned and operated by Twitter Inc., which offers a social networking and microblogging service, enabling its users to send and read messages called tweets. These are text-based posts of up to 140 characters: the creators of Twitter chose this length because the number was close to the 160 characters typical of an SMS, with the extra 20 characters used for a username. By default, tweets are publicly visible, but senders can restrict message delivery to their followers. Users may subscribe to other users' tweets, which is known as following, and subscribers are known as followers. Since its creation in March 2006 and launch in July 2006, by Jack Dorsey, Twitter has gained popularity worldwide, with over 500 million registered users as of 2012, generating over 340 million tweets daily and handling over 1,6 billion search queries per day. Twitter official (verified) corporate accounts enjoy greater acceptance.

Pinterest is a pinboard-style photo-sharing Website that allows users to create and manage theme-based image collections such as events, interests, and hobbies. Users can browse other pinboards for images, "re-pin" images to their own pinboards, or they can "like" photos. Pinterest was founded by Ben Silbermann, Paul Sciarra, and Evan Sharp; development began in December 2009, and the site launched as a closed beta in March 2010. In December 2011, the site became one of the top 10 largest social network services, according to Hitwise data, with 11 million total visits per week. Pinterest also allows businesses to create pages aimed at promoting their businesses online: business pages can include prices of products, ratings and reviews. In February 2013, Reuters and ComScore stated that Pinterest had 48,7 million users globally.

Google+ (pronounced and sometimes written as Google Plus) is a social networking site and identity service owned and operated by Google Inc. It is the second-largest SNS in the world, and is said to have overtaken Twitter in January 2013 with approximately 359 million users, although these figures are contested.

Retailing is increasingly a high-tech industry with retailers using communications and information systems technologies to increase operating efficiencies and improve customer service (Levy & Weitz, 2012). These new applications and virtual presences include the use of Websites to sell products and services to customers, providing a seamless multichannel interface, activating co-creation processes, building a more rewarding shopping experience in store and out of store and creating a new interactive and real time relationship through Social networking Sites (Burton et al., 2011). The result is that customers can interact with retailers anytime, anywhere.

Despite rapid growth in marketing use of SNSs, there is a little theoretical or empirical research examining how retailers, belonging to different sectors, use those popular sites. Andzulis, Panagopoulos and Rapp (2012) proposed a review of Social Media and their implications for the sale process and in the sales force, but with a producers point of view.

Catching the Social Media networking wave is neither as easy nor as straightforward as might seem at first. It is a low-cost but high-energy strategy. Many companies have built up experience in managing it, but as yet there are few retailers among them.

Retailers today however are starting to use Social networking Sites for several reasons:

- Social networking presence gives retailers a more personal identity, which can differentiate it from competitors. As customers grow tired of one-sided marketing messages, Social Media provides a new way for retailers to engage customers in conversations. On April 27, 2011, IKEA in Hong Kong ran their "Happy Inside" campaign through a "Bedroom Makeover" Facebook contest, offering a 90-second shopping spree to the person who submitted the best photos to show how IKEA helped "turn his/her bedroom nightmare around." The IKEA Website shows a video of the three lucky IKEA fans sweeping up $10,000 in products in seconds;
- Social networking accounts can be used to promote new products and services or new stores, and to publicize promotions. Retailers are using Pinterest to display grouped and curated selections of their products in a visual and creative way (Sevitt & Samuel, 2013).
- The new relationship means firms can gather customer insight and incorporate it into strategy. SNSs also allow retailers to engage honest feedback, both solicited and unsolicited. SNSs allow retailers to monitor comments, understand how messages are perceived, what information custom-

ers want, highlight purchasing and buying preferences (Casteleyn et al., 2009; Patino et al., 2012). Trough surveys and pools retailer can test new services or assortments. It was pressure from online responses that forced fashion retailer Gap to withdraw its planned logo redesign in October 2010;

- Retailers can also sell on Social networking Sites (social commerce, or f-commerce). New functions on Facebook allow retailers to launch secure, transactional stores as APPs, so that customers can buy from within the site. Transactional Facebook stores give a purpose and measurability to f-commerce, although the market is still relatively small. There are however companies such as Blooming which offer social-focused capabilities to firms aiming to sell through these sites.

Geolocation

Customers are increasingly armed with mobile devices, such as smartphones and tablets. Inside the store, in an instant, they can thus find out everything they want to know about what is on the shelves, and whether any friends are in the store or have been there. They can read, and rate, reviews of the products and assortments, opinions about employees courtesy, and they can make price comparisons with the nearest shop.

Singh (2012) identifies in geo-socialisation one of the mega-mega trends of today. "The next platform of social networking will rely on geographic services and capabilities such as geocoding and geotagging to allow social network to connect and co-ordinate users with local people or events that match their interest" (p. 81).

Retailers need to take advantage of this sharing. Quoting Salt (2011), "Social location sharing is happening to your product, service, venue, and location whether you are active or not."

"Social location marketing" is the process of utilizing social location sharing tools as a mar-

keting channel, while "social location sharing" defines the platforms and applications used for sharing the information about locations. What differentiates social location sharing from much of the rest of SNSs is that it is specific to a location. And retailers well know that is all about "Location Location Location." When a customer "checks in" in a specific location, a supermarket or a clothes shop, s/he is telling the network where s/he is. This is a public declaration of approval or affinity for the place. This is earned media. A customer checking in at an Apple Store is stating a preference for that brand, and advocating it as a social location sharer. From a user perspective, social location sharing sites are often a sort of game, including rewards and prizes. Foursquare, for example, awards check-in badges and points.

Retailers are thus able to promote check-in into a store, or a single department of the store. Segmented offers also allows rewards to be tied to in-store promotions - especially those offered in partnership with third party suppliers.

At the time of writing, *Foursquare* is the most important social location mobile site (SoLoMo). It is a free APP that helps people make the most of where they are and share and save the places they visit. People use it to find the best place to go based on what their friends and experts recommend. They check in at store in the real world and leave tips to tell others what they like, or dislike. People can also receive personalized recommendations and deals based on where they are, or where their friends are, or where people with the same tastes have been. Foursquare co-founders Dennis Crowley and Naveen Selvadurai met in 2007 in New York City: they began building the first version of Foursquare in fall 2008, and launched it at South by Southwest Interactive in Austin, Texas in March 2009. Today (January, 2013) the community consists of over 30 million people worldwide, with over 3 billion check-ins, one million every day. Over a million businesses use the Merchant Platform. Retailers may promote news, events, and discounts with Foursquare Local

Updates, or set up a Foursquare Special to attract and reward visitors. Foursquare free analytics informs retailers about customers checking in to their business – they can see who customers are, when they come, how much they're talking about the brand across other SNSs, and more.

Social location marketing is an activity very close to gaming. Many retailers organize treasure hunts into the shop, inviting customers to interact with, rate and snap pictures in various shop areas.

Finally, some social location APPs are being rolled out to integrate with retailers loyalty programs.

Social Networking Strategy and Plans

This section examines the components of a Social Networking Plan. Social networking sites have the potential to effect many strategy, in different ways. Listening is the primary step in engaging a customer.

1.   Listen first! Monitoring

One of the most exciting aspect of SNSs for retailers is the opportunity 1) to identify consumer preferences and use this information to shape business strategy through customer endorsement and 2) to monitor what people is thinking of them and have the chance to effectively manage brand reputation.

Those opportunities have already given certain retailers a significant and long-lasting competitive advantage. Rick Bendel, Global Chief Marketing Officer of Walmart, said: "Social Media is a free, massive focus group, taking place in real time. And it is taking place with or without your permission."

Retailers need to monitor conversations and respond to them, especially if the commentary is negative. The three steps of Social Media Monitoring, which underpin Social CRM are: listening (first!), understanding, and reporting.

Listening gives retailers the appropriate baseline and credibility to join the conversation. Before a retailer can face the social networking arena, needs to identify and understand the value proposition for the customer. In a context in which "Markets are conversations" (first thesis of the The Cluetrain Manifesto, Levine et al, 1999), hearing is not enough: listening is a technique used in conversations, which requires a person to pay attention to the speaker and provide feedback.

Quoting Qualman (2013, p. 36), "Negative comments and posts are easier for companies to find with Social Media. Hence, those companies have more time to focus on the solution rather than spending time finding the problem. (…) Ineffective companies spend time attempting to obfuscate or manipulate negative comments within Social Media." Once a retailer starts to monitor what is being said about its brand/products/services, they should get to know their audience. They need to know who they are, where they hang out online, how they use the Web and their expectations as well as which competitors' page/accounts they follow.

Zarrella's advice (2010) is to "Lurk, lurk, and lurk some more; get to know the community before you start posting."

A very interesting new qualitative marketing research technique for providing consumer insight has been developed by Kozinets: the "Netnography," a market-oriented ethnography conducted on online communities dedicated to marketing-relevant topics. It uses the information publicly available in online forums and communities to identify, and understand, the needs and decision influences of relevant online consumer groups. (Kozinets, 2010)

2.   Know the global marketing strategy of the company, aiming for total integration

Retailer Social Media strategy should fit with the retailers established identity and core values. Selective retailers, for example, need to offer the same level of service and conversational tone on Social Networking Sites as they do offline.

3.   Identify the right strategy

Strategy and tactics are inseparable, but strategy must come before tactics. Before opening a page on Facebook, retailers need to identify their goals and strategy. The majority of Social Media Marketing handbooks today describe tactics and Facebook micro-marketing tools, which, however, are changing day by day. Strategic thinking, according to Drucker (1999), is knowing the right questions to ask. Before learning how to manage a Facebook page or a Twitter account, a retailer should answer a few basic questions: What is the purpose of using SNSs? What resources do we have? Where are customers talking about their preferences, commenting on shops and services? Where are our competitors? Which are expected threats, and our weaknesses in Web 2.0?

To answer these questions, it is helpful to make a SWOT analysis, highlighting retailers' strengths and weaknesses in approaching Web 2.0 and the opportunities and threats of facing Social Networking Sites.

4.   Set the goal of the strategy and Key Performance Indicators (KPI)

Using free Social Media tools and placements is more time- and cost-effective than traditional advertising, but retailers must remember that Social Media marketing is a low-cost, high-energy type of strategy. Opening an official page on Facebook is free, although it can be costly in terms of time and money to create appropriate content and respond rapidly to customer queries and so on.

It is difficult to measure the return on investment (ROI) of Social Media (Hoffman, 2010). Some companies even state, "We aren't doing Social Media because there isn't any ROI." But this leads to the more urgent question of the cost of doing nothing. As Qualman (2013) states, "The

ROI of Social Media is that in five years your company will still exist."

There are some aspects of advertising campaigns that can be measured (Avinash, 2009) through key performance indicators (KPI). Paid media and Owned media are traceable, like more traditional forms of media. But Earned media, the most effective form, is not. To calculate the ROI of Social Media, retailers deduct the cost of their financial and time investment from the income generated. But not all the fans who visit the retailer's Facebook page turn into customers or leads. The open question is how to measure effective engagement rates. Simply counting the number of fans or followers does not work: first of all, not all fans are active and, secondly, at the time of writing, it is possible to buy targeted fans for few cents on eBay. The numbers of customer posts, retweets, sharing and reviews are on the other hand useful metrics.

A further aspect not covered by traditional KPI is the cultural change brought about by social networking marketing. Catching the Social Media wave, retailers abandon one-way communication and embrace a new conversational paradigm where communication between retailers and customers flows in two directions.

Most SNSs makes control dashboards available to retailers in freemium: basic insights are offered free while fees are charged for more sophisticated marketing instruments.

5.   Build up the team, and invest in training. Create and share the social media policy

Retailers must synchronize their strategic and tactical activities to create, deliver, and communicate customer value trough SNSs. One of the most common error is to delegate to the last incoming stagers the Social Media marketing activities, only because "they're young." Social Media marketing requires high level of planning, commitment and competence. Retailers need to pay attention selecting the Social Media marketing team, and an ongoing training is required. Moreover, SNSs also make it possible to search for new human resources, in line with the mood of the brand. As well as more traditional sites such as Linkedin, Facebook can also be used, as in the Jobs APP from Zara on their official Facebook page.

The Social Media Policy (SMP) of a company is a corporate code of conduct (Negri, 2013). An internal SMP provides guidelines for employees who post online either as part of their job or as a private person. An external SMP regulates the relationship between company/fans-followers and fans-followers/fans-followers in the social networking context. The main goal of an SMP is to set standards for appropriate behavior and ensure that an employee posts will not expose the company to legal problems or public embarrassment. The SMP is one of the most important parts of a social network plan. The Walmart SMP is very interesting and covers employees, customers and associates. The main points are shown Box 1 (source: Walmart).

Box 1. Walmart's social media guidelines

We engage with our customers and stakeholders beyond the walls of our stores: you can find us on Facebook, Twitter, YouTube, Flickr and Foursquare. This page will give you a better idea on how to engage with us in social media, what you can expect from us, and where to find more information.

Walmart's Twitter Engagement Guidelines

Twitter asks a very basic question of its users: "What's happening?" And we know the answer to that question – we're working every day to help people save money so they can live better.

Through our Twitter account we aim to provide you with information on Walmart's major activities and initiatives - from sustainability to diversity, from healthier foods to charitable giving. We welcome your thoughts on any and all of those topics.

Please note that we won't be able to reply to store or service issues through Twitter. If you would like to comment about customer service or other issues please visit our Walmart Facebook feedback app, leave a comment through our Contact Us page or call 1-800-WALMART.

Here are a couple of things you should know about our Twitter engagement:

All official Walmart Twitter users are identified at walmart.com/twitter.

We are committed to having a dialogue with our followers. We count on you to use @ messages in a way that contributes to the dialogue. Please support any claims with links to information sources whenever possible. We love opinions; we love them even more when you back them up with facts.

We strive to respond to as many relevant questions and comments as possible, but we reserve the right to use our judgment in selecting the messages we respond to.

Following a Twitter account or including an account in a Twitter list does not constitute an endorsement; the same applies to re-tweeting messages posted on accounts that Walmart does not own, or marking them as "favorites."

The posting and presence of content on Twitter and on this site does not necessarily mean that Walmart agrees with the content, ensures its accuracy or otherwise approves of it. Nothing in any Twitter page constitutes a binding representation, agreement or an endorsement on the part of Walmart. Please review Twitter's terms of use carefully when engaging on the site.

Walmart's Facebook Engagement Guidelines

We're excited that you've joined us on our Facebook Fan page, and we know you've got plenty to say. At Walmart, our mission is our purpose: we save people money so they can live better.

While you're with us, we hope you'll take a moment to read the following guidelines we ask you to follow when contributing to our Facebook Fan page:

Don't do anything that breaks the law.

Be polite and courteous, even if you disagree. Excessive name calling, profanity, fighting words, discriminatory epithets, sexual harassment, bullying, gruesome language or the like, will not be tolerated.

Stay on topic. Keep the conversation relevant to the community and contribute to the dialogue. We reserve the right to remove off-topic, out of context, spam or promotional postings.

Keep it real. All wall postings should come from a real person and Facebook profile. Postings from fake or anonymous profiles will be deleted when discovered.

There is a place for customer service-related questions, complaints, concerns or ideas from customers. If you are a customer and have a customer service comment, complaint, concern or idea, we encourage you to post it on Walmart's Facebook Feedback tab, to ensure that we can respond in a timely manner. Please note that any customer service posts published on a Walmart page by customers will be removed when discovered. As always, if you would like to comment about customer service or any other issue you can visit our Contact Us page or call 1-800-WALMART.

We reserve the right to remove content posted to Facebook that violates these guidelines.

---

continued on following page

Box 1. Continued

If you are a Walmart associate, please follow these additional guidelines:

Know the rules. Before engaging on Facebook, or on any other social media property, make sure you read and understand Walmart's Social Media Policy and Walmart Information Policy. In any and all interactions make sure that you don't share confidential or private information about the Company's business operations, products, services, or customers; respect financial disclosure laws; and do not say you speak for the Company without express written authorization from the Company to do so.

Remember that we have a dedicated FB team tasked with responding to customer inquiries or criticism. Our Official Walmart Facebook team is responsible for engaging customers through our page. To avoid confusion, we ask that you not attempt to respond to customer inquiries or comments directed specifically to the Company or asking for an official Company response on this site.

Consider using company established channels for job-specific issues. While we encourage associates to join our Facebook community and participate in conversations with our customers and other users, we encourage you to direct your complaints or concerns about your job or working environment to your store management team using the established Open Door Process or MyWalmart.com.

For Walmart managers: If you are a manager, please make sure you are familiar with our Social Media Management Guidelines, available on the Walmart Wire.

Guidelines for Associates' Use of Walmart-Sponsored Location Based Promotions

Walmart is currently experimenting with in-store promotional campaigns for users of location-based services like Foursquare and Facebook Places. If you are an associate using these services, you may have the opportunity to check in at your store's location every day, which could give you an unfair advantage over our customers. That's why we ask you not to participate in location based-promotions for your own store. Please feel free to take advantage of location-based promotions when you check in at other Walmart stores offering these promotions.

---

6. Select the Social Networking Sites where you want operate, and choose the right tools.

Retailers need to know their target and their audience, and select SNSs where these can be found. They should understand the special features offered by each SNSs and use them. Social Networking Sites vary greatly based on their feature sets, but there are some common elements across most of them.

Accounts: Pinterest, YouTube, Linkedin, Facebook and Twitter offer special accounts and tools for businesses. For example, it is not possible for retailers or other businesses to have a profile on Facebook, but they can manage a page showing information about the company, its history, contact information, and so on.

Social networking sites allow retailers to operate multiple accounts that can target specific groups of shoppers, for example by location, store or private labels.

Some retailers are targeting local customers. In the UK, Waterstones has Twitter accounts for individual stores, and can notify customers of book signing and other local events. Other retailers are tailoring communications to user interests. Amazon, for example, manages various different Twitter accounts and various Facebook pages including Amazon Student, Amazon Mom, Amazon Fashion, Amazon Kindle and Amazon Tech Deals. In 2011, with the launch of Facebook.com/SearsLatino and its Twitter handle @SearsLatino, Sears added a Sears Latino Social Media channel so that it could engage culturally and strengthen relationships with Hispanic customers. In order to make online shopping more accessible and convenient, these customers are encouraged to share stories and ideas, provide feedback and learn more about Sears' Latino initiatives.

If the retailer has a recognizable spokesperson, a profile for him/her, or for the Social Media team, can be created, endowed with photo and signage.

Connecting: The most important action on a SNS is the act of two people connecting. Facebook reserves the term "friending" for individuals, and uses the term "fanning" when people connect with a brand. Twitter term is "following." Retailers must conduct active efforts to drive prospects and customers to their Social Media pages, starting from their Websites, flyers or store. In the search for a two-way relationship, retailers would be well-advised to follow everyone who follows their brand on Twitter.

7.   Set the style of your presence, and the editorial plan. Create interesting contents, promotions, events, and share.

Retailers must invest in a good editorial plan, looking for interesting content and good design, and establish a regular activity of pasting and sharing. Different types of content can be combined on SNSs, and multimedia, such as APPs and videos can be added. Retailers need to regularly update their status, pin on their board and tweet. Every SNS requires particular content. There should be content that is exclusive to Social Media, not only the replica of Website/flyers. Fans/followers should be motivated to create content on SNSs themselves: organic content is much more convincing.

To make a content more viral, it should be posted to media-sharing sites using effective tags. Media-sharing sites make it easy to distribute multimedia content to thousands or millions of viewers. It is important to use open licensing and embedding features to encourage viewers to share media. Where possible, voting badges should be used to make it easy to vote so content can be rated. Social media make it easier to launch seasonal and promotional campaigns in conjunction with external events in the real world, for example Thanksgiving or Father's Day.

Events: The majority of SNSs allows retailers to create an event and invite their fans/followers to attend it. These events most commonly occur in the real world/store, but some are online-only events. RSVP function is included, as are commenting and photo uploads.

Pricing strategy and promotion: Literature presented Social Media as the new hybrid element of the promotion mix (Glynn Mangold & Faulds, 2009). SNSs are a good context to test pricing policies and promotions, as shown by the experiences of Marks and Spencer (M&S) and Tesco. M&S in May 2009 backed down from charging extra for larger bra sizes (£2 more for bras with a cup size above DD) after a consumer-led Facebook protest against the so called "tit-tax." More than 14,000 consumers joined a Facebook group calling for an end to differential pricing. Under the headline "We boobed" M&S's adverts on Facebook page say: "We were wrong, so as of Saturday 9th May the storm in a D cup is over."

In November 2011 Tesco allowed Facebook fans to vote on items they wanted to see as part of its Big Price Drop promotion, converting fans into brand advocates through customer involvement and endorsement. As part of the promotion, Tesco introduced the Big Price Drop Vote on its Facebook page, giving fans the option to vote for the items they wanted to see reduced in the next stage of the offer. In addition, customers could enter a photo competition based on spotting Tesco's promotional lorry and playing the Price Drop Challenge.

This is coherent with Planet Retail intuition (2012) about one of the biggest changes to have occurred in the FMCG sector in recent times: the rise of customer endorsement, as retailers increasingly involve shoppers in the decision-making process. Social Networking Sites are particularly suitable for this. Walmart, again, has used CrowdSaver since November 2010 to trial price reductions based on a voting system. If the required number of fans "like" an offer on Facebook, it goes live, driving participation and increasing loyalty. The first item, a plasma television, required 5,000 "likes" for a reduction from USD488 to USD398 – this was achieved in around 12 hours, generating great brand loyalty and publicity for the company (Planet Retail).

Price promotions are used by retailers to educate customers in new shopping process. The e-commerce site Yoox, for example, offered an extra 15% off on its collection when customers shop via a smartphone or tablet.

SNSs learn about customer' preferences and their buying habits, so they can plan advertising (Facebook paid media) and suggest other products or brands. This recorded history permits to provide real time pricing offers on selected items coherently with customers' preferences. Dell successfully implemented promotional offers and discounts trough Twitter.

And, maybe in a later future, SNSs could intersect data belonging from fidelity cards with social networking' data set. At the time of this writing, Facebook said that is considering the possibility.

Applications (APPs): Social networking sites have increased their functions through Application Programming Interfaces (APIs) which allow them to create new Apps to plug into their site. As noted above, Facebook now offers an App by which a complete purchasing transaction can take place on Facebook.

Calls to Action (CTAs): A call to action (CTA) is "an invitation you make to your Website visitors to engage in some type of action that benefits your business aims–and hopefully theirs, too" (Zarrella, 2010, p. 201). There are two kinds of CTAs: sticky and conversion. Sticky CTAs turn ephemeral waves of traffic into return visitors, for example, asking them to fill in a form or a newsletter. Whereas conversion-based CTAs lead a visitor into the sales funnel: these are more intrusive and useful for promotion.

8. Responding to fans (See also the section on social customer care).

Retailers must always answer online greetings and criticisms. Their answers will stay on the Internet forever, having an amplifying effect. When responding to a post, tweet or a review, the protocols of the SMP and/or crisis management guidelines must always be followed, even if the user has posted incorrect or grossly misleading information. The retailer should ask the customer if there is anything specific that can be done to remedy the situation, and perhaps offer a discount.

9. Monitor continuously and make the necessary fine tuning. Plan crisis management (See also the section on crisis management).

"Set-it-and-forget-it" is not a good social network marketing strategy. Retailers should be active with updates and interaction. Real time marketing is required on Web 2.0. Monitoring Social Networking Sites, and Social Media in general, is an ongoing process. Retailers can use dedicated software and programs like Google Alerts, or spiders. It is important to remember that although data collection can be managed by programs, analysis needs to be performed by a person. Spiders and analytical software cannot in fact read sarcasm, very informal/urban slang, plays on words, mistyped words and emoticons. Monitoring can be initially based on keywords related to the retailer's brand, products, sector, competitor and key employees' names.

Retailers today are mostly trying out different strategies, ranging from using SNSs for marketing and promotions, to localization, customer endorsement and full integration.

Coming to the conclusion, strongly emerges that this social strategy requires substantial commitment and continuous monitoring activity. Social strategy must be managed as an explicit strategic activity, and requires a unique strategy and a coherent framework for implementations.

Social Customer Care

Social sites like Facebook and Twitter are key sources of information about customers, and can provide insight into what customers are saying about private label products, competitors and employees. Customers often appear keen to share their experiences and opinions on their social network accounts, and the penetration and diffusion of Social Networking Sites have led to big changes and opportunities for customer service. Retailers and consumers no longer have to rely on a busy call center agent to solve a problem, check the status of an order or get advice on choosing the right store address (Fraticelli & Negri, 2013). Today there is an array of digital customer service tools at their disposal, including live chat, Social Networking Sites and smartphones. Alongside traditional customer care services, such as dedicated phone numbers, call centres, email and online contact forms or in store desk, retailers now can plan a social customer service: the so called social caring. Customers often demand an immediate and sympathetic response to their complaints, and the online social network context is perfect for that. Twitter is the most suitable Social Media. Responsiveness, the ability to help customers and provide prompt service, is one of the benefits it offers: the microblogging service is a simple and efficient way of sending messages far and wide, offering the added value of the human touch. Customer experience is enhanced by the use of informal friendly tones, and signing-off with the employee's name, putting a name to a voice, provides reassurance.

Best Buy, the American multinational consumer electronics corporation, is one of the many firms today to manage effective customer care on Twitter. It offers the verified account "Best Buy Support" - @BestBuySupport

"Have questions about @BestBuy? Need Support? Let us know! We're here to help 24x7." is the promise. The account currently has a tweet count of over 46,882.

Conversocial (2012) highlights that many businesses - an estimated 71% - claim to use Social Media for customer service, but many do not appear to be using it to its full potential, with only a small percentage fulfilling customer expectations for having their issues solved online.

Social customer service brings two main benefits:

- Off line customer care becomes lighter, involving fewer queues, calls and emails to manage;

- Visibility is gained through helping customers. All the followers/friends of the customer see the prompt solutions offered. Simply letting customers know that Social Media is a channel they can turn to for help and queries makes a great impression. It offers an opportunity to please even the unhappiest of customers.

Companies often turn customers to a dedicated Facebook App as an alternative to collecting customer queries. Walmart has a Feedback APP where all questions are responded to and its invitation on Facebook reads: "For all of us here at Walmart, there's only one boss, the customer. So let us know if you've got a question, concern or idea. I look forward to hearing your feedback."

Other companies have found the maximum of 140 characters to be a limitation in responding to complicated customer questions. Responses to individual customer queries can thus be recorded on video, uploaded to YouTube, and tweets replied to with a link to the video. These videos have received favorable response, and have been retweeted (becoming earned media), creating a positive word of mouth and a "sense of community" around the brand.

Leveraging Social Media for customer service gives daily opportunities to make a highly visible impact which can be positive or negative. Research by eMarketer (2013) underlines that delivering good customer service does not necessarily come cheap, but it is one of the few remaining ways retailers can hold on to customers without cutting deeply into margins. It finds that consumers are willing to pay more if a retailer appears to act in their best interest, helps them to get more value out of the products they purchase, creates convenient new ways to shop, and lets them know when to expect delivery of an order.

Crisis Management

Retailer mistakes are clearly identifiable. And partly because retailers are part of the everyday experience for consumers, the retail landscape is invariably rich in failures and near failures, increasingly so in the current global economic downturn – (Palmer et al., 2009). The retail sector receives a large amount of media coverage, particularly where there are accusations of wrongdoing, and this can provide a reputation decline. When a retailer finds, or creates, an unhappy customer, this should be used as a customer service opportunity; the consumer should be engaged and efforts made to remedy the situation. By proactively engaging with its customers, a retailer can build stronger relationships (Levy & Weitz, 2012).

But the speed and depth of Social Media means a crisis can explode and spread like wildfire. There are several examples of companies whose involvement in social networks and online communities has done them more harm than good. And there is nothing that bloggers and efolks love more than a story of a company that has screwed up its "social capital" by misusing the Social Media tools available to it.

One of the most recent cases showing how social marketing can be a positive force for crisis management was Tesco's management of the frozen beef burger outrage: a crisis born on the shelves, but immediately arrived on the net. Tesco private label burgers, like many other similar products from numerous manufacturers, were involved in a scandal when government scientists in Ireland, where many burgers are produced, found traces of horse DNA. Tesco and other retail chains were widely blamed for the contamination.

Tesco immediately cleared its shelves in store, and on line, on its Facebook fanpage, laid out the facts. Fans' reaction was not slow. On 16 January 2013 Tesco posted "We Apologise":

We apologise.

You have probably read or heard that we have had a serious problem with three frozen beef burger products that we sell in stores in the UK and Ireland.

The Food Safety Authority of Ireland (FSAI) has told us that a number of products they have recently tested from one of our suppliers contained horsemeat.

While the FSAI has said that the products pose no risk to public health, we appreciate that, like us, our customers will find this absolutely unacceptable.

The products in our stores were Tesco Everyday Value 8 x Frozen Beef Burgers (397g), Tesco 4 x Frozen Beef Quarter Pounders (454g) and a branded product, Flamehouse Frozen Chargrilled Quarter Pounders.

We have immediately withdrawn from sale all products from the supplier in question, from all our stores and online.

If you have any of these products at home, you can take them back to any of our stores at any time and get a full refund. You will not need a receipt and you can just bring back the packaging.

We and our supplier have let you down and we apologise.

If you have any concerns, you can find out how to contact us at the bottom of this page, or go to any of our customer service desks in-store, or ask to speak to your local Store Manager.

So here's our promise. We will find out exactly what happened and, when we do, we'll come back and tell you.

And we will work harder than ever with all our suppliers to make sure this never happens again.

This post is part of a complete and careful Social Media strategy (https://www.ourtesco.com).

Tesco replied to customer complaints on an individual basis, even posts which were tasteless and offensive. Customer care employees were tactful, down-to-earth and apologetic. All Tesco posts were signed by a single employee, as "Matt from Customer Care." On the fanpage there was a conversation rather than one-way communication. As the weeks passed, Tesco brought fans up to date, posted news and reassured people. Finally, Tesco declared the end of the emergency with a post.

The first 6,649 posts were analyzed using netnography (Negri, 2013). The findings show a range of fans' reactions: from the joking to the blaming. The majority of them are positive in tone. The data shows there was overall positive reaction to the apology post. Tesco was able to use Social Media monitoring to stay on top of what people and fans were saying. It apologized publicly and engaged people with a simple apologetic message which was perceived as authentic and honest. Fans and clients served as Tesco's advocates, actually helping to contain and manage the crisis. Tesco received more visibility and trust than any traditional paid-for advertising could have achieved.

Tesco's experience, as well as relative literature, allows us to formulate the following guidelines for 2.0 crisis management by retail firms.

- Monitor Social Networking Sites to unveil potential crises. It is important to realize that the warning signs of a potential crisis probably do not usually show up as a spike in the volume of conversation, but as a shift in sentiment.
- Prepare a Social Media Policy, a Crisis Management Plan and organize a crisis team: the more prepared you are, the more active you can be.
- Take action to remove contaminated products from store shelves as soon as possible.
- Do not under- or over-react, and keep your tone appropriate to every situation,

personal, simple, and authentic. Humor can be used lightly in response to satirical comments.
- Act quickly and decisively: apologize before being discovered and attacked. The real-time Web requires real time marketing.
- Make sure to apologize for and solve any customer service problems as soon as possible. Reply to customer complaints on an individual basis.
- Pay attention to what followers/fans are saying and show that you are listening and considering their opinions.
- Communicate continually with customers and contact media to advise them about what is going on.
- Document your actions.
- Evaluate material/immaterial compensations.
- Declare the end of the crisis.

Unlike the past, crises today move at speed, and follow the rules of Social Media. Retailer reputation depends among other things on responses made to those who highlight mistakes.

SOLUTIONS AND RECOMMENDATIONS

Recommendations for Retailers

The most common mistakes in Social Media Marketing are listed below, along with suggestions on how they can be avoided.

1. Not setting realistic goals or knowing how to measure results. Results are not immediate: building networks, getting credibility and becoming trustworthy takes time, resources and patience.
2. Misunderstanding or, worse, ignoring the peculiarities of Social Networking Sites and their marketing tools. Retailers must

research and understand the platforms they are interested in using, and choose the tools that work best for the goals and the audience they are trying to reach. Retailers need to follow the rules of the context, communities and Social Networking Sites.

3. Don't be inconstant: using a Social Media platform once then never again makes it seem that you are ignoring your customers. Interact appropriately, positively and frequently. The real-time Web requires real time marketing. If you only intend to reserve your brand name to avoid fakes, keep your profile/page/account hidden. Create a venue on Foursquare, a page on Facebook, a channel on YouTube or a group on Linkedin is the same of being listed in the Yellow Pages. Customers can find you, but to engage a relationship with them, retailers need to interact and create consistent contents.

4. Be transparent and personal, and not (only) promotional. People become fans on Facebook or follow firms on Twitter because they love your work and want to connect with you as a person. Automated responses and impersonal messages are counter-productive. Post and share original, relevant and interesting contents. Contribute, rather than pitch.

5. Rewards and special offers. Literature has shown (Palmatier et al, 2009) that relationship marketing investments generate short-term feelings of gratitude that drive long-lasting performance benefits based on gratitude. As the conversation is bi-directional, the benefits cannot be unidirectional: customers need to receive value from their Social Media efforts. And customers expectations are increasing. They also desidered to be rewarded for their loyalty to the store, and for fanning and following the retailer presence on SNSs. They also start to find couponing sales (Auchan in Italy, and WholeFoods in

UK trough Groupon) in a deal-of-the-day Websites. Retailer need to plan special offers not available to the general customers, dedicated to fans and followers, in the forms of reductions that customers can request on line and use in store. For example, Carrefour is offering a discount to customers that made a "chek-in" on Foursquare, Lidl offered a special bonus to its fans on Facebook once reaching the 500.000 fans. Other retailers are giving virtual badges (made of an HTML code), a social proof of their loyalty.

6. Basic errors in spelling or grammar are the best way to alienate fans in Social Media Marketing communications. This type of mistake harms opinion of a brand. Double check your spelling and grammar. Once you publish a post in your wall, it's out there forever.

7. Posting too often (over-exposure), or trying too hard to be funny. Before rushing in to an aggressive Social Media push, retailers should bear in mind that social networks have been set up to be just that – social. Keep the post short, and remember that fans prefer infographics, video, gaming APPs and image.

8. Censorship or redirection might be a temptation for those focused on brand image. A mistake often made by companies on Facebook is disabling the ability for fans to post on their official page. Although at first this may sound like a good idea to preserve the "good name" of the retailer and to prevent negative comments being displayed for the world to see, in the medium term it can cause more damage to your brand reputation. Customers, fans, competitors and employees will not be discouraged from speaking about your company if they have something to say, and they will go in another page, or blog, that you're not able to monitor and manage.

And of course, retailers, like anyone else using the Internet and Social Networking Sites, need to remember that it has downsides relating to issues like privacy and security management, scamming, cookies policy, and fake identities or trolls.

FUTURE RESEARCH DIRECTIONS

The following lines try to highlight the next Social Media trends.

Changing of Social Networking Sites: SNSs are constantly changing, and appear to follow a sort of lifecycle: Facebook usage is currently stable, and it is still the largest social networking site, but there are many more local sites as well. Google+ is struggling to take off. Visual social networks, such as Pinterest and YouTube are expanding rapidly. The only thing that is constant is change.

Peer review sites can determine your reputation and business. Yelp is today becoming more widely established, while TripAdvisor is declining slightly. Retailers need to check and revise Social Media plans and budgets considering these rapid shifts.

Mobile: The fastest growing marketplace on the planet is unfolding in the palms of our hands on smartphones. "M-commerce" has arrived. With the proliferation of mobile devices and tablets, retailers are facing increasingly new ways of shopping. There is an urgent need to develop APPs and sites optimized for mobiles. Retailers can yet use QR codes and new shopping Apps that deliver customized coupons based on past spending habits when the shopper is in the store, or permit to create a shopping list.

Big data: Digital information is exploding in the form of information, tweets, posts, reviews pictures, and video. The site http://onesecond. designly.com/reveals new developments on internet. Retailers have the possibility to collect and use big data to fine tune services for their customers, linking loyalty card data with other sources. But it will be an expensive investment.

F-commerce is at present a niche. British online fashion retailer ASOS operates a transactional f-commerce APP, allowing customers to buy from within Facebook. However, the majority of retailers, including Gap, recently removed their transactional Facebook stores, indicating that it is a niche market with limited ROI. Most retailers are opting to add "Like," "Pin" and "Tweet" social buttons to their existing e-commerce and m-commerce sites. On the other hand, digital and virtual goods such as music and streamed or downloaded content can be purchased more simply using Facebook Credits. The Spotify Facebook APP allows users to play music from within the social site and share it with their friends.

There are also numerous area and trends for further research that were uncovered in this Chapter, including the role of devices in the purchasing behaviour, privacy and security management, augmented reality, co-creation opportunities, and fakes management. The additional reading section offers some follow-up materials.

CONCLUSION

With the rise of mobile devices and an increasing number of Internet users worldwide, retailers are beginning to experiment with their presence on Social Networking Sites such as Facebook, Pinterest and Twitter. Best Buy, for example, is managing a fully-transactional store on Facebook. Costly television advertising and traditional communicational channels are no longer the best way to reach and retain shoppers. Customers themselves, referring and reviewing products, shops and services via Social Media tools, are the new retail marketing frontier. They can do all of this from the sofa through tablets (while TV is broadcasting advertisements), or directly inside stores with smartphones.

The difference between online and offline experience is fading: customers standing into the store are at the same time on line through their tablets, mobiles and, will soon be using new devices like augmented reality glasses. So business models based on the distinction between online/off line marketing need to shift, and simply digitizing old business models and marketing plans is not sufficient.

In-store integration is already happening as retailers introduce click and collect services (E.g. Mango), kiosks and mobile devices (E.g. Burberry) and build offers around check-in rewards (E.g. Carrefour through Foursquare). There will be an increased blurring of channels between brick and mortar and online stores. Increasing mobile usage will continue to drive this transition.

Retailers will soon need to be equipped with new ICT and infrastructure to take advantage of geo-socialisation opportunities, and create touch points for digitally equipped customers.

Retailers need an integrated approach to the new media, and recognize and respect the specific characteristics of each type. Entire retail organizations, including the most senior levels, need to be involved, not only the digital marketing office or PR: the "Talking Shop" blog was recently launched by Philip Clark, the chief executive of Tesco.

Social Networking sites are a retail marketing channel, a customer service instrument, an engagement opportunity and a crisis management tool – and retailers need to bear all of these aspects in mind to engage customers through an exciting and high-value experience.

REFERENCES

Andzulis, J., Panagopoulos, N. G., & Rapp, A. (2012). A review of Social Media and implications for the sale process. *Journal of Personal Selling & Sales Management, 3*, 305–316. doi:10.2753/PSS0885-3134320302

Avinash, K. (2009). *Web Analytics 2.0: The Art of Online Accountability and Science of Customer Centricity.* Indianapolis, IN: Wiley Publishing, Inc.

Baer, J. (2010). Operationalizing in 2010. *Marketing in 2010: Social Media Becomes Operational.* Retrieved August 2013, from http://conversationagent.typepad.com/Marketingin2010.pdf

Barefoot, D., & Szabo, J. (2010). *Friends with Benefits: A Social Media Marketing Handbook.* San Francisco, CA: No Starch Press, Inc.

Boyd, D. M., & Ellison, N. B. (2007). Social network sites: Definition, history, and scholarship. *Journal of Computer-Mediated Communication, 13*(1), 11. doi:10.1111/j.1083-6101.2007.00393.x

Burton, S., & Soboleva, A. (2011). Interactive or reactive? Marketing with Twitter. *Journal of Consumer Marketing, 28*(7), 491–499. doi:10.1108/07363761111181473

Byfield-Green, L. (2012). *Retail & Social Media: How and why are successful retailers tapping into social networking channels?* Planet Retail.

Casteleyn, J., Mottart, A., & Rutten, K. (2009). How to use Facebook in your market research. *International Journal of Market Research, 51*(4), 439–447. doi:10.2501/S1470785309200669

Conversocial. (2012). *Evolving Social Customer Service.* Retrieved May, 2013, from http://www.conversocial.com/resources/whitepapers

Corcoran, S. (2009). Defining Earned, Owned and Paid Media. *Forrester Research Blogs.* Retrieved November 2011, from http://blogs.forrester.com/interactive_marketing/2009/12/defining-earned-owned-and-paid-media.html

Divol, R., Edelman, D., & Sarrazin, U. (2012). Demystifying social media. *McKinsey Quarterly.* Retrieved August, 2012, from http://www.mckinsey.com/insights/marketing_sales/demystifying_social_media

Doherty, N. F., & Ellis-Chadwick, F. (2010). Internet retailing: the past, the present and the future. *International Journal of Retail & Distribution Management, 38*(11/12), 943–965. doi:10.1108/09590551011086000

Drucker, P. (1999). *Management Challenges for 21st Century*. New York, NY: Harper Business.

eMarketer. (2013). *Multichannel Customer Service*. Retrieved July, 2013, from https://www.emarketer.com/go/multichannelcustomerservice

Fraticelli, F., & Negri, F. (2013). Twittering organizations' customer service: evidences from top 100 companies. In *Proceedings of 10th SIM Conference*. SIM.

Glynn Mangold, W., & Faulds, D. J. (2009). Social media: The new hybrid element of the promotion mix. *Business Horizons, 52*, 357–365. doi:10.1016/j.bushor.2009.03.002

Gummerus, J., Liljander, V., Weman, E., & Pihlstrom, M. (2012). Customer engagement in a Facebook brand community. *Management Research Review, 35*(9), 857–877. doi:10.1108/01409171211256578

Harris, L., & Dennis, C. (2011). Engaging customers on Facebook: Challenges for e-retailers. *Journal of Consumer Behaviour, 10*, 338–346. doi:10.1002/cb.375

Harvey, C. G., Stewart, D. B., & Ewing, M. T. (2011). Forward or delete: What drives peer-to-peer message propagation across social networks? *Journal of Consumer Behaviour, 10*, 365–372. doi:10.1002/cb.383

Hinchcliffe, D., & Kim, P. (2012). *Social Business by Design*. San Francisco, CA: Jossey-Bass, a Wiley Imprint.

Hoffman, D. L., & Fodor, M. (2010). Can You Measure the ROI of Your Social Media Marketing? *MIT Sloan Management Review, 52*(1), 41–49.

Kozinets, R. V. (2010). *Netnography. Doing ethnographic research online*. Thousand Oaks, CA: Sage.

Levine, R., Locke, C., Searls, D., & Weinberger, D. (1999). *The Cluetrain Manifesto*. Retrieved November, 2013, from http://www.cluetrain.com/

Levy, M., & Weitz, B. A. (2012). *Retailing Management* (8th ed.). New York, NY: McGraw-Hill Companies, Inc.

McKinsey Global Institute. (2012). *The social economy: Unlocking value and productivity through social technologies*. Retrieved September, 2012, from http://www.mckinsey.com/insights/high_tech_telecoms_internet/the_social_economy

Negri, F. (2013). NetworkCracy. Giappichelli Ed.

Nielsen. (2012). *State of the Media: The Social Media Report*. Nielsen.

O'Reilly, T. (2006). *Web 2.0 Principles and Best Practices*. Retrieved June 2011, from http://oreilly.com/catalog/web2report/chapter/web20_report_excerpt.pdf

Palmatier, R. W., Burke Jarvis, C., Bechkoff, J. R., & Kardes, F. R. (2009). The Role of Customer Gratitude in Relationship Marketing. *Journal of Marketing, 73*, 1–18. doi:10.1509/jmkg.73.5.1

Palmer, M., Simmons, G., & de Kervenoael, R. (2009). Brilliant mistake! Essays on incidents of management mistakes and mea culpa. *International Journal of Retail & Distribution Management, 38*(4), 234–257. doi:10.1108/09590551011032072

Patino, A., Pitta, D. A., & Quinones, R. (2012). Social media's emerging importance in market research. *Journal of Consumer Marketing, 29*(3), 233–237. doi:10.1108/07363761211221800

Qualman, E. (2013). *Socialnomics* (2nd ed.). Hoboken, NJ: John Wiley & Sons, Inc.

Richter, F. (2013). *Coca-Cola is the No. 1 Brand on Facebook*. Retrieved August 2013, from http://www.statista.com/markets/14/media-advertising/chart/1377/most-talked-about-brands-on-facebook/

Salt, S. (2011). Social Location Marketing. Indianapolis, IN: Que.

Sevitt, D., & Samuel, A. (2013, July-August). How Pinterest Puts People In Stores. *Harvard Business Review*, 26–27.

Singh, S. (2012). *New Mega Trends*. New York, NY: Palgrave MacMillan. doi:10.1057/9781137008091

Walker Naylor, R., Poynor Lamberton, C., & West, P. M. (2012). Beyond the Like Button: The Impact of Mere Virtual Presence on Brand Evaluations and Purchase Intentions in Social Media Settings. *Journal of Marketing*, 76, 105–120. doi:10.1509/jm.11.0105

Wirtz, B. W., Schilke, O., & Ullrich, S. (2010). Strategic development of business models: implications of the web 2.0 for creating value on the Internet. *Long Range Planning*, 43(2/3), 272–290. doi:10.1016/j.lrp.2010.01.005

Zarrella, D. (2010). *The social media marketing book*. Sebastopol, CA: O'Reilly Media, Inc.

ADDITIONAL READING

Ailawadi, K. L., Beauchamp, J. P., Donthu, N., Gauri, D. K., & Shankar, V. (2009). Communication and Promotion Decisions in Retailing: A Review and Directions for Future Research. *Journal of Retailing*, 85(1), 42–55. doi:10.1016/j.jretai.2008.11.002

Anderson, C. (2006). *The Long Tail: Why the Future of Business is Selling Less of More*. New York, NY: Hyperion.

Anderson, C. (2009). *Free: How Today's Smartest Businesses Profit by Giving Something for Nothing*. New York, NY: Hyperion.

Anderson, C. (2012). *Makers: The New Industrial Revolution*. New York, NY: Hyperion.

Anderson, E. (2010). *Social Media Marketing. Game Theory and the Emergence of Collaboration*. Heidelberg: Springer.

BCG, The Boston Consulting Group (2011). *The Digital Manifesto. How Companies and Countries Can win in the Digital Economy.*

Benkler, Y. (2006). *The Wealth of Networks*. CT: Yale University Press.

Blanchard, O. (2011). *Social Media ROI*. Boston, MA: Pearson Education, Inc.

Capozzi, L., & Berlin Zipfel, L. (2012). The conversation age: the opportunity for public relations. *Corporate Communications: An International Journal*, 17(3), 336–349. doi:10.1108/13563281211253566

Chatfield, T. (2013). Netymology. UK: Quercus Ed.s Ltd.

Cross, R., Liedtka, J., & Weiss, L. (2005). A Practical Guide to Social Networks. *Harvard Business Review*, (march): 124–132. PMID:15768681

Fiorito, S., Gable, M., & Conseur, A. (2010). Technology: advancing retail buyer performance in the twenty-first century. *International Journal of Retail & Distribution Management*, 38(11/12), 879–893. doi:10.1108/09590551011085966

Furht, B. (Ed.). (2010). *Handbook of Social Network Technologies and Applications*. New York, NY: Springer. doi:10.1007/978-1-4419-7142-5

Heinonen, K. (2011). Consumer activity in social media: Managerial approaches to consumers' social media behavior. *Journal of Consumer Behaviour*, 10, 356–364. doi:10.1002/cb.376

Kaplan, A., & Haenlein, M. (2010). Users of the World, Unite! The Challenges and Opportunities of Social Media. *Business Horizons*, 53(1), 59–68. doi:10.1016/j.bushor.2009.09.003

Kozinets, R. V. (2002). The Field Behind the Screen: Using Netnography for Marketing Research in Online Communities. *JMR, Journal of Marketing Research*, 39(1), 61–72. doi:10.1509/jmkr.39.1.61.18935

Kozinets, R. V., de Valck, K., Wojinicki, A. C., & Wilner, S. J. S. (2010). Networked Narratives: Understanding Word-of-Mouth marketing in Online Communities. *Journal of Marketing, 74,* 71–89. doi:10.1509/jmkg.74.2.71

Kumar, V., & Rajan, B. (2012). Social coupons as a marketing strategy: a multifaceted perspective. *Journal of the Academy of Marketing Science, 40,* 120–136. doi:10.1007/s11747-011-0283-0

Lovink, G. (2008). *Zero Comments: Blogging and Critical Internet Culture.* London, UK: Routledge.

Lovink, G. (2011). *Networks Without a Cause: A Critique of Social Media.* Cambridge, UK: Polity Press.

Ludwig, S., de Ruyter, K., Friedman, M., Bruggen, E. C., Wetzels, M., & Pfann, G. (2013). More Than Words: The Influence of Affective Content and Linguistic Style Matches in Online Reviews on Conversion Rates. *Journal of Marketing, 77*(January), 87–103. doi:10.1509/jm.11.0560

Masum, H., & Tovey, M. (Eds.). (2011). *The Reputation Society.* MA: The MIT Press.

Negri, F. (2011). Retail 2.0, or not? *Proceedings of 16th International EAERCD Conference on Research in the Distributive Trades, Parma.*

Piskorski, M. J. (2013). *Networks as Covers: Evidence from an On-Line Social Network.* Working paper 13-083, Harvard Business School.

Sennet, F. (2012). *Groupon's Biggest Deal Ever: The Inside Story of How One Insane Gamble, Tons of Unbelievable Hype.* New York, NY: St. Martin's Press.

Smith, T. (2009). The Social Media Revolution. *International Journal of Market Research, 51*(4), 559–561. doi:10.2501/S1470785309200773

Sridhar, S., & Srinivasan, R. (2012). Social Influence Effects in Online Product Ratings. *Journal of Marketing, 76*(September), 70–88. doi:10.1509/jm.10.0377

Thai, M. T., & Pardalos, P. M. (Eds.). (2012). *Handbook of Optimization in Complex Networks. Communication and Social Networks.* New York, NY: Springer.

Trusov, M., Bucklin, R. E., & Pauwels, K. (2009). Effects of Word-of-Mouth Versus Traditional Marketing: Findings from an Internet Social Networking Site. *Journal of Marketing, 73,* 90–102. doi:10.1509/jmkg.73.5.90

Van Dijk, J. (2006). *The Network Society* (2nd ed.). London: SAGE.

Venkatesan, R., & Farris, P. W. (2012). Measuring and Managing Returns from Retailer-Customized Coupon Campaigns. *Journal of Marketing, 76*(January), 76–94. doi:10.1509/jm.10.0162

Walker Naylor, R., Poynor Lamberton, C., & West, P. M. (2012). Beyond the Like Button: The Impact of Mere Virtual Presence on Brand Evaluations and Purchase Intentions in Social Media Settings. *Journal of Marketing, 76*(November), 105–120. doi:10.1509/jm.11.0105

Weinschenk, S. M. (2009). *Neuro Web Design: What Makes Them Click?* Berkeley, CA: New Riders.

KEY TERMS AND DEFINITIONS

Check-In: The process whereby a person announces their arrival to a physical place trough a mobile application and the phone's GPS to find the current location. At the same time, users share their locations with their friends.

Mobile Application (APP): A software application designed to run on smartphones, tablet computers and other mobile devices.

Paid, Owned and Earned Media (POEM): Refers to the different means for a brand to gain visibility on the Internet.

Social Currency: Is information shared which encourages further social encounters, in a viral loop.

Social Gamification: The process of using Social Media features and behaviors to amplify gamification effects and experience of Social Media.

Social Networking Sites: Platforms that allow people to manage and to expand online their social network.

SoLoMo: Integration of social, local and mobile platforms.

Tag: A non-hierarchical keyword or term assigned to a piece of information that helps to describe an item and allows it to be found again by browsing or searching.

Web 2.0: A Web 2.0 site may allow users to interact and collaborate with each other in a Social Media dialogue as creators of user-generated content in a virtual community.

Chapter 24
Singapore's Online Retail Deviants:
Analyzing the Rise of Blogshops' Power

Ronan de Kervenoael
Sabanci University, Turkey & Aston University, UK

Alan Hallsworth
Portsmouth University, UK

David Tng
Singapore Institute of Management, Singapore

ABSTRACT

Geography, retailing, and power are institutionally bound up together. Within these, the authors situate their research in Clegg's work on power. Online shopping offers a growing challenge to the apparent hegemony of traditional physical retail stores' format. While novel e-formats appear regularly, blogshops in Singapore are enjoying astonishing success that has taken the large retailers by surprise. Even though there are well-developed theoretical frameworks for understanding the role of institutional entrepreneurs and other major stakeholders in bringing about change and innovation, much less attention has been paid to the role of unorganized, nonstrategic actors–such as blogshops–in catalyzing retail change. The authors explore how blogshops are perceived by consumers and how they challenge the power of other shopping formats. They use Principal Components Analysis to analyze results from a survey of 349 blogshops users. While the results show that blogshops stay true to traditional online shopping attributes, deviations occur on the concept of value. Furthermore, consumer power is counter intuitively found to be strongly present in the areas related to cultural ties, excitement, and search for individualist novelty (as opposed to mass-production), thereby encouraging researchers to think critically about emerging power behavior in media practices.

DOI: 10.4018/978-1-4666-6074-8.ch024

INTRODUCTION

Blogshops are defined as online stores that use blogging technology and platforms such as blogspot.com and livejournal.com. Fletcher and Greenhill (2009) describe blogshops as "virtual shops that utilize hosted blogging systems." As such, the blogshop or blog shop is an online shopper/consumer based retail business using hosting platforms (often free) to discuss, promote and sell goods. Blogshops may sell standardized mass merchandise such as clothes and accessories (blogshop as aggregator) but of more interest to us is that they also sell less common items such as handmade, personalized and customized products including one-off pieces. Blogshops tend to specialize in certain markets (type of goods and market catchment) where they reach recognition for the quality of the products sold and services offered. Examples include, at category level, organic or fair-trade products, at market level, small scale producers' items only, and one off specialty products (often considered as real pieces of art) that also leverage collaboration between bloggers to create innovative products.

The literature stresses that flexibility and desire for distinction are critical to differentiate such services from other retail formats. Advantages include short lead-times, payment by cash on delivery (CoD) and, often, endless possibilities to personalize the items. We also recognize that some blogshops start as a swapping and exchanging platform allowing teenagers to maximize their economic and social power. An increasing number of blogshop owners monetize their passion by hawking their products (clothes, bags, shoes and other accessories) at weekend flea markets (Eisen, 2013). Blogshops have, however, evolved into the start-up of choice for many 'would-be entrepreneurs'; not just teenagers, students but also anybody with online access. They seek to supplement their lifestyle with novel unique experiences linked to individual preferences, tailored and often unique services and products that bypass the main retailer market orientation strategies, mass production methods and power. Consequently, both retailers (blogshop manager) and users are presented as socially active, highly interconnected, and often technically competent. As such they are homophilious to each other in terms of lifestyle, power and status leading to the flow of influence being not one way but two ways. Blogshop managers and users improve their efficiency by managing structured and unstructured information assets and business processes in a unified environment to increase collective intelligence and power compared to traditional 'static pre-defined offered experience' of most retail formats. Over time, individual users can develop a "folksonomy" that allows the entire blogshop to benefit from this new collective intelligence: creating a 'blogshop level' knowledge repository that encourages flow between the nodes in the ecosystem and propose new added values. Folksonomy is defined, in our context, as a user generated classification system using their 'own' lexical approach and set of practices to increase the power of the emerging retail format. Importantly, the more users participate, the easier it is to reach a critical mass and encourage potential new users to share (Wasko & Faraj, 2005). From this perspective, information is provided from a richer variety of sources based on current social experiences of the users allowing previously unknown or restricted alternatives or substitutes on a global scale to emerge shifting the traditional marketer balance of power.

In Singapore, our area of interest, LiveJournal, a popular blogging platform, reported S$100 million worth of transactions in 2011, roughly 8% of Singapore's total e-commerce transactions. Statistics from the LiveJournal survey also show that in Asia 10% of the blogshops make S$2,000 per month with the highest making S$20,000 (SupMedia, 2012). LiveJournal hosts more than 50,000 blogshops with over 480,000 users every month (Wee, 2013). According to LiveJournal (2013) blogshops have on average eight transactions a month with a per-item sales price of S$20 equating to about S$8 million worth of blogshop transactions per month. Yet, 80% of Singapore's blogshops earn less than S$500 a month (www. livejournal.sg). Blogshops typically use bank transfer or cash on delivery (CoD) as a mode of payment. This allows an additional form of payment instead of the regular credit card and paypal options. However, it is worth noting that blogshops are not usually registered businesses – which carries legal implications, or lack of them, for users. Regarding day-to-day activities, Social Media are seen as synergistic to blogshop's business. They provide a rich source of potential consumers, free advertising via e-WOM, and are the main portal for affiliate marketing links (Laroche et al, 2013). Social media also allow a more experiential shopping experience with the use and sharing of photos and videos directly made by users. Comments and feedback form the main strategic mechanism. The strength of social network's reach in Singapore is highlighted by ComScore media (2010) showing that 82% of internet users not only are on social media but share reviews, comments, photos and videos: 12% higher than the rest of the world - making them truly active participants. Many Web sites claim to list the best blogshop in Singapore e.g. Choo, (2013), the most popular blogshosp (2012). This phenomenal success was underlined by Roshni Mahtani, CEO of Tickled Media, the publisher of LiveJournal in the South-East Asian markets, who claimed that:

With the total e-commerce market estimated at S$1.6 billion this year, we are proud to see that LiveJournal transactions might represent a staggering 6% of that, re-affirming us as one of the largest e-commerce players in Singapore. The world is bound for an economic slowdown in 2012, but we believe blogshopping will continue to grow here as e-commerce truly represents the most cost-effective way to do business (Wee, 2011).

From a theoretical perspective, our core concern is with power: explicitly, the potential for non-organized actors to reach sufficient field level momentum that they can even re-shape the retail industry. We debate the increasing organic engagement (co-creation) of non-organized non-institutionalized actors within the channel. They are fostering innovation from outside the main retail firms by engaging more holistically with their users (Bijker & Law, 1997). The chapter proposes that thus far, current operational practices do not adequately reflect demand-led models. We will not pursue institutional theory but note the view of Ansari and Phillips (2011) that it has yet to appropriately integrate the role of post-modern consumers in creating, developing, encouraging and legitimizing micro-practices (see also Galvin et al, 2005; Castells, 2001; Dacin et al 2002). That said, Weick et al (2005) argue that the macro-micro divide in institutional retail theory can be bridged by paying more attention to field-level actors' practices and behaviors – as we do here.

The rest of the chapter is organized as follows. We review the background of blogshops and the impact of new media on lifestyles and behaviors. From a theoretical perspective, Clegg's Circuits of Power are examined and leveraged to present the opportunities and challenges face when innovating in the retail sector. The next section describes the methodology, followed by the results and discussion. The last section presents theoretical and managerial implications as well avenues for future research.

BACKGROUND

From the Network Society to Blogshops

It is important to first remember that networked communication technologies materialize the emergence of new values: the central tenet to contemporary understanding of democracy and freedom of speech. Information Communication Technologies (ICTs) have been widely appropriated by the general population but, in particular, the emerging middle-classes who have higher than average levels of education and income. Alienation from the traditional circuits of power, both political and from large global retailers, is encouraging a new style of entrepreneurs who leverage social media to meet their rising expectations, re-defining retail choice and opportunities (Clarke et al, 2006; Elms et al 2010). Such middle class individuals are much more likely to engage with social media to get their way. Insofar as they are networked, these emerging behaviors are generating novel business models that are rapidly reaching critical mass as they are adopted in real time all around the world. Following Dean (2010, p. 29), blogging is defined as "the practices of posting, linking, commenting, reacting, measuring and circulating [making] mediated reflexivity available to virtually everyone who wants to bother." Core to this rising networked culture is the conceit of authenticity (against computer generated spamblogs or splogs that intend to generate higher search engine ranking by copying and pasting content) co-creation, and co-production of value (Vargo & Lush, 2008a; b; Vargo et al 2008). At this point, it is important to underline the diversity that exists within the many blogospheres (e.g. personal blog, microblogging, corporate blogs, by genre and media type, social bookmarking etc) and type of bloggers (e.g. hedonist, tekkie, professional, preacher, maven, life improver, beauty hunter, life stager etc).

Note, too, that Social Media are synergistic with Blogshop's business model. If blogshops are the 'free' alternative to retail outlets, social media marketing are the 'free' advertising platform for such businesses (Laroche et al, 2013). According to Sashittal et al., (2012) blogshop shopping allows users to satisfy their needs to brand themselves and broadcast their identities on social networks. This is encouraged by blogshop tools and strategies of sharing photos/videos, using local models

(e.g. students, users) and often metropolitan settings (capturing the moment – ephemerality - of a particular discussion or item usage within the dynamically evolving urban landscape (Toder-Alon et al, 2005). As the movement towards searching online for recommendations and reviews goes upward, the significance and impact of discussions - e-WOM - on blogshops has led to the monetization of such a large follower base by dynamic new entrepreneurs (Yang & Peterson, 2003). The rise of e-mails, brand communities, blogs, and consumer-generated platforms of various types are in many case surpassing the oral, face-to-face, informal WOM structure (Pantelidis, 2010).

Power, Technology Acceptance, and Blogshop Strategies

Geography forms a significant dimension in retailing and is a particularly interesting context in which power relations are played out (Hallsworth & Taylor, 1996; Hallsworth, 1997; Dearden & Wilson, 2011). Major retailers possess market power but power itself is a complex concept – hence our interest in the landmark work of Stewart Clegg who has argued that power manifests itself in circuits of differing scales. Applied to retail, we utilize the work of Clegg (1987; 1989; 1991) as a template for the analysis of the short-term and long-term retail strategic change that led to the emergence of blogshops. Clegg's Circuits of power are, in ascending order of generality, causal, dispositional and facilitative and were further exemplified in geography by the work of Hallsworth and Taylor (1996).

Hallsworth (1997) built on this work to summarize past conceptions of power as provided by Hobbes, Weber, Machiavelli, Foucault, Giddens and others. In Clegg's typology,

The Hobbesian view of power is taken to underpin Clegg's causal, or, episodic circuit that relates to the day-to-day interactions of all types of agents: business enterprises, individuals, institutions, and

governments. Agents are seen to interact within an established framework of social relations. The basis of interaction between agents in this causal circuit is the control of resources [...] Power within these enduring, stable, day-to-day relationships is exercised only occasionally, and may be met with resistance (Hallsworth, 1997 p. 331).

If we seek the essence of established power as expressed by traditional retailers it most typically is found in the dispositional circuit. The dispositional circuit of power involves the social integration of agents (business enterprises, individuals, or regulatory institutions etc.) through the formulation and fixing of 'the rules of the game' at a particular time and in a particular place. As Hallsworth, 1997) notes, "They are the obligatory passage points discussed by Callon (1986): the line that may not be crossed and the line drawn by legal frameworks, labour regulations, planning requirements, and environmental controls" (Hallsworth, 1997 p. 332).

As many researchers have demonstrated, in countries such as England - where a handful of major retailers dominate the sale of goods from shops – they are actively engaged on lobbying to ensure that "the system" suits their practices or can be modified to assist them (Pal et al, 2001; Sparks, 2008). Controls over land use and a relatively stable political system (Ekinsmyth et al, 1995) have contributed to market-leading Tesco building up property worth some £30 billion. Store property is both a major asset – against which revenue streams can be released – but also a huge sunk cost. It is to avoid the risky expense of sunk costs of retail stores that many operators sell online. However, unlike our Blogshops, what is sold is usually standardized mass merchandise often also available in retail stores. It is vital to note, however, that the sheer expense of large stores constitutes a 'barrier to entry' to rivals and cements the local power of the already powerful. Accordingly, the activities that take place in Clegg's dispositional circuit of power are central to understanding how

Land Use regulations over retail stores actually operate in the real world. Note, incidentally that in the English land use planning system there is no provision for local individuals to stop a store development simply because they do not want it. Here we underline the rapidly changing lifestyle and the growing importance of the online channel that is rarely taken into account in real world, local planning decisions. At a recent new store application by Tesco (which gained national media coverage because, unusually, it was turned down) local protesters complained that the store might cause valued local shops – and their suppliers- to close. Many local residents realized that e-shopping behavior, while not discussed during planning applications, ought to be taken into account at some stage as it is increasingly expanding choice and altering the balance of power. Pro-local arguments *per se* are not valid evidence and so the practices of big powerful retailers, operating in Clegg's dispositional circuit of power, usually leave local consumers powerless. Note, too, that the huge infrastructural changes that have facilitated global online retailing fit comfortably in Clegg's widest, facilitative, circuit. Essentially, forces of digitalization are socially redrawing traditional industry boundaries and disrupting deeply embedded market conventions and geographical scales (Krider & Putler, 2013; DiMaggio & Powell, 1983; Galvin et al, 2005; Castells, 2001).

Our interest lies in the way that corporate power can be challenged by everyday, mundane, yet collectively powerful, non-institutionalized actors such as bloggers. The power of individuals acting collectively has largely been regarded as insignificant or taken-for-granted. In this paper, we argue that events at the field-level may arise from the cumulative behavior of dispersed actors who sit beyond any one firm's control: just people who are attempting to solve everyday problems in their daily lives (Dorado, 2005). They bring change through 'partaking' activities that are generated by dispersed actors' behaviors and where 'no individual or organization can be identified as responsible for the change' (Dorado, 2005).

Power from a consumer perspective is grounded on the general claim that consumers are empowered by technologies (Pitt et al, 2002), by wider choice and global competition (Nelson, 2002; Clegg, 1989). Yet power's conceptual elusiveness makes it difficult to delimit (Denegri-Knott et al, 2006). Three different models of power are traditionally presented in the consumer behavior and culture literature:

1. The consumer sovereignty model, based on consumer rationality and freedom of choice (Zureik & Mowshowits, 2005); This model echoes economistic notions of rationality, full information and un-constrained choice;
2. The consumer culture model, focusing on the influence of culture on non-market needs (e.g. group affiliation, self-esteem, identity, excitement) leading to a subjective evaluation and perception of the value proposition (see Cross (2000), on the jeremiad against consumerism). This model focuses on consumer centric marketing and the role of branding, hedonistic consumption and emotion and lastly
3. The discursive power model, where notions of consumer resistance are not merely destructive and reactive but productive and proactive. This model is often grounded in the new service-driven digital economies where the role of external agent has become critical to innovation.

Some viewed consumer as 'pro-sumer' (producer and consumer) and power as constitutive in the sense that power builds upon knowledge, constructs truths, and forms subjectivities (Schilling, 2010; Shankar, et al, 2006; Mikkonen et al, 2011). With a focus on the discursive co-production of the market, this model rejects consumer apathy and sees them as actively engaging in social innovation construction and - promoted by the consumer culture model – refute the opposition between powerful marketers and resisting consumers (Clegg, 1989; Hindess, 1996). The discursive model represents power as a (co)creative force structuring fields of (inter)action and exchange of free agents (Denegri-Knott et al., 2006 p. 954 for a map of power). As such the definition of power cannot be fully investigated by just asking consumers about empowerment. The mere fact of asking about power too often creates a reaction against current large players (e.g. supermarket giants) even if they are used daily by the majority. Research has shown that consumer behavior can be altered in very fundamental ways when researching power. This is one reason why we avoided questions on power – it is too multi-faceted to cover in ways that are understandable by most consumers. If power is mentioned overtly, consumers may want to react to what is perceived as the right to protest (global retailers are often blamed for global issues beyond their reach). This links too easily to the David and Goliath Syndrome (which explains why so many of us root for underdogs) whereas we seek evidence of wider changes in the balance of power in the total system. Second, this study considers the fact that on blogshops three concurrent sources of activity are present [blogging, purchasing and the collective power of the participation itself]. As such, the survey design attempts to consider how marketing managers might envision their role in the subtle movement from a passive to an active willingness by consumers to regain some control. We feared it may lead to stereotyping if power was mentioned overtly.

Another relevant field concerns the adoption of technological innovations. The Technology Acceptance Model (TAM), developed by Davis (1989), and based on the theory of reasoned action (Fishbein & Ajzen, 1975) is often portrayed as the traditional tool to assess user engagement in any new ICT behavior. TAM followed by the Unified Theory of Acceptance and Use of Technology (Venkatesh et al, 2003) (see Figure 1) posits that perceived ease of use and perceived usefulness are the predictors of usage. TAM analysis has been successfully conducted in many settings, for example, adoption of technological innovation (Gao et al, 2012), spreadsheet applications (Mathieson, 1991), e-mail (Szajna, 1996), Websites (Koufaris, 2002) and multi-purpose online services (Wang & Lin, 2012). Linking TAM to power, some scholars recognize that firms ought to empower their employees to make independent knowledge based decisions that serve the firm's broader mission through value creation at every point of the customer life cycle (Schilling, 2010). Accordingly, the discursive power model in Holt's (2002) view allows consumer/employee tensions and deviance to be interpreted not as a loss of control by firms but as a welcome behaviour that "assist(s) entrepreneurial firms to tear down the old branding paradigm and create opportunities for companies that understand emerging new principles." As such Kozinets and Handelman (2004) emphasis that consumers and firms, in the increasingly multi-level nature of service-driven digital economies, have strategies that in the long term ought to be far more overlapping, mutual and interdependent than is usually depicted in the media or consumer groups. This change mirrors recent evolutions on the interaction between consumers and Technology in co-creating and reproducing the market (Denegri-Knott, 2006; Denegri-Knott et al., 2006; Lusch et al, 2007). According to the dominant social capital theory, social knowledge is defined as 'resource that actors derive from specific social structures and then use to pursue their interest; it is created by changes in the relationship among actors' (Baker, 1990

Construct Definitions:

- **Behavioral Intention:** The degree to which a person has formulated conscious plans to perform [or not] some specified future behavior. We assume that these behaviors will lead to greater control and influence for users.

Figure 1. Unified theory of acceptance and use of technology (UTAUT)
Source: Venkatesh, et al, 2003

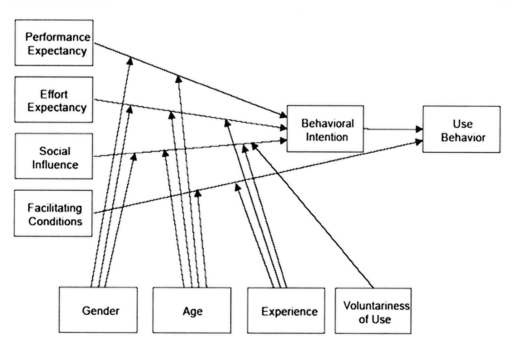

- **Facilitating Conditions:** The degree to which an individual believes that an organizational and technical infrastructure exists to support use of the system. In our case this concept is also linked to co-creation and co-production agendas.
- **Effort Expectancy:** Is the degree of convenience perceived for using system that in our context increase users' agency.
- **Performance Expectancy:** The degree to which an individual believes that using the system will help him or her to attain gains in job performance. As such, self-identity and the power derived from taking control of one's identity building are particularly relevant.
- **Social Influence:** The degree to which an individual perceives that important others believe he or she should use the new system. Power here is indirectly derived from being in the know and able to influence and shape the outcome.
- **Voluntariness:** The extent to which potential adopters perceive the adoption decision to be non-mandatory hence having choices.

Unpacking some key variables, convenience - the state of being able to proceed with a task with little effort or difficulty - is usually identified as a significant factor that affects online shopping behavior. Blogshops ought to be well placed to offer such convenience and flexibility as they are in constant contact with their users and are small and flexible enough to provide a really customized service (e.g. home delivery, large varieties and recent product reviews, personal relationships with, and knowledge of, users). Indirectly, the power that firms have over users' 'time' will decrease, just as advertisers are facing when consumers choose when and where to interact with communication campaigns (in the case of active engaged users). Consumers' risk,

however, may be greater than with traditional online firms that are regulated by clearer legal guidelines (Liu & Forsyth, 2010). Also a greater level of professionalism may be expected by those users who regularly order online and can benchmark service provision. While risk-averse individuals are more likely to purchase offline, blogshops face other issues beyond traditional monetary risk, value proposition, ease of use (e.g. easy Web-layouts and user-friendly formats) and security (e.g. frauds and privacy infringements). The additional factors include: communication types and styles regarding comment/discussion posting appropriateness, language register used (formal, informal, urban). The above are being used in practice within a wide set of cultures, social knowledge, ICT skills and overall social mannerism understanding (Constantinides, 2004). In Singapore four official languages and a multitude of lingo are an intrinsic part of the society. As such, power is taken away from retailers by consumers who are more anti-conformist and independent. Reactance is felt by many users who are increasingly deprived from freedom of choice as they are being force to choose among listed items and services only. Power is derived from engaging in unusual experiences that increase creativity: establishing a unique identity by deliberately not buying from traditional retail formats.

Social knowledge is defined as 'a resource that actors derive from specific social structures .... use to pursue their interests..... created by changes in the relationship among actors' (Baker, 1990). As such, in marketing central to consumer responsiveness is the concept of market orientation (Harris, 2000). It is defined by Harris (1998) as "...a dynamic orientation, attitudes and actions are geared towards the market." Market orientation creates the 'necessary behavior' including interfunctional co-ordination, customer orientation and competitor orientation (Narver & Slater, 1990). Many studies also show that market orientation rests primarily on cultural knowledge (Gebhardt et al, 2006). Yet, culture is portrayed as "fragmented across groups and inconsistent across its manifestation" (DiMaggio, 1997). Particularly relevant for blogshops' development is the notion of a 'cultural toolkit' - introduced by Swidler (1986) - which proposes that "culture provides the materials from which individuals and groups construct strategies of action." Accordingly, culture is neither everywhere nor one-sided but surfaces from the amalgamation of resources (e.g. norms, values, beliefs) across different institutional settings. Blogshops' users can take up resources and derive power from several registers (field level resources) and repertoires (actor level resources) without concern for apparent contradictions.

Moreover, and particularly significant for the emerging business model associated with blogshops, Levitt et al, (1999:1483) advocate that "interpersonal dynamics between individual actors can profoundly impact organizational performance and quality." Identifying these dynamics can be facilitated by understanding the social-knowledge-sharing strategies deployed by actors that justify deviant practices as a power bridging function (Levi, 2011). Indeed, within an increasingly service-driven economy, Johnson et al (2007) show that "technical communicators influence technology use and the transfer of knowledge about these technologies" and thereby facilitate the emergence of new business models (Surowiecki, 2004).

Finally, blogshops can also been seen as retail deviants. Collinson (1994) describes deviance as attempts to "challenge, disrupt or invert prevailing assumptions, discourses and power relations." Drawing further on Fleming and Spicer (2008), four key practices of deviance have been analyzed; refusal, voice, escape and creation:

Refusal overtly blocks the effects of power by undermining the flow of domination. Voice demands that those in control change particular aspects of power relations to favor those being affected by them. Escape reflects processes of mental disengagement from the workplace: cynicism, skepticism and dis-identification. Creation refers to the way that alternative identities and discursive systems of representation emerge within domination.

Thus, according to Penaloza and Price (1993) deviance is "trouble with the sudden intrusion, the unanticipated agency of a consuming subject which inexplicitly reverses the marketer's gaze and contests the place and authority of the marketing position." Consequently, retail deviance, as indirect power appropriation by blogshops owner/users is marked by "the way individuals and groups practice a strategy of appropriation in response to structures of domination" (Poster, 1992). Finally, associated with the concept of computer playfulness in the UTAUT model, the concept of entertainment value is relevant in this context. Entertainment value refers to the satisfaction of emotional and hedonic powers, such as fun, joy and excitement derived from participating in a task (Sahney et al., 2005; Carpenter & Fairhurst, 2005; Schau et al, 2009, Wang & Lin, 2012).

Overall, this review highlights some important factors. First, blogshops are evolving in a dynamic environment, often from *outside* traditional retail firm boundaries and traditional marketer power, via non-institutionalized agents. Second, despite the preconception that deviance from traditional retail format and TAM may be risky, little research exists that explores the indirect rising power of online social knowledge sharing that fosters sources of management innovation and new business opportunities.

METHODOLOGY

A convenience sample was utilized with the empirical study confined to blogshoppers who purchased from blogshops in Singapore in the first 4 months of 2012. Links for the survey were posted on three different blog shop sites namely:

- http://wonderstellar.livejournal.com/;
- http://www.facebook.com/vanillacrystals. Blogshop;
- http://www.facebook.com/rrazzleDdazzle.

Qualtrics was selected as the online questionnaire hosting Website. 349 surveys in total were collected during the period and 58% of the respondents were aged 22-30 years old, and 39.1% were between 17-21 years old. About 66.5% of the respondents were students and 23.8% were employed.

A large proportion of the respondents were degree holders (56.9%) or had completed vocational school (34.4%), demonstrating high levels of computer literacy. 65.6% of the respondents were female. The reasons which led to shopping on blogshops were firstly convenience [the main reason with a mean rank of 1.95 on a scale 1 strongest to 7 weakest], followed by pricing/ discounts 2.31, selection 3.5, ability to compare different shops 3.61, privacy 4.67 and better shopping experience 5.09. 78.5% of the respondents also reported spending S$100 or less per month on Blogshops (Table 1).

All constructs (41 statements in total) in the survey were adapted from existing scales for the blogshop context. Constructs were derived from Carpenter and Fairhurst (2005) regarding convenience; Prasad et al (2009) regarding enjoyment/experience, Fletcher, and Greenhill, (2009) regarding payment; Eastman, et al (2009) regarding trendiness, image; Wells and Tigert (1971) regarding opinion, Lumpkin and Darden (1982), Sahney, Shrivastava, and Bhimalingam (2008) regarding variety and choice and Wolfinbanger and Gilly (2001) regarding experiential power. Most constructs were measured on a seven point Likert scale. In order to minimize response bias some constructs were reverse scored. To test reliability and validity of the constructs PCA - using Varimax rotation - was used to reduce the items (Tabachnick & Fidell, 2001). A cutting point factor loading above the coefficient of 0.6 was chosen (Hair et al., 1998). Table 2 and 3 present the final 15 rotated items, the cumulative percentage of variance accounted for was 69.54% demonstrating a good set of variables to explain the phenomenon. Also, it is noted that the last 3 components have 2 only factors each, demonstrating the need to develop, in future research, new scales better adapted to the blogshop situation. Two interviews with blogshop owners are also provided to allow better understanding and interpretation of power shift from a retail perspective in the discussion section: thereby encouraging researchers to think critically about emerging power behavior in media practices.

RESULTS AND DISCUSSION

As can be seen in Table 3, the research shows six predictor variables, underlying a role in the subtle

Table 1. What are the attributes which lead to you shopping on Blogshops compared to other retail formats

	N	Mean	Std. Deviation	Variance
Convenience	349	1.95	1.232	1.517
Pricing/Discounts	349	2.31	1.322	1.748
Selection/choice	349	3.50	1.442	2.078
Ability to compare different shops	349	3.61	1.317	1.733
Privacy/reputation	349	4.67	1.290	1.665
Better shopping experience	349	5.09	1.225	1.501
Others	349	6.88	.613	.376

Table 2. PCA factor loading coefficients

	Component					
	1	**2**	**3**	**4**	**5**	**6**
1.Trust3	.791					
2.Trust2	.760					
3.Trust4	.720					
4.Unique2		.790				
5.Unique3		.777				
6.Unique1		.740				
7.Enter7			.809			
8.Enter8			.778			
9.Enter6			.715			
10.Cs2				.888		
11.Cs1				.870		
12.Unique6					.875	
13.Unique4					.796	
14.Conv6						.776
15.Conv4						.728

%variance explained
Component 1: 25.54.
Component 2: 11.236
Component 3: 9.32
Component 4: 8.96
Component 5: 7.70
Component 6: 6.77

movement from a passive to an active willingness by consumers to regain some control which is not commonly seen in traditional online shops.

One important feature of the results is the realization that building a culture for participation starts with providing the power of doing and enjoying. A key trait of these young entrepreneurs is rapid learning from mistakes so as to generate future value for their blogshops. The first component underlines the importance of leveraging the power of the local, including skill sets to facilitate the sharing of knowledge and expertise that in turn matches expectations and inspirations that are relevant. While the first two statements are related to mechanical transactional aspects (no currency conversion, no surprise in taxes and final price) the last statement is, in our opinion, particularly significant regarding power. Though using a global medium, local language customs and forms are found to remain crucial to engagement. In a multicultural society such as Singapore, the development and sustainability of blogshops is related to the ability to reduce mis-communication risks during the online interaction. Language and dialogue transparency stimulates activities and allows visible and open progresses to be made hence empowering users beyond what is possible in traditional retail formats. The use of 'local lingo' encourages actions and active users that become the consistent catalyst to develop the new business model and retail format. 'Lingo', such as Singlish and local slang, can generate loyalty through its inherently local terminology that foreign shoppers simply may not understand. Indeed, the best blogshops were said, in our two complementary interviews, to be run by entrepreneurs who focus on fostering trust by allowing users the power to truly participate in the business model strategy, tactic and development with an emphasis to protect their local users' views and preferences. This is particularly interesting in the context of Clegg's analysis because the owners are operating in the lowest, causal circuit of power: where relationships are formed. Most major retailers, whilst claiming to be 'in touch' with their customers (sometimes using loyalty cards) do not really operate at this level. Trust is derived from the local societal structure that results in a given appreciation of power and was described as the new currency among friends and followers. Users trust their friends and other participants before making purchase decisions, making relationships that are developed through appropriate understanding of local language nuances and local traditions are more valuable. Furthermore, not all forms of communication are created equal. Locally-made videos, photos and audio recordings provide a way for users to see the personal side of the blogshops' experiment and empower real user material as opposed to carefully constructed marketing imagery.

Table 3. PCA results and Cronbach's Alpha

Components	Items	Short-Form	Cronbach Alpha
1. Close Cultural Ties/ Localness	• I trust blogshops because Blogshops allows local form of payment methods (such as bank transfer) compared to the typical online shops • I trust blogshops because Blogshops are under the same Singapore legal system as me compared to the typical online shops • I trust blogshops because Blogshops uses my language (english,singlish) compared to the typical online shops	Trust 2 Trust 3 Trust 4	0.705
2. Novelty	• I like blogshops because It makes me feel trendy compared to typical online shops • I like blogshops because It gives me more clothing variety compared to typical online shops • I like blogshops because It provides access to unique clothing designs compared to typical online shops	Unique 1 Unique 2 Unique 3	0.712
3. Excitement	• I like blogshops because Blogshop give me a different experience compared to the typical online shops • I like blogshops because Blogshops are exilarating to buy limited quantity clothings when a new season comes out compared to the typical online shops • I like blogshops because I enjoy the fast paced changes in "seasons" in blogshops compared to the typical online shops	Enter 6 Enter 7 Enter 8	0.705
4. Customer Service	• I like blogshops because I can directly contact the manager through sms, Facebook compared to the typical online shops • I like blogshops because It is easier to contact the manager due to being in the same time zone compared to the typical online shops	CS1 CS2	0.804
5. Value	• I like blogshops because It offers me better promotions compared to typical online shops • I like blogshops because It is cheaper compared to typical online shops	Unique 4 Unique 6	0.683
6. Convenience	• I like blogshops because I save more time buying from them compared to the typical online shops • I like blogshops because I get my clothes/items quicker than conventional online shopping compared to the typical online shops	Conv 4 Conv 6	0.421

We use words that are understandable by Singaporeans, like us [empowerment of the masses not the elite]. Maybe that creates a homely feel. Mostly blogshops have loyal supporters, so this creates trust and supporters which come back to buy from the same blogshop even though other blogshops have the same items at a cheaper price. That is customer retention (Theo)"

The second component is related to the idea of nurturing the power of novelty and social innovation. The notion of uniqueness for any given item is closely related to the building of identity and personal growth of participants. Sharing insightful information through e-WOM on what is really new and how an item has evolved enables blogshops' owners to form a relationship with the ecosystem's users rather than promoting items in a traditional marketing sense. Through the concepts of crowdsourcing, co-creation and co-productions, the blogshops community shapes the development of new items, categories and, most of all, the direction of blogshops' improvement strategies: enhancing the sense of presence within computer generated environment. Here within blogshops, power is at the same time conflictive and consensual or pertains to the 'power over' or 'power to' types. Blogshop owners are motivated by shared goals and pride (passion-centric individuals) towards innovative and novel ways to discuss and share knowledge about products and services. As suggested by one of the interview respondent:

Some of the designs that we have are only exclusive to theia, so another blogshop might not have it, and thus people will come and get it from us instead (Makoto).

The third component is related to the notion of excitement. This is very particular to blogshops and is often at best a subdued variable in traditional online shopping Websites where speed and standardization of the shopping process are more important via finished and immutable products. Excitement is often powered by a sense of belonging so that each member can influence decisions on purchasing and/or further participation. Blogshops' users feel that excitement value is provided by more user input and diversity of debate. Tippers and mavens provide the foundation for excitement and accelerate content creation, constantly refreshing the discussion and providing a tempo to product and discussion cycles. Excitement as a new value proposition allows consumer empowerment to be seen as the outcome of a collaborative process.

Basically there is very little demand for tubes, for girls, in the market, participants would ask the blogshop's owner to design a tube or something equivalent. Basically you can do a request. And if the blogshop owner reviews the comment, they would try to respond to the customer's request. So in the next collection, or whatever, you may find that kind of product added. That is one of the good aspects of blogshops excitement, flexibility and innovative responses (Theo).

As such, the fifth component: customer service is not a surprise. The key in most blogshop successes was described as the reinvention of the customer relationship through allowing and fostering greater customer engagement, moving away from the lip service provided by most e-firm's market orientation that de-empower users through a myriad of administrative loops and obscure processes. Being able to engage with the original entrepreneur, the co-creator and co-producers offer meaningful connections and personal identification that respond to the different levels of expectations in term of engagement. The importance of the daily experiences and real-time sharing of sometimes complex mundane activities that humanize the relationship were underlined as decisive in the follow-up interviews. Re-empowering users by encouraging the feedback, sharing desired experiences and finding shared solutions were at the forefront of the networked service experience that leverage collective intelligence. These advanced forms of CRM allow forward-thinking solutions rather than standardized responses.

I engage in really constructive discussions, these influence my next move and list of items I am selling. I know my users. I have met them face to face during delivery…. It is like a big group of friends. I provide the level of service I will provide for my others friends. I also prefer to say no, sorry, rather than risk to sell an item that I know will not meet expectations (Makoto).

The last component, 'convenience' demonstrates that basic business acumen must not be forgotten. Users, most of them middle class and well educated, are nevertheless looking for better functional value. Often understood as financial value it, however, also encompasses the idea of fair value and more importantly fair sharing of the profit with the agent/user that created the value. At a functional level, the results suggest that price is a big issue as participants want to maximise their personal economic power. Blogshops provide payment alternatives to the traditional credit card system via CoD or free of charge local bank transfers - allowing participants such as students, who do not own a credit card due to age limitations or income, to enjoy online shopping. Furthermore, just as in England, large retail corporations, in the two interviews, were criticized for withdrawing too much wealth from local communities and abusing market power in their supply chain. Re-defining convenience, it was associated with a shorter supply cycle allowing participation (customer empowerment in the firm's process), production, customization and delivery in line with expectations (within the same day) to come up with the best solution, moving away from selling and numbers. Users and entrepreneurs can be described as being motivated by challenges that feel inherently worthwhile. This behavior has also been associated in the gamification phenomenon literature where both blogshops participant/buyers and non-participant/non-buyers want to create an experience that is compelling and empowering for all parties.

When blogshops' owners choose the clothes, they have to choose the best, because it is very competitive. It's not just one or two blogshops around. So to attract customers, blogshops have to choose the nicer pieces, up to date pieces. But it's based on the taste of the blogshop owner that has to reflect a certain style and beliefs. So when some people do not know what to go for, they would just rely on the blogshop owner's taste and purchase the clothes which the blogshops' owner thinks are good. It maybe is because I have something to support my claims. I have a favorite style and little by little I have demonstrated that I am reliable (Makoto).

CONCLUSION

Blogshops' business models are still evolving in this rapidly-changing field. The overall thrust of this research is not about the specific technologies used but rather the shift in mind-set towards an increasingly socially-networked world that relies on non-institutional actors to generate innovation in turn empowering consumers and users and undermining the traditional retailers' domination of retail format.

The social graph generated by the network economy is creating new possibilities and re-shaping every aspect of both professional retailing and personal lives. Expectations and norms, both local and global, are altering power bases that, together with increasing user participation, are re-defining how firms are organized. In effect, blogshops are urging a) traditional online firms to become more people-centric rather than technology centric and b) traditional global players to really understand local specificity (emotional power level) rather than pushing through a world-wide standardization of the shopping experience. Our 'experiential' survey of Singaporeans stressed excitement and 'buzz' - feelings and emotions that are now largely absent from standardized, mass-merchandised store formats as a key variable that empowers the retail experience.

The preference for 'local' resonates everywhere. The debate is shifting from the simple *who are we* as shoppers online to *how we are* amongst other e-shoppers. Yet certain aspects remain troublesome for the nascent blogshops industry. First, social networking services appear to be consolidating and as such are more likely to wipe away local specificity and concentrate power in the hand of few gatekeepers. Second, real time devices together with geo-location applications have yet to permeate the blogshops phenomenon. This may lead to an hybrid retail format whereby a number of blogshops group together to have an offline presence (shop). Third, traditional brands and retailers are already working hard to identify and lobby 'influencers'. In a sense an institutionalization process of a new kind is at work that can be related to skunkwork firms that, through a small and loosely structured group of people, research and develop a project primarily for the sake of radical innovation (common in the pharmaceutical industry or Lockheed's World War II projects). If successful, however, they may eventually be bought out and integrated into larger corporations (as has happened with many of Coca-Cola's recent 'new' products).

In such situations, issues with the monetization of users' private information or voluntary, not-for-profit participation remain unanswered. However, such collaborative participation is a world away from the top-down exploitation of market power that can give store-based retailers local spatial monopolies and massive property assets.

Our findings stress the inherently anti-local nature of mass, standardized retailing – something to which the Blogshops are reacting. Their customers find empowerment and are even influencing the products that are sold because there are real links at Clegg's causal level of power. Yet this is made possible by e-technology – vast changes within Clegg's facilitative circuit of power. The biggest retailers, conversely, use dispositional-circuit market power (over shoppers, rivals, suppliers and even local governments) that many characterize as abuse of power. It remains to be seen how much real power ordinary shoppers and their chosen suppliers can take back through use of e-channel Blogshops.

REFERENCES

Ansari, S., & Phillips. (2011). Text me! New consumer practices and change in organizational fields. *Organization Science*, *22*(6), 1579–1599. doi:10.1287/orsc.1100.0595

Baker, W. (1990). Market networks and corporate behavior. *American Journal of Sociology*, *96*(3), 589–625. doi:10.1086/229573

Bijker, W., & Law. (1997). *Shaping technology/ building society*. MIT Press.

Callon, M. (1986). Some Elements of a Sociology of Translation: Domestication of the Scallops and the Fishermen of St. Brieuc Bay. In J. Law (Ed.), *Power Action and Belief A New Sociology of Knowledge?* (pp. 196–233). London: Routledge.

Carpenter, J. M., & Fairhurst, A. (2005). Consumer Shopping Value, Satisfaction, and Loyalty for Retail Apparel Brands. *Journal of Fashion Marketing and Management*, *9*(3), 256–269. doi:10.1108/13612020510610408

Castells, M. (2001). *Internet Galaxy: Reflections on the internet, business, and society*. Oxford, UK: Oxford University Press. doi:10.1007/978-3-322-89613-1

Choo, B. (2013). *The Best BlogShops in Singapore 2013- The most popular and highest rated!* Retrieved March 30, 2013, from http://www.thesmartlocal.com/read/the-best-blogshops-in-singapore-2013

Clarke, I., Hallsworth, A., Jackson, P., de Kervenoael, R., Del Aguila, R., & Kirkup, M. (2006). Retail restructuring and consumer choice: Long-term local changes in consumer behaviour: Portsmouth, 1980-2002. *Environment & Planning A*, *38*(1), 25–46. doi:10.1068/a37207

Clegg, S. (1987). The Power of Language, the Language of Power. *Organization Studies*, *8*, 60–70. doi:10.1177/017084068700800105

Clegg, S. (1989). *Frameworks of Power*. London: Sage. doi:10.4135/9781446279267

Clegg, S. (1991). Postmodern Management? *Journal of Organizational Change Management*, *5*, 31–49. doi:10.1108/09534819210014869

Collinson, D. (1994). Strategies of resistance: Power, knowledge and subjectivity in the workplace. In J. M. Jermier, D. Knights, & W. R. Nord (Eds.), *Resistance and Power in Organizations* (pp. 25–68). New York, NY: Routledge.

Constantinides, E. (2004). Influencing the online consumer's behavior: The Web experience. *Internet Research*, *14*(2), 111–126. doi:10.1108/10662240410530835

Cross, G. (2000). *An All-Consuming Century: Why Commercialism Won in Modern America*. New York: Columbia University Press.

Dacin, T., Goldstein, J., & Scott, W. R. (2002). Institutional theory and institutional change. *Academy of Management Journal*, *45*, 45–56. doi:10.5465/AMJ.2002.6283388

Davis, F. D. (1989). Perceived usefulness, perceived ease of use and user acceptance of information technology. *Management Information Systems Quarterly, 13*(3), 319–339. doi:10.2307/249008

Dean, J. (2010). *Blog Theory*. Cambridge, MA: Polity Press.

Dearden, J., & Wilson, A. (2011). A Framework for Exploring Urban Retail Discontinuities. *Geographical Analysis, 43*, 172–187. doi:10.1111/j.1538-4632.2011.00812.x

Denegri-Knott, J., Zwick, D., & Schroeder, J. E. (2006). Mapping consumer power: an integrative framework for marketing and consumer research. *European Journal of Marketing, 40*, 950–971. doi:10.1108/03090560610680952

DiMaggio, P. (1997). Culture and cognition. *Annual Review of Sociology, 23*, 263–287. doi:10.1146/annurev.soc.23.1.263

DiMaggio, P., & Powell, W. (1983). The iron cage revisited: Institutional isomorphism and collective rationality in organizational fields. *American Sociological Review, 48*, 147–160. doi:10.2307/2095101

Dorado, S. (2005). Institutional entrepreneurship, partaking, and convening. *Organization Studies, 26*(3), 385–414. doi:10.1177/0170840605050873

Eastman, J. K., Iyer, R., & Randall, C. (2009). Understanding internet shoppers: an exploratory study. *Marketing Management Journal, 19*(2), 104–117.

Eisen, T. (2013). Blogshops move to real world for serious cash. *The Straits Times*. Retrieved November 20, 2013, from http://www.divaasia.com/article/4807

Ekinsmyth, C., Hallsworth, A. G., Leonard, S., & Taylor, M. (1995). Stability and change in Economic Geography. *Area, 27*(4), 289–299.

Elms, J., Canning, C., de Kervenoael, R., Whysall, P., & Hallsworth, A. (2010). 30 years of retail change: Where (and how) do you shop? *International Journal of Retail and Distribution Management, 38*(11/12), 817–827. doi:10.1108/09590551011085920

Fishbein, M., & Ajzen, I. (1975). *Belief, attitude, intention and behavior: an introduction to theory and research*. Addison-Wesley.

Fleming, P., & Spicer, A. (2008). Beyond power and resistance. *Management Communication Quarterly, 21*(3), 301–309. doi:10.1177/0893318907309928

Fletcher, G., & Greenhill, A. (2009). Blog/shop: it is authentic so don't worry. *Journal of Information. Communication and Ethics in Society, 7*(1), 39–53. doi:10.1108/14779960910938089

Galvin, T., Ventresca, & Hudson, M.B. (2005). Contested Industry Dynamics. New directions in the study of legitimacy. *International Studies of Management and Organization, 34*(4), 57–84.

Gao, T., Rohm, A. J., Sultan, F., & Huang, S. (2012). Antecedents of consumer attitudes toward mobile marketing: A comparative study of youth markets in the United States and China. *Thunderbird Int'l Bus Rev, 54*, 211–224. doi:10.1002/tie.21452

Gebhardt, G. F., Carpenter, G. S., & Sherry, J. J. F. (2006). Creating a market orientation: a longitudinal, multifirm, grounded analysis of cultural transformation. *Journal of Marketing, 70*(4), 37–55. doi:10.1509/jmkg.70.4.37

Hair, J. F. J., Anderson, R. E., Tatham, R. L., & Black, W. C. (1998). *Multivariate Data Analysis*. Prentice-Hall.

Hallsworth, A. G. (1997). Rethinking Retail Theory: Circuits of Power as an Integrative Paradigm. *Geographical Analysis, 29*(4), 329–338. doi:10.1111/j.1538-4632.1997.tb00968.x

Hallsworth, A. G., & Taylor, M. (1996). 'Buying' power' interpreting retail change in a circuits of power framework. *Environment & Planning A, 28*, 2125–2137. doi:10.1068/a282125

Harris, L. C. (1998). Cultural domination: the key to a market oriented culture? *European Journal of Marketing, 32*(3/4), 354–373. doi:10.1108/03090569810204643

Harris, L. C. (2000). The organizational barriers to developing market orientation. *European Journal of Marketing, 34*(5-6), 354–373.

Hindess, B. (1996). *Discourses of Power: From Hobbes to Foucault*. Oxford, UK: Blackwell Publishers Ltd.

Johnson, G., Langley, A., Melin, L., & Whittington, R. (2007). *Strategy as Practice: Research Directions and Resource*. Cambridge, MA: Cambridge University Press. doi:10.1017/CBO9780511618925

Koufaris, M. (2002). Applying the technology acceptance model and flow theory to online consumer behavior. *Information Systems Research, 13*(2), 205–223. doi:10.1287/isre.13.2.205.83

Kozinets, R. V., & Handelman, J. M. (2004). Adversaries of consumption: Consumer movements, activism, and ideology. *The Journal of Consumer Research, 31*(3), 691–704. doi:10.1086/425104

Krider, R. E., & Putler, D. S. (2013). Which Birds of a Feather Flock Together? Clustering and Avoidance Patterns of Similar Retail Outlets. *Geographical Analysis, 45*, 123–149. doi:10.1111/gean.12005

Laroche, M., & Habibi, M, R., & Richard, M.O. (2013). To be or not to be in social media: How brand loyalty is affected by social media? *International Journal of Information Management, 33*, 76–82. doi:10.1016/j.ijinfomgt.2012.07.003

Levi, A. (2011). *How Apple (unintentionally) revolutionized corporate IT*. Retrieved March 15, 2012, from http://tech.fortune.cnn.com/2011/08/02/apples-unintentional-corporate-it-revolution/

Levitt, R. E., Thomsen, J., Christiansen, T. R., Kunz, J. C., Jin, Y., & Nass, C. (1999). Simulating Project Work Processes and Organizations: Toward a Micro-Contingency Theory of Organizational Design. *Management Science, 45*, 1479–1495. doi:10.1287/mnsc.45.11.1479

Liu, C., & Forsythe, S. (2010). Sustaining Online Shopping: Moderating Roles of Online Shopping Motives. *Journal of Internet Commerce, 9*(2), 83–103. doi:10.1080/15332861.2010.503848

Lounsbury, V., & Crumley, E. T. (2007). New practice creation: An institutional perspective on innovation. *Organization Studies, 28*(7), 993–101. doi:10.1177/0170840607078111

Lumpkin, J. R., & Darden, W. R. (1982). Relating Television Preference Viewing to Shopping Orientations, Lifestyles, and Demographics. *Journal of Advertising, 11*(4), 56–67. doi:10.1080/00913367.1982.10672822

Mathieson, K. (1991). Predicting user intentions: Comparing the technology acceptance model with theory of planned behavior. *Information Systems Research, 2*(3), 173–191. doi:10.1287/isre.2.3.173

Mikkonen, H., Dholakia, N., Moisander, J., & Valtonen, A. (2011). Consumer resistance as struggle over subjectivity. *University of Rhode Island Working paper series*, 2011/2012 no 6.

Narver, J. C., & Slater, S. F. (1990). The effect of a market Orientation on business profitability. *Journal of Marketing, 54*, 20–35. doi:10.2307/1251757

Nelson, W. (2002). All power to the consumer? Complexity and choice in consumers' lives. *Journal of Consumer Behaviour, 2*, 185–195. doi:10.1002/cb.99

Pal, J., Bennison, D., Clarke, I., & Byrom, J. (2001). Power, policy, networks and planning: the involvement of the major grocery retailers in the formulation of Planning Policy Guidance Note 6 since 1988. *International Review of Retail, Distribution and Consumer Research, 11*, 225–246. doi:10.1080/09593960122876

Pantelidis, I. S. (2010). Electronic Meal Experience: A Content Analysis of Online Restaurant Comments. *Cornell Hospitality Quarterly, 51*(4), 483–491. doi:10.1177/1938965510378574

Penaloza, L., & Price, L. (1993). Consumer Resistance: A Conceptual Overview. In *Advances in Consumer Research*. Provo, UT: Association for Consumer Research.

Pitt, L. F., Berthon, P. R., Watson, T. R., & Zinkhan, G. (2002). The internet and the birth of real consumer power. *Business Horizons, 45*(6), 7–14. doi:10.1016/S0007-6813(02)00220-3

Poster, M. (1992). The question of agency: de Certeau and the history of consumption. *Diacritics, 22*(2), 94–107. doi:10.2307/465283

Prasad, C. J. S., & Aryasri, A. R. (2009). Determinants of Shopper Behavior in E-tailing: An Empirical Analysis. *Paradigm, 13*(1), 73.

Sangeeta, S., Shrivastava, A., & Bhimalingam, R. (2008). Consumer Attitude Towards Online Retail Shopping in the Indian Context. *Journal of Consumer Behaviour, 3*(4).

Sashittal, H. C., Sriramachandramurthy, R., & Hodis, M. (2012). Targeting college students on Facebook? How to stop wasting your money. *Business Horizons, 55*(5), 495–50. doi:10.1016/j.bushor.2012.05.006

Sawhney, M., Verona, G., & Prandelli, E. (2005). Collaborating to Create: The Internet as a Platform for Customer Engagement in Product Innovation. *Journal of Interactive Marketing, 19*(4), 4. doi:10.1002/dir.20046

Schau, H. J., Muniz, A. M., & Arnould, E. J. (2009). How Brand Community Practices Create Value. *Journal of Marketing, 73*, 30–51. doi:10.1509/jmkg.73.5.30

Schilling, M. A. (2010). *Strategic Management of Technological Innovation*. Boston: McGraw Hill.

Shankar, A., Cherrier, H., & Canniford, R. (2006). Consumer empowerment: A Foucauldian Interpretation. *European Journal of Marketing, 9-10*, 1013–1030. doi:10.1108/03090560610680989

Sparks, L. (2008). Commentary: when Tony met Bobby. *Environment & Planning A, 40*, 2793–2799. doi:10.1068/a41271

SupMedia. (2012). *LiveJournal upgrades Singapore's 50,000 Blogshops to premium e-commerce stores*. Retrieved December 9, 2012, from: http://www.sup.com/en/news_399.html

SupMedia. (2012). *LiveJournal.sg stages Singapore's first Blogshop fashion show*. Retrieved from http://www.sup.com/en/news_388.html

Surowiecki, J. (2004). *The Wisdom of Crowds*. New York: Anchor Books.

Swidler, A. (1986). Culture in Action: Symbols and Strategies. *American Sociological Review, 51*, 273–286. doi:10.2307/2095521

Szajna, B. (1996). Empirical evaluation of the revised technology acceptance model. *Management Science, 42*(1), 85–92. doi:10.1287/mnsc.42.1.85

Tabachnick, B. G., & Fidell, L. S. (2001). *Using multivariate statistics* (4th ed.). Needham Heights, MA: Allyn & Bacon.

Toder-Alon, A., Brunel, F. F., & Schneier, W. L. (2005). Ritual Behaviour and Community Change: Exploring the Social-Psychological Roles of Net Rituals in the Developmental xi Processes of Online Consumption Communities. In Online Consumer Psychology: Understanding and Influencing Consumer Behavior in the Virtual World (pp. 7–35). Lawrence Erlbaum Associates, Inc.

Vargo, S. L., & Lusch, R. F. (2008a). Service-Dominant Logic: Continuing the Evolution. *Journal of the Academy of Marketing Science, 36*(1), 1–10. doi:10.1007/s11747-007-0069-6

Vargo, S. L., & Lusch, R. F. (2008b). Why Service? *Journal of the Academy of Marketing Science, 36*(1), 25–38. doi:10.1007/s11747-007-0068-7

Vargo, S. L., Maglio, P. P., & Akaka, M. A. (2008). On Value and Value Co-Creation: A Service Systems and Service Logic Perspective. *European Management Journal, (26)*: 145–152. doi:10.1016/j.emj.2008.04.003

Venkatesh, V., Morris, M. G., Davis, G. B., & Davis, F. D. (2003). User acceptance of information technology: Toward a unified view. *Management Information Systems Quarterly, 27*, 425–478.

Wang, K., & Lin, C. L. (2012). The adoption of mobile value-added services: Investigating the influence of IS quality and perceived playfulness. *Managing Service Quality, 22*(2), 184–208. doi:10.1108/09604521211219007

Wasko, M. M., & Faraj, S. (2005). Why should I share? Examining the social capital and knowledge contribution in electronic networks of practice. *Management Information Systems Quarterly, 29*(1), 35–57.

Wee, J. (2011). *What Singaporeans do on Live-Journal*. Retrieved December 23, 2011, from http://e27.co/?p=17110

Weick, K., Sutcliffe, K., & Obstfeld, D. (2005). Organizing and the process of sensemaking. *Organization Science, 16*(4), 409–421. doi:10.1287/orsc.1050.0133

Wells, W. D., & Tigert, D. J. (1971). Activities, Interest, and Opinions. *Journal of Advertising Research*, 27–35.

Wolfinbarger, M., & Gilly, M. (2001). Shopping online for freedom, control and fun. *California Management Review, 43*(2), 34–55. doi:10.2307/41166074

Yang, Z., & Peterson, R.T. (2003, Winter). I read about it online. *Marketing Research*, 26-31.

Zureik, E., & Mowshowitz, A. (2005). Consumer Power in the Digital Society. *Communications of the ACH, 48*, 46–51. doi:10.1145/1089107.1089136

ADDITIONAL READING

Agriculture & Agrifood Canada. (2010). *Global Trends Grocery Retailing Implications for suppliers and Manufacturers*. Her Majesty the Queen in Right of Canada.

Alexander, A., Nell, D., & Bailey, A, R., & Shaw, G. (2009). The Co-Creation of a Retail Innovation: Shoppers and the Early Supermarket in Britain. *Enterprise and Society, 10*(3), 529–558. doi:10.1093/es/khp016

Angelides, M. C. (1997). Implementing the Internet for Business: A Global Marketing Opportunity. *International Journal of Information Management, 17*(6), 405–419. doi:10.1016/S0268-4012(97)00024-8

Aoyama, Y., & Sheppard, E. (2003). The Dialectics of Geographic and Virtual Space. *Environment and Planning., 35*(7), 1151–1156. doi:10.1068/a3623

Bell, D., & Lattin, J. (1998). Shopping Behaviour and Consumer Preference for Store Price Format: Why Large Basket Shoppers Prefer EDLP. *Marketing Science, 17*(1), 66–68. doi:10.1287/mksc.17.1.66

Burt, S., & Sparks, L. (2003). E-commerce and the Retail Process: A Review. *Journal of Retailing and Consumer Services, 10*(5), 275–286. doi:10.1016/S0969-6989(02)00062-0

Cairncross, F. (2001). *The Death of Distance 2.0: How the Communications Revolution will Change our Lives*. London: Texere.

Cherrier, H., Black, I., & Lee, M. (2011). Intentional non-consumption for sustainability: Consumer Resistance and/or anti-consumption? *European Journal of Marketing, 45*(11), 1757–1767. doi:10.1108/03090561111167397

Clark, G., & Wrigley, N. (1995). Sunk Costs: A Framework for Economic Geography. *Transactions of the Institute of British Geographers, 20*(2), 204–212. doi:10.2307/622432

Clarke, I. (2000). Retail Power, Competition and Local Consumer Choice in the UK Grocery Sector. *European Journal of Marketing, 34*(8), 975–1002. doi:10.1108/03090560010331469

Couclelis, H. (2004). Pizza over the Internet: E-commerce, the Fragmentation of Activity and the Tyranny of the Region. *Entrepreneurship and Regional Development*. 16, 41 – 54. Doi:1080/08985620042000205027

Davies, A., & Elliott, R. (2006). The evolution of the empowered consumer. *European Journal of Marketing, 40*(9/10), 1106–1121. doi:10.1108/03090560610681032

De Kervenoael, R., Soopramanien, D., Elms, J., & Hallsworth, A. (2006). Exploring value through integrated services solutions: The case of e-grocery shopping. *Managing Service Quality, 16*(2), 348–45. doi:10.1108/09604520610650646

Dieberger, A. (2003). Social Connotations of Space in the Design for Virtual Communities and Social Navigation. In K. Hook, D. Benyon, & A. Munro (Eds.), *Designing Information Spaces: The Social Navigation Approach* (pp. 293–313). London: Springer. doi:10.1007/978-1-4471-0035-5_13

Doherty, N., & Ellis-Chadwick, F. (2010). Internet Retailing: The Past, the Present and the Future. *International Journal of Retail & Distribution Management, 38*(11/12), 943–965. doi:10.1108/09590551011086000

Elms, J., Canning, C., de Kervenoael, R., Whysall, P., & Hallsworth, A. G. (2010). 30 years of retail change: where (and how) do you shop? *International Journal of Retail and Distribution Management, 38*(11/12), 817–827. doi:10.1108/09590551011085920

Everts, J., & Jackson, P. (2009). Modernisation and the Practices of Contemporary Food Shopping. *Environment and Planning. D, Society & Space, 27*(5), 917–935. doi:10.1068/d11908

Fernie, J., & Sparks, L. (2009). *Logistics and Retail Management: Emerging Issued and Challenges* (3rd ed.). London: Kogan Page.

Gronow, J., & Warde, A. (2001). Introduction. In J. Gronow, & A. Warde (Eds.), *Ordinary Consumption* (pp. 1–8). London: Routledge.

Hand, C., Dall'Olmo Riley, F., Harris, P., Singh, J., & Rettie, R. (2009). Online Grocery Shopping: The Influence of Situational Factors. *European Journal of Marketing, 43*(9/10), 1205–1219. doi:10.1108/03090560910976447

Hogg, M. K. (1998). Anti-constellations: exploring the impact of negation on consumption. *Journal of Marketing Management, 14*(1/3), 133–158. doi:10.1362/026725798784959354

Hogg, M. K., & Michell, P. C. N. (1996). Identity, self and consumption: a conceptual framework. *Journal of Marketing Management, 12*(7), 629–644. doi:10.1080/0267257X.1996.9964441

IGD. (2011). *On-line Shopping, Letchmore Heath*. Watford: IGD.

Iyer, R., & Muncy, J. A. (2009). Purpose and object of anti-consumption. *Journal of Business Research*, *62*(2), 160–168. doi:10.1016/j.jbusres.2008.01.023

Jackson, P., & Holbrook, B. (1995). Multiple meanings: shopping and the cultural politics of identity. *Environment & Planning A*, *27*(12), 1913–1930. doi:10.1068/a271913

Kwan, M. (2002). Time, information technologies and the geographies of everyday life. *Urban Geography*, *23*, 471–482. doi:10.2747/0272-3638.23.5.471

Lee, M., Roux, D., Cherrier, H., & Cova, B. (2011). Anti-consumption and consumer resistance: concepts, concerns, conflicts and convergence. *European Journal of Marketing*, *45*(11/12), 1680–1687.

MacKenzie, D., & Wajcman, J. (Eds.). (1999). The Social Shaping of Technology, Milton Keynes, Buckinghamshire: Open University Press.

Miller, D., Jackson, P., Thrift, N., Holbrook, B., & Rowlands, M. (1998). *Shopping, Place and Identity*. London: Routledge.

Mintel, (2011).*Online Grocery Shopping*, Mintel Oxygen Reports, London.

Penaloza, L., & Price, L. L. (1993). Consumer resistance: a conceptual overview. *Advances in Consumer Research. Association for Consumer Research (U. S.)*, *20*, 123–128.

Weber, K. (2005). A toolkit for analyzing corporate cultural toolkits. *Poetics*, *33*, 227–252. doi:10.1016/j.poetic.2005.09.011

Wrigley, N., Lowe, M., & Currah, A. (1998). Retailing and e-retailing. *Urban Geography*, *23*(2), 180–197. doi:10.2747/0272-3638.23.2.180

KEY TERMS AND DEFINITIONS

Empowerment: Involving external, non-institutionalized agents, including consumers to participate and voice their views in the current and future strategy of the firm. Co-creation and co-production of services allows control, excitement, enjoyment to be felt by all parties. This has become of pre-requisite in digital driven society as information is freely flowing among individual while firms have come to recognize that sources of innovation are diffused in the environment beyond the RandD department.

Entrepreneur: An individual or group of individuals with a passion for creating and innovating. Someone who exercises initiative and rapidly recognizes new opportunities/gaps in changing market conditions.

Folksonomy: a user generated classification system using their 'own' lexical approach and set of practices. Importantly, the more users participate, the easier it is to reach a critical mass and encourage potential new users to share. From this perspective, information is provided from a richer variety of sources based on current social experiences of the users allowing previously unknown or restricted alternatives or substitutes on a global scale to emerge.

Retail Change: Evolution in consumer lifestyle and lifecycle that pushes retailers (traditional and new comer) to innovate. In doing so, they answer more precisely emerging needs and wants towards providing customer delight.

Retail Format: The type of shop and channel a retailer is choosing to operate in. Retail formats help to define strategy for overall store design (place), product range and depth (including the approach taken to pricing and promotion), and significantly the customer type and experience. E.g. Website, supermarket, hypermarket, market, farm shop.

Social Media: Consumer generated media (CGM) reflect the experience that consumers are now producing and publishing online. Consumer generated multimedia (CGM2) refers to content that goes beyond text and includes audio, images, animation and videos. Examples include the "I love my Ipod" advertisement on Youtube. This new form of participation is described as following three main patterns: (a) consumer solicited media (CSM) that capture invited but non-incentivised user advertising; (b) incentivized consumer generated media (iCGM) that include prize money and chances to win competitions; (c) consumer fortified media (CFM) that captures the phenomenon of consumer content (e.g. discussion on forum and blogs) created around the existence of other marketer led and legitimate content; and (d) compensated consumer generated media (cCGM) where consumers are paid for the use of their creation, a practice allowing particular bloggers and artists to participate as third party providers. The CSM process allows interactive participation and discussion triggering a democratization process of the brand, leveraging crowd sourcing capabilities leading to advertising stickiness that is necessary to spark the spread of an idea.

Chapter 25
Is Multichannel Integration in Retailing a Source of Competitive Advantage?
A Consumer Perspective

Daniela Andreini
University of Bergamo, Italy

Giuseppe Pedeliento
University of Bergamo, Italy

ABSTRACT

Multichannel integration in retailing is the ability of retailers to combine physical infrastructures (stores) and virtual channels (catalogues, Internet, and mobile shopping) in order to sell and distribute products and the related post-sales services. The purpose of this chapter is to investigate how shoppers perceive three different multichannel integration models in retailing: independent, database, and full-integrated models. The results of a qualitative enquiry and a quantitative survey reveal that when consumers choose among different multichannel retailers, the retailer's brand reputation, the experience with other shopping channels of the same retailer, and the Website design are the most cited factors influencing their purchasing decision. Even though findings disclose that respondents do not perceive multichannel integration as a driver of their shopping choices, the qualitative data indicates the existence of a respondents' attitude towards the multichannel integration, measured in this chapter through an exploratory and a confirmatory factor analysis in the quantitative survey.

INTRODUCTION

Multichannel integration is defined as the activity of retailers to combine physical infrastructures (e.g. stores) and virtual channels (e.g. catalogues, Internet and mobile shopping) in order to sell, distribute and provide products and related post-sales services (Müller-Lankenau et al., 2005; Rangaswamy & Van Bruggen, 2005).

In the multichannel retailing literature researchers have identified three different multichannel models corresponding to as many degrees of

DOI: 10.4018/978-1-4666-6074-8.ch025

integration between sale channels (Andreini, 2012; Müller-Lankenau et al., 2005; Steinfield et al., 2005):

1. **Independent Model:** Where sales channels are independent and even belonging to different organizations, e.g. Darty and Zara.
2. **Database Model:** Where sales channels exploit digital technologies to share the same customer database, e.g. Apple and Media Market.
3. **Full-Integrated Model:** Where retailers mirror the physical store in other channels, integrating two or more channels with highly integrated services, such as: booking or ordering online and pick-up the purchased items in store, returning products to stores and searching the inventory in each retail outlet, e.g. Fnac and Auchan Drive.

These different levels of multichannel integration involve different degrees of investments in IT, process integration, organizational structure and human resources.

Many authors suggested the full-integrated model in retailing as an effective strategy to achieve a competitive advantage and to gain higher revenues (Müller-Lankenau et al., 2005; Rangaswamy & Van Bruggen, 2005; Steinfield et al., 2005; Zhang et al., 2010).

Multichannel customers, in fact, are generally considered to be more profitable than single-channel customers are (Kumar & Venkatesan, 2005; Venketesan et al., 2007; Gensler et al., 2012), especially for specific product categories (Kushwaha & Shankar, 2013).

For these reasons, most of the research on multichannel retailing focused on the characteristics of multichannel customers (Dholakia et al., 2010), on their preferences (Neslin & Shankar, 2009; Verhoef et al., 2007), and on the drivers that induce shoppers to purchase in more than one channel (Balasubramanian et al., 2005; Montoya-Weiss et al., 2003; Noble et al., 2005; Venketesan et al., 2007).

In spite of a wider scholars' interest in multichannel integration and the related cross-effects between sales channels, still little is known about consumers' attitudes towards different levels of retailers' multichannel integration.

Such understanding is of vital importance for retailers since customers' attitude contributes to set the basis for a competitive advantage (Zeithaml, 1988) and can be applied as an input of managerial decisions concerning the most effective level of multichannel integration.

In this stance, the research questions this study addresses can be put forward as follows: how do consumers perceive different levels of multichannel integration in retailing? Is the multichannel integration a driver of shoppers' purchasing decisions? How can we measure the consumer attitude towards the multichannel integration in retailing?

In order to answer these research questions, we performed two empirical studies (a first, qualitative and a second quantitative) by focusing on two different retailing industries: consumer electronics and grocery.

The results of the first qualitative study revealed that when consumers choose among different retailers characterized by different degrees of multichannel integration, the retailer's brand reputation, the experience with other shopping channels of the same retailer, and the website design, are the factors which influence the most their purchasing decisions. The level of multichannel integration, instead, has been revealed irrelevant in shoppers' decisions.

In spite of these results, the findings of the qualitative study enlightened the existence of a consumers' attitude towards the multichannel integration in retailing, tested in a further quantitative analysis.

A survey to 214 Italians and 48 Swedish customers has been administered in order to verify and to measure the existence of a consumer attitude toward three different levels of multichannel integration, namely independent, database and full-integrated. An exploratory and a confirmatory factor analysis indicate the existence of a consumer attitude towards retailers pursuing a full-integrated multichannel model.

The contribution of this study to the multichannel retailing literature is twofold. First, it shows that even though shoppers do not take into account the retailers' level of multichannel integration in their purchasing decisions, the multichannel experience affects their choices (e.g. the experience with other shopping channels of the same retailer and the website design). Second, it defines and tests a new construct that measure the consumer attitude towards the full-integrated multichannel model in retailing.

From a managerial perspective, understanding and measuring the consumers' attitude towards the multichannel integration helps retailers to more carefully evaluate the investments for the integration of their sales channels. Moreover, the research presented demonstrates how multichannel integration is a strategy more suitable to retain and maintain existing customers than to attract new shoppers.

The remainder of this chapter is structured as follows. The first part provides a review of the literature of multichannel integration in retailing and of multichannel consumers. The second part describe the qualitative and the quantitative studies conducted. Finally, in the third part, results, managerial implications and limitations are discussed.

LITERATURE REVIEW

Multichannel integration is not a new phenomenon in retailing. Sears, the former largest US retailer, can be considered as the first multichannel organization since 1925, when it opened its first physical store after about thirty years of catalogue-based retailing.

Even though the current literature highlights the strategic importance of multichannel strategies,

multichannel retailing is still at an early stage. In the US, as instance, retailers combining both physical and the online stores account for about 40 per cent (Badrinarayanan et al., 2012), while in the European Union, multichannel retailers account for just 14 per cent, showing significant differences among the 27 countries forming the EU (EU Economic and Scientific Policy, 2011). Furthermore, according to a recent market research conducted by Aberdeen Group (2011), the majority of multichannel retailers still have weak capabilities in combining marketing and operations across retail channels, i.e. have a low level of multichannel integration.

As far as the way in which multichannel integration is realized in retailing, Steinfield et al., (2005) and Müller-Lankenau et al., (2005) developed forerunning exploratory studies aimed at revealing the level of retailers' multichannel integration respectively in the US and in Europe.

Steinfield et al., (2005) conducted a content analysis of the major US based retailers' websites in different product categories. Müller-Lankenau et al., (2005) observed the grocery chains leaders in the European markets. Both researches identified three different models of multichannel integration in retailing:

1. **Independent Channels:** Distribution channels are independent from each others, often displaying different assortment and pricing policies. Accordingly, the customer experience is channel specific, e.g. customers can pick up or return the products they bought only by using the channel through which they purchased. Thus, the integration of the retailing channels is related to the use of the same retailer's brand name. This strategy generally allows the avoidance of possible overlapping and conflicts between channels.

2. **Database Integration:** The level of integration among retailing channels is funded on the customer and product databases. In this case, customers can use their fidelity card and

their discount coupons in each sales channel of the same retailer. Therefore, shoppers benefit from a more interactive purchase experience and, at the same time, retailers minimize the investments in integration.

3. **Full-Integration:** Retailers pursuing a full-integrated model, mirror the physical store in other channels, integrating sales channels with advanced services. Some examples are: booking or ordering online and picking up in physical store, returning products to physical stores and searching the inventory in each retail outlet.

The concept of multichannel integration, hence, does not refer only at simply creating interactions between different sales channels, but also - and foremost - at providing superior customer value and thus a superior retailers' competitive advantage *vis-à-vis* competitors, through the exploitation of the actual and potential synergies between channels. In this perspective, multichannel integration is not just a viable and suitable way to reach specific segments of shoppers, but it is also a strategy to reinforce and enrich customers' purchasing experiences (Rangaswamy & Van Bruggen, 2005).

Müller-Lankenau et al., (2005) identified three drivers of influence on retailers' multichannel integration choices: the product characteristics, the structure of the retailing sector, and the consumers' behavior. Zhang et al., (2010) instead, proposed a conceptual model in which the main benefits stemming from a retailing multichannel integration are: the access to new markets, the higher level of customer satisfaction and loyalty, the competitive advantage towards the main competitors. According to these authors, there are three the main challenges retailers have to overcome in order to benefit from the advantages of multichannel integration. First, the customers' resistance in adopting alternative retailing channels, other than the physical store; second, the significant amount of investments required to set up new retailing channels; third, the conspicuous amount of resources that retailers have to direct to reach the desired level of integration among channels. Andreini (2012) analyzed the endogenous and the exogenous factors influencing different multichannel integration models in the European retailing. By content analyzing 84 websites belonging to the top ten European retailing brands in the grocery and in the consumer electronics sectors, findings reveled a strong correlation between the endogenous factors (relative channel power and ownership) and the level of multichannel integration displayed by the retailers investigated. The unique exogenous factor correlated with the retailers' level of multichannel integration was the pressure of local competition. On the contrary, consumers' IT maturity was not significantly correlated with the level of multichannel integration investigated in each national retailing market.

MULTICHANNEL INTEGRATION AND MULTICHANNEL SHOPPERS

Kumar and Venkatesan (2005) defined multichannel shoppers as individuals who purchase in more than a single channel in a given period of time.

In the current literature, three research streams studying the consumer multichannel behavior can be identified: the first, focused on factors influencing shoppers' purchasing decision among different retailing channels; the second, focused on the impact of multichannel shoppers' behaviors on retailers' financial performances; the third, on the identification of clusters of customers according to their level of multichannel shopping experiences.

Among the scholars belonging to the first stream of research, Montoya-Weiss et al., (2005) unveiled that the website design (i.e. navigation structure, content and graphic style) affects the perceived service quality of the retailer, the perceived risk related to the online shopping and, thus, the online channel choice. Moreover, these authors revealed that the online and the in-store service quality affect the customer overall satisfaction in a synergic, but competitive way. These findings suggest that retailers should carefully recognize and balance the cross-channel influences and tensions to deliver an effective service to customers.

By investigating the customer database of a US multichannel retailer, Kumar & Venkatesan (2005) have shown that pricing, product categories, shopper-store physical distance, and retailers' communication investments influence the customers' decision to purchase online instead of choosing the physical store of the same retailer.

Balasubramanian et al., (2005) presented and tested a conceptual framework aimed at clarifying the reasons why consumers choose one specific retailing channel in a multichannel-retailing context. They concluded that, at different stages of the purchasing process, shoppers choose a sale channel according to:

- Their economic goals,
- Their quest for self-affirmation,
- Their quest for symbolic meanings associated with the product and with the shopping process,
- Their quest for social interaction and experiential impact, and
- Their reliance on schemas and scripts for shopping.

They thus revealed that different consumers' goals are at play across different stages of the purchasing process as well as in the choice of the purchasing channel.

Focusing on a single US based retailer, Dholakia et al., (2005) analyzed if and how customers' purchasing behavior changed after the introduction of the online channel in addition to established channels (i.e. catalogue and physical stores) of the same retailer. Three are the main results of this research. First, customers are more willing to purchase in the sales channel where they already had positive purchasing experiences; second, shoppers are more likely to add channels than to substitute them; third, consumers switch easier between similar sales channels (e.g. from catalogue to Internet), than between dissimilar sales channels (e.g. from stores to Internet). Furthermore, they show that the use of multiple channels is greater among those who entered as Internet customers, reflecting their lower risk-aversion and their lower learning costs.

As far as the studies focused on the impact of multichannel shoppers on retailers' performances is concerned, Kumar and Venkatesan (2005) investigated the customer database of a high technology hardware and software manufacturer. These authors found that multichannel shoppers provide higher revenues and share of wallet, have higher past customer value, and are more active than single-channel customers are.

In the same vein, Venketesan et al., (2007) provided evidence that multichannel shoppers of an apparel retailer are associated with higher profitability and higher levels of loyalty than single channel shoppers. Gensler et al., (2012), focusing on the European bank sector, demonstrated that multichannel customers are cheaper to maintain in the long run, allowing to obtain a higher profitability in comparison with traditional customers.

Kushwaha and Shankar (2013) instead, contrary to conventional wisdom that all multichannel customers are more valuable than single-channel customers, have shown that differences in customers' profitability are tightly linked with the nature of product purchased. Their findings suggest that multichannel customers are the most valuable segment for hedonic product categories, while catalog or store-only customers provide higher monetary for low-risk product categories. For utilitarian products perceived as high risky, Internet shoppers emerged as the most valuable segment, while catalog or store-only shoppers were found to be more valuable for low risk product categories.

Finally, in the third stream of research, researchers clustered shoppers according to their level of multichannel shopping behavior.

Among these studies, Keen et al., (2004) identified four consumer segments in the US retailing market.

1. **Generalists:** Who consider the channel choice part of their overall shopping experience.
2. **Formatters:** Who are averagely risk adverse and buy only through physical stores.
3. **Price Sensitive:** Who do not care about the channel choice and simply purchase from the cheapest one.
4. **Experiencers:** Who prefer to use a channel that they had successfully used before.

In a more recent study conducted in the Dutch retailing market, Konuş et al., (2008) proposed three multichannel segments.

1. **Multichannel Enthusiasts:** Who have a positive attitude towards all sales channels. These customers display a high level of innovativeness and consider shopping a pleasurable experience.
2. **Store Focused Consumers:** Who are oriented towards brick-and mortar stores and show the highest levels of channel and brand loyalty.
3. **Uninvolved Shoppers:** Who have little interest in any channel and a low degree of shopping involvement.

The studies mentioned so far, focused on the organizational perspective and, when consumer behavior is of primer concern, on the multichannel influence on purchasing behaviors.

In spite of the growing interest toward multichannel retailing and its influence on consumer behavior, the literature still lacks significant contributions aimed at shedding light on how customers perceive different levels of multichannel integration in retailing and on how these perceptions are able to influence the retailer's choice.

EMPIRICAL STUDIES

This study is aimed at answering to the following research questions: how do consumers perceive different levels of multichannel integration in retailing? Is the multichannel integration a driver of shoppers' purchasing decisions? How can we measure the consumer attitude towards the multichannel integration in retailing?

In order to reach these objectives, the authors opted for a mixed method approach. Tashakkori and Teddlie (1998) defined mixed models designs as representing studies that combine quantitative and qualitative approaches within different stages of the research process. The mixed method approach is especially suitable to expand the knowledge about new emergent phenomena (Creswell and Clark, 2007). Moreover, the combination of qualitative and experimental data reinforces the validity and reliability of the research (Tashakori & Teddlie, 1998).

In particular, a first qualitative study was aimed at enlightening how shoppers perceive the multichannel integration in retailing, and at verifying if and how different levels of multichannel integration affect the customers' purchasing behaviors. In this qualitative study we focused on two product categories: consumer electronics and groceries. The aforementioned product categories were chosen because in both markets, players have been developing multichannel strategies for a decade (Steinfield et al., 2005; Müller-Lankenau et al., 2005). Furthermore, in these markets, both customers and suppliers are accustomed to use multiple channels to sell and purchase products and services (Grosso et al., 2005).

A following survey-based study, instead, was aimed at demonstrating the existence of a consumer attitude towards multichannel integration in retailing and at developing a suitable measurement scale to measure such attitude. This last study was conducted by involving a sample of Italians and a sub-sample of Swedish consumers experienced with online shopping. We thus controlled for the validity of the results reached by comparing two populations which are very different in terms of e-commerce usage: according to the European Commission (2013) in fact, in 2012 just 17 per cent of Italians purchased online against 74 per cent of the Swedish.

Swedish are comparatively more likely to purchase online than Italians for two main reasons: first of all for the differences between the two countries in terms of Internet penetration. In fact, while in Sweden the Internet penetration rate is approaching universal access, in Italy it remains at 51.7 per cent of the population, against the 67.6 per cent of European Union (EU27) (Internet World Stats, 2010; European Commission, 2012). Second, for the existence of significant cultural differences between the two countries: Italy is traditionally a more low-trust and risk-adverse society than Sweden (Fukuyama 1995), resulting in a halting development and in a lower customers' adoption of the e-commerce (Dholakia et al., 2005; Dinev et al., 2006).

Methodological issues and related results of each of the study conducted are extensively reported on the following.

Qualitative Study

The literature to date does not offer tested and reliable scales to measure customers' perception of different levels of retailers' multichannel integration. For this reason we started with a qualitative analysis consisting in open-ended questions and in a brief online purchasing simulation (Strauss & Corbin, 1990; Denzin & Lincoln, 1994).

The interview canvas was set up by using both substantive and specific questions. The former are questions which provoke an answer that requires the expression of a meaningful explanation, such as "how was your first online purchasing experience?"; the latter, are questions on specific details concerning channel choices, such as "does the presence of a physical store affect your decision in purchasing in a specific retailer online?"

In order to validate and sustain the results of the interviews, the authors decided for a purchasing simulation, a method which has been successfully applied also in previous studies – e.g. Burke (2002) and Dholakia et al., (2010) - allowing to grasp the consumer behavior when he/she actually purchases online.

The aim of the online simulation was to identify if and how different levels of multichannel integration affected the interviewees' decision of buying among different multichannel retailers. In particular, during the purchasing simulation, the interviewer asked each interviewee to simulate the purchasing of low-risk/low involvement products (Kushwaha & Shankar, 2013) in both consumer electronics and grocery, by using three different websites corresponding to as many configurations of multichannel integration: independent channels, database integration and full-integration (Steinfield et al., 2005; Müller-Lankenau et al., 2005). For each of the product categories we asked the participants to simulate the online purchasing of the following items: a 10 inches digital pictures frame, a one Giga-byte USB stick and a 500 Giga-byte external hard disk, for the consumer electronics retailing. A 500 gram spaghetti pack, a 500 gram tomato sauce and a bottle of one liter of olive oil instead, were chosen for the grocery retailing.

At the end of the simulation, we asked the participant three questions for each of the product categories: "Which online retailer would you select to finalize the purchase of each item?," "Why?" "Have you noticed that in some retailers you can benefit from multichannel integration services, like the pick-up in store? Do these purchasing options influence your choice? If yes, how?."

The sample of participants has been formed by using a snowball technique (Goodman, 1961) and by making sure that all the participants possessed the relevant characteristics required to understand the phenomena under study (Denzin & Lincoln, 1994) - i.e. that they have had previous experiences of online purchasing of both consumer electronics and grocery products.

The composition of the sample is as follows: all the participants are aged between 20 and 45 years old, hold at least a high school diploma and have previous experiences of online shopping of both consumer electronics and groceries. The number of observations has been defined *in itinere* by applying the saturation criteria; we thus stopped to collect further data when the answers to the qualitative interviews and the outcome of the purchasing simulations became repetitive (Weiss, 1994). 21 interviews and as many simulations have been collected. All the interviews were recorded and transcribed within 24 hours (Yin, 1994). The work gave rise to about 100 pages of interviews transcripts and field notes, which were codified through a transversal thematic analysis. In this way, we were able to isolate the recurring thematic discourses concerning the multichannel integration and to create a discourse on the theme (Ricolfi, 2006).

The identification of some "key expressions" and "key sentences" allowed for a systematic benchmark of the content of each interview collected.

The codification process of the qualitative and of the experimental data collected, allowed identifying some predominant thematic categories concerning the criteria of choice followed by the consumers involved in the study.

These predominant thematic categories, are summarized in the following:

1. **Inconsistency of the full-integrated model:** none of the interviewees cited the retailers' full-integration (when occurring) as a purchasing driver neither in consumer electronics, nor in grocery. During the purchasing simulation, none of the participants have made explicit considerations about the possibility to purchase the product online and pick-up it in store. We thus explicitly asked them if and how the multichannel integration

services displayed by some online retailers were perceived and considered. Most of the respondents declared they were not interested in this opportunity and underlined a general disagreement toward the retailers' choice to "hybridize" their distribution channels:

If I decide to buy online is because I want the product to be delivered directly to my place. I don't see any reason that drives me to the store and pick-up the product there. I have bought it online! (P.S. 22 years old)

Yes, sometimes can be useful, especially if the store is near to my place. Anyway, if prices online and offline are the same, why should I purchase online? If there are not differences in prices there are no incentives to buy online ... (P.C. 38 years old)

Other consumers expressly declared to dislike the full-integrated retailing services:

I think that buying online and picking-up in store is totally useless. If I buy online I want the products to be shipped to my place! (C.A. 23 years old).

2. **The importance of the brand:** the consumers' familiarity with the retailers' brand is an important driver of choice among multichannel retailers.

When I shop online the familiarity with the brand of the retailer is of primer importance. The brand is a criterion I take into account because a well-known brand is more trustworthy (F.C. 27 years old).

I feel safer when purchasing in a well-known retailer than in a small and unknown one. You will actually get the products you ordered and you will receive them on time (M.C. 36 years old)

The retailer XY is widely known. I wouldn't have chosen an unknown grocery (L.S. 31 years old).

3. **Past purchasing experiences in other channels of the same retailer:** the past purchasing experiences in physical stores strongly affect the online purchasing choice.

I have chosen this online retailer because I generally buy in its stores (F.D. 22 years old).

I trust more the website XYZ because I often buy in their shops (M.B. 35 years old).

I'm trying to find some reasons to choose the website of the store where I usually shop. However, I have to say that the best website is another one. But I think that in the end I will choose the one I'm more familiar with (S.M. 40 years old).

I always choose this website because I have always had good experiences in their stores. I trust them (M.C. 23 years old).

4. **The website design:** the website design and the layout are important drivers of choice among multichannel retailers.

I will choose this website because is more pleasant and more colorful. The others are more essential, less pleasant (M.G. 21 years old).

The website of the retailer ZYX is charming. I loved to browse it. The others were more boring, more aseptic. Even though the product was not available I think I would have selected that website anyway (C.G. 30 years old).

The website is featured by several products information as well as by different criteria the consumer can use to compare different products and select the one that fits his/her needs (D.A. 29 years old).

I would never buy from that website. It is awful. Products should be also divided by brands while in this website they are just divided by product type even though they are not homogeneous in terms of quality (R.G. 25 years old).

The results reached in this first study have shown that the different levels of multichannel integration and the related services are not recognized and perceived as drivers of choice among different multichannel retailers. Shoppers do not take into account the multichannel integration and the related services when deciding the multichannel retailer where to purchase.

Relevant factors affecting the retailers' choice emerging from the interviews conducted are the consumers' level of familiarity with the retailers' brand, past purchasing experiences had in traditional brisk and mortar store and the technical characteristics (ease of use, layout, pleasantness, content) of the retailer's website.

In spite of this, although multichannel integration did not emerge as a relevant factor, the fact that respondents considered the retailers' brand awareness and shoppers' positive experience stores as drivers of their online purchasing choices, suggest a customers' generalized positive attitude towards multichannel integration. In the light of these findings, the researchers developed a further study aimed at generating a scale to measure consumers' attitude towards the multichannel integration in retailing.

Quantitative Study

The survey-based study was aimed at demonstrating the existence of a consumer attitude according to the levels of multichannel integration of retailers: independent, database and full-integrated multichannel models. To assist in reaching this objective, we administered a web-based survey and we performed and exploratory factor analysis (EFA) and a subsequent confirmatory factor analysis (CFA) on the data gathered. This procedure allowed to test for the suitability of the measurement scales developed by Steinfield et al., (2005) and Müller-Lankenau et al., (2005), and applied in organizational multichannel behaviors.

The questionnaire was divided into two sections. In the first section, we collected demographic information and the frequency of online shopping. In the second section, we measured the attitude towards the three aforementioned models of multichannel integration in retailing, on a five-point Likert scale. The final scales were comprised of 14 items (see Table 1): three items measuring the consumer attitude toward the independent multichannel integration model, four items measuring the consumer attitude towards the database multichannel integration model, seven items, measuring the consumer attitude towards the full-integrated multichannel model.

The questionnaire was emailed to 1,000 graduate students of an Italian university in June 2012, inviting them to share the questionnaire with the members of their families. We also involved a group of exchange students from Sweden that were temporarily resident in Italy to cross-check the results obtained from the sample of Italians. The involvement of Swedish respondents allowed us to control for the validity and reliability of the results according to respondents level of familiarity with e-commerce. After four weeks, we received 495 questionnaires. Of these 495 questionnaires, 233 were unusable because respondents had not purchased any physical product online in the last six months.

The composition of the final sample (n= 262) is represented in Table 2 according to respondents'

demographic information (nationality, gender, education, age) and frequency of online shopping.

We applied a factor analysis (using the maximum likelihood extraction and the orthogonal varimax rotation) and reliability tests to assess the trustworthiness of the 14 proposed items.

We identified only one valid and reliable construct explaining the customers' attitude towards the full-integrated multichannel retailing. The construct was composed by the following items:

I prefer to purchase in online retailers which own also physical stores; When I buy a product online it is important to know that I can pick-up the purchased item in retailer's physical stores if needed When I buy a product online it is important to know that I can return the purchased item in-store if needed; It would be great to reserve a product through the retailer's Website but pick-up and pay it in-store.

Thus, of the seven items originally composing the construct labeled as "attitude towards the full-integrated multichannel model," three had to be deleted (factor loading ≤ 0.45). The factor analysis was applied to the final four items reported above (using the maximum likelihood extraction and the orthogonal varimax rotation). The reliability

Table 1. Constructs and items

Attitude towards the independent multichannel integration model:
• When I buy online, I prefer to receive products at home than pick-up them in store
• I usually purchase online because prices are lower than in-store
• I like purchasing online because I can find product difficult to find in store
Attitude towards the database multichannel integration model:
• Being able to use a loyalty card in all the sale channels of the same retailer, is very important to me
• Having an in-store technical assistance while I'm shopping online, is very important to me
• Having an in-store commercial assistance while I'm shopping online, is very important to me
• I like shopping in stores that offer also online services, e.g. technical assistance, gift coupons and loyalty programs
Attitude towards the full-integrated multichannel model:
• I prefer to purchase in online retailers which own also physical stores
• I prefer to purchase in online retailers which have physical stores near to my place
• The Website and the physical stores of a multichannel retailer must offer the same products
• The Website and the physical stores of a multichannel retailer must offer the same prices
• When I buy a product online it is important to know that I can pick-up the purchased item in retailer's physical stores if needed
• When I buy a product online it is important to know that I can return the purchased item in-store if needed
• It would be great to reserve a product through the retailer's Website but pick-up and pay it in-store

Table 2. Composition of the sample (n=262)

	%
Nationality	
Italian	81.7
Swedish	18.3
Gender	
Male	45
Female	55
Education	
High school diploma	42.4
University degree	55.3
Doctorate	2.3
Age	
18-30	76.7
31-40	11.8
>40	11.4
Frequency of online shopping	
Once a week	4.2
Once every two weeks	2.7
Monthly	5.7
Once every two month	17.6
Once a quarter	44.8
Once every six months	26

analysis supported the internal consistency of this measurement scale (Cronbach's α =.785, and item-to-total correlations higher than .532), higher than the .70 threshold suggested by Nunnally (1978). In addition, composite reliability (CR) and average variance extracted (AVE) of the construct were above the recommended threshold of .6 for the former and .5 for the latter (Bagozzi & Yi, 1988; Fornell & Larcker, 1981).

The results of the factor analysis (Cronbach's Alpha, Eigenvalues, explained variances, standardized loadings, means and standard deviations) are summarized in Table 3.

As shown in Table 3, the exploratory and the factor analysis have identified a unique construct suited to measure the customer attitude towards the full-integrated multichannel model.

In order to understand if different consumers' profiles are related to a different attitude towards the full-integrated multichannel model in retailing, we correlated the construct "attitude towards the full-integrated multichannel model" with the socio-demographic variables of respondents (i.e. gender, age, education, online shopping frequency and nationality). The results have shown that only the frequency of online shopping is significantly – but negatively - correlated with the construct (r= -.276, p<.001). This finding underlines that a positive attitude towards a full-integrated multichannel model in retailing is connected with a store-oriented segment of shoppers and in particular to those consumers less inclined to shop online.

Finally, we conducted a *t-test* on the construct "attitude towards the full-integrated multichannel model" to check differences in the sample. The mean value of the construct, did not differ significantly between Italians and Swedish (p=.95). Thus, such attitude seems to not be linked to a cultural propensity to purchase online.

Table 3. Composition of measures and items descriptive statistics

Factors and items (α = Cronbach's alpha; EV = Eigenvalue; VAR = % of explained variance)	Std. Loading	Mean (min: 1; max: 5)	Std. Deviation
Attitude towards the full-integrated multichannel model (α =.785; EV = 1.975; VAR = 49.35%)			
I prefer to purchase in online retailers which own also physical stores	.894	3.13	1.38
When I buy a product online it is important to know that I can pick-up the purchased item in retailer's physical stores if needed	.662	3.87	1.21
When I buy a product online it is important to know that I can return the purchased item in-store if needed	.616	3.53	1.26
It would be great to reserve a product through the retailer's Website but pick-up and pay it in-store	.598	3.44	1.34

RESULTS AND FUTURE RESEARCH DIRECTIONS

The research here presented was aimed at giving answers to the following research questions: how do consumers perceive different levels of multichannel integration in retailing? Is the multichannel integration a driver of shopper purchasing decisions? How can we measure the consumer perception of multichannel integration in retailing?

The authors provided answers to the aforementioned questions by means of mixed method research design performing a first qualitative, and a second quantitative study.

In particular, the first study unveiled the drivers of consumer purchasing behavior among different retailers characterized by different degrees of multichannel integration, i.e. independent, database and full-integrated (Müller-Lankenau et al., 2005; Steinfield et al., 2005). Findings reached through one-to-one interviews were deepened through online purchasing simulation, which allowed to increase the validity and reliability of the qualitative data collected.

The results reached partially contradict the established idea that a higher level of multichannel integration leads to a greater differentiation, and that the pursue of a full-integrated model in retailing drives to higher value delivered to consumers. Participants in fact, gave greater importance to factors other than multichannel integration, such as the retailers' brand awareness, past positive purchasing experiences in other channels of the same retailer, and the Website quality and usability. Thus, shoppers select a multichannel retailer for their online purchase when they are familiar with the retailer's brand, when they already had a positive past experience in another sales channel of the same retailer, and when the Website is sufficiently informative and easy to use. Even though consumers did not mention the multichannel integration as a driver of their choice, the attitude towards the multichannel integration strongly emerged.

Interviews transcripts and purchasing simulations confirm this statement. This means that the multichannel integration is not related to possible advantages that consumers can gain by combining different services. Rather, it is connected with the spill-over effects converging from one channel to another. Customers who have had positive in-store purchasing experiences are more willing to use also the online sales channel. In the same vein, customers who were dissatisfied with their in store experiences are reluctant to purchase from the same retailer also online. Moreover, well-established retailers' reputation and image, emerged as strong drivers of shoppers' choices among different multichannel retailers.

These findings support the thesis that the multichannel integration in retailing is not related to consumers' utilitarian benefits; rather to support the retailers' image and the reputation in retailing markets.

In light of these results, the authors explored the possibility to create a scale suited to measure the attitude towards different levels of multichannel integration (independent, database and full-integrated). To reach this objective, the authors used and adapted the measurement scales developed by Steinfield et al., (2005) and Müller-Lankenau et al., (2005), designed to measure the level of retailers multichannel integration. The scale was tested on the basis of the data collected on a sample of Italian shoppers and cross checked by involving a sub-sample of Swedish consumers: the latter more incline to online shopping than the former (European Commission, 2013). The scale's validity and reliability were measured through a first exploratory and a subsequent confirmatory factor analysis.

The results revealed the existence of a single construct which is suited to measure the customers' attitude towards a full-integrated multichannel model in retailing. This result suggests that customers perceive only the highest level of multichannel integration, while not perceiving intermediate levels of integration such as the possibility to use loyalty card or discount coupons in different channels.

In particular, of the seven items composing the construct labeled as "attitude towards the full-integrated multichannel model," four were retained while three were discarded. The four items retained were all related to product distribution, such as the possibility to pick up or to return a product purchased online in traditional brick and mortar stores. Differently, items related to the congruence of the assortment and/or of the pricing policy across channels where dropped for inconsistency. In contrast with what generally stated in the multichannel literature (Neslin et al., 2006), the alignment of pricing policies and of products assortment in each sales channel do not contribute to the formation of consumers' attitude towards the retailers' multichannel integration. This means that, for the respondents, multichannel integration is more a matter of distribution than of pricing, assortment and communication.

In alliance with this result, the existence of a negative correlation between the construct "attitude towards the full-integrated multichannel model" and online shopping frequency suggest that multichannel integration is perceived more by store-oriented customers (Keen et al., 2004), than by those shoppers more inclined to online shopping.

Thus, a higher level of integration among retailing channels, via the exploitation of distribution and logistics synergies, is suggested as a viable strategy retailers can pursue to stimulate cross-channel behaviors of store-oriented consumers.

Accordingly, multichannel integration mostly seems to be a suitable strategy to maintain actual customers and make them loyal, rather than a way to attract new customers from the Web. This challenges the established idea that multichannel integration is particularly effective to attract Web-oriented customers.

In spite of the contributions this research brought into being, some limitations should be underlined. First, since the retailing literature still lacks constructs and measurement scales aimed at measuring consumers' attitude toward multichannel integration, we adapted and applied a measurement scale originally developed to measure the organizational level of integration in retailing (Steinfield et al., 2005; Müller-Lankenau et al., 2005). Thus, future research is needed to develop specific measures of consumers' multichannel attitude fitting the very characteristics of multichannel retailing and of multichannel shoppers.

Second, even though the t-test reveals that Italian and Swedish consumers demonstrate the same attitude towards the full-integrated model in retailing, this findings should be confirmed by involving a larger sample of respondents. Hence, cross-cultural research is needed to deepen the analyses and the results reported in the present study and to evaluate in which way cultural forces affect customers' attitude toward different models of multichannel integration.

Third, an additional limitation of the study which deserves to be mentioned is related to the composition of the sample of respondents to the survey which is predominantly composed by youngsters. Although youngsters are generally considered as the most interesting target of consumers for online shopping (Dholakia, 1999; Social Networks, 2007; Nadeem et al., 2012), replications of the study conducted are needed by involving a wider range of "ordinary people."

CONCLUSION

The marketing literature underlined the advantages that retailers can obtain by achieving a higher level of integration among sales channels. Therefore scholars have generally outlined in their managerial implications that retailers should exploit the synergies and complementarities between sales channels in order to reach a wider and richer audience.

While the literature abounds in studies demonstrating a higher profitability of multichannel than of single channel customers (Kumar & Venkatesan, 2005; Venketesan et al., 2007; Gensler et al., 2012; Kushwaha & Shankar, 2013), contributions focusing on consumers' attitude toward different levels of multichannel integration are in short supply.

Given this lack, this research has been designed to understand how consumers perceive different levels of multichannel integration in retailing and if such integration is an actual driver of shoppers' purchasing choices and decisions. Moreover, the establishment of a measure of consumer attitude towards the multichannel integration in retailing has been tempted by applying and adapting already existing measurement scales (Steinfield et al., 2005; Müller-Lankenau et al., 2005).

The results reached in two different studies can be summarized as follows:

- Consumers do not perceive different levels of multichannel integration developed by retailers, except for the highest level, i.e. the full-integrated model. Nevertheless, the full-integrated model in retailing does not drive purchasing choices, i.e. does not give a competitive advantage to retailers. Consumers' choose the online retailer where to buy according to their familiarity with the retailers' brand, their past purchasing experiences in other channels and the quality of the retailers' Website.
- The results of the qualitative study have been confirmed by the quantitative survey. The development and test of a measurement scale aimed at identifying consumers' attitude toward different level of retailers' multichannel integration (independent, data base and full-integrated) unveiled the statistical inconsistency of the first two (independent and database), while the statistical significance of a single construct suited to measure the customers' attitude of a full-integrated multichannel model in retailing.

- The existence of a negative correlation between the construct "attitude towards the full-integrated multichannel model" and online shopping frequency, suggests that a higher level of multichannel integration is perceived more by store-oriented customers, than by those shoppers more incline to online shopping.

In light of the results briefly displayed above, the managerial implications stemming from this research are twofold: first, multichannel integration is not an aspect that customers' actually take into account in their online purchasing decisions. Multichannel integration hence, is not an element of competitive differentiation and a possible source of competitive advantage. Rather, is a viable strategy to sustain and support a pre-existing retailers' image and reputation in the market.

Second, past positive purchasing experiences were found to strongly influence the choice among multichannel retailers. Thus, multichannel integration seems to be more suited for store-oriented customers than for those more accustomed to online purchasing. In-store promotional initiatives to incentivize consumers' cross-purchasing are hence supposed to be more effective than those propelling in-store promotions to online customers.

REFERENCES

Aberdeen Group. (2011). *State of multi-channel retail marketing: a paradigm shift for reaching new customers*. Retrieved from http://www.aberdeen.com

Andreini, D. (2012). I fattori esogeni ed endogeni influenti sulle strategie di integrazione multicanale: un'analisi nel retailing in Europa. *Mercati e Competitività, 3*, 13–31.

Badrinarayanan, V., Becerra, E. P., Kim, C. H., & Madhavaram, S. (2012). Transference and congruence effects on purchase intentions in online stores of multi-channel retailers: initial evidence from the US and South Korea. *Journal of the Academy of Marketing Science, 40*(4), 539–557. doi:10.1007/s11747-010-0239-9

Bagozzi, R. P., & Yi, Y. (1988). On the evaluation of structural equation models. *Journal of the Academy of Marketing Science, 16*(1), 74–94. doi:10.1007/BF02723327

Balasubramanian, S. R., & Raghunathan, V., & Mahajan. (2005). Consumers in a multichannel environment: product utility, process utility, and channel choice. *Journal of Interactive Marketing, 19*(2), 12–15. doi:10.1002/dir.20032

Burke, R. R. (2002). Technology and the customer interface: what consumers want in the physical and virtual store. *Journal of the Academy of Marketing Science, 30*(4), 411–432. doi:10.1177/009207002236914

Creswell, J. W., & Clark, V. L. P. (2007). *Designing and conducting mixed methods research.* Thousand Oaks, CA: Sage Publications.

Denzin, N. K., & Lincoln, Y. S. (1994). *Handbook of qualitative research.* London: Sage Publications.

Dholakia, R. R. (1999). Going shopping: key determinants of shopping behaviors and motivations. *International Journal of Retail and Distribution Management, 27*(4), 154–165. doi:10.1108/09590559910268499

Dholakia, R. R., Zhao, M., & Dholakia, N. (2005). Multichannel retailing: a case study of early experiences. *Journal of Interactive Marketing, 19*(2), 63–74. doi:10.1002/dir.20035

Dholakia, U. M., Kahn, B. E., Reeves, R., Rindfleisch, A., Stewart, D., & Taylor, E. (2010). Consumer behavior in a multichannel, multimedia retailing environment. *Journal of Interactive Marketing, 24*(2), 86–95. doi:10.1016/j.intmar.2010.02.005

Dinev, T., Bellotto, M., Hart, P., Russo, V., Serra, I., & Collauti, C. (2006). Privacy calculus model in e-commerce: A study of Italy and the United States. *European Journal of Information Systems, 15*(4), 389–402. doi:10.1057/palgrave.ejis.3000590

EU Economic and Scientific Policy. (2011). *Consumer behavior in a digital environment.* European Parliament.

European Commission. (2012). Consumers' attitudes towards cross-border trade and consumer protection. Flash barometer 332, May 2012, Brussels.

European Commission. (2013). The consumer conditions scoreboard - consumers at home in the single market (9th Ed.). July 2013, Brussels.

Fornell, C., & Larcker, D. F. (1981). Evaluating structural equation models with unobservable variables and measurement error. *JMR, Journal of Marketing Research, 18*(1), 39–50. doi:10.2307/3151312

Fukuyama, F. (1995). *Trust: the social virtues and the creation of prosperity.* Free Press.

Gensler, S., Verhoef, P. C., & Böhm, M. (2012). Understanding consumers' multichannel choices across the different stages of the buying process. *Marketing Letters, 23*(4), 987–1003. doi:10.1007/s11002-012-9199-9

Goodman, L. A. (1961). Snowball sampling. *Annals of Mathematical Statistics, 32*(1), 148–170. doi:10.1214/aoms/1177705148

Grosso, C., McPherson, J., & Shi, C. (2005). Retailing: what's working online. *The McKinsey Quarterly*, *3*(18), 18–20.

Internet World Stats. (2010). Retrieved from http://www.internetworldstats.com/stats9.htm#eu

Keen, C., Wetzels, M., De Ruyter, K., & Feinberg, R. (2004). E-tailers versus retailers: which factors determine consumer preferences. *Journal of Business Research*, *57*(7), 685–695. doi:10.1016/S0148-2963(02)00360-0

Konuş, U., Verhoef, P. C., & Neslin, S. A. (2008). Multichannel shopper segments and their covariates. *Journal of Retailing*, *84*(4), 398–413. doi:10.1016/j.jretai.2008.09.002

Kumar, V., & Venkatesan, R. (2005). Who are the multichannel shoppers and how do they perform? Correlates of multichannel shopping behavior. *Journal of Interactive Marketing*, *19*(2), 44–62. doi:10.1002/dir.20034

Kushwaha, T., & Shankar, V. (2013). Are Multichannel Customers Really More Valuable? The Moderating Role of Product Category Characteristics. *Journal of Marketing*, *77*(4), 1–19. doi:10.1509/jm.11.0297

Montoya-Weiss, M. M., Voss, G. B., & Grewal, D. (2005). Determinant of online channel use and overall satisfaction with a relational, multichannel service provider. *Journal of the Academy of Marketing Science*, *31*(4), 448–458. doi:10.1177/0092070303254408

Müller-Lankenau, C., Wehmwyer, K., & Klein, S. (2005). Multi-channel strategies: capturing and exploring diversity in the European retail grocery industry. *International Journal of Electronic Commerce*, *10*(2), 85–122. doi:10.2753/JEC1086-4415100204

Nadeem, W., Iqbal, N., Hussain, Z., & Bilal, A. (2012). Affinity with computers and perceived trustworthiness as determinants of internet purchase in fashion outlets. *Actual problems of economics*, (130), 350-356.

Neslin, S. A., Grewal, D., Leghorn, R., Shankar, V., Teerling, M. L., Thomas, J. S., & Verhoef, P. C. (2006). Challenges and opportunities in multichannel customer management. *Journal of Service Research*, *9*(2), 95–112. doi:10.1177/1094670506293559

Neslin, S. A., & Shankar, V. (2009). Key issues in multichannel customer management: current knowledge and future directions. *Journal of Interactive Marketing*, *23*(1), 70–81. doi:10.1016/j.intmar.2008.10.005

Networks, S. (2007). *Gender and Friending: An Analysis of Myspace Member Profiles*. Retrieved from http://www.scit.wlv.ac

Noble, S. M., Griffith, D. A., & Weinberger, M. G. (2005). Consumer derived utilitarian value and channel utilization in a multi-channel retail context. *Journal of Business Research*, *58*(12), 1643–1651. doi:10.1016/j.jbusres.2004.10.005

Nunnally, J. C. (1978). *Psychometric Theory*. New York, NY: McGraw-Hill.

Rangaswamy, A., & Van Bruggen, G. H. (2005). Opportunities and challenges in multichannel marketing: an introduction to the special issue. *Journal of Interactive Marketing*, *19*(2), 5–11. doi:10.1002/dir.20037

Ricolfi, L. (2006). *La ricerca qualitativa*. Roma: Carocci Editore.

Steinfield, C., & Adelaar, T., & Liu. (2005). Click and mortar strategies viewed from the web: a content analysis of features illustrating integration between retailers' online and offline presence. *Electronic Markets*, *15*(3), 199–212. doi:10.1080/10196780500208632

Strauss, A., & Corbin, J. (1990). *Basics of Qualitative Research: Grounded Theory Procedures and Techniques*. Newbury Park, CA: Sage Publications.

Tashakkori, A., & Teddlie, C. (1998). *Mixed methodology: combining qualitative and quantitative approaches*. London: Sage Publications.

Venkatesan, R., Kumar, V., & Ravishanker, N. (2007). Multichannel shopping: causes and consequences. *Journal of Marketing, 71*(2), 114–132. doi:10.1509/jmkg.71.2.114

Verhoef, P. C., Neslin, S. A., & Vroomen, B. (2007). Multichannel customer management: Understanding the research-shopper phenomenon. *International Journal of Research in Marketing, 24*(2), 129–148. doi:10.1016/j.ijresmar.2006.11.002

Weiss, R. S. (1994). *Learning from strangers: The art and method of qualitative interviewing*. New York: Free Press.

Yin, R. K. (1994). *Case study research: design and methods*. London: SAGE Publications.

Zeithaml, V. A. (1988). Consumer perceptions of price, quality, and value: a means-end model and synthesis of evidence. *Journal of Marketing, 52*(3), 2–22. doi:10.2307/1251446

Zhang, J., Farris, P. W., Irvin, J. W., Kushwaha, T., Steenburgh, T. J., & Weitz, B. A. (2010). Crafting integrated multichannel retailing strategies. *Journal of Interactive Marketing, 24*(2), 168–180. doi:10.1016/j.intmar.2010.02.002

ADDITIONAL READING

Ahn, T., Ryu, S., & Han, I. (2005). The impact of the online and offline features on the user acceptance of Internet shopping malls. *Electronic Commerce Research and Applications, 3*(4), 405–420. doi:10.1016/j.elerap.2004.05.001

Ancarani, F., & Shankar, V. (2004). Price levels and price dispersion within and across multiple retailer types: Further evidence and extension. *Journal of the Academy of Marketing Science, 32*(2), 176–187. doi:10.1177/0092070303261464

Anderson, C. (2006). *The long tail: why the future of business is selling less of more*. New York: Hyperion.

Boaretto, G., Noci, A., & Pini, F. M. (2011). Marketing Reloaded: Leve e Strumenti per la Co-Creazione di Esperienze Multicanale, Ed. Il Sole24Ore.

Brynjolfsson, E., Smith, M. D., & Hu, Y. J. (2006). From niches to riches: the anatomy of the long tail. *Sloan Management Review, 47*(4), 67–71.

Chen, P. Y., Wu, S. Y., & Yoon, J. (2004). The impact of online recommendations and consumer feedback on sales. In *Proceedings of the International Conference on Information Systems*, ed. ICIS. Seattle: Association for Information Systems, 711–724.

Choi, J., & Park, J. (2006). Multichannel retailing in Korea: Effects of shopping orientations and information seeking patterns on channel choice behavior. *International Journal of Retail & Distribution Management, 34*(8), 577–596. doi:10.1108/09590550610675912

Frambach, R. T., Roest, H. C., & Krishnan, T. V. (2007). The impact of consumer internet experience on channel preference and usage intentions across the different stages of the buying process. *Journal of Interactive Marketing, 21*(2), 26–41. doi:10.1002/dir.20079

Grewal, D., & Levy, M. (2007). Retailing research: past, present, and future. *Journal of Retailing, 83*(4), 447–464. doi:10.1016/j.jretai.2007.09.003

Inman, J. J., Shankar, V., & Ferraro, R. (2004). The roles of channel-category associations and geodemographics in channel patronage. *Journal of Marketing, 68*(2), 51–71. doi:10.1509/jmkg.68.2.51.27789

Jarvis, C. B., MacKenzie, S. B., & Podsakoff, P. M. (2003). A critical review of construct indicators and measurement model misspecification in marketing and consumer research. *The Journal of Consumer Research, 30*(2), 199–218. doi:10.1086/376806

Kilcourse, B., & Rowen, S. (2008). Finding the integrated multi-channel retailer. *Benchmark Study.*

Kwon, W. S., & Lennon, S. J. (2009). Reciprocal effects between multichannel retailers' offline and online brand images. *Journal of Retailing, 85*(3), 376–390. doi:10.1016/j.jretai.2009.05.011

Kwon, W. S., & Lennon, S. J. (2009). What induces online loyalty? Online versus offline brand images. *Journal of Business Research, 62*(5), 557–564. doi:10.1016/j.jbusres.2008.06.015

Lee, H. H., & Kim, J. (2008). The effects of shopping orientations on consumers' satisfaction with product search and purchases in a multi-channel environment. *Journal of Fashion Marketing and Management, 12*(2), 193–216. doi:10.1108/13612020810874881

McGoldrick, P. J., & Collins, N. (2007). Multichannel retailing: profiling the multichannel shopper. *International Review of Retail, Distribution and Consumer Research, 17*(2), 139–158. doi:10.1080/09593960701189937

Oueslati, H. (2011). Réactions des consommateurs face à différents niveaux d'intégration dans le cadre d'une stratégie de distribution multicanal, *International Conference Marketing Trends.*

Park, D. H., Lee, J., & Han, I. (2007). The effect of on-line consumer reviews on consumer purchasing intention: The moderating role of involvement. *International Journal of Electronic Commerce, 11*(4), 125–148. doi:10.2753/JEC1086-4415110405

Schoenbachler, D. D., & Gordon, G. L. (2002). Multi-channel shopping: understanding what drives channel choice. *Journal of Consumer Marketing, 19*(1), 42–53. doi:10.1108/07363760210414943

Schröder, H., & Zaharia, S. (2008). Linking multi-channel customer behavior with shopping motives: An empirical investigation of a German retailer. *Journal of Retailing and Consumer Services, 15*(6), 452–468. doi:10.1016/j.jretconser.2008.01.001

Shankar, V., & Winer, R. S. (2005). Interactive marketing goes multichannel. *Journal of Interactive Marketing, 19*(2), 2–3. doi:10.1002/dir.20038

Steinfield, C., Bouwman, H., & Adelaar, T. (2002). The dynamics of click-and-mortar electronic commerce: opportunities and management strategies. *International Journal of Electronic Commerce, 7*(1), 93–120.

Thomas, J. S., & Sullivan, U. Y. (2005). Managing marketing communications with multichannel customers. *Journal of Marketing,* 239–251. doi:10.1509/jmkg.2005.69.4.239

Van Baal, S., & Dach, C. (2005). Free riding and customer retention across retailers' channels. *Journal of Interactive Marketing, 19*(2), 75–85. doi:10.1002/dir.20036

Van Birgelen, M., de Jong, A., & de Ruyter, K. (2006). Multi-channel service retailing: the effects of channel performance satisfaction on behavioral intentions. *Journal of Retailing, 82*(4), 367–377. doi:10.1016/j.jretai.2006.08.010

Van der Heijden, H., & Verhagen, T. (2004). Online store image: conceptual foundations and empirical measurement. *Information & Management, 41*(5), 609–617. doi:10.1016/j.im.2003.07.001

Verhagen, T., & Van Dolen, W. (2009). Online purchase intentions: A multi-channel store image perspective. *Information & Management, 46*(2), 77–82. doi:10.1016/j.im.2008.12.001

Wallace, D. W., Giese, J. L., & Johnson, J. L. (2004). Customer retailer loyalty in the context of multiple channel strategies. *Journal of Retailing, 80*(4), 249–263. doi:10.1016/j.jretai.2004.10.002

Wilson, H., Street, R., & Bruce, L. (2008) The Multichannel Challenge: Integrating Customer Experiences for Profit, Ed. Elsevier.

Zhu, F., & Zhang, X. (2010). Impact of online consumer reviews on sales: The moderating role of product and consumer characteristics. *Journal of Marketing, 74*(2), 133–148. doi:10.1509/jmkg.74.2.133

KEY TERMS AND DEFINITIONS

Consumer Attitude: Consumer's favorable or unfavorable inclination toward an object (e.g. a person, a place, a retailer). Attitude influences individual's choices and responses to stimuli. Attitude is often considered to be composed by four major component: (1) Affective: emotions or feelings. (2) Cognitive: belief or opinions held consciously. (3) Conative: inclination for action. (4) Evaluative: positive or negative response to stimuli.

Ecommerce: Buying and selling of products or services over electronic systems such as the Internet and other computer networks.

Full-Integrated Multichannel Model: Organizational configuration pursued by those retailers which mirror the physical store in other channels, integrating channels with advanced services.

Multichannel Integration: The ability of retailers to combine physical and virtual channels in order to sell and distribute products and the related post-sales services.

Multichannel Retailing: The adoption of more than a single channel by a retailer. Possible channels can be: brick-and-mortar stores, online stores, mobile stores, mobile app stores, telephone sales, catalogues and any other method of transacting with a customer.

Multichannel Shoppers: Consumers who purchase in more than a single channel in a given period of time.

Retail: The sale of goods or commodities in small quantities directly to consumers.

Store Shopping: Buying and selling of products or services over traditional brick-and-mortar stores.

Chapter 26
About the Challenges to Start E-Commerce Activity in SMEs:
Push-Pull Effects

Rauno Rusko
University of Lapland, Finland

Joni Pekkala
University of Lapland, Finland

ABSTRACT

This chapter introduces the challenges that SMEs face while starting e-commerce activity in the Northern Finland context. Based on the project results, six interviews, and the preliminary outcomes of the questionnaire, this study focuses on push-pull effects to start e-commerce activities. Following this framework, the structure of this study is twofold. At first, the authors ask why a firm, which already has an existing traditional brick-and-mortar shop, would develop its business exploiting digital solutions and e-commerce. In other words, what is the attainable incremental value for this kind of firm via e-commerce? Second, what kinds of attractive possibilities will e-commerce provide for the business of the firm? Both of these perspectives are concentrated on the phase in which the firm takes in the use e-commerce activities. The authors study this phase, basing the analysis on the literature review, questionnaire, and six interviews of SME entrepreneurs. The outcomes of this chapter show the relevance of push-pull perspective in the studies about the first steps of e-commerce.

INTRODUCTION

Especially in the branches of migration, tourism and entrepreneurship the Push-Pull effects are typical research subjects (Tata, 1977; Edgar et al., 2004; Singer, 2009; Buhalis & Main, 1998; Qian et al., 2011). In tourism, the studies are emphasizing, in addition to challenges faced while starting advanced information technology (Buhalis & Main, 1998), Push-Pull perspective in the context of tourists and destination: what are the reasons for a tourist to travel away from his/her home in order to meet new destinations?, or what are those factors of tourism destination, which will attract tourists to that destination? (Murillo, et al., 2008). In entrepreneurship, there are also Push-

DOI: 10.4018/978-1-4666-6074-8.ch026

Pull factors: what kinds of reasons in the current situation of life are pushing individuals towards to establish a new firm?, and on the contrary: which factors and opportunities are tempting individuals for entrepreneurship? One forms of push effect in entrepreneurship is business incubator (Qian et al., 2011; Rusko, 2011).

Similarly, this chapter considers E-commerce via these two perspectives: What kinds of reasons there are in the current business of brick-and-mortar shop, which requires the enlargement of business activities towards E- commerce? (push –effect), and What are the factors for business, which are tempting to establish an E-commerce unit? (pull –effect). We consider these two perspectives using qualitative materials (interviews) by emphasizing strategies and business practices in the analysis.

This study is based on the combination of literature review about E-commerce emphasizing especially the noticed challenges faced while starting E-commerce activity and its multi-channel marketing possibilities (see, e.g. Bhile et al., 2002; Yang, et al., 2012; Neslin et al., 2006; Zhang, et al., 2010), associated especially with Push-Pull dichotomy. These practical perspectives are based on interviews of six Finnish SME entrepreneurs, which have established E-commerce activities.

This chapter has the following structure: after this introduction follows literature review about E-commerce and especially its features emphasizing first steps towards E-commerce. Then we introduce research design of this chapter. The empirical outcomes of the research have been presented after that. Discussion –part of chapter combines the outcomes of literature review, questionnaire and interviews. Finally we have concluding remarks with recommendation for further study subjects.

LITERATURE REVIEW

This part of the chapter is basing on two parts. At first, it is focused on the literature introduc-

ing first steps of E-commerce and then literature emphasizing the reasons for E-commerce. We are interested these themes generally and in the context of Small and Medium Enterprises (SME) especially.

The Models about the First Steps of E-Commerce

ICT literature contains several alternative ways to categorize the development of E-commerce (See, e.g. Aranyossy, 2011; Daniel et al., 2002; Levy and Powell, 2003; Mendo & Fitzgerald, 2005; Rao et al., 2003). At first, we consider a very popular stage model for E-commerce, introduced by Rao, Metts & Monge (2003). According to them, there are four stages in E-commerce development:

1. Presence
2. Portals
3. Transactions integration
4. Enterprises integration

Each of these stages has own facilitators and barriers. Their perspective covers possible long-term development of an enterprise associated with E-commerce, although Rao and colleagues do not suppose that all firms will follow all these stages in their E-commerce development. This development contains, for example, high level collaboration between customers and suppliers (Enterprises integration). This stage is somewhat of an ideal concept for the "e-world" environment (ibid., 20-21). However, for the study here the first two stages, Presence and Portals, are the most interesting ones.

Presence –stage contains initial steps that organizations do to get involved in digital environment, that is, they have a window to the Web (Rao et al., 2003, 16). At this stage, Web-pages contain one-way information about the organization. Rao and colleagues name the commitment of the most important facilitator, which means the commitment of strategy towards Internet as a tool for achieving strategic aims, such as increasing sales, better services for customers, more available information and cost savings. Except cost savings, which is a push factor, the other variables, such as increasing sales, better services for customers, more available information are pull factors of commerce. Of course, the distinction between push or pull factors depends also on the current stage of the business in the firm (internal factors): if the economic or financial situation of the firm is challenging, then it is possible that the current situation pushes towards E-commerce in order to achieve all of these: more sales and savings and more customers via improved business strategy. If the financial situation is stable without E-commerce, then there is not any necessity for E-commerce. In this case, however, an entrepreneur might find tempting to start first steps towards E-commerce because of the possibilities which it provides, such as better services for customers and therefore, perhaps, higher turnover, that is mainly external potential factors.

According to Rao and colleagues (2003), the second stage, portal –stage, has following facilitators: internal organizational changes, investment and usability. Portal –stage contains introduction to two-way communication: customer or supplier order placing, the use of profiles and cookies. It also enables developed customizing activities (Rao et al., 2003, 17). Although the Portal stage is the second stage of development path introduced by Rao and colleagues (2003), its features of E-commerce could also be as an impulse to start E-commerce activities. Again, it might be firm-specific whether these features are associated push- or pull-effects of E-commerce.

Rao and colleagues (2003) also list several barriers to different stages of E-commerce development. In the Presence –stage there might be several organizational reasons not to introduce E-commerce functions, such as technological resistance, acceptance of growth strategy, financial investments and development of telecommunication infrastructure. In the Portals -stage

there are following barriers: the development of B2B interfaces and cultural and/or language issues. Of course the power of these barriers has an essential role while an entrepreneur and/or managers of the firms are deciding whether or not to take E-commerce in use and in what form in the enterprise. The strategic decisions are often based on some kinds of cost-benefit analysis (see, e.g. Schwenk, 1984; Shrivastava & Grant, 1985; Klingebiel & Meyer, 2013). In this case, the strategists are deliberating the attractions and barriers associated with E-commerce activities.

One alternative way to consider the stages of SMEs in E-commerce is to use questionnaire and its results in cluster analysis and cluster SMES in groups basing on these results (Daniel et al., 2002). Daniel and colleagues (2002) found following groups: developers, communicators, Web presence and transactors.

Developers are at the start of their E-commerce adoption developing their services, such as email communication with customers and suppliers, providing (Web) information about company, its products and services and using Web for advertising and brand building. "Communicators" also use email for communication for between employees and electronically exchanging documents and designs with customers and suppliers. At this stage the most important development activity is focused on Websites in order to provide company, product and service information. (Daniel et al., 2002, 260). After these steps is following "presence" phase, which one is already the first step in the typology of Rao and colleagues (2003). However, these two studies define the contents of these steps differently. According to Daniel and colleagues (2003), in this phase the two-way orders are possible, but Rao and colleagues (2003) see for "presence" step essential the one-way information about the organization and two-way orders are typical for the "portal" stage.

Furthermore, there are some other studies considering the first steps of the E-commerce. For example, also Aranyossy (2011) introduce the first steps of e-commerce development in her working paper. According to her, these steps are building information capabilities, using the company Web-site as a marketing tool – affecting the firm performance through the sales volume. In addition, transactional e-commerce function works as a new sales channel having effects on the sales revenue and the cost of administration and sales or inventory turnovers as well. Furthermore, E-commerce has a connection with the building activities of a loyal customer base. In addition, Aranyossy see that these features "are more like future options or intangible assets, their effect on the company performance is more strategic, future-centric and elusive." (Aranyossy, 2011, 11).

Generally, the perspectives of Rao and colleagues (2003), Daniel and colleagues (2003) and Aranyossy (2011) about the first steps of E-commerce development are nearly similar: these studies emphasize the possibilities of E-commerce as a tool of information and a source for the enlargement of turnover. Generally, E-commerce studies consider the following aims of enterprises while studying the first steps of E-commerce: relatively simple technologies, such as e-mail, to dispense and gather information. Then, there is next the own static homepage containing basic information. After that, there are wider range of information and attempts to market products and after-support. (Mendo & Fitzgerald, 2005, 679). According to Mendo and Fitzgerald (2005), traditionally in the most mature E-commerce stages of the E-commerce development models, the Web site is claimed to be totally integrated with several back office systems, such as ERP, CRM and SCM applications. Also Rao and colleagues (2003) mention customer relationship management (CRM) and supply chain management (SCM) in their enterprises integration –the stage of E-commerce development model.

Levy and Powell (2003) introduce four roles for Web technologies in SMEs: brochureware, support, opportunity and development. They emphasize the role of different business, entrepreneur and his/her attitudes related to E-commerce in the context of this role selection. Furthermore, their model is not associated any growth model with the particular order of phases and it is in that way resembles the model of Rao and colleagues (2003). However, in some models the stages of E-commerce are sequential and activities in them cumulative, that is each stage or cluster is undertaking all of the activities of the previous cluster (see, e.g. Daniel and colleagues, 2003, 260).

Reasons for E-Commerce Adoption According to Some Literature

According to Grandon and Pearson (2004), there are in the literature of E-commerce three factors affecting the strategic value of information technologies: operational support, managerial productivity and strategic decision aids. In addition, they identified four factors that influence electronic commerce adoption: organizational readiness, external pressure, perceived ease of use and perceived usefulness. Grandon and Pearson (2004) also studied the linkages between the strategic value of E-commerce and adoption of E-commerce. As a result, they noticed that those top managers who perceived E-commerce as adding strategic value to the firm are adopting more easily E-commerce for use.

Among these factors, which Grandon and Pearson (2004) mention, "external pressure" is possible to categorize among the push factors and some of them among the pull factors of E-commerce: operational support, managerial productivity and strategic decision aids. Some of these factors are generally easing the adoption of E-commerce, such as perceived usefulness, organizational readiness and perceived ease of use, but them are difficult to divide into push or pull factors.

Stephen Drew (2003) has also noticed the strategic importance of E-commerce in his study about eastern England. E-commerce is both threat and opportunity for SME business strategies. E-commerce is at the centre of technology and corporate strategies, and associated with trans-formational change (Drew, 2003). Drew (2004) find four key management issues of E-commerce: opening new markets, improving the quality of products and services, reducing costs and improving efficiencies and growing the volume of the business. Furthermore, Drew lists relevant driving forces for the adaption of E-commerce:

1. Pressures from suppliers of other business partners
2. Customers demanding the deal on the Internet
3. Need to increase the value of the business
4. Orders of top management
5. Industry changes and trends
6. Opportunity to expand and grow
7. Threat of competitors taking the business
8. Need to keep up with existing competitors

Only point (6) "opportunity expand and grow" is a pull factor and the rest of the factor are push factors. Among the key management issues push factor is only "reducing costs and improving efficiencies" and pull factors are opening new markets, improving the quality of products and services and growing the volume of the business.

Actually, these two studies differentiate with each other: Drew (2003) emphasizes pull factors of E-commerce and Grandon and Pearson (2004)

push factors of E-commerce. On Table 1 is the list of the pull and push factors basing on the literature review. Furthermore, there are some general factors promoting E-commerce, which are difficult to divide between these two categories.

RESEARCH DESIGN

The research method of this chapter is based on case study strategy. Case study strategy covers several methods and materials in order to achieve the research objectives (See, e.g. Yin, 2003; Eriksson & Kovalainen, 2008). The research material is based on the results of the project, which focused on the themes sales management. Material covers both qualitative and quantitative sources: six interviews and preliminary results of questionnaire with 132 respondents of managers or owners. Questionnaire was transmitted via the regional organization of Federation of Finnish Enterprises to about 1800 firms. Thus, the response rate is 7.3 per cent. Practically all of the respondents are SMEs from the Northern Finland.

The target group of interviews was chosen carefully: all interviewed six enterprises have E-commerce functions in their business model. The qualitative material of the case study consists of six recorded face to face interviews of entre-preneurs and six enterprises. These interviews

Table 1. Push and pull factors of e-commerce (Aranyossy 2011; Drew, 2003; Grandon & Pearson, 2004; Rao et al., 2003)

Push Factors	General Promoting Factors	Pull Factors
• Pressures from suppliers or other business partners • Customers demanding the deal on the Internet • Need to increase the value of the business • Orders of top management • Industry changes and trends • Threat of competitors taking the business • Need to keep up with existing competitors • Reducing costs and improving efficiencies • External pressure • Cost savings.	• Perceived usefulness; usability • Organizational readiness • Perceived ease of use • internal organizational changes, • Investment • Marketing tool	• Opportunity to expand and grow • Opening new markets • Improving the quality of products and services • Growing the volume of the business. • Operational support • Managerial productivity • Strategic decision aids • Increasing sales • Better services for customers • More available information and cost savings.

implemented during spring 2013 by one of the authors of this chapter. On average, these interviews lasted between 0.5 hours to one hour. The number of tthe ranscribed words of interviews varies between 1850 words to 4300 words. The basic structure of these interviews was the same for all interviews, but the interviewer adapted the nuances and content of the questions during each interview basing on the answers and emphasis of interviewees.

We decided to study the forms of E-commerce of SMEs in addition to the questionnaire by using interviews, because they provide more specific material for research questions compared with the questionnaire. An interviewer is able to react to the answers of the interviewee in order to find more information about the appearing interesting themes during the process of interviews. Furthermore, the structured questionnaire restricts the form of the information coming from the respondents. The interviewees are all entrepreneurs and representing various branches of business in Northern Finland. Although all enterprises have their main office in Northern Finland, their clientele is in some cases even very international. Furthermore, the role of Web and the E-commerce is very advanced in all of these firms making them the ideal research object for this study. This was the main criterion for the selection of research population.

Thus, the interviews have been recorded, transcribed, read carefully and encoded manually by the authors of this chapter in order to find the most important underlying themes of E-commerce which these interviewees have met. The analysis is based on qualitative interview material containing micro-stories of these companies and especially content analysis, which is focused on the first steps of E-commerce of the respondents. The respondents are owners or co-owners of the companies. The aim of the content analysis is to investigate the most essential features associated with push- and pull-effects of E-commerce among the research population.

In addition to the questionnaire, interviews and content analysis are typical tools and methods of studying the features of E-commerce in SMEs (see, e.g. McGowan et al., 2001; Koh & Kim, 2004; AlGhamdi et al., 2012; Mavlanova, et al., 2012). In the study of McGowan and colleagues (2001) the firms come from different sectors including manufacturing, services and retail. Also the study here in this chapter covers all these sectors in the questionnaire, but emphasis on the interviews is in the branch of retail and services.

EMPIRICAL OUTCOMES

The Results of the Questionnaire

This study exploits the preliminary outcomes of the questionnaire, which is a part of the results of the project, which focused on the sales management in Northern Finland. The questionnaire contained, for example, the battery of questions about promoting the factors of E-commerce. Among 132 respondents, between 111-116 of them, answered these questions. The most important promoting factors of E-commerce are (in this particular order):

1. Better service to customer (Pull –effect)
2. New customers (Pull -effect)
3. Customers want to use E-commerce (Push –effect)
4. Higher sales (Pull –effect)
5. More appearance and new customers to brick-and-mortar (Pull –effect)
6. Competitors have E-commerce (Push -effect)
7. Higher productivity (Pull –effect)
8. Entry to new markets (Pull –effect)
9. Achievement of competitive advantage (Pull –effect)
10. Synergy effect (Pull –effect)
11. Rationalizing via E-commerce (Push effect)
12. Passing intermediary (Pull –effect)

The most of the promoting factors of E-commerce is possible to locate in the category of pull effect, only three variables "Customers want to use E-commerce," "Competitors have E-commerce" and "Rationalizing via E-commerce" presents clearly push effects. (Table 2)

RESULTS OF THE INTERVIEWS

In order to achieve in-depth –case study perspective, quantitative results are completed with the interviews of entrepreneurs, which currently have E-commerce activities in their business. Quantitative analysis revealed that there is, among the SMEs of Northern Finland, both push- and pull-effects during the first steps of E-commerce. The aim of the qualitative part of this chapter is to find more descriptive details associated with Push-Pull effects in E-commerce start.

General Underlying Information about the Case Study Enterprises

In order to ensure the anonymity of the respondents we call these firms as A, B, C, D, E and F. All these firms are relatively small: several of them have only a couple of workers, including entrepreneur(s), the largest ones have about 20 workers. The age of the firms fluctuates between 2-40 years. All of these firms have E-commerce activities, which was the main criterion for research population and some of them have even the pioneering role in E-commerce in their branches. Table 3 summarizes some basic details about these firms.

The First Steps of E-Commerce

The reasons to start E-commerce activities fluctuate remarkably among the case study enterprises. Furthermore, some interviewees express these reasons more completely than the other ones. Often this theme has been passed quickly, but during the

interviews also these underlying reasons to take to use E-commerce as a part of their business model have usually appeared.

Better Services to the Customers

One of the discourses among the case study material directed towards the better services to customers via E-commerce activities. On Table 1 this feature is located in the pull –site of E-commerce. This factor was the most important pull factor of E-commerce in the questionnaire. Also, interviews showed the importance to achieve better services to customers via E-commerce. Among both qualitative and quantitative case material, one important detail is that many of these SMEs are located in the areas which are nearly unoccupied, which fact might have general effects on the contents of the answers of the interviewees and questionnaire.

The difference is mostly there that in our brick-and-mortar shop visit both local and tourists and travelers and then E-commerce, what we have looked, that it is let's say, that almost 100% it is only in the use of Finnish. (E)

And then we have those... in Web is a lot of already in the beginning of 21ˢᵗ century and before the blogs have been invented, that there is discussion groups and hobby groups and.. and we have had a politics in which we take care of this magazine and then we have updated those own Web pages. And then we support these kinds of hobby groups and discussion groups and so on in a way, that we will answer their questions, they will other ways do their own business. (D)

For our own Web pages, we have constructed online reservation which as if.. customer is able to direct from there to reserving and then so.. there as producing gradually then more services which means we will not satisfy only for that, that

Table 2. Promoting factors of e-commerce in SMES according to the results of the questionnaire (Scale 1-5)

Do you have now E-commerce?		Higher sales	Synergy effect	Rationalization via E-commerce	Higher productivity	Passing intermediary	Achievement of competitive advantage	Competitors have E-commerce	Incremental value for current products	Possibility to sell totally new products	Wider product range	Customer data via E-commerce	Better service to customer	Customers want use E-commerce	More appearance and new customers to brick-and-mortar	New customers	Entry to new markets
No E-Commerce	Mean	3,44	3,04	2,87	3,46	2,77	3,05	3,40	2,76	2,35	2,27	2,72	3,57	3,46	3,48	3,49	3,15
	N	82	80	82	81	79	81	82	80	79	81	80	84	83	83	84	84
	Std. Dev.	1,297	1,409	1,447	1,415	1,458	1,457	1,404	1,407	1,396	1,379	1,312	1,235	1,262	1,476	1,427	1,468
E-Commerce	Mean	4,23	3,69	3,56	4,00	3,78	4,16	4,19	3,50	3,34	3,41	3,47	4,00	4,19	4,06	4,16	4,03
	N	31	32	32	32	32	32	32	32	32	32	32	32	32	32	32	32
	Std. Dev.	,990	1,230	1,268	1,164	1,362	1,081	,998	1,320	1,405	1,266	1,077	1,191	1,120	1,190	1,019	,999
Total	Mean	3,65	3,22	3,06	3,61	3,06	3,36	3,62	2,97	2,64	2,59	2,94	3,69	3,66	3,64	3,67	3,40
	N	113	112	114	113	111	113	114	112	111	113	112	116	115	115	116	116
	Std. Dev.	1,266	1,387	1,428	1,366	1,497	1,446	1,346	1,417	1,463	1,437	1,289	1,233	1,263	1,422	1,356	1,407

497

Table 3. The cases analyzed

Firm	Firm A	Firm B	Firm C	Firm D	Firm E	Firm F
Industry	Tourism/services/ Retail	Retail	Retail, B2B	Content provider, retail	Retail	Retail (and manufacturing)
Age of firm	About 40 years	5 years	Nearly 20 years	About 30 years	2 years	About 30 years
Establishment of E-commerce (First domain)	2005	2009	Over 10 years (At first pages of chain)	About 30 years	2 years (Chain)	About 30 years
The forms of E-commerce	Several sales channels in Web including several international portals	Own Web pages and Web store (with the help of ICT provider)	Most of the sales via traditional shop; Web store is e.g. marketing channel	Most of the sales via own international Web store. Free partial content in Web store (marketing)	Finnish Web bases and Web store upkeeping by international chain.	Several Web shops
Number of domains	Over five	Under five	Under five	Under five	Under five	Over five
Brick-and-mortar shop and Web shop?	Brick-and-mortar shop and Web shop	Brick-and-mortar shop and Web shop	Brick-and-mortar shop and Web shop	Brick-and-mortar shop and Web shop	Brick-and-mortar shop and Web shop	Web shop (initially mail-shop with manufacturing)

the customer reserve accommodation from here. Now there is build such a package, that you can.. it is basic price package and then the customer can reserve special package/product, in which belongs in addition to accommodation also meal and.. <taken away because of anonymity>.. And in the future meaning to produce also different packages in order to provide option what it can.. wants to buy ready while being in home.. planning the trip. (A)

E-commerce has bring that kind of.. Let's say that we are able to jump to the so called present time which means, we can achieve different clientele more efficiently and we get customers also to the brick-and-mortar shop. It is actually bipartite there is (1) direct delivery, direct deal in which we have not any contact with customer in spite of via E-commerce, but then we have those (2) consumers, who use it (E-commerce) as a tool in order to become acquainted with products and visit then in the brick-and-mortar shops. E-commerce

is absolutely necessity today in retail business. Especially, because of the service, that we are able to service to the customers and being active where, however, all customers, are using most of their media time.(C)

Most of these comments above show the possible synergy effect about having both brick-and-mortar shop and Web shop at the same time in Northern Finland. This kind of multi-channel feature seems to increase, according to interviewees, the total quality of services for the contemporary customers by providing several service combinations between the brick-and-mortar shop and E-commerce. Especially, the feature of E-commerce will reduce the costs of customers in the sparsely inhabited areas such as Northern Finland.

Wider Product Selection

It is also possible that the selection of products is wider in the E-commerce compared with the selection of products in brick-and-mortar shop. This feature is associated with pull factor "growing the volume of the business" on Table 1.

Perhaps in that, that we have wider selection of products there (in E-commerce) because we do not those e.g. <...> products will not keep in the front of brick-and-mortar shop, because of the miscellaneous clientele of this center... (B)

However, also in this case (B) above some of the selection, which is not in the front of the brick-and-mortar shop is possible to find for customers in the warehouse of the same shop building for the visitors of the shop. However, separated service and product selection between and brick-and-mortar shop and E-commerce might generally cause confusion for customers, but this feature did not come up among the case study material. It is noteworthy that in questionnaire wider product selection was not very important factor during the first steps of E-commerce.

Tool of Marketing and Sales

In interviews, the entrepreneurs of SMEs see that E-commerce in its different forms is a necessary tool for marketing and for the growth of sales. "Tool for marketing" generally promotes E-commerce, but growth of sales is pull -factor "Growing the volume of the business" on Table 1. Furthermore, "Higher sales" was important reason for E-commerce also in the questionnaire. The E-commerce strategies and business models of the SMES deviate among the population of the interviewees. Some of them already have long history in marketing via Web pages and the other ones have just started their path with E-commerce. For example, the attitudes of respondents about Facebook deviate:

Facebook, I will not see that it is as a marketing channel any excellent or something like that when thinking about sales. It more like parade tool and

of course one of them... but it is true that in the side of E-commerce Google has autocrat at least I see so. Google is totally incomparable. (C)

Well, it (Facebook pages) has been constructed lately. And generally we are involved with as if in relatively small effort and other ways we start with so... in practice... We have Facebook–pages, I think that they are constructed during last year. If we think about what our enterprise has, so we has basic Web pages, where we introduce our <products> and from where you can order <...> and also other products. Then we have... Specific blog and it's this kind of official blog of editor, which we will not update so often. About once a two week, or three times a week. Generally we launch new <products> or inform some kinds of changes. But it is such an official as if noticeboard, information channel. Then we have those of Facebook pages, where there is practically plenty of same content as in the blog. D

The importance of E-commerce as a part of the firms' strategy varies among firms according to the interviewees from very first small steps to advanced level, where the firm has several separated shops in Web. In the case of (E) the presence in Web is the most important character of E-commerce. In the case of F the firms have several Web shops for different product selection. Actually, they have the whole family of products in Web.

Yes, the sales come from this brick-and-mortar shop, absolutely. That, the E-commerce is such an extra... But also in E-commerce there is always it, that the updating of E-commerce, it is not free. All the time there are costs running also, that is not free, but absolutely it (E-commerce) must be and always it benefits... Yes, E-commerce always pays, but absolutely the main volume is here (in brick-and-mortar shop). Absolutely. (E)

Yes, in a sense that if we open, in a way, new shop (in Web) then it is not near big news because it is in the same pole of products as if all and technologically all of them are from our point of view together and in the same. For customer it seems to be separated. But the reason why do so is, of course, that if you have very narrow... So at first, the search engine visibility is, of course, better when there is for very narrow index-word visibility specialized Web shop and then these all other factors... Credibility is easier to achieve in that way. Another way is to then to provide those supermarkets (in Web) where you have all possible (products). Both of these perspectives are robust, but in some conditions it is more efficient to provide small niche-shop (in Web). (F)

We achieve most of our customers via Web. (F)

How to Promote E-Commerce for SMEs?

Some of the respondents provided also some general suggestions how to launch new Web pages of the firm. Especially important is that these pages are "genuine" for the entrepreneur. Furthermore, interviewees encourage to treat E-commerce technology open-eyed without any afraid. The technology might be as easy as possible to use for entrepreneurs.

That the assumption is that the entrepreneur produces Web page and supposes that we will do this one suitable for me and hopefully someone else also will like this my perspective. It is one way and surely most of them are doing so. And it is a starting point and from that it will start. But after that it would be do it the other way around, so that it is based on the development feedback from the customers. (F)

I would encourage (entrepreneur) so that it should be start from concrete and deep in that way that when the entrepreneurs might be afraid of tech-

nology and ICT... it will fallen when we start to think about that it is nevertheless so complicated all in all for them who do not know about these (technology) in that way. It should be possible to provide ... to entrepreneurs that: "sign this paper and we will provide for you an E-commerce." In other words it is important to make the threshold as low as possible to start (C)

If the decision is based on about the minds of the 50 years old persons, them it is a big threshold to start the E-commerce. (C)

And it is really big matter, to choose these systems it is really big matter from the point of view of E-commerce development in the future. It gains to investigate very carefully when you are establishing and planning the Web shop. So good to familiarize, that what is the suitable technical platform and solution for my needs and whether we need the co-integration of ERP and E-commerce or not. If we do not need today, what is the situation in the future after five years. Whether it is good to establish ERP, which is integrated with Web shop at same time. These are the details which I will chose now afterward differently, if possibly. (C)

The latter comment shows the importance of integrated technology associated with E-commerce: Enterprise Resource Planning (ERP) might be integrated with E-commerce as soon as possible, then the need for re-engineering the systems of enterprise will be smaller in the future.

Location

E-commerce provides several advantages which are based on the fact that it is mostly location-free activity. This question is very important in scarcely populated Northern Finland. Location is an important reason to establish Web-store among the case study material. Mostly it is possible to interpret as a push –factor, because it is basing on the current "weak" conditions of business. The decision is based on the aim to service customers carefully in scarcely-populated area of Northern Finland. Thus, this discourse is also possible to include in pull-factor "better service for customers" on Table 1, but only partly. In the questionnaire, this factor was missing in the battery of questions.

Well, Web shop is similar to whatever other shop. For example, there is no difference whether you establish a new shop for example in the corner of the municipality of Utsjoki shop, some kinds of special retail shop. It needs placement, production machinery and it needs warehouse. It needs in other words money.(F)

And generally electronic commerce, it enables... At least I think that it is in one form of customer service, I think it is good to have, that those people who like the product, that they have possibility to get them also in other ways as they start to drive it from here. I think that it as a service as more to customer. That if they want, if they like some of the products, so they need not to stop to use it. And it will not mean that you must to drive 500 kilometers and come here to get new but that then you can order it via Web, and easily order. I think that it is as if such an added value for customer. That it has not any disadvantages, either. If you have the energy to update them. Or well, have the energy and have the energy, but I mean that you feel like it. It has nothing else. (E)

DISCUSSION

The general aim of this chapter is to find out the reasons why the small and medium enterprises (SME), especially in Northern Finland, will start E-commerce, that is, why they will enlarge their activities from brick-and-mortar shops towards E-commerce. Furthermore, we focus our consideration on two types of reasons to start E-commerce: push and pull factors: the current conditions of business in brick-and-mortar shops which are

not satisfactory without any remarkable changes and, on the other hand, the attracting possibilities which multi-channel sales and marketing (brick-and-mortar and E-commerce) might provide compared with one-channel sales.

The results of the questionnaire about promoting the factors of E-commerce are mainly parallel with the outcomes of literature review. This chapter completes the outcomes with the interviews of the owners of SMEs from Northern Finland. According to the interviews, literature review and questionnaire, a brick-and-mortal shop, completed with different forms of E-commerce, provides better services for customers. It is even so that entrepreneurs in interviews see the business without Web pages and E-commerce to be incomplete. The business is not credible without E-commerce, which fact is especially one of the push factors of E-commerce. At the same time, E-commerce is tempting because of its several possibilities for services, such as better option with buying channels, after-sales support and service via Web, familiarize with products before buying them from brick-and-mortar shop and possibility to save transportation costs by ordering the product via Web. All of these sub-factors is possible to describe with synergy effect basing on the opportunities of multi-channel strategy. Furthermore, some enterprises among the interviewees notice after-sale participation and services, e.g. in the forms and platforms of social media, the important features of E-commerce (Table 4).

One important pull factor for E-commerce, basing on literature and sample cases, is the possibility to enlarge markets nationally and even internationally. For example according to interviews, most of the enterprises and entrepreneurs emphasize the opportunities to enlarge their markets via Internet pages and E-commerce.

There were also enterprises, which have tight connection with tourism in their business. For them, the branch and its surrounding conditions create a situation, where they have to focus their marketing via Internet pages and to have multi-

Table 4. Push and pull factors of e-commerce basing on literature review (L), questionnaire (Q) and interviews (I)

Push Factors	L	Q	I	Pull Factors	L	Q	I
Pressures from suppliers or other business partners	L			Opportunity to expand and grow	L		
Customers demanding (the deal on the Internet)	L	Q	I	Opening new markets	L	Q	I
Need to increase the value of the business	L			Improving the quality of products and services	L		I
Orders of top management	L			Growing the volume of the business	L		
Industry changes and trends	L		I	Operational support	L		
Threat of competitors taking the business	L	Q		Managerial productivity (ERP, CRM,...)	L		I
Need to keep up with existing competitors	L			Strategic decision aids	L		
Reducing costs and improving efficiencies	L		I	Increasing sales	L	Q	I
External pressure	L			Better services for customers	L	Q	I
Cost savings/Rationalizing	L	Q		More available information and cost savings	L		
Location			I	More appearance and new customers to brick-and mortal		Q	I
The business is not credible without E-commerce			I	Higher productivity		Q	
Demand is coming abroad			I	After-sale participation and services (Social media)			I
				Synergy effect (multi-channel marketing)		Q	I
				Passing intermediary		Q	
				Achievement of competitive advantage		Q	

channel marketing strategy. In other words, that fact that demand is coming from outside the local area is one of the push factors for E-commerce.

One of the push factors of E-commerce, according to the interviews, is the fact that the firms have electric systems in order to coordinate their business, such as ERP, SCM and CRM. These systems are possible to integrate in the flows of products and information coming from E-commerce. Thus, at its best, E-commerce provides synergy effect with these existing systems of enterprise. Furthermore, for example warehouse activities are possible to combine efficiently between E-commerce and brick-and-mortar shops by using these systems, such as ERP and CRM, which have effects on the managerial productivity. However, typically this kind of robust outcome needs several years and long multiform paths for enterprises. Obviously, it is challenging to establish system

which is already initially suitable for the multi-faceted needs of the firm with its multi-channels sales. This possibility is potentially a pull factor, but practically this is not so obvious.

The empirical material of this study has several connection points with the theoretical discussions introduced in the literature review as Table 4 shows. However, empirical analysis reveals some factors which were not so evident in the literature review, such as the importance of location and the general fact that business is not so credible without E-commerce. Both of them are push factors for E-commerce. Furthermore, empirical analysis emphasizes some pull factors, which are not so typical in the literature of E-commerce: possibility to shorten distribution channels by passing intermediaries via E-commerce and the high importance of after-sale participation and services.

CONCLUSION

As a result, this study provides new viewpoints for E-commerce, which fact is based on several reasons:

It provides

- Completed Push-Pull perspective for E-commerce
- New pieces of knowledge about SMES and E-commerce
- Perspectives of SMEs in Northern Finland about E-commerce

Our study shows that it is possible to divide the first steps of E-commerce into two categories:

1. **Pull Factors:** The reasons for E-commerce coming from the current conditions of the business, that is: why is the firm not satisfied the current state of business, which forces to seek new channels, such as E-commerce
2. **Push Factors:** The features of E-commerce, which are so tempting that it attracts enterprises to start E-commerce.

The processes of the firms associated with E-commerce are multifaceted. Some firms have established their Web pages and E-commerce via national or international business chain. This is a relatively easy way to come in E-commerce business. Another example to create E-commerce business is based on long-term learning. This kind of path of E-commerce is long and challenging, but the firms have independent strategy generally and in the context of E-commerce. The latter case suits well in the ideas of learning school and emergent strategy (Mintzberg et al., 1998), which perspective has reflections also in strategy as practice perspective. (See, e.g. Rusko, 2011).

This chapter contains several restrictions and possibilities for further studies. The empirical part of this study is based on questionnaire and six interviews of entrepreneurs in Northern Finland. Although the themes were rather universal associated with E-commerce, this geographical background has effects on the empirical results: for example the role of location proved to be especially important for the respondents. This study revealed the possibility to consider the first steps of E-commerce via division between push- and pull factors. This chapter is only the experiment for this perspective. This theme, focused on this division, provides several possibilities for further studies in the future. Similarly, the practical actions of entrepreneurs and personnel have effects on the E-commerce strategies of the firm. Also, this kind of "strategy-as-practice" perspective provides possibilities for further studies in the field of E-commerce.

ACKNOWLEDGMENT

The authors want to thank the project of Lapland Sales Academy for their support and three anonymous referees of the chapter for their constructive advice.

REFERENCES

AlGhamdi, R., Nguyen, J., Nguyen, A., & Drew, S. (2012). Factors Influencing e-commerce Adoption by Retailers in Saudi Arabia: A quantitative analysis. *International Journal of Electronic Commerce Studies*, 3(1), 83–100.

Aranyossy, M. (2011). *Resource-based Analysis of E-commerce Business Value*. Working paper.

Bhide, M., Deolasee, P., Katkar, A., Panchbudhe, A., Ramamritham, K., & Shenoy, P. (2002). Adaptive Push-Pull: Disseminating dynamic web data. *Computers. IEEE Transactions on*, 51(6), 652–668.

Buhalis, D., & Main, H. (1998). Information technology in peripheral small and medium hospitality enterprises: strategic analysis and critical factors. *International Journal of Contemporary Hospitality Management, 10*(5), 198–202. doi:10.1108/09596119810227811

Drew, S. (2003). Strategic uses of e-commerce by SMEs in the east of England. *European Management Journal, 21*(1), 79–88. doi:10.1016/S0263-2373(02)00148-2

Edgar, B., Doherty, J., & Meert, H. (2004). *Immigration and homelessness in Europe*. Policy Pr.

Eriksson, P., & Kovalainen, A. (2008). Qualitative methods in business research. *Sage (Atlanta, Ga.)*.

Grandon, E. E., & Pearson, J. M. (2004). Electronic commerce adoption: an empirical study of small and medium US businesses. *Information & Management, 42*(1), 197–216. doi:10.1016/j.im.2003.12.010

Klingebiel, R., & De Meyer, A. (2013). Becoming aware of the unknown: decision making during the implementation of a strategic initiative. *Organization Science, 24*(1), 133–153. doi:10.1287/orsc.1110.0726

Koh, J., & Kim, Y. G. (2004). Knowledge sharing in virtual communities: an e-business perspective. *Expert Systems with Applications, 26*(2), 155–166. doi:10.1016/S0957-4174(03)00116-7

Levy, M., & Powell, P. (2003). Exploring SME Internet adoption: towards a contingent model. *Electronic Markets, 13*(2), 173–181. doi:10.1080/1019678032000067163

Mavlanova, T., Benbunan-Fich, R., & Koufaris, M. (2012). Signaling theory and information asymmetry in online commerce. *Information & Management, 49*(5), 240–247. doi:10.1016/j.im.2012.05.004

McGowan, P., Durkin, M. G., Allen, L., Dougan, C., & Nixon, S. (2001). Developing competencies in the entrepreneurial small firm for use of the Internet in the management of customer relationships. *Journal of European Industrial Training, 25*(2/3/4), 126-136.

Mendo, F. A., & Fitzgerald, G. (2005). A multidimensional framework for SME e-business progression. *Journal of Enterprise Information Management, 18*(6), 678–696. doi:10.1108/17410390510628382

Mintzberg, H., Ahlstrand, B. W., & Lampel, J. (1998). *Strategy Safari: the Complete Guide Trough the Wilds of Strategic Management*. London: Financial Times Prentice Hall.

Murillo Viu, J., Romani Fernandez, J., & Surinach Caralt, J. (2008). The impact of heritage tourism on an urban economy: the case of Granada and the Alhambra. *Tourism Economics, 14*(2), 361–376. doi:10.5367/000000008784460481

Neslin, S. A., Grewal, D., Leghorn, R., Shankar, V., Teerling, M. L., Thomas, J. S., & Verhoef, P. C. (2006). Challenges and opportunities in multichannel customer management. *Journal of Service Research, 9*(2), 95–112. doi:10.1177/1094670506293559

Qian, H., Haynes, K. E., & Riggle, J. D. (2011). Incubation push or business pull? Investigating the geography of US business incubators. *Economic Development Quarterly, 25*(1), 79–90. doi:10.1177/0891242410383275

Rao, S. S., Metts, G., & Monge, C. A. M. (2003). Electronic commerce development in small and medium sized enterprises: A stage model and its implications. *Business Process Management Journal, 9*(1), 11–32. doi:10.1108/14637150310461378

Rusko, R. (2011). Virtual Business Incubations: An Alternative Way to Develop and Service Peripheral Areas. [IJIDE]. *International Journal of Innovation in the Digital Economy*, 2(3), 48–64. doi:10.4018/jide.2011070104

Rusko, R. (2012). Strategic Processes and Turning Points in ICT Business: Case Nokia. [IJIDE]. *International Journal of Innovation in the Digital Economy*, 3(3), 25–34. doi:10.4018/jide.2012070103

Schwenk, C. R. (1984). Cognitive simplification processes in strategic decision-making. *Strategic Management Journal*, 5(2), 111–128. doi:10.1002/smj.4250050203

Shrivastava, P., & Grant, J. H. (1985). Empirically derived models of strategic decision-making processes. *Strategic Management Journal*, 6(2), 97–113. doi:10.1002/smj.4250060202

Singer, A., Hardwick, S. W., & Brettell, C. B. (2009). *Twenty-first century gateways: Immigrant incorporation in suburban America*. Brookings Institution Press.

Tata, R. J. (1977). Uruguay: Population geography of a troubled welfare state. *The Journal of Geography*, 76(2), 46–51. doi:10.1080/00221347708980880

Yang, D.-J., Chou, D.-H., & Liu, J. (2012). A Study of Key Success Factors when Applying E-commerce to the Travel Industry. *International Journal of Business and Social Science*, 3(8), 114–119.

Yin, R. K. (2003). *Case study research: Design and methods* (Vol. 5). Sage.

Zhang, J., Farris, P. W., Irvin, J. W., Kushwaha, T., Steenburgh, T. J., & Weitz, B. A. (2010). Crafting integrated multichannel retailing strategies. *Journal of Interactive Marketing*, 24(2), 168–180. doi:10.1016/j.intmar.2010.02.002

ADDITIONAL READING

Amorós, J. E., Fernández, C., & Tapia, J. (2012). Quantifying the relationship between entrepreneurship and competitiveness development stages in Latin America. *The International Entrepreneurship and Management Journal*, 8(3), 249–270. doi:10.1007/s11365-010-0165-9

Anderson, R., Wielicki, T., & Anderson, L. (2010). Barriers to Application of E-learning in Training Activities of SMEs. *International Journal on E-Learning*, 9(2), 159–167.

Applegate, L. M. (2001). Emerging e-business-models. *Harvard Business Review*, 79(1), 79–87. PMID:11189465

Applegate, L. M., Austin, R. D., & McFarlan, F. W. (2003). *Corporate information strategy and management* (6th ed.). New York: McGraw Hill.

Applegate, L. M., Austin, R. D., & Soule, D. L. (2009). *Corporate information strategy and management* (8th ed.). Burr Ridge, IL: McGraw-Hill/Irwin.

Ashurst, C., Cragg, P., & Herring, P. (2012). The role of IT competences in gaining value from e-business: An SME case study. *International Small Business Journal*, 30(6), 640–658. doi:10.1177/0266242610375703

Baviera-Puig, A., Buitrago-Vera, J., & Mas-Verdú, F. (2012). Trade areas and knowledge-intensive services: The case of a technology centre. *Management Decision*, 50(8), 1412–1424. doi:10.1108/00251741211262006

Bellman, S., Potter, R. F., Treleaven-Hassard, S., Robinson, J. A., & Varan, D. (2011). The effectiveness of branded mobile phone apps. *Journal of Interactive Marketing*, 25, 191–200. doi:10.1016/j.intmar.2011.06.001

Buhalis, D., & Law, R. (2008). Progress in information technology and tourism management: 20 years on and 10 years after the Internet–the state of eTourism research. *Tourism Management, 29*(4), 609–623. doi:10.1016/j.tourman.2008.01.005

Buhalis, D., & Licata, M. C. (2002). The future etourism intermediaries. *Tourism Management, 23*(3), 207–220. doi:10.1016/S0261-5177(01)00085-1

Caskey, K., & Subirana, B. (2010). Supporting SME e-commerce migration through blended e-learning. *Journal of Small Business and Enterprise Development, 14*(4), 670–688. doi:10.1108/14626000710832767

Cavalcante, S., Kesting, P., & Ulhøi, J. (2011). Business model dynamics and innovation:(Re) establishing the missing linkages. *Management Decision, 49*(8), 1327–1342. doi:10.1108/00251741111163142

Daniel, N. E. (2011). *The effective measurement of SME e-commerce performance in the Western Cape* (Doctoral dissertation, University of Technology).

Deakins, D., & Frese, M. (1998). Entrepreneurial learning and the growth process in SMEs. *The Learning Organization, 5*(3), 144–155. doi:10.1108/09696479810223428

Dubosson-Torbay, M., Osterwalder, A., & Pigneur, Y. (2001). E-businessmodel design, classification and measurements. *Thunderbird International Business Review, 44*(1), 5–23. doi:10.1002/tie.1036

Eisenmann, T. R. (2002). *Internet business models: Text and cases.* New York: Irwin/McGraw-Hill.

Eriksson, L. T., Hultman, J., & Naldi, L. (2008). Small business e-commerce development in Sweden–an empirical survey. *Journal of Small Business and Enterprise Development, 15*(3), 555–570. doi:10.1108/14626000810892346

Fuchs, M., Scholochov, C., & Höpken, W. (2009). E-Business adoption, use and value creation: An Austrian hotel study. *Information Technology & Tourism, 11*(4), 267–284. doi:10.3727/109830510X12670455864168

Gilmore, A., Gallagher, D., & Henry, S. (2007). E-marketing and SMEs: Operational lessons for the future. *European Business Review, 19*(3), 234–247. doi:10.1108/09555340710746482

Goffee, R., & Scase, R. (1995). *Corporate realities: The dynamics of large and small organizations.* London: Routledge.

Gorling, S., & Rehn, A. (2008). Accidental ventures – A materialist reading of opportunity and entrepreneurial potential. *Scandinavian Journal of Management, 24*, 94–102. doi:10.1016/j.scaman.2008.03.001

Grizelj, F. (2003). Collaborative knowledge management in virtual service companies–approach for tourism destinations. *Tourism, 51*(4), 371–385.

Huarng, K.-H. (2011). A comparative study to classify ICT developments by economies. *Journal of Business Research, 64*(11), 1174–1177. doi:10.1016/j.jbusres.2011.06.018

Huarng, K.-H., & Yu, T. H.-K. (2011a). Internet software and services: Past and future. *Service Industries Journal, 31*(1), 79–89. doi:10.1080/02642069.2010.485193

Huarng, K.-H., & Yu, T. H.-K. (2011b). Entrepreneurship, process innovation and value creation by a non-profit SME. *Management Decision, 49*(2), 284–296. doi:10.1108/00251741111109160

Ivanov, D. (2012). *The impact of e-commerce on small-size companies in Sweden* (Doctoral dissertation, Karlstad University).

Javalgi, R. G., Todd, P. R., Johnston, W. J., & Granot, E. (2012). Entrepreneurship, muddling through, and Indian Internet-enabled SMEs. *Journal of Business Research, 65*, 740–744. doi:10.1016/j.jbusres.2010.12.010

Kelliher, F., Foley, A., & Frampton, A. (2009). Facilitating small firm learning networks in the Irish tourism sector. *Tourism & Hospitality Research, 9*(1), 80–95. doi:10.1057/thr.2008.36

Kim, S.-H., & Huarng, K.-H. (2011). Winning strategies for innovation and high-technology products management. *Journal of Business Research, 64*(11), 1147–1150. doi:10.1016/j.jbusres.2011.06.013

Kuttainen, C., & Lexhagen, M. (2011). Overcoming Barriers to Sme E-Commerce Adoption using Blended Learning: A Swedish Action Research Case Study. *Information Technology & Tourism, 13*(1), 13–26. doi:10.3727/109830511X13167968595660

Laudon, K. C., & Traver, C. G. (2011). *E-Commerce 2011: Business, technology* (7th ed.). New York, NY: Pearson.

Lawrence, J. E. (2011). The Growth of E-Commerce in Developing Countries: An Exploratory Study of Opportunities and Challenges for SMEs. [IJICTRDA]. *International Journal of ICT Research and Development in Africa, 2*(1), 15–28. doi:10.4018/jictrda.2011010102

Machfud, A. K., & Kartiwi, M. (2013, March). E-commerce adoption by Indonesian small agribusiness: Reconsidering the innovation-decision process model. In *Information and Communication Technology for the Muslim World (ICT4M), 2013 5th International Conference on* (pp. 1-6). IEEE.

Mariotti, S. (2006). *Entrepreneurship: Starting and operating a new business, Pearson education.* Upper Saddle Rivers, NJ: Pearson Education, Inc.

Mason, K., & Spring, M. (2011). The sites and practices of business models. *Industrial Marketing Management, 40*(6), 1032–1041. doi:10.1016/j.indmarman.2011.06.032

Meyer, M. H., & Crane, F. G. (2010). *Entrepreneurship: An innovator's guide to startups and corporate ventures.* Thousand Oaks, CA: SAGE Publication Inc.

Mohapatra, S. (2013). Sustainability in E-Commerce Adoption in Small and Medium Enterprises (SMEs), A Case Study in Odisha, India. [IJGC]. *International Journal of Green Computing, 4*(2), 12–23. doi:10.4018/jgc.2013070102

Morris, M., Schindehutte, M., & Allen, J. (2005). The entrepreneur's business model: Toward a unified perspective. *Journal of Business Research, 58*, 726–735. doi:10.1016/j.jbusres.2003.11.001

Petrovic, O., Kittl, C., & Teksten, R. D. (2001). *Developing business models for e-business.* Vienna: International Electronic Commerce Conference.

Rayport, J. F., & Jaworski, B. J. (2001). *E-commerce.* New York: McGraw-Hill/Irwin.

Ribeiro, D., & Montoro-Sánchez, M. Á. (2011b). Introduction: The challenges of defining and studying contemporary entrepreneurship. *Canadian Journal of Administrative Sciences, 28*, 297–301. doi:10.1002/cjas.217

Sawhney, M., Wolcott, R. C., & Arroniz, I. (2006). The 12 different ways for companies to innovate. MIT. *Sloan Management Review, 47*(3), 75–81.

Shane, S. (2003). *A general theory of entrepreneurship: The individual-opportunity nexus.* Northampton, MA: Edward Elgar. doi:10.4337/9781781007990

Siegel, D. S., & Renko, M. (2012). The role of market and technological knowledge in recognizing entrepreneurial opportunities. *Management Decision, 50*(5), 797–816. doi:10.1108/00251741211227500

Stockdale, R., & Standing, C. (2006). A classification model to support SME e-commerce adoption initiatives. *Journal of Small Business and Enterprise Development*, *13*(3), 381–394. doi:10.1108/14626000610680262

Todd, P., & Javalgi, R. (2007). Internationalization of SMEs in India: Fostering entrepreneurship by leveraging information technology. *International Journal of Emerging Markets*, *2*(2), 166–180. doi:10.1108/17468800710739234

Trimi, S., & Berbegal-Mirabent, J. (2012). Business model innovation in entrepreneurship. *The International Entrepreneurship and Management Journal*, *8*(4), 449–465. doi:10.1007/s11365-012-0234-3

Vesper, K. H. (1994). *New venture experience*. Seattle, WA: Vector Books.

Wielki, J. (2010). The impact of the Internet on the development of web-based business models. *Journal of Internet Banking and Commerce*, *15*(3), 1–9.

Zucchella, A., & Hagen, B. (2012). The International Growth of e-Commerce Ventures. *International Business: New Challenges, New Forms. New Perspectives*, *19*, 137.

KEY TERMS AND DEFINITIONS

Brick-and-Mortar Shop: Traditional shop where the customers have possibility to buy products and services.

E-Commerce: Commercial activities associated with Internet or Web-based platforms in different forms.

Emergent Strategy: Strategy, which is not actually planned. Emergent strategy is part of the "learning school" among the strategy schools.

ERP: Enterprise resource planning.

Push-Pull Effect: Factors which push from the initial state towards better opportunities and factors which pull because of their attractive characteristics towards the future state of business.

SCM: Supply chain management.

SMEs: Small and medium sized enterprises.

Compilation of References

Aaker, D. A. (1996). *Building Strong Brands*. Free Press.

Aaker, D. A. (2004). *Brand Portfolio Strategy: Creating Relevance, Differentiation, Energy, Leverage and Clarity*. Free Press.

Aaker, D. A. (2004a). Leveraging the Corporate Brand. *California Management Review*, *46*(3), 6–18. doi:10.2307/41166218

Aaker, D. A. (2007). Innovation: Brand it or lose it. *California Management Review*, *50*(1), 8–24. doi:10.2307/41166414

Aaker, D. A. (2009). *Strategic Market Management*. New York: Wiley.

Aaker, D. A., & Keller, K. L. (1990). Consumer evaluation of brand extensions. *Journal of Marketing*, *54*(1), 27–41. doi:10.2307/1252171

Aaker, D. A., Kumar, V., & Day, G. S. (2001). *Marketing Research* (7th ed.). New York: John Wiley and Sons.

Aaker, J. (1997). Dimensions of brand personality. *JMR, Journal of Marketing Research*, *34*(3), 347–356. doi:10.2307/3151897

Aberdeen Group. (2011). *State of multi-channel retail marketing: a paradigm shift for reaching new customers*. Retrieved from http://www.aberdeen.com

Abrams, D. (2005, September 6). You're considered old when you reach 49. *Evening Standard*.

Abrams, D., Russell, P. S., Vouclair, C.-M., & Swift, H. (2011). Ageism in Europe – Findings from the European Social Survey. *European Research Group on Attitudes to Age Report*. Retrieved November 30th, 2013, from http://www.ageuk.org.uk/Documents/EN-GB/For-professionals/ageism_across_europe_report_interactive.pdf?dtrk=true

Adams, S. J. (2004). Age discrimination legislation and the employment of older workers. *Labour Economics*, *11*, 219–241. doi:10.1016/j.labeco.2003.06.001

Agergaard, E., Olsen, P. A., & Allpass, J. (1970). The interaction between retailing and the urban center structure: A theory of spiral movement. *Environment and Planning*, *2*, 55–71. doi:10.1068/a020055

Agrawal, R. (2009). Threat of a me too perception: a case of Café Coffee Day. *The Marketing Review*, *9*(3), 251–271. doi:10.1362/146934709X467811

Aguirre-Rodriguez, A., Bosnjak, M., & Sirgy, J. M. (2012). Moderators of the self-congruity effect on consumer decision-making: a meta-analysis. *Journal of Business Research*, *65*, 1179–1188. doi:10.1016/j.jbusres.2011.07.031

Ahearne, M., Bhattacharya, C. B., & Gruen, T. (2005). Antecedents and consequences of customer– company identification: expanding the role of relationship marketing. *The Journal of Applied Psychology*, *90*, 574–585. doi:10.1037/0021-9010.90.3.574 PMID:15910151

Ahmed, P. K., & Machold, S. (2004). The quality and ethics connection: toward virtuous organizations. *Total Quality Management & Business Excellence*, *15*(4), 527–545. doi:10.1080/1478336042000183604

Aiello, A. Jr, Czepiel, J. A., & Rosenberg, L. J. (1977). Scaling the heights of consumer satisfaction: an evaluation of alternative measures. In R. Day (Ed.), *Consumer satisfaction, dissatisfaction, and complaint behavior* (pp. 43–50). Bloomington, IN: Indiana University School of Business.

Ailawadi, K. L., & Harlam, B. (2004). An empirical analysis of the determinants of retail margins: the role of store brand share. *Journal of Marketing*, *68*(1), 147–166. doi:10.1509/jmkg.68.1.147.24027

Ailawadi, K. L., Neslin, S. A., & Gedenk, K. (2001). Pursuing the value-conscious consumer: store brands versus national brand promotions. *Journal of Marketing*, 65(1), 71–89. doi:10.1509/jmkg.65.1.71.18132

Ailawadi, K., Pauwels, K., & Steenkamp, J.-B. (2008). Private-label use and store loyalty. *Journal of Marketing*, 72(6), 19–30. doi:10.1509/jmkg.72.6.19

Akerlof, G., & Shiller, R. (2009). *Animal Spirit: How Human Psychology Drives the Economy, and Why It Matters for Global Capitalism*. Princeton University Press.

Albanese, P. J. (1988). The intimate relations of the consistent consumer: Psychoanalytic object relations theory applied to economics. In P. J. Albanese (Ed.), *Psychological foundations of economic behavior* (pp. 59–79). New York: Praeger.

Alexandru, P. N., & Cristian, D. D. (2008). Tendencies of internationalization in retailing. *The Journal of the Faculty of Economics*, 4(1), 1099–1105.

AlGhamdi, R., Nguyen, J., Nguyen, A., & Drew, S. (2012). Factors Influencing e-commerce Adoption by Retailers in Saudi Arabia: A quantitative analysis. *International Journal of Electronic Commerce Studies*, 3(1), 83–100.

Aliawadi, K. L., & Keller, K. L. (2004). Understanding retail branding: conceptual insights and research priorities. *Journal of Retailing*, 80, 331–342. doi:10.1016/j.jretai.2004.10.008

Allen, J., & Root, J. (2004, September 7). The new brand tax. *Wall Street Journal*.

Alpert, J. I., Alpert, M. I., & Maltz, E. N. (2005). Purchase occasion influence on the role of music in advertising. *Journal of Business Research*, 58(3), 369–376. doi:10.1016/S0148-2963(03)00101-2

Altis, I. (2006). *CSR Manager within Italian companies*. Third Report on Corporate Social Responsibility in Italy.

Altman, B. W. (1998). Corporate Community Relations in the 1990s: A Study of Transformation. *Business & Society*, 37(2), 221–227. doi:10.1177/000765039803700205

Altmann, M. (2007). *Coffee Shop Industry – A Strategic Analysis. Scholarly Research Paper Katz-Graduate School of Business Pittsburgh/USA Doc. N. V111348*. Retrieved August 19, 2013, from http://www.grin.com

Amato, L. H., & Amato, C. H. (2012). Retail Philanthropy: Firm Size, Industry, and Business Cycle. *Journal of Business Ethics*, 1(7), 435–448. doi:10.1007/s10551-011-1048-x

Amodio, L. V. (1998). Mood makers: an in-depth look at how scents claim to boost your spirit and de-stress your nerves. *Good Housekeeping (New York, N.Y.)*, 227(5), 53–55.

Anderson, P. (1986). Personality, perceptions and emotion-state factors in approach-avoidance behaviours in the store environment. In *Proceedings of AMA*, (pp. 35-39). Chicago: American Marketing Association.

Anderson, J. C., & Gerbing, D. W. (1988). Structural equation modelling in practice: a review and recommended two-step approach. *Psychological Bulletin*, 103, 411–423. doi:10.1037/0033-2909.103.3.411

Andersson, T. D., & Mossberg, L. (2004). The dining experience: do restaurants satisfy customer needs? *Food Service Technology*, 4(4), 171–177. doi:10.1111/j.1471-5740.2004.00105.x

Andrade, C. F., Palmeira, M., & Kato, H. T. (2010). Private Brands and Brazilian Supermarkets. In *Proceedings of British Academy of Management Conference*. Sheffield, UK: BAM.

Andrade, E. B., Kaltcheva, V., & Weitz, B. (2002). Self-Disclosure on the Web: The Impact of Privacy Policy, Reward and Company Reputation. *Advances in Consumer Research. Association for Consumer Research (U. S.)*, 29(1), 350–353.

Andreassen, T. W., & Olsen, L. L. (2012). Customer Service: Does It Matter? In J. Kandampully (Ed.), *Service Management: The New Paradigm in Retailing*. New York: Springer. doi:10.1007/978-1-4614-1554-1_3

Andreini, D. (2012). I fattori esogeni ed endogeni influenti sulle strategie di integrazione multicanale: un'analisi nel retailing in Europa. *Mercati e Competitività*, 3, 13–31.

Andreu, L., Sanchez, I., & Mele, C. (2010). Value co-creation among retailers and consumers: new insights into the furniture market. *Journal of Retailing and Consumer Services*, 17(4), 241–250. doi:10.1016/j.jretconser.2010.02.001

Andrews, F. M., & Withey, S. B. (1976). *Social indicators of well-being: America's perception of life quality.* New York, NY: Plenum Press. doi:10.1007/978-1-4684-2253-5

Andzulis, J., Panagopoulos, N. G., & Rapp, A. (2012). A review of Social Media and implications for the sale process. *Journal of Personal Selling & Sales Management, 3,* 305–316. doi:10.2753/PSS0885-3134320302

Ang, S. H. (2001). Personality Influences on Consumption: Insight from the Asian Economic Crisis. *Journal of International Consumer Marketing, 13*(1), 5–21. doi:10.1300/J046v13n01_02

Ang, S. H., Leong, S. M., & Kotler, P. (2000). The Asian apocalypse: crisis marketing. *Long Range Planning, 33*(1), 97–119. doi:10.1016/S0024-6301(99)00100-4

Anitsal, I., & Anitsal, M. M. (2011). Emergence of Entrepreneurial Retail Forms. *Academy of Entrepreneurship Journal, 17*(2), 1–17.

Annett, J. (1996). Olfactory memory: A case study in cognitive psychology. *The Journal of Psychology, 130*(3), 309–319. doi:10.1080/00223980.1996.9915012 PMID:8667286

Anon. (2013a). European Consumers Want Choices and Convenience When Shopping Online. *ComScore.* Retrieved October 27, 2013, from http://pressroom.ups.com/Press+Releases/Current+Press+Releases/ci.European+Consumers+Want+Choices+And+Convenience+When+Shopping+Online.print

Anon. (2013b). Majority care about high street decline, but parking prevents use. *AMT.* Retrieved October 27, 2013, from http://towns.org.uk/2013/06/10/majority-care-about-high-street-decline-but-parking-prevents-use/

Ansari, S., & Phillips. (2011). Text me! New consumer practices and change in organizational fields. *Organization Science, 22*(6), 1579–1599. doi:10.1287/orsc.1100.0595

Anselmsson, J., & Johansson, U. (2007). Corporate social responsibility and the positioning of grocery brands. *International Journal of Retail and Distribution Management, 35*(10), 835–856. doi:10.1108/09590550710820702

Anselmsson, J., & Johansson, U. (2009). Retailer brands and the impact on innovativeness in the grocery market. *Journal of Marketing Management, 25*(1-2), 75–95. doi:10.1362/026725709X410043

Apelbaum, E., Gerstner, E., & Naik, P. A. (2003). The Effects of Expert Quality Evaluations Versus Brand Name on Price Premiums. *Journal of Product and Brand Management, 12*(2–3), 154–165. doi:10.1108/10610420310476915

Aranyossy, M. (2011). *Resource-based Analysis of E-commerce Business Value.* Working paper.

Areni, C. S., & Kim, D. (1993). The Influence of Background Music on Shopping Behavior: Classical Versus Top-Forty Music in a Wine Store. *Advances in Consumer Research. Association for Consumer Research (U. S.), 20,* 336–340.

Areni, C. S., & Kim, D. (1994). The influence of in-store lighting on consumers' examination of merchandise in a wine store. *International Journal of Research in Marketing, 11*(2), 117–125. doi:10.1016/0167-8116(94)90023-X

Arnett, D. B., German, S. D., & Hunt, S. D. (2003). The identity salience model of relationship marketing success: the case of nonprofit marketing. *Journal of Marketing, 67*(2), 89–105. doi:10.1509/jmkg.67.2.89.18614

Arnett, D. B., Laverie, D. A., & Meiers, A. (2003). Developing parsimonious retailer equity indexes using partial least squares analysis: a method and applications. *Journal of Retailing, 79,* 161–170. doi:10.1016/S0022-4359(03)00036-8

Arnold, M. J., & Reynolds, K. E. (2003). Hedonic shopping motivations. *Journal of Retailing, 79*(2), 77–95. doi:10.1016/S0022-4359(03)00007-1

Arnold, M. J., & Reynolds, K. E. (2012). Approach and avoidance motivation: Investigating hedonic consumption in a retail setting. *Journal of Retailing, 88*(3), 399–411. doi:10.1016/j.jretai.2011.12.004

Arnold, M. J., Reynolds, K. E., Ponder, N., & Lueg, J. E. (2005). Customer delight in a retail context: Investigating delightful and terrible shopping experience. *Journal of Business Research, 58,* 1132–1145. doi:10.1016/j.jbusres.2004.01.006

Arnould, E. J., & Price, L. L. (1993). River magic: Extraordinary Experience and the extended service encounter. *The Journal of Consumer Research, 20*(1), 24–45. doi:10.1086/209331

Arnould, E. J., & Price, L. L. (2000). Authenticating Acts and Authoritative Performances: Questing for Self and Community. In D. G. Mick, S. Ratneshwar, & C. Huffman (Eds.), *The Why of Consumption: Contemporary Perspectives on Consumer Motives, Goals and Desires* (pp. 140–163). London: Routledge.

Arnould, E. J., Price, L. L., & Tierney, P. (1998). Communicative staging of the Wilderness serviceescape. *The Service Industries Journal*, *18*(3), 90–115. doi:10.1080/02642069800000034

Arnould, E. J., & Thompson, C. J. (2005). Consumer Culture Theory (Cct), Twenty Years of Research. *The Journal of Consumer Research*, *31*(4), 868–882. doi:10.1086/426626

ASSIFERO. (2010). *La filantropia istituzionale in Italia. Le fondazioni private di erogazione: Crescita e Ruolo* [Institutional Philanthropy in Italy. Private Foundations: Development and Role] Report.

Atinc, M., & Walton, M. (1998). *Social Consequences of the East Asian Financial Crisis.* Retrieved Jun 16, 2013, from http://citeseerx.ist.psu.edu/viewdoc/download?doi=10.1.1.198.2871&rep=rep1&type=pdf

Avinash, K. (2009). *Web Analytics 2.0: The Art of Online Accountability and Science of Customer Centricity.* Indianapolis, IN: Wiley Publishing, Inc.

Azevedo, S. G., & Carvalho, H. (2012). Contribution of RFId Technology to Better Management of Fashion Supply Chains. *International Journal of Retail & Distribution Management*, *40*(2), 128–156. doi:10.1108/09590551211201874

Babakus, E., Bienstock, C. C., & Van Scotter, J. R. (2004). Linking Perceived Quality and Customer Satisfaction to Store Traffic and Revenue Growth. *Decision Sciences*, *35*(4), 713–737. doi:10.1111/j.1540-5915.2004.02671.x

Babin, B. J., & Attaway, J. S. (2000). Atmospheric affect as a tool for creating value and gaining share of customer. *Journal of Business Research*, *49*, 91–99. doi:10.1016/S0148-2963(99)00011-9

Babin, B. J., & Darden, R. D. (1995). Consumer Self-Regulation in a Retail Environment. *Journal of Retailing*, *71*(1), 47–70. doi:10.1016/0022-4359(95)90012-8

Babin, B. J., Hardesty, D. M., & Suter, T. A. (2003). Colour and shopping intentions: The intervening effect of price pairness and perceived affect. *Journal of Business Research*, *56*, 541–551. doi:10.1016/S0148-2963(01)00246-6

Babin, B., Darden, W., & Griffin, M. (1994). Work and/or fun: Measuring hedonic and utilitarian shopping value. *The Journal of Consumer Research*, *20*(4), 644–656. doi:10.1086/209376

Baccarani, C., Ugolini, M., & Bonfanti, A. (2010). *A Conceptual Service Quality Map: The Value of a Wide Opened Perspective.* Paper presented at the Organizational Excellence in Service, 13th Toulon-Verona Conference. Coimbra, Portugal.

Backstrom, K. (2006). Understanding recreational shopping: A new approach. *International Review of Retail, Distribution and Consumer Research*, *16*(2), 143–158. doi:10.1080/09593960600572167

Bäckström, K., & Johansson, U. (2006). Creating and Consuming Experiences in Retail Store Environments: Comparing Retailer and Consumer Perspectives. *Journal of Retailing and Consumer Services*, *13*(6), 417–430. doi:10.1016/j.jretconser.2006.02.005

Badrinarayanan, V., Becerra, E. P., Kim, C. H., & Madhavaram, S. (2012). Transference and congruence effects on purchase intentions in online stores of multi-channel retailers: initial evidence from the US and South Korea. *Journal of the Academy of Marketing Science*, *40*(4), 539–557. doi:10.1007/s11747-010-0239-9

Baer, J. (2010). Operationalizing in 2010. *Marketing in 2010: Social Media Becomes Operational.* Retrieved August 2013, from http://conversationagent.typepad.com/Marketingin2010.pdf

Bagdare, S. (2012). Managing Employee Effectiveness for Retail Customer Experience. *Asia Pacific Marketing Review*, *1*(1), 98–106.

Bagozzi, R. P. (1980). *Causal Models in Marketing.* New York: Wiley.

Bagozzi, R. P. (1992). The self-regulation of attitudes, intentions, and behavior. *Social Psychology Quarterly*, *55*(2), 178–204. doi:10.2307/2786945

Bagozzi, R. P., Bergami, M., Marzocchi, G., & Morandin, G. (2012). Customer–organization relationships: Development and test of a theory of extended identities. *The Journal of Applied Psychology, 97*(1), 63–76. doi:10.1037/a0024533 PMID:21766998

Bagozzi, R. P., & Yi, Y. (1988). On the evaluation of structural equation models. *Journal of the Academy of Marketing Science, 16*(1), 74–94. doi:10.1007/BF02723327

Bailey, N., & Areni, C. S. (2006). When a few minutes sound like a lifetime: Does atmospheric music expand or contract perceived time? *Journal of Retailing, 82*(3), 189–202. doi:10.1016/j.jretai.2006.05.003

Baker, J. (1987). The Role of the Environment in the Marketing Service: The Consumer Perspective. In J. A. Czepiel, C. A. Congram, & J. Shanahan (Eds.), *The Services Challenge: Integrating for Competitive Advantage* (pp. 79–84). Chicago: American Marketing Association.

Baker, J., Grewal, D., & Parasuraman, A. (1994). The Influence of Store Environment on Quality Inferences and Store Image. *Journal of the Academy of Marketing Science, 22*(4), 328–339. doi:10.1177/0092070394224002

Baker, J., Levy, M., & Grewal, D. (1992). An Experimental Approach to Making Retail Store Environmental Decisions. *Journal of Retailing, 68*(4), 445–460.

Baker, J., Parasuraman, A., Grewal, D., & Voss, G. B. (2002). The influence of multiple store environment cues on perceived merchandise value and patronage intentions. *Journal of Marketing, 66*(2), 120–141. doi:10.1509/jmkg.66.2.120.18470

Baker, M. J. (2000). Writing a literature review. *The Marketing Review, 1*, 219–247. doi:10.1362/1469347002529189

Baker, R. G. (1965). Explorations in Ecological Psychology. *The American Psychologist, 20*(1), 1–14. doi:10.1037/h0021697 PMID:14251988

Baker, W. (1990). Market networks and corporate behavior. *American Journal of Sociology, 96*(3), 589–625. doi:10.1086/229573

Balasubramanian, S. R., & Raghunathan, V., & Mahajan. (2005). Consumers in a multichannel environment: product utility, process utility, and channel choice. *Journal of Interactive Marketing, 19*(2), 12–15. doi:10.1002/dir.20032

Baldinger, A. L., & Ruben, J. (1996). Brand loyalty: The link between attitude and behaviour. *Journal of Advertising Research, 36*(2), 22–34.

Ballantine, P. W., & Creery, S. (2010). The Consumption and Disposition Behaviour of Voluntary Simplifiers. *Journal of Consumer Behaviour, 9*(1), 45–56. doi:10.1002/cb.302

Ballantyne, D. (2004). Dialogue and its role in the development of relationship specific knowledge. *Journal of Business and Industrial Marketing, 19*(2), 114–123. doi:10.1108/08858620410523990

Balmer, J. M. T. (2008). Identity based views of the corporation: Insights from corporate identity, organisational identity, social identity, visual identity, corporate brand identity and corporate image. *European Journal of Marketing, 42*(9/10), 879–906. doi:10.1108/03090560810891055

Baltas, G. (1997). Determinants of store brand choice: a behavioral analysis. *Journal of Product and Brand Management, 6*(5), 315–324. doi:10.1108/10610429710179480

Baltas, G., & Argouslidis, P. C. (2007). Consumer characteristics and demand for store brands. *International Journal of Retail & Distribution Management, 35*(5), 328–341. doi:10.1108/09590550710743708

Baltas, G., Doyle, P., & Dyson, P. (1997). A model of consumer choice for national vs store brands. *The Journal of the Operational Research Society, 48*(10), 988–995. doi:10.1057/palgrave.jors.2600454

Bamfield, J. A. N. (2012). *Shopping and crime.* New York: Palgrave Macmillan. doi:10.1057/9780230393554

Bamfield, J. A. N. (2013). *Retail futures 2018: Shop numbers, online and the High Street, A guide to retailing in 2018.* Nottingham, UK: Centre for Retail Research.

Banat, A., & Wandebori, H. (2012). Store Design and Store Atmosphere Effect on Customer Sales per Visit. In *Proceedings of Planetary Scientific Research Center Proceeding of the 2nd International Conference on Business, Economics, Management and Behavioural Sciences.* Retrieved June 30, 2013, from http://psrcentre.org/images/extraimages/1012545.pdf

Barefoot, D., & Szabo, J. (2010). *Friends with Benefits: A Social Media Marketing Handbook.* San Francisco, CA: No Starch Press, Inc.

Barile, S., & Pastore, A. (2002). Forme, caratteri e divenire sistemico dei rapporti con la distribuzione ed il consumo. In G. M. Golinelli (Ed.), L'approccio sistemico al governo dell'impresa, (vol. 3, pp. 187-225). Padova, Italy: Cedam.

Barile, S., & Saviano, M. (2010). *S-DL, VSA and SS – Highlighting Convergences.* Paper presented at the International CooperLink Workshop the emerging Perspective of Service Science for Management and Marketing Studies. Naples, Italy.

Barile, S. (1996). *Le formule di distribuzione al dettaglio.* Padova, Italy: Cedam.

Barile, S. (2000). *Contributi sul pensiero sistemico in Economia d'Impresa.* Salerno, Italy: Arnia.

Barile, S. (2008). *L'impresa come sistema: Contributi sull'Approccio Sistemico Vitale (ASv)* (2nd ed.). Torino, Italy: Giappichelli.

Barile, S. (2009). *Management sistemico vitale.* Torino, Italy: Giappichelli.

Barile, S., Montella, M., & Saviano, M. (2012). A Service-Based Systems View of Cultural Heritage. *Journal of Business Market Management, 5*(2), 106–136.

Barile, S., Pels, J., Polese, F., & Saviano, M. (2012). An Introduction to the Viable Systems Approach and its Contribution to Marketing. *Journal of Business Market Management, 5*(2), 54–78.

Barile, S., & Polese, F. (2010). Linking the viable system and many-to-many network approaches to service-dominant logic and service science. *International Journal of Quality and Service Science, 2*(1), 23–42. doi:10.1108/17566691011026586

Barile, S., & Saviano, M. (2011). Foundations of systems thinking: the structure-system paradigm. In *Contributions to theoretical and practical advances in management: A Viable Systems Approach (VSA)* (pp. 1–26). Avellino, Italy: International Printing.

Barile, S., & Saviano, M. (2012). Oltre la partnership: un cambiamento di prospettiva. In S. Esposito De Falco, & C. Gatti (Eds.), *La consonanza nel governo dell'impresa: Profili teorici e applicazioni.* Milano, Italy: Franco Angeli.

Barile, S., Saviano, M., Polese, F., & Di Nauta, P. (2012). Reflections on Service Systems Boundaries: A Viable Systems Perspective: The case of the London Borough of Sutton. *European Journal of Management, 30,* 451–465. doi:10.1016/j.emj.2012.05.004

Barile, S., Saviano, M., Polese, F., & Di Nauta, P. (2013). Il rapporto impresa-territorio tra efficienza locale, Efficacia di contesto e sostenibilità ambientale. *Sinergie, 90,* 25–49.

Barnes, J. G. (2003). Establishing meaningful customer relationships: why some companies and brands mean more to their customers. *Managing Service Quality, 13*(3), 178–186. doi:10.1108/09604520310476445

Barnes, J. G., & Wright, J. W. (2012). A Framework for Applying Customer Insight and Context to the Development of a Shopping Experience Strategy. In J. Kandampully (Ed.), *Service Management: The New Paradigm in Retailing* (pp. 43–65). New York: Springer. doi:10.1007/978-1-4614-1554-1_4

Barnes, L., & Lea-Greenwood, G. (2006). Fast fashioning the supply chain: shaping the research agenda. *Journal of Fashion Marketing and Management, 10*(3), 259–271. doi:10.1108/13612020610679259

Barone, M. J., Norman, A. T., & Miyazaki, A. D. (2007). Consumer response to retailer use of cause-related marketing: Is more fit better? *Journal of Retailing, 83,* 437–445. doi:10.1016/j.jretai.2007.03.006

Bartoccini, E., & Di Fraia, G. (2004). Le comunità virtuali come ambienti. In e-Research: Internet per la ricerca sociale e di mercato. Roma: Laterza.

Bart, Y., Shankar, V., Sultan, F., & Urban, G. L. (2005). Are The Drivers And Role Of Online Trust The Same For All Web Sites And Consumers? A Large-Scale Exploratory Empirical Study. *Journal of Marketing, 69*(4), 133–152. doi:10.1509/jmkg.2005.69.4.133

Bates, A. D. (1989). The Extended Specialty Store: A Strategic Opportunity for the 1990s. *Journal of Retailing, 65*(3), 379–389.

Bateson, J. E. G. (1985). Retailing and Services Marketing: Friends or Foes? *Journal of Retailing, 61*(4), 11–13.

Batra, R., & Ahtola, O. (1991). Measuring the hedonic and utilitarian sources of consumer attitudes. *Marketing Letters, 2*, 159–170. doi:10.1007/BF00436035

Batra, R., Ahuvia, A., & Bagozzi, R. P. (2012). Brand Love. *Journal of Marketing, 76*, 1–16. doi:10.1509/jm.09.0339

Batra, R., & Sinha, I. (2000). Consumer-level factors moderating the success of private label brands. *Journal of Retailing, 76*(2), 175–191. doi:10.1016/S0022-4359(00)00027-0

Bauman, Z. (2007). *Liquid Times: Living in an Age of Uncertainty*. Cambridge, MA: Polity Press.

Baur, D., & Schmitz, P. H. (2012). Corporations and NGOs: When Accountability Leads to Co-optation. *Journal of Business Ethics, 106*, 9–21. doi:10.1007/s10551-011-1057-9

Beatty, S. E., & Ferrell, M. E. (1998). Impulse buying: Modeling its precursors. *Journal of Retailing, 74*(2), 169–191. doi:10.1016/S0022-4359(99)80092-X

Beckmann, S. C., & Roy Langer, C. (2005). *Netnography: Rich insights from online research*. Retrieved August 20, 2013, from http://frontpage.cbs.dk/insights/pdf/670005_beckmann_langer_full_version.pdf

Beem, E. R., & Oxenfeldt, A. R. (1966). A Diversity Theory for Market Processes in Food Retailing. *Journal of Farm Economics, 48*, 69–95. doi:10.2307/1236319

Beerli, A., Díaz Meneses, G., & Gil, S. M. (2007). Self-congruity and destination choice. *Annals of Tourism Research, 34*(3), 571–587. doi:10.1016/j.annals.2007.01.005

Beer, S. (1972). *Brain of the firm: a development in management cybernetics*. Herder and Herder.

Bekin, C., Carrigan, M., & Szmigin, I. (2005). Defying Marketing Sovereignty: Voluntary Simplicity at New Consumption Communities. *Qualitative Market Research: An International Journal, 8*(4), 413–429. doi:10.1108/13522750510619779

Belch, G. E., & Belch, M. A. (2009). *Advertising and Promotion: An Integrated marketing communication Perspective*. New York: McGraw-Hill.

Belk, R. W. (1985). Materialism: Trait aspects of living in the material world. *The Journal of Consumer Research, 12*(3), 265–279. doi:10.1086/208515

Belk, R. W. (1988). Possessions and the extended self. *The Journal of Consumer Research, 15*, 139–168. doi:10.1086/209154

Belk, R. W., Guliz, G., & Soren, A. (2003). The Fire of Desire: A Multisited Inquiry into Consumer Passion. *The Journal of Consumer Research, 30*, 326–352. doi:10.1086/378613

Bellizzi, J. A., & Hite, R. E. (1992). Environment Color, Consumer Feelings, and Purchase Likelihood. *Psychology and Marketing, 9*, 347–363. doi:10.1002/mar.4220090502

Bellizzi, J. A., Krueckeberg, H. F., Hamilton, J. R., & Martin, W. A. (1981). Consumer Perceptions of National, Private, and Generic Brands. *Journal of Retailing, 57*(4), 56–70.

Bennison, D., Warnaby, G., & Pal, J. (2010). Local shopping in the UK: Towards a synthesis of business and place. *International Journal of Retail & Distribution Management, 38*(11/12), 846–864. doi:10.1108/09590551011085948

Berman, B., & Evans, J. R. (1995). *Retail Management*. Englewood Cliffs, NJ: Prentice-Hall, Inc.

Berman, B., & Evans, J. R. (2010). *Retail Management: A Strategic Approach* (11th ed.). Pearson Education, Inc.

Berry, L. L., & Barnes, J. A. (1987). Retail Positioning Strategies in the USA. In G. Johnson (Ed.), *Business Strategy and Retailing* (pp. 107–115). Chichester, UK: John Wiley and Son Ltd.

Berry, M., & Linoff, G. (1999). *Mastering Data Mining: The Art and Science of Customer Relationship Management*. New York: John Wiley & Sons, Inc.

Bertoldi, G., Giachino, C., & Marenco, S. (2012). Bringing gourmet coffee to India: lessons of an Italian firm in an emerging market. *Business Strategy Review, 33*, 32–43. doi:10.1108/02756661211282777

Bertoli, G., & Resciniti, R. (Eds.). (2012). *International Marketing and the Country of Origin Effect*. Cheltenham, UK: Edward Elgar.

Bettencourt, L., & Gwinner, K. (1996). Customization of the service experience: the role of the frontline employee. *International Journal of Service Industry Management, 7*(2), 3–20. doi:10.1108/09564239610113442

Bettman, J. R. (1974). Relationship of information-processing attitude structures to private brand purchasing behavior. *The Journal of Applied Psychology, 59*(1), 79–83. doi:10.1037/h0035817

Beverland, M. B. (2006). The real thing: branding authenticity in the luxury wine trade. *Journal of Business Research, 59*(2), 251–258. doi:10.1016/j.jbusres.2005.04.007

Beverland, M. B., & Farrelly, F. J. (2010). The Quest for Authenticity in Consumption: Consumers' Purposive Choice of Authentic Cues to Shape Experienced Outcomes. *The Journal of Consumer Research, 36*(5), 838–856. doi:10.1086/615047

Bharadwaj, L., & Wilkening, E. A. (1977). The prediction of perceived well-being. *Social Indicators Research, 4*(1), 421–439. doi:10.1007/BF00353143

Bhattacharya, C. B., & Sen, S. (2003). Consumer-company identification: a framework for understanding consumers' relationships with companies. *Journal of Marketing, 67*, 76–88. doi:10.1509/jmkg.67.2.76.18609

Bhide, M., Deolasee, P., Katkar, A., Panchbudhe, A., Ramamritham, K., & Shenoy, P. (2002). Adaptive Push-Pull: Disseminating dynamic web data. *Computers. IEEE Transactions on, 51*(6), 652–668.

Bigné, J. E., & Andreu, L. (2004). Modelo cognitivo-afectivo de la satisfacción en servicios de ocio y turismo. *Cuadernos de Economía y Dirección de la Empresa, 21*, 89–120.

Bignell, P., & Lefty, M. (2013). High Street blues: the slow death of retail Britain. *The Independent*. Retrieved March 27, 2013, from http://www.independent.co.uk/news/business/analysis-and-features/high-street-blues-the-slow-death-of-retail-britain-8458766.html

Bijker, W., & Law. (1997). *Shaping technology/building society*. MIT Press.

Billings, W. L. (1990). Effects of Store Atmosphere on Shopping Behaviour. *Honors Projects*. Retrieved June 30, 2013, from http://digitalcommons.iwu.edu/busadmin_honproj/16

Binkley, J., Eales, M., Jekanowski, M., & Dooley, R. (2001). Competitive behavior of national brands: the case of orange juice. *Agribusiness, 17*, 139–160. doi:10.1002/1520-6297(200124)17:1<139::AID-AGR1007>3.0.CO;2-4

Binninger, A. S. (2008). Exploring the relationships between retail brands and consumer store loyalty. *International Journal of Retail & Distribution Management, 36*(2), 94–110. doi:10.1108/09590550810853057

Bishop, D. (2013). Customer service lessons from the High Street. *The Marketing Donut*. Retrieved August 6, 2013, from http://www.marketingdonut.co.uk/marketing/customer-care/understanding-your-customers/customer-service-lessons-from-the-high-street

Bitner, M. J. (1992). Servicescapes: The Impact of Physical Surroundings on Customers and Employees. *Journal of Marketing, 56*(2), 57–71. doi:10.2307/1252042

Black, D., Clemmensen, N. J., & Skov, M. B. (2009). Supporting the supermarket shopping experience through a context-aware shopping trolley. In *Proceedings of the 21th Annual Conference on the Australian Computer-Human Interaction* (pp. 33-40). ACM Press.

Black, D. W. (1996). Compulsive buying: A review. *The Journal of Clinical Psychiatry, 57*, 50–55. PMID:8698681

Black, D. W. (2007). A review of compulsive buying disorder. *World Psychiatry; Official Journal of the World Psychiatric Association (WPA), 6*(1), 14–18. PMID:17342214

Blasco, L., Hernandez, B., & Jimenez, J. (2011). Co-creation processes and engagement: an empirical approach. In E. Gummesson, C. Mele, & F. Polese (Eds.), *Service Dominant logic, Network & Systems Theory and Service Science*. Napoli, Italy: Giannini.

Bloch, P., & Richins, L. (1983). Shopping without purchases: An investigation of consumer browsing behaviour. In R. Bagozzi, A. Tybout, & A. Arbor (Eds.), *Advances in consumer research* (pp. 389–393). Association for Consumer Research.

Bloemer, J. M., & Kasper, H. D. (1995). The complex relationship between consumer satisfaction and brand loyalty. *Journal of Economic Psychology*, *16*, 311–329. doi:10.1016/0167-4870(95)00007-B

Bloemer, J., & De Ruyter, K. (1998). On the relationship between store image, store satisfaction and store loyalty. *European Journal of Marketing*, *32*(5/6), 499–513. doi:10.1108/03090569810216118

Blombäck, A., & Ramírez-Pasillas, M. (2012). Exploring the logics of corporate brand identity formation. *Corporate Communications: An International Journal*, *17*(1), 7–28. doi:10.1108/13563281211196335

Bluestein, A. (2013, September). You sign, companies listen. *Fast Company*, 34-36.

Bock, G.-W., Lee, J., Kuan, H.-H., & Kim, J.-H. (2012). The progression of online trust in the multi-channel retailer context and the role of product uncertainty. *Decision Support Systems*, *53*(1), 97–107. doi:10.1016/j.dss.2011.12.007

Boeck, H., & Wamba, S. F. (2008). RFID and buyer-seller relationships in the retail supply chain. *International Journal of Retail & Distribution Management*, *36*(6), 433–460. doi:10.1108/09590550810873929

Boedeker, M. (1995). New-Type and Traditional Shoppers: A Comparison of two Major Consumer Groups. *International Journal of Retail & Distribution Management*, *23*(3), 17–26. doi:10.1108/09590559510083966

Bohl, P. (2012). The effects of store atmosphere on shopping behaviour – A literature review. *Corvinus Marketing Studies*, *1*.

Boletín Información Comercial Española (BICE). (2011). La distribución comercial en España en 2010. *Boletín Económico de ICE*, *3015*. Retrieved August 3, 2013, from http://www.revistasice.com/es-ES/BICE/Paginas/ultimo-boletin.aspx?numero=3015

Bollen, K. A. (1989). *Structural Equations with Latent Variables*. New York, NY: Wiley Interscience.

Bolton, L. E., & Reed, A. II. (2004). Sticky priors and identification based judgments. *JMR, Journal of Marketing Research*, *41*, 397–410. doi:10.1509/jmkr.41.4.397.47019

Bolton, R. N., Lemon, K. N., & Verhoef, P. C. (2004). The theoretical underpinnings of customer asset management: A framework and propositions for future research. *Journal of the Academy of Marketing Science*, *32*(3), 271–292. doi:10.1177/0092070304263341

Bolton, R. N., & Saxena-Iyer, S. (2009). Interactive Services: A Framework, Synthesis and Research Directions. *Journal of Interactive Marketing*, *23*(1), 91–104. doi:10.1016/j.intmar.2008.11.002

Bone, P. F., & Ellen, P. S. (1999). Scents in the marketplace: explaining a fraction of olfaction. *Journal of Retailing*, *75*(2), 243–262. doi:10.1016/S0022-4359(99)00007-X

Bone, P. F., & Scholder, E. P. (1998). Does it matter if it smells? Olfactory stimuli as advertising executional cues. *Journal of Advertising*, *27*(4), 29–40. doi:10.1080/00913367.1998.10673567

Bonfanti, A. (2013). Towards an Approach to Signage Management Quality (SMQ). *Journal of Services Marketing*, *27*(4), 312–321. doi:10.1108/08876041311330780

Bonfanti, A., Centomo, N., & De Stefani, E. (2013). Checkpoint Systems: prevenire i furti nei punti vendita. *Micro & Macro Marketing*, *3*, 549–574.

Borghini, S., Diamond, N., Kozinets, R. K., McGrath, M. A., Muñiz, A. M. Jr, & Sherry, J. F. Jr. (2009). Why are Themed Brand Stores so Powerful? Retail Brand Ideology at American Girl Place. *Journal of Retailing*, *85*(3), 363–375. doi:10.1016/j.jretai.2009.05.003

Botsman, R., & Rogers, R. (2010). *What's mine is yours: How collaborative consumption is changing the way we live*. Harper Collins Publisher.

Boyd, D. M., & Ellison, N. B. (2007). Social network sites: Definition, history, and scholarship. *Journal of Computer-Mediated Communication*, *13*(1), 11. doi:10.1111/j.1083-6101.2007.00393.x

Brammer, S. J., & Pavelin, S. (2006). Corporate Reputation and Social Performance: The Importance of Fit. *Journal of Management Studies*, *43*(3), 435–455. doi:10.1111/j.1467-6486.2006.00597.x

Brando, C. H. J. (2013). Trends in new coffee consuming markets – Out of Home consumption. *P&A International Marketing*. Retrieved April 20, 2013, from http://www.ico.org/event_pdfs/seminar-consumption/peamarketing-e.pdf

Bravo, M., Vasquez-Parraga, A. Z., & Zamora, J. (2005). Loyalty in the air: Real and fictitious factors in the formation of loyalty of airline passengers. *Studies and Perspectives in Tourism, 14*(2), 101–126.

Brehm, J. A. (1966). *Theory of Psychological Reactance.* New York: Academic Press.

Brehm, S. S., Kassin, S. M., & Fein, S. (1999). *Social psychology.* New York, NY: Houghton Mifflin.

Brennan, C., Carmichael, F., & Ingham, B. (2007). Ageism and Employment: A Survey of the Literature in the Context of Current Research Agendas. *University of Salford, European Social Fund project on Ageism and Employment.* Retrieved February 12th, 2012, from http://www.mams.salford.ac.uk/PWO/Projects?Ageism-Employment

Briggs, F. (2013). Local shops and town centres are top choice for European shoppers, CBRE finds. *Retailtimes.* Retrieved October 27, 2013, from http://retailtimes.co.uk/local-shops-and-town-centres-are-top-choice-for-european-shoppers-cbre-finds/#

British Academy of Management (BAM). (2012). The Future of the Retail Fashion Store: Setting a New Research Agenda. *Retail Fashion Seminar.* British Academy of Management.

Brodie, R. (2009). Empirical Evidence about the Service Dominant Logic. In E. Gummesson, C. Mele, & F. Polese (Eds.), *Service science, S-D logic and network theory.* Napoli, Italy: Giannini.

Broeckelmann, P. (2010). Exploring consumers' reactions towards innovative mobile services. *Qualitative Market Research: An International Journal, 13*(4), 414–429. doi:10.1108/13522751011078827

Broekemier, G., Marquardt, R., & Gentry, J. W. (2008). An exploration of happy/sad and like/disliked music effects on shopping intentions in a women's clothing store service setting. *Journal of Services Marketing, 22*(1), 59–67. doi:10.1108/08876040810851969

Browne, G. J., Durrett, J. R., & Wetherbe, J. C. (2004). Consumer reactions to towards clicks and bricks: Investigating buying behavior on-line and at stores. *Behaviour & Information Technology, 23,* 237–245. doi:10.1080/01449290410001685411

Browne, M. W., & Cudeck, R. (1993). Alternative ways of assessing model fit. In K. A. Bollen, & J. S. Long (Eds.), *Testing structural equation models.* Newbury Park, CA: Sage Publications.

Brown, M., Pope, N., & Voges, K. (2003). Buying or Browsing? An exploration of shopping orientations and online purchase intention. *European Journal of Marketing, 37*(11/12), 1666–1684. doi:10.1108/03090560310495401

Brown, S. (1987). Institutional Change in Retailing: A Review and Synthesis. *European Journal of Marketing, 21*(6), 5–36. doi:10.1108/EUM0000000004701

Brown, S. (1990). The Wheel of Retailing: Past and Future. *Journal of Retailing, 66*(2), 143–149.

Brown, S. (1991). Variations on a Marketing Enigma: The Wheel of Retailing Theory. *Journal of Marketing Management, 7*(2), 131–155. doi:10.1080/0267257X.1991.9964146

Brown, S., & Burt, S. (1992). Retail Internationalization: Past Imperfect, Future Imperative. *European Journal of Marketing, 26*(8-9), 80.

Bruce, Moore, & Birtwistle. (2004). *International Retail Marketing – a case study approach.* Oxford, UK: Elsevier.

Bruner, G. C. II. (1990). Music, mood and marketing. *Journal of Marketing, 54*(4), 94–104. doi:10.2307/1251762

Brunetti, F. (2004). *Pervasività d'Impresa e Relazioni di Mercato: Quale Futuro?* Torino: Giappichelli.

Bryaman, A. (2004). *Social Research Methods.* Oxford University Press.

Buckley, P. G. (1987). The Internal Atmosphere of a Retail Store. *Advances in Consumer Research. Association for Consumer Research (U. S.), 14*(1), 568.

Bucklin, L. P. (1972). *Competition and Evolution in the Distributive Trades.* Englewood Cliffs, NJ: Prentice Hall.

Buechler, S. M. (2010). *Understanding Social Movements: Theories from the Classical Era to the Present.* Boulder, CO: Paradigm Publishers.

Buhalis, D., & Main, H. (1998). Information technology in peripheral small and medium hospitality enterprises: strategic analysis and critical factors. *International Journal of Contemporary Hospitality Management, 10*(5), 198–202. doi:10.1108/09596119810227811

Bunker, M. P., & Ball, D. (2006). Causes and Consequences of Grudge-Holding in Service Relationships. *Journal of Services Marketing, 22*(1), 37–47. doi:10.1108/08876040810851941

Burger, P. C., & Schott, B. (1972). Can private brand buyers be identified? *JMR, Journal of Marketing Research, 9*, 219–222. doi:10.2307/3149961

Burke, R. R. (2002). Technology and customer interface: What consumers want in the physical and virtual store. *Journal of the Academy of Marketing Science, 30*(4), 411–432. doi:10.1177/009207002236914

Burns, D. J., Manolis, C., & Keep, W. W. (2010). Fear of Crime on Shopping Intentions: An Examination. *International Journal of Retail & Distribution Management, 38*(1), 45–56. doi:10.1108/09590551011016322

Burton, S., & Soboleva, A. (2011). Interactive or reactive? Marketing with Twitter. *Journal of Consumer Marketing, 28*(7), 491–499. doi:10.1108/07363761111181473

Burt, S. (2000). The strategic role of retail brands in British grocery retailing. *European Journal of Marketing, 34*(8), 875–890. doi:10.1108/03090560010331351

Burt, S. L., & Davies, K. (2010). From the retail brand to the retail-er as a brand: themes and issues in retail branding research. *International Journal of Retail & Distribution Management, 38*(11/12), 865–878. doi:10.1108/09590551011085957

Business Monitor International (BMI). (2013). *United States Food & Drink Report 2013*. BMI.

Butcher, K. et al. (2001). Evaluative and relational influences on service loyalty. *International Journal of Service Industry Management, 12*(4), 310–327. doi:10.1108/09564230110405253

Butler, M. (2013). Showrooming: are retailers ready to embrace it? *The Guardian*. Retrieved June 8, 2013, from http://www.guardian.co.uk/media-network/media-network-blog/2013/may/09/showrooming-retail-solution-e-commerce

Buttle, F. (1984). Merchandising. *European Journal of Marketing, 18*(6-7), 104–124. doi:10.1108/EUM0000000004795

Byfield-Green, L. (2012). *Retail & Social Media: How and why are successful retailers tapping into social networking channels?* Planet Retail.

Calhoun, B. (2008). Shaping the Public Sphere: English Coffeehouses and French Salons and the Age of the Enlightenment. *Colgate Academic Review, 3*, 74–99.

Callon, M. (1986). Some Elements of a Sociology of Translation: Domestication of the Scallops and the Fishermen of St. Brieuc Bay. In J. Law (Ed.), *Power Action and Belief A New Sociology of Knowledge?* (pp. 196–233). London: Routledge.

Campbell, A., Converse, P. E., & Rodgers, W. L. (1976). *The quality of American life: perceptions, evaluations, and satisfactions*. New York, NY: Russell Sage Foundation.

Cardinali, M. G. (2009). The strategic options of modern retailers in the development of new formats. In *Proceedings of XV European Association of Education and Research in Commercial Distribution Conference* (pp. 1-28), Guildford, UK: Surrey University.

Carducci, V. (2006). Culture Jamming: A Sociological Perspective. *Journal of Consumer Culture, 6*(1), 116–139. doi:10.1177/1469540506062722

Caritas Data. (2012). *Top 3000 Charities 2012*. London: Sarasin & Partners.

Carpenter, J. M. (2008). Consumer shopping value, satisfaction and loyalty in discount retailing. *Journal of Retailing and Consumer Services, 15*, 358–363. doi:10.1016/j.jretconser.2007.08.003

Carpenter, J. M., & Fairhurst, A. (2005). Consumer Shopping Value, Satisfaction, and Loyalty for Retail Apparel Brands. *Journal of Fashion Marketing and Management, 9*(3), 256–269. doi:10.1108/13612020510610408

Carrefour, S. A. (2013). *Corporate Website*. Retrieved on August 15, 2013 from http://www.fondation-carrefour.org

Carrol, A. B. (1991). The pyramid of corporate social responsibility: toward the moral management of organizational stakeholders. *Business Horizons, 34*, 39–48. doi:10.1016/0007-6813(91)90005-G

Carroll, B. A., & Ahuvia, A. C. (2006). Some antecedents and outcomes of brand love. *Marketing Letters, 17*(2), 79–89. doi:10.1007/s11002-006-4219-2

Cartner-Morley, J. (2012). Burberry designs flagship London shop to resemble its Website. *The Guardian.* Retrieved June 8, 2013, from http://www.theguardian.com/fashion/2012/sep/12/burberry-london-shop-Website

Carù, A., & Cova, B. (2003). Revisiting Consumption Experience: A More Humble but Complete View of the Concept. *Marketing Theory, 3*(2). doi:10.1177/14705931030032004

Casalegno, C., Pellicelli, M., & Civera, C. (2012). Social Values and Ethics for Communicating the Corporate Identity. *The China Business Review, 11*(7), 656–671.

Castaldo, S. (2007). *Trust in Marketing Relationships.* Cheltenham, UK: Edward Elgar. doi:10.4337/9781847208576

Castaldo, S. (Ed.). (2001). *Retailing & innovazione.* Milano, Italy: Egea.

Castaldo, S., & Cillo, P. (2001). Le strategie di accrescimento delle risorse fiduciarie nel retailing: il ruolo delle carte fedeltà. *Industria & Distribuzione, 1*, 33–45.

Castaldo, S., & Mauri, C. (Eds.). (2008). *Store Management.* Milano, Italy: Franco Angeli.

Castañeda, A. J., & Montoro, F. J. (2007). The effect of Internet General Privacy Concern on Customer Behavior. *Electronic Commerce Research, 7*(2), 117–141. doi:10.1007/s10660-007-9000-y

Casteleyn, J., Mottart, A., & Rutten, K. (2009). How to use Facebook in your market research. *International Journal of Market Research, 51*(4), 439–447. doi:10.2501/S1470785309200669

Castells, M. (2001). *Internet Galaxy: Reflections on the internet, business, and society.* Oxford, UK: Oxford University Press. doi:10.1007/978-3-322-89613-1

Castro, E., & Navarro, A. (2003, March-April). Disposición del punto de venta. *Distribución y Consumo,* 5-22.

Centre for Corporate Citizenship. (2012). Commitment to value: The state of corporate citizenship 2012 highlights. *Boston College Carroll School of Management.* Retrieved on July 31, 2013 from www.bccorporatecitizenship.org

Cespedes, F. V., & Smith, H. J. (1993). Database Marketing: New Rules for Policy and Practice. *Sloan Management Review, 34*(4), 8–12.

CGAP (Center for Charitable Giving and Philanthropy). (2011). How generous is the UK? Charitable giving in the context of household spending. *Tom McKenzie and Katie Pharoah, CGAP Briefing Note 7.*

Chahal, M. (2013). Open all hours: the future of the High Street. *Marketing Week.* Retrieved March 27, 2013, from http://www.marketingweek.co.uk/trends/open-all-hours-the-future-of-the-high-street/4005606.article

Chai, L. G. (2009). A Review of Marketing Mix: 4Ps or More? *International Journal of Marketing Studies, 1*(1), 1–14.

Chapman, P., & Templar, S. (2006). Scoping the Contextual Issues that Influence Shrinkage Measurement. *International Journal of Retail & Distribution Management, 34*(11), 860–872. doi:10.1108/09590550610710255

Charity Retail Association. (2013). *Corporate Website.* Retrieved on August 29, 2103 from http://www.charity-retail.org.uk

Chase, S. (2012). The rise of the Mall in Brazil. *The Globe and Mail.* Retrieved August, 25, 2013, from http://www.theglobeandmail.com/report-on-business/international-business/latin-american-business/the-rise-of-the-mall-in-brazil/article593004/

Chattaraman, V. (2012). Multicultural Consumers and the Retail Service Experience. In J. Kandampully (Ed.), *Service Management: The New Paradigm in Retailing.* New York: Springer. doi:10.1007/978-1-4614-1554-1_10

Chaudhuri, A., & Holbrook, M. B. (2001). The chain of effects from brand trust and brand affect to brand performance: the role of brand loyalty. *Journal of Marketing, 65*(2), 81–93. doi:10.1509/jmkg.65.2.81.18255

Chebat, J. C., Chebat, B. G., & Vaillant, D. (2001). Environmental background music and in-store selling. *Journal of Business Research, 54*, 115–123. doi:10.1016/S0148-2963(99)00089-2

Chebat, J. C., & Michon, R. (2003). Impact of ambient odors on mall shoppers' emotions, cognition, and spending, a test of competitive causal theories. *Journal of Business Research, 56*, 529–539. doi:10.1016/S0148-2963(01)00247-8

Chebat, J.-C., & Morrin, M. (2007). Colors and cultures: exploring the effects of mall decor on consumer perceptions. *Journal of Business Research*, 60(3), 189–196. doi:10.1016/j.jbusres.2006.11.003

Chebeň, J., & Hudáčková, L. C. (2010). *Influence of the Global Economic Crisis on Consumer Behaviour in Slovakia*. Retrieved Jun 16, 2013, from http://vz.fmv.vse.cz/wp-content/uploads/9_2010.pdf

Chen, H.-S., & Hsieh, T. (2011). The effect of atmosphere on customer perceptions and customer behaviour responses in chain store supermarkets. *African Journal of Business Management*, 5(24), 10054–10066.

Chen, W. Y., & Jim, C. Y. (2008). Assessment and valuation of the ecosystem services provided by urban forests. In M. M. Carreiro, Y. C. Song, & J. Wu (Eds.), *Ecology, planning, and management of urban forests* (pp. 53–83). New York, NY: Springer. doi:10.1007/978-0-387-71425-7_5

Chernev, A., Hamilton, R., & Gal, D. (2011). Competing for consumer identity: limits to self-expression and the perils of lifestyle branding. *Journal of Marketing*, 75, 66–82. doi:10.1509/jmkg.75.3.66

Cherrier, H. (2007). Ethical Consumption Practices: Co-Production of Self-Expression and Social Recognition. *Journal of Consumer Behaviour*, 6(5), 321–335. doi:10.1002/cb.224

Cherrier, H. (2009a). Anti-Consumption Discourses and Consumer-Resistant Identities. *Journal of Business Research*, 62(2), 181–190. doi:10.1016/j.jbusres.2008.01.025

Cherrier, H. (2009b). Disposal and Simple Living: Exploring the Circulation of Goods and the Development of Sacred Consumption. *Journal of Consumer Behaviour*, 8(6), 327–339. doi:10.1002/cb.297

Cheung, C. M. K., & Thadani, D. R. (2012). The impact of electronic word-of-mouth communication: a literature analysis and integrative model. *Decision Support Systems*, 54(1), 461–470. doi:10.1016/j.dss.2012.06.008

Childres, T. L., Carr, C. L., Peck, J., & Carson, S. (2001). Hedonic and utilitarian motivations for online retail shopping behavior. *Journal of Retailing*, 77, 511–535. doi:10.1016/S0022-4359(01)00056-2

Chiou, J. S., & Droge, C. (2006). Service quality, trust, specific asset investment, and expertise: Direct and indirect effects in a satisfaction-loyalty framework. *Journal of the Academy of Marketing Science*, 34(4), 613–627. doi:10.1177/0092070306286934

Choi, S. T., & Coughlan, A. T. (2006). Private label positioning: quality versus feature differentiation from the national brand. *Journal of Retailing*, 82(2), 79–93. doi:10.1016/j.jretai.2006.02.005

Choo, B. (2013). *The Best BlogShops in Singapore 2013-The most popular and highest rated!* Retrieved March 30, 2013, from http://www.thesmartlocal.com/read/the-best-blogshops-in-singapore-2013

Christenson, G. A., Faber, R. J., de Zwaan, M., & Raymond, N. C. (1994). Compulsive buying: Descriptive characteristics and psychiatric comorbidity. *Journal of Clinical Psychiatry*, 55, 5-1 1.

Christodoulides, G., Jevons, C., & Blackshaw, P. (2011). The voice of the consumer speaks forcefully in brand identity: user-generated content forces smart marketers to listen. *Journal of Advertising Research*, 51(1), 101–111. doi:10.2501/JAR-51-1-101-111

Churchill, G. A., & Surprenant, C. (1982). An Investigation into Determinants of Customer Satisfaction. *JMR, Journal of Marketing Research*, 19, 491–504. doi:10.2307/3151722

Cicala, J. E., Smith, R. K., & Bush, A. J. (2012). What makes sales presentations effective- a buyer-seller perspective. *Journal of Business and Industrial Marketing*, 27(2), 78–88. doi:10.1108/08858621211196958

Citrin, A. V., Stern, D. E., Spangenberg, E. R., & Clark, M. J. (2003). Consumer Need for Tactile Input: An Internet Retailing Challenge. *Journal of Business Research*, 56(11), 915–922. doi:10.1016/S0148-2963(01)00278-8

Civera, C., & Musso, G. (2012). Corporate Social Responsibility and Social Economy: A closer look on financial tools into the Italian Context. In Instrumentos Solidarios en tiempo de crisis. Bosch Editor and Santander Universidades.

Clarke, I. I. (2001). Emerging value propositions for m-commerce. *The Journal of Business Strategy*, 18(2), 133–149.

Clarke, I., Hallsworth, A., Jackson, P., de Kervenoael, R., Del Aguila, R., & Kirkup, M. (2006). Retail restructuring and consumer choice: Long-term local changes in consumer behaviour: Portsmouth, 1980-2002. *Environment & Planning A*, 38(1), 25–46. doi:10.1068/a37207

Clark, T. (2009). *Starbucks: Il buono e il cattivo del caffè*. Milano: Egea.

Clegg, S. (1987). The Power of Language, the Language of Power. *Organization Studies*, 8, 60–70. doi:10.1177/017084068700800105

Clegg, S. (1989). *Frameworks of Power*. London: Sage. doi:10.4135/9781446279267

Clegg, S. (1991). Postmodern Management? *Journal of Organizational Change Management*, 5, 31–49. doi:10.1108/09534819210014869

Coe, B. D. (1971). Private versus national preference among lower and middle-income consumers. *Journal of Retailing*, 4, 61–72.

Coe, N. M., & Wrigley, N. (2009). *The Globalization of Retailing* (Vol. 1-2). Cheltenham, MA: Edward Elgar Publishing Ltd.

Coleman, P. (2006). *Shopping Environments: Evolution, Planning and Design*. Architectural Press.

Collins-Dodd, C., & Lindley, T. (2003). Store brands and retail differentiation: the influence of store image and store brand attitude on store brand own perceptions. *Journal of Retailing and Consumer Services*, 10(4), 345–352. doi:10.1016/S0969-6989(02)00054-1

Collinson, D. (1994). Strategies of resistance: Power, knowledge and subjectivity in the workplace. In J. M. Jermier, D. Knights, & W. R. Nord (Eds.), *Resistance and Power in Organizations* (pp. 25–68). New York, NY: Routledge.

Coltman, T. (2007). Why build a customer relationship management capability? *The Journal of Strategic Information Systems*, 16, 301–320. doi:10.1016/j.jsis.2007.05.001

Constantin, J. A., & Lusch, R. F. (1994). *Understanding resource management: How to deploy your people, products, and processes for maximum productivity*. Paper presented at The Planning Forum. Oxford, OH.

Constantinides, E. (2004). Influencing the online consumer's behavior: The Web experience. *Internet Research*, 14(2), 111–126. doi:10.1108/10662240410530835

Conversocial. (2012). *Evolving Social Customer Service*. Retrieved May, 2013, from http://www.conversocial.com/resources/whitepapers

Cooper, K. (2012). High Street plunges into triples dip. *The Sunday Times*. Retrieved March 27, 2013, from http://www.thesundaytimes.co.uk/sto/business/Retail_and_leisure/article1184780.ee

Copeland, M.V., & Malik, O. (2005, July). How to Ride the Fifth Wave. *Business 2.0*.

Corciolani, M. (2010). *La ricerca di autenticità nei processi di consumo*. Pisa: Edizioni PLUS.

Corcoran, S. (2009). Defining Earned, Owned and Paid Media. *Forrester Research Blogs*. Retrieved November 2011, from http://blogs.forrester.com/interactive_marketing/2009/12/defining-earned-owned-and-paid-media.html

Cornelius, B., Natter, M., & Faure, C. (2010). How store front displays influence retail store image. *Journal of Retailing and Consumer Services*, 17, 143–151. doi:10.1016/j.jretconser.2009.11.004

Corstjens, M., & Lal, R. (2000). Building store loyalty through store brands. *JMR, Journal of Marketing Research*, 37(3), 281–291. doi:10.1509/jmkr.37.3.281.18781

Corstjens, M., & Lal, R. (2012). Retail Doesn't Cross Borders: Here's Why and What to Do About It. *Harvard Business Review*, 90(4), 104–111. PMID:22299510

Costabile, M. (2001). *Il capitale relazionale*. Milano, Italy: McGraw-Hill.

Costanza, R., d'Arge, R., De Groot, R., Farber, S., Grasso, M., & Hannon, B. et al. (1997). The value of the world's ecosystem services and natural capital. *Nature*, 387(6630), 253–260. doi:10.1038/387253a0

Costa, P. Jr, & McCrae, R. (1992). Normal personality assessment in clinical practice: The Neo Personality Inventory. *Psychological Assessment*, 4, 5–13. doi:10.1037/1040-3590.4.1.5

Cotterill, S. (2013). 43% of Europeans shop online. *InternetRetailer*. Retrieved October 27, 2013, from http://www.Internetretailer.com/2012/06/07/43-europeans-shop-online

Countryman, C. C., & Jang, S. (2006). The effects of atmospheric elements on customer impression: the case of hotel lobbies. *International Journal of Contemporary Hospitality Management, 18*(7), 534–545. doi:10.1108/09596110610702968

Cova, B., & Dalli, D. (2009). Working Consumers: The Next Step in Marketing Theory? *Marketing Theory, 9*(3), 315–339. doi:10.1177/1470593109338144

Cova, B., Kozinets, R. V., & Shankar, A. (Eds.). (2007). *Consumer Tribes*. Burlington, MA: Butterworth-Heinemann.

Cowper, R. J. (1992). Shopping Centre Management for the 'Nineties'. *Property Management, 10*(4), 329–337. doi:10.1108/02637479210030466

Cox, R., & Brittain, P. (2004). *Retailing: An introduction*. Financial Times, Prentice Hall.

Cozens, P., Saville, G., & Hillier, D. (2005). Crime Prevention through Environmental Design (CPTED), Are View and Modern Bibliography. *Journal of Property Management, 23*(5), 328–356. doi:10.1108/02637470510631483

Creswell, J. W. (2009). Research design: Qualitative, quantitative, and mixed methods approaches. *Sage (Atlanta, Ga.)*.

Creswell, J. W., & Clark, V. L. P. (2007). *Designing and conducting mixed methods research*. Thousand Oaks, CA: Sage Publications.

Cronin, J. J., & Taylor, S. A. (1992). Measuring service quality: A reexamination and extension. *Journal of Marketing, 56*(3), 55–68. doi:10.2307/1252296

Cross, G. (2000). *An all-consuming century: Why commercialism won in modern America*. New York: Columbia University Press.

Culnan, M. J. (1993). How Did They Get My Name? An Exploratory Investigation Of Consumer Attitudes Toward Secondary Information Use. *Management Information Systems Quarterly, 17*(3), 341–363. doi:10.2307/249775

Cunningham, I., Hardy, A. P., & Imperia, G. (1982). Generic Brands Versus National Brands and Store Brands. *Journal of Advertising Research, 22*, 25–32.

Cunningham, R. M. (1956). Brand loyalty- What, where, how much. *Harvard Business Review, 34*, 116–128.

d'Astous, A., Maltais, J., & Roberge, C. (1990). *Compulsive buying tendencies of adolescent consumers*. Paper presented at Advances in Consumer Research Conference. Provo, UT.

Dabholkar, P. A., Bobbitt, L. M., & Lee, E.-J. (2003). Understanding consumer motivation and behaviour related to self-scanning in retailing. *International Journal of Service Industry Management, 14*(1), 59–95. doi:10.1108/09564230310465994

Dacin, T., Goldstein, J., & Scott, W. R. (2002). Institutional theory and institutional change. *Academy of Management Journal, 45*, 45–56. doi:10.5465/AMJ.2002.6283388

Dailey, L. (2004). Navigational web atmospherics: Explaining the influence of restrictive navigation cues. *Journal of Business Research, 57*(7), 795–803. doi:10.1016/S0148-2963(02)00364-8

Dakoumi Hamrouni, A., & Touzi, M. (2011). Technique of collage for store design atmospherics. *Qualitative Market Research: An International Journal, 14*(3), 304–323. doi:10.1108/13522751111137523

Dalli, D., & Corciolani, M. (2008). Collective Forms of Resistance: The Transformative Power of Moderate Communities: Evidence from the Bookcrossing Case. *International Journal of Market Research, 50*(6), 757–775. doi:10.2501/S1470785308200195

Dancey, C. P., & Reidy, J. (2002). *Statistics Without Maths for Psychology* (2nd ed.). Pearson Education Ltd.

Darden, W. R., Erdem, O., & Darden, D. K. (1983). A Comparison and Test of Three Causal Models of Patronage Intentions. In W. R. Darden, & R. F. Lusch (Eds.), *Patronage Behavior and Retail Management*. New York: North-Holland.

Davidson, W. R., Bates, A. D., & Bass, S. J. (1976, November-December). The Retail Life Cycle. *Harvard Business Review*, 89–96.

Davies, G. (1999). The Evolution of Marks and Spencer. *The Service Industries Journal*, *19*(3), 60–73. doi:10.1080/02642069900000030

Davis, D. F., Golicic, S. L., & Boerstler, C. N. (2010). Benefits and Challenges of Conducting Multiple Methods Research in Marketing. *Journal of the Academy of Marketing Science*, *39*(3), 467–479. doi:10.1007/s11747-010-0204-7

Davis, F. D. (1989). Perceived usefulness, perceived ease of use, and user acceptance of information technology. *Management Information Systems Quarterly*, *13*, 319–340. doi:10.2307/249008

Davis, L., & Dyer, B. (2012). Consumers' value perceptions across retail outlets: Shopping at mass merchandisers and department stores. *International Review of Retail, Distribution and Consumer Research*, *22*(2), 115–142. doi:10.1080/09593969.2011.634074

Dawar, N., & Stornelli, J. (2013). Rebuilding the relationship between manufacturers and retailers. *MIT Sloan Management Review*, *54*(2), 83–90.

Dawson, J. (2000). Viewpoint: Retailer Power, Manufacturer Power, Competition and Some Questions of Economic Analysis. *International Journal of Retail & Distribution Management*, *28*(1), 5–8. doi:10.1108/09590550010306700

Dawson, J. A. (2001). Is there a New Commerce in Europe? *International Review of Retail, Distribution and Consumer Research*, *11*(3), 287–299. doi:10.1080/713770598

Dawson, S. (1993). Consumer Responses to Electronic Article Surveillance Alarms. *Journal of Retailing*, *69*(3), 353–362. doi:10.1016/0022-4359(93)90011-7

Day, G. S. (1969). A two-dimensional concept of brand loyalty. *Journal of Advertising Research*, *9*, 29–35.

Day, R. L. (1978). Beyond social indicators: quality of life at the individual level. In *Marketing and the quality of life*. Chicago, IL: American Marketing Association.

Day, R. L. (1987). Relationship between life satisfaction and consumer satisfaction. In A. C. Samli (Ed.), *Marketing and quality-of-life interface* (pp. 289–311). Westport, CT: Greenwood Press.

De Farias, S. A. (2010). *Store Atmospherics and Experiential Marketing: a conceptual framework and research propositions for an extraordinary customer experience*. Retrieved October 30, 2013, from http://www.anpad.org.br/diversos/trabalhos/EMA/ema_2010/2010_EMA27.pdf

De Kervenoael, R., Aykac, D. S. O., & Bisson, C. (2008). The influence of social E-Atmospherics in practice: A website content analysis perspective. In *Proceedings of the 7th International Congress, Marketing Trend*. Retrieved June 30, 2013, from http://research.sabanciuniv.edu/7430/

de Luca, P. (2009). Atmosfera del punto vendita ed esperienza di shopping nel commercio al dettaglio. In S. Sciarelli & R. Vona (Eds.), Management della distribuzione commerciale: Elementi di economia e gestione delle imprese commerciali. Milano: McGraw-Hill.

de Luca, P., & Pegan, G. (2012). *La percezione del Made in Italy sui mercati internazionali: primi risultati di una ricerca netnografica sulle comunità online di consumatori di caffè*. Paper presented at IX Convegno Annuale della SIM - Società Italiana di Marketing. Benevento, Italy.

de Luca, P., & Pegan, G. (2013). *I coffee shop italiani nel quadro competitivo internazionale: una ricerca qualitativa sul mercato USA*. Paper presented at X° Convegno Annuale della SIM - Società Italiana di Marketing. Milano, Italy.

de Luca, P., Vianelli, D., & Marzano, F. C. (2013). Entry Strategies and Distribution Channels of Italian SMEs in the Chinese Market. In B. Christiansen., E. Turkina & N.Williams N. (Eds.), Cultural and Technological Influences on Global Business. Hershey, PA: IGI Global.

de Luca, P. (2000). Gli effetti dell'atmosfera del punto vendita sul comportamento d'acquisto del consumatore: verifica empirica di un modello di psicologia ambientale. *Industria & Distribuzione*, *2*, 11–22.

de Luca, P., & Vianelli, D. (2004). Coinvolgimento del consumatore e valutazione dell'atmosfera del punto vendita. *Micro&Macro Marketing*, *3*, 581–594.

De Nisco, A., & Warnaby, G. (2013). Shopping in downtown. The effect of urban environment on service quality perception and behavioural intentions. *International Journal of Retail & Distribution Management*, *41*(9), 654–670. doi:10.1108/IJRDM-05-2013-0106

De Toni, A. F., & Tracogna, A. (2005). *L'industria del caffè: Analisi di settore, casi di eccellenza e sistemi territoriali: Il caso Trieste*. Milano: Il Sole 24 Ore.

De Wulf, K., Odekerken-Schroder, G., & Iacobucci, D. (2001). Investments in consumer relationships: A cross-country and cross-industry exploration. *Journal of Marketing, 65*, 33–50. doi:10.1509/jmkg.65.4.33.18386

De Wulf, K., Odekerken-Schroëder, G., Goedertier, F., & Van Ossel, G. (2005). Consumer perceptions of store brands versus national brands. *Journal of Consumer Marketing, 22*(4), 223–232. doi:10.1108/07363760510605335

Dean, J. (2010). *Blog Theory*. Cambridge, MA: Polity Press.

Dearden, J., & Wilson, A. (2011). A Framework for Exploring Urban Retail Discontinuities. *Geographical Analysis, 43*, 172–187. doi:10.1111/j.1538-4632.2011.00812.x

DeCew, J. (1997). *In Pursuit of Privacy: Law, Ethics, and the Rise of Technology*. Ithaca, NY: Cornell University Press.

Dekimpe, M. G., Steenkamp, J. B. E. M., Mellens, M., & Vanden Abeele, P. (1997). Decline and variability in brand loyalty. *International Journal of Research in Marketing, 14*(5), 405–420. doi:10.1016/S0167-8116(97)00020-7

Delgado-Ballester, E., Munuera-Alemàn, J. L., & Yagüe-Guillén, M. J. (2003). Development and validation of a brand trust scale. *International Journal of Market Research, 45*(1), 35–53.

Deloitte & Stores Media. (2013). 2012 Top 250 Global Retailers. *16ᵗʰ Annual Global Powers of Retailing Report*. Retrieved on August 25, 2013 from http://www.stores.org/2012/Top-250-List

Demetriou, M., Papasolomou, I., & Vrontis, D. (2009). Cause-related Marketing: Building the corporate image while supporting worthwhile causes. *Journal of Brand Management, 17*, 266–278. doi:10.1057/bm.2009.9

Denegri-Knott, J., Zwick, D., & Schroeder, J. E. (2006). Mapping consumer power: an integrative framework for marketing and consumer research. *European Journal of Marketing, 40*, 950–971. doi:10.1108/03090560610680952

Dennis, C., Harris, L., & Sandhu, B. (2002). From bricks to clicks: Understanding the e-consumer. *Qualitative Market Research: An International Journal, 5*(4), 281–290. doi:10.1108/13522750210443236

Denzin, N. K., & Lincoln, Y. S. (1994). *Handbook of qualitative research*. London: Sage Publications.

Denzin, N. K., & Lincoln, Y. S. (1998). *Collecting and interpreting qualitative materials*. Thousand Oaks, CA: Sage Publications.

Department for Communities and Local Government. (2013). *The Future of High Streets: Progress since the Portas Review*. London: Crown.

DeSarbo, W. S., & Edwards, E. A. (1996). Typologies of compulsive buying behavior: A constrained clusterwise regression approach. *Journal of Consumer Psychology, 5*(3), 231–262. doi:10.1207/s15327663jcp0503_02

Desinger, C., Dekhil, M., Ghosh, R., Jain, J., & Hsu, M. (2010). Transforming retail customer shopping experiences using mobile devices, open architectures, and operational business intelligence. *HP Laboratories*, 36.

Desmond, J., McDonagh, P., & O'Donohoe, S. (2000). Counter-Culture and Consumer Society. *Consumption. Markets & Culture, 4*(4), 241–279. doi:10.1080/10253866.2000.9670358

Deutschen, E., De Ruyter, K., Wetzels, M., & Ooterveld, P. (2004). Response Rate and Response Quality of Internet-Based Surveys: An Experimental Study. *Marketing Letters, 15*(1), 21–36. doi:10.1023/B:MARK.0000021968.86465.00

Dewey, J. (1966). *Theory of valuation*. Chicago, IL: The University of Chicago Press.

Dhar, R., & Nowlis, S. M. (1999). The effect of time pressure on consumer choice deferral. *The Journal of Consumer Research, 25*(4), 369–384. doi:10.1086/209545

Dhar, S. K., & Hoch, S. J. (1997). Why store brand penetration varies by retailer. *Marketing Science, 16*, 208–227. doi:10.1287/mksc.16.3.208

Dhar, S. K., Hoch, S. J., & Kumar, N. (2001). Effective category management depends on the role of the category. *Journal of Retailing, 77*(2), 165–184. doi:10.1016/S0022-4359(01)00045-8

Dholakia, R. R. (1999). Going shopping: key determinants of shopping behaviors and motivations. *International Journal of Retail and Distribution Management, 27*(4), 154–165. doi:10.1108/09590559910268499

Dholakia, R. R., Zhao, M., & Dholakia, N. (2005). Multichannel retailing: a case study of early experiences. *Journal of Interactive Marketing, 19*(2), 63–74. doi:10.1002/dir.20035

Dholakia, U. M., Kahn, B. E., Reeves, R., Rindfleisch, A., Stewart, D., & Taylor, E. (2010). Consumer behavior in a multichannel, multimedia retailing environment. *Journal of Interactive Marketing, 24*(2), 86–95. doi:10.1016/j.intmar.2010.02.005

Díaz, L., & Flores, E. (2001). La estructura de la emoción humana: un modelo cromático del sistema afectivo. *Salud Mental, 24*(4), 20–35.

Dick, A. S., & Basu, K. (1994). Customer loyalty: Toward an integrated conceptual framework. *Journal of the Academy of Marketing Science, 22*, 99–113. doi:10.1177/0092070394222001

Dick, A. S., Jain, A. K., & Richardson, P. (1995). Correlates of store brand proneness: some empirical observations. *Journal of Product and Brand Management, 4*(4), 15–22. doi:10.1108/10610429510097663

Dick, A. S., Jain, A. K., & Richardson, P. (1996). How consumers evaluate store brands. *Journal of Product and Brand Management, 5*(2), 19–28. doi:10.1108/10610429610119405

Diener, E. (1984). Subjective well-being. *Psychological Bulletin, 95*, 542–575. doi:10.1037/0033-2909.95.3.542 PMID:6399758

Dilley, J., & Wolf, K. L. (2013). Homeowner interactions with residential trees in urban areas. *Arboriculture and Urban Forestry, 39*(6), 267–277.

DiLonardo, R. L. (2004). Got an Eye on Your Inventory? *Aftermarket Business, 114*(12), 34–38.

DiMaggio, P. (1997). Culture and cognition. *Annual Review of Sociology, 23*, 263–287. doi:10.1146/annurev.soc.23.1.263

DiMaggio, P., & Powell, W. (1983). The iron cage revisited: Institutional isomorphism and collective rationality in organizational fields. *American Sociological Review, 48*, 147–160. doi:10.2307/2095101

Dinev, T., Bellotto, M., Hart, P., Russo, V., Serra, I., & Collauti, C. (2006). Privacy calculus model in e-commerce: A study of Italy and the United States. *European Journal of Information Systems, 15*(4), 389–402. doi:10.1057/palgrave.ejis.3000590

Dirks, D. (2004). *It comes with the territory: Women Restaurant Workers' Experiences of Sexual Harassment and Sexual Objectification.* (Unpublished doctoral dissertation). Graduate School of the University of Florida.

Dittmar, H. (2005). A new look at 'compulsive buying': Self-discrepancies and materialistic values as predictors of compulsive buying tendency. *Journal of Social and Clinical Psychology, 24*(5), 832–859. doi:10.1521/jscp.2005.24.6.832

Divol, R., Edelman, D., & Sarrazin, U. (2012). Demystifying social media. *McKinsey Quarterly.* Retrieved August, 2012, from http://www.mckinsey.com/insights/marketing_sales/demystifying_social_media

Doherty, N. F., & Ellis-Chadwick, F. (2010). Internet retailing: the past, the present and the future. *International Journal of Retail & Distribution Management, 38*(11/12), 943–965. doi:10.1108/09590551011086000

Dolich, I. J. (1969). Congruence relationships between self images and product brands. *JMR, Journal of Marketing Research, 6*(1), 80–84. doi:10.2307/3150001

Dominiczak, P. (2013). Pay day lenders 'could replace independent shops' in High Street reforms. *The Telegraph.* Retrieved August 6, 2013, from http://www.telegraph.co.uk/lifestyle/reinvent-the-high-street/10088028/Pay-day-lenders-could-replace-independent-shops-in-high-street-reforms.html

Doney, P. M., & Cannon, J. P. (1997). An examination of the nature of trust in buyer-seller relationships. *Journal of Marketing, 61*(2), 35–51. doi:10.2307/1251829

Donovan, R. J., Rossiter, J. R., Marcoolyn, G., & Nesdale, A. (1994). Store atmosphere and purchasing behavior. *Journal of Retailing, 70*(3), 283–294. doi:10.1016/0022-4359(94)90037-X

Donovan, R., & Rossiter, J. (1982). Store atmosphere: an environmental psychology approach. *Journal of Retailing, 58*, 34–57.

Dorado, S. (2005). Institutional entrepreneurship, partaking, and convening. *Organization Studies, 26*(3), 385–414. doi:10.1177/0170840605050873

Douglas, M., & Isherwood, B. (1984). *Il mondo delle cose. Oggetti, valori, consumo*. Bologna: Il Mulino.

Dou, X., Walden, J. A., Lee, S., & Lee, J. Y. (2012). Does source matter? Examining source effects in online product reviews. *Computers in Human Behavior, 28*(5), 1555–1563. doi:10.1016/j.chb.2012.03.015

Dowden, C. (2013, August 8). Is it better for business to actually do good or to just look like it's doing good? *Financial Post*. Retrieved August 10, 2013 from http://business.financialpost.com/2013/08/09/is-it-better-for-business-to-actually-do-good-or-to-just-look-like-its-doing-good/

Dowdy, C. (2008). *One-off: Independent Retail Design*. Laurence King Publishing Ltd.

Dragun, D. (2004). The financial implications of retail strategy. In J. Reynolds, & C. Cuthbertson (Eds.), *Retail strategy: The view from the bridge*. Oxford, UK: Elsevier Butterworth-Heinemann. doi:10.1016/B978-0-7506-5696-2.50009-X

Dreesman, A. C. R. (1968). Patterns of Evolution in Retailing. *Journal of Retailing, 44*, 64–81.

Drew, S. (2003). Strategic uses of e-commerce by SMEs in the east of England. *European Management Journal, 21*(1), 79–88. doi:10.1016/S0263-2373(02)00148-2

Drollinger, T., & Comer, L. B. (2013). Salesperson's listening ability as an antecedent to relationship selling. *Journal of Business and Industrial Marketing, 28*(1), 50–59. doi:10.1108/08858621311285714

Drucker, P. (1999). *Management Challenges for 21st Century*. New York, NY: Harper Business.

Du, J.-G., & Fan, X.-C. (2006). A model of salesperson's trust and satisfaction based on the high-priced products selling in retailing. In *Proceedings of the international conference on management science and engineering* (1055-1060). Academic Press.

Dube, L., & Morin, S. (2001). Background music pleasure and store evaluation Intensity effects and psychological mechanism. *Journal of Business Research, 54*, 107–113. doi:10.1016/S0148-2963(99)00092-2

Duncan, T., & Mulhern, F. (2004). *A White Paper on the Status, Scope and Future of IMC*. New York: McGraw-Hill.

Dunne, P. M., Lusch, R. F., & Griffith, D. A. (2002). Retailing (4th ed.). South-Western, Thomson Learning.

Dupuis, M. (2000). *Retail Innovation: Towards a Framework of Analysis*. Paper presented at the EAERCD Conference on Retail Innovation. Barcelona.

Dutt, P., & Padmanabhan, V. (2009). *When to Hit the Panic Button? Impact of Currency Crisis on Consumer Behaviours*. Retrieved May 7, 2011, from http://faculty.edu/dutt/Research/Paddy_Pushan.pdf

Duygan, B. (2005). *Aggregate Shocks, Idiosyncratic Risk, and Durable Goods Purchases: Evidence from Turkey's 1994 Financial Crisis*. European University Institute Finance and Consumption Program. Retrieved Jun 16, 2013, from http://www.econbiz.de/en/search/detailed-view/doc/all/aggregate-shocks-idiosyncratic-risk-and-durable-goods-purchases-evidence-from-turkeys-1994-financial-crisis-duygan-burcu/10005069449/?no_cache=1

Eastman, J. K., Iyer, R., & Randall, C. (2009). Understanding internet shoppers: an exploratory study. *Marketing Management Journal, 19*(2), 104–117.

East, R., Harris, P., Wittson, G., & Lomax, W. (1995). Loyalty to supermarkets. *International Review of Retail, Distribution and Consumer Research, 5*, 99–109. doi:10.1080/09593969500000006

Economist. (2003). *Coffee Houses: The Internet in a cup*. Retrieved August 19, 2013, from http://www.economist.com/node/2281736/print

Edgar, B., Doherty, J., & Meert, H. (2004). *Immigration and homelessness in Europe*. Policy Pr.

Ehrenberg, A. S. C., & Goodhardt, G. J. (2000). New brands: near instant loyalty. *Journal of Marketing Management, 16*, 607–617. doi:10.1362/026725700785045912

E-Imports. (2012). *Coffee Statistics*. Retrieved May 5, 2013, from http://www.e-importz.com/Support/specialty_coffee.htm

Eisen, T. (2013). Blogshops move to real world for serious cash. *The Straits Times*. Retrieved November 20, 2013, from http://www.divaasia.com/article/4807

Ekinsmyth, C., Hallsworth, A. G., Leonard, S., & Taylor, M. (1995). Stability and change in Economic Geography. *Area, 27*(4), 289–299.

Ellis, L., & Ficek, C. (2001). Colour preferences according to gender and sexual orientation. *Personality and Individual Differences, 31*, 1375–1379. doi:10.1016/S0191-8869(00)00231-2

Elmadağ, A. B., Ellinger, A. E., & Franke, G. R. (2008). Antecedents and Consequences of Frontline Service Employee Commitment to Service Quality. *The Journal of Marketing Theory and Practice, 16*(2), 95–110. doi:10.2753/MTP1069-6679160201

Elms, J., Canning, C., de Kervenoael, R., Whysall, P., & Hallsworth, A. (2010). 30 years of retail change: Where (and how) do you shop? *International Journal of Retail and Distribution Management, 38*(11/12), 817–827. doi:10.1108/09590551011085920

eMarketer. (2013). *Multichannel Customer Service*. Retrieved July, 2013, from https://www.emarketer.com/go/multichannelcustomerservice

EMEA. (2013). *How we shop: Inside the minds of Europe's consumers. EMEA*. London: CBRE Ltd.

Engel, J., Blackwell, R., & Miniard, P. (1990). *Consumer Behavior*. Orlando, FL: The Dryden Press.

En, X., Hock-Hai, T., & Wen, W. (2006). Volunteering Personal Information On The Internet: Effects Of Reputation, Privacy Notices, And Rewards On Online Consumer Behavior. *Marketing Letters, 17*(1), 61–74. doi:10.1007/s11002-006-4147-1

Eriksson, P., & Kovalainen, A. (2008). Qualitative methods in business research. *Sage (Atlanta, Ga.)*.

Ernst, H., Hoyer, Krafft, & Soll. (2010). *Consumer Idea Generation*. Vallendar.

Eroglu, S. A., Machleit, K. A., & Chebat, J. C. (2005). The Interaction of Retail Density and Music Tempo: Effects on Shopper Responses. *Psychology and Marketing, 22*(7), 577–589. doi:10.1002/mar.20074

Eroglu, S. A., Machleit, K. A., & Davis, L. M. (2001). Atmospheric qualities of online retailing: a conceptual model and implications. *Journal of Business Research, 54*(2), 177–184. doi:10.1016/S0148-2963(99)00087-9

Escalas, J. E., & Bettman, J. R. (2003). You Are What They Eat: The Influence of Reference Groups on Consumers' Connections to Brands. *Journal of Consumer Psychology, 13*(3), 339–348. doi:10.1207/S15327663JCP1303_14

Escalas, J. E., & Bettman, J. R. (2005). Self-construal, reference groups, and brand meaning. *The Journal of Consumer Research, 32*, 378–389. doi:10.1086/497549

Espinoza, F., Liberali, G., & D'Angelo, A. C. (2004). Testing the influence of retail atmosphere on store choice criteria, perceived values, and patronage intentions. *American Marketing Association (AMA) Winter Educators` Conference Proceedings, 15*, 120-125.

Etgar, M. (2008). A Descriptive Model of the Consumer Co-Production Process. *Journal of the Academy of Marketing Science, 36*, 97–108. doi:10.1007/s11747-007-0061-1

Etsell, C., & Hinton, M. (2013). How the UK will shop: 2013. *Verdict in Association with SAS*. Retrieved August 6, 2013, from http://www.siicex.gob.pe/siicex/documento-sportal/alertas/documento/doc/773247859rad0250B.pdf

Ettenson, R., Conrado, E., & Knowles, J. (2013). Rethinking the 4 Ps. *Harvard Business Review, 91*(1), 26.

EU Economic and Scientific Policy. (2011). *Consumer behavior in a digital environment*. European Parliament.

Euromonitor International. (2012). *Cafés/Bars in the US*. Author.

Euromonitor International. (2013). *Coffee in the US*. Retrieved August 8, 2013, from http://www.euromonitor.com/coffee-in-the-us/report

European Commission. (2012). Consumers' attitudes towards cross-border trade and consumer protection. Flash barometer 332, May 2012, Brussels.

European Commission. (2013). The consumer conditions scoreboard - consumers at home in the single market (9th Ed.). July 2013, Brussels.

European Corporate Social Responsibility Award Scheme. (2013). *Corporate website*. Retrieved on August 30, 2013 from www.europeancsrawards.eu

Ewing, M. T. (2000). Brand and retailer loyalty: Past behaviour and future intentions. *Journal of Product and Brand Management*, 9(2), 120–127. doi:10.1108/10610420010322161

Faber, R. J., & O'Guinn, T. C. (1988). *Dysfunctional consumer socialization: A search for the roots of compulsive buying*. Paper presented at the 13th annual International Association for Research in Economic Psychology Colloquium. Leuven, Belgium.

Faber, R. J., & O'Guinn, T. C. (1992). A clinical screener for compulsive buying. *The Journal of Consumer Research*, 19, 459–469. doi:10.1086/209315

Faber, R. J., O'Guinn, T. C., & Krych, R. (1987). Compulsive consumption. In M. Wallendorf, & P. Anderson (Eds.), *Advances in consumer research* (Vol. 14, pp. 132–135). Provo, UT: Association for Consumer Research.

Falk, J. L. (1981). The environmental generation of excessive behavior. In S. J. Mule (Ed.), *Behavior in excess: An examination of volitional disorders* (pp. 313–337). New York: Free Press.

Falk, R. (1999). *Predatory Globalization: Critique*. Cambridge, MA: Polity Press.

Feick, L., & Price. (1987). The Market Maven: A Diffuser of Marketplace Information. *Journal of Marketing*, 51(1), 83–97. doi:10.2307/1251146

Ferguson, L. W. (1941). A Study of the Likert Technique of Attitude Scale Construction. *Mead Project*. Department of Psycology, University of Connecticut. Retrieved November 24th, 2013, from http://www.brocku.ca/MeadProject/sup/Ferguson_1941.html

Ferguson, R., & Goldman, S. M. (2010). The Cause Manifesto. *Journal of Consumer Marketing*, 27(3), 283–287. doi:10.1108/07363761011038356

Ferrin, D. L., Bligh, M. C., & Kohles, J. C. (2007). Can I Trust You to Trust Me? A Theory of Trust, Monitoring, and Cooperation in Interpersonal and Intergroup Relationships. *Group & Organization Management*, 32(4), 465–499. doi:10.1177/1059601106293960

Ferrin, D. L., Bligh, M. C., & Kohles, J. C. (2008). It Takes Two to Tango: An Interdependence Analysis of the Spiraling of Perceived Trustworthiness and Cooperation in Interpersonal and Intergroup Relationships. *Organizational Behavior and Human Decision Processes*, 107(2), 161–178. doi:10.1016/j.obhdp.2008.02.012

Findlay, D. (2013). High Street retailers must rediscover that emotional connection with customers. *Marketing Magazine*. Retrieved August 6, 2013, from http://www.marketingmagazine.co.uk/article/1186124/high-street-retailers-rediscover-

Fiore, A. M., & Kim, J. (2007). An integrative framework capturing experiential and utilitarian shopping experience. *International Journal of Retail & Distribution Management*, 35(6-7), 421–442. doi:10.1108/09590550710750313

Firat, A. F., & Venkatesh, A. (1995). Liberatory Postmodernism and the Reenchantment of Consumption. *The Journal of Consumer Research*, 22(3), 239–267. doi:10.1086/209448

Fishbein, M., & Ajzen, I. (1975). *Belief, attitude, intention, and behavior: An introduction to theory and research*. Reading, MA: Addison-Wesley.

Fisher, L. (2012). Top retailers at channel crossroads. *Marketing Magazine*. Retrieved March 27, 2013, from http://www.marketingweek.co.uk/trends/top-retailers-at-channel-crossroads/4003348.article

Fiszbein, A., Giovagnoli, P. I., & Adúriz, I. (2003). The Argentinean crisis and its impact on household welfare. *CEPAL Review*, 79, 143–158.

Fitzsimmons, J. A. (2003). Is self-service the future of services? *Managing Service Quality*, 13(6), 443–444. doi:10.1108/09604520310506496

Fitzsimons, G. J. (2000). Consumer response to stockouts. *The Journal of Consumer Research*, 27(2), 249–266. doi:10.1086/314323

Flatters, P., & Willmott, M. (2009). Understanding the post-recession consumers. *Harvard Business Review*, 7(8), 106–112.

Flavián, C., Martínez, E., & Polo, Y. (2001). Loyalty to grocery stores in the Spanish market of the 1990s. *Journal of Retailing and Consumer Services, 8*(2), 85–93. doi:10.1016/S0969-6989(99)00028-4

Fleming, P., & Spicer, A. (2008). Beyond power and resistance. *Management Communication Quarterly, 21*(3), 301–309. doi:10.1177/0893318907309928

Fletcher, G., & Greenhill, A. (2009). Blog/shop: it is authentic so don't worry. *Journal of Information. Communication and Ethics in Society, 7*(1), 39–53. doi:10.1108/14779960910938089

Florida, R. (2002). *The Rise of the Creative Class.* New York: Basic Books.

Forbes. (2011). *Steps to More Honest Business.* Retrieved from http://www.forbes.com/sites/thebigenoughcompany/2011/09/21/3-steps-to-a-more-honest-business/

Fornari, D. (2012). *New factors in channel relationships.* Milano, Italy: Egea.

Fornell, C., & Larcker, D. F. (1981). Evaluating structural equation models with unobservable variables and measurement error. *JMR, Journal of Marketing Research, 18*(1), 39–50. doi:10.2307/3151312

Fournier, S. (1991). Meaning-based framework for the study of consumer-object relations.[Provo, UT: Association for Consumer Research.]. *Advances in Consumer Research. Association for Consumer Research (U. S.), 18,* 736–742.

Fournier, S. (2009). Lessons learned about consumers' relationships with brand. In *Handbook of brand relationships.* N.Y. Society for Consumer Psychology and M.E. Sharp.

Foxall, G. (1997). Affective Responses to Consumer Situations. *International Review of Retail, Distribution and Consumer Research, 7*(3), 191–225. doi:10.1080/095939697342996

Foxall, G. R. (1997). The Emotional Texture of Consumer Environments: A Systematic Approach to Atmospherics. *Journal of Economic Psychology, 18*(4), 505–523. doi:10.1016/S0167-4870(97)00021-4

Foxall, G. R., & Greenley, G. E. (1999). Consumers' Emotional Responses to Service Environments. *Journal of Business Research, 46*(2), 149–158. doi:10.1016/S0148-2963(98)00018-6

Foxall, G. R., & Greenley, G. E. (2000). Predicting and Explaining Responses to Consumer Environments: An Empirical Test and Theoretical Extension of the Behavioural Perspective Model. *The Service Industries Journal, 20*(2), 39–63. doi:10.1080/02642060000000019

Fram, E. H. (1965). Application of the Marketing Concept to Retailing. *Journal of Retailing, 41*(2), 19–26.

Frankenberg, E., James, P., & Duncan, T. (2003). Economic Shocks, Wealth, and Welfare. *The Journal of Human Resources, 38*(2), 280–321. doi:10.2307/1558746

Frank, R. E., & Boyd, H. W. (1965). Are private-brand prone grocery customers really different? *JMR, Journal of Marketing Research, 4,* 27–35.

Fraticelli, F., & Negri, F. (2013). Twittering organizations' customer service: evidences from top 100 companies. In *Proceedings of 10th SIM Conference.* SIM.

Freeman, R. E., & Phillips, R. A. (2002). Stakeholder theory: a libertarian defence. *Business Ethics Quarterly, 12*(3), 331–333. doi:10.2307/3858020

Friedman, M. (1970). The social responsibility of firms is to increase its profits. *New York Times Magazine.*

Friend, L. A., Costley, C. L., & Brown, C. (2010). Spirals of Distrust vs Spirals of Trust in Retail Customer Service: Consumers as Victims or Allies. *Journal of Services Marketing, 24*(6), 458–467. doi:10.1108/08876041011072573

Frith, H., & Gleeson, G. (2004). Clothing and Embodiment: Men Managing Body Image and Appearance. *Psychology of Men & Masculinity, 5*(1), 40–48. doi:10.1037/1524-9220.5.1.40

Fukuyama, F. (1995). *Trust: the social virtues and the creation of prosperity.* Free Press.

Fullerton, R. A., & Punj, G. N. (2004). Repercussions of Promoting an Ideology of Consumption: Consumer Misbehavior. *Journal of Business Research, 57*(11), 1239–1249. doi:10.1016/S0148-2963(02)00455-1

Fullerton, R., & Punj, G. (1993). Choosing to Misbehave: A Structural Model of Aberrant Consumer Behavior. *Advances in Consumer Research. Association for Consumer Research (U. S.)*, *20*, 570–574.

Galvin, T., Ventresca, & Hudson, M.B. (2005). Contested Industry Dynamics. New directions in the study of legitimacy. *International Studies of Management and Organization*, *34*(4), 57–84.

Gao, T., Rohm, A. J., Sultan, F., & Huang, S. (2012). Antecedents of consumer attitudes toward mobile marketing: A comparative study of youth markets in the United States and China. *Thunderbird Int'l Bus Rev*, *54*, 211–224. doi:10.1002/tie.21452

Garbarino, E., & Johnson, M. S. (1999). The different roles of satisfaction, trust and commitment in customer relationships. *Journal of Marketing*, *63*(2), 70–87. doi:10.2307/1251946

Gardner, B. B., & Levy, S. J. (1955). The product and the brand. *Harvard Business Review*, *33*(2), 33–39.

Gardner, T. (2014). *Glasgow High Street* [Image]. Retrieved from Toni Gardner.

Garling, T., Kirchler, E., Lewis, A., & van Raaij, F. (2009). Psychology, Financial Decision Making, and Financial Crisis. *Psychological Science in the Public Interest*, *10*, 1–47. doi:10.1177/1529100610378437

Garretson, J., Fisher, D., & Burton, S. (2002). Antecedents of private label attitude and brand promotion attitude: similarities and differences. *Journal of Retailing*, *78*(2), 91–99. doi:10.1016/S0022-4359(02)00071-4

Gaur, S. S., Herjanto, H., & Bathula, H. (2012). Does buyer–seller similarity affect buyer satisfaction with the seller firm? *International Review of Retail, Distribution and Consumer Research*, *22*(3), 315–335. doi:10.1080/09593969.2012.682597

Gebhardt, G. F., Carpenter, G. S., & Sherry, J. J. F. (2006). Creating a market orientation: a longitudinal, multifirm, grounded analysis of cultural transformation. *Journal of Marketing*, *70*(4), 37–55. doi:10.1509/jmkg.70.4.37

Geddes, I. (2011). The store of the future: The new role of the store in a multichannel environment. *Deloitte*. Retrieved August 6, 2013, from http://www.deloitte.com/assets/Dcom-UnitedKingdom/Local%20Assets/Documents/Industries/Consumer%20Business/uk-cb-store-of-the-future-report.pdf

Gefen, D., Karahanna, E., & Straub, D. W. (2003). Trust and TAM in online shopping: An integrated model. *Management Information Systems Quarterly*, *27*(1), 51–90.

Gelbrich, K. (2011). I Have Paid Less Than You! The Emotional and Behavioral Consequences of Advantaged Price Inequality. *Journal of Retailing*, *87*(2), 207–224. doi:10.1016/j.jretai.2011.03.003

Gensler, S., Verhoef, P. C., & Böhm, M. (2012). Understanding consumers' multichannel choices across the different stages of the buying process. *Marketing Letters*, *23*(4), 987–1003. doi:10.1007/s11002-012-9199-9

Gentile, C., Spiller, N., & Noci, G. (2007). How to Sustain the Customer Experience: An Overview of Experience Components that Co-create Value With the Customer. *European Management Journal*, *25*(5), 395–410. doi:10.1016/j.emj.2007.08.005

Ger, G., & Belk, R. W. (1996). Cross-cultural Differences in Materialism. *Journal of Economic Psychology*, *17*(1), 55–77. doi:10.1016/0167-4870(95)00035-6

Geuens, M., Brengman, M., & S'Jegers, R. (2001). An exploratory study of grocery shopping motivations. In A. Groeppel-Klien, & F.-R. Esch (Eds.), *European advances in consumer research* (vol. 5, pp. 135-140). Provo, UT: Association for Consumer Research.

Ghemawat, P. (2007). Managing Differences: The Central Challenge of Global Strategy. *Harvard Business Review*, *85*(3), 58–68. PMID:17348170

Gil, A. C. (2002). *Como elaborar projetos de pesquisa* [How to do research projects]. Sao Paulo: Atlas. (in Portuguese)

Gilbert, L. A., & Han, H. (2005). Understanding mobile data services adoption: demography, attitudes or needs? *Technological Forecasting and Social Change*, *72*, 327–337. doi:10.1016/j.techfore.2004.08.007

Gilboa, S., & Rafaeli, A. (2003). Store Environment, Emotions and Approach Behavior: Applying Environmental Aesthetics to Retailing. *International Review of Retail, Distribution and Consumer Research, 13*(2), 195–211. doi:10.1080/0959396032000069568

Gill, M. (2007). *Shoplifters on Shop Theft: Implications for Retailers.* Leicester, UK: Perpetuity Research & Consultancy International.

Gill, M., Bilby, C., & Turbin, V. (1999). Retail Security: Understanding what Deters Shop Thieves. *Journal of Security Administration, 22*(1), 29–39.

Gilmore, J. (2004). *Quantitative Trends in the North American Coffee Market 2004, Datamonitor Inc.* Paper presented at the 93rd National Coffee Association Conference. Dana Point, CA.

Gilmore, J. H., & Pine, B. J. II. (2007). *Authenticity: What consumers really want.* Boston: Harvard Business School Press.

Gist, R. R. (1968). *Retailing: Concepts and decisions.* New York: Wiley.

Glenday, J. (2013). Study warns one in five High Street shops could be shuttered by 2018. *The Drum.* Retrieved March 27, 2013, from http://www.thedrum.com/news/2013/05/28/study-warns-one-five-high-street-shops-could-be-shuttered-2018

Global Consumer Confidence, Concerns and Spending. (2009). *A global Nielsen consumer report.* Retrieved from http://pt.nielsen.com/documents/tr_0905NelsenGlobalConsumerConfidenceReport1stHalf09.pdf

Global Consumer Confidence, Concerns and Spending. (2010). *A global Nielsen consumer report.* Retrieved from http://lk.nielsen.com/site/documents/CCI1stQuater10.pdf

Glynn Mangold, W., & Faulds, D. J. (2009). Social media: The new hybrid element of the promotion mix. *Business Horizons, 52*, 357–365. doi:10.1016/j.bushor.2009.03.002

Glynn, M. S., & Chen, S. (2009). Consumer-factors moderating private label brand success: further empirical results. *International Journal of Retail & Distribution Management, 37*(11), 896–914. doi:10.1108/09590550910999343

Gold, J. (2008, March 12). La Mill: The Latest Buzz. *LA Weekly.*

Goldman, A. (1975). The role of trading up in the development of the retailing system. *Journal of Marketing, 39*(1), 54–62. doi:10.2307/1250803

Goleman, D. (2003). *Destructive Emotions.* London: Bloomsbury Publishing PLC.

Golinelli, G. M., Barile, S., Spohrer, J., & Bassano, C. (2010). *The Evolving Dynamics of Service Co-creation in a Viable Systems Perspective.* Paper presented at the 13th Toulon-Verona Conference. Coimbra, Portugal.

Golinelli, G. M. (2000). *L'approccio sistemico al governo dell'impresa: La dinamica evolutiva del sistema impresa tra economia e finanza* (Vol. 2). Padova, Italy: Cedam.

Golinelli, G. M. (2010). *Viable Systems Approach (VSA): Governing Business Dynamics.* Padova, Italy: CEDAM Kluwer.

Golinelli, G. M., Barile, S., Saviano, M., & Polese, F. (2012). Perspective Shifts in Marketing: Toward a Paradigm Change? *Service Science, 4*(2), 121–134. doi:10.1287/serv.1120.0015

Gómez, M., & García, C. (2012, March-April). Marketing sensorial: cómo desarrollar la atmósfera del establecimiento comercial. *Distribución y Consumo*, 30-39.

Gómez, M., & García, C. (2010). *Nuevas tendencias en el punto de venta: el marketing sensorial. Distribución comercial y comportamiento del consumidor, Ramón Areces Foundation.* University of Oviedo.

Gómez, M., & Rozano, M. (2008). La influencia del aroma en la percepción del establecimiento comercial. *Revista Portuguesa de Marketing, 23*(2), 59–68.

González-Benito, O., & Martos-Partal, M. (2012). Role of retailer positioning and product category on the relationship between store brand consumption and store loyalty. *Journal of Retailing, 88*(2), 236–249. doi:10.1016/j.jretai.2011.05.003

Goodman, L. A. (1961). Snowball sampling. *Annals of Mathematical Statistics, 32*(1), 148–170. doi:10.1214/aoms/1177705148

Goodwin, C. (1991). Privacy: Recognition of a Consumer Right. *Journal of Public Policy & Marketing, 10*(1), 149–166.

Grabner-Kraeuter, S. (2002). The Role of Consumers' Trust in Online-Shopping. *Journal of Business Ethics*, *39*(1-2), 43–50. doi:10.1023/A:1016323815802

Grandinetti, R. (Ed.). (2008). *Marketing: Mercati, prodotti e relazioni*. Roma, Italy: Carocci.

Grandon, E. E., & Pearson, J. M. (2004). Electronic commerce adoption: an empirical study of small and medium US businesses. *Information & Management*, *42*(1), 197–216. doi:10.1016/j.im.2003.12.010

Grayson, K., & Martinec, R. (2004). Consumer Perceptions of Iconicity and Indexicality and Their Influence on Assessments of Authentic Market Offerings. *The Journal of Consumer Research*, *31*(2), 296–312. doi:10.1086/422109

Grayson, R. A. S., & McNeill, L. S. (2009). Using atmospheric elements in service retailing: understanding the bar environment. *Journal of Services Marketing*, *23*(7), 517–527. doi:10.1108/08876040910995301

Greenley, G. E., & Shipley, D. D. (1988). An Empirical Overview of Marketing by Retailing Organisations. *Service Industries Journal*, *8*(1), 49–66. doi:10.1080/02642068800000005

Grewal, D., Baker, J., Levy, M., & Voss, G. B. (2003). The effects of wait expectations and store atmosphere evaluations on patronage intentions in service-intensive retail stores. *Journal of Retailing*, *79*, 259–268. doi:10.1016/j.jretai.2003.09.006

Grewal, D., Krishnan, R., Baker, J., & Borin, N. (1998). The effect of store name, brand name and price discounts on consumers' evaluations and purchase intentions. *Journal of Retailing*, *74*(3), 331–352. doi:10.1016/S0022-4359(99)80099-2

Grewal, D., Krishnan, R., Levy, M., & Munger, J. (2010). Retail success and key drivers. In *Retailing in the 21st Century* (pp. 15–30). Springer. doi:10.1007/978-3-540-72003-4_2

Grewal, D., & Levy, M. (2009). Emerging Issues in Retailing Research. *Journal of Retailing*, *85*(4), 522–526. doi:10.1016/j.jretai.2009.09.007

Grewal, D., Levy, M., & Kumar, V. (2009). Customer Experience Management in Retailing: An Organizing Framework. *Journal of Retailing*, *85*(1), 1–14. doi:10.1016/j.jretai.2009.01.001

Grohmann, B., Spangenberg, E., & Sprott, D. (2007). The Influence of Tactile Input on the Evaluation of Retail Product Offerings. *Journal of Retailing*, *83*(2), 237–245. doi:10.1016/j.jretai.2006.09.001

Grönroos, C. (1994). Quo vadis, marketing? Towards a relationship marketing paradigm. *Journal of Marketing Management*, *10*(4), 347–360. doi:10.1080/0267257X.1994.9964283

Grönroos, C. (2000). *Service Management and Marketing: A Consumer Relationship Management Approach*. Chichester, UK: John Wiley & Sons.

Grönroos, C. (2008). Service Logic Revisited: Who Creates Value? And Who Co-Creates? *European Business Review*, *20*(4), 298–314. doi:10.1108/09555340810886585

Grönroos, C. (2011). A service perspective in business relationships: The value creation and marketing interface. *Industrial Marketing Management*, *40*(1), 240–247. doi:10.1016/j.indmarman.2010.06.036

Grosso, C., McPherson, J., & Shi, C. (2005). Retailing: what's working online. *The McKinsey Quarterly*, *3*(18), 18–20.

GRTB. (2007). *The Global Retail Theft Barometer*. Nottingham, UK: Centre for Retail Research.

Grzeskowiak, S., Sirgy, M. J., Lee, D. J., & Claiborne, C. B. (2006). Housing well-being: Developing and validating a measure. *Social Indicators Research*, *79*(3), 503–541. doi:10.1007/s11205-005-5667-4

Guilt Free Consumption. (2013). Retrieved from http://www.trendwatching.com

Guiry, M., Magi, A. W., & Lutz, R. J. (2006). Defining and measuring recreational shopper identity. *Journal of the Academy of Marketing Science*, *34*(1), 74–83. doi:10.1177/0092070305282042

Gulas, C. S., & Bloch, P. H. (1995). Right under our noses: ambient scent and consumer responses. *Journal of Business and Psychology*, *10*(1), 87–98. doi:10.1007/BF02249272

Gummerus, J., Liljander, V., Weman, E., & Pihlstrom, M. (2012). Customer engagement in a Facebook brand community. *Management Research Review*, *35*(9), 857–877. doi:10.1108/01409171211256578

Gummesson, E. (2002). *Total Relationship Marketing.* Oxford, UK: Butterworth-Heinemann.

Gummesson, E. (2004). *Many-to-Many Marketing.* Malmö, Sweden: Liber.

Gummesson, E., Mele, C., & Polese, F. (2009). Service science, S-D logic and network theory: Integrating the perspectives for a new research agenda. In E. Gummesson, C. Mele, & F. Polese (Eds.), *Service science, S-D logic and network theory.* Napoli, Italy: Giannini.

Gummesson, E., Mele, C., & Polese, F. (2011). Integrating the 3 Pillars of the 2011 Naples Forum on Service: S-D logic, Network & Systems Theory and Service Science. In E. Gummesson, C. Mele, & F. Polese (Eds.), *Service-Dominant Logic, Network & Systems Theory and Service Science.* Napoli, Italy: Giannini.

Gummesson, E., & Polese, F. (2009). B2B Is Not an Island. *Journal of Business and Industrial Marketing, 24*(5/6), 337–350. doi:10.1108/08858620910966228

Gurel-Atay, E., Giese, J. L., & Godek, J. (2010). Retailer evaluation: The crucial link between in-store processes and shopping outcomes. *International Review of Retail, Distribution and Consumer Research, 20*(3), 297–310. doi:10.1080/09593969.2010.491202

Gurel-Atay, E., Giese, J., & Godek, J. (2008). Exploring the role of shopping efficacy on customer satisfaction and behavioral intentions. In A. Y. Lee, & D. Soman (Eds.), *NA - Advances in Consumer Research* (pp. 964–965). Duluth, MN: Association for Consumer Research.

Gustafsson, A., Johnson, D. M., & Ross, I. (2005). The effects of customer satisfaction, relationship commitment, dimensions, and triggers on customer retention. *Journal of Marketing, 69*(4), 210–218. doi:10.1509/jmkg.2005.69.4.210

Guy, C. M. (1998). Classifications of retail stores and shopping centres: some methodological issues. *GeoJournal, 45,* 255–264. doi:10.1023/A:1006960414161

Hair, J., Black, W., Babin, B., & Anderson, R. (2010). *Multivariate data analysis* (7th ed.). Upper Saddle River, NJ: Pearson Prentice Hall.

Håkansson, H., & Snehota, I. (1995). *Developing Relationships in Business Marketing.* London, UK: Routledge.

Hall, J. (2011). Mary Portas: High Streets destined to 'disappear forever'. *The Telegraph.* Retrieved March 20, 2013, from http://www.telegraph.co.uk/finance/newsbysector/retailandconsumer/8951411/Mary-Portas-high-streets-destined-to-disappear-forever.html

Hall, J. (2013, June 12). Four tips for giving to the right nonprofit. *Forbes.* Retrieved on August 7, 2013 from http://www.forbes.com/sites/johnhall/2013/06/12/4-tips-for-choosing-a-philanthropic-partner/

Hallowell, R. (1996). The relationships of customer satisfaction, customer loyalty, and profitability: An empirical study. *International Journal of Service Industry Management, 7*(4), 27–42. doi:10.1108/09564239610129931

Hallsworth, A. G. (1997). Rethinking Retail Theory: Circuits of Power as an Integrative Paradigm. *Geographical Analysis, 29*(4), 329–338. doi:10.1111/j.1538-4632.1997.tb00968.x

Hallsworth, A. G., & Taylor, M. (1996). 'Buying' power'interpreting retail change in a circuits of power framework. *Environment & Planning A, 28,* 2125–2137. doi:10.1068/a282125

Hanappi, H. (2004). *The Survival of the Fattest: Evolution of needs, lust and social value in a long-run perspective.* Paper presented at the European Association for Evolutionary Political Economy Conference. Crete.

Hannerz, U. (1996). *Transnational Connections.* New York: Routledge.

Haralambos, M., & Holborn, M. (2008). *Sociology – Themes and perspectives.* London, UK: Collins.

Harris, L. C. (1998). Cultural domination: the key to a market oriented culture? *European Journal of Marketing, 32*(3/4), 354–373. doi:10.1108/03090569810204643

Harris, L. C. (2000). The organizational barriers to developing market orientation. *European Journal of Marketing, 34*(5-6), 354–373.

Harris, L. C., & Goode, M. M. H. (2004). The Four Levels Of Loyalty And The Pivotal Role Of Trust: A Study Of Online Service Dynamics. *Journal of Retailing, 80*(2), 139–158. doi:10.1016/j.jretai.2004.04.002

Harris, L., & Dennis, C. (2011). Engaging customers on Facebook: Challenges for e-retailers. *Journal of Consumer Behaviour, 10*, 338–346. doi:10.1002/cb.375

Hart, C. (1999). The Retail Accordion and Assortment Strategies: an Explanatory Study. *International Review of Retail, Distribution and Consumer Research, 9*(2), 111–126. doi:10.1080/095939699342598

Hartman, K. B., & Spiro, R. L. (2005). Recapturing store image in customer-based store equity: a construct conceptualization. *Journal of Business Research, 58*, 1112–1120. doi:10.1016/j.jbusres.2004.01.008

Harvey, C. G., Stewart, D. B., & Ewing, M. T. (2011). Forward or delete: What drives peer-to-peer message propagation across social networks? *Journal of Consumer Behaviour, 10*, 365–372. doi:10.1002/cb.383

Hassanein, K., & Head, M. (2007). Manipulating perceived social presence through the web interface and its impact on attitude towards online shopping. *International Journal of Human-Computer Studies, 65*(8), 689–708. doi:10.1016/j.ijhcs.2006.11.018

Hauser, J., Tellis, G. J., & Griffin, A. (2006). Research on Innovation: A Review and Agenda for Marketing Science. *Marketing Science, 25*, 686–717. doi:10.1287/mksc.1050.0144

Hayes, R., & Blackwood, R. (2006). Evaluating the Effects of EAS on Product Sales and Loss: Results of a Large-Scale Field Experiment. *Security Journal, 19*(4), 262–276. doi:10.1057/palgrave.sj.8350025

Hayes, R., & Downs, D. M. (2011). Controlling Retail Theft with CCTV Domes, CCTV Public View Monitors, and Protective Containers: A Randomized Controlled Trial. *Security Journal, 24*(3), 237–250. doi:10.1057/sj.2011.12

Hayes, R., Johns, T., Scicchitano, M., Downs, D., & Pietrawska, B. (2011). Evaluating the Effects of Protective Keeper Boxes on 'Hot Product' Loss and Sales: A Randomized Controlled Trial. *Security Journal, 24*(3), 357–369. doi:10.1057/sj.2011.2

Headey, B., Holmstrom, E., & Wearing, A. (1985). Models of well-being and ill-being. *Social Indicators Research, 7*(3), 211–234. doi:10.1007/BF00319311

Heath, J., & Potter, A. (2005). *Nations of Rebels: How the Counter Culture Became Consumer Culture.* New York: Harper Business.

Hee-Woomg, K., Xu, Y., & Koh, J. (2004). A Comparison of Online Trust Building Factors Between Potential Customers and Repeat Customers. *Journal of the Association for Information Systems, 5*(10), 392–420.

He, H., & Mukherjee, A. (2007). I am, ergo I shop: does store image congruity explain shopping behaviour of Chinese consumers? *Journal of Marketing Management, 23*(5-6), 443–460. doi:10.1362/026725707X212766

Heide, M., & GrØnhaug, K. (2006). Atmosphere: Conceptual Issues and Implications for hospitality management. *Scandinavian Journal of Hospitality and Tourism, 6*(4), 271–286. doi:10.1080/15022250600979515

Helgeson, J. G., & Supphellen, M. (2004). A conceptual and measurement comparison of self-congruity and brand personality: The impact of socially desirable responding. *International Journal of Market Research, 46*(2), 205–233.

Heskett, J. L. et al. (1997). *The service profit chain: How leading companies link profit and growth to loyalty, satisfaction and value.* New York: The Free Press.

Heskett, J. L., Jones, T. O., Loveman, G. W., Sasser, W. E. Jr, & Schlesinger, L. A. (1994, March-April). Putting the service profit chain to work. *Harvard Business Review.*

Hill, J. (2013). High Street chain store closures soar, says research. *BBC News Business.* Retrieved November 15, 2013, from http://www.bbc.co.uk/news/business-21611772

Hillson, D., & Webster, R. (2004). Understanding and managing risk attitude. In *Proceedings of 7th Annual Risk Conference.* Retrieved April 22, 2010, from http://www.kent.ac.uk/scarr/events/finalpapers/Hillson%20%2B%20Murray-Webster.pdf

Hillson, D., & Webster, R. (2006). *Managing Risk Attitude using Emotional Literacy.* Retrieved April 22, 2013, from http://www.ashgate.com/pdf/white_papers/Gower_White_Paper_Managing_Risk_Attitude_Emotional_Literacy.pdf

Hinchcliffe, D., & Kim, P. (2012). *Social Business by Design.* San Francisco, CA: Jossey-Bass, a Wiley Imprint.

Hindess, B. (1996). *Discourses of Power: From Hobbes to Foucault*. Oxford, UK: Blackwell Publishers Ltd.

Hine, T. (2002). *I want that! How we all became shoppers*. New York: Harper Collins Press.

Hingley, M., Taylor, S., & Ellis, C. (2007). Radio Frequency Identification Tagging. Supplier Attitudes to Implementation in the Grocery Retail Sector. *International Journal of Retail & Distribution Management*, 35(10), 803–820. doi:10.1108/09590550710820685

Hirschman, E. C., & Holbrook, M. B. (1982). Hedonic Consumption: Emerging Concepts, Methods and Propositions. *Journal of Marketing*, 46, 92–101. doi:10.2307/1251707

Hoch, S. J., & Banerji, S. (1993). When Do Private Labels Succeed? *Sloan Management Review*, 34, 57–67.

Hoeffler, S., & Keller, K. L. (2002). Building brand equity through corporate societal marketing. *Journal of Public Policy & Marketing*, 21, 78–89. doi:10.1509/jppm.21.1.78.17600

Hoffman, D. (1999). Information privacy in the marketspace: implications for the commercial uses of anonymity on the web. *The Information Society*, 15(2), 129–140. doi:10.1080/019722499128583

Hoffman, D. L., Kopalle, & Novak. (2010). The "Right" Consumers for Better Concepts: Identifying and Using Consumers High in Emergent Nature to Further Develop New Product Concepts. *JMR, Journal of Marketing Research*. doi:10.1509/jmkr.47.5.854

Hoffman, D. L., & Fodor, M. (2010). Can You Measure the ROI of Your Social Media Marketing? *MIT Sloan Management Review*, 52(1), 41–49.

Hoffman, D., Novak, T. P., & Peralta, M. A. (1999). Building Consumer Trust Online Environment: The Case For Information Privacy. *Communications of the ACM*, 42(4), 80–85. doi:10.1145/299157.299175

Hofstede, G. (2004). *Hofstede Dimension Data Matrix*. Retrieved August 22, 2010, from http://www.geerthofstede.nl

Hofstede, G., & McCrae, R. (2004). Personality and culture revisited: linking traits and dimensions of culture. *Cross-Cultural Research*, 38(1), 52–88. doi:10.1177/1069397103259443

Holbrook, M. B., & Hirschmann, E. C. (1982). The experiential aspects of consumption: consumer fantasies, feelings, and fun. *The Journal of Consumer Research*, 9, 132–140. doi:10.1086/208906

Hollander, S. C. (1960). The Wheel of Retailing. *Journal of Marketing*, 25(1), 37–42. doi:10.2307/1249121

Hollander, S. C. (1966). Notes on the Retail Accordion. *Journal of Retailing*, 43, 24–40.

Hollenbeck, C. R., Peters, C., & Zinkhan, G. M. (2008). Retail Spectacles and Brand Meaning: Insights from a Brand Museum Case Study. *Journal of Retailing*, 84(3), 334–353. doi:10.1016/j.jretai.2008.05.003

Hollenbeck, C. R., & Zinkhan, G. M. (2010). Anti-Brand Communities, Negotiation of Brand Meaning, and the Learning Process: The Case of Wal-Mart. *Consumption. Markets & Culture*, 13(3), 325–345. doi:10.1080/10253861003787056

Holt, D. B. (2002). Why Do Brands Cause Trouble? A Dialectical Theory of Consumer Culture and Branding. *The Journal of Consumer Research*, 29(1), 70–90. doi:10.1086/339922

Holt, D. B. (2004). *How Brands Become Icons: The Principles of Cultural Branding*. Boston: Harvard Business School Press.

Holt, D. B. (2005). How societies desire brands: Using cultural theory to explain brand symbolism. In S. Ratneshwar, & D. G. Mick (Eds.), *Inside consumption* (pp. 273–291). London: Routledge.

Holton, G. (2004). Defining Risk. *Financial Analysts Journal*, 60(6), 19–25. doi:10.2469/faj.v60.n6.2669

Homburg, C., Hoyer, W. D., & Fassnacht, M. (2002). Service Orientation of a Retailer's Business Strategy: Dimensions, Antecedents, and Performance Outcomes. *Journal of Marketing*, 66(4), 86–101. doi:10.1509/jmkg.66.4.86.18511

Hosay, S., & Martin, D. (2012). Self-image congruence in consumer behaviour. *Journal of Business Research*, 65, 685–691. doi:10.1016/j.jbusres.2011.03.015

Hosch, S. J., & Loewenstein, G. F. (1991). Time-inconsistent preferences and consumer self-control. *The Journal of Consumer Research*, 17, 492–507. doi:10.1086/208573

Hoyer, W. D., Chandy, R., Dorotic, M., Kraff, M., & Singh, S. S. (2010). Consumer Cocreation in New Product Development. *Journal of Service Research, 13*(3), 283–296. doi:10.1177/1094670510375604

Hsiang-Fei, L., & Sheng-Hshiung, T. (2011). Customers' perceptions of service quality: do servers' age stereotypes matter? *International Journal of Hospitality Management, 30*, 283–289. doi:10.1016/j.ijhm.2010.09.002

Huang, M. (2001). The theory of emotions in marketing. *Journal of Business and Psychology, 16*(2), 239–247. doi:10.1023/A:1011109200392

Huang, Y., & Huddleston, P. (2009). Retailer premium own-brands: creating customer loyalty through own-brand products advantage. *International Journal of Retail & Distribution Management, 37*(11), 975–992. doi:10.1108/09590550910999389

Huffman, C., & Kahn, B. E. (1998). Variety for Sale: Mass Customization of Mass Confusion. *Journal of Retailing, 74*(4), 491–513. doi:10.1016/S0022-4359(99)80105-5

Hu, H., & Jasper, C. R. (2006). Social cues in the store environment and their impact on store image. *International Journal of Retail and Distribution Management, 34*(1), 25–48. doi:10.1108/09590550610642800

Hui, K. L., Teo, H. H., & Lee, S. Y. T. (2007). The value of privacy assurance: an exploratory field experiment. *Management Information Systems Quarterly, 31*(1), 19–33.

Hui, M. K., & Bateson, J. E. G. (1991). Perceived Control and the Effects of Crowding and Consumer Choice on the Service Experience. *The Journal of Consumer Research, 18*(2), 174–184. doi:10.1086/209250

Hui, M. K., Laurette, D., & Chebat, J.-C. (1997). The impact of music on consumers` reactions to waiting for services. *Journal of Retailing, 73*(1), 87–104. doi:10.1016/S0022-4359(97)90016-6

Hu, L. T., & Bentler, P. M. (1995). Evaluating model fit. In R. H. Hoyle (Ed.), *Structural equation modeling: concepts, issues, and applications*. Thousand Oaks, CA: Sage Publications.

Hultén, B. (2012). Sensory Cues and Shoppers' Touching Behaviour: The Case of IKEA. *International Journal of Retail & Distribution Management, 40*(4), 273–289. doi:10.1108/09590551211211774

Hulten, B., Broweus, N., & van Dijk, M. (2008). *Sensory Marketing*. Palgrave Macmillan.

Hunter, B. T. (1995). The sales appeal of scents (using synthetic food scents to increase sales). *Consumer Research Magazine, 78*(10), 8–10.

Hunt, S. D. (2010). *Marketing Theory: Foundations, Controversy, Strategy, Resource-Advantage Theory*. Armonk, NY: M.E. Sharpe.

Hyman, M. R., Kopf, D. A., & Lee, D. (2010). Review of literature – future research suggestions: private label brands: benefits, success factors and future research. *Journal of Brand Management, 17*(5), 368–389. doi:10.1057/bm.2009.33

IBISWorld. (2013). Coffee & Snack Shops in the US. *IBISWorld Industry Report 72221b*. Retrieved August 20, 2013, from www.ibisworld.com

IfM & IBM. (2008). *Succeeding through Service Innovation: A Service Perspective for Education, Research, Business and Government*. Cambridge, UK: University of Cambridge Institute for Manufacturing.

Insider. (2012). *White paper*. Retrieved from http://www.mediacom.com/media/2088012/mediacom%20the%20insider_the%20empowered%20consumer_whitepaper.pdf

Interbrand. (2011). *Best global brands*. Retrieved August 3, 2013, from http://www.interbrand.com/es/best-global-brands/Best-Global-Brands-2011.aspx

Internet World Stats. (2010). Retrieved from http://www.internetworldstats.com/stats9.htm#eu

Izard, C. E. (1977). *Human emotions*. New York: Plenum Press. doi:10.1007/978-1-4899-2209-0

Izraeli, D. (1973). The Three Wheels of Retailing: A Theoretical Note. *European Journal of Marketing, 7*(1), 70–74. doi:10.1108/EUM0000000005101

Janakiraman, N., Meyer, R. J., & Morales, A. C. (2006). Spillover Effects: How Consumers Respond to Unaspected Changes in Price and Quality. *The Journal of Consumer Research, 33*, 361–369. doi:10.1086/508440

Jarvenpaa, S. L., Tractinsky, J., & Vitale, M. (2000). Consumer Trust In An Internet Store. *Information Technology Management, 1*(1/2), 45–71. doi:10.1023/A:1019104520776

Jarvenpaa, S. L., & Tractinsky, N. (1999). Consumer trust in an internet store: a cross-cultural validation. *Journal of Computer-Mediated Communication, 5*(2), 1–35.

Jasiulewicz, A. (2011). Economic Crisis Influence on the Polish Consumer Behaviour. In *Overcoming the Crisis: Economic and Financial Developments in Asia and Europe*, (pp. 77-88). Retrieved June, 24, from http://www.hippocampus.si/ISBN/978-961-6832-32-8/papers/jasiulewicz.pdf

Jasper, C., & Klassen, M. (1990). Stereotypical Beliefs about Appearance: implications for retailing and consumer issues. *Perceptual and Motor Skills, 71*, 519–528. doi:10.2466/pms.1990.71.2.519 PMID:2251085

Javalgi, R., & Moberg, C. (1997). Service loyalty: Implications for service providers. *Journal of Services Marketing, 11*(3), 165–179. doi:10.1108/08876049710168663

Jensen, J. M. (2011). Consumer loyalty on the grocery product market: an empirical application of Dick and Basu's framework. *Journal of Consumer Marketing, 28*(5), 333–343. doi:10.1108/07363761111149983

Jensen, J. M., & Hansen, T. (2006). An empirical examination of brand loyalty. *Journal of Product and Brand Management, 15*(7), 442–449. doi:10.1108/10610420610712829

Jiang, J.-C., Chen, C.-A., & Wang, C.-C. (2008). Knowledge and trust in e-consumers' online shopping behavior. In *Proceedings of the International Symposium on Electronic Commerce and Security* (pp. 652-656). IEEE.

Jin, B., & Sternquist, B. (2004). Shopping is truly a joy. *The Service Industries Journal, 24*(6), 1–18. doi:10.1080/0264206042000299158

Jinfeng, W., & Zhilong, T. (2009). The impact of selected store image dimensions on retailer equity: Evidence from 10 Chinese hypermarkets. *Journal of Retailing and Consumer Services, 16*, 486–494. doi:10.1016/j.jretconser.2009.08.002

Johnson, D., & Grayson, K. (2005). Cognitive and affective trust in service relationships. *Journal of Business Research, 58*(4), 500–507. doi:10.1016/S0148-2963(03)00140-1

Johnson, E. J., Bellman, S., & Lohse, G. L. (2002). Defaults, framing, and privacy: Why opting in opting out. *Marketing Letters, 13*(1), 5–15. doi:10.1023/A:1015044207315

Johnson, E. J., & Payne, J. W. (1985). Effort and accuracy in choice. *Management Science, 31*(4), 395–414. doi:10.1287/mnsc.31.4.395

Johnson, G., Langley, A., Melin, L., & Whittington, R. (2007). *Strategy as Practice: Research Directions and Resource.* Cambridge, MA: Cambridge University Press. doi:10.1017/CBO9780511618925

Jones, M. A. (1999). Entertaining Shopping Experiences: An Exploratory Investigation. *Journal of Retailing and Consumer Services, 6*(3), 129–139. doi:10.1016/S0969-6989(98)00028-9

Jones, M. A., & Suh, J. (2000). Transaction-specific satisfaction and overall satisfaction: an empirical analysis. *Journal of Services Marketing, 14*(2), 147–159. doi:10.1108/08876040010371555

Jones, P., Clarke-Hill, C., Shears, P., Comfort, D., & Hillier, D. (2004). Radio Frequency Identification in the UK: Opportunities and Challenges. *International Journal of Retail & Distribution Management, 32*(3), 164–171. doi:10.1108/09590550410524957

Joye, Y., Willems, Brengman, & Wolf, K. (2010). The effects of urban retail greenery on consumer experience: Reviewing the evidence from a restorative perspective. *Urban Forestry & Urban Greening, 9*, 57–64. doi:10.1016/j.ufug.2009.10.001

Kacen, J. J., & Lee, J. A. (2002). The influence of culture on consumer impulsive buying behavior. *Journal of Consumer Psychology, 12*(2), 163–176. doi:10.1207/S15327663JCP1202_08

Kacker, M. (1986). Coming to Terms with Global Retailing. *International Marketing Review, 3*(1), 7. doi:10.1108/eb008295

Kahneman, D. (2003). Maps of bounded rationality: Psychology for behavioral economics. *The American Economic Review, 93*(5), 1449–1475. doi:10.1257/000282803322655392

Kaikati, J. D. (1985). Don't discount off-price retailers. *Harvard Business Review, 63*(3), 85–92.

Kajalo, S., & Lindblom, A. (2010a). The Perceived Effectiveness of Surveillance in Reducing Crime at Shopping Centers in Finland. *Property Management, 28*(1), 47–59. doi:10.1108/02637471011017172

Kajalo, S., & Lindblom, A. (2010b). Surveillance Investments in Store Environment and Sense of Security. *Facilities, 28*(9/10), 465–474. doi:10.1108/02632771011057198

Kajalo, S., & Lindblom, A. (2011a). Effectiveness of Formal and Informal Surveillance in Reducing Crime at Grocery Stores. *Journal of Small Business and Enterprise Development, 18*(1), 157–169. doi:10.1108/14626001111106488

Kamakura, W. A., Mittal, V., de Rose, F., & Mazzon, J. A. (2002). Assessing the Service-Profit Chain. *Marketing Science, 21*(3), 294–317. doi:10.1287/mksc.21.3.294.140

Kandampully, J. (2012b). Service as the New Paradigm in Retailing. In J. Kandampully (Ed.), *Service Management: The New Paradigm in Retailing* (pp. 1–6). New York: Springer. doi:10.1007/978-1-4614-1554-1_1

Kandampully, J. (Ed.). (2012a). *Service Management: The New Paradigm in Retailing.* New York: Springer. doi:10.1007/978-1-4614-1554-1

Kang, J., Tang, L., Lee, J. Y., & Bosselman, R. H. (2012). Understanding customer behavior in name-brand Korean coffee shops: The role of self-congruity and functional congruity. *International Journal of Hospitality Management, 31*, 809–818. doi:10.1016/j.ijhm.2011.09.017

Kang, S. J., & Sawada, Y. (2008). Credit crunch and household welfare, the case of the Korean financial crisis. *The Japanese Economic Review, 59*, 438–458. doi:10.1111/j.1468-5876.2008.00429.x

Kano, N., Seraku, N., Takahashi, F., & Tsuji, S. (1984). Attractive Quality and Must-Be Quality. *Journal of Japanese Society for Quality Control, 14*(2), 39–48.

Kaplan, R., & Kaplan, S. (1989). *The experience of nature: A psychological perspective.* New York, NY: Cambridge University Press.

Karababa, E., & Ger, G. (2010). Early Modern Ottoman Coffeehouse Culture and the Formation of the Consumer Subject. *The Journal of Consumer Research, 37*, 737–760. doi:10.1086/656422

Kaufman, S. (1985). Coping with Rapid Retail Evolution. *Journal of Consumer Marketing, 2*(1), 17–27. doi:10.1108/eb038817

Kay, M. (2010). Marketing During a Recession: Social Effects and Marketing Opportunities. In *Proceedings of the Northeast Business & Economics Association*, (pp. 587-589). Academic Press.

Kaynak, E. (1979). A refined approach to the wheel of retailing. *European Journal of Marketing, 13*(7), 237–245. doi:10.1108/EUM0000000004957

Keen, C., Wetzels, M., De Ruyter, K., & Feinberg, R. (2004). E-tailers versus retailers: which factors determine consumer preferences. *Journal of Business Research, 57*(7), 685–695. doi:10.1016/S0148-2963(02)00360-0

Keiningham, T. L., Aksoy, L., & Williams, L. (2012). Why Loyalty Matters in Retailing. In J. Kandampully (Ed.), *Service Management: The New Paradigm in Retailing* (pp. 67–82). New York: Springer. doi:10.1007/978-1-4614-1554-1_5

Kellaris, J. J., & Kent, R. J. (1992). The influence of music on consumer's temporal perceptions: does time fly when you're having fun? *Journal of Consumer Psychology, 1*(4), 365–379. doi:10.1016/S1057-7408(08)80060-5

Kellaris, J. J., & Rice, R. C. (1993). The influence on tempo, loudness, and gender of listener on responses to music. *Psychology and Marketing, 10*(1), 15–28. doi:10.1002/mar.4220100103

Keller, K. L. (1993). Conceptualizing, measuring, and managing customer-based brand equity. *Journal of Marketing, 57*(1), 1–22. doi:10.2307/1252054

Kellert, S. R., & Wilson, E. O. (Eds.). (1993). *The biophilia hypothesis.* Washington, DC: Island Press.

Kelley, E., & Schewe, L. (1975). Buyer behaviour in a stagflation-shortages economy. *Journal of Marketing, 39*, 44–60. doi:10.2307/1250114

Kelly, J. (2013a). *Dundee High Street* [Image]. Retrieved from James Kelly.

Kelly, J. (2013b). *High Street decline* [Image]. Retrieved from James Kelly.

Kennedy, M.S., & Ferrell, L.K., Thorne, & LeClair, D. (2001). Consumers' trust of salesperson and manufacturer: an empirical study. *Journal of Business Research, 51*, 73–86. doi:10.1016/S0148-2963(99)00039-9

Kerfoot, D., & Korczynski, M. (2005). Gender and Service: New Directions for the Study of 'Front-line' Service Work. *Gender, Work and Organization, 12*(5), 387–399. doi:10.1111/j.1468-0432.2005.00280.x

Kim, A. C., Dongchul, H., & Aeung-Bae, P. (2001). The effect of brand personality and brand identification on brand loyalty: applying the theory of social identification. *The Japanese Psychological Research, 43*, 195–206. doi:10.1111/1468-5884.00177

Kim, H., Fiore, A. M., Niehm, L. S., & Jeong, M. (2010). Psychographic characteristics affecting behavioral intentions towards pop-up retail. *International Journal of Retail & Distribution Management, 38*(2), 133–154. doi:10.1108/09590551011020138

Kim, M., & Kandampully, J. (2012). The Service Imperative in the Retailing Industry. In J. Kandampully (Ed.), *Service Management: The New Paradigm in Retailing* (pp. 7–24). New York: Springer. doi:10.1007/978-1-4614-1554-1_2

Kim, N., Cho, E., Kim, Y., & Lee, M. (2011). Developing an effective strategic mix of corporate philanthropy. *The Service Industries Journal, 31*(7), 1049–1062. doi:10.1080/02642060903079428

Kinnear, T. C., Bernhardt, K. L., & Krentler, K. A. (1995). *Principles of marketing*. New York, NY: Harper Collins.

Kjeldegard, D., & Ostberg, J. (2007). Coffee Grounds and the Global Cup: Glocal Consumer Culture in Scandinavia. *Consumption. Markets and Culture, 10*(2), 175–187. doi:10.1080/10253860701256281

Klatzky, R. L., & Lederman, S. J. (1992). Stages of manual exploration in haptic object identification. *Perception & Psychophysics, 52*(6), 661–670. doi:10.3758/BF03211702 PMID:1287570

Kleine, S. S., Kleine, R. E., & Allen, C. T. (1995). How is possession 'me' or 'not me'? Characterizing types and an antecedent of material possession attachment. *The Journal of Consumer Research, 22*, 327–343. doi:10.1086/209454

Kliatchko, J. (2008). Revisiting the IMC construct: a revised definition and four pillars. *International Journal of Advertising, 27*(1), 133–160.

Kligman, A. M., & Graham, J. A. (1986). *The Psychology of Appearance in the Elderly*. Retrieved February 12th, 2012, from http://www.ncbi.nlm.nih.gov/pubmed/3521995

Klingebiel, R., & De Meyer, A. (2013). Becoming aware of the unknown: decision making during the implementation of a strategic initiative. *Organization Science, 24*(1), 133–153. doi:10.1287/orsc.1110.0726

Kniazeva, M., & Venkatesh, A. (2007). Food for Thought: A Study of Food Consumption in Postmodern Us Culture. *Journal of Consumer Behaviour, 6*(6), 419–435. doi:10.1002/cb.232

Koh, J., & Kim, Y. G. (2004). Knowledge sharing in virtual communities: an e-business perspective. *Expert Systems with Applications, 26*(2), 155–166. doi:10.1016/S0957-4174(03)00116-7

Kondawar, D., & Jadhav, P. (2012). Global economic crisis & consumer behavior. *ABHINAV, 1*(12), 82–87.

Konuş, U., Verhoef, P. C., & Neslin, S. A. (2008). Multichannel shopper segments and their covariates. *Journal of Retailing, 84*(4), 398–413. doi:10.1016/j.jretai.2008.09.002

Kotler, P. (1973-1974). Atmospherics as a Marketing Tool. *Journal of Retailing, 49*(4), 48–64.

Kotler, P. (1986). The prosumer movement: A new challenge for marketers. *Advances in Consumer Research. Association for Consumer Research (U. S.), 13*(1), 510–513.

Kotler, P. (2000). *Marketing Management: Analysis, Planning, Implementation, and Control* (10th ed.). Upper Saddle River, NJ: Prentice Hall.

Kotler, P. (2005). *According to Kotler: the world's foremost authority on marketing answers your questions*. New York, NY: Amacon.

Kotler, P., Kartajaya, H., & Setiawan, I. (2010). *Marketing 3.0: From Products to Customers to the Human Spirit*. John Wiley & Sons Inc. doi:10.1002/9781118257883

Kotler, P., & Keller, K. L. (2006). *Administracao de Marketing* [Marketing Management]. Sao Paulo: Pearson Prentice Hall. (in Portuguese)

Kotler, P., & Keller, K. L. (2006). *Marketing Management* (12th ed.). Pearson Education, Inc.

Koufaris, M. (2002). Applying the technology acceptance model and flow theory to online consumer behavior. *Information Systems Research*, *13*(2), 205–223. doi:10.1287/isre.13.2.205.83

Koufaris, M., & Hampton-Sosa, W. (2004). The Development Of Initial Trust In An Online Company By New Customers. *Information & Management*, *41*(3), 377–397. doi:10.1016/j.im.2003.08.004

Kozinets, R. (2002, February). The field behind the screen: Using netnography for marketing research in online communities. *JMR, Journal of Marketing Research*, 61–72. doi:10.1509/jmkr.39.1.61.18935

Kozinets, R. (2010). *Netnography: Doing ethnographic research online*. Thousand Oaks, CA: Sage Publications.

Kozinets, R. V. (2007). Inno-Tribes: Star Trek as Wikimedia. In B. Cova, R. V. Kozinets, & A. Shankar (Eds.), *Consumer Tribes*. Burlington, MA: Butterwoth-Heinemann.

Kozinets, R. V. (2010). *Netnography. Doing ethnographic research online*. Thousand Oaks, CA: Sage.

Kozinets, R. V., & Handelman, J. M. (2004). Adversaries of Consumption: Consumer Movements, Activism, and Ideology. *The Journal of Consumer Research*, *31*(3), 691–704. doi:10.1086/425104

Krafft, M., & Mantrala, M. K. (Eds.). (2010). *Retailing in the 21st century: current and future trends*. Springer. doi:10.1007/978-3-540-72003-4

Kremer, F., & Viot, C. (2012). How store brands build retailer brand image. *International Journal of Retail & Distribution Management*, *40*(7), 528–543. doi:10.1108/09590551211239846

Krider, R. E., & Putler, D. S. (2013). Which Birds of a Feather Flock Together? Clustering and Avoidance Patterns of Similar Retail Outlets. *Geographical Analysis*, *45*, 123–149. doi:10.1111/gean.12005

Krishna, A., & Morrin, M. (2008). Does Touch Affect Taste? The Perceptual Transfer of Product Container Haptic Cues. *The Journal of Consumer Research*, *34*(6), 807–818. doi:10.1086/523286

Krishnamurthi, L., & Raj, S. P. (1991). An empirical analysis of the relationship between brand loyalty and consumer price elasticity. *Marketing Science*, *10*, 172–183. doi:10.1287/mksc.10.2.172

Krugman, D. M., Reid, L. N., Dunn, S. W., & Barban, A. M. (1994). *Advertising: Its Role in Modern Marketing*. Fort Worth, TX: Dryden Press.

Kuenzel, S., & Halliday, V. S. (2008). Investigating antecedents and consequences of brand identification. *Journal of Product and Brand Management*, *17*, 293–304. doi:10.1108/10610420810896059

Kuepfer, J., & Papula, J. (2010). Corporate social responsibility–the dilemmas behind the popular concept and how to best address them! *International Journal of Sustainable Society*, *2*(3), 291–305. doi:10.1504/IJSSOC.2010.034765

Kukar-Kinney, M., Ridgway, N. M., & Monroe, K. B. (2009). The relationship between consumers' tendencies to buy compulsively and their motivations to shop and buy on the Internet. *Journal of Retailing*, *85*(3), 298–307. doi:10.1016/j.jretai.2009.05.002

Kulas, J. T., Mcinnerney, J. E., Demuth, R. F., & Jadwinski, V. (2007). Employee Satisfaction and Theft: Testing Climate Perceptions as a Mediator. *The Journal of Psychology*, *141*(4), 389–402. doi:10.3200/JRLP.141.4.389-402 PMID:17725072

Kumar, N., & Steenkamp, J.-B. E. M. (2007). *Private Label Strategy*. Cambridge, MA: Harvard Business School Press.

Kumar, V., Pozza, I. D., & Ganesh, J. (2013). Revisiting the satisfaction-loyalty relationship: Empirical generalizations and directions for future research. *Journal of Retailing*, *89*(3), 246–262. doi:10.1016/j.jretai.2013.02.001

Kumar, V., & Venkatesan, R. (2005). Who are the multichannel shoppers and how do they perform? Correlates of multichannel shopping behavior. *Journal of Interactive Marketing*, *19*(2), 44–62. doi:10.1002/dir.20034

Kushwaha, T., & Shankar, V. (2013). Are Multichannel Customers Really More Valuable? The Moderating Role of Product Category Characteristics. *Journal of Marketing*, *77*(4), 1–19. doi:10.1509/jm.11.0297

Kwak, H., Zinkhan, G. M., & Crask, M. R. (2003). Diagnostic screener for compulsive buying: Applications to the USA and South Korea. *The Journal of Consumer Affairs*, *37*, 161–171. doi:10.1111/j.1745-6606.2003.tb00445.x

Kwong-Leung, T. (2000). Ageism and Sexism at Work: The Middle-Aged Women of Hong Kong. *Gender, Technology and Development*, *4*(2), 225–253. doi:10.1177/097185240000400203 PMID:12179949

La Cour, A., & Kromann, J. (2011). Euphemisms and hypocrisy in corporate philanthropy. *Business Ethics (Oxford, England)*, *20*(3), 267–279. doi:10.1111/j.1467-8608.2011.01627.x

Ladhari, R., Souiden, N., & Ladhari, I. (2011). Determinants of loyalty and recommendation: the role of perceived service quality, emotional satisfaction and image. *Journal of Financial Services Marketing*, *16*(2), 111–124. doi:10.1057/fsm.2011.10

Lafferty, B. A., Goldsmith, R. E., & Hult, G. I. (2004). The impact of the alliance on the partners: A look at cause-brand alliances. *Psychology and Marketing*, *21*, 509–531. doi:10.1002/mar.20017

Lai, F., Hutchinson, J., & Zhang, G. (2005). Radio Frequency Identification (RFID) in China: Opportunities and Challenges. *International Journal of Retail & Distribution Management*, *33*(12), 905–916. doi:10.1108/09590550510634639

Lambert, C. (2006). The marketplace of perceptions. *Harvard Magazine*, *108*(4), 50–60.

Lamey, L., Deleersnyder, B., Dekimpe, M. J., & Steenkamp, J.-B. E. M. (2007). How Business Cycles Contribute to Private-Label Success: Evidence from the United States and Europe. *Journal of Marketing*, *71*(1), 1–15. doi:10.1509/jmkg.71.1.1

Lamey, L., Deleersnyder, B., Steenkamp, J.-B. E. M., & Dekimpe, M. J. (2012). The Effect of Business-Cycle Fluctuations on Private-Label Share: What Has Marketing Conduct Got to Do with It? *Journal of Marketing*, *76*, 1–19. doi:10.1509/jm.09.0320

Lam, S. K., Ahearne, M., Hu, Y., & Schillewaert, N. (2010). Resistance to brand switching when a radically new brand is introduced: a social identity theory perspective. *Journal of Marketing*, *74*, 128–146. doi:10.1509/jmkg.74.6.128

Lam, S. Y. (2001). The effects of store environment on shopping behaviors: a critical review. *Advances in Consumer Research. Association for Consumer Research (U. S.)*, *28*, 190–197.

Langston, P. (2012). Will click and collect save the High Street? *Retail Week*. Retrieved June 9, 2013, from http://www.retail-week.com/multichannel/comment-will-click-and-collect-save-the-high-street/5039566.article

Laroche, M., & Habibi, M, R., & Richard, M.O. (2013). To be or not to be in social media: How brand loyalty is affected by social media? *International Journal of Information Management*, *33*, 76–82. doi:10.1016/j.ijinfomgt.2012.07.003

Laroche, M., Ueltschy, L. C., Abe, S., Cleveland, M., & Yannopoulos, P. P. (2004). Service quality perceptions and customer satisfaction: Evaluating the role of culture. *Journal of International Marketing*, *12*(3), 58–85. doi:10.1509/jimk.12.3.58.38100

LaRosa, C., & Campbell, J. (2010). *Your Frontline Employees Are Your Brand: How Do You Hire The Right Ones?* Retrieved February 12th, 2012, from http://www.fastcodesign.com/1665464/your-frontline-employees-are-your-brand-how-do-you-hire-the-right-ones

Law, D., Wong, C., & Yip, J. (2012). How does Visual Merchandising Affect Consumer Affective Response? An Intimate Apparel Experience. *European Journal of Marketing*, *46*(1/2), 112–133. doi:10.1108/03090561211189266

Lee, D. J., & Sirgy, M. J. (1995). Determinants of involvement in the consumer/marketing life domain in relation to quality of life: a theoretical model and research agenda. In H. L. Meadow, M. J. Sirgy, & D. Rahtz (Eds.), *Development in quality of life studies in marketing* (pp. 13–18). Dekalb, IL: Academy of Marketing Science.

Lee, D. J., Sirgy, M. J., Larsen, V., & Wright, N. D. (2002). Developing a subjective measure of consumer well-being. *Journal of Macromarketing*, *22*(2), 158–169. doi:10.1177/0276146702238219

Lee, H. J. et al. (2010). The influence of consumer traits and demographics on intention to use retail self-service checkouts. *Marketing Intelligence & Planning*, *28*(1), 46–58. doi:10.1108/02634501011014606

Lee, J., & Qualls, W. J. (2010). A dynamic process of buyer-seller technology adoption. *Journal of Business and Industrial Marketing, 25*(3), 220–228. doi:10.1108/08858621011027812

Lee, M. K. O., & Turban, E. (2002). A Trust Model for Consumer Internet Shopping. *International Journal of Electronic Commerce, 6*(1), 75–91. doi:10.1023/A:1013340118965

Lee, M. S. W., Fernandez, K. V., & Hyman, M. R. (2009). Anti-Consumption: An Overview and Research Agenda. *Journal of Business Research, 62*(2), 145–147. doi:10.1016/j.jbusres.2008.01.021

Lee, Y.-I., & Trim, P. R. J. (2006). Retail marketing strategy: the role of marketing intelligence, relationship marketing and trust. *Marketing Intelligence & Planning, 24*(7), 730–745. doi:10.1108/02634500610711888

Leigh, T. W., Peters, C., & Shelton, J. (2006). The Consumer Quest for Authenticity: The Multiplicity of Meanings within the Mg Subculture of Consumption. *Journal of the Academy of Marketing Science, 34*(4), 481–493. doi:10.1177/0092070306288403

Leroux, M., & Ralph, A. (2013). Retailers will shine if customers can click and collect. *The Times*. Retrieved March 14, 2013, from http://www.thetimes.co.uk/tto/business/industries/retailing/article3660985.ece

Levi, A. (2011). *How Apple (unintentionally) revolutionized corporate IT*. Retrieved March 15, 2012, from http://tech.fortune.cnn.com/2011/08/02/apples-unintentional-corporate-it-revolution/

Levine, R., Locke, C., Searls, D., & Weinberger, D. (1999). *The Cluetrain Manifesto*. Retrieved November, 2013, from http://www.cluetrain.com/

Lévi-Strauss, C. (1992). *Antropologia strutturale*. Milano: Mondadori.

Levitt, R. E., Thomsen, J., Christiansen, T. R., Kunz, J. C., Jin, Y., & Nass, C. (1999). Simulating Project Work Processes and Organizations: Toward a Micro-Contingency Theory of Organizational Design. *Management Science, 45*, 1479–1495. doi:10.1287/mnsc.45.11.1479

Levy, M., Grewal, D., Peterson, R. A., & Connolly, B. (2005). The concept of the big middle. *Journal of Retailing, 81*(2), 83–88. doi:10.1016/j.jretai.2005.04.001

Levy, M., & Powell, P. (2003). Exploring SME Internet adoption: towards a contingent model. *Electronic Markets, 13*(2), 173–181. doi:10.1080/1019678032000067163

Levy, M., & Weitz, B. A. (2012). *Retailing Management* (8th ed.). McGraw-Hill/Irwin.

Levy, S. J. (1959). Symbols for sale. *Harvard Business Review, 37*, 117–124.

Lewis, D., & Bridger, D. (2005). Market researchers make increasing use of brain imaging. *Advances in Clinical Neuroscience & Rehabilitation, 5*(3), 36–37.

Leyens, J. P., & Fiske, S. T. (1994). Impression formation: From recitals to symphonie fantastique. In P. G. Devine, D. L. Hamilton, & T. M. Ostrom (Eds.), *Social cognition: Impact on social psychology*. San Diego, CA: Academic Press.

Liao, S., Shao, I. P., Wang, H., & Chen, A. (1999). The adoption of virtual banking: an empirical study. *International Journal of Information Management, 19*(1), 63–74. doi:10.1016/S0268-4012(98)00047-4

Liaw. (2007). *The Influence of Multiple Store Environment Cues on Shopping Mood and Patronage Satisfaction*. Paper presented at the 7th Global Conference on Business & Economics. Rome, Italy.

Ligas, M. (2000). People, products, and pursuits: exploring the relationship between consumer goals and product meanings. *Psychology and Marketing, 17*(11), 983–1003. doi:10.1002/1520-6793(200011)17:11<983::AID-MAR4>3.0.CO;2-J

Liljander, V., Polsa, P., & van Riel, A. (2009). Modelling consumer responses to an apparel store brand: store image as a risk reducer. *Journal of Retailing and Consumer Services, 16*(4), 281–290. doi:10.1016/j.jretconser.2009.02.005

Lillya, D. (2011). *The guide to UK Corporate Giving* (8th ed.). DSC.

543

Lincoln, K., & Thomassen, L. (2008). *Private label: Turning the retail threat into your biggest opportunity.* London: Kogan Page.

Lindblom, A., & Kajalo, S. (2011). The Use and Effectiveness of Formal and Informal Surveillance in Reducing Shoplifting: A Survey in Sweden, Norway, and Finland. *International Review of Retail, Distribution and Consumer Research, 21*(2), 111–128. doi:10.1080/095939 69.2011.562677

Lindquist, J. D. (1975). Meaning of image: A survey of empirical and hypothetical evidence. *Journal of Retailing, 50*(4), 29–38.

Liston-Heyes, C., & Liu, G. (2010). Cause-related marketing in the retail and finance sectors. *Nonprofit and Voluntary Sector Quarterly, 39*(1), 77–96. doi:10.1177/0899764008326680

Liu, C., & Forsythe, S. (2010). Sustaining Online Shopping: Moderating Roles of Online Shopping Motives. *Journal of Internet Commerce, 9*(2), 83–103. doi:10.10 80/15332861.2010.503848

Liu, G., & Ko, W. W. (2011). An analysis of cause-related marketing implementation strategies through social alliance: Partnership conditions and strategic objectives. *Journal of Business Ethics, 100*(2), 253–281. doi:10.1007/s10551-010-0679-7

Liu, T. C., & Wang, C. Y. (2008). Factors affecting attitudes toward private labels and promoted brands. *Journal of Marketing Management, 24*(3-4), 283–298. doi:10.1362/026725708X306103

Livesey, F., & Lennon, P. (1978). Factors affecting consumers' choice between manufacturer brands and retailer own labels. *European Journal of Marketing, 12*(2), 158–170. doi:10.1108/EUM0000000004965

Lohr, V. I., Pearson-Mims, C. H., Tarnai, J., & Dillman, D. (2004). How urban residents rate and rank the benefits and problems associated with trees in cities. *Journal of Arboriculture, 30*(1), 28–35.

Lounsbury, V., & Crumley, E. T. (2007). New practice creation: An institutional perspective on innovation. *Organization Studies, 28*(7), 993–101. doi:10.1177/0170840607078111

Lovelock, C., & Wirtz, J. (2004). *Services Marketing: People, Technology, Strategy.* Prentice Hall, Pearson.

Lovelock, C., & Wright, L. (2007). *Servicos: marketing e gestao* [Services: marketing and management]. Sao Paulo: Saraiva. (in Portuguese)

Lugli, G. (1976). *Economia della distribuzione commerciale.* Milano, Italy: Giuffrè.

Lumpkin, J. R., & Darden, W. R. (1982). Relating Television Preference Viewing to Shopping Orientations, Lifestyles, and Demographics. *Journal of Advertising, 11*(4), 56–67. doi:10.1080/00913367.1982.10672822

Luo, X. (2002). Trust Production And Privacy Concerns On The Internet: A Framework Based On Relationship Marketing And Social Exchange Theory. *Industrial Marketing Management, 31*(2), 111–118. doi:10.1016/S0019-8501(01)00182-1

Lusch, R. F., Vargo, L. S., & O'Brien, M. (2007). Competing through service: Insights from service-dominant logic. *Journal of Retailing, 83*(1), 5–18. doi:10.1016/j.jretai.2006.10.002

Lusch, R. F., & Vargo, S. L. (Eds.). (2006). *The Service-Dominant Logic of Marketing - Dialog, Debate, and Directions.* Armonk: ME Sharpe.

Lusk, J. L., & Coble, K. H. (2005). Risk Perceptions, Risk Preference and Acceptance of Risky Food. *American Journal of Agricultural Economics, 87*(2), 393–421. doi:10.1111/j.1467-8276.2005.00730.x

Machleit, K. A., Eroglu, S. A., & Mantel, S. P. (2000). Perceived retail crowding and shopping satisfaction: What modifies this relationship? *Journal of Consumer Psychology, 9*(1), 29–42. doi:10.1207/s15327663jcp0901_3

Machleit, K. A., Kellaris, J. J., & Eroglu, S. A. (1994). Human versus spatial dimensions of crowding perceptions in retail environments: A note on their measurement and effect on shopper satisfaction. *Marketing Letters, 5*(2), 183–194. doi:10.1007/BF00994108

Macintosh, G., & Lockshin, L. S. (1997). Retail relationships and store loyalty: a multi-level perspective. *International Journal of Research in Marketing, 14*, 487–497. doi:10.1016/S0167-8116(97)00030-X

Macleod, S. (2001). Why worry about CSR. *Strategic Communication Management, 5*(5), 8–9.

Maglio, P. P., & Spohrer, J. (2008). Fundamentals of service science. *Journal of the Academy of Marketing Science, 36*(1), 18–20. doi:10.1007/s11747-007-0058-9

Magnusson, P. R., Matthing, & Kristensson. (2003). Managing User Involvement in Service Innovation: Experiments With Innovating End Users. *Journal of Service Research, 6*(2), 111–124. doi:10.1177/1094670503257028

Majfud, J. (2009). The pandemic of consumerism. *UN chronicle*. Retrieved from http://institucional.us.es/araucaria/otras_res/2009_11/resegna_1109_6.htm#_ftn1

Malhotra, N. K. (1988). Self concept and product choice: an integrated perspective. *Journal of Economic Psychology, 9*, 1–28. doi:10.1016/0167-4870(88)90029-3

Malhotra, N. K. (2001). *Pesquisa de marketing: uma orientacao aplicada* [Marketing Research: an applied approach]. Porto Alegre: Bookman. (in Portuguese)

Malhotra, N. K., Kim, S. S., & Agarwal, J. (2004). Internet Users' Information Privacy Concerns (IUIPC), the Construct, the Scale, and a Causal Model. *Information Systems Research, 15*(4), 336–355. doi:10.1287/isre.1040.0032

Manasseh, T., Müller-Sarmiento, P., Reuter, H., von Faber-Castell, C., & Pallua, C. (2012). Customer Inspiration–A Key Lever for Growth in European Retail. *Marketing Review St. Gallen, 29*(5), 16–21. doi:10.1365/s11621-012-0159-9

Manganari, E. E., Siomkos, G. J., & Vrechopoulos, A. P. (2009). Store atmosphere in web retailing. *European Journal of Marketing, 43*(9/10), 1140–1153. doi:10.1108/03090560910976401

Mano, H., & Oliver, R. L. (1993). Assessing the Dimensionality and Structure of the Consumption Experience: Evaluation, Feeling, and Satisfaction. *The Journal of Consumer Research, 20*(3), 451–466. doi:10.1086/209361

Mansoor, D., & Jalal, A. (2011). The Global Business Crisis and Consumer Behaviour: Kingdom of Bahrain as a Case Study. *International Journal of Business and Management, 6*(1), 104–115.

Mantrala, M. K., Levy, M., Kahn, B. E., Fox, E. J., Gaidarev, P., Dankworth, B., & Shah, D. (2009). Why is Assortment Planning so Difficult for Retailers? A Framework and Research Agenda. *Journal of Retailing, 85*(1), 71–83. doi:10.1016/j.jretai.2008.11.006

Maple, P. (2008). The Spectrum of Philanthropy. *Caritas London, 5*, 34–36.

Markin, R. J., & Duncan, C. P. (1981). The Transformation of Retailing Institutions: Beyond the Wheel of Retailing and Life Cycle Theories. *Journal of Macromarketing, 1*(1), 58–66. doi:10.1177/027614678100100110

Markin, R. J., Lillis, C. M., & Narayana, C. L. (1976). Social-psychological significance of store space. *Journal of Retailing, 52*(1), 43–54.

Markman, E. (2006). *The Coffee House: A Cultural History*. London: Weidenfeld and Nicolson.

Maronick, T. J., & Walker, B. J. (1974). The dialectic evolution of retailing. In B. Greenberg (Ed.), *Proceedings of the Southern Marketing Association*. Atlanta, GA: Georgia State University.

Marshall, G. W., Goebel, D. J., & Moncrief, W. C. (2003). Hiring for success at the buyer-seller interface. *Journal of Business Research, 56*, 247–255. doi:10.1016/S0148-2963(02)00435-6

Martenson, R. (2007). Corporate brand image, satisfaction and store loyalty: a study of the store as a brand, store brands and manufacturer brands. *International Journal of Retail & Distribution Management, 35*(7), 544–555. doi:10.1108/09590550710755921

Martinelli, E. (2009). Service-dominant logic and retail convergence. In E. Gummesson, C. Mele, & F. Polese (Eds.), *Service science, S-D logic and network theory*. Napoli, Italy: Giannini.

Massara, F. (2003). Store atmosphere: still a fledgling art. *ECR Journal, 3*(2), 47–52.

Mathieson, K. (1991). Predicting user intentions: Comparing the technology acceptance model with theory of planned behavior. *Information Systems Research, 2*(3), 173–191. doi:10.1287/isre.2.3.173

Matos, F., & San Martin, S. (2007). La confianza, la intención de compra, la reputación y las emociones en la relación del consumidor con la marca: aplicación al caso de la marca Mundo Maya-México. In *Nuevas tendencias en dirección de empresas*. Departamento de Economía y Administración de Empresas, Universidad de Burgos.

Mattar, F. N. (2007). *Pesquisa de Marketing* [Marketing Research]. Sao Paulo: Atlas. (in Portuguese)

Mattila, A. S., & Wirtz, J. (2001). Congruency of scent and music as a driver of in-store evaluations and behaviour. *Journal of Retailing*, 77(2), 273–289. doi:10.1016/S0022-4359(01)00042-2

Mavlanova, T., Benbunan-Fich, R., & Koufaris, M. (2012). Signaling theory and information asymmetry in online commerce. *Information & Management*, 49(5), 240–247. doi:10.1016/j.im.2012.05.004

McAfee, A. (2006). Enterprise 2.0: The Dawn of Emergence Collaboration. *MIT Sloan Management Review*, 47(3), 21–28.

McAfee, A. (2009). *Enterprise 2.0: New Collaborative Tools for Your Organization's Toughest Challenges*. Boston: Harvard Business Press.

McBride, S. (1980). *Many voices, one world: Communication in society, today and tomorrow*. New York: UNESCO.

McCabe, D. B., & Nowlis, S. (2003). The Effect of Examining Actual Products or Product Descriptions on Consumer Preference. *Journal of Consumer Psychology*, 13(4), 431–439. doi:10.1207/S15327663JCP1304_10

McCarthy, E. J. (1964). *Basic Marketing: A Managerial Approach*. Richard D. Irwin.

McCarville, R. E., Shaw, S. M., & Ritchie, M. (2013). *Shopping as leisure: A study of avid shoppers*. World Leisure Journal.

McCracken, G. (1986). Culture and Consumption: A Theoretical Account of the Structure and Movement of the Cultural Meaning of Consumer Goods. *The Journal of Consumer Research*, 13(1), 71–84. doi:10.1086/209048

McDonald, M., Rogers, B., & Woodburn, D. (2000). *Key Customers: How to Manage them Profitably*. Butterworth-Heinemann.

McDonald, S., Oates, C. J., Young, C. W., & Hwang, K. (2006). Toward Sustainable Consumption: Researching Voluntary Simplifiers. *Psychology and Marketing*, 23(6), 515–534. doi:10.1002/mar.20132

McGoldrick, P. (2002). *Retail Marketing*. McGraw-Hill Education.

McGoldrick, P. J., & Davies, G. (Eds.). (1995). *International Retailing: Trends and Strategies*. Glasgow, UK: Pitman Publishing.

McGowan, P., Durkin, M. G., Allen, L., Dougan, C., & Nixon, S. (2001). Developing competencies in the entrepreneurial small firm for use of the Internet in the management of customer relationships. *Journal of European Industrial Training*, 25(2/3/4), 126-136.

McKinsey Global Institute. (2012). *The social economy: Unlocking value and productivity through social technologies*. Retrieved September, 2012, from http://www.mckinsey.com/insights/high_tech_telecoms_internet/the_social_economy

McKnight, D. H., Choudhury, V., & Kacmar, C. (2002). The Impact of Initial Consumer Trust on Intention to Transact with a WebSite: A Trust Building Model. *The Journal of Strategic Information Systems*, 13(4), 297–323. doi:10.1016/S0963-8687(02)00020-3

McKnight, D. H., Kacmar, C., & Choudhury, V. (2004). Shifting Factors and the Ineffectiveness of Third Party Assurance Seals: A Two-Stage Model of Initial Trust in a Web Business. *Electronic Markets*, 14(3), 252–266. doi:10.1080/1019678042000245263

McNair, M. P. (1958). Significant Trends and Development in the Postwar Period. In A. B. Smith (Ed.), *Competitive Distribution in a Free, High-level Economy and its Implications for the University*. Pittsburgh, PA: University of Pittsburgh Press.

McNeill, L., & Wyeth, E. (2011). The private label grocery choice: consumer drivers to purchase. *International Review of Retail, Distribution and Consumer Research*, 21(1), 95–109. doi:10.1080/09593969.2011.537822

Meadow, H. L. (1988). The satisfaction attitude hierarchy: Does marketing contribute? In S. Shapiro (Ed.), *Proceedings of the 1988 American Marketing Association Winter Educators' Conference* (pp. 482-483). Chicago, IL: American Marketing Association.

Mehrabian, A., & Russel, J. A. (1974). *An approach to environmental psychology.* Cambridge, MA: MIT Press.

Mendelson, J., & Mello, N. (1986). *The addictive personality.* New York: Chelsea House.

Mendo, F. A., & Fitzgerald, G. (2005). A multidimensional framework for SME e-business progression. *Journal of Enterprise Information Management, 18*(6), 678–696. doi:10.1108/17410390510628382

Merci. (2013). *Corporate Website.* Retrieved on August 29, 2013 from http://www.merci-merci.com

Metro Group AG. (2013). *Corporate Website.* Retrieved on August 25, 2013 from http://www.metrogroup.de

Meuter, M. L. et al. (2000). Self-service technologies: understanding customer satisfaction with technology-based service encounters. *Journal of Marketing, 64,* 50–64. doi:10.1509/jmkg.64.3.50.18024

Michael, S. C., & Kim, S. M. (2005). The organizational ecology of retailing: A historical perspective. *Journal of Retailing, 81*(2), 113–123. doi:10.1016/j.jretai.2005.03.005

Micheletti, M. (2003). *Political Virtue and Shopping: Individuals, Consumerism, and Collective Action.* New York: Palgrave Macmillan. doi:10.1057/9781403973764

Michelli, J. (2007). *The Starbucks Experience: 5 Principles for Turning Ordinary Into Extraordinary.* New York: McGraw Hill.

Mick, D. G., & Buhl, C. (1992). A Meaning-Based Model of Advertising Experiences. *The Journal of Consumer Research, 19*(3), 317–338. doi:10.1086/209305

Mieres, C. G., Martin, A. M., & Gutierrez, J. A. T. (2006). Influence of perceived risk on store brand proneness. *International Journal of Retail & Distribution Management, 34*(10), 761–772. doi:10.1108/09590550610691347

Mihm, B. (2010). Fast Fasion In A Flat World: Global Sourcing Strategies. *International Business & Economics Research Journal, 9*(6), 55–63.

Mikkonen, H., Dholakia, N., Moisander, J., & Valtonen, A. (2011). Consumer resistance as struggle over subjectivity. *University of Rhode Island Working paper series,* 2011/2012 no 6.

Miller, D., & Reilly, J. (1994). *Food scares in the media.* Glasgow University Media Group. Retrieved April 04, 2010, from http://www.dmiller.info/food-scares-in-the-media

Miller, G. (2013). Is the prime reason customers shop online price or convenience? Which one? Are you sure? *The Retail Intelligence Company.* Retrieved August 12, 2013, from http://upstreamcommerce.com/blog/2013/08/07/ptime-reason-customers-shop-online-

Miller, D. (1988). Relating Porter's Business Strategies to Environment and Structure: Analysis and Performance Implications. *Academy of Management Journal, 31*(2), 280–308. doi:10.2307/256549

Miller, D. (1998). *A theory of shopping.* New York: Cornell University Press.

Miller, D., & Dröge, C. (1986). Psychological and Traditional Determinants of Structure. *Administrative Science Quarterly, 31*(4), 539–560. doi:10.2307/2392963

Miller, M. B. (1995). Coefficient alpha: introduction from the perspectives of classical test theory and structural equation modeling. *Structural Equation Modeling, 2*(3), 255–273. doi:10.1080/10705519509540013

Miller, P. (1980). Theoretical and practical issues in substance abuse assessment and treatment. In W. R. Miller (Ed.), *The addictive behaviors* (pp. 265–290). Oxford, UK: Paragon.

Milliken, J. (2012). Mobile phones are changing the world of retail – at a remarkable rate. *The Guardian.* Retrieved March 20, 2013, from http://www.guardian.co.uk/media-network/media-network-blog/2012/jun/26/mobile-retail-technology-consumer

Milliman, R. (1986). The influence of background music on the behaviour of restaurant patrons. *The Journal of Consumer Research, 13,* 286–289. doi:10.1086/209068

Milliman, R., & Fugate, D. (1993). Atmospherics as an Emerging Influence in the Design of Exchange Environments. *Journal of Marketing Management, 3*(1), 66–75.

Millman, R. E. (1982). Using background music to affect the behavior of supermarkets shoppers. *Journal of Marketing, 46,* 86–91. doi:10.2307/1251706

Milne, G. R. (2000). Privacy And Ethical Issues In Database/Interactive Marketing And Public Policy: A Research Framework And Overview Of The Special Issue. *Journal of Public Policy & Marketing, 19*(1), 1–6. doi:10.1509/jppm.19.1.1.16934

Milne, G. R., & Boza, M. E. (1999). Trust and Concern in Consumers' Perceptions of Marketing Information Management Practices. *Journal of Interactive Marketing, 13*(1), 5–24. doi:10.1002/(SICI)1520-6653(199924)13:1<5::AID-DIR2>3.0.CO;2-9

Milne, G. R., & Gordon, M. E. (1993). Direct Mail Privacy-Efficiency Trade-offs Within an Implied Social Contract Framework. *Journal of Public Policy & Marketing, 12*(2), 206–215.

Minton, A., et al. (2013). How can we save the High Street? *The Guardian.* Retrieved June 9, 2013, from http://www.guardian.co.uk/commentisfree/2013/jan/15/how-can-we-save-high-street

Mintzberg, H., Ahlstrand, B. W., & Lampel, J. (1998). *Strategy Safari: the Complete Guide Trough the Wilds of Strategic Management.* London: Financial Times Prentice Hall.

Min-Young, L., Fairhurst, A., & Wesley, S. (2009). Corporate Social Responsibility: A Review of the Top 100 US Retailers. *Corporate Reputation Review, 12*(2), 140–158. doi:10.1057/crr.2009.10

Miquel, S., Caplliure, E. M., & Aldas-Manzano, J. (2002). The effect of personal involvement on the decision to buy store brands. *Journal of Product and Brand Management, 11*(1), 6–18. doi:10.1108/10610420210419513

Miranda, M. J., Konya, L., & Havrila, I. (2005). Shoppers' satisfaction levels are not the only key to store loyalty. *Marketing Intelligence & Planning, 23*(2), 220–232. doi:10.1108/02634500510589958

Mitchell, J. E., Burgard, M., Faber, R., Crosby, R., & De Zwaan, M. (2006). Cognitive behaviour therapy for compulsive buying disorder. *Behaviour Research and Therapy, 44*, 1859–1869. doi:10.1016/j.brat.2005.12.009 PMID:16460670

Mittal, S., & Gera, R. (2013). Relationship between service quality dimensions and behavioural intentions: An SEM study of public sector retail banking customers in India. *Journal of Service Research, 12*(2), 147–171.

Mohan, G., Sivakumaran, B., & Sharma, P. (2012). Store environment's impact on variety seeking behavior. *Journal of Retailing and Consumer Services, 19*(4), 419–428. doi:10.1016/j.jretconser.2012.04.003

Mohr, B. A., Webb, D. J., & Harris, K. E. (2001). Do consumers expect companies to be socially responsible? The impact of corporate social responsibility on buying behavior. *The Journal of Consumer Affairs, 35*(1), 45–72. doi:10.1111/j.1745-6606.2001.tb00102.x

Montoya-Weiss, M. M., Voss, G. B., & Grewal, D. (2005). Determinant of online channel use and overall satisfaction with a relational, multichannel service provider. *Journal of the Academy of Marketing Science, 31*(4), 448–458. doi:10.1177/0092070303254408

Moore, G. (1991). *Crossing the Chasm: Marketing and Selling High-Tech Products to Mainstream Customers.* New York, NY: Harper Business Essentials.

Moore, R. L., & Moschis, G. P. (1981). The role of family communication in consumer learning. *The Journal of Communication, 31*, 42–45. doi:10.1111/j.1460-2466.1981.tb00449.x

Moorman, C., Zaltman, G., & Deshpandé, R. (1992). Relationships Between Providers and Users of Market Research: The Dynamisc of Trust Within and Between Organizations. *JMR, Journal of Marketing Research, 29*(3), 314–328. doi:10.2307/3172742

Moraes, C., Szmigin, I., & Carrigan, M. (2010). Living Production-Engaged Alternatives: An Examination of New Consumption Communities. *Consumption Markets & Culture, 13*(3), 273–298. doi:10.1080/10253861003787015

Morgan, R. M., & Hunt, S. D. (1994). The commitment-trust theory of relationship marketing. *Journal of Marketing, 58*, 20–38. doi:10.2307/1252308

Morgan, T. (2008). *Visual Merchandising: Window and in-store displays for retail.* Laurence King Publishing.

Morgeson, F. V. III, Mithas, S., Keiningham, T. L., & Aksoy, L. (2011). An investigation of the cross-national determinants of customer satisfaction. *Journal of the Academy of Marketing Science, 29*(2), 198–215. doi:10.1007/s11747-010-0232-3

Morier, M. (2005). *The sweet sound and smell of success: consumer perceptions as mediators of the interactive effects of music and scent on purchasing behaviour in a shopping mall.* (Thesis). Universidad de Concordia, Montreal, Canada.

Morin, C. (2011). Neuromarketing: The new science of consumer behavior. *Society, 48*(2), 131–135. doi:10.1007/s12115-010-9408-1

Morin, S., Dube, L., & Chebat, J. C. (2007). The role of pleasant music in servicescapes: A test of the dual model of environmental perception. *Journal of Retailing, 83*(1), 115–130. doi:10.1016/j.jretai.2006.10.006

Morrin, M., & Ratneshwar, S. (2000). The effects of retail store environment on retailer performance. *Journal of Business Research, 49*, 167–181. doi:10.1016/S0148-2963(99)00005-3

Morrin, M., & Ratneshwar, S. (2000). The impact of ambient scent on evaluation, attention and memory for familiar and unfamiliar brands. *Journal of Business Research, 49*, 157–165. doi:10.1016/S0148-2963(99)00006-5

Morris, J. (2012). *Coffee House Formats Compared.* Paper presented at the CHORD Conference Retailing and Distribution History. Wolverhampton, UK.

Morris, J. (2013). Why Espresso? Explaining changes in European coffee preferences from a production of culture perspective. *European Review of History: Revue europeenne d'histoire, 20*(5), 881-901.

Moschis, G. P., & Cox, D. S. (1988). Deviant consumer behavior. *Advances in Consumer Research. Association for Consumer Research (U. S.), 16*, 732–737.

Moss, M. (2007). *Shopping as an entertainment experience.* Lanham, MD: Lexington Books.

Moulds, J. (2013). UK GDP shrank by 0.3% in fourth quarter. *The Guardian.* Retrieved March 27, 2013, from http://www.guardian.co.uk/business/2013/jan/25/uk-gdp-crunch-time-osborne

Mourali, M., & Yang, Z. (2013). The Dual Role Of Power In Resisting Social Influence. *The Journal of Consumer Research, 40*(3), 539–554. doi:10.1086/671139

Mower, J. F., Kim, M., & Childs, M. L. (2012). Exterior atmospherics and consumer behaviour: Influence of landscaping and window display. *Journal of Fashion Marketing and Management, 16*(4), 442–453. doi:10.1108/13612021211265836

Moye, L., & Kincade, D. H. (2002). Influence of Usage Situations and Consumer Shopping Orientations on the Importance of the Retail Store Environment. *International Review of Retail, Distribution and Consumer Research, 12*(1), 59–79. doi:10.1080/09593960110103823

Mueller, A., Mueller, Albert, Mertens, Silbermann, Mitchell, et al. (2007). Hoarding in a compulsive buying sample. *Behaviour Research and Therapy, 45*(11), 2754–2763. doi:10.1016/j.brat.2007.07.012 PMID:17868641

Mukherjee, A., & Nath, P. (2007). Role of electronic trust in online retailing: A re-examination of the commitment-trust theory. *European Journal of Marketing, 41*(9/10), 1173–1202. doi:10.1108/03090560710773390

Mulhern, F. J. (1997). Retail Marketing: From Distribution to Integration. *International Journal of Research in Marketing, 14*(2), 103–124. doi:10.1016/S0167-8116(96)00031-6

Muller, A. (2008, December) Self-service shopping: Advantages for both retailers and customers. *The Retail Digest*, 50-53.

Müller-Lankenau, C., Wehmeyer, K., & Klein, S. (2005). Multi-Channel Strategies: Capturing and Exploring Diversity in the European Retail Grocery Industry. *International Journal of Electronic Commerce, 10*(2), 85–122. doi:10.2753/JEC1086-4415100204

Murillo Viu, J., Romani Fernandez, J., & Surinach Caralt, J. (2008). The impact of heritage tourism on an urban economy: the case of Granada and the Alhambra. *Tourism Economics, 14*(2), 361–376. doi:10.5367/000000008784460481

Murphy, P. E. (1978). The effect of social class on brand and price consciousness for supermarket products. *Journal of Retailing, 54*, 33–42, 89.

Musso, F. (2010). Innovation in Marketing Channels: Relationships, Technology, Channel Structure. *Symphonya: Emerging Issues in Management, 1*, 1–19.

Myers, J. G. (1967). Determinants of private brand attitude. *JMR, Journal of Marketing Research, 4*(1), 73–81. doi:10.2307/3150168

Nadeem, W., Iqbal, N., Hussain, Z., & Bilal, A. (2012). Affinity with computers and perceived trustworthiness as determinants of internet purchase in fashion outlets. *Actual problems of economics*, (130), 350-356.

Nakken, C. (1988). *The addictive personality: Understanding compulsion in our lives.* San Francisco: Harper & Row.

Nambisan, S., & Baron. (2009). Virtual Customer Environments: Testing a Model of Voluntary Participation in Value Co-creation Activities. *Journal of Product Innovation Management, 26*(4), 388–406. doi:10.1111/j.1540-5885.2009.00667.x

Naquin, C. E., & Paulson, G. D. (2003). Online Bargaining and Interpersonal Trust. *The Journal of Applied Psychology, 88*(1), 113–120. doi:10.1037/0021-9010.88.1.113 PMID:12675399

Narasimhan, C., & Wilcox, R. (1998). Private labels and the channel relationship: A cross-category analysis. *The Journal of Business, 71*(4), 573–600. doi:10.1086/209757

Narver, J. C., & Slater, S. F. (1990). The effect of a market Orientation on business profitability. *Journal of Marketing, 54*, 20–35. doi:10.2307/1251757

Nasar, J. L. (1998). *The evaluative image of the city.* Thousand Oaks, CA: Sage Publications.

Naylor, G., Kleiser, S. B., Baker, J., & Yorkston, E. (2008). Using Transformational Appeals to Enhance the Retail Experience. *Journal of Retailing, 84*(1), 49–57. doi:10.1016/j.jretai.2008.01.001

Neal, J., Sirgy, M. J., & Uysal, M. (2004). Measuring the Effect of Tourism Services on Travelers' Quality of Life: Further Validation. *Social Indicators Research, 69*, 243–277. doi:10.1007/s11205-004-5012-3

Neate, R., & Moulds, J. (2012). More High Street name will collapse in New Year, warns retail body. *The Guardian.* Retrieved March 27, 2013, from http://www.guardian.co.uk/business/2012/dec/31/high-street-names-collapse-new-year

Negri, F. (2013). NetworkCracy. Giappichelli Ed.

Neilson, L. A. (2010). Boycott or Buycott? Understanding Political Consumerism. *Journal of Consumer Behaviour, 9*(3), 214–227. doi:10.1002/cb.313

Nelson, W. (2002). All power to the consumer? Complexity and choice in consumers' lives. *Journal of Consumer Behaviour, 2*, 185–195. doi:10.1002/cb.99

Neslin, S. A., Grewal, D., Leghorn, R., Shankar, V., Teerling, M. L., Thomas, J. S., & Verhoef, P. C. (2006). Challenges and opportunities in multichannel customer management. *Journal of Service Research, 9*(2), 95–112. doi:10.1177/1094670506293559

Neslin, S. A., & Shankar, V. (2009). Key issues in multichannel customer management: current knowledge and future directions. *Journal of Interactive Marketing, 23*(1), 70–81. doi:10.1016/j.intmar.2008.10.005

Netemeyer, R. G., Krishnan, B., Pullig, C., Wang, G., Yagci, M., & Dean, D. et al. (2004). Developing and validating measures of facets of customer-based brand equity. *Journal of Business Research, 57*, 209–224. doi:10.1016/S0148-2963(01)00303-4

Networks, S. (2007). *Gender and Friending: An Analysis of Myspace Member Profiles.* Retrieved from http://www.scit.wlv.ac

Newholm, T., McGoldrick, P., Keeling, K., Macaulay, L., & Doherty, J. (2004). Multi-story trust and online retailer strategies. *International Review of Retail, Distribution and Consumer Research, 14*(4), 437–456. doi:10.1080/0959396042000260889

Newholm, T., & Shaw, D. (2007). Studying the Ethical Consumer: A Review of Research. *Journal of Consumer Behaviour, 6*(5), 253–270. doi:10.1002/cb.225

Newman, M. (2012). Customers want convenience. *RetailWeek.* Retrieved August 12, 2013, from http://www.retail-week.com/comment/customers-want-convenience/5033060.article

Newman, A. J., & Cullen, P. (2002). *Retailing: environment & operations.* Thomson Learning.

Newman, A., Foxall, J., & Gordon, R. (2003). In-store customer behaviour in the fashion sector: some emerging methodological and theoretical directions. *International Journal of Retail & Distribution Management, 31*(11), 591–600. doi:10.1108/09590550310503311

Nie, B., Zhao, F., & Yu, J. (2010). *The Impact of the Financial Crisis on Consumer Behaviour and the Implications of Retail Revolution*. Retrieved July, 08, 2013, from http://www.seiofbluemountain.com/upload/product/201008/2010shcyx06a12.pdf

Nielsen Company. (2008, October 30). *Consumer Reaction to the Banking Crisis, Comments about Economy*. Retrieved from http://www.claritas.com/eDownloads/webinar/Nielsen-Claritas-Webinar-Consumer-Reaction-Banking-Crisis-103008.pdf

Nielsen. (2010). *Perception of the Protection & Security Elements of Products*. Neilsen.

Nielsen. (2011). *Global Private Label Report: The Rise of the Value-Conscious Shopper*. Retrieved from http://www.nielsen.com/us/en/newswire/2011/global-private-label-report-the-rise-of-the-value-conscious-shopper.html

Nielsen. (2012). *State of the Media: The Social Media Report*. Nielsen.

Nies, S., & Natter, M. (2012). Does Private Label Quality Influence Consumers' Decision on Where to Shop? *Psychology and Marketing*, 29(4), 279–292. doi:10.1002/mar.20521

Noble, S. M., Griffith, D. A., & Weinberger, M. G. (2005). Consumer derived utilitarian value and channel utilization in a multi-channel retail context. *Journal of Business Research*, 58(12), 1643–1651. doi:10.1016/j.jbusres.2004.10.005

Noordhoff, C., Pauwels, P., & Odekerken-Schröder, G. (2004). The effect of customer card programs: A comparative study in Singapore and The Netherlands. *International Journal of Service Industry Management*, 15(4), 351–364. doi:10.1108/09564230410552040

Norberg, P. A., Horne, D. R., & Horne, D. A. (2007). The Privacy Paradox: Personal Information Disclosure Intentions versus Behaviors. *The Journal of Consumer Affairs*, 41(1), 100–126. doi:10.1111/j.1745-6606.2006.00070.x

North, A. C., Hargreaves, D. J., & McKendrick, J. (1999). The Influence of In-Store Music on Wine Selections. *American Psychological Association*, 217-275.

Norum, P. (2008). The role of time preference and credit card usage in compulsive buying behavior. *International Journal of Consumer Studies*, 32(3), 269. doi:10.1111/j.1470-6431.2008.00678.x

Nunnally, J. C. (1978). *Psychometric Theory*. New York, NY: McGraw-Hill.

Nunnally, J. C., & Bernstein, I. H. (1994). *Psychometric theory* (3rd ed.). New York: McGraw-Hill.

NYCEDC-New York City Economic Department Corporation. (2013). *Coffee and tea in New York City*. Retrieved May 30, 2013, from http://www.nycedc.com/blog-entry/coffee-and-tea-new-york-city

O' Brien, H. L. (2010). The influence of hedonic and utilitarian motivations on user engagement: the case of online shopping experiences. *Interacting with Computers*, 22, 344–352. doi:10.1016/j.intcom.2010.04.001

O'Brien, P. (2013). Click and collect cannot save the High Street analyst. *InternetRetailing*. Retrieved June 9, 2013, from http://Internetretailing.net/2013/04/click-and-collect-cannot-save-the-high-street-analyst/

O'Guinn, T. C., & Faber, R. J. (1989). Compulsive buying: A phenomenological exploration. *The Journal of Consumer Research*, 16, 147–157. doi:10.1086/209204

O'Hern, M. S., & Rindfleisch. (2009). Customer Co-Creation: A Typology and Research Agenda. *Review of Marketing Research*, 6, 84–106.

O'Reilly, L. (2012). Digital will save the High Street. *Marketing Week*. Retrieved March 27, 2013, from http://www.marketingweek.co.uk/news/digital-will-save-the-high-street/4004029.article

O'Reilly, T. (2006). *Web 2.0 Principles and Best Practices*. Retrieved June 2011, from http://oreilly.com/catalog/web2report/chapter/web20_report_excerpt.pdf

O'Shea, L. S., & Awwad-Rafferty, R. (2009). *Design and Security in the Built Environment*. New York: Fairchild Books.

O'Sullivan, E., & Spanger, K. J. (1998). *Experience Marketing. Strategies for the New Millennium. State College*. PA: Venturing Publishing.

Oakes, S. (2003). *Psychology and Marketing*. McGraw-Hill.

Oates, D. (2011). The changing face of UK retail in today's multi-channel world. *An Experian white paper*. Retrieved March 27, 2013, from http://www.experian.co.uk/assets/business-strategies/white-papers/RWC-whitepaper2.pdf

Odekerken-Schroëder, G., de Wulf, K., Kasper, H., Kleijnen, M., Hoekstra, J., & Commandeur, H. (2001). The impact of quality on store loyalty: a contingency approach. *Total Quality Management, 12*(3), 307–322. doi:10.1080/09544120120034474

Ofir, C., & Simonson, I. (2007). The Effect of Stating Expectations on Customer Satisfaction and Shopping Experience. *JMR, Journal of Marketing Research, 44*, 164–174. doi:10.1509/jmkr.44.1.164

Ogawa, S., & Piller. (2006). Reducing the Risks of New Product Development. *Sloan Management Review, 47*, 65–72.

Oh, H., & Petrie, J. (2012). How do storefront window displays influence entering decisions of clothing stores? *Journal of Retailing and Consumer Services, 19*, 27–35. doi:10.1016/j.jretconser.2011.08.003

OIFB-Osservatorio Internazionale Food Beverage. (2013). *Globalizzazione dei consumi*. Retrieved May 10, 2013, from http://www.oifb.com/index.php?option=com_content&view=article&id=109

Okazaki, S., Navarro, A., & Campo, S. (2013). Media integration of QR code: a preliminary exploration. *Journal of Electronic Commerce Research, 14*(2), 137–148.

Olahut, M. R., El-Murad, J., & Plaias, I. (2012). Store atmosphere: Conceptual Issues and It`s Impact on Shopping Behaviour. In *Proceedings of International Conference Marketing – from information to decision*, (pp. 317-343). Academic Press.

Oliver, R. L. (1980). A Cognitive Model of the Antecedents and Consequences of Satisfaction Decisions. *JMR, Journal of Marketing Research, 17*, 460–469. doi:10.2307/3150499

Oliver, R. L. (1993). Cognitive, affective, and attribute bases of the satisfaction response. *The Journal of Consumer Research, 20*, 418–430. doi:10.1086/209358

Oliver, R. L. (1999). Whence consumer loyalty? *Journal of Marketing, 63*, 33–44. doi:10.2307/1252099

Oliver, R. L. (2010). *Satisfaction: A Behavioral Perspective on the Consumer* (2nd ed.). Armond, NY: M.E. Sharpe.

Oliver, R. L., Rust, R. T., & Varki, S. (1997). Customer delight: Foundations, findings, and managerial insight. *Journal of Retailing, 73*(3), 311–336. doi:10.1016/S0022-4359(97)90021-X

Oliver, R. L., & Swan, J. E. (1989). Equity and disconfirmation perceptions as influences on merchant and product satisfaction. *The Journal of Consumer Research, 16*, 372–383. doi:10.1086/209223

Ooi, J., & Sim, L.-L. (2007). The Magnetism of Suburban Shopping Centers: Do Size and Cineplex Matter? *Journal of Property Investment & Finance, 25*(2), 111–135. doi:10.1108/14635780710733816

Osservatorio Socialis. (2010). *L'impegno sociale delle aziende in Italia*. [The social effort in Italian Companies]. Report.

Overstreet, J., & Clodfelter, R. (1995). Safety and Security Concerns of Shopping Center Consumers and the Effect of these Concerns on Shopping Behavior. *Journal of Shopping Center Research, 2*(1), 91–109.

Oxford Brookes University. (2007). *Unit 23 Recognise diversity when delivering customer service*. Retrieved February 12th, 2012, from http://www.brookes.ac.uk/services/ocsld/staffcourses/nvq/standards/customer_service/level2/unit23.html

Oyserman, D. (2009). Identity-based motivation and consumer behaviour. *Journal of Consumer Psychology, 19*, 276–279. doi:10.1016/j.jcps.2009.06.001

Pal, J., Bennison, D., Clarke, I., & Byrom, J. (2001). Power, policy, networks and planning: the involvement of the major grocery retailers in the formulation of Planning Policy Guidance Note 6 since 1988. *International Review of Retail, Distribution and Consumer Research, 11*, 225–246. doi:10.1080/09593960122876

Palmatier, R. W., Burke Jarvis, C., Bechkoff, J. R., & Kardes, F. R. (2009). The Role of Customer Gratitude in Relationship Marketing. *Journal of Marketing, 73*, 1–18. doi:10.1509/jmkg.73.5.1

Palmatier, R. W., Dant, R. P., Grewal, D., & Evans, K. R. (2006). Factors influencing the effectiveness of relationship marketing: a meta-analysis. *Journal of Marketing, 70*, 136–153. doi:10.1509/jmkg.70.4.136

Palmeira, M., Santos, C., & Palmeira, D. (2012). Frontline Employees' Self-perception of Ageism, Sexism, and Appearance Discrimination – comparative analysis in Fashion and Food Retailing. In *Proceedings of British Academy of Management Conference*. Cardiff, UK: BAM.

Palmeira, M., Palmeira, D., & Santos, C. (2012). A Perception of Prejudice in the Face-to-face Retail Services: comparative analyses of age and gender. *International Journal of Applied Behavioral Economics, 1*(4), 22–40. doi:10.4018/ijabe.2012100103

Palmer, M., Simmons, G., & de Kervenoael, R. (2009). Brilliant mistake! Essays on incidents of management mistakes and mea culpa. *International Journal of Retail & Distribution Management, 38*(4), 234–257. doi:10.1108/09590551011032072

Pandelica, A., & Pandelica, I. (2011). The change of consumers' behaviour in crisis conditions: A psychological approach to the empirical evidence from Romania. *African Journal of Business Management, 5*(28), 11399–11412.

Pantano, E. (2013). Ubiquitous retailing innovative scenario: from the fixed point of sale to the flexible ubiquitous store. *Journal of Technology Management and Innovation, 8*(2), 84–92. doi:10.4067/S0718-27242013000200007

Pantano, E., & Naccarato, G. (2010). Entertainment in Retailing: the influences of advanced technologies. *Journal of Retailing and Consumer Services, 17*(3), 200–204. doi:10.1016/j.jretconser.2010.03.010

Pantano, E., & Timmermans, H. J. P. (2011). *Advanced Technologies Management for Retailing: Frameworks and Cases*. IGI Global. doi:10.4018/978-1-60960-738-8

Pantelidis, I. S. (2010). Electronic Meal Experience: A Content Analysis of Online Restaurant Comments. *Cornell Hospitality Quarterly, 51*(4), 483–491. doi:10.1177/1938965510378574

Pan, Y., & Zinkhan, G. M. (2006). Determinants of retail patronage: A meta-analytical perspective. *Journal of Retailing, 82*(3), 229–243. doi:10.1016/j.jretai.2005.11.008

Pappu, R., & Quester, P. (2006). A consumer-based method for retailer equity measurement: Results of an empirical study. *Journal of Retailing and Consumer Services, 13*, 317–329. doi:10.1016/j.jretconser.2005.10.002

Pappu, R., & Quester, P. (2006). Does customer satisfaction lead to improved brand equity? An empirical examination of two categories of retail brands. *Journal of Product and Brand Management, 15*(1), 4–14. doi:10.1108/10610420610650837

Parasuraman, A., Zeithaml, V. A., & Berry, L. L. (1996). The behavorial consequences of service quality. *Journal of Marketing, 60*, 31–46. doi:10.2307/1251929

Parente, J. (2000). *Varejo no Brasil – Gestao e Estrategia* [Retailing in Brazil – Management and Strategy]. Atlas. (in Portuguese)

Park, C. W., Iyer, E. S., & Smith, D. C. (1989). The effects of situational factors on in-store grocery shopping behavior: The role of store environment and time available for shopping. *The Journal of Consumer Research, 15*(4), 422–433. doi:10.1086/209182

Park, C. W., MacInnis, D. J., Priester, J., Eisingerich, A. B., & Iacobucci, D. (2010). Brand attachment and brand attitude strength: conceptual and empirical differentiation of two critical brand equity drivers. *Journal of Marketing, 74*, 1–17. doi:10.1509/jmkg.74.6.1

Park, C. W., & Young, S. M. (1986). Consumer response to television commercials: the impact of involvement and background music on bran attitude formation. *JMR, Journal of Marketing Research, 23*(1), 11–24. doi:10.2307/3151772

Parker, B. T. (2009). A comparison of brand personality and brand user-imagery congruence. *Journal of Consumer Marketing, 26*(3), 175–184. doi:10.1108/07363760910954118

Park, H.-J., & Burns, L. D. (2005). Fashion orientation, credit card use, and compulsive buying. *Journal of Consumer Marketing, 22*(2/3), 135–141. doi:10.1108/07363760510595959

Pastore, A. (1996). *I nuovi rapporti tra industria e distribuzione*. Padova, Italy: Cedam.

Patino, A., Pitta, D. A., & Quinones, R. (2012). Social media's emerging importance in market research. *Journal of Consumer Marketing*, 29(3), 233–237. doi:10.1108/07363761211221800

Pavlou, P. A. (2003). Consumer Acceptance Of Electronic Commerce - Integrating Trust And Risk With The Technology Acceptance Model. *International Journal of Electronic Commerce*, 7(3), 69–103.

Payne, A., & Frow, P. (2005). A Strategic Framework for Customer Relationship Management. *Journal of Marketing*, 69, 167–176. doi:10.1509/jmkg.2005.69.4.167

Peck, J., & Childers, T. (2008). If it Tastes, Smells, Sounds, and Feels Like a Duck, then it must be a …: Effects of sensory factors on consumer behaviours. In *Handbook of Consumer Psychology*. Psychology Press.

Peck, J., & Childers, T. L. (2003). Individual differences in haptic information processing: the need for touch scale. *The Journal of Consumer Research*, 30(3), 430–442. doi:10.1086/378619

Peck, J., & Childers, T. L. (2003). To Have and to Hold: The Influence of Haptic Information on Product Judgements. *Journal of Marketing*, 67, 35–48. doi:10.1509/jmkg.67.2.35.18612

Peck, J., & Childers, T. L. (2007). If it tastes, smells, sounds, and feels like a duck, then it must be a…: effects of sensory factors on consumer behaviours. In F. Kardes, C. Haugtvedt, & P. Herr (Eds.), *Handbook of Consumer Psychology*. Mahwah, NJ: Erlbaum.

Peck, J., & Wiggins, J. (2006). It just Feels Good: Customers' Affective Response to Touch and its Influence on Persuasion. *Journal of Marketing*, 70, 56–69. doi:10.1509/jmkg.70.4.56

Peele, S. (1990). The meaning of addiction: Compulsive experience and its interpretation. Lexington, MA: Lexington.

Pegan, G., & Vianelli, D. (2013). *Il ruolo degli importatori nella valorizzazione del country of origin: un'indagine qualitativa sul vino italiano nel mercato statunitense.* Paper presented at X° Convegno Annuale della Società Italiana di Marketing Smart-Life: Dall'innovazione tecnologica al mercato. Milan, Italy.

Peirce, C. S. (1998). *Collected Papers of Charles Sanders Peirce*. Bristol, UK: Thoemmes.

Pellegrini, L. (2008). I rapporti industria-distribuzione: modelli integrati e ricerca di cooperazione. *Economia e Politica Industriale*, 3, 12–31.

Penaloza, L., & Price, L. (1993). Consumer Resistance: A Conceptual Overview. In *Advances in Consumer Research*. Provo, UT: Association for Consumer Research.

Peñaloza, L., & Venkatesh, A. (2006). Further Evolving the New Dominant Logic of Marketing: From Services to the Social Construction of Markets. *Marketing Theory*, 6(3), 299–316. doi:10.1177/1470593106066789

Pennings, J., Wansink, B., & Meulenberg, M. (2002). A Note on Modeling Consumer Reaction to a Crisis: The Case of the Mad Cow Disease. *International Journal of Research in Marketing*, 19, 91–100. doi:10.1016/S0167-8116(02)00050-2

Pentecost, R., & Andrews, L. (2010). Fashion retailing and the bottom line: The effects of generational cohorts, gender, fashion fanship, attitudes and impulse buying on fashion expenditure. *Journal of Retailing and Consumer Services*, 17(1), 43–52. doi:10.1016/j.jretconser.2009.09.003

Perner, L. (2008). *Consumer behaviour: the psychology of marketing*. Univ. of Southern California. Retrieved Jun 6, 2013, from http://www.consumerpsychologist

Perrigot, R., Basset, G., & Cliquet, G. (2007). Does the retailing wheel still work? The case of the hard discount stores in France. In J. Zentes, D. Morschett, & H. Schramm-Klein (Eds.), *XIV European Association of Education and Research in Commercial Distribution Conference Proceedings* (pp. 1328-1353). Saarbruecken, Germany: Saarland University.

Perriman, H., Ramsaran-Fowdar, R., & Baguant, P. (2010). The impact of the global financial crisis on consumer behavior. In Z. Haqq (Ed.), *Proceedings of Annual London Business Research Conference*. Retrieved July, 18, 2013, from http://www.wbiconpro.com/06-Priya.pdf

Persaud, A., & Azhar, I. (2012). Innovative Mobile Marketing via Smartphones: Are Consumers Ready? *Marketing Intelligence & Planning*, 30(4), 418–443. doi:10.1108/02634501211231883

Peterson, P. (2012). Merci: a Parisian store to be thankful for. *Huffington Post*. Retrieved on August 28, 2013 from http://www.huffingtonpost.com/pam-peterson/merci-paris-store_b_2276982.html

Phelps, J., Nowak, G. J., & Ferrell, E. (2000). Privacy Concerns and Consumer Willingness to Provide Personal Information. *Journal of Public Policy & Marketing, 19*(1), 27–4. doi:10.1509/jppm.19.1.27.16941

Phillips, S., Alexander, A., & Shaw, G. (2005). Consumer Misbehavior: The Rise of Self-Service Grocery Retailing and Shoplifting in the United Kingdom c. 1950-1970. *Journal of Macromarketing, 25*(1), 66–75. doi:10.1177/0276146705275715

Piercy, N. F., Cravens, D. W., & Lane, N. (2010). Marketing Out Of The Recession: Recovery Is Coming, But Things Will Never Be The Same Again. *Marketing Review, 10*(1), 3–23. doi:10.1362/146934710X488915

Pine, B. J. II, & Gilmore, J. H. (1999). *The Experience Economy: Work is Theatre & Every Business a Stage*. Boston: Harvard Business School Press.

Pine, B. J. II, & Gilmore, J. H. (2002). Customer Experience Places: The New Offering Frontier. *Strategy and Leadership, 30*(4), 4–11. doi:10.1108/10878570210435306

Pine, J. B. II, & Gilmore, J. H. (1998, July-August). Welcome to the Experience Economy. *Harvard Business Review*, 97–105. PMID:10181589

Pitt, L. F., Berthon, P. R., Watson, T. R., & Zinkhan, G. (2002). The internet and the birth of real consumer power. *Business Horizons, 45*(6), 7–14. doi:10.1016/S0007-6813(02)00220-3

PlanetRetail. (2011). *Country report Western Europe*. London: Author.

Plassman, H. ODoherty, J., Shiv, B, & Rangel, A. (2007). Marketing actions can modulate neural representations of experienced pleasantness. *Proceedings of the National Academy of Sciences of the United States of America, 105*(3), 1050-1054.

Pliner, P., Chaiken, S., & Flett, G. (1990). *Gender Differences in Concern with Body Weight and Physical Appearance Over the Life Span*. Retrieved February 12th, 2012, from http://psp.sagepub.com/content/16/2/263.short

PLMA (Private Label Manufacturer's Association). (2012). *Private Label Today*. Retrieved May 15, 2013, from http://plmainternational.com/en/private_label12_en.htm

Plouffe, C. R., Sridharan, S., & Barclay, D. W. (2010). Exploratory navigation and salesperson performance: investigating selected antecedents and boundary conditions in high-technology and financial services contexts. *Industrial Marketing Management, 39*(4), 538–550. doi:10.1016/j.indmarman.2009.02.003

Plutchik, R. (1980). *Emotion: a psycho evolutionary synthesis*. New York: Harper & Row.

Ponte, S. (2002). The 'Latte Revolution'? Regulation, Markets and Consumption in the Global Coffee Chain. *World Development, 30*(7), 1099–1122. doi:10.1016/S0305-750X(02)00032-3

Pooler, J. (2003). *Why we shop: Emotional rewards and retail strategies*. London: Praeger Publishers.

Poon, P., Albaum, G., & Chan, P. S.-F. (2012). Managing trust in direct selling relationships. *Marketing Intelligence & Planning, 30*(5), 588–603. doi:10.1108/02634501211251070

Portas, M. (2011). The Portas Review: An independent review into the future of our High Streets. *BIS*. Retrieved March 27, 2013, from http://www.bis.gov.uk/assets/BISCore/business-sectors/docs/p/11-1434-portas-review-future-of-high-streets.pdf

Porter, M. (1980). *Competitive Strategy*. New York: Free Press.

Porter, M., & Kramer, M. (2011). Creating Shared Value: How to reinvent capitalism and unleash a wave of innovation and growth. *Harvard Business Review, 89*(1/2), 62–77.

Porter, M., & Kramer, R. M. (2002). The Competitive Advantage of Corporate Philanthropy. *Harvard Business Review, 80*(12), 57–68. PMID:12510538

Poster, M. (1992). The question of agency: de Certeau and the history of consumption. *Diacritics, 22*(2), 94–107. doi:10.2307/465283

Potter, B. (2013). The future High Streets forum launches: Why no mention of digital? *Econsultancy*. Retrieved August 6, 2013, from http://econsultancy.com/uk/blog/62483-the-future-high-streets-forum-launches-why-no-mention-of-digital

Poulter, S. (2012). Dying High Street shops where up to a third is empty. *The Daily Mail*. Retrieved March 27, 2013, from http://www.dailymail.co.uk/news/article-2097383/Dying-high-streets-shops-empty.html

Prahalad, C. K., & Ramaswamy, V. (2004). Co-creation experiences: The next practice in value creation. *Journal of Interactive Marketing*, 18(3), 5–14. doi:10.1002/dir.20015

Prahalad, C. K., & Ramaswamy, V. (2004). *The Future of Competition: Co-creating Unique Value with Consumers*. Boston: Harvard Business School Press.

Prasad, A., Prasad, P., & Mir, R. (2011). One mirror in another: Managing diversity and the discourse of fashion. *Human Relations*, 64(5), 703–724. doi:10.1177/0018726710386511

Prasad, C. J. S., & Aryasri, A. R. (2009). Determinants of Shopper Behavior in E-tailing: An Empirical Analysis. *Paradigm*, 13(1), 73.

Premazzi, K., Castaldo, S., Grosso, M., Raman, P., Brudvig, S., & Hofacker, C. (2010a). Customer information sharing with e-vendors: The role of initial trust and incentives. *International Journal of Electronic Commerce*, 14(3), 63–91. doi:10.2753/JEC1086-4415140304

Premazzi, K., Castaldo, S., Hofacker, C., & Grosso, M. (2010b). Supporting retailers to exploit online settings for internationalization: the different role of trust and compensation. *Journal of Retailing and Consumer Services*, 17(3), 229–240. doi:10.1016/j.jretconser.2010.03.006

Pretious, M., Stewart, R., & Logan, D. (1995). Retail Security: A Survey of Methods and Management in Dundee. *International Journal of Retail & Distribution Management*, 23(9), 28–35. doi:10.1108/09590559510098681

Pringle, C. D., Jannings, D. F., & Longeneckr, J. G. (1988). *Managing Organizations: Functions and Behaviors*. Columbus, OH: Merrill.

Prus, R., & Dawson, L. (1991). Shop 'til you drop: Shopping as recreational and laborious activity. *Canadian Journal of Sociology*, 16(2), 145–164. doi:10.2307/3341271

Puccinelli, N. M., Goodstein, R. C., Grewal, D., Price, R., Raghubir, P., & Stewart, D. (2009). Customer experience management in retailing: Understanding the buying process. *Journal of Retailing*, 85(1), 15–30. doi:10.1016/j.jretai.2008.11.003

Putsis, W. P. Jr, & Cotterill, R. W. (1999). Share, price and category expenditure – geographic market effects and private labels. *Managerial and Decision Economics*, 20(4), 175–187. doi:10.1002/(SICI)1099-1468(199906)20:4<175::AID-MDE928>3.0.CO;2-I

Qian, H., Haynes, K. E., & Riggle, J. D. (2011). Incubation push or business pull? Investigating the geography of US business incubators. *Economic Development Quarterly*, 25(1), 79–90. doi:10.1177/0891242410383275

Qualman, E. (2013). *Socialnomics* (2nd ed.). Hoboken, NJ: John Wiley & Sons, Inc.

Quelch, J., & Jocz, K. (2009). How to market in a Downturn. *Harvard Business Review*. Retrieved February 8, 2010, from http://hbr.harvardbusiness.org/2009/04/how-tomarket-in-a-downturn/ar/1

Quelch, J., & Harding, D. (1996). Brands versus private labels: fighting to win. *Harvard Business Review*, 74(1), 99–109.

Quester, P. G., Karunaratna, A., & Goh, L. K. (2000). Self-congruity and product evaluation: a cross-cultural study. *Journal of Consumer Marketing*, 17(6), 525–535. doi:10.1108/07363760010349939

Quinn, I. (2013). Independent stores 'should team up on click & collect offers'. *The Grocer*. Retrieved June 9, 2013, from http://www.thegrocer.co.uk/companies/independent-stores-should-team-up-on-click-and-collect-offers/343174.article

Rafiq, M., Fulford, H., & Lu, X. (2013). Building customer loyalty in online retailing: The role of relationship quality. *Journal of Marketing Management*, 29(3-4), 494–517. doi:10.1080/0267257X.2012.737356

Rai, S. (2010). *Oxford dictionary or Politics*. Retrieved February 12th, 2012 from http://www.answers.com/topic/sexism

Raju, J. S., Srinivasan, V., & Lal, R. (1990). The effects of brand loyalty on competitive price promotional strategies. *Management Science*, 36(3), 276–304. doi:10.1287/mnsc.36.3.276

Raju, J., Sethuraman, R., & Dhar, S. (1995). National Brand: Store Brand Price Differential and Store Brand Market Share. *Pricing Strategy and Practice*, 3(2), 17–24.

Raman, P., & Pashupati, K. (2005). Online Privacy: Consumer Concerns and Technological Competence. In S. Krishnamurthy (Ed.), *Contemporary Research in E-Marketing* (pp. 200–225). Hershey, PA: Idea Group Publishing.

Ramaswamy, S. (2013). Shopping then and now: Five ways retail has changed and how businesses can adapt. *Google Think Insights*. Retrieved August 6, 2013, from http://www.google.com/think/articles/five-ways-retail-has-changed-and-how-business

Rangaswamy, A., & Van Bruggen, G. H. (2005). Opportunities and challenges in multichannel marketing: an introduction to the special issue. *Journal of Interactive Marketing, 19*(2), 5–11. doi:10.1002/dir.20037

Rao, S. S., Metts, G., & Monge, C. A. M. (2003). Electronic commerce development in small and medium sized enterprises: A stage model and its implications. *Business Process Management Journal, 9*(1), 11–32. doi:10.1108/14637150310461378

Rattam, E. (1998). *Novo modelo de estratificacao socioeconomica para marketing e pesquisas de marketing.* [New Social Classification Approach for Marketing and Marketing Research] (In Portuguese). Retrieved July 1st, 2008, from http://www.anpad.org.br/enanpad/1998/dwn/enanpad1998-mkt-27.pdf

Raykov, T. (1998). Coefficient alpha and composite reliability with interrelated nonhomogeneous items. *Applied Psychological Measurement, 22*(4), 375–385. doi:10.1177/014662169802200407

Reddy, B. K., & Reddy, J. S. (2012). Atmospherics: a silent sales person in organized retailing. *International Journal of Sales. Retailing and Marketing, 1*(1), 23–29.

Reed, A. II, Forehand, M. R., Puntoni, S., & Warlop, L. (2012). Identity-based consumer behaviour. *International Journal of Research in Marketing, 29*, 310–321. doi:10.1016/j.ijresmar.2012.08.002

Reichheld, F. (1993). Loyalty-based management. *Harvard Business Review, 71*(2), 64–73. PMID:10124634

Reichheld, F. F. (1996). *The Loyalty Effect.* Boston: Harvard Business School Press.

Reimers, V., & Clulow, V. (2009). Retail centres: It's time to make them convenient. *International Journal of Retail & Distribution Management, 37*(7), 541–562. doi:10.1108/09590550910964594

Reitberger, W., Obermair, C., Ploderer, B., Meschtscherjakov, A., & Tscheligi, A. (2007). Enhancing the shopping experience with ambient displays: a field study in a retail store. *Lecture Notes in Computer Science, 4794*, 314–331. doi:10.1007/978-3-540-76652-0_19

Rekik, Y., Sahin, E., & Dallery, Y. (2009). Inventory Inaccuracy in Retail Stores due to Theft: An Analysis of the Benefits of RFID. *International Journal of Production Economics, 118*(1), 189–198. doi:10.1016/j.ijpe.2008.08.048

Resciniti, R. (2004). *Il marketing orientato all'esperienza: L'intrattenimento nella relazione con il consumatore.* Napoli: Edizioni Scientifiche Italiane.

Reynolds, J., & Cuthbertson, C. (2004). *Retail Strategy – the view from the bridge.* Oxford, UK: Elsevier Butterwork-Heinemann.

Reynolds, J., Howard, E., Cuthbertson, C., & Hristov, L. (2007). Perspectives on retail format innovation: relating theory and practice. *International Journal of Retail & Distribution Management, 35*(8), 647–660. doi:10.1108/09590550710758630

RGA. (2009). *Etica o etichetta? Primo report su responsabilità sociale e competitività.* [Ethics or brand? Firts report on social responsibility and competitiveness]. Report.

Richardson, P. S., Dick, A. S., & Jain, A. K. (1994). Extrinsic and intrinsic cue effects on perceptions of store brand quality. *Journal of Marketing, 58*(4), 28–36. doi:10.2307/1251914

Richardson, P. S., Jain, A. K., & Dick, A. (1996). Household Store Brand Proneness: A Framework. *Journal of Retailing, 72*(2), 159–185. doi:10.1016/S0022-4359(96)90012-3

Richins, M. L., & Dawson, S. (1992). A consumer values orientation for materialism and its measurement: Scale development and validation. *The Journal of Consumer Research, 19*, 303–316. doi:10.1086/209304

Richter, F. (2013). *Coca-Cola is the No. 1 Brand on Facebook.* Retrieved August 2013, from http://www.statista.com/markets/14/media-advertising/chart/1377/most-talked-about-brands-on-facebook/

Ricolfi, L. (2006). *La ricerca qualitativa.* Roma: Carocci Editore.

Ridgeway, N. M., Kukar-Kinney, M., & Monroe, K. B. (2008). An expanded conceptualization and a new measure of compulsive buying. *The Journal of Consumer Research*, *35*(4), 622–639. doi:10.1086/591108

Rifon, N. J., LaRose, R., & Choi, S. M. (2005). Your Privacy Is Sealed: Effects of Web Privacy Seals on Trust and Personal Disclosures. *The Journal of Consumer Affairs*, *39*(2), 339–362. doi:10.1111/j.1745-6606.2005.00018.x

Rintamaki, T., Kanto, A., Kuusela, H., & Spence, M. (2006). Decomposing the value of department store shopping into utilitarian, hedonic and social dimensions: Evidence from Finland. *International Journal of Retail & Distribution Management*, *34*(1), 6–24. doi:10.1108/09590550610642792

Ritzer, G. (1998). *The McDonaldization Thesis.* London: Sage.

Riverside, City of. (2006). *City Report.* California - USA.

Rizkalla, A. N. (1989). Sense of time urgency and consumer well-being: Testing alternative causal models. In T. K. Srull (Ed.), *NA - Advances in Consumer Research* (pp. 180–188). Provo, UT: Association for Consumer Research.

Roberts, J. A., & Sepulveda, C. J. M. (1999). Money attitudes and compulsive buying: An exploratory investigation of the emerging consumer culture in Mexico. *Journal of International Consumer Marketing*, *11*(4), 53–74. doi:10.1300/J046v11n04_04

Robertson, J. (2003). *Knowledge management for frontline staff.* Retrieved February 12th, 2012, from http://www.steptwo.com.au/papers/kmc_frontline/index.html

Robertson, R. (1995). Glocalization: Time-Space and Homogeneity-Heterogeneity. In M. Featherstone, S. Lash, & R. Robertson (Eds.), *Global Modernities* (pp. 25–44). London: Sage. doi:10.4135/9781446250563.n2

Robins, F. (2005). The Future of Corporate Social Responsibility. *Asian Business & Management*, *4*, 95–115. doi:10.1057/palgrave.abm.9200125

Robles, F., Simon, F., & Haar, J. (2002). *Winning strategies for the new Latin markets.* Financial Times/Prentice Hall.

Rodie, A. R., & Kleine, S. S. (2000). Customer Participation in Services Production and Delivery. In T. A. Swartz, & D. Iacobucci (Eds.), *Handbook of Services Marketing and Management.* Thousand Oaks, CA: Sage Publications. doi:10.4135/9781452231327.n10

Rohm, A. J., & Swaminathan, V. (2004). A typology of online shoppers based on shopping motivations. *Journal of Business Research*, *57*, 748–757. doi:10.1016/S0148-2963(02)00351-X

Rojek, C. (2006). Representation. In C. Rojek, S. M. Shaw, & A. J. Veal (Eds.), *A handbook of leisure studies* (pp. 459–474). London, UK: Palgrave-Macmillan. doi:10.1057/9780230625181

Roland Berger. (2013). What the customer really wants. *Roland Berger.* Retrieved October 27, 2013, from http://www.rolandberger.com/press_releases/513-press_archive2013_sc_content/What_the_customer_really_wants.html

Rousey, S. P., & Morganosky, M. A. (1996). Retail format change in US markets. *International Journal of Retail & Distribution Management*, *24*(3), 8–16. doi:10.1108/09590559610147883

Roy, M., Dewit, O., & Aubert, B. A. (2001). The impact of interface usability on trust in web retailers. *Internet Research: Electronic Networking Applications and Policy*, *11*(5), 388–398. doi:10.1108/10662240110410165

Ruddick, G. (2013). Government should freeze business rates for two years to help the High Street. *The Telegraph.* Retrieved March 27, 2013, from http://www.telegraph.co.uk/finance/newsbysector/retailandconsumer/10069475/Government-should-freeze-business-rates-for-two-years-to-help-high-street.html

Ruimei, W., Shengxiong, W., Tianzhen, W., & Xiling, Z. (2012). Customers e-trust for online retailers: a case in China. In *Proceedings of the 8th International Conference on Computational Intelligence and Security* (pp. 573-577). IEEE Computer Society Press.

Rumbo, J. D. (2002). Consumer Resistance in a World of Advertising Clutter: The Case of Adbusters. *Psychology and Marketing*, *19*(2), 127–148. doi:10.1002/mar.10006

Rumsey, N., & Harcourt, D. (2005). *The Psychology of Appearance.* Retrieved February 12th, 2012, from http://www.lavoisier.fr/livre/notice.asp?id=O22WA3AR3LLOWE

Rundle-Thiele, S., & MacKay, M. M. (2001). Assessing the performance of brand loyalty measures. *Journal of Services Marketing, 15*(7), 529–546. doi:10.1108/EUM0000000006210

Rusko, R. (2011). Virtual Business Incubations: An Alternative Way to Develop and Service Peripheral Areas. [IJIDE]. *International Journal of Innovation in the Digital Economy, 2*(3), 48–64. doi:10.4018/jide.2011070104

Rusko, R. (2012). Strategic Processes and Turning Points in ICT Business: Case Nokia.[IJIDE]. *International Journal of Innovation in the Digital Economy, 3*(3), 25–34. doi:10.4018/jide.2012070103

Ryssel, R., Ritter, T., & Gemunden, H. G. (2004). The impact of information technology deployment on trust, commitment and value creation in business relationships. *Journal of Business and Industrial Marketing, 19*(3), 197–207. doi:10.1108/08858620410531333

Salt, S. (2011). Social Location Marketing. Indianapolis, IN: Que.

Sampson, J. (2013). Why the High Street isn't dying. *Huffington Post.* Retrieved March 27, 2013, from http://www.huffingtonpost.co.uk/josie-sampson/why-the-high-street-isnt-dying_b_2811337.html?icid=hp_search_art

Sánchez Pérez, M., Estrella Ramón, A. M., Ruiz Real, J. L., & García Ramírez, A. (2011). Retailing in Europe: Situation and trends. *Revista de Estudios Empresariales, 2*, 67–95.

Sangeeta, S., Shrivastava, A., & Bhimalingam, R. (2008). Consumer Attitude Towards Online Retail Shopping in the Indian Context. *Journal of Consumer Behaviour, 3*(4).

Sansone, C., & Smith, J. L. (2000). Interest and self-regulation: The relation between having to and wanting to. In C. Sansone, & J. M. Harackiewicz (Eds.), *Intrinsic and extrinsic motivation: The search for optimal motivation and performance* (pp. 343–374). San Diego, CA: American Press. doi:10.1016/B978-012619070-0/50034-9

Saraceno, P. (1970). La gestione dell'impresa alla luce dell'analisi dei sistemi. *Ricerche economiche, 3/4*, 256-273.

Sashittal, H. C., Sriramachandramurthy, R., & Hodis, M. (2012). Targeting college students on Facebook? How to stop wasting your money. *Business Horizons, 55*(5), 495–50. doi:10.1016/j.bushor.2012.05.006

Sathish, A. S., & Venkatesakumar, R. (2011). Coffee Experience and Drivers of Satisfaction, Loyalty in a Coffee outlet – With specially reference to Café Coffee Day. *Journal of Contemporary Management Research, 5*(2), 1–13.

Saunders, D. et al. (1992). Employee voice to supervisors. *Employee Responsibilities and Rights Journal, 5*, 241–259. doi:10.1007/BF01385051

Saviano, M. (2013). *The Viable Systems Approach (vSA), what it is, what it is not.* Paper presented at the 2013 Naples Forum on Service-Service Dominant logic, Network & Systems Theory and Service Science: integrating three perspectives for a new service agenda. Ischia, Italy.

Saviano, M. (2001). Il fenomeno della globalizzazione verso un'interpretazione in chiave sistemica vitale. *Esperienze d'Impresa, 1*, 41–68.

Saviano, M. (2003). *Analisi sistemico vitale della distribuzione commerciale.* Torino, Italy: Giappichelli.

Sawhney, M., Verona, G., & Prandelli, E. (2005). Collaborating to Create: The Internet as a Platform for Customer Engagement in Product Innovation. *Journal of Interactive Marketing, 19*(4), 4. doi:10.1002/dir.20046

Sayman, S., & Raju, J. S. (2004). Investigating the cross-category effects of store brands. *Review of Industrial Organization, 24*(2), 129–141. doi:10.1023/B:REIO.0000033349.67467.b7

SBDCN-Small Business Development Center Network. (2012). *Coffee Shop Business Overview & Trends 2012.* Retrieved May 10, 2013, from http://www.sbdcnet.org/small-business-research-reports/coffee-shop-2012

Schaefer, A., & Crane, A. (2005). Addressing Sustainability and Consumption. *Journal of Macromarketing, 25*(1), 76–92. doi:10.1177/0276146705274987

Schau, H. J., Muniz, A. M., & Arnould, E. J. (2009). How Brand Community Practices Create Value. *Journal of Marketing, 73*, 30–51. doi:10.1509/jmkg.73.5.30

Schein, E. (2010). *Organizational culture and leadership.* Wiley and Sons.

Scherhorn, G., Reisch, L. A., & Raab, G. (1990). Addictive buying in West Germany: An empirical study. *Journal of Consumer Policy, 13*, 355–387. doi:10.1007/BF00412336

Schilling, M. A. (2010). *Strategic Management of Technological Innovation*. Boston: McGraw Hill.

Schirrmacher, F. (2004). *A Revolucao dos Idosos* [The Methuselah Complot]. Rio de Janeiro, Brazil: Campus / Elsevier. (in Portuguese)

Schlosser, A. E., White, T. B., & Lloyd, S. M. (2006). Converting Web Site Visitors into Buyers: how Web Site Investment Increases Consumer Trusting Beliefs and Online Purchase Intentions. *Journal of Marketing, 70*(2), 133–148. doi:10.1509/jmkg.70.2.133

Schlosser, S., Black, D. W., Repertinger, S., & Freet, D. (1994). Compulsive buying: Demography, phenomenology, and comorbidity in 46 subjects. *General Hospital Psychiatry, 16*, 205–212. doi:10.1016/0163-8343(94)90103-1 PMID:8063088

Schmitt, B. (1999). Experiential Marketing. *Journal of Marketing Management, 15*(1-3), 53–67. doi:10.1362/026725799784870496

Schmitt, B. H. (2003). *Customer Experience Management*. Wiley & Sons.

Schmitt, N. (1996). Uses and abuses of coefficient alpha. *Psychological Assessment, 8*(4), 250–353. doi:10.1037/1040-3590.8.4.350

Schoder, D., & Yin, P. L. (2000). Building firm trust online. *Communications of the ACM, 43*(12), 73–79. doi:10.1145/355112.355127

Schoenbachler, D. D., & Gordon, G. L. (2002). Trust and Customer Willingness to Provide Information in Database-Driven Relationship Marketing. *Journal of Interactive Marketing, 16*(3), 2–16. doi:10.1002/dir.10033

Schor, J. B. (1991). *The overworked American: The unexpected decline of leisure*. New York: Basic Books.

Schor, J. B. (2004). *Born to buy*. New York: Scribner.

Schultz, D. E., Tannenbaum, S. I., & Lauterborn, R. F. (1993). *Integrated marketing communications*. Chicago: NTC Business.

Schumpeter, J. A. (1950). *Capitalism, Socialism and Democracy*. New York: Harper & Brothers Publishers.

Schwenk, C. R. (1984). Cognitive simplification processes in strategic decision-making. *Strategic Management Journal, 5*(2), 111–128. doi:10.1002/smj.4250050203

Scollon, C. N., Diener, E., Oishi, S., & Biswas-Diener, R. (2004). Emotions across cultures and methods. *Journal of Cross-Cultural Psychology, 35*(3), 304–326. doi:10.1177/0022022104264124

Scott, J., & Marshall, G. (2009). *Oxford dictionary of sociology* (3rd ed.). Oxford, UK: Oxford University Press. doi:10.1093/acref/9780199533008.001.0001

Seaford, B. C., Culp, R. C., & Brooks, B. W. (2012). Starbucks: Maintaining A Clear Position. *Journal of the International Academy for Case Studies, 18*(3), 39–57.

Sebastiani, R., Montagnini, F., & Dalli, D. (2013). Ethical Consumption and New Business Models in the Food Industry: Evidence from the Eataly Case. *Journal of Business Ethics, 114*(3), 473–488. doi:10.1007/s10551-012-1343-1

Seiders, K., Voss, G. B., Grewal, D., & Godfrey, A. L. (2005). Do satisfied customers buy more? Examining moderating influences in a retailing context. *Journal of Marketing, 69*(4), 26–43. doi:10.1509/jmkg.2005.69.4.26

Sellitto, C., Burgess, S., & Hawking, P. (2007). Information Quality Attributes Associated with RFID-Derived Benefits in the Retail Supply Chain. *International Journal of Retail & Distribution Management, 35*(1), 69–87. doi:10.1108/09590550710722350

Semeijn, J., van Riel, A. C. R., & Ambrosini, A. B. (2004). Consumer evaluations of store brands: effects of store image and product attributes. *Journal of Retailing and Consumer Services, 11*(4), 247–258. doi:10.1016/S0969-6989(03)00051-1

Sen, S., & Bhattacharya, C. B. (2001). Does doing good always lead to doing better? Consumer reactions to corporate social responsibility. *JMR, Journal of Marketing Research, 38*(2), 225–243. doi:10.1509/jmkr.38.2.225.18838

Sen, S., Block, L. G., & Chandran, S. (2002). Window displays and consumer shopping decisions. *Journal of Retailing and Consumer Services, 9*, 277–290. doi:10.1016/S0969-6989(01)00037-6

Sethuraman, R., & Cole, C. (1999). Factors influencing the price premiums that consumers pay for national brands over store brands. *Journal of Product and Brand Management, 8*(4), 340–351. doi:10.1108/10610429910284319

Sevitt, D., & Samuel, A. (2013, July-August). How Pinterest Puts People In Stores. *Harvard Business Review*, 26–27.

Shama, A. (1978). Management and Consumers in Era of Stagflation. *Journal of Marketing, 42*(3), 43–52. doi:10.2307/1250533

Shama, A. (1980). *Marketing in a slow growth economy: the impact of stagflation on consumer psychology.* New York: Praeger Publishers.

Shankar, A., Cherrier, H., & Canniford, R. (2006). Consumer empowerment: A Foucauldian Interpretation. *European Journal of Marketing, 9-10,* 1013–1030. doi:10.1108/03090560610680989

Shankar, V., Urban, G. L., & Sultan, F. (2002). Online Trust: A Stakeholder Perspective, Concepts, Implications and Future Directions. *The Journal of Strategic Information Systems, 11*(4), 325–344. doi:10.1016/S0963-8687(02)00022-7

Sharma, A. (2001). Consumer decision-making, salespeople's adaptive selling and retail performance. *Journal of Business Research, 54,* 125–129. doi:10.1016/S0148-2963(99)00090-9

Sheehan, K. B. (2005). Public Opinions of Online Privacy: Definitions, Assessment and Implications for Industry and Public Policy. In S. Krishnamurthy (Ed.), *Contemporary Research in E-Marketing* (pp. 186–199). Idea Group Publishing.

Sheehan, K. B., & Hoy, M. G. (1999). Flaming, Complaining, Abstaining: How Online Users Respond to Privacy Concerns. *Journal of Advertising, 28*(3), 37–51. doi:10.1080/00913367.1999.10673588

Sheehan, K. B., & Hoy, M. G. (2000). Dimensions of Privacy Concern among Online Consumers. *Journal of Public Policy & Marketing, 19*(1), 62–73. doi:10.1509/jppm.19.1.62.16949

Shembri, S., Merrilees, B., & Kristiansen, S. (2010). Brand Consumption and Narrative of the Self. *Psychology and Marketing, 27*(6), 623–638. doi:10.1002/mar.20348

Shen, P. (2010). A Study on the Multi-Dimensional Relationship Between Consumer Shopping Value and Retailer Brand Equity. In *Proceedings of Marketing Science Innovations and Economic Development - Proceedings of 2010 Summit International Marketing Science and Management Technology Conference* (pp. 128-132). Retrieved August 3, 2013, from http://www.seiofbluemountain.com/upload/product/201008/2010shcyx02a9.pdf

Sherman, E., Mathur, A., & Belk Smith, R. (1997). Store Environment and Consumer Purchase Behaviour: Mediating Role of Consumer Emotions. *Psychology and Marketing, 14*(4), 361–378. doi:10.1002/(SICI)1520-6793(199707)14:4<361::AID-MAR4>3.0.CO;2-7

Sherman, E., & Smith, R. B. (1986). Mood states of shoppers and store image: promising interactions and possible behavioural effects. In P. Anderson (Ed.), *Advances on consumer research.* Provo, UT: Association for Consumer Research.

Sheth, J., Newman, B., & Gross, B. (1991). Why we buy what we buy: A theory of consumption values. *Journal of Business Research, 22*(2), 159–170. doi:10.1016/0148-2963(91)90050-8

Sheth, J., & Sisodia, R. (2012). *The 4 As of marketing: Creating value for customer, company and society.* New York, NY: Routledge.

Shields, R. (2013). Google touts retail solutions. *Marketing Week.* Retrieved March 27, 2013, from http://www.marketingweek.co.uk/news/google-touts-retail-solutions/4005513.article

Shin, G., & Shim, S. S. Y. (2002). A service management framework for m-commerce applications. *Mobile Networks and Applications, 7*(3), 199–212. doi:10.1023/A:1014574628967

Shneiderman, B. (2000). Designing Trust Into Online Experiences. *Communications of the ACM, 43*(12), 57–59. doi:10.1145/355112.355124

Shoemaker, S., & Lewis, R. C. (1999). Customer loyalty: the future of hospitality marketing. *International Journal of Hospitality Management, 18,* 345–370. doi:10.1016/S0278-4319(99)00042-0

Shrivastava, P., & Grant, J. H. (1985). Empirically derived models of strategic decision-making processes. *Strategic Management Journal*, 6(2), 97–113. doi:10.1002/smj.4250060202

Siegel, S., & Castellan, J. Jr. (2006). *Estatistica Naoparametricapara ciencias do comportamento* [Nonparametric Statistics for the Behavioral Sciences]. Porto Alegre: Bookman. (in Portuguese)

Sierra, D. B., Alier, E., & Falces, C. (2000). Los efectos de las variables ambientales sobre la conducta del consumidor. *Distribución y Consumo*, 54, 5–23.

Sikora, D. (2013). Online or Offline Shopping? Its Not Either or Neither –It's Both. *Insights*. Retrieved October 27, 2013, from http://insights.wired.com/profiles/blogs/online-or-offline-shopping-it-s-not-either-or-neither-it-s-both#axzz2ixud0ZSn

Simon, H. (2009). The crisis and customer behaviour: eight quick solutions. *Journal of Customer Behaviour*, 8(2), 177–186. doi:10.1362/147539209X459796

Singer, A., Hardwick, S. W., & Brettell, C. B. (2009). *Twenty-first century gateways: Immigrant incorporation in suburban America*. Brookings Institution Press.

Singh, S. (2006). Impact of color on marketing. *Management Decision*, 44(6), 783–789. doi:10.1108/00251740610673332

Singh, S. (2012). *New Mega Trends*. New York, NY: Palgrave MacMillan. doi:10.1057/9781137008091

Sirgy, M. J. (1982). Self-concept in consumer behavior: a critical review. *The Journal of Consumer Research*, 9, 287–300. doi:10.1086/208924

Sirgy, M. J. (1985). Using self-congruity and ideal congruity to predict purchase motivation. *Journal of Business Research*, 13, 195–206. doi:10.1016/0148-2963(85)90026-8

Sirgy, M. J. (2002). *The psychology of quality of life*. Dordrecht, The Netherlands: Kluwer Academic Publishers. doi:10.1007/978-94-015-9904-7

Sirgy, M. J., Grewal, D., & Mangleburg, T. (2000). Retail environment, self-congruity, and retail patronage: an integrative model and a research agenda. *Journal of Business Research*, 49, 127–138. doi:10.1016/S0148-2963(99)00009-0

Sirgy, M. J., Grewal, D., Mangleburg, T. F., Park, J., Chon, K., & Claiborne, C. B. et al. (1997). Assessing the predictive validity of two methods of measuring self-image congruence. *Journal of the Academy of Marketing Science*, 25(3), 229–241. doi:10.1177/0092070397253004

Sirgy, M. J., Hansen, D. E., & Littlefield, J. E. (1994). Does hospital satisfaction affect life satisfaction? *Journal of Macromarketing*, 14, 36–46. doi:10.1177/027614679401400204

Sirgy, M. J., Johar, J. S., Samli, A. C., & Claiborne, C. B. (1991). Self-congruity versus functional congruity: predictors of consumer behaviour. *Journal of the Academy of Marketing Science*, 19(4), 363–375. doi:10.1007/BF02726512

Sirgy, M. J., Kruger, S. P., Lee, D. J., & Yu, G. B. (2011). How does a travel trip affect tourists' life satisfaction? *Journal of Travel Research*, 50(3), 261–275. doi:10.1177/0047287510362784

Sirgy, M. J., Lee, D. J., & Bae, J. (2006). Developing a subjective measure of internet well-being: Nomological validation. *Social Indicators Research*, 78(2), 205–249. doi:10.1007/s11205-005-8209-1

Sirgy, M. J., Lee, D. J., Grzeskowiak, G., Chebat, J.-C., Johar, J. S., Herman, A., & Montana, J. (2008). An extension and further Validation of a community-based consumer well-being measure. *Journal of Macromarketing*, 28(3), 243–257. doi:10.1177/0276146708320447

Sirgy, M. J., Lee, D. J., & Kressmann, F. (2006). A need-based measure of consumer well-being (CWB) in relation to personal transportation: Nomological validation. *Social Indicators Research*, 79(2), 337–367. doi:10.1007/s11205-005-4920-1

Sirgy, M. J., Rahtz, D., & Lee, D. J. (2004). Further validation and extension of the quality of life community healthcare model and measures. *Social Indicators Research*, 69(2), 167–198. doi:10.1023/B:SOCI.0000033592.58120.9b

Sirohi, N. E., McLaughlin, W., & Wittink, D. R. (1998). A model of consumer perceptions and store loyalty intentions for a supermarket retailer. *Journal of Retailing*, 74(2), 223–245. doi:10.1016/S0022-4359(99)80094-3

Sit, J., Merrilees, B., & Birch, D. (2003). Entertainment-seeking shopping centre patrons: The missing segments. *International Journal of Retail & Distribution Management, 31*(2), 80–94. doi:10.1108/09590550310461985

Sitkin, S., & Weingart, L. (1995). Determinants of risky decision making behaviour: A test of mediating role of risk perception and propensity. *Academy of Management Journal, 38*, 1573–1592. doi:10.2307/256844

Sivadas, E., & Baker-Prewitt, J. L. (2000). An examination of the relationship between service quality, customer satisfaction, and store loyalty. *International Journal of Retail and Distribution Management, 28*(2), 73–82. doi:10.1108/09590550010315223

Slovic, P., Finucane, M., Peters, E., & MacGregor, D. (2004). Risk as Analysis and Risk as Feeling: Some Thoughts about Affect, Reason, Risk and Rationality. *Risk Analysis, 24*(2), 311–322. doi:10.1111/j.0272-4332.2004.00433.x PMID:15078302

Smith, J. (2013, July 16). America's most generous companies. *Forbes*. Retrieved on August 29, 2013 from http://www.forbes.com/sites/jacquelynsmith/2013/07/16/americas-most-generous-companies/

Smith, K. (2013). 6 challenges retailers face. *EDIDT*. Retrieved November 11, 2013, from http://editd.com/blog/2013/04/6-challenges-retailers-face/

Smith, N. (2013, June 5). Corporate social responsibility: Power to the people. *Marketing Week*. Retrieved on August 23, 2013 from http://www.marketingweek.co.uk/trends/corporate-social-responsibility-power-to-the-people/4006810.article

Smith, A. et al. (2004). Delivering customer loyalty schemes in retailing: Exploring the employee dimension. *International Journal of Retail & Distribution Management, 32*(4), 190–204. doi:10.1108/09590550410528962

Smith, R. B., & Sherman, E. (1993). Effects of store image and mood on consumer behavior: a theoretical and empirical analysis. In L. McAlister, & M. L. Rothschild (Eds.), *Advances in Consumer Research* (Vol. 20). Provo, UT: Association for Consumer Research.

Smith, S., & Wheeler, J. (2002). *Managing the Customer Experience: Turning Customers into Advocates*. Harlow, UK: Prentice Hall.

Snyder, C. R., & Fromkin, H. L. (1977). Abnormality as a positive characteristic: The development and validation of a scale measuring need for uniqueness. *Journal of Abnormal Psychology, 86*(5), 518–527. doi:10.1037/0021-843X.86.5.518

Soars, B. (2009). Driving Sales through Shoppers' Sense of Sound, Sight, Smell and Touch. *International Journal of Retail & Distribution Management, 37*(3), 286–298. doi:10.1108/09590550910941535

Solomon, M. R. (1988). Mapping product constellations: a social categorization approach to consumption symbolism. *Psychology and Marketing, 5*, 233–258.

Solomon, M. R. (2008). *Consumer Behavior: buying, having and being* (8th ed.). Prentice Hall.

Solomon, M. R., & Rabolt, N. J. (2009). *Consumer Behavior in Fashion*. Pearson Education.

Son, J.-Y., & Kim, S. S. (2008). Internet Users' Information Privacy-Protective Responses: A Taxonomy and A Nomological Model. *Management Information Systems Quarterly, 32*(3), 503–529.

Sorescu, A., Frambach, R. T., Singh, J., Rangaswamy, A., & Bridges, C. (2011). Innovations in Retail Business Models. *Journal of Retailing, 87S*(1), S3–S16. doi:10.1016/j.jretai.2011.04.005

Spangenberg, E. R., Crowley, A. E., & Henderson, P. (1996). Improving the store environment: Do olfactory cues affect evaluations and behaviors? *Journal of Marketing, 60*(2), 67–80. doi:10.2307/1251931

Spangenberg, E., Herramann, A., Zidansek, M., & Sprott, D. (2013). The Power of Simplicity: Processing Fluency and the Effects of Olfactory Cues on Retail Sales. *Journal of Retailing, 89*(1), 30–43. doi:10.1016/j.jretai.2012.08.002

Sparks, L. (2008). Commentary: when Tony met Bobby. *Environment & Planning A, 40*, 2793–2799. doi:10.1068/a41271

Spies, K., Hesse, F., & Loesch, K. (1997). Store Atmosphere, Mood and Purchasing Behavior. *International Journal of Research in Marketing, 14*(1), 1–17. doi:10.1016/S0167-8116(96)00015-8

Spiggle, S. (1994). Analysis and Interpretation of Qualitative Data in Consumer Research. *The Journal of Consumer Research, 21*(3), 491. doi:10.1086/209413

Spohrer, J., Golinelli, G. M., Piciocchi, P., & Bassano, C. (2010). An Integrated SS-VSA Analysis of Changing Job Roles. *Service Science, 2*(1), 1–20. doi:10.1287/serv.2.1_2.1

Spohrer, J., Maglio, P. P., Bailey, J., & Gruhl, D. (2007). Steps Toward a Science of Service Systems. *Computer, 40*, 71–77. doi:10.1109/MC.2007.33

Statista. (2013). *Market share of the leading coffee chains in the United States in 2011.* Retrieved May 9, 2013, from http://www.statista.com/statistics/250166/market-share-of-major-us-coffee-shops

Statistic Brain. (2013). *Coffee Drinking Statistics.* Retrieved May 11, 2013, from http://www.statisticbrain.com/coffee-drinking-statistics

Stebbins, R. A. (2006). Shopping as leisure, obligation, and community. *Leisure, 30*(2), 467–474. doi:10.1080/14927713.2006.9651367

Steenkamp, J. B. E. M., Van Heerde, H., & Geyskens, I. (2010). What makes consumers willing to pay a price premium for national brands over private labels? *JMR, Journal of Marketing Research, 47*(6), 1011–1024. doi:10.1509/jmkr.47.6.1011

Steenkamp, J. B., & van Trijp, H. (1991). The use of LISREL in validating marketing constructs. *International Journal of Research in Marketing, 8*(4), 283–299. doi:10.1016/0167-8116(91)90027-5

Steenkamp, J.-B. E. M., & Dekimpe, M. G. (1997). The increasing power of store brands: building loyalty and market share. *Long Range Planning, 30*(6), 917–930. doi:10.1016/S0024-6301(97)00077-0

Steiner, R. (2013). No stopping the online shopping revolution as 'omni-channel' retailers offer more options than ever before. *Thisismoney.* Retrieved June 6, 2013, from http://www.thisismoney.co.uk/money/markets/article-2317260/The-omni-channel-online-shopping-revolution.html

Steinfield, C. (2004). The Missing Link: Connecting Physical And Virtual Channels Through Click & Mortar Electronic Commerce. In K. Stanoevska-Slabeva (Ed.), *Digital Economy* (pp. 141–157). Anspruch und Wirklichkeit. doi:10.1007/978-3-642-17032-4_10

Steinfield, C., & Adelaar, T., & Liu. (2005). Click and mortar strategies viewed from the web: a content analysis of features illustrating integration between retailers' online and offline presence. *Electronic Markets, 15*(3), 199–212. doi:10.1080/10196780500208632

Stern, L. W., & El-Ansary, A. I. (1977). *Marketing Channels.* Englewood Cliffs, NJ: Prentice Hall.

Stiglitz, J. (2008, September 16). The fruit of hypocrisy. *The Guardian.* Retrieved February 10, 2010, from http://www.guardian.co.uk/commentisfree/2008/sep/16/economics.wallstreet

Stock, R. M., & Hoyer, W. D. (2005). An Attitude-Behavior Model of Salespeople's Customer Orientation. *Journal of the Academy of Marketing Science, 33*(4), 536–552. doi:10.1177/0092070305276368

Stokburger-Sauer, N., Ratneshwar, S., & Sankar, S. (2012). Drivers of consumer–brand identification. *International Journal of Research in Marketing, 29*, 406–418. doi:10.1016/j.ijresmar.2012.06.001

Stokols, D. (1978). Environmental psychology. *Annual Review of Psychology, 29*, 253–259. doi:10.1146/annurev.ps.29.020178.001345 PMID:341781

Stokos, D. (1972). On the distinction between density and crowding: some implications for future research. *Psychological Review, 79*(3), 275–277. doi:10.1037/h0032706 PMID:5056743

Storbacka, K., & Nenonen, S. (2009). Customer relationships and the heterogeneity of firm performance. *Journal of Business and Industrial Marketing, 24*(5/6), 360–372. doi:10.1108/08858620910966246

Strauss, A., & Corbin, J. (1990). *Basics of Qualitative Research: Grounded Theory Procedures and Techniques.* Newbury Park, CA: Sage Publications.

Stryker, S. (1968). Identity Salience and Role Performance. *Journal of Marriage and the Family, 4,* 558–564. doi:10.2307/349494

Stryker, S., & Burke, P. J. (2000). The past, present, and future of an identity. *Social Psychology Quarterly, 63*(4), 284–297. doi:10.2307/2695840

Summers, T., & Hebert, P. (2001). Shedding Some Light on Store Atmospherics: Influence of Illumination on Consumer Behaviour. *Journal of Business Research, 54,* 145–150. doi:10.1016/S0148-2963(99)00082-X

Sun, P.-C., & Lin, C.-M. (2010). Building customer trust and loyalty: an empirical study in a retailing context. *The Service Industries Journal, 30*(9), 1439–1455. doi:10.1080/02642060802621478

Sun, T., Tai, Z., & Tsai, K.-C. (2009). The role of interdependent self-construal in consumers' susceptibility to retail salespersons' influence: a hierarchical approach. *Journal of Retailing and Consumer Services, 16*(5), 360–366. doi:10.1016/j.jretconser.2009.04.002

SupMedia. (2012). *LiveJournal upgrades Singapore's 50,000 Blogshops to premium e-commerce stores.* Retrieved December 9, 2012, from: http://www.sup.com/en/news_399.html

SupMedia. (2012). *LiveJournal.sg stages Singapore's first Blogshop fashion show.* Retrieved from http://www.sup.com/en/news_388.html

Su, Q., & Adams, C. (2010). *Consumers' Attitude Toward Mobile Commerce: A Model to Capture the Cultural and Environment Influences.* Hershey, PA: IGI Global.

Surchi, M. (2011). The temporary store: a new marketing tool for fashion brands. *Journal of Fashion Marketing and Management, 15*(2), 257–270. doi:10.1108/13612021111132672

Surowiecki, J. (2004). *The Wisdom of Crowds.* New York: Anchor Books.

Swan, J. E. (1974). A Functional Analysis of Innovation in Distribution Channels. *Journal of Retailing, 50*(1), 9–23.

Swan, J. E. et al. (1999). Customer trust in a salesperson: An integrative review and meta-analysis of the empirical literature. *Journal of Business Research, 44*(2), 93–107. doi:10.1016/S0148-2963(97)00244-0

Sweeney, J. C., & Soutar, G. N. (2001). Consumer perceived value: The development of a multiple item scale. *Journal of Retailing, 77*(2), 203–220. doi:10.1016/S0022-4359(01)00041-0

Swidler, A. (1986). Culture in Action: Symbols and Strategies. *American Sociological Review, 51,* 273–286. doi:10.2307/2095521

Swoboda, B., Haelsig, F., Schramm-Klein, H., & Morschett, D. (2009). Moderating role of involvement in building a retail brand. *International Journal of Retail & Distribution Management, 37*(11), 952–974. doi:10.1108/09590550910999370

SymphonyIRIgroup. (2012). *Le Private Label in Europa-2012.* Esiste un limite alla crescita, Ottobre.

Szajna, B. (1996). Empirical evaluation of the revised technology acceptance model. *Management Science, 42*(1), 85–92. doi:10.1287/mnsc.42.1.85

Szmigin, I., & Bourne, H. (1998). Consumer Equity in Relationship Marketing. *Journal of Consumer Marketing, 15*(6), 544–557. doi:10.1108/07363769810240545

Szymanski, D. M., & Busch, P. S. (1987). Identifying the generics-prone consumer: a meta-analysis. *JMR, Journal of Marketing Research, 24,* 425–431. doi:10.2307/3151391

Tabachnick, B. G., & Fidell, L. S. (2001). *Using multivariate statistics* (4th ed.). Needham Heights, MA: Allyn & Bacon.

Tai, H. C., & Fung, A. M. C. (1997). Application of an environmental psychology model to in-store buying behavior. *International Review of Retail, Distribution and Consumer Research, 7*(4), 311–337. doi:10.1080/095939697342914

Tajfel, H., & Turner, J. C. (1986). The social identity theory of inter-group behavior. In S. Worchel, & W. G. Austin (Eds.), *Psychology of intergroup relations.* Chicago, IL: Nelson-Hall.

Takei, H., Kudo, K., Miyata, T., & Ito, Y. (2006). Adaptive Strategies for Japan's Retail Industry Facing a Turning Point. *Nomura Research Institute Papers, 110,* 1–13.

Tarasewich, P. (2002). Issues in mobile e-commerce. *Communications of the Association for Information Systems, 8,* 41–64.

Tashakkori, A., & Teddlie, C. (1998). *Mixed Methodology:Combining Qualitative and Quantitative Approaches*. Thousand Oaks, CA: Sage Publication.

Tata, R. J. (1977). Uruguay: Population geography of a troubled welfare state. *The Journal of Geography, 76*(2), 46–51. doi:10.1080/00221347708980880

Tauber, E. M. (1972). Why do people shop? *Journal of Marketing, 36*(4), 46–49. doi:10.2307/1250426

Tauber, E. M. (1995). Why do People Shop? *Marketing Management, 4*(2), 58–60.

Teller, C., & Dennis, C. (2012). The Effect of Ambient Scent on Consumers' Perception, Emotions and Behaviour – a Critical Review. *Journal of Marketing Management, 28*(1/2), 14–36. doi:10.1080/0267257X.2011.560719

Tepper Tian, K., Bearden, W. O., & Hunter, G. L. (2001). Consumers' need for uniqueness: scale development and validation. *The Journal of Consumer Research, 28*(1), 50–66. doi:10.1086/321947

Tesco, P. L. C. (2013). *Corporate Website*. Retrieved on August 22, 2013 from http://www.tescoplc.com

The Kroger Co. (2013). *Corporate Website*. Retrieved on August 16, 2013 from http://www.kroger.com

Thompson, N. J., & Thompson, K. E. (2007). Marketing and the Ageing Consumer Population: the Future is Not as Clear as the Past. In *Proceedings of British Academy of Management Conference*. Warwick, UK: BAM.

Thompson, C. J., & Arsel, Z. (2004). The Starbucks Brandscape and Consumers' (Anti-Corporate) Experiences of Glocalization. *The Journal of Consumer Research, 31*, 631–643. doi:10.1086/425098

Thompson, C. J., & Coskuner-Balli, G. (2007). Countervailing Market Responses to Corporate Co-Optation and the Ideological Recruitment of Consumption Communities. *The Journal of Consumer Research, 34*(2), 135–152. doi:10.1086/519143

Thompson, C. J., Rindfleisch, A., & Arsel, Z. (2006). Emotional branding and the strategic value of the Doppelgänger brand image. *Journal of Marketing, 70*(1), 50–64. doi:10.1509/jmkg.2006.70.1.50

Thompson, S. A., & Sinha, R. K. (2008). Brand Communities and New Product Adoption: The Influence and Limits of Oppositional Loyalty. *Journal of Marketing, 72*(6), 65–80. doi:10.1509/jmkg.72.6.65

Thomson, M., MacInnis, J. D., & Park, C. W. (2005). The ties that bind: measuring the strength of consumers' emotional attachments to brands. *Journal of Consumer Psychology, 15*, 77–91. doi:10.1207/s15327663jcp1501_10

Thornton, J. (1992, February). Shoplifting - girls who steal. *Seventeen*, 86-87.

Timothy, D. (2005). *Shopping, tourism, retailing, and leisure*. Toronto, Canada: Channel View Publications.

Titus, P., & Everett, P. B. (1995). The consumer retail search process: A conceptual model and research agenda. *Journal of the Academy of Marketing Science, 23*(2), 106–119. doi:10.1177/0092070395232003

Tiwari, R., Buse, S., & Herstatt, C. (2006, September-October). From electronic to mobile commerce: Opportunities through technology convergence for business services. *Tech Monitor*, 38-45.

Tiwari, R. S. (2009). *Retail Management, Retail Concepts and Practices*. Mumbai: Global Media.

Toder-Alon, A., Brunel, F. F., & Schneier, W. L. (2005). Ritual Behaviour and Community Change: Exploring the Social-Psychological Roles of Net Rituals in the Developmental xi Processes of Online Consumption Communities. In Online Consumer Psychology: Understanding and Influencing Consumer Behavior in the Virtual World (pp. 7–35). Lawrence Erlbaum Associates, Inc.

Tonglet, M. (2000). Consumer Misbehaviour: Consumers' Perceptions of Shoplifting and Retail Security. *Security Journal, 13*(4), 107–122. doi:10.1057/palgrave.sj.8340063

Tonglet, M. (2002). Consumer Misbehaviour: An Exploratory Study of Shoplifting. *Journal of Consumer Behaviour, 1*(4), 336–354. doi:10.1002/cb.79

Tonglet, M., & Bamfield, J. (1997). Controlling Shop Crime in Britain: Costs and Trends. *International Journal of Retail & Distribution Management, 25*(9), 293–300. doi:10.1108/09590559710185772

Torres, A., Bijmolt, T., Tribo', J., & Verhoef, P. (2012). Generating global brand equity through corporate social responsibility to key stakeholders. *International Journal of Research in Marketing, 29*(1), 13–24. doi:10.1016/j.ijresmar.2011.10.002

Toufaily, E., Souiden, N., & Ladhari, R. (in press). Consumer trust toward retail websites: comparison between pure click and click-and-brick retailers. *Journal of Retailing and Consumer Services.*

Turley, L. W., & Chebat, J. C. (2002). Linking Retail Strategy, Atmospheric Design and Shopping Behaviour. *Journal of Marketing Management, 18*(1/2), 125–144. doi:10.1362/0267257022775891

Turley, L. W., & Milliman, R. E. (2000). Atmospheric effects on shopping behaviour: A review of the experimental evidence. *Journal of Business Research, 49*, 193–211. doi:10.1016/S0148-2963(99)00010-7

Turner-Mitchell, P. (2012). Don't abandon retail: People will always want the High Street. *The Guardian*. Retrieved August 6, 2013, from http://www.theguardian.com/uk/the-northerner/2012/sep/21/manchester-salford-high-street-retail-mary-portas-shops

Tuškej, U., Golob, U., & Podnar, K. (2013). The role of consumer–brand identification in building brand relationships. *Journal of Business Research, 66*, 53–59. doi:10.1016/j.jbusres.2011.07.022

Twing-Kwong, S., Albaum, L. G., & Fullgrabe, L. (2013). Trust in customer-salesperson relationship in China's retail sector. *International Journal of Retail & Distribution Management, 41*(3), 226–248. doi:10.1108/09590551311306264

Uncles, M. D., & Ellis, K. (1989). The buying of own labels. *European Journal of Marketing, 23*(3), 57–70. doi:10.1108/EUM0000000000561

Underhill, P. (1999). *Why we buy: the science of shopping.* New York: Simon and Schuster.

Urban, G. L., Sultan, F., & Qualls, W. J. (2000). Placing trust at the center of your internet strategy. *Sloan Management Review, 42*(1), 39–48.

Urbonavicius, S., & Pikturnien, I. (2010). Consumer in the face of economic crisis: Evidence from two generations in Lithuania. *Economics and Management, 15*, 827–834.

Utz, S., Kerkhof, P., & van den Bos, J. (2012). Consumer rule: how consumer reviews influence perceived trustworthiness of online stores. *Electronic Commerce Research and Applications, 11*(1), 49–58. doi:10.1016/j.elerap.2011.07.010

Vaccaro, V. (2001). *In-store music's influence on consumers responses: the development and test of a music-retail environment model.* (Thesis). City University, New York.

Vaccà, S. (1963). *I rapporti industria-distribuzione nei mercati dei beni di consumo.* Milano, Italy: Giuffrè.

Vahie, A., & Paswan, A. (2006). Private label brand image: its relationship with store image and national brand. *International Journal of Retail and Distribution Management, 34*(1), 67–84. doi:10.1108/09590550610642828

Valdani, E. (2009). *Cliente & Service Management.* Milano, Italy: Egea.

Valence, G., d'Astous, A., & Fortier, L. (1988). Compulsive buying: Concept and measurement. *Journal of Consumer Policy, 11*, 419–433. doi:10.1007/BF00411854

Valenzuela, A., Mellers, B., & Strebel, J. (2008). Cross cultural differences in delight. In A. Y. Lee, & D. Soman (Eds.), *NA - Advances in Consumer Research* (pp. 678–679). Duluth, MN: Association for Consumer Research.

Vallaster, C., Lindgreen, A., & Maon, F. (2012). Strategically Leveraging Corporate Social Responsibility: A Corporate Brand Perspective. *California Management Review, 54*(3), 34–60. doi:10.1525/cmr.2012.54.3.34

Van den Poel, D., & Leunis, J. (1999). Consumer acceptance of the internet as a channel of distribution. *Journal of Business Research, 45*(3), 249–256. doi:10.1016/S0148-2963(97)00236-1

van Riel, A. C. R. (2012). Strategic Service Innovation Management in Retailing. In J. Kandampully (Ed.), *Service Management: The New Paradigm in Retailing* (pp. 83–95). New York: Springer. doi:10.1007/978-1-4614-1554-1_6

Varaldo, R. (1971). *Potere e conflitti nei canali di distribuzione.* Pisa, Italy: Editrice tecnico scientifica.

Varaldo, R., & Dalli, D. (2003). Le relazioni strategiche tra industria e distribuzione. *Sinergie, 61-62*, 255–297.

Varaldo, R., & Fornari, D. (1998). La evoluzione dei rapporti industria-distribuzione. Dalla cooperazione al conflitto. *Sinergie, 46,* 21–49.

Vargo, S. L., & Lusch, R. F. (2006). Service-Dominant Logic: What it is, What it is not, What it might be. In R. F. Lusch, & S. L. Vargo (Eds.), *The Service-Dominant Logic of Marketing: Dialog, Debate, and Directions.* Armonk: M.E. Sharpe.

Vargo, S. L., & Lusch, R. F. (2008). Why service? *Journal of the Academy of Marketing Science, 36,* 25–38. doi:10.1007/s11747-007-0068-7

Vargo, S. L., & Lusch, R. F. (2008a). Service-Dominant Logic: Continuing the Evolution. *Journal of the Academy of Marketing Science, 36*(1), 1–10. doi:10.1007/s11747-007-0069-6

Vargo, S. L., Maglio, P. P., & Akaka, M. A. (2008). On value and value co-creation: A service systems and service logic perspective. *European Management Journal, 26*(3), 145–152. doi:10.1016/j.emj.2008.04.003

Various Authors. (2011). *Contributions to theoretical and practical advances in management: A Viable Systems Approach (vSA).* Avellino, Italy: International Printing.

Varley, R. (2001). *Retail Product Management: Buying and Merchandising.* Routledge. doi:10.4324/9780203358603

Vásquez Casielles, R., Suárez Álvarez, L., & Díaz Martín, A. M. (2005). Trust as a key factor in successful relationships between consumers and retail service providers. *The Service Industries Journal, 25*(1), 83–101. doi:10.1080/0264206042000302423

Vasquez-Parraga, A. Z., & Alonso, S. (2000). Antecedents of customer loyalty for strategic intent. In J. P. Workman Jr, & W. D. Perreault (Eds.), *Marketing Theory and Applications.* Chicago: American Marketing Association.

Velarde Fuertes, J. (2011). Problemática actual de la distribución comercial española (un estado de la cuestión). *ICADE. Revista cuatrimestral de las Facultades de Derecho y Ciencias Económicas y Empresariales, 83-84,* 393-411.

Veloutsou, C., Gioulistanis, E., & Moutinho, L. (2004). Own labels choice criteria and perceived characteristics in Greece and Scotland: factors influencing the willingness to buy. *Journal of Product and Brand Management, 13*(4/5), 228–241. doi:10.1108/10610420410546943

Venkatesan, R., Kumar, V., & Ravishankar, N. (2007). Multichannel Shopping: Causes and Consequences. *Journal of Marketing, 71*(2), 114–132. doi:10.1509/jmkg.71.2.114

Venkatesh, V., & Davis, F. D. (1996). A model of the antecedents of perceived ease of use: development and test. *Decision Sciences, 27*(3), 451–481. doi:10.1111/j.1540-5915.1996.tb01822.x

Venkatesh, V., Morris, M. G., Davis, G. B., & Davis, F. D. (2003). User Acceptance of Information Technology: Toward a Unified View. *Management Information Systems Quarterly, 27*(3), 425–478.

Venkatesh, V., Thong, J. Y. L., & Xu, X. (2012). Consumer acceptance and use of information technology: extending the unified theory of acceptance and use of technology. *Management Information Systems Quarterly, 36*(1), 157–178.

Verhoef, P. C., Lemon, K. N., Parasuraman, A., Roggeveen, A., Tsiros, M., & Schlesinger, L. A. (2009). Customer Experience Creation: Determinants, Dynamics and Management. *Journal of Retailing, 85*(1), 31–41. doi:10.1016/j.jretai.2008.11.001

Verhoef, P. C., Neslin, S. A., & Vroomen, B. (2007). Multichannel customer management: Understanding the research-shopper phenomenon. *International Journal of Research in Marketing, 24*(2), 129–148. doi:10.1016/j.ijresmar.2006.11.002

Veryzer, R. W. (1999). A nonconscious processing explanation of consumer response to product design. *Psychology and Marketing, 16*(6), 497–522. doi:10.1002/(SICI)1520-6793(199909)16:6<497::AID-MAR4>3.0.CO;2-Z

Vesel, P., & Zabkar, V. (2010). Comprehension of relationship quality in the retail environment. *Managing Service Quality, 20*(3), 213–235. doi:10.1108/09604521011041952

Vianelli, D., de Luca, P., & Pegan, G. (2012). *Modalità d'entrata e scelte distributive del made in Italy in Cina.* Milano: Franco Angeli.

Vieira, V. A. (2013). Stimuli-Organism-Response Framework: a meta-analytic review in the store environment. *Journal of Business Research, 66*(9), 1420–1426. doi:10.1016/j.jbusres.2012.05.009

Viswanathan, S. (2005). Competing across Technology-Differentiated Channels: The Impact of Network Externalities and Switching Costs. *Management Science, 51*(3), 483–496. doi:10.1287/mnsc.1040.0338

Völckner, F., & Sattler, H. (2006). Drivers of Brand Extension Success. *Journal of Marketing, 70*(2), 18–34. doi:10.1509/jmkg.70.2.18

von Bertalanffy, L. (1968). *General System Theory: Foundations, Development, Applications.* New York: George Braziller.

von Hippel, E. (1986). Lead Users: A Source of Novel Product Concepts. *Management Science, 32*, 791–805. doi:10.1287/mnsc.32.7.791

Wagner, J. A., Klein, N. M., & Keith, J. E. (2003). Buyer-seller relationships and selling effectiveness: the moderating influence of buyer expertise and product competitive position. *Journal of Business Research, 56*, 295–302. doi:10.1016/S0148-2963(02)00441-1

Wakefield, K. L., & Baker, J. (1998). Excitement at the mall: Determinants and effects on shopping response. *Journal of Retailing, 74*(4), 515–539. doi:10.1016/S0022-4359(99)80106-7

Walker Naylor, R., Poynor Lamberton, C., & West, P. M. (2012). Beyond the Like Button: The Impact of Mere Virtual Presence on Brand Evaluations and Purchase Intentions in Social Media Settings. *Journal of Marketing, 76*, 105–120. doi:10.1509/jm.11.0105

Walker, W. G. (1975). Marketing research is important in retailing, now, more than ever. *Marketing News, 8*(17), 9.

Wallop, H. (2013). Click and collect- the new way to go shopping. *The Telegraph.* Retrieved March 27, 2013, from http://www.telegraph.co.uk/finance/newsbysector/retailandconsumer/9785532/Click-and-collect-the-new-way-to-go-shopping.html

Walmart. (2013). *Corporate Website.* Retrieved on August 2, 2013 from http://corporate.walmart.com

Walter, A., Ritter, T., & Gemunden, H. G. (2001). Value Creation in Buyer-Seller Relationships: Theoretical Considerations and Empirical Results from a Supplier's Perspective. *Industrial Marketing Management, 30*, 365–377. doi:10.1016/S0019-8501(01)00156-0

Walters, D. (1981). The 1970s in retailing: a retrospective view. *International Journal of Retail & Distribution Management, 9*(2), 8–15. doi:10.1108/eb018090

Wanger, T. (2007). Shopping motivation revised: A means-end chain analytical perspective. *International Journal of Retail & Distribution Management, 35*(7), 569–582. doi:10.1108/09590550710755949

Wang, H., Wei, Y., & Yu, C. (2008). Global brand equity model: combining customer-based with product-market outcome approaches. *Journal of Product and Brand Management, 17*(5), 305–316. doi:10.1108/10610420810896068

Wang, K., & Lin, C. L. (2012). The adoption of mobile value-added services: Investigating the influence of IS quality and perceived playfulness. *Managing Service Quality, 22*(2), 184–208. doi:10.1108/09604521211219007

Ward, P., Davies, B., & Kooijman, D. (2003). Ambient smell and the retail environment: relating olfaction research to consumer behavior. *Journal of Business and Management, 9*(3), 289–302.

Waring, P. (2011). Keeping up appearances: Aesthetic Labour and Discrimination Law. *The Journal of Industrial Relations, 53*(2), 193–207. doi:10.1177/0022185610397141

Warman, M. (2013). The future of shopping: From high street to iStreet. *The Telegraph.* Retrieved August 6, 2013, from http://www.telegraph.co.uk/technology/news/9821702/The-future-of-shopping-from-h...

Wasko, M. M., & Faraj, S. (2005). Why should I share? Examining the social capital and knowledge contribution in electronic networks of practice. *Management Information Systems Quarterly, 29*(1), 35–57.

Wearn, R. (2013). Online shops take stock and move into the High Street. *BBC News.* Retrieved August 8, 2013, from http://www.bbc.co.uk/news/business-22404652?print=true

Weber, E., & Milliman, R. (1997). Perceived risk attitudes: Relating risk perception to risky choice. *Management Science, 43*, 123–144. doi:10.1287/mnsc.43.2.123

Wee, J. (2011). *What Singaporeans do on LiveJournal*. Retrieved December 23, 2011, from http://e27.co/?p=17110

Weick, K., Sutcliffe, K., & Obstfeld, D. (2005). Organizing and the process of sensemaking. *Organization Science, 16*(4), 409–421. doi:10.1287/orsc.1050.0133

Weiss, R. S. (1994). *Learning from strangers: The art and method of qualitative interviewing*. New York: Free Press.

Wellhoff, A., & Masson, J. E. (2005). *Le Merchandising: Bases, Techniques, Nouvelles Tendances*. Paris: Dunod.

Wells, R., Kleshinski, C. E., & Lau, T. (2012). Attitudes Toward and Behavioral Intensions to Adopt Mobile Marketing, Comparisons of Gen Y in the United States, France and China. *International Journal of Mobile Marketing, 7*(2), 5–24.

Wells, W. D., & Tigert, D. J. (1971). Activities, Interest, and Opinions. *Journal of Advertising Research*, 27–35.

Werther, W. B., & Chandler, B. (2005). Strategic corporate social responsibility as global brand insurance. *Business Horizons, 48*, 317–324. doi:10.1016/j.bushor.2004.11.009

Westbrook, T. (2013). High Street needs e-tail therapy: Lack of vision as much to blame for retailers' failures as the rise of e-commerce. *Insight*. Retrieved August 6, 2013, from http://www.cio.co.uk/insight/strategy/high-street-needs-e-tail-therapy/

Wheeler, A. (2009). *Designing Brand Identity: An Essential Guide for the Whole Branding Team*. Wiley.

Whiteaker, J. (2012). Feature: Is the UK a click & collect nation? *Retailgazette*. Retrieved August 6, 2013, from http://www.retailgazette.co.uk/articles/23311-feature-is-the-uk-a-click-collect-nation

Wieland, H., Polese, F., Vargo, S. L., & Lusch, R. F. (2012). Toward a Service (Eco)Systems Perspective on Value Creation. *International Journal of Service Science, Management, Engineering, and Technology, 3*(3), 12–25. doi:10.4018/jssmet.2012070102

Wilk, R. (1995). Learning to Be Local in Belize: Global Systems of Common Difference. In D. Miller (Ed.), *Worlds Apart: Modernity Through the Prism of the Local* (pp. 110–131). London: Routledge.

Willems, K., & Swinnen, G. (2011). Am I cheap? Testing the role of store personality and self-congruity in discount retailing. *International Review of Retail, Distribution and Consumer Research, 21*(5), 513–539. doi:10.1080/0959 3969.2011.618888

Williams, C. (2006). Shopping as Symbolic Interaction: race, class, and gender in the Toy Store. *Symbolic Interaction, 28*(4), 459–472. doi:10.1525/si.2005.28.4.459

Williamson, S. C. (1991). Comparative Economic Organization: The Analysis of Discrete Structural Alternatives. *Administrative Science Quarterly, 36*(2), 269–296. doi:10.2307/2393356

Wirtz, B. W., Schilke, O., & Ullrich, S. (2010). Strategic development of business models: implications of the web 2.0 for creating value on the Internet. *Long Range Planning, 43*(2/3), 272–290. doi:10.1016/j.lrp.2010.01.005

WiseGeek. (2013). *What is a coffee shop*. Retrieved August 19, 2013, from http://www.wisegeek.org/what-is-a-coffee-shop.htm

Withers, C., & De Judicibus, D. (2013). Augmented Aisles: the online invasion. *The Guardian*. Retrieved June 6, 2013, from http://www.guardian.co.uk/media-network/media-network-blog/2013/mar/14/online-technology-high-street-innovation

Wolfinbarger, M., & Gilly, M. (2001). Shopping online for freedom, control and fun. *California Management Review, 43*(2), 34–55. doi:10.2307/41166074

Wolf, K. (2003a). Public response to the urban forest in inner-city business districts. *Journal of Arboriculture, 29*(3), 117–126.

Wolf, K. L. (2003b). Freeway roadside management: The urban forest beyond the white line. *Journal of Arboriculture, 29*(3), 127–136.

Wolf, K. L. (2004a). Nature in the retail environment: Comparing consumer and business response to urban forest conditions. *Landscape Journal, 23*(1), 40–51. doi:10.3368/lj.23.1.40

Wolf, K. L. (2004b). Trees and business district preferences: A case study of Athens, Georgia, US. *Journal of Arboriculture, 30*(6), 336–346.

Wolf, K. L. (2005a). Business district streetscapes, trees, and consumer response. *Journal of Forestry, 103*(8), 396–400.

Wolf, K. L. (2005b). Trees in the small city retail business district: Comparing resident and visitor perceptions. *Journal of Forestry, 103*(8), 390–395.

Wolf, K. L. (2006). Assessing public response to the freeway roadside: Urban forestry and context sensitive solutions. *Transportation Research Record, 1984*, 102–111. doi:10.3141/1984-12

Wolf, K. L. (2007). The environmental psychology of trees. *International Council of Shopping Centers Research Review, 14*(3), 39–43.

Wolf, K. L. (2008a). Metro nature: its functions, benefits and values. In E. L. Birch, & S. M. Wachter (Eds.), *Growing greener cities: Urban sustainability in the twenty-first century* (pp. 294–315). Philadelphia, PA: University of Pennsylvania Press.

Wolf, K. L. (2008b). Community context and strip mall retail: Public response to the roadside landscape. *Transportation Research Record, 2060*, 95–103. doi:10.3141/2060-11

Wolf, K. L. (2009a). Strip malls, city trees, and community values. *Arboriculture & Urban Forestry, 35*(1), 33–40.

Wolf, K. L. (2009b). Trees mean business: city trees and the retail streetscape. *Main Street News, 263*, 1–9.

Wolf, K. L. (2012). The changing importance of ecosystem services across the landscape gradient. In D. N. Laband, B. G. Lockaby, & W. C. Zipperer (Eds.), *Urban-rural interfaces: Linking people and nature* (pp. 127–146). Madison, WI: Soil Science Society of America.

Wolf, K. L. (2013a). Why do we need trees? Let's talk about ecosystem services. *Arborist News, 22*(4), 32–35.

Wolf, K. L. (2013b). The urban forest. *Communities & Banking, 24*(2), 25–27.

Wong, J. (2010). *Aussie café culture accounts for 'biggest growth in coffee AFN March 4*. Retrieved August 25, 2013, from http://www.ausfoodnews.com.au/2010/03/04/aussie-cafe-culture-accounts-for-biggest-growth-in-coffee.html

Wong, A. (2004). The role of emotional satisfaction in service encounters. *Managing Service Quality, 14*(5), 365–376. doi:10.1108/09604520410557976

Wong, A., & Sohal, A. S. (2003). Service quality and customer loyalty perspectives on two levels of retail relationships. *Journal of Services Marketing, 17*(5), 495–513. doi:10.1108/08876040310486285

Wong, A., & Sohal, A. S. (2006). Understanding the quality of relationships in consumer services. *International Journal of Quality & Reliability Management, 23*(3), 244–264. doi:10.1108/02656710610648215

Wonnacott, T. H., & Wonnacott, R. J. (1981). *Estatística Aplicada A Economia e a Administracao* [Applied Statistics for Economy and Business]. Rio de Janeiro, Brazil: LTC Publishers. (in Portuguese)

Workman, L., & Paper, D. (2010). Compulsive buying: A theoretical framework. *The Journal of Business Inquiry, 9*(1), 89–126.

World Health Organization. (2011). *Impact of economic crises on mental health*. Retrieved from http://www.euro.who.int/data/assets/pdf_file/0008/134999/e94837.pdf

Wright, L. T., Newman, A., & Dennis, C. (2006). Enhancing consumer empowerment. *European Journal of Marketing, 40*(9/10), 925–935. doi:10.1108/03090560610680934

Wu, F., Yeniyurt, S., Kim, D., & Cavusgil, S. T. (2006). The impact of information technology on supply chain capabilities and firm performance: A resource-based view. *Industrial Marketing Management, 35*(4), 493–504. doi:10.1016/j.indmarman.2005.05.003

Yalch, R., & Spangenberg, E. (1990). Effects of Store Music on Shopping Behaviour. *Journal of Services Marketing, 4*, 31–39. doi:10.1108/EUM0000000002502

Yalch, R., & Spangenberg, E. (1993). Using store music for retail zoning: a field experiment. *Advances in Consumer Research. Association for Consumer Research (U. S.), 20*, 632–636.

Yalch, R., & Spangenberg, E. (2000). The Effects of Music in a Retail Setting on Real and Perceived Shopping Times. *Journal of Business Research*, *49*, 139–147. doi:10.1016/S0148-2963(99)00003-X

Yang, Z., & Peterson, R.T. (2003, Winter). I read about it online. *Marketing Research*, 26-31.

Yang, D.-J., Chou, D.-H., & Liu, J. (2012). A Study of Key Success Factors when Applying E-commerce to the Travel Industry. *International Journal of Business and Social Science*, *3*(8), 114–119.

Yang, D., & Wang, X. (2010). The effects of 2-tier store brands' perceived quality, perceived value, brand knowledge, and attitude on store loyalty. *Frontiers of Business Research in China*, *4*(1), 1–28. doi:10.1007/s11782-010-0001-7

Yang, J. (2013). Harnessing value in knowledge management for performance in buyer–supplier collaboration. *International Journal of Production Research*, *51*(7), 1984–1991. doi:10.1080/00207543.2012.701774

Yang, K. (2010). Determinants of US consumer mobile shopping services adoption, implications for designing mobile shopping services. *Journal of Consumer Marketing*, *27*(3), 262–270. doi:10.1108/07363761011038338

Yin, R. K. (2003). *Case study research: Design and methods* (3rd ed.). Thousand Oaks, CA: Sage.

Yoo, C., Park, J., & MacInnis, D. J. (1998). Effects of Store Characteristics and In-Store Emotional Experiences on Store Attitude. *Journal of Business Research*, *42*, 253–263. doi:10.1016/S0148-2963(97)00122-7

Yoon, S. J. (2002). The Antecedents And Consequences Of Trust In Online Purchase Decisions. *Journal of Interactive Marketing*, *16*(2), 47–63. doi:10.1002/dir.10008

Yu, H., & Fang, W. (2009). Relative impact from products quality, service quality, and experience quality on customer perceived value and intention to shop for the coffee shop market. *Total Quality Management*, *20*(11), 1273–1285. doi:10.1080/14783360802351587

Yu, W., & Ramanathan, R. (2008). An assessment of operational efficiencies in the UK retail sector. *International Journal of Retail & Distribution Management*, *36*(11), 861–882. doi:10.1108/09590550810911656

Zamora, J., Vasquez-Parraga, A. Z., Morales, F., & Cisternas, C. (2004). Formation process of guest loyalty: Theory and an empirical test. *Studies and Perspectives in Tourism*, *13*(3-4), 197–221.

Zamora, J., Vasquez-Parraga, A. Z., Rodriguez, A., & Gonzalez, A. (2011). Road travelers' motivations and loyalty: Train versus bus services. *Journal of Travel & Tourism Marketing*, *28*, 541–555. doi:10.1080/10548408.2011.588119

Zarantonello, L. (2009). Gli spazi di consumo temporanei: un'analisi esplorativa attraverso cinque casi di studio. *Micro & Macro Marketing*, *18*(1), 19–40.

Zarrella, D. (2010). *The social media marketing book*. Sebastopol, CA: O'Reilly Media, Inc.

Zeithaml, V. (1988). Consumer perceptions of price, quality, and value: A means-end model and synthesis of evidence. *Journal of Marketing*, *52*(3), 2–22. doi:10.2307/1251446

Zentes, J., Morschett, D., & Schramm-Klein, H. (2007). *Strategic Retail Management: Text and International Cases*. Wiesbaden, Germany: Gabler.

Zhang, J., Farris, P. W., Irvin, J. W., Kushwaha, T., Steenburgh, T. J., & Weitz, B. A. (2010). Crafting integrated multichannel retailing strategies. *Journal of Interactive Marketing*, *24*(2), 168–180. doi:10.1016/j.intmar.2010.02.002

Zhu, Z., Nakata, C., Sivakumar, K., & Grewal, D. (2013). Fix it or leave it? Customer recovery from self-service technology failure. *Journal of Retailing*, *89*(1), 15–29. doi:10.1016/j.jretai.2012.10.004

Ziliani, C. (2010, Spring). Loyalty marketing in Italy: a decade of customer cards and clubs in food retailing. *Retail Digest*, 54-57.

Zohar, D. (1990). *The Quantum Self: Human Nature and Consciousness Defined by the New Physics*. New York: Quill.

Zorrilla, P. (2000). Política de merchandising en la empresa de distribución detallista. In Marketing En Sectores Específicos. editorial Pirámide.

Zurawicki, L., & Braidot, N. (2005). Consumer during the crisis: responses from the middle class in Argentina. *Journal of Business Research*, *58*(8), 1100–1109. doi:10.1016/j.jbusres.2004.03.005

Zureik, E., & Mowshowitz, A. (2005). Consumer Power in the Digital Society. *Communications of the ACH*, *48*, 46–51. doi:10.1145/1089107.1089136

About the Contributors

Fabio Musso is Professor of Business Management in the Department of Economics, Society, and Politics, and Chairman of the M.S. in Marketing and Communication at the University of Urbino (Italy). He has over 20 years of experience in teaching and research. Prior to entering the university, he worked as marketing manager in the automotive and furniture industry. His research interests include marketing channels, retailing, trade marketing, international strategy, international marketing, logistics, and CSR. He has more than 120 research publications in various refereed international journals/conferences, and he has published 9 books. He is Editor in Chief of the *International Journal of Economic Behavior*, Associate Editor of the *International Journal of Applied Behavioral Economics*, and member of the scientific board of several academic journals. He has been visiting scholar in the Institute for Retail Studies, University of Stirling (Scotland, UK). He is member of the European International Business Academy (EIBA). He received several awards for his research achievements.

Elena Druică is a Full Professor of Economics and the Head of the Department of Economics and Administrative Sciences in the Faculty of Business and Administration, University of Bucharest, with 20 years of teaching and research experience and 7 years of managerial experience. She graduated from a faculty of Mathematics of the same university in 1994; she got a master diploma in Armonic Analysis and another one in Financial and Risk Management. She earned a PhD degree in Mathematics and another one in Economics. Her teaching area of expertise is in Game and Decision Theory and Behavioral Economics. She has been conducting interdisciplinary research activity, in which she brought together inputs from the two areas of specializations aforementioned. She is author and co-author of 4 books printed in Romania, of 2 chapters included in international editorial projects, and the editor of another book published in the USA. Her academic portfolio includes 22 papers published in international, peer-reviewed journals, 22 other papers published in conference proceedings, and 8 conference presentations to prestigious international events.

* * *

Daniela Andreini is Assistant Professor in the Department of Management, Economics, and Quantitative Methods at the University of Bergamo (Italy) and visiting professor at the University of Washington Bothell, Seattle (USA). She holds a doctorate in marketing from "La Sapienza" University of Rome. During her doctorate program, she was visiting scholar at Ryarson University of Toronto. Her research on marketing includes the introduction of e-commerce channels in the commerce of typical Italian products, the return on investment in internet activities for click and mortar firms, multi-channel retail businesses, industrial marketing, and consumer behavior. Since 2013, she is member of the research staff of ELab-OPRI, the permanent research center on professional service firms of the University of Bergamo.

Kenneth D. Bahn, Ph.D, was a professor of marketing at James Madison University. His research has been published in the *Journal of Consumer Research, Journal of Retailing*, and *Journal of the Academy of Marketing Science*, among others. His research interests included children's consumer behavior, nutrition and physical fitness, and product variety. He served as a proceedings editor for Academy of Marketing Science, and an editorial review board member of *Journal of Retailing*. He also served as a director of MBA programs in James Madison University from 1997-2008.

Sergio Barile is full professor of business management at Sapienza, University of Rome, Italy. He is a member of the Board of Directors of the Italian Academy of Business Administration and Management (AIDEA). He is also a member of the Editorial Board of significant Italian journals dealing with business management and economics science. He serves as a member of the scientific committee and referee for national and international workshops and conferences. He published several books and articles in international journals, including the *European Management Journal, Journal of Service Management, International Journal of Quality and Service Sciences, Journal of Business Market Management, Service Science*. He has contributed to the theoretical and practical foundation and diffusion of the Viable Systems Approach (vSA). His main research interests are business governance and management, decision theory, complexity theory. He received several awards for his research achievements. He is a consultant for relevant public institutions and private companies.

Gloria Berenguer-Contrí (PhD, University of Valencia, Spain) is Professor in the Marketing Department of University of Valencia. She has been a visitant researcher at different universities and her studies are published in several international journals (e.g. *International Journal of Hospitality Management, International Journal of Contemporary Hospitality Management, International Journal of Retail & Distribution Management, Journal of Retailing and Consumer Services, Journal of Wine Research, Journal of Foodservice Business Research*, among others). Her current research interests are consumer behaviour and services marketing.

Angelo Bonfanti is Researcher ad Assistant Professor in Business Management at the University of Verona (Italy), Department of Business Administration. He received his PhD from the "Parthenope" University of Naples (Italy) and is a member since 2004 of the editorial review team of *Sinergie Italian Journal of Management*, edited by CUEIM, contributing with editorial and organizational activities. His current research interests include service management and marketing, business communication, and retail management.

Barbara Borusiak is Associate Professor at Poznan University of Economics (Poland), in the Department of Commerce and Marketing within the Faculty of Management. She specializes in models of retail growth and retail internationalization, delivering lectures on Retail Management, Retail Growth Strategies, and International Business for bachelor and master studies at Poznan University of Economics. She is a member of the programme committee for "Handel wewnętrzny w Polsce" (Commerce in Poland) – a report edited annually by the Institute for Market, Consumption, and Business Cycles Research in Warsaw (Poland). She is the Polish coordinator for the triple diploma master study programme in Marketing Innovation Management organized by the European University Viadrina in Frankfurt (Germany) together with Poznan University of Economics (Poland) and Lorraine University Nancy-Metz (France). She is the Head of the Ph.D. study programme for the Faculty of Management at Poznan University of Economics.

Elena Candelo is Associate Professor in Strategic Management at University of Turin (Italy), Department of Management. She took a degree in Economics with 110 and Honorable mention at the Faculty of Economics, Turin University, and PhD in Business Management. Her main research areas include strategic management, brand management, corporate social responsibility, management of tourist destinations, and automotive industry.

Cecilia Casalegno took her Master degree in International Management at the Faculty of Economics, University of Turin (Italy), in 2003. She has a PhD degree in business administration, and from 2008, she has been researcher and lecturer at the Department of Management, University of Turin. She teaches in Marketing, Firm Strategy, and Communication courses at the University of Turin, and she is professor of Marketing and product fashion design at the Politecnic of Turin. Her main fields of research concern integrated marketing communication, strategic human resource management, and leadership development strategy. She is author of national and international publications (books and papers).

Sandro Castaldo is professor at Bocconi University (Italy). He holds a PhD in Management from Bocconi University. He teaches Channel Marketing, Trade Marketing and Retailing at graduate (Master of Science) and postgraduate level (MBA and executive education). His research is mainly focused on collaborative channel relationships, multichannel management (on line vs. off line), and consumer trust. He has published many articles on international journals and books. *Trust in Market Relationships* (Edward Elgar, 2007), *Coopetition: Winning Strategies for the 21st Century* (edited book, Edward Elgar, 2010), and *Channel and Retail Marketing* (with Monica Grosso and Katia Premazzi, Edward Elgar, 2013) are his most recent books.

Philip Cheng (Australian Catholic University, Faculty of Law and Business) has more than 25 years of experience in university teaching, research, and administration (including members of Academic and Faculty Boards, Dean, Head of Department, members of Learning and Teaching Committee, and other committees). During that time, he has assumed responsibilities in Australia, Singapore, Hong Kong, and China. Philip has been teaching in various disciplines, finance, and accounting included. He has been an active researcher with close to 80 research outcomes, including quality refereed journal articles and conference papers. Philip is a member of the editorial board of two journals. Philip's recent interest is in multidisciplinary behavioural research in finance, accounting, marketing, and neuroscience.

Chiara Civera holds a Bachelor Degree in Business Economics with Marketing specialization and took a Master Degree in Business Administration in 2009 both from University of Turin (Italy), Faculty of Economics. She got a PhD in Business and Management from University of Turin, Faculty of Economics in 2013, after having spent two years at London South Bank University in London as PhD and research student, while she was also working as business analyst for a consulting company based in London. The main subjects of her interest and research are marketing, branding, social marketing, corporate-social responsibility, non-profit sector management, and fundraising strategies. During the academic year 2009-2010, Chiara was a lecturer of marketing and branding at University of Turin. She worked as researcher for the International Labour Organization (United Nation) in Turin from January to September 2011.

Ronan de Kervenoael is a Marketing Lecturer at Sabanci University in Turkey and network Lecturer at Aston University, UK. His wider research interests lie under the umbrella of consumer behaviour and retailing, including the study of social, cultural, and technological transformations in how consumers (re)organize their lives and become producers of their experiences. His work has been published in *Environment & Planning A, World Development, Service Industries Journal, Telecommunication Policy.*

Patrizia de Luca, PhD, is Professor at the University of Trieste (Italy), where she teaches Marketing and Research Methodology for Management Decisions. She is Deputy Director of the Department of Economics, Business, Mathematics, and Statistics, and member of some academic committees. Her research focus is on distribution channels, retail marketing, and consumer behavior. She authored many refereed publications in national and international books and journals. She is referee for several Italian journals and international books. She has recently participated in two large programs on distribution and sales of Italian products in emerging and developed countries, sponsored by the Italian Ministry of Education, University, and Research, and in other research projects on international marketing. Now, she is also working on a research project financed by UE on cooperation and innovation in the Adriatic Area.

Amalia Duţu is Associate Professor at the University of Pitesti (Romania), Faculty of Economic Sciences, Department of Management and Business Administration, and a member of collaborative teaching staff at Academy of Economic Studies, Bucharest. Currently she is member of the managerial team of Economics Faculty, Dean Assistant and Marketing Manager of the Businesses Incubation and Technology Transfer Centre, University of Pitesti. She holds the doctorate from the Academy of Economic Studies, Bucharest in the field of Marketing, since 2006. Her teaching experience is in domains like Marketing, Marketing Research, International Marketing, and Strategic Planning. Her key competences are quantitative and qualitative researches, quantitative data analysis using SPSS, strategic planning. She is also working as freelance consultant in marketing research and strategic planning, since 2010. She is author or co-author of more than 40 publications in national and international peer-reviewed journals and conference proceedings.

Ahmet Ekici, Ph.D, is Assistant Professor of marketing at Bilkent University, Ankara (Turkey). His research mainly focuses on issues of related to macromarketing (quality of life studies, consumer well-being, business ethics, developing markets, and poverty) and public policy and marketing with a special emphasis on food safety, institutional trust, vulnerable groups, and poverty and consumption. His research has been published in *Journal of Public Policy and Marketing, Journal of Business Research, Journal of Macromarketing, Journal of Business Ethics, Industrial Marketing Management, Social Indicators Research, Journal of Research for Consumers,* and *Advances in Consumer Research.*

Pablo Jose Escobedo is a JD candidate at Indiana University Maurer School of Law. He holds a double-bachelor degree, a Bachelor of Arts in Communication – Mass Communication and a Bachelor of Business Administration in Marketing, both earned at the University of Texas-Pan American between 2011 and 2013. He worked as an intern at the UTPA-COBA Dean's Office from 2011 to 2013, and as a research assistant of Dr. Arturo Vasquez-Parraga for the customer loyalty project in stores of the Rio Grande Valley during 2011.

Cristina García Gumiel, born in Madrid, has more than 10 years of experience working in marketing within the retail sector. She holds currently the position of Head of Marketing and Brand Events for Spain at Unibail-Rodamco, Europe's leading listed commercial property company. Cristina started her career in the retail market in 2005 as a market research manager at Sonae Sierra, the biggest Portuguese retail company, specialized in shopping centres. In 2007, she was appointed Head of Strategic Marketing for Spain and Portugal. In 2009, she joined Unibail-Rodamco Spain, as a Strategic Marketing manager, being promoted to Head of Marketing and Brand Events for Spain in 2012. Member of the technical committee in the Spanish Shopping Centre Association Cristina has focused her career to the customer analysis and satisfaction. Degree in Business Management and in Market Research, both from the Universidad Autonoma de Madrid (UAM), Cristina has published several articles related to consumer behavior and sensorial marketing. Cristina is also teacher in Marketing in the Business Management School at UAM.

Toni Gardner graduated in 2013 from Abertay University (Scotland, UK) with an Honours degree in Marketing and Business. During her studies, Toni completed modules in retail marketing, marketing communications, international marketing, market research, and consumer behaviour, completing a dissertation on the decline of the UK High Street. Toni engaged with business as part of her studies through real business scenarios, providing creative marketing solutions to the problems and challenges facing local and national businesses, and participated in extracurricular activities including membership of Abertay University Marketing Society. Following graduation, Toni was employed as a marketer for a Web developer, providing online marketing solutions for e-commerce and non-e-commerce businesses throughout Scotland specialising in relationship building and e- and m-commerce marketing.

Irene Gil-Saura (PhD, University of Valencia) is Professor of Marketing at the University of Valencia (Spain). Her main teaching and research interests include business-to-business marketing, services marketing, consumer behavior, and retailing. She has taught these topics in undergraduate and postgraduate courses. She has published articles in several international journals as the *Annals of Tourism Research, The International Review of Retail, Distribution and Consumer Research, Industrial Marketing Management, International Journal of Hospitality Management, Tourism Management, International Journal of Service Industry Management, The Service Industries Journal, International Journal of Contemporary Hospitality Management, Journal of Marketing Channels, International Journal of Culture, Tourism and Hospitality Research, Industrial Management & Data Systems Journal, International Journal of Retail & Distribution Management, Tourism Review*, among others.

Mónica Gómez is Associate Professor of Marketing at Universidad Autónoma de Madrid (PhD, Universidad Autónoma de Madrid). Her research interests are power in marketing channels: national vs. store brands; consumer behaviour and in-store atmosphere; brand equity and customer equity. She has published more than 50 research articles. Most of them are published in international journals such as the *European Journal of Marketing, International Journal of Market Research, Innovar Journal, Journal of Retailing and Consumer Services, the International Journal of Retailing and Distribution Management*, and the *Journal of Euromarketing*, among others. She has also published in prestigious Spanish Journals, such as the *Revista Española de Investigación de Marketing ESIC, Cuadernos de Economía Española*, and the *Revista Europea de Dirección y Administración de Empresas*. She has presented several conferences in EMAC, EIRASS, and EUNIP, among others.

Monica Grosso is Assistant Professor of Marketing at EMLYON Business School, France. She holds a PhD in Management from Bocconi University. She teaches Essentials of Marketing, Go to Market Strategy, Retail Management, and Category Management both at the graduate (Master of Science) and post-graduate level (EMBA and executive education). Her research focuses on vertical channel relationships, with a focus on private labels and brand competition, partnerships between manufacturers and retailers, retailers' relationship management with their shoppers, shoppers' perceptions of the store and privacy issues in the digital channels. Coopetition, satisfaction, trust, and loyalty are the key variables investigated in her studies.

Eda Gurel-Atay, PhD, serves the marketing community by researching and teaching in the consumer behavior area. Her research interests center on the impact of social values on various consumer behaviors; lifestyles and psychographics; celebrity endorsements and advertising effectiveness; and materialism. Shopping process and its impact on retailer evaluation and shopping well-being of consumers are other topics that attract her attention. Her current studies explore the relationship between celebrity values, brand values, and consumer vales; impact of lifestyles on health-related behaviors; impact of values (such as materialism and happiness) on consumer well-being; and the relationship between self-expressiveness in shopping, shopping well-being, and overall subjective well-being. Her work appeared in peer-reviewed journals such as *Journal of Advertising Research, Social Indicators Research*, and *The International Review of Retail, Distribution, and Consumer Research*.

Alan Hallsworth was formerly a Professor in the Department of Retailing and Marketing at Manchester Metropolitan University (UK) and is currently visiting researcher at Portsmouth Business School. His interests in retail range widely: from EU competition policy to local food. His work has been published in *Environment & Planning A, Economic Geography, Service Industries Journal*, etc.

Alicia Izquierdo-Yusta, PhD, is Associate Professor at the Department of Marketing of the University of Burgos (Spain). She has participated in different Conferences and Seminars worldwide and has written several articles in different high standing international journals in different international journals (*Total Quality Management and Business Excellence; Service Business; Innovar, European Journal of Marketing*, etc.). Her main research lines are e-commerce, technology adoption, marketing communications, sales promotions, and product and services innovation. She is a member of the following associations: European Marketing Academy (EMAC) and The European Association for Education and Research in Commercial Distribution (EAERCD).

Ana Isabel Jimenez-Zarco, PhD, is Associate Professor at the Economic and Business Studies Department of the Open University of Catalonia (Spain). She has participated in different Conferences and Seminars worldwide and has written several articles in different international journals (e.g. *Computers in Human Behaviour, Academy of Marketing Science Review, Journal of Marketing Channels, The Marketing Review, European Journal of Innovation Management, Innovar, European Journal of Marketing*, etc.). Her main research lines are brand identity, image management, product innovation and ICT applications in management and marketing. She is a member of the following associations: Product Development Management Association (PDMA), European Marketing Academy (EMAC), a reviewer of some journal and international congress and associate editor of journals such as *Innovar, Journal of*

Marketing Trends, and *Revista da Micro e Pequena Empresa*. She is a member of the research group i2TIC (UOC) focused on the interdisciplinary analysis of the interaction between ICT use and information, communication, and knowledge flow on individuals and organizations.

Dong-Jin Lee, PhD, is Professor of marketing at Yonsei University, Korea. His research has been published in the *Journal of Marketing, Journal of the Academy of Marketing Science, International Journal of Research in Marketing, Journal of Advertising, Journal of Business Research*, and *Journal of Business Ethics,* among others. His research interests include relationship marketing, business ethics, and quality-of-life studies. He has served as the vice president for the ISQOLS and director of Academy of Marketing Science.

Isabella Maggioni is a PhD candidate in Management at the Catholic University of Milan, Italy. Her research interests include the following topics: customer loyalty and loyalty-building initiatives, retail marketing, identity-based consumer behaviour, destination branding, ethical and sustainable consumption. Her PhD thesis focuses on the role of identity-based motivations and self-concept in consumer behaviour, analyzing the relationship among store environment, self-congruity, and customer loyalty in grocery retail. She has been a visiting fellow at the University of New South Wales and at Monash University. She has also worked as a teaching assistant at the Catholic University of Milan, Italy. From April 2014, she is research fellow at the Australian Centre for Retail Studies, Monash University.

Elisa Martinelli, PhD, is Assistant Professor at the Department of Economics Marco Biagi of the University of Modena and Reggio Emilia, where she teaches Trade Marketing and Sales Management. Her main research interests are concerned with retailing and channel management, customer loyalty, and the Country Of Origin (COO) effect. On these topics she published a number of papers in national (e.g. *Micro&Macro Marketing, Mercati e Competitività, Sinergie*) and international journals (e.g. *The Service Industries Journal, The International Review of Retail, Distribution and Consumer Research*), as well as some books and book chapters with leading editors (e.g. Edward Elgar, Il Mulino). She has been awarded by the Royal Society of Edinburgh (Scotland, UK) with the 2013 CRF/RSE European Visiting Research Fellowships – Visits from Europe to Scotland. She has been visiting scholar in the Institute for Retail Studies, University of Stirling (Scotland, UK).

María Pilar Martínez-Ruiz, PhD, is Associate Professor at the Department of Marketing of the University of Castilla-La Mancha (Spain). She has participated in different Conferences and Seminars worldwide and has written several articles in different high standing international journals (e.g., *Journal of the Operational Research Society, European Journal of Marketing, The International Journal of Market Research, European Journal of Operational Research*, etc.). Her main research lines are retailing, marketing communications, sales promotions and product and services innovation. Member of the following associations: Academy of Marketing Science (AMS), European Marketing Academy (EMAC), and The European Association for Education and Research in Commercial Distribution (EAERCD). She was co-track chair of the Pricing and Retailing Track at the 75 edition of the Summer´s Educators AMA Conference (celebrated in 2012 in Chicago).

Francesca Montagnini is Assistant Professor of Management at University of Milan-Bicocca (Italy). She received her PhD. from Catholic University, Milan, where she served also as a research fellow and an adjunct professor of marketing. Her research interests include service innovation and its relationships with new consumption trends. Recently, she focused her studies on corporate sustainability particularly in retailing. She presented on these topics at major international conferences and published in international journals.

Francesca Negri, PhD, is Researcher at the Department of Economics – Marketing Area, University of Parma, Italy. Her work explores retail and trade marketing themes, and in particular is focused on how retailers are facing the Web 2.0. Additional projects look at customer complaint handling and social caring, social networking site business models, and how to make qualitative research online, trough content analysis and netnography. She has involved in various research project on retail, and has participated in several international events and conferences. In the last years, she is holder of the courses of "Social Media Marketing" and "Crisis Communication & Reputation Management." Updates and augmentations of her research can be found on her Facebook page (Social Media Marketing Unipr) and Twitter (Retail Is Detail – @FNegriUnipr).

Mirian Palmeira is Associate Professor in the Business School, Federal University of Parana, Brazil. Member of the Scientific Advisory Board of the *International Journal of Economic Behavior* (IJEB), author of different articles related to the fields of retailing and services, fashion, experiential marketing, and information and integrated marketing communication. Her education levels are Fashion Design (2012) at Centro Europeu, Curitiba, Parana, PhD (1995) and Master (1988) degrees in Marketing at Fundacao Getulio Vargas, Sao Paulo, Brazil.

Eleonora Pantano, is a Post-Doc Research Fellow at University of Calabria (Italy) in cooperation with Technical University of Eindhoven (The Netherlands). She earned a PhD in "Psychology of Programming and Artificial Intelligence" in 2008 and a Master Degree in Management Engineering in 2005. Her research interests are related to the innovation and technologies and in retailing and e-tailing, with emphasis on the investigation of human behavior in advanced technology-based environments. Furthermore, she is member of the Editorial Board and hoc reviewer of numerous international journals. Her works appear in numerous international journals such as the *Journal of Marketing Management* and the *Journal of Retailing and Consumer Services* (she was also guest editor of two special issue of this journal in innovation and technologies for retailing).

Giuseppe Pedeliento is a Post Doctoral Research Fellow in the Department of Management, Economics, and Quantitative Methods at the University of Bergamo (Italy) and holds a Doctorate in Marketing from the same university. Former visiting researcher and lecturer in Product and Brand Management at the Aalto University School of Economics in Helsinki (Finland), and visiting scholar at the University of Washington Bothell, Seattle (USA), he is member of the research staff of ELab-OPRI, the permanent research center on professional service firms of the University of Bergamo. His research include multichannel retailing, industrial marketing, project marketing, consumer behavior, and professional service firms.

Giovanna Pegan is Assistant Professor at the University of Trieste, Italy, where she teaches International Marketing and Communication Management. At the end of 2013, she received the National Scientific Qualification to function as Associate Professor in Italian Universities. She is local coordinator for the "Italian Marketing Competition" of the SIM (Italian Marketing Association) and she is referee for several Italian Journals and International Books. She has authored refereed publications in national and international books and journals. Her research focus is on consumer behavior, international marketing, and communication management. She has recently participated in two large research programs on distribution and sales of Italian products in the Chinese and American markets, sponsored by the Italian "Ministry of Education, University, and Research," and in other research projects on international marketing. Now, she is also working on a research project financed by UE on cooperation and innovation in the Adriatic Area.

Joni Pekkala is a recent University of Lapland (Finland) graduate. He graduated as a Master of Social Sciences majoring in management and marketing. In the latter part of his studies, he worked two years as a researcher in the Social Sciences department in several different projects. One of his main interests is e-commerce and marketing and his research in the Lappish companies doing e-commerce spawned his article. Currently, he works as a project manager in one of the biggest advertisement firms in Lapland.

Sanda Renko is Professor at the Department of Trade of the Faculty of Economics and Business at the University of Zagreb, Croatia. She has carried out research on topics such as retailing and wholesaling, category management, logistics, channels of distribution, etc. She was the editor of the book "Challenges for the Trade in Central and Southeast Europe," published by Emerald Group. In addition, she was the guest editor in journals such as the *British Food Journal, Journal of Food Products Marketing, World Journal of Retail Business Management*. She has presented papers at several conferences such as CIRCLE, EUROMED, International Retailing Conference, Oxford Retail Futures Conference, etc. She is involved in FP7 EU Project "Focus Balkans."

Janice Rudkowski is Principal and Owner of Helianthus Consulting and Instructor with Ted Rogers School of Retail Management at Ryerson University (Canada). Her 18+ years' experience spans private, public, and non-profit sectors across diverse industries including consumer packaged goods, retail, fashion, healthcare, technology, and education. Recognized for her marketing and communications expertise, she has elevated the growth of global brand names such as Barbie, Dove, and One-A-Day Multivitamins. Janice has forged a unique and entrepreneurial career path by merging together all of her professional passions: consulting, teaching, facilitating, researching, writing, and designing curriculum. When not pursuing her professional endeavours, she can be found planning her next global travel adventure, canning pickles, practicing yoga, learning to play the piano, or cross-country skiing. Janice holds a BAA from the School of Fashion at Ryerson University and an MBA, Marketing from the Schulich School of Business at York University. She lives in Toronto, Canada.

María-Eugenia Ruiz-Molina (PhD, University of Valencia) is Associate Professor in the Marketing Department of University of Valencia, where she earned her PhD in Business Administration and Management. Her studies are published in several international journals (e.g. *Industrial Management and Data Systems, International Review of Retail, Distribution and Consumer Research, International*

Journal of Retail & Distribution Management, International Journal of Hospitality Management; International Journal of Contemporary Hospitality Management, etc.). Her current research interests are consumer behavior, retailing, and ICT business solutions.

Rauno Rusko, PhD, is a Lecturer of Management at the University of Lapland (Finland). His research interests are in the cooperative, competitive, and coopetitive features of business and management, especially in the branches of ICT, forest industry, and tourism. In addition to several book chapters, his articles have been published in the following journals: *Forest Policy and Economics, the International Journal of Business Environment, International Journal of Technoentrepreneurship, the International Journal of Tourism Research, Industrial Marketing Management, European Management Journal, International Journal of Innovation in the Digital Economy*, and in *Global Business and Management Research: An International Journal.*

Miguel Angel Sahagun is a Doctoral Candidate at the University of Texas Pan-American (UTPA). He holds a Master of Business Administration (MBA) from the University of Texas at Brownsville (UTB), and a Bachelor of Industrial Engineering from Instituto Tecnologico y de Estudios Superiores de Occidente (ITESO). He has pursued his PhD as well as working as research assistant and academic instructor at UTPA from 2010 to present. He was the MBA Program Director at the Instituto Internacional de Estudios Superiores (IIES) from 2008 to 2010, and taught undergraduate and graduate courses at IIES in addition to designing curricula for several business majors from 2006 to 2008. He worked for different worldwide manufacturing companies in the automobile industry in various positions from Industrial Engineer to Plant Manager from 1994 to 2005.

Marialuisa Saviano, PhD, is Associate Professor of Business Management at the University of Salerno, Italy. She is President of the Association for research on Viable Systems (ASVSA) and Vice President of the Italian Association for Sustainability Science (IASS). She participates in researches and studies contributing to the development of the Viable Systems Approach (VSA). She has published several articles in international journals, including the *European Management Journal, Journal of Service Management, Journal of Business Market Management*, and *Service Science*. She serves as referee for several Italian and international journals. She received the best paper award at the 2011 Naples Forum on Service and at the XXIV Sinergie Annual Conference. She is also finalist in the 2012/2013 Emerald/EMRBI Business Research Award for Emerging Researchers. Her main research interests include the Viable Systems Approach, service science, service marketing, retailing, healthcare, knowledge management, complexity, and cultural heritage management.

Roberta Sebastiani is Associate Professor of Management at the Catholic University of S.H. (Italy) and Assistant Director of Centrimark – Center of Research in Marketing, Catholic University. Her research interests include service innovation, value co-creation and corporate sustainability. She has had papers presented at major international conferences and published in international books and management journals, including *The Service Industries Journal* and the *Journal of Business Ethics.*

M. Joseph Sirgy, PhD, is Professor of Marketing and Virginia Real Estate Research Fellow at Virginia Tech. He has published extensively in the area of marketing, business ethics, and quality of life (QOL). He co-founded the International Society for Quality-of-Life Studies (ISQOLS) in 1995, served as its Executive Director/Treasurer from 1995 to 2011, and as Development Director (2011-12). In 2003, ISQOLS honored him as the Distinguished QOL Researcher. He also served as President of the Academy of Marketing Science.

Harry Timmermans is Chair of the Urban Planning Group of the Eindhoven University of Technology (The Netherlands). He has research interests in modeling decision-making processes and decision support systems in a variety of application domains. His main current research project is concerned with the development of a dynamic model of activity-travel behavior. He is editor of the *Journal of Retailing and Consumer Services*, and serves on the board of several other journals in transportation, geography, urban planning, marketing, artificial intelligence, and other disciplines. He is Co-Chair of the International Association of Travel Behavior Research (IATBR), and member of several scientific committees of the Transportation Research Board. He has also served as member of conference committees in transportation and artificial intelligence. He has been co-author of more than 500-refereed articles in international journals.

David Tng Zi Jun received his Diploma in Electronics with a focus on Business from Temasek Polytechnic, Singapore, in 2009. He earned his Bachelor of Science Degree in Business Management from University of Birmingham in 2013. He is the recipient of the Student Champion award by the University of Birmingham. While pursuing his degree, David worked along with multiple online retailing start-ups ranging from clothing to food products. He is currently a full-time marketing executive at ETS Solutions seeking to improve the engineering company's online presence.

Jason Turner (PhD) is the Programme leader of the MBA (Master of Business Administration) at the University of Abertay (Scotland, UK), specialising in marketing research, consumer buying behavior, and customer loyalty in the retail sector. He has worked in the area of retail and the customer/client interface for over 15 years and has published in and edited and reviewed for national and international journals and conferences as well as writing for industry marketing publications. He provides consultancy to SMEs, specifically in the areas of relationship marketing, product assortment, branding, and marketing research, and is actively involved in leading initiatives to improve the experience and employability prospects of university students and young learners in secondary schools through the use of real business scenarios.

Arturo Z. Vásquez-Párraga (PhD) is Professor of Marketing and International Business at the University of Texas-Pan American (UTPA). He holds a PhD degree in Economics from the University of Texas at Austin, and a PhD degree in Marketing and International Business from Texas Tech University. He has performed scientific research in strategic marketing, customer loyalty, marketing and business ethics, and strategies of Latin American companies in the United States, and has extensively published in leading journals such as the *Journal of Marketing Research, Journal of Business and Industrial Marketing, Journal of Consumer Marketing, Journal of Retailing and Consumer Services, Journal of Business Research, Journal of Travel Research, Journal of Euromarketing*, and *Health Marketing Quarterly*. In addition to his regular teaching at UTPA, Dr. Vásquez teaches graduate courses in Chilean, Peruvian, Colombian, and Mexican universities during the summer months, and trains executives and professionals using comprehensive workshops dedicated to ethics auditing, competency-based learning, and scientific research for journal publications.

Donata Tania Vergura received her PhD in Economics from the University of Parma (Italy). She is a Researcher at the Department of Economics of the University of Parma and she teaches Social Marketing. Her research interests include topics related to consumer behaviour, neuromarketing, and social marketing, but her main area of research is gambling. She started studying it when she was a PhD student, writing a thesis on recreational gamblers' motives and beliefs. She is currently carrying out research projects aimed at investigating gamblers' behaviour and identifying marketing strategies to promote responsible gambling.

Kathleen Wolf (PhD) is a Research Social Scientist with the College of the Environment, University of Washington (Seattle, USA). She is also a key collaborator with the USDA Forest Service, Pacific Northwest Research Station in the development of a program on Urban Natural Resources Stewardship. Kathy's studies are based on the principles of environmental psychology; her professional mission is to discover, understand, and communicate human behavior and benefits, as people experience nature in cities. She is also interested in how scientific information can be integrated into local government policy and planning. An overview of Dr. Wolf's research programs can be found at www.naturewithin. info; additional research findings on Green Cities: Good Health: www.greenhealth.washington.edu.

Grace B. Yu, PhD, is an assistant professor of marketing at Duksung Women's Univeristy, Korea. Her research has been published in *Advances in Consumer Research*, *Journal of Business Ethics*, *Journal of Business Research*, *Journal of Travel Research*, and *Social Indicators Research*, among others. Her research interests include consumer behaviors, customer relationship management, and quality-of-life studies. Before joining the university, she had worked as an Account Executive (AE) at Saatchi & Saatchi, a multinational advertising company.

Index

CPSIA information can be obtained at www.ICGtesting.com
Printed in the USA
BVOW06*2057230614

356649BV00002B/3/P